Strategy

Strategy

Theory, Practice, Implementation

Professor Brad MacKay, Dr Mikko Arevuo, Professor David Mackay, and Professor Maureen Meadows

Great Clarendon Street, Oxford, OX2 6DP,
United Kingdom

Oxford University Press is a department of the University of Oxford.
It furthers the University's objective of excellence in research, scholarship,
and education by publishing worldwide. Oxford is a registered trade mark of
Oxford University Press in the UK and in certain other countries

Impression: 1

Published in the United States of America by Oxford University Press
198 Madison Avenue, New York, NY 10016, United States of America

British Library Cataloguing in Publication Data
Data available

Library of Congress Control Number: 2019957257

ISBN 978–0–19–877942–1

Printed in Great Britain by
Bell & Bain Ltd., Glasgow

ABOUT THE AUTHORS

Brad MacKay is Professor of Strategy in the University of St Andrews School of Management, and Senior Vice-Principal and Vice-Principal (International Strategy and External Relations) on the University senior management team. Brad's research, teaching and consultancy interests include strategy development, execution and implementation, contingency planning, scenario planning, the political economy of strategy-making, and scaling sustainability. He has published in a range of leading scholarly journals, and his research has been widely covered in the press, including the Financial Times and Wall Street Journal. He is a regular commentator on business-related issues in the media.

Mikko Arevuo is Reader in Strategy at Regent's University London. His background includes senior business experience in global financial services and management consulting; academic research; and university, graduate, and executive-level teaching. His research and teaching expertise is in strategy as managerial practice, competitive strategy, senior management and group decision-making processes, and the application of visual methods in organizational research. Mikko has also consulted widely in the UK public and private sectors. He worked with Fortune 500 companies as a facilitator providing evidence-based tools and frameworks to support strategic decision-making processes. A native of Finland, Mikko earned his BA in Economics from University of Michigan, Ann Arbor, and his MBA and PhD from Cranfield University.

David Mackay is Professor of Strategy at the Strathclyde Business School in Glasgow. Previously he held business management roles in multi-national, SME and entrepreneurial start-up organisations in the UK. He has a continuing research interest in developing understanding of effective strategic management and organisational leadership practices and knowledge. As a practitioner, Dave has engaged with a wide range of private, public, and charitable organisations, supporting their strategy work and development of implementable, practical outcomes. Dave has taught and consulted internationally in locations including the USA, India, Hong Kong, Malaysia, Singapore, Oman, Bahrain, Jordan, and the UAE.

Maureen Meadows is Professor of Strategic Management at the Centre for Business in Society at Coventry University. Formerly with the Open University Business School and Warwick Business School, Maureen's research interests include the use of strategy tools such as scenario planning and visioning by senior managers, and the post-merger integration phase following M&A deals. With a background in mathematics, statistics, and operational research, Maureen has many years' experience of working with 'big data' and customer analytics, both as a practitioner in the financial services sector and as an academic. She has published on the progress and problems experienced by organisations working on strategic projects such as market segmentation, relationship marketing, and customer relationship management.

ACKNOWLEDGEMENTS

The authoring process has been a most rewarding journey for us. In keeping with custom, we would like to acknowledge and thank people who have given us their time, shared their wisdom, and supported us during the writing process. First and foremost, we would like to thank each of the strategy practitioners who gave the author team his or her time. Your invaluable contribution makes this book different from other strategic management texts and allows the reader to learn from your experience.

We have been supported throughout the writing process by a magnificent team at Oxford University Press. In particular, we would like to thank the book's Commissioning Editor Nicola Hartley and Development Editor Stephanie Southall. This 'dynamic duo' went beyond their call of duty to support the writing team and we are grateful for the editorial support, encouragement, and guidance provided throughout. Also, we owe a debt of gratitude to Jon Crowe and the wider team at Oxford University Press for the professional services and positive scholarly environment they have provided. From start to finish, it has been a pleasure to be associated with OUP.

To the many anonymous academic colleagues who reviewed various versions of the chapters, we cannot thank you enough for your extensive constructive feedback which guided us in our address of mainstream strategy theory and pushing the boundaries of contemporary topics. We hope you can detect how your inputs have benefited the finished article. To the anonymous practice reviewers, we appreciate the positivity and advice as to how to reflect the multiplicity of ways in which strategy is encountered or practised in organizational life.

To our colleagues, friends, and families, we thank you for bearing with us as we put many other aspects of life on pause to complete the project. For our closest families, we have a few specific things to say.

From Dave: *To Jen, Jack, and Matthew, thank you for your continual support and infinite patience in evenings, weekends, and holidays in the face of the seemingly endless promises of 'I'll just be a few more minutes'—made it in the end!*

From Mikko: *I am forever indebted to and in awe of the most important people in my life, my wife Erika and my children Max and Eva. Your love, support, and unwavering belief in me kept me going and endure to the end.*

From Maureen: *To Matthew, Tom, and Joe, your love, patience, and support make everything possible!*

And from Brad: *I am ever thankful for the encouragement, sage advice, well-placed sympathy and support of my wife and partner Rebecca Sweetman, and for the laughter, love, wisdom, and indulgence of my two boys, Conor and Aidan, who have taught me that good strategy does indeed walk on two feet.*

Brad, Mikko, Dave, and Maureen, July 2019

The authors and Oxford University Press would like to sincerely thank our two contributors who worked tirelessly and determinedly in writing the online resources for this text, providing excellent material for students and instructors that will add insurmountable pedagogical value to the learning experience of business strategy:

Dr Knowledge Chinyanyu Mpofu, Senior Lecturer in Strategy, Bloomsbury Institute London in collaboration with the University of Northampton

Dr Mark Toon, Lecturer in Marketing and Strategy and Deputy Head of Learning and Teaching, Cardiff University

The authors and Oxford University Press would like to sincerely thank our dedicated editorial consultants who provided exceptionally detailed feedback to help provide specialist direction and insight throughout the development process.

Garry Carr, Course Director at Leeds Business School, Leeds Beckett University

Dr Mariya Eranova, Lecturer in Strategic Management, University of Greenwich

Dr Knowledge Chinyanyu Mpofu, Senior Lecturer in Strategy, Bloomsbury Institute London in collaboration with the University of Northampton

Dr Mark Toon, Lecturer in Marketing and Strategy and Deputy Head of Learning and Teaching, Cardiff University

We are also immensely grateful to all other academics and strategy practitioners who gave their time and expertise to review draft material throughout the writing process. Your help in shaping the book, and sharing your experiences, was invaluable.

Academic Editorial Review Panellists

Dr Mark Bailey, Senior Lecturer in Economics, Ulster University

Dr Mian Ajmal, Associate Professor of Management, Abu Dhabi University

Professor Ken Russell, Deputy Principal – Academic Development, Inverness College, University of the Highlands and Islands

Dr Gerry Urwin, Associate Professor at the School of Strategy and Leadership, Coventry University

Dr Federica Brunetta, Assistant Professor in the Department of Business and Management, Luiss Guido Carli University, Rome

Dr Richard Godfrey, Lecturer in Strategy, University of Leicester

Dr Mike Kennard, Senior Lecturer in Innovation, Strategy and Entrepreneurship, University of Manchester

Dr Krystin Zigan, Lecturer in Strategy and Director of BA Business and Management at Kent Business School, University of Kent

Professor Marc Day, Strategy and Operations Management, Henley Business School

Dr Sara Fisher, Lecturer in Management, Division of Strategy and Enterprise, Lancashire School of Business and Enterprise, University of Central Lancashire

Dr Jagannadha Pawan Tamvada, Associate Professor at the Department of Strategy, Innovation, and Entrepreneurship, Southampton Business School, University of Southampton

Dr Alistair Bowden, Senior Lecturer at Newcastle Business School, Northumbria University
Mr Clayton Davies, Senior Lecturer in Strategy and Enterprise, University of the West of England
Mr Marcus Thompson, Lecturer in Business Strategy, Entrepreneurship, and International Marketing, University of Aberdeen
Dr Wyn Morris, Lecturer in Management, Aberystwyth University
Dr Dane Anderton, Senior Lecturer, Alliance Manchester Business School, University of Manchester
Dr Selwyn S. Seymour, Senior Lecturer in Strategic Management, University of Bedfordshire Business School
Dr Killian McCarthy, Associate Professor of Strategy, University of Groningen
Dr Humphrey Bourne, Senior Lecturer in Management and Faculty Education Director, University of Bristol
Dr Krishna Venkitachalam, Associate Professor of Strategy, Stockholm University
Dr Andrew Wild, Associate Professor in Strategy, Nottingham University Business School
Dr Saleema Kauser, Lecturer in Organisational Strategy and Business Ethics, Alliance Manchester Business School, The University of Manchester
Professor Patrick Reinmoeller, Professor of Strategic Management, Cranfield University School of Management
Mr Adrian Pryce, Senior Lecturer in Strategy and International Business, University of Northampton
Ms Andrea Benn, Principal Lecturer, University of Brighton
Professor Martin Friesl, Professor of Business Administration and Organization at Otto-Friedrich-University Bamberg
Ms Marie Kerr, Senior Lecturer in Business Strategy, Operations, and Enterprise, Leeds Business School, Leeds Beckett University
Dr Ivan Zupic, Lecturer in Entrepreneurship, Institute of Management Studies, Goldsmiths, University of London
Dr Vasiliki Bamiatzi, Senior Lecturer in Strategy and Innovation, Liverpool Management School, University of Liverpool
Mr James B Johnston, Lecturer in Management, Strategy, and Leadership, University of the West of Scotland
Dr Ayfer Ali, Assistant Professor of Strategy and International Business at Warwick Business School, University of Warwick
Dr Scott Lichtenstein, Associate Professor of Strategy and Strategic Leadership, Birmingham City University
Dr Igor Pyrko, Lecturer in Strategic Management, Aston Business School
Dr Omar Al-Tabbaa, Senior Lecturer in Strategy and International Business, Kent Business School, University of Kent
Dr Mark Crowder, Senior Lecturer, Manchester Metropolitan University
Mrs Catherine Cai, Senior Lecturer in Strategy and International Management, University of the West of England

Practitioner Editorial Review Panellists

Paul L. Hart, Chief Financial Officer (contract), Toronto, Canada
Edward Regula, Integration Policy Advisor, US Federal Government
Stephen Lin, Strategic Management Consultant/CSO Coach, Singapore
Katherine Crisp, Strategy and Innovation Consultant, International Development, UK
Niko Karjalainen, Director of Corporate Ventures, Investment Management, UAE

To the generous *individuals* who have contributed their time and expertise to our Practitioner Insights, we thank you especially for working with us and for your unique perspectives on strategy in practice. In order of appearance in the book:

Marianne Meehan, Entrepreneur, Strategy Consultant, and Business Mentor
Robert Chia, Professor of Management, Adam Smith Business School, University of Glasgow
Professor Bernie Bulkin, OBE, Professor of Chemistry, former Chief Scientist and senior executive at BP, venture capitalist, and radio broadcaster and columnist
Gordon Ramsay, Plant leader, P&G
Dick Howeson, CEO of uTalk
Alan Wright, Central Operations Director, Arcus
Julie Moret, Head of ESG, Franklin Templeton
Dr Ibrahim Saif, CEO of the Jordan Strategy Forum
David McGinley, Group Managing Director for A&P Group
Kieran Phelan, Global Sustainability and Compliance Director, William Grant & Sons
Ned Phillips, Founder and CEO, Bambu
Fiona Logan, CEO, Insights
Terry A'Hearn, CEO, SEPA
Kathryn Kerle, Chair of Greater London Mutual Limited (GLM)
Sam Smith, CEO of C-Change
Sandy Wilson, Independent Strategy Consultant, Educator, and Executive Coach
Ann-Maree Morrison, Business Owner and Chair, Women in Enterprise, Scotland
Tariq Ibrahim, Strategy Consultant, Oman
Dr Steve Graham, CEO, Royal College of Physicians and Surgeons
Catherine Tilley, Former Director of Operations at the Strategy & Trend Analysis Centre, McKinsey
Aileen McLeod, Head of Business Planning, Commercial and Performance, Transmission at SSE plc

And finally, many thanks to our student panellists who also provided insightful feedback on draft chapter material and our Process–Practice Framework of Strategy.

PREFACE

Dear Reader

Thanks for picking up *Strategy: Theory, Practice, Implementation*! In the crowded market for strategy textbooks, we appreciate that you have identified with our aim of helping students to think, talk, and act like strategists.

Our approach to writing this book has emerged from our shared experiences in teaching, consulting, researching, and leading strategy work in different settings. In particular, we noticed a gap between the formal theoretical approaches to strategy typically taught at undergraduate and postgraduate levels and the practices and processes of strategy adopted by organizational practitioners. It may be that those we were working with had internalized previously studied theoretical frameworks, or that through practice and experience they had developed an ability to think strategically without making an explicit reference to theoretical constructs in their work. Our feeling though was that there was a missing 'middle ground' in which the realities of addressing strategic issues and opportunities could be connected with the theories that can help frame, explain, and resolve strategy challenges in an effective way.

Responding to strategic problems, issues, and opportunities always involves decision-making. However, in practice, the assumptions of rationality and decision-making conditions that we know from economics often bear little resemblance to what takes place on the ground. Strategists commonly have to operate in complex, dynamic environments, making decisions with limited information under conditions of uncertainty and ambiguity. In such situations the optimal way forward may not be knowable, and decisions may be subject to managerial biases and political motivations. Rather than rational derivation of clear plans, strategy becomes a continuing process of negotiation, (re)action, interpretation, and learning. How this is continually enacted by practitioners—over time, in context, using practices, tools, and activities—is the focus of this book.

In adopting this view of strategy, we believe that this book has several distinct features. Firstly, what people do and experience in strategy is a recurring focus in each chapter, to set a platform for learning about how strategy happens in a range of settings and situations. We believe that this is a key aspect of developing knowledge, skills, and behaviours in strategy that enhance student employability—graduate practical abilities are high on the agenda for most potential employers! Further, there is a burgeoning body of strategy process and practice theory with which we wanted to connect, share, and exemplify.

To meet our aim of developing students' abilities to think, talk, and act as effective strategy practitioners we have shaped the latest strategy theory into a 'process–practice' framework which draws all elements of the book together. To bring the process–practice framework to life, we have covered classic strategy topics that will allow you to deepen your knowledge of scholarly thought and discuss and collaborate with students and practitioners of strategy from around the world. Equally, we have embraced topics of high relevance to contemporary strategy, such as the opportunities and threats associated with trends in digital transformation and platform innovation, sustainable development and growth, and internationalization and globalization. We have included a diverse set of case examples from all manner of industries and from all continents, and from public sector and third-sector organizations alongside private firms large and small. For each case, we have asked a range of questions to test and extend your thinking on what people actually do in strategy, and how theory can be used to interrogate practice.

A further distinctive feature of the book is the extent to which we have placed the practitioner at the centre of the strategy-making and strategic decision-making processes. In each chapter, in addition to theory and case examples we include a 'practitioner perspective'—an unvarnished view of how strategy is implemented in practice from an experienced individual's unique history. There is a written summary in each chapter and an accompanying video interview in the online resources. The practitioners have a wide range of backgrounds and identities, and we have represented their views exactly as they expressed them. Whilst we have tried to select practitioners with an interest in the topic addressed in each chapter, they all also offer general insights about their own theories-in-use of strategy practice. This extensive engagement with practitioners is a unique feature of this book. Emphasizing human action in strategic management draws widely from the work of some of the greatest minds of management, economics, psychology, managerial cognition, behavioural and evolutionary economics, decision-making, and strategizing activities and practices literature. We are excited about the potential of these practitioner resources to support learning for students who have yet to gain strategy experience or those looking to broaden their perspectives as to what really happens in strategy practice. For colleagues designing strategy modules, we are equally looking forward to learning about—and possibly collaborating on—innovative teaching and pedagogical applications of these resources to meet the needs and interests of the modern strategy student.

We have also developed what we believe are the most comprehensive method guides available for the application of mainstream theories of strategy and common strategy tools (and a few lesser known approaches too!). We have engaged with methods or theories in such a way that you should be able to interpret, explain, or do the work of strategy differently as an outcome of reading each chapter. We had previously found ourselves drawing such guides out for students at all levels during courses without a reference text to support them. These guides should allow you to build confidence and capabilities in the application of well-established views of strategy as a platform to then engaging with more specialized and nuanced considerations in the field. We have used all the method guides reported in the chapters in consultancy practice, in teaching, and even in our own companies or business activities. However, we have tried to write them in such a way that they are a non-prescriptive starting point for undertaking strategy work. Our wish is that students and teachers can creatively 'make the tools their own' according to personal preference and the needs of the situations they face.

Indeed, throughout the book we have attempted to engage with strategy as a 'situated' activity. For us, this means that how strategy is best understood, approached, and enacted will depend on the history and circumstances of those involved. Thus we have written about how strategy 'might be', rather than what strategy 'is', in order that the student can engage in, or the tutor facilitate, learning about strategy that embodies their own interests and experiences. To support this personal engagement with the subject, we present a wide range of relevant theories and how they might be useful in practice, case examples to provoke enquiry and reflection, and practitioner perspectives as examples of how others grapple with the subject matter.

We start the book by offering multiple interpretations of what strategy might mean, whilst resisting firm commitment to any particular definition, and conclude by describing multiple ways in which you can continue your own unique lifelong learning journey about strategy-in-practice through reflection. For colleagues, whilst we lean towards pedagogies that help students build deep process and practice understanding, we have endeavoured to write in an open way which means that you can adopt chapter combinations and interpretations of the text that fit the needs of your teaching philosophy.

We hope you enjoy using the book, exploring the online resources, and of course trying to apply the learning. Good luck in your journey to think, talk, and act like a strategist!

The Author Team, July 2019

GUIDE TO THE BOOK

LEARNING OBJECTIVES

- A list of clear outcomes, using key terms from the chapter, indicates what you can expect to learn
- You can use this list to navigate the chapter content, making your learning experience focused and efficient.

TOOLBOX

- Key concepts, theories, frameworks, and models are highlighted in this feature and accompanied by short annotations to help you build your knowledge of strategic tools.
- This very practical feature also provides a handy revision resource for later study.

OPENING CASE STUDY

Based on a range of small, medium, and large organizations across a variety of sectors and geographies, this feature opens each chapter to set the scene. Carefully-paced questions for discussion accompany the opening case, asking you to identify the key themes and critically consider the strategy discussed as you progress through the chapter.

CASE EXAMPLES

Shorter case vignettes within the chapter focus on key concepts and also cover a vast range of organizations. The case examples allow you to pause and consider how the illustration relates to the concepts discussed, and through further questions for discussion, help check your developing understanding of the topic or encourage you to discuss and debate with classmates.

PRACTITIONER INSIGHTS

Based on first-hand interviews with exceptional strategy experts from across the globe, practitioner insights provide you with unique insight into how the strategic tools and concepts discussed within the chapter are applied in the real world. These in-chapter interviews are accompanied by online video interviews with each practitioner.

CHAPTER SUMMARY

- Chapter summaries provide a brief outline of the important concepts to take away, helping you to consolidate your learning before you move on.
- They also contextualize each subject area within the bigger picture of the Process-Practice Model of Strategy.

END-OF-CHAPTER QUESTIONS

1. Recall questions and application questions enable you to remind yourself of the key points of the chapter, and then apply your knowledge to practise deeper strategic thinking.
2. Here you are encouraged to put yourself in the position of a professional, pick organizations you are interested in, and consider how you would think, talk, and act like a strategist in those scenarios.

FURTHER READING

Seminal and cutting-edge research is listed, along with brief annotations of each, to support you in reading beyond the chapter and to facilitate easy navigation of the key academic perspectives in the field.

Research Insights and more Further Reading references are provided online to further broaden your academic reading.

GUIDE TO THE ONLINE RESOURCES

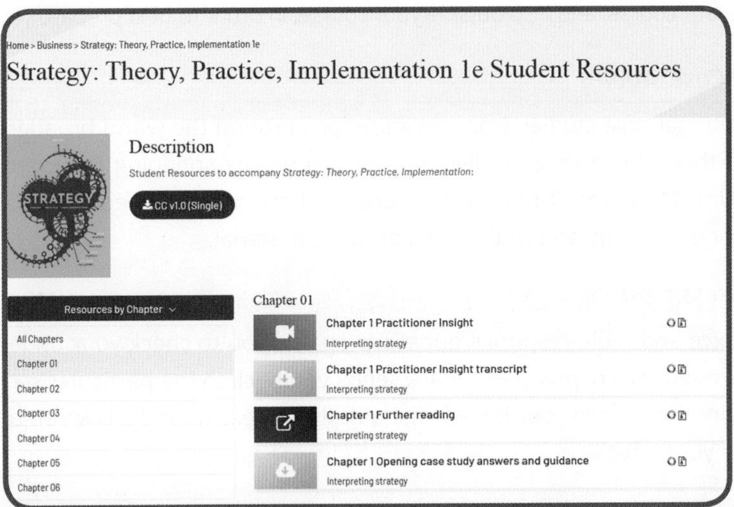

www.oup.com/he/mackay1e

For students

Enhanced eBook

An interactive version of the text includes selected online resources at your fingertips to enhance the learning experience. Accessible via a unique access code on the inside cover of the book, the enhanced eBook enables on-the-go assessment, video viewing, and further reading and research, all in one place.

Practitioner Insights

Uniquely filmed for this text, practitioner insight videos award students with an exciting glimpse into the world of professionals from a diverse range of organizations. Sixteen outstanding strategists talk about their experiences throughout their career in relation to the corresponding chapter topic. These videos offer deeper insight into the tools they use in their day-to-day working life and offer students the chance to examine the implementation of strategy theory in the professional world. Practitioner insights also provide a chance to appreciate how studying strategy will help support future careers, following in the footsteps of experts.

Research Insights

Abstracts for key pieces of research to accompany each chapter serve to broaden your perspective of the academic field, accompanied by author insights into how each paper can support your study. The research insights help support you to become the most well-rounded strategy graduates of the future, ensuring that the practice of strategy is balanced with academic rigour.

Career Insights

A bespoke video of each practitioner offering employability guidance, including skills you can develop throughout your course, and also outside your course, in order to best prepare you for your career.

Additional Case Studies

Sixteen additional case studies from organizations around the world broaden students' learning even further. These case studies include companies spanning five continents, including Deliveroo, Uniqlo, Thomas Cook, and BritBox, and are accompanied with learning outcomes, questions for discussion, and multimedia ancillary material.

Student Assessment

Multiple-choice and multi-response questions enable you to check your understanding as you progress through the chapters. Feedback sends you back to the particular section of the chapter to pinpoint the gaps in your knowledge quickly and easily, and allow you to revisit the topic according to your needs.

Further Reading

Additional further reading recommendations ensure you are well-informed as you refine your own strategic thinking beyond the text.

Flashcard Glossary

Key terms and phrases are provided in a flashcard glossary to quickly test understanding.

For lecturers

Teaching Notes for In-Chapter Opening Cases and Case Examples

Teaching ideas for class work using the Opening Case Studies and Case Examples in each chapter. Potential approaches to the Questions for discussion that accompany each Opening Case and Case Example in the book are also included.

PowerPoint Teaching slides

PowerPoint slides for lecturers support teaching by providing all the tables and figures in a presentation-style suite of slides.

Teaching Notes to accompany additional case studies

Teaching notes and suggested approaches to answering the questions for discussion in class, to accompany each additional online case study.

Test Bank

Additional assessment is provided in the tutor test bank.

Boardroom Challenge, including Teaching Notes

CONTENTS

DETAILED CONTENTS

OPENING CASES, CASE EXAMPLES, AND PRACTITIONER INSIGHTS

FIGURES

TABLES

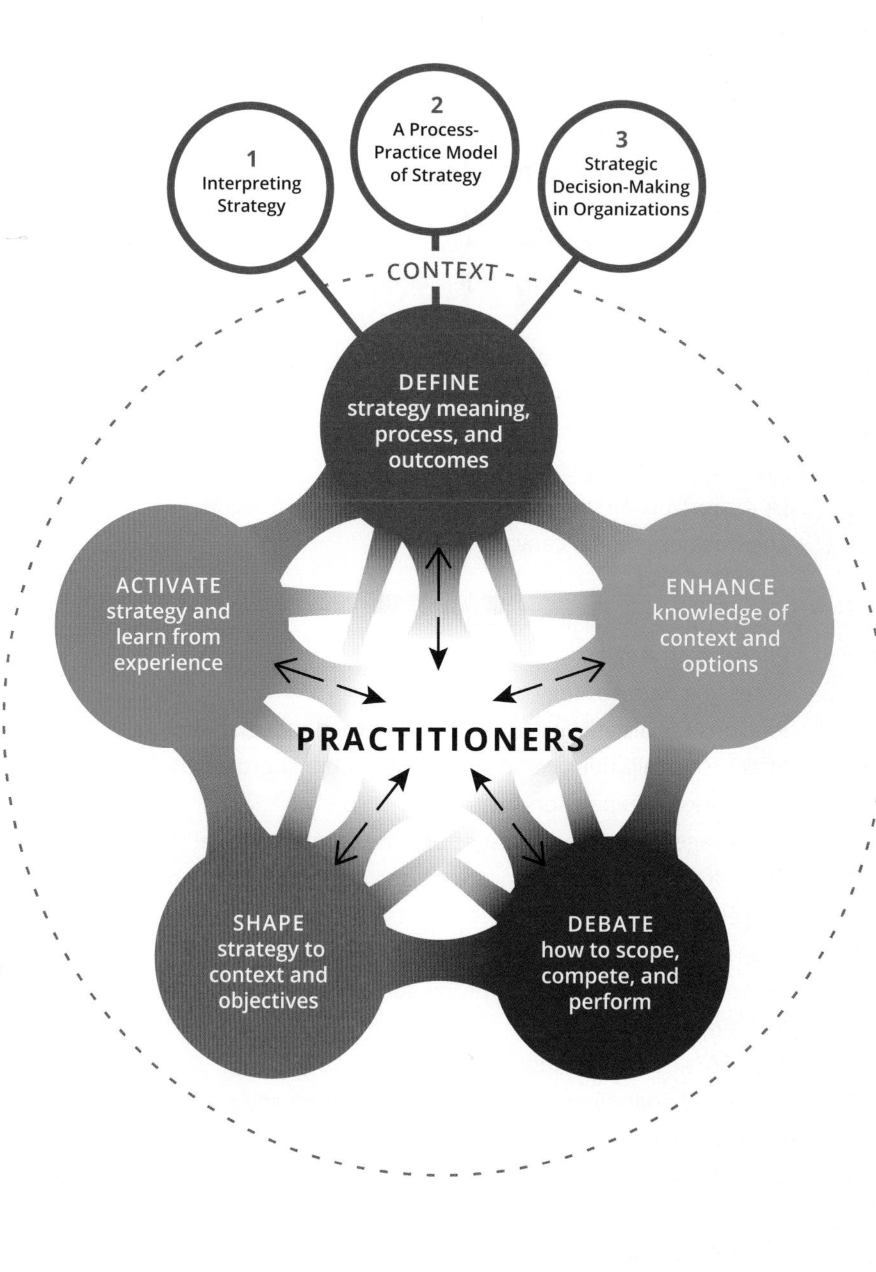

1
Interpreting Strategy
2
A Process-Practice Model of Strategy
3
Strategic Decision-Making in Organizations
CONTEXT
DEFINE
strategy meaning, process, and outcomes
ACTIVATE
strategy and learn from experience
ENHANCE
knowledge of context and options
PRACTITIONERS
SHAPE
strategy to context and objectives
DEBATE
how to scope, compete, and perform

PART ONE

Define strategy meaning, process, and outcomes

We start by addressing how you can clarify and agree what strategy means to those involved and identify related appropriate approaches to strategy activity and decision-making. To build your understanding and vocabulary, in Chapter 1 we introduce a wide range of interpretations of strategy you might encounter, in Chapter 2 we examine process and practice theories and how they might be used in combination to explain activity, and in Chapter 3 we review decision-making theories of high relevance to strategy work. To support your capacity to apply these insights, Chapter 1 describes a method for agreeing what strategy means to those involved, Chapter 2 offers frameworks for selecting categories of strategy activity that can drive progress, and Chapter 3 shows how you can adopt decision-making principles—as individuals or groups—that match the needs of any situation you face.

By the end of Part 1, you should have enhanced abilities to think, talk, and act like a practitioner, defining strategy meaning, approaches, and outcomes.

CHAPTER ONE

Interpreting Strategy

CONTENTS

1

LEARNING OBJECTIVES

By the end of this chapter, you should be able to:

- Explain how strategy can be interpreted in multiple ways
- Comprehend the challenges and benefits of agreeing a shared understanding of strategy with key stakeholders
- Critically assess the usefulness of strategy in different organizational situations and from different stakeholder perspectives
- Appreciate the value of strategy as a mechanism for coordinating organizational effort and decision-making
- Apply a simple mechanism for clarifying how strategy is interpreted within and between stakeholder groups

TOOL BOX

- **12Ps of strategy**
  A framework that highlights different ways in which strategy might be interpreted. Provides a method to discuss and explore what strategy means to stakeholders in different settings.
- **Strategy scoping method**
  A method to support structured discussion and clarification of shared meaning of strategy between stakeholders in any given context.

1.1 Introduction

Strategy is a mainstay in the management of organizational, civic, and personal life. It is rare to find an organization that doesn't have a strategy either explicitly or implicitly. Further, at a country level, industrial strategies abound that are intended to grow the economies and productivity of nations. Companies vie to help us develop personal financial strategies to save for later life. And the role of political strategies in determining the outcome of elections and influencing public opinion is becoming increasingly important, to cite just a few examples.

Yet for all its widespread usage, the meaning of the term strategy is hard to pin down. As we will explore, strategy can be interpreted in many ways according to the experience and perspective of individuals. The academics, consultants, gurus, and practitioners jostling to advise organizations rarely agree on the definition or even the nature of strategy. If you ask ten people what they mean by strategy, you will likely receive ten different explanations! According to historian Sir Lawrence Freedman (2013:ch. 1), **strategy** defies precise definition yet is the best word we have to describe efforts to:

> *'maintain a balance between ends, ways and means'; 'identifying objectives and the resources and methods available for meeting such objectives' within the context of the 'drama and challenge' of the 'inherent unpredictability of human affairs'.*

This lack of clear definition of strategy presents us with a fundamental issue. When working with others in the development and implementation of strategy, how can we be sure that we hold compatible views about what strategy means? And how can we know we are working towards the same outcomes if we understand strategy differently?

Relatedly, there are varied opinions as to the value of strategy. Strategy theoretically provides us with a way of coordinating activities, messages, and decisions across groups of individuals towards achieving shared long-term aims. However, these outcomes assume that when presented with a strategy, all individuals will be ready, willing, and able to interpret that strategy consistently, and enact it without error. When the volatility, uncertainty, ambiguity, and complexity (VUCA) of our ever-changing context is factored in (see Frynas et al. 2018), the question does arise as to how valuable strategy might be for individuals, organizations, institutions, or nations.

Given these challenges, to explain how strategy can benefit an organization we will focus on examining strategy practice—what is actually done—and strategy process—how activities relating to strategy occur in context and over time. To do so requires us to consider the role of people—their knowledge, abilities, and behaviours—and the way in which the flow of strategy work might occur. As Henry Mintzberg (Mintzberg and Hunsicker 1988:73) notes, 'to manage strategy is to craft thought and action, control and learning, stability and change'.

Our intention here is to create a reference text which enables the application of what we know about strategy from research to how it might occur in practice. For students in a classroom setting, the book will give insights about how to think, talk, and act like a strategist. Drawing on the methods from across the chapters you will be able to build your skills in undertaking meaningful strategy analysis and recommendations as suits your future needs when faced with real-world situations.

In this opening chapter, we review what strategy might mean to **stakeholders**—those individuals or groups affected by, and with the power to influence, strategy. By building awareness of possible interpretations of strategy, you will be equipped to discuss strategy with others regardless of their perspective. Stakeholder views can then be reconciled through collective conversation to express a shared meaning of strategy that meets the needs of a situation. In being able to lead this sort of 'strategy scoping' work in your future career, you become able to move from telling others what strategy 'is'—its meaning, form, function, and outputs—to enabling a group to agree and activate strategy work in a way that fits their needs.

To aid you in this task, after introducing a range of concepts and interpretations of strategy, we introduce a strategy scoping method (see the Tool Box for an explanation of this) that can help you initiate strategy conversations and shared meaning making. By the conclusion of this chapter, you should be aware of a range of ways in which strategy might be understood, discussed, or enacted.

1.2 Strategy in modern organizations

Entire books have been written about the history of strategy and the development of approaches to strategy in different parts of the world (for instance, Freedman (2013) and Jullien (2004) as recommended at the end of this chapter). Indeed, writing on strategy dates back millennia, with early treatises such as the *Art of War*, attributed to the Chinese military strategist Sun Tzu some 2500 years ago, and *How to Survive Under Siege*, written by the Greek writer Aeneas Tacticus around 2400 years ago.

To set the scene for examining current interpretations of strategy, we will review how the usage of strategy has evolved in modern organizations (see Mackay and Zundel (2017) for a further examination of how concepts of strategy and tactics have developed from various influences). Whilst the historical roots of the word strategy itself can be traced to the military and political position in Ancient Athens of *strategos*, and the Athenian war council known as *strategoi* in about 500 BCE (Cummings 1993), we focus here on describing the changing ways in which strategy has been part of organizational life in recent decades. Thereafter, we review the benefits that different 'types' of strategy are expected to bring to an organization.

The evolving use of strategy

Strategy as a focus of management interest in modern business life came to the fore in the 1960s. Prior to this time, annual financial reviews and budgeting activities were the main planning activities in an organization. Since then, however, strategy as a management interest and consultancy industry mainstay has blossomed.

According to Pettigrew et al. (2006), the modern usage of the term strategy in organizational management has its foundations in academic and consultancy practice from the United States. Work by US academics such as Alfred Chandler, Kenneth Andrews, and Igor Ansoff did much to establish the modern usage of the concept of strategy. In the 1960s, on both sides of the Atlantic, specific ideas of strategy started to enter business school teaching and research, a trend which increasingly gathered pace until a focus on strategy emerged as a stand-alone discipline from business policy in the late 1970s.

In early incarnations of strategy, it was associated with the formulation of rational plans, policies, and organizational designs intended to deliver long-term business performance. This concept of strategy was catalysed by the emergence of US consultancy firms—such as McKinsey and the Boston Consulting Group—specializing in developing tools, terminology, and managerial support for rational analytical strategy work. These consultancy firms rapidly grew outside the United States, exporting the emerging concept of strategy as an elaborately planned procedure around the world.

Through the 1970s and 1980s, the academic and practitioner strategy communities turned more towards the ideas of industrial economics and organization (I/O), as exemplified by the work of Michael Porter (1980, 1984) in developing further tools and concepts. These ideas stemmed originally from industrial economists grappling with a concern of how large organizations achieve monopoly positions. Porter's key insight was to turn this concern on its head, arguing that in competitive environments the strategies employed by such organizations can form the bases of competitive strategy. This brought into focus the idea of **competitive advantage**—the capacity to outperform competitors—based on the relationship between industry structure, organizations' conduct, and superior financial performance. Strategy became associated with analysis of environmental conditions and the adoption of a defensive and profitable market 'position' in which the organization might outperform its competitors—known as the **'market-based' view (MBV)** of strategy.

The market-based view was augmented in the 1980s by the **resource-based view (RBV)**, becoming the dominant research focus in the 1990s. Finding its roots in the work of the American-born British economist Edith Penrose (1959), from an RBV perspective competitive advantage is understood to arise from possessing distinctive bundles of resources that can be used to create outcomes valued by customers. In essence, organizations that have resources which are relatively rare, difficult to imitate, and can be used to create outcomes valued by customers will have an advantage over their competitors lacking such resources. According to the RBV, strategy is about identifying unique value-creating resources—which are difficult to replicate and at the organization's disposal—and organizing effectively to exploit them and deliver superior performance. An overview of the MBV and the RBV is presented in Table 1.1. In Chapters 5 and 6, we will examine in depth how these influential views of strategy can be put into practice.

In one sense, the MBV and the RBV are complementary as it is beneficial to understand both the external context and the resource base of the organization during strategy work. In another sense, the MBV and the RBV both examine the world from a 'rational' perspective and thus have shared limitations. Through the 1970s and 1980s, widespread adoption of these economics-grounded works into MBA teaching and consultancy practice meant that strategy as a rational business planning activity became further promoted in management language and literature.

A significant limitation of analytical planning approaches typified by the RBV and MBV is that human aspects of strategy are marginalized (Bartlett and Ghoshal 1994). By underplaying the role of **agency**—the ability of humans to be creative and exhibit independently minded choice—purely analytical theories of strategy don't necessarily match practice (see Franco-Santos et al. 2017). In reaction to this missing human factor, academic enquiry into 'process' aspects of how

TABLE 1.1 **A brief comparison of market-based and resource-based views**

	Market-based view	Resource based view
Means	Organizational conduct in the external environment can create competitive advantage	Configuration of distinctive and ordinary resources can create competitive advantage
Also known as	The 'outside-in' approach—making decisions based on external factors	The 'inside-out' approach—organizing internal factors to create external value
Important concepts	Macro trends Industry structure Market position Competitor activities Organizational conduct	Resource base Configuration / bundles Distinctiveness Capabilities Value creation
Benefits	Generates deep insights about the current and future external context	Helps better exploit what the organization already has available
Limitations	Based on assumption that market position is a matter of choice—not always possible to react to external context in an ideal way	Having resources and being able to organize to exploit them does not necessarily create benefits—value is determined by external factors

strategy is made and managed in practice emerged in the mid-1980s. To varying degrees, **process studies** address how human factors, such as errors, learning, culture, habit, power, and politics, play a role in how strategy happens. Process studies examine how, over time, strategy happens through the activities and approaches of fallible human beings operating within a complex and ever-changing world (e.g. MacKay and Chia 2013). As Mintzberg and Waters (1985) observe, what is realized through strategy is a product of deliberate and emergent activity. This means that strategy is a combination of what is planned, how those involved decide to act, and what the changing context enables.

Through the 1990s and 2000s, strategy theory and practice turned towards investigating how strategy might enable organizations to cope with competitive challenges and disruption arising from increasing globalization and accelerating technological advances (Kerr 2016). Consequently, topics such as internationalization, innovation, and collaboration have become increasingly intertwined with the strategy literature. Strategy studies and consultancy practice increasingly focused on how organizations might predict and cope with evolving contexts, preparing for the future by developing capacities for adaptability, agility, and entrepreneurship. Strategy as a practice that can be learned and improved through coaching, training, study, and reflection also emerged as a topic of significant interest.

Strategy theory and practice continue to evolve. At the time of writing, a contemporary focus on language, methods, and concepts of strategic resilience and sustainability permeate strategy journals and consultancy offerings. Topics such as **big data**—the vast volumes of information available to organizations—**digitalization**—taking action to benefit from digital technology—and **sustainability**—competing within the ecological limits of our planet—are at the fore for strategic managers in many organizations (e.g. Loonam et al. 2018). We address these contemporary themes in Part 4 of the book.

CASE EXAMPLE 1.1 OPEN SESAME! THE RISE OF ALIBABA

Alibaba is a giant of e-commerce in China and an increasing presence in internet trading activities around the world. Founded in 1998 in Hangzhou, China, by Jack Ma and 18 collaborators, from humble beginnings Alibaba has experienced rapid growth.

Like Uber with ride-hailing and Airbnb with accommodation services, Alibaba is an internet platform company which doesn't stock any products. Instead, Alibaba provides a virtual marketplace for safe, reliable, and direct transactions between customers and businesses of any size or type. On its basic service, there is no charge to businesses selling on Alibaba's platform. Instead, the Alibaba.com site makes money by selling targeted advertising space, exploiting Alibaba's data analytics capabilities and customer information. To maximize its revenue from advertisers, growing and maintaining the biggest user base possible is an important focus for the organization.

The Alibaba Group also operates a range of companies supporting user needs on the platform which do charge for their services. Additional Alibaba Group commercial offerings include secure payments, financial services, distribution, and cloud computing services. In combination, this eco-system of companies creates conditions in which it is easy for all different types of user to transact.

Alibaba Group sums up its mission as 'make it easy to do business anywhere' by allowing businesses to 'transform the way they market, sell and operate' through the provision of 'fundamental technology infrastructure and marketing reach'. Over the last 20 years, the effective implementation of this mission has richly rewarded Alibaba's owners and investors. In June 2017, Alibaba became the most valuable Asian company, and was placed within the top ten most valuable Fortune 500 firms. In the fiscal year ending 31 March 2019, Alibaba reported consolidated revenues of 376.8 billion yuan, an increase of 50.5% from 2017–18. This revenue was generated from an active user base of 443 million buyers on its marketplace, in which 75% of transactions were conducted on mobile devices. Key growth areas include Alibaba's cloud computing services, which recorded 104% year-on-year growth in 2017, and mobile-related services.

It is impossible to know for sure whether Alibaba will achieve its aim of existing for at least 102 years (a number picked to enable the claim of existing within the twentieth, twenty-first, and twenty-second centuries!). For now, Alibaba is taking many steps to diversify and grow operations to sustain its market leading e-commerce position. Focus areas include continuing to invest in technology and infrastructure in its operations, exploring international opportunities to reach new consumers, and searching for external organizations with which to partner or add to the Group. In building a varied network of related organizations—in China and abroad—it would seem that Alibaba is accumulating the resources and potential to survive and grow in the long term.

Questions for discussion

Based on the information above and considering the modern development of strategy:

1. How would you describe Alibaba's strategy?
2. What do you think different stakeholders—employees, shareholders, customers, trading partners—want from Alibaba's strategy?
3. What factors will influence what is 'in' the strategy at Alibaba?
4. How important is flexibility of strategy to a company like Alibaba? Explain your answer.

Sources

Alibaba.com (2019) https://www.alibabagroup.com/en/about/overview (accessed 8 June 2019)

Banjo, S. and Ramli, D. (2018) https://www.bloomberg.com/news/articles/2018-04-02/alibaba-buys-ele-me-in-deal-that-implies-9-5b-enterprise-value (accessed 8 June 2019).

Hahn, L. (2018) https://investorplace.com/2018/03/alibaba-stock-india-expansion/ (accessed 8 June 2019).

Hsu, J.W. (2018) http://www.alizila.com/alibaba-invests-us2-billion-lazada-accelerate-regions-e-commerce/ (accessed 8 June 2019).

Jing, M. (2017) http://www.scmp.com/tech/enterprises/article/2097570/alibabas-market-value-soars-record-us360-billion-bullish-2018-sales (accessed 8 June 2019).

Statista.com (2019) https://www.statista.com/statistics/225614/net-revenue-of-alibaba/ (accessed 8 June 2019).

It is useful for you, as a student of strategy, to have a sense of the recent history of the concept. As you learn to think, talk, and act as a strategist, you will encounter concepts and theories arising from each of the time periods described. Knowing the context in which the tool or theory was developed will help you understand how to use it, and its limitation or benefits. Older tools and theories are still in use, as new developments in the field have tended to add to, rather than replace, the pool of methods and concepts used in strategy (Vuorinen et al. 2018). Thus, strategy is a field of interest with multiple, competing interpretations of the central concept and methods (Seidl 2007). As you study strategy, becoming conversant with a wide variety of tools and theories will increase your capacity to engage with stakeholders of all backgrounds and perspectives in undertaking strategy work.

It is also worth noting that as the field has developed, strategy has been subject to recurring criticisms (see Farjoun 2007; Barnett 2016). Strategy literature and consultancy advice is often observed to be overly positive in outlook. The potential for failure, and the practical limitations and consequences of strategy approaches, are frequently understated—putting pressure on practitioners to achieve ideal outcomes that may not be possible. As a subject area, strategy is regularly identified as being subject to fads and fashions, as previous methods are discarded for the latest solution or remedy that rewards originators and innovators. Over time, cynicism and change weariness about the latest and greatest way of making strategy takes hold. And where it doesn't, slavish adherence to single ways of making, managing, or researching strategy limit the possibilities of strategy effectiveness. We will attempt to address this matter by offering critical summaries of bodies of strategy literature, highlighting limitations of concepts and theories, exemplifying practical challenges with case illustrations and possible alternative perspectives. You can play your part too, by engaging with the questions throughout and at the end of chapters to challenge your thinking about what strategy means and how useful it might be in practice.

Strategy in organizational life has evolved in the last 60 years into a complex field which the strategist must navigate and take others with them whilst doing so. However, this challenging set of circumstances is also a major source of opportunity for you as a student. Throughout this book, we will cover many of the themes, theories, and methods that have accrued over the years in strategy academia and practice. With awareness of the rich options available for how to engage with strategy, you will be able to progress your own capabilities in thinking, talking, and (in your future careers) acting as a strategist in an effective and flexible way.

1.3 Expectations of strategy in organizations

We have discussed how the use of the term 'strategy' has evolved. But what does strategy mean in the context of organizations today? And in what ways does strategy benefit an organization? To provide a grounding for examining interpretations of strategy in the following section, we first explain the different types and anticipated benefits of strategy you may encounter. Being aware of these common categories and expectations will help you interpret the strategy literature and engage in debate about what strategy might mean.

Organizational strategy

Our focus is on strategy theory and practice as it might be applied in organizations. Arguably the core long-term aim of any organization is to survive (Poulis and Poulis 2016) and preferably thrive. This survival can happen when, over the long term, the organization is able to create value for stakeholders in a way which is less than the cost of doing so. Adapting the high-level description of strategy from the chapter introduction:

> **Organizational strategy** *is about maintaining a balance between ends, ways, and means of surviving and thriving—providing a framework for making choices and trade-offs; and identifying resources, methods, actions, and value-creating objectives that sustain the organization over time within an ever-changing context.*

When we describe organizational strategy, we refer to ongoing efforts to act and react in a way that secures organizational survival. Whilst growth is often a key additional aim (i.e. survive and grow), it is worth noting that not every organization seeks to grow. For many owner–managers of 'lifestyle' businesses (where the organization exists to suit the owner's needs), growth would change the nature and purpose of their organization (Kammerlander and Ganter 2015). Organizational strategy, then, is closely related to organizational purpose. Many public and third-sector organizations, for instance, do not pursue a growth agenda either, instead seeking to deliver a specific mandate within the context of the resources available to them. Organizational strategy is no less valuable in these non-profit-focused settings.

Corporate, business, and functional strategy types

There are many ways in which types of organizational strategy can be explained and discussed. Three important types of strategy are corporate, business, and functional strategy.

Corporate strategy addresses the question of 'where to operate?'—identifying the industrial sectors and locations in which an organization will focus its energy and efforts. Corporate strategy can be used to articulate the intended scope of the whole organization. With this scope, an appropriate organizational structure can be implemented and reporting lines, finance/resource flows, and physical locations identified. Referring to Case Example 1.1, Alibaba's decision to expand internationally (geographical scope) is a corporate strategy decision, as is the decision to enter the logistics and distribution sector (sectoral scope).

Business strategy addresses the question of 'how to meet customer needs?' to gain an advantage over competitors in selected geographies and sectors. For example, Alibaba's decision to provide its main platform free of charge to users for the basic service, but to charge advertisers to reach customers, is a business strategy decision intended to give the organization a competitive advantage over its rivals. Jack Ma, the ex-CEO of Alibaba, identifies this business strategy decision as one of the key reasons why Alibaba was able to effectively drive eBay (who charged a transaction fee to customers) from the Chinese market in 2004. This term applies beyond 'businesses' to public or third-sector organizations too as they compete for resources, funding, and attention whilst fulfilling a societal need (e.g. Hansen and Jacobsen 2016).

Functional strategy addresses the question of 'how to operate?' in order to deliver an optimal contribution to corporate and business strategy from functions such as human resources, finance, and operations. Functional strategy balances efficiency gains from standardized working with a need for effective delivery of local functional needs determined by where and how an organization is in operation. For example, rather than standardize on one way of working, decisions about how to staff, locate, and invest in infrastructure for the high-growth cloud computing services division of Alibaba might be different from how the same decisions are taken in the heavily regulated financial services division.

The commonality between these categories is that strategy is about reading the organizational situation and identifying the 'best' options for purposeful action that might move towards specific desired outcomes. This purposeful action offers the promise of **efficacy**—achieving desired outcomes—and **efficiency**—achieving those outcomes with minimal use of resources.

The terms corporate, business, and functional strategy provide useful ways of talking about complementary aspects of organizational strategy. When we discuss corporate strategy, our attention is directed towards the markets and geographical locations in which the organization has the best fit, and the best way in which to structure the organization to reach those markets and locations. Within those markets, business strategy challenges us to find the most effective and cost-efficient ways to fulfil customer needs. And functional strategy organizes resources in order to best deliver business and corporate strategy aims.

Whilst each type of strategy can be planned separately, better overall outcomes might be realized when they are considered as part of an organizational strategy system (Figure 1.1). This means that corporate, business, and functional strategy are related, each creating possibilities and limitations for the rest of the system (Sull et al. 2018a). For example, a change in corporate strategy may require an amendment to functional strategy; a change in functional strategy may open up new possibilities for business strategy, etc. Being aware of this system can help you understand organizational strategy in a holistic way. Equally, it enables you to critique the coherence of organizational strategy. If business strategy intentions are to move in a direction not supported by functional strategy, it is highly likely that business strategy initiatives will fail. Challenging the extent to which corporate, business, and functional strategies align is an important step when evaluating organizational strategy.

Anticipated benefits of organizational strategy

To produce and maintain organizational strategy takes (often significant) effort and attention from a wide range of stakeholders. Why would an organization incur this cost? Quite simply, organizational strategy is understood to provide performance benefits that outweigh the costs involved. Organizational strategy offers the potential for enhanced managerial decision-making, resource

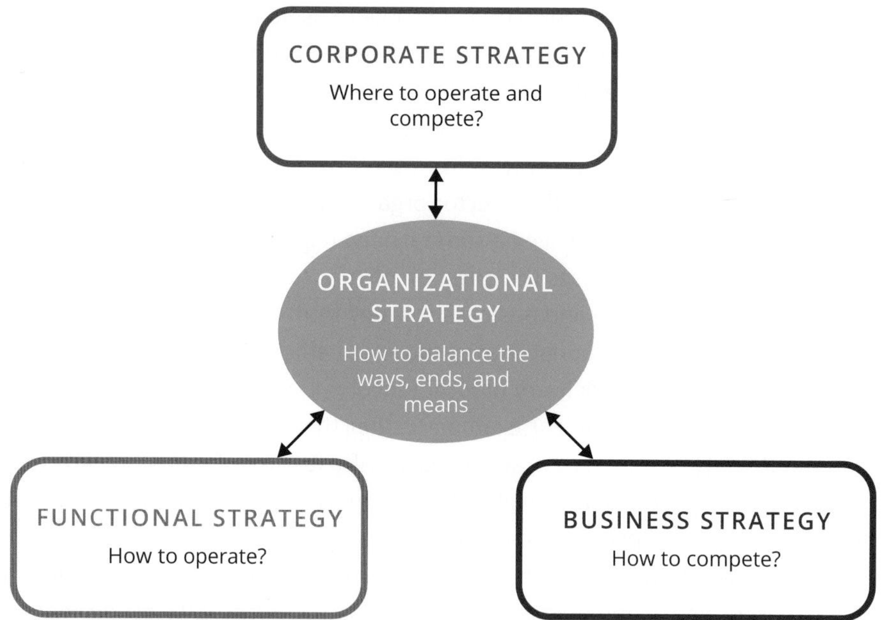

FIGURE 1.1 Components of organizational strategy.

deployment, stakeholder management, and coordinated action (Grant 2003). In turn, enhanced business performance enables the organization to survive, grow (if that is an aim), and prosper.

Managerial decision-making

Strategy can act as a set of boundaries which guide managerial decision-making. Imagine that the Alibaba Group is presented with the opportunity to purchase a logistics firm in Spain, an innovative digital marketing firm in China, or a highly profitable manufacturer of oil and gas products in Brazil. Which of these, if any, should Alibaba pursue? Organizational strategy provides a decision-making mechanism and frame of reference with which to evaluate and, if required, choose between available options (see Chapter 3).

Resource deployment

Strategy provides a blueprint for the deployment of organizational resources. Once decisions are made about where and how to operate, resources can then be deployed in a focused way to try to deliver those decisions. For example, Alibaba's investment of financial resources in automated warehousing technology makes sense as a means by which to deliver logistics revenue, and support platform operations, whilst delivering long-term efficiencies that best ensure organizational survival and growth.

Stakeholder management

Strategy acts as a social and a political tool to manage and engage stakeholders. Having a strategy allows communication, engagement, and the building of shared meaning about its current and future activities with all those who might have a stake in the organization (e.g. employees, suppliers, local community, investors, customers, etc.). Having a clear, articulated strategy creates a sense that the organization is competent and well managed. A published strategy

CASE EXAMPLE 1.2 **STRATEGY FOR TRANSPORT FOR LONDON**

Transport for London (TfL) is the integrated transport authority responsible for meeting the Mayor of London's transport strategy and promises. Employing c.27,500 people, TfL runs London's public transport network and main road systems, handling 31 million separate journey segments across the network daily. The organization aims to 'do all we can to keep the city moving, working and growing and to make life in our city better'.

Covering the 1569 km^2 of Greater London, TfL operates a vast transport network which includes the London Underground, London Buses, Docklands Light Railway, London Overground, TfL Rail, London Trams, London River Services, London Dial-a-Ride, Victoria Coach Station, Santander Cycles, and the Emirates Air Line (cable car). It has a long-term mission, guided by the *Mayor's Transport Strategy*, to work towards 80% of all journeys being made on foot, by cycle, or using public transport by 2041.

The organization's £10.4bn annual budget comes from four main funding sources: fares income (47%), grants (33%), other income such as congestion charging (12%), and borrowing (8%) (based on the profile for 2018). Funding is deployed by an extended management team in line with TfL's strategy, overseen by a board of governors.

TFL's strategy identifies a shared focus for the organization entitled the 'Healthy Streets Approach'—this operating philosophy aims to improve Londoners' health and their quality of life, clean up the city's air and enhance its environment, reconnect communities, and help provide new homes and jobs in places that work well for people.

The organizational strategy details how, over a time horizon to 2041, TfL will 'change the transport mix across London, providing viable and attractive alternatives that will allow Londoners to reduce their dependence on cars'. According to Mayor Sadiq Khan, this 'aim is simple but ambitious, and has important implications for our streets, public places and future growth as a city'. Valerie Shawcross CBE, Deputy Mayor for Transport, further comments that to deliver the strategy 'is a big ask and achieving it won't be easy ... TfL and its partners will need to change the way they operate, making every decision with this strategy in mind'.

TfL continues to innovate its operations and undertake strategic initiatives to deliver the 2041 objectives. It is engaged in a number of projects exploring how journeys can be made easier through the application of technology and data-based operations. Partnering with technology firms, live travel information drives apps and in-network timetabling and journey planning services. The use of accessible low-friction payment systems, such as Oyster and contactless, are constantly being upgraded to help move locals and tourists around London more easily. TfL is also implementing one of the world's largest capital investment portfolios. It is building the Elizabeth Line, modernizing Tube services and stations, transforming the road network, and investing in safety infrastructure to protect vulnerable road users such as pedestrians and cyclists.

TfL's latest strategy document—published in 2018—was developed by a consultative process involving TfL staff, board members, multiple partner organizations, and 'thousands of Londoners who took the time to comment on the draft document'. The document is also interwoven with insights and evidence drawn from an extensive bank of research data, presented in full in an online repository. The strategy narrative includes explanation of decisions and visualization methods (such as maps and charts) to communicate rationale.

The main organizational strategy document is supported by a series of action plans addressing functional areas of TfL responsibility or strategic concerns (e.g. freight and servicing action plan, zero deaths or serious injury action plan, etc.). These plans outline initiatives and actions that must target a contribution to the aims of the main strategy. The organizational strategy also informs the boundaries and content of policy and business plans for TfL's organizational units.

TfL's strategy is seen as vital to the future prosperity of London, and the mayor's vision for 'a fairer, greener, healthier and more prosperous city'. Through the coordinated activity of TfL's workforce and partner network, how well the

Continued

strategy is delivered will go a long way towards determining if citizens in 2041 have access to 'active, efficient and sustainable transport choices that support the health and wellbeing of Londoners, but also the city as a whole by reducing congestion and enabling the most efficient use of valuable street space'.

Questions for discussion

1. Summarize the strategic objectives for TfL and explain how the initiatives that are being undertaken will help deliver these objectives.
2. What value might the organizational strategy bring to TfL? How will having the document help the organization achieve its aims?
3. Why do you think the strategy was prepared in the way described? Why didn't the mayor just set a vision and plan himself?
4. In what ways is the organizational strategy apparently leading to coordination of effort amongst TfL stakeholders?

Sources

Mayor of London (2018) Mayor's Transport Strategy. https://www.london.gov.uk/what-we-do/transport/our-vision-transport/mayors-transport-strategy-2018 (accessed 8 June 2019).

TFL (2019) Travel in London Reports. https://tfl.gov.uk/corporate/publications-and-reports/travel-in-london-reports#mtsevidence (accessed 8 June 2019).

TFL (2019) How We Work. https://tfl.gov.uk/corporate/about-tfl/how-we-work (accessed 8 June 2019).

might also be required to unlock funding for organizations of all sizes and types. For example, without an appropriate strategy, it is unlikely that Alibaba would have achieved sufficient investor confidence to become the most valuable Asian company in June 2017.

Coordinated action

Strategy enables collaborative working between different functions, divisions, and locations of an organization. Through organizational strategy, it is in all stakeholders' interests that the best overall organizational performance is achieved. This can require optimal contribution, rather than maximized performance, from organizational 'components' such as divisions, business units, and teams. For example, organizational strategy might clarify how customer data gathered in the platform division of Alibaba is shared with other divisions—the platform division incurs a cost for this work which benefits other divisions, enhancing overall performance, even though the platform division's operating costs are not minimized.

These are high-level general benefits of organizational strategy. Throughout the book, we have included many examples of further benefits to an organization or individuals engaged in specific strategy activities.

1.4 **Interpretations of strategy**

When you work with strategy in practice in your future career, how strategy is understood by stakeholders in any given situation will be a key consideration for you as either a participant in, or a leader of, strategy activity. However, as identified earlier in this chapter, the field of strategy has evolved over the years to include many competing methods, concepts, and interpretations (Arend 2016).

So, how can strategy be understood in any given situation? How can we navigate through such a wide variety of interpretations? Mintzberg et al. (2009) note that whilst it is human nature to search for **the** definition of 'strategy', strategy—in their view—requires at least five different definitions—plan, pattern, perspective, position, and ploy. As shown in Figure 1.2, we have extended these interpretations to propose 12 possible components of strategy, based on our practical experience and themes we have detected in the academic and practitioner literature.

The 12 components describe what strategy can mean to different people, but not necessarily what it does mean to any individual nor what is relevant to any group of people in any given situation.

These interpretations are not mutually exclusive categories but rather strands of thinking that might be woven together into a customized view of strategy. For example, a colleague may hold a view that strategy is about defining **purpose** and setting an actionable **plan** for delivery through a clear organizational strategy **process**. This colleague may believe, with conviction, that this is how everyone understands strategy! They also may not have considered or be aware of further possible interpretations. For you as a student of strategy, being aware of a range of possible interpretations will increase your ability to engage stakeholders from different backgrounds and adapt your approach to strategy to suit the specific needs of a situation (Jalonen et al. 2018).

Each interpretation of strategy can be associated with a form of output and potential benefits to the organization. Also, each interpretation is subject to limitations in practice, of which it is helpful to be mindful. Further, certain conditions are required to be in place for each interpretation of strategy work to be undertaken effectively.

In the following sections we describe and explain each of the interpretations of strategy. Building on Case Example 1.2, we will draw on extracts from TfL strategy to illustrate how you might encounter each perspective in practice. In addition, we have provided supporting references and further reading for each of the Ps in a bibliography in the online resources, should you wish to dig further into any of the interpretations. For further detailed examples of how the perspectives appear in practice, you can refer to the 'practitioner insights' section at the end of each chapter (see also the practitioner videos in the **online resources**).

You will be able to use your knowledge of the 12Ps to analyse theories, concepts, and practitioner insights in the rest of the book, deepening your knowledge of how strategy might be understood in different settings. This approach should allow you to learn about and prepare to engage with strategy in practice, even if you have yet to acquire any practical experience yourself.

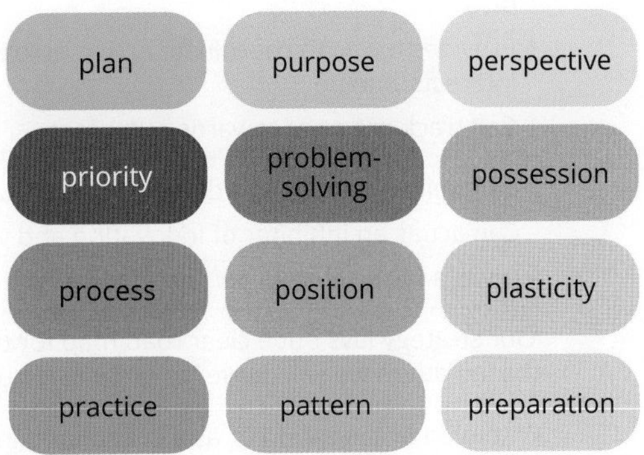

FIGURE 1.2 Interpretations of strategy.

Strategy as a plan

When asking students or practitioners 'What does strategy mean?', a common response is that strategy is a plan or roadmap for how to deliver target objectives with available resources. When subsequently asked 'Is every plan a strategy?', the answer is 'No'. Whilst strategy typically carries an implication, in part, of planning, strategy is also more than a simple plan. A strategic plan appears to be distinguished from daily plans of an operational nature by its all-encompassing (holistic) nature, a time horizon that is longer than regular operational considerations, and a foundation in a non-routine consideration of often complex circumstances (Arend et al. 2017).

As described in Table 1.2, strategy as a plan can act as a coordinating mechanism to guide the prescribed activities of individuals and teams towards common objectives. Those objectives need to be defined in order that this organizing effect can be achieved, and relevant activities identified and initiated. Plans need not be in any particular format or even written down. However, those leading strategy work in an organization should anticipate stakeholder expectations that there will be a component of strategy work or output that relates to planning. Strategic planning can also be a key mechanism for assuring external stakeholders, such as investors, that the organization is well run (e.g. Baginski et al. 2017).

Examples of strategy as a plan from the TfL document are shown in Figures 1.3 and 1.4. As can be seen, the format of strategic plans can be highly varied in terms of timescale, topic, categories, formats, and information embedded in the plan.

TABLE 1.2 **Strategy as a plan**

Strategy as ...	Plan
Interpretation	A deliberate course of action towards desired objectives
Function for the organization	Acts as a coordinating mechanism or guide to map out a path from where an individual/organization is today to where they/it wants to be in future
What is needed to work with this interpretation in practice	An articulation of what the end-points/objectives are In order to make a plan, you need to know where you are going There needs to be a sense of the constraints and resources available
Benefits	+ A commonly understood definition of strategy that is easy to discuss + Provides a way to coordinate action across a wide range of interests/people + Can track progress towards outcomes
Limitations	– Can quickly become outdated as circumstances change – Can act as an inhibitor of innovation and valuable opportunism – Gives a false sense of certainty/security
Might be expressed as ...	'Our strategy lays out a clear road map for the next three years, and the initiatives we will deliver to grow as a business'
When you are likely to encounter this interpretation	Within an organization or as a consultant; in any formal strategy exercise some sort of plan is normally expected as part of the outputs

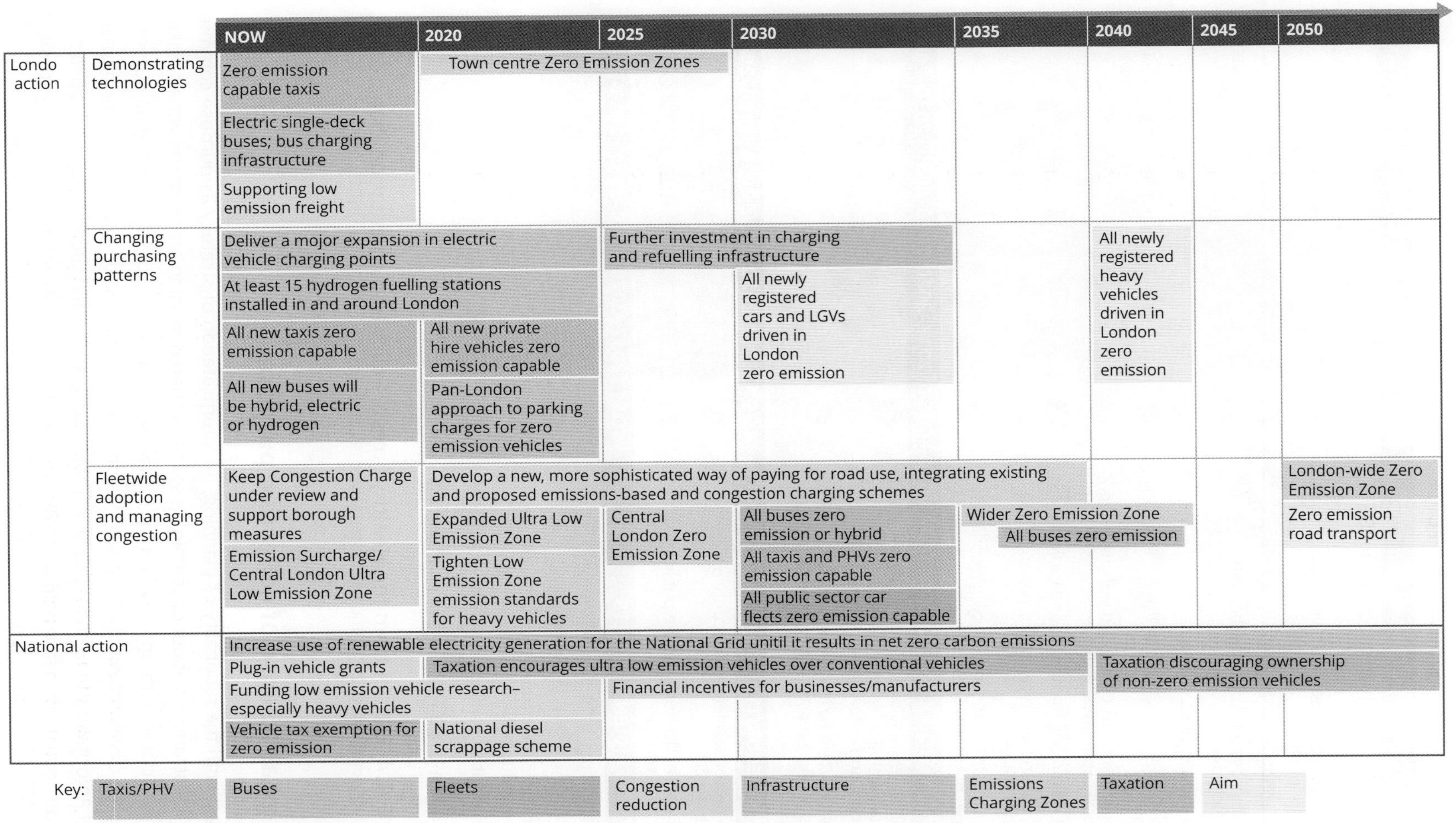

		NOW	2020	2025	2030	2035	2040	2045	2050
Londo action	Demonstrating technologies	Zero emission capable taxis	Town centre Zero Emission Zones						
		Electric single-deck buses; bus charging infrastructure							
		Supporting low emission freight							
	Changing purchasing patterns	Deliver a mojor expansion in electric vehicle charging points		Further investment in charging and refuelling infrastructure					
		At least 15 hydrogen fuelling stations installed in and around London			All newly registered cars and LGVs driven in London zero emission		All newly registered heavy vehicles driven in London zero emission		
		All new taxis zero emission capable	All new private hire vehicles zero emission capable						
		All new buses will be hybrid, electric or hydrogen	Pan-London approach to parking charges for zero emission vehicles						
	Fleetwide adoption and managing congestion	Keep Congestion Charge under review and support borough measures	Develop a new, more sophisticated way of paying for road use, integrating existing and proposed emissions-based and congestion charging schemes						London-wide Zero Emission Zone
			Expanded Ultra Low Emission Zone	Central London Zero Emission Zone	All buses zero emission or hybrid	Wider Zero Emission Zone			Zero emission road transport
		Emission Surcharge/ Central London Ultra Low Emission Zone	Tighten Low Emission Zone emission standards for heavy vehicles		All taxis and PHVs zero emission capable	All buses zero emission			
					All public sector car flects zero emission capable				
National action		Increase use of renewable electricity generation for the National Grid unitil it results in net zero carbon emissions							
		Plug-in vehicle grants	Taxation encourages ultra low emission vehicles over conventional vehicles				Taxation discouraging ownership of non-zero emission vehicles		
		Funding low emission vehicle research–especially heavy vehicles		Financial incentives for businesses/manufacturers					
		Vehicle tax exemption for zero emission	National diesel scrappage scheme						

Key: Taxis/PHV | Buses | Fleets | Congestion reduction | Infrastructure | Emissions Charging Zones | Taxation | Aim

Green key not present on original

FIGURE 1.3 Zero emission road transport plan. Source: Mayor's Transport Strategy 2018. Courtesy of the Mayor of London.

HEALTHY STREETS AND HEALTHY PEOPLE

POLICY 2–ACTIVE TRAVEL	COST	2017–2020	2020–2030	2030–2041
Improve local walking routes, including routes to schools	L			
Transform Oxford Street and investigate options for Parliament Square	L			
Deliver a London-wide strategic cycle network	M			
Protect, improve and promote the Walk London Network	L			
Develop and support Cycle Hire	M			
Support and encourage cycling and walking to school	L			
Promote and support cycling and walking to work and in local communities	L			
Improve wayfinding for walking and cycling	L			
Improve walking and cycling information in TfL Journey Planner	L			
Embed accessibility and inclusivity in planning and design of Healthy Streets	L			
POLICY 3–VISION ZERO FOR ROAD DANGER	**COST**	**2017–2020**	**2020–2030**	**2030–2041**
Deliver Vision Zero by encouraging safer road user behaviours with a programme of education, engagement and enforcement initiatives	L			
Deliver Vision Zero by improving vehicle safety (includes banning most dangerous HGVs/HGV Direct Vision)	L			
POLICY 4–SECURITY	**COST**	**2017–2020**	**2020–2030**	**2030–2041**
Improve personal safety and security on London's streets	L			
Ensure safety and security on the public transport network	L			
POLICY 4–EFFICIENT STREETS	**COST**	**2017–2020**	**2020–2030**	**2030–2041**
Encourage more freight consolidation	M			
Reduce, re-time and re-mode deliveries	L			
Work with boroughs to develop traffic reduction strategies, including workplace parking levies	L			
Improve customer communication for road users	L			

L low (<£100m) M medium (£100m-£1bn) H high (>£1bn)

FIGURE 1.4 Extract from the Healthy Streets Policy Implementation Plan. Source: Mayor's Transport Strategy 2018. Courtesy of the Mayor of London.

Strategy as a sense of collective purpose

In contrast with the rationality of planning, an interpretation of strategy as purpose communicates that strategy is about developing a sense of shared mission amongst the varied stakeholders associated with an organization (Ackermann and Eden 2011a). Strategy as purpose concerns the development of a long-term vision and sense of mission grounded in the intrinsic values of an organization. As described in Table 1.3, this interpretation of strategy appeals to the human need to do meaningful work (Birkinshaw et al. 2014). An interest in defining strategy as purpose is very often found in top management teams and during boardroom discussions

TABLE 1.3 **Strategy as purpose**

Strategy as ...	Purpose
Interpretation	A guiding sense of the long-term vision, mission, values, and intentions of an individual or organization
Function for the organization	Provide a motivating and unifying sense of direction for the whole organization, based around a shared set of values, which can be translated into meaningful ambitions at all levels of the organization
What is needed to work with this interpretation in practice	Understanding of the intrinsic values of the organization, agreement as to the markets, products, structure, and operating approach that will be adopted by the organization, and an ability to combine these insights into a meaningful narrative that connects with hearts and minds
Benefits	+ Gives a broad framework to unite effort whilst enabling local creativity/innovation + Provides a motivating sense of meaning with which individuals can identify + Is less susceptible to being rendered irrelevant by changing circumstances
Limitations	- If words don't match actions, can be a source of inertia and resistance - Hard to achieve in larger organizations in an effective, authentic way - Difficult to change/alter, restricting leadership options and decision-making
Might be expressed as ...	'Our strategy defines who we are as an organization—our aims and shared values—that guide everything we do'
When you are likely to encounter this interpretation	This is typically an interest of senior leaders across private, public, and third-sector organizations; appears in 'high-level', 'long-term' strategy conversations concerning the whole organization.

(Bartlett and Ghoshal 1994). Once formulated, the purpose of the organization can be raised in strategy conversations at all different levels as a reference point for decision-making.

When a convincing long-term vision is articulated that aligns with the values of an organization and its purpose, it can provide a motivating and unifying effect for employees and stakeholders across all levels (Quinn and Thakor 2018). It appeals to an increasing need of people to do meaningful work, and to go 'above and beyond'. The long-term vision and sense of mission may act as a guiding framework, providing a reference point against which objectives can be set in the short, medium, and long term for individuals and teams. This framework need not be as specific as a firm plan. Instead, a vision outlines principles and a long-term direction for the organization which might be used to evaluate the suitability of proposed activities as they arise.

For example, a vision for TfL is to 'create a future London that is not only home to more people but is a better place for all those people to live in' (*Mayor's Transport Strategy*, p.19). The boundaries of this statement are so broad that all TfL employees should be able to relate their job role to it. It is also inherently positive and with the potential to be meaningful to Londoners.

More specifically, aspirational outcomes are outlined for transport:

> *... the success of London's future transport system relies upon reducing Londoners' dependency on cars in favour of increased walking, cycling and public transport use. This simple aim of a shift away from the car will help address many of London's health problems, by reducing inactivity and cleaning up the air. It will help to eliminate the blight of road danger. It will limit the city's contribution to climate change and help to develop attractive local environments. It will reconnect communities by creating places where people are prioritised*

over cars. It will revitalise local high streets and attract international businesses and their employees to more pleasant urban centres.

Mayor's Transport Strategy, p.19

This vision statement paints a future picture of meaningful positive change without prescribing the specific initiatives that might be contained in a plan. It also gives a 'sense of mission', and these two things combined help to articulate a unifying purpose.

Strategy as a holistic perspective

A strategic perspective implies a long-term holistic view of circumstances, enabling decisions and actions that yield maximum advantage, as described in Table 1.4. Individuals and organizations might be referred to as being strategic, implying an ability to look beyond the immediate and obvious when interpreting a situation. By being aware of the totality of their circumstances, and the potential short-, medium-, and long-term consequences of their actions, strategic individuals or groups seem able to make decisions that create advantageous outcomes in the long run (Felin and Zenger 2019).

A commonly used example of this is the expert chess player thinking through the combinations and permutations of acting on any of the options available to them (e.g. Graber 2009). They may appear to incur short-term losses that don't make sense to an untrained eye, but which prove to be decisions that deliver victory by positioning the whole game board to their

TABLE 1.4 **Strategy as a holistic perspective**

Strategy as ...	Perspective
Interpretation	A capacity to take a holistic long-term view of circumstances—beyond the immediate and obvious—towards maximal advantage
Function for the organization	Enables thinking about the consequences and broader implications of actions, interactions, and trends affecting an individual or group
What is needed to work with this interpretation in practice	The capacity to think beyond the short-term, close at hand, immediate demands or options in any given situation; requires an openness to the ideas and possible actions of others, the trajectories of events, and contextual drivers
Benefits	+ aids decision-making for long-term benefit of the individual or organization + helps avoid knee-jerk reactions that consume resource and limit future options + can be inspirational to others/supportive of strategic leadership
Limitations	- without like-minded peers, strategic thinking can breed frustration/conflict - organizational life doesn't always allow time for reflection/strategic thought - being labelled strategic can encourage arrogance in leaders
Might be expressed as ...	Individuals or groups being referred to as 'strategic thinkers' that can see the whole organizational situation—current and possible futures—in a way that colleagues struggle to achieve
When you are likely to encounter this interpretation	This sort of evaluation of personal capability appears in organizational recruitment and selection processes for promotion, involvement in strategy, or commissioning of external advice

long-term advantage. However, Teece et al. (2016) point out that chess is a 'closed' system where the rules are well established, and the metaphor for strategic thinking underplays the extent to which dynamism and unexpected events have to be accommodated. Therefore adopting a strategic perspective means being able to influence opponents' actions towards one's own long-term gain and an ability to cope with immersion in complex and dynamic circumstances plus an openness to new thoughts, ideas, and actions (Powell 2017).

In the TfL strategy, the 'whole journey' plan concept represents a strategic perspective on improving public transport services:

> *London's public transport services can be improved for all Londoners and also become a more appealing option than car use by:*
>
> **(a)** *Improving safety, affordability and customer service so the whole public transport network becomes easier and more convenient to use for more people.*
>
> **(b)** *Improving public transport accessibility so that disabled and older people can travel spontaneously and independently.*
>
> **(c)** *Shaping and growing the bus network to provide convenient, reliable, accessible public transport options where they are needed.*
>
> **(d)** *Making rail services the most efficient way for people to travel longer distances by tackling crowding and improving the reliability, comfort and appeal of rail travel.*
>
> *A good public transport experience means catering for the whole journey, with all its stages, from its planning to the return home. All public transport journeys start or finish on foot or by cycle, and half of all walking in London is done to or from public transport stations or stops. It is essential to integrate bus, Tube, rail and tram services with improvements to street environments to provide Londoners with attractive alternatives to car use.*
>
> *The areas around and within stations, however, can be cluttered and difficult to navigate, provision for cycle parking can be inconsistent, and interchanges between services can be complex. Stations and stops will be designed for active, efficient and sustainable onward journeys. The first things passengers will see on emerging from the station will be clear walking directions and maps, cycle hire facilities, bus connections and an attractive, accessible and inclusive public realm, rather than car parking and pick-up/drop-off spaces.*
>
> *Mayor's Transport Strategy*, p.131

The strategic perspective expressed here is that unless all aspects of the journey experience are improved simultaneously, the conversion of citizens to non-car journeys will be sub-optimal. Thus, in planning to improve the transport network, holistic investment is required to give the best chance of realizing the strategic vision.

Strategy as prioritization

Strategy can be interpreted as a form of collective focus and prioritization of effort. Faced with conflicting demands on the use of limited resources, choices must be made on a regular basis by managers as to what to do and what not to do in pursuit of organizational results (Sull et al. 2018b). An interpretation of strategy as prioritization is that managers and their teams have a shared sense of focus for their efforts, emotions, resources, and time (see Table 1.5). The intention of this focus is to give the greatest return on resource investment in terms of beneficial organizational outcomes.

To adopt strategy as prioritization means to be aware of options for action and use of resources, and to be selective in the options that are identified for implementation. Knowing what not to do is as important as addressing specific interests (Collis 2016). This interpretation of strategy has at its heart the concept of capacity management. Strategy as prioritization is a recognition that organizational performance is a function of available capabilities **and** finite resources. This is perhaps easiest to understand in terms of financial resources. Imagine that our organization has £1 million, and we have the skills to follow two investment opportunities of £500,000 and £700,000. Both are possible but, because of limited finances, pursuing one option will mean that the other cannot be achieved. Therefore we must make a choice as to which option to prioritize. When there is more opportunity than our resource capacity can support, deciding how to allocate our resources is the process of prioritization. Having a shared sense of clear strategic priorities can guide employees and coordinate activity without prescribing exactly how they need to do their work (Gulati 2018).

For example, to build a future-ready transport system, the TfL strategy identifies 23 focus areas in which resources and initiatives will be prioritized, such as walking and cycling, opportunities to reduce car use, and climate change resilience in natural and built environments. In each of these areas, plans, investments, and initiatives are identified that prioritize walking, cycling, and public transport over car use.

TABLE 1.5 **Strategy as prioritization**

Strategy as ...	Priority
Interpretation	Where energy, efforts, emotions, and resources are focused
Function for the organization	Concentrate the allocation of resources and effort on those initiatives that will give biggest payback to the organization and address the most pressing challenges
What is needed to work with this interpretation in practice	An awareness of the options for action and the resources at disposal, the relative value of opportunities facing the organization and the risks posed by current challenges, and a means of selecting the options to prioritize to realize the best outcomes for the organization
Benefits	+ Strategy can be made that is realistic and impactful, even with limited resources + Helps clarify what 'not to do' and thus enables coherent decision-making + Connects strategy with action that makes sense given the current context
Limitations	– May focus on immediate needs at the expense of long-term investment – Can be highly political, as those involved want their interests prioritized – Needs to be regularly revised to reflect shifting organizational context
Might be expressed as ...	'We will focus our efforts and resources on these three strategic priorities—all other activities will have to wait until these are achieved'
When you are likely to encounter this interpretation	This is often a concern for those making functional strategies or heading up organizational units as they attempt to convert high-level ambitions into local plans, with limited resources, that deliver maximum return on effort

Strategy as a problem-solving mechanism

Strategy is sometimes described as a mechanism for organizational level problem-solving. The sorts of challenges that face an organization, potentially threatening its survival, will often fit the definition of a **wicked problem**. Wicked problems are over-determined, meaning that they are complex, subject to a system of influences, and don't seem to have any easy or obvious solution. For example, delivering fully sustainable operations is a wicked problem for multinational consumer goods firms. Conventional approaches to problem-solving won't adequately address wicked problems (McMillan and Overall 2016). As described in Table 1.6, strategy activity can be approached in a way that stabilizes the conditions for decision-making and implementation of policy towards coping better with wicked problems (Wright et al. 2019).

Strategy as problem-solving requires firstly a diagnostic phase in which, as far as is possible, the nature of the challenges facing the organization are described and defined through data collection and analysis. Secondly, as the challenges become clearer, organizational policy is agreed for how to respond to the specific nature of the challenge facing the organization. This will likely require debate and consensus agreement between stakeholders based on limited data. Finally, once organizational policy is agreed (for instance, setting a policy in relation to a disruptive new technology), a coherent set of actions to implement the policy across organizational teams and functions is agreed to cope with or mitigate wicked problems (Daviter 2017).

TABLE 1.6 **Strategy as problem-solving**

Strategy as ...	Problem-solving
Interpretation	A mechanism by which to solve problems and address challenges threatening the sustainability of an organization and the attainment of its goals
Function for the organization	As either a one-off event or a continuing process, strategy fulfils an organizational function of solving problems with limited information and uncertainty about the direction of unfolding circumstances
What is needed to work with this interpretation in practice	A diagnosis which describes and defines the nature of the challenges facing the organization, an agreed policy for how best to respond to the specific nature of the challenges, and a coherent set of actions to implement the policy
Benefits	+ Brings a clarity of expected response to uncertainty about the future + Can build coping skills and organizational resilience + Connects data analytics, intuition, governance, and performance interests
Limitations	– Strategic problems tend to be 'wicked'—complex, uncertain, and without easy/obvious solutions – 'Paralysis by analysis'—can over-analyse options and responses – 'Best guess' data analysis can create false certainty about future
Might be expressed as ...	'Our strategy prepares us to continue to deliver on the expectations of our shareholders, employees, customers, and communities in these challenging times'
When you are likely to encounter this interpretation	When in a context that is perceived as volatile, uncertain, ambiguous, changing, or under threat of disruption, strategy is often discussed by management teams as a means of finding solutions to threats to organizational sustainability

The TfL strategy addresses a 'wicked problem' for London relating to how to move an ever-growing and ageing population around an already congested transport network:

> *This growth is expected to generate about 6 million additional trips each day by 2041. Unless new ways are found to plan the city as it grows, overcrowding will see some public transport lines and stations grinding to a halt, air quality will get worse and streets and public places will become ever-more dominated by motor traffic. And it is important also to plan for an ageing population, with increasing accessibility needs.*
>
> *Mayor's Transport Strategy*, p.15

Strategy as an organizational possession

If many in organizational life are asked 'What is your strategy?' they will refer to the content of a polished piece of media, such as a document, a web page, a poster on the wall, a reference card carried in the pocket, etc. In this way, strategy can be understood as a possession—something the organization has—which is evidenced by a collection of artefacts and materials communicating a coherent message (see Table 1.7).

TABLE 1.7 **Strategy as a possession**

Strategy as ...	Possession
Interpretation	A collection of artefacts, materials, and 'things' that can be used for the benefit of the organization
Function for the organization	Creates the potential for strategy to be shared, for the clarification of what is meant by strategy, and to evidence that strategy work has been completed
What is needed to work with this interpretation in practice	Agreed content with which to populate the artefacts, agreed formats and designs for the artefacts, and production and distribution mechanisms to turn them into reality
Benefits	+ Provides a visible tangible reminder of identity and mission to employees + Gives an impression to external stakeholders of a well-run organization + Legitimizes and coordinates the work of strategic managers
Limitations	- Having fixed artefacts can encourage inertia/avoidance of strategy renewal - Artefacts don't deliver performance outcomes - Hard to create artefacts which are meaningful across stakeholder groups
Might be expressed as ...	'Our strategy masterplan document is laid out on our website, and is summarized in the annual report and on cue cards distributed to all employees'
When you are likely to encounter this interpretation	External and internal communications professionals often own the 'artefacts' of strategy, to be used to influence stakeholder views

Strategy as a set of possessions recognizes the importance of the content and format of strategy communication to the impact that strategy work might have on organizational stakeholders (Dameron et al. 2015). For strategy to act as a coordinating mechanism and decision-making aid, unambiguous information needs to be communicated through strategy media in an appealing way. It is unlikely that one medium or method of communication will suffice to best meet the needs of different stakeholders and the nature of various strategic messages. Therefore the creation of a range of appropriate artefacts and possessions—which communicate consistent messages in different ways—is often required in large-scale strategy dissemination efforts (Arnaud et al. 2016). Online methods, including social media, are now a particular concern to those working in strategy communication (Plesner and Gulbrandsen 2015).

For example, the outline for the London *Mayor's Transport Strategy* can be found online (https://tfl.gov.uk/corporate/about-tfl/the-mayors-transport-strategy) (see Figure 1.5). The famous London Underground map imagery is used to communicate strategy ideas about future route developments (Figure 1.6). Visually appealing posters, such as the healthy streets indicators in Figure 1.7, summarize and communicate action plans.

Strategy as an organizational process

Thinking of strategy as an organizational process brings attention to the continuing social and political interactions and organizational learning that shape strategy content and action over time (see Table 1.8). Strategy can be considered a social process, as the content of strategy emerges through conversations and debates between organizational stakeholders

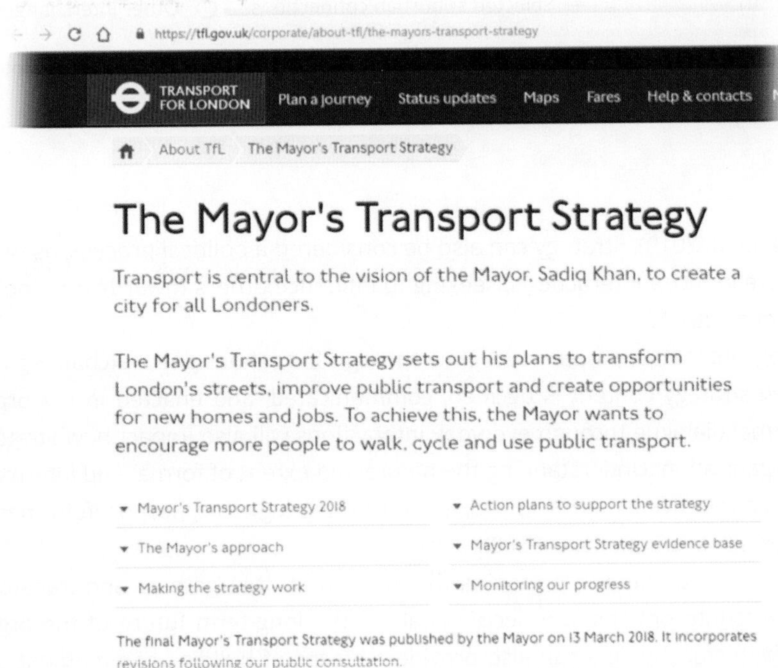

FIGURE 1.5 The TfL strategy website. Source: Courtesy of the Mayor of London.

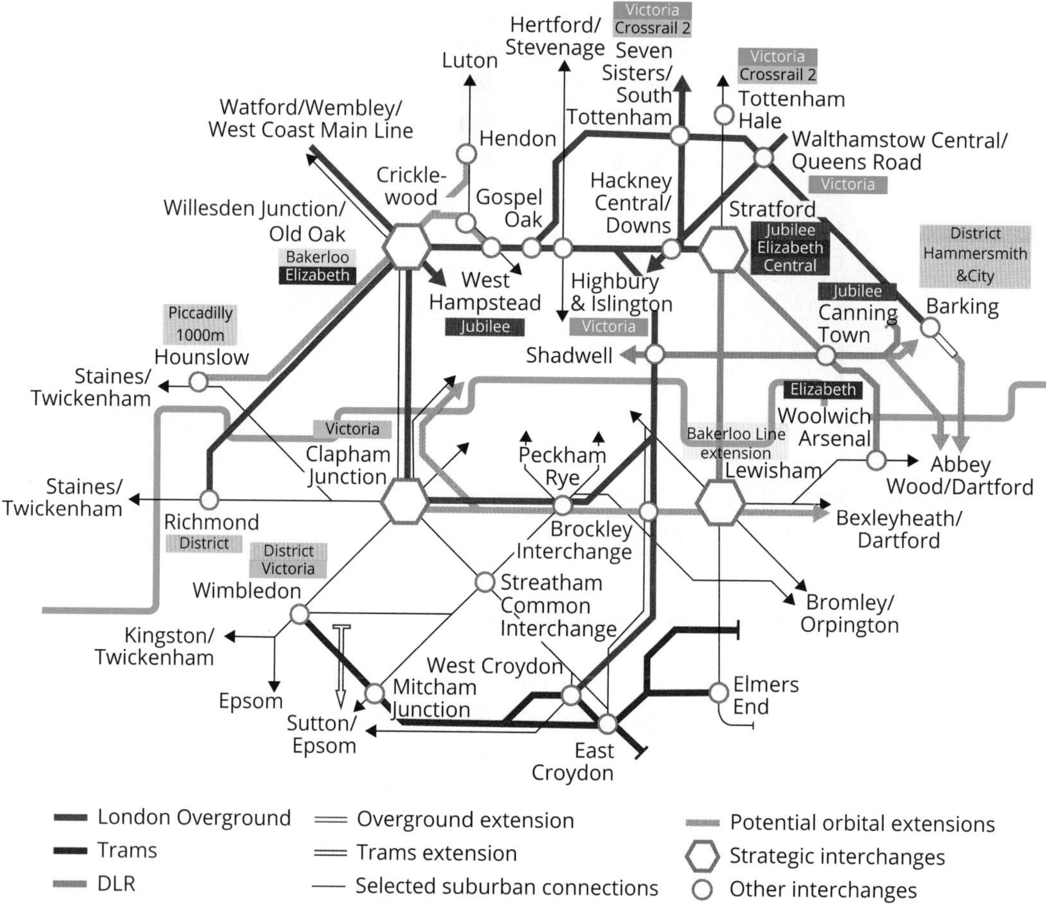

FIGURE 1.6 Strategic infrastructure initiatives. Source: Courtesy of the Mayor of London.

(e.g. Dobusch et al. 2019). Strategy can also be considered a political process, as vested interests participate in those interactions, seeking to influence others towards their point of view (e.g. Conroy et al. 2017).

How strategy interactions occur over time through formal designed exchanges will directly influence how strategy content is decided, communicated, and enacted in the organization. Equally, informal dialogue through everyday interactions will also impact how strategy is realized in the organization. Understanding the nature and extent of formal and informal strategy conversations and activities can help you, in a future strategy role, purposefully manage strategy as a process (Vilà and Canales 2008).

Strategy process can be interpreted as the mechanism that gathers and transforms organizational inputs into options and decisions about the long-term future of the organization. Interactions with stakeholders can also provide a means of building commitment to strategy outcomes. The extent to which this is possible depends on involvement of key stakeholders in

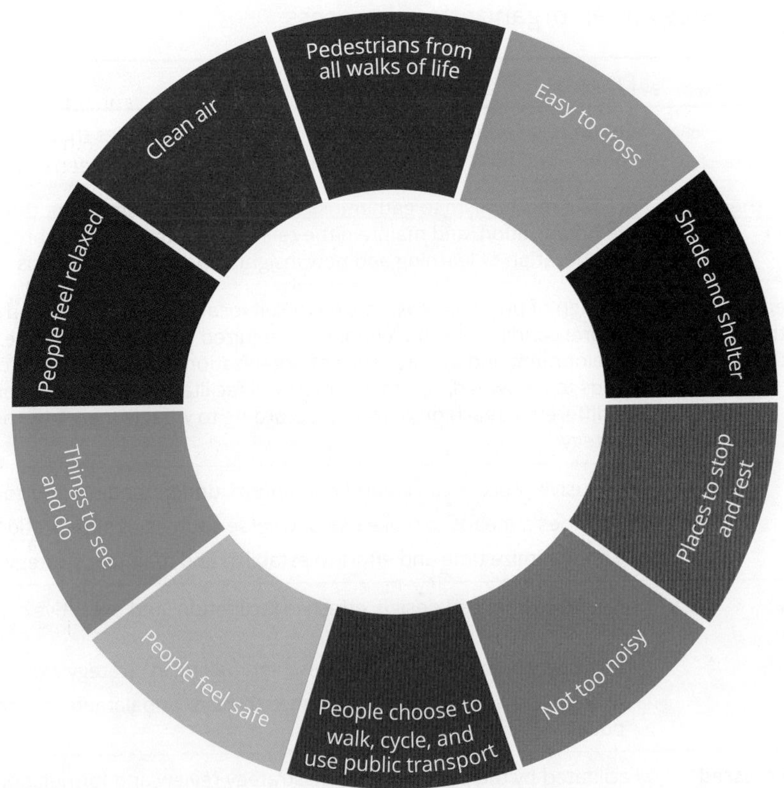

FIGURE 1.7 Healthy streets indicators. Sources: From Transport for London. (2017). Healthy Streets for London; Lucy Saunders.

the process (Ackermann and Eden 2011b). Ongoing strategy processes also enable the renewal of strategy content, based on what has been learned from taking action or monitoring the shifting organizational context.

The TfL strategy process is defined in a number of ways. An overall strategy process architecture for London, of which the TfL strategy is part, is depicted in Figure 1.8. In this high-level process, it can be seen how the TfL strategy will influence and be influenced by other aspects of London administration, how it will drive outcomes through business planning, and then service and delivery action planning, and how monitoring will be used to trigger renewal activities. At a lower level of detail, the monitoring activity is described in Figure 1.9 as a continuing process. A collaborative approach to enacting the process cycles in Figures 1.8 and 1.9 to deliver target outcomes is also described:

> *Achieving this magnitude of change across London will require the Mayor and TfL to work with, among others, the Government, London's boroughs, other transport operators, businesses, and everyone who makes this city their home. As such, the aims of this strategy will be pursued collaboratively, using wide consultation and developing the right solutions to London's transport challenges for each borough, neighbourhood and street. Alongside a new London Plan and the Mayor's other new strategies, this document provides a blueprint for a better London. By working together we can create a city for all Londoners.*
>
> *Mayor's Transport Strategy*, p.35

1

TABLE 1.8 **Strategy as an organizational process**

Strategy as ...	Process
Interpretation	Continuing social and political interactions and activities that shape strategy content and how it is communicated, enacted, and revised
Function for the organization	Act as a mechanism to gather insights and build commitment throughout the organization, and maintain the relevance of the strategy through incorporation of learning and new insights on a continuing basis
What is needed to work with this interpretation in practice	A design of process—customized to suit local, organizational, and cultural conditions—that enables all required contributions to the development and maintenance of organizational strategy. The process needs to be owned, communicated, and facilitated. How this is done will be different in each organization according to what is meant by the term strategy
Benefits	+ Inclusive process can create momentum, understanding, and commitment + Provides a means to make use of diverse sources of organizational wisdom + Can minimize time and effort to establish and maintain strategy
Limitations	- Needs customized design, effective facilitation, and executive sponsorship - Inclusivity opens potential for mischief-making in strategy work - May generate insights and outcomes that are unpalatable for those in power
Might be expressed as ...	Facilitated by the policy group, the strategy review and formulation process happen on six-monthly cycles, with implementation meetings every month to track progress
When you are likely to encounter this interpretation	Strategy 'owners'—those responsible for strategy outputs for their area/organization—will be concerned with process. External consultants/facilitators often have their own designs of process, methods, and tools that they offer to clients for strategy work

Strategy as a target market position

When considering how value is created by the organization, strategy can be interpreted as a desired state or position in the mind of relevant stakeholders (Markides 2000). If value means 'relative worth', the value of products or services of an organization will be compared with those of competitors in the minds of customers. As a desired market position, it then follows that strategy will be how an organization attempts to be perceived by customers as having products or services that are more valuable than those of competitors (Chew and Osborne 2009). What constitutes value will depend on the target audience. This may mean utility of the offering (i.e. some products/services offer greater functionality than others); it may be the image or reputation of the product or service; it may be the price/perceived value for money, etc.

Strategy as a desired position has roots in the modern industrial economics and organization-based development of strategy theory described in Section 1.1. It also aligns well with concepts of marketing strategy in which strategy considers how adjusting pricing, product design, placement, and promotional activities in order to best reach customers according to

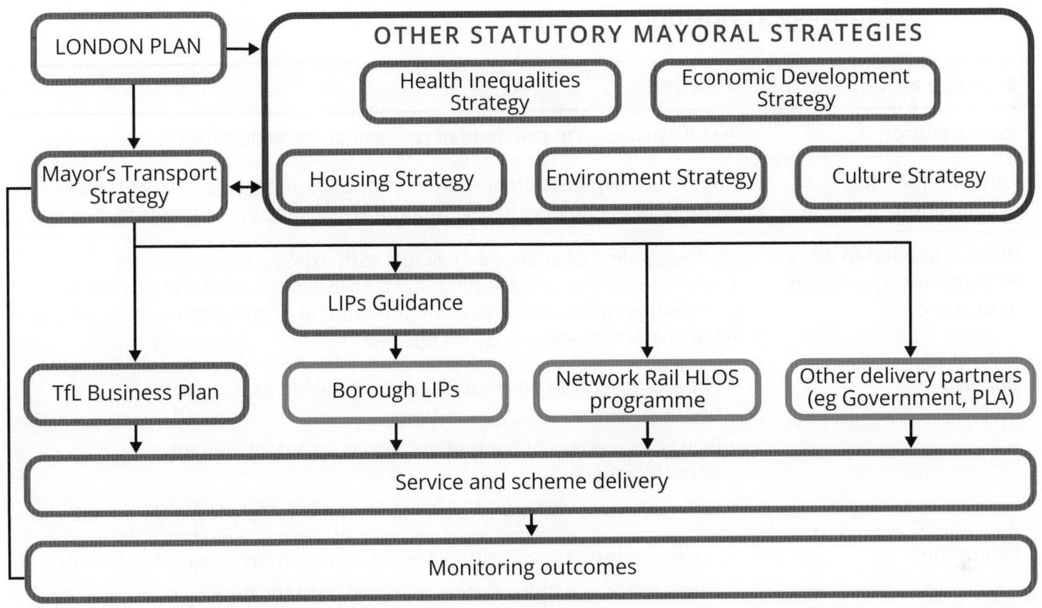

FIGURE 1.8 Transport strategy delivery process. Source: Mayor's Transport Strategy 2018. Courtesy of the Mayor of London.

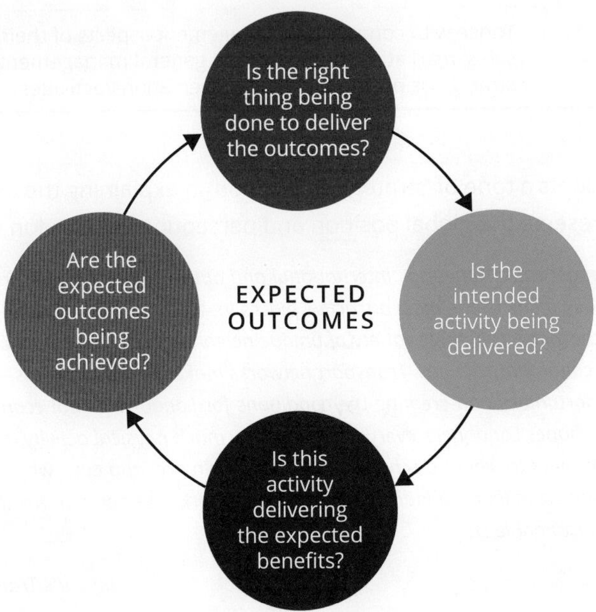

FIGURE 1.9 Monitoring, appraisal, and evaluation cycle. Source: Mayor's Transport Strategy 2018. Courtesy of the Mayor of London.

what they value (e.g. Guo et al. 2018). Whatever the definition of value adopted, strategy as position refers to the organizational conduct required to achieve a desired perceived state in the minds of stakeholders based on the space it attempts to occupy in a competitive environment (see Table 1.9).

TABLE 1.9 **Strategy as position**

Strategy as ...	Position
Interpretation	A state occupied in the mind of relevant stakeholders
Function for the organization	Enables an explanation of how an individual or organization will create value for stakeholders in relation to the activities of competitors
What is needed to work with this interpretation in practice	Understanding of what is achievable with existing resources and external environmental realities such as industry-structural and macro-environmental factors. A keen understanding of competitor activities and what customers value are also needed
Benefits	+ Focuses attention on creating customer value as a driver of performance + Brings awareness of competitor activity as a determinant of performance + Connects well with brand- and marketing-led organizational visions
Limitations	– Factors determining position are not all within organizational control – Tends to focus within existing markets, perhaps missing disruptive new sectors – Can breed complacency/arrogance when leading position achieved
Might be expressed as ...	'We offer the most profitable 'super-premium' brand in our sector in Western Europe, the Middle East, and North America'
When you are likely to encounter this interpretation	Those with commercial management aspects of their job roles, such as sales, marketing, branding, and general management, will likely address strategy as position in their conversations/activities

The TfL strategy adopts a tone of 'strategy as position' in explaining the importance of investing in transport to preserve the global position and perceptions of London versus other cities:

> *London is one of the most entrepreneurial, international and outward-looking cities in the world. Its dynamism and diversity make it one of the most attractive places in which to live and work. It is home to people from every corner of the globe, to a huge variety of unique neighbourhoods and public spaces and to some of the world's leading cultural attractions. Transport networks make the city what it is—connecting communities, opening up opportunities and creating the conditions for London's global economy to flourish. The transport system also shapes Londoners' everyday lives—how much physical activity they do, how long and pleasant their daily journeys to work, to school and around town are, and even where they choose to live. Careful planning can enable millions of individual decisions to work together in a way that creates a healthy and environmentally sustainable city.*
>
> *Mayor's Transport Strategy*, p.11

The TfL strategy communicates the need to achieve an enhanced transport network, proposing a 'world-leading strategy' to get ahead of other locations as destinations of choice for global citizens, as 'major cities around the world are grappling with the same challenges we face in London' (*Mayor's Transport Strategy*, p.11). Also, it is careful to point out how the strategy will deliver enhanced value for native Londoners, politicians, public officials, and funding bodies.

Strategy as plasticity

Strategy as a plasticity describes an approach to strategy synonymous with agility, entrepreneurship, and opportunism (Table 1.10). As circumstances change for an individual or organization, strategy can be a way of coordinating activities that enables the best to be made of the situation (Isenberg 1987). Strategy as plasticity describes an entrepreneurial capacity to sense and seize opportunity as presented by circumstances, moulding priorities and activities on a continuing basis according to the wisdom and expertise of those making decisions (Munro 2010). By staying attuned to their evolving circumstances and remaining open to new possibilities, opportunities and threats can be managed in as short a time as possible.

Strategy as a plasticity aligns with the concept of the agile organization, in which 'small, entrepreneurial groups are designed to stay close to customers and adapt quickly to changing conditions' (Rigby et al. 2018:90). By maintaining loose reporting structures, simple decision criteria, flexible resources, and adaptable processes and procedures, agile teams can react swiftly to unexpected localized opportunities in order to maximize gains for the organization. (Denning 2018).

TABLE 1.10 **Strategy as a plasticity**

Strategy as ...	Plasticity
Interpretation	A means to opportunistically handle or gain advantage from a situation
Function for the organization	A way of operating which allows the individual or organization to cope with, or capitalize on, unfolding circumstances
What is needed to work with this interpretation in practice	An entrepreneurial capacity to recognize opportunities and the best way of seizing those opportunities for an organization or individual. Agility and flexibility of individual or organizational practice is also required
Benefits	+ High connectivity with context allows opportunities to be sensed and seized + Fosters organizational capacity for flexibility and agility that enables survival + Encourages high relevance and efficacy of decision-making and resource use
Limitations	– Very hard to execute ongoing in large firms without a destabilizing effect – Incompatible with predictability focus of performance management cultures – Requires flexible operating systems and mindset throughout whole organization
Might be expressed as ...	'We are a fluid and adaptable organization, willing to take calculated risks and always on the lookout for the next opportunity'
When you are likely to encounter this interpretation	This strategic mode of operating is often seen as a defining characteristic of entrepreneurial individuals or organizations; also found to varying degrees in some national cultures (e.g. wayfinding, nomadic life, American dream)

Pockets of entrepreneurial intent can be detected in the TfL strategy. For example, a proposal is put forward that:

> *The Mayor, through TfL, will explore and trial demand-responsive bus services as a possible complement to 'conventional' public transport services in London. This will include consideration of trials that could unlock otherwise difficult-to-serve areas of outer London.*
>
> *Mayor's Transport Strategy*, p.282

The language of this proposal is highly tentative and exploratory, unlike the firm commitments made elsewhere in the document. The proposal recognizes the need to find new ways to serve parts of outer London without saying what those ways will specifically be. This suggestion is framed in the terms of strategy as plasticity.

Further, in relation to the rapidly shifting nature of available technology, the TfL strategy aims to retain a responsive agile approach that can evolve to keep pace with opportunity:

> *Recent years have seen major technological developments, including the rapid uptake of mobile technology ... Technology will continue to advance rapidly, and across the world billions of pounds will be invested in the development of 'new mobility services' ... By tracking and shaping new technological developments as they emerge, London will continue to benefit from one of the most comprehensive and integrated transport networks in the world ... The Mayor, through TfL, will work to ensure its information systems and payment platforms take account of technological advances and evolve to remain fit for purpose.*
>
> *Mayor's Transport Strategy*, p.276

Strategy as a practice

Interpreted as a practice, strategy arises from what people do rather than something an organization has (Johnson et al. 2008). As a continuing accomplishment emerging from human effort, the nature of strategy work depends on factors such as the personal characteristics of all of those contributing to and involved in strategy inside and outside the organization, embedded ways of working that have evolved over time, and methods available to formulate ideas and attempt to implement them (e.g. Breene et al. 2007). Underpinning this human effort is the experience and wisdom of practitioners, their specific practices, the flow of knowledge and information through relationships, and the biases and limitations of how those involved think (Johnson et al. 2003). We explore this perspective in depth in Chapter 2.

Strategy as a practice helpfully provides insight as to how strategy can be better achieved through education and organizational design work (see Table 1.11). As an activity people do, there is potential to modify the way strategy is understood and enacted over time through learning and development for practitioners. Further, by considering the full set of strategy practices used or available within an organization, adjustments to team composition and strategy process design might help organizational strategy to be conducted in more effective ways (e.g. Lee 2019).

The TfL strategy contains many instances of guidance for how the transport strategy should be developed and delivered. For example, to implement the vision, the TfL strategy mandates

TABLE 1.11 **Strategy as a practice**

Strategy as ...	Practice
Interpretation	An activity people do rather than something organizations have
Function for the organization	Recognizes that strategy relies on human effort, and that effort is shaped by the experience and wisdom, knowledge flows, human connections, and the ways of thinking of the people involved
What is needed to work with this interpretation in practice	Awareness of the preferred/dominant activities and practices, the range of experiences, and the ways of thinking of the people/team involved in strategy work. An ability to minimize the downsides of established practice whilst playing to the individual's/team's strengths during strategy activities
Benefits	+ Capacity for effective strategy can be developed through HR and organizational design work, and learning and development activity + A focus on diversity of experience brings strength and depth to strategy work + Encourages criticality of strategy practices and outcomes, reducing arrogance
Limitations	– Engrained practices can be harmful/sub-optimal for strategy work – Strategy practice that is at odds with organizational culture is likely to fail – Strategy is vulnerable to the biases and limited capacities of people
Might be expressed as ...	'Our strategy draws on the strengths of our diverse senior management team, bringing a long history of organizational leadership and strategic management experience in our chosen sectors'
When you are likely to encounter this interpretation	Consultants, educators, academics, and HR professionals will often have a view on effective strategy practices and how they might be recruited, nurtured, and enhanced in an organization

HR, human resources.

'including local people in local decisions to provide the greatest benefit for everyone' (*Mayor's Strategy for London*, p.26), the use of 'an evidence-based programme of measures to adapt existing, and to design and build new, transport infrastructure' (*Mayor's Strategy for London*, p.125), and to 'use the healthy streets approach to deliver coordinated improvements to public transports and streets' (*Mayor's Strategy for London*, p.132).

Strategy as a pattern in a stream of activity

The management scholar Henry Mintzberg famously described strategy as 'a pattern in a stream of activities'. This interpretation of strategy highlights the importance of recognizing culture when articulating strategy. Like the perspective of strategy as a practice, this can include the management team culture, their established ways of working, and their approach to engaging with others (Groysberg et al. 2018). However, this perspective goes further, also incorporating the norms, routines, and patterned ways of working in an organization as part of what might be referred to as strategy and strategic change (Beynon-Davies et al. 2016) (see Table 1.12).

TABLE 1.12 **Strategy as a pattern in a stream of activity**

Strategy as ...	Pattern
Interpretation	Recurring aspects of an individual or organization's activity
Function for the organization	Draws attention to the cultural norms and habitual activity which, if tapped, could constitute a powerful resource for competitive advantage
What is needed to work with this interpretation in practice	A deep sense of how work happens within an organization and its setting, developed through immersion in that context. An ability to work through rather than against natural patterns of behaviour
Benefits	+ Cultural norms that generate customer value can be a source of sustainable competitive advantage + Aligning with norms reduces resistance to strategy implementation efforts + Aligning with culture reduces the variables the strategist must consider
Limitations	- Often have to 'live' in the organization to grasp intangible aspects of culture - Culture may vary in emphases in different parts of an organization - Strategy based on culture may harm an organization if it doesn't fit with evolving competitive realities
Might be expressed as ...	'Our proud history and expertise in this industry is at the core of our strategy and the foundation upon which we build for the future'
When you are likely to encounter this interpretation	Culture may be considered in varying degrees during strategy making, but the fit between strategy and culture inevitably comes to the fore in 'implementation' work

The implication of this view of strategy is that an effective culture—where effective means able to contribute to the delivery of organizational objectives—might be a source of competitive advantage (see Wu et al. 2019). No individual has full control over culture, it is very hard to replicate, and changing culture, even if possible in an intended way, is a long-term endeavour. Therefore, if an established way of working in an organization creates valuable outcomes, competitors may not be able to replicate or imitate the effect of that culture. Also, this perspective highlights the folly of deliberately strategizing in a way that is out of alignment with culture—as the management guru Peter Drucker proclaimed, 'culture eats strategy for breakfast'. Strategy as a pattern in a stream of activity challenges the strategic management team to utilize cultural norms and habitual activity productively as a basis for planning and delivering strategic initiatives (Powell 2017).

The TfL strategy highlights that 'making walking and cycling more appealing to Londoners requires a big change in the city's culture'. In responding to this challenge, it is recognized that the TfL remit covers differing patterns of needs and behaviours in London which must be taken account of through a varied portfolio of strategy initiatives:

Central London is a global cultural and economic centre, with a dynamic financial and commercial hub, a vibrant West End, emerging tech quarters and a rich heritage. Most of the capital's employment growth will occur here as well as Canary Wharf so to compete for jobs on the world stage, it must remain very well connected, with a world-class public realm and safe air quality levels. Insufficient rail and Tube services for central London will constrain future economic growth—a capacity increase of about 80 per cent is required to tackle crowding on today's services and to cater for growth between now and 2041.

An intense mix of urban challenges exists in inner London—severe congestion, poor air quality, excessive noise, high levels of deprivation and limited access to green space ... Bus use is particularly important in inner London as it offers low-cost, accessible transport for everyone. Improving the quality of this most affordable form of public transport will help to reduce health inequalities through reduced car use.

The majority of the city's residents live in outer London ... At present, many people have no choice but to drive, particularly for trips around outer London, rather than into the city centre. Rail services must be improved to make the most efficient public transport option for longer journeys more appealing. Improved bus routes—particularly services that could replace existing car journeys—will also be vital, and where traditional bus routes are not appropriate, this could include new models for 'demand-responsive' bus services.

Mayor's Strategy for London, pp.29–33

Basing strategic proposals on understanding of the patterns and associated needs of each geographical area will increase the likelihood of TfL strategy outcomes being realized whilst minimizing resistance to implementation, as residents can identify with the value-add of strategic changes.

Strategy as preparation for the future

As preparation for the future, strategy can be interpreted as a mechanism for identifying and taking action today that builds options and capabilities that will enable an organization to respond to opportunities and challenges in the future (Birkinshaw et al. 2016). Adopting this view, strategy and strategic management methods enable management teams to look beyond short-term performance pressures and build capability for sustaining the organization in the long term (Bungay 2019). A major responsibility for a strategic management team is to prepare the organization adequately to meet future competitive and operating requirements (Schoemaker et al. 2018). This is particularly challenging given that the future is very difficult to predict! So what are these requirements, and what action needs to be taken now to be ready in the future? How do we 'future-proof' strategy and, by extension, the organization?

For strategy to be an organizational mechanism for preparing for the future, it requires a set of methods and mentalities to be available for strategy work (see Table 1.13). Firstly, there must exist systems for both environmental scanning and the monitoring of external trends, and internal review of available resources and capabilities. These systems must make data available wherever relevant in the organization as an input to strategy work. With this data available, methods are required to enable management teams to step away from operational life and interrogate, debate, and decide on future organizational needs. With the insights from these strategic conversations, adequate change management capabilities must be available to implement actions that build resources and capabilities as required. These sensing, seizing, and

TABLE 1.13 **Strategy as preparation for the future**

Strategy as ...	Preparation
Interpretation	A way of anticipating possible future challenges and preparing now to be ready to meet those challenges
Function for the organization	Defines and guides learning processes that read internal and external trends and anticipate possible future scenarios. Builds organizational resilience through taking actions today that nurture the resources and capabilities required to meet future challenges
What is needed to work with this interpretation in practice	Management tools and systems for environmental scanning and internal monitoring; agreed strategic management methods to enable management teams to interrogate, debate, and decide on future organizational needs; change management capabilities to develop resources and capabilities as required; and flexibility to respond to needs as they arise
Benefits	+ Fosters managerial vigilance and constant re-evaluation of strategic needs + Generates valuable shared management learning that informs action + Enables necessary capabilities that fit the organization to be built and maintained
Limitations	– Requires a significant investment of management time – Foresight can be unsettling if not accompanied by action planning – Can give a false sense of confidence about 'knowing' the future perfectly
Might be expressed as ...	'By asking ourselves "What if?" and connecting with all manner of external data sources, we develop strategic insights and contingency plans that provide assurance of our continuing success as an organization'
When you are likely to encounter this interpretation	Management teams in industries with long planning horizons (such as energy and defence) and civil servants considering national interests will often be interested in this perspective. Further, management teams sensing likely disruption in their industry will also be interested in this view

reconfiguring mechanisms (Teece 2007) describe the dynamic capability of the organization—'the organizational capability to purposefully create, extend or modify its resource base' (Helfat et al. 2007:4) (see Chapter 6). Consequently, there must also be an element of adaptability and flexibility built in, as well as a healthy dose of good judgement.

The TfL strategy, with its horizon to 2041, is arguably written with a strong emphasis on planning for the future. Projected population growth is used as the basis for evaluating the actions required in the next 20 years to be able to service the transport needs of Londoners in 2041.

The strategy notes that 'by 2041, rising public transport demand means that, without further action, in morning peak conditions 71% of travel on London Underground and 67% of national rail travel will be in crowded conditions'.

In defining the action to take, broader trends are taken into consideration:

Within the timescales of this strategy, changes in consumer behaviours, lifestyles and technology could have a profound effect on the ways cities work. Between now and 2041, two new generations will enter the workforce, new economic models based on shared access rather than private ownership will continue to evolve, and new technologies and increasing digital connectivity could significantly change the way people live and work. Engaging with these trends will allow the implementation of this strategy to adapt as needed to achieve its aims.

Mayor's Transport Strategy, p.16

Embedded in this view is the ongoing need for managerial vigilance and capabilities to adapt the strategy to changing circumstances. By so doing, TfL will be able to best prepare for the future through a strategic approach that is revised on an ongoing basis.

1.5 **Strategy scoping method**

In the previous section, we outlined 12 interpretations of strategy. As noted, these '12Ps' provide different ways of thinking about strategy, which might be used in different circumstances, in different contexts, or at different points in time, but can be woven together into a customized view of strategy. Mintzberg et al. (2009:15) highlight that, despite differences in available interpretations, there are a number of high-level points of agreement in strategy theory and practice. Namely, strategy (a) concerns both organization and environment, (b) is typically a complex matter, (c) affects the long-term welfare of the organization, (d) involved issues of content (what is agreed) and process (how it is agreed), (e) is not purely deliberate, (f) exists on different levels, and (g) involves a range of thought processes.

Building on this common ground, how can you, in your future career, agree with stakeholders what strategy means, how to work with strategy, and what a strategy process should yield in an organizational setting? In this section we review a simple descriptive method that can be used to map the meaning of strategy in any given context.

This strategy scoping method uses a descriptive mechanism to engage stakeholders. By asking those involved in strategy to describe what it means—and what it does not mean—an appropriate scope can be placed on strategy activities. We can use the '12Ps' as a guide to ask strategy stakeholders relevant questions as part of this approach.

Using a scoping method sets a solid foundation for effective interactions between participants in strategy work (Mitreanu 2006). It is important to repeat the method when moving between stakeholder groups involved in strategy. For example, what strategy means to the board of a multinational corporation might be significantly different from what strategy means to the managers of a production facility at one of the same organization's subsidiary locations. Clarifying the interpretations held by each group of stakeholders is an enabler of effective strategy work.

To illustrate how scoping works, we will offer a guide and exercise below aimed at students of strategy. To deepen your understanding of how a strategy scoping method can help individuals create a shared view of strategy, work through the exercise with two or three other students on your course.

Step 1: Clarify the focus of the exercise

Select an organization you all know well, such as the institution at which you are studying, a company or NGO where you have all studied recently, a sports team you all follow, or even a band or musician you have an interest in (this is the equivalent of identifying the boundaries of the strategy exercise if you were doing this in an organization). In this example, we will consider three students—John, Shakeel, and Lucia—reflecting on what they think strategy means for a local multi-sports venue used by students for swimming, football, basketball, and athletics.

Step 2: Identify your individual views

Each complete the simple rating exercise shown in Table 1.14 to reflect individual interpretations of what organizational strategy should lead to for the focus organization.

TABLE 1.14 **Scoping strategy through the 12Ps**

Strategy as ...	For me, strategy activity for the focus organization should result in ...	Not relevant or important		Relevant but not important		Important and relevant
Plan	... a guiding plan	1	2	3	4	5
Purpose	... an inspiring vision	1	2	3	4	5
Perspective	... a broader view	1	2	3	4	5
Priority	... focus of attention and resources	1	2	3	4	5
Problem-solving	... actionable solutions to complex issues	1	2	3	4	5
Possession	... physical outputs which can be shared	1	2	3	4	5
Process	... a design of activities and agreed outputs	1	2	3	4	5
Position	... a market identity	1	2	3	4	5
Plasticity	... agility and clever moves	1	2	3	4	5
Practice	... effective ways to do strategy	1	2	3	4	5
Pattern	... strategy to fit with how we work	1	2	3	4	5
Preparation	... actions today to prepare for tomorrow	1	2	3	4	5

Step 3: Combine your views into a single diagram

Take the scoring for each set of individual views and transfer them into a single diagram. In this case we will use a bar graph (see Figure 1.10). However, you can use whatever format you prefer. We suggest using a diagram format so that it is easy to compare where you agree or disagree about strategy.

Step 4: Identify where you agree about what strategy means

In Figure 1.10, the three participants all agree that strategy should result in a guiding plan, including actions today to prepare for tomorrow that fit with how we currently work, and physical outputs which can be shared. They also agree that there is little need to focus on agility and clever moves, or actionable solutions to complex issues. These views can already be articulated as part of your shared understanding of strategy.

Step 5: Discuss how to address differences of opinion

Focus conversations on how diverging views should be addressed in strategy. For example, John thinks that identifying a future market position is vital, whereas Shakeel and Lucia don't see the relevance. John should explain his thinking to Shakeel and Lucia, and vice versa, and they can debate whether to undertake strategy activities that result in an intended market focus. This focused discussion allows learning to occur between participants, and the negotiation of a meaningful outcome.

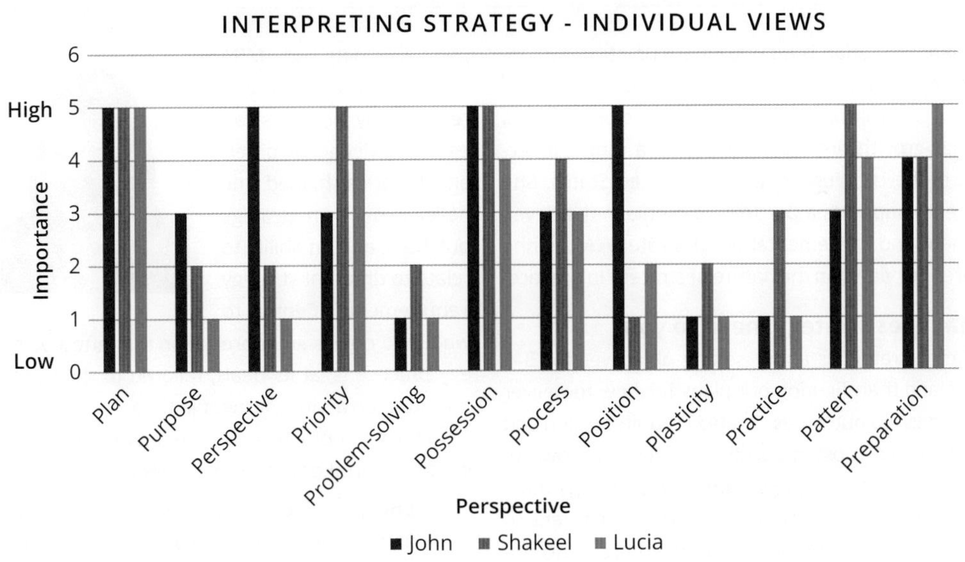

FIGURE 1.10 Representing individual views of strategy.

Step 6: Articulate a final agreed statement of strategy scope

Write down a final statement of the shared meaning of strategy which captures the outcomes of the debate. In this example, after discussion John, Shakeel, and Lucia agree that the organizational strategy should be developed by a transparent set of designed activities, resulting in a guiding plan that brings focus to the use of resources, including actions today to prepare for tomorrow which fit with how the facility currently works, and physical outputs which can be shared.

There are several features of this method which deliver practical benefits. The 12P-based questionnaire challenges participants to think widely and articulate what they take for granted. It also provides a common set of ideas and terminology for comparing interpretations. Focusing firstly on where participants are mainly in agreement sets a positive platform for further group discussions, and debating the scope of strategy allows learning to occur between participants.

If you would like to develop your understanding of the strategy scoping method, see the guide in the **online resources** for how to conduct scoping for organizational strategy. As it is derived and illustrated from practice, it shows how the method can benefit practitioners in a live organizational setting. This guide has been developed from our work with organizations we have supported in their strategy activities.

Finally, consider applying the strategy scoping method to any strategy assignment given in your module. By checking the required outputs against the 12P framework, you will be able to ensure that your submission is delivering all that is expected of you, and that you are connecting with the relevant theories and concepts of strategy.

PRACTITIONER INSIGHT: **MARIANNE MEEHAN**

Marianne Meehan is an entrepreneur, strategy consultant, and business mentor. She has held operational, general management, and directorship roles in high-growth organizations across a range of sectors in the UK, Europe, and the United States. She currently supports a portfolio of clients in the development and implementation of strategy. Marianne shares her views on the nature of strategy in practice.

What does strategy mean to you?

For me, strategy is about setting objectives for 3–5 years and then figuring out plans for how to deliver those desired outcomes. Strategy requires vision and planning, but most importantly a focus on how implementation will happen. At its core, strategy must be about action. Without a shared commitment to some sort of future work together there is no implementation and no delivery of outcomes. I realize that strategy can mean different things to different people. Doing an MBA helped me deepen and reframe my view of strategy. Knowledge of different theories helped me develop my own strategy practices, and an ability to relate to different strategy 'requirements'. Central to what I do now is an appreciation that effective strategy practice is, at its heart, tailored to the needs of the situation at any moment in time.

In terms of practice, I would advise anyone seeking to undertake work to think about:

- **Engagement**—work in a way the draws others in, for their ideas, energy, and commitment
- **Implementation**—always push towards answering 'So what are we going to do?' when

considering problems, opportunities, or options for the future

- **Be realistic**—deal as much as you can in an unvarnished view of the world. Take multiple data sources and opinions into account to better understand the way the world is, rather than how you'd like it to be, when undertaking strategy development or planning for implementation.

Career path that now informs strategy perspectives

My first role was for a firm of accountants, in which I picked up basic accountancy and finance skills, seeing academic learning come to life. When I reflect back, that first role nurtured my interest in operations, processes, and strategy implementation. I then joined a small company called Water at Work in 1995. The firm provided 19-litre bottles of water and cooler machines to companies in the UK. It was a new concept in the UK market at the time—the founder saw the opportunity to import the idea from America. I was there for ten years over a period of high growth. When I joined, we had 2000 customers and 20 employees—ten years later there were 600 employees serving 120,000 customers! It was an incredible learning experience. There was significant organic growth and we also grew through acquisition. In 1997 we were bought by a Canadian company called Sparkling Spring Water Group—a move that brought cash and resources to grow. Danone acquired Sparkling Spring Water Group in 2003 and entered into a joint venture with Eden Springs in 2004.

I left Eden Springs in 2005 to take up a Chief Financial Officer role running a Family Office for a high net worth family setting up an office in the Netherlands and Connecticut, USA. The main aspects of the role were to manage the family assets, develop the investment portfolio, identify and integrate other business investments, and manage all operational aspects for the family members. In 2007 we acquired a Canadian company that designed and manufactured capital equipment—I was given the task of leading the strategic change process and operations transformation. The project was a success, after which I came back to the UK in 2010 to do an MBA specializing in strategy. After graduating, I took up the newly created role of MBA Operations Director for three years, before setting up my own consultancy business. I have a passion for strategy and am supporting a continuing portfolio of ten clients on a range of projects to deliver strategic enhancement. Further, in 2015, a colleague I met through the MBA and I opened up the award-winning Tribe Yoga Studios in Edinburgh—we now have three facilities (including a spin studio) and are thinking strategically about where to go next!

How was strategy perceived or viewed in these different environments?

In Water at Work, there was no formal strategy—we were just doing whatever seemed necessary to grow at breakneck speed, manage cash, and survive. A strategy evolved when we connected with bigger organizations. But initially the strategy corresponded to whatever could be accommodated in the budget–financial planning cycle. There was no concrete long-term plan, and we didn't have a formal shared view of where we were going together.

The Family Office was very different—the head had an eye for opportunity. He developed a long-term strategy focused on return on investment. He built a highly diverse portfolio through projects that (a) were interesting and (b) had high possible returns. He had many options as he was often approached by acquisition prospects because of his wealth. He took a long-term patient approach rather than quarterly-focused decisions about returns on investment. In that business, strategy was a continuing process—effective management of what we had in hand, but continual readiness to react to opportunities. We had protocols that we used to keep us fit for the future. The over-arching corporate strategy guided all activity; then we had specific business strategies for different work streams, and by asking 'How do we make that happen?', functional strategies were developed to deliver operational outcomes. Within the parameters of the owner's strategic vision, we all knew how to work with each other—there was trust, high understanding, positive relationships, consistent ways of working, support for each other, recognition, and reward.

As a consultant, I've noticed that strategy as a possession is vital to keeping people engaged. Documents and materials—plans, visions, write-ups—are brought out time and time again to help everyone pay attention, track progress, and think in a focused way. I've found that strategy can be a scary or confusing prospect at all levels of an organization—clear and simple documentation during

1

a strategy episode is vital to demystifying, learning, and building a shared sense of meaning. Strategy 'possessions' can give a sense of achievement and a key reference resource, and are an important sign of tangible contribution as a consultant.

Across all my roles, I've found that strategy work can help surface and resolve problems that matter—enabling improvements to be realized that engage employees as it improves their lives. To allow this to happen, the practices of senior leaders in relation to strategy are crucial. If they choose to overwrite what colleagues suggest, engagement potential is harmed and the reputation of 'strategy' as a type of work is damaged. If you invite people to contribute, you have to listen to what they say and take it seriously. Otherwise don't invite them.

When we started up the business, I used a combination of my experiences to lead development of the objectives and a vision for the company through workshop sessions. The business owners set the initial view, and then we got the whole team together in Dublin and invited participation in setting implementation priorities and plans. We use the strategy to this day and continue to update it when we feel it is necessary, such as when we have achieved an objective or we want to do something significant and new.

CHAPTER SUMMARY

In this chapter we addressed the following learning outcomes.

- **Explain how strategy can be interpreted in multiple ways**
  Strategy was described at a high level as the best word we have to capture the balancing of ways, means, and objectives for an individual or organization. However, strategy has been shown to resist precise definition. Instead, there are multiple possible interpretations of strategy that different stakeholders may adopt to varying degrees according to their personal views and understanding of the needs of a situation.

- **Comprehend the challenges and benefits of agreeing a shared understanding of strategy with key stakeholders**
  The main challenge that the strategist faces is to work with the stakeholders involved to discuss and agree what strategy means and set an appropriate scope of strategy work/target outcomes. Doing this well increases the likelihood of buy-in to the process and outcomes, and also the quality of strategy work as a wider range of inputs are gathered to highly relevant activities.

- **Critically assess the usefulness of strategy in different organizational situations and from different stakeholder perspectives**
  Possible interpretations of strategy have accrued over the last 60 years with different intellectual and practical heritages. For example, early academic thoughts on strategy as a rational plan grounded in analytical methods are now complemented by process and practice theories which connect with the human aspects of making and managing strategy. With limitations and within practical constraints, each interpretation of strategy has the potential to contribute to how a group of stakeholders work together on organizational strategy. It is valuable for you to be aware of possible interpretations of strategy and to be able to guide the scoping of strategy work effectively.

- **Appreciate the value of strategy as a mechanism for coordinating organizational effort and decision-making**
  Organizational strategy can add value as a mechanism that guides decision-making, resource allocation, stakeholder management, and coordinated actions. This mechanism will rarely be most effective when it produces fixed outcomes on a one-off basis. It will work best when it is kept relevant through continuing managerial attention and incorporation of new learning and insights from the evolving organizational context.
- **Apply a simple mechanism for clarifying how strategy is interpreted within and between stakeholder groups**
  A simple scoping method based on the 12P framework was reviewed. The scoping method creates a customized definition of strategy to suit stakeholder needs and incorporate their views. Through questions that relate to established strategy interpretations, structured dialogue between stakeholders can reveal the extent to which a shared understanding of strategy is held. If what is meant by strategy is surfaced and resolved at the start of strategy work, then target outcomes can be identified and stakeholder perspectives effectively managed.

END OF CHAPTER QUESTIONS

Recall questions

1. How has the concept of strategy developed over the twentieth century, and how does this developmental path influence how it is understood today?
2. What might we mean by organizational strategy?
3. What are the main differences between corporate, business, and functional strategies?
4. What benefits might organizational strategy yield?
5. Summarize the range of possible interpretations of strategy covered in this chapter. What are they and what do they mean?
6. Why might we choose to start a strategy process by scoping a strategy with those involved?

Application questions

A) Imagine you have been assigned to lead a strategy team within a business unit of a multinational corporation. What actions would you take initially to build stakeholder engagement in the strategy process? Draft a short plan of action, with explanatory comments as to why each action should be undertaken.

B) Ask five people who have a connection with strategy (either leading, participating in, or implementing strategy work) the question 'What does strategy mean to you?' Use the scoping method to explore their interpretation in detail and map their responses onto a diagram (in which the emphases of their responses can be compared).

1

C) Pick two or three organizations that are of interest to you and explore how strategy is described and used in their externally facing media (website, advertising, annual report, etc.). Note which interpretations of strategy are evident in their media, and also the messages which seem to be portrayed by the styling of their media (strategy as a possession). Reflecting on the organizations' contexts and histories, suggest some explanations for the similarities and differences between the organizations approaches.

ONLINE RESOURCES

www.oup.com/he/mackay1e

FURTHER READING

Strategy: A History, by Sir Lawrence Freedman

Freedman, L. (2013). *Strategy: A History*. Oxford: Oxford University Press.

This extensive text traces the history of the development and use of strategy. It is an engaging well-written book that takes the reader from the roots of strategy in ancient civilisations, through military applications and developments, up to the modern incarnations and interpretations of strategy used in organizational life today. It will be helpful to students looking to understand strategy beyond functional methodological interpretations.

A Treatise on Efficacy, by Françoise Jullien (transl. Janet Lloyd)

Jullien, F. (2004). *A Treatise on Efficacy: Between Western and Chinese Thinking* (transl. J. Lloyd). Honolulu, HI: University of Hawaii Press.

Françoise Jullien's text compares and contrasts interpretations of strategy as originating in Ancient Greek and Chinese thought. Our modern usage of strategy—in the business press and academic life—seems strongly linked to Ancient Greek teachings and influences. As laid out in this book, there is much to learn from the processual thinking and philosophies of Ancient Chinese thought on strategy, which offers different ideas as to what it means to be strategic. This book presents these two ancient influences side by side, challenging us to ask how we can be more effective in our strategy work. It will be of use to those struggling to make strategy more impactful, and to understand how we can manage strategy as a process, through people, in a complex and ever unfolding world.

Strategy Safari, by Henry Mintzberg, Bruce Ahlstrand, and Joseph Lampel

Mintzberg, H., Ahlstrand, B., and Lampel, J. (2009). *Strategy Safari: Your Complete Guide Through the Wilds of Strategic Management*. Harlow: Prentice Hall.

Strategy Safari *is a popular text that offers a review of academic perspectives available in the strategy literature. It makes a neat complement to the different practice-focused interpretations raised in this chapter. Mintzberg and colleagues offer insights as to how a range of schools of thought in strategy—such as design, culture, power, planning, cognition—have developed, and how associated research might be used separately and in combination. It will be of use to those seeking to understand how academic perspectives of strategy have emerged over the years, and why there are different 'tribes' or types of strategy academic.*

Good Strategy/Bad Strategy, by Richard Rumelt

Rumelt, R.P. (2011). *Good Strategy/Bad Strategy: The Difference and Why It Matters*. London: Profile Books.

Richard Rumelt has been a highly influential American strategy academic over the past 30 years. He offers his insights as to what makes a 'good' strategy, and how it might add value to strategic managers and organizations. He writes about the importance of having a core, or kernel, idea of strategy around which all other interpretations and actions can be developed in a coherent way. It will be helpful to those looking for ideas about how strategy can be used as a problem-solving mechanism, and to further understand the importance of strategy as priority.

REFERENCES

Ackermann, F. and Eden, C. (2011a). *Making Strategy: Mapping Out Strategic Success*. London: Sage.

Ackermann, F. and Eden, C. (2011b). Strategic management of stakeholders: theory and practice. *Long Range Planning*, **44**(3), 179–96.

Arend, R.J. (2016). Divide and conquer, or the disintegration of strategic management: it's time to celebrate. *Strategic Organization*, **14**(2), 156–66.

Arend, R.J., Zhao, Y.L., Song, M., and Im, S. (2017). Strategic planning as a complex and enabling managerial tool. *Strategic Management Journal*, **38**(8), 1741–52.

Arnaud, N., Mills, C.E., Legrand, C., and Maton, E. (2016). Materializing strategy in mundane tools: the key to coupling global strategy and local strategy practice? *British Journal of Management*, **27**(1), 38–57.

Baginski, S.P., Bozzolan, S., Marra, A., and Mazzola, P. (2017). Strategy, valuation, and forecast accuracy: evidence from Italian Strategic Plan disclosures. *European Accounting Review*, **26**(2), 341–78.

Barnett, M.L. (2016). Strategist, organize thyself. *Strategic Organization*, **14**(2), 146–55.

Bartlett, C.A. and Ghoshal, S. (1994). Changing the role of top management: beyond strategy to purpose. *Harvard Business Review*, **72**(6), 79–88.

Beynon-Davies, P., Jones, P., and White, G.R.T. (2016). Business patterns and strategic change. *Strategic Change*, **25**(6), 675–91.

Birkinshaw, J., Foss, N.J., and Lindenberg, S. (2014). Combining purpose with profits. *MIT Sloan Management Review*, **55**(3), 49–56.

Birkinshaw, J., Zimmermann, A., and Raisch, S. (2016). How do firms adapt to discontinuous change? *California Management Review*, **58**, 36–58.

Breene, R.T.S., Nunes, P.F., and Shill, W.E. (2007). The chief strategy officer. *Harvard Business Review*, **85**(10), 84–93.

Bungay, S. (2019). 5 myths about strategy. *Harvard Business Review Digital Articles*, https://hbr.org/2019/04/5-myths-about-strategy.

Chew, C. and Osborne, S.P. (2009). Exploring strategic positioning in the UK charitable sector: emerging evidence from charitable organizations that provide public services. *British Journal of Management*, **20**(1), 90–105.

Collis, D. (2016). Lean strategy. *Harvard Business Review*, **94**(3), 62–8.

Conroy, K.M., Collings, D.G., and Clancy, J. (2017). Regional headquarter's dual agency role: micro-political strategies of alignment and self-interest. *British Journal of Management*, **28**(3), 390–406.

Cummings, S. (1993). Brief case: the first strategists. *Long Range Planning*, **26**(3), 133–5.

Dameron, S., Lê, J.K., and LeBaron, C. (2015). Materializing strategy and strategizing materials: why matter matters. *British Journal of Management*, **26**, S1–12.

Daviter, F. (2017). Coping, taming, or solving: alternative approaches to the governance of wicked problems. *Policy Studies*, **38**(6), 571–88.

Denning, S. (2018). The emergence of Agile people management. *Strategy and Leadership*, **46**(4), 3–10.

Dobusch, L., Dobusch, L., and Müller-Seitz, G. (2019). Closing for the benefit of openness? The case of Wikimedia's open strategy process. *Organization Studies*, **40**(3), 343–70.

Farjoun, M. (2007). The end of strategy? *Strategic Organization*, **5**(3), 197–210.

Felin, T. and Zenger, T. (2018). What sets breakthrough strategies apart: innovative strategies depend more on novel, well-reasoned theories than on well-crunched numbers. *MIT Sloan Management Review*, **59**(2), 86–8.

Franco-Santos, M., Nalick, M., Rivera-Torres, P., and Gomez-Mejia, L. (2017). Governance and well-being in academia: negative consequences of applying an agency theory logic in higher education. *British Journal of Management*, **28**(4), 711–30.

Freedman, L. (2013). *Strategy: A History*. Oxford: Oxford University Press.

Frynas, J.G., Mol, M.J., and Mellahi, K. (2018). Management innovation made in China: Haier's Rendanheyi. *California Management Review*, **61**(1), 71–93.

Graber, R.S. (2009). Business lessons from chess: a discussion of parallels between chess strategy and business strategy. *Academy of Educational Leadership Journal*, **13**(1), 79–85.

Grant, R.M. (2003). Strategic planning in a turbulent environment: evidence from the oil majors. *Strategic Management Journal*, **24**(6), 491–517.

Groysberg, B., Lee, J., Price, J., and Cheng, J.Y-J. (2018). The leader's guide to corporate culture. *Harvard Business Review*, **96**(1), 44–52.

Gulati, R. (2018). Structure that's not stifling. *Harvard Business Review*, **96**(3), 68–79.

Guo, C., Wang, Y.J., Hao, A.W., and Saran, A. (2018). Strategic positioning, timing of entry, and new product performance in business-to-business markets. Do market-oriented firms make better decisions? *Journal of Business-to-Business Marketing*, **25**(1), 51–64.

Hansen, J.R. and Jacobsen, C.B. (2016). Changing strategy processes and strategy content in public sector organizations? A Longitudinal case study of NPM reforms' influence on strategic management. *British Journal of Management*, **27**(2), 373–89.

Helfat, C.E., Finklestein, S., Mitchell, W., et al. (2007). *Dynamic Capabilities: Understanding Strategic Change in Organisations*. Oxford: Blackwell.

Isenberg, D.J. (1987). The tactics of strategic opportunism. *Harvard Business Review*, **65**(2), 92–7.

Jalonen, K., Schildt, H., and Vaara, E. (2018). Strategic concepts as micro-level tools in strategic sensemaking. *Strategic Management Journal*, **39**(10), 2794–826.

Johnson, G., Langley, A., Melin, L., and Whittington, R. (2008). *Strategy as Practice: Research Directions and Resources*. Cambridge: Cambridge University Press.

Johnson, G., Melin, L., and Whittington, R. (2003). Micro strategy and strategizing: towards an activity-based view. *Journal of Management Studies*, **40**(1), 3–22.

Jullien, F. (2004). *A Treatise on Efficacy: Between Western and Chinese Thinking* (Trans J. Lloyd). Honolulu, HI: University of Hawaii Press.

Kammerlander, N. and Ganter, M. (2015). An attention-based view of family firm adaptation to discontinuous technological change: exploring the role of family CEOs' noneconomic goals. *Journal of Product Innovation Management*, **32**(3), 361–83.

Kerr, W.R. (2016). Harnessing the best of globalization. *MIT Sloan Management Review*, **58**(1), 58–67

Lee, Y.W. (2019). Enhancing shared value and sustainability practices of global firms: the case of Samsung Electronics. *Strategic Change*, **28**(2), 139–45.

Loonam, J., Eaves, S., Kumar, V., and Parry, G. (2018). Towards digital transformation: lessons learned from traditional organizations. *Strategic Change*, **27**(2), 101–9.

Mackay, D. and Zundel, M. (2017). Recovering the divide: a review of strategy and tactics in business and management. *International Journal of Management Reviews*, **19**(2), 175–94.

MacKay, R.B. and Chia, R. (2013). Choice, chance, and unintended consequences in strategic change: a process understanding of the rise and fall of Northco Automotive. *Academy of Management Journal*, **56**(1), 208–30.

McMillan, C., and Overall, J. (2016). Wicked problems: turning strategic management problems upside down. *Journal of Business Strategy*, **37**(1), 34–43.

Markides, C.C. (2000). *All the Right Moves: A Guide to Crafting Breakthrough Strategy*. Boston, MA: Harvard Business School Press.

Mintzberg, H. and Hunsicker, J.Q. (1988). Crafting strategy. *McKinsey Quarterly* (3), 71–90.

Mintzberg, H. and Waters, J.A. (1985). Of strategies, deliberate and emergent. *Strategic Management Journal*, **6**(3), 257–72.

Mintzberg, H., Ahlstrand, B., and Lampel, J. (2009). *Strategy Safari: Your Complete Guide Through the Wilds of Strategic Management*. Harlow: Prentice Hall.

Mitreanu, C. (2006). Is strategy a bad word? *MIT Sloan Management Review*, **47**(2), 96–96.

Munro, I. (2010). Nomadic strategies in the network society: from Lawrence of Arabia to Linux. *Scandinavian Journal of Management*, **26**(2), 215–23.

Penrose, E. (1959). *The Theory of The Growth of the Firm*. Oxford: Basil Blackwell.

Pettigrew, A., Thomas, H., and Whittington, R. (2006). Strategic management: the strengths and limitations of a field. In: Pettigrew, A., Thomas, H., and Whittington, R. (eds), *Handbook of Strategy and Management*, pp. 1–30. London: Sage.

Plesner, U. and Gulbrandsen, I.T. (2015). Strategy and new media: a research agenda. *Strategic Organization*, **13**(2), 153–62.

Porter, M.E. (1980). *Competitive Strategy: Techniques for Analyzing Industries and Competitors*. New York: Free Press.

Porter, M.E. (1984). *Competitive Advantage: Creating and Sustaining Superior Performance*. New York: Free Press.

Poulis, K. and Poulis, E. (2016). Problematizing fit and survival: transforming the law of requisite variety through complexity misalignment. *Academy of Management Review*, **41**(3), 503–27.

Powell, T.C. (2017). Strategy as diligence: putting behavioural strategy into practice. *California Management Review*, **59**(3), 162–90.

Quinn, R.E. and Thakor, A.V. (2018). Creating a purpose-driven organization. *Harvard Business Review*, **96**(4), 78–85.

Rigby, D.K., Sutherland, J., and Noble, A. (2018). Agile at scale. *Harvard Business Review*, **96**(3), 88–96.

Rumelt, R.P. (2011). *Good Strategy/Bad Strategy: The Difference and Why It Matters*. London: Profile Books.

Schoemaker, P.J.H., Heaton, S., and Teece, D. (2018). Innovation, dynamic capabilities, and leadership. *California Management Review*, **61**(1), 15–42.

Seidl, D. (2007). General strategy concepts and the ecology of strategy discourses: a systemic-discursive perspective. *Organization Studies*, **28**(2), 197–218.

Sull, D., Turconi, S., Sull, C., and Yoder, J. (2018a). Four logics of corporate strategy. *MIT Sloan Management Review*, **59**(2), 38–44.

Sull, D., Turconi, S., Sull, C., and Yoder, J. (2018b). How to develop strategy for execution. *MIT Sloan Management Review*, **59**(2), 47.

Teece, D., Peteraf, M., and Leih, S. (2016). Dynamic capabilities and organizational agility: risk, uncertainty and strategy in the innovation economy. *California Management Review*, **58**(4), 13–35.

Teece, D.J. (2007). Explicating dynamic capabilities: the nature and microfoundations of (sustainable) enterprise performance. *Strategic Management Journal*, **28**(13), 1319–50.

Vilà, J. and Canales, J.I. (2008). Can strategic planning make strategy more relevant and build commitment over time? The case of RACC. *Long Range Planning*, **41**(3), 273–90.

Vuorinen, T., Hakala, H., Kohtamäki, M., and Uusitalo, K. (2018). Mapping the landscape of strategy tools: a review on strategy tools published in leading journals within the past 25 years. *Long Range Planning*, **51**(4), 586–605.

Wright, G., Cairns, G., O'Brien, F.A., and Goodwin, P. (2019). Scenario analysis to support decision making in addressing wicked problems: pitfalls and potential. *European Journal of Operational Research*, **278**(1), 3–19.

Wu, L.-F., Huang, I.-C., Huang, W.-C., and Du, P.-L. (2019). Aligning organizational culture and operations strategy to improve innovation outcomes: an integrated perspective in organizational management. *Journal of Organizational Change Management*, **32**(2), 224–50.

CHAPTER TWO

A Process–Practice Model of Strategy

CONTENTS

2

LEARNING OBJECTIVES

By the end of this chapter, you should be able to:

- Explain how strategy can be understood from a process–practice view
- Explain what is meant by practice, practitioners, practices, tools, activity, and process in the context of strategy work
- Evaluate the usefulness of the attention-based view as an aid to understanding what people do in relation to strategy
- Critically assess the limitations of adopting rigid approaches to strategy
- Articulate how the strategy process–practice framework can guide your learning about how to think, talk, and act as a strategy practitioner

TOOL BOX

- **Combinatory model of strategy as process and practice**
  This model illustrates how strategy—as a continuous stream of activity—occurs over time and in context through an interplay of strategy formulation and implementation efforts.
- **Attention-based view**
  A set of concepts and theoretical contributions that help explain how organizations behave, adapt to changing environments, develop capabilities, and strategize according to how decision-makers' attention is informed and directed. A valuable complement to the process–practice framework.
- **Strategy process–practice framework**
  A guiding framework that can be used as a checklist and reference point for learning how to think, talk, and act like a strategist, in line with understanding of strategy as process and practice.

2

OPENING CASE STUDY AN ENGINE FOR GROWTH AT EPIC GAMES

Epic Games' Fortnite, with an estimated 200 million players, is the world's most popular video game. It has a variety of game options built around a Battle Royale format, in which players seek to scavenge resources and weapons to eliminate all other contenders on a mystical island. Played online, it has cross-platform capability, meaning that players from all manner of devices and gaming systems can play together. In 2018, Fortnite generated a reported $1 billion through in-game microtransactions, where players pay for cosmetic upgrades, according to Nielsen company SuperData. CEO Tim Sweeney commented that Epic 'wants to have a direct relationship with our customers on all platforms where possible. Physical storefronts and middlemen distributors are no longer required'.

So far, Fortnite is proving highly lucrative. Key competitors Activision Blizzard and Take Two Interactive have suffered major share price falls over investor concerns about the revenue generating exploits of Epic's in-game 'V-Bucks' system. The cash being generated by Epic is allowing it to innovate well beyond Fortnite.

Epic is 48% owned by Chinese internet giant Tencent, which bought its stake for $330 million in 2012. This is looking an excellent investment as Epic Games was recently valued at $15 billion and attracted $1.25 billion in a 2018 funding round. Surprisingly, given Fortnite's success, the success of this investment call is attributed more to the Unreal Engine. The Unreal Engine is Epic's proprietary core gaming code. It has underpinned Fortnite's rise to a viral video game sensation. But Epic believe that it is on a path to be a widespread licensed technology in sectors as diverse as medical research, automotive development, and architecture.

'In a way, the Unreal Engine is to Epic Games what Amazon Web Services is to Amazon. Both companies monetize the proprietary infrastructure used to support their core businesses. Over time, these infrastructure offerings have become core businesses of their own,' comments Jud Waite, a senior analyst at CB Insights.

Now in its fourth version, Epic's software platform the Unreal Engine was originally developed for its own series of games (first powering a title called Unreal, hence the name). Developers can use the Engine's features for tasks such as rendering graphics and controlling actions in a game's environment to build all manner of applications. Unreal Engine's technological developments are showcased through Fortnite, which is helping to bolster their marketing campaign to promote its cross-platform capabilities to allow gamers to play on devices from smartphones to high-end PCs.

The game's success also allows Epic to experiment with new ways to make money, from a proprietary game store to 'e-sports'. Epic does not charge companies to use Unreal Engine, but instead takes a 5% cut of all gross revenue on applications (primarily games) created using the engine, but only once they make $3000 per quarter. In fact, Epic is even earning money from Fortnite's main competitor, Player Unknown's Battlegrounds, developed using Unreal Engine by South Korea's Bluehole.

According to Epic data, the latest version, Unreal Engine 4, is currently licensed to over seven million hobbyists and professional designers for both gaming and enterprise use. Since releasing this version free in 2015, the company has grown an enterprise team of dozens of employees which supports non-gaming markets such as architecture and automotive design. Sweeney highlights that this line of work has blossomed since computer graphics technology developed sufficiently to enable photorealistic images to be generated in real time.

While consumers have been slow to adopt virtual reality hardware, enterprise applications in the corporate world are on the rise. Unreal Engine has been used in building design (for example, in 2007 it was used to produce a virtual prototype of the new Dallas Cowboys stadium that could be taken on tour). Medical research is also showing potential as a market for the Unreal Engine. UK-based pharmaceutical research firm C4X Discovery recently starting using Unreal Engine technology to visualize and manipulate 3D molecules in virtual reality, with the potential to let scientists collaborate remotely in the virtual environment. And several car manufacturers including Audi, BMW, and McLaren recently attended an

Unreal Engine enterprise technology event in Germany to explore automotive development potential.

Most enterprise users are using the free version of Unreal Engine, but optional paid support services, such as onsite visits and access to a community of developers and third-party developers, allow Epic to make money from its enterprise effort. However, Epic is currently working on building features and developing new technology within the Unreal Engine that will create a wide range of possible corporate client offerings and make Epic a potential player in many new sectors.

Sweeney predicts that game users will be overtaken by enterprise users of Unreal Engine by the end of 2019, and he thinks that ultimately industry-specific and entertainment uses will converge as part of a bigger digital industry. There is no doubt that the digital playing field is shifting, driven by platform-oriented firms like Epic and a growing demand for digitally enabled innovation in a wide range of sectors. The challenge for developers, clients, and platform providers will be keeping pace with the continually evolving circumstances as pioneers—or at least relevant players—in the dynamic world of digital industries.

Questions for discussion

Imagine you are the CEO of Epic Games.

1. What external trends, factors, and opportunities do you think that you will have to address in your strategy work over the next 3–5 years?
2. What stakeholders are likely to (a) have an influence on your strategy and (b) want to be participants in your strategy work?
3. How realistic is it for you to set and stick exactly to a five-year strategy plan for Epic? Explain your answer.
4. What sort of activities would you carry out in order to make and manage strategy effectively?

This case is based on https://www.cnbc.com/2018/12/14/the-reason-epic-landed-a-15-billion-valuation-is-not-fortnite-success.html with extracts from https://www.theguardian.com/games/2018/oct/28/fortnite-company-epic-games-valued-15bn

2.1 **Introduction**

In this chapter, we focus on what people actually do in relation to strategy over time and in context. We explore how strategy can be understood as a continuing accomplishment of practitioner activity. Henry Mintzberg (1987:66) highlights the practical value of being able to 'craft strategy', drawing on 'skill, dedication and mastery of detail ... a feeling of intimacy and harmony with the materials at hand'. Using the image of a potter artfully shaping an output from clay—working and reworking materials—Mintzberg describes the practice of strategy as a continual effort in which 'formulation and implementation merge into a fluid process of learning through which creative strategies emerge'.

In line with a crafting metaphor, we introduce a dynamic 'process–practice' framework of strategy. This framework accommodates the interpretations of strategy highlighted in Chapter 1. Drawing on the latest theorizing about how strategy occurs over time in context, the process–practice framework should help you understand and explain:

- the central importance of practitioners and what they do in strategy
- how you can cope when strategy ideas don't work out as planned in reality
- the ways in which strategy can be considered as a continual stream of activity

- how we can responsively revise our practices, crafting strategy to meet situational needs
- how different theories, data sources, and interpretations can be incorporated into collective strategy practices.

Being able to think in terms of a flexible process–practice framework is beneficial as strategy activity rarely, if ever, occurs in an orderly repeatable fashion. It is on this issue that linear prescriptive models of strategy fail. If strategy activity occurs in rigid sequence, regardless of the situation, contextual factors are likely to diminish the efficiency and effectiveness of practitioner efforts. As an alternative, a process–practice framework highlights how practitioners can draw on a range of learned and improvised **practices** to meet the changing strategy requirements of an organization over time. Through awareness and practice of different types of strategy activity, you can improve your ability to craft strategy according to circumstances. You can also learn how to reflect on experience, read situations, and adapt your practices over time to improve your effectiveness as a strategy practitioner.

We will explore how the process–practice framework can help you work with strategy as a 'fluid process' without any artificial divide between formulation and implementation activities. This is a valuable insight to learn as in an organizational setting you are likely to encounter a divided view of strategy formulation and implementation. Formulation is typically seen as the responsibility of only a select few individuals, such as the top team or a strategy function. Conventional thinking dictates that this small group of leaders formulate strategy as a guiding vision or masterplan, and then roll out their ideas for implementation to the rest of the organization. The communication of strategy—through 'town hall' meetings, email newsletters, performance management systems, etc.—aligns the rest of the organization, with each team or individual receiving their part to play. Implementation then follows, guided and tracked by performance management systems and scorecards.

This accepted convention of separating strategy formulation and implementation activities seems at odds with the realities of strategy in practice. There is no doubt that the ideas and activities of senior leaders are crucial in strategy work. However, as shown in Figure 2.1, studies of strategy success rates find that conventional strategy implementation efforts are more likely to fail than succeed in meeting intended outcomes. A review of strategy implementation failure by Sull et al. (2015) highlights several key issues prevailing across organizational strategy work that limit the possibilities of strategic success and impact:

- **(a)** an emphasis on installing top-down 'alignment' of strategy rather than lateral coordination and agreement
- **(b)** sticking rigidly to strategy plans rather than acting opportunistically within a set of shared principles
- **(c)** investing time in one-way communication rather than building shared meaning and understanding of strategy
- **(d)** performance management cultures that reward 'more of the same' behaviours rather than measured risk-taking in pursuit of change and innovation
- **(e)** concentrating strategy responsibility and involvement in a few leaders rather than distributing it across the organization.

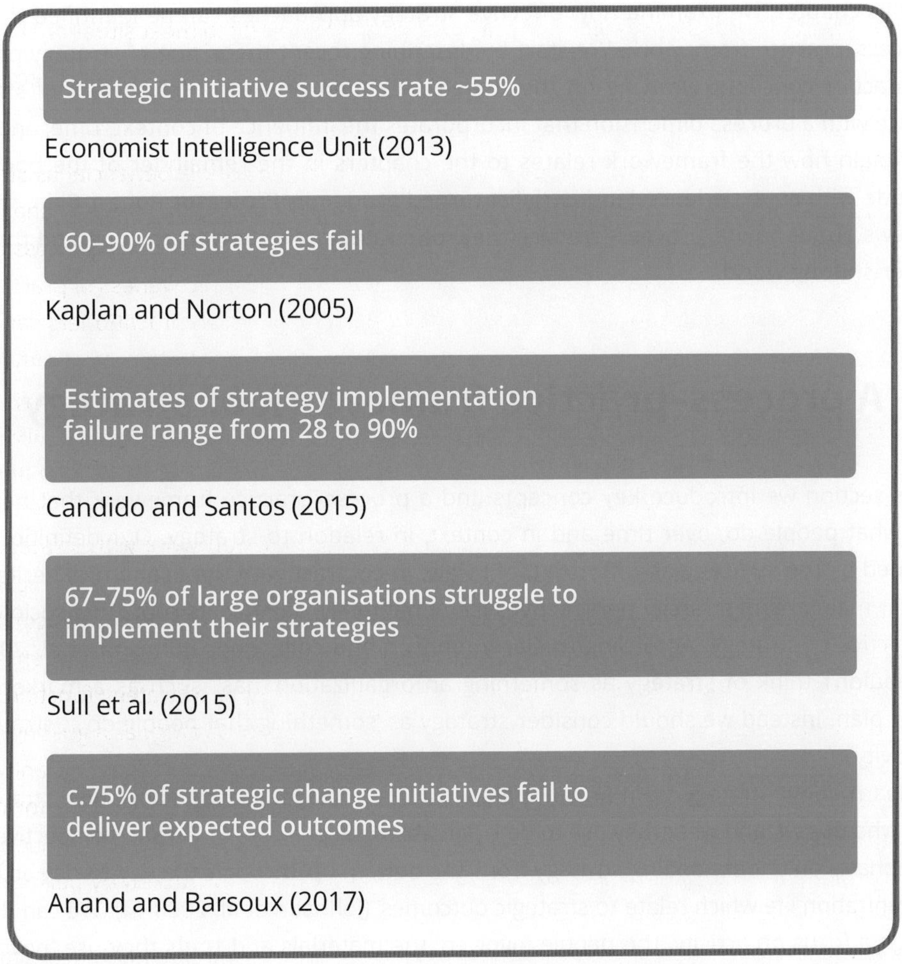

Strategic initiative success rate ~55%
Economist Intelligence Unit (2013)
60–90% of strategies fail
Kaplan and Norton (2005)
Estimates of strategy implementation failure range from 28 to 90%
Candido and Santos (2015)
67–75% of large organisations struggle to implement their strategies
Sull et al. (2015)
c.75% of strategic change initiatives fail to deliver expected outcomes
Anand and Barsoux (2017)

FIGURE 2.1 **Estimated strategy implementation failure rates.**

What might you do to make and manage strategy in a way that increases the likelihood of strategy delivering valuable outcomes? Reversing the issues described by Sull et al. (2015) would be an approach to strategy that builds coordination, cooperation, and engagement, encourages alertness, reflection, and responsiveness, enables the seizing of unanticipated opportunities, builds shared meaning-making of strategy across stakeholders, rewards and recognizes appropriate risk-taking and novelty, and spreads the responsibility for strategy-making and management throughout the organization. Through such an approach, any fixed separation between strategy formulation and implementation activities dissolves.

To address strategy in this way doesn't mean ignoring established methods and approaches, such as creating strategy plans and targets, using environmental analysis and business information, communicating through emails, 'town hall' meetings, and involving the top team. Instead, these activities are used to the extent that they are productive in a given situation, augmented by any additional practices and stakeholder involvement required at that moment in time.

In this chapter, we examine how effective strategy approaches can be identified through a process–practice framework. We start by describing recent theorizing of strategy process and practice concepts. Drawing on these ideas, we then present a framework of strategy practice with a process dimension that incorporates the influence of context, time, and flow. We explain how the framework relates to the chapters in the remainder of the book. We conclude with an experienced industrialist turned academic, Professor Robert Chia, sharing his views about how a 'process–practice' view of strategy can allow us to cope and thrive in an ever-shifting world.

2.2 A process–practice framework of strategy

In this section we introduce key concepts and a process–practice framework that help explain what people do, over time and in context, in relation to strategy. Our definitions are informed by the **strategy-as-practice** (SaP) view. In contrast with the economics heritage of popular mainstream strategy perspectives (see Chapter 1), SaP has its roots in a sociological perspective of strategy. According to Gerry Johnson and colleagues (Johnson et al. 2008:3), we shouldn't think of strategy as something an organization 'has', such as a market position or plan. Instead we should consider strategy as 'something that people do ... strategy is an activity'.

To learn about strategy from an SaP perspective is to ask questions about how strategy is done, who does it, and what they use to do it (Jarzabkowski et al. 2016). An SaP perspective puts an emphasis on understanding strategy from 'the bottom up' through 'the day-to-day activities of organization life which relate to strategic outcomes' (Johnson et al. 2003:14). We can do this through a focus on activity, the people involved, the materials and **tools** they use, novel and routine ways of working, common habitual approaches, and the influence of efforts and interactions of individuals, organizations, and institutions over time.

Key definitions

Practice

Underpinning SaP is a definition of **practice** **as the 'on-going stream of activity' that constitutes organizational life** (Jarzabkowski 2003:24). As a matter of organizational relevance, strategy-as-practice can be considered as 'a situated, socially accomplished flow of organizational activity' (Jarzabkowski, 2005:7). The elements of this definition are instructive. 'Situated' means that the strategy **activity** undertaken occurs within context at a moment in time that will, in part, shape what is done. 'Socially accomplished' means that strategy results from the actions and interactions of practitioners. 'Flow' indicates that strategy is an ongoing concern that is always moving and shifting.

In Epic Games, practice describes the totality of continuing actions and interactions between colleagues in different functions, divisions, and locations, and their engagements with external parties such as customers, investors, and contractors. This practice encompasses the delivery of daily operations and attainment of organizational outcomes, such as revenue generation and new product development. Strategy, as practice, describes the stream of activity within Epic's organizational practice that makes and implements decisions that relate to strategic outcomes. This might include how to continue to develop Fortnite in the face of competitor activity and investor expectations; how to invest the financial gains in new product lines based on Unreal Engine, etc. Over time, the focus of strategy practice will evolve as the organizational context also shifts.

Practitioners

Practitioners are those individuals and groups of individuals whose efforts and activities contribute to strategy (Paroutis and Pettigrew 2007). We may also refer to practitioners as **actors**, as they are actively involved in the accomplishment of strategy on an ongoing basis.

The characteristics of practitioners—their history, education, experience, skills, connections, relationships, knowledge, biases, hidden agendas, etc.—influence how they think, make decisions, and act in any given situation, and thus the way in which they play a part in strategy activities (Adner and Helfat 2003). Practitioners might be internal staff, such as the senior management team, department heads, functional representatives, and operators. Practitioners can also be external to the organization, such as consultants, advisers, government officials, etc.

Practitioners influence strategy through the action they take, in which they allocate their time, attention, and effort towards trying to accomplish some manner of outcome. Tim Sweeney and his senior management team are practitioners who will have a recurring involvement in strategy practice in Epic Games. How Sweeney and his team focus their attention, and draw on their know-how and situational insights, will shape formal strategy activities. Equally, investors, the development community, prospective enterprise customers, and Fortnite users are all examples of other actors that may be involved in strategy practice at different moments.

Practices

Practices describe the ways of working adopted by practitioners when trying to accomplish a type of task. For example, we can use communication practices to share or receive information. Communication practices cover a wide range of acting, include writing, texting, gesturing, speaking, listening, reading, etc. (Ocasio et al. 2018). In relation to strategy, practices refer to 'regular, shared and legitimate ways of doing strategy work' (Burgelman et al. 2018:542). Strategy practices describe all the ways of working that we know and might draw on towards achieving strategy-related outcomes such as practices for debating the scope of strategy, practices for gathering and analysing strategic data, etc.

The format of practices can vary widely. Practices may be solo activities or involve interacting with others; practices might draw on physical supporting materials, or theories and concepts to shape ways of thinking and talking. We may undertake practices consciously or automatically depending on our familiarity with circumstances. We can deploy practices according to our preferences, skills, and understanding of the needs of a situation. As summarized by Jarzabkowski and Spee (2009:82) practices are 'complex bundle[s] involving social, material and embodied ways of doing that are interrelated and not always articulated or conscious to the actor involved in doing'.

In the Epic example, strategic practices for sensing the external environment include hosting technology events for non-customers, gathering feedback through the enterprise sales team, examining how rivals use the Unreal Engine, regular discussions with investors and analysts, use of customer/gamer feedback forums. These practices have evolved and been added over time as 'regular, shared, legitimate ways of working' in Epic under a general category of practices of 'gathering external data'.

Activity

Activity is that which is actually done by practitioners. As we direct individual and organizational resource towards action and interaction on a daily basis, we are said to undertake activity. Organizational activity is the aggregation of what individual practitioners from inside and outside the organization do, in context, towards some matter of collective interest.

Strategic activity refers to work done towards attaining some sort of strategy-related outcome. According to Jarzabkowski (2003:24), we use our practices, in routine or creative ways, on a continuing basis to contribute to an ongoing stream of strategic activity. To enable us to make sense of strategy, it is helpful to examine 'episodes' in the ongoing stream of strategic activity. An 'episode' is a period of time, with a defined start and end point, within which a set of activity involving practitioners, practices, context, and outcomes can be examined. To consider a strategizing episode means to focus attention on the strategic activity that occurred within a defined time period.

As described in the case study, a pivotal moment for Epic was when computer graphics technology became sufficiently advanced to allow photorealistic virtual reality offerings to be created through the Unreal Engine. The subsequent strategizing episode responded to this change in context by investment in an enterprise sales team and initiation of product research activity, amongst other decisions. Regardless of how circumstances change in future, this strategizing activity should be evaluated and interpreted in the context of the external development as it occurred within the timescale of the episode.

Tools

During strategy activity and as part of their strategy practices, practitioners may draw on strategy tools. **Tools describe the techniques, methods, models, and frameworks which support interactions and decision-making in strategy activity** (Clark 1997). Examples of strategy tools with academic roots are PESTEL, 5 Forces, SWOT, etc., which we will examine in later sections (see Vuorinen et al. (2018) for a review of the usage of research-led tools in strategy).

Tools can also include common technologies such as PowerPoint which, depending on how they are used, can have a significant influence on how strategy interactions and decisions occur (Knight et al. 2018). Further, as Jalonen et al. (2018) describe, the concepts and terms that we use when talking with others about strategy can also be considered tools, as they help us progress shared thinking and decide on actions to take. It is not uncommon for organizations to create new phrases or words that reflect their own strategy needs and interests.

Strategy tools 'provide a common language for strategic conversations between managers across hierarchical, functional, and geographic boundaries' (Jarzabkowski and Kaplan 2015:544). To better suit the situational needs of strategic activity, tools may be deployed in creative ways by practitioners beyond their formal designed scope. The actual boundaries and possibilities of strategy tools are known as **affordances**—all the possible ways in which a user might use a tool or object in everyday strategy activity (Demir 2015). As you seek to use tools effectively, being mindful of affordances can help you create '**tools-in-use**' that bring people together, spur creativity, provide legitimacy, incorporate local suggestions, and drive action in strategy practice (Giraudeau 2008). The adaption of strategy tools to suit local needs and situations can also reflect the social norms, politics, and culture of an organization, helping acceptance and engagement with strategy outcomes (Spee and Jarzabkowski 2009:224).

Throughout this book, we will challenge you to think of how you might creatively use the mainstream strategy tools that we introduce to give maximum benefit in different situations you might face. We will also ask you to think about the possible influences—beneficial and negative—on strategy activity that your selection and modification of strategy tools might have.

Strategy tools are not covered in the Epic case, but the Unreal Engine gives us an example of affordances. The Unreal Engine was originally designed as the technical platform to meet in-house needs, but Epic are constantly finding creative ways in which to use it as the basis for commercial offerings and revenue generation. The affordances of the Unreal Engine are continually enabling Epic to diversify its client base and sources of income.

Context

Context—the circumstances which form the setting for strategy activity to occur—matters in our understanding of strategy as it influences what practitioners decide and do in relation to strategy (Mahoney and McGahan 2007).

For ease of analysis, context is often described in terms of internal and external circumstances. Internal context refers to the cultural and historical context of an organization, its size and structure, the resources accrued over time, and existing strategic objectives, initiatives, and vision. In Chapters 4 and 6, we will consider how these elements of each organization's unique internal context can be better understood.

External context refers to the competitive or institutional settings in which an organization is embedded. The competitive setting refers to the nature, extent, and relationships of entities with which an organization vies directly for its continuing existence. The broader institutional environment in which organizations are embedded is 'a dynamic and self-renewing system, framed by state, international, and nongovernmental forces and populated by corporations large and small, interest groups, and individuals striving to have their voices heard' (Doh et al. 2012:36)

As we will explore in Section 2.3, knowing, responding to, and exploiting the internal and external contexts is vital to making appropriate strategy decisions (Frynas et al. 2018:88). Context also matters in terms of 'fit'—the extent to which there is a match between what external circumstances demand and what an organization does. As Markides (2000:194) comments, 'the right strategy for any firm must account for its unique evolution as well as the evolution of its industry'—a holistic view of context can help support strategy decisions and activity that ensures continuing fit.

The internal context for Epic includes the entrepreneurial and agile culture that has driven the organization thus far, its support from Tencent, and the strong financial resources and growing capabilities of its human resources in supporting multiple diverse market offerings. The external context includes factors such as the evolving needs of customers and potential new markets in which the organization can compete as technological progress occurs. Strategic decision-making and activity are situated in this dynamic and ever-evolving context.

2

Process

Process **refers to the continual unfolding of events, experiences, and activities over time**. The effects of time are crucial to this definition. Like a flowing river, the context in which strategy activity occurs is constantly changing. Strategic ideas and activity that seem appropriate at one time can prove disastrous at a later juncture as events intervene (MacKay and Chia 2013). This challenge is amplified by strategic initiatives often varying in terms of duration how they need to be managed (Ancona et al. 2001).

Our strategic practices and priorities are also constantly evolving as we observe shifting circumstances and learn from experience. When we achieve a strategic outcome, such as developing a new product, it represents a temporary advantage that we can attempt to exploit and maintain through ongoing activity (such as production and distribution, sales, or further innovation activity).

Tsoukas and Chia (2002) describe this understanding of process through the metaphor of a tightrope walker. From a distance, the tightrope walker looks to be standing still, whereas up close the walker is continually expending energy in making many small movements to stay in balance on the tightrope. The implication of this process view is that in organizational life, even staying the same requires energy, effort, and activity. Strategy process might then be understood as the continuing, coordinated activities of stakeholders to create ideas, artefacts, plans, priorities, etc. that sustain or change the organization, to the benefit of those involved with it.

For Epic, from a process perspective it would not make sense to become fixed on a set strategy when new applications for the Unreal Engine are being revealed all the time through either their own efforts or shifting customer needs. Instead, remaining vigilant for new market possibilities, and actively exploring those that show promise, seems a sensible continuing approach to strategy. This activity should sit alongside continuing to generate cash through regular updates of Fortnite. Whilst such ongoing development requires effort and resource usage, the revenue generated enables the company to continue to operate whilst funding new product and market options.

It is worthwhile noting that the above definition of process reflects what is known as 'strong process theorizing' (Langley et al. 2013). If you are reading strategy literature or examining organizational processes, you are likely to come across different interpretations of strategy process, typically concerning the mechanisms, factors, and activity steps involved in how strategy decisions are made and implemented. For an overview of these alternative interpretations, see Van de Ven (1992).

From across these definitions, we can summarize that from a process–practice view of strategy:

- strategy is accomplished ongoing, in context, through the activities of practitioners
- strategy practices are ways of working that practitioners draw upon in routine or creative ways as they attempt to act strategically
- strategy practices often draw on the use of tools, the design of which can be creatively adapted to suit local needs, to help undertake strategy activity in an effective way
- strategic outcomes, once achieved, will be temporary. Practitioners can seek to maintain desired outcomes through continuing activity
- strategy as a process is never 'complete' as events and experiences continue to unfold around and through us over time

CASE EXAMPLE 2.1 **FOSTERING STRATEGY PRACTICES IN NHS ENGLAND**

The National Health Service (NHS) is the publicly funded healthcare provider within each of the nations of the UK. The NHS in England is divided into organizational units known as Trusts, which serve a healthcare specialism or geographical territory. The regulator of health service Trusts in England is called Monitor, and aims to provide 'patients consistently safe, high quality, compassionate care within local health systems that are financially sustainable'.

In a 2013 report, Monitor noted that the ability of NHS Trusts to 'develop and implement strategic and operational plans is critical if they are to deliver effective and sustainable responses to current and future challenges'. The report defined strategic planning as 'the process of developing an organization's purpose, aims and objectives, including the allocation of related resources and responsibilities, drawing on robust evidence and setting challenging but feasible timescales for achieving goals ... Carrying out strategic planning at relevant points in the development of an organization will guide it through decision-making about service provision and resource allocation, and help executives and non-executives to govern effectively'.

However, based on field research in 30 Trusts, Monitor found that there were many instances of a lack of strategy capabilities and effective strategic practices in Trust leadership teams. Monitor recommended an initiative to develop 'the guidance, tools and support that [health] organizations need to strengthen their internal processes and capacity for [strategic] planning'. A toolkit developed in collaboration with the consultancy firm PWC to support all NHS providers in developing clear and well thought out strategies was published free to use in 2014.

A strategy framework was proposed in a toolkit format based on seven categories of strategy practice, as illustrated in Figure 2.2. Underpinning the model is a definition of strategy as 'a set of choices designed to work together to deliver the long-term goals of an organization in the face of uncertainty'. Each category of practice is intended to provide guidance for Trust leadership teams in their strategy work. The framework guidance notes point out that, without being prescriptive, the tools can be adapted according to the specific needs of a Trust's situation.

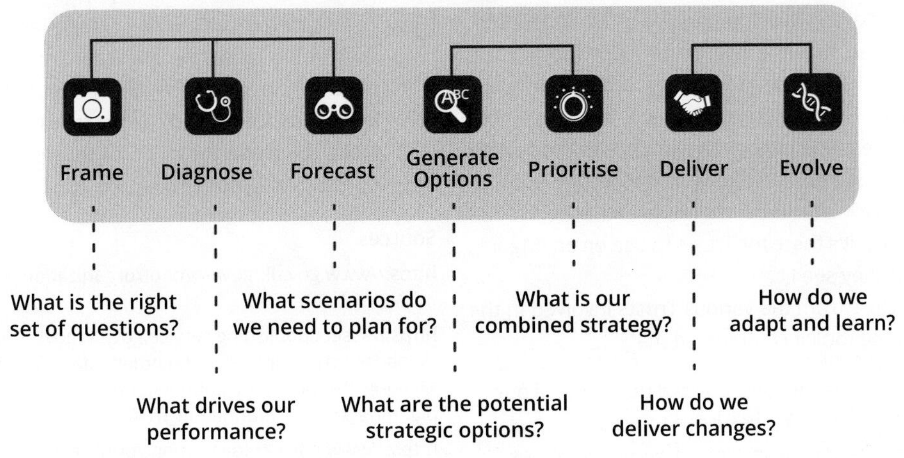

FIGURE 2.2 **NHS Trust strategy practices toolkit.** Source: Strategy development toolkit, p. 3. https://assets.publishing.service.gov.uk/government/uploads/system/uploads/attachment_data/file/456099/Monitor_TDA_developing_strategy_flyer_FINAL.pdf

Continued

2

Frame: establish the scope of the strategy development process by identifying the important strategic choices and decisions to be made and the criteria for making them.

Diagnose: understand current performance in detail at an overall and functional level.

Forecast: create a view of what the future might look like, including trends and technologies that may affect the organization.

Generate options: explore alternative ideas for acting to improve current services or introduce new ways of working that help improve strategic performance.

Prioritize: choose which strategic initiatives to pursue and check that they make sense as a coherent system.

Deliver: Allocate resources and defining the activities, milestones, measurements, and key performance indicators as to how strategy will be realized.

Evolve: monitor outcomes of activities, re-evaluating the strategy regularly, or when unexpected changes occur, and recommit to or refresh existing direction as required.

The toolkit was developed based on researching effective strategy practices within healthcare organizations from within the UK and internationally, as well as strategy practices deemed to be effective in a business setting. The toolkit was piloted with five Trusts to prove and refine the guidance offered for a 'health' setting.

Suzie Baillie, Development Director of Monitor, commented that the use of the pilot tool kit 'depends on the organization's stage of development—not every Trust would seek to use every tool. The idea of the guide is that you can dip into the section that is most applicable to you. We'll refine it based on feedback over time. It's not prescriptive, it's not regulatory, it's there for Trusts to use on an ongoing basis as they see fit'.

Directors from the various Trusts involved in the pilot of the toolkit commented that:

> 'In trying the tools, we realised that some of our strategic planning has been too rigid, perhaps too focused on investments, whereas we need an approach that it is much more dynamic that can reflect changes in the local health economy and our expectations as to what our role should be nationally within the NHS. We've learnt from the framework and have applied aspects to decision-making already.'
>
> 'The practices in the toolkit worked well in board discussions as an enabler of constructive challenge to assumptions and decisions. Importantly, the framework provides a means to ensure that functional strategies are in alignment and tied in to organizational strategy needs.'
>
> 'The use of refined practices helps keep a focus on patients and their needs "as all too often in strategy development, it can become abstract and you can lose sight of what you are really trying to deliver".'
>
> 'Mindful strategy practices will keep you focused on needs of all stakeholders—such as clinicians, patients, suppliers and local communities—and will lead strategists to engage them in discussions to understand operational reality, generate options and make good decisions.'

Questions for discussion

1. What do you imagine might trigger strategizing episodes for NHS Trust leaders? With whom do they need to work?
2. Drawing on the definitions of process, practice, practices, and practitioners, comment on the possible advantages and disadvantages of proposing a strategy practices toolkit for an organization such as an NHS Trust.
3. To what extent might the categories of practices in the toolkit be applicable to any organization? In guidance documentation, how important is it to keep the practices generic or make them specific to a healthcare organization? Explain your answer.

Sources

https://www.gov.uk/government/organizations/monitor/about

https://assets.publishing.service.gov.uk/government/uploads/system/uploads/attachment_data/file/286327/Meeting_the_needs_of_patients__Improving_strategic_planning_in_NHS_foundation_trusts.pdf

https://www.gov.uk/government/publications/strategy-development-a-toolkit-for-nhs-providers

https://assets.publishing.service.gov.uk/government/uploads/system/uploads/attachment_data/file/363273/Monitor_-_Developing_Strategy_-_a_guide_for_board_members.pdf

2.3 **Dynamic frameworks of strategy**

With a set of concepts defined that explain parts of the jigsaw of how strategy can be understood from a process-practice perspective, how can we draw these concepts together into a framework? In this section, we first describe an established theoretical perspective—the attention-based view—which explains how decision-makers behave in relation to strategy. We then introduce a complementary set of dynamic frameworks which integrate process and practice considerations.

Attention-based view of strategy

A useful perspective we can draw on to help explain what people do in relation to strategy is the attention-based view. The **attention-based view (ABV)** is a set of concepts and theoretical contributions that help explain how organizations behave, adapt to changing environments, develop capabilities, and make strategy according to how the limited attention of decision-makers is informed and directed. Influenced by the work of Cyert and March (1963) and Simon (1947) on behavioural theories of the firm, William Ocasio is a key proponent of the ABV.

According to Ocasio (1997:189), attention 'encompass(es) the noticing, encoding, interpreting, and focusing of time and effort by organizational decision-makers on both (a) issues: the available repertoire of categories for making sense of the environment: problems, opportunities, and threats; and (b) answers: the available repertoire of action alternatives: proposals, routines, projects, programs, and procedures'.

What are known as **attentional structures**—communication channels, knowledge flows, organizational procedures, and opportunities for interaction with others—influence how information reaches decision-makers' attention about the issues and answers relevant to their current context (Barnett 2008). Based on their processing of information received, decision-makers will advocate strategic initiatives that Ocasio (1997:201) describes as organizational moves: 'the myriad of actions undertaken by the firm and its decision-makers in response to or in anticipation of changes in its external and internal environment'.

The ABV is useful to us in building understanding of strategy activities over time. What managers do—what they discuss and focus on—is driven by the information they receive, their personal backgrounds and experience, and the situation/context of the organization (Gebauer 2009). As we develop our insights about how strategy activity occurs, it is helpful to consider how information is brought to the attention of decision-makers through strategy practices and tools. Joseph and Wilson (2018) suggest that **attentional design**—using tools and procedures to deliberately channel the attention of decision-makers—will have a major influence on how strategic choices are made (we will explore this further in Chapter 15). Ocasio et al. (2018) note that this may be through simple actions such as considering the language used in communications such as strategic planning documents. For example, adding the term 'strategic' can divert executive attention towards considering material, decisions, or resources (Gond et al. 2018). Strategy tools can equally increase the scope of information reaching decision-makers; for example, environmental scanning and debate involving a diverse range of stakeholders can be used to influence strategic decision-makers' attention (Galbreath 2018).

The personal characteristics of practitioners can play a part in the focus of their attention. For example, the emotions of managers at different levels in Nokia played a role in the organization's fall from grace. When negative signals started emerging from the market about Nokia's products and offerings, research uncovered that senior managers were scared of shareholders' reactions, just as middle managers were scared of peers' reactions. This led to a biasing of information shared within the organization, and ultimately decision-makers paying attention to the 'wrong' things (Vuori and Huy 2016).

However, according to Ocasio (1997), practitioners will vary their focus of attention depending on the situations they face, and their decisions and activities will be more influenced by the context in which they are operating than their individual characteristics. Thus, from an ABV, the influence of context on the direction of attention (known as **situated attention**) is a crucial factor to consider when seeking to understand what decision-makers focus on and what they do (Ferreira 2017).

Strategy as process and practice

Burgelman et al. (2018:541) propose the integration of process and practice concepts and perspectives, as defined in this chapter so far, through the model shown in Figure 2.3.

In this model, strategy is crafted through a continual interplay of strategizing episodes and efforts to convert strategy ideas and initiatives into reality. Strategizing episodes refer to deliberate strategy-making efforts, such as board meetings or strategy workshops. Strategizing may occur on a scheduled basis, as part of habitual organizational practice. Equally, as indicated by the ABV, strategizing may be triggered by the identification of what decision-makers consider to be significant external events (Martin 2014). Decisions arising from strategizing episodes lead to organizational moves in which practitioner activities, attention, and resources attempt strategic initiatives to deliver desired outcomes. However, the strategic outcomes realized through

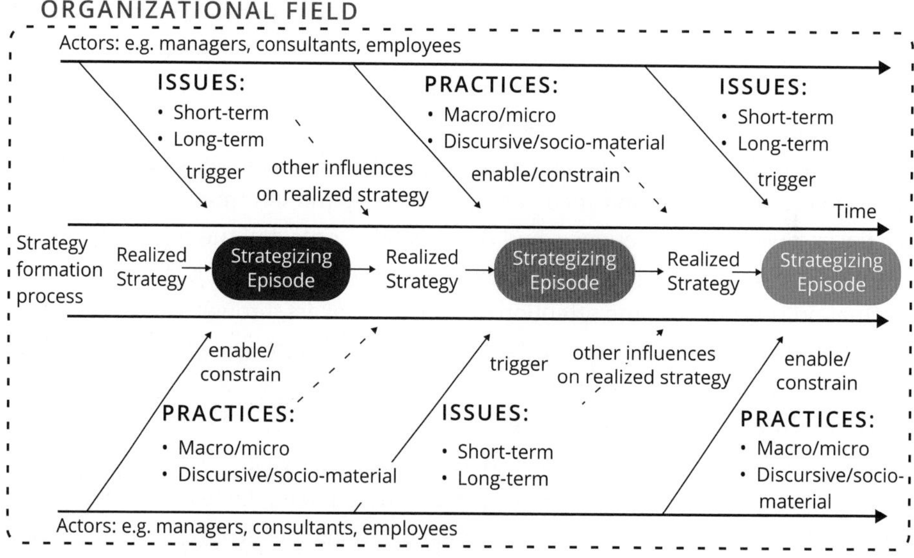

FIGURE 2.3 Combinatory model of strategy as process and practice (SAPP). Source: Reproduced with permission from Burgelman, R. et al. (2018). Strategy processes and practices: dialogues and intersections. *Strategic Management Journal*, **39**(3): 531–558. https://doi.org/10.1002/smj.2741. © John Wiley & Sons, Ltd.

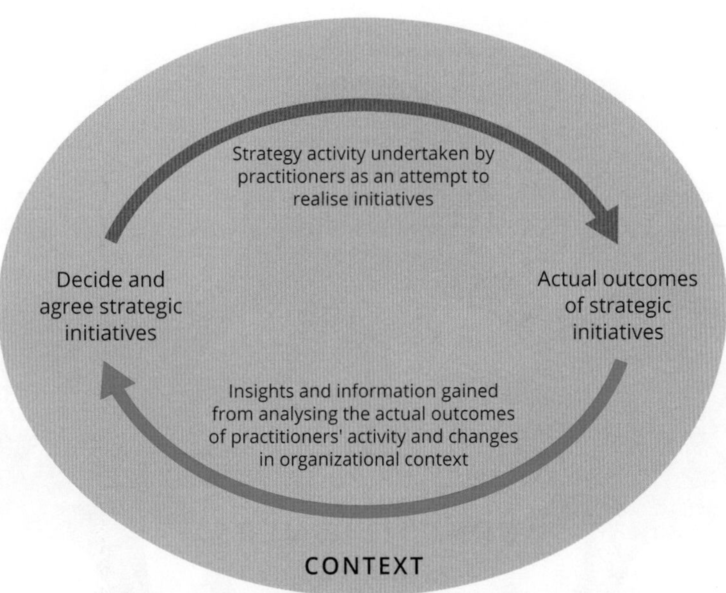

FIGURE 2.4 Interplay of strategizing, practitioner activity, and realized outcomes.

organizational moves are a product of practitioner activity and contextual forces. Insights arising from the strategic outcomes actually achieved plus new information about the internal and external context then inform the next strategizing episode.

This continuing interplay of strategizing, practitioner activity, and realized outcomes, summarized in Figure 2.4, explains how strategy is crafted over time (Gond et al. 2018). Figures 2.3 and 2.4 reflect the view that strategy practitioners have to be aware of the effects of time, the flow of events, and the possibilities of the current context when deciding what to do, and how to do it. Tracking how the context is unfolding can allow for timely intervention through strategy practices, such that advantage (albeit temporary) can be realized (Hansen and Jacobsen 2016). Through practitioner activity and practices, short- and long-term issues might be addressed as they are encountered, and sufficient gains realized from strategy work, in order that the organization might survive and possibly thrive.

The interplay of strategizing, activity, and outcomes in Figure 2.4 also serves to explain how practical experiments might be conducted in highly uncertain environments to improve the quality of strategic decision-making (Pettus et al. 2018). By taking limited strategic action, observing the realized outcomes, and reflecting on the insights gained, new learning can be used to inform a subsequent round of strategizing. By doing a little, you can learn a lot that helps decision-making during strategizing (Ashkenas 2013).

The process–practice framework of strategy

Building on the combinatory model, we propose a process–practice framework of strategy as shown in Figure 2.5 as a guiding reference to further explain what people do, over time and in context, in relation to strategy. At the centre of the framework are practitioners—the people

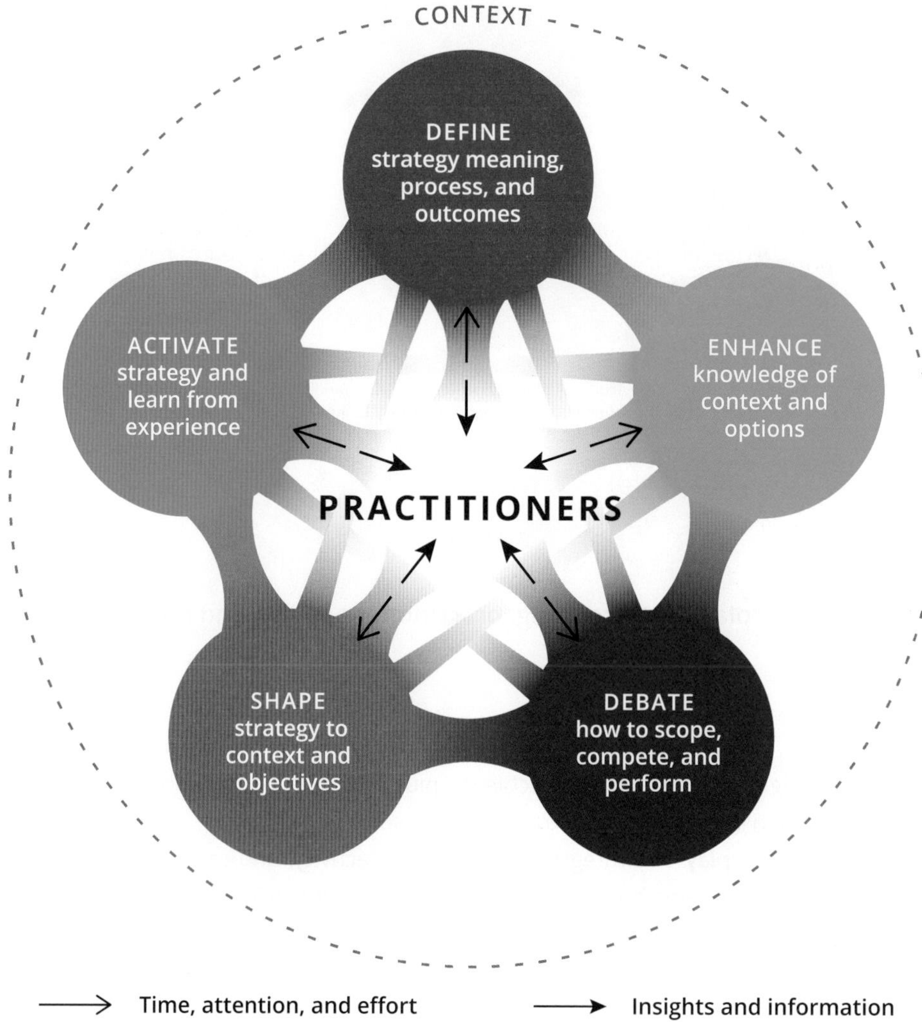

FIGURE 2.5 Strategy process–practice framework.

involved in the 'doing' of strategy. Thoughout the book we will retain a focus on building understanding of how practitioners think, talk, and act as they engage in strategy activity. We will ask you to play your part too—as a current or future practitioner—by continually challenging yourself to reflect on how the theories, concepts, methods, and examples might be of use to you in understanding or practising strategy.

The middle layer of the model shows categories of strategy practices. We propose these categories to enable discussion and exploration ways of working that you will encounter as you participate in or lead strategizing episodes. Practices are deployed in strategy activity as practitioners allocate their time, attention, and resources to trying to do something, in turn being able to observe the consequences of their actions and gather feedback information. The outer layer of the model indicates that practitioners deploy strategy practices within context—the unfolding circumstances, events, and experiences in which strategy activity occurs over time.

Categories of practices

We have identified five main categories of strategy practices that will be explored throughout the book as shown in Figure 2.5. These categories are described by their intended outcome/contribution to strategy activity.

Define strategy meaning, approach, and outcomes: Ways of working intended to establish what strategy means to stakeholders in the current context, agreeing an approach and target outcomes for strategy work, including who to involve, and how, in making decisions.

Enhance knowledge of context and options: Practices concerning collection and analysis of data about strategy options, opportunities, and constraints arising from organizational context, environmental trends and resources, capabilities, and organizational activities.

Debate how to scope, compete and perform: Practices that review the sectors and locations in which the organization could or should operate, how it competes, and how to organize and deploy resources for optimal performance.

Shape strategy to context and objectives: Practices that evaluate and refine strategy ways, means, and objectives according to collaboration, innovation, and growth needs; influences of digitalization and possibilities of disruption; internationalization considerations; and sustainability attitudes, obligations, and opportunities.

Activate strategy and learn from experience: Ways of leading the planning and organizing of strategizing episodes and strategic change, engaging stakeholders and building momentum behind realization activities, and continually improving understanding of how to make and manage strategy in practice.

Regulating flow

The flow of activity in strategy is underpinned by the knowledge and insights of practitioners, and their interpretation of the needs, possibilities, and constraints of the context. We represent the flow of the strategy process by a two-way relationship between practitioners and practices. As explained in Figure 2.3, practitioners deploy practices during strategy activity, consciously or unconsciously. At the same time, practitioners receive new information about the effectiveness and impact of their practices, in context, from participating in or observing strategy activity. This information may be ignored, encourage continuing activity, provoke a change in practice or type of activity, or bring activity to a stop. In effect, practitioners regulate the flow of strategy activity and decide how, if at all, practices should be deployed. Figure 2.6 further explains how the elements of the process–practice framework interface.

Responsiveness to situational needs

It is possible that practitioners might address a strategic issue by collectively deploying strategy practices in a logical sequence from 'Define Strategy' round to 'Activate Strategy'. Most consultants and strategy process designers will attempt to instigate this sort of orderly collaborative working in strategy. However, the deployment of strategy practices happens in a far more varied and reactive manner in practice.

According to their appraisal of the needs of a situation, practitioners might turn their attention and efforts towards any type of strategy practice. When practitioner attention is focused on

2

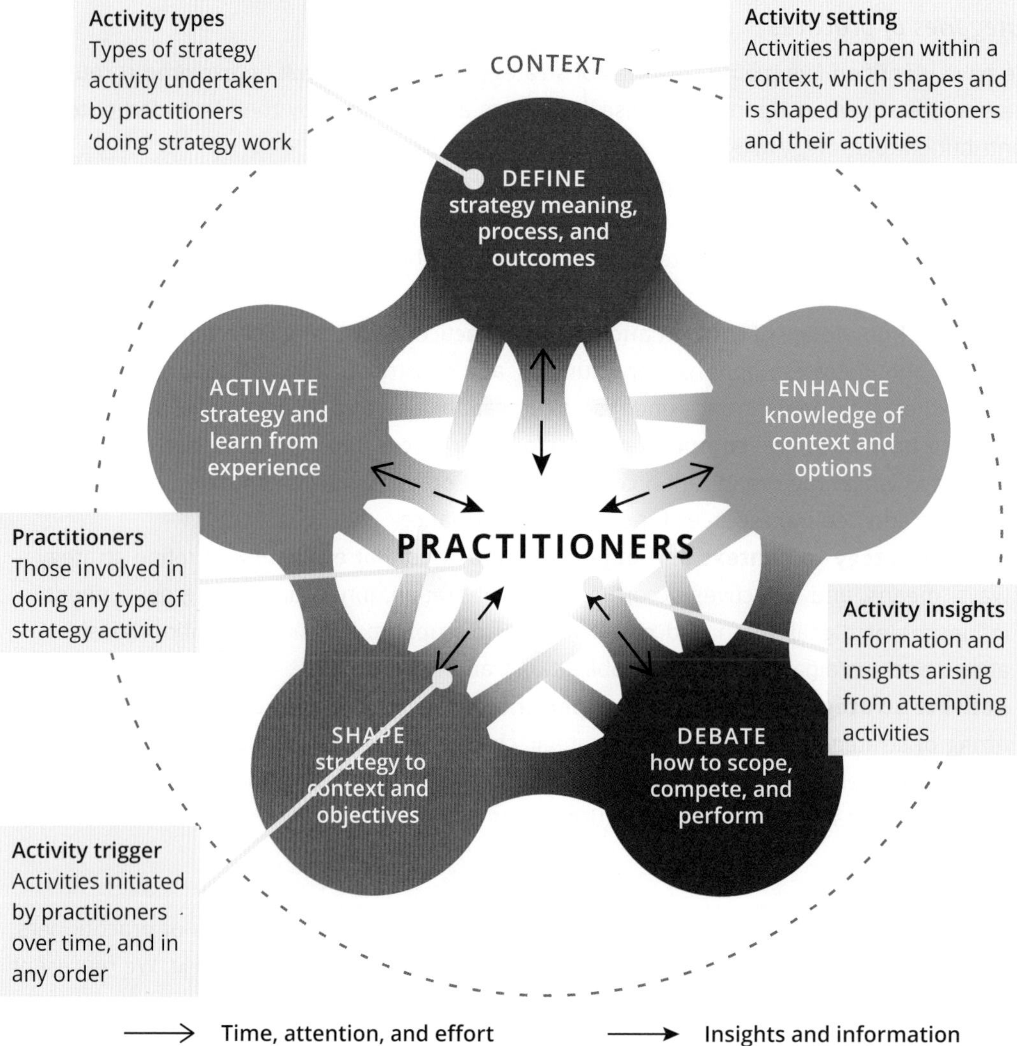

FIGURE 2.6 The process–practice model explained.

a strategizing episode, information flows to practitioners which, as they interpret it, influences what they do next. This information may relate to the usefulness of their practices, the reality and needs of the context in which strategy activity is occurring, or both.

As new information from immersion in strategy activity is digested, insights about appropriate activities to undertake next can be gleaned (see Chapter 16 where we discuss this capacity for responsiveness in terms of reflection-in-practice). When practitioners perceive that their activities have led to intended outcomes, and that their interpretation of the context is accurate and complete, their working theories about what needs to be done are reinforced. However, when the outcomes of activity differ from expectations and/or changes in the operating context are detected, practitioners may trigger the deployment of strategy practices in response (see Table 2.1).

TABLE 2.1 **Insight from learning from doing and contextual awareness**

Responsive practices	Strategizing triggered by learning by doing	Strategizing triggered by contextual awareness
Define strategy meaning, approach, and outcomes	'We need to clarify the parameters of our strategy activity'	'Our prior agreement of what was required from strategy activity no longer fits with the demands of the context'
Enhance knowledge of context and options	'We need to build a shared understanding of our current and possible future context and the options we have available to us for taking action'	'We need to understand better how the possibilities, constraints, opportunities, and threats in our operating context have changed, and the implications of trajectories of change'
Debate how to scope, compete, and perform	'We need to agree on our scope and form, how we compete, and how we organize to optimize performance'	'At an organizational level, we need to revise what we are currently doing and/or how we are doing it to avoid performance issues in a shifting context'
Shape strategy to context and objectives	'We need to prioritize and enact initiatives which make sense for us as an organization, given the specific context in which we are operating'	'We need to review our prior decisions about priority actions and resource deployments as they may no longer be optimal given the changing context'
Activate strategy and learn from experience	'We need to find optimal ways of carrying out the focused use of resources and change projects corresponding to our strategic decisions'	'The difference between anticipated and actual strategy implementation results suggest that we need to re-evaluate our assumptions about context and related decisions and resource usage'

In effect, practitioners are constantly deciding whether to continue with or revise the strategy activity they plan to do next, based on their reading of the organizational context and realities (Denning 2019).

In the NHS example, this tendency is recognized in the comments from the Monitor director that strategy practitioners should 'dip into the section [of the guide] that is most applicable to you' and that not every Trust will need to use every tool during their strategy work. This is an example of strategy as a 'situated' activity. Practitioner interpretations of the specific context and how it changes over time influence the practices used during strategy activity. Responsiveness and flexibility in practices give practitioners the ability to cope when strategy outcomes are not realized as planned. If practitioners can increase their knowledge of possible practices, and improve their ability to read strategic situations, their context-sensitive deployment of practices will likely deliver more effective strategy outcomes than any prescriptive approach. This responsiveness in approach is valuable, as it is normal for continuing strategy activities to require re-evaluation as practitioners disagree about what needs to be done in the context of new insights and a changing organizational context (Kaplan and Orlikowski 2013).

Facilitating strategy activity

Responsive approaches from practitioners does not mean that strategy decisions, directions, and objectives are written anew every time something changes for the organization. Rather, the process–practice models shown in Figs 2.4–2.6 describe how a continuing interplay happens between the plans and ideals of strategy formulation and the realities of implementation practice and changing circumstances as sensed by practitioners. This interplay enables formal strategy plans, visions, possessions, and priorities to be incrementally adjusted in order to remain fitting to the organizational context. In between formal updates of strategy work, the skills and capacities of strategy practitioners are required to realize outcomes in the best way possible within the constraints of the situation.

It is both possible and often necessary to plot a high-level roadmap and timetable for strategy whilst at the same time engaging in continually revised strategy practices grounded in practitioner wisdom and insights. It would be naive to ignore the pressure on most senior management teams to run a visible and logical strategy process. Equally, senior management teams and organizational leaders will be evaluated on the results that they deliver over time. Therefore remaining open to revisiting strategy thinking and practices on a continuing basis, driven by learning from doing and awareness of contextual changes, appears vital to ensuring organizational performance in the long run. This way of engaging in strategy work can be termed as planned **emergence**—'where preparation meets opportunism' (King 2008:362).

As you develop your own strategy experience and capabilities, you will typically have to navigate between formal published strategy plans and the realities faced by those having to take action in context over time. To become a successful strategist, you will need to develop your capacity to manage the tensions between the ideas of strategy theory and the realities of strategy practice. We can think of this as 'facilitating' strategy—where facilitation means enabling strategy process to flow in an effective way. Facilitation is required for both the (re)formulation of strategy plans, and the effective deployment of those plans in practice. The process–practice framework in Figure 2.6 can give you a useful checklist to think through when building your repertoire of strategy practices that enable you to facilitate strategy in practice.

2.4 **Applying the process–practice framework**

Learning how to think, talk, and act like a strategist

When the world changes around an organization, and change, innovation, and strategy become vital for organizational survival, 'how leaders think, speak, and act becomes paramount' (Schoemaker et al., 2018:35). Our aim in this book is to equip you with the know-how of language, tools, and theories that will enable you to deal with the formalities and realities of strategy in your future career. By so doing, you will enhance your ability to think, talk, and act like a strategist. The knowledge of strategic practices you acquire might help you grow and improve your personal practice, as well as the effectiveness of group decision-making and project work with which you are involved. In this section we offer some suggestions as to how you can use this book to maximum effect.

CASE EXAMPLE 2.2 **DRIVENMEDIA—BUILDING A BUSINESS AS A YOUNG ENTREPRENEUR**

DrivenMedia—formerly The Advert Man—was established by Ed Hollands, then a 21-year-old business studies graduate, in 2016. DrivenMedia's aim is to allow organizations to 'advertise in a normally unreachable space'—namely the sides of many of the vans, lorries, and articulated vehicles that populate the UK's densely occupied road network. DrivenMedia turns the sides of these vehicles into mobile billboards for brands, organizations, and businesses. This generates 'highly visible, flexible and colourful marketing opportunities across the UK, Europe and overseas'.

Business inspiration came for founder Ed Hollands during his studies whilst walking through Derby near a large roundabout. Approaching the junction, he saw 'a line of around 200 cars with nothing to look at but the side of these huge commercial vehicles'. Ed had previously considered starting a business based on mounting digital advertising boards next to congested road spaces. The legality of such billboards is a grey area, and upon seeing the lorries interspersed with the cars, Ed had a eureka moment that haulage companies might be willing to lease out the space to advertisers to achieve the same effect, and more.

To explore the potential of the business idea, Ed started noting the contact details on trucks and phoning the haulage companies to ask their views. It was a tough start, with scepticism and uncertainty from many firms. But one haulier with a fleet of over 100 commercial trailers agreed to participate and others followed, creating potential advertising space. Since selling his first space, Ed has gone on to run campaigns for a wide range of organizations. He also works with a range of hauliers and marketing agencies who have become strategic partners.

Ed acknowledges that he started in a haphazard way by cold-calling organizations, and he quickly realized the need to upskill his selling tactics. Taking business mentor advice from a local entrepreneur, Ed added structure to his business development and sales practices—improving how he was able to make relevant contacts and avoid wasting time. Ed has learned how to manage cash flow, highlighting that it was a big challenge for DrivenMedia given the time required to prove the concept to clients and haulage firms alike. In his perspective, 'When you finish university it's the best time to start a business as you're used to eating and living with a limited income and you aren't likely to have additional responsibilities'.

In 2018, Ed appeared on *Dragon's Den*, a BBC show in which venture capitalists evaluate investment opportunities. Ed's efforts to build a £250,000 annual turnover business in just two years impressed the dragons and won him the financial backing and involvement of Jenny Campbell. Ed commented: 'To have someone so distinguished give [your business] the seal of approval gives you a real lift. The passion the dragons have for business and the confidence they have when making decisions—I've been able to leech off it.'

In preparing to run the business, Ed reflects: 'I studied business at university so that I'd have the right skills when I had that right idea. And I've learned more about trucks in the last few years than I ever thought I'd want to know. I then dived straight in.' Ed comments that being able to tap into the experience of his mentors is vital to being able to successfully grow the business. He adds that if he was starting again, 'I would take more opportunities and get more experiences that you can spark ideas from. I don't do this enough'.

In giving advice to any other graduates wanting to start their own business, Ed comments: 'The first thing I'd do is go and speak to your customers. If you talk to them and find out exactly what they want, what they want to pay, and how they want it to look, work, taste—you're going to create a product that customers want. I did it the other way around. I had the idea, knew it would work, and talked to hauliers before going to customers. Initially we only offered the sides of the trucks, but it transpired that they wanted the backs too. And I resisted that for a while before finally committing. We lost about seven months in the process.'

Looking to the future, Ed says: 'The plan is to grow as fast as we can. We're working in an exciting space and we've got a lot of innovations in the pipeline. We're looking at other potential ways of helping hauliers and advertisers, too. I'd like to create a

Continued

DrivenGroup in the future. To grow DrivenMedia and get someone else in to play with it, and then set up a supporting business in a completely different space.'

Questions for discussion

1. In Ed's story, what events occurred that he couldn't fully control, and what did he do on purpose in order to develop his ability to think, talk, and act like a strategist and business leader?
2. When Ed started DrivenMedia, he had the strategic insight that the side of trucks represented an untapped marketing space that could form the basis of a viable business. Describe how this insight informed what he did (his practice), and how what he did led to a revision of his strategic insight.
3. What sources of information seem important in shaping Ed's activities and plans?
4. How might Ed's context shift in the next few years? What external or internal factors might trigger strategizing episodes for him?

Sources

https://www.drivenmedia.co.uk/

https://www.clearskyaccounting.co.uk/graduates/success-story-ed-hollands/

https://www.businessleader.co.uk/meet-ed-hollands-the-young-entrepreneur-building-a-business-with-the-help-of-a-dragon/65107/

https://businessadvice.co.uk/from-the-top/dragons-den-success-was-nothing-compared-to-learning-to-sell-for-this-young-entrepreneur/

Think like a strategist

The theory that we will lay out in each of the chapters will build comprehension of the concepts, language, and possibilities of strategy in a wide range of practical situations that you are likely to encounter. Better understanding of strategy theory will give you new ways to order your thoughts, direct your attention, understand organizational contexts, and read the flow of situations from a strategic perspective. Parts 1 and 3 will equip you to be able to comprehend the major theories and perspectives by which strategy is understood. Part 2 will enable you to understand strategy analysis and evaluation methodologies, and how you can deploy tools to help you better understand the context and options for strategy. Part 4 will provide you with knowledge of nuanced strategy theory and contemporary considerations that most practitioners involved in strategy activity will have to face. Part 5 will give you insights into how the activation and realization of strategy can be approached and improved through leading change, design of activities, and learning and reflection.

Talk like a strategist

Much of strategy activity involves interacting with others through discursive practices of debate and discussion (Garbuio et al. 2015). To prepare you for this, we will provide many examples of how practitioners talk and write about strategy. All chapters conclude with practitioner insights, in which we share practitioners' views in their own words to give you examples of strategy 'talk'. In addition, in all sections we share case examples and illustrations of how strategy has been interpreted and reported in real organizational settings. Through these examples you will be able to pick up insights that enable you to discuss strategy in a credible and meaningful way. Through development of a strategy vocabulary and exposure to dialogue that is generally applicable across strategy settings, you will be in a strong position to engage practitioners in strategy-related discussions. A crucial skill in leading strategy activity is being able to ask constructive questions in order to challenge the thinking and direct the attention of other practitioners (Kahneman et al. 2019). By working through the cases in each chapter, you should be able to enhance your capacity to question others productively as part of strategy activity.

Act like a strategist

To support you in learning to act like a strategist, we have included method guides, worked examples, and application advice from our own experiences as strategists. We have focused on fundamental guides in the main text for all readers and included a range of extended guides in the online resources for those who want to build deeper insights. The main method guides can be found in Part 2 where we present ways in which you can approach analytical aspects of strategy-making. Throughout the other parts, we have included method guides wherever relevant to ensure that the reader is always able to do something new or differently as a result of engaging with the section.

As your capacity to think, talk, and act like a strategist grows, so too will your ability to engage with the process–practice framework. The better able you are to think like a strategist, the more you will be able to read context and information flows. The better able you are to talk like a strategist, the more comprehensively you will be able to engage others in defining, debating, and shaping discursive practices, and constructively challenge their engagement in strategy with effective questioning. And the better able you are to act like a strategist, the more effectively you will be able to analyse situations and design, lead, and learn from strategic activity.

Engaging with the process–practice framework in this book

This textbook is organized according to the different categories of strategy practices identified in the process–practice framework (see Figure 2.7). As you adopt your own approach to learning about strategy, the book is constructed in a manner that reflects the process–practice framework. Chapters can be read in any order that interests you and should still make sense.

In Part 1 we examine how to define strategy meaning, approach, and outcomes. We have already explored how strategy can be interpreted, and how we can build a shared meaning of strategy through a scoping exercise. The process–practice framework (Figure 2.6) and the combinatory model (Figure 2.3) gives us two complementary ways of building our understanding of strategy activity and practices. In the next chapter, we consider the process–practice model from a decision-making perspective, shedding light on how strategizing episodes and strategic decisions punctuate organizational life.

In Part 2 we cover methods that might be used to collect and analyse data that better informs practitioners about the organizational context. Data can inform our view of the historical context and matters of internal importance such as the culture, values, objectives, and purpose of the organization. Data might raise our understanding of the institutional, market, and competitive contexts in which the organization is embedded, or the resource and capability context—including current activities and possible future activities. According to the focus of your strategy work, exploring some or all of these types of contextual data will aid identification of options for strategic action and strategic decision-making.

In Part 3 we review different types of strategy conversation that may occur—examining the sorts of concepts, theories, and mental framings that practitioners might adopt to have different types of strategizing episodes. Corporate strategy concerns the scope and structure of the organization, business strategy examines how the organization chooses to compete in its chosen markets, and functional strategy, implementation, and performance examines how projects or business units are organized and executed to deliver optimal results for the whole organization.

FIGURE 2.7 The process–practice framework of strategy chapter map.

In Part 4 we consider contemporary influences that might need to be examined by practitioners refining strategy options to suit context. For many organizations, growth—through mergers and acquisitions, collaborations, or innovative means—is a target outcome for those making strategy. Increasingly, organizations will experience market disruption, discontinuous change, and impacts of digitalization; there are few organizations that are not affected by international options and flow of goods, and sustainability is an increasingly important feature in the life of organizations and practitioners.

Finally, in Part 5 the plans and agreements of strategy decision-making processes need to be enacted. How strategic change is managed and led, and how outcomes can be negotiated through social and political processes of strategy are key topics for you to understand. How strategy activities and strategizing episodes are designed can increase the likelihood of successful outcomes. And as we describe strategy as a continuing accomplishment, enacted by practitioners, it is also possible through reflection and discussion to identify points of learning and improvement that will enhance future strategy performance.

PRACTITIONER INSIGHT: **ROBERT CHIA**

Robert Chia is a Professor of Management at the Adam Smith Business School, University of Glasgow. He entered academia following an extensive technical and managerial career in industry beginning with the Singaporean Air Force and ending with Metal Box, a multinational manufacturer of cans and metal containers. He fulfilled technical, engineering, and manufacturing management roles, before becoming director of human resources for the Metal Box group in the Asia–Pacific region.

Robert shares his practitioner academic views on strategy, process, and practice.

Strategy

I've observed down the years that three-quarters of the world gets on fine in business and organizational life without ever hearing or worrying about the term 'strategy'. It doesn't mean that leaders and managers don't 'strategize' or do things that we in academia identify as 'strategic practices'. But in my experience, people in industry don't worry too much about the definition of strategy—they just get on and do it. They live out the essence of strategy, which for me is how you fundamentally extract advantage in any situation you find yourself in. To do this, you must have an acute sense of what is going on and develop knowing about where and how to act in order to give you a momentary advantage. If you can do that well over time, those advantages accrue and become sustainable.

From my experience of working with and in organizations, the tools and methods of strategy are useful when you are trying to enter new markets or new domains with which you are not familiar. Theories, concepts, frameworks—they can help you pay attention to the right kinds of things. But you can't have effective strategy without a heightened sensitivity to local needs. For those running organizations, you need to be aware of the realities of the world around you—spend time immersed in the direct operations of the organization and acquiring valuable insights of its inner workings. I would call this operational immersion a vital part of being able to know how to act decisively in a strategic way. All too often strategy is just a word coined by people on the outside to describe something that they don't fully understand.

It puzzles me that in academia and practice we can be so seduced by analysis and reports when we know that change is permanently happening around us. I think that those who are more adaptable and agile than others are less attached to such static representations of what is going on. For me, a capacity for strategy arises from becoming finely tuned to our surroundings. One of the ideas I like is the notion of 'management by walking around', described by Tom Peters in *In Search of Excellence*. It is something which resonates with what I tried to practise at Metal Box, and on many occasions surprisingly viable solutions to seemingly impossible strategic challenges were found simply by being in close-quarter contact and immersing oneself in the operational day-to-day activity and engaging with those at the coal face who have a detailed understanding of what it means to serve our customers on a daily basis.

Process

Everyone uses the word process. But 99% talk about the 'process of ...', such as the 'process of making a strategy'. This is using process as a descriptor for 'activity in stages'. It is not how I understand process. For me, more fundamentally 'process is ... reality'. It means that everything is in flow, in flux, and always changing—a 'blooming, buzzing confusion' as the philosopher William James put it. We can then think of artefacts such as strategic plans as attempts to temporarily stabilize this incessant flow to produce a 'surrogate' reality so that we can meaningfully act on it—they are islands of temporary order in a churning sea of chaos. This perspective helps us to be less attached to these representations and hence less committed to a fixed view of the world, thereby making us more effectively strategic in our responses to environmental changes.

Strategy practice is about the gradual aggregation of our actions into a stabilized form. Strategy emerges sometimes unexpectedly through our local coping acts over time. We also refine how we act by staying closely connected to the changing situation and striving to learn from reality with humility. And we must accept

Continued

2

that strategy is never finished. The idea that you can have a fixed strategy is only conceived by those detached from the grind of everyday operations, such as senior leaders or academics who have never got their hands dirty. The more detached you are from the local scene, the more you talk in generalizable terms. The more you are at the coal face, the more you realize the little details that make up strategy. Very often, from a perspective of 'process as reality', strategy is incremental and what might even be considered mundane and operational is vital to strategy emergence.

The one topic that most strategy discussions don't touch on is timing, timeliness, and temporality. With awareness of reality as flow, when you act is so crucial. Timing is everything; don't pluck the fruit before it has ripened. If you act too early, you may need more effort and the results will be less satisfactory. If you can learn how to read closely the tendencies and trajectories of a situation, you will be more effective in developing an internalized strategy that gives you the capacity to cope and survive whatever environmental surprises you face.

At Metal Box, we built production capabilities centred on flexibility and responsiveness to customer needs; we had to because virtually all our products were exported all over the world. We had learned that when the market is volatile, as it was in Singapore in the 1980s, inventory control systems have limited use. You can have all the charts, models, and computerized tracking systems you want, but if you are really in a rapidly changing context, being able to respond quickly to the immediacy of situations is what counts. For those in strategy, you must work hard to build your capacity to make decisions 'on the hoof', in situ, on the go, and with limited information.

Practice

Practices are our raw material for managing flow and coping with uncertainty in our lives. Strategy practices help us to create advantage in any situation that we face as individuals or collectives. Practices are largely embodied knowings—how we orient ourselves or approach or act in any situation. Over time, we learn how certain practices can produce valuable outcomes that we desire. We also become sensitized to the fact that situations are always changing. So, our practices have to be malleable and adaptable. I may inherit and learn a set of practices—through an apprenticeship, or from doing a degree, or from working in an organization—but learning from others doesn't mean that I'm a clone or that I'm going to mindlessly reapply a practice I've seen elsewhere. This is why a refined sensitivity to goings-on is crucial. Intelligently, we can challenge ourselves to adapt and creatively deploy practices according to the needs of a situation in order to increase our efficacy. In attempting to work with strategy, immersion in the reality of our context and a tool box of learned practices—that we are willing to adapt to the needs of our situation—give us potential to make the best of the circumstances. It is a learning journey that never ends! Oftentimes, however, we have to let go of what we know first and let the situation itself dictate our appropriate response.

CHAPTER SUMMARY

In this chapter we addressed the following learning outcomes.

- **Explain how strategy can be understood from a process–practice view**
  From a process–practice view, strategy is understood as a continuing accomplishment of practitioner activity over time and in context. Even strategies that advocate no change will still require effort if the status quo is to be maintained. What is crucial from this view is that strategy is something people do. This puts a focus on understanding practitioners—their characteristics, decisions, and actions—in order to understand how strategy happens. Avoiding false separation between strategy formulation and implementation practices will increase the potential for effective attainment of strategy outcomes.

- **Explain what is meant by practice, practitioners, practices, activity, and process in the context of strategy work.**

  We defined key concepts from a strategy-as-practice (SaP) perspective (a sociological take on strategy).

  Practice: an 'ongoing stream of activity' that constitutes organizational life

  Practitioners: the individuals and groups of individuals whose efforts and activities contribute to strategy

  Practices: the ways of working adopted by practitioners when trying to accomplish a type of task

  Tools: the techniques, methods, models, and frameworks which support interactions and decision-making in strategy activity

  Activity: that which is actually done by practitioners

  Process: the continual unfolding of events, experiences, and activities over time

  Strategy practice: the ongoing stream of strategy-related activity in an organization—arises from practitioners drawing on practices over time and in context.

- **Evaluate the usefulness of the attention-based view as an aid to understanding what people do in relation to strategy**

  The attention-based view (ABV) was introduced as a set of concepts and theoretical contributions that help explain how organizations behave, adapt to changing environments, develop capabilities, and strategize according to how decision-makers' attention is informed and directed. By understanding and purposefully designing attentional structures (ways of flowing information to decision-makers), we can improve the quality of insights on which decision-makers base their selection of strategic initiatives to match the needs of the context they face.

- **Critically assess the limitations of adopting rigid approaches to strategy**

  We noted that strategy activity rarely, if ever, plays out in a linear fashion in reality. We noted that those designing strategy activities—such as consultants or organizational leaders—will propose an orderly arrangement of strategy practices. However, it was suggested that flexibility and responsiveness of approach to strategy work is crucial to being effective within a shifting context over time.

- **Articulate how learning how to think, talk, and act as a strategy practitioner enhances your ability to engage with the strategy process–practice framework**

  We noted that the better able you are to think like a strategist, the more you will be able to read context and information flows. The better able you are to talk like a strategist, the more comprehensively you will be able to engage others in defining, debating, and shaping discursive practices. And the better able you are to act like a strategist, the more effectively you will be able to analyse situations and design, lead, and learn from strategic activity. As you develop these capacities, you will grow as a strategy practitioner who is able to craft strategy in context over time through responsive and intelligent deployment of practices.

END OF CHAPTER QUESTIONS

Recall questions

1. What are some of the main issues associated with separating strategy formulation and implementation activities and responsibilities?
2. Define what is meant by the terms 'practices', 'practitioners', and 'activity'? How do these terms relate to 'process' and 'practice' as defined in this chapter?
3. What does it mean when we describe strategy as a 'situated' activity?
4. Describe the five different types of practices identified in the process–practice framework.
5. What is meant by 'facilitating strategy'?

Application questions

A) Think of a situation in which you have either made a personal strategy (such as a career strategy) or been part of an organizational strategy (as part of a job role, as a member of a club or society). Recall the activities that were involved and try to write them down in the order that they happened. Try to write the activities for the time period from when you first started thinking about the strategy, through to the delivery of results. Place the activities you have written down into the categories of the process–practice framework. How linear is the process? (i.e. does it flow neatly from defining parameters to activating the strategy?) Can you identify activities for each of the categories? Why do you think the activities played out the way that they did? What would you do differently if you were involved in that strategy process again?

ONLINE RESOURCES

www.oup.com/he/mackay1e

FURTHER READING

Strategy processes and practices, by Robert A. Burgelman et al.

Burgelman, R.A., Floyd, S.W., Laamanen, T., et al. (2018). Strategy processes and practices: dialogues and intersections. *Strategic Management Journal*, **39**(3), 531–58.

This paper provides a useful resource to further explore and deepen insights into the process–practice framework. The authors draw together many insights, literature references, and a model, which is presented in Figure 2.2 in this chapter. You may wish to refer to this article for further academic references in support of viewing strategy process as a phenomenon which occurs in context over time, enabled and constrained by the practices of those involved.

Process studies of change in organisation and management, by Ann Langley et al.

Langley, A., Smallman, C., Tsoukas, H., and Van de Ven, A.H. (2013). Process studies of change in organization and management: unveiling temporality, activity and flow. *Academy of Management Journal*, **56**(1), 1–13.

Whilst written about change, this paper provides detailed insight for those who are interested in studying strategy as a flow of activities occurring over time in context. The authors highlight the temporary nature of stability in organizational affairs, and how a continuing flow of activities in context leads to the emergence, development, growth, and termination of organizational features. The philosophical underpinnings of this paper are consistent with the process–practice framework outlined in this chapter, and the 'third' definition of strategy in the Van de Ven paper suggested below.

Suggestions for studying strategy process, by Andrew H. Van de Ven

Van de Ven, A.H. (1992). Suggestions for studying strategy process: a research note. *Strategic Management Journal*, **13**, 169.

This classic paper provides insights into how strategy process might be interpreted: as a way of building explanations of causality (if X happens, then Y will follow); as a set of concepts that refer to the actions of individuals or organizations (strategy is a kind of work that people or groups do); as a sequence of events that describe how change happens over time (as a flow of activity). These different expressions of how strategy process is understood will help you connect with and interpret the different schools of thought 'out there' in the strategy academic literature focusing on strategy process studies.

Strategy Without Design, Robert C.H. Chia and Robin Holt

Chia, R.C.H. and Holt, R. (2009). *Strategy Without Design: The Silent Efficacy of Indirect Action*. Cambridge: Cambridge University Press.

This book was co-authored by the 'practitioner insights' contributor for this chapter. The book provides deep insights as to how strategy might be understood from a 'strong process' philosophy. We asked Robert to summarize the key message of the book; his response was: 'Build strategy from the bottom up through small acts and modest adjustments. Don't try grand schemes—they don't work! Only when you have a solid foundation of practical insight are you able to build. Don't be tempted to do otherwise, there is too much impatience for quick answers.'

REFERENCES

Adner, R. and Helfat, C.E. (2003). Corporate effects and dynamic managerial capabilities. *Strategic Management Journal*, **24**(10), 1011–25.

Anand, N. and Barsoux, J.-L. (2017). What everyone gets wrong about change management. *Harvard Business Review*, **95**(6), 78–85.

Ancona, D.G., Goodman, P.S., Lawrence, B.S., and Tushman, M.L. (2001). Time: a new research lens. *Academy of Management Review*, **26**(4), 645–63.

Ashkenas, R. (2013). Four tips for better strategic planning. *Harvard Business Review Digital Articles*, https://hbr.org/2013/10/four-tips-for-better-strategic-planning

Barnett, M.L. (2008). An attention-based view of real options reasoning. *Academy of Management Review*, **33**(3), 606–28.

Burgelman, R.A., Floyd, S.W., Laamanen, T., et al. (2018). Strategy processes and practices: dialogues and intersections. *Strategic Management Journal*, **39**(3), 531–58.

Candido, C.J.F. and Santos, S.P. (2015). Strategy implementation: what is the failure rate? *Journal of Management & Organization*, **21**(2), 237–62.

Chia, R.C.H. and Holt, R. (2009). *Strategy Without Design: The Silent Efficacy of Indirect Action*. Cambridge: Cambridge University Press.

Clark, D.N. (1997). Strategic management tool usage: a comparative study. *Strategic Change*, **6**, 417–27.

Cyert, R.M. and March, J.G. (1963). *A Behavioral Theory of the Firm*. Englewood Cliffs, NJ: Prentice Hall.

Demir, R. (2015). Strategic activity as bundled affordances. *British Journal of Management*, **26**, S125–41.

Denning, S. (2019). The ten stages of the Agile transformation journey. *Strategy & Leadership*, **47**(1), 3–10.

Doh, J.P., Lawton, T.C., and Rajwani, T. (2012). Advancing nonmarket strategy research: institutional perspectives in a changing world. *Academy of Management Perspectives*, **26**(3), 22–39.

Economist Intelligence Unit (2013) Why good strategies fail. https://www.pmi.org/-/media/pmi/documents/public/pdf/learning/thought-leadership/why-good-strategies-fail-report.pdf (accessed 20 July 2019).

Ferreira, L.C. (2017). Sense and sensibility: testing an attention-based view of organizational responses to social issues. *Business Ethics: A European Review*, **26**(4), 443–56.

Frynas, J.G., Mol, M.J., and Mellahi, K. (2018). Management innovation made in China: Haier's Rendanheyi. *California Management Review*, **61**(1), 71–93.

Galbreath, J. (2018). Do boards of directors influence corporate sustainable development? An attention-based analysis. *Business Strategy & the Environment*, **27**(6), 742–56.

Garbuio, M., Lovallo, D., and Sibony, O. (2015). Evidence doesn't argue for itself: the value of disinterested dialogue in strategic decision-making. *Long Range Planning*, **48**(6), 361–80.

Gebauer, H. (2009). An attention-based view on service orientation in the business strategy of manufacturing companies. *Journal of Managerial Psychology*, **24**(1), 79–98.

Giraudeau, M. (2008). The drafts of strategy: opening up plans and their uses. *Long Range Planning*, **41**(3), 291–310.

Gond, J.-P., Cabantous, L., and Krikorian, F. (2018). How do things become strategic? 'Strategifying' corporate social responsibility. *Strategic Organization*, **16**(3), 241–72.

Hansen, J.R. and Jacobsen, C.B. (2016). Changing strategy processes and strategy content in public sector organizations? A longitudinal case study of NPM Reforms' influence on strategic management. *British Journal of Management*, **27**(2), 373–89.

Jalonen, K., Schildt, H., and Vaara, E. (2018). Strategic concepts as micro-level tools in strategic sensemaking. *Strategic Management Journal*, **39**(10), 2794–826.

Jarzabkowski, P. (2003). Strategic practices: an activity theory perspective on continuity and change. *Journal of Management Studies*, **40**(1), 23–55.

Jarzabkowski, P. (2005). *Strategy as Practice: An Activity-Based Approach*. London: Sage Publications.

Jarzabkowski, P. and Kaplan, S. (2015). Strategy tools-in-use: a framework for understanding 'technologies of rationality' in practice. *Strategic Management Journal*, **36**(4), 537–58.

Jarzabkowski, P. and Spee, P.A. (2009). Strategy-as-practice: a review and future directions for the field. *International Journal of Management Reviews*, **11**(1), 69–95.

Jarzabkowski, P., Kaplan, S., Seidl, D., and Whittington, R. (2016). If you aren't talking about practices, don't call it a practice-based view: rejoinder to Bromiley and Rau in *Strategic Organization*. *Strategic Organization*, **14**(3), 270–4.

Johnson, G., Langley, A., Melin, L., and Whittington, R. (2008). *Strategy as Practice: Research Directions and Resources*. Cambridge: Cambridge University Press.

Johnson, G., Melin, L., and Whittington, R. (2003). Micro strategy and strategizing: towards an activity-based view. *Journal of Management Studies*, **40**(1), 3–22.

Joseph, J. and Wilson, A.J. (2018). The growth of the firm: an attention-based view. *Strategic Management Journal*, **39**(6), 1779–1800.

Kahneman, D., Lovallo, D.A.N., and Sibony, O. (2019). A structured approach to strategic decisions: reducing errors in judgment requires a disciplined process. *MIT Sloan Management Review*, **60**(3), 67–73.

Kaplan, R.S. and Norton, D.P. (2005). The office of strategy management. *Harvard Business Review*, **83**(10), 72–80.

Kaplan, S. and Orlikowski, W.J. (2013). Temporal work in strategy making. *Organization Science*, **24**(4), 965–95.

King, B.L. (2008). Strategizing at leading venture capital firms: of planning, opportunism, and deliberate emergence. *Long Range Planning*, **41**(3), 345–66.

Knight, E., Paroutis, S., and Heracleous, L. (2018). The power of PowerPoint: a visual perspective on meaning making in strategy. *Strategic Management Journal*, **39**(3), 894–921.

Langley, A., Smallman, C., Tsoukas, H., and Van de Ven, A.H. (2013). Process studies of change in organization and management: unveiling temporality, activity, and flow. *Academy of Management Journal*, **56**(1), 1–13.

Mackay, R.B. and Chia, R. (2013). Choice, chance, and unintended consequences in strategic change: a process understanding of the rise and fall of Northco Automotive. *Academy of Management Journal*, **56**(1), 208–30.

Mahoney, J.T. and McGahan, A.M. (2007). The field of strategic management within the evolving science of strategic organization. *Strategic Organization*, **5**(1), 79–99.

Markides, C.C. (2000). *All the Right Moves: A Guide to Crafting Breakthrough Strategy*. Boston, MA: Harvard Business School Press.

Martin, R.L. (2014). The big lie of strategic planning. *Harvard Business Review*, **92**(1/2), 78–84.

Mintzberg, H. (1987). Crafting strategy. *Harvard Business Review*, **65**(4), 66–75.

Ocasio, W. (1997). Towards an attention-based view of the firm. *Strategic Management Journal*, **18**(S1), 187–206.

Ocasio, W., Laamanen, T., and Vaara, E. (2018). Communication and attention dynamics: an attention-based view of strategic change. *Strategic Management Journal*, **39**(1), 155–67.

Paroutis, S. and Pettigrew, A. (2007). Strategizing in the multi-business firm: strategy teams at multiple levels and over time. *Human Relations*, **60**(1), 99–135.

Pettus, M.L., Kor, Y.Y., Mahoney, J.T., and Michael, S.C. (2018). Sequencing and timing of strategic responses after industry disruption: evidence from post-deregulation competition in the US railroad industry. *Strategic Organization*, **16**(4), 373–400.

Schoemaker, P.J.H., Heaton, S., and Teece, D. (2018). Innovation, dynamic capabilities, and leadership. *California Management Review*, **61**(1), 15–42.

Simon, H.A. (1947). *Administrative Behavior: A Study of Decision-making Processes in Administrative Organizations*. Chicago, IL: Macmillan.

Spee, A.P. and Jarzabkowski, P. (2009). Strategy tools as boundary objects. *Strategic Organization*, **7**(2), 223–32.

Sull, D., Homkes, R., and Sull, C. (2015). Why strategy execution unravels—and what to do about it. *Harvard Business Review*, **93**(3), 57–66.

Tsoukas, H. and Chia, R. (2002). On organizational becoming: rethinking organizational change. *Organization Science*, **13**(5), 567–82.

Van de Ven, A.H. (1992). Suggestions for studying strategy process: a research note. *Strategic Management Journal*, **13**, 169–88.

Vuori, T.O. and Huy, Q.N. (2016). Distributed attention and shared emotions in the innovation process. *Administrative Science Quarterly*, **61**(1), 9–51.

Vuorinen, T., Hakala, H., Kohtamäki, M., and Uusitalo, K. (2018). Mapping the landscape of strategy tools: a review on strategy tools published in leading journals within the past 25 years. *Long Range Planning*, **51**(4), 586–605.

CHAPTER THREE

Strategic Decision-Making in Organizations

CONTENTS

3

LEARNING OBJECTIVES

By the end of this chapter, you should be able to:

- Distinguish strategic decisions from routine decisions
- Analyse the differences between rational and cognitive approaches to decision-making in organizations
- Evaluate the impact of common heuristics and biases on organizational decision-making
- Examine the tools and techniques available for managers to improve the quality of their decision-making processes
- Understand the practical application of decision-making tools in collective decision-making

TOOL BOX

- **Devil's advocacy**
  A decision-making technique designed to overcome groupthink (a practice of thinking or making decisions as a group in a way that discourages creativity or joint and several responsibility). One or more people in the group takes the 'devil's advocate' role, and works to point out all the flaws and risks with an option under consideration.
- **Dialectical enquiry**
  A group decision-making technique that attempts to overcome groupthink. Groups using this technique divide into two camps—those advocating for an idea and those advocating against it. Both sides highlight the advantages of their assigned decision and outline the disadvantages of the opposing idea.
- **Delphi method**
  The Delphi method is a forecasting framework based on the results of multiple rounds of questionnaires sent to a panel of experts.
- **Causal mapping**
  A causal map is a cognitive map in which the links between nodes represent causality or influence as understood by strategists. Causal mapping is used as a tool to aid strategic thinking and decision-making.

3

OPENING CASE STUDY TO LEND OR NOT TO LEND?

First National Bank (FNB) in Kitchener (in Ontario, Canada) specializes in commercial real estate loans. They have a major branch in Kitchener which writes on average over $1 billion in new loans every year, primarily to local developers and private investors. In order to secure a loan from FNB, a borrower must provide certain documents before their contract-to-buy expires. If these requirements are not fulfilled, the bank can refuse the approval of the loan.

The painstaking process of securing a commercial real estate loan is normally made up of two stages: competitive bidding, followed by closing. During the bidding stage, the buyer solicits quotes from lenders. Then the lenders bid by sending a letter of intent, offering a loan at a stated rate of interest. The final loan itself is dependent on completion of due diligence paperwork and approvals. Finally, the buyer chooses an offer and signs the letter of intent. To confirm the offer, the buyer pays 0.25%–0.5% of the loan value to the lender (the bank) as a non-refundable deposit.

During the closing stage, to finalize the loan agreement, the legal documents and approvals are completed. According to FNB's due diligence, the documents required are financial statements from the buyer, copies of leases from the seller, and bonded property appraisals, among other documents. The approvals come from two FNB representatives: the vice president, who manages the bank's loan portfolio, and FNB's risk manager, who reports directly to corporate headquarters.

Therefore, to successfully close on a property, the buyer needs to coordinate a complex three-way deal between the seller, the buyer, and the lender. All three parties must cooperate in the preparation of several required documents, and typically the closing process takes around a month to a month and a half, but is limited by an expiration date in the contract-to-buy between the seller and the buyer.

Within this process, the skilled negotiation and execution of commercial real estate loans is carried out by the business development managers at FNB. They meet prospective borrowers, determine an appropriate interest rate for the size and the risk of the transaction, secure preliminary approvals, prepare the letter of intent, and then process the loan through the closing process.

One of the senior business development managers at the Kitchener branch of FNB is John Hamond. He specializes in loans over $1 million, and single-handedly writes more than $100 million of new business each year, making him one of the most experienced and highest-grossing business development managers at FNB in Kitchener. His success is largely thanks to his ability to establish solid working relationships both within the company, as well as outside FNB, in addition to his reputation for consistently successfully closing transactions.

In November 2018, Hamond began working on a loan for the Kitchener Group, a privately held company that was new to commercial real estate. Although the loan was relatively small, at $1 million, because of the unusually low loan-to-value ratio of the planned amount Kitchener wanted to borrow, FNB saw this opportunity as potentially very lucrative in terms of future business from Kitchener. To put that into perspective, of the appraised value of the $3 million property, Kitchener only planned to borrow $900,000. To add pressure for this deal, FNB was bidding against a former colleague, which made Hamond's manager, the vice president of commercial banking, especially keen to win the bidding war. Kitchener Group was becoming a strategically important prospective client for FNB.

By December 2018, the Kitchener Group made a successful offer on a property and entered a contract-to-buy with the seller; a month later, Kitchener invited lenders to bid on the loan, and several submitted aggressive bids. By February 2019, FNB had submitted a relatively low bid, but Hamond had to lower it even more on Kitchener's request. Another month down the loan, Kitchener signed a letter of intent with FNB. Kitchener then asked FNB to accelerate the closing process, according to the looming deadline for their contract-to-buy, which expired on 29 March 2019, leaving less than half the usual time for closing. To try and close the deal, Hamond agreed to work closely with the Kitchener Group's attorney Paul Talley who, like the Kitchener Group, was new to commercial real estate transactions.

Hamond speeded up the FNB approvals as agreed and sent the draft loan agreement to Talley on 14 March 2019. Talley returned the draft loan agreement on 21 March 2019. Talley was finding it difficult to procure some of the due diligence documents, and asked for leeway. Hamond agreed to be as flexible as possible.

Talley submitted a set of due diligence documents on 28 March 2019, one day before the expiration of the Kitchener Group's contract-to-buy. But the set of documents was incomplete. As we know, if a client does not provide all key documents, despite months of skilled negotiation and careful execution, the bank's risk manager may be forced to refuse the approval of the million-dollar real estate loan. In this case, Talley had not provided any 'tenant acknowledgements'. These are routine, but essential, documents procured by the seller from his tenants, stating that the tenants do in fact have leases. Hamond contacted the FNB risk manager who, in line with protocol, said that the loan would indeed be rejected if it lacked tenant acknowledgements.

On Friday 29 March 2019, Talley and Hamond spent the morning frantically contacting their clients to procure tenant acknowledgements in order to salvage the deal. Unfortunately, they only managed to acquire one barely legible faxed tenant acknowledgement, which they knew was insufficient. Despite this, Talley wanted Hamond to seek approval of the loan with the paperwork they had, and offered to provide FNB with a document guaranteeing that, within the month, Kitchener would produce the missing tenant acknowledgements. On this basis, he asked for FNB to release the money so that the closing could be agreed.

By now it was 1:00 p.m. on Friday 29 March 2019. The Kitchener Group's contract-to-buy would expire at the end of business that day ...

Questions for discussion

Imagine you are in John Hamond's position as a senior business development manager.

1. Could you find a way to completed the transaction? What steps could you take?
2. Should you walk away from the transaction? Why/Why not?
3. What, if anything, could you have done differently had you been John Hamond?

Source

Adapted from: Harrison, M. (2007) John Hamond at First National Bank, Daniel Webster College. Case from The Case Centre, Cranfield, UK.

3.1 **Introduction**

Rigorous analysis can usefully underpin strategy, but analysis itself does not lead to action. Agreed strategies have to be put into practice, and this involves managerial judgement and decision-making that set the course of action for an organization.

As outlined in the dynamic frameworks of strategy in Chapter 2, decision-making is a crucial recurring feature of strategy practice. In addition to featuring as a core aspect of strategizing episodes, decisions made about how to approach implementation, how to learn from realized outcomes, and where to focus managerial attention are highly influential on the form and effectiveness of strategy activity. As such, to conclude this first part of the book, we examine the role of decision-making on strategy process and practices in detail.

Decision-making is relatively easy if we assume that human beings are fully rational decision-makers, relevant information is freely available to inform the decision, and the decision outcomes are predictable and the risks quantifiable. Hence, when we are confronted with a problem that requires us to choose between alternatives, we consider the nature and

3

the impact of the options that are available to us in order to find a solution. We analyse the options we have come up with and then select the one that seems the most effective and optimal solution to the problem. Powerful advanced data analytics and intelligent algorithms have been developed to help us in decision-making with the aim of reducing uncertainty and risk. However, if decision-making was as simple as theory implies, and if managerial judgement could be left to mathematical modelling and algorithms, why in real life do businesses keep getting decisions wrong?

The aim of this chapter is to help you appreciate the complexity of strategic decision-making and consider how it can be improved. Sound strategic decision-making and good business performance are intrinsically linked. No individual or organization can achieve perfect decision outcomes all the time. Nevertheless, strategists are tasked to make decisions in volatile, uncertain, and ambiguous environments which should benefit the firm and its stakeholders. These decisions have to take into account the plurality of human effort and activity as a collective organizational phenomenon, as well as incorporate the cognitive processes of individual decision-makers and decision-making groups. In this chapter we consider the many decision-making traps that lurk in the minds of decision-makers and decision-making groups in the form of **cognitive biases**. Research into biases in decision-making has its roots in **prospect theory**. We also outline some of the frameworks and tools that practitioners can use to improve their decision-making processes and the quality of the decision outcomes. Finally, we outline the challenges of making decisions in groups, and the role of strategic leaders in organizational decision-making.

3.2 **Routine decisions and strategic decisions**

Before we consider decision-making processes and how they can be improved, it is important that we define the types of decisions that we are interested in here. We all make tens if not hundreds of decisions every day. Most of them are routine, such as what we are going to wear when we get ready for work in the morning, or what route we are going to take to work. Similarly, organizations make routine decisions, such as placing a replenishment order for stationery from an approved office supplies provider, or sales managers approving sales force travel expenditure within set guidelines. In fact, most routine managerial decisions are governed by some type of decision-making guidelines or policies that require limited managerial time and effort. Indeed, algorithms are increasingly used to make previously time-consuming decisions more routine. For example, the assessment of consumer loans, credit cards, car loans, and even mortgages by financial institutions are now managed using algorithms which require limited human judgemental intervention.

In contrast with some routine problems, most strategic problems do not have simple solutions. Such problems are often characterized by volatility, uncertainty, complexity, and ambiguity (together referred to as **VUCA**) that require managerial judgement, and it is often the errors in these judgement calls that can produce poor decision outcomes (Schoemaker et al. 2018). In fact, it is estimated that half of all business decisions end in failure (Nutt 2002). McKinsey, a global strategic management consulting firm, found in a survey that 60% of senior executives thought that bad strategic decision outcomes were about as frequent as good ones, and 12% thought that good decision outcomes were altogether infrequent (McKinsey Global Survey Results 2009). Poor decisions can even result in disaster; for example, investment bank Lehman Brothers' monumental mistakes in their investment strategies that triggered the global financial crises of 2007–2008, and oil giant BP's decision-making flaws that led to the Deepwater Horizon drilling rig disaster.

Moreover, in contrast with routine decisions, strategic decisions have an organization-wide impact. Mintzberg et al. (1976) consider strategic decisions as large, expensive, and precedent-setting decisions that are made under conditions of ambiguity and uncertainty about the final decision outcome. Once a strategic decision is made and implemented, it is difficult to reverse, as both financial and human resources have been committed to the decision, at least in the short term, and subsequent decisions are based on these strategic decisions.

According to Nutt and Wilson (2010), strategic decisions have the following characteristics:

- They deal with complex problems which are hard to define.
- The outcomes are risky and shrouded in uncertainty and ambiguity.
- They require an understanding of the problem before a viable solution can be formulated.
- They rarely have one best solution, but rather a series of possible solutions.
- They involve trade-offs and the setting of organizational priorities, as scarce resources have to be allocated to a possible solution to the problem.
- They are influenced by competing political interests that may bias decision-makers towards a solution that aligns with their preferences.
- They are often connected with other organizational problems, which warrant additional decision-making, especially once the original strategic decision is being implemented in the organization.

As this list suggests, treating strategic decision-making as a simple and singular decision between two known alternatives does not fully capture the complexity of strategic decision problems. Although we have mechanisms to assess risk through probability theory, dealing with strategic decision problems is much more difficult when the information we gather to support a decision and the actual decision outcomes are uncertain and ambiguous. We do not live in a perfect world where the future is knowable and where the outcomes of our decisions unfold in a predictable way. Think about the decision involving the proposed high-speed rail link investment between London and the North of England, known as HS2. The first phase of this project is conservatively estimated to cost close to £60 billion and the link will not be ready until 2026 at the earliest, with subsequent links being planned to be introduced in 2032–2033. The magnitude of this strategic decision does not impact only one organization, or even multiple organizations, but the United Kingdom as a whole, as this investment would need to be prioritized over other worthy projects by the current as well as future governments.

Critics of the HS2 project have questioned the assumption that for several decades, or even longer, people will still conduct business and live their lives in a way that requires faster travel links between London and the North. Such a high degree of uncertainty about the future of the UK economy and the way people will conduct their affairs in the future makes decision-making more of an art than a science. The best a strategist can do under such circumstances is to focus on the quality of the decision-making processes, and accept that it is impossible to predict the outcome of the decision.

Not all strategic decisions are identical, although they share some common characteristics as highlighted by Nutt and Wilson (2010). In the opening case study of this chapter John Hamond faced a strategic decision, as he considered the prospective client as strategically important to his bank and to him individually as a star business development manager. He needed to decide whether to pursue the good business potential of the Kitchener Group or to stop spending his time on this small transaction and move on to more lucrative business opportunities. The time frame for the outcomes of Hamond's decision could be considered in years. In contrast, the decision that the UK government ministers had to make regarding the HS2 investment was of a totally different magnitude, and the impact of that decision would be felt by the whole economy for decades to come with a much greater degree of uncertainty and ambiguity.

Therefore strategic decisions require a great deal of judgement that has far-reaching consequences not only for the decision-makers but also for the organizations and stakeholders that are affected by these decisions. Moreover, as the future is unknowable, strategists need to make decisions based on what they anticipate might happen in the future. The best any decision-maker can hope for is that the quality of their decision-making process is as good as possible, given the information available to them at the time when the decision is made.

3.3 How do we make strategic decisions?

Before we take a closer look at how decision-making processes can be improved, we start our discussion by first asking what specifically constitutes strategic decision-making. To begin thinking about this question, let's first consider the following two scenarios:

1. You are about to finish your business degree from a well-known university. Your grades are good and you expect to receive a number of offers from leading consulting firms.

What steps will you take to select the right job?

2. You work in the corporate acquisition department of a large multinational technology firm. Your company is interested in acquiring a promising start-up in a growing marketing analytics industry.

Which firm, if any, will you advise the company to acquire?

Although the context of these two scenarios is very different, they do have things in common: each scenario constitutes a problem with a number of alternative solutions, and both require a decision to be made, and a strategic action to be taken.

Let's next consider the steps to take when applying a 'rational' decision-making process to the above scenarios. The 'rational' decision-making model has its origins in economics. It assumes that humans are what economists call 'homo economicus' or 'economic man', persons who make rational decisions in order to achieve their most preferred, optimum outcome given the constraints upon choice (Black et al. 2017). The 'rational' decision-making model prescribes us to apply the following six steps to each scenario (Bazerman and Moore 2008).

The six-step rational decision-making model

1. Define the problem
2. Identify decision criteria
3. Weigh the criteria
4. Generate alternatives
5. Rate each alternative on each criterion
6. Compute the optimal decision

Source: Bazerman and Moore 2008

Once a decision-maker has defined the problem (Step 1), he or she needs to identify the decision criteria that will be important in solving the problem (Step 2). During Step 2, the decision-maker must determine what is relevant in making the decision, which brings the decision-maker's interests, values, and personal preferences into the process. In Step 3, the decision-maker weighs the previously identified criteria in order to give him or her the correct priority in the decision. The decision-maker generates possible alternatives (Step 4) which could succeed in resolving the problem. No attempt is made in this step to appraise these alternatives, only to list them. In Step 5 the decision-maker must critically analyse and evaluate each alternative. The strengths and weaknesses of each option become evident as they are compared with the criteria and weightings established in Steps 2 and 3. In the final step (Step 6) each alternative is ranked according to its weighted criteria and the alternative with the highest score is selected. Assuming that decision-makers are fully rational, and that they have all information available and are able to assign objective weightings to each alternative, decision-making can be a rather simple mechanistic exercise.

Although we should approach decision-making as rationally as possible, there are limitations to the rational model. Considering the above six-step rational decision-making model, let's go through each step and identify the difficulties strategists may come across when applying this six-step rational model in practice.

Define the problem

Practitioners often unintentionally act without a thorough understanding of the problem to be solved, which can lead them to solve the wrong problem. For example, managers could erroneously believe that a firm's poor sales performance is due to the underperforming sales force rather than the quality of a product itself. Having invested significant amounts of money on developing Nokia's mobile communications platform Symbian, the managers blamed the rapidly falling sales on problems with the physical attributes of the Nokia phones and on marketing, while refusing to believe that the problem was the very operating platform in which they had made strategic investments. Accurate judgement is needed to identify and define the problem. Managers can easily go wrong by defining the problem in terms of a proposed solution, missing a bigger problem, or diagnosing the problem in terms of its symptoms.

Identify the decision criteria

Most decisions require us to accomplish more than one objective. When selecting a job we consider the reputation of the firm, the type of work we want to do, the distance from our home, the salary, opportunities for advancement, and so on. A rational decision-maker will be able to identify all relevant criteria in the decision-making process and organize them in some sort of priority order of importance, but in reality this is almost impossible to determine objectively. For example, what one person thinks is relevant, another may not, and vice versa. Organizations frequently confront this problem in budgeting decisions. As resources are finite, not every worthy activity can be accommodated and trade-offs are necessary. Hence, budgeting decisions may become influenced by non-quantifiable considerations such as organization political and power considerations rather than return on investment analysis.

Weigh the criteria

Rational decision-makers will know the relative value they place on each of the criteria that were identified in the Step 2. For example, when selecting a possible new employer they are able to accurately assign a weighting to the reputation of the firm, a different weighting to the opportunities for advancement, etc. The weighting is based on the value the decision-maker places on each of the criteria, which may be quantifiable in monetary terms or whatever scoring criteria are being used by the decision-maker. Again, it is doubtful whether we are able to make such a calculation objectively.

Generate alternatives

This step requires the decision-maker to define the possible course of action. Decision-makers often spend too much time seeking alternatives and collecting ever more information to evaluate the options. This can create a barrier to effective decision-making. An optimal search for alternative solutions should continue only until the cost of the search outweighs the value of added information to be used in the considering the alternative solutions. Very few of us, if any, are able to ascertain this break-even point where the cost of the search equals the benefit gained.

Rate each alternative on each criterion

This is often the most difficult step in the decision-making process as it typically requires the decision-maker trying to anticipate future events. In rational decision-making, potential consequences of each identified alternative should be considered and anticipated. But, as Henry Mintzberg observed (Mintzberg et al. 1976), the future is unknowable. As such there are serious concerns about any decision-maker's ability to anticipate the future with any degree of accuracy.

Compute the optimal decision

A rational decision-maker would have developed a criterion to evaluate the alternatives in order to make the most optimal decision. This would entail multiplying the ratings for each alternative by the weight for each criterion and then choosing the solution with the highest sum of the weighted ratings. But as we have seen there are serious limitations to the rationality in developing objectively defined criteria and a rating system for the criteria. Although the mathematical calculation is relatively simple, the result is false if the component parts of the calculation are not accurate.

We have seen that the rational decision-making model assumes that decision-makers approach the decision-making task in an orderly fashion and that full rationality is achievable, including the availability of all information that is relevant for the decision. The six-step list provides you with a useful order for thinking about what an optimal decision-making process might look like. In your future career it will be important to make an effort to approach strategic decision-making in an orderly way.

3.4 **The bounds of human rationality**

The rational decision-making model describes how a decision **should** be made, but it fails to describe how a decision **is** made in practice. So what are the boundaries that prevent us from applying this rational model? Two main factors that constrain our ability to engage in purely rational decision-making are the bounds to our rationality and the uncertainty that is particularly pertinent for strategic decisions that can unfold far in the future. All strategic decisions feature evaluative human judgement, and making tough calls requires people to distill vast amounts of complex and ambiguous information into a decision. As human judgement is unreliable, all evaluations are susceptible to errors (Kahneman et al. 2019). In this section we discuss the limitations of rational decision-making.

Nobel laureate Herbert Simon suggested that all human judgement is bounded (or limited) in its rationality, and we can better understand decision-making by describing and explaining actual decisions rather than by focusing on what should be done rationally in decision-making processes (March and Simon 1958). While Simon's framework of 'bounded rationality' views people as attempting to make rational decisions, it acknowledges that there are limitations that prevent us from making rational decisions as prescribed by the rational decision-making model. These include limitations in information:

- a lack of important information that would help to define the problem
- a lack of clarity in the relevant decision criteria
- uncertainty and ambiguity about the decision outcome, due to the long time frame.

There are also a number of limitations in the following individual abilities:

- the amount of information decision-makers can hold in their memory
- their level of intelligence
- errors in how the decision problem is perceived, which can inhibit the decision-maker's ability to calculate the optimal choice accurately from a number of alternatives.

Finally, Eisenhardt and Zbaracki (1992) propose politics and power as additional limitations that hinder optimum decision-making. Decision-makers may hold different and often conflicting goals in organizations (see Case Example 3.1). This makes decision-making a political process and the final decision reflects the preference of the most powerful decision-maker or a coalition.

Recent research has shown that even if the use of decision-making algorithms were the best alternative for a given decision problem, people are still reluctant to use them (Dietvorst et al. 2015). For example, if decision-makers know that a specific forecast goal is hard to achieve, and the previous use of an algorithm in forecasting did not fully meet the expected forecast goal in the past, decision-makers revert to using human judgement. However, research shows that doing this often results in a worse performance than when the algorithm is applied. In fact, on average, algorithms are about 10–15% better than human judgement alone (Michelman 2017). A simple example of a highly accurate algorithm is a university admissions algorithm which models student performance in the USA. A combination of test scores, grade point averages, etc. are assigned an equal weighting, which significantly outperforms admissions experts in predicting student performance.

All of these limitations prevent decision-makers from making the optimal decision assumed by the rational model. The decisions that result from these limitations typically overlook the full range of possible consequences and decision-makers forgo the best solution in favour of one that is acceptable or reasonable (Bazerman and Moore 2008). Such decision-making is referred to by Simon as **satisficing**—rather than examining all possible alternatives, people simply search until a **satisfactory** solution is found which will **suffice** because it achieves an acceptable, but not necessarily an optimum, level of performance.

Uncertainty

Perceived environmental uncertainty (Milliken 1987) is another major factor that makes managerial decision-making difficult, especially when dealing with strategic decision problems. Milliken identifies three types of uncertainty that managers face in their organizations:

1. State uncertainty—uncertainty about the organization's future environment and key trends.
2. Effect uncertainty—uncertainty as to how these events or trends will impact the organization.
3. Response uncertainty—uncertainty as to how the organization should respond.

Research (Sund et al. 2016; Milliken 1987) indicates that these three types of uncertainty have important, and at times paradoxical, implications for organizations. It would be easy to assume that the practitioners' uncertainty about their firm's future environment and the key trends that could affect it (state uncertainty) would correlate with volatility in the firm's macro and competitive environment. Such uncertainty would increase both decision-makers' uncertainty as to what impact this volatility would have on their organization (effect uncertainty) and how to respond to such changes (response uncertainty). In other words, it is often presumed that high state uncertainty leads into high effect and response uncertainty, and when the uncertainty over future trends is low, it should reduce the degree of effect and response uncertainty. For example, we often make the assumption that companies in relatively stable industries such as agriculture and food production possess a low degree of effect and response certainty as strategists are able to plan their organizations' activities with a high degree of certainty.

In reality, however, low 'state uncertainty' may have an adverse impact on the levels of other types of uncertainty. An example of this could be an increasing usage of robotics and artificial intelligence (AI) in manufacturing and everyday life. Organizations know that robotics and AI are a key future trend (low state uncertainty), but the strategists do not necessarily know what impact the increased use of robotics would have on the organization (high effect uncertainty) or how to respond to this perceived threat or opportunity (high response uncertainty). Practitioners may,

CASE EXAMPLE 3.1 **WHERE WILL THE AXE FALL?**

A department within a well-known university was faced with a major strategic problem: it had to find savings that would inevitably include redundancies across academic and administrative staff departments. Student numbers of the university's degree programmes had declined steadily over the previous three years.

The university's board of governors and trustees had become increasingly concerned about the university's finances. At a recent board meeting, it had been agreed that every faculty, including this one, would need to implement permanent savings of £2 million by the end of the following academic year.

The principal of the department was tasked with forming a working group to identify savings at the university. It consisted of four academic departments as well as departments for academic quality, information systems and administration, and library and information services. The working group consisted of the heads of all departments and academic union representatives.

The atmosphere at the first working group meeting was tense, but everyone present agreed that the university had to implement the cost-savings programme, and collectively they would find the required £2 million of savings. It was agreed that all department heads would consult with their staff members and present their cost reduction plans at the next meeting.

At the next meeting, it became obvious that the cost reduction plans would not add up to the required amount of savings. The department heads for finance and economics and human resource management were not present at the meeting. They had sent their cost savings projections in advance, and the principal had noticed that their proposed savings were marginal at best. At the meeting, the head of academic quality argued that her department could not afford any savings as the department was short-staffed already. Furthermore, academic quality was a top priority for the university in order for the institution to maintain its reputation as a top-quality teaching and research institution. She suggested that the main brunt of the savings should be borne by specialist academic departments, as the specialist programmes had seen the greatest reduction in student numbers.

In the absence of the two department heads whose degree programmes were identified by the head of academic quality, the other heads of academic departments objected strenuously. They argued that the academic staff were the lifeline of any university, and job cuts would cause irreparable reputational damage to the university as a whole and to the departments in question in particular, which were well-known for high-quality research output. The academic heads were very clear that any reduction in academic staff would result in large class sizes that would damage student satisfaction, and the loss of teaching and research staff would damage the school's standing in international league tables. Any cuts should come from administrative support services which could be streamlined by reducing unproductive and needless bureaucracy, including over-zealous quality control systems.

At this point the union representatives stated that they did not agree with any cost savings through staff cuts. They felt that in comparison with other universities, this department was too top heavy. Any cost savings through staff cuts would stretch the already hard-working staff across academic and administrative departments beyond breaking point. Instead, the axe should fall on the university's management layers as there were many managers who did not make a contribution to teaching, research, or the day-to-day operation of the university beyond their managerial responsibilities.

The meeting ended in deadlock. No future meeting date was set as all department heads insisted that they had given their best cost-savings projections. The total of proposed savings that included some early retirement of pension-aged staff and a reduction in contractor and visiting academic staff amounted to £800,000, £1.2 million short of the set target.

Questions for discussion

1. Apply the rational decision-making model to this decision problem.
2. Identify what the participants of the meeting think would limit the rationality of the decision-making process and outcome.
3. Consider how the principal could explore other solutions to this strategic problem.

Details of the case have been written in a way that hides the identity of the organization. However, the decision problem is real.

in fact, be most motivated to pay attention to their organizations' environments when they are pretty certain that significant changes are occurring. Despite being uncertain about the impact of these changes and how to respond, the perceived high level of environmental uncertainty will force them to consider how the organization might become vulnerable to the environmental changes, and then to develop a response. Under low levels of environmental uncertainty, managers could become complacent and be caught out by disruptive radical changes in the environment that could have been predictable in advance, had that management remained more rigorous in scanning their external environment for possible disruptions. No matter what type of uncertainty is perceived by the managers, the experience of uncertainty is fundamental to the managerial sense-making of decision problems (Sund et al. 2016).

Later in this chapter we will look at various tools that are available to managers to improve the quality of their decision-making processes in order to develop a capability in dealing with the uncertainty that surrounds complex decision problems. Although the future will always remain uncertain, there are tools that enable managers to collectively make sense of the decision problems by sharing diverse views and developing shared courses of action.

3.5 **Managerial heuristics**

Bounded human rationality and our satisficing behaviour in decision-making together indicate that although we wish to think that we are rational, we do not behave according to the prescriptive rational decision-making model. These concepts help us realize that we make decisions with imperfect information, and that the behaviours, political agendas, and preferences of others may not allow us to make optimal decisions. But is our judgement and decision-making biased? And if so, in what ways? Where finding an optimal solution to a problem is impossible or impractical, heuristic methods can be used to speed up the process of finding a satisfactory solution. Heuristics are often mental shortcuts that ease the cognitive burden of making a decision. Examples of heuristics include the use of a rule of thumb, an educated guess, an intuitive judgement or gut feeling, or common sense. In this section we consider a number of heuristics that are common in managerial decision-making.

System One and System Two thinking

According to cognitive scientists (Kahneman et al. 1982), humans possess two modes of thinking: intuitive and reflective. In intuitive thinking, impressions, associations, feelings, intentions, and the urgency for action flow effortlessly without us having to assess our actions. This type of intuitive thinking, where initial observations made within the first few seconds create a lasting impression of the observed by the observer, is referred to as thin-slicing (Ambady and Rosenthal 1992). Intuitive thinking produces a constant representation of the world around us that allows us to do things almost automatically and simultaneously, such as walking, noticing things around us, and thinking at the same time. This is known as System One thinking. It leads to action; it is effortless, and it leads us to do things and form opinions.

In contrast, System Two thinking is slow, deliberate, and requires effort. This type of reflective thinking is activated when we are faced with problems where the stakes are high, when we detect an obvious error that requires us to correct our actions, or when we have to follow certain rules (such as the prescriptive model of 'rational' decision-making). But because System Two thinking requires a concerted effort, our effortless System One thinking tends to be the dominant force in decision-making. We need to make a conscious effort to fight against the siren calls of the System One thinking that offers us instantaneous solutions to problems or pushes us to form opinions without any further consideration.

System One thinking is part of our biological make-up—the 'flight or fight' reflex. It is good at making us react instantaneously when we are confronted with a problem or when we are faced with a serious threat to our immediate well-being. However, even when we are confronted with a complex analytical problem without any threat to our physical well-being, System One thinking produces an instantaneous answer to the problem—a solution that we often refer to as 'gut feeling'. Our 'gut feeling' short circuits the need to engage the System Two thinking, saving us the effort to work through the analysis. This can be a tremendous advantage for managers who have accumulated significant experience and can draw on that experience to come up with instantaneous solutions to problems. However, 'gut feeling' can lead us astray with disastrous consequences when it signals a solution to a problem that cannot be extrapolated from past experiences. The two systems are summarized in Table 3.1.

Tversky and Kahneman (1974) identified systematic biases that influence our judgement and decision-making which result from the powerful prevalence of System One thinking. They found that we use a number of simplifying strategies, or **heuristics**, when making decisions. Heuristics allow us to cope with difficult and complex environments that surround decisions. Kahneman (2011) has proposed a general 'law of least effort' which applies to cognitive as well as physical exertion. His 'law' asserts that if there are several ways of achieving the same goal, people will eventually gravitate to the least demanding course of action. In the economy of action, effort is a cost, and the acquisition of a skill is driven by the balance of benefits and costs. In other words, people will eventually opt for the easiest option, which requires the least amount of effort. However, even in complex decision-making situations, people still revert to an action that requires the least effort. Rather than having to work through a problem, our cognitive and physiological make-up lead us to make decisions using decision-making heuristics to find a short cut to the decision problem.

TABLE 3.1 **System One and System Two thinking**

System One thinking	System Two thinking
Intuitive	Reflective
Automatic	Requires a concerted effort
Produces a constant representation of the world around us Examples: Simultaneous actions, such as walking, noticing things around us, and thinking	Activated when we are faced with problems where the stakes are high Examples: When we detect an obvious error that requires us to correct our actions When we have to follow certain rules (such as the prescriptive model of 'rational' decision-making)
Leads to action: effortless, and leads us to do things, and form instant opinions	Slow, deliberate, and requires conscious effort

3

CASE EXAMPLE 3.2 A VIRTUAL REALITY DRESSING ROOM

Nicola is about to finish her master's degree in luxury brand management. She initially trained as a fashion designer, and as part of her master's final year project she has produced a business start-up plan to form a company that rents expensive evening wear and jewellery to women who may have to attend formal occasions, but do not have the means or the wish to spend considerable sums of money on fashion items. To differentiate her offer from the competition, she wants to create a virtual dressing room for women to try on the clothes before renting them. The outfits will be couriered to customers, who are usually time poor, without them having to try on the clothing items first in real life. The functionality of the virtual dressing room is the core of the company's competitive advantage. It is critical that the virtual dressing room accurately reflects the fit of the clothes, as they would in a real life changing room.

To create a virtual reality dressing room, Nicola needs to hire a virtual reality expert to design the dressing room functionality before approaching venture capitalists with her idea. Nicola knows that there are 12 universities with degree programmes in virtual reality and web design, but in order to save time she decides to limit her search to the top three technology universities to find a new graduate to help her out.

Questions for discussion

1. In light of our discussion so far in this chapter, what do you think of Nicola's strategy for finding the best candidate for the virtual reality design task?

From the view of the rational decision-making model, Nicola's strategy in Case Example 3.2 is deficient. She uses satisficing behaviour as she decides to focus her search on the top three universities only, although she knows that there are 12 universities that produce designers with the skill sets required for her business. Narrowing her search may exclude excellent candidates who do not attend the top universities. However, although using the heuristic method of focusing on only the top three universities may eliminate the best candidate, the time that Nicola saves on narrowing her search may outweigh the potential loss. The likelihood that Nicola's limited search will produce a satisfactory candidate from the top universities is high. Economists would probably support Nicola's strategy for finding a designer for her business as they would argue that people use heuristics because the time saved often outweighs the costs of any potential reduction in the quality of a decision that is being made (Bazerman and Moore 2008).

Common heuristics in managerial decision-making

In addition to the satisficing behaviour demonstrated by Nicola in Case Example 3.2, there are a number of heuristics that research (Bazerman and Moore 2008) has shown to apply across all peoples, genders, and cultures. Table 3.2 lists the most commonly found heuristics in managerial decision-making.

The use of heuristics may produce correct or partially correct judgements (Bazerman and Moore 2008). The use of partially correct judgements should not always be discouraged, and arguably it might not even be possible to discourage it entirely, as we have explored the idea

TABLE 3.2 **Common heuristics in managerial decision-making**

Heuristic	Definition	Example
Representativeness	A tendency to assume that what we see or will see is typical of what can occur	Assumption that colleagues who act in a friendly manner are genuinely friendly and cooperative
Availability	A tendency to assume that what could happen in a new situation will be the same as what we have seen or experienced in the past	Assumption that the acquisition under consideration will work out as well as our previously well executed acquisition
Anchoring and adjustment	A tendency to make judgements based on an initial assessment as an anchor, but failing to make sufficient adjustments later on as new information is revealed	Contract price negotiation becomes anchored on the initial cost quoted by the contractor rather than on a fully objective cost assessment
Affect	A tendency to allow emotions such as fear and pleasure to guide our decision-making	Negative feelings about nuclear power may lead to overstating its risks and understating its benefits

in Sections 3.3 and 3.4 that people will inevitably always use some simplifying mechanisms to make complex decisions under uncertainty and ambiguity. But we have to realize that the use of heuristics in decision-making can create serious problems, primarily because people are not aware that they rely on them in making decisions. It is important to understand, in your study of strategy, that it is this unawareness that may lead practitioners to make costly mistakes by applying heuristics in inappropriate contexts, which can lead to biased decision-making.

Hot and cold reflection and reflexion

As we have mentioned, an intuitive judgement or gut feeling might be a managerial heuristic used in strategic decision-making. But to what level of success? Whilst the field of strategic management has relied largely on behavioural and cognitive assumptions about how strategists strategize, it has tended to privilege analytical, linear, and rational approaches over emotional intuitive alternatives. The limits of knowing and learning have been assumed to be a function of the limits of the ability of the strategist or strategic systems to process information, but rational processes have been a central idea. Increasingly, however, researchers argue that emotion sometimes plays a decisive role in decision-making and intuitive judgements. The role of emotion is particularly important when considering the emphasis on analysis and dispassionate reasoning in strategy processes.

This is particularly critical given the prevalence of surveys that suggest that many organizational leaders rely on 'gut feel' or 'intuition' in their strategic decisions. An *Economist Intelligence Unit* survey, sponsored by Applied Predictive Technologies in February 2014, revealed some interesting findings. Of the 174 executives from around the world that they surveyed, the majority described themselves as 'data-driven' or 'empirical'. Only 10% of the survey respondents described themselves as 'intuitive'. Yet, when they were asked what they do when the data contradicts their gut instinct, the majority replied that they would reanalyse the data or collect more data. Only 10% said that they would follow the course of action set out by the data, and 73% said that they trust their own intuition.

These findings are not surprising when one considers, as Argyris (1991) has argued, that senior executives in particular have often reached their step on the career ladder by exercising good judgement. They are, as a consequence, confident in their 'gut instincts' and, because they are also generally intelligent, they are also capable of justifying and rationalizing them. For example, consider leaders who have made successful decisions that might have seemed unusual or a poor choice, but were a result of gut instinct: Henry Ford doubling his worker's wages in 1914 to combat falling demand for his cars; Anita Roddick's mixing of business and environmental activism with the founding of the Body Shop; Richard Branson selling his Virgin music label to support his fledgling airline; or Steve Jobs bet on the iPod and then the iPad. These were all decisions, to quote legendary GE CEO Jack Welch, which came 'straight from the gut'. However, on the other hand, such emotionally involved gut-feeling judgements have also led to significant mistakes. Think of Decca Records turning down the Beatles, former Daimler-Benz CEO Jürgen Schrempp's disastrous merger with Chrysler, HP's former CEO Carly Fiorina's questionable acquisition of Compaq Computer, or former RBS CEO Fred Goodwin's decision to acquire ABN Amro just as the 2008 financial crises was beginning.

Decision-making and judgement is not, then, just a function of the pure computational processing or cognitive abilities of people. It also has an emotional component. Many of the experiences and patterns stored in memory that form the bases for intuitive judgements and the decisions that follow have been ascribed with emotional or psychological markers. They can be positive or negative, but their importance is that they influence one's 'gut feeling'. Some scholars, such as Hodgkinson and Healey (2011), argue that the emotional dimension of judgement and decision-making—while primarily unconscious—is particularly important for dynamic capabilities such as the sensing (and shaping) of opportunities, the seizing of opportunities, and the reconfiguring of assets and structures to maintain competitiveness. What we see and how we act—our categorizations, stereotypes, and biases—are as much a function of our unconscious emotional responses as they are of our reasoning ability.

3.6 **Cognitive biases and strategic decision processes**

In the previous section we discussed a number of heuristics commonly used by managers. Since strategic decisions are shrouded in ambiguity and uncertainty, there is no reason to expect that strategists are exempt from various biases (Schwenk 1988, 1995). But what kind of biases do managers express in their strategic decision-making? And is there any way to avoid these biases or to reduce their negative impact? In this section we consider common managerial biases in strategic decision-making before discussing how strategists can improve the quality of their decision-making processes to mitigate these biases.

According to Tversky and Kahneman (1974), each heuristic (representativeness, availability, anchoring and adjustment, and affect, as listed in Table 3.2) may create cognitive biases that lead decision-makers into decision traps. Hogarth (1981) has identified 29 separate biases that are likely to occur in decision-making, while Bazerman and Moore (2008) discuss 13 types of cognitive biases found in managerial decision-making. As some biases are closely related to each other, we will concentrate on the most common biases that have been identified as impacting managerial decision-making.

Lovallo and Sibony's cognitive bias typology

Lovallo and Sibony (2010) and Kahneman et al. (2011) propose a typology of cognitive biases in organizations that is by no means exhaustive, but focuses on those decisions that occur most frequently and that may have the largest impact on business decision outcomes. These researchers identify four groups of biases:

- **Action-orientation:** this bias results from intuitive decision-making that enables managers to take action rather than spend time on complex analysis.
- **Interest-seeking:** this bias results from a form of self-preservation as a decision-maker will choose an alternative that is most advantageous to him or her.
- **Pattern-recognition:** seasoned practitioners pride themselves on pattern-recognition skills that are the product of years of experience giving them confidence and trust in their decision-making capabilities to extrapolate from past experiences.
- **Stability-seeking and social biases:** most people prefer stability to change and consensus to confrontation, which may prevent the decisions being challenged enough before the final decision is made.

In the opening case study, John Hamond had to make a decision whether to spend more time with his prospective client. Kitchener Group, an inexperienced real estate borrower, seemed not to be able to produce the required documentation which would allow the transaction to be concluded. Moreover, the transaction was small, but Hamond was keen to pursue it as he was under the impression that Kitchener Group could become a major client in the future. Finding a new client with significant upside potential would serve his career well, and hence Hamond was tempted to focus on the positives of the transaction only, rather than asking himself if Kitchener's behaviour was a reflection of the firm's management that could become problematic should the bank enter into a long-term lending relationship with Kitchener. Moreover, having already spent a significant amount of time on the transaction, Hamond could be unwilling to move on from it as he would feel that without a deal he would have wasted a lot of his time and effort. The decision to keep pursuing the deal, even against all odds, which manifests itself as unwillingness to move on and accept the loss of time spent is known as an escalation of commitment bias and a sunk-cost fallacy.

Prospect theory

Loss aversion, one of the stability-seeking biases, is a particularly destructive bias. Prospect theory is a behavioural model developed to explain decision-making involving uncertainty and risk and its relation to perceived gains and losses of decisions (Kahneman and Tversky 1979). Prospect theory can be considered as ground-breaking research in decision-making that highlights that human judgement is fallible and subject to biases. As much current research on improving the quality of decision-making processes is largely grounded in prospect theory, we will discuss it in more detail before moving on to a summary of the most common biases in each of the four groups.

Prospect theory (Kahneman and Tversky 1979) describes how people choose between different options, prospects, and how they estimate the perceived likelihood of each of these options.

Consider a simple bet. You are offered a choice between receiving $900 or taking a bet that has a 90% chance of winning $1000 and a 10% chance of winning $0. Research shows that when dealing with gains, people are risk averse and will choose the sure gain ($900) over a riskier prospect (90% chance of winning $1000). Using rational decision-making theory, the expected value of both options is $900 (for the second option the expected value is ($1000 × 0.9) + ($0 × 0.1) = $900).

Now consider a slightly different bet. You are asked to choose between losing the $900 that you already have, and taking a bet where you have a 90% chance of losing $1000. Research shows that losses are treated in the opposite manner to gains. When aiming to avoid a loss, people become risk-seeking and take the gamble (the second option) over a sure loss.

These types of behaviour cannot easily be explained by the expected-utility approach. In both the above situations, the expected utility of both choices is the same (±$900): the probability multiplied by the expected win. Yet people largely prefer one option over the other. Prospect theory explains that people demonstrate certainty and loss aversion biases when they make such decisions. People tend to overweigh options that are certain, and are risk averse for gains. We would rather get an assured lesser win than take the chance of winning more, but also risk possibly winning nothing. The opposite is true when dealing with certain losses; people engage in risk-seeking behaviour to avoid a bigger loss.

People's reaction to loss is more extreme than their reaction to gain. In financial investment decisions, even experienced investors can get caught in loss aversion traps. As losses feel more extreme than gains, investors are often unwilling to cut their losses in their investment portfolios. Rather than cutting their losses, investors allow unrealized losses to accumulate in the hope that the investment will turn round as time goes by.

Typology of managerial biases

The most common biases are (Lovallo and Sibony 2010):

- action-orientation biases
- interest-seeking biases
- pattern-recognition biases
- stability-seeking biases.

Table 3.3 describes each of these common biases, alongside an example of each.

Because cognitive biases are deeply embedded into the human psyche, they are difficult to detect in our own behaviours. In fact, Kahneman (2011) states that being aware of heuristics and biases does not de-bias one's own behaviour. However, while we may not be able to control our own intuitions, we are able to apply rational thought to detect biases in others' decision-making. In order to do this, we need to first understand the nature and the context of biases, and then develop processes to challenge the recommendations of others. Senior managers are often expected to review recommendations and make a final call. When reviewing recommendations, practitioners often add a rather crude safety margin for biases or errors, but they very rarely undertake a systematic review of recommendations put forward to them that challenges the assumptions and the projected outcomes of the recommended decisions.

3

TABLE 3.3 **The most common biases**

	Description	Example
Action-orientation biases		
Overoptimism	The tendency for managers to be overoptimistic about the outcome of planned actions, to overestimate the likelihood of positive events, and to underestimate the likelihood of negative ones	Overoptimistic financial projections
Overconfidence	Overestimating our skill level relative to those of others, leading managers to overestimate their ability to affect future outcomes, take credit for past outcomes, and neglect the role of chance	Overestimate our ability to turn a failing company around when successive management teams have failed in the past
Competitor neglect	The tendency to plan without factoring in competitive responses	Launch of aggressive promotion campaigns without fully considering competitor response
Interest-seeking biases		
Misaligned individual incentives	Incentives for managers to adopt views or to seek outcomes favourable to their unit or themselves, at the expense of the overall interest of the company; these self-serving views are often held genuinely, not cynically	Misaligned performance bonus payments that may lead to self-serving behaviour
Inappropriate attachments	Emotional attachment of individuals to people or elements of the business, creating misaligned of interests	Legacy products or brands that no longer add value to the organization
Misaligned perception of corporate goals	Disagreements (often not spoken) about the hierarchy or relative weight of objectives pursued by the organization and the trade-offs between them	Passive–aggressive behaviour of managers in implementing strategic objectives
Pattern-recognition bias		
Confirmation	The overweighting of evidence consistent with a favoured belief, underweighting of evidence against a favoured belief, or failure to search impartially for evidence	Decision-making process focuses mainly on gathering supporting evidence for the favoured option
Management by example	Generalizing based on examples that are particularly recent or memorable	Recent successful high-profile advertising campaign becomes a template for all future campaigns
False analogies	Relying on comparisons with situations that are not directly comparable	A business practice that works in one geographic market is assumed to work in another market location
Champion bias	The tendency to evaluate a plan or proposal based on the track record of the person presenting it, more than on the facts supporting it	Halo effect—a high performing manager will continue to perform well in whatever they want the organization to do next

Continued

3

TABLE 3.3 *Continued*

	Description	Example
Stability-seeking biases		
Anchoring and adjustment	Managers root themselves to an initial value, leading to insufficient adjustments of subsequent estimates	The initial acquisition price of an acquisition becomes the negotiating anchor regardless of whether subsequent evaluations would indicate a significantly different value
Loss aversion	The tendency to feel losses more acutely than gains of the same amount, making us more risk averse than a rational calculation would suggest	Unwillingness to cut losses in the hope that things will turn around; loss aversion is a particularly destructive bias that results from prospect theory, which was covered in more detail earlier in this section
Sunk-cost fallacy	Managers pay attention to historical costs that are not recoverable when considering future course of action	Money already spent on the project may lead into an 'escalation of commitment' by committing more funds into a project that may be failing; this is closely linked to loss aversion
Status quo bias	Managers have a preference for the status quo in the absence of pressure to change it	Managers are unwilling to adopt to changing market conditions until it may be too late
Social biases		
Groupthink	Striving for consensus at the cost of a realistic appraisal of alternative courses of action	In a group meeting, one is not willing to express a concern or a contrary view to what is being discussed in order to preserve consensus
Sunflower management	Tendency for groups to align with the views of their leaders, whether expressed or assumed	Unwillingness to express a contrary view for the fear that such a view could be perceived as having a negative attitude

Source: Lovallo, D. and Sibony, O. (2010). The case for behavioural strategy. *McKinsey Quarterly on Behavioral Strategy*, Spring (mckinseyquarterly.com).

How can practitioners detect biases in decisions?

Based on research with senior executives, Kahneman et al. (2011) developed a rigorous process aimed at identifying cognitive biases which may have influenced the people putting recommendations forward for senior manager approval. The aim of the process outlined in Table 3.4 is to help managers retrace steps back in the decision process where heuristics may have steered people or groups astray. Senior executives are often tasked with approving what has been recommended by working groups. It is at this stage that senior practitioners should offer a final challenge to the decision that has been put in front of them for approval, which is also a means of safeguarding themselves against their own biases.

Embedding these practices into formal organizational decision-making procedures ensures that managers become familiar with processes that may improve the quality of their own decision-making in situations where they have the final say in a decision. As the processes become part of the organization's way of conducting business, they are used with regularity, not

TABLE 3.4 **The final challenge: a process for evaluating recommendations for strategic decisions**

Check	Question to ask	Action to take
1. Check for interest-seeking bias	Is there any reason to expect that the team is making a recommendation based on self-interest?	Review the proposal, paying special attention to overoptimism bias
2. Check for affect heuristic and interest-seeking bias	Has the team fallen in love with their proposal?	Check the process by which the proposed recommendation was formulated
3. Check for groupthink	Were there dissenting opinions within the team?	Check whether dissenting opinions were explored adequately Solicit dissenting views if in doubt
4. Check for false analogies bias	Could the recommendation be overly influenced by analogy with a memorable success?	Ask for more analogies, and rigorously analyse their similarity to the current situation
5. Check for conformation bias	Are credible alternatives included with the recommendation?	Request additional options
6. Check for availability heuristic	If this decision were to be made a year from now, what information would be required and can it be obtained now?	Create a checklist of the data needed for an informed decision
7. Check for anchoring bias	Where do projections come from? Are there any unsubstantiated numbers, extrapolation from the past, a motivation to use some base line as an anchor?	Re-anchor with figures generated from other models or benchmarks, and request a new analysis
8. Check for champion bias	Is the team assuming that a person, organization, or a particular approach that is successful in one area can be just as successful in another?	Eliminate false interferences, and ask the team to seek additional comparable examples
9. Check for sunk-cost fallacy	Is the team overly attached to a history of past decisions?	Consider the issue if you had just joined the organization with the decision-making responsibility
10. Check for overoptimism	Is the base case overly optimistic?	Have the team built a case taking an outside view Consider war-gaming the decision
11. Check for overconfidence	Is the worst case scenario bad enough?	Have the team conduct a pre-mortem: imagine that the worst has happened, and develop a story about the causes of the failure
12. Check for loss aversion	Is the recommending team overly cautious?	Realign incentives to share responsibility for the risk, or consider how to reduce or eliminate risk

only when managers are unsure of which way to call a decision. Another important reason for adopting such decision-making procedures is to safeguard against overconfidence and overoptimism biases of senior decision-makers themselves.

3.7 Collective decision-making

The process for evaluating strategic decisions outlined in Table 3.4 is targeted at senior executives who may have the ultimate say in a decision. But how should we understand and improve the processes for working on and evaluating strategic problems and identifying diverse solutions to such problems? As most strategic decision problems are worked on in groups, in this section we explore the nature of collective decision-making. We also look at how organizations can effectively use collective decision-making practices to improve the overall quality of their problem identification and solution development capabilities.

In complex decision situations, groups have been shown to have better problem-solving capabilities than individuals acting alone (Daft et al. 1993; van Ginkel and van Knippenberg 2009). This may be because group members bring a variety of information, critical judgement, solution strategies, and a wide range of perspectives to the decision problem. However, groups can be subject to conflict and, just as individuals, they can be subject to cognitive biases. Conflict and biases may hinder the quality of decision outcomes and group members' decision acceptance. In this section of the chapter, we will start by discussing different manifestations of conflict, and go on to discuss different group biases (Arevuo 2015).

Cognitive and affective conflict

Research into group decision-making has shown that group member interaction may lead to **cognitive conflict** (Hambrick 1994; Amason 1996). Cognitive conflict arises when a number of possible solutions are suggested by different group members. These solutions compete against each other when group members debate the relative merits of each solution. We can think of cognitive conflict as a competition of ideas among the group members.

Pioneering work by Amason (1996) provided a convincing argument that cognitive conflict is beneficial in collective decision-making, and this has become widely accepted by scholars. The accepted assumption is that cognitive conflict improves decision-making quality. Therefore this has prompted researchers to explore how to create cognitive conflict in collective decision-making situations. A great deal of research has accumulated on techniques, such as devil's advocacy and **dialectical enquiry**, which encourage critical interaction between decision-making group members. We will discuss each in turn.

Devil's advocacy

Devil's advocacy involves a group developing a solid argument for a recommended course of action, and subjecting that recommendation to an in-depth formal critique. The critique calls into question the assumptions and recommendations presented to the **devil's advocate**, and attempts to show why the recommendations should **not** be adopted.

Because good recommendations based on solid assumptions will survive even the most forceful and effective criticism, this approach is likely to yield sound judgements or recommendations.

There are seven steps for groups to follow in using the devil's advocacy approach to solve strategic problems (adapted from Schweiger et al. 1986):

1. Identify a problem needing group analysis and decision-making.
2. Divide the group or team into two subgroups of equal size.
3. Assign one subgroup to play devil's advocate (DA subgroup) and the other to develop a consensus recommendation for the decision problem (CO subgroup).
4. After separating into subgroups, instruct the CO group to develop a set of recommendations and build an argument for them, supported by all the key assumptions, facts, and data that underlie them. This group writes out the recommendations, assumptions, facts, and data on a whiteboard or large piece of paper. Meanwhile, instruct the DA subgroup to prepare for their critique by discussing the case and identifying critical assumptions, data, and facts that the other group might miss. Then, bring the subgroups together.
5. Instruct the CO subgroup to present its recommendations and assumptions to the DA subgroup.
6. The DA subgroup critiques the recommendations, attempting to uncover all that is wrong with the recommendations, assumptions, facts, and data and explaining why the recommendations should not be adopted.
7. Separate the subgroups again so that the CO group revises its recommendations to answer the critiques, while the DA group works to find more critiques that would strengthen the recommendation.

Repeat Steps 4 and 5 until both subgroups can accept the recommendations, assumptions, and data. Once both subgroups agree on a recommended solution, move forward and enact the recommendations.

A group may appoint a devil's advocate to argue against the prevailing ideas, position, or decision of the group. While a devil's advocate can simply play a contrary role, someone who argues against a particular idea can also stimulate discussion which can identify weak points in an argument that need to be addressed. Therefore one could consider this approach extremely useful, albeit stressful for someone advocating alone against an accepted idea in a group. However, while devil's advocacy takes into consideration many alternatives, it is true to say that it concentrates quite heavily on the shortcomings, or negatives, of the approach to an idea.

Dialectical enquiry

Dialectical enquiry is a more balanced approach than devil's advocacy, as it gives equal importance to the positives and the negatives of alternatives. Like devil's advocacy, dialectical enquiry is another approach to collective decision-making. The technique can be traced back to the dialectic school of philosophy in ancient Greece. Plato and his followers attempted to define what constitutes a truth by exploring opposite positions, called thesis and antithesis. Essentially, dialectical enquiry is a debate between two opposing sets of viewpoints. Although it stimulates programmed conflict, it is a constructive approach because it elicits the benefits and limitations of opposing sets of ideas.

Organizations that use dialectical enquiry create teams of decision-makers. Each team is instructed to generate and evaluate alternative courses of action and then recommend the best one. After hearing each team's alternative courses of action, the teams and the organization's top managers meet together and select the best parts of each plan and synthesize a final plan that provides the best opportunity for success. The process can be broken down to five steps (adapted from Schweiger et al. 1986):

1. The process begins with the formation of two or more divergent groups to represent the full range of views on a specific problem. Each group is made as internally homogeneous as possible. However, the groups should be as different from one another as possible. Collectively, they cover all positions that might have an impact on the ultimate solution to a problem.
2. Each group meets separately, identifies the assumptions behind its position, and rates them on their importance and feasibility. Each group then presents a 'for' and an 'against' position to the other groups.
3. Each group debates the other groups' positions and defends its own. The goal is not to convince others, but to confirm that what each group expresses as its position is not necessarily accepted by others.
4. Information that is provided by all the groups is analysed. This results in the identification of information gaps and establishes guidelines for further research on the problem.
5. An attempt is made to achieve consensus among the positions. Strategies are sought that will best meet the requirements of all positions that remain viable. This final step permits further refinement of information needed to solve the problem.

Consensus decision-making

Another approach to group decision-making is the consensus approach where the agreement of the whole group is sought for a decision. Devil's advocacy and dialectical enquiry have been shown to create more cognitive conflict in decision-making groups compared with the consensus approach. Research by Schweiger et al. (1986) indicated that both dialectical enquiry and devil's advocacy led to higher-quality assumptions and decision outcomes than the consensus approach to decision-making. However, decision-makers in consensus groups expressed more satisfaction and desire to continue to work with their groups, and indicated a greater level of decision acceptance than those groups who were asked to apply dialectical enquiry and devil's advocacy in their decision-making process.

The Delphi method

Another popular decision-making technique is the Delphi method. This technique is used to achieve group consensus, but the group does not physically come together to find an answer to a given problem. The Delphi method has similarities with devil's advocacy and dialectical enquiry, and it is most commonly used in forecasting. It was originally conceived in the 1950s by the Rand Corporation, and the name refers to the Oracle of Delphi, a priestess at a temple of Apollo in ancient Greece known for her prophecies. The Delphi method allows experts to work towards a mutual agreement by conducting and circulating series of questionnaires and releasing related feedback to further the discussion with each subsequent round. The experts' responses shift as rounds are completed, based on the information produced by other experts participating in the analysis. The steps of the Delphi method are as follows:

1. A group of experts are selected to examine a decision problem or task.
2. Each expert member is sent a questionnaire with the instructions to comment on the decision problem or task based on their personal opinion, experience, or previous research.
3. The questionnaires are returned, collated, and analysed.
4. A copy of the compiled comments is sent to each expert participant and they are given an opportunity to make further comments.
5. All questionnaires and additional comments are returned for further analysis and a decision is made if another round is necessary or if the results are ready to be acted on.

The questionnaire rounds can be repeated as many times as necessary to achieve a general consensus.

The Delphi method seeks to aggregate opinions from a diverse set of experts, and it can be done without having to bring everyone together for a physical meeting. Since the responses of the participants are anonymous, individual panellists do not have to worry about repercussions for their opinions. Consensus can be reached over time as opinions are swayed. While the Delphi method allows commentary from a diverse group of participants, it does not result in the same sort of interaction as a live discussion. Response times can be long, which slows the rate of discussion.

Increased cognitive conflict can result in affective conflict

As we have seen, the manipulation of decision-making groups through various techniques is designed to increase the level of cognitive conflict in order to improve the quality of the decision-making processes. This is achieved as groups are required to consider a number of diverse perspectives. However, more recent research suggests that although cognitive conflict may increase performance through better quality decision-making, there is a danger that the beneficial cognitive conflict spills into a dysfunctional **affective conflict** (Parayitam and Dooley 2011). Affective conflict arises when the competition of ideas spills over into a personal conflict. The conflict is no longer limited to the competition between ideas but a conflict between individuals who hold opposing views. Affective conflict, or a conflict between group members, can become very destructive to the functioning of the group as a cohesive unit. Cognitive conflict has been shown to improve decision-making quality, while affective conflict has been demonstrated to have a negative impact on decision acceptance by group members, as individuals become so wedded to their opinions that the group cannot make a decision on which all members agree

(Parayitam and Dooley 2007, 2009). In other words, the high level of cognitive conflict may result in the best possible decision outcome in the given circumstances, but the stressful or pressurized environment created by the process of reaching the decision may also have resulted in tensions amongst the group members.

Devil's advocacy and dialectical enquiry are particularly vulnerable to the emergence of affective conflict. Decision-making group members become so deeply wedded to their own views that they perceive other group members with differing or challenging positions with hostility. If this hostility is allowed to escalate it may result in a dysfunctional group and the group members may become unwilling to work or collaborate with each other in this particular situation or, worse still, in any future group work situations.

Affective conflict tends to be emotional and focuses on personal incompatibilities or disputes. These disputes result from group members' personal judgements that they are not fully able to articulate to other decision-making group members. The more these personal judgements influence decisions, the more there is potential for decision-making group members to speculate and find reasons to distrust the motivation and hidden agendas of their fellow members. Hence, too much affective conflict may hinder overall group performance as the decision is not accepted by some decision-making group members regardless of the quality of the decision outcome. Research by Parayitam and Dooley (2011) indicates that too much cognitive conflict in a decision-making group may breed contempt. Therefore they suggest that moderate levels of cognitive conflict should be maintained to ensure high-quality decision outcomes but, in order to maintain group cohesion, managers should be mindful that cognitive conflict is positively correlated with affective conflict (Arevuo 2015).

Group decision-making biases

In addition to the cognitive biases that affect individual decision-making (discussed in Section 3.6) there are a number of biases which pose specific challenges for group decision-making. The growing recognition of the prevalence of cognitive biases in strategic decision-making has resulted in an increased interest in how biases affect strategic thinking in collective decision-making situations.

Groups tend to make riskier decisions than individuals because risk is perceived to be shared by the group as a collective, rather than one individual decision-maker alone (Stoner 1968). In addition, the Abilene paradox (Harvey 1988) and 'groupthink' are two of the ever-present biases that lurk in the background in most group decision-making situations. In the Abilene paradox, a group collectively decides on a course of action that is counter to the preferences of many or all of the individuals in the group. It involves a common breakdown of group communication in which each member mistakenly believes that their own preferences are counter to those of the group and therefore does not raise objections. A common phrase relating to the Abilene paradox is a desire not to 'rock the boat'. This differs from **groupthink** in that the Abilene paradox is characterized by the group members 'guessing' what decision the others might prefer, without actually exploring options, so they may reach a decision that nobody had any preference for. Groupthink occurs within a group in which the desire for harmony or conformity results in an irrational or dysfunctional decision outcome (Janis 1972). This means that group members try to minimize conflict and reach a consensus decision without undertaking a critical evaluation of alternative viewpoints, by both actively suppressing dissenting viewpoints and isolating themselves from outside influences.

Groupthink requires individuals to avoid raising controversial issues or alternative solutions, and there is a loss of individual creativity, uniqueness, and independent thinking. Dysfunctional group dynamics produce an 'illusion of invulnerability', an inflated feeling of certainty that the right decision has been made. As a result of this dysfunctional dynamic, the group can significantly overrate its own abilities in decision-making as well as significantly underrating the abilities of its opponents. This relates to our discussion about overconfidence bias in Section 3.6.

So, how do groups avoid the Abilene paradox and groupthink? Nutt (2002), in his research into 'failed' decisions, has pointed out that the development of sound group decision-making processes is critical in order for groups to achieve meaningful decision outcomes. He considers the effective decision-making process to comprise five stages (Arevuo 2015).

1. Collecting information to understand the claims calling for action.
2. Establishing a direction that indicates the desired result.
3. Engaging in a systematic search for ideas.
4. Evaluating these ideas with the direction in mind.
5. Managing the social and political barriers that can block the preferred course of action during the decision implementation stage.

We have seen how complex decision-making is in practice. There are many decision-making traps that lurk beneath the surface. They range from our cognitive limitations and biases to group dynamics and behaviours. Therefore the development and adoption of tools to help decision-makers in eliciting multiple perspectives, providing the means for groups to produce substantive decision outcomes, and achieving agreement and decision buy-in is critical to successful strategy development and implementation. One such tool is causal mapping.

Causal mapping

Bryson et al. (2014) have developed a visual decision-making technique called 'causal mapping' that is designed to help groups improve their strategic decision-making processes. Visual tools are particularly useful in strategy work, as strategic decisions are often made collectively in group working situations.

In a **causal map**, ideas are causally linked to one another through the use of arrows and nodes. The arrows indicate how one idea or action leads to another in a means to ends relationship. In effect, the maps are word-and-arrow diagrams where the arrows mean 'might cause', 'might lead to', or 'might result in'. Causal mapping facilitates a visual articulation of a large number of ideas, actions, and their consequences (Bryson et al. 2004). An example of a fully developed strategy map is shown in Figure 3.1. This map incorporates the collective understanding of a decision problem (our opening case study 'To lend or not to lend?') by a decision-making group. The group used a whiteboard and sticky notes to develop a solution to the problem.

FIGURE 3.1 Causal map of the case study 'To lend or not to lend?'. Adapted from: Arevuo, M., Reinmoeller, P., & Huff, A.S. (2017). How maps are made matters: enacting artifacts in collective decision making. *Academy of Management Annual Meeting Proceedings*, **2017**(1), 1.

Note how the map has been constructed in a non-linear way with groups of clustered sticky notes. All causal maps are non-linear as they reflect how we really think and the clustered notes reflect the critical issues in the decision problem. Although a fully developed causal map may seem disorganized, the mapping process follows a logical structure.

Mapping starts by identifying the problem. Once the problem has been identified, our attention turns to thinking about possible solutions. The critical aspect of this step is not only to identify possible solutions, but also to assess their feasibility. If a possible solution cannot be implemented for whatever reason, it should be rejected at the early stage of the discussion. An example of a possible solution to competitor threat is acquisition of the competing firm. However, if the company lacks the financial resources to execute this, acquisition as a possible solution is unfeasible and another solution to competitor threat must be found.

Once feasible solutions have been identified, the decision-makers need to consider the consequences of the alternative solutions. For example, if the firm has the financial resources to carry out the acquisition of the competing firm, the decision-makers should consider what consequences such an action would have on the firm more widely. For example, the acquisition could require a significant commitment of management and financial resources. If these resources were to be used for the acquisition, what would be the trade-offs and their consequences for the other operational aspects of the firm? Given the consequences of this option, is it still the best possible option in view of the resource constraints and the overall strategy of the firm? The answers to these types of question involve 'laddering' up and down between the solutions and their consequences until all possible options and their consequences have been exhausted.

Causal maps that have been created in groups bring together the thinking of many people, including conflicting views, subtly different slants on the same issues, and different perspectives held by individual group members. Such group causal maps provide simplified representations of the beliefs of the greater group. They may not necessarily be a representation of the reality perceived by any one individual or all of the group members. Rather, a group map is a collectively constructed and shared account of a given situation by all group members (Arevuo 2015).

Group mapping could be perceived simplistically as a form of brainstorming. However, Eden and Ackerman (2010) draw a distinction between group maps and a free-flowing brainstorming of ideas. Group mapping that is used for decision-making is focused on raising issues and concerns. These are usually activities or events that can either support or challenge the decision-making aspiration of the group. In contrast with eliciting 'off-the-wall' ideas in group brainstorming sessions as the means of unleashing creativity, group mapping focuses on bringing together the current wisdom and experience of the group members, as well as issues surrounding the problem situation. Therefore group mapping is a process of engaging in a dialogue to uncover the causality between the problem and a number of potential solution outcomes, represented as a map. This process provides the means for the decision-making group to structure and merge differing perspectives that should eventually lead to a shared understanding of the issue in a holistic manner. Eden and Ackerman (2010: 243) argue '... not only is a better understanding derived from seeing the whole and thus a better outcome, but a better appreciation of the organization's context is also elicited'.

Effective group causal maps

Eden and Ackermann (2010) have built on Nutt's (2002) effective decision-making processes by suggesting that the causal mapping process prevents decision-making groups from talking over each other and going around in circles. It helps group members to speak and be heard. The mapping process produces a lot of ideas, promotes causal reasoning, and ultimately clarifies the most suitable course of action.

According to Eden and Ackermann (2010), the achievement of both substantive and process outcomes of group maps can be viewed as meeting Nutt's (2002) criteria for effective decision-making: collecting information to understand the claims calling for action; establishing a direction that indicates the desired result; mounting a systematic search for ideas; evaluating ideas with a direction in mind; and managing and measuring social and political barriers that can block the preferred course of action.

In addition, Eden and Ackermann (2010) state that the shared and collective construction of the group map increases individual ownership, acceptance, and the feeling of fairness of the decision outcomes. This is because the map shows evidence that all decision-making group members have been listened to, and their claims have been displayed on the map. There is additional evidence that the collective enactment of the strategy map eliminates groupthink and cognitive biases such as the escalation of commitment bias (Maule and Hodgkinson 2002).

PRACTITIONER INSIGHT: **PROFESSOR BERNIE BULKIN OBE**

3

Drawing on his varied and impressive career as Professor of Chemistry, former chief scientist and senior executive at BP, venture capitalist, and radio broadcaster and columnist, Professor Bernie Bulkin OBE shares his thoughts on management and decision-making through his life experiences. In our discussion he tells us that one should not only focus on organizational and business activities to gain insight to many aspects of leadership and management, but learning should be derived through a life that is well lived and keenly observed.

Many executives try to avoid jury service, as serving in a trial could take them away from their business commitments for a protracted period of time. Professor Bulkin says that this is a mistake, not only because we have certain civic duties, but also because such service presents an opportunity to learn aspects of decision-making and team-building that one would not learn on any course.

Most business teams are established for the long term, but diverse teams have, from time to time, to come together for short periods of intense work to find a solution to a problem or get a deal done. This is what a jury has to do, as Professor Bulkin reflected when he found himself serving in a gang murder trial in New York City. However, unlike in business, where the final decision is made by the leader based on discussions among peers or recommendations from front-line managers, but who will ultimately be accountable for it, in a jury room everyone has to be in on the decision, stand up, and support the verdict. It can be quite instructive how people from all walks of life can come together and collectively reach a unanimous agreement on what constitutes a strategic decision, reflects Professor Bulkin. A verdict in a murder trial is obviously an important strategic decision as it will have far-reaching consequences for the defendant.

The testimony lasted for nine days including the final prosecution and defence statements. On the morning of day 10 the judge addressed the jurors, explaining the need for proof beyond reasonable doubt. He also explained circumstantial evidence and under what circumstance the jury could accept it as a consideration of innocence or guilt. Finally, he moved on to discuss what, in New York State law, constituted self-defence. 'Having sat through nine days of a vast amount of testimony it was not until the very end of the proceedings that we heard this crucial bit of law on self-defence, the organizing principle according to which we had to assess the evidence', says Professor Bulkin. 'Do we sometimes do this in our meetings, in a lead-up to a decision? Do we keep back the key point until the last, perhaps to increase its impact or because we see it as a way of increasing our own impact on the group?'

The jury was dismissed to consider the evidence and the members were instructed that if they were still debating at 10 p.m. that evening they would be taken to a hotel overnight and brought back the following morning. Nine days of evidence and the judge's instructions on law were narrowed down to perhaps an hour of evidence that was relevant to the question of innocence or guilt. The majority of the jurors favoured a 'not guilty' verdict but some were wavering. 'At 8.30 p.m. a court police officer came to the jury room to inform us that we had to give him the names and telephone numbers of our families, given that if we had not reached a verdict within the next 90 minutes we would be sent to a hotel for the night.'

'The judge must have been very familiar with juror behaviour, and knew that sending the officer in might catalyse a decision', says Professor Bulkin. So it proved, and the jury reached a unanimous 'not guilty' verdict. Without a time limit, groups can keep debating for ever, but as the 10 p.m. deadline loomed the jurors in this case were motivated to get off the fence and make a decision.

When we work on important decisions, we need to be able to see the wood from the trees and focus on what is critical information for the decision—the rest is noise. Professor Bulkin says that the consideration of 'business risks' is on the agenda of every board meeting, but the evidence for ineffectual risk management in big corporations is all around us. One of the main problems is that we focus on wrong things entirely by not identifying the real underlying risks. For example, a manager might identify the failure to deliver promised growth as a major risk. In response they might strengthen the sales force in order to deliver growth. However, this is basic management, not risk management.

Another reason why corporations fail in risk management is by not paying attention to past performance. Although past performance is not an indicator of the future in everything, it can be an indicator of a trend. Have there been two or three environmental incidents that have resulted in fines or an increasing frequency of minor incidents? An increase in the frequency of such incidents is a good indicator of a higher probability of a major incident. Boards must have the data to enable them to probe this with the management.

Finally, slick processes should not be a substitute for substantive presentation. The management has access to numerous beautiful graphics programmes for the board risk discussion agenda item. Among the papers for the board meeting there is a big fold-out chart in many colours, displaying the risks. These charts are things of beauty and when they come out board members are lulled into thinking that everything is under control. 'It isn't. The thing that is under control is the use of the graphics programme.'

Source

More insights on business and leadership are covered in Professor Bulkin's collection of vignettes:

Bulkin, B. (2015). *Crash Course: One Year to Become a Great Leader in a Great Company*. London: Whitefox.

CHAPTER SUMMARY

In this chapter we addressed the following learning outcomes:

- **Distinguish strategic decisions from routine decisions**
  Most of our decisions are routine decisions that do not require much effort. In contrast, strategic decisions involve problems that do not have simple solutions. Strategic decisions are large, expensive, and precedent-setting, complex decisions that are made under conditions of volatility, ambiguity, and uncertainty of the final decision outcome. Once a strategic decision is made and implemented, it is difficult to reverse, as both financial and human resources have been committed to the decision, at least in the short term.
- **Analyse the differences between rational and cognitive approaches to decision-making in organizations**
  Rational decision-making is a multistep process for making optimal choices between alternatives. The rational decision-making process is based on logic, objectivity, and analysis over subjectivity, insight, and judgement. In contrast, cognitive decision-making models suggest that decision-making requires judgement that is bounded in its rationality, and we can better understand decision-making by describing and explaining actual decisions rather than by focusing on what should be done rationally in decision-making processes. Even if we were able to identify an optimum decision outcome, other people in our organizations may have agendas that prevent us from pursuing the optimum decision. In practice, we aim to make decisions that are based on sufficient analysis and which produce a satisfactory outcome for all key stakeholders.
- **Evaluate the impact of common heuristics and biases to organizational decision-making**
  Heuristics are useful for practitioners as they can reduce the need for, or totally circumvent, the search for information to support a decision. However, they can result in biases that can lead into adverse consequences and decision outcomes. Human judgement is unreliable and susceptible to errors that can stem from cognitive biases or random errors.

3

- **Examine the tools and techniques available for managers to improve the quality of their strategic decision-making processes**
  As the outcomes of strategic decisions unfold in an uncertain future, the key challenge for decision-makers is to improve their strategic decision-making processes so that the decision that is made is the best possible within the limitations of bounded rationality. We identified a number of tools that decision-makers can apply to improve their decision-making processes by debiasing their decision-making and increasing the degree of cognitive conflict in collective decision-making, while at the same time reducing the potential for the emergence of affective conflict.

- **Understand the practical application of decision-making tools in collective decision-making**
  Most strategic decision-making takes place in groups. We introduced a number of decision-making tools that groups can use to improve the quality of their collective decision-making processes: devil's advocacy, dialectical enquiry, the Delphi method, and causal mapping. We noted that while consensus decision-making may demonstrate the highest degree of collective buy-in into a decision, collective decision-making tends to be the least creative and innovative decision-making process.

END OF CHAPTER QUESTIONS

Recall questions

1. What are the key differences between routine and strategic decisions?
2. What are the characteristics of strategic decisions?
3. What are the most common heuristics and biases in managerial decision-making?

Application questions

A) You and your team are working on a problem that has far-reaching consequences for your firm. You decide to bring your team together to work on the problem. How could you organize the team to ensure that the potential solutions to the problem have been fully analysed and that all team members agree to the solution?

B) In your role as the head of the marketing department you have the final say on the firm's decision on future advertising strategy and the budget. How would you evaluate the recommendation that has been presented to you?

C) Can you give examples of any biases you have experienced when making decisions in your personal life? In hindsight, do you feel that you made the right decision? Strategy mapping is a tool to create a visual representation of a problem. What do you think are the benefits and difficulties of using strategy maps in collective decision-making and why?

ONLINE RESOURCES

www.oup.com/he/mackay1e

FURTHER READING

3

Visual Strategy: Strategy Mapping for Public and Nonprofit Organizations, by John M. Bryson, Fran Ackermann, and Colin Eden

Bryson, J.M., Ackermann, F., and Eden, C. (2014). *Visual Strategy: Strategy Mapping for Public And Non-Profit Organizations*. San Francisco, CA: John Wiley.

This is a how-to book on causal mapping. The authors show how causal mapping prevents groups of people from talking over one another and going round in circles. It helps people to speak and be heard, produce lots of ideas and understand how they fit together, make use of causal reasoning, and clarify ultimately what they want to do in terms of mission, goals, strategies, and actions.

A structured approach to strategic decisions, by Daniel Kahneman, Dan Lovallo, and Olivier Sibony

Kahneman, D., Lovallo, D., and Sibony, O. (2019). A structured approach to strategic decisions. *MIT Sloan Management Review*, **60**(3).

The article suggests a practical and broadly applicable approach to reducing errors in strategic decision-making. This can be accomplished through the Mediating Assessments Protocol (MAP) that is a structured approach to grounding strategic decisions, like interviews, on mediating assessments.

Thinking, Fast and Slow, by Daniel Kahneman

Kahneman, D. (2011). *Thinking, Fast and Slow*. New York: Macmillan.

The book gives a tour of the mind and explains the two systems that drive the way we think. System 1 is fast, intuitive, and emotional; System 2 is slower, more deliberative, and more logical. The impact of overconfidence on corporate strategies, the difficulties of predicting what will make us happy in the future, the profound effect of cognitive biases on everything from playing the stock market to planning our next holiday, each of these can be understood only by knowing how the two systems shape our judgements and decisions.

Prospect theory: an analysis of decision under risk, by Daniel Kahneman and Amos Tversky

Kahneman, D. and Tversky, A. (1979). Prospect theory: an analysis of decision under risk. *Econometrica*, **47**(2), 263–91.

This seminal article was published in the journal Econometrica *and it has become that journal's most cited article of all time. In 2002 Kahneman was awarded the Nobel Prize in Economics for their work (Tversky had sadly died before the prize was awarded). It describes Kahneman and Tversky's prospect theory, an explanation of how people choose between different options and how they estimate the perceived likelihood of each of these options. Prospect theory can be considered as ground-breaking research in decision-making which highlights that human judgement is fallible and subject to biases.*

The structure of 'unstructured' decision processes, by Henry Mintzberg, Duru Raisinghani, and André Théorêt

Mintzberg, H., Raisinghani, D., and Théorêt, A. (1976). The structure of 'unstructured' decision processes. *Administrative Science Quarterly*, **21**(2), 246–75.

A field study of 25 strategic decision processes, together with a review of the related empirical literature, suggests that a basic structure underlies these 'unstructured' processes. This structure is described in terms of 12 elements: three central phases, three sets of supporting routines, and six sets of dynamic factors. This paper discusses each of these elements in turn, and then proposes a general model to describe their interrelationships. The 25 strategic decision processes studied are then shown to fall into seven types of path configurations through the model.

3

Handbook of Decision Making, edited by Paul C. Nutt and David C. Wilson

Nutt, P.C. and Wilson, D.C. (eds) (2010). *Handbook of Decision Making*. Chichester: John Wiley.

The book is an important reference text for all students of and professionals in management, organization, and decision-making. It offers a wide range of theoretical and empirical approaches to the understanding of organizational and strategic decisions. The chapters bring together a critical mass of writing on decision-making as an organizational and research activity. The book offers an appraisal of the field and suggestions for research, as well as the current status of decision-making practice and suggestions for improvement.

REFERENCES

Amason, A.C. (1996). Distinguishing the effects of functional and dysfunctional conflict on strategic decision-making: resolving a paradox for top management teams. *Academy of Management Journal*, **39**, 123–48.

Ambady, N. and Rosenthal, R. (1992). Thin slices of expressive behavior as predictors of interpersonal consequences: a meta-analysis, *Psychological Bulletin*, **111**(2), 256–74.

Arevuo, M. (2015). Epistemic objects in collective decision-making: a practice perspective on the use of causal maps as situated material artifacts. PhD Thesis, Cranfield School of Management, Cranfield CERES, http://www.dspace.lib.cranfield.ac.uk/handle/1826/9879 (accessed 16 July 2019).

Arevuo, M., Reinmoeller, P., & Huff, A.S. (2017). How maps are made matters: enacting artifacts in collective decision making. *Academy of Management Annual Meeting Proceedings*, **2017**(1), 1.

Argyris, C. (1991). Teaching smart people how to learn. *Harvard Business Review*, May–June, 99–109.

Bazerman, M.H. and Moore, D.A. (2008). *Judgment in Managerial Decision Making* (7th edn). New York: John Wiley.

Black, J., Hashimzade, N., and Myles, G. (2017). *Oxford Dictionary of Economics*. Oxford: Oxford University Press.

Bryson, J., Ackermann, F., Eden, C., and Finn, C. (2004). *Visible Thinking: Unlocking Causal Mapping for Practical Business Results*. Chichester: John Wiley.

Bryson, J.M., Ackermann, F., and Eden, C. (2014). *Visual Strategy: Strategy Mapping for Public and Nonprofit Organizations.* San Francisco, CA: John Wiley.

Daft, R.L., Bettenhausen, K.R., and Tyler, B.B. (1993). Implications of top managers' communication choices for strategic decisions. In: Huber, G.P. and Glick, W.H. (eds), *Organizational Change and Redesign: Ideas and Insights in Improving Performance*. Oxford: Oxford University Press.

Dietvorst, B.J., Simmons, J.P., and Massey, C. (2015). Algorithm aversion: people erroneously avoid algorithms after seeing them err. *Journal of Experimental Psychology*, **144**(1), 114–26.

Eden, C. and Ackermann, F. (2010). Decision-making in groups: theory and practice. In: Nutt, P.C. and Wilson, D.C. (eds), *Handbook of Decision Making*, pp. 231–72. Chichester: John Wiley.

Eisenhardt, K.M. and Zbaracki, M.J. (1992). Strategic decision making. *Strategic Management Journal*, **13**, 17–37.

Hambrick, D.C. (1994). Top management groups: a conceptual integration and reconsideration of the 'group' label. In: Staw, B.M. and Cummings, L.L. (eds), *Research in Organizational Behavior*, pp. 171–214. Greenwich, CT: JAI Press.

Harvey, J. (1988). The Abilene paradox: the management of agreement. *Organizational Dynamics*, Summer, 17–34.

Hodgkinson, G. and Healey, M. (2011). Psychological foundations of dynamic capabilities: reflexion and reflection in strategic management. *Strategic Management Journal*, **32**(13), 1500–16.

Hogarth, R.M. (1981). Beyond discrete biases: functional and dysfunctional aspects of judgmental heuristics. *Psychological Bulletin*, **90**(2), 197–217.

Janis, I.L. (1972). *Victims of Group Think*. New York: Free Press.

Kahneman, D. (2011). *Thinking, Fast and Slow*. New York: Macmillan.

Kahneman, D. and Tversky, A. (1979). Prospect theory: an analysis of decision under risk. *Econometrica*, **47**(2), 263–91.

Kahneman, D., Lovallo, D., and Sibony, O. (2011). The big idea: before you make that big decision. *Harvard Business Review*, June, 51–60.

Kahneman, D., Lovallo, D., and Sibony, O. (2019). A structured approach to strategic decisions. *MIT Sloan Management Review*, **60**(3).

Kahneman, D., Slovic, P., and Tversky, A. (eds) (1982). *Judgment Under Uncertainty: Heuristics and Biases*. Cambridge University Press: Cambridge.

Lovallo, D. and Sibony, O. (2010). The case for behavioural strategy. *McKinsey Quarterly*, January, https//:www.mckinseyquarterly.com.

McKinsey Global Survey Results (2009). Flaws in strategic decision-making. *McKinsey Quarterly*, January, https//:www.mckinseyquarterly.com.

March, J.G. and Simon, H.A. (1958). *Organizations*. New York: John Wiley.

Maule, A.J. and Hodgkinson, G.P. (2002). Heuristics, biases, and strategic decision making. *Psychologist*, **15**, 68–71.

Michelman, P (2017). When people don't trust algorithms. *MIT Sloan Management Review*, **59**(1), 11–13.

Milliken, F.J. (1987). Three types of perceived uncertainty about the environment: state, effect, and response uncertainty. *Academy of Management Review*, **12**, 133–43.

Mintzberg, H., Raisinghani, D., and Théorêt, A. (1976). The structure of 'unstructured' decision processes. *Administrative Science Quarterly*, **21**(2), 246–75.

Nutt, P.C. (2002). *Why Decisions Fail: Avoiding the Blunders and Traps that Lead to Debacles*. San Francisco, CA: Berrett-Kohler.

Nutt, P.C. and Wilson, D.C. (eds) (2010). *Handbook of Decision Making*. Chichester: John Wiley.

Parayitam, S. and Dooley, R.S. (2007). The relationship between conflict and decision outcomes: moderating effects of cognitive- and affect-based trust in strategic decision-making teams. *International Journal of Conflict Management*, **18**(1), 42–73.

Parayitam, S. and Dooley, R.S. (2009). The interplay between cognitive and affective conflict and cognition- and affect-based trust in influencing decision outcomes. *Journal of Business Research*, **62**(8), 789–96.

Parayitam, S. and Dooley, R.S. (2011). Is too much cognitive conflict in strategic decision-making teams too bad? *International Journal of Conflict Management*, **22**, 342–57.

Schoemaker, P.J.H., Heaton, S., and Teece, D. (2018). Innovation, dynamic capabilities, and leadership. *California Management Review*, **61**(1), 15–42.

Schweiger, D., Sandberg, W., and Ragan, J. (1986). Group approaches for improving strategic decision making: a comparative analysis of dialectical inquiry, devil's advocacy, and consensus. *Academy of Management Journal*, **29**(1), 51–71.

Schwenk, C.R. (1988). *Essence of Strategic Decision Making*. Lexington, MA: Lexington Books.

Schwenk, C.R. (1995). Strategic decision making. *Journal of Management*, **21**, 471–93.

Stoner, J.A.F. (1968). Risky and cautious shifts in group decisions: the influence of widely held values. *Journal of Experimental Psychology*, **4**, 442–59.

Sund. K.J., Galvan, R.J., and Huff, A.S. (eds) (2016). *Uncertainty and Strategic Decision Making*. Bingley: Emerald Group.

Tversky, A. and Kahneman, D. (1974). Judgment under uncertainty: heuristics and biases. *Science*, **185**, 1124–31.

van Ginkel, W.P. and van Knippenberg, D. (2009). Knowledge about the distribution of information and group decision making: when and why does it work? *Organizational Behavior and Human Decision Processes*, **108**(2), 218–29.

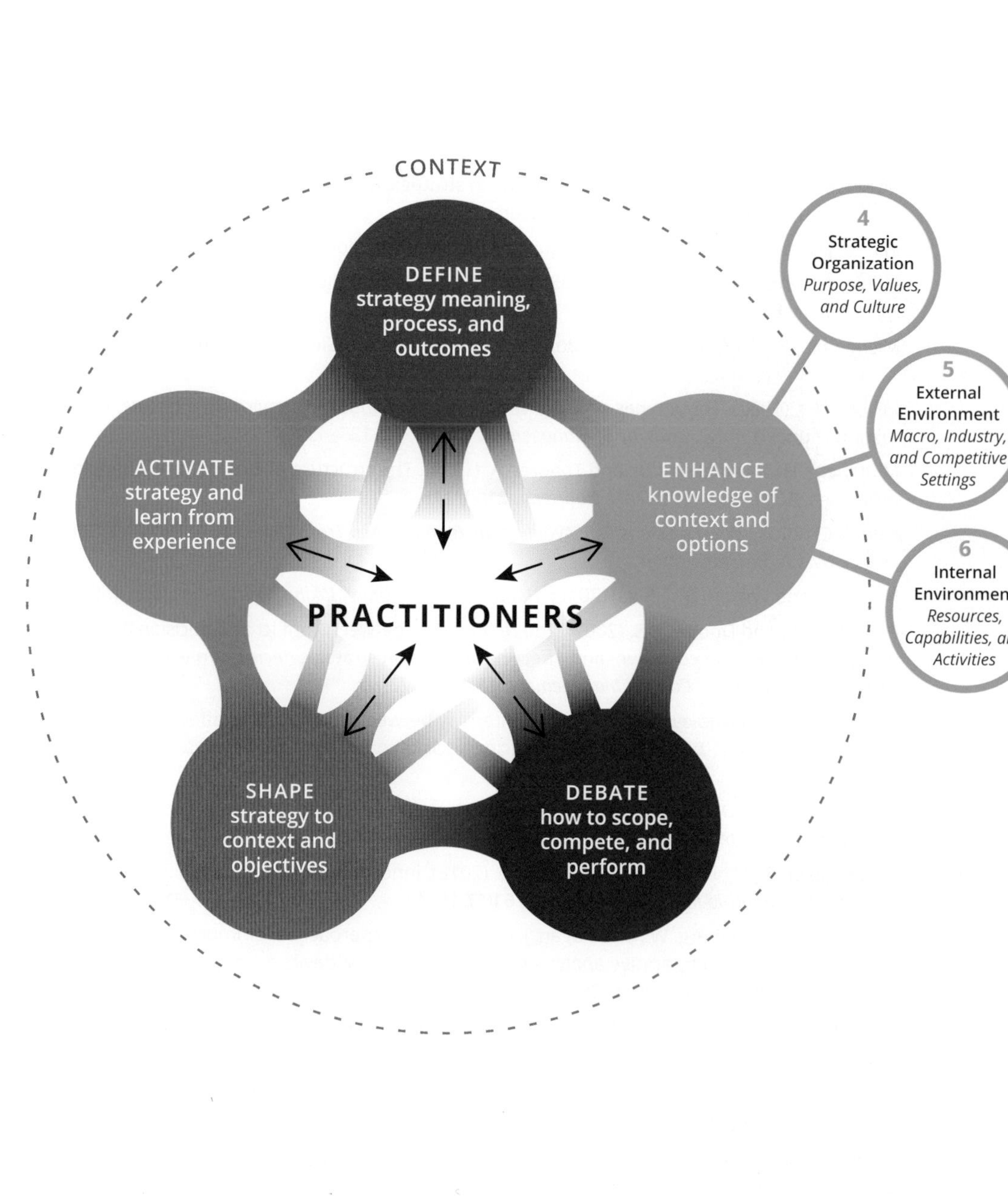

CONTEXT
DEFINE
strategy meaning, process, and outcomes
ENHANCE
knowledge of context and options
DEBATE
how to scope, compete, and perform
SHAPE
strategy to context and objectives
ACTIVATE
strategy and learn from experience
PRACTITIONERS
4
Strategic Organization
Purpose, Values, and Culture
5
External Environment
Macro, Industry, and Competitive Settings
6
Internal Environment
Resources, Capabilities, and Activities

PART TWO

Enhance knowledge of context and options

Organizations are integral participants in societal, industrial, and competitive settings. In Part 2 we examine how the historical, internal, and external context of an organization might be investigated, analysed, and understood as an informant of strategizing activity. We start our discussion in Chapter 4 by considering the purpose of the organization and the values that guide its operations. These values form the basis of all organizational activity. In Chapter 5 we assess the nature and impact of the external context of the firm, presenting analytical frameworks to identify and assess trends, opportunities, and threats. Finally, in Chapter 6 we look inside the organization at its internal resources and capabilities. For a firm to survive and flourish in a competitive environment it requires resources, capabilities, and processes, and an ability to renew them, to support its value-adding activities. The composition of the organization's internal resource base and architecture are critical building blocks of competitive strategy.

By the end of Part 2, you should have enhanced abilities to think, talk, and act like a practitioner, investigating and enhancing knowledge of context and options.

CHAPTER FOUR

Strategic Organization

Purpose, Values, and Culture

CONTENTS

LEARNING OBJECTIVES

4

By the end of this chapter, you should be able to:

- Identify the importance of organizational purpose, vision, mission, and values in strategy development
- Evaluate how vision, mission, and values translate to deliverable performance targets and objectives
- Critically assess the concepts of shareholder and stakeholder value maximization
- Examine how a firm can effectively engage with stakeholders who have conflicting interests
- Recognize the importance of an organization's history as a creator of path dependence and its role in both formal and informal organization culture
- Interpret the multifaceted nature of organization culture and its relationship with a firm's competitive advantage

TOOLBOX

- **Mission statement development**
  A framework that can be applied to develop forward-looking statements that communicate the purpose, values, and mission of the organization to both internal and external stakeholders.
- **Theory of shareholder and stakeholder value maximization**
  An important analysis of the overall purpose of the organization: whose interests does the organization serve?
- **Concept of corporate social responsibility**
  A consideration of the role of the organization in wider society and the development of business models that add value to both shareholders and the wider society.
- **Stakeholder mapping**
  An analytical framework to identify and prioritize the organization's stakeholders.
- **Cultural Web of the organization**
  An analytical framework to identify the components of the organization's culture.

OPENING CASE STUDY MCKINSEY & CO—MISSION AND VALUES

McKinsey & Company is a global management consulting firm. The firm conducts qualitative and quantitative analysis to evaluate management decisions across public, not-for-profit, and private sectors. McKinsey is widely considered as one of the most prestigious management consultancy firms, with a clientele including some of the world's largest corporations as well as governments and nonprofit organizations. Most organizations articulate their vision and values in a mission statement. The aim of such statements is to inform in a concise way the organization's customers, employees, suppliers, and even competitors on what the guiding principles of the firm are. McKinsey's vison and values are stated below.

Our mission

Our mission is to help our clients make distinctive, lasting, and substantial improvements in their performance and to build a great firm that attracts, develops, excites, and retains exceptional people.

We believe we will be successful if our clients are successful.

Solving the hardest problems requires the best people. We think that the best people will be drawn to the opportunity to work on the hardest problems. We build our firm around that belief. These two parts of our mission reinforce each other and make our firm strong and enduring.

We are a values-driven organization. Our values reflect the thinking of our founder, James O. McKinsey, and Marvin Bower, managing director from 1950 to 1967, who was a major force in shaping the firm. Our values have been updated in small ways to reflect the changing times. They inform both our long-term strategy as a firm and the way we serve our clients on a daily basis. We put aside one day a year to reflect as a group on what our values mean to both our work and our lives.

Our values

***Adhere to the highest professional standards*:**

- put client interests ahead of the firm's;
- observe high ethical standards;
- preserve client confidences;
- maintain an independent perspective;
- manage client and firm resources cost-effectively;

Improve our clients' performance significantly

- follow the top-management approach;
- use our global network to deliver the best of the firm to all clients;
- bring innovations in management practice to clients;
- build client capabilities to sustain improvement;
- build enduring relationships based on trust;

Create an unrivalled environment for exceptional people

- be non-hierarchical and inclusive;
- sustain a caring meritocracy;
- develop one another through apprenticeship and mentoring;
- uphold the obligation to dissent;
- govern ourselves as a 'one firm' partnership.

Questions for discussion

1. How does the statement describe McKinsey & Co's values and the way that they are applied to the firm's business proposition?
2. How does the statement describe the intended value of the firm's contribution to its clients and wider society?
3. McKinsey & Co is a profit-seeking business, but the mission statement does not explicitly mention profits. Why do you think this is?
4. Visit Coca-Cola's and Google's corporate websites and read their vison and mission statements and compare and contrast them with the McKinsey & Co statement. Is there a difference in the way the statements describe how the companies articulate their business and values? Which company's statement do you think gives the best description of the firm's values, vison, and mission? Why?

Source

https://www.mckinsey.com/about-us/overview/our-mission-and-values (accessed 1 March 2019)

4.1 **Introduction**

From a process–practice perspective, strategizing occurs within an organizational context that encompasses its history, culture, values, objectives, and directions of travel. As discussed in Chapter 2, this organizational context can be a trigger for and an enabler of constraint on strategy activity. In this chapter, we consider how those involved in strategy can build knowledge of internal organizational context as an aid to effective strategizing. We begin by considering how the concept of organizational purpose differs from other statements of organizational direction and how this affects those delivering and managing strategy. We present a process model of how to deliver the organization's stated purpose in practice. We also evaluate two different perspectives on the question of who the firm serves: shareholders, stakeholders, or both? We then expand our discussion to consider the role of the firm in a wider societal and organizational context in terms of its stakeholders. Most organizations possess stakeholders with conflicting interests, so it is imperative that we consider the mechanisms that firms can use to manage the various stakeholder groups that have an interest in the activities of the firm.

Finally, we turn our attention to understanding how organizational history and path dependence act as the basis of informal and formal aspects of organization culture. We introduce the concept of the Cultural Web as a way of describing and evaluating organizational culture, and we consider how organization culture relates to a firm's competitive advantage.

4.2 **Organizational purpose**

An organization's purpose (also described as its raison d'être) is an affirmation of the reason for its existence; for example, what does the organization do, who does it serve, and where does the organization expect to be in the future? These activities and aspirations are often articulated in forward-looking statements about the organization's activities.

According to Ratan Tata, the retired CEO of Tata Group, the purpose of any organization is 'a spiritual and moral call for action; it is what a person or company stands for' (Tata et al. 2013). Commercial enterprises exist to make a profit, but they are also integral participants in communities and society, both locally and globally. Some state that there is a persistent myth that the ultimate purpose of a firm is to maximize shareholder value (Tata et al. 2013). However, profit maximization is not a purpose; it is an outcome that results from offering a valuable customer proposition and playing a positive ethical role in the community in which it exists rather than the other way around.

For example, consider Nestlé's purpose statement: 'Nestlé's purpose is enhancing quality of life and contributing to a healthier future. We want to help shape a better and healthier world. We also want to inspire people to live healthier lives. This is how we contribute to society while ensuring the long-term success of our company' (https://www.nestle.com/aboutus, accessed 9 October 2018). Note how Nestlé's purpose statement does not focus on the firm's products and services, or even on the customers and employees of the firm. It articulates a forward-looking aspiration that inspires and motivates employees to work towards a better and healthier world.

This gives the organization, and its employees, a role that contributes to society, and in so doing ensures the long-term success of the firm. Naturally, for any organization to survive it has to offer products and services that customers find valuable and that will enhance their quality of life in terms of either their health and wellbeing, or some other tangible or intangible criteria. In our opening case, McKinsey & Co consider that the firm's aim is to 'help our clients make distinctive, lasting, and substantial improvements in their performance'.

Many companies do not have explicitly articulated purpose statements, but instead have a number of other statements that describe organizational direction: vision, mission, and value statements.

Kenny (2014) has produced a typology to distinguish various statements as a first step in helping organizations to produce forward-looking documents that are both motivational and achievable (see Table 4.1).

TABLE 4.1 **Kenny's typology of forward-looking statements**

Kenny's typology	Definition	Aim	Example
A vision statement	What the organization wishes to become in some years' time	To elevate thinking beyond the organization's day-to-day activities in a clear and memorable way It is usually articulated by the firm's senior management	The vision statement of the charity Save the Children is very short and therefore memorable Save the Children's vision is to create 'a world in which every child attains the right to survival, protection, development, and participation'
A mission statement	What are the business activities that the organization engages in (and what are those that it doesn't) now and in the future?	To provide focus for the managers and the employees	Google defines its mission statement in terms of what the company does: 'To organize the world's information and make it universally accessible and useful'
A value statement	The organization's desired culture	To act as a behavioural compass for all the employees and managers of the firm by articulating a set of principles which govern both the inward and outward conduct of all organizational participants	Disney's value statement articulates honesty integrity, respect, courage, openness, diversity, and balance as the fundamental values of the organization: 'These values are demonstrated through such traits and behaviours like making guests happy, caring about fellow cast members, working as a team, delivering quality, fostering creativity, paying attention to every detail, and having an emotional commitment to Disney'
A purpose statement	The heartbeat of the organization	To connect the heart of the organization with the head by putting managers and employees in customers' shoes and considering the role of the organization as a member of society	Oxfam clearly states the reason (or purpose) for the charity's existence: 'Oxfam strives to help create lasting solutions to the injustice of poverty. We are part of a global movement for change, one that empowers people to create a future that is secure, just, and free from poverty'

Many firms do not produce separate documents for each forward-looking statement within the typology outlined in Table 4.1. Unfortunately, these forward-looking statements are often a confused mix of vision and mission, and in some cases the statements may sound inspirational, but are so general as to have little practical value, or so aspirational that they are undeliverable in practice. On the other hand, with quarterly performance pressures, especially for publicly quoted companies, the forward-looking aspirations are overshadowed by short-term considerations and quick fixes. However, whatever statement is produced to guide the organization it should be aspirational, memorable, inspirational, and, most importantly, achievable by the organization.

Many organizations articulate purpose, vision, and mission statements in their corporate documents and websites. However, just because an organization has a forward-looking statement, this does not guarantee that it or its employees adhere to those recorded aspirations, or whether this translates to their target audience. When managers attempt to impose a vision, employees do not take the message to heart. Employees must make the connection from the meaningfulness of their work to the company vision and mission to internalize and imbed them in their daily work (Cable and Vermeulen 2018).

There are numerous ways of measuring the success of an organization in delivering on the stated purpose, vision, and mission, and adhering to its own standards set in their forward-looking statement. For example, some of the more common measurement criteria include the sustainability of the firm's profitability over an extended period of time, market share, brand value and customer perception, employee satisfaction surveys, etc. In addition, the social impact of most large companies is monitored by corporate social responsibility agencies including UN Global Compact, an organization that monitors and helps companies to adhere to and advance the universal principles of human and labour rights, environmental protection, and anti-corruption practices. It should be noted that these indicators are retrospective measurements. However, most firms conduct competitor intelligence analysis, and many branding and corporate social responsibility agencies produce annual rankings of companies on a set of criteria. Strategists use such rankings to evaluate their firm's performance against that of the competitors.

Some companies do not publish forward-looking vision or mission statements at all. For example, Apple Inc. does not have a mission statement link on their website. Instead, Apple tells people what the firm has accomplished, and what 'amazing' things the firm's products can do. Therefore, rather than articulating a mission statement, Apple shows people what mission they are currently on: 'Apple designs Macs, the best personal computers in the world ... Apple leads the digital music revolution ... Apple is reinventing the mobile phone with its revolutionary iPhone and AppStore' (Palotta 2011). Rather than making an attempt to predict the future of computing and the digital world, Apple chooses to emphasize their commitment to producing products and services that allow people to do 'amazing' digital things now, regardless of how the future unfolds.

Whatever the nature of aspirational forward-looking statements in terms of their detail, organizations must be able to develop processes and inspire employees to live up to the publicly stated or internally established standards to deliver, go on a mission, and show the world that they are doing what they have set out to accomplish.

4.3 **Delivering on vision, mission, and values**

We have discussed a number of forward-looking statements used in many firms, including vision, mission, value, and purpose statements. How do organizations ensure that they live up to these statements? What processes can strategists develop to help their organization live up to its values and deliver the vision and mission? To realize the vision and mission of the organization, consistent with corresponding values, the strategist might engage with goals, objectives, and initiatives, tracking progress using key performance indicators and targets. In this section, we examine what these terms mean and how they might influence the strategy process. As you study strategy, it is important to understand these terms, as they are used widely in literature. Further, you will almost certainly be required to work towards personal and team objectives if you are employed in a managerial role. Building your understanding of these key terms will enable you to participate effectively in discussions about how strategy can be used to coordinate the organization and drive performance outcomes in practice.

Goals, objectives, and initiatives

Organizations use goals, objectives, and initiatives to help them achieve their vision.

Goals

As described by Ackermann and Eden (2011), goals are the long-term aims of an organization—the 'ends' it might try to achieve. Goals can be common to all organizations in an industry; for example, all publicly listed organizations will aim to maximize shareholder return, and increasingly sustainability is becoming embedded as an essential component of long-term organizational aims (see Chapter 13). Equally, goals might be specific to a smaller number of organizations in a sector, such as 'be a leading research institute in Canada'. Such a goal might be a high-level long-term aim for some Canadian universities, but other universities might aspire to alternative goals, such as teaching excellence and quality of student experience.

The combination of general and specific goals held by an organization can be envisaged as its goal system. This system should be **coherent**; in other words, the goals should make sense individually, and as a combined set. Where goals are mutually exclusive—for example, having the lowest marketing spend in the sector, as well as having the highest brand awareness and market presence—the goal system can become a source of conflict between different groups in the organization. In this example, it would be difficult to spend the least amount possible on marketing, and still have the highest brand awareness within the market. This can have a negative impact on collaborative working and, ultimately, harm the performance of the organization.

Goals can be expressed as a 'future state' of the organization, describing a vision of how the organization aspires to be and to operate at a later point in time. The goal system should be consistent and tied to the vision statement of the organization. Goals may have a quantitative component (e.g. be the number one or two organization by revenue in our sector) or be wholly qualitative (e.g. be renowned for our philanthropy and social responsibility).

Objectives

Objectives can be considered as intermediate outcomes towards achieving goals. In comparison with goals, objectives are more specific statements of future intent that are tied to the organization's mission statement. For example, an objective for the goal 'be a leading research institute in Canada' might be 'increase the number of *Financial Times* (FT) ranked journal articles submitted each year to 100 by 2022', and another objective might be 'grow annual research council funding to $10 million by 2021'.

The format of these example objectives conforms to what is known as SMART criteria. SMART means:

Specific—target a specific area for focus of effort/resource allocation
Measurable—can be associated with an indicator of progress
Achievable—is realistic to believe that it can be delivered in the current context with available resources
Relevant—can be connected to the goals and current situation of the organization
Time-related—has an associated time-frame for delivery.

Although a well-recognized format that is used widely in practice, SMART objectives are also criticized for setting a ceiling on achievement. In other words, by setting SMART objectives that are too conservative, and rewarding people for achieving them, organizational performance can be diminished. As an alternative, Sull and Sull (2018) recommend that objectives should be FAST—Frequently discussed, Ambitious, Specific, and Transparent—to ensure that organizational goal attainment is not unintentionally limited.

Objectives are equivalent to milestones on the road to delivery of goals. Objectives might be revised on a more regular basis than goals, as an organization's context unfolds.

Initiatives

Initiatives are projects to which specific organizational resources are deployed. Initiatives can be considered the specific practical means by which objectives are achieved. For example, in order to 'grow annual research council funding to $10 million by 2021', initiatives the organization might undertake could be:

- create a peer review system for the internal evaluation of draft grant applications
- retain an external grant application writer to be made available as a resource for all draft applications more than $2.5 million in value
- implement a grant-writing progress tracking system.

Initiatives can be quantified in terms of an associated budget, timescale, and organizational accountability (such as a department or individual being given responsibility for making the initiative happen). Initiatives can typically be triggered, revised, or cancelled at short notice.

The value of an initiative might be explained in relation to the objectives that are supported by delivering the initiative.

Key performance indicators and targets

4

Often referred to by the acronym KPIs, key performance indicators describe the ways in which progress towards objectives will be evaluated. For example, for the objective 'grow annual research council funding to $10 million by 2021' listed above, KPIs might include 'number of research grant applications submitted every year', 'average value of research grant applications', and 'grant submission win rate'.

KPIs are often referred to in terms of leading or lagging indicators. Leading indicators are concerned with predicting **future** performance, whereas lagging indicators focus on reacting to **prior** performance. For example, a leading indicator might be 'number of colleagues completing safety evaluations'. Where performance against the indicator is high, it is likely that future safety performance will be enhanced. In contrast, 'number of lost time incidents' is a backward-looking measure that tracks how successful safety performance has been in the past.

For each KPI, there can be an associated target to which organizational performance might aspire and against which it might be evaluated. Targets that push for performance that exceeds historical attainment levels are referred to as 'stretch targets'. For example, the targets for the research income KPIs could be as set out in Table 4.2.

Targets and KPIs provide a means of tracking the overall performance of the organization as well as progress against achieving specific goals and objectives. Targets may be accompanied by what are known as 'control limits' and 'glide paths'.

Control limits are the levels of performance which will trigger a corrective action in an organization. For example, if the average application value in Table 4.2 is tracking at $1.5 million halfway through the year, action may be required with those applying for grants in order to improve progress towards the target. Control limits might be high (e.g. when the rate of employee absence goes above 4%) or low (e.g. when production line efficiency drops below 85%). When control limits are breached, a managerial response will typically be required. If you are

TABLE 4.2 **Examples of targets associated with KPIs**

KPI	Target	Rationale
Number of research grant applications submitted every year	10 applications per year	An evaluation of historical grant application activity shows the institution averaging 8–12 applications per year; therefore, this seems a realistic target
Average value of research grant applications	Average application value $2.5 million	Considering win and application rate, an average research grant value of $2.5 million is required to achieve the overall goal; reviewing prior bid activity, the range of submission goes from $1 million to $4 million, so $2.5 million is achievable
Grant submission win rate	Win rate 40%	Historical performance in this KPI has been tracking at 35%, so to aim for 40% can be considered a stretch target

responsible for an area of organizational performance, this may mean that you have to provide a root-cause analysis of any issues and propose a corrective action plan. This is equally true for operational and strategic control limits (see Practitioner Insight in Chapter 9 for an example of how strategic initiatives and daily operations are monitored and managed through targets).

An issue with control limits is that progress towards achieving KPIs for targets may not always be linear. For example, if the research councils in the example in Table 4.2 only accept applications every four months, the institution will deliver no applications for the first three months of the year. Therefore a 'glide path', which is a chart of anticipated progress against meeting a target that is constructed based on knowledge of organizational activity and context, is used to enable more nuanced management of KPIs and targets. Glide paths should be constructed on the basis of knowledgeable evaluation of possible progress against a target. Glide paths will be less helpful when a straight line is drawn between a starting level of performance and a desired end state. Figure 4.1 is an example of a glide path for research grant applications over a year. Rather than draw a straight line from 0 in January to 10 in December, the anticipated number of applications reflects the timescales for submission anticipated by the authors. The horizontal lines represent months in which no submissions should be anticipated.

Associated with KPIs in strategy practice is the term **Balanced Scorecard** first proposed by Kaplan and Norton (1992). As discussed in Chapter 9, a Balanced Scorecard is a set of both leading and lagging KPIs for an organization which address performance holistically (i.e. not just on financial performance). A Balanced Scorecard should comprise indicators selected according to the specific context and needs of the organization, as outlined in Table 4.3.

Imagining, monitoring, and delivering organizational aims

Figure 4.2 shows how the concepts of goals, objectives, initiatives, KPIs, and targets operate in combination in order to imagine, monitor, and deliver organizational aims. It can be seen how work on specific initiatives can contribute to realizing the aims of the organization. Initiatives

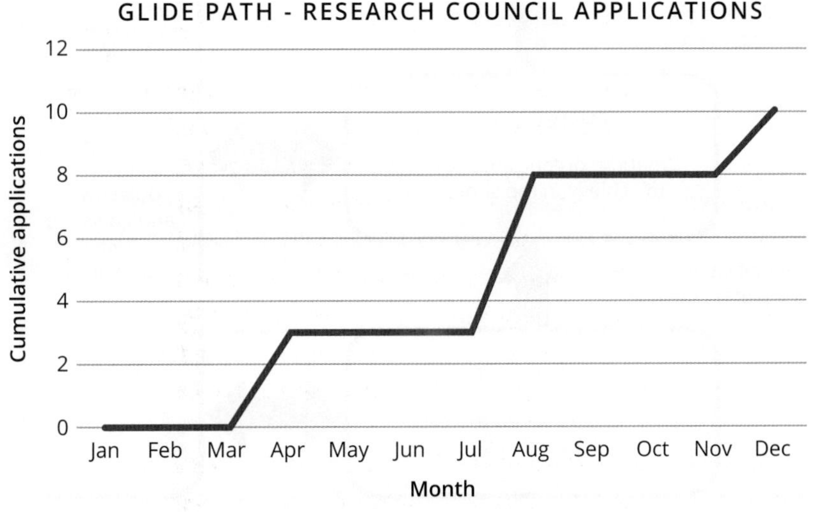

FIGURE 4.1 An example of a glide path for a target.

4

TABLE 4.3 **Measures relating to the balanced scorecard**

KPI	Indicator
Financial and business performance	Running a financially viable and sustainable organization, meeting the needs of shareholders and stakeholders
Customer and commercial performance	Understanding and meeting the needs of customers, competing effectively and generating revenue
Operations and infrastructure	Buildings, equipment, systems, and processes that create and deliver customer value and employee services
People, learning, and development	Building human capacity to meet current and future needs

provide a means through which to meet objectives. Equally, objectives justify the investment of resources behind an initiative by providing target outcomes to which the initiative will contribute. Similarly, short-term objectives (e.g. 1 year targets) show the paths through which longer-term goals (e.g. 3–5 years) will be realized over time, and goals help to explain how achieving objectives will help the organization.

A single initiative can support multiple objectives, as shown in Figure 4.3. For example, an initiative to 'create a peer review system for the internal evaluation of draft grant applications' could contribute to the objective 'grow annual research council funding to $10 million by 2021', and also support another objective such as 'double the number of multi-disciplinary committees by 2020'. Further, objectives can be connected with multiple goals. Using the same example,

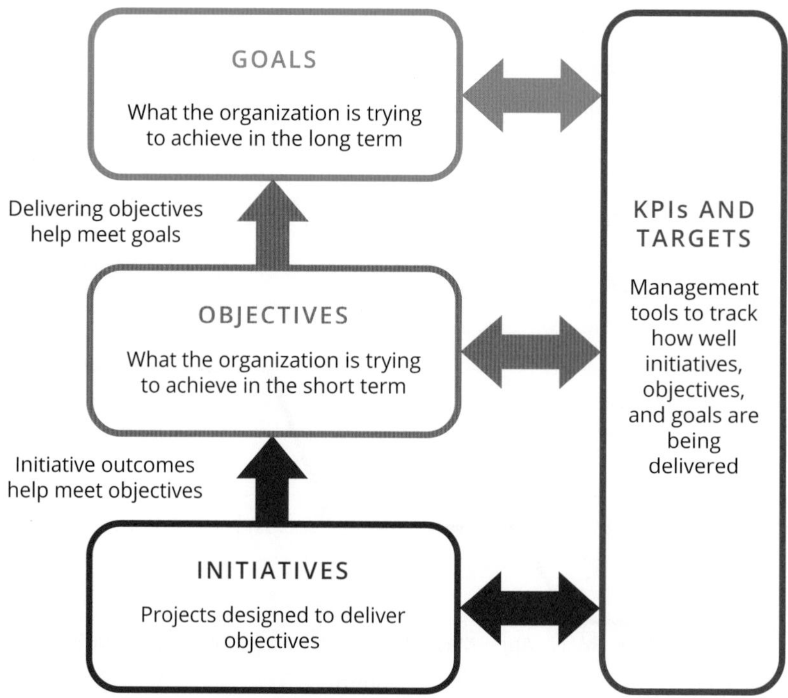

FIGURE 4.2 **Imagining, monitoring, and delivering organizational aims.**

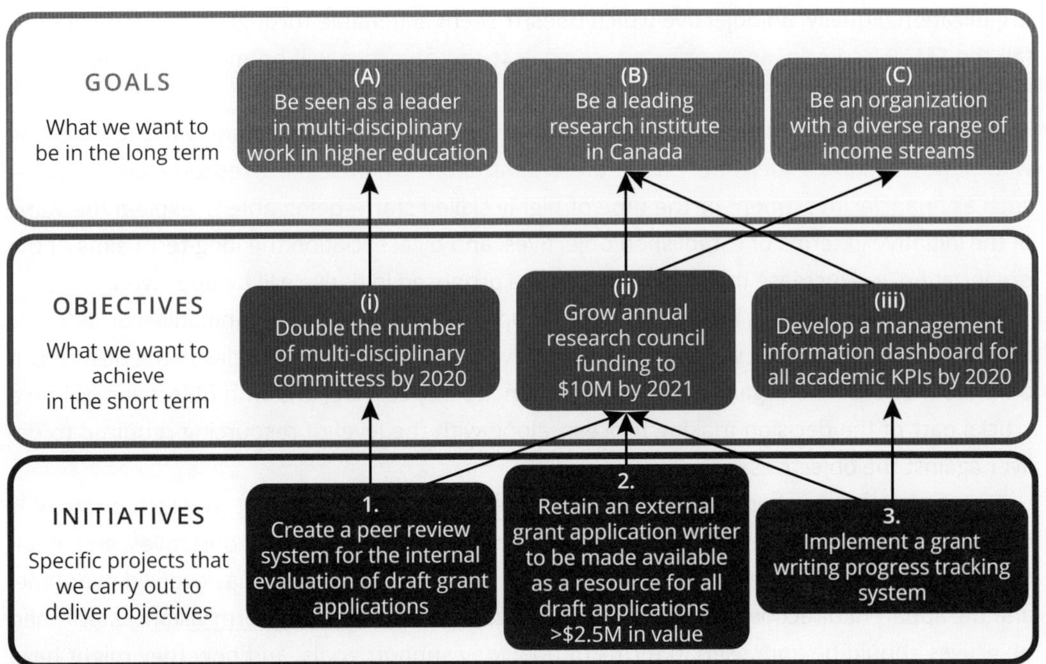

FIGURE 4.3 **Connections between initiatives, objectives, and goals.**

'grow annual research council funding to $10 million by 2021' will contribute to attainment of the goal 'be a leading research institute in Canada' and also 'be an organization with a diverse range of income streams'.

When evaluating strategic initiatives and options for action, it is valuable to understand these relationships in order to identify the best use of organizational resources. If you can map the objectives that might be supported by the initiatives under consideration, you will be able to identify the initiatives that might give the best return on investment. You will also be able to articulate how goals are anticipated to be achieved through objectives and associated initiatives.

If you work as a strategist later, you may need to prioritize deployment of resources as part of your strategy work. Having a sense of the relationships between initiatives, objectives, and goals can help you make choices about which projects to work on first in order to deliver most benefit to the organization. The map in Figure 4.3 could be enhanced by further examining the links between the elements. Knowing the extent of the contribution represented by each arrow, or the certainty with which we can claim that an initiative will deliver on an objective, could add further nuance to our decision-making.

Organizational goals, objectives, and initiatives as an input to the strategy process

When learning about strategy, it is important to understand existing goals, objectives, and initiatives as enablers and constraints of what might be done. A new initiative that can't be connected with existing organizational objectives might be difficult to justify—part of making the business case for such an initiative would be to explain how it adds relevant value to the organization. Equally, an objective which doesn't seem actionable through initiatives will likely fail the SMART criteria, and performance against the objective will be more about luck than purposeful action.

Initiatives that are clearly linked to one or more objectives have an instant way of connecting with powerful stakeholder interests in the organization. When seeking resource allocations—such as financial investment or the time of highly skilled staff—being able to explain the value of the initiative in terms of established objectives, and by association the long-term aims of the organization, will increase the likelihood that the proposed initiative will be approved.

Where a new initiative is proposed that overlaps in scope with existing initiatives or different options for taking action, it will be necessary to evaluate which initiative delivers the best return on investment for the organization. When this happens, connections with objectives will be a crucial part of the decision-making process, along with the level of resourcing required to deliver against the objectives.

Therefore, when gathering information on the organizational context in which strategy is occurring it is crucial to develop an appreciation of existing goal systems, objectives, and initiatives. This data-gathering exercise should consider how the goal system has evolved over time, and the apparent direction of travel of the organization towards a long-term vision. Established objectives should be appraised in terms of how they support goals, and how they might have evolved over time, and existing and proposed initiatives should be charted in terms of the intent to deliver objectives.

4.4 **Shareholder or stakeholder value maximization?**

So far in this chapter, we have discussed the role and purpose of organizations and considered their role and sphere of influence more widely than solely focusing on generating revenue and profit. We then outlined the processes that strategists can apply to deliver the firm's purpose. But let's go back to our explanation of an organization's purpose as an affirmation of the reason for its existence. For example, what does the organization do, who does it serve, and where does it expect to be in the future? We will now focus on one of these questions: Whose interests does the firm serve?

The answer to this fundamental question is far from straightforward. For example, should firms simply serve their shareholders' interest, or should they have a responsibility to the communities they operate in and society more generally? The debate over whether firms should have a wider social responsibility beyond the organization's business activities has historically been controversial. Professor Milton Friedman, a Nobel Laureate in Economics, famously stated that the only social responsibility of business is to use its resources and engage in activities designed to increase its profits. Friedman's position has become known as the shareholder model of business. Friedman argued that having a wider social responsibility beyond maximizing returns to the shareholders (the owners of a business) was an immoral idea that violates the rights of the shareholders (Friedman 1970). Friedman and his University of Chicago colleagues argued that shareholders who had invested in a firm were expecting the business (through its agents and corporate managers) to engage in activities that would maximize returns for their investment, and to use corporate resource to solve non-business social problems would effectively amount to theft from shareholders. Should shareholders wish to solve wider social problems, they should do so privately through their own charitable contributions, not through contributions by the business that shareholders had invested in with the expectation of earning a return on their investment. Friedman and his colleagues also pointed out that successful firms already make a wider social contribution as a normal course of their business activities by providing employment and through taxes on their profits that are paid to both local and central governments.

The critics of shareholder value maximization are many. For example, Stout (2012) states that shareholder value thinking leads corporate managers to focus on short-term performance at the expense of long-term value creation. Jensen (2002) argues that in order to maximize value, corporate managers must both satisfy and enlist the support of all corporate stakeholders—customers, employees, managers, suppliers, financiers, and local communities. This wider concern for other stakeholders beyond the narrow focus on shareholders has become knowns as the stakeholder value view. According to this view, instead of striving to maximize shareholder wealth, managers should strive to balance all stakeholder interests (Freeman 1984). In contrast with the shareholder view, the stakeholder view posits that the essence of the firm is to create value for all stakeholders, not just the firm's shareholders alone.

So, are shareholder and stakeholder perspectives incompatible? van der Linden and Freeman (2017) state that Friedman never thought that corporate managers should ignore other stakeholder interests. But his concern for stakeholder interests was limited, to the extent that they were instrumental to the interest of shareholders. However, as van der Linden and Freeman (2017) discuss, Friedman's thinking was not opposed to the stakeholder view if it is accepted that the primary responsibility of corporate managers is to create as much value as possible for stakeholders, because this is how one creates as much value as possible for the shareholders. In other words, what's good for all stakeholders is good for the firm's ultimate owners—the shareholders.

In addition, we should note that it's hard to create value for all stakeholders without making a profit, unless the organization is a charity or an aid organization that relies on donations and benefactors to sustain its activity (Birkinshaw et al. 2014). Therefore the profit motive that is the cornerstone of any firm's raison d'être is good for the wider society. As we saw earlier in this chapter, Nestlé's corporate purpose is to help shape a better and healthier world by inspiring people to live healthier lives. Nestlé ranked second in the Food Products industry sector of the 2018 Dow Jones Sustainability Index (DJSI), an indicator of the firm's contributions to wider societal concerns. The DJSI evaluates the sustainability performance of the largest 2500 companies listed on the Dow Jones Global Stock Market Index. Nestlé achieved a full score for Health and Nutrition performance criteria and holds the leadership scores in the Environmental and Social dimensions (https://www.sustainability-indices.com). So, making a contribution to the wider society makes good business sense as it will also ensure the long-term success of the company.

Stakeholder management

As we have seen, business has evolved beyond shareholder value maximization towards a view that the interests of business and society are inextricably linked. Corporations are today expected to take into consideration not only shareholders' interests, but also those of other groups, organizations, and individuals that have a stake or an interest in the firm. The greater the stakeholders' understanding of the firm, and the closer the firm's ties to its stakeholders, the easier it is to create sustainable value, both for the firm and the firm's stakeholder groups (including the wider society).

Stakeholders, to use a definition put forward by Freeman (1984), are any one group or individual who can affect or is affected by the achievement of an organization's purpose, principally financiers, customers, suppliers, employees, and communities. Freeman argues that stakeholders can have a significant impact on firm performance that is beyond their role as factors of production or consumption (e.g. employees or customers). Therefore it is important that managers identify key stakeholders and engage with them when setting the firm's strategic direction and making strategic decisions. This is particularly critical for firms that have invited customers and suppliers to participate directly in the design of products and services through co-creation initiatives. Research indicates that stakeholders do not actively participate in co-creation unless they are allowed to generate value for themselves as well (Ramaswamy and Gouillart 2010). So, how does a firm manage its stakeholders, to maximize the benefit for everyone?

Stakeholder mapping

In order to effectively manage stakeholders and engage them strategically, it is important for a firm to understand who their key stakeholders are, where they come from, and their level of interest in and power over the organization.

Stakeholder mapping is a process that aims to identify a list of key stakeholders across the whole stakeholder spectrum. Mapping can be broken into four phases:

1. **Stakeholder identification**: listing of relevant groups, organizations, and people.
2. **Stakeholder analysis**: understanding stakeholder perspectives, interests, and power.
3. **Stakeholder map generation**: visualizing a relationship between the firm and the stakeholders.
4. **Stakeholder ranking**: ordering of stakeholder importance and their influence on the firm.

A number of different frameworks for undertaking stakeholder mapping and analysis are available. The most common mapping framework was developed by Mendelow (1981,1986). His framework identifies stakeholders in terms of their interest and power. This is a particularly useful tool for understanding political priorities, as stakeholder groups often have conflicting interests. For example, in Western market economies, the interests of shareholders and managers often conflict with the interests of labour unions over salaries. Similarly, environmental and community groups are often in conflict with natural resource extraction firms, such as the highly politicized and emotional disagreement over the use of fracking to extract natural gas or oil from deep-rock formations.

The two dimensions of Mendelow's power–interest matrix are shown in Figure 4.4. The matrix depicts stakeholders relative to the power they hold, and the extent to which they are likely

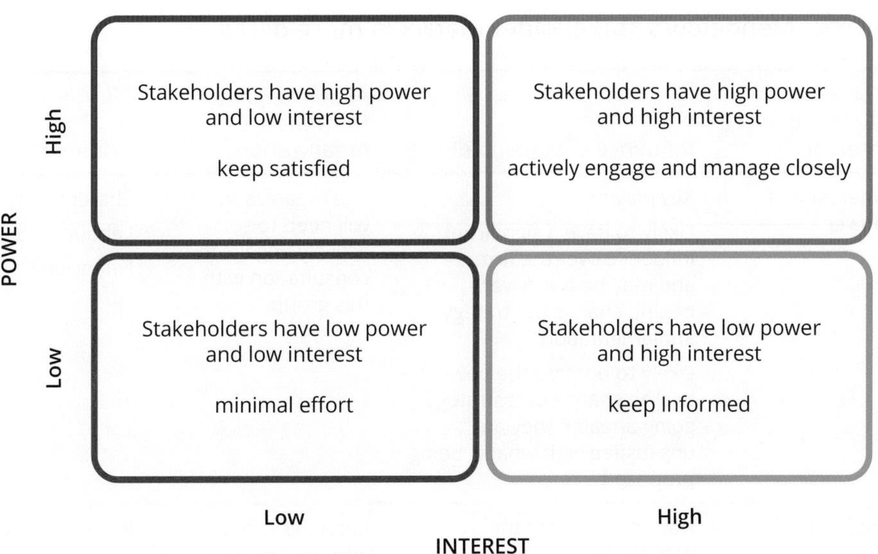

FIGURE 4.4 Mendelow's stakeholder power–interest matrix.

to demonstrate interest in either supporting or opposing a particular strategy of the firm. The four boxes from the matrix are considered in more detail in Table 4.4.

Stakeholder mapping enables the firm to understand its stakeholders and potentially move its relationship with them beyond transactional relationships towards understanding, engagement, and respect. The key questions that management should ask when developing a stakeholder engagement strategy are as follows (Kourdi 2015):

1. Which stakeholders are the most significant for the organization? Whose input will be valuable when strategy is being developed, and who are instrumental in its implementation?
2. How do the firm's stakeholders relate to each other, and how could these relationships be strengthened or leveraged further?
3. What do the firm's stakeholder groups value? What do they want of the firm and how effective are they at getting it?
4. How will the firm be able to strengthen and manage the stakeholder relationships?
5. How should the firm communicate with its various stakeholder groups, with what frequency, message, and communications channel?

In conclusion, stakeholder management is not an easy task, especially as it is a political process with a number of conflicting interests. However, engaged stakeholders can be an important resource for the firm to generate sustainable advantage, earn the company a solid reputation for sound business practices in the community, and successfully fulfil the firm's purpose.

TABLE 4.4 **Mendelow's stakeholder matrix in more detail**

Level of stakeholder power and interest	Influence of stakeholder	Action required from the organization	Example
High interest and high power	Key players Likely to have a significant influence over the firm and may be the driver behind change or strategy implementation Likely to possess the power to stop change or a strategy going ahead if they are unsatisfied with what is being proposed	The organization will need to actively engage in consultation with this group	Shareholders Labour unions Financiers
High Interest and low power	Has an interest in the organization Unlikely to have the power to influence change Can attempt to join forces with a group with power (such as the press, media, and the government who normally do not have much interest in the day-to-day activities of an individual firm) and become a key player as a result	Keep this group informed of the firm's operations and performance	Pressure groups Other non-governmental organizations with a high interest in the firm
Low interest and high power	Has the potential to become a 'high interest and high power' stakeholder group	It is essential that this group is kept satisfied that the firm is operating within the accepted norms of the law, so that they are less likely to gain interest and exercise their power	The media is unlikely have a significant interest in day-to-day activities of the firm but may become a powerful stakeholder if the firm is discovered to have engaged in unethical activities
Low interest and low power	Unlikely to have an interest in the organization and its direction This may be due to their lack of power to influence the organization and they are likely to accept the prevailing situation and show little if any resistance to the strategy or the changes in the organization	Limited effort by the firm beyond ensuring that any contractual agreements are properly discharged	Contractors who are working in the firm on a specific assignment for a predetermined contract period

CASE EXAMPLE 4.1 GAP INC. STAKEHOLDER MAPPING

Gap's commitment to social responsibility was first articulated in 1992 when the company published one of the earliest sets of ethical sourcing principles in the garment industry. Despite 100 people operating globally to police and enforce Gap's code, which covered labour, environmental and health, and safety standards across the firm's suppliers and subcontractors in its global supply chain, Gap's local suppliers failed to implement the code's requirements.

When a number of serious labour and environmental protection violations were uncovered, Gap came under pressure from advocacy groups in the USA and the UK. There was much media attention surrounding protests outside Gap's head office in San Francisco for several weeks—especially when the groups protested with no clothes on. Executives realized that there was a legal problem with the way in which Gap assessed risk to ethical trade, and they identified that the level of change required to improve their risk mitigation approach to ethical trade and reassure their critics necessitated a major overhaul.

As the first step to deeper engagement with its stakeholders, Gap undertook a stakeholder mapping exercise by listing as many stakeholders as possible and then ranking them by their importance. 'We recognized that it would not be possible for us to have a strategic relationship with each of the stakeholders, so we highlighted those who we deemed to be the most key', recalled Deanna Robinson, Gap's head of monitoring and vendor development.

Prioritizing stakeholders allowed the firm to focus on developing transparent relationships with a few of the most influential organizations. 'We will never be able to engage at the same level of depth with every organization that exists', explained Daryl Knudsen, Gap's director of public policy and stakeholder engagement, 'but by engaging with organizations who themselves have extensive networks, we have managed to receive some level of input and influence from those networks.'

An external consultancy firm facilitated this mapping process at Gap. They involved participants from different function groups across the organization, including legal, public relations, government affairs, and global compliance in the stakeholder mapping process, in order to create a map of stakeholders that was customized and prioritized by those participating. This not only enabled Gap to ensure that employees were engaged with the new process and strategy, but it also facilitated a development opportunity for those employees to get to know who the key stakeholders were, and additionally enabled the executives to better understand how the decisions they make and their relationships with stakeholders impact the lives of labourers making their clothes.

This acitivity meant that Gap's approach was starting to evolve from a risk-averse legalistic strategy to one based on proactive engagement which could tease out stakeholder needs, positions, and motivations. It was a significant change in the company's approach which meant that many of the senior decision-makers were learning about stakeholder theory and discovering who their stakeholders were for the first time.

Once Gap had identified its stakeholders, the company set about getting to know them better and consulting them on how they thought they could improve their labour practices. There was one particular meeting which had important consequences for the company. Gap's executives met Lynda Yanz, of the Maquila Solidarity Network (MSN) in Toronto, Canada, which is an influential workers' rights group concerned with labour rights issues in the Americas, and a key sourcing market for the company. Yanz advised that Gap should work to engage stakeholders more holistically, and this would mean that stakeholders could communicate directly about emerging issues with corporate responsibility team members.

This meeting made one other thing clear to the executives: in order to improve labour conditions, they could not do this alone, but needed to develop partnerships with relevant stakeholders and participate in emerging multi-stakeholder initiatives. After meeting with MSN, Gap joined two multi-stakeholder initiatives (MSIs): the New-York-based Social Accountability International in 2003, and the London-based Ethical Trading Initiative (ETI) in 2004. By joining these MSIs, executives felt that they had provided a safe platform for tackling issues with various stakeholders,

Continued

as well as gaining their insights and perspectives on the best ways to handle those issues raised.

Questions for discussion

1. What were the main differences between Gap's legalistic risk mitigation and stakeholder mapping approaches?
2. Gap executives admitted that they were mistaken in trying to 'go it alone' in their efforts to improve labour conditions. Why is this admission significant?
3. What groups emerged as key stakeholders in the case, why, and how did Gap address their concerns?

Sources

Smith, N.C., Ansett, S., and Erez, L. (2011). How Gap Inc. engaged with its stakeholders. *MIT Sloan Management Review*, Summer.

Smith, N.C., Ansett, S., and Erez, L. (2019). How Gap engaged with its stakeholders. In: Lenssen, G. and Smith, N. (eds), *Managing Sustainable Business*. Dordrecht: Springer.

4

4.5 **Culture: history and path dependency**

In this chapter we have focused on the purpose and values of organizations. But how does the history and culture of an organization impact on its purpose and values? And how do the purpose and values of an organization provide a framework for its culture? Organizational values and the ways that a business operates are to a great extent influenced by its past. Many organizations have long histories, and the values of the founders are often deeply embedded in the psyche of the organization. History, as well as established processes that have evolved over many years, can often shape strategy that can lead to success, but can also act as a barrier for change, which can in turn negatively impact the organization. In this section we will explore the influence of history, path dependency, and culture, and the impact they may have on strategy.

The history and cultural heritage of an organization can be a source of advantage because it cannot easily be replicated by competitors. For example, Tesco, a British multinational groceries and general merchandise retailer, was founded in 1919 by Jack Cohen as a group of market stalls. The Tesco name first appeared in 1924, after Cohen purchased a shipment of tea from T.E. Stockwell and combined those initials with the first two letters of his surname. The firm still carries the founder's name, and his ethos of 'pile it high and sell it cheap' is embedded in the operating principles of the firm. For many years Tesco was the leading discount chain.

However, it can be argued that Tesco's leading position as a high-value discount retailer has become challenged by Aldi and Lidl. As relatively new entrants to the UK market, Aldi and Lidl seem to have created a business proposition that delivers higher value at a lower price to the UK consumer, and this has eaten into Tesco's dominance. Hence the organization's history and heritage can also be problematic, as they can act as barriers for change. Either way, managers cannot ignore the role of the organization's heritage and culture in understanding the firm's strategy or in making an attempt to change the culture or develop new capabilities.

Path dependency

Path dependency is a useful concept for thinking about the influence of history on a business and is integral to shaping a business's culture. Path dependency stresses the importance of past events for future action or, more precisely, the role of foregone decisions for current and future decision-making in an organization (Schreyogg and Sydow 2010). This means that current and future decisions are historically conditioned: 'bygones are rarely bygones' (Teece et al. 1997:522). This is because an organization's decisions are often made within and with reference to the cultural and operating framework and processes that have evolved over its history and are unique to that organization.

Path dependency can be used to explain the development of strategic resources and organizational capabilities. As will be explored further in Chapter 8, a firm's existing capabilities are the sum total of past decisions taken by managers in accruing resources and developing the firm's strategy and position in a competitive marketplace. For example, the competitive advantage of the world's largest retailer, Wal-Mart Inc., is based on its supply chain logistics capabilities and low prices. However, the firm's super-efficient warehousing operations, distribution, and supplier network was not a result of careful strategic planning; it evolved gradually over time from the trading conditions that the firm faced during its early years in rural Arkansas. Sam Walton, the founder of Wal-Mart, could not afford to locate his stores in expensive in-town retail locations with high footfall. Instead, he had to accept locations in small rural towns that were deemed unattractive by other retailers. However, these locations became strategic assets as they provided enough space for parking for shoppers and very large hypermarkets. Moreover, as Wal-Mart was the first to establish a presence in these rural locations, it became evident that that the locations chosen by Sam Walton could not support more than one hypermarket.

As suppliers were not keen to deliver merchandise to Walton's out-of-town locations, he was forced to develop his own distribution system, and in order to attract customers to these locations from major towns, he had to find ways to make his prices so low that customers deemed them worthy of a journey to the Wal-Mart store. This example illustrates how path dependency can support a successful strategy by creating a set of processes and development of strategic assets that are unique to the firm and difficult, if not impossible, for the competitors to copy and that may serve as the basis of competitive advantage.

However, path dependency can be a double-edged sword. While a firm's competitive advantage may be based on culture and/or capabilities that have evolved from the very early stages of its life, is it possible for a business to develop radically new capabilities or adapt to new competitive realities? The prevailing culture and existing capabilities can become barriers to change, especially in fast-moving competitive environments where the continuous renewal of capabilities is a prerequisite for sustaining a competitive advantage. Leonard-Barton (1992) posits that if an organization is unable to develop new capabilities in response to future competitive developments, its existing core capabilities are simultaneously core rigidities that limit the firm's ability to respond to competitive changes. For example, Dell Computers' direct sales business model was so highly developed and recognized that the firm had difficulties in developing a complementary business model of selling its computers through retailers. Customers associated Dell with low-cost built-to-order systems, rather than computers that they could see and feel at retail outlets.

The challenges of managing change are discussed in more detail in Chapter 14. Our focus in the rest of this chapter is to understand the strategic importance of the culture of the organization which is a product of the environment where the organization operates, its history, and the sum total of the processes and competencies that have evolved throughout its past activities. The key point to remember is that while the firm's past may give it a competitive advantage, if the organization is not able to renew itself in an evolving competitive marketplace, it may lose the advantage by attempting to rely on its past competencies.

Organization culture

Organizations can be considered as complex cultural systems which interact with the environments in which they operate and from which they recruit their employees. Multinational corporations such as Unilever or Sony Corporation may operate differently from country to country, but they also have their own distinctive characteristics and styles which do not vary from one geographical location or national culture to another.

For example, Chase Manhattan Bank (JPMorgan Chase of today), one of the pathfinders of global banking, understood the importance of corporate and national cultures to the bank's business operations in the 1980s, ahead of its closest competitors, which made Chase the leading global corporate bank. The bank recruited employees from different cultures to their local international offices. Because Chase realized that their employees had been socialized in their own native cultures, management recruits had to attend a year-long management training programme at the bank's headquarters in New York and London, where they were instilled with the 'Chase way of doing business', including how to dress and interact with corporate clients. Moreover, the bank employed facilities managers who travelled to Chase's international locations to ensure that the office furniture, artwork, and even the managers' desk name plates were compliant with corporate standards. This meant that the bank's global clients, such as General Motors, would receive the same level of customer service regardless of the international location.

Culture can be perceived to be strategically important, as a strong culture in an organization may provide a firm with a competitive advantage. It is worthwhile emphasizing that what makes a particular culture successful for an organization is that the values are widely shared and acted on by all organizational participants (as a reminder of this, refer to Table 4.1 about our discussion of forward-looking statements in Section 4.3). When organizational values are fully aligned with participants' personal values, drives, and needs, culture can unleash tremendous amounts of energy towards a shared purpose and foster the organization's capacity to thrive (Groysberg et al. 2018).

However, in large and diverse companies with complex operations, cultures can give rise to subcultures. Subcultures can be thought of as a subset of the firm's members who identify themselves as a distinct group with their own values and norms that may be separate from the overall corporate culture of the organization. Subcultures may form around shared interests within the organization or they may reflect similar professional, gender, ethnic, or national cultural identities. If an organization has a number of subcultures with values that are not

CASE EXAMPLE 4.2 GOLDMAN SACHS' BUSINESS CULTURE CRITICIZED BY US OFFICIALS

Criminal charges filed by the US government in the 1MDB (Malaysian Ministry of Finance-owned strategic development company) scandal represented bad news for the defendants, a Malaysian financier and two former investment bankers at Goldman Sachs, a Wall Street investment bank.

The charges were also a blow for Goldman itself, which faced fresh scrutiny over its role in underwriting about $6.5bn of bond offerings for 1MDB in three deals during 2012 and 2013. Much of that money was siphoned off and spread around a web of officials, ending up in Van Gogh paintings, Beverly Hills properties, and investment in the hit movie, *The Wolf of Wall Street*, according to an earlier US Department of Justice indictment.

Since the furore began to intensify, a few years previously, the Wall Street bank tried to put distance between itself and the affair, maintaining that it knew nothing about how the proceeds of the bond offerings would be spent. A former star Goldman Sachs dealmaker in south-east Asia pleaded guilty to conspiring to commit money laundering and bribe foreign officials. Other Goldman bankers were arrested or indicted on similar money-laundering charges and accused of violating US laws against bribing foreign officials, according to the Department of Justice.

Recently, however, more staff at the bank have found themselves implicated. According to the indictment, 'other employees and agents' at the New York-based financial institution at the centre of the affair (which the Department of Justice did not name) knew that bribes and kickbacks had been promised to officials to secure business for the bank. It is alleged that those people conspired to conceal that information from the compliance and legal departments.

The bank's 'business culture, particularly in south-east Asia, was highly focused on consummating deals; at times prioritising this goal ahead of the proper operation of its compliance functions', the Department of Justice alleged. In response to the accusations made, Goldman Sachs is considering a special surveillance programme to monitor higher-risk employees in far-flung locations, so the bank can demonstrate that 'lessons have been learned' from the 1MDB scandal.

Questions for discussion:

1. In your opinion, do you consider Goldman Sachs to have a problem with its business culture? If so, how would such a problem have emerged?
2. Do you consider that a surveillance programme is an appropriate intervention to deal with the 1MDB scandal? Why/Why not?
3. Do you think that it is possible to create a homogenous organization culture that is shared by all? If so, how could this be achieved?
4. Consider what you have learned so far in this chapter. What advice would you offer Goldman Sachs in terms their corporate culture?

Sources

Financial Times, 2 November 2018.

'Goldman's business culture criticised by US officials', 2 December 2018, https://www.ft.com/content/763db0c4-ddff-11e8-9f04-38d397e6661c (accessed 2 November 2018).

'Goldman eyes monitoring of high-risk staff after 1MDB', https://www.ft.com/content/68ca9f7a-f4b5-11e8-9623-d7f9881e729f (accessed 2 December 2018).

commonly shared, this may result in a fragmented culture, and these subcultures may evolve into behaviours and attitudes that are in conflict with the overall values and purpose of an organization. A fractured or fragmented culture may hinder the organization from reaching its goals or cause serious damage to the business and its reputation. The damage that fractured cultures can cause became evident during the Great Recession of 2008 which implicated many financial institutions globally. According to the UK's Financial Conduct Authority (FSA), 'toxic cultures were a key cause of the failings that harmed consumers and markets' (*Financial Times*, 1 November 2018).

Schein's three dimensions of culture

Edgar Schein (1997) defines culture as deeply embedded fundamental assumptions and beliefs that are shared by the members of the organization. Culture represents the basic assumptions and frameworks that organizational actors use to make sense of challenges and opportunities, both internally and externally, and how they deal with them. These 'taken for granted assumptions' may have a physical and visual manifestation in artefacts such as logos. The assumptions and frameworks that make up culture are grounded on the purpose and the values of the organization that guide its mission and on the activities conducted to realize the organization's mission (Deal and Kennedy 1982; Schein 1997).

Schein classifies culture in three dimensions:

1. The first dimension of culture is built around artefacts that represent the visible organizational features such as logos, uniforms, buildings, architecture, and workplace designs. The firm's customers may interact with some of the artefacts, such as a customer placing a hamburger order at one of the new Macdonald's self-service kiosks before being served by a uniformed employee. Inside the organization, the way workspace is configured may have a significant impact on the way that employees interact with each other. Apple's new Campus2 in Cupertino, California, houses 12,000 employees, and the circular building is divided into modular sections, known as pods, which are used for office work, teamwork, and social activities. Everyone, from the CEO to summer interns, will be placed into these pods, helping employees build connections, collaborate, and discover mentorship opportunities, as employees of all levels of experience and seniority frequently come into contact with each other.
2. Schein's second dimension of culture encompasses the firm's **articulated values**. These values are made explicit in the purpose, value, and mission statements that we studied at the beginning of this chapter. The objective of these statements is to get the whole organization to work towards common shared goals and objectives.
3. The third dimension of Schein's culture classification includes the **deeply held beliefs and assumptions** that are not explicitly articulated in artefacts or statements. Often, this level is hidden as mental (or cognitive) maps of organizational actors that provide them with the implicit means of interpreting the world and making decisions (Weick 2001, 2009; Huff 1990). An example of this sort of cognitive mapping is known as causal mapping, which is used by strategists as a means of improving the quality of managerial decision-making processes by making decision-makers' assumptions of a strategic problem more explicit. (You can develop your understanding of causal mapping in Chapter 3.)

These deep cognitive structures of culture are difficult to articulate. They have emerged over a long period of time throughout the history of the organization, and if they are not visible, they will be difficult to manage and change. However, cognitive maps are vitally important in managerial practice as they implicitly guide thinking and decision-making in organizations.

According to Schein, these three dimensions of artefacts, articulated values, and deeply held beliefs and assumptions together make up the culture of an organization,.

The Cultural Web

As you study strategy, it is important to understand not just the different aspects of organizational culture, but also how, in your future career, you might analyse organizational culture. The Cultural Web (Johnson 1992) has become the most commonly used tool to analyse organizational culture. (There are also a number of different frameworks for assessing organizational cultures, such as Groysberg's Eight Distinct Culture Styles, which is included in the **online resources** (Groysberg et al. 2018)). The Cultural Web is an attempt to incorporate Schein's dimensions of culture which depict the behavioural, physical, and symbolic manifestations of culture forming the 'paradigm' of an organization (see Figure 4.5).

The Cultural Web identifies six interlinked elements that make the 'paradigm' of an organization. The paradigm (e.g. 'the way we do things around here': Johnson 1992) at the centre of the Cultural Web is the set of assumptions that are shared and taken for granted in the organization. It is likely that the assumptions of the paradigm are very basic. For example, the paradigm of the UK National Health Service (NHS) is to treat the sick. It is often difficult to identify the elements that constitute the paradigm, especially for those who work inside the organization. The six elements of the Cultural Web are a means of guiding strategic conversations about organizational culture:

1. **Stories.** The past events that people talk about inside and outside the organization, including stories about employee and manager behaviours. Who and what the company chooses to immortalize says a great deal about what the organization values, and what is perceived as exemplary behaviour. For example, does the organization revere stories about successful sales deals or about innovations by factory-level workers that reduced the firm's production costs? 'Stories capture organizational life in a way that no compilation of facts ever can. This is because they are carriers of life itself, not just reports on it' (Czarniawska 1997:21).

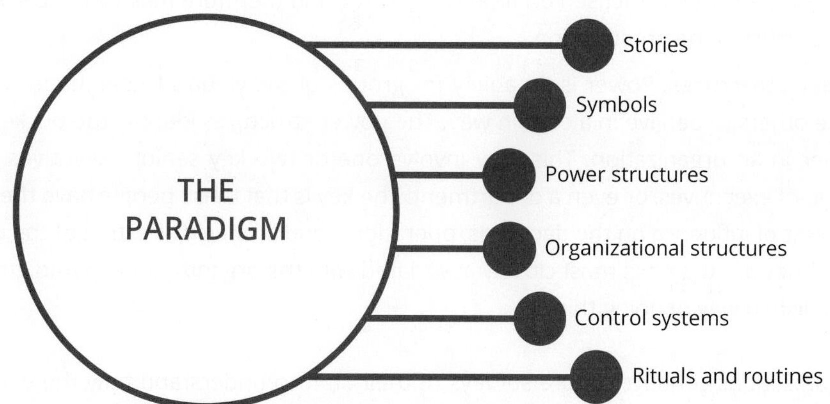

FIGURE 4.5 The Cultural Web of organization. Source: Reproduced with permission from Johnson, G. (1992) Managing strategic change—strategy, culture and action. *Long Range Planning*, **25**(1):28–36. https://doi.org/10.1016/0024-6301(92)90307-N. Copyright © 1992 Published by Elsevier Ltd.

2. **Rituals and routines.** The daily organizational behaviours and actions of people that are deemed acceptable. This determines what is expected to happen in given situations, and what is valued by the management. Rituals and routines can be both formal and informal. Examples of formal rituals and routines include events such as annual performance appraisals, promotion or disciplinary processes, sales conferences, and so on. Impromptu birthday celebrations with cake, drinks after work, or gossiping around the water cooler are examples of informal rituals or routines.
3. **Symbols.** The visual representations of the company including logos, how upmarket the offices are, size and location of offices for different levels of staff, formal or informal dress codes, etc. Job titles have a functional purpose in an organization, but they also have a symbolic meaning in communicating status or power. Consider the symbolic meaning of two different office layouts: some organizations may have separate dining facilities and private elevators that are reserved for exclusive use by the senior managers to take them to their offices at the top of the building; in contrast, some firms design their senior management offices to be modest with 'lots of glass walls for the executives who have offices, and most people working in open plan' (Bulkin 2015:134). Although symbols are depicted as a separate element in the Cultural Web, it should be noted that many other elements of the web also have a symbolic meaning.
4. **Organizational structure.** This includes the roles, responsibilities, and reporting relationships that are defined by the organization chart, as well as the unwritten lines of power and influence that indicate whose contributions are most valued. Fewer formal reporting lines may be a manifestation of a less hierarchical organization, which may indicate that the organization culture is more collaborative than an organization with deep and rigid reporting relationships.
5. **Control systems.** The formal and informal ways that the organization and people are monitored and supported. These include financial, product, and service quality control and assurance, and employee reward systems. The nature and design of the systems indicate what is important to the organization. An expenditure approval process that requires a number of signatories up the organizational structure may be representative of a company that is focused on financial control, and therefore may be indicative of the lack of trust in the organization.
6. **Power structures.** Power is an ability for groups or individuals to persuade, induce, or force others to behave in a certain way. The power structures identify the pockets of real power in an organization. This may involve one or two key senior executives, a whole group of executives, or even a department. The key is that these people have the greatest amount of influence on the decisions, operations, and strategic direction of the organization. They are the ones most closely associated with the organizational paradigm and the established way of doing things.

Many organizations conduct culture surveys of their staff to understand how the existing culture is perceived by organizational members and how it relates to an ideal culture that organization members would prefer. Such surveys resemble student satisfaction surveys that you may have taken.

A number of culture analysis tools are employed by change management consultants, but many of them are built around the Cultural Web framework, or a variation thereof, such as the Organizational Culture Inventory® by Human Synergistics (https://www.humansynergistics.com). A wide gap between the perceived and the ideal culture may signal a need for cultural change.

Constructing a Cultural Web

A starting point for organizations to understand their culture is to construct a Cultural Web of the organization. This can be accomplished for the organization as a whole, or for independent subsidiaries and divisions. As a strategist would do, in order to develop your understanding of this process, you can start by looking at each element of the Cultural Web separately and asking questions that help to determine the dominant factors in each element. Cultural Web elements and related questions are as follows.

Stories

- How do people currently describe the organization?
- What is the reputation of the organization among its customers and other stakeholders?
- How do these stories describe what the organization believes in?
- How do employees think about and describe the history of the organization?
- What stories do employees tell new recruits who join the company?
- Who are the heroes, villains, mavericks, or rebels in these stories?

Rituals and routines

- What rituals and routines do customers experience when dealing with the organization?
- What are the daily and special occasion routines among the employees in the organization?
- Would a change in rituals and routines be immediately obvious if they were changed?
- What behaviours are embedded in the organization's rituals and routines?
- What core beliefs of the organization are embedded in its rituals and routines?
- When confronted with a new problem, what rules do employees apply when trying to solve it?

Symbols

- Does the organization use specific jargon or language that is often only understood by the people in the firm?
- Are there specifc status symbols that are used to connote seniority or special positions in the organization?
- What imagery, including logos, trademarks, and photos, are associated with the organization and how are they perecievd by employees, customers, and other stakeholders?

Organizational structure

- Is the organization structure flat or hierarchical?
- Does the organization operate using formal or informal communication practices?
- Does the organization rely on formal or informal lines of authority?

Control systems

- Which of the organization's processes or procedures have the strictest levels of control? Which processes and procedures have the loosest levels of control?
- Are employees rewarded for doing good work or following set procedures?
- What reports are produced, and to whom are they circulated, to keep control of operations, finance, etc.?

Power structures

- Is there a concentration of power in the organization and who exercises it?
- What do those in power believe in and champion in the organization?
- Who are the decision-makers in the organization and who are able to influence decision-making?
- How do employees perceive those in power? Is power being used for the good of the organization or abused for personal gain?

As a strategist answers these questions, a picture of organizational culture begins to emerge, allowing them to describe the culture and identify the dominant factors across the Cultural Web. After completing the existing organizational Cultural Web, the process should be repeated with the aim of understanding what an ideal culture would look like if everything were correctly aligned. This allows the strategist to make a direct comparison between the perceived and ideal cultures of the organization and understand any gaps.

Mapping the differences

After comparing the existing and the ideal Cultural Webs of the organization and having identified the differences between the two, the next step is to consider the organization's strategic aims and objectives and develop a programme to align the organization's culture with these aims and objectives.

- What cultural strengths and weaknesses have been highlighted by the analysis of the current culture?
- What factors are hindering strategy or are misaligned with one another?
- What factors are detrimental to the health and productivity of the workplace?
- What factors should be encouraged and reinforced?
- Which elements need to change?
- What new beliefs and behaviours are needed?

Can culture be managed?

The steps involved in constructing a Cultural Web show that culture is clearly an important element in any organization. However, the question that we need to address is that if culture is such an important element and possibly a source of competitive advantage, can it be effectively managed?

Two McKinsey & Co consultants, Peters and Waterman, in their book *In Search of Excellence* (Peters and Waterman 1982) argued that the answer to this question is 'Yes'. They stated that truly great companies have excellent cultures which are the sources of their financial success. Such successful cultures are built around core values that are widely shared and acted on by organizational participants. Peters and Waterman's book and other works by academics, such as Deal and Kennedy (1982) and Schein (1997), elevated organizational culture to the forefront of academic minds as well as the minds of managers and consultants. This led to the emergence of a group of strategy culture theorists and academic studies that argued for a link between culture and competitive advantage (Hall 1993).

This view came under scrutiny not least because some of the firms that Peters and Waterman had listed as truly excellent lost their leading competitive positions shortly after publication of their book, but also because questions were raised over Peters and Waterman's data integrity and analysis. Early on in the debate, Jay Barney, in a seminal article (Barney 1986), questioned whether culture could be a source of competitive advantage. Basing his argument on the tenets of the resource-based view (RBV), which will be explored in depth in Chapter 8, Barney argued that if organization culture could be a source of sustainable competitive advantage, it would have to meet the criteria of being valuable, rare, inimitable, and non-substitutable (VRIN).

Barney (1986) identified three requirements for culture to form the basis of competitive advantage. The first is that a firm's culture must enable it to do things and behave in ways that add economic **value** to the firm, which is clearly a prerequisite for generating even normal economic performance. If a firm's culture enables it to behave in ways that are inconsistent with a firm's competitive situation, that culture cannot be a source of superior financial performance, sustained or otherwise.

The second requirement is that valuable cultures must be **rare**. If many firms have similar cultures that allow them to behave and compete in approximately the same way, none will possess a culturally based competitive advantage, and above-normal economic performance cannot be expected.

Finally, even if the above conditions are met, it is still necessary for a firm's culture to be **inimitable** for it to generate sustained superior financial performance. Imitable cultures, even if they are valuable, and even if they are currently rare, remove any competitive advantages they may provide. The culture-driven success of one firm creates an incentive for other firms to modify their cultures to duplicate that success.

Barney questioned whether culture could be created intentionally by strategists, because if culture could be designed and implemented as a result of managerial intervention, it would not be inimitable (meaning that it could be copied by competitors), and therefore not a source of sustainable advantage. Barney concluded his argument by stating that, while culture was important, it was the beyond the reach of strategists to create because if a superior culture could be engineered, it could be replicated by the firm's competitors. Barney's view offers us added

PRACTITIONER INSIGHT: **JULIE MORET, FRANKLIN TEMPLETON**

> Environmental, social, and governance (ESG) considerations represent a structural shift in asset management industry that is here to stay.
>
> Julie Moret, Head of ESG, Franklin Templeton

4

This practitioner insight demonstrates how the strong corporate values of Franklin Templeton are being translated into a business proposition for the firm to assist their clients in managing environmental, social, and governance (ESG) risks.

Franklin Templeton is a California-based global investment management firm. The company is committed to ESG responsible investing, is a signatory of the Principles for Responsible Investing and several regional stewardship codes, and is an Investor Advisory Group member of SASB (Sustainability Accounting Standards Board).

The company invokes the name and philosophy of Benjamin Franklin, one of the founding fathers of the USA, in the firm's corporate value statements:

> Benjamin Franklin's ideas of frugality and prudence, when it came to saving and investing, inspired the name of our firm back in 1947. His valuable wisdom has continued to shape other aspects of the culture here at Franklin Templeton, including our commitment to Corporate Citizenship.
>
> Often credited with popularizing the saying 'Do well by doing good', Ben Franklin's spirit of civic engagement and citizenship has left a legacy around the world and also has helped shape society's modern notion of Corporate Citizenship.
>
> At Franklin Templeton, we believe that being a good corporate citizen is good business. Strong economies and societies around the world help fuel the growth of our business, while integrity, trust and responsibility are essential to our continued success as a premier global investment management organization.

In the following, Julie Moret, Head of Franklin Templeton ESG, discusses how investors should manage ESG risks and opportunities in practice.

Many of the biggest global challenges are issues such as inequality, climate change, and population growth. We believe that harnessing frameworks like the United Nations Sustainable Development Goals (SDG) can support new investment opportunities.

Over the years, as new information has emerged and evolved, investors have found innovative means to harness new insights to help inform their investment decisions. Today, more forward-looking investors are turning to ESG analysis to provide additional perspectives to complement existing investment research efforts.

ESG analysis traces its roots to the 1960s, when some faith-based organizations adopted ethical screens to identify and exclude companies from their investment portfolios that did not meet their moral values. Typical so-called 'sin' stocks included tobacco and alcohol. As the emergence of heightened social and political awareness grew in the 1970s, the practice of screening extended to encompass conduct, behaviour, and violations of internationally accepted norms and standards. Today, a more nuanced approach has evolved that can incorporate a broad range of techniques from positive screening and/or the use of ESG analysis to manage risks and open new investment opportunities.

At Franklin Templeton we make a clear distinction that ESG is different from ethical investing and doesn't require a trade-off in terms of performance. We define ESG factors as a set of performance indicators that provide a measure of sustainability to assess the future preparedness of issuers managing what are longer-term strategic risks which can reshape competitive advantage. We take an economic-based approach to integrating ESG analysis alongside financial analysis, which is to say we look to assess the impact of ESG factors on an issuer's long-term business model and resilience to adapt to ESG driven changes. By employing an ESG lens investors should look to understand ESG-related business risks and opportunities. ESG-informed investing is compatible with the principles of prudent investing.

As a result of the 2015 United Nations Climate Change Conference in Paris there is likely to be increased focus on finding ways to reduce carbon emissions. Over the long term, this may have implications for businesses using and producing fossil fuels that could find themselves structurally challenged by new rules or targets. Investors employing an ESG lens should examine metrics such as a company or country's carbon emissions, intensity, reserves, or energy mix, and may find themselves better able to identify those that are more flexible and able to adapt. ESG analysis is not just about identifying and measuring risk; there are also investment opportunities. Across the world, some significant demographic trends, such as growing populations, are apparent which put a strain on natural resources including water. Companies that can capitalize on the growing demand for efficient water solutions as well as those that demonstrate sustained growth while reducing water use appear well positioned to adapt their business models to changing ESG issues that can be material for their long-term success.

As the business rationale for ESG crystallizes, we expect that investment managers will increasingly be forced to engage in this space as a matter of fiduciary duty as policy-makers and regulators turn their attention to sustainability. The direction of travel is clear: there is a growing expectation that investment managers and investors should deepen their understanding of the scope and impact these issues pose to long-term operational business resiliencies and new avenues for future growth potential.

Sources

Moret, J. (2019). Understanding the evolution of ESG, *ESGCLARITY*, 5 March. https://esgclarity.com/understanding-the-evolution-of-esg/

Moret, J. (2019). Five key ESG themes for the coming year, *Investment Week*, 5 March. https://www.investmentweek.co.uk/investment-week/analysis/3071834/five-key-esg-themes-for-the-coming-yearfranklintempleton.com

insight to Case Example 4.2 on destructive subcultures that are deemed to coexist with the Goldman Sachs' overarching corporate culture. Surely, a firm with Goldman Sachs's resources could have created a homogenous culture if it were possible?

An organization's ability to create a homogenous culture is questioned by Stanford academic Joanne Martin (2001). Her research challenges the functional perspective held by the strategic culture theorists that a homogenous and widely accepted culture can in fact be designed and implemented by managers. Martin contends that culture is not as uniform as originally thought, but more differentiated and fragmented, and the perception that ideal culture is something that can be shared and managed is not the case in everyday organizational life. In reality, organizations are more differentiated on national, gender, or divisional lines.

Martin's critique of organizational culture leaves a strategist little room for action beyond creating an environment where members of an organization can try to make sense of the challenges and opportunities, given the firm's circumstances, processes, and organization politics that need to be untangled and negotiated. Martin's assertions complicate the life of a strategist by removing the practitioners' ability to manage culture as an organizational function. In particular, this is problematic in instances where the organization is faced with a need for change. The need for change may result from a requirement to stay at the forefront of competitive market developments, or to avoid a significant deterioration in the firm's competitive position, necessitating radical change in order to survive as a going concern. A full discussion of how organizational actors can make sense of and attempt to manage the complex challenges of strategic change is given in Chapter 14.

From a process–practice perspective, it is crucial for those involved in strategizing or implementation activity to develop an understanding of the organization's social, cultural, and historical context. Directing managerial attention towards participation in and learning from tools such as the Cultural Web can generate valuable insights into the organizational setting. Reflecting on realized outcomes from strategizing decisions (as per the strategizing cycle in Chapter 2, Figure 2.5) can also help deepen organizational context knowledge. Better understanding of the organizational context enables effective strategy decisions to be made which align with enabling aspects of organizational culture, exploit historically accrued resources, avoid running against embedded ways of working, and/or challenge 'rigidities' that might threaten organizational survival.

CHAPTER SUMMARY

In this chapter we addressed the following learning outcomes.

- **Identify the importance of organizational purpose, vision, mission, and values in strategy development**

  An organization's purpose is the affirmation of the reason for its existence: for example, what does the organization do, who does it serve, and where does it expect to be in the future? These questions are articulated in forward-looking statements about the organization's activities and are used to give direction to the organization's participants as well as to communicate what the organization stands for to external stakeholders.

- **Evaluate how vision, mission, and values translate to deliverable performance targets and objectives**

  For the organization to realize its vision and mission consistent with corresponding values, the practitioners need to engage with goals, SMART objectives, and initiatives. In order to ensure that the vision and mission are delivered, strategists must track progress using key performance indicators and targets.

- **Critically assess the concepts of shareholder and stakeholder value maximization**

  Commercial enterprises exist to make a profit, but they are also an integral participant in society and global community. Modern business practice has evolved from a narrowly focused shareholder value maximization to wider stakeholder value maximization. Being a good corporate citizen makes good business sense.

- **Examine how a firm can effectively engage with stakeholders who hold conflicting interests**

  All organizations possess stakeholders with conflicting interests. Not all stakeholders have the same degree of power and interest in the organization's activities. Stakeholder mapping is a tool for strategists to group stakeholders based on their relative power and interest and to develop strategies to manage these diverse power and interest groups.

- **Recognize the importance of an organization's history as a creator of path dependence and its role in both formal and informal organization culture**
An organization's values and the ways that the firm operates are to a great extent influenced by its history. History and its cultural heritage can be a source of advantage for the organization because it cannot easily be replicated by competitors. The way the organization operates is said to be path dependent on its history and practices that have evolved and accumulated over time. However, we must remember that while the firm's past may give it a competitive advantage, if the organization is not able to renew itself in an evolving competitive marketplace, it may lose this advantage by attempting to rely solely on its past competencies and activities.

- **Interpret the multifaceted nature of organization culture and its relationship with the firm's competitive advantage**
The organization's culture incorporates both tangible manifestations and intangible tacit elements that make up the overall culture of the organization. Culture can be analysed by tools such as the Cultural Web. It is generally accepted that culture can be an important value-creating strategic asset for the organization. However, there is a debate as to what extent an organization's culture can be designed by strategists and to what extent culture can be considered as a source of the firm's sustainable competitive advantage.

? END OF CHAPTER QUESTIONS

Recall questions

1. List and define an organization's forward-looking statements.
2. What are the elements of a stakeholder map?
3. What is understood by path dependence?
4. Define organizational culture.
5. Identify the components of the Cultural Web model.

Application questions

A) Why do you think organizations should have clearly articulated vision, mission, and value statements?

B) The only responsibility of a firm is to make a profit. Do you agree with this statement? If yes, why? If not, why not?

C) Critically discuss the role of path dependence as a source of sustainable competitive advantage.

D) Critically consider whether organizational culture can be effectively designed and managed.

E) Organizational culture is a source of sustainable competitive advantage. Do you agree with this statement? If yes, why? If not, why not?

ONLINE RESOURCES

www.oup.com/he/mackay1e

FURTHER READING

4

Organizational culture: can it be a source of sustained competitive advantage?, by Jay Barney

Barney, J.B. (1986). Organizational culture: can it be a source of sustained competitive advantage? *Academy of Management Review*, **11**(3), 656–65.

This seminal article explains Barney's argument that if organization culture could be a source of sustainable competitive advantage, it would have to meet the criteria of being valuable, rare, and inimitable.

The social responsibility of business is to create value for stakeholders, by R. Edward Freeman and Heather Elms

Freeman, R.E. and Elms, H. (2018). The social responsibility of business is to create value for stakeholders. *MIT Sloan Management Review*, January. https://sloanreview.mit.edu/article/the-social-responsibility-of-business-is-to-create-value-for-stakeholders/ (accessed 5 May 2019).

This article proposes that the stakeholder approach aims to create a new narrative about business that enables companies to make the lives of communities and people better through the creation of stakeholder value, rather than simply profit to shareholders. The article suggests a recognition that if we want the outcome of business to be a more responsible form of capitalism, stakeholders are required to value business responsibility.

The leader's guide to corporate culture: how to manage the eight critical elements of organizational life, by Boris Groysberg et al.

Groysberg, B., Lee, J., Price, J., and Cheng, J. (2018). The leader's guide to corporate culture: how to manage the eight critical elements of organizational life. *Harvard Business Review*, January–February.

The article argues that when culture is properly managed, it can help strategists to achieve change and build organizations that will thrive in even the most trying times. The authors describe eight distinct culture styles: caring, focused on relationships and mutual trust; purpose, exemplified by idealism and altruism; learning, characterized by exploration, expansiveness, and creativity; enjoyment, expressed through fun and excitement; results, characterized by achievement and winning; authority, defined by strength, decisiveness, and boldness; safety, defined by planning, caution, and preparedness; order, focused on respect, structure, and shared norms.

Managing strategic change—strategy, culture, and action, by Gerry Johnson

Johnson, G. (1992). Managing strategic change—strategy, culture, and action. *Long Range Planning*, **25**(1), 28–36.

This seminal paper develops a number of explanatory frameworks, including the Cultural Web, which address the links between the development of strategy in organizations, dimensions of corporate culture, and managerial action. In considering such linkages, and by illustrating them with examples from work undertaken in companies, the paper also seeks to advance our understanding of the problems and means of managing strategic change.

Why making money is not enough, by Ratan Tata et al.

Tata, R., Hall, S.L., Sharma, A., and Sarkar, C. (2013). Why making money is not enough. *MIT Sloan Management Review*, Summer.

The authors argue that it is possible to build and lead companies that retain a deeper purpose. Ratan Tata, one of the article's authors, writes that Tata Group's founder, Jamsetji N. Tata, believed that acquiring wealth was not the primary purpose of life; he considered that his company's mission was to help the communities in which it operated. Even today, despite the growing wealth of the Tata Group, company leaders are not featured in the listings of the richest people in India or the world. This is because two-thirds of the shares of Tata Sons, the holding company of the Group, belong to the Tata Trusts, one of the largest and oldest Indian philanthropic foundations.

Isolating mechanisms as sustainability factors of resource-based competitive advantage, by Karolina Mazur

Mazur, K. (2013). Isolating mechanisms as sustainability factors of resource-based competitive advantage. *Management*, **17**(2), 31–46.

This paper discusses isolating mechanisms as key factors of resource-based competitive advantage. Strategic resources which fulfil the conditions of being valuable, rare, inimitable, and non-substitutable can generate extraordinary profits for organizations. The possibility of these long-term profits being achieved can be protected by isolating mechanisms. There are different types of these mechanisms, but the most important are causal ambiguity, lead time, path dependency, the role of history, socially complex links, and time compression diseconomies.

REFERENCES

Ackermann, F. and Eden, C. (2011). *Making Strategy: Mapping Out Strategic Success*. London: Sage.

Barney, J.B. (1986). Organizational culture: can it be a source of sustained competitive advantage? *Academy of Management Review*, **11**(3), 656–65.

Birkinshaw, J., Foss, N.J., and Lindenberg, S. (2014). Combining purpose with profits. *MIT Sloan Management Review*, Spring.

Bulkin, B. (2015). *Crash Course: One Year to Become a Great Leader of a Great Company*. London: Whitefox.

Cable, D. and Vermeulen, F. (2018). Making work meaningful: a leader's guide. *McKinsey Quarterly*, October.

Czarniawska, B. (1997). *Narrating the Organization*. Chicago, IL: Chicago University Press.

Deal, T.E. and Kennedy, A.A. (1982). *Corporate Cultures: The Rites and Rituals of Corporate Life*. Reading, MA: Addison-Wesley.

Freeman, R.E. (1984). *Strategic Management: A Stakeholder Approach*. Boston, MA: Pitman,

Friedman, M. (1970). The social responsibility of business is to increase profits. *New York Times Magazine*, 13 September.

Groysberg, B., Lee, J., Price, J., and Cheng, J. (2018). The leader's guide to corporate culture: how to manage the eight critical elements of organizational life. *Harvard Business Review*, January–February.

Hall, R. (1993). A framework linking intangible resources and capabilities to sustainable competitive advantage. *Strategic Management Journal*, **14**(8), 607–18.

Huff, A.S. (1990). *Mapping Strategic Thought*. Chichester: John Wiley.

Jensen, M.C. (2002). Value maximization and the corporate objective function. In: Andriof, J., Waddock S., Rahman, S., and Husted. B. (eds), *Unfolding Stakeholder Thinking: Theory, Responsibility, and Engagement*, pp. 65–84. Sheffield: Greenleaf.

Johnson, G. (1992). Managing strategic change—strategy, culture, and action. *Long Range Planning*, **25**(1), 28–36.

Kaplan, R.S. and Norton, D.P. (1992). The Balanced Scorecard—measures that drive performance. *Harvard Business Review*, **70**, 71–9.

Kenny, G. (2014). Your company's purpose is not its vision, mission, or values. *Harvard Business Review*, September.

Kourdi, J. (2015). *Business Strategy: A Guide to Effective Decision-Making* (3rd edn). London: Economist.

Leonard-Barton, D. (1992). Core capabilities and core rigidities. *Strategic Management Journal*, **13**, 111–26.

Martin, J. (2001). *Organizational Culture: Mapping the Terrain*. London: Sage.

Mendelow, A. (1981). Environmental scanning: the impact of the stakeholder concept. In: ICIS 1981 Proceedings.

Mendelow, A. (1986). In: Proceedings of the Second International Conference on Information Systems, Cambridge, MA.

Palotta, D. (2011). Do you have a mission statement, or are you on a mission? *Harvard Business Review*, January.

Peters, T. and Waterman, R. (1982). *In Search of Excellence: Lessons from America's Best Run Companies*. New York: Harper & Row.

Ramaswamy, V. and Gouillart, F. (2010). Building the co-creative enterprise. *Harvard Business Review*, **88**(10), 100–9.

Schein, E.H. (1997). *Organizational Culture and Leadership* (2nd edn). San Francisco, CA: Jossey Bass.

Schreyogg, G. and Sydow, J. (2010). *The Hidden Dynamics of Path Dependence: Institutions and Organizations*. Basingstoke: Palgrave Macmillan.

Smith, N.C., Ansett, S., and Erez, L. (2011). How Gap Inc. engaged with its stakeholders. *MIT Sloan Management Review*, Summer.

Smith N.C., Ansett S., and Erez L. (2019). How Gap engaged with its stakeholders. In: Lenssen, G. and Smith, N. (eds), *Managing Sustainable Business*. Dordrecht: Springer.

Stout, L. (2012). *The Shareholder Value Myth: How Putting Shareholders First Harms Investors, Corporations, and the Public*. San Francisco, CA: Berrett-Koehler.

Sull, D. and Sull, C. (2018). Research insight: with goals, FAST beats SMART. https://sloanreview.mit.edu/article/with-goals-fast-beats-smart/

Tata, R., Hall, S.L., Sharma, A., and Sarkar, C. (2013). Why making money is not enough. *MIT Sloan Management Review*, Summer.

Teece, D.J., Pisano, G., and Shuen, A. (1997). Dynamic capabilities and strategic management. *Strategic Management Journal*, **18**(7): 509–33.

van der Linden, B. and Freeman, E. (2017). Profit and other values: thick evaluation in decision making. *Business Ethics Quarterly*, **27**(3), 353–79.

Weick, K.E. (2001). *Making Sense of the Organization*. Oxford: Blackwell.

Weick, K.E. (2009). *Making Sense of the Organization*, Vol. 2 *The Impermanent Organization*. Chichester: John Wiley.

CHAPTER FIVE

External Environment

Macro, Industry, and Competitive Settings

CONTENTS

LEARNING OBJECTIVES

By the end of this chapter, you should be able to:

- Explain how the two-way relationship between an organization and the external environment impacts on strategy and competitive advantage through concepts of structure, position, conduct, and performance
- Evaluate the non-market macro-environmental drivers shaping an organization and the ecosystem in which it resides
- Interrogate market structures, dynamics, and trends, explaining the implications for buyers, competitors, and suppliers
- Critically assess the direct competitive context for an organization, identifying the customer value creation and competitive characteristics most likely to enable survival and growth
- Argue the benefits of using combinations of external environmental analysis tools
- Agree a refined set of external environmental analytical outcomes by triangulating findings from across levels of analysis, and testing ideas through scenario thinking

5

TOOLBOX

- **Market-based view**
  A theoretical perspective that helps explain how organizations can gain or sustain competitive advantage based on their position, conduct, and performance within external structures. Also known as the 'outside-in' perspective.
- **Ecosystems view**
  A theoretical perspective that considers organizations as embedded in a complex network of relationships. An ecosystem arises through the activities of all participants, and it may be in an organization's best interests to act in a way that improves the ecosystem.
- **PESTEL**
  A method for analysing the macro-level trends and factors affecting an organization and its broad ecosystem. Helps build understanding of the wide context in which an organization is embedded.
- **Industry analysis**
  A method for analysing the current attractiveness and future potential of the markets in which an organization operates. Examines forces and factors that shape market profitability and sustainability for organizations.

- **Strategic group analysis**
  A method for identifying clusters of competitors in a market that are following broadly similar strategies to serve similar groups of customers. Enables identification of performance criteria that an organization can use to compare themselves with competitors.
- **Competitor profiling**
  A method that guides evaluation of how competitors operate, and how they might act/react to future strategic initiatives by your own organization.
- **Integrative review**
  A method for consolidating and improving initial insights and options generated by external analysis techniques.
- **Scenario thinking**
  Building on external analysis outcomes, a method of exploring the possible future implications for an organization of current trends and trajectories. Helps you think about what strategic initiatives might be needed today in order to be ready for future challenges.

OPENING CASE STUDY **A BUMPY RIDE AHEAD FOR THE AUTOMOTIVE INDUSTRY**

Organizations in the global automotive industry are facing an external environment in flux. New opportunities and threats from the changing industrial landscape are influencing strategic decision-making processes and organizational performance for all involved in the automotive supply chain.

Globalization continues to exert an influence as automotive firms headquartered in emerging economies change their competitive approach. For example, Chinese car manufacturers are increasing exports, offering their own challenger products to luxury imports, while technology firms are collaborating with automotive firms in pioneering new models and features (such as Microsoft's Automotive Cloud in partnership with VW). Their revised conduct is boosting their own performance at the expense of more established automotive firms such as Ford, Toyota, and VW, which rely on China for profitable sales. Further, the dynamics of competition are likely to be altered by an upcoming wave of mergers and acquisitions, as established firms seek to deliver greater efficiencies and grow capacity to respond to shifting consumer tastes on a global scale. As traditional automotive organizations consolidate on a grand scale, the potential for suppliers, consumers, and governments to benefit from the automotive industry will be altered.

The industry is also being shaken by unprecedented disruption in the technological landscape. Firstly, autonomous vehicles—also known as 'self-driving' cars—are nearing commercial launch. This new generation of automotive product promises to improve transport network efficiencies, and create new freedoms for commuters in general, and for young, old, and disabled passengers in particular. Tesla, BMW, Ford, and Volvo have all confirmed plans to sell autonomous vehicles by 2022, with most major firms following suit in the subsequent decade. Autonomous vehicles have also attracted new market entrants. Google and Apple are two notable examples of firms seeking to disrupt the competitive dynamics of the automotive industry through autonomous vehicles. Lacking a legacy car business to protect or defend, their cash-rich status means that they have the power to acquire a medium-scale, or even large-scale, auto manufacturer such as Ford or PSA.

Many hurdles facing the commercialization of autonomous vehicles remain—from clarifying insurance and liability for accidents on an industrial scale, revisiting requirements to hold drivers' licences, and overcoming public health and safety concerns to mapping of requisite government assets such as highways. Technology-based lawsuits are becoming ever more common in the industry, as firms converge on superior designs of both electric and autonomous vehicles. Further, as cars become increasingly technologically enhanced, connected to the internet of things, cybersecurity becomes an increasing risk and liability for automotive manufacturers. However, it seems likely that these challenges will be overcome as firms and governments vie to profit from this new technology.

In addition to the emergence of autonomous vehicles, the rise of electric vehicle technology as a substitute for the internal combustion engine is also shaping the external context. Grants from governments are incentivizing established firms such as VW, BMW, and Renault–Nissan to pursue electric vehicle manufacture (e.g. UK government grants). For example, in Norway, the largest oil and gas exporter in Western Europe, 58% of new cars were electric in March 2019, and only electric vehicles will be on sale from as early as 2025. The Norwegian government is also currently engaged in a massive infrastructure investment to build the charging stations required to sustain electrical vehicle usage, and has legislated to remove vehicle duties, road tolls, and bus lane usage penalties for electric vehicles. Changes in consumer behaviour in China—the largest automotive market—is also driving global adoption of electric vehicles.

At the intersection of electric and autonomous vehicles, Tesla is investing in 'Giga-factories' that change the economics of car production, creating politically popular high-paying jobs and reducing production costs. This new manufacturing approach may disrupt the operational set-up required by large incumbents whilst demanding new competencies in digital innovation, technology platform management, and external collaboration. Further, new entrants, such as those selling equipment to retrofit a vehicle to be self-driving, are appearing at all stages of the supply chain, affecting incumbents beyond the main manufacturers.

As established forces of industrial evolution meet technological disruption, tracking changes in the external environment, and exerting favourable influence wherever possible, has never been more important for strategic managers in the automotive industry.

Questions for discussion

1. What trends seem to be occurring at a global level that will influence the strategy of all firms in the automotive industry in the next five years?
2. What factors within the electric vehicle industry will shape how firms compete as the industry grows?
3. If Google decided to compete directly with Tesla, what main strategic initiatives might they undertake?
4. Imagine you are head of the government department for transport in Norway. What policy would you look to undertake in the next 5–10 years that would influence automotive firms?

Sources

Cheap's no longer chic for China's carmakers. *Bloomberg Businessweek*, 5 December 2016:29.

Wheels in motion, *Economist*, 15 April 2017:61–2.

https://waymo.com/ (accessed 1 May 2019)

Kicking the self-driving tyres. *Bloomberg Businessweek*, 9 January 2017:26–7.

https://www.theguardian.com/technology/2017/jun/13/apple-self-driving-car-technology-tim-cook (accessed 1 May 2019).

https://www.wsj.com/articles/off-the-map-the-rough-road-ahead-for-self-driving-cars-in-china-1499938205 (accessed 1 May 2019).

Fury road. *Bloomberg Businessweek*, 20 March 2017:54–7.

The myth of cyber-security. *Economist*, 8 April 2017:9.

http://www.autoexpress.co.uk/car-tech/85183/driverless-cars-everything-you-need-to-know-about-autonomous-vehicles (accessed 1 May 2019).

https://www.gov.uk/plug-in-car-van-grants/what-youll-get (accessed 1 May 2019).

Norway ditches the 'Fossil Car'. *Bloomberg Businessweek*, 5 June 2017:31–3.

Tesla makes a U-Turn in China. *Fortune*, 15 June 2017:48–55.

Rebuilding the factory. *Fortune*, 1 September 2016:16.

Tunnel vision, *Bloomberg Businessweek*, 20 February 2017:52–5.

Mastering the digital innovation challenge. *MIT Sloan Management Review*, Spring 2017:14–16

Driven in the valley. *Fortune*, 1 October 2016:38–45.

5.1 **Introduction**

5

Individuals and organizations don't exist in a vacuum. They are embedded in relationships, systems, and structures that inform and constrain their activity and which are, in turn, sustained or changed by organizational activity. In this chapter, we examine methods and theories that can be used to build understanding of our external context. We consider how this external context influences and is influenced by our own strategy activities—now and in the future.

We start by unpacking the market-based view (MBV), first introduced in Chapter 1, and an ecosystems perspective. The MBV—also known as the 'outside-in' approach—is a well-known theoretical perspective in strategy literature. An ecosystems perspective is a contemporary view of an external context in which organizations are an active part. Understanding the concepts and arguments of MBV and ecosystems perspectives will give you new ways of thinking about the nature and implications of the external context in which an organization is embedded.

We then introduce a set of methods for enquiring about and analysing the external context. Many methods are available to aid strategic managers' examination of relevant aspects of their external context. Directed at different levels and scales of enquiry, these methods encourage practitioners to organize data about the external environment and draw possible implications for strategy activity. We will first review a range of methods to help you sense changes and trajectories in external context, and to draw insights and implications from any information you discover.

- At a 'macro' level of enquiry, the **PESTEL** framework will be used to identify and analyse the priority factors and trends that affect wide groups of broadly related organizations.
- At a 'market' level of enquiry, an industry forces framework will be used to evaluate the structure, dynamics, and profitability of groups of organizations interacting in the provision and consumption of similar products and services.
- At a 'micro' level of enquiry, competitive analysis methods generate insights about direct competitor activities and specific customer needs facing an organization.

These methods use concepts and frameworks to enable you to gather, organize, and interpret a core set of data about the external context. The use of complementary methods enables you to evaluate and possibly combine data generated by analysis. Where information from different levels of enquiry corresponds to the same external phenomena (Figure 5.1), you can compare insights arising, enhancing your ability to build a rich picture of what is happening in the external context (this approach is referred to as 'triangulation', which we will discuss later in this chapter). For example, macro-analysis might detect a technology trend with the potential to open up a market to new entrants that currently has high barriers to entry. If close competitors are also exploring the use of this new technology, there is a set of deep insights to be derived relating to the technology trend that could influence our strategy activity.

Variations of PESTEL, industry forces, and competitive analysis methods are taught extensively across strategic management programmes around the world. As we address these methods,

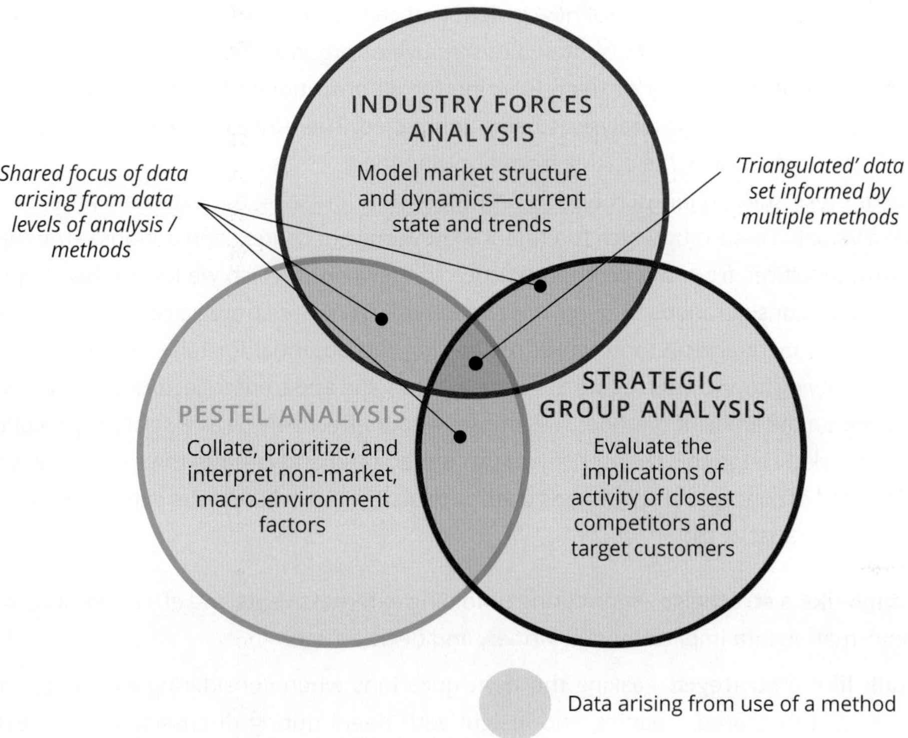

FIGURE 5.1 Complementary methods of analysis.

you will build understanding of terminology, theory, and practices of external environmental analysis that will allow you to engage widely with other strategists.

Building knowledge of how to interpret the external context is useful in strategy practice. A need to examine the external context might be part of formal strategy activity or might arise in an ad hoc way from events encountered during day-to-day operations. Theories and concepts helpfully direct our attention to aspects of our external context that we might not otherwise have considered. As we gather and organize data guided by method frameworks, we may become aware of changing trajectories or new factors in the external environmental context. Through discussion and debate, we can establish possible implications of individual or systemic changes in the external context, maintaining our ability to respond (Morton et al. 2018). It is then up to those involved in strategy to decide whether there is a need to respond to these implications by triggering a strategizing episode. Deciding to take the step from awareness to action will be a matter of judgement based on practitioner wisdom, experience, preferences, and biases. Insights from well-executed external analysis can usefully inform these decisions.

As we proceed through the chapter, it is wise to remember the practical limitations of external enquiry. Each theory and method focuses on a limited aspect of the external context and can only ever provide an approximation of actual events and trajectories. The way in which you choose to interpret concepts and customize analysis methods will shape the external context insights achieved. So too will the accuracy and comprehensiveness of information used to populate frameworks. The degree of initial understanding of practitioners—of the context and methods—influences the degree of new insight that can be achieved through external analysis. The completion of a framework is often a descriptive or organizing activity and won't automatically trigger strategic activity or deep learning for all practitioners. And the external context continually unfolds, even as analysis is being conducted. Therefore it is vital that we are aware of the shelf-life of any insights arising from applying tools.

Despite these shortcomings, the tools and theories addressing the external context can still provide a valuable means by which to 'enhance knowledge of context and options'—the category of strategic practices from the process–practice framework in which we locate this chapter. By keeping these considerations in mind, we can benefit from the strategic conversations and insights enabled by analytical tools whilst minimizing the potential for false certainty and static thinking. Knowing how to interrogate the current 'state' and apparent trajectories of your external context, within the limits of methods, will improve your effectiveness as a strategy practitioner.

As you work through this chapter, if you can understand and critique the market-based view and the range of concepts and methods used to describe and evaluate the external context, you will grow your capacity to:

- **think like a strategist**—monitoring unfolding external events and effectively interpreting information into implications, priorities, and decision acts
- **talk like a strategist**—asking the right questions when considering external data and talking with shared meaning and insight with peers during discussions of the external context
- **act like a strategist**—applying methods, leading others through analysis, recording justified implications, and using insights as an informant of further strategy practices.

Necessarily, this chapter focuses on explaining foundational 'generic' versions of external analysis methods. The knowledge you gain of these methods can usefully be combined, contrasted, and extended with theories and methods from other chapters. The methods and theories of the 'inside-out' resource-based view covered in Chapter 6 make an obvious, strong complement to the 'outside-in' approach detailed in this chapter (see the commentary at the end of Chapter 6 on this matter). Further, the methods and theories of Part 4, addressing topics such as growth potential, internationalization, sustainability, and digitalization, have the potential to create hybrid strategy practices and methods when combined with generic external analysis tools. We encourage you to experiment with this potential to make your own innovative strategic approaches to 'enhancing knowledge of context and options'.

5.2 **Analysing the external context**

What do we mean by the external context?

The external context—or external environment—refers to all aspects of an organization's situation which exist beyond the boundaries of its direct control. For the sake of enabling 'easy' analysis, the external environment is often treated as a separate entity acting on the organization. This understanding of the organization and its environment is referred to as an

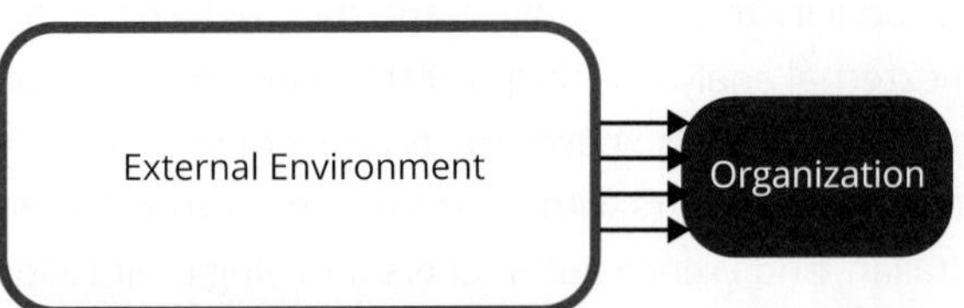

Isolated interpretation—organization separate to environment

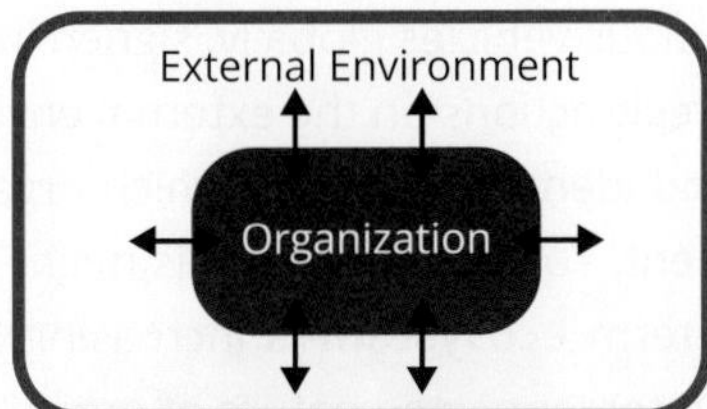

Embedded interpretation—organization as part of environment

FIGURE 5.2 Isolated and embedded interpretations of organization external context.

isolated interpretation in Figure 5.2. This isolated interpretation corresponds to what Kim and Mauborgne (2009) describe as a **structuralist approach** to strategy. In our experience, it is common practice in strategy analysis to conduct external environmental analysis which focuses only on the impact of the external environment on an organization.

An incomplete picture of the opportunities and threats presented by the external environment will emerge from this isolated approach to analysis. As an alternative, the organization can be thought of as a constituent part of its context, embedded in a broader system of external interactions and events. This is illustrated as an **embedded approach** to external analysis in Figure 5.2. Our practical experience of working with organizational strategy suggests that different strategic insights will be developed through analysis depending on how the relationship between an organization and its external environment is interpreted.

It is widely accepted that events occurring in the external environment will constrain and enable strategic options for an organization. However, it can also be argued that the strategic choices enacted by organizations will in turn shape the external environment. For example, as a broad non-market factor the legislative environment acts on individuals and organizations, constraining their activity. However, organizations need not be passive recipients of legislative forces. For instance, in the UK, community groups have successfully lobbied local government to delay or ban shale gas fracking activity in their county (Nyberg et al. 2018). Through individual or collective lobbying activities, an organization can play an active part in shaping the legislative context in which it operates.

An ecosystems perspective of the external context

As described in Chapter 2, process theorists such as Chia and Holt (2009) have long advocated an embedded interpretation of the organization–environment relationship. Further, the rise in popularity of dynamic capability theory (see Chapter 6), and the associated notion that organizations may have a capacity to proactively shape their external context, has challenged structuralist thinking and external analysis. Thus, whilst the external environment provides the context for organizational activity, it is also partly the product of previous organizational activity through relationships with external others within external structures. For instance, the collaborative action of German, Italian, and French automakers lobbying their respective governments has fast-tracked the preparation of autonomous vehicle-friendly domestic legislative environments. In turn, the German, Italian, and French governments led the modification of a 46-year-old UN automotive treaty to support autonomous vehicles globally, signed into law in 2014.

Being able to anticipate the impact of strategic actions on the external environment can help organizational decision-making processes and identify routes by which organizational activity can favourably shape the external environment. To imagine how this might happen, as an expression of an embedded perspective, the term **ecosystem** is increasingly used in strategy theory and practice to draw attention to the interconnected nature of organizational existence.

According to Moore (2006), a business ecosystem refers to intentional communities of economic actors whose individual business activities share in some large measure the fate of the whole community. It is rare now for an organization not to have some sort of collaboration with other organizations. As collaborative relationships multiply, a network of organizations co-creating value emerges, in which structures, relationships, and ways of working co-evolve over time. The external structures and relationships in which an organization is embedded can be described as the organization's **business ecosystem**.

Use of the ecosystems concept has grown and expanded in recent years as a way of imagining the external context of an organization. Indeed, the notion of an ecosystem now challenges the notion of an 'industry' as the most relevant external label for organizational context (Fuller et al. 2019) As shown in Figure 5.3, in a review of the academic literature, Tsujimoto et al. (2018) identified that the notion of an ecosystem might be applied to describe all the actors attached to single industries (such as mass-market electric vehicles), related industries (all types of car manufacturer), or broad ecosystems of 'multi-actor' networks (the business ecosystem plus further actors such as governments, consumers, and universities). We also note that all ecosystems exist within the natural environment.

In this chapter, for a focal organization we will explore how to analyse the industrial and broad ecosystems context (as shown in Figure 5.3) through market-level and macro-level methods respectively. In Chapter 10, we will examine how you can develop business ecosystems to sustain or grow the organization. In Chapter 13, we will reflect on the relationship between an organization and its ecosystems and the natural environment. In Chapter 11, we will explore how platform strategy, leadership, and innovation can be approached as part of organizational strategy.

A market-based view of strategy

A focus on the external context and its importance as a determinant of organizational strategy is often referred to as a market-based view (MBV) of strategy. It is also known as an 'outside-in' perspective on strategy and organizational performance. According to the tenets of the MBV, external environmental structures provide the context for organizational activity in an industry/market. As described in the seminal texts by Michael Porter—*Competitive Strategy* (Porter 1980) and *Competitive Advantage* (Porter 1984)—the choices organizations make for how they position

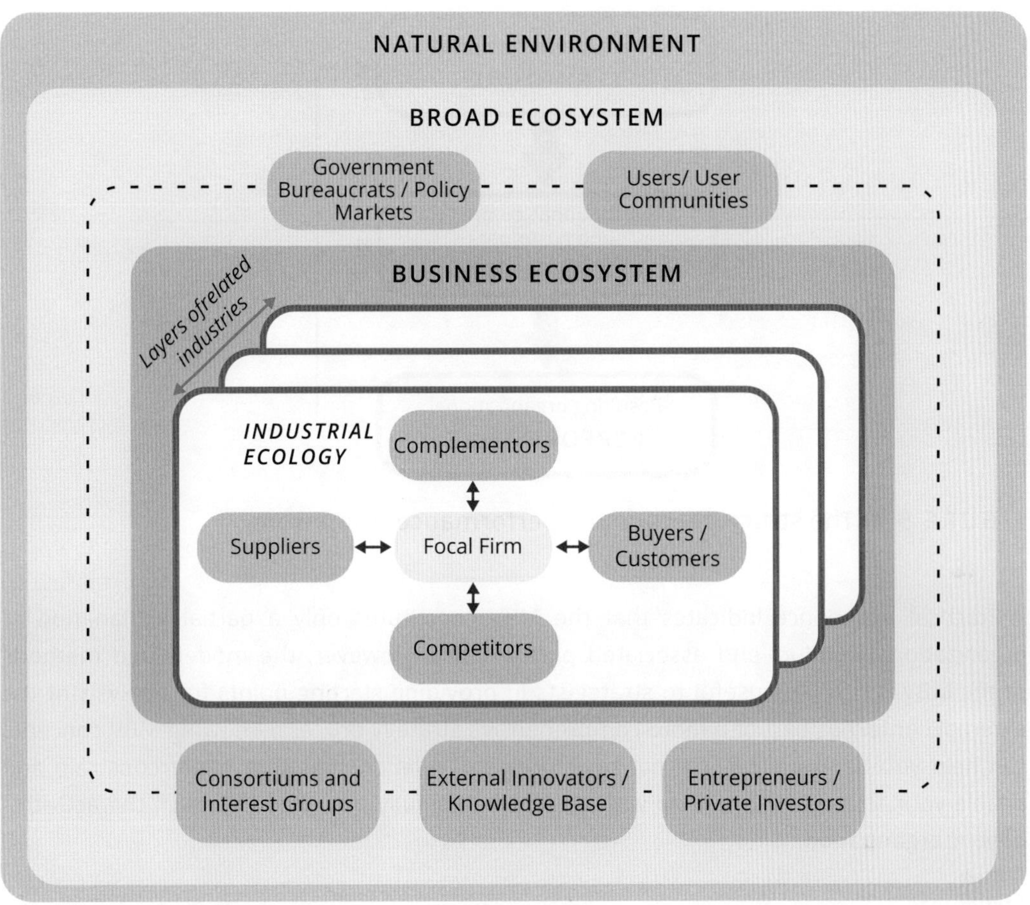

FIGURE 5.3 Ecosystem interpretations of organizational external context. Adapted with permission from Tsujimoto, M. et al. (2018). A review of the ecosystem concept—Towards coherent ecosystem design. *Technological Forecasting and Social Change*, **136**, 49–58. doi:https://doi.org/10.1016/j.techfore.2017.06.032. © 2017 The Authors. Published by Elsevier Inc.

themselves in that market will result in differential performance according to how well their conduct matches the needs of customers relative to the competitive alternatives. This structure–conduct–performance (**SCP**) model is at the heart of MBV thinking (Figure 5.4). In this figure, an embedded interpretation of the SCP framework is represented, showing the feedback effects and two interactions between an organization and the external environment.

The MBV has roots in industrial economics theory which holds that the position an organization adopts in the minds of its customers, relative to its competitors, will be a key determinant of its survival and success in the long run. There are practical limitations to this theorizing as a sole explanation for strategic performance. For example, MBV theorizing assumes that all organizations have equal access to resources and can execute repositioning activities as a matter of strategic choice. Customers are assumed to act in a rational manner, selecting the best positioned organizations to meet their needs based on access to perfect information about the market alternatives. With awareness of the limitations of these underlying assumptions, tools associated with the MBV can form a useful part of a well-balanced portfolio of methods that improve strategy work, without leaving you vulnerable to the limitations of any single theoretical perspective.

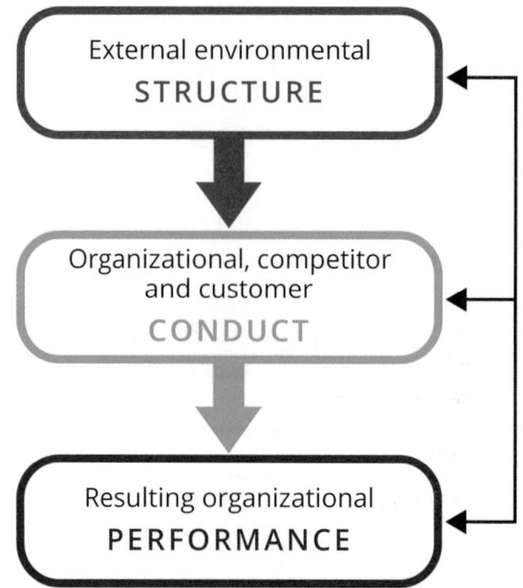

5

FIGURE 5.4 The structure–conduct–performance framework.

Practical experience indicates that the MBV constitutes only a partial explanation of organizational conduct and associated performance. However, the models and methods of the MBV can still be useful to strategists in providing starting points for analysis of the external context as part of a more comprehensive strategy process. Knowing MBV concepts can help you be aware of external structures and relationships that might constrain and enable your strategic choice, and which might be usefully influenced through the activities of your organization.

Structures

The external environment can be understood as a complex arrangement of overlapping structures. Structures refer to the enduring physical, social, and institutional settings in which an organization's activity occurs.

- **Physical environment** The geography, terrain, and place in which the organization is located. The Scotch whisky industry, for instance, is highly impacted by geographical boundaries—producers need to operate within appropriate terrain in Scotland for their output to be considered a Scotch brand (see Chapter 10, Practitioner Insight).
- **Social environment** The stakeholders—employees, communities, suppliers, customers, competitors, etc.—which the organization directly interacts with. For example, Tesla's 'Giga-factory' in Reno required engagement with potential employees, local government, community representatives, and supplier organizations to enable effective and successful development of the facility.
- **Institutional environment** The intra-organizational setting for the organization—government bodies, industry sectors, customer groups, national cultures, etc.—within which the organization is embedded. Emirates Airlines, for instance, has to take action within the rules and legislation of trading blocs such as the EU as well as the Open Skies policy and the laws of the countries in which it operates. It is also required to conform with common technical and operational practices of the global airline industry.

A useful binary distinction you can draw when examining the external context is between market and non-market structures (see also Doh et al. 2012).

- Market structures refer to the arrangement of competitors, suppliers, and customers that are interested in a type of product of service. Market structures have a direct impact on organizational competitive advantage and can be profiled by industry forces and competitive analysis methods as described later in this chapter.
- Non-market structures refer to all other enduring aspects of the external environment—government and non-governmental organizations, local communities, the natural environment, universities, etc.—in which organizational activity takes place. The impact of non-market structures on competitive advantage for an organization can be analysed using PESTEL analysis as detailed later in this chapter.

Structures constitute an organizational landscape which can be mapped through strategic analysis. Harvard professor and ex-McKinsey consultant Pankaj Ghemawat argues for mapping business landscapes—plotting different strategic choices in terms of their potential contribution to economic profitability given structures in the external context (Ghemawat 2017). According to Ghemawat, the aim of strategy is to find 'high points' on this landscape where strategic choices offer high economic returns for an organization, given its context.

Relationships

Focusing on analysing structures or market/non-market factors is a convenient way of dividing up the external context. Equally, paying attention to the connectedness of these structures and factors can yield valuable insights for you. As Mahoney and McGahan (2007:12) suggest, organizations exist 'in a nexus of relationships between governments, individuals, markets, and other social institutions'. By interpreting the nature of relationships between different aspects of the external environment, you can learn about unfolding trends in the external context. For example, for energy companies, understanding of research developments in fracking technology has to be accompanied by awareness of social and governmental attitudes to the environmental impact of such extractive techniques. Without understanding how governments, consumers, and researcher initiatives are developing in combination, a balanced sense of the commercial potential of fracking and related strategic options for action by the firm will not be possible.

Evaluating the implications of how the organization relates to its external environment can build arguments in support of strategic action. In aspects of the external environment which command managerial attention on a frequent basis, such as the direct competitive environment, enhanced understanding of the relationships between competitors and customer groups is vital information. For instance, if an organization learns that, after a series of quality failures, a previously loyal customer no longer trusts a competitor that has been supplying them exclusively, it may represent an opportunity to be pursued. As described in Chapter 7, an organization may map their own external environmental stakeholder relationships by thinking through 'With whom do we interact?' Further, reflecting on 'who is interacting in our external environment, and how might it affect us?' will build up a sense of how the external environmental context will unfold more generally. In both cases, analysis of relationships and interactions through and beyond the boundaries of the organization can yield valuable strategic insights.

CASE EXAMPLE 5.1 COMPETITIVE ADVANTAGE IN WHITE GOODS SUPPLY

5

Headquartered in Turkey, Arçelik is a manufacturer of white goods such as fridges, freezers, ovens, and dishwashers. In 2018 it generated global sales of $7.4 billion with a 12.2% pre-tax profit. Over 68% of this revenue came from sales outside Turkey.

Several factors relating to Arçelik's position in the external environment contributed to its competitive advantage and continuing success. On 31 December 1995, Turkey became part of the EU customs union, allowing Turkish firms to reach nearly 300 million consumers on far more favourable terms of trade. Arçelik responded rapidly to this change in the macro-environmental landscape, and is now established as a leading supplier of budget appliances in Western Europe. This brand has benefited from a move by Western European consumers towards lower-priced domestic goods following the global financial crisis. A visible symbol of its expanded status can be seen as its Beko brand appears as the shirt sleeve sponsor of the world-famous Barcelona football club.

Arçelik has also exploited a global shift in supply chain possibilities, as information technology and trade liberalization has created many opportunities for creating international production operations. To minimize production costs whilst maximizing closeness to consumers, Arçelik now operates 21 factories in eight countries, employing 30,000 staff. Given Turkey's geographic position at the East of Europe and the West of Asia, Arçelik is in a favourable location to manage the flow of goods between a wide range of production facilities and consumer markets.

Arçelik is pursuing long-term expansion in Asia's growing markets. Despite variation in local government, consumer tastes, and competitive landscapes according to country, the white goods industry is consistently in a hyper-competitive state. In response, Arçelik is taking a carefully considered range of strategic actions to target different markets in different ways, according to the needs of each country. It has long operated factories in China and has recently opened a new fridge factory in Thailand. It purchased a domestic white goods manufacturer in Pakistan in 2016, and it is partnering with Tata in India in a $100 million joint venture to sell under a local brand, Voltas, and import goods made in Turkey. In March 2019, Arçelik purchased a majority stake in Singer Bangladesh, the country's largest retailer of consumer durables with 385 stores and 720 wholesale dealers. 'Singer Bangladesh is a strategic fit for us, and this deal is a unique opportunity to invest in Bangladesh, a market which holds great untapped potential', said Hakan Bulgurlu, Arçelik's CEO. These actions are designed to maintain favourable relationships with local governments and suppliers, whilst positioning the firm as a reliable value-for-money brand which profitably meets the needs of consumers in each market it serves.

Arçelik is also preparing to profit from shifts in macro-trends in technology and consumer behaviour. It is investing heavily in technological innovation which might exploit development in sensor technology and the 'internet of things', reportedly developing internet-connected fridges which can detect when food is going off and automatically order replacements.

Questions for discussion

1. Explain how the physical location of Arçelik's headquarters has been of benefit to its recent success.
2. Discuss what seem to be crucial macro-environmental trends that will benefit Arçelik on a continuing basis.
3. If you were the CEO of Arçelik, what sort of external environmental data would be helpful to you as you develop or review your strategy?

Source

This vignette is based on information in 'Cleaning up', *Economist*, 3 June 2017:68, updated with insights from 'Majority stake in Singer Bangladesh for Arçelik', 24 March 2019. https://www.aa.com.tr/en/asia-pacific/turkey-majority-stake-in-singer-bangladesh-for-arcelik/1427587

Competitive advantage from a market-based view

Developing insights into the structures and relationships in the external environment can help strategic managers understand their competitive advantage. According to Peteraf and Barney (2003), competitive advantage describes a firm's potential to best its rivals in any outcome of interest. An organization can be described as having a competitive advantage if it is able to create more value than the marginal (break-even) competitor in a market. For private sector organizations, competitive advantage is typically equated to profit potential. For public- and third-sector organizations, competitive advantage might be gauged by different criteria, such as the ability of the organization to access funding.

A principal aim of strategy is to enable an organization to gain or sustain competitive advantage through the planned allocation of resources and purposeful action. With competitive advantage, a firm will be able to deliver a return for its owners, or a non-private organization will be able to deliver its mandate. From an MBV, competitive advantage arises by adopting a position in external structures from which perceived benefits for customers can be created that they are willing to pay more for than the economic costs of producing those benefits. An MBV thus directs strategists' attention to the dynamics and trajectories of non-market and market structures in which the organization is embedded. Strategic choices can then be made about how to attempt to maintain or adjust an organization's position in the external environment with the intent of enhancing or sustaining competitive advantage.

From an ecosystems perspective, competitive advantage might also arise through playing a pivotal role in a network of organizations, acting as a 'keystone'. Keystone organizations 'provide a stable and predictable set of common assets', such as Alibaba's ecommerce platform (see Chapter 1) or Android by Google, which allows other organizations to build their own offerings (Lansiti and Levien 2004). By enhancing the ecosystem, keystone organizations can enhance their own prospects of survival and success. Thus the focus of organizational strategy broadens to consider how initiatives might develop the whole ecosystem to the benefit of all organizations. For example, should you aim to undertake initiatives that might result in 50% of a market of £10 million, or initiatives that lead to 20% of a market that you've supported growing to £100 million? We will explore keystone advantage as we examine a related concept—platform leadership—in Chapter 11.

Competitive advantage and a market-based view can be applied not just to a whole organization, but also to components of an organization. In Chapter 6 we will review ways in which functions, business units, or teams might strategize. Applying the concept of competitive advantage at a business unit or team level can help you identify how a business unit or team sustains its contribution to the broader organization. Through this approach you will be able to evaluate whether the work carried out by the team or business unit remains more valuable to the organization than alternative internal options (e.g. sister units) or external options (e.g. outsourcing).

5.3 **Developing a core dataset on the external environment**

As noted by Vuorinen et al. (2018), there are hundreds of tools available for conducting strategy environmental analysis. Each examines some aspect of the external context with a different scope and focus of review. Faced with such a dizzying array of options, where should you start trying to build your knowledge of the external context? In this section, we discuss how a set of three methods—PESTEL, industry forces, and competitive analysis—might be used to probe the external context in complementary ways. Consistent with the advice of Hambrick and Fredrickson (2001), each method directs attention to distinct aspects of the external environment and, using a theoretically informed structured approach, develops a set of implications specific to the focal organization under review. As described in Table 5.1, each method is subject to inherent strengths and limitations, of which you should be mindful when undertaking strategic analysis.

When used in combination, these methods generate a foundational set of data about the external environment as a strong starting point for strategy conversations (Kaplan and Norton 2008). In terms of return on effort, this core dataset will suffice for many a strategy team. For others who wish to conduct a nuanced analysis according to the perceived needs of the organization's situation, the core dataset forms a strong platform for that work.

As outlined in Section 5.1, the methods we will review can be described in terms of the level of analysis. In other words, each operates with a different scope when prompting a review of the external context. We will consider each in turn—defining the framework, considering supporting theory, reviewing its application, and highlighting its limitations. We will then review how the insights emerging from each tool can be used in combination to derive a useful external environmental core dataset (as shown in Figure 5.1).

Analysing non-market factors in the macro-environment

PESTEL analysis

PESTEL refers to a method for examining trends in the macro-environment and how they might influence and be influenced by an organization. It brings scrutiny to the non-market structures in which organizational activities occur and in which the organization is embedded. For the strategist, PESTEL is useful as a thought-provoking complement to the implications of market structures uncovered through industrial and competitive analysis.

PESTEL is an acronym for six macro-environmental factors which can be used to organize a description of the broad external context:

Political—the local, national, and supra-regional political trends that shape the operating environment for the organization. This will take into consideration how the political will of powerful individuals, political parties, campaign groups, and local, national, and regional governments might have a direct or indirect impact on the operating environment for the organization. The strategist may wish to consider how they can individually, or collectively with others, find a voice in the political process. For example, President Trump's approach to business and environmental policy marked a change in direction from the Obama administration, altering the landscape of opportunities and threats for those working or trading in the USA in many industries (Wright et al. 2019).

Economic—the health and trends (often cyclical) of economic activity which have an impact on organizational activity. This will address factors such as energy prices, interest rates, foreign exchange, national growth, etc. in the economic settings in which the organization operates. For the strategist, awareness of macro-economic conditions is a key informant of risk management and decision-making in relation to investments and capacity

TABLE 5.1 **Purpose, advantages, and limitations of a range of external analysis tools**

Method	Purpose	Advantages	Limitations
Macro-level PESTEL analysis	Identify the high-level trends in the external context that will impact on the broad ecosystem in which the organization operates Gain insight about how to meet these challenges in the future or attempt to influence the macro-environment	+ Can provide foresight of threats to the organization's relevance/ existence + Helps identify where long-term investment and capability building should be directed + Highlights the possibilities of shaping the ecosystem in a way which is favourable to the organization + Reduces the likelihood of being caught out by blind spots in strategy team thinking	- Significant volumes of data tend to need to be managed and prioritized - Will yield different results according to where the boundaries for analysis are drawn - Reviews external factors in isolation: the macro-environment results from complex combinations of PESTEL factors - Does not review the market specifics of competition for an organization
Market-level industry forces analysis	Evaluate the attractiveness of the markets and industries in which the organization competes Direct energy and effort to markets where there will be maximum potential of returns for the organization	+ Brings order to analysis of the attractiveness of the markets in which the organization is competing + Provides a means of identifying where markets need to be exited in a controlled manner + Identifies actions which might be taken to extend favourable market conditions for an organization	- Implications can be highly sensitive to where market boundaries are drawn - Does not address nuances of how market segments are serviced - Can be misleading at a high level of aggregation and more meaningful focus on individual product or geographic markets is time-consuming for a strategy team
Micro-level competitive analysis	Focus on developing deep insights about the activities of direct competitors, and what is valued by target customers Assess the likelihood of the organization being able to compete effectively in this context	+ Generates strategic insights of high relevance to 'daily' operations + Focuses on customer value creation, bringing attention to competitive advantage + Brings rigour and structure to analysis of direct competition, controlling for 'commonly held beliefs' about factors for competitive success in the strategy process	- Only focuses on market-segment-related insights - Does not factor in trends and future trajectories well - Requires high levels of discipline in execution, as it addresses factors which many in the organization believe they know much about already - May uncover politically sensitive insights about the realities of how well the organization is able to compete

management. For instance, the economics of the global airline industry, and the viability of many firms competing in the industry, are affected by the impact of oil price fluctuations. As a consequence, many airlines engage in a financial risk management activity called hedging when purchasing fuel.

Social—trends in attitudes and demographics within society at large which shape the products, services, and way of operating of the organization. Reviewing macro-social conditions will consider how customer demands and needs are evolving in the long term and how employee expectations and availability are shifting. For the strategist, this factor raises questions about capabilities and capacities that need to be invested in now in order to be able to meet future customer demands in a sustainable way. For example, shifting consumer attitudes towards data, technology, mobile devices, and openness of information has created whole new markets and industries based on social media platforms.

Technological—developments in product, process, and service-enabling technologies, and the associated possibilities and impacts on the value the organization creates and how it operates. This will consider how technological developments in all walks of life and locations might cross over to the domain of the organization. Trends in investment, research, and development activities through the knowledge base (universities, institutes, colleges, etc.), other industries, and in different geographies are all reviewed here. For the strategist, this can be an unsettling piece of analysis to conduct as the potential implications of technological progress are digested (from a game-changing opportunity, which to be seized requires organizational transformation, to possible extinction events for the current organizational set-up). As illustrated in the opening case study, macro-level technological trends in autonomous vehicles and electric power technology are likely to transform the automotive industry, and transportation more generally, in the decades to come.

Environmental—a macro-review of how the changing state of the natural environment will affect the activities of all within an organization's ecosystem. Broadly, this will address the implications of climate change on the natural environment and acceptable organizational practices, regulation of environmental impact (e.g. waste, emissions, carbon footprint), and incentives and opportunities for progressive environmental practices. The environmental angle has a clear cross-over with all other PESTEL categories, but is worth isolating as a recurring influential macro-factor that will shape the future operating context for industries. For the strategist, this factor draws attention to an organization's sustainability agenda, and how that might permeate strategy. Increasingly, organizational opportunity and competitive advantage appear to be available for those willing to go 'beyond compliance' in sustainability practice, argues the Scottish Environment Protection Agency.

Legislative—direction of travel and scheduled developments in the laws, legislation, and regulation affecting all stakeholders in the localities in which an organization operates. By considering the current, and likely future, formal parameters within which an organization operates, decisions can be made about how to optimally organize activity, and how to reconfigure products/services to exploit opportunity and avoid the costs of non-compliance presented by the legislative context. For example, changes in minimum wage legislation can impact on the scope of services which can be offered by charitable organizations, as funding sources fail to keep pace with statutory obligations.

PESTEL is widely used as a basis for macro-environmental analysis. Variations of the acronym exist—such as STEP, STEEP, STEEPL—reflecting different interpretations of the scope of each of the underlying categories (e.g. some integrate the legislative category into the Political category). Provided that due consideration is given to all relevant aspects of the macro-environmental context, the specific variation of PESTEL used is arbitrary.

How to apply PESTEL

This section explains how PESTEL can be used to conduct macro-environmental analysis with maximum return on effort. It is important to remember that a perfect model of the external environment is not a feasible outcome. Instead, this analysis can be used to uncover trends in the broad ecosystem which might require a strategic response by the organization. The descriptions in this section, and the full worked example of a PESTEL analysis in Figure 5.5, reflect the most efficient and effective applications of PESTEL we have encountered in our consultancy experience.

Step 1. Agree the operating principles for the boundaries of PESTEL factors

Whilst PESTEL is intended to help you think about the broad ecosystem in which your organization exists, it is also important to define limits on the scope of that analysis. Where the line is drawn for inclusion in PESTEL analysis will influence the effort involved in conducting research. For example, imagine you are examining trends in the macro-environment for an Indian airline serving only the domestic market. Do you run PESTEL analysis for the airline industry for India, Asia, or the world?

We advise that the boundary for each PESTEL factor is set according to organizational relevance. This matter of judgement may lead to different outcomes for each factor by each team conducting strategy. The key question for you to ask is 'What macro-environmental trends might impact on us in the future?' In the case of the Indian airline, global trends in aircraft technology might have to be considered, as the diffusion of any new technology in the future will likely make it relevant to the organization. In terms of macro-social trends, however, limiting that analysis to India makes more sense given the domestic focus of the airline.

Step 2. Create a research plan to investigate the PESTEL factors

To keep the PESTEL exercise manageable, it is useful to create an initial research plan. This starts with identifying the sources and resources which might be reviewed about macro-trends, applying the 'relevance' principle from Step 1 to set appropriate limits. Possible sources include, but are not limited to, the publications of government bodies and trade associations, industry and academic journals, third-sector and non-governmental organizations, business press, and the mainstream media, most of which is available through the internet or by direct approach. Further specialist research may be available at a price, or through libraries.

Step 3. Populate a table with descriptions of relevant factors from the external analysis

Create a table as shown in Figure 5.5 in which you compile the findings of your PESTEL research. It is advised that the descriptions are kept brief with supporting information and sources reserved for a separate document. Where there are options for categories into which to allocate an identified trend, select the most appropriate fit. However, do not duplicate the entry across more than one category. Provided that the point is captured once within the table, the framework has served its purpose.

(A) PREPARE TEMPLATE

Create a blank table ready for population with descriptive data.

Note, only 2 descriptions have been included in this example. This is only for the sake of space. Include as many entries as seem relevant in practice.

Factor	Description	Priority
Political		
Economic		
Social		
Technological		
Environmental		
Legislative		

(B) ADD DESCRIPTIONS

Based on research of the macro-environmental context, add in descriptions of trends and influences that may affect the organization.

Keep these description in a summary format for usability, citing headline facts and figures but reserving details for a separate explanatory document.

Factor	Descriptions	Priority
Political	Favourable policies in USA and European nations for domestic players	
	Political intervention in trading bloc terms likely as a consequence of Brexit	
Economic	Over-capacity in industry (25–30%)	
	Emergence of 'middle class' in many developing economies main growth area	
Social	Strong global demand for 'luxury' brands	
	Gen Y pushing demand for sustainable products	
Technological	Emergence of hybrid & electrical technologies	
	Autonomous vehicles nearing commercialisation	
Environmental	Air pollution/emissions control part of public debate globally	
	Carbon footprint of production under scrutiny	
Legislative	European legislation governing emissions regulation tightening	
	Global legislation imminent on recyclability of material usage	

(C) PRIORITIZE DESCRIPTIONS

Informed by the research activity, debate the relative priority of all descriptive entries in the table. This prioritization will be specific to the strategy team's organization.

A visual indicator is used in this example – the more the quadrants are filled in, the higher the priority. Numbers, letters or a simple priority/not priority categorisation would also work.

Factor	Descriptions	Priority
Political	Favourable policies in USA and European nations for domestic players	
	Political intervention in trading bloc terms likely as a consequence of Brexit	
Economic	Over-capacity in industry (25–30%)	
	Emergence of 'middle class' in many developing economies main growth area	
Social	Strong global demand for 'luxury' brands	
	Gen Y pushing demand for sustainable products	
Technological	Emergence of hybrid & electrical technologies	
	Autonomous vehicles nearing commercialisation	
Environmental	Air pollution/emissions control part of public debate globally	
	Carbon footprint of production under scrutiny	
Legislative	European legislation governing emissions regulation tightening	
	Global legislation imminent on recyclability of material usage	

FIGURE 5.5 Completion of PESTEL for a global automotive firm.

Factor	Descriptions	Priority
Political	Favourable policies in USA and European nations for domestic players	
	Political intervention in trading bloc terms likely as a consequence of Brexit	
Economic	Over-capacity in industry (25–30%)	
	Emergence of 'middle class' in many developing economies main growth area	
Social	Strong global demand for 'luxury' brands	
	Gen Y pushing demand for sustainable products	
Technological	Emergence of hybrid & electrical technologies	
	Autonomous vehicles nearing commercialisation	
Environmental	Air pollution/emissions control part of public debate globally	
	Carbon footprint of production under scrutiny	
Legislative	European legislation governing emissions regulation tightening	
	Global legislation imminent on recyclability of material usage	

(D) DECIDE CUT-OFF

As a team, debate where to draw the line in evaluating strategic implications of priorities.

In this case, the top 5 factors are selected as the topics for developing implications and action options.

Implications	Options for Action
Over-capacity means that consolidation is highly likely – a wave of mergers and acquisitions are imminent which the org must prepare to defend or exploit	
If growth is going to come from the middle classes in developing economies, essential to maintain a strong presence in these markets	
Major technological disruption from autonomous vehicles and electrical power technology demand an investment in competences required to deal with the new landscape	
New EU laws on tighter emission control will have to be prepared for, affecting all players in the European market	

(E) DEVELOP IMPLICATIONS

Discussing the identified priorities in combination, identify implications for the future of the organization.

Where appropriate combine factors together in drawing implications. In this example, the technological disruption from two priority factors is addressed through a single implication

Implications	Options for Action
Over-capacity means that consolidation is highly likely – a wave of mergers and acquisitions are imminent which the org must prepare to defend or exploit	Arrange and manage financial position to fend off takeovers
	Commission scanning of market for merger & acquisition targets
If growth is going to come from the middle classes in developing economies, essential to maintain a strong presence in these markets	Explore joint venture options in top 10 growing emerging markets
	Invest in marketing intelligence for all emerging markets
Major technological disruption from autonomous vehicles and electrical power technology demand an investment in competences required to deal with the new landscape	Prioritise investment in electric vehicle R&D activity
	Source tech partner firms for AV technology
New EU laws on tighter emission control will have to be prepared for, affecting all players in the European market	Lobby for long timescales to meet new emissions standards
	Increase staffing in emissions compliance function

(F) OPTIONS FOR ACTION

For each of the implications, develop potential organizational responses under the heading "options for action".

These options are not a commitment to follow through. Instead, they will be fed into the strategy process as options for action for consideration, supported by macro-environmental analysis.

FIGURE 5.5 *Continued*

Step 4. Prioritize the macro-trends identified based on potential future impact

PESTEL analysis will generate a multitude of possible macro-environmental influences on the organization. Not all of these will be of equal relevance or importance to the future of the organization. Prioritizing identified trends is an important act in converting PESTEL research into a useful strategy outcome.

Through debate and discussion with those you are working with, use your judgement to allocate a priority status to each of the macro-factors identified. This should result in a simple priority/non-priority label for each factor, and a shared understanding of the supporting rationale. In the table, capture the prioritization outcomes for each of the identified trends. Prioritized trends might be highlighted in bold and/or ranking scoring displayed if appropriate. We have also seen teams use visual indicators to good effect in this task. We offer an option in the applied PESTEL example for a global original equipment manufacturer (OEM) in the automotive industry (Figure 5.5). These prioritized trends are sometimes referred to as key drivers—specific non-market factors which are believed to have most influence on the organization's future performance.

Step 5. Develop organizational implications for priority trends

In keeping with the aims of this type of strategy practice, build your knowledge of the external context by discussing the possible organizational implications of the priority factors. To do so you should debate the question 'If this trend continues as anticipated, what does it imply for our organization in the short, medium, and long term?' A priority trend may have several implications, and each implication may be supported by more than one priority trend. You might find that the organizational implications are supported by multiple PESTEL factors. This is normal and highlights that the macro-context is only divided into separate categories for our convenience when conducting analysis. We find it helpful to create a separate table of implications at this point, as shown in illustration E in Figure 5.5.

Step 6. Identify options for action in response to organizational implications

If you decide that the implications might require an organizational response, the final step in PESTEL analysis is to identify options for strategic initiatives/action. Listing such options is not a commitment to follow through with action. Rather, this step creates a useful input to strategic decision-making which reflects macro-environmental trends and considerations. For example, imagine you have identified an implication of macro-trends that 'our current products are likely to become obsolete within three years'. Your corresponding options for strategic action could be 'Exit the product market within the next year', 'Invest in R&D towards creating a new generation of products', and 'Lobby for tighter regulation on emergent technology'.

Options for action might focus on how to maintain or enhance competitive advantage or keystone advantage through intelligent responses to macro-trends. Options for action might address how to attempt to shape macro-trends, as well as how to react to the consequences of changes in the broad ecosystem. Identifying options for action helps you to avoid feeling powerless when faced with the implications of external environmental forces. Concluding your PESTEL analysis with a set of options for action keeps a focus on activity and creates a 'common currency' that can be built on by other methods of analysis.

Analysing market structure and dynamics

In this section, we review a method for examining the structure and dynamics of the markets in which an organization offers its products or services. A market is defined as the individuals, organizations, and activities involved in the provision or consumption of a product or service within a defined geography. An industry can be defined as related markets which can be grouped together according to either similarity in products (e.g. the mobile computing industry) and/or geographies (e.g. Australian industry). Industry forces analysis provides a means of examining the organizational implications of how a market is structured and interacts now and in the future. Whilst this analysis can be applied to a whole industry, we will examine how it can be applied to a specific geographic or product market.

Markets can and do vary significantly in size and characteristics. Organizations may also seek to compete across a range of product or geographical markets, each with its own distinctive characteristics. Within a market, there may be many ways in which organizations seek to compete and operate. Industry forces analysis helps the strategist decide if the organization should continue to operate in a market and, if so, what actions might usefully shape the configuration of the market structure to the organization's advantage. Industry forces analysis should not be confused with competitive analysis (addressed in the next section on 'micro-level' analysis).

A foundation in the 'Five Forces'

Michael Porter's framework—the 'Five Forces' (depicted in Figure 5.6)—is reported by Grundy (2006) as the most commonly used analytical framework in market-based strategic analysis (see the latest reprint of his highly influential *Harvard Business Review* article—Porter (2008)). Although it has been subject to extensive critique, it is a mainstay of strategy theory and practice.

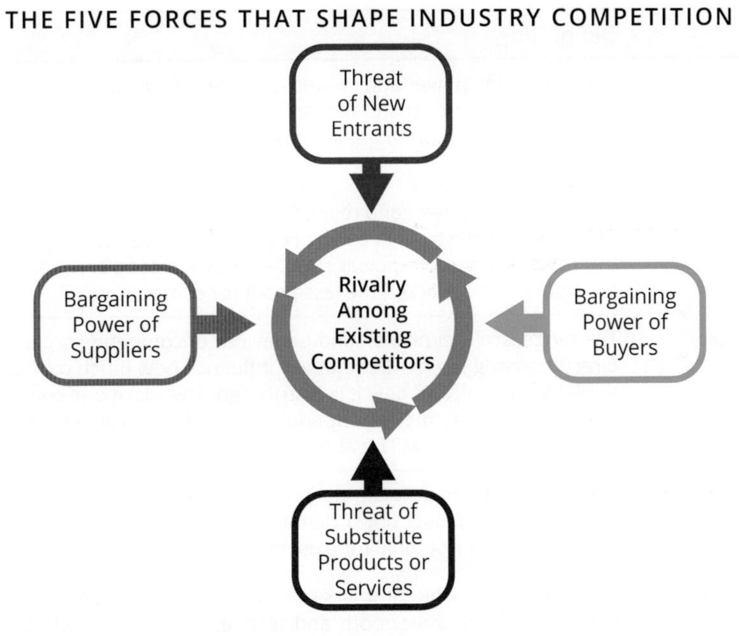

THE FIVE FORCES THAT SHAPE INDUSTRY COMPETITION

Threat of New Entrants

Bargaining Power of Suppliers

Rivalry Among Existing Competitors

Bargaining Power of Buyers

Threat of Substitute Products or Services

FIGURE 5.6 The Five Forces (5F) framework. Source: Porter, M.E. (2008). The five competitive forces that shape competitive strategy. *Harvard Business Review* (January), 25–41. By permission of Harvard Business Publishing.

In defining what we mean by industry forces, we aim to build on the thinking of the **Five Forces**, addressing the limitations of Porter's model by adding further components.

The Five Forces framework is intended to describe and analyse the effect of market structure on profitability, and therefore attractiveness, for organizations. It is not merely about defining a market as attractive or not, but rather modelling the structure and dynamics of the market so that you can better understand options for remaining and influencing in a market, or exiting it at the appropriate time. As Brandenburger (2002) describes it, if the amount of possible profit in a market is a 'pie', Five Forces helps us to understand how big the pie is and how it will be divided up. The model prompts you to identify how the relationship between buyers, suppliers and customers, potential new market entrants, and substitute offerings shapes the profitability, and appropriation of profit, in a market. The meaning of each of these forces is described in Table 5.2.

5

The profit potential for competitors in the market will be determined by the extent to which bargaining power exists over buyers and suppliers. For example, if an organization is the only provider of a vital service in a particular market, it has very high bargaining power over its buyers (a monopoly situation). Therefore it can set a price which contains a high profit margin as the customer doesn't have any further options—pay the price or don't get the service. This also applies in reverse for an organization in relation to its own suppliers. If an organization is the only buyer of a product or service from multiple sellers, it will have high bargaining power (a monopsony situation). It can then offer to pay a price that is close to cost for the supplier. Most organizations will face a situation where they are neither facing nor holding monopoly or monopsony levels of bargaining power in their relationships with buyers and suppliers. Understanding the extent of bargaining power with buyers and suppliers can generate valuable insights about the potential for competitive advantage in a market.

TABLE 5.2 **Description of each of the Five Forces**

Force	Definition
Buyer power	The bargaining power and related attitudes of customers which will determine the price customers are willing to pay for the goods/services in this market. The more bargaining power customers have, the less profit for competitors.
Supplier power	The bargaining power and related attitudes of suppliers which will determine the extent to which profit can be retained by those offering goods/services in this market. The more power suppliers have to control supply and set prices for inputs to the market, the less profit for competitors.
Competitive rivalry	The range, scale, similarity, and behaviour of competing organizations directly serving the market that will influence how much profitability is available in total, and how it is distributed. The more one competitor has power over rivals (through superior competitive advantage), the more of the available profit they will be able to appropriate.
Threat of new entrants	The likelihood that new competitors will enter an industry, bringing with them capacity to meet buyer demands and a desire to compete in a way that will erode profit potential for existing competitors.
Threat of substitutes	The extent to which customers may be tempted to abandon this market in favour of alternative goods and services providing comparable utility by different means. If viable substitutes are available, the price competitors can charge in this market will be limited.

A relevant further force to consider in understanding market attractiveness is the extent of direct competition. The more competition in a sector, the greater the likelihood that profit potential will be reduced for an organization. Many organizations competing in a market does not mean that every competitor cannot be profitable (i.e. all organizations can hold some sort of competitive advantage in a market). For instance, competitors operating in a growing market where demand outstrips supply might all be profitable. From an ecosystems perspective, there is a logic to collaborating with competitors to grow the overall market to the benefit of all. However, where there is intense competition, overall profit which might be created in a market will be divided amongst more players, and competitor activity can influence the behaviour of buyers and suppliers through negotiation, advertising, collaboration, etc., altering the balance of bargaining power for an organization with its buyers and suppliers. Therefore profiling the competitive forces in a market—intensity and interactions with buyers and suppliers—provides relevant insights for an organization about the attractiveness of the market to the organization.

There are two further factors advocated in Michael Porter's framework which influence the buyer–supplier–competitor forces. Barriers to entry is an assessment of the extent to which it is feasible for new competitors to join the market. If a market is observed to have high profitability, as evidenced by the success of current competitors, others will be attracted to enter that market if it is more profitable than their current situation. If there are high barriers to entry, the effort required to enter the market is prohibitive for many organizations. High barriers to entry will protect the profitability of the industry for current incumbents. Low barriers to entry will lead to a quick erosion of the profit for current players as new entrants increase the level of competition. Profiling this force can be useful for you in building understanding of how competition and bargaining power aspects of the market may change in the future.

Availability of substitutes is the final force suggested by Porter. The concept of a substitute refers to the availability of alternative markets through which customers can achieve sufficiently similar outcomes to the focus market. For example, bicycle hire is a substitute market to the car hire industry. They both provide similar utility of being able to lease a mechanism for moving from A to B. However, the technology involved, the cost base, and the supply chain differ substantially between the two markets, and the customer realizes the utility of the offerings by distinctive means. Thus, whilst these markets have some commonalities, the organizations operating in them are substitutes rather than direct competitors.

Understanding the extent to which substitutes might be attractive to a customer base will provide insights about the profitability potential of a market. The more attractive available substitutes are, the less able prices are to rise in a market without driving current customers to that substitute. In our experience, it is normal for the concept of substitutes to be misapplied in practice. The common mistake is to evaluate substitutes as only marginally different direct competitors. For example, it would be an error to consider Facebook search and Google search as substitutes, rather than competing organizations. It may be true their main product or service—the offering that made them famous—is in different markets. But in the market being evaluated (online search) they are in direct competition through similar technological means. A substitute for this market would be encyclopaedias; the availability of which is unlikely to have any impact on the structure or interactions of the online search market. Note that the reverse argument does not apply, as the rise of the online search market as a substitute for encyclopaedias has significantly altered the attractiveness of that market.

Limitations of Five Forces analysis

According to Michael Porter, when interviewed by Argyres and McGahan (2002), the original Five Forces model was intended to be a specific aid to decision-making. However, it has been critiqued extensively, particularly for being treated as a holistic tool of strategic evaluation, perhaps more so than any other strategic management framework (cf. Grundy 2006). Identified limitations of Five Forces include the following.

- **Five Forces is too static** By taking only a snapshot of the current situation, Five Forces doesn't capture the trajectory of the market. On the basis that the structures, relationships, and activities within a market may change over time, Five Forces might generate analytical insights with a very short shelf-life. This challenge can be mitigated by tracing historical paths and analysing trends in industry forces. Further, reflecting on the market life cycle and any enduring structural characteristics of the market can improve the strategist's understanding of market attractiveness and appropriate options for strategic action.
- **Five Forces insights are highly dependent on where the market boundaries are drawn** How the market boundaries are defined within an industry can have a huge bearing on the analytical outcomes from Five Forces. Considerations of the application of Five Forces to the luxury car market, or the second-hand car market, or the second-hand luxury car market will all yield different outcomes. And where should geographical boundaries be drawn to deliver the most useful outcomes for those making strategic decisions? To address this limitation, it may be necessary to create multiple models of industry forces for a focal market, re-running analysis with narrower and broader market boundaries.
- **Five Forces doesn't represent all the factors that impact on market profitability** A recurring point of critique is that Five Forces rarely tells the whole picture of market profitability. Non-market factors such as government interests or labour union activity can impact on the structure and attractiveness of a market—these are not represented in the Five Forces. This observation partly explains the value of undertaking strategic analysis using complementary methods. By combining the outcomes of industry forces analysis with macro- and micro-level analytical outcomes, a more comprehensive picture of the external environment facing the organization can be established.
- **Five Forces ignores the effects of non-competitive products and services that influence profitability** Five Forces analysis focuses attention on the direct supplier, buyer, and competitor relationships in a specific market. However, just as individuals and organizations don't exist within a vacuum, nor does a market exist in isolation. Brandenburger and Nalebuff (1996) observe that non-competitive, non-substitutable products and services from alternative markets can have a significant influence on the profitability and attractiveness of an industry. For example, the development of a vehicle charging infrastructure market will impact the profitability and dynamics of the Norwegian electric vehicle (EV) market. These complementary effects are not addressed in the Five Forces framework.
- **Five Forces doesn't take into consideration of the potential importance of networks on market attractiveness** The dynamics and structure of a market may be influenced by what are known as network effects. This refers to how the customer value of a product or service is dependent on the size and availability of a relevant network. For example, if the purpose of

a telephone is to enable remote conversation, the usefulness of a telephone to a customer (and the price they are willing to pay for it) will depend on how many of the customer's contacts also have telephones which are networked together. The more relevant contacts that are connected to that network, the more valuable the telephone is to the customer.

An industry forces analysis framework

To conduct valuable analysis of the market-level context, we advocate that you draw an industry forces framework as illustrated in Figure 5.7. This framework incorporates the Five Forces as identified by Porter. It also challenges the management team to consider further factors which mitigate the limitations of Five Forces and incorporate industrial ecology thinking (Figure 5.3). Porter (2008:86) identifies many of these additional factors, pointing out that they are not forces that determine a market's structure, but rather factors that influence the Five Forces. In practice, for a strategy team seeking to conduct market-level analysis, it is less important whether a consideration is labelled a force or a factor, and more important that organizational implications of a matter of relevance is addressed.

Influence of complementarities

Complementarities are offerings from a separate market—providing a different utility to customers—which will influence the dynamics of the focus market. For example, video games producers are complementors to console hardware manufacturers. They are not in active competition, nor are they substitutes, and they are not buyers or suppliers to console manufacturers. However, the activities of video games manufacturers will be highly influential on the structure and attractiveness of the console hardware market. Without a library of available games or a pipeline of game development activity, a console is unlikely to attract much customer interest. Equally, the development of the console hardware market influences the structure and interactions of the video games market. Many commentators describe complementarities as the sixth force, such is their potential relevance to insightful market-level analysis.

Influence of industry life cycle

It can be useful to consider the historical development of a market when seeking to profile industry forces (Lei and Slocum 2005). Figure 5.8 depicts a typical life cycle curve for a market. As the market emerges, competition is between a limited number of innovative competitors for early adopting customers. As the interested customer base grows over time, revenues rise and potentially more competition is attracted into the market. Eventually a stage of maturity is reached where revenues level out, before the market goes into decline as the customer base moves on to alternative products and interests.

Considering the position of a market on this life cycle curve can provide a useful input to industrial forces analysis and strategic decision-making. For example, imagine an organization innovating in two new markets A and B, both in the emergence phase. Reflecting on the 'barriers to new entry' force, how easy is it for new competitors to enter the market? Market A appears to have higher growth potential but lower barriers to entry than market B. The organization may choose to pursue market B as it is recognized that many competitors will probably join market A as it enters the growth phase, whereas competition will be more limited in market B, offering

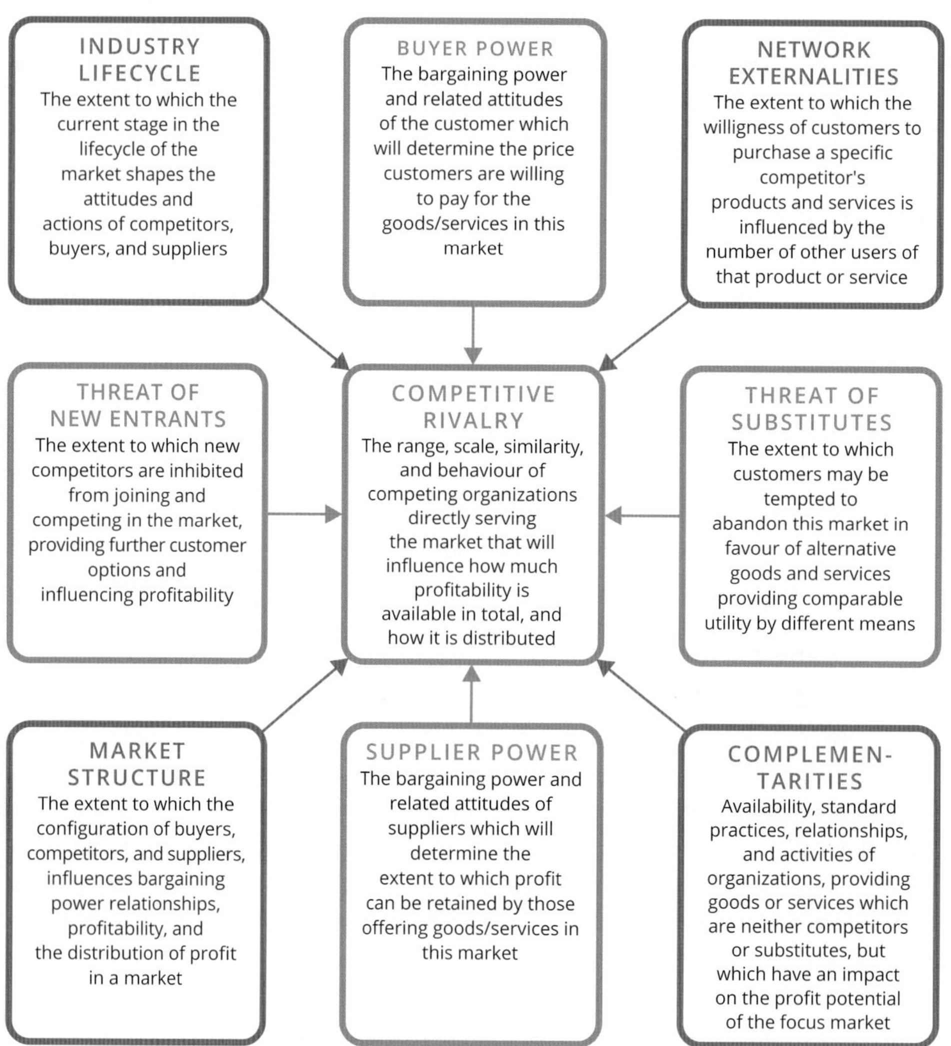

FIGURE 5.7 Industry forces framework.

a greater return on organizational effort. Alternatively, if market B had been in decline rather than emergence, the organization would choose to prioritize market A instead.

Table 5.3 shows relevant questions about and implications of industry life cycle positioning that the strategist may wish to consider when undertaking industry forces analysis.

Influence of market configuration

Within industry forces analysis, the configuration of competitors, buyers, and suppliers—the market structure—can be useful to focus on during strategic conversations. The nature of the market structure—as illustrated in Figure 5.9, can be a major influence on the perceived attractiveness for strategic decision-makers. In a market where an organization is a monopoly

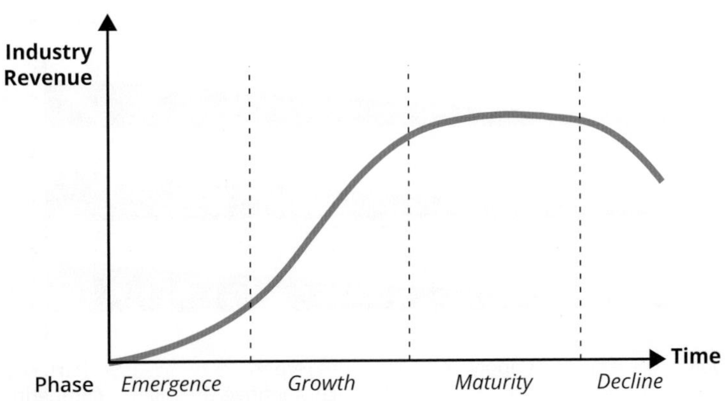

FIGURE 5.8 Industry life cycle curve.

TABLE 5.3 **Interpreting industry life cycle**

Life cycle stage	Potential implications for competing organizations	Questions to consider
Emergence	It is unlikely that any one standard or competitor will dominate. Likely scope for experimentation, innovation, and shaping market characteristics.	How can we innovate in a way that shapes this market in our favour? Does this market have potential to develop and grow?
Growth	Scalability of offering and operations is required to keep pace and maintain or grow market share in this phase. New entrants may be attracted if profit potential is high. Network externalities may start to show here if there are buyer and supplier benefits from focusing on a single-platform/standard offering.	How can we take actions to increase our capture of market share? What can we do to advantageously grow the total market size? Can we do anything (on our own, or collaborating with competitors) to deter new competitors from entering the market? Are any network externalities developing? What can we do to become the preferred option for buyers?
Maturity	Growth levels off and competition becomes more intense. Likely that industry will not attract many more entrants at this point. Those with high market share and effective operations will likely seek to remain; other organizations may start seeking alternative uses of resources.	How well do we stack up against the competition? Are we making enough profit to justify staying in this market, or should we seek new sources of growth? Can we reduce our costs to improve our profitability, even if total market profit isn't increasing?
Decline	Organizations start to leave the market as reducing volume impacts the attractiveness of the market as a focus of organizational resources. However, profit potential may be sustained for organizations that remain, provided that a sufficient number of competitors leave.	Should we exit this market? If we are remaining, how can we capture the market share of exiting firms? How should we review our prices in this declining market? What is the remaining lifespan of the market, and how should we plan our time in it?

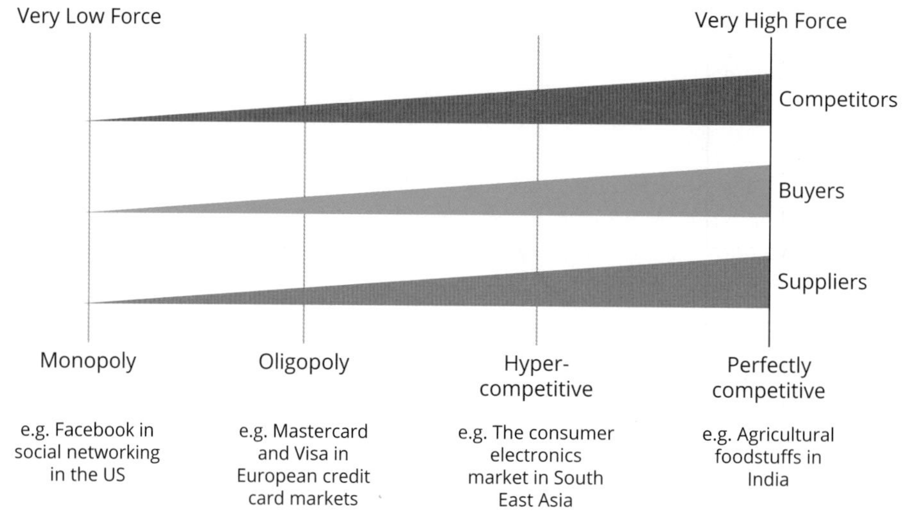

FIGURE 5.9 **Impacts of differing market structures.**

or oligopoly competitor, even temporarily, actions which preserve and exploit this status will be desirable. In hyper-competitive and (near) perfectly competitive markets, finding alternative markets with greater profit potential will likely be a focus of strategic conversations.

An increasingly common term used to describe market structures with high or very high competitor, buyer, and supplier forces is 'red ocean markets'. The metaphor was first proposed by INSEAD academics Kim and Mauborgne (2005) to illustrate the red ink accounting losses and threats to survival of organizations operating in highly competitive markets (like blood in shark-infested waters!). Kim and Mauborgne suggest that organizations should constantly be seeking the temporary monopolies of 'blue oceans'—markets for customer needs which are currently unserved (i.e. lack competition) and which hold high profit potential. The strategic mindset and methods required to pursue blue ocean market innovation are addressed fully in Chapter 11.

Influence of network externalities

Network externality—also known as the network effect—describes a situation where the market structure aligns around a dominant standard, platform, or product. This can have a profound influence on market structure and attractiveness (Chatterjee and Matzler 2019). It often leads to a monopolistic market structure, such as with Uber as a ride-hailing platform in many cities. There is a network effect as customers are attracted to the Uber platform because it has most drivers (suppliers), and drivers are attracted to the Uber platform as it has most customers. For both drivers and customers, there is less utility in using less populated platforms (i.e. the value of the platform is a function of the number of customers associated with it). Over time, this self-reinforcing dynamic (or virtuous cycle) maintains a monopoly situation for Uber. As a result of network externalities, those holding the largest network in certain markets can achieve a sustainable competitive advantage, aided by customer and supplier behaviour. For markets in emergence or growth phases, it is worthwhile for the strategy team to be vigilant for any signs of network externalities during market-level analysis. Unless the organization is the beneficiary of a network externality, exiting a market early where network externality is developing can be a prudent option for strategic action.

Non-market external factors

Whilst PESTEL analysis highlights macro-trends in the external environment, it can also draw attention to non-market factors which have an influence on the attractiveness of an industry. For example, government views of a market can have a major influence on the attractiveness of an industry. This might be represented directly in the original Five Forces through government-enforced legislative barriers to entry. Further though, what if a government owns a stake in one of the competing firms or decides to take a lax approach to the enforcement of intellectual property law? Awareness of how government might influence market structure, relationships, and activity can generate valuable insights about the attractiveness of an industry. Indirectly, activities in the broad ecosystem from institutions such as universities, governmental organizations, and non-governmental organizations may have an impact on the attractiveness of a market. Thus, when completing industry forces analysis, a practical step can often be to check the findings from PESTEL analysis for non-market factors which may indirectly affect the attractiveness of a market.

Applying industry forces analysis

This section explains how an industry forces framework can be used to conduct market-level analysis. As with PESTEL, the aim is not to create an exact model of the markets in which an organization is operating. Instead, this analysis should deepen your awareness and enable informed decision-making of the market context of the organization.

Step 1. Define the boundaries for industry forces analysis and identify relevant iterations

Before starting to gather data, it is important to define the product market and geographical boundaries that will be examined. Without identified boundaries, industry forces analysis can quickly become muddled. For many organizations, it will be necessary to conduct more than one industry forces analysis. Exactly how many times the analysis is required will be determined by their situation. For every combination of distinctive product groupings and geographic market boundaries that apply to an organization, a new industry forces analysis will be required. This can also apply to any markets (products or geographies) that an organization is considering entering.

Step 2. For each market scope under review, populate the descriptive industry forces framework

Seek data to populate this framework from a combination of internal expertise (if available) and external sources such as trade publications, legislation, and the websites of competitors, suppliers, and buyers. Complete two tables organizing data relating to the market factors and Five Forces categories for the agreed product and geographic market scope. A worked example of this applied industry framework is shown in Figure 5.10. A further common format for organizing data is to make a version of Porter's diagram (Figure 5.6) with additional notes recording further factors of relevance. As long as the data is organized and represented in a clear way, you should pick an approach to organizing data that suits your preferences.

Step 3. Categorize each force based on the data collected

With a rich set of descriptive data collected and organized, the next step is to evaluate the 'force' being exerted that is shaping market competition (see Table 5.2 for a guide to interpreting the forces). For each force, note the decision (e.g. Low, Very High, etc.) in the table.

CASE EXAMPLE 5.2 SATISFYING A GROWING GLOBAL APPETITE FOR ONLINE TAKEAWAY MARKETS

5

As indicated by the share prices of emerging firms, investors are being drawn to the profit potential of online takeaway markets across the world. For example, the value of Delivery Hero, a takeaway ordering firm headquartered in Berlin, rose to $5 billion in the three months following a $3.1 billion initial valuation in March 2017, and has since risen to $8.77 billion (May 2019). Equivalent firms in the UK (Just Eat—$5.3 billion), the Netherlands (Takeaway.com—$4.7 billion), and the USA (Grub Hub—$5.73 billion) have seen major rises in valuations as consumers increasingly transact through online takeaway ordering hubs. The number of orders placed with Delivery Hero grew from 81.6 million in 2017 to 117.3 million in 2018.

The high valuation of these relatively new firms can be in part explained by their emergence as the dominant platforms in their local markets. Food takeaway markets are characterized by a 'winner takes all' structure, in which, after an initial period of equal competition for consumer attention, one firm in a geographical territory will emerge as the preferred site of both consumers and suppliers during the growth phase of the industry life cycle. With most orders placed online through mobile devices, research has shown that consumers tend to install only one food ordering app. Thus, once a firm starts to gain more consumers than its competitors, it is favoured by more suppliers (as they are concerned with maximizing their own revenue). This in turn attracts more consumers wanting more choice, and a virtuous cycle of growth is established for one dominant firm, yielding profits of up to 20% per transaction. In the takeaway ordering markets, it is observed that a 'reverse network effect' also takes place, where the non-dominant firms struggle to retain suppliers and users of their customer app.

There are challenges for leading firms to maintaining this highly profitable position in the long term. First, online platform giants such as Amazon, Uber, and Alibaba are configured to profit from mass online transactions in different markets, and are showing interest in entering online takeaway competition. Second, as consumer interest in technology and health shifts, platform firms must also keep pace with consumers lifestyle preferences. For example, how will wearable technology such as Google glass shape consumers' use of takeaway ordering in the future? Third, governments are also increasingly paying attention to activities in the takeaway ordering market. Apart from encouraging consumers to eat healthy foods, governments are scrutinizing the employment practices of platform operators using 'zero hours' contracts in their supply chain. Takeaway platform companies typically organize casual delivery workers in their thousands, treating them as independent agents. Legislation around this human resourcing approach could disrupt the profit potential of the market.

The strategic management team at Delivery Hero is discovering that an understanding of local nuance and legislation is as vital as financial resources when expanding into new markets such as Saudi Arabia and Hong Kong. To continue to grow in a global industry estimated at $72 billion, organizations such as Delivery Hero must remain vigilant as to the specific industry forces at play in each of their target markets.

Questions for discussion

1. Referring back to the concept of a keystone organization earlier in this chapter, explain how Delivery Hero's success since the initial public offering (IPO) has been helped by 'keystone advantage'.
2. How likely is it that Delivery Hero will be challenged by a major competitor in its home country market of Germany? Explain your answer
3. If you were CEO of Delivery Hero, what knowledge of the external context would you value most as you make your strategy?

Source

This case vignette is based on 'We can be heroes', p.58, *The Economist*, 8 July 2017, updated with information from https://www.deliveryhero.com/blog_post/one-year-after-ipo/ and https://www.infrontanalytics.com/fe-EN/42675ED/Delivery-Hero-AG/market-valuation

Factors of market relevance	
Factor	**Description**
Industry lifecycle	Industry in early growth phase: 2% of new vehicle registrations electric in 2017—up 80% from 2016. High levels of innovation
Market structure	Hyper-competitive at present: 55 plug in models and differentiated variants available. No platform standard established yet
Network externalities	No network externalities in evidence yet
Complementarities	Double digit growth of charging infrastructure market year on year. 13,000 charging points UK-wide as of Aug 2017
Non-market contextual factors	High levels of government incentives to competitors and buyers of electric vehicles. Political pressure to reduce emissions

Forces shaping market competition			
Category	**Description**	**Force**	**Trajectory**
Buyer power	Charging network growing, buyers incentivized to adopt vehicles, grants widely available so deman now outstripping supply	Low	↓
Supplier power	Supply to automotive OEMs is highly competitive; proprietary EV technology being developed and held by OEMs	Low	↔
Competitive rivalry	13 major automotive firms offering EVs in UK. Market demand growing rapidly—supply struggling to meet demand	Mid	↑
Threat of new entrants	Government incentives and maturing supply chain generating start-ups and further entry into EV market from existing auto industry	High	↔
Threat of substitutes	Vast improvements in hybrid technology and 'clean' internal combustion engine; continued presence of public transport	Mid	↑

Implications	Options for action
It is to the organization's advantage that bargaining power remains weak for buyers and suppliers, so actions should be considered to contribute to maintaining these currently low forces	Lobby the government to keep incentive schemes in place (maintaining high adoption)
	Continue to invest in 'in-house' R&D for EV-specific components and technology
Whilst there are many competitors, the market is growing fast so it is still potentially profitable. Need to be mindful that this force is likely to intensify as new entrants continue to be attracted, and market share and profitability will come under pressure in the future	Ramp up efforts to capture market share, building brand reputation and customer loyalty where possible during early growth phase
	Urge government to back existing players with financial incentives
Threat of substitutes suggests alternative markets will continue to keep a downward pressure on the EV market for some time to come. Not committing to EV alone could help manage the risk associated with this pressure	Continue to invest in alternative technological options—hybrid and clean internal combustion engine (ICE—as part of R&D portfolio)

FIGURE 5.10 Worked example of applied market-level analysis.

Step 4. Review the history of each force to build understanding of trends

An element of dynamism is introduced to the framework by consideration of the industry life cycle. Identifying if and how all forces are changing over time can provide a further valuable set of inputs to the strategist's deliberations. This activity counteracts the 'static' limitation of a single iteration of the framework.

How this is executed will vary for each organization. Broadly, the steps involved are:

(a) identifying a suitable length of time for review of organizational history

(b) examining trends in the descriptive data relating to each force from the past to the present

(c) making a set of arguments to support a claim about the direction of travel for each force.

The length of time for review, the clarity of data required to claim a trend, and the required depth of supporting arguments will be a matter of judgement and agreement for you according to the organization's situation. In practice, we find that discussions of trends in industry forces analysis can benefit from insights from PESTEL analysis. In the table, the overall anticipated direction of travel, and a short statement of the supporting arguments, should be noted for each force (a trajectory column has also been added in Figure 5.10).

Step 5. Draw organizational implications from the findings

The next step is to convert the descriptive model of the forces and factors operating in the market into organizational implications. This involves asking the overarching question: 'Given the current state, and direction of travel, of these industry forces and the underlying market factors, what are the implications for our organization in the short, medium, and long term?'

You may wish to ask, 'Is this a market in which we want to remain?' If analysis shows that profitability is falling, and the forces are working against any sort of recovery of profitability, an organization may wish to consider exiting the market. This means a controlled withdrawal in a way that does minimal harm to the organization, and the diversion of resources towards alternative, more valuable activities or markets. This can be a tough call to make, as organizational inertia and historical emotional attachment to a market can be hard to overcome. However, it can also be a matter of organizational survival: for example, despite an extensive history in the industry, IBM's exit from the business of manufacturing mainframes is considered a vital action in recovering from the negative effects of its Roadmap 2015 strategy (see the vignette 'When fixed strategy goes wrong' in the **online resources**).

Further issues are worth considering in discussions of industry forces. What capacity might the organization have to drive down forces that are currently 'high' and harming profitability? Does the organization have any ability to contribute to keeping forces 'low' that are currently enabling industry profitability? Should you avoid taking any action in relation to industry forces? If analysis suggests that industry profitability is acceptable now and appears to be so in the future, a sensible outcome from analysis could be to 'do nothing'. This strategic inaction is quite different from thoughtless inaction. Recognizing that intervention isn't required, or might not help, or is even wasteful, and that resources are better deployed elsewhere is an entirely plausible outcome from industry forces analysis.

The agreement of implications is achieved through informed debate by you and the strategy team, referring to the data and arguments gathered in previous steps. Implications should be noted in the table.

Step 6. Identify options for action in response to organizational implications

As with PESTEL analysis, the final step in this analysis is to identify options for strategic action as an input to strategic decision-making. Steps 2–6 can then be repeated for all relevant market and geographical parameters identified in Step 1.

Undertaking market analysis can lead practitioners to a shared understanding of the markets where efforts will be focused in the future, and a sense of the options available for them to manage their participation in those markets in an effective way.

Competitive analysis

The final form of external analysis we will consider is what might be termed 'micro-level' or competitive analysis. When undertaking micro-level analysis, insights are drawn from exploring an organization's immediate relationships and interactions with customers and competitors. Anticipating the future actions, demands, and responses of external parties to which the organization is closely coupled aids strategic management conversations and decision-making at a level of detail below market-level analysis. In this section, we will explain how strategic group analysis might be used as a method to examine the influences of, and on, the organization from direct competition and customers.

Strategic group analysis

Strategic group analysis is a method which identifies direct competitors that should be studied as part of micro-level analysis. As reported by Cool and Schendel (1987), a **strategic group** is defined as the collection of organizations adopting broadly the same strategy to service the needs of the same group of customers. Strategic groups can be identified by mapping the position of competitors in an industry against two competitive criteria, as illustrated in Figure 5.11.

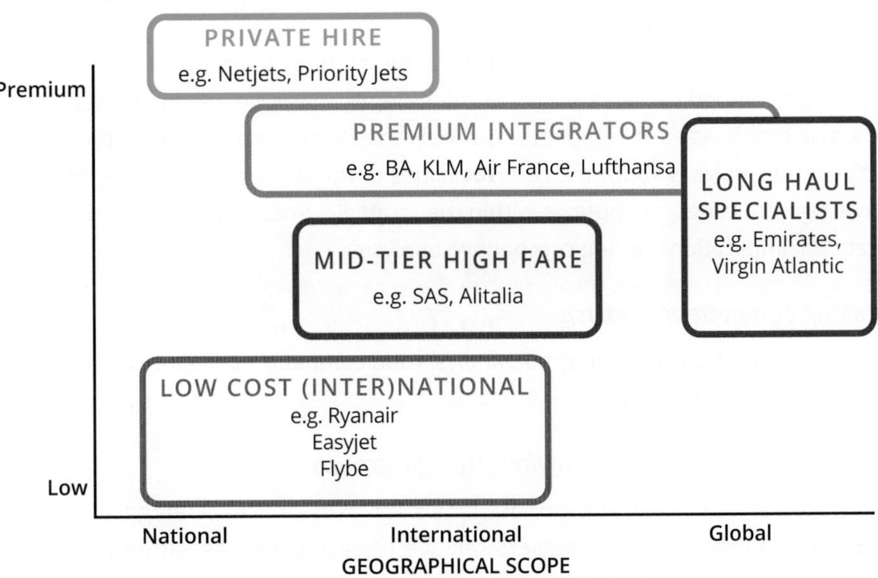

FIGURE 5.11 Strategic group analysis for the UK airline industry.

For example, in the UK airline industry, arguably Ryanair, EasyJet, and Flybe form a strategic group, offering low-cost flights to a wide range of domestic and European destinations from multiple regional and international airports. They are targeting holidaymakers and price-conscious business travellers. This renders them distinctive from, for example, British Airways and KLM, which provide short, medium, and long-haul flights at a higher price point, targeting less cost-conscious business and holiday travellers.

If Ryanair is our focus organization, in conducting competitive analysis it makes sense that priority consideration is given to the actions of their direct competitors EasyJet and Flybe. Without ignoring other strategic groupings, this focus on a limited, highly relevant set of competitors enables the organization to develop nuanced competitive insights. Strategic group analysis also enables an exploration of the expectations and buying criteria of the specific customer segments targeted by the organization. By building up a picture of what it takes to meet the needs of target customers in a superior way to competitors, micro-level analysis can allow you to identify options for actions which might be required to sustain or improve competitive performance.

Competitor profiling

Focusing your attention on profiling direct competitors will generate valuable insights as to the likely actions and reactions of your organization's closest rivals to changing circumstances, including those instigated by your own strategic activities. This may be supported by competitive intelligence—'legal practices of gathering market information that have sometimes been associated with legal infringements and espionage' (Reinmoeller and Ansari 2016:117).

In practice, much may be known about direct competitors by a management team through experience of running the organization on a daily basis. However, adopting a structured approach to competitor profiling can ensure well-rounded thinking, and avoid blind spots. Table 5.4 illustrates a structured approach which can be used to evaluate the likely activities of competitors based on what they have done in the past, how they aspire to operate, and what they are ultimately seeking to achieve.

Considering a range of factors and indicators, the strategy team can use a structured competitor profiling method to develop a coherent in-depth analysis of all the direct competitors in their strategic group. As each competitor is reviewed using the same criteria, the strategy team will also generate insights about the commonalities of the strategic group. Identifying patterns of recurring goals, values, or routines within the strategic group will assist the identification of organizational implications during competitive analysis.

Undertaking competitive analysis

This section explains how strategic group analysis and competitor profiling can be used to enact micro-level environmental analysis.

Step 1. Decide on criteria for identifying strategic groups

It is first necessary to select appropriate labels for axes on the strategic group chart that can be used to position industry players relative to each other. As with the industry forces analysis, it may be necessary to run this exercise more than once, preparing a selection of

TABLE 5.4 **Competitor profiling**

Factors	Reason for profiling	What do competitors really want?	How do competitors aspire to operate?	What have competitors traditionally done?
Strategic dimensions	These strategic factors shape competitor strategy. Understanding them will help us predict competitor actions.	What goals, published and unpublished, does the organization have?	What are the stated beliefs, ethics and values of the organization that will influence decision-making and action?	What routines, capabilities, and standard practices define and constrain strategic actions?
Characteristics	Key questions to ask about the strategic dimensions.	What governance and ownership structure is in place, and how will this affect strategic action?	How embedded are the stated values in the operating approach and historical actions of the competitor?	How do culture, information flow, size, maturity, leadership stability, and organizational complexity shape actions?
Top management	Pay attention to how the top management team operates. As the strategic decision-makers, they will be key in determining how the competitor acts.	How are the top team compensated? How credible are they in the pursuit of organization goals? What is their reputation for action?	What are the life experiences of the top team? To what extent do they role model and seek external advice in a manner consistent with stated organizational values?	To what extent do egos and self-justification define the top management team approaches? Are they reported as micro-managers? Or is power devolved in the organization?
Strategic organization	Review the structure and scale of the competitor to evaluate how its actions might be constrained or enabled by how it is organized.	What are the scale and diversity of the business, overall business priorities, market position and competitive advantage of the competitor?	Do all aspects of the business, functions, business units, and divisions share common values? How ethical is the behaviour of the competitor at all levels?	Are there any patterns in the strategic actions enacted by the organization? Is there any history of blind spots in thinking or organizational politics shaping strategic action?
Capabilities strategies	Consider the long-term commitments to growing and exploiting specific capabilities. These will shape what it can do.	What is the stated intent about the capabilities on which the competitor will be based in the long term?	What key capabilities are emphasized in the long term? Does the competitor commit to investing in improvements consistent with their values?	To what extent does the organization continually invest in new capabilities and/or capability renewal?
Performance results and attitude	The way in which the organization performs, and even interprets success, will have an impact on how it competes.	How well has the competitor performed in delivering profitability, growth, revenue, sustainability, and non-economic outcomes?	How well is risk managed for the benefit of all stakeholders? What is the attitude to external threats, opportunities, and use of funds?	How do performance management approaches and commitment to non-economic goals seem to influence strategic choice?

strategic group analysis charts to identify the closest competitors. The famous 4Ps model of marketing (McCarthy 1960) can provide a useful starting point for consideration as labels for each axis.

Price: compare organizations according to the prices they charge for their products/service (e.g. low—medium—premium—super-premium prices).

Product: compare organizations according to the variation in their product/service lines (e.g. single products vs multiple products, fixed products vs customizable offerings, etc.).

Placement: compare the geographic range or availability of the products/services (e.g. widely available vs exclusively stocked, regional vs national vs international geographic availability).

Promotion: compare the approach to communicating with customers (e.g. mass marketed vs targeted promotion).

According to the characteristics of the markets in which the organization competes, different dimensions of comparison will make sense. For example, in the airline example above, price and placement are highly relevant variables for comparing firm activities. On the other hand, promotion—whilst not totally irrelevant—is far less useful. However, in the drinks industry, promotion is a highly relevant variable with which to compare the activities of different firms.

Step 2. Map competitors onto the strategic group analysis charts, identifying clusters

Plot all competitors in the market onto the strategic group analysis chart according to how they correspond to the selected axes. The position of your own organization should also be marked. Identify clusters of firms that are located in similar positions. These clusters represent 'strategic groups'. It can be helpful for conversations following the charting activity to give a name to each of the clusters.

The charting activity can be repeated against alternative axes labels. Aside from checking the allocation of strategic groups, this analysis can generate further insights as to how the organization's own strategic group operates. The outcome of this step is a description of the strategic group(s)—direct competitors and target customers—in which the organization operates.

Step 3. Describe the characteristics and expectations of the customer segments targeted by this strategic group

Evaluating the implications of an organization's strategic grouping, customer value creation is explored first. The key question to be posed in this step is 'What do customers value from the offerings of organizations in this strategic grouping?' This requires discussion of what seems to be valued by the customer segments served by the strategic group. Market reports/intelligence, insights from internal expertise, and a review of competitor market facing material can all contribute to this conversation. A common mistake in this step is to list strengths or achievements of the organization—focus only on what is valued by the customers served by the strategic group.

The outcomes of this conversation should be documented in a table. An example is given in Figure 5.12 which captures the implications of a strategic group analysis completed for Nissan and its Leaf electric vehicle in the UK. By the end of this step, the strategy team should have a description of points of customer value for the focal strategic group.

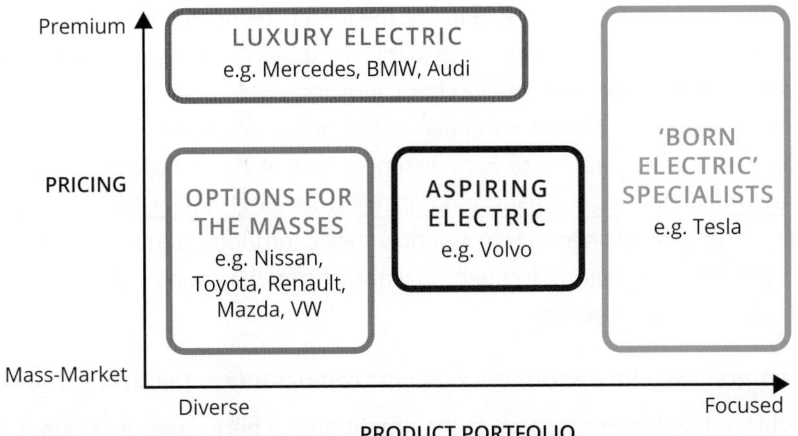

Characteristics of customer value	Common competitive characteristics	Relative performance (5 high)
Access to government incentives/tax breaks	Compliance with government requirements	5
Range of EV vehicle that meets my needs	Reliable technical performance and >100 mile range for battery	4
The look, feel, and features of a mainstream car	Common aesthetics with mainstream product lines	3
An accessible price for purchase	Benefits of economies of scale and lean knowledge	4
Low maintenance costs	High reliability designs	4

Implications	Options for action
The organization is leading competitors in compliance with government requirements, which in turn benefits (and attracts) cost-conscious customers. This is an advantage to be protected and exploited.	Lobby the government to keep the pace of new EV-friendly legislation high
	Build superior compliance and funding access message into marketing dialogue with potential customers
Technical performance in EV technology and regular vehicle reliability and low-cost production is strong—action needs to be taken to reinforce and seek improvements in these customer valued features.	Maintain investment in range performance technology and EV reliability R&D activity
	Create an operations team to transfer lean knowledge to EV production
There is scope to bring the look, feel, and features of the EV more in line with customers' expectations of what is involved in a mainstream car. This could ward off competitor attacks in the future.	Invest in aesthetic design teams and R&D activity to move EV beyond 'prototypical' look, feel, and features towards a mainstream design

FIGURE 5.12 Worked example of competitive analysis.

Step 4. Identify the characteristics for competitive success in the strategic grouping

What are the commonalities in the strategic grouping as to how organizations make profit whilst creating value for target customers? A 'recipe' of common characteristics for creating customer value in a sustainable way can be uncovered through a review of organizational and competitor activities. It should be possible to explain any aspect of the group recipe in terms of how it contributes to profitably creating value for the target customers. It might be useful to consider the prompts listed in Table 5.4 as an aid to this discussion. Findings should be noted in the analysis table under 'common competitive characteristics'.

For example, considering the budget European airline operators, low-cost culture, modern aircraft fleet, lean operations, mass customer awareness, and effective digital customer interfaces might all be common factors in organizations in this strategic grouping. Each of these common characteristics can be explained in terms of how they contribute to the airline being able to operate profitably whilst delivering frequent low-price flights to a wide range of European destinations (what the customer seeks).

Step 5. Evaluate organizational performance against competitors in the strategic grouping

As far as is possible, an objective appraisal of the organization's performance versus strategic group competitors is required based on the common competitive characteristics noted in the previous step. Working through each competitive characteristic, the question to be asked is: 'What is our performance, relative to competitors, against this competitive criterion?'

You should note, in a consistent way, the outcomes of this evaluation activity in column 3, labelled 'relative performance'. Simple numeric scoring or qualitative descriptors (5, leading performance; 3, average; 1, lagging performance) are adequate for this task. It is a good idea to make some short supporting notes and reserve any detailed analysis of relative performance to a separate document.

Step 6. Draw organizational implications from the findings

As with previous methods, the next activity is to convert the evaluation of relative performance in the strategic grouping into organizational implications. If relative performance is strong, the straightforward implication for the organization is likely to be that it is worthwhile to continue to operate in this strategic grouping. If relative performance could be improved, the effort and resources required to raise performance could be discussed. And if relative performance is poor, does it make sense for the organization to continue to operate in this strategic grouping? Or should the organization attempt to reposition towards an alternative strategic grouping with a different set of competitive criteria? Capture the outcomes of this discussion in a separate table (as shown in the example in Figure 5.12).

Step 7. Develop options for strategic action connected to organizational implications

Based on the organizational implications identified, options for strategic action can be derived for your organization. If the organization has decided that it will no longer compete within a strategic industry grouping, it may choose to take actions to move towards a different strategic grouping, or to seek a new competitive space (attempting to serve a group of customers in a novel way). This sort of repositioning activity requires a significant investment of transformative organizational effort. Such a bold initiative is not unheard of as a deliberate strategic manoeuvre. There was a trend in UK manufacturing organizations in the 2000s to attempt repositioning towards 'higher-value' strategic groups. As reported by the OECD (2007), 'moving up the value chain' through a process of 'servitization', the high-value manufacturing movement involved augmenting product supply with additional services or changing the way in which customer demands were met. For example, power organizations such as Rolls Royce and Aggreko moved from the provision of physical power generation units to selling clients 'power by the hour'.

Under this arrangement, the client paid for the power they received, and the responsibility for maintaining and even operating equipment was handled by the supplier for a fee.

If an organization is confident in its ability to compete within an industry grouping, the options for action will then correspond to sustaining or improving its ability to do so. This will likely mean investment and attention directed towards initiatives that consolidate performance in the defining characteristics for the strategic industry grouping. For example, in the budget airline industry, Ryanair prioritized a campaign called 'always getting better' to drive continuous improvement whilst protecting its low-cost efficient operating model. In parallel, it invested heavily in upgrading its digital customer interface, began advertising on television to grow customer awareness, and continued to invest in new fleet. In combination, these initiatives maintained the competitive edge for the organization versus its competitors in the UK budget airline strategic industry grouping. Any options for strategic action should be noted in the final column of the table.

5.4 **Combining insights and options from external context analysis**

An integrative review comparing, combining, and refining insights arising from complementary methods can deliver several benefits. First, by comparing the outcomes from each method, contradictions and tensions can be highlighted for further evaluation and debate. Second, reflective review highlights opportunities to merge related options for strategic action into 'better' options supported by a range of arguments. Third, through discussion and reflection, you and your colleagues can develop narratives for sharing with others as a result of your analysis.

Integrative review of external analysis outcomes

To prepare for an integrative review the findings arising from each method are compiled into a master table. In a reversal of previous approaches, we suggest that the first column is the options for action, the second column lists associated organizational implications, and the third column refers to supporting data from each analysis method. A partial worked example is shown in Table 5.5.

When compiling the table, arrange the options for action next to other options addressing the same 'theme' or topic. It doesn't matter if the options for action are in direct contradiction. For example, in preparing the table, you would locate 'increase in-house investment in the development of electric vehicles' and 'reduce in-house investment in the development of electric vehicles' next to each other (see Dialectic enquiry in Chapter 3). In Table 5.5, findings included relate to a theme of technological developments arising from the worked examples earlier in this chapter.

With all options for strategic action arranged in the table, the strategy team can proceed to reflect on and review the outcomes. Identical options for action can be consolidated into single entries in the table, and supporting arguments compiled. If an option for action is implied by PESTEL, industry forces, and competitive analysis, you have a strong argument for giving that option priority consideration in decision-making. This does not mean that

TABLE 5.5 **Integrative review: example of an initial table of compiled insights**

Options for action	Organizational implications	Supporting data
Prioritize investment in electric vehicle R&D activity	Prepare technical competence and production capabilities for new era of auto	Technology development trends—PESTEL
Continue to invest in 'in-house' R&D for EV-specific components and technology	Prevent bargaining power drifting towards the EV supply chain, and enhance ability to compete against rivals	Low supplier power and trending rise—industry forces
Invest in aesthetic design teams to move EV towards a mainstream design	Address a customer need that is currently not well served, and avoid becoming a competitive disadvantage in future	Customer value of aesthetics—competitive analysis
Continue to invest in alternative technological portfolio options—hybrid and clean ICE	Manage risk of price–performance trade-off switches for customers to substitute to electric vehicles	Threat of substitutes—industry forces
Maintain investment in range performance technology and EV reliability R&D activity	Keep pace with competitors and preserve strong technical performance that positions products well	Competitive performance—competitor analysis
Source tech partner firms for audio-visual (AV) technology	Prepare technical competence and production capabilities for new era of auto	Technology development trends—PESTEL

an option for action implied by one piece of analysis only isn't worthy of consideration. It might be that the action option has emerged from a nuanced insight that would only be detected by one type of analysis. However, corroboration from different levels of analysis—particularly from reviewing market and non-market structures—is a signal to which you should pay attention.

You may decide to retain all options until further analysis can be conducted. Equally, where different options have arisen for a topic or theme, a **triangulation** approach can be used for creative development of new options. Triangulation is originally a navigational technique, where the selection of three landmarks can be used to orient a map and determine the map-holder's current location. In strategic analysis and business research, we can use the process of triangulation to develop new options, informed by the implications of different methods (Tassabehji and Isherwood 2014). Figure 5.13 illustrates this process.

For example, imagine PESTEL analysis suggests macro-environmental trends that will become increasingly hostile to an industry sector in the long term (implying that preparations should be started for industry exit), whereas industry forces and competitive analysis suggest that the organization is performing well and should invest in defending its currently profitable industry position. Figure 5.14 shows such an example in relation to electric vehicle technology development for a firm currently performing well with superior internal combustion engine technology. PESTEL analysis suggests that environmental pressures, changes in government and consumer attitudes, and progress in technological performance will direct the future of the

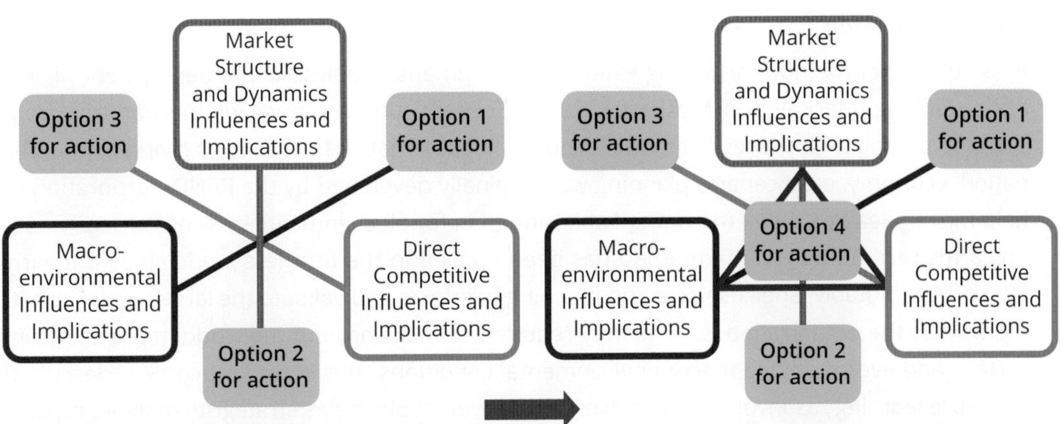

FIGURE 5.13 Development of new options through triangulation.

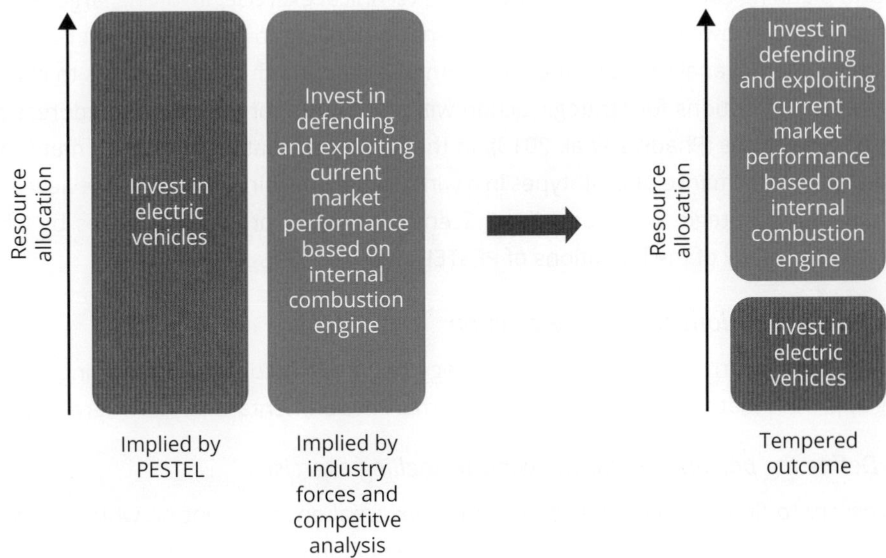

FIGURE 5.14 Worked example of option triangulation.

mass automotive industry strongly towards electrical vehicles. However, the industry forces and strategic group analysis show that there remains significant profit potential from continuing to exploit the current market performance in the short term.

Bringing the different modes of analysis together can create a tempered set of implied actions. In this automotive case, immediate investment actions to defend the industry position might still be proposed, but appropriately scaled to organizational risk/opportunity posed by the potential change in long-term direction. At the same time, investing in developing capabilities and technology in electric vehicle manufacture prepares the organization to be ready for long-term change.

By the end of the integrative review process, a refined set of external analyses—descriptive models, organizational implications, and justified options for strategic action—will be available to support subsequent strategy practices. Along with a core 'internal' analysis dataset (see Chapter 6), this data will also feed directly into the strategic decision-making process.

Scenario thinking

A useful further method for testing external environmental analysis is the deployment of scenario thinking (MacKay and McKiernan 2018). Scenario thinking borrows mechanisms from scenario planning—a process of modelling plausible alternative futures for a market, industry, nation, economy, etc. Scenario planning was originally developed by the RAND Corporation to help military leaders 'think the unthinkable' and plan for all eventualities as the nuclear weapons arms race unfolded. The method has been applied in the business world since the early 1980s. Most notably, Shell use scenario planning to inform and validate the large capital investments that the organization is frequently required to make around the world in complex, uncertain, and ever-changing macro-environmental conditions. This sort of outcome is described as 'future learning', as involvement in scenario conversations helps strategists to avoid myopia and blind spots in their current thinking, and to retain flexibility to respond to future external environmental change by making a range of investments in the here and now (Grant 2003).

Scenario planning can be a highly involved and technical exercise, involving large teams and months of activity. However, we can borrow scenario thinking to run an efficient review of external environmental analysis outcomes. The aim of a scenario thinking review is to check how well the full set of options for strategic action will prepare the organization to address plausible alternative futures (Phadnis et al. 2015). In the same way that an aerospace manufacturer would test the performance of prototypes in a wind-tunnel machine, this sort of review exercise is referred to as strategic 'wind-tunnelling'. Scenario thinking provides a means by which to compensate for many of the limitations of PESTEL analysis.

Wind-tunnelling options for strategic action

To give the best return on effort for the strategy team, we recommend following a scenario thinking approach that re-uses insights from external environmental analysis wherever possible.

Step 1. Define the parameters for the wind-tunnelling exercise

It is necessary to first agree the trends from the external environment on which to construct scenarios. The strategy team is advised to revisit the outcomes of their work in PESTEL analysis identifying priority trends, or key drivers, from the macro-environment. Select initially the top two trends (the exercise can be repeated for further combination of trends) as a starting point. For example, in the automotive case, trend 1 could be the commercialization of autonomous vehicle technology and trend 2 could be the mass adoption of electric vehicles.

For each of these priority trends, two polar opposite futures are defined: (i) the trend happens as predicted; (ii) the trend doesn't happen/occurs only in a minor way. Applied to the autonomous vehicle trend, two polar opposites could be (i) autonomous vehicles are widely adopted and (ii) autonomous vehicle technology fails to be realized; for electric vehicles, the polar opposites could be (i) electric vehicles achieve mass adoption and (ii) electric vehicles attract only limited adoption.

These priority trends and their associated predictability/unpredictability polarities are used to set a template for the scenario conversation. Figure 5.15 shows the template for the automotive example. Note that each axis corresponds to a priority trend, and the polar opposites align with one half of the template. Ideally the axes in the grid will be independent, i.e. one will not significantly depend on the other happening.

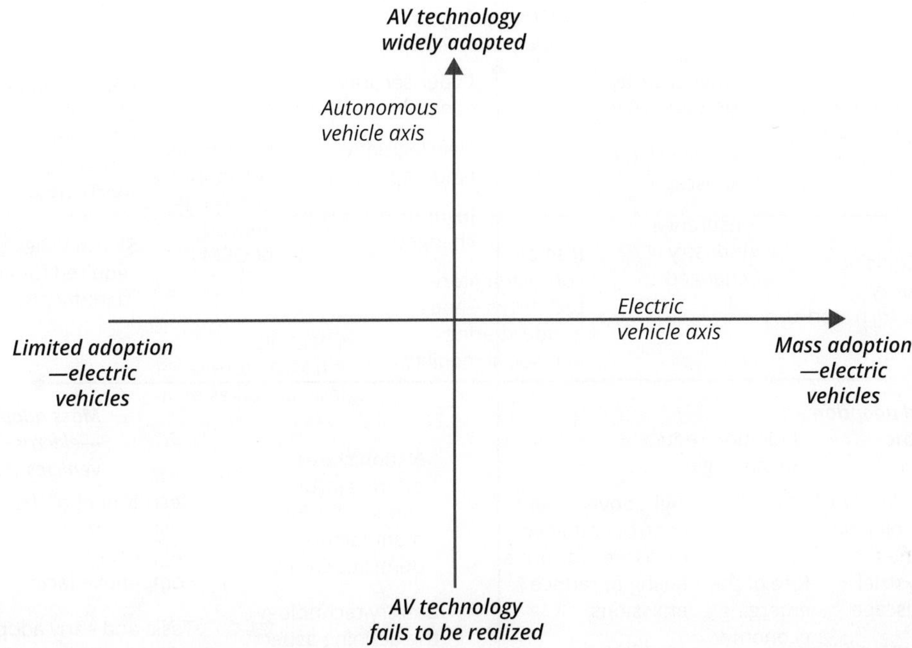

FIGURE 5.15 Example scenario template for the automotive industry.

With the subject matter for the first scenario thinking conversation defined, the strategy team can also set the timescale to be discussed. We advise that this selection is made according to what makes sense given the two axes. In the automotive example, findings in PESTEL work suggested that both widespread commercialization of AV technology and mass adoption of electric vehicles could be achieved by 2025. Therefore adopting this as a timescale would make sense.

2. Populate the scenario template with data from analysis

With the template prepared, the strategy team then engages in an open discussion about each of the quadrants on the grid. Each quadrant frames the range of possibilities that could emerge within the parameters as defined by the two axes. All themes of interest emerging from any level of external environmental analysis should be reviewed. How these themes of interest might manifest in each of the quadrants mapped on the template is discussed, and insights are noted.

For example, talent recruitment/management was a theme of interest arising from external environmental analysis in the automotive case. Consider the top left quadrant of the grid. What kind of talent is required in a future with widespread AV technology, but limited adoption of electric vehicles? Traditional automotive engineers will be required, but so will many software and electronic engineers. In the top right quadrant, the nature of the automobile has shifted significantly, and software, electrical, and electronic engineers will be in high demand in the industry. In the bottom left quadrant, traditional talent approaches should be continued, and in the bottom right, electrical engineers will be in high demand.

Figure 5.16 shows the scenario template populated for a range of themes of interest in the automotive example.

AV technology widely adopted

Dominance of tech firms in automotive

Acquisition frenzy for tech start-ups

Cyber security competence vital

New legislative landscape

Insurance industry changed

Rise of complementary tech firms—apps in ride sharing and social mobility

Cyber security competence vital

New legislative landscape

Insurance industry changed

Co-branded collaborative enterprises instead of OEMs

Cars redefined as electrical / electronic systems rather than mechanical

Silicon Valley talent required for auto manufacturers

Charging infrastructure industry takes off

Limited adoption —electric vehicles

Mass adoption —electric vehicles

Pollution-reducing technologies critical

High level of consolidation define the industrial landscape

Alternate fuels power vehicles

Rise of the emerging economy manufac-turers

Tight government control / punitive measures for firms failing to reduce emissions

Traditional recruitment approaches continue

Nation states offering strong support for EV manufacture to domestic OEMs

Battery technology the defining aspect of vehicle manufacture

Recruitment of the best electrical engineers a competitive factor

Tesla and early adopter OEMs as dominant automotive global players

AV technology fails to be realized

FIGURE 5.16 Populated scenarios for the automotive industry.

3. Create the labels and narratives for each quadrant of the template

Once the template is populated, a set of narratives describing the future can be created by joining together the imagined future details in each quadrant. Each quadrant is also given a label which summarizes the key implication for the industry. Our experience tells us that this is a non-trivial matter. The creative act of summarizing and articulating plausible alternative futures is a key step in helping the management team to avoid myopic thinking. The automotive example is developed as illustrated in Figure 5.17.

4. Review, and where appropriate adjust, options for strategic action based on the emergent scenarios

To complete the wind-tunnelling exercise, the final scenario conversation should use the four alternatives as a frame of reference to review the completeness of the set of options for strategic action. The questions for the strategy team to ask, for each scenario, are:

(a) 'If this scenario were to happen, which of our current options for strategic action would be most relevant?'

(b) 'Do we have any major gaps in how our options for strategic action could prepare us for dealing with this scenario?' If yes, 'How could we amend or augment our options for strategic action to help us better prepare for this scenario?'

In this way, the scenarios play the role of the wind-tunnel, using plausible alternative futures to test how well the identified options for strategic action might prepare the organization to survive and grow.

High adoption —autonomous vehicles

RISE OF THE MACHINES
Technology firms pressurize the automotive sector, taking over struggling traditional manufacturers. The core abilities required to create a vehicle now extend to cyber security, complex software engineering, and systems integration. The legislative landscape shifts too, and manufacturers have to take on liability for their machines from cradle to grave.

AUTOMOTIVE REVOLUTION
The automotive industry as we know it is changed radically. Cars are more of a technology product now, requiring a Silicon Valley-like skills base. Non-market factors are reinvented for insurance, emissions, and safety performance. Collaborative capabilities and networked organizations are required to manage the complexity of production.

Limited adoption —electric vehicles

Mass adoption —electric vehicles

A NEW ICE AGE
The internal combustion engine has to be reinvented to handle new fuels and significantly lower emissions. Manufacturers that don't have this focus on ICE efficiency and performance face heavy penalties and trade restrictions from governments and legislators.

GREEN CREDENTIALS RULE
Driving a step change in electrical performance will give firms competitive advantage as zero emission vehicles become the norm. The dominant firms in the industry will be those that are furthest down this developmental path. Early adopters such as Tesla will likely be at the vanguard.

Limited adoption—AV

FIGURE 5.17 Future narratives for the automotive industry.

PRACTITIONER INSIGHT: DR IBRAHIM SAIF

Dr Ibrahim Saif is the CEO of the Jordan Strategy Forum. Previously, he served in Jordan as the Minister of Energy & Mineral Resources from March 2015 to June 2017, and the Minister of Planning and International Cooperation from March 2013 until March 2015. Prior to his appointment as a minister, Dr Saif was a senior scholar at the Carnegie Middle East Center, and served as a consultant to the World Bank, the International Monetary Fund, and other international organizations. Dr Saif was also a former director of the Centre for Strategic Studies at the University of Jordan, and served as the Secretary General of the Economic and Social Council in Jordan.

He shares his views on (national) strategy, collective analysis, and the external environment.

What does strategy mean to you?

Strategy involves defining actionable steps that

Continued

enable you to achieve practical targets. In various strategic leadership positions I've held, strategy activity required figuring out what we needed to do, and then quickly moving into the practicalities of assigning jobs and responsibilities, and getting people behind what needed to be achieved. Having a long-term vision is also important in strategy, although that can often be a shared vision with other entities. For example, in one of my ministerial roles, setting vision for energy and mineral resources was part of my strategy remit, but clearly this needed to connect into the direction for the country. At a national level, it was important when making strategy to work in harmony with the needs and interests of multiple different stakeholders and institutions, bearing in mind their own targets and influences. In Jordan, we also had to consider how our own vision meshed with the vision of surrounding countries.

I believe that strategy work can only succeed if you are constantly reconsidering your actions and keeping your targets under perpetual check and review. You build your strategy on certain assumptions and scenarios. For example, the cost of production—domestic or external—is a key factor influencing government policy and business activity in Jordan at present. But such factors can change at any moment, and your plans and initiatives needed to be reviewed accordingly. At a higher level too, you may have to revisit your long-term vision when faced with significant change. It is important to shape your strategy practice accordingly when the external environment is characterized by unpredictability and uncertainty. You could work through an elaborate process to calculate strategy or define a strategy tied to leading individuals. But any fixed long-term strategy in a volatile context would lack credibility. Instead, using targets and indicators to trigger flexible responses in your strategy initiatives is a far more fruitful approach.

How does the Jordan Strategy Forum (JSF) enable its members to better understand their external context?

The JSF is a 'think tank', fully funded by a consortium of private sector organizations that want to create jobs, encourage competition, and raise governance standards. The vision of the JSF is to promote the private sector as a leading player in the national ecosystem that delivers benefit for the country. The JSF isn't dominated by any one firm. Instead, it is comprised of small, medium, and large organizations from across industries and stakeholder groups. Participants come together to debate and learn about events, trends, success stories, and cross-sectoral issues defining the business landscape. In addition to private organizations, we work with representatives of trade partners, the World Bank, the International Monetary Fund, etc. to objectively assess the business environment in Jordan and the surrounding region.

When members of the JSF meet, they value simple methods, common sense debates, and discussion as the main mechanisms for generating insights. Discussion themes that we explore can be self-generated—members are very active in raising topics relating to the emergence and implications of new technologies, for example. Alternatively, we might use credible sources, such as the annual World Economic Forum report on global competitiveness to stimulate forum members to re-examine aspects of the business environment. We also engage in benchmarking and undertake survey work. We manage a tool called the Investment Confidence Index based on data gathered from a wide range of stakeholders in the business environment in Jordan. We use The Investment Confidence Index findings to provoke a response from our members, and to encourage them to stay attuned to reality.

What is your experience of strategy at a national level?

When I was leading strategy planning in a ministerial role, I worked on multiple scenarios to prepare my thinking about possible futures. Jordan imports 98% of the materials required to satisfy its energy needs. Requirements at a national level are susceptible to shifts in three macro-factors in particular—energy technology development, volatility of energy prices, variations in patterns of consumption. Moreover, these factors may all be in motion at the same time. Being able to read and react quickly to systemic changes was crucial to our national strategic capability and being able to meet our national energy needs on an ongoing basis.

At a national level, there are many players who must be considered when formulating strategies, including the private sector, non-governmental organizations, citizens, and parliamentary and legislative interests. We were also very aware of regional politics and trends, and a need to bear in mind what is happening with our neighbours when setting our own plans. In government, a key aim is to create the right ecosystem between legislators, regulators, and the private sector in a transparent way. If done well, this system can deliver major contributions to national level performance and progress.

What advice would you give others involved in making organizational strategy?

I would advise any colleague seeking to engage in making strategy for an organization to thoroughly examine the local market and the associated socio-political environment. You need to look at these together. I would also check, at a national level, the relationship between your country and the regional environment, to understand your future trading context. And I think it is vital to check and evaluate your resources objectively—knowing how to access adequate financial and human capital to achieve your aims is crucial.

And one main thing I've learned is that it takes constant attention to see a strategy through. It is difficult to keep people to strategies, especially politicians.

CHAPTER SUMMARY

Against the target learning outcomes, in this chapter we have addressed the following ideas.

- **Explain how the two-way relationship between an organization and the external environment impacts on strategy and competitive advantage through concepts of structure, position, conduct, and performance**
  We reviewed how the position of an organization in external environmental structures, through relationships and interactions with other organizations, will impact its competitive advantage (its potential to do better than break-even competitors). Organizational performance will be influenced by the strategic conduct of the firm as choices are made about how to act in response to, and attempting to influence, external structures.
- **Evaluate the non-market, macro-environmental drivers shaping an organization and the ecosystem in which it resides**
  PESTEL (political, economic, social, technological, environmental, and legislative) factors offer a useful framework to evaluate the forces acting on all organizations in an industry. Not all PESTEL factors will have equal influence on an organizational ecosystem—identifying the priority forces, also known as key drivers, allows the identification of the relevant options for strategic action.
- **Interrogate market structures, dynamics, and trends, explaining the implications for buyers, competitors, and suppliers**
  Industry forces analysis is a method which enables a strategy team to review the attractiveness of different product or geographic markets in which it operates. Industry forces analysis augments Porter's Five Forces framework with further factors—complementarities, network externalities, market structure, industry life cycle, and non-market indirect effects. Industry forces analysis can be used to develop organizational implications of underlying structures, dynamics, and trends for market competitors, buyers, and suppliers.

- **Critically assess the direct competitive context for an organization, identifying the customer value creation and competitive characteristics most likely to enable survival and growth**
  Competitive analysis focuses on how the needs of target groups of customers are serviced by the closest competitors of the organization following broadly similar strategies. This is known as the strategic group of the organization. By identifying common factors for success within the strategic group, competitive analysis enables the identification of actions that can enhance the competitive performance of the organization, or seek to reposition it within a different competitive space.

- **Argue the benefits of using combinations of external environmental analysis tools**
  Each environmental analysis tool has a specific purpose, providing the strategist with insights to a bounded aspect of the external context. Thus external environmental analysis tools have strengths and limitations. The strategist is well advised to use tools from across levels of analysis to generate a balanced set of insights into the external environmental context facing the organization.
- **Agree a refined set of external environmental analytical outcomes by triangulating findings from across levels of analysis, and testing ideas through scenario thinking**
  To gain maximum benefit from using a combination of external environmental analysis tools, options for action identified across levels of analysis should be pooled and reconciled. This may involve finding new options for action through a process of triangulation. The combined and revised set of options for action can be tested and refined through the application of scenario thinking, drawing on key drivers from the macro-environment identified through PESTEL analysis. This sort of reflective practice—conducted as part of strategic conversations between organizational decision-makers—can significantly benefit efforts to craft informed robust strategies.

END OF CHAPTER QUESTIONS

Recall questions

1. What is the main difference between an isolated interpretation and an embedded interpretation of an organization and its external environment?
2. Explain what is meant by the SCP framework of the market-based view and its implications for organizational strategy.
3. Explain what is meant by a business ecosystem.
4. What is meant by market and non-market external environmental factors?
5. What macro-environmental factors does the acronym PESTEL stand for?
6. What are the purpose, advantages, and disadvantages of PESTEL, industry forces, and competitive analysis?
7. What does scenario planning add to the process of conducting external environmental analysis?

Application questions

A) Imagine that you are leading a strategy development team within a privately owned firm that sells one main product line into the UAE and Oman. Describe and justify the process you would advocate to the owners of the firm for conducting external environmental analysis.

B) Select an organization that is familiar to you, and develop a statement of the strategic group(s) associated with the organization. Who are the direct competitors? What do the target customers seem to value? What are the factors for success for organizations operating within that strategic group?

C) Pick an industry you know well, and work through a scenario development process for that industry based on two priority trends from the macro-environment. What outcomes were delivered by the process which would be of interest to organizations in that industry? What did you learn from conducting the process about the benefits and limitations of scenario planning?

ONLINE RESOURCES

www.oup.com/he/mackay1e

FURTHER READING

Competitive Strategy and *Competitive Advantage*, by Michael Porter

Porter, M.E. (1980). *Competitive Strategy: Techniques for Analyzing Industries and Competitors*. New York: Free Press.

Porter, M.E. (1984). *Competitive Advantage: Creating and Sustaining Superior Performance*. New York: Free Press.

Michael Porter has been recognized as the most influential strategy author via his publication of several seminal textbooks written from a market-based view. These two books are the original source of many theories and frameworks of market-based analysis still popular today in strategy education and consultancy practice.

Scenarios: The Art of Strategic Conversation, by Kees van der Heijden

van der Heijden, K. (2008). *Scenarios: The Art of Strategic Conversation* (2nd edn). Chichester: John Wiley.

This book is a well-regarded text written by a leading scholar with extensive scenario planning practical experience at Shell. It is a helpful reference for any strategist seeking to know more about how to mitigate the limitations of macro-environmental analysis in practice through scenario-based strategic conversations with a team.

Strategy and the Business Landscape, by Pankaj Ghemawat

Ghemawat, P. (2017). *Strategy and the Business Landscape*. London: Pearson.

Combining examples from global organizations and market-based theorizing, this text offers further insights into how a consultant might apply tools of strategic analysis with a market-based emphasis.

The myths and realities of business ecosystems, by Jack Fuller, Mark Jacobides, and Martin Reeves

Fuller, J., Jacobides, M.G., and Reeves, M. (2019). The myths and realities of business ecosystems. *MIT Sloan Management Review*, 25 February, 2–10.

An excellent primer on the current state of business ecosystems thinking. Explains the concepts of ecosystems in comparison with alternative market arrangements, dispels multiple myths grounded in commonly held beliefs about ecosystems, and gives advice about how to start to deploy ecosystems thinking.

REFERENCES

5

Argyres, N. and McGahan, A.M. (2002). An interview with Michael Porter. *Academy of Management Executive*, **16**(2), 43–52.

Brandenburger, A. (2002). Porter's added value: high indeed! *Academy of Management Executive*, **16**(2), 58–60.

Brandenburger, A. and Nalebuff, B. (1996). *Co-Opetition*. New York: Crown Publishing Group.

Chatterjee, S. and Matzler, K. (2019). Simple rules for a network efficiency business model: the case of Vizio. *California Management Review*, **61**(2), 84–103.

Chia, R.C.H. and Holt, R. (2009). *Strategy Without Design: The Silent Efficacy of Indirect Action.* Cambridge: Cambridge University Press.

Cool, K.O. and Schendel, D. (1987). Strategic group formation and performance: the case of the US pharmaceutical industry, 1963–1982. *Management Science*, **33**(9), 1102–24.

Doh, J.P., Lawton, T.C., and Rajwani, T. (2012). Advancing nonmarket strategy research: institutional perspectives in a changing world. *Academy of Management Perspectives*, **26**(3), 22–39.

Fuller, J., Jacobides, M.G., and Reeves, M. (2019). The myths and realities of business ecosystems. *MIT Sloan Management Review*, 25 February, 2–10.

Ghemawat, P. (2017). *Strategy and the Business Landscape*. London: Pearson.

Grant, R.M. (2003). Strategic planning in a turbulent environment: evidence from the oil majors. *Strategic Management Journal*, **24**(6), 491–513.

Grundy, T. (2006). Rethinking and reinventing Michael Porter's Five Forces model. *Strategic Change*, **15**(5), 213–29.

Hambrick, D.C. and Fredrickson, J.W. (2001). Are you sure you have a strategy? *Academy of Management Executive*, **15**(4), 48–59.

Iansiti, M. and Levien, R. (2004). Strategy as ecology. *Harvard Business Review*, **82**(3), 68–78.

Kaplan, R.S. and Norton, D.P. (2008). Mastering the management system. *Harvard Business Review*, **86**(1), 62–77.

Kim, W.C. and Mauborgne, R. (2005). *Blue Ocean Strategy*. Boston, MA: Harvard Business Review Press.

Kim, W.C. and Mauborgne, R. (2009). How strategy shapes structure. *Harvard Business Review*, September, 73–80.

Lei, D. and Slocum, J.W., Jr (2005). Strategic and organizational requirements for competitive advantage. *Academy of Management Executive*, **19**(1), 31–45.

McCarthy, J. (1960). *Basic Marketing: A Managerial Approach*. Momewood, IL: Richard D. Irwin.

MacKay, B. and McKiernan, P. (2018). *Scenario Thinking*. Cambridge: Cambridge University Press.

Mahoney, J.T. and McGahan, A.M. (2007). The field of strategic management within the evolving science of strategic organization. *Strategic Organization*, **5**(1), 79–99.

Moore, J.F. (2006). Business ecosystems and the view from the firm. *Antitrust Bulletin*, Spring (51), 31–75.

Morton, J., Stacey, P., and Mohn, M. (2018). Building and maintaining strategic agility: an agenda and framework for executive IT leaders. *California Management Review*, **61**(1), 94–113.

Nyberg, D., Wright, C., and Kirk, J. (2018). Dash for gas: climate change, hegemony, and the scalar politics of fracking in the UK. *British Journal of Management*, **29**(2), 235–51.

OECD (2007). Moving up the value chain: staying competitive in the global economy. https://www.oecd.org/sti/ind/38558080.pdf (accessed 1 May 2019).

Peteraf, M.A. and Barney, J.B. (2003). Unraveling the resource-based tangle. *Managerial and Decision Economics*, **24**(4), 309–23.

Phadnis, S., Caplice, C., Sheffi, Y., and Singh, M. (2015). Effect of scenario planning on field experts' judgment of long-range investment decisions. *Strategic Management Journal*, **36**(9), 1401–11.

Porter, M.E. (1980). *Competitive Strategy: Techniques for Analyzing Industries and Competitors*. New York: Free Press.

Porter, M.E. (1984). *Competitive Advantage: Creating and Sustaining Superior Performance*. New York: Free Press.

Porter, M.E. (2008). The five competitive forces that shape competitive performance. *Harvard Business Review*, January, 78–93.

Reinmoeller, P. and Ansari, S. (2016). The persistence of a stigmatized practice: a study of competitive intelligence. *British Journal of Management*, **27**(1), 116–42.

Tassabehji, R. and Isherwood, A. (2014). Management use of strategic tools for innovating during turbulent times. *Strategic Change*, **23**(1/2), 63–80.

Tsujimoto, M., Kajikawa, Y., Tomita, J., and Matsumoto, Y. (2018). A review of the ecosystem concept: towards coherent ecosystem design. *Technological Forecasting and Social Change*, **136**, 49–58.

van der Heijden, K. (2008). *Scenarios: The Art of Strategic Conversation* (2nd edn). Chichester: John Wiley.

Vuorinen, T., Hakala, H., Kohtamäki, M., and Uusitalo, K. (2018). Mapping the landscape of strategy tools: a review on strategy tools published in leading journals within the past 25 years. *Long Range Planning*, **51**(4), 586–605.

Wright, G., Cairns, G., O'Brien, F.A., and Goodwin, P. (2019). Scenario analysis to support decision making in addressing wicked problems: pitfalls and potential. *European Journal of Operational Research*, **278**(1), 3–19.

CHAPTER SIX

Internal Environment

Resources, Capabilities, and Activities

CONTENTS

LEARNING OBJECTIVES

By the end of this chapter, you should be able to:

- Explain the importance of building understanding of resources, capabilities, and activities in organizational strategy
- Explain how an organization can compete through the deployment of distinctive resources using the concepts and ideas of the resource base view
- Evaluate the potential of an organization to manage its resource base over time through dynamic capability
- Appraise the configuration of an organization as a set of supporting and value-adding activities
- Critically assess the value of internally focused analytical tools in strategy work

6

TOOL BOX

- **Resource-based view (RBV)**
  A theoretical perspective that helps explain how organizations can gain or sustain competitive advantage based on the distinctive resources to which they have access, and how they configure to use them; also known as the 'inside-out' perspective.
- **Dynamic capabilities view**
  An extension of the resource-based view—a theoretical perspective that helps explain how organizations can purposefully create, extend, or modify their resource base over time.
- **Resource-based inventory**
  A checklist-based approach to building shared views about the current resource base for an organization; generates valuable insights through focused discussion and sets a strong foundation for more nuanced resource-based view analysis.
- **VRIO analysis**
  A framework for identifying resources which might act as a source of competitive advantage for an organization, by the extent which they are **v**alued by the customer, **r**are, **i**mperfectly imitable, and can be used within the **o**rganization.
- **Capability audit**
  Working backwards from what an organization has actually done, model the different types of capabilities and competences that are supported by the organization's resource base. Enables discussion of how these capabilities and competences are used.
- **Dynamic capability analysis**
  Reviews the possibilities of modifying the organization's resource base to support a revised set of capabilities that meet future strategic needs.
- **Value chain analysis**
  Models an organization's direct activities that create value and indirect activities that shape the environment for value creation, as the basis for identifying improvements to those activities that might boost organizational performance.

OPENING CASE STUDY 'THE SUBLIME THAT IS THE STUFF OF OUR DREAMS ...'

Louis Vuitton Moët Hennessy (LVMH) is a global organization offering super-premium branded, high-quality products. The group bears the name of some of its most famous brands—Louis Vuitton fashion, Moët wines, and Hennessy spirits. However, it operates more broadly across five key sectors: wines and spirits, fashion and leather goods, perfumes and cosmetics, watches and jewellery, and selective retailing. According to the group annual report, in 2018 LVMH recorded revenues of €46.8 billion, profit from operations of €10 billion, and a free cash flow of €5.5 billion, allowing it to claim a solid financial position despite global economic uncertainty.

In the last 25 years, a main contributor to the continued revenue growth of the group has been a series of acquisitions of historically grounded luxury brands. On the LVMH website, it is noted that 'the group brings together truly exceptional Houses (of brands). Each of them creates products that embody unique savoir-faire, a carefully preserved heritage and a dynamic engagement with modernity. These creations make our Houses ambassadors of a distinctively refined art de vivre'. Brands controlled by the group include Moët & Chandon, Krug, Veuve Clicquot, Hennessy, Louis Vuitton, Parfums Christian Dior, Givenchy, Guerlain, Benefit Cosmetics, TAG Heuer, Hublot, Zenith, and Bulgari.

Explaining the way in which the organization competes and performs, Francesco Trapani, president of Watchmaking and Jewellery at LVMH commented:

> When you buy a brand watch or jewellery item, you don't just buy a product but also a dream of sorts. This dream is a result of several things. Today the story of the brand is important—this is why brands are increasingly spending time and money on telling the public their history and the different stages of that history. The dream stems from both the fame of the brand and from its history. And whilst it is obvious we sell a product it is more and more important that we offer a product that is recognisable in style with a strong, innovative and high-quality character. This is why every year significant investment is made in developing new materials to launch new products. A client distinguishes between a brand with 20 years of experience and a brand with 150 years of experience. Brands with long histories gear their product launches to the past—they RE-launch products that are more interesting than mere new products.

Mr Trapani's comments embody the creativity and innovative spirit encouraged in the organization, in which brand houses are challenged to 'continually renew their offerings, resolutely looking to the future whilst always respecting their unique heritage'. In delivering super-premium goods on a global scale, LVMH operates a tightly controlled network of suppliers, production facilities, and distribution channels.

> At LVMH, we never compromise on quality. Because we embody the world of craftsmanship in its most noble and accomplished form, we pay meticulous attention to detail and to perfection.

Further, to allow decision-making and brand management according to the needs of its heritage, sectoral changes, and in-country requirements:

> LVMH has an agile and decentralized organization that encourages efficiency and responsiveness. It stimulates individual initiative by entrusting each person with significant responsibilities. Our entrepreneurial spirit encourages both risk-taking and perseverance. It requires pragmatic thinking and an ability to motivate teams, leading them to achieve ambitious objectives.

As an example of creating competitive advantage through unique resources, there are few organizations that can match the performance and effectiveness of LVMH. Its ability to continue to perform in this way seems to rely on continual dynamic reconfiguration of its resource base to exploit the heritage, distinctiveness, and customer loyalty of its brands. For this, insightful and nuanced strategic awareness of the resource base is required.

Questions for discussion

1. Why might customers purchase products from an LVMH brand? What are the implications for the pricing and revenue generating opportunities for the group?
2. What resources seem to allow the organization to perform effectively in the super-luxury segment? How do these resources contribute to performance?
3. How would you describe the management priorities and concerns for organizational leaders in LVMH? To which factors do they pay most attention?

Sources

https://www.lvmh.com/news-documents/press-releases/record-results-for-lvmh-in-2018/

https://www.lvmh.com/group/about-lvmh/the-lvmh-spirit/

https://www.youtube.com/watch?v=WA1vHeMOHqQ (Mr Trapani interview)

http://www.thefashionlaw.com/home/lvmh-a-time-line-behind-the-building-of-a-conglomerate

6.1 Introduction

What an organization has available to use—its **resources**—and what it is able to do—its **capabilities**—are crucial considerations in strategy as part of the internal context. The decisions and activities an organization engages in, now and in the future, will be enabled and constrained by the resources and capabilities it has at its disposal (Garbuio et al. 2015). From a process–practice perspective, developing awareness of these resources and capabilities and the implications for what is possible through strategy is a vital part of knowing the organizational context. In this chapter, we explore theories and methods that can help you build your knowledge of an organization's resources and capabilities, and the options that are available to improve the effectiveness of how these are deployed through activity.

We also explore how distinctive resources might enable competitive advantage using the theory and concepts of what is known as the resource-based view (RBV). The RBV is a way of thinking that focuses on how an organization might grow and survive by exploiting distinctive **value-creating** resources at its disposal. The ideas of the RBV are extended through the **dynamic capability view (DCV)** which explains how organizational resources can be created, modified, or divested over time. These theoretical perspectives will give you ways of thinking that are complementary to the market-based view (MBV) and ecosystems perspectives outlined in Chapter 5.

In this chapter we will explain how to interpret and work with RBV and DCV concepts to build knowledge of the 'internal' context and related options for strategic action in an organization. The RBV is often called the 'inside-out' approach, as it focuses on the implications of the resources within an organization's control, and how those resources can be used most effectively to meet the needs of customers or outperform competitors. The DCV brings into focus the potential to adapt resources—through learning, innovation, reorganization, acquisition, etc.—to ensure that it can compete and survive as its context changes.

Building knowledge of resources is crucial, as each organization has access to a unique 'stock' of resources, accrued over time, which need to be managed according to situational needs (Dierickx and Cool 1989). Diversity in the resource stocks between firms means that they have the potential to undertake different activities and achieve differing levels of performance (Peteraf 1993).

However, having superior potential, and converting potential into superior performance, are two separate matters. The RBV draws on the thinking of Penrose (1959) in suggesting that entrepreneurial management of the resource base is crucial to continuing organizational performance. Evaluating the gap between what an organization might be able to do to its optimal advantage, and what it currently does, will generate valuable insights for you for resource-related strategic initiatives (Wernerfelt 1984, 1995). Further, understanding how resources are ebbing and flowing to the organization over time—deliberately or otherwise—can give a sense of future performance potential and resilience.

Building understanding of how well resources and capabilities are being used to create value requires a customer focus. Just as with competitor analysis, customers ultimately decide whether the activities of a for-profit organization are worth paying for, or are worth continuing to fund for not-for-profit organizations. Examining how well the resources of the organization are being used to deliver outcomes valued by customers will provide highly relevant insights for organizational strategy.

We can also gain insight into competitive advantage through the RBV. The uniqueness and configuration of an organization's resources and capabilities in part determine its competitive advantage (Peteraf and Barney 2003). We will examine the possibilities of nurturing and exploiting distinctive resources in ways that might create and sustain competitive advantage. To aid you in this task, we will review a range of methods for conducting analysis of the resources, capabilities, and activities of the organization.

- **Resource-base profiling**—build up a clear shared picture of what the organization currently has available in terms of resources.
- **VRIO analysis**—VRIO stands for 'valuable, rare, inimitable, and organization', the characteristics of resources which might give an organization competitive advantage.
- **Capability audit**—identifying the capabilities currently being used by the organization to undertake activities and deliver outcomes.
- **Dynamic capability analysis**—figuring out how new resource configurations might be created to develop a capability profile that is fit for the future.
- **Value chain analysis**—identify how organizational activities might be revised and improved to better create customer value and organizational performance.

The RBV has often been criticized for being too theoretical and of limited value to practising managers (e.g. Connor 2002). In this chapter, we address these criticisms by introducing you to methods which have been developed through applied research and consultancy practice underpinned by RBV and DCV theory. Using these methods in combination will allow you to build knowledge of resources and capabilities, and to identify options for improving resource-based performance in the future.

As with external context analysis, we will reflect on the relative strengths and limitations of the different resource-based analysis methods. With this critical edge to our use of analytical tools, we might uncover insights about the resources, capabilities, and activities of the organization that add value to organizational strategy practice.

6.2 Analysing an organization's resources, capabilities, and activities

The RBV has received sustained attention from strategy academics for over 35 years. Consequently, there are many RBV concepts, and an equally wide range of applications of those concepts are available in the literature. For clarity, before discussing the RBV we define our interpretation of a range of relevant concepts.

Key definitions

Resources describe **what the organization has that can be used**. There are many ways to classify resources—tangible, intangible, human, tradeable/non-tradeable. In this chapter, we will work with categories of resources as defined in Table 6.1. These categories are intended to help you identify the resources that an organization has at its disposal. Please note, if you are reading about the resource-based view, many journal articles will use the term 'asset' to mean what we describe here as 'resources'. For LVMH, resources can be identified across all the different categories: reputational resources include its famous brands such as Moët & Chandon, Benefit Cosmetics, and TAG Heuer; it has extensive physical resources in the form of production facilities and high-end retail outlets; its highly trained artisanal workforce represent a skills resource; the intense focus on quality across the organization is a cultural resource, etc.

The **resource base** refers to **all the resources directly owned or available to the organization on a preferential basis**. The organization will have a set of resources that it owns outright, such as buildings, brand names, and equipment. It will also have exclusive rights to access the capacities of people through employment contracts. Further, through collaborative agreements with other organizations (e.g. suppliers, research institutes, partner firms), an organization might have access to the resources of others which is not available to all firms. The sum total of all these resources is described as the resource base of the organization (Helfat et al. 2007). In the LVMH case, the resource base describes all its wholly owned resources (brands, buildings, cash reserves, etc.) and preferentially accessed resources (the people who choose to continue to work there, the exclusive supplier network, etc.). LVMH can draw on any aspect of this resource base to try to achieve its aims on a continuing basis.

Resource stocks refers to **the current level of resources available to the organization**. Like the stocks of different types of food in a store cupboard, resource stocks describe the available capacity of different types of organizational resources. Resource stocks are a crucial consideration for those making strategy. At any given time, resource stocks might be allocated—deployed through organizational activities—or held in reserve (i.e. available for deployment). Having a resource base that is fully committed to activities means that the organization has no capacity for additional initiatives. Equally, having a high level of resource stocks that are not deployed means that the organization is not engaging in productive activity. Both these extremes carry risks for organizational resilience and survival (Dierickx and Cool 1989). The financial resources (e.g. cash, available credit) of LVMH have allowed it to acquire a range of brands over recent years. Having uncommitted stocks of financial resources means that at any

6

TABLE 6.1 **Categories of resources**

Category	Description	Such as ...	For example ...
Physical	Tangible resources that can be bought and sold on the open market	Buildings, equipment, vehicles, raw materials, IT infrastructure	Emirates' fleet of long range aircraft
Natural	Natural resources linked to location and geographic conditions	Rich soil, water supply, clean air, minerals, renewable energy potential, location in economic zone	Highland Spring's access to naturally occurring water springs arising from its geographical location
Financial	Monetary assets and liabilities as recorded on a balance sheet	Creditors, debtors, funding, cash	Apple's accrued overseas 'cash pile'
Informational	Raw and refined data about the organization or its ecosystem	Customer data, supplier data, competitor data, organizational performance data	Fitbit's biometric user data—reportedly the largest such database in the world
Knowledge	Understanding of technical or commercial value	Intellectual property, trade secrets, trademarks, organizational learning	Dyson's vacuum cyclone technology incorporated in a wide product range
Reputational	The way in which the organization is perceived by stakeholders	Brand assets and awareness, trust, loyalty, goodwill towards organization	Coca-Cola's global brand reputation and symbols
Cultural	The norms and habitual ways of working in the organization	Shared employee attitudes and values, internal relationships, operational routines, engrained priorities	Hyundai's deeply engrained commitment to value engineering and reliability
Organizational	The structuring of resources, reporting, legal entities, and financial flows in the organization	Legal structure, stock market listing, tax registration, transfer pricing arrangements, HQ–subsidiary relations	Starbuck's organizational structure enables financial flows for tax efficiency in its global operations
Managerial	The capacities of the individuals and teams with resource allocation powers	Leadership charisma, accumulated experience of management team, decision-making biases	Jack Ma's charisma, connections, and approach to investment as key assets underpinning the growth of Alibaba
Skills	The specific expertise, talents, and abilities in the human resource base of the organization	Professional expertise, manual crafts, staff qualifications	The expertise of Tata Global Beverages staff as tea scientists, blenders, growers, distributors, and marketeers
Relational	The connections and assets available on a preferential basis through external stakeholders	Supplier base, government ties, customer relationships, network/ecosystem position, collaborations	Goldman Sachs' highly developed relationships with government and tax authorities across the world
Motivational	The drive, interest, and morale of staff to work towards organizational aims	Employee morale in functions or locations, incentive schemes, positivity of attitude to organizational strategy	Google's use of non-monetary rewards, recognition schemes, and on-site facilities to spur productivity

moment it has the potential to pursue new acquisitions. If the financial resources are already allocated to initiatives in a time period, it may be unable to pursue acquisition opportunities that arise unexpectedly.

Capabilities refers to **individual or collective potential to take action to a threshold level of performance**. Capabilities are best described as 'the ability to ...' perform an activity to a minimum threshold of performance. For example, having 'the ability to legally drive' means that an individual can meet the minimum legal performance levels to drive on a public road. Capabilities arise from deploying resources, often in combinations described as 'bundles' (Lampel and Shamsie 2003); for example, a combination of a government issued licence, practical driving skills, and a theoretical knowledge of road systems and car operation combine to enable a capability to legally drive. However, having the capability to drive legally doesn't imply exceptional performance and doesn't mean that the individual will choose to do so at any time. Ability to manage supplier networks, ability to execute acquisitions, and ability to communicate with consumers are all examples of capabilities at LVMH.

Competences refers to **individual or collective potential to take action to a superior level of performance**. As a subset of capabilities, competences refers to the capabilities in which the individual or organization can demonstrate superior performance (relative to the minimum required performance standard). Continuing the driving example, through advanced driver training, a safety track record, expert evaluation, etc., an individual may make a claim to be a competent legal driver. This means that relative to other legal drivers, they exceed the minimum expected performance levels. Again, having such a competence doesn't mean that the individual will choose to use it at any given time. There are several competences in the LVMH example in which the organization consistently demonstrates superior performance, such as 'the ability to relaunch modernised yet historical brands' and 'the ability to deliver the highest standards of artisanal production on a global scale'.

Activities refer to **that which is actually done by the organization**. In Chapter 2, we defined activity in relation to the process–practice framework as 'that which is actually done by practitioners'. In discussing the RBV we can also understand that an organization carries out activities, drawing on its resource base. Activities are often configured to connect together in an organizational process, where over time, by design, activity outcomes feed into or trigger subsequent activities. Activities may be routine—recurring actions with familiar features between occurrences. Equally, activities may be novel, where an unfamiliar innovative act is undertaken. Day-to-day operational activities involve the sourcing and conversion of materials into products, which are then distributed to customers around the world and sold through LVMH facilities. At the same time, entrepreneurial activities involve experimenting with the novel relaunch of heritage brands—trying out new materials and engaging customers in novel dialogue about their 'dreams'.

Activity outcomes refers to **the consequences of organizational activities**. Over time, organizational activities may result in a range of outcomes that affect stocks of resources. Activities may lead to the supply of products or services, generating inventory and revenue. Activities might result in a change in the resource base, such as creating, consuming, replenishing, and divesting resources. Activities may result in informational outcomes—creating triggers for further activities, or providing new insights and learning for those involved with the organization. Activity outcomes may be intentional or unintentional, and known or unknown to those involved with the organization. For example, in LVMH, a main outcome of day-to-day activities is significant financial returns (an activity outcome of €10 billion profit being achieved in 2018). Acquisition activities result in extended reputational resources (brands with heritage) being at the organization's disposal.

Resource flows refers to ***the incremental changes in resource stocks that occur over time***. As activities occur and outcomes are achieved, resources flow into and out of the resource base. Resource flows describe the changes in available organizational resource stocks occurring over time. These changes can be either an increase or a decrease in stock levels at a rate determined by circumstances. Some resource stocks will be affected by organizational activities; for example, regular financial outflows have to occur for the purchase of production materials. Others will be unaffected—using a knowledge resource such as a product recipe doesn't limit its use in future. Understanding, monitoring, and influencing resource flows may be a vital activity for the future performance of the organization (Dierickx and Cool 1989). LVMH achieved free cash flows of €5.5 billion into its financial reserves in 2018, and also reported 'exceptional harvests', meaning a very high flow into the future liquid material resource stocks for its wine and spirits division.

An organization's resource, capability, and activity system

Consistent with the process–practice framework and the combinatory model (see Chapter 2), we propose that you consider organizational resources, capabilities, and activities as a connected system, as depicted in Figure 6.1. Over time, available stocks of resources in the resource base create or sustain the capabilities to perform a range of activities. When capabilities are deployed, resources are allocated to execute selected activities, and the consequences of those activities may result in flows to or from the resource base stock (Markides 2000).

As we have seen from the LVMH example, the resource base contains diverse types and stock levels such as financial reserves, production facilities, a 'high-quality' culture, a 'house of brands', a skilled workforce, global supplier network, etc. In combination, these resources create a potential to relaunch super-luxury heritage products across a wide range of products on a global scale. Activating this potential uses up resource stocks, as cash, availability of staff and facilities, etc. are allocated to product relaunch activities, reducing available stocks of resources for alternative activities such as pursuing acquisition targets.

When the product relaunch activity is executed, all may happen as intended, resulting in a successful launch and beneficial flows to the resource base of more cash from sales, new intellectual property, enhanced brand and market knowledge, new product design skills, strengthened supplier relationships, etc. Equally, should activities not work out as planned, the consequences might be negative for the resource base, such as loss of cash (e.g. on a product recall), diminished brand reputation (from poor product performance), etc. The eroding effect of these negative flows on the resource base may limit the future capabilities of the firm, as foundational resource stocks are depleted.

As the resource, capability, and activity system operates, the selection and execution of specific activities in practice will create a unique profile of resources for the organization. At any moment in time, the types and characteristics of resources within the resource base and the stock levels available for deployment will be a function of the historical path followed by the organization (Vergne and Durand 2011). Put in a different way, what an organization is capable

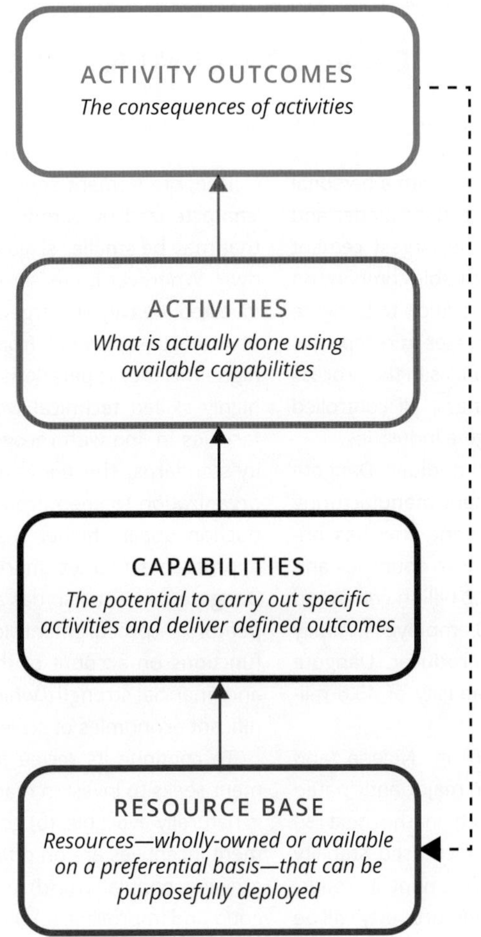

FIGURE 6.1 Resources, capabilities, and activities as a system.

of doing in the present is a function of what has happened in the past (Teece et al. 1997). As introduced in Chapter 4, this is known as organizational **path dependency**.

Path dependency raises several queries for those involved in strategy work. What resource stocks have we accrued in our resource base? What capabilities and activities might we deploy today in order build a valuable/relevant resource base in the future? By undertaking certain activities today, are we putting at risk, or even constraining, our capacity to act in the future? To understand how you can engage with these questions, later in this chapter we will consider the topic of dynamic capability—the capacity to purposefully create, extend, and modify the resource base of the organization (Helfat et al. 2007:4).

A resource-based view of strategy

We can build on our definitions of resources, capabilities, and activities by considering the RBV, or inside-out view, of competitive advantage and organizational strategy. The RBV can provide us with theoretical insights as to how the organization is able to compete and survive (Wernerfelt 1984).

CASE EXAMPLE 6.1 DANGOTE CEMENT PREPARES FOR THE FUTURE

6

Aliko Dangote is Africa's richest man with a personal net worth of over $10 billion. He is the founder and chairman of Dangote Cement, the largest cement producer in Africa and the most valuable company on the Nigerian Stock Exchange. In addition to Dangote Cement, Mr Dangote also owns stakes in companies producing salt, sugar, and flour, and is in the process of growing an oil refining business, all controlled through a parent company, Dangote Industries.

Originally an importer of commodities, Dangote Industries transitioned into cement manufacturing during the 1990s. Dangote Cement now has on-the-ground operations in ten African countries and annual revenues in excess of $2.2 billion generated through the work of over 24,000 employees. A fully integrated quarry-to-customer producer, Dangote has a pan-African production capacity of 45.6 million tonnes per annum (Mta).

More factories are planned in Nigeria and throughout Africa to capitalize on major anticipated population and economic growth in the next 30 years. As countries experience increased stability and development, extensive investment in roads, buildings, urban infrastructure, and property will be required. Dangote Industries anticipate that this will drive a demand for cement that will far outweigh the current supply capacity.

At present, Nigeria is Sub-Saharan Africa's largest market for cement, consuming more than 18.6 Mt in 2017, of which Dangote supplied 12 Mt (c.40% of its Nigerian production capacity) at profit margins of c.60%. Also benefiting from tax holidays and investment incentives, Dangote Cement's Nigerian operations return significant financial flows to Dangote Industries. Cement is a bulky product, and Dangote Cement benefits from being in close proximity to Nigeria's substantial limestone deposits. It exports tariff free to countries in the West African trading bloc ECOWAS, increasing the capacity utilization, efficiency, and profitability of its Nigerian plants. Indeed, through the activities of Dangote Cement, Nigeria has shifted from being a net importer to a net exporter of cement (the only country in ECOWAS to achieve this status).

Dangote Cement seeks to stand out in markets 'characterized by competitors with older factories that may be smaller-scale or less efficient than our own'. Wherever it has set up, Dangote Cement has invested heavily in large-scale plants using state of the art equipment from Europe and China for high-efficiency operations. It invests in hiring a highly skilled technical workforce which operates facilities in line with recognized international quality standards. These investments have allowed the organization to keep product costs lower and production quality higher than competitors, winning a profitable market share in its target markets. Dangote Cement also has advantages over its competitors in procurement, logistics, and distribution functions on account of the Dangote Group's size and financial strength, which allow it to achieve significant economies of scale.

To continue its recipe for success, Dangote Cement seeks to invest in markets where (a) limestone is naturally available, (b) government backed investment incentives are on offer, (c) there is a large and growing population, (d) transport infrastructure is good and improving, (e) the price of energy and fuel are low, (f) there is a 'cement deficit', (g) government policy is to invest in housing and infrastructure, and (h) existing competition use older and smaller production plants.

In future, the company is also planning to float shares on the London Stock Exchange. This is partly a statement of its global ambition, and partly an aid to the adoption of improved governance and business culture. The organization is already steered by a formidable board and executive team with significant global leadership experience and strong political connections across Africa. The subsequent reputational gains and corporate capability of a London listing would help Dangote compete outside its current markets. In the meantime, it is likely that the Dangote Group will continue its development of the Nigerian industrial landscape. Mr Dangote comments 'Nigeria is one of the best-kept secrets. A lot of foreigners are not investing because they're waiting for the right time. There is no right time'.

Questions for discussion

1. Describe the resource base underpinning Dangote Cement's operations. Identify what you consider to be the most crucial resource combinations underpinning Dangote Cement's success. Explain your answer.
2. How are Dangote Cement, and Dangote Industries, aiming to adapt their resource base to be ready for the future?
3. Comment on Dangote's criteria for selecting new markets. To what extent does it make sense, given current organizational capabilities? Are there any long-term vulnerabilities associated with this approach?

Sources

https://www.theguardian.com/cities/2019/feb/25/concrete-the-most-destructive-material-on-earth

https://www.forbes.com/profile/aliko-dangote/

https://uk.reuters.com/article/nigeria-dangote-cement-ipo/update-1-nigerias-dangote-cement-says-london-listing-likely-to-be-2020-idUKL5N20O4BS

http://www.dangotecement.com/about-us

https://www.economist.com/business/2014/04/12/building-on-concrete-foundations

https://www.bloomberg.com/news/articles/2019-05-16/a-5-billion-listing-makes-mtn-nigeria-s-number-two-firm-chart

The RBV is a way of thinking about how organizations use their resources to endure, and possibly succeed, over time. According to RBV theorizing, it is the difference in the resource bases of organizations—what they have, and how they use it—that is the key to explaining organizational performance differentials over time (Peteraf 1993). This contrasts with the market-based view (MBV) (see Chapter 5), in which it is assumed that all firms have equal access to equivalent resources.

At the centre of RBV theorizing is a search for resources that comply with a set of characteristics that give the organization a possible competitive edge. This crucial conceptual framework, known as the VRIO framework, is shown in Table 6.2.

Each characteristic in the VRIO framework is a test for whether a resource might be a source of competitive advantage for an organization. A resource that can be described by all four characteristics has the potential to be a source of sustainable competitive advantage (meaning advantage that endures despite competitor efforts). In the LVMH example at the start of the chapter, luxury brands with iconic histories are resources that meet all four VRIO criteria. The

TABLE 6.2 **The VRIO framework**

Resource characteristic	Description
Valuable	Can be used to create outputs of value to customers that they are willing to pay for (or fund, in the case of not for profit)
Rare	In limited supply; not available to all organizations
Imperfectly imitable	It is not possible to copy or create the resource, or obtain the same value from other means
Organization	Available in a format in which it can actually be used, if required, by the organization in its specific context

Source: adapted from Barney (1991, 1995).

relaunched brands for Bulgari are valuable to customers to the extent they are willing to pay a super-premium price for the associated watches and jewellery, the brand is rare as it is wholly owned by LVMH and therefore is unavailable to competitors, the history of the brand is impossible to imitate, and the brand assets are deployed through a number of products. Because the V, R, I, and O criteria are all met, the relaunched Bulgari brands create a source of sustainable competitive advantage for LVMH.

A resource that meets the V and R criteria might be a source of temporary competitive advantage that is vulnerable to the activities of competitors. For example, the smartphone industry was initially dominated by Blackberry (a trading name of Research-In-Motion). These products were highly valued by business customers and in short supply (rare), as other mobile manufacturers focused on fashion or mass-produced simple functionality models. Over time, however, others were able to imitate the technology of Blackberry through their own research and development (R&D) efforts, and the same mobile business computing functionality became available through mobile-enabled tablets, laptops, and wearable tech. In other words, Blackberry's technological resources eventually failed the 'imperfectly imitable' test. As a consequence, Blackberry's initial market dominance was eroded by firms such as Samsung and Apple.

These examples illustrate the argument made by Barney (1991) that VRIO resources, and thus sources of sustainable competitive advantage, are likely to be 'socially embedded'. This means that resources which have a history with customers, such as brands, or resources associated with organizational history, such as culture, are the most likely to pass all four VRIO criteria tests. If a resource can be traded on the open market, such as technological components, products, or equipment, it may give a short-term advantage but will likely be vulnerable to competitor activities (Augier and Teece 2009).

If the intention of organizational strategy is to ensure survival, from the RBV it is most important to understand what the organization can do differently and the extent to which that difference is utilized (Bachmann 2002). A common error that we have found in consultancy practice is strategists describing what an organization does well—its competences—as sources of competitive advantage. What the organization does well certainly matters in terms of performance, as will be discussed later in the chapter. However, in terms of creating competitive advantage and thus the potential to do better than break-even competitors, resource difference matters more than excellence.

For example, Toyota once enjoyed a competitive advantage over American vehicle manufacturers because of its lean production systems. This advantage endured over several decades because of the cultural embeddedness of the lean approach translating into low-price high-reliability vehicles valued by many customers that rivals could not match. However, lean production systems as a source of advantage has now eroded as rivals have caught up, or new rivals have entered the market with equally strong lean production systems embedded in their organizational culture. It remains vital for Toyota to sustain excellent lean performance. To not do so would be to put the organization at a competitive disadvantage. However, the excellent lean approach of Toyota no longer sets it apart from its rivals. For Toyota, difference—and thus competitive advantage—now arises from brand and technological innovation resources.

This search for distinctive resources, or resource 'asymmetries' (Miller 2003), that are valued by the customer is at the heart of the resource-based view. Understanding where valuable resource distinctiveness can be exploited today or nurtured for the future is the central ambition of the RBV.

Resource bundles and complementarities

The RBV highlights that VRIO resources are rarely, if ever, deployed on their own. Instead, resources tend to be configured in 'bundles' during use (Miller and Shamsie 1996). On its own a resource might enable no, or a very limited range of, capabilities. In combination with other resources, the potential for taking action can be significantly enhanced. There need be nothing special about the resources being combined to create potential for action. Equally, the value of distinctive resources might only be unlocked in the presence of 'ordinary' resources providing **complementarity**. Complementarity refers to when two separate resources enhance the qualities and usefulness of each other when present together. In the case of Dangote Cement (see Table 6.3), having highly skilled technicians enhances the output that can be achieved by modern equipment. Equally, having modern equipment will increase the productivity potential of the highly skilled staff. This is comparable to the idea of complementary firms unlocking the profit potential of an industry as discussed in Chapter 5. The example in Table 6.3. is a simple combination of two resources. In practice, it is normal to find highly complex combinations of resources in organizational life.

When undertaking resource-based analysis, it is important to understand how distinctive resources are combined with complementary resources to unlock value-creating capabilities and competitive advantage. The extent to which an organization is able to do this is described by the O criterion of VRIO (Barney 1995). If a distinctive resource cannot be made operational because of a lack of complementary resources, the distinctive resource cannot create competitive advantage. For example, a start-up firm might develop an innovative renewable energy technology that meets the VRI criteria, but runs out of financial resource to commercialize it. The VRI resource was owned by the firm but was not operationalized and no competitive advantage was achieved in practice.

Understanding complementarities in relation to VRIO resources is crucial for organizations that outsource aspects of their operation. As will be discussed in a later chapter, outsourcing is when an external firm is contracted to carry out a business process for the organization, rather than it being completed internally. For example, many automotive firms have outsourced the movement of parts within their assembly plants to third-party logistics firms. If complementary resources needed to realize the benefit of VRIO resources are outsourced, any issues with the outsourced service provider might directly impact on the competitive advantage of the organization (Barthelemy and Adsit 2003).

Distinctive and threshold capabilities

VRIO resources, along with complementary resources, will create **distinctive capabilities** for the organization. Distinctive capabilities refer to the potential to take value-creating actions that are not available to all competitors. For a capability to be considered distinctive, it doesn't have

TABLE 6.3 **Example of complementarity: Dangote Cement**

	Highly skilled technicians	Low skilled technicians
Modern, high tech equipment	Optimal performance	Moderate performance
Old, low tech equipment	Moderate performance	Low performance

to be unique, just 'not common' or shared amongst competitors. When deployed effectively, distinctive capabilities may result in products and services of value to customers that generate profit for the organization.

Equally, many capabilities arising from the resource base will not be distinctive and therefore not part of a direct explanation of organizational competitive advantage. However, non-distinctive capabilities may be vital to an organization's survival, and therefore organizational strategy, because of the enabling role they play for operations. **Threshold capabilities** are capabilities that an organization is required to maintain to a minimum performance level. Threshold capabilities create the conditions in which distinctive capabilities can be exploited. For example, all chemicals manufacturers in Europe must maintain threshold capabilities in compliance with health, safety, and environmental legislation. Without these capabilities being available to the minimum required performance level, a chemicals manufacturer will not be permitted to operate. The enactment of these threshold capabilities will likely be tracked and audited against regulatory and voluntary standards (e.g. ISO14001, ISO18001, etc.). However, as these capabilities are required of all manufacturers, they are not a source of distinctiveness and therefore competitive advantage for any organization. Also, the value delivered to customers is not directly linked to these capabilities.

Threshold capabilities should not be neglected when reviewing the organizational resource base. In terms of strategy, threshold capabilities will have a negative impact on organizational performance when they are not maintained and enacted to a minimum required standard. As you prepare to analyse the resource base of the organization, do not feel pressure to focus on VRIO resources only. Understanding threshold capabilities is equally important.

Analysing competences

We defined competence as being able to achieve superior performance relative to competitors in some matter of interest. Distinctive competences are those competences which draw on distinctive resources to achieve outcomes that are prized by the customer (Ackermann and Eden 2011). For example, LVMH's 'ability to relaunch modernised yet historical brands' delivers outcomes at a superior level of performance. As this competence is underpinned by distinctive reputational resources in the form of heritage brands, it is arguably a distinctive competence.

Distinctive competences provide potential to act in unique ways to superior performance levels in comparison to what competitors can do. As you conduct analysis of the resource base, looking for opportunities to make new resource combinations that combine competences with VRIO resources is a useful focus. For example, LVMH has a competence in creating artisanal outputs to the highest quality standards (i.e. LVMH is able to achieve these outputs in a superior way to competitors). When LVMH adds iconic brands to their portfolio, combining these brands with their artisanal production competence creates significant new sources of customer value creation, competitive advantage, and growth in sales revenue.

Competence can also aid organizational performance, and survival, through achieving threshold capabilities with efficiency. In LVMH, supply chain management competence (above average performance for the luxury goods sector) improves the financial results of the organization. Every luxury goods manufacturer needs to move materials and finished products around the world. To lack supply chain capabilities would be to go out of operation. However, availability of products in store is a minimum expectation of customers, and is not an outcome for which they are willing to pay additional money. For LVMH, lowering costs and cash tied up in inventory holdings in the supply chain does not affect the price customers are willing to pay, meaning that the financial benefits of competence in threshold capabilities can be retained in the organization. In turn, this means that the organization has more available financial resources to invest or deploy towards other initiatives.

In the 1990s, a trend emerged in strategy consultancy towards advising on core competences for competitive advantage. Drawing on the influential work of Prahalad and Hamel (1990), core competences describe competences that recur throughout an organization, underpinning value creation and strategy across all aspects of operations. For example, a core competence for the budget airline Ryanair could be cost minimization. This means that all activities undertaken by the organization might incorporate a superior (versus competitors') ability to minimize the costs incurred. Where these core competences create outcomes valued by the customer (as opposed to being valued by the organization), the organization might claim core distinctive competences and sustainable competitive advantage. In this example, low-cost flights would be the outcome valued by Ryanair's customers. The theoretical proposition of core competence is that strategy work should identify core (distinctive) competences and organize operations and initiatives to best exploit and sustain the core (distinctive) competences. In practice, this can be a challenging exercise to achieve in a value-adding way during strategy work, as core competences are not obvious or easily articulated for most organizations.

As you think about conducting internal analysis, you can combine analysis of capabilities and competences with competitive analysis (Chapter 5). As competitive analysis helps you to define what an organization needs to be able to do to succeed in servicing a group of customers, you can use insights about competences, and threshold and distinctive capabilities, to evaluate the performance of your organization against competitors.

Legacy issues in the resource base

A challenge in strategy work is to remain vigilant for changes in circumstances that need to be reflected in managerial thinking whilst the organization is experiencing success. As Peter Drucker suggested, success can be a curse as complacency is the biggest killer of businesses (Ashkenas 2011). In particular, it is important to continue to evaluate resources and capabilities that are considered sources of competence or competitive advantage. From a process–practice perspective, as the organizational context continues to unfold, are the resources and capabilities that were once assets now turning into liabilities?

As introduced in Chapter 4, Dorothy Leonard-Barton (1992) used the term core rigidities to describe resources which were once valuable, and are still considered so in strategy work, but which are in actuality a hindrance to organizational performance. Rigidities and inertia arise when those with decision-making powers 'become emotionally attached inappropriately to the people, places, and things associated closely with the strategic status quo' (Healey and Hodgkinson 2017:121). According to the decisions taken, the consequences of this type of emotional attachment may be fatal to the long-term survival prospects of the organization.

Kodak is an example of core rigidities leading to organizational demise. At one point in 1976, Kodak sold 95% of the world's camera film and was ranked in the top five global brands. The preceding year, Kodak had also invented a 0.01 megapixel digital camera. Over the subsequent decades, those responsible for strategic management in Kodak invested poorly in building digital photography resources and capabilities, hindered by a belief that it would harm competences, competitive advantage, and revenue in film and photo paper technologies. Despite these views, the customer and competitive environment was changing around Kodak, and digital photography was gradually destroying the mass market for photo film. By the time that the core rigidity commitment to film was acknowledged, it was too late for Kodak. On 19 January 2012, trading in Kodak's shares were suspended at 36 cents as the organization filed for bankruptcy protection. Thousands of jobs were lost, and vast amounts of shareholder value destroyed (shares were trading at $90 in 1997) by a failure to embrace a technology that the company had once invented as a VRIO resource.

The same story can be found in many different industries as changes in customer interests, competitor activities, and available technology redefine the size and shapes of markets: for example, HMV in branded music sales, Nokia in mobile phones, and Barnes and Noble in book stores. The consequences of complacent decisions made by powerful incumbents at the peak of their success can result in once valuable resources and capabilities turning into liabilities that destroy the organization.

As you undertake analysis of the resource and capability context, including a diversity of data sources, seeking the voice of the customer and inviting critical voices alongside existing organizational narratives can improve the objectivity of your appraisal work, and guard against you unwittingly or uncritically adopting legacy managerial thinking.

Dynamic capability

The RBV examines what an organization has in the present. But how can an organization purposefully adjust its resource base in order to react to, or instigate, change in its environment over time? And can the ability to adjust the resource base enable an organization to survive and grow? These questions are addressed by the dynamic capability perspective. In a seminal article, Teece et al. (1997) describe the dynamic capability perspective as an extension of the resource base view, incorporating evolutionary mechanisms to provide a means of explaining how some organizations can adapt and survive, and how others fail. Teece et al. (1997) connect with the idea of path dependency in proposing the paths, positions, processes (PPP) framework for the role of dynamic capability in organizational survival (see Figure 6.2).

In the framework, processes refer to how, over time, resource stocks ebb and flow according to decisions and activities, historical paths determine an organization's current resource position, and decisions made about how to manage the resource base in the present will create possible paths/options for the organization in the future (Adner and Levinthal 2004). In relation to the activity system shown in Figure 6.1, historical paths describe previous cycles of the system, the resource base describes the current position, and dynamic capability is the potential to take purposeful action now in order to create a desired resource base profile in the future (Teece et al. 2016).

Dynamic capability can be defined as the 'organizational capacity to create, extend or modify the resource base' (Helfat et al. 2007:4). Dynamic capability can be used to adjust the resource base in reaction to environmental changes, or to modify the resource base to build new or

CASE EXAMPLE 6.2 **SIX SIGMA GIVES WAY TO RENDANHEYI**

Weeks after sealing a $5.4 billion deal to buy General Electric Appliances (GEA) in 2016, Zhang Ruimin, chairman of China's Haier Group, stood before 500 anxious GE white-collar workers asking questions about their futures. The irony wasn't lost on Zhang, revered in China as a pioneering corporate titan but mostly anonymous to the outside world. When Zhang was struggling in the 1990s to transform Haier from a collective village enterprise into a world-class manufacturer, he idolized General Electric Co. because of its reputation for corporate excellence. 'We went for courses at Crotonville, studying Six Sigma', he says, referring to GE's management training centre in New York and its famous data-driven process-improvement strategy. 'Now they were looking at me, asking: "What can you do for us?" '

As it turned out, quite a lot. Zhang may have initially embraced Six Sigma, but as Haier became the biggest appliance maker in the world, he sought a different approach to eliminate the sluggish bureaucracy that comes with size. So he created a management philosophy he calls Rendanheyi, which translates loosely to 'employees and customers become one'. The ideology seeks to make big companies operate like a collection of start-ups, emphasizing flexibility and risk-taking—and no middle managers (Frynas et al. 2018). Zhang thought the approach would help revitalize a stagnant GEA, where sales growth was 1% in 2014 and only 4% the next year as its once mighty parent General Electric floundered.

The company says it's working so far. GEA's revenue in US dollars grew by 11% in the first half of 2018 with the help of new products such as front-control ranges with Wi-Fi connectivity and its Café brand, which features customizable knobs and handles. 'We finally feel we have a parent who supports us and wants us to win', says Kevin Nolan, CEO of Louisville-based GEA. 'We view ourselves as part of the biggest appliance company in the world, and we are very proud of that.'

According to Zhang, Haier helped bring GEA 'back to life' and as a result 'our GE Appliances employees are feeling fortunate that Haier acquired this company. If not, they might have been laid off'. Haier's remaking of GEA reverses a typical narrative that cash-rich Chinese companies fail when trying to assimilate Western acquisitions. Such deals include TCL's acquisition of France's Thomson Electronics, SAIC Motors' takeover of South Korea's SsangYong Motor, and Ping An Group's investment in Fortis. 'Seventy percent of acquisitions fail, and 70 percent of that is because of culture', Zhang says. 'What we are is an example to follow.'

Zhang implemented Rendanheyi in 2010 at Haier. It advocates dividing monolithic business units into micro-enterprises that essentially act as start-ups with quarterly targets. Base salaries are low, with performance-based bonuses added on. 'The key tenet of the structure is that every micro-enterprise has "zero distance" to the customer', he says. Haier organizes business units around individual products instead of traditional functions such as supply chain, factory operations, and distribution. For example, everyone involved, from start to finish, in making a washing machine—from sourcing materials to manufacturing to sales—works in the same micro-enterprise. Haier is now described as 'a case study in what can be accomplished when an established company is willing to challenge bureaucracy's authoritarian structures and rule-choked practices' (Hamel and Zanini 2018:59).

At Haier Group, where the phrase 'middle manager' is almost an expletive, 10,000 people were dismissed after Rendanheyi was implemented, even as the company created jobs in growing businesses such as internet-connected appliances, logistics, and delivery. But GEA's job cuts have been modest, with only two middle managers let go so far. Others were redeployed and more workers were hired as sales increased, the company says.

GEA's old management structure created risk-averse silos that crippled the company's ability to launch products such as water heaters and packaged air conditioners, Nolan says. If a product wasn't in one of the core businesses—cooking, laundry, refrigeration, and dishwashing—it didn't receive the company's full attention or resources. 'Before, every business unit was focused on optimizing themselves', Nolan says. 'Now, everyone is focused on

Continued

the outside marketplace and focused on how to get their products to win—which can also mean taking risks on new types of products', he says. 'It's a huge culture difference.'

Questions for discussion

1. Evaluate the extent to which the management philosophy Rendanheyi is a VRIO resource.
2. It seems that GEA has undergone a successful cultural transformation from a Six Sigma to a Rendanheyi operating approach. To what extent did the GEA context before acquisition help this transformation? Explain your thinking.
3. What capabilities and competences do you detect in Haier's approach? How do they create value for customers? Do you think that any of these capabilities or competences are distinctive?
4. To what extent is GEA increasing or decreasing its readiness to face future challenges?

Sources

Based on Chang R. (2019). A Chinese farewell to Six Sigma. *Bloomberg Businessweek European Edition*, 11 February: 20–1.

See also Frynas et al. (2018) and Hamel and Zanini (2018) for further insights.

modified capabilities for anticipated future needs (Schoemaker et al. 2018). As per the framework in Figure 6.2, with a sense of your previous paths, current position, and future options, dynamic capability would be deployed to alter the resource base in the present to be ready for future needs. Dynamic capabilities are the subset of organizational capabilities associated with managing or manipulating the resource base. For example, dynamic capabilities were deployed by Haier to acquire GEA—using a combination of financing, change management, and leadership capabilities to purchase and integrate the GEA resource base into the Haier resource base (Frynas et al. 2018).

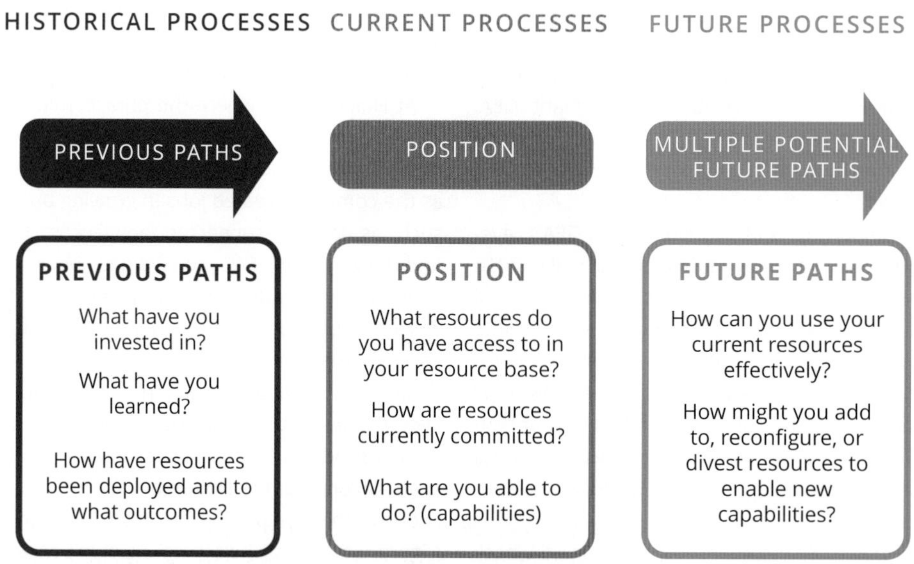

FIGURE 6.2 Paths, positions, processes (PPP) framework. Source: Adapted with permission from Teece, D. J., Pisano, G. and Shuen, A. (1997), Dynamic capabilities and strategic management. *Strategic Management Journal,* **18**: 509–533. doi:10.1002/(SICI)1097-0266(199708)18:7<509::AID-SMJ882>3.0.CO;2-Z. Copyright © 1997 John Wiley & Sons, Ltd.

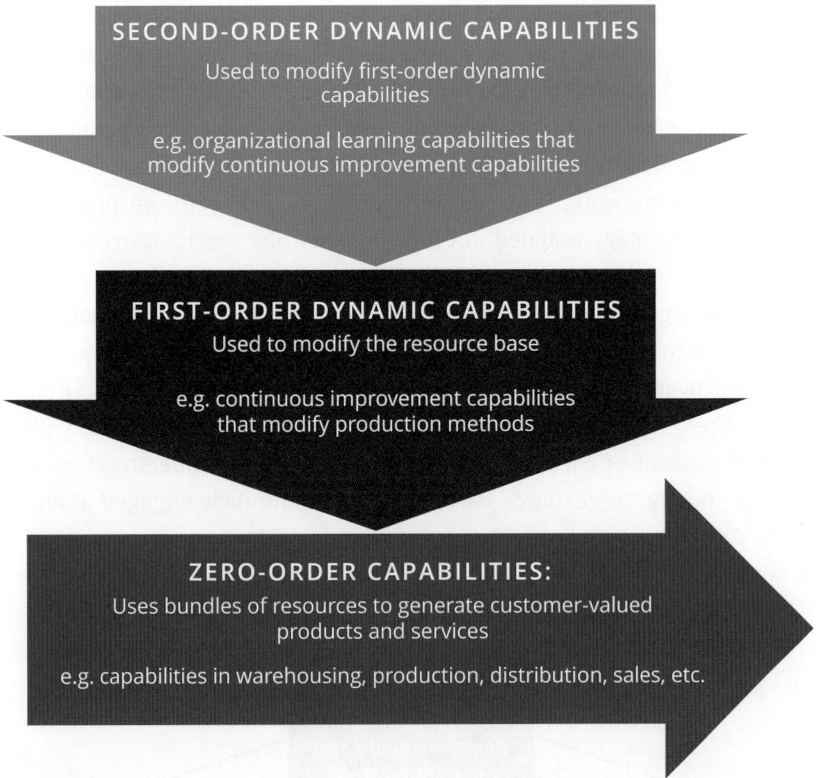

FIGURE 6.3 Orders of capabilities.

Winter (2003) describes ordinary capabilities as the 'zero order' of the organization—the operational routines and activities that directly create value for customers through product or service provision. Dynamic capabilities are referred to as 'first order' when they are used to modify ordinary capabilities (see Figure 6.3). Dynamic capabilities do not directly create products or services, so only indirectly enable competitive advantage. However, by favourably reconfiguring the resource base, dynamic capabilities revise ordinary capabilities and create new options for action and contributing to the survival of the organization (Teece 2014).

For example, the supply chain and manufacturing processes at a shampoo production facility reflect zero-order capabilities, as they produce finished goods that can be sold to customers. For efficiency gains, these zero-order processes will tend to occur in a routine way once established. The R&D capabilities that create a new variant of shampoo, or the project and change management processes that introduce that variant to the production facility might be referred to as 'first-order' dynamic capabilities—changing the way in which the **zero-order capabilities** arise from the resource base. The altered zero-order capabilities then result in either revised production techniques or production of a different range of finished goods.

First-order dynamic capability can also be nurtured through organizational learning (Zollo and Winter 2002). Therefore it can be argued that learning is a 'second-order' dynamic capability, i.e. learning (second order) alters dynamic capability (first order) which alters operational processes (zero order), as illustrated in Figure 6.3. Imagine that the change team of an insurance company engage in a management development programme which increases their innovation implementation skills. The programme has nurtured the team's capacity to implement innovation, and thus enhanced the dynamic capability in the organizational resource base. In other words, the experience of programme learning (second order) built the team's innovation skills, enhancing the organizational capacity to intentionally modify (first order) the service operations (zero order).

Teece (2007) further elaborates the processes underpinning dynamic capability in a sensing–seizing–reconfiguring framework. These strategic practices align with the 'preparing for the future' interpretation of strategy outlined in Chapter 1. Sensing mechanisms and processes put organizational decision-makers data about the current and possible future resource base requirements facing an organization in context. Seizing mechanisms are decisional processes which help determine to which insights from sensing data the organization will respond. Reconfiguring mechanisms then activate the relevant capabilities to manage flows to the resource base.

Building on Teece's sensing–seizing–transforming framework, and in line with a process–practice view, the concept of **core dynamic capabilities** can be understood as capabilities to create, extend, or modify the resource base which are continually engaged in an organization (see Figure 6.4). Core dynamic capabilities are underpinned by a constant focus of managerial attention to sensing and interpreting relevant aspects of the organizational context (Zeng and

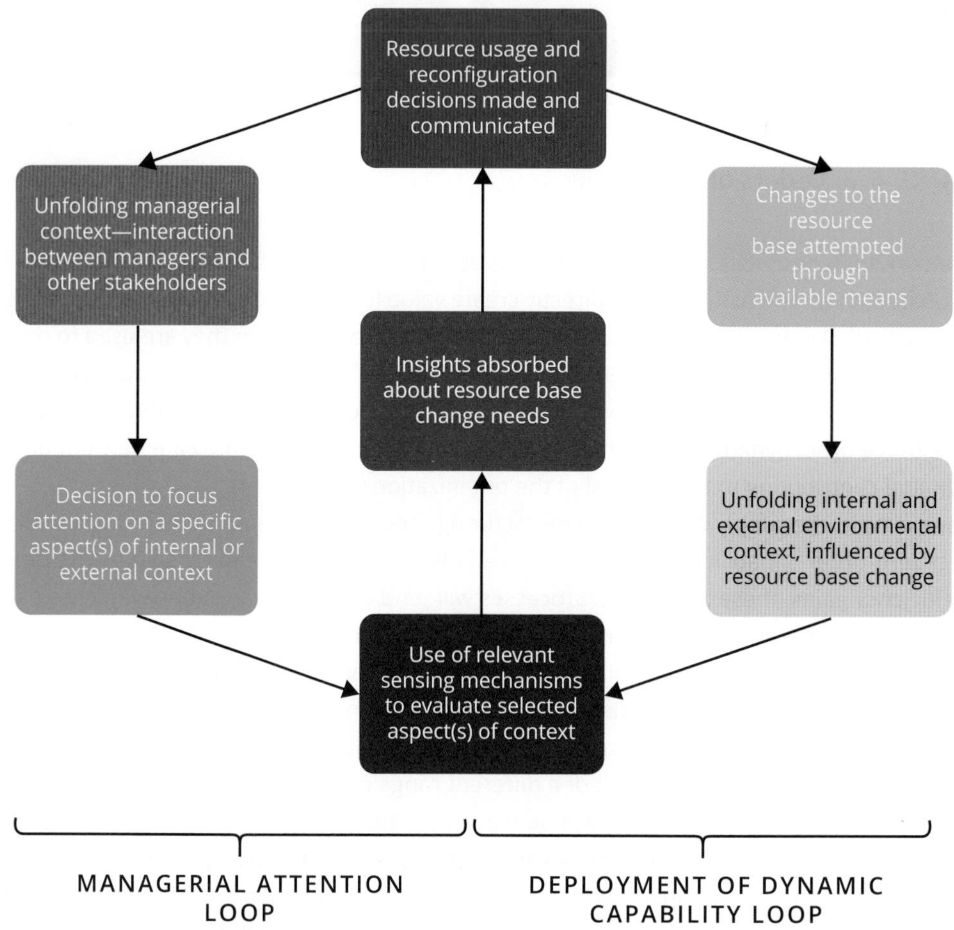

FIGURE 6.4 Core dynamic capabilities.

Mackay 2019). For example, in LVMH, R&D processes that are continually adding new knowledge resources about materials science might be considered core dynamic capabilities. As sources of renewal in the resource base, core dynamic capabilities should be nurtured and exploited. An organization may possess dynamic capabilities which are used intermittently, if at all—referred to as contingent dynamic capabilities. Those making strategy may wish to consider if and how contingent dynamic capabilities might be deployed for the benefit of the organization.

As already described in this chapter, analysis of the resource base, distinctiveness, threshold and distinctive capabilities, competences, and core rigidities might align with the 'sensing' element of Teece's (2007) framework. In other words, collecting data and evaluating the current status of these resource base concepts is a form of dynamic capability 'sensing' activity. If missed opportunities or potential weaknesses are detected in relation to these concepts, remedial options for actions might be identified. The options for action will then feed into the option evaluation process, which aligns with dynamic capability 'seizing'. Once evaluated, any modifications arising to the resource base are implemented, which corresponds to Teece's concept of 'reconfiguration'.

Table 6.4 summarizes and illustrates the key concepts relating to 'what an organization is able to do', which we will draw on in conducting capability analysis.

6.3 **Developing insights about resources, capabilities, and activities**

To put resource base theory into practice to create insights and strategy inputs about the internal context, we can deploy a set of analysis tools as listed in Table 6.5. We have selected methods which can be used by an external party, such as a student of strategy, to build knowledge of the resource base context and options for action. We illustrate the methods based on the LVMH case. These illustrations are to provide examples of how to apply the methods, rather than a prescription of the level of data you need to include. How you apply the methods will be determined by the specific nature of the organization you are examining and the volume and quality of data available to you.

Resource base inventory

Creating an inventory of existing resource stocks is a valuable starting point for internal analysis. A shared view of the resource base can be derived through stakeholder dialogue and research. The typology of resources depicted in Table 6.1 provides a useful checklist to ensure that exploration of available resources is broad enough. Once a resource base inventory is created, it can form a platform for further analytical techniques.

Step 1. Uncover initial data

To answer the question 'What does the organization have that it can use?', research the organization from multiple sources, such as the company website, news articles, and industry reports. You can often find useful information in the 'about us' and 'media relations' section of an organization's website. Search also for reports or interviews from current or ex-employees

6

TABLE 6.4 **Summary of capability types**

Type	Meaning we are	Illustrations from case vignettes
Threshold capability	Able to carry out an activity necessary to operate in the industry at a level of performance similar to competitors	'Able to maintain fertility of land for growing grapes' if you can't do this, then there is no possibility of competing in the wine business ... therefore all competitors, including LVMH, have this capability
Threshold competence	Able to deliver superior operational performance in an activity required to operate in the industry	'Able to run cement production operations efficiently' Using highly skilled staff and modern equipment, Dangote can produce cement at a lower unit cost than its competitors
Distinctive capability	Able to create value for customers for which they are willing to pay us/fund us—and we continue to strive towards optimized performance	'Able to organize around customer needs' By adopting the Rendanheyi management philosophy, GEA is delivering outcomes that customers are valuing, and financial performance is improving. However, this adoption is not yet at the level of the Haier group, and efforts are continuing to exploit the distinctive cultural resource of Rendanheyi
Distinctive competence	Able to create value for customers—for which they are willing to pay us/fund us—at an optimized performance level	'Able to deliver heritage products that fulfil customer dreams' The LVMH 'houses' deliver highly valued customer outcomes—e.g. product that meets consumer expectations of perfection and individual dreams for which they are willing to pay a super-premium. LVMH aim to sustain and exploit what is industry-leading, optimized performance in this area
Dynamic capability	Able to modify our resource base and adapt our capabilities when required	'Able to expand cement production operations into new territories' Dangote cement have consistently demonstrated an ability to extend their resource base through new on-the-ground operations in new countries, following a clear set of strategic guidelines whilst doing so
Core dynamic capability	Able to continually modify and adapt our resource base and capabilities	'Able to grow through acquisition' LVMH is in perpetual acquisition mode—scanning for, and maintaining resource stocks to be able to respond to, opportunities of extending its 'house of brands' by acquisition
Core rigidity	Maintaining a capability that was once useful but might now be a liability	Whilst part of GE, the once successful function-oriented organizing approach was stifling business performance. When a customer-centric approach was adopted on moving to Haier, the improved financial performance revealed the extent to which the 'ability to organize in a functionally optimal way' had been a core rigidity for GEA

TABLE 6.5 **Resource base analysis methods**

Method	Purpose
Resource-base inventory	Agree the existing 'stocks' of organizational resources
VRIO analysis	Identify resources with the potential for creating competitive advantage from within the resource base
Capability audit	Profile the main capabilities and competences that the organization currently uses
Dynamic capability analysis	Identify how new resource configurations and capabilities can be arranged in order to meet shifting organizational needs
Value chain analysis	Identify options for enhancing the configuration of value-creating activities in the organization or its network

to gain access to insider views. Do not be concerned with the strength of any possible resource features such as 'distinctiveness', 'superior performance', or 'excellence'. Try to think broadly about what an organization has.

Step 2. Capture and organize resource and capability data

As information is accumulated, capture and organize suggestions against the resource categories suggested in Table 6.1. Ideas should be written in as summarised a way as possible without being too general. For example, rather than listing individual pieces of production machinery, or writing one-word entries such as 'equipment', the facilitator might note 'cutting-edge production machinery utilizing technology XYZ' as an available resource. Table 6.6 shows an example of an initial resource inventory for LVMH.

Step 3. Reflect on completeness of inventory

Once the table is initially populated, review your combined thinking with participants, and challenge yourselves to answer the question 'What resources have we missed?' If a category of resources is not deemed relevant as a response to the question, then it need not be included. There may be no further resources to add.

This initial method may lead to some straightforward strategy options being identified that are intended to address gaps in the resource profile. However, the main intention of this inventory is to form the basis of a range of subsequent analysis, exploring in greater detail the characteristics, possibilities, and implications of the organizational resource base.

VRIO analysis

The resource base inventory was prepared without any consideration of characteristics such as distinctiveness of resources. We can now use the VRIO criteria to evaluate identified resources as potential sources of competitive advantage.

Step 1. Prepare a VRIO template

Transfer the organizational resources into the left column of a table (such as Table 6.7), where the remaining columns are labelled with the VRIO category headings.

6

TABLE 6.6 **Illustrative resource base inventory for LVMH**

Category	Description	Resources (what the organization has that it can use)
Physical	Tangible resources that can be bought and sold on the open market	Extensive portfolio of owned locations in prime sites for luxury shopping
Natural	Natural resources linked to location and geographic conditions	Vineyards in the Champagne region
Financial	Monetary assets and liabilities as recorded on a balance sheet	Free cashflow from highly profitable operations
Informational	Raw and refined data about the organization or its ecosystem	Customer database; extensive supply chain data
Knowledge	Understanding of technical or commercial value	Materials science patents; luxury supply chain process knowledge
Reputational	Way in which the organization is perceived by stakeholders	Extensive luxury brand portfolio grounded in natural heritage
Cultural	Norms and habitual ways of working in the organization	Engrained focus on the highest level of quality and uncompromising commitment to brand values
Organizational	Structuring of resources, reporting, legal entities, and financial flows in the organization	French corporate headquarters; globally distributed separate legal entities for each brand headquarter
Managerial	Capacities of the individuals and teams with resource allocation powers	Bernard Arnault as a figurehead; highly experienced management team for each brand
Skills	Specific expertise, talents, and abilities in the human resource base of the organization	Artisanal craft skills in selected luxury sectors; brand management skills; lean production expertise
Relational	Connections with, and assets available on a preferential basis through, external stakeholders	Extensive supplier network supported by LVMH experts; strong government relations in key markets
Motivational	Drive, interest, and morale of staff to work towards organizational aims	Committed staff base; non-monetary recognition schemes

Step 2. Evaluate each entry in the table against the VRIO criteria

For each of the resources in the table, work through the column headings, responding to the questions raised in Table 6.8.

Step 3. Identify possible sources of competitive advantage

As described earlier in this chapter, resources that are valuable and rare might be a source of temporary competitive advantage for organizations; resources that satisfy all the VRIO criteria might be a source of sustainable competitive advantage. Review the evaluation outputs in the table, highlighting the possible sources of temporary and sustainable competitive advantage.

Table 6.9 shows a sample of VRIO analysis applied to a selection of the resources identified in Table 6.6 for LVMH. The distinctive resources underpinning sustainable competitive advantage

TABLE 6.7 **VRIO template**

Resource	Valuable	Rare	Inimitable	Organization
Resource 1				
Resource 2				
...				
Resource *N*				

TABLE 6.8 **VRIO evaluation prompts**

Resource characteristic	Description	Question to ask
Valuable	Can be deployed to create outputs of value to the customers	Is the customer willing to pay money for the direct output of this resource? If YES = Valuable
Rare	In limited supply; not available to all organizations	Is this resource available to only a limited subset of those competing in the sector? If YES = Rare
Imperfectly imitable	It is not possible to copy or create the resource	Is this resource impossible to substitute or copy in a way that is of equal value to the customer? If YES = Imperfectly imitable
Organization	Can be deployed effectively within the organization	Is it possible for the organization to use this resource in a purposeful way? If YES = Organization ready

for LVMH appear to be the historically embedded super-luxury brand portfolio, the artisanal craft skills of the workforce, and selected locational resources such as vineyards in the Champagne region. Temporary advantage might arise from store locations (vulnerable to trends towards online shopping and reselling alternatives) and materials science patents (vulnerable to being superseded by competitor R&D activities).

The challenge with this method is to remain focused on distinctiveness rather than excellent performance. For example, lean production expertise might be highly valuable to LVMH in maximizing profitability by reducing operating costs. However, this doesn't translate into an output for which the customer is willing to pay more. Therefore lean production expertise doesn't meet the V of the VRIO criteria.

Step 4. Identify options for actions to create, protect, or exploit VRIO resources

With insights generated about possible sources of temporary or sustainable competitive advantage identified, possible options for action can be identified. Table 6.10 shows an example of a range of options for how possible sources of competitive advantage might be protected or exploited within LVMH.

6

TABLE 6.9 **An extract from VRIO analysis for LVMH**

Resource	Valuable	Rare	Inimitable	Organization
Vineyards in the Champagne region	Yes	Yes	Yes	Yes
Extensive luxury brand portfolio grounded in natural heritage	Yes	Yes	Yes	Yes
Artisanal craft skills in selected luxury sectors	Yes	Yes	Yes	Yes
Extensive property portfolio in prime sites for luxury shopping	Yes	Yes	No	Yes
Material science patents	Yes	Yes	No	Yes
Free cash flow from highly profitable operations	No	No	No	Yes
Extensive customer database of wealthy clients	No	Yes	Yes	Yes
Extensive supply chain data	No	No	No	Yes
...	...	...	...	...
Engrained focus on the highest level of quality	Yes	No	No	Yes
Non-monetary recognition schemes	No	No	No	Yes

This is a quick and easy method of challenging participants to think about the competitive advantage potential in the resource base. However, it does have some significant limitations. First, by focusing on individual resources, the effect of complementarities and resource combinations is lost. This matters as competitive advantage might arise from capabilities created from combinations of resources. Secondly, this analysis focuses on what the organization currently

TABLE 6.10 **Options for action to create, protect, or exploit competitive advantage**

Resource	Option for action to create, protect, or exploit competitive advantage
Extensive property portfolio in prime sites for luxury shopping	Use legal action to prevent reselling of LVMH products Build online presence but refrain from online selling
Vineyards in the Champagne region	Lobby to protect 'Champagne' label status as only being created by grapes from the Champagne region
Materials science patents	Continue to invest in materials science R&D Explore ways to exploit materials science patents across product categories
Extensive luxury brand portfolio grounded in natural heritage	Continually search for acquisition opportunities for super-luxury brands with established histories
Artisanal craft skills in selected luxury sectors	Invest extensively in apprenticeship training schemes in all product categories

has or has access to in the resource base. What the organization could be in the future is not addressed. This 'present focus' may limit creative and entrepreneurial thinking. Thirdly, examining distinctive resources doesn't necessarily cover how competences can deliver strategically important operational performance gains. The following methods—with a focus on current and potential capabilities—enable us to mitigate these issues.

Capabilities audit

To develop a sense of how resources are used in combination, we can conduct a capabilities audit. Informed by the outcomes achieved by the organization in the recent past, or what it is currently delivering, we can identify the strengths and development opportunities of the organization's capability profile. We can use emerging insights from a capabilities audit as an input to strategic decision-making. This method also provides a foundation for dynamic capability analysis, exploring creative ways in which to manage the resource base.

Step 1. Collate information about the activity outcomes achieved by the organization

To build an evidence base for auditing capabilities, we use the concepts of the activity system (from Figure 6.1) in reverse, starting with activity outcomes, to drive our research activities. Consider the outcomes that an organization currently achieves or has achieved in its recent history. What products and services does it offer? What business results has it achieved? What adjustments to its resource base has it made, such as new partnerships, new international locations, updated technology, new hires, etc.?

Compile a list of any outcomes you identify in either a table or a shared location. Figure 6.5 shows a free-form record of quantitative and qualitative, current and recent outcomes identified from analysing the 2018 summary statement to shareholders for LVMH.

Step 2. Identify how activity outcomes were achieved

The information in Figure 6.5 is helpful, as identifying capabilities is a subjective task. By starting with what we know the organization has actually done—activity outcomes—we can then turn our focus to the activities that delivered the outcome. These activities represent the 'doing' of capabilities—relating capabilities to activities and outcomes helps you discuss and agree capabilities with colleagues.

Once a set of outcomes has been collated, respond to the question, 'What activities did the organization do to achieve these outcomes?' Consider each outcome in turn and note the activities through which the outcome was achieved and the underlying capabilities that enabled the activities. Table 6.11 shows a selection of capabilities identified for LVMH.

It is natural when you start this exercise to identify capabilities that are high level or generically worded. Challenge yourself to break these down further, as it will help further analysis as to how we can build the capability base for the future. For example, 'ability to lower operating costs' is a generic high-level capability. This might be broken down further into capabilities such as 'ability to implement lean thinking in production', 'ability to manage a just-in-time global supply chain', 'ability to sustain a quality culture focused on zero defects', etc.

You might also find that different outcomes are achieved through the same capability. For example, the capability 'ability to flow financial resources throughout the group' might support a

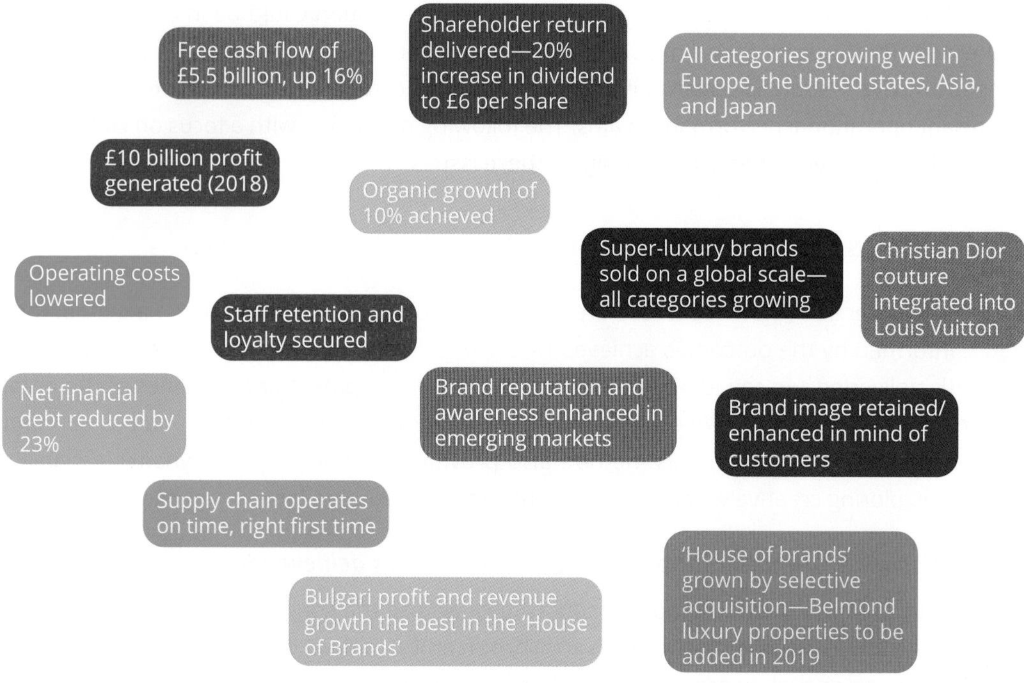

FIGURE 6.5 Example activity outcomes from LVMH.

TABLE 6.11 **Example capabilities for LVMH**

Ability to:
Manage each brand according to the needs of its specific heritage
Acquire super-premium brands across luxury sectors
Influence and inspire a luxury brand organization consistently
Apply latest material standards to historical products
Consistently take decisions and actions that preserve brand quality and integrity
Maintain drive and commitment of staff to sustaining super-luxury standards
Benefit from corporate scale whilst preserving individual brand identity
Raise funds to back major acquisitions
Maintain the fertility of land for cultivating grapes
Maintain perfect retail availability of quality assured products
Operate global product supply network with minimal disruption

number of outcomes such as 'Belmond luxury properties acquired', 'Dividend improved for shareholders', and 'Net debt reduced by 23%'. Only record the capability once in your list. However, it is also helpful to make a note of where a capability delivers multiple outcomes for future discussion.

Step 3. Organize the capabilities into categories

Organize the capabilities you have identified according to categories as per Table 6.12.

In this example, no core rigidities were revealed for LVMH from the initial data sources reviewed. This may change with further research, or upon interviewing insiders. Review the

TABLE 6.12 **Types of capability: illustrations from LVMH**

Type	Illustrations from LVMH case example Ability to:
Threshold capability	Sustain the fertility of the land for grape growing Maintain retail availability of products
Threshold competence	Integrate lean thinking into artisan-oriented production Benefit from corporate scale whilst preserving individual brand identity
Distinctive capability	Manage a global network of super-luxury retail outlets Take business decisions that preserve brand integrity
Distinctive competence	Deliver heritage products that fulfil customer dreams Manage brands according to the needs of specific categories
Dynamic capability	Research and apply materials science to heritage products Arrange funding to support acquisitions
Core dynamic capability	Grow through acquisition

categorized list of capabilities and ask the question: 'Given the activity outcomes identified, what capabilities have we missed?'

Step 4. Draw implications and options for action

Once you have a completed list, discuss implications for what the organization might do in future with existing capabilities. Use the category headings to help you think about the possibilities. For example, if the organization has an extensive set of threshold competences, how might these be deployed to deliver enhanced organizational performance?

Dynamic capability analysis

The data developed through the capability audit approach can be used as the basis for dynamic capability analysis. Using this method, you can explore how the resource base might be purposefully modified to enhance the set of capabilities available to the organization.

Step 1. Evaluate the existing profile of capabilities

Starting with the capabilities identified for each type (such as in Table 6.12), consider capabilities that you think the organization would benefit from:

- **(a)** adding to the portfolio
- **(b)** revising to increase range or performance potential
- **(c)** extending into new applications
- **(d)** retiring from the portfolio.

In a table template such as Table 6.13, make a note of any adjustments to the capability profile that, in your view, might benefit the organization.

TABLE 6.13 **Dynamic capability analysis**

Capability change	Target capabilities	Resource base change	Dynamic capability needed	Appraisal of existing dynamic capability (DC)
Add	Ability to serve the luxury foods market with a heritage brand	Add a 'luxury food company' to the house of brands	Acquisition	Acquisition DC available
Modify	Ability to apply sustainable materials science to heritage brands	Add 'sustainability' expertise to R&D base Licence sustainable materials database	Talent recruitment Innovation management Procurement	Talent management and procurement DCs available Investment in training required to adequately develop innovation management DC
Extend	Ability to apply lean thinking to operation of luxury retail outlets	Add 'lean retail' knowledge Hire 'lean retail' human resource	Talent recruitment Change management	Talent recruitment DC available Change management DC requires external input to add domain expertise
Remove	Ability to supply luxury lifestyle magazines	Sell luxury lifestyle magazine brands	Divestiture	Not present—seek to contract external experts to manage sale

Step 2. Identify resource base changes to enable revised capability profile

Identify the adjustments to the resource profile that would be required to deliver the revised capability profile. To help you identify what might need to be done, look back at the resource base inventory. Think about the types of resource stocks, and also the extent to which they are currently committed. It may be necessary to create additional capacity of existing stocks in order to enable capability revisions. Additional capacity might also be made available by divesting current resources or retiring existing capabilities to free up allocated resource stocks.

Step 3. Evaluate the adequacy of existing dynamic capabilities

Evaluate whether the organization has adequate dynamic capabilities to deliver the required resource base changes. To do so, work through the adjustment in resources identified in Table 6.13. Against each resource, identify the dynamic capabilities from Table 6.13 that will be deployed to deliver the change. If the required first-order dynamic capability isn't available in the organization, either identify the second-order dynamic capability that will be used to develop the first-order dynamic capability or reconsider whether to pursue the resource base change.

Step 4. Draw implications and options for action

To complete the analysis, consider the possible implications of the deployment of dynamic capabilities in terms of future capabilities for the organization. Consider how a revised capability profile could enhance the exploitation of distinctive resources and/or enhance organizational performance.

Resource and capability analysis is challenging to complete in a way that reflects reality when you are an outsider to an organization. However, without expecting perfection, conducting such an analysis will still generate valuable contextual insights; you will learn methods that prepare you to conduct such an analysis once you are on the inside of an organization. Being able to conduct this sort of analysis will greatly increase your ability to contribute to strategic decision-making conversations.

Value chain analysis

The final method we consider, known as value chain analysis, complements resource and capability analysis by focusing on strategic activities. Value chain analysis examines the configuration of activities in an organization, searching for alternative arrangements that improve business performance (Kaplan and Norton 2008). As the title suggests, the focus of analysis is on how activities add value, or relative worth, to the customer as part of a sequence or chain. It is important to understand what value means to the customers of the organization under review, as it may differ in different situations (Kornberger 2017). Where the chain of activities can be ordered more effectively or efficiently, customer service and organizational performance can be improved.

The generic value chain framework is shown in Figure 6.6. First proposed by Michael Porter (1985) in his seminal book on competitive advantage, value chain is a strategy tool that is widely taught on management programmes. In his initial text, Porter described different categories of value chain activity, and exemplified the concept with an example of a white goods manufacturer. He identified two main types of activity—primary and support. Primary activities correspond to zero-order capabilities (see Figure 6.3) and the sequence of operational activities through which products and services are directly created. Support activities are those organizational activities that create the conditions in which primary activities occur. Within primary and support activities, Porter identified a series of organizing categories as explained in Table 6.14.

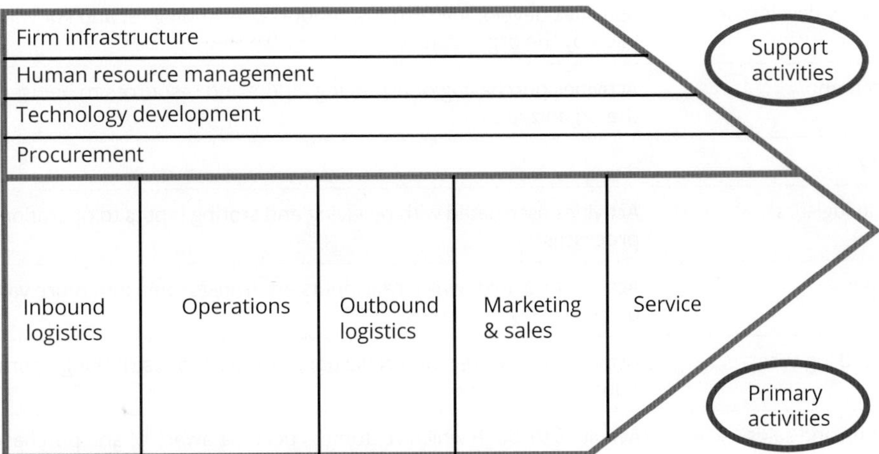

FIGURE 6.6 Generic value chain framework. Source: Reproduced with permission from Porter, M. E. (1985). *Competitive Advantage: Creating and Sustaining Superior Performance*. New York: Free Press, p. 46, Figure 2.3.

Step 1. Set the boundaries for your analysis

As with other forms of strategy analysis, you need to set appropriate boundaries for modelling value-creating activities. For example, it may be more appropriate to create several value chain analyses for different divisions of a multinational rather than trying to create a single analysis for the whole organization. Once your boundary has been selected, ensure that all participants in the analytical process are following the same parameters.

Step 2. Identify support and primary activities

List the primary and support activities that the organization currently undertakes in either table or diagram format. Remember to focus on activities—that which is done—rather than resources—what the organization has. It can be helpful here to refer to resource and capability analysis for coherence and relevant activities. Table 6.15 shows a summary version of this task for LVMH (the tighter the boundaries, the more detailed and useful the value chain will be).

For organizations which combine services and manufacturing, or only provide services, it will be necessary to modify the definitions/categories in the direct operation to better suit the nature of the customer offering. This is particularly true for third-sector or public-sector organizations. It is good practice to redefine the descriptions of the organizing categories to suit the nature of the organization, whilst not forgetting to examine primary and support activities.

TABLE 6.14 **Value chain organizing**

Category	Description
Support	
Firm infrastructure	Activities governing, managing, and arranging the environment in which all other activities occur
Human resources management	Activities organizing human resources: hiring, firing, remunerating, developing employees, etc.
Technology development	Activities developing systems, products, technologies, and knowledge used by the organization
Procurement	Activities purchasing or arranging inputs and resources to be used by the organization
Primary	
Inbound logistics	Activities associated with receiving and storing inputs to operational processes
Operations	Activities through which raw inputs are transformed into more valuable outputs using resources
Outbound logistics	Activities associated with collecting, storing, and distributing operational outputs to customers
Marketing and sales	Activities through which customers become aware of and purchase operational outputs
Services	Activities through which the post-sale value of operational outputs is maintained or enhanced

TABLE 6.15 **Value chain analysis for LVMH**

Component	Content
Firm infrastructure	Group leadership by Bernard Arnault, brand governance by industry expert managers, maintenance of super-premium stores
Human resource management	Deployment of talent management programmes, value systems, brand education for employees
Technology development	R&D activities exploring heritage-based product development technologies, implementation of lean production systems
Procurement	Execution of mergers and acquisitions (M&A) processes, maintenance of super-premium material sourcing/procurement systems, rigorous management of high-quality supply chain
Inbound logistics	Coordination with global supply network, material conformance processes
Operations	Craft-based production processes, staffed by artisans, manual operations, 100% inspection regime
Outbound logistics	Non-internet distribution through wholly owned network of luxury stores
Marketing and sales	Celebrity endorsements, active limitation of product supply, implementation of destroy remnants policy, exclusive event sponsorship
Services	No questions asked after-care, integrated portfolio for major clients

For service organizations, inbound logistics can be understood as receiving customer requests. For example, call-handling systems in an insurance contact centre could be considered as part of inbound logistics services; and outbound logistics could describe activities in which call outcomes are communicated to the customer by email and text.

Step 3. Evaluate the current configuration of the value chain

Work through each nominated activity in each of the organizing categories and challenge the extent to which primary activities are required to create value, or support activities are necessary to allowing the direct operation to function properly. If activities are not required to sustain customer value creation, they might be considered for elimination to boost operational performance and to free up resource stocks.

If activities are confirmed as being required, work through the activities and identify whether those activities might be modified or outsourced to a third party to boost performance and/or enhance customer value creation. Further, any potential vulnerabilities in activities that are identified from this scrutiny might be captured for an action response.

Step 4. Draw implications and options for action

Based on the analysis of activities, draw implications on the potential benefits and risks of modifying the value chain. This may include the identification of value-adding activities that are critical to defend/maintain in house so that they can be protected and customer value creation potential preserved. For many organizations, the direct operation is finely tuned, and many of the benefits of value chain will be yielded by analysing support activities.

PRACTITIONER INSIGHT: **DAVID MCGINLEY, A&P INDUSTRIES**

6

David McGinley is group managing director for A&P Group, a global ship repair, conversion, and marine specialist. A&P operate from four locations around the UK, and also have an operation in Sydney which delivers on behalf of the Commonwealth of Australia. The organization has revenues of about £140 million per annum, and employs around 900 staff. At the start of his career, David served in the British Royal Navy for 24 years, rising to the rank of warrant officer. In his subsequent civilian career, David has held senior positions with several organizations, including business development director and director of Commercial Port Operations for Babcock Marine. David is a past president of the UK Shipbuilders and Ship Repairers Association, and is also a Council member of the Society of Maritime Industries. David shares his views on resources, capabilities, and strategy.

If resources are 'what an organization has that it can use', what are the crucial resources for A&P for the long term?

Crucial resources for us are our people, facilities, and reputation. Reputation is paramount in our industry where clients rely on us to complete safety critical work on complex equipment. We have worked hard to develop a reputation for delivering on time with zero defects in a fully HSE compliant manner. Our reputation is a key reason why clients continue to entrust us with their critical assets. We rely on our people to deliver on our commitments to our clients in the manner they expect. Our technical staff are highly trained experts who work in a systematic, safe manner, whilst always seeking innovative ways to meet client needs. Our client-facing commercial staff must be able to communicate transparently and manage stakeholders effectively, setting the highest standards in ethical conduct during all phases of relationship management. Those in positions of leadership have a responsibility to set organizational expectations and ensure we adhere to our obligations. Through these behaviours and towards fully delivering a client brief, we are then able to make effective use of our technical facilities.

If capabilities are 'what an individual or organization can do', what capabilities matter most to A&P? How do you build, maintain and deploy these capabilities?

As you might expect, our capabilities in servicing client needs arise from combinations of our critical resources of people, facilities, and reputation. We are able to have effective working relationships with clients because of our trusted reputation. We have advanced technical capabilities in ship repair, conversion, and fabrication that we can match to client needs. Our workforce capabilities arise from the skills and experience of our staff, channelled through comprehensive organizational systems (which comply with a range of internationally recognized ISO standards) to make sure that we work in a safe consistent way. As a leadership team, we work hard to build a positive forward-looking culture that ties these capabilities together into an organization that clients want to work with.

To protect and grow our capabilities, we invest heavily in training and succession planning. Training-wise, we are always looking to improve our work systems and capabilities in safe efficient operations, often through partnering with local education providers. We are also permanently engaged in recruiting into our workforce—with an average workforce age of 54, this is a crucial task for us. We are trying to ensure a future talent pipeline through a portfolio of activities. We have invested significantly in apprenticeships across every site to create a local supply of the technical skills we need. We hire graduate managers to bring external perspectives and business function knowledge. Having a blend of apprenticeship- and degree-trained individuals is important for us. And we will support any staff member looking to better themselves through education and progress through the business, without forcing anyone to do so. Finally, we are continually investing in our technical facilities to ensure that we can deliver all the client asks of us in a safe, reliable, and profitable manner.

How do you ensure that A&P's resource and capability base is kept relevant to the strategic needs of the organization in the future?

I receive many internal reviews and industry reports as inputs to strategic decision making. At present, fluctuations in oil prices and the difficult political climate associated with Brexit are impacting our industry and business. In addition, personally I try to be 'present' in the business as much as possible to help me decide what to do. Any time I'm at a site, I'll do a walk-around myself. I like to take the chance to talk to people informally and listen to what they have to say. I also organize regular breakfast meetings with a cross-section of staff. I give them some views as to what is happening, but then I stop talking and ask their opinions. We also have formal suggestion schemes for technical and business process improvements. When solutions work, those who originated the ideas receive a financial reward. Opening up multiple channels for social interaction at all levels is so important to knowing the reality of what needs adjusted in the organization.

What does strategy mean to you?

Strategy is how you live your life in a high-level arc towards end-goals of some sort. If your goals are achievable, how you get there is a strategy. If they aren't achievable, then you don't have a strategy. It is your responsibility as a business leader to define a path that people can follow. You need to ground your aims and plans in reality without stifling aspiration. If you want a business to perform, then you have to look at its capabilities, determine what it can do, and set your strategy accordingly.

You can be specific with interim targets without being too fixed on strategy. For me, it is best to use strategy as a set of boundaries within which you can manoeuvre as an organization. You use initiatives and activities to move you forward but you have to be prepared to change as circumstances change around you. There are many outside influences into which you have no input to which you might need to respond.

To make this work, as a leader, I think that you need to feel a deep connection to the business and your staff. If you don't nurture people so they can feel that they can fail and learn, then you won't push on as a collective—communications falter, colleagues go into themselves, and you will under-achieve. For me, it is just as crucial to never deny issues or problems as it is to recognize and celebrate successes. We are all human at the end of the day. To appropriate a famous saying, by successfully working well, together, we increase the ability for us all to 'live long and prosper'.

CHAPTER SUMMARY

In this chapter we addressed the following learning outcomes.

- **Explain the importance of building understanding of resources, capabilities, and activities in organizational strategy**

  Understanding the interplay of resources, capabilities, and activities is valuable in organizational strategy. Resources are defined as what an organization has that it can use. Capabilities are defined as what the organization can do to a minimal performance threshold. Available capabilities emanate from bundles of available resources. When capabilities are deployed we can refer to this as organizational activity. Activity results in outcomes that affect the organizational context (customers, competitors, local communities, etc.). Activity can also result in incremental changes to the resource base (e.g. selling a product generates cash, which tops up financial resources). The consumption and replenishment of resource stocks are referred to as flows.

- **Explain how an organization can compete through the deployment of distinctive resources, using concepts and ideas of the resource-based view**

  From a resource-based view, competitive advantage arises from the possession of resources that meet the VRIO—valuable, rare, inimitable, and organization—criteria.

Competitive advantage from VRIO is only a potential. For competitive advantage to lead to organizational performance, VRIO resources need to be deployed—typically in bundles with complementary resources—in a way that creates differential performance from competitors, and at a cost that is less than the customer is willing to pay.

- **Evaluate the potential of an organization to manage its resource base over time through dynamic capability**
  Dynamic capability describes the capacity to purposefully create, extend, or modify the resource base of the organization. For an organization to have dynamic capability, capacities must exist to sense the possibilities of resource base change, decide which resource base change opportunities to seize, and reconfigure the resource base in response. Dynamic capability emanates from the resource base—what an organization has achieved in the past can give a strong indication as to what it can do in the present. Analysing the knowledge, processes, capabilities, and capacities in the resource base will enable the strategist to evaluate the potential for purposeful resource base change over time.

- **Appraise the configuration of an organization as a set of supporting and value-adding activities**
  If value means 'relative worth', i.e. a product or service that the customer is willing to pay for, then analysis of the activities that create value can be important for the strategist. Customer willingness to pay can be understood as arising from a series of activities which, to varying degrees, add value. Value chain analysis examines the activities in an organization which might create value directly (primary activities) or shape an environment in which value can be created (support activities). Enhancing primary or supporting activities through improvement, outsourcing, or reconfiguration actions, or the elimination of non-value-adding activities, can improve the performance of the organization.

- **Critically assess the value of internally focused analytical tools in strategy work**
  As with all tools and perspectives, RBV has the potential to add value to our thinking, depending on how we use it. It is also subject to limitations. In the academic literature, RBV is criticized for being too static, having limited predictive power, being of limited use to managers, having a grounding in circular logic, and being subject to confusion from causal ambiguity. In this chapter we have proposed methods that might mitigate some of these effects and enable valuable insights for strategists through the application of RBV thinking. We encourage students and practitioners to try the methods for themselves, and judge the value of the RBV on the usefulness of the insights gathered.

? END OF CHAPTER QUESTIONS

Recall questions

1. Define resources, capabilities, competences, and activities. Explain how these concepts operate together in an organization, using the terms stocks and flows.
2. Describe the key components of the resource base framework commonly referred to as VRIO. Explain how each component contributes to competitive advantage.

3. What is meant by dynamic capability? How might dynamic capability be useful to an organization?
4. Explain the potential value of threshold capabilities to an organization.
5. Explain the difference between primary and support activities, and explain how each of these categories are used in value chain analysis.

Application questions

A) Select an organization that is familiar to you and complete a resource and capability audit based on available information. What seem to be the main sources of competitive advantage from a resource base view? What dynamic capability does the organization appear to have? How could the organization creatively adapt its resource base to be fit for the future?

B) Pick a product or service you know well and sketch out a value chain analysis for how it is delivered and supported. How could the value chain be modified or reconfigured in order to improve the performance of the organization delivering the product/service or to improve customer value creation?

C) Reflecting on the application of resource base analysis, what are the main limitations you find of using resource base tools as stand-alone methods? How easy is it to understand an organization's resource base and activities as an outsider? How feasible is it to undertake resource base analysis in a meaningful way without complementary market-based analysis?

ONLINE RESOURCES

www.oup.com/he/mackay1e

FURTHER READING

Firm resources and sustained competitive advantage, by Jay Barney

Barney, J. (1991). Firm resources and sustained competitive advantage. *Journal of Management*, **17**(1), 99–120.

This paper is required reading for students of the resource-based view topic. It introduces the VRIO framework and has been highly influential in the development of the resource-based perspective in strategy research ever since. The main concepts are covered in this chapter, but students are strongly encouraged to explore the original arguments in this seminal paper.

Mapping distinctive competencies: a systemic approach, by Colin Eden and Fran Ackermann

Eden, C. and Ackermann, F. (2000). Mapping distinctive competencies: a systemic approach. *Journal of the Operational Research Society*, **51**(1), 12–20.

The approach advocated in this chapter for auditing the resource base, capabilities, and activity outcomes is based on an interpretation of Eden and Ackermann's principles for the use of mapping methods to support strategy work. This paper explains how the use of a systematic approach to mapping of the resource base can lead to understanding of distinctiveness and competitive advantage from patterns of resources. Note that Eden and Ackermann's use of competences is synonymous with how capabilities have been defined in this chapter. For a further, detailed example of how to map the resource base, you can see also Chapter 7 of Making Strategy *(Ackermann and Eden 2011).*

Dynamic Capabilities: Understanding Strategic Change in Organisations, by Constance Helfat et al.

Helfat, C.E., Finklestein, S., Mitchell, W., et al. (2007). *Dynamic Capabilities: Understanding Strategic Change in Organisations*. Oxford: Blackwell.

Dynamic capability remains a hot topic in strategy academia. With the high level of research interest shown in the concept since Teece et al.'s seminal publication in 1997, multiple competing views of dynamic capability emerged in the literature. This book by Helfat et al. is an attempt to draw together dynamic capability thinking from leading authors in order to progress understanding and a research agenda for understanding strategic change. Drawing on a range of considerations, it explains dynamic capability in a coherent way and offers valuable insights into resource-based competitive advantage that will benefit students of strategy in general, as well as those interested in knowing more about dynamic capability.

REFERENCES

Ackermann, F. and and Eden, C. (2011). *Making Strategy: Mapping Out Strategic Success*. London: Sage.

Adner, R. and Levinthal, D.A. (2004). What is not a real option: considering boundaries for the application of real options to business strategy. *Academy of Management Review*, **29**(1), 74–85.

Ashkenas, R. (2011). When the invincible become 'vincible'. *Harvard Business Review*. https://hbr.org/2011/03/when-the-invincible-become-vin.html

Augier, M. and Teece, D.J. (2009). Resource, capabilities, and Penrose effects. In: Teece, D.J. (ed), *Dynamic Capabilities and Strategic Management: Organising for Innovation and Growth*, pp. 113–35. Oxford: Oxford University Press.

Bachmann, J.W. (2002). Competitive strategy: it's OK to be different. *Academy of Management Executive*, **16**(2), 61–5.

Barney, J. (1991). Firm resources and sustained competitive advantage. *Journal of Management*, **17**(1), 99–120.

Barney, J.B. (1995). Looking inside for competitive advantage. *Academy of Management Executive*, **9**(4), 49–61.

Barthelemy, J. and Adsit, D. (2003). The seven deadly sins of outsourcing: executive commentary. *Academy of Management Executive*, **17**(2), 87–100.

Connor, T. (2002). The resource-based view of strategy and its value to practising managers. *Strategic Change*, **11**(6), 307–16.

Dierickx, I. and Cool, K. (1989). Asset stock accumulation and sustainability of competitive advantage. *Management Science*, **35**(12), 1504–13.

Eden, C. and Ackermann, F. (2000). Mapping distinctive competencies: a systemic approach. *Journal of the Operational Research Society*, **51**(1), 12–20.

Frynas, J.G., Mol, M.J., and Mellahi, K. (2018). Management innovation made in China: Haier's Rendanheyi. *California Management Review*, **61**(1), 71–93.

Garbuio, M., Lovallo, D., and Sibony, O. (2015). Evidence doesn't argue for itself: the value of disinterested dialogue in strategic decision-making. *Long Range Planning*, **48**(6), 361–80.

Hamel, G. and Zanini, M. (2018). The end of bureaucracy: how a Chinese appliance maker is reinventing management for the digital age. *Harvard Business Review Digital Articles*, Nov/Dec, 50–9.

Healey, M.P. and Hodgkinson, G.P. (2017). Making strategy hot. *California Management Review*, **59**(3), 109–34.

Helfat, C.E., Finklestein, S., Mitchell, W., et al. (2007). *Dynamic Capabilities: Understanding Strategic Change in Organisations*. Oxford: Blackwell.

Kaplan, R.S. and Norton, D.P. (2008). Mastering the management system. *Harvard Business Review*, **86**(1), 62–77.

Kornberger, M. (2017). The values of strategy: valuation practices, rivalry, and strategic agency. *Organization Studies*, **38**(12), 1753–73.

Lampel, J. and Shamsie, J. (2003). Capabilities in motion: new organizational forms and the reshaping of the Hollywood movie industry. *Journal of Management Studies*, **40**(8), 2189–210.

Leonard-Barton, D. (1992). Core capabilities and core rigidities: a paradox in managing new product development. *Strategic Management Journal*, **13**(Special Issue), 111–25.

Markides, C.C. (2000). *All the Right Moves: A Guide to Crafting Breakthrough Strategy*. Boston, MA: Harvard Business School Press.

Miller, D. (2003). An asymmetry-based view of advantage: towards an attainable sustainability. *Strategic Management Journal*, **24**(10), 961–76.

Miller, D. and Shamsie, J. (1996). The resource-based view of the firm in two environments: the Hollywood film studios from 1936 to 1965. *Academy of Management Journal*, **39**(3), 519–43.

Penrose, E. (1959). *The Theory of The Growth of The Firm*. Oxford: Basil Blackwell.

Peteraf, M. (1993). The cornerstones of competitive advantage: a resource-based view. *Strategic Management Journal* (1986–1998), **14**(3), 179–91.

Peteraf, M.A. and Barney, J.B. (2003). Unraveling the resource-based tangle. *Managerial and Decision Economics*, **24**(4), 309–23.

Porter, M.E. (1985). *Competitive Advantage: Creating and Sustaining Superior Performance*. New York: Free Press.

Prahalad, C.K. and Hamel, G. (1990). The core competence of the corporation. *Harvard Business Review*, **68**(3), 79–91.

Schoemaker, P.J.H., Heaton, S., and Teece, D. (2018). Innovation, dynamic capabilities, and leadership. *California Management Review*, **61**(1), 15–42.

Teece, D.J. (2007). Explicating dynamic capabilities: the nature and microfoundations of (sustainable) enterprise performance. *Strategic Management Journal*, **28**(13), 1319–50.

Teece, D.J. (2014). The foundations of enterprise performance: dynamic and ordinary capabilities in an (economic) theory of firms. *Academy of Management Perspectives*, **28**(4), 328–52.

Teece, D.J., Pisano, G., and Shuen, A. (1997). Dynamic capabilities and strategic management. *Strategic Management Journal*, **18**(7), 509–33.

Teece, D., Peteraf, M., and Leih, S. (2016). Dynamic capabilities and organizational agility: risk, uncertainty, and strategy in the innovation economy. *California Management Review*, **58**(4), 13–35.

Vergne, J.-P. and Durand, R. (2011). The path of most persistence: an evolutionary perspective on path dependence and dynamic capabilities. *Organization Studies*, **32**(3), 365.

Wernerfelt, B. (1984). A resource-based view of the firm. *Strategic Management Journal*, **5**(2), 171–80.

Wernerfelt, B. (1995). The resource-based view of the firm: ten years after. *Strategic Management Journal*, **16**(3), 171–4.

Winter, S.G. (2003). Understanding dynamic capabilities. *Strategic Management Journal*, **24**(10), 991–5.

Zeng, J. and Mackay, D. (2019). The influence of managerial attention on the deployment of dynamic capability: a case study of internet platform firms in China. *Industrial and Corporate Change*, **28**(5), 1173–92.

Zollo, M. and Winter, S.G. (2002). Deliberate learning and the evolution of dynamic capabilities. *Organization Science*, **13**(3), 339–51.

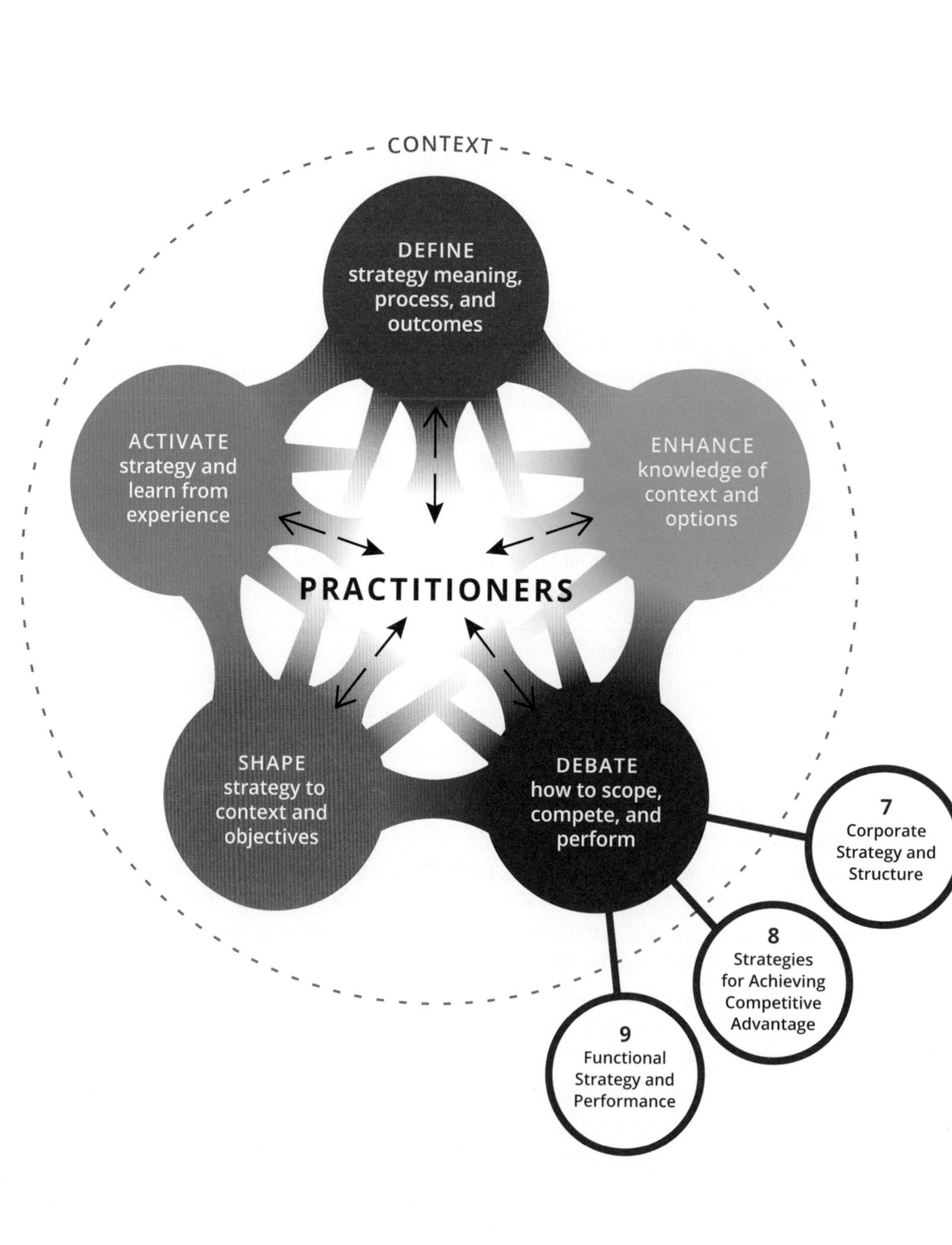

CONTEXT
DEFINE
strategy meaning, process, and outcomes
ACTIVATE
strategy and learn from experience
ENHANCE
knowledge of context and options
PRACTITIONERS
SHAPE
strategy to context and objectives
DEBATE
how to scope, compete, and perform
7
Corporate Strategy and Structure
8
Strategies for Achieving Competitive Advantage
9
Functional Strategy and Performance

PART THREE

Debate how to scope, compete, and perform

In Part 3 of the book, we explain how strategy might be debated, understood, and scoped within an organization by looking at how questions of competition and strategic performance can be addressed. In Chapter 7 we explore corporate strategy and the relationship between an organization's structure and its strategy. We consider the different ways in which activities can be organized in order to help an organization to achieve its goals. In Chapter 8 we address the important question of competitive advantage. We explore the nature and sources of competitive advantage, and how it might be sustained over time through business strategy. Chapter 9 investigates functional strategy; we discuss how strategy work occurs within organizational units, in alignment with corporate and business strategy demands, and in conjunction with strategic performance management approaches.

By the end of Part 3, you should have enhanced abilities to think, talk, and act like a practitioner, debating how to scope, compete and perform through strategy.

CHAPTER SEVEN

Corporate Strategy and Structure

CONTENTS

LEARNING OBJECTIVES

By the end of this chapter, you should be able to:

- Describe the main organizational structural types which sit in the simple, complex, and innovation-oriented categories
- Analyse the main organizational structural types in terms of their strengths and weaknesses
- Evaluate the suitability of a range of structural types for organizations against a number of design tests
- Appreciate the role of systems and culture in supporting the delivery of an organization's strategy
- Discuss the relationship between internationalization and organizational structure
- Examine the advantages and disadvantages of internationalization for MNCs

TOOLBOX

- **Mintzberg's six ideal structural types**
  Henry Mintzberg identifies a number of possible structural configurations adopted by organizations. He suggests that these structural types can result from the strategy an organization adopts and the extent to which it practises that strategy.
- **Simons' basic control levers**
  A framework which can help managers to understand the different ways in which they can exercise control in organizations that require flexibility, creativity, and innovation.
- **Deal and Kennedy's corporate cultures**
  A model which identifies four types of corporate culture, based on two key dimensions—the degree of risk associated with the company's activities, and the speed at which feedback is received on whether decisions or strategies are successful.
- **The OLI framework**
  OLI stands for **o**wnership, **l**ocation, and **i**nternalization, three potential sources of advantage that may underlie a firm's decision to become a multinational. This framework helps us to explore the reasons why a firm may decide to do so.
- **The Stopford and Wells matrix**
  A model that explores the typical stages of development for companies that are moving towards an international organizational structure. It suggests that the process is driven by both the number of products sold internationally and the importance of international sales to the company.
- **Porter's configuration/coordination matrix**
  A framework proposed by Michael Porter, which gives his view of the relationship between the organization's configuration (i.e. where value chain activities are performed) and coordination (i.e. how the organization's value chain is managed).

7

OPENING CASE STUDY **ROLLS-ROYCE RESTRUCTURING**

In 2018, Warren East, CEO of Rolls-Royce Holdings, announced plans to radically transform the UK engineering firm. His plans to change the organization involve significant job cuts. Over two years, Rolls-Royce is to cut 4600 jobs (mainly office and middle-management roles) in an effort to generate around £1.9 billion in free cash flow in the next five years, aiming to achieve a target of £1 billion in only two years (by 2020).

Rolls-Royce has a history of enduring restructures. Longer-serving staff have experienced similar shake-ups. In 2014 the plan to reduce head count by 2600 was never fully realized, as after a year the company had hired back 1000 employees, although this was partly to do with the fact that organization needed to hire staff with different skills to those they had made redundant in order to put Rolls-Royce in a better position to take advantage of new opportunities (such as in digital-led services). The overall reduction from that restructure was only 600 roles. Rolls-Royce claimed that the organization simply wasn't robust enough in 2014 and 2015 to fully see through their drastic restructuring plans—they had had five profit warnings by that point. Suppliers and employees have been known to express frustration at the bureaucratic nature of the organization, with the *Financial Times* reporting that:

> The latest plan to cut 4600 middle-management jobs, largely in the UK, is an acknowledgment that those previous attempts to reshape the group underestimated the scale of the effort required to change fossilized processes that have built up over decades. 'This all comes back to the culture of the organization', said one Rolls-Royce engineer. The bureaucracy 'just finds ways of reintroducing itself to make sure this doesn't happen'.

Whilst some employees and suppliers remain sceptical about the planned changes, the promise of such sent shares soaring—after details of the restructuring plan emerged, the shares traded 3% higher. The *Financial Times* explains further:

> Rolls-Royce's problem in investors' eyes has long been that financial results have been opaque and volatile. It has traditionally achieved margins far below those of its bigger competitors, such as General Electric of the US, giving it less investment firepower. Investors were heartened to see details of the transformation plan that the group hopes will finally deliver on its promises.

There is widespread recognition that the problems the firm are facing cannot be solved by 'cutting a few costs here and there'. Managers believe that fundamental changes are needed, to reduce the levels of complexity that Rolls-Royce appears to be wedded to. The *Financial Times* notes, based on a recent consultancy study, that:

> A number of project managers had been left to their own devices without direct reports and, as a result, with little accountability. Out of 18,000 job functions examined, 2000 could simply be stopped. And there were 4500 posts in a corporate centre that had 'almost endless ... rights' to meddle in the business divisions, imposing extra cost for services they neither needed nor wanted.

On a positive note, the firm claims to be making progress, for example in cutting out unnecessary rules and procedures. Managers intend to make further improvements, including introducing a more dynamic budgeting cycle that will help the firm to plan for and respond to changes in the external environment. The overall aim of the restructuring is to simplify the ways in which the firm does business—and for some managers, this is driven by the fear that 'if we do not do this, someone else will'.

The strategy brings with it some significant risks. At a time when the firm needs to increase the production of aircraft engines to record levels, it cannot afford to find that managers and employees are distracted by the changes going on in the business. Redundancy plans are, of course, likely to have a negative impact on staff morale, and management will be keen to ensure that employees are focused on the future of the firm rather than its past difficulties.

Questions for discussion

1. How would you describe Rolls-Royce's strategy, according to the article extracts quoted above?

2. What do you think are the main factors driving the strategic choices that Rolls-Royce is making?
3. What do you think the main benefits of a restructuring will be for Rolls-Royce? What might be the barriers to the company achieving those benefits?
4. How will the attitudes and actions of employees affect the implementation of the strategy? Explain your answer.

Sources

Peggy Hollinger, Industry Editor, *Financial Times*, 15 June 2018.

https://www.reuters.com/article/us-rolls-royce-hldg-restructuring/rolls-royce-cuts-4600-jobs-at-pivotal-moment-for-business-idUSKBN1JA0JD (accessed 22 May 2019).

7.1 Introduction

At heart, organizations exist to enable us to do things that it would be difficult, if not impossible, to do alone. These organizations form intricate networks through which exchange happens readily; we rely on these networks to satisfy our daily needs and wants. Even if we were more self-sufficient and lived in a world in which we produced everything we needed for ourselves, we would still need organizations of some form—for example, at a family or community level—for our basic social needs to be met.

Organizations exist to facilitate joint action, with their structures being determined both by the way in which tasks that need to be completed are divided, and by the way that sub-tasks are managed to fulfil overall goals. The way that these tasks are broken down and reintegrated is called structuring; the particular structure adopted by a given organization is known as its **organizational structure**.

An organization's structure enables activities to be carried out in a way that is consistent with its overall purpose. As such, it represents a control mechanism that helps to keep the organization on track.

For a large organization in particular, we can consider its structure to operate at several levels—at the top level, the form of the overall organization, then cascading down through sub-units and functions to the level at which products are made or services are delivered.

In this chapter we consider organizational structure at these different levels. We explore the role of structure in the implementation of strategic change, and we consider how managers can evaluate and choose between alternative structures. We also discuss the concepts of systems and organizational cultures as alternative control mechanisms, and we consider the relationship between internationalization and organizational structure.

7.2 The relationship between strategy and structure

When discussing the relationship between an organization's strategy and its structure, the contribution of Alfred Chandler—an American professor of business history, and probably one of the most influential strategic thinkers of his time—should not be overlooked. In his book *Strategy and Structure* (Chandler 1962) he described his research in four large US companies. In it he argued that they all faced essentially the same internal and external pressures for change. He charted their evolution, and demonstrated that they had all developed similar types of divisionalized multi-business unit structures (known as **M-form structures** (see section on multidivisional complex structures). A divisionalized organization is one that is typically organized around a number of different products or services, markets, or geographies. This led Chandler to offer two propositions. First, fundamental environmental changes require an adaptive response. Secondly, the strategies that are put into practice eventually produce a 'fit' between the new types of organization which develop and their competitive environments.

In describing their developmental paths, Chandler showed how each company had taken a different route to reach the new structural form. They had faced different types of difficulties along the way, and used different strategy processes to get there, but they had all arrived at the same end-point.

Chandler's case studies showed that growth created administrative problems. The companies responded by formalizing techniques for administration and work allocation. He described how they adapted internally by amending and revising their organizational structures and channels of control. The internal strategies they adopted to respond to external environmental change led to the development of new structural forms of organization.

Therefore Chandler put forward a suggestion that became one of the most famous dictums in the history of strategic management: 'Structure follows strategy'. It has become self-evident in today's environment that organizations need to adapt to environmental change. The idea that strategy is in part about an organization achieving and maintaining a 'fit' with its environment has also been highly influential, and still retains considerable currency.

In this section we will start by considering the relationship between strategy and structure, the main elements of organizational structure, and Mintzberg's influential theories on organizational structure. We will consider the strengths and weaknesses of the main structural forms that are widely recognizable in contemporary organizations (including simple, complex, and innovation-oriented structures), before concluding by considering how to choose an effective structure for an organization.

Structure, systems, and culture

Today, we might challenge Chandler's view. Does structure always follow strategy? The Rolls-Royce case study that opened this chapter might lead us to reflect on an ongoing tension between an organization's high-level goals and the need, over time, to create an appropriate structure that is likely to help deliver the espoused strategy. The role of structure in operational effectiveness is widely discussed in the existing management literature (e.g. Nadler et al. 1997; Bennet and Bennet 2004). The discussion is typically based on the assumption that an organization relies on its structure in order to coordinate its activities; the right organizational structure may also help to deliver a unique mix of values.

Structural mechanisms include the ways in which people interface and interact while doing their work, the flow of information through the organization, and the coordination and control

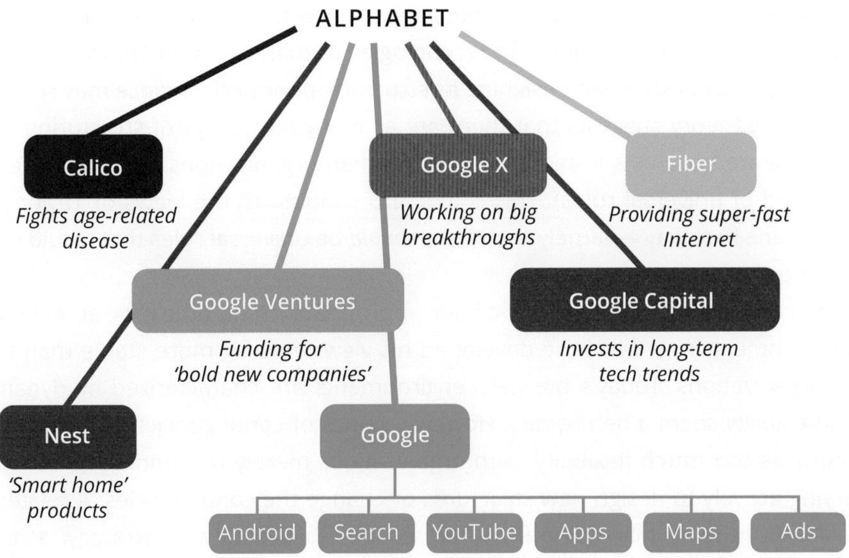

FIGURE 7.1 The different 'Alphabet companies', which are subsidiaries of Alphabet Inc. Source: Courtesy of Seeking Alpha. Full article: https://seekingalpha.com/article/4213384-alphabet-berkshire-tomorrow-part-1

of essential activities and practices. For example, Google Inc. was restructured in 2015 to become Alphabet Inc., after which Google's search product became a wholly owned subsidiary of a new parent company Alphabet. Google's other projects and teams were spun out into separate 'Alphabet companies', each with its own CEO (Alphabet Inc. is a holding company with no business operations of its own). Figure 7.1 shows the different 'Alphabet companies', which are now subsidiaries of Alphabet Inc.

It was reported that the main aim behind this restructuring was to help entrepreneurs build and run companies with the autonomy and speed they need. In other words, the company engaged in a diversification strategy by restructuring to move beyond the search engine business (e.g. Dudovskiy 2017).

Such an example may seem to support Chandler's (1962) logic that 'structure follows strategy', and that organizations choose their structures to support their strategic direction. However, the opposing view is that strategy follows structure. This means that an organization's structure, culture, and operational practices can dictate future strategy. Put simply, our view of what is desirable, or even possible, in terms of future strategy can be affected if an organization's structure, culture, and operational practices become the norm without further question or comment.

In Chandler's view, strategy needs to be developed first; only then do we ask ourselves what structure might be needed to ensure that the strategy can be implemented successfully. For example, a new strategy may create new resource demands in terms of staff, machinery, or infrastructure; these demands could change the way the organization operates, making a new structure necessary.

Chandler's arguments influenced the development of **contingency theory**. Contingency theory (e.g. Donaldson 2001) views the structure of an organization as a response to the particular circumstances or events it faces (the contingencies), which collectively affect its strategy. These contingencies may include changes in technologies or markets. If an organization fails to consider such contingencies when designing its structure, poor performance may result.

Contingency theory suggests that there are as many right ways of structuring an organization as there are situations it might face (rather than organizations being designed according to some kind of universal rules). This is in sharp contrast to the views of Taylor (1911), who advocated 'one best way'—namely that there *should* be universal rules that would underpin the success of *any* organization.

Taylor's recommendations may have been appropriate for his time if we accept that the business environment from which he developed his views was far more stable than those facing today's organizations. Today's business environments are characterized by dynamic change, making flexibility seem a better idea. However, critics of contingency theory might argue that it encourages **too much** flexibility, with organizations merely responding to situations rather than trying actively to design new structures or change the contingencies. A related challenge to contingency theory may come from the resource-based view of strategy, as discussed in Chapter 6; here we see organizations thinking proactively about their internal resources and capabilities, and hence adopting strategies that can change their external environments, for example creating new markets.

The main elements of organizational structure

Let us now consider the many configurations organizations can adopt on their path to success. A key idea here is that key elements of structure combine to form natural clusters (or 'configurations'). Here the term 'configurations' refers to the natural clusters or groupings that result when the key elements of structure are combined. The idea behind this is that formal structures and processes need to be aligned so that they can more comprehensively influence the informal processes and relationships that occur in all organizations. This is based on the belief that if the formal and informal sides of an organization are closely connected, it becomes easier to undertake more effective strategy work.

A configuration consists of both the broader and the more micro structures within an organization, and includes the processes and relationships through which an organization's strategy is developed.

There are three essential aspects of an organization's configuration: its structural design, processes, and relationships.

- **Structural design** influences the way in which knowledge and skills are developed within an organization. The wrong (or an inappropriate) structural design can result in essential knowledge and skills not being developed, or strategies not being implemented. As such, structural design lies at the heart of the advantage a particular organization may offer. However, an appropriate structure alone is not enough.
- **Processes** drive and support what people do, both within and around an organization. As such, they strongly influence an organization's likelihood of success (or failure). They help define how strategies are created, and they determine how employees interact when implementing a strategy.

- **Relationships** connect people within an organization to each other, and to those outside the organization who have an impact on its success. In larger organizations, relationships form internally between those in the corporate 'hub' and those located in dispersed organizational units. Externally, relationships are developed through routine interactions with consultants, shareholders, and other stakeholders.

Managers typically describe their organizations in terms of **organization charts**, which are a useful way of depicting formal relationships. Organization charts represent the different 'levels' within larger organizations, and typically indicate reporting lines. Redrawn organization charts often lie at the heart of restructuring attempts by signifying the introduction of a new set of skills which may be seen to be crucial to the future success of the organization. For example, a new organization chart which includes a 'director of strategy' role that did not previously appear makes a clear statement that strategy has become more of a concern for the organization and is considered more important to its future success.

Mintzberg on organizational structure

Henry Mintzberg is a Canadian business and management academic and author, and an influential contemporary thinker about strategic management (e.g. Mintzberg 1979, 1989, 1993). Like the contingency theorists, Mintzberg does not believe that there is always 'one best way' to design an organization. However, he goes beyond the contingency argument, which posits that context determines structure, to suggest that characteristics of organizations appear to fall into natural clusters or configurations. He argues that when structures are designed, organizations need to be viewed as a whole. He suggests (Mintzberg 1979) that the structure of any organization has two essential elements: (i) the **parts** of the structure, and (ii) the **mechanisms** that hold them together.

First, he identifies six basic parts, which are illustrated in Figure 7.2:

- the operating core
- the strategic apex
- the middle line
- the technostructure
- support staff
- ideology.

He then lists six mechanisms, which link the basic parts together:

- direct supervision
- mutual adjustment
- standardization of work processes
- output
- skills
- norms.

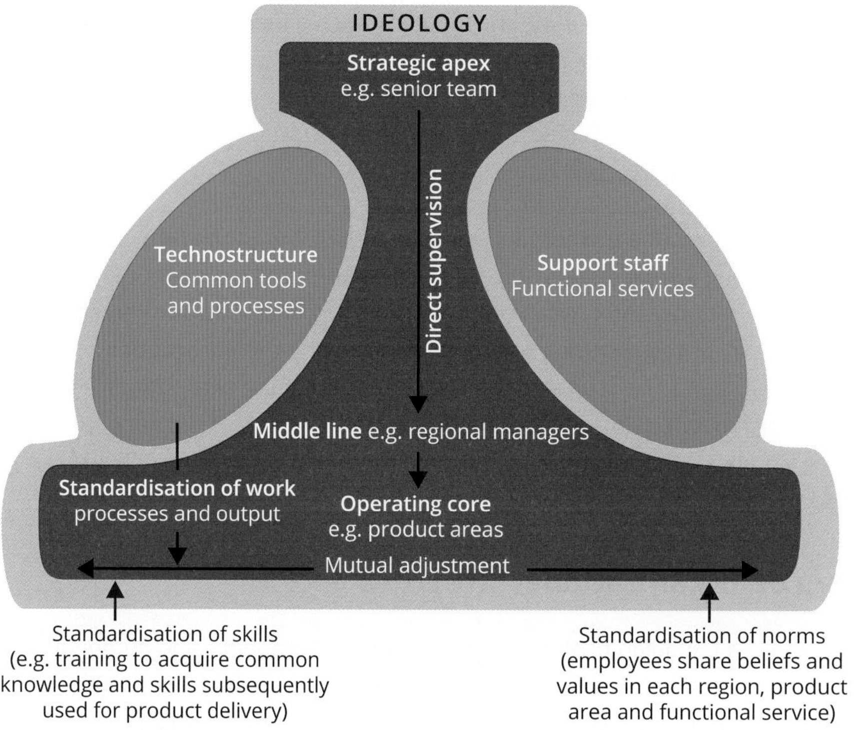

7

FIGURE 7.2 Mintzberg's six parts of the organization. Source: After Mintzberg, H. (1979). *The Structuring of Organisations*, adapted in Segal-Horn, S. (2004). *The Strategy Reader* Blackwell, p, 247, Figure 13.1. Reproduced with permission of John Wiley & Sons Limited.

These mechanisms form the 'glue' that brings together the work of every employee or team in getting the overall work done.

Mintzberg suggests that the combination of these two elements with the centralization or decentralization of power in an organization results in six structural configurations, illustrated in Figure 7.3. 'Centralization' implies that the decision-making power rests at a single point in the organization, while 'decentralization' implies that the power is relatively dispersed among many individuals or levels within the organization. So, what are these six structural configurations?

Mintzberg's six ideal structural types

Mintzberg develops six structural configurations (or 'types') by considering the consequences of emphasizing each of the six basic parts listed above in turn. This leads us to the six structural configurations described in Table 7.1. The first, 'simple structure', will typically be seen in a small organization, or one that is at a relatively early stage in its development, where the 'strategic apex' remains the key part of the organization. As we move across the six structures described in Table 7.1, we see that the size and complexity of the organization can develop in a range of ways, with different parts of the organization seen to be behind the ways in which it develops. We discuss this further as we provide our own summary of organizational forms below, under the headings 'simple', 'complex', and 'innovation-oriented'. Think about the characteristics of Mintzberg's six types depicted in Table 7.1 as you read the discussion of various organizational structures in the following section.

TABLE 7.1 **Mintzberg's six ideal structural types**

	Simple structure	Machine bureaucracy	Professional bureaucracy	Divisionalized form	Adhocracy	Missionary
Key part	Strategic apex	Technostructure	Operating core	Middle line	Support staff	Ideology
Coordinating mechanism	Direct supervision	Standardization of work processes	Standardization of skills	Standardization of outputs	Mutual adjustment	Standardization of norms
Dominant pull to:	Centralize	Standardize	Professionalize	Balkanize	Collaborate	Evangelize
Decentralization	None (centralized)	Limited horizontal	Horizontal	Limited vertical	Selective horizontal and vertical	Full decentralization
Planning and control	Little	Action planning	Little	Much performance control	Limited action planning	Little
Liaison devices	Few	Few	In administration	Few	Many throughout	Few
Situational factors	Age and size, technical system, environment, power					
Examples	Small owner–manager organizations undertaking simple activities, e.g. small shops	Fast-food chains, airlines, telephone banking	Hospitals, colleges, law firms (or other professional service firms or partnerships)	Large conglomerates	Creative advertising agencies, bespoke software boutiques	Evangelical churches, revolutionary movements

Simple, complex, and innovation-oriented structures

We now move from Mintzberg's account of organizational structure to our own list of structural forms—forms that are widely reflected in contemporary organizations. We will summarize them under three main categories:

- simple structure (functional)
- complex structure (multidivisional, holding, matrix, network, and transnational)
- innovation-oriented structure (project-based structure and adhocracy).

We should stress, however, that many organizations have characteristics of more than one structure, and that innovation and strategic change can of course take place through more than one category of structure. As you read the descriptions of each form, try to relate them to any organizations that you are familiar with—including any 'hybrid' structures that seem to incorporate aspects of more than one form. An understanding of different organizational structures is very valuable as you reflect on the different strategies that organizations are pursuing, and the barriers that they may encounter as they work on strategy implementation.

Simple structure

An organization is likely to have a simple structure during its early stages, with work divided between a number of sections/departments according to their function. This is known as a functional structure (Figure 7.3).

The functional structure is perhaps the simplest form of organizational structure, and may reflect responsibilities including operations, finance, marketing, and human resources. This type of configuration is usually found in smaller companies, or those with narrow (rather than diverse) product ranges. Organizations of this type may evolve into larger, more complex entities that adopt multidivisional structures (which we will discuss later in this section); each of these divisions may retain their functional configuration.

What are the advantages of a functional structure?

- The CEO can keep in touch will all functions and operations relatively easily.
- Control mechanisms are reduced and remain simple.
- Responsibilities and reporting mechanisms are clearly defined and easily understood.
- Specialists are located at senior and middle management levels, and are clearly identified within the overall structure.

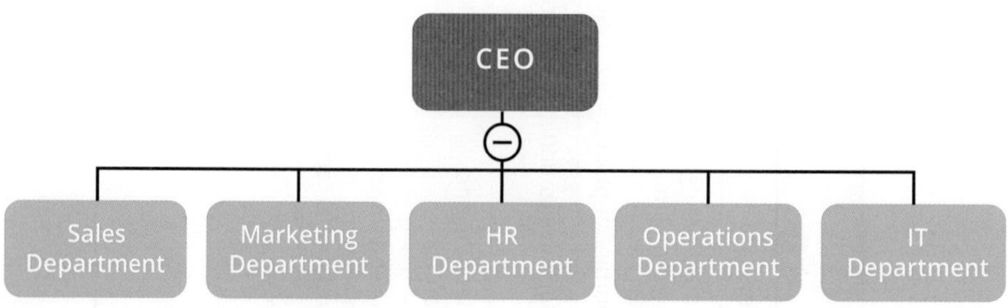

FIGURE 7.3 Example of a simple organizational chart with a functional structure.

However, there may be disadvantages.

- Senior managers can become overburdened with routine matters and operational detail as they focus on their functional responsibilities, and may fail to monitor the external environment if they become too inward-looking.
- Diversity can become difficult to cope with, as functional lines become rigid.
- It may be difficult to coordinate between functions as functional barriers are reinforced.
- It may be difficult for an organization with this configuration to adapt to changes in its size and changes in the external environment.

The advantages and disadvantages listed here both stem from an organization's basic and simple form.

Complex structures

Most organizations become larger and more complex over time, and their structures also tend to evolve, as the organization begins to employ more staff, operate in more locations, provide a wider range of products and services, and so on. We will look at a number of **complex structures** that reflect these changes in how activities can be organized: **multidivisional structure**, **holding structure**, **matrix structure**, **network structure**, and **transnational structure**. We begin with the multidivisional structure.

The multidivisional structure

As noted above, organizations often become more complex in structure as they develop. The multidivisional structure, or the M-form, is a configuration built up by multiple divisions defined by products, services, or geographical areas, and a central head office organized by function. For example, Figure 7.4 illustrates the organization chart of the industrial group Bouygues, which shows their interests in construction, roads, property, TV, and telecommunications.

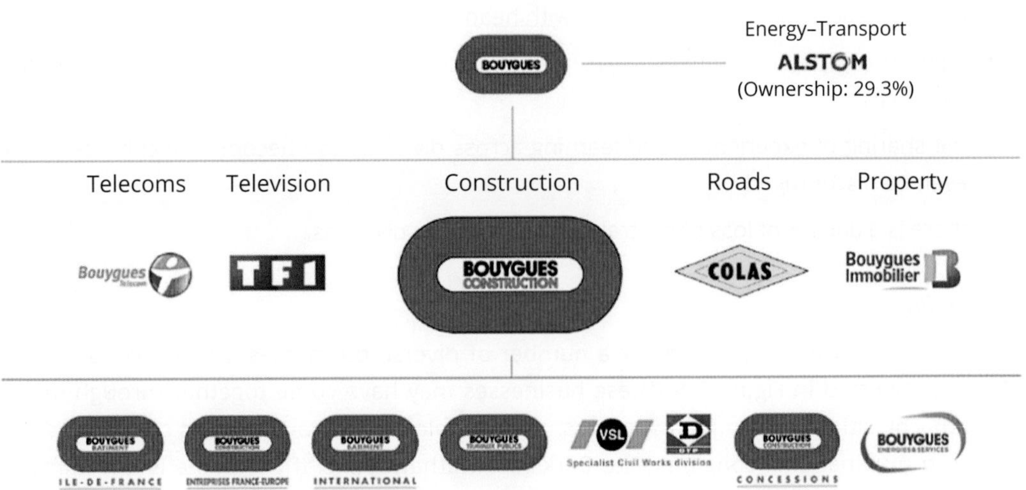

FIGURE 7.4 Example of multidivisional structure. Source: Courtesy of BOUYGUES Group

The introduction of divisions often stems from problems that functional structures experience when dealing with diversity or expansion, as noted when we discussed the disadvantages of a simple structure above. Divisions are often introduced when domestic organizations expand into other geographical markets. The intention is that each division in a multidivisional structure will be better able to respond to the specific requirements of its product/market strategy, using its own set of functional departments.

This type of configuration also exists in many public services, where the organization is structured around service departments such as education, social services, recreation, and so forth. For example, in the health sector, it has been argued that the potential benefits of a more decentralized M-form structure, such as flexibility, can outweigh the potential disadvantages, such as a possible increase in costs due to some duplication of effort (Bustamante 2016).

The multidivisional structure has a number of advantages:

- divisions can be added or divested (removed) as appropriate, giving an organization a high degree of operational flexibility
- each division can be managed by monitoring selected performance indicators, and therefore accountability at the divisional level can be increased
- divisional managers have greater ownership of their own divisional strategies
- growth areas can be clearly identified and nurtured
- conflicts between functional areas can be reduced
- career progression is promoted: divisional managers can adopt a strategic leadership role within their division that equips them with the skills and experience needed for a move to the corporate centre.

However, the multidivisional structure also has some potential disadvantages:

- central and divisional activity can become duplicated as functions behave more like independent businesses
- divisional priorities may overshadow those coming from the corporate centre, leading to fragmentation and potential conflict with head office
- internal competition between divisions can occur as they 'compete' for scarce central resources
- the sharing of experiences and learning across divisions can become difficult—and may even be discouraged
- there is a danger of loss of central 'control' over the divisions.

The holding structure

A holding structure groups together a number of diverse businesses under a central head office, as depicted in Figure 7.5. These businesses may have come together through mergers and acquisitions, or via joint ventures. An example of a famous holding company is the American multinational conglomerate Berkshire Hathaway Inc. If the name is not immediately familiar to you, many of the brands owned by Berkshire Hathaway are certainly household names in many parts of the world, and cover a diverse spread of industries, including

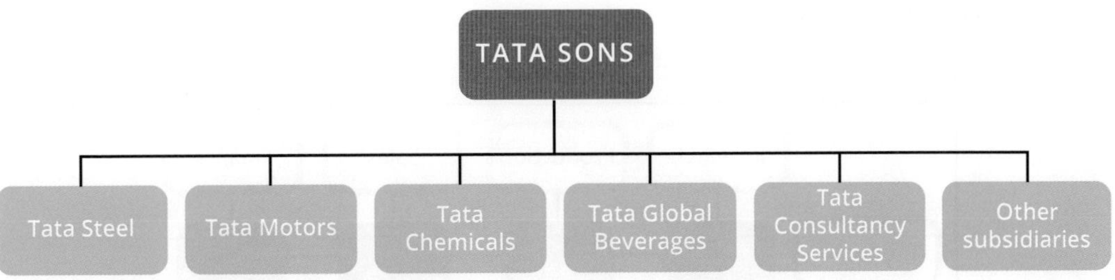

FIGURE 7.5 Example of a holding structure: Tata Group. Source: Reproduced with permission from *The Economist* (2017). Tata's governance is still faulty. [online] Available at: https://www.economist.com/business/2017/02/09/tatas-governance-is-still-faulty [Accessed 31 Jan. 2020]. © The Economist Group Limited, London 2017.

Duracell (batteries and smart power systems), Dairy Queen (restaurants), and Fruit of the Loom (textiles and clothing).

In a holding structure, every division operates autonomously as a **strategic business unit (SBU)**, with the head office acting as a central coordinator. Holding structures can be adopted by organizations of differing sizes: smaller organizations may adopt 'holding' structures as part of a strategy of rapid growth predicated upon the exploitation of new opportunities.

A holding structure has a number of advantages:

- it allows for multiple ownership, and hence a greater spread of risk around the companies making up the group
- the SBUs benefit from being exposed to a wider range of knowledge and expertise through their collaboration
- the organization has the flexibility to tap into new market opportunities.

Some of the potential disadvantages of a holding structure are:

- minimal control, or intervention over strategic issues, by the corporate parent
- the possibility that under-performing SBUs become isolated and difficult to manage
- the potential for conflicts and competition to emerge between SBUs.

The matrix structure

The matrix structure combines elements of the different structures we have already seen—for example, product divisions and geographical territories, or product divisions and functional specialisms (Figure 7.6). As such, it can combine aspects of functional and holding structures to yield a more complex hybrid structure.

Matrix structures are often adopted by multiproduct, multinational, and multifunctional organizations, as they make them adept at coordinating resources and capabilities across projects, completing routine production and engineering tasks, and achieving economies of scale (Hobday 2000). Some form of matrix structure has been adopted over the years by a long list of major corporations, including General Electric (GE), Bechtel, Citibank, Dow Chemical, Shell Oil, Texas Instruments, and TRW (Davis and Lawrence 1978).

It can be highly challenging to implement a strategy within an organization that has adopted a matrix structure, not least because of the need to coordinate the needs of different businesses

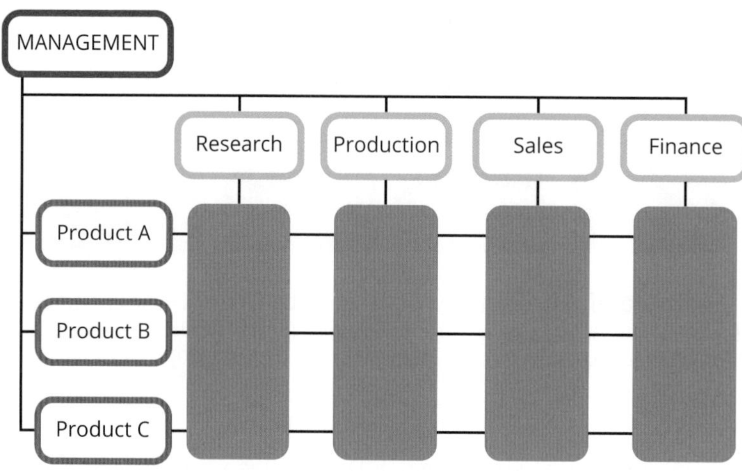

FIGURE 7.6 Example of a matrix structure.

CASE EXAMPLE 7.1 KEIRETSU

Keiretsu is the term given to a form of structure in which a set of organizations link together, usually through business relationships (often as suppliers) and by holding a small portion of shares in each other. Keiretsu is a Japanese word which translates literally as 'headless combine'.

The structure of keiretsu can resemble a spider's web, in that as members of the keiretsu, companies own a portion of their supplier, and suppliers own a bit of the company, which creates a sort of symbiotic relationship which means that those companies are much more likely to work together in a way that is mutually beneficial than if they were not connected in this way. Some might argue that this way of working together creates a culture of sharing information within the keiretsu, which can increase efficiency. By sharing information among customers, suppliers, and employees, quicker investment decisions can be made, and suppliers, employees, and customers will better understand the purposes and goals of those investments.

Others might argue that by linking together in this way, keiretsu creates an environment wherein there is limited competition, which in turn might actually lead to inefficiency. By having easy access to capital, companies within the keiretsu might take more strategic risks, which might result in too much debt. Furthermore, American trade officials have historically been critical of Japan's keiretsu as they view it as restrictive in terms of trade. This could arguably be problematic in terms of globalization and technological developments, both of which would allow the keiretsu to identify new markets.

However, despite its government's disapproval at the time, in the 1990s corporate America became very interested in the benefits of a corporate community that reflected the keiretsu structure. Keiretsu tradition was referenced in the *Harvard Business Review* in 1996 by Jeffrey Dyer, who described Chrysler as 'an American keiretsu'. After reducing the number of suppliers, Chrysler's relationship with its remaining suppliers had improved greatly, as 'the two sides [began to] strive together to find ways to lower the costs of making cars and to share the savings'.

Dyer wasn't the only corporate figure seeing the value in the keiretsu tradition. At about the same time, Richard Branson, founder of the UK's Virgin Group, wrote in *The Economist*: 'At the centre of our keiretsu brand will be a global airline and city-centre megastores acting like flag-ships for the brand around the world'. Similarly, in *The New Yorker* in 1997, journalist Ken Auletta mapped out the interwoven connections of six of the world's most influential media, entertainment, and software companies, which he likened to a keiretsu. He included in this Microsoft, Disney, Time Warner, News Corporation, TCI, and GE/NBC. Meanwhile, closer to the original home of the keiretsu, a similar structure of companies based in South Korea was building its industrial grouping run by the chaebol.

However, the American keiretsu style was fundamentally different from the Japanese model. First, the Japanese keiretsu are regulated by specific laws, and structured to ensure almost mandatory cooperation. Secondly, unlike a traditional tight grouping of Japanese keiretsu companies like Mitsubishi and Sumitomo, outside Japan the word 'keiretsu' is used to describe any loose network of alliances between more than two organizations. This reflects American companies' motives for linking together, which is described by Auletta: the American style of keiretsu works 'to create a safety net of sorts, because technology is changing so rapidly that no one can be sure which technology or which business will be ascendant'.

Auletta even went as far as to predict that the keiretsu would become 'the next corporate order'. But was he right? Today, many liken the global domination of tech firms, such as Google, Apple, Facebook, and Microsoft (still), and their presence in many key technology sectors, such as internet searching, smartphone software, social media, and operating systems, as a modern-day American version of keiretsu. For example, these companies have almost unlimited access to capital, which means they can take strategic risks without too much risk of financial damage. They can also share advanced tech expertise and credibility, as the traditional keiretsu allows, which may be seen to provide that safety net Auletta described 30 years ago.

However, it could be argued that Google's search function or Microsoft's code are actually not significantly different today from what they were three or even five years ago, and even as they move into new technologies like robotics, driverless cars, mapping, and energy, some argue that digital innovation and competition is potentially stifled by such a small group of companies dominating the tech world. Perhaps it is the new corporate order, but nevertheless, even with this new style of keiretsu, arguably the same challenges remain.

Questions for discussion

1. What advantages may be offered to a firm that is a member of a keiretsu or similar grouping?
2. Why is the idea of keiretsu a controversial concept for some commentators?
3. How to you think the idea of keiretsu might continue to evolve in the twenty-first century, for instance as a result of modern communications and technology?

Sources

Adapted from *The Economist*, 16 October 2009.

https://hbr.org/2013/09/the-new-improved-keiretsu

https://www.investopedia.com/articles/economics/09/japanese-keiretsu.asp

https://www.thedailybeast.com/how-a-few-monster-tech-firms-are-taking-over-everything-from-media-to-space-travel-and-what-it-means-for-the-rest-of-us?ref=scroll (accessed 18 July 2019).

and different countries or regions. However, such a structure brings with it potential benefits; knowledge management can be particularly effective under a matrix structure because it allows separate areas of knowledge to be integrated across organizational boundaries. This is reflected in the organizational structure of Starbucks, the American coffee company, which has a matrix structure that has evolved over time to meet the needs of the business, as we discuss in Case Example 7.2.

Case Example 7.2 provides a good illustration of a matrix structure in practice, and as with each different structural type there are associated advantages and disadvantages.

CASE EXAMPLE 7.2 STARBUCKS COFFEE COMPANY'S ORGANIZATIONAL STRUCTURE

Starbucks is a world-famous coffee house chain which has over 24,000 stores in 70 countries, making it the largest in the world. The organizational structure of Starbucks has been identified as a major part of its success. Starbucks has quite a unique organizational structure that has evolved over time to suit changing business needs; it is a matrix structure which, as we saw earlier in this section, is a hybrid structure combining different structural dimensions.

The main features of Starbucks Coffee's organizational structure are:

- functional hierarchy
- geographic divisions
- product-based divisions
- teams.

Functional hierarchy indicates how the company's structure is grouped according to function, or department, such as human resources, marketing, and finance. Each of these departments is led from the company's headquarters, which means that any decision made in the HR department in the company's headquarters impacts all the Starbucks cafés. This makes the company's functional structure hierarchical, and facilitates a top-down management of the whole company, directed by the CEO.

Geographic divisions. Starbucks organizational structure also involves geographic divisions, which allows it to offer a higher level of flexibility in order to respond to varying geographical needs to support the market conditions. This geographical structure is made up of three regional divisions to support Starbucks' global market. The three regions are China and Asia–Pacific, the Americas, and Europe, the Middle East, Russia, and Africa. However, Starbucks has also implemented sub-divisions in the Western, Northwest, Southeast, and Northeast United States, each led by a senior vice president. This enables each manager to report to two superiors: the geographic head (e.g. President of US Operations) and the functional head (e.g. Corporate HR Manager).

Product-based divisions. A further way of dividing the company's organizational structure is by product, which allows Starbucks to focus their innovation and product development within specialized areas of the company. For example, apart from coffees and other beverages, Starbucks has other divisions for merchandise and for baked goods.

Teams. Providing a personalized service to customers is a valuable asset of Starbucks' team structure. This structure, which is implemented at the lowest organizational level, means that, day-to-day in each Starbucks branch, teams are organized to deliver the service to customers that Starbucks is renowned for.

Incremental changes have been made to Starbucks' structure in response to quick expansion to a global level in recent decades. This led the company to shift its focus away from the individual customer, to concentrate on growing their global presence. However, this resulted in a decline in sales in 2007, which inevitably meant that Starbucks had to reassess. The decline was attributed to the lack of focus on customer experience, which they re-established as a key priority within their organizational structure in 2008. To implement this change, new regional divisions were set up, and better training was provided for the teams at Starbucks cafés. The current organizational structure is a result of this prioritization of the customer experience, and resulting improved financial performance.

Questions for discussion:

1. This case outlines how Starbucks' organizational structure aims to meet the firm's current business needs. Considering the advantages and disadvantages of the range of structures we have discussed so far, comment on how successfully Starbucks' organizational structure appears to help the company to achieve its strategic objectives.
2. What do you think are the possible advantages and disadvantages of the organizational structure that the firm has

adopted—for example, choosing a form of hybrid structure?

3. How do think that the organizational structure of Starbucks might have to evolve in the future? Explain your answer.

Sources

Meyer, P., http://panmore.com/starbucks-coffee-company-organizational-structure, 14 February 2019.

Starbucks company profile: https://www.starbucks.com/about-us/company-information

The advantages of a matrix structure are that it can:

- encourage overlapping businesses to collaborate to address relevant opportunities, (e.g. developing strategies that bring together the range of product lines at Starbucks)
- integrate knowledge and learning across locations (e.g. Starbucks' senior team can take an overview of geographic locations, while local managers can adapt their activities to meet local needs)
- enable the flexibility required to adapt to changing strategic conditions (e.g. creating a renewed focus on customer experience in the case of Starbucks)
- enable two or more individuals to be responsible for strategic decision-making and accountability (e.g. at Starbucks, managers report to both a geographic head and a functional head).

Some of the disadvantages of a matrix structure are that it can:

- be confusing and slow if strategic decision-making involves several participants
- lead to unclear job and task allocation if there is confusion around roles and responsibilities
- lead to unclear responsibilities for costs and profits
- generate tension and potential conflict between individuals in teams if they feel they have divided loyalties.

Some large international organizations have chosen to adopt different structures in different parts of the world, perhaps driven by changes in their senior team at a particular time. For example, in 2012 GE moved away from a matrix structure in India, while retaining that structure in other parts of the world (Ganguly 2012). For GE, moving away from a matrix structure represented a decentralization of power in India, giving its managers on the ground permission to 'localize the business'. It allowed GE to try something different in a country that represented a very small percentage of its global business at that time.

However, such a decision can also lead to local managers feeling that they have lost the prestige that comes with reporting directly to the company's global headquarters. They may also feel that they have lost some autonomy, as their strongest reporting line is now to the head of the local country, rather than to an executive on the other side of the world. This illustrates the various complexities and tensions involved in designing an appropriate organizational structure for a very large organization operating in multiple businesses in multiple locations around the world.

The network structure

The network structure is a flexible non-hierarchical structure in which a series of independent organizations or SBUs are grouped together. As such, it may comprise numerous individuals, project groups, or collaborations who are collectively designing, producing, and marketing a given product or service. All the participating entities are linked by formal or informal relationships (Figure 7.7). The essential feature of a network structure is that the boundaries of the organization are permeable and less distinct, so that the organization becomes 'boundaryless' (Arthur and Rousseau 1996).

The majority of the productive activities of an organization with a network structure are outsourced to suppliers and distributors. As a result, its activities may be spread worldwide. Staff may not be employed on a long-term basis; they may instead be hired for specific projects for particular periods of time based on the skills and competencies they offer.

The network structure is common in dynamic and complex environments in which an organization needs to be responsive in terms of its creativity and innovation if it is to be effective, and to be able to demonstrate a clear competitive advantage.

The advantages of the network structure are that it gives an organization the flexibility needed to respond to rapid changes, and allows it to focus on its areas of particular competence, while drawing on distinct areas of expertise and benefiting from efficiencies exhibited by other firms.

What are the possible disadvantages of the network structure?

- Relationships are transitional, unstable, and subject to tensions.
- High levels of trust are required.
- Cultures may diverge as the organizations making up the network evolve over time.

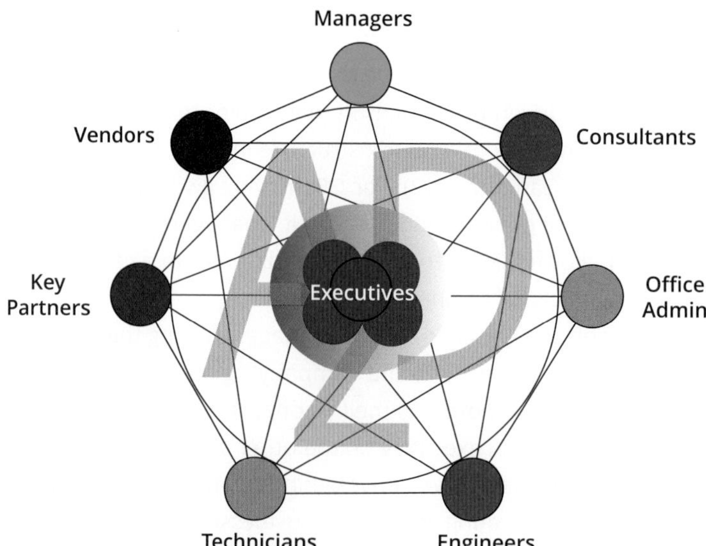

FIGURE 7.7 Example of a network structure.

- The coordination required to make the parties operate collaboratively can be time consuming and resource intensive, but such coordination must happen if economies of scale and scope are to be achieved
- An organization may inhibit its own development and operational optimization by continually outsourcing activities.

The transnational structure

This configuration enables an organization to operate effectively on an international scale, and can help to spread knowledge across geographic borders. The transnational structure seeks to maximize the benefits from two extreme international strategies: the multidomestic strategy and the global strategy.

- A **multidomestic strategy** involves a portfolio of separate national companies with a coordinating centre, where the separate national companies have little contact or interaction with each other.
- A **global strategy** involves an organization making the same product available in many different national markets (Segal-Horn and Faulkner 2010). In so doing, the organization attempts to benefit from economies of scale by standardizing its product offer.

A global strategy is supported by global product divisions (e.g. worldwide manufacturing systems), whereas a multidomestic strategy is supported by local subsidiaries, each with a substantial amount of autonomy with respect to the design, manufacture, and marketing of products.

A transnational structure seeks to combine the best of both global and multidomestic approaches. A famous example is HSBC. Its advertising campaign positions HSBC as 'The World's Local Bank'; it tries to set itself apart as a bank that has many global connections, yet is still flexible enough to care for the needs of local customers (Renteria 2010). The term 'glocalization' has been coined to describe this approach, which essentially aligns high local responsiveness with high global coordination—in other words, the benefits of globally coordinated operation, particularly in terms of scale and scope, are coupled with the merits of being flexible enough to adapt to local market needs.

The transnational configuration has the following characteristics.

- Each national unit operates independently, but is a source of ideas and capabilities for the whole corporation. For example, in the oil and gas sector, new technologies developed in one location can then be rolled out around the world. BP points to the recent deployment of its 'big data' Argus platform for use at 99.5% of its wells, aiming to support critical decisions with state-of-the-art analytical tools (Looney 2017).
- National units achieve greater scale economies through specialization on behalf of the whole corporation, or at least by dividing operations into large regions. Again, BP provides an interesting example of a firm with its roots in a particular location, but key activities around the world. BP is a British multinational oil and gas company headquartered in London, yet nearly a third of its global business interests are in the USA, and it has important

operations in Rotterdam, Russia, Iraq, Canada, Egypt, Angola, India, the South China Sea, Indonesia, Australia, Azerbaijan, Brazil, and Trinidad and Tobago, as well as other locations around the world.

- The corporate centre manages the global network by first establishing the role of each business unit, and then sustaining the systems, relationships, and culture to make the network of business units operate effectively. In the HSBC example, the intention was to provide a familiar customer experience around the world, despite national variation in the features of products and services.

What are the disadvantages of a transnational structure?

- It requires managers to be willing to focus their work on both local *and* international responsibilities simultaneously, which can be demanding.
- Responsibilities at the local and the global level can be both complex and confusing, and potentially even in conflict, placing additional strain on individuals.
- Internal politics may overshadow effective work.

Innovation-oriented structures

The final two configurations described here are the project-based structure and adhocracies. Both structures are associated with a particular intention on the part of an organization to innovate. They share many of the characteristics of network organizations, as described in the section on the network structure, but they go even further in pursuit of dynamic flexibility.

The project-based structure

In this configuration, teams are created, undertake their work (e.g. on a contract basis), usually for a fixed time-span, and then dissolve. Such a structure can be particularly appropriate for organizations that deliver large and expensive goods or services (such as major projects in the fields of civil engineering or information technology), or those delivering time-limited events (such as sporting events, festivals, or large consultancy engagements). The organization structure comprises a constantly changing collection of project teams that are overseen by a small corporate group. Many organizations use such teams on an impromptu basis to complement the 'main' organizational structure. For instance, high tech companies such as Vodafone, Sharp, Sony, NTT, Mitsubishi Electric, and Matsushita Electric often exhibit project-based structures (Kodama 2007).

What are the advantages of a project-based structure?

- It is highly flexible—projects can be established and dissolved as required. This can be vital in a fast-moving environment where organizations need to bring together and exploit individual knowledge and competencies quickly and in novel ways.
- It makes accountability and control mechanisms transparent because project teams have defined tasks to achieve with defined timescales.
- Knowledge exchange is effective because project members can be drawn from different departments within an organization.

- Individuals may be more willing to work in different locations around the world because of the relatively short timelines involved, hence making it possible to assemble teams that draw from an organization's global talent pool.

The project-based structure also has potential disadvantages.

- The success of project-based structures can lead to them being used inappropriately, whereby there is an attempt to use them to sort out any and every problem.
- If projects do not have strong programme management they may drift in focus or activity.
- The constant formation and disbanding of project teams—and associated movement and reassignment of individuals from across an organization—can hinder the development of specialist knowledge and expertise, which may delay organizational learning.

Adhocracies

Mintzberg (1989) suggests that adhocracies are innovation-oriented organizational forms. They have a flexible organic structure with few formal constraints, thereby offering the maximum potential for innovation. They encourage diverse experts to interact, and focus on client needs and best practices (Dolan 2010). The emphasis is on an organization's ability to innovate and be creative, in an environment in which knowledge is the key strategic asset.

Adhocracies rely on a variety of expertise to win business, and are primarily organized around experts or areas of expertise. They may be young firms that rely on one or more charismatic and entrepreneurial founding members to lead the organization. It has been suggested that NASA functioned as an **adhocracy** in its first dozen or so years (Desveaux 2012). It was created in the wake of failures and conflicts between branches of the US military, and was given considerable autonomy and a clear problem-solving mandate—to land people safely on the Moon within a decade.

Adhocracies have also been described as 'cellular' (Miles et al. 1997) because they must be highly fluid and adaptive to change while performing complex tasks.

Adhocratic organizations may feature the coordinated operation of multifunctional teams. For example, the UK-based pharmaceutical firm GlaxoSmithKline has broken its drug discovery operation into about 40 units that compete with one another for funding (Birkinshaw and Ridderstale 2015). These configurations are similar to the project-based structure discussed above, as their focus is driven by the design, development, and delivery of tailor-made projects. The key difference is timescale: project teams tend to be set up for a specific purpose for a fixed period of time, while adhocracies are ongoing configurations.

Adhocracies tend to remove hierarchical layers and 'flatten' the organization wherever possible, with the point of contact with the customer assuming particular importance. For instance, Zappos, the online shoe and clothing retailer, is famous for its ability to deliver an excellent customer experience, based partly on the ability of the customer service staff to understand and deliver what the client wants (Glassman 2013). Adhocracies also strive to respond quickly and responsively to customer needs. For example, Zappos offers thousands of product lines and the ability to customize the product to meet the needs of an individual customer. Such an approach requires a departure from the centralized command and control mode that we typically see in complex structures.

Organizational structures: the reality

It is important to note that, in reality, few organizations adopt a structure that is exactly like one of the pure structural configurations we have discussed. Similarly, it would be an oversimplification to say that a company adopts one form and has no traces of any of the other types within its structure. In practice, an organization may exhibit many micro-structures within one or more macro-structures. As a consequence, an organization may adopt a blend of different structures that have either been consciously formed, or have evolved as the organization has faced and responded to new challenges.

How does an organization choose its structure?

We have discussed a range of structural configurations (with the caveat that companies often use a blend of these types). But how do organizations choose which structure to adopt? Goold and Campbell (2002) offer nine design tests for those organizations making a conscious decision to adopt a specific structure. Managers can evaluate their proposals for possible organizational structures against these nine tests in order to identify a suitable configuration for their organization. This can be a useful way for managers to assess whether the formal structure they are working to establish is appropriate and covers the main issues they are seeking to address. The first four tests emphasize the need for a good fit between the proposed structure and the key goals of the organization.

- **The market advantage test**
  If we think of Chandler's dictum that 'structure follows strategy', we can see that this test, which represents a test of fit between the firm's structure and its market strategy, is very important. For example, if coordination between two steps in a production process is important to market advantage, then these steps should probably be placed in the same structural unit.
- **The parenting advantage test**
  This test holds that there should be a good fit between the organization's structure and the parenting role of the corporate centre. For example, if the corporate centre aims to add value as a manager of synergy, it should design a structure that places important integrative specialisms (such as marketing or research) at the centre. Recall the case study of Rolls-Royce that opened this chapter: interviewees characterized the actions of the 'corporate centre' as 'meddling' in the business divisions, creating extra costs for unwanted services.
- **The people test**
  This maintains that there must be a good fit between the organization's structure and the people available to fill key roles. For example, it is dangerous to switch completely from a functional structure to a multidivisional structure if, as is likely, the organization lacks managers with competence in running decentralized business units.
- **The feasibility test**
  This test can be seen as a catch-all category. It reminds us that the structure must fit with a range of constraints that the organization has to address—perhaps including legal constraints, or pressures from important stakeholders such as trade unions. Rumelt (2011)

gives the example of International Harvester's new strategic plan which involved structural changes such as cutting costs and strengthening networks. Unfortunately, the plan did not mention important obstacles such as the firm's very poor labour relations or its very inefficient production facilities—and most of the business was sold off a few years later.

The above four tests are an important starting point when choosing an appropriate structural design, as they highlight a range of important aspects that should not be overlooked. However, Goold and Campbell (2002) go further in identifying five more tests, with the aim of exploring whether the proposed organizational structure appears to be based on good general design principles.

- **The specialized cultures test**
  This test is based on the notion that a good organizational design brings together specialist staff. This is important as it allows specialists to develop their expertise in close collaboration with each other. Therefore a structure will fail this test if it breaks up important specialist cultures.
- **The difficult links test**
  This tests asks us to consider whether a proposed structure will set up links between parts of the organization where good relationships are important, but such relationships are also likely to be strained. For example, extreme decentralization to profit-accountable business units may strain relationships with a central R&D department. This kind of structure may fail if compensating mechanisms are not put in place.
- **The redundant hierarchy test**
  This test reminds us that a proposed structure should be checked in case it has too many layers of management. Redundant levels of hierarchy can cause unnecessary blockages and associated costs for the firm.
- **The accountability test**
  This test stresses the importance of clear lines of accountability. The aim is to ensure that managers throughout the organizational structure are totally committed to achieving the organization's goals, and are accountable for delivery against the organizational strategy. For example, matrix structures are sometimes accused of lacking clear accountability, as managers tend to have dual lines of reporting under such structures.
- **The flexibility test**
  Another important test is the extent to which an organizational design will allow for change in the future, perhaps in response to changes in a fast-moving external environment. For example, divisional domains should be specified in a sufficiently broad manner to allow divisional managers to follow new opportunities as they emerge.

Kranias (2000) gives a good example of a situation where we can put the nine tests into practice by discussing the case of Japanese multinational companies entering the UK, and the choices that they have made with regard to their organizational structure and its fit with their strategy. Table 7.2 explains why establishing a subsidiary in the UK (typically following a transnational structure, as discussed in this chapter) represents a fit between strategy and structure for the company.

TABLE 7.2 **Examples of 'fit' for a Japanese multinational company**

Test	Examples of 'fit' for a Japanese multinational company
The **market advantage** test	• The Japanese firm depends on foreign markets for the supply of raw materials and as export markets for its production • A UK subsidiary may protect the firm against increasing land prices and labour costs in Japan • It may also protect the firm from any increase in protectionism against Japanese products in the world market, and against currency fluctuations
The **parenting advantage** test	• The corporate parent controls all operations worldwide and is the source of competitive advantage • Information flows from the centre to the subsidiaries • All subsidiaries are part of the corporate value chain and participate in corporate strategy • Strong centralization is necessary for the coordination of global operations
The **people** test	• Japan is a unique country, relatively isolated from the rest of the world, and with a unique culture • The prospect of long-term employment changes both the attitude of the employee towards the company, and also the attitude of the company towards the employee, i.e. the company considers the employee to be an asset
The **feasibility** test	• Many Japanese firms have seen the UK not only as a big market but also as a gateway to European markets • The UK economy has been seen as stable • UK legislation and taxes have been seen as favourable • The UK has also been seen as an attractive location because of the language, and the availability of knowledge-based resources
The **specialized** cultures test	• Japanese firms tend to have non-specialized career paths which are seen as immersing the employee in the overall philosophy of the organization • Through rotation to different functional areas, the employees encounter and absorb the corporate ideology
The **difficult links** test	• The traditional separation of sales and manufacturing in Japanese multinational companies is one of the reasons why this configuration is appropriate • The separation is motivated by the desire to improve information sharing, achieve better customer service, and a general preference for keeping specialized activities separate
The **redundant hierarchy** test	• Japanese expatriate managers tend to assume the top positions in the management hierarchy of the subsidiary company • Expatriates also tend to play a connecting role between the corporate centre in Japan and the subsidiary in the UK • Expatriates attempt to pass on the corporate philosophy to the subsidiary; their presence in the overseas subsidiary is typically temporary (e.g. not exceeding 3 years) • Local managers may assume (for example) second and third places in the hierarchy of the UK subsidiary company

TABLE 7.2 *Continued*

Test	Examples of 'fit' for a Japanese multinational company
The **accountability** test	• Although the control exercised by the centre is typically rather flexible, the system of reporting to the centre is detailed • These companies tend to focus on planning procedures, both formal and informal, long-term and short-term • The centre takes a proactive role by setting strategic priorities and actively participating in business-level strategies
The **flexibility** test	• The strategic goal of the company is to increase its flexibility in the face of demands from European markets • The European market is felt to be quite complex, e.g. consisting of multiple languages, which in practice may mean that a range of different products have to be produced in relatively small volumes • Flexibility can also be translated into a reduction in stock levels. The proximity of customers can reduce lead times and stock levels may be kept as low as possible (e.g. with customers holding just a few days' worth of stock), hence production occurs in small and specific quantities as ordered • The centre tends to reduce its pressure on its overseas operations in the UK over time. The management tends to become more localized, and the subsidiaries more oriented towards meeting the needs of the European market. The centre, and consequently the subsidiaries, tend to realize that their role is to satisfy a different market and not necessarily to attempt to implement the espoused corporate strategy even at the cost of adopting the flexibility required

Goold and Campbell's nine tests provide a useful screening device for forming an effective configuration. However, even if a structural design passes these tests, the structure still needs to match with other aspects of the organization's configuration, processes, relationships, and culture.

7.3 The impact of systems on strategy

We have looked at the link between strategy and structure and considered the main structural forms in organizations. But within any given organizational structure, how do things get done? All organizations, whatever their broad structural form, will have a number of systems and routines in place. Systems can be thought of as the micro-structures that make organizations work. In this section we look at what systems are, and why they are so important to the practice of strategy. We explore different types of operational and control systems, and we introduce levers of control (Simons 1995)—a comprehensive approach to the establishment of control systems in organizations that operate in environments where they experience rapid and continuous change. We end the section by discussing 'control via simple rules', as advocated for organizations in turbulent environments where high levels of flexibility and creativity are also required (Eisenhardt and Sull 2001).

What are systems?

In organizational terms, a system can be described as a micro-structure that actually makes an organization work. A system tells people and machines what to do, it monitors performance, and it provides a means by which to evaluate an organization's overall performance. As such, systems are the building blocks from which capabilities develop; they can make important connections between long-term strategy and short-term actions, supporting communication, planning, feedback, and learning (Kaplan and Norton 1996).

Routines are a particularly important subset of systems in strategic terms because they can be the source of competitive advantage for an organization. At an organizational level, a routine can be considered 'the way we do things around here'; they tend to persist over time and guide people's behaviour. We can think of them as being to the organization what skills are to the individual. A routine increases efficiency and effectiveness by encapsulating the knowledge that is necessary for the standardized performance of a task. Systems provide the link between strategy and operational effectiveness.

Systems perform in two ways.

- **As operational systems**—that is, those mechanisms, including working practices and routines, that underlie the efficient use and deployment of resources and capabilities; for instance, the order fulfillment system in a warehouse, where customer orders that have been placed online are picked and prepared for distribution.
- **As control systems**—that is, those mechanisms that monitor the achievement of strategic goals; for instance, a system that monitors the number of items manufactured per week that meet the required quality standards, or the proportion of an airline's flights that arrive at their destination on time.

Why are systems important?

Systems enable, specify, guide, and control behaviours in an organization. They allow the resources and capabilities of an organization to interact in order to create value. They both facilitate activity and control it. As such, they are key to the implementation of strategy. Examples include cost control systems, performance evaluation systems, and reward systems to incentivize staff to focus on certain tasks.

If an organization's strategy and systems don't align, the organization will struggle to implement its planned strategy successfully. For example, a business may be growing so fast that its systems have difficulty keeping up, or they develop in directions which are less than ideal; a performance management system may encourage staff to continue to pursue good scores on previously defined performance metrics, even when those metrics are no longer aligned with the organizational strategy. Pongatichat and Johnston (2008) point out that this is an important problem in public sector organizations as well as private ones:

> *With three or four tiers of government and elections for each tier every three or four years, new and sometimes distinctly different political agendas may be suddenly forced on the organization. Indeed a change in the political domination in a council (city, borough, county, region or central) may lead*

> *to the complete reversal of some policies which will not only affect that level but also all the tiers below it.*
>
> Pongatichat and Johnston (2008: 210–11)

In dynamic environments, operational systems must include features that allow the organization to change core capabilities over time—for example, in production, technology, or marketing. Without such an ability to change, an organization will be unable to learn, innovate, and seize emerging opportunities in products and markets. Operational systems that embody these qualities may be genuine sources of distinctiveness.

We now look at how operational systems can help or hinder an organization to learn and develop.

Operational systems as learning

We know from everyday experience that we learn some things through word of mouth and simply 'having a go', while other learning is more structured: we learn by reading things that are written down (they are 'codified'). The former type of learning encapsulates the acquisition of tacit knowledge, i.e. knowledge that is less easily written down.

Organizations face challenges when it comes to the development of systems because the knowledge underlying some skills is largely tacit in nature; it is difficult to articulate and is more easily expressed through performance (Tsoukas 2005). For example, a customer service representative may learn how to deal with difficult customers by experiencing many interactions over time. Through these experiences, the representative can learn how to respond in certain situations. Customer service training can help to a certain extent, but it typically takes experience and practice to learn successful responses. It is difficult to give every example in training, so having an experienced person on hand to mentor new employees can help transfer that knowledge and experience to them.

Tacit systems are ways of doing things that are essentially assumed knowledge: members of an organization take the knowledge needed to do that thing for granted, to the point where that knowledge is never written down. Codified systems, on the other hand, are explicitly documented. One could argue that this difference distinguishes routines from systems: routines often embody tacit knowledge, while systems tend to be more explicit.

Implementing strategy requires the integration of many types of knowledge embodied in people and practices across the organization (Open University 2010). In a dynamic environment, it can be difficult for organizations to achieve this integration while preserving their operational efficiency. Operational systems can contribute to making the process of integrating knowledge more efficient, and also enable the organization to use its knowledge to adapt to its changing circumstances. This is achieved through organizational learning. Routines are key: firms may use routines to help support decisions such as the choice of product designs or the setting of production levels.

The process of learning is likely to be different for every organization. A small organization with a flat hierarchy may be able to achieve close and frequent face-to-face contact between the key people that work there. This means that operational systems need to be flexible to support these interactions. In contrast, in large organizations with complex structures, there is a danger that the operational systems can become sources of inefficiency. In other words, they become such a routine part of day-to-day working that, over time, the organization becomes slow and unresponsive to change as bureaucratic rigidity gradually takes hold. Garvin suggests that this points to a dual challenge: 'a learning organization is an organization skilled at creating, acquiring, and transferring knowledge, and at modifying its behavior to reflect new knowledge and insights' (Garvin 1993: 80). This suggests that the successful management of strategy can require processes of unlearning (Nystrom and Starbuck 1984), and that managers must recognize this. Existing capabilities can become obsolete because of significant environmental shifts; they need to be unlearned in order to adapt new and better ways of doing things.

Montgomery (2008) makes a similar point when she argues that the search for competitive advantage can leave organizations blinkered: they fail to evolve their activities over time. Unless organizations are prepared to evolve—to give up old ways of doing things and adopt new ones—they risk becoming locked into an outmoded view of their own success. For newer recruits, the problem may be less about unlearning, and more about ensuring that they really 'get' the organization's strategy—a concept sometimes referred to as 'embeddedness', which is affected by job conditions (such as training opportunities and a clear development path), and also by perceptions of and trust in top management (Galunic and Hermreck 2012).

Control systems

Having considered the different ways in which an organization can be structured, we may find ourselves asking: within a given structure, how does an organization ensure that its employees act in a way that is consistent with its agreed strategy? To answer this question, we explore how control systems help an organization to remain focused on its strategic goals.

Control systems align individuals, locations, and activities with strategic decisions and provide ways to monitor performance against strategic goals. Control systems take different shapes and forms, with some being imposed by outside stakeholders and others being chosen by management. As we see for structural configurations, different organizations require different control systems: it is not a case that 'one size fits all'. We illustrate this by looking at two different types of control systems—financial and dynamic. We finish with an alternative to a control system—control via simple rules.

Financial control systems

In many organizations, the management of performance focuses on the monitoring of finances and budgets, with 'numbers' being used to define budgetary activities and set financial targets. As such, the budgetary process involves setting and monitoring financial estimates—in relation to both income and expenditure—for a fixed period (e.g. a financial year) for the organization as a whole and often for different levels within the organization.

Budgets can be considered to have three purposes: they provide a forecast of future income and expenditure, they represent targets against which required financial performance can be measured, and they represent limits of authority (levels of expenditure up to which spending has been approved).

Budgets are often reviewed and established annually: the previous year's performance is reviewed, and future forecasts are set out (typically over an agreed time period such as three years, for example). The budgetary process may also be a vehicle for analysing the impact of implementing strategic initiatives. While conventional accounting practices and policies exist, organizations vary when it comes to presenting their financial plans. This diversity makes the use of financial plans potentially ambiguous. Generally, the more complex the organization, the more sophisticated and formalized the financial control processes are likely to be.

Such financial planning and budgetary control processes also apply to not-for-profit organizations where financial integrity and accountability are of paramount importance. In order to remain fully informed of financial performance, the trustees of most charitable organizations (being accountable to the relevant authority, such as the Charity Commission for England and Wales) will require regular statements covering the financial health of the organization. Examples of such reports include income and expense statements, balance sheets, and cash flow statements.

If financial control is mismanaged in any way, the consequences for an organization can be disastrous. In the third sector, which includes charitable organizations, financial control mismanagement is perhaps particularly catastrophic because of the potential loss of trust which can ensue. For example, the reasons behind the closure of Kids Company in the UK in 2015 received a great deal of analysis in the media. When the charity closed, it said its finances had become stretched because of the number of children needing help. But donors had apparently been withdrawing their support, alarmed by stories of alleged mismanagement (BBC 2016). Earlier that summer, the charity had said that it wanted to restructure and had sought new funds from the UK government and donors. But when it finally closed in August 2015, government ministers said that they wanted to recover a £3 million grant given to the charity a week before. Criticisms included lavish spending and mismanagement, and—in the eyes of the media—the charity's chief executive, formerly seen as an inspirational leader, was labelled a 'disgrace' (Renegade Inc. 2017). The charity was accused of a 'chronic failure of governance' and 'insularity', i.e. resisting peer-led scrutiny (Ilott 2016). This illustrates that control must be rigorous; and any assessment of strategic performance must be open to the inclusion of issues other than financial criteria alone, such as the ethical behaviour of employees and their achievements.

Dynamic control systems

There is obviously a balance to be struck between the control needed to maintain an organization's activities within agreed strategic parameters, and the flexibility needed to foster creativity and innovation, particularly in organizations faced with continuous change. Robert Simons (1995) argues that an effective control mechanism is one that promotes the strategic flexibility and innovative capabilities that the organization needs to adapt to change, but in a controlled manner.

Unlike the financial control systems discussed in the previous section, Simons' approach to control brings together both feedback and feedforward mechanisms according to broader organizational criteria, such as an organization's culture. Using strong empirical evidence, he describes four 'levers' of control which, when used collectively, can reconcile the conflict between

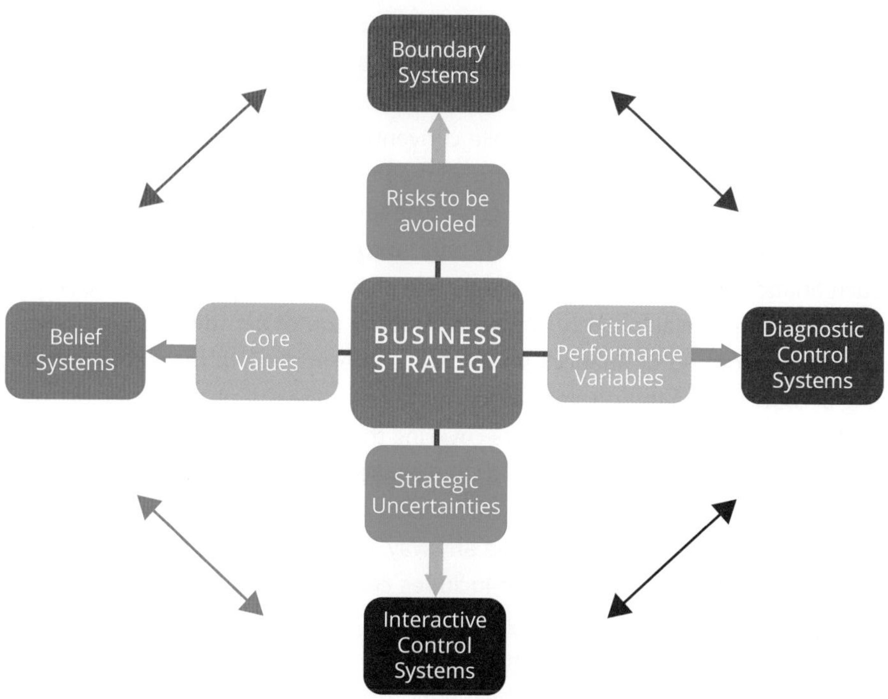

FIGURE 7.8 Levers of control. Source: From Simons, R. (1995). *Levers of Control: How Managers Use Innovative Control Systems to Drive Strategic Renewal*. Boston, MA: Harvard Business School Press. By permission of Harvard Business Publishing.

7

flexibility and control. The interrelationships between these levers are shown in Figure 7.8. We can explore each of these four levers in a little more detail, as follows.

- **Belief systems** are the explicit values of the organization, encapsulated in its mission statement. They inspire and guide the strategy process and provide a framework for implementation decisions. Typically, expressions of belief systems are concise and inspirational. For example, Twitter say that they 'believe in free expression and think every voice has the power to impact the world' (Twitter 2019). Belief systems promote the commitment of employees to the organization's core values in pursuing its strategic goals.
- **Boundary systems** indicate the boundaries of the 'acceptable domain of activity' of an organization, and can be closely associated with its belief system. Codes of conduct and ethical principles are examples of 'business conduct boundaries', while planning documents, which define the scope of an organization's activities, are 'strategic boundary systems'. Simons (1995) suggests that these act as an 'organization's brakes', and that every organization needs them to avoid both activities that are off-limits and unacceptable risks. A famous example is Bill Gates' statement of what Microsoft was *not* going to be: they weren't going into hardware (e.g. Brant 2016).
- **Interactive control systems** stimulate search and learning, permitting new strategies to develop throughout the organization as individuals respond to perceived opportunities and threats. Here the focus is on strategic uncertainties and challenging existing assumptions. Typically an effective interactive control should include four distinct features:

- it keeps strategic information up-to-date for management
- the information is organized and accessible to managers at all levels in the organization
- it encourages strategic decision-making in a process of dialogue between superiors, subordinates, and peers
- it serves as a catalyst for ongoing debate and critical thinking about underlying data, assumptions, and action plans.

For example, Tata Steel is proud to report that it has implemented environmental management systems that provide it with 'a framework for managing compliance and achieving continuous improvement' (Tata Steel Europe 2019). The data is widely accessible and used as a basis for critical debate. The company requires appropriate strategic information in order to minimize its environmental impact 'wherever practicable and cost-effective to do so'. Tata Steel's environmental management systems enable them to monitor its main potential environmental impacts (from emissions to air of particulates, oxides of nitrogen, sulphur dioxide, and carbon dioxide, and to water of hydrocarbons and suspended solids), as well as to report annually on its energy usage and waste treatment activities.

- **Diagnostic control systems** allow managers to measure outputs and compare them with expected standards of performance over defined time periods. Managers can then adjust and modify inputs and processes in the light of these analyses to ensure that future outputs more closely match organizational targets. Such diagnostic systems help managers to track the progress of individuals and divisions towards the achievement of strategically important goals. An example is the formal review of performance in regular meetings at board, departmental, and team level, commonly referred to as appraisals.

Control via simple rules

Is Simons' model sufficiently flexible to be applied in highly turbulent and relatively creative environments? Eisenhardt and Sull (2001) argue that such environments require an altogether different perspective on control. They give examples of organizations which have done remarkably well in highly chaotic environments despite few apparent resources, and which have used constantly evolving strategies to make the most of unanticipated one-off opportunities. Sull and Eisenhardt (2012) give the example of ALL (América Latina Logística), which prioritized capital expenditure by asking whether proposals:

- removed obstacles to growing revenues
- minimized up-front expenditure
- provided benefits immediately (rather than paying off in the long term)
- reused existing resources.

Examples such as ALL suggest that the organization succeeded by learning to handle strategy as a set of simple rules. Such an approach could work for a wide range of organizations, not least because of the profound impact the new economy has had on all manner of firms whereby they must now capture unanticipated opportunities in order to succeed. Managers of such companies—like Yahoo!, according to Eisenhardt and Sull (2001)—know that the greatest opportunities for competitive advantage lie in market confusion, so they jump into chaotic markets and shift flexibly among opportunities as circumstances dictate. Yahoo! had a clear focus on product innovation, supported by simple rules such as know the priority rank of each product in development and ensure that every engineer can work on every project (Eisenhardt and Sull 2001).

Control by simple rules rather than complicated systems is an approach most suited to organizations in the new economy—organizations that have to survive in markets that are both rapidly changing and ambiguous. Sull and Eisenhardt (2012) give the example of Skrill, a provider of online payment services. Skrill decided to woo business from digital service providers like Skype and Facebook. Skrill was faced with hundreds of ideas for payment options it could develop for such customers, and had to weigh up complex trade-offs when deciding which opportunities to pursue. Selecting which payment options to adopt became Skrill's critical bottleneck. A cross-functional team was convened; before the meeting, each team member articulated the rules that his or her function would use to evaluate alternatives. The team negotiated all the ideas down to a handful of rules, such as 'The customer can complete payment in fewer than five steps' and 'More than one existing customer requested the payment option'.

It is important to note, then, that simple strategy rules are not broad or vague. Rather, they are specific and flexible, so that managers can approach each opportunity in a controlled and disciplined manner. The simple rules proposed by Eisenhardt and Sull (2001: 114) fall into five broad categories:

- **How-to rules** spell out key features of how a process is executed (in the Skrill example, the firm focused on payment options that could be completed in less than five steps).
- **Boundary rules** encourage managers to focus on which opportunities can be pursued and which are outside the organization's scope (again, in the Skrill example, they chose options that were requested by more than one existing customer as being within the scope).
- **Priority rules** help managers rank the accepted opportunities (see the ALL example).
- **Timing rules** help managers synchronize the pace of emerging opportunities with other parts of the organization; this might include prioritizing projects where a strong cross-functional team can be put together, and pulling out of projects where key skills may be lacking or key members of staff are leaving the organization.
- **Exit rules** help managers to decide when to pull out of yesterday's opportunities; this might include cancelling a project when financial returns do not come in according to previously agreed plans.

To be effective, simple rules must relate to a single process, and must be frequently reviewed to keep in step with the rapidly changing contexts they are put in place to operate within. It is also important to minimize the number of rules: Eisenhardt and Sull (2001) recommend between two and seven rules. Their research found that young companies often had too few rules to be effective, and more mature companies often had too many.

7.4 The impact of culture on strategy

How would you describe culture and why is it important for strategy? In this section we suggest that 'culture', a set of shared values and beliefs, is created as the organization learns and evolves over time—for instance, as strategy is formulated and implemented, as the organization adapts to its external environment and seeks to integrate individuals into an effective whole (Schein 2004). Hence there is an important interrelationship between strategy and culture.

We begin this section by discussing what culture is. In short, it can be described as the personality and practices of the whole organization and, importantly, it reminds us to focus on the 'people' aspects of strategic management. We reflect on why culture is a critical issue from the perspective of the practice of strategy. In order to build a successful organization, the willing participation, commitment, and satisfaction of its people are highly desirable dimensions, if not essential to success. We review different types of organizational culture, and explore how organizations might go about changing their culture as this can be an important dimension of successful strategy implementation, influencing the behaviour of its people in desirable ways.

What is culture?

We have seen that an organization's structure and systems affect not only its operational efficiency but the people who work in it. Within a given structure, people need to come together in a coordinated and controlled manner in order to work effectively. To achieve this, the organization becomes a social system in which people establish their behaviours, relationships, and social groupings alongside those formally defined by management. Think back to the case study on restructuring at Rolls-Royce that opened this chapter; interviewees pointed to previous attempts to reshape the firm, when managers had underestimated the effort required to change fossilized processes that had built up over decades, and commented that the bureaucracy 'just finds ways of reintroducing itself to make sure this doesn't happen'.

Building a successful organization requires the willing participation, commitment, and satisfaction of its people. This shapes the personality and practices of the whole organization—in short, its culture. Before we proceed, we should try to be clear about what we mean by this complex, and at times elusive, idea. Culture is a multilayered, highly interconnected construct (Watkins 2013). We can consider culture at the level of national culture and identity, at the level of professions and occupations, and at the level of personal networks and social groups. However, organizations often operate simultaneously at all of these levels; they represent a coming together of different nationalities, professions and/or occupations, and (of course) individuals. Once we appreciate this, we can begin to get a sense of the complexity of the concept of culture as applied to the development and implementation of strategy.

Culture is something that we can't see—but we can sense it and we can see its effects. A key question in organizational analysis (Denison 1996) has become: Is culture something that an organization has or something that it is? There are a range of possible answers to that question. At one end, authors like Deal and Kennedy (see sections on 'How do we change culture?' and 'Examples of generic cultures') seem to suggest that organizations have a lever (or set of levers) called 'culture' that managers can pull in order to achieve change. At the other end, some authors argue that culture is created and re-created by the members of the organization themselves (e.g. Denison and Mishra 1995). Culture is constructed by individuals, but it may or may not be shared by all members of the organization.

Why is culture important?

Schein (2004) argues that organizations face two basic challenges as they evolve over time: they must (i) integrate individuals into an effective whole, and (ii) adapt to meet the needs of the external environment they operate in. As an organization addresses these challenges, it will develop a set of shared values and beliefs that we might call its 'culture'.

Schein (2004: 1) suggests that 'culture is both a dynamic phenomenon that surrounds us at all times, being constantly enacted and created by our interactions with others, and shaped by leadership behaviour, and a set of structures, routines, rules and norms that guide and constrain behaviour'. This idea that culture is both a guide and a constraint on behaviour is crucial for us to understand, if we are interested in how strategic change is implemented in organizations. Equally key is understanding the idea that culture is both enacted by peers and created by leaders. In fact, Schein argues that 'leadership and culture are two sides of the same coin', explaining that:

> *cultures begin with leaders who impose their own values and assumptions on a group. If that group is successful, and the assumptions come to be taken for granted, we then have a culture that will define for later generations what kinds of leadership are acceptable (Schein 2004: 2).*

In time, then, this leads to a situation in which culture effectively defines leadership.

If the organization loses sight of the needs of its external environment, effective leadership will both detect this fact and be prepared to change things to remedy the situation. Thus leadership goes back to defining what acceptable culture is, and the process continues. Therefore Schein argues that the 'ability to perceive the limitations of one's own culture and to evolve the culture adaptively is the essence and ultimate challenge of leadership' (Schein 2004: 2).

The concept of culture as something that develops at specific moments, in response to particular challenges and driven by particular charismatic individuals, emphasizes its dynamic nature. If culture is subject to change, then perhaps managers can deliberately change it in order to facilitate new strategic directions. However, Schein warns that this is far from easy—and we will discuss this further in relation to Deal and Kennedy's (1982) typology of four generic cultures (see later in this section).

Schein maintains that culture manifests itself at three levels in an organization:

- **The level of observable artefacts**—corporate identity, dress code, buildings, etc. This level is very easy to observe, but it can still be difficult to interpret by an 'outsider' to the organization.
- **The shared espoused beliefs and values of the organization** ('espoused' because they are the ones that people will claim they have, even though their actual behaviour may suggest otherwise). These beliefs and values, while significant, may be aspirations rather than reality.
- **The shared basic assumptions of the organization** which are the bedrock of culture. They do tend to guide behaviour, but can be so 'taken for granted' that it is very difficult to change them without changing the cognitive structures which keep them in place.

For a further discussion of culture and Schein's three dimensions, see Chapter 4.

Schein argues that the only way to fully understand corporate culture is to engage with the third level—with inevitable difficulty.

> *If one does not decipher the pattern of basic assumptions that may be operating, one will not know how to interpret the artefacts correctly, or how much credence to give to the articulated values. In other words, the essence of a culture lies in the pattern of basic underlying assumptions, and once one understands those one can easily understand the more surface levels and deal appropriately with them.*
>
> Schein (2004:36)

It is possible to distinguish between corporate and organizational cultures by asking the question 'Is culture something that an organization **is**, or something that an organization **has**?' If culture is something that an organization 'has', then it can be treated as any other variable that has an impact on structures and processes. As such, it can be changed by the organization's management in order to improve efficiency or effectiveness.

However, if culture is something that an organization 'is', then it emerges from personal and social interactions within the organization; it is continuously created and re-created by its participants rather than being imposed by management.

'Corporate culture' refers to and reflects managers' values, interpretations, and preferred ways of doing things. 'Organizational culture' is a much broader concept; it may embrace subcultures and it is almost impossible to define in concrete terms. The problem for managers is that they may assume that their understanding of the corporate culture is fully reflected in the organizational culture, whereas the former is only part of the latter. Managers may also confuse compliance with the organizational culture with the existence of a homogeneous organizational culture.

While culture shapes the way that people in an organization behave, every culture is distinct in terms of intensity (its 'depth') and integration (its 'breadth').

Cultural intensity is the degree to which members of a unit accept the norms, values, or other cultural content associated with the unit (Wheelen and Hunger 2012). Mature organizations may promote particular values strongly (for instance, Google, founded in 1997–1998, has perhaps become synonymous with strong corporate culture) or may have more intensive cultures (in which employees are expected to behave more consistently) compared with new start-ups whose values may be less well established.

Cultural integration is 'the extent to which units throughout an organization share a common culture (Wheelen and Hunger 2012: 89). In a hierarchical structure where there is a single hierarchy of command and control, culture is likely to be highly integrated (the armed forces would be an extreme example). We can contrast this with a matrix structure which is composed of diverse sub-divisions, each with its own possible subculture.

Therefore culture fulfils several important functions in an organization:

- it reflects and reinforces a shared sense of identity, possibly both internally and externally
- it aligns employees' values and norms with those of the organization
- it enables the organization to work as a social system

- it provides a frame of reference for employees to draw upon when undertaking productive activities, and serves as a guide for appropriate behaviour.

From a strategic point of view, a strong culture can help to reinforce an organization's sources of advantage. If an organization has a culture that promotes flexibility and responsiveness, it is better placed to adapt to changes in its external environment. When an organization's resources and capabilities are embedded in its culture in this way, they will become a seamless part of its operational effectiveness—and this can be difficult for competitors to imitate.

How do we change culture?

We can argue that control of behaviour through culture can be seen as an important alternative to the control of behaviour via structuring. For example, on your first day in a new job, your line manager or mentor and your new coworkers will provide you with important clues in terms of how the organization works, what you are expected to do, how you are expected to perform and act, what stance to take if faced with any unethical practices, and so on. Culture can therefore be an important lever for implementing strategy. Yet can cultures be changed in the same way as structures can?

The strategy literature has a range of views on the extent to which culture can be managed. Some see culture as a controllable organizational variable that is prone to manipulation. Some see it as partly controllable—that is, management can influence it only in given circumstances. Let us now reflect further on this debate and the process of culture change.

As we have suggested, the culture–strategy relationship implies that organizational culture is a variable that can be controlled to support the implementation of a strategy as effectively as possible. Researchers have explored the ideas that, first, culture and performance are linked and, secondly, that culture can be manipulated in line with management intentions (Ogbonna and Harris 2002). The strategy literature tends to accept that the overall performance of an organization depends on the strength of its culture. Writers such as Deal and Kennedy (1982) and Ouchi (1981) became known as the 'trait writers', as they were interested in the impact of cultural traits on strategic performance. They put forward the notion of a set of universally appropriate cultural characteristics, such as 'closeness to the customer' or 'constant innovation', as sources of competitive advantage.

However, critics have since challenged the notion that all organizations exhibit universal cultural characteristics, arguing that such research downplays the inherent differences that can exist between societies, industries, and even organizations as a result of their different cultures. For example, critics, including Barney (1986, 1991) and Kotter and Heskett (1992) argue that the degree of impact of an organization's culture on its performance depends on how readily that culture can adapt to change (see Chapter 4 for more details).

Even though culture may not be **completely** controlled by management, it may be manipulated under certain circumstances in order to align it more effectively with strategy. In other words, it is 'partly controlled' (e.g. Johnson 1988, 2000; Schein 2004). While exploring the management of strategic change, Johnson (1992, 2000) developed a 'cultural web' (see Figures 4.5 and 7.9) and applied it to organizations in diverse settings such as health and chemicals.

Our discussion here demonstrates that there is no clear consensus when it comes to agreeing the extent to which culture can be changed as part of a strategy being implemented, and

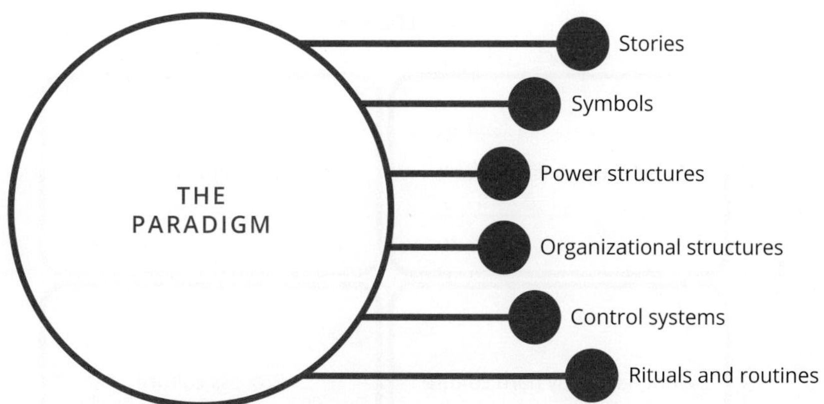

FIGURE 7.9 The cultural web of organization. Source: Reproduced with permission from Johnson, G. (2000). Strategy through a cultural lens: learning from managers' experience. *Management Learning*, **31**(4), 403–26. Copyright © 2000, © SAGE Publications.

it reinforces the complexity of the culture–strategy relationship. The reality is that, while it is possible for culture to be changed, it is a challenging and time-consuming process. Therefore it is important that any attempt to bring about change is considered carefully. In particular, an organization should:

- evaluate what a particular change in strategy means in terms of its culture
- assess if a change in culture is needed at all
- decide if an attempt to change the culture is worth the likely costs to the whole strategy process (see Wheelen and Hunger 2012).

Ogbonna and Harris (2002) argue that the management of culture may be seen as a dynamic process, which could involve establishing an entirely new culture or keeping, modifying, or discarding an existing one. Ultimately, an organization's culture is a powerful tool; it can lead to advantage or to failure depending on how its management choose to develop or sustain it in pursuit of the implementation of strategy.

Examples of generic cultures

Deal and Kennedy (1982) identified four generic cultures which are still recognizable in many organizations today.

- **The tough-guy macho culture:** organizations dominated by rugged individualists who thrive on risk and quick results. For example, at Apple under Steve Jobs, employees were reported to be working under great pressure, with very high expectations in terms of both innovation and secrecy.
- **The work hard, play hard culture:** very busy, with activity and the short term emphasised. Examples include Zappos, the online shoe and clothing retailer: 'All of us at Zappos .com live the "work hard, play hard" mentality!' (Zappos 2019).
- **The bet-your-company culture:** epitomized by high-risk decisions with long-term consequences. BP's culture has been criticized as contributing to the Gulf Oil Crisis: 'BP's culture

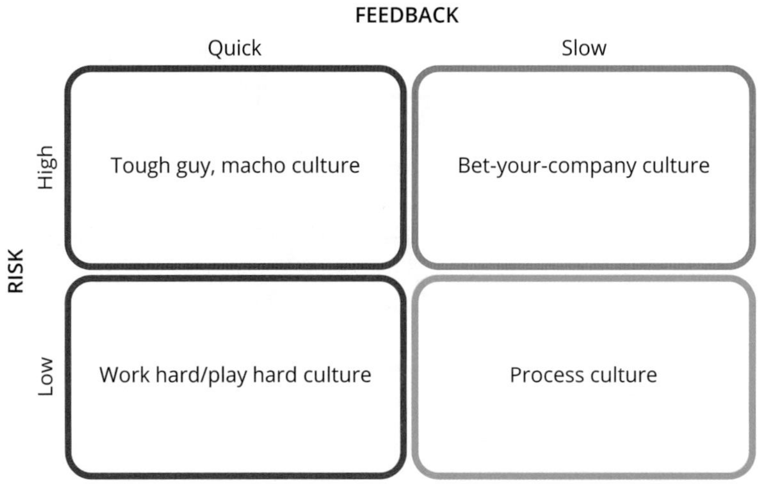

		FEEDBACK: Quick	FEEDBACK: Slow
RISK	High	Tough guy, macho culture	Bet-your-company culture
	Low	Work hard/play hard culture	Process culture

FIGURE 7.10 Corporate cultures. Source: adapted from Deal, T.E. and Kennedy, A.A. (1982). *Corporate Cultures: The Rites and Rituals of Corporate Life*. Reading, MA: Addison Wesley, pp.107–8.

allowed extreme shortsightedness in pursuit of profit at the cost of safety or environmental stewardship' (Edersheim 2010).

- **The process culture:** characterized as low risk, with slow feedback. Examples might include financial services firms such as Lloyd's of London, the world's leading insurance market: 'To protect themselves businesses should spend time understanding what specific threats they may be exposed to and speak to experts who can help' (Beale 2017).

This classification can also be expressed as a 2×2 matrix, as illustrated in Figure 7.10.

In keeping with our earlier discussion, Deal and Kennedy (1982) support the notion that cultures can indeed be modified, but they strike a note of caution by describing the process of changing culture as a 'black art'. However, they go on to offer the following five principles in support of successful cultural change:

- Recognize that peer group **consensus** will be the major influence on acceptance or willingness to change.
- Convey and emphasize **two-way trust** in all matters (and especially communications) relating to change.
- Think of change as **skill-building**, and concentrate on training as part of the change process.
- Be **patient**: allow enough time for the change to take hold.
- Be **flexible**: encourage people to adapt the basic idea of the change to fit the real world around them (i.e. allow cultural change to be modified and adapted by the people concerned, rather than imposing it on them).

These five principles reinforce the advice from Hickson et al. (2003), which emphasizes the importance of an organization being prepared for change if that change is to be successfully implemented. To that end, Hickson et al. identify the following factors, which can make the implementation of strategy more successful if considered:

- 'acceptability'—to what extent do people **accept** what's being done?
- 'receptivity'—to what extent are they **receptive** to what's being done?
- 'priority'—is this implementation considered a priority relative to other business goals?

Notice how these factors have clear parallels with Deal and Kennedy's list.

Ultimately, it is hard to escape the fact that cultural change is hard—yet the culture of an organization is so central to the successful execution of strategy that it cannot be ignored. The topic of culture is also covered in Chapter 4, where we discuss the purpose and values of an organization.

7.5 International strategy and structure

Why do many firms wish to internationalize and what are the perceived economic, operational, and competitive drivers and potential benefits? We will consider these questions, review the different ways in which firms can go about internationalizing, and look at the different conditions under which internationalization may or may not be a robust strategy. We discuss international strategy in greater depth in Chapter 12, when we explore globalization. However, the key themes for this chapter are the international configuration of the international firm and a process approach to internationalization.

Why internationalize?

Until the end of the nineteenth century, international trade was dominated by trading companies or investment houses. Since then, international trade has become increasingly dominated by **multinational corporations (MNCs)**. The difference between the former and the latter is that while the activities of the former were conducted from a base in their domestic markets, the activities of MNCs are based on **foreign direct investment (FDI)**, i.e. locating part of the firm's activities—perhaps design, manufacturing, assembly, sales, distribution, or R&D—in other countries (countries that are not the firm's home country). What is more, these investments tend to be actively managed as single operational entities within a unified corporation.

MNCs are complex organizations. They are difficult to manage, they may decline into dysfunctional bureaucracies, they can be inflexible, unresponsive, and slow to change, they sometimes attract negative coverage in the media, and they can be unpopular with the public. So what is the purpose of the MNC in the twenty-first century?

Perhaps the main strategic benefit in being an MNC is that it should provide the organization with flexibility—with a range of strategic options. The firm can choose between a range of ways of pursuing its international strategy. Much domestic market strategy is likely to be defensive, i.e. trying to protect existing positions. However, an increasing proportion of world trade is across borders. MNCs have a wider range of strategies open to them because they are international and operate across borders. Despite some cross-border global and regional integration, international integration is incomplete, and this allows MNCs to benefit from market imperfections—making international strategy different from national strategy.

Ghemawat (2003) calls this incomplete state of cross-border integration 'semi-globalization'. He makes the point that international strategies take account of such market imperfections in their formulation and implementation. If the world really were one 'global village', global strategies would be irrelevant—they would be the same as domestic strategy.

Governments and MNCs

Governments and supra-national organizations can erect regulatory, institutional, and tariff barriers to trade, while MNCs can attempt to configure their international operations to exploit those barriers which favour them and avoid those which do not. Such trade barriers may include:

- high tariffs
- import quota systems
- refusal to sanction licences
- nationalistic purchasing and ownership policies
- centralized 'command' economies
- excessively nationalistic domestic demand.

Governments tax immobile assets and nationally based consumption, and try to set corporation taxes at levels which will provide them with useful sources of tax revenue without forcing corporations to shift their investments in jobs, buildings, research, or technology to other locations. Governments seek to attract high-quality inward investment by MNCs into their countries by offering capital gains, regional grants (e.g. in employment 'black spots'), tax-free zones, and so on.

MNCs: what, when, and why?

MNCs are companies which have part of their activities located outside their home country and operate in international markets. In MNCs, comparative costs, risks, and regulatory context may influence where a particular activity is carried out. International trade may be carried out in different ways. The four main types of international trade are:

- exporting
- FDI—the defining characteristic of MNCs
- licensing
- joint ventures, strategic alliances, and the like.

The theory of FDI, and of alternative organizational forms to develop business across frontiers, is set out in a simple way via the OLI framework (Collinson et al. 2017). The OLI framework (Figure 7.11) is a decision model which we can use to explore the potential sources of advantage that a domestic firm may have when it considers whether to become a multinational. OLI stands for Ownership, Location, and Internalization, three potential sources of advantage which may underlie a firm's decision to become a multinational. We discuss the three questions that make up the decision model below.

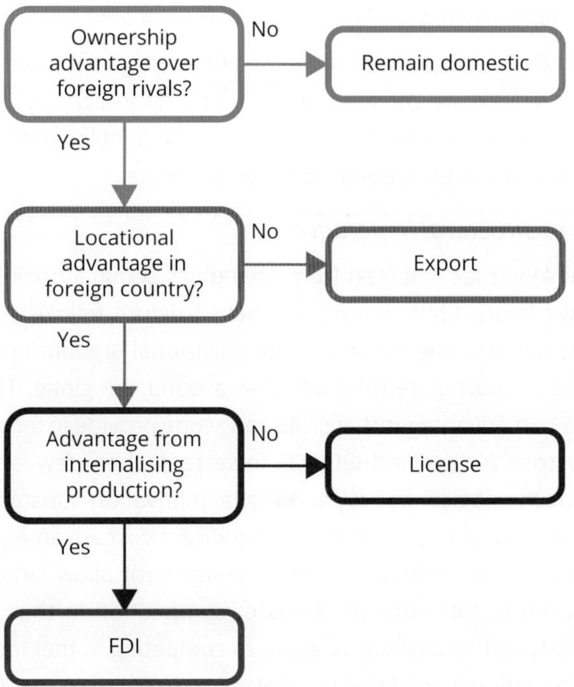

FIGURE 7.11 The OLI Framework. Source: Reproduced with permission from Collinson, S. et al. (2017). *International Business*, Seventh Edition. Harlow: Pearson. © Pearson Education Limited, 2012, 2017.

7

1. Ownership advantages address the question of why some firms, but not others, go abroad, and suggest that a successful MNC has some firm-specific advantages which allow it to overcome the costs of operating in a foreign country. This approach views firms as collections of resources and capabilities (see Chapter 6 for a full discussion), and suggests that if a firm has no such advantages, it might be wise to consider remaining domestic.
2. Location advantages focus on the question of where an MNC chooses to locate. Consider the example of whether a firm should locate its manufacturing facilities in another country where it hopes to reach customers. The framework suggests that if there is no advantage to be gained by going international, such as locating its manufacturing operations near an overseas source of raw materials, it may be better for the firm to remain domestic and export its products to overseas locations, rather than manufacturing overseas.
3. Internalization advantages influence how a firm chooses to operate in a foreign country. The firm needs to consider the advantages and disadvantages of keeping its activities internal via an FDI (e.g. setting up a wholly owned subsidiary in an overseas location) compared with other entry modes such as exports, licensing, or a joint venture. For instance, a firm may wish to keep production activities internal because it can keep costs down or maintain control of quality. A joint venture may not be appropriate if the firm has major concerns about avoiding 'leakage' of competitive advantage to rival firms, for example via proprietary knowledge.

Reasons for internationalization

We live in a world of MNCs—corporate entities selling on a global scale and with activities in many parts of the world. Next we consider two different approaches you need to understand which explain why organizations internationalize: the first is internationalization as structural imperative, and the second is internationalization as process.

Internationalization as structural imperative

Here we return to thinking that emerged from Chandler's seminal book *Strategy and Structure* (Chandler 1962). As we know, Chandler argued that 'structure follows strategy'; he described how major companies adopted the M-form or multidivisional organizational structure in order to cope with the need to coordinate their activities around the globe. The economic basis of Chandler's work is 'the cost advantages that scale and scope provide in technologically advanced, capital intensive industries' (Chandler 1990: 32). In sectors where few large firms appeared, it was because neither technological nor organizational innovation substantially increased minimum efficient scale, i.e. large plants did not offer significant cost advantages over smaller ones.

Investments in scale, scope, distribution, and management allow large firms to build dominant positions, sufficient to influence the basis of competition in their industry in terms of structure, key resources, and capabilities relevant to competing in that industry. Advantages of scale and scope lead to national and international concentration, so that competition becomes oligopolistic (i.e. competition is limited to a few, usually large, competitors). Growth becomes a continuous search for improved quality, sourcing, distribution, and marketing, and is rooted in continuously enhanced cost structures. Some growth can come from acquisition, but the main emphasis for long-term growth is likely to be twofold:

- **geographic expansion into international markets** in the continuous drive for increments in scale and cost advantages
- **expansion into related product markets** in the pursuit of enhanced scope economies.

Together, these can create a dynamic spiral of volume, scale, scope, and cost curves, reinforced by organizational capabilities developed to cope with fierce oligopolistic competition. The opportunity to create first-mover investments is short-lived (e.g. Chandler 1990). Therefore the logic of sustainable international competition is to make long-term scale investments to create organizational capabilities and then to continue to reinvest in them.

In a similar vein, Stopford and Wells (1972) developed a simple model to illustrate the typical stages of development for companies that are moving towards an international organizational structure. They saw this as a process driven by two dimensions (see Figure 7.12):

- foreign product diversity, i.e. the number of products sold internationally
- the importance of international sales to the company, i.e. foreign sales as a percentage of total sales.

Stopford and Wells (1972) suggested that international divisions were set up at an early stage of internationalization when the figures for both product diversity and percentage of foreign sales were low. Then, those companies which found that international expansion led to substantial product diversity tended to adopt a worldwide product division structure (Pathway A

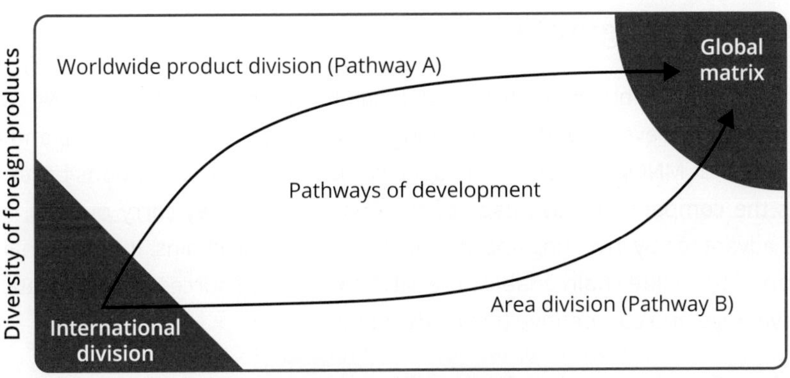

FIGURE 7.12 The Stopford and Wells matrix: pathways for international development.
Source: Stopford, J.M. and Wells, L.T. (1972). *Managing the Multinational Enterprise: Organization of the Firm and Ownership of the Subsidiary*. New York: Basic Books. Adapted by Segal-Horn, S. and Faulkner, D. (2010). *Understanding Global Strategy*. Andover: Cengage Learning EMEA, Figure 7.2.

in Figure 7.12). Or, if companies expanded overseas without increasing product diversity, they tended to adopt a geographical area structure (Pathway B in Figure 7.12). Finally, when both foreign sales and the diversity of products were high, a global matrix emerged. Thus the grid structure of the MNC with a geographic axis and a product group axis emerged.

Internationalization as a process

The internationalization process model (Johanson and Vahlne 1977), also known as the Uppsala model or the 'stages' model, suggests that the process by which a firm increases its international involvement should occur in **stages**. Johanson and Vahlne envisaged a firm gradually internationalizing through increased commitment to, and knowledge of, foreign markets. Therefore the firm is most likely to enter markets with **successively greater psychic distance** (e.g. Perlmutter 1969), where **psychic distance** is a subjective notion of distance based on the **perceived** differences between a 'home' country and 'foreign' country (regardless of time and spatial factors). At the outset, it sells to countries culturally most similar to its own, before gradually broadening out.

The model depends on the notion that uncertainty, and hence risk, increases with greater psychic distance and unfamiliarity. The problem with this model is that it is very formal; it assumes that a firm is starting out with no existing international organization. However, there are many examples of internationalizing companies which have gone for large rather than familiar markets—and also for many markets at the same time. Consider the expansion of Ikea into China, or Carrefour's expansion across countries in Europe, Asia, and South America. The contrast is between a 'waterfall' pattern of global expansion (one country at a time) and a 'sprinkler' pattern (many countries at a time). In current markets with shortening product life cycles, and the strategic importance of rapid time to market, there is often insufficient time to adopt the waterfall approach.

The 'stages' model of the internationalization process is highly sequential and also rather deterministic. Its contribution to theory is to demonstrate how internationalization can cause production to gradually move from the home country. The two approaches described above are about the process of **becoming** international. However, they can also help us to understand some of the problems that MNCs may face when they are locked into the structures and processes of an earlier stage of internationalization than the stage they have currently reached.

International configuration

We have discussed how and when MNCs may begin to become international. We can now look at what MNCs can achieve as part of becoming an international organization, and why. Kogut (1985) suggests that MNCs are able to win against most domestic operations because they can both access the comparative advantage of nations in which they carry out FDI, and achieve competitive advantage by investing appropriately in their value chains. International location or configuration of the value chain enables the MNC to identify sources of comparative (country/location) advantage and competitive (firm) advantage.

Configuration of the international value chain

An organization that competes internationally must decide how to spread the activities in its value chain among countries (Porter 1986: 23). In our earlier discussion of organizational structure, we used the term 'configuration' to describe the structural design and processes of an organization. In international strategy, 'configuration' refers to where the various value chain activities are performed. It is about **where** we do what we do, and **why**. Such decisions result in differing configurations for different organizations and industries. The location of activities in an international value chain is one of the most important concepts in international strategy, because it is how MNCs benefit from the geographic dispersion of their activities. It is the means by which large organizations can make the most of the potential advantages identified by Kogut (1985), mentioned earlier. Organizations typically have a wide choice of possible configurations of their activities; organizations that operate across borders should use their choice of configuration as a source of advantage.

Configuration and coordination

Figure 7.13 shows Porter's (1986) view of the relationship between **configuration** (where value chain activities are performed) and **coordination** of the organization's value chain configuration (how it is managed). To get to the heart of the message, let's start by considering the horizontal axis—where are the organization's key activities configured? Many organizations will begin with a value chain that is geographically concentrated, for example to achieve economies of scale. However, over time, this concentration may become 'less necessary' (in Porter's language) because modularization of production technologies or variety at low cost means that scale is no longer so important to that organization. On the other hand, a geographic concentration of key activities may become 'less possible', for example because the organization needs to be closer to its markets and customers (e.g. for R&D or market research). The other arrow in Figure 7.13 makes the same basic point: if you disaggregate your value chain away from being geographically concentrated (top right), you must become very efficient at coordination (i.e. it becomes 'more important') in order to make the disaggregated value chain work. It is also more feasible to do this with modern information and communication technology (ICT); before modern ICT existed, configurations had to be more concentrated.

The high level of coordination required to manage complex global supply chains may result in higher costs. These additional costs must be weighed against the cost savings in other parts of the value chain. Additional potential non-financial costs, such as risk to reputation or brand, can arise from international configuration of value chains.

CONFIGURATION OF ACTIVITIES

Geographically dispersed | Geographically concentrated

COORDINATION OF ACTIVITIES: High / Low

Concentration less necessary or possible

Coordination more important and feasible

FIGURE 7.13 Porter's configuration–coordination matrix. Source: Reproduced with permission from Porter, M.E. (1986). *Competition in Global Industries*. Boston, MA: Harvard Business School Press, Figure 1.7. By permission of Harvard Business Publishing.

PRACTITIONER INSIGHT: **GORDON RAMSAY, PLANT LEADER, P&G, WEST VIRGINIA**

Procter & Gamble (P&G) is a fast-moving consumer goods company (FMCG) headquartered in Cincinnati, Ohio. Founded in 1837, P&G has a portfolio of ten main product categories organized into five 'segments', generating $67 billion turnover in 2018 through sales in over 180 countries, supported by operations in 70 countries employing 92,000 people. We spoke to Gordon Ramsay, plant leader for P&G in their West Virginia operations. He has been involved in the start-up of this multi-category site servicing the Beauty Care and the Fabric and Home Care segments. The plant is the biggest supply chain initiative in P&G's history, comprising the introduction of 42 lines in the new facility. Gordon shares his views on corporate strategy, structure, and culture within this multinational setting.

Corporate strategy and structure

As I see it, there are three main components to P&G's corporate structure.

(a) A go-to-market structure within a region that presents a single customer-facing organization. This function interacts with our main customers, such as Walmart, Target, Costco etc., to offer them the full P&G product range from one point of contact.

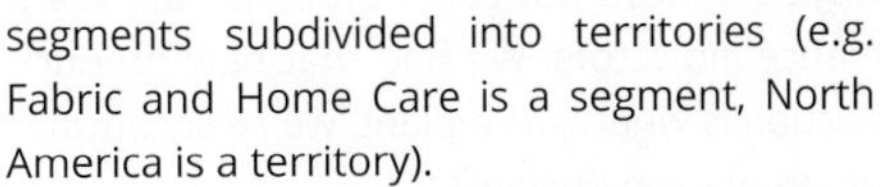

(b) In terms of financial flows and reporting lines, we are organized internally in defined segments subdivided into territories (e.g. Fabric and Home Care is a segment, North America is a territory).

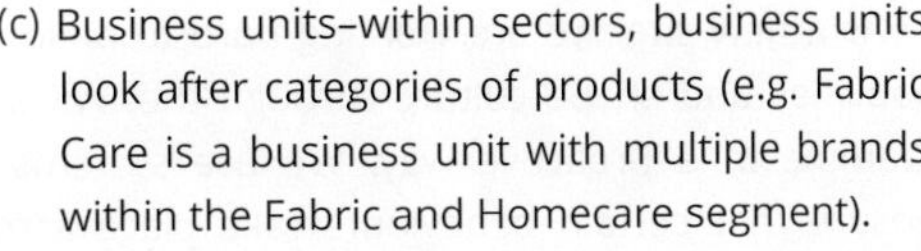

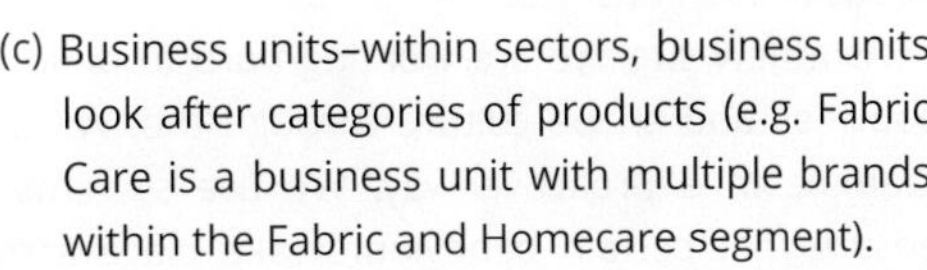

(c) Business units–within sectors, business units look after categories of products (e.g. Fabric Care is a business unit with multiple brands within the Fabric and Homecare segment).

This isn't a static picture—P&G ebbs and flows in terms of its corporate structure. At present, the corporate strategy is moving away from a highly centralized structure—moving from horizontal functions (e.g. centralized purchasing) to tightly integrated 'verticals' (e.g. more autonomy for sectors). This move will increase the extent to which business unit performance can be enhanced by

Continued

working in a way that suits the needs of the sector. For me, strategy defines your long-term goals and how you're planning to achieve them. It is our job as a leadership team in the plant to set and implement strategy that steers the site in line with corporate expectations, accommodating the needs of multiple existing and changing structures.

Corporate culture and systems

A focus for the site leadership team is to meet the preferences and ways of working for each sector and business unit. It is advantageous for us to have one way of working on site, but that could take us out of alignment with how work is happening at other locations within the sector. The site leadership team play a key role in making sure we do what is best for the overall business, adopting the practices that will give the best outcomes, whilst keeping our approach simple, consistent, and locally relevant for colleagues.

A vitally important feature in how we manage our organization is IWS—Integrated Work Systems. IWS is our continuous improvement system—the A–Z guide as to how you run a world-class production site. All the tools, processes, and systems to deliver operational excellence are defined in that programme documentation and knowledge. That is our guiding operations strategy for the site. I have a strategy document specifically for my leadership team, on which item number one is 'IWS is the way we do the work'. Having that shared methodology gives us a common way of working, supported by a central corporate team and resources, that allows us to meet the needs of each business unit. For continuing operations, we harmonize around the IWS way to achieve our common corporate key performance indicators. We find that new product introduction is where, as a plant, we really attune to the needs of each business.

As a new site, we are working hard to build capabilities and shape culture through the IWS programme in a proactive way. We use systems to ensure that certain behaviours take place across leadership, operational, and technical roles. For example, IWS explains how leadership should spend time on the shop floor talking to colleagues; how to systemize the information flow and communication throughout the site on a weekly basis; how to receive feedback through a range of scheduled employee forums; how to deploy regular corporate surveys. The key activities you need to do to shape culture are engrained in the IWS programme. For me, it is so important for every member of the leadership team to spend time in the operation 'sensing' reality! We need to have our finger on the pulse if we are to be able to deal with actual events, manage the organization effectively, and build a high-performance culture.

Effects on strategic performance of corporate culture versus national culture

I've worked for P&G in the UK, Switzerland, and the USA. I've been really surprised by the difference in the cultures between the different centres. The business processes and work systems are consistent, and colleagues are generally all results focused. However, there are major differences between localities in the norms for how people interact, communication protocols, and the expectations about how decisions should be made. It is hugely important not to cause unintentional offence when operating between different locations. You need to find a way to navigate cultural differences, changing your approach to optimize personal effectiveness, in order to implement strategy and lead the delivery of great results in a multinational context.

Extending to supply chain partners

In a respectful manner, we are increasingly working with our supply chain partners in an IWS way. We can hold them accountable for results, but we can't, and wouldn't, stipulate exactly how we want them to work. What we have started doing as a company though is to 'sell' IWS. We are using Ernst & Young as a consultancy partner. We bring their people into advanced IWS P&G sites where we train them, and then they can sell IWS on our behalf. We have two suppliers co-located on this site providing materials, an arrangement that allows us to carry zero inventory in a high-volume line. One of those suppliers has bought IWS from Ernst & Young, and as they build their capability in our way of working, the supply chain partnership is getting stronger and stronger, and the mutually beneficial performance gains are increasing.

Being effective in a corporate setting

New employees and graduates coming into a complex and fast-paced business such as ours will succeed if they bring capabilities in collaboration and team-working, tenacity and solutions focus, and problem-solving and analytical thinking. An ability for reflection is important too. I think of it as self-feedback. I am non-stop critiquing what I'm doing, and everything we are doing as a leadership team, in order to check that we are performing as well as we can and achieving our targets. In our leadership team meetings, we discuss our approach, we debate and listen, and we try to reality check our different points of view. I think that people—individual or collective—who have the ability to assess themselves and give themselves feedback will progress, learn, and grow faster.

CHAPTER SUMMARY

In this chapter we have addressed the following ideas against the target learning outcomes.

- **Analyse the main organizational structural types in terms of their strengths and weaknesses**
  The relationship between strategy and structure was introduced, followed by the main aspects of structure and the coordinating elements that link them. We discussed the 'ideal types' of organizational structure, with examples of simple, complex, and innovation-oriented structures—with an analysis of their main strengths and weaknesses in each case.
- **Evaluate the suitability of a range of structural types against a number of design tests**
  We introduced nine design tests (Goold and Campbell 2002) which can help an organization to select or move towards an appropriate organizational structure. The first four tests fit with the key objectives of the organization—market advantage, parenting advantage, people, and feasibility. The remaining five tests are based on more general principles of good design—specialized cultures, difficult links, redundant hierarchy, accountability, and flexibility.
- **Appreciate the role of systems and culture in supporting the delivery of an organization's strategy**
  We have discussed what we mean by both systems and culture in the context of the practice of strategy, and why they are such important elements of successful strategy implementation. Different types of operational and control systems were reviewed, alongside Simons' (1995) levers of control as a comprehensive approach to the establishment of control systems in organizations that operate in environments where they experience rapid and continuous change. 'Control via simple rules' was also explored, as advocated for organizations in turbulent environments where high levels of flexibility and creativity are also required. Examples of generic cultures were set out, and some of the issues around changing cultures in the context of the practice of strategy were also reviewed.
- **Comprehend the relationship between internationalization and organizational structure**
  Finally, we discussed why firms might wish to internationalize, and examined some of the drivers and potential benefits of internationalization. We reviewed the different ways in which firms can go about internationalizing, and the different conditions under which internationalization may or may not be a robust strategy. We also explored a process approach to international strategy.

7

END OF CHAPTER QUESTIONS

Recall questions

1. How would you describe the relationship between an organization's strategy and its structure? Do you agree with Chandler that 'structure follows strategy'?
2. Give a brief description of a 'simple' organizational structure and its main advantages and disadvantages.
3. Summarize the key differences between the main types of 'complex' organizational structure—multidivisional, matrix, holding, network, transnational, and innovation-oriented (project-based and adhocracy).
4. How would you define the 'culture' of an organization? How does culture manifest itself, and what function does it perform?
5. Explain why a firm might want to internationalize, and what benefits internationalization might bring.

Application questions

A) Ask five people who work in different organizations to describe the structure of their organization (or alternatively, research five different organizations online). Draw a diagram for each organization that summarizes its organizational structure; compare and contrast the diagrams with Mintzberg's six ideal structural types, noting similarities and differences.

B) Choose an organization that you can research online, and draw a picture of its organizational structure—at a good level of detail if possible. Use Goold and Campbell's nine design tests to evaluate whether the organization's configuration is appropriate or not. Reflecting on the organization's context and history, suggest some explanations for any discrepancies that you observe.

C) Imagine you have been assigned to lead a strategy team within an organization that is currently based in a single country, but is considering moving to an international strategy. What are the key issues that you would consider relating to changes in organizational structure, systems, and culture? Make brief notes to share with colleagues about the possible benefits and risks, and key actions to take.

ONLINE RESOURCES

www.oup.com/he/mackay1e

FURTHER READING

Structure in Fives: Designing Effective Organizations, by Henry Mintzburg

Mintzberg, H. (1993). *Structure in Fives: Designing Effective Organizations*. Englewood Cliffs, NJ: Prentice-Hall.

This book synthesizes messages from research on what it takes to design an effective organization, presented in a form that will be read by managers, staff specialists, and consultants who are concerned with the structuring of organizations.

Good Strategy, Bad Strategy: The Difference and Why It Matters, by Richard Rumelt

Rumelt, R.P. (2011). *Good Strategy, Bad Strategy: The Difference and Why It Matters*. New York: Crown Business.

In this book the author lists some of the hallmarks of bad strategy, and argues that the kernel of a good strategy contains three elements—a diagnosis, a guiding policy, and a set of coherent actions.

Organizational Behaviour, by Daniel King and Scott Lawley

King, D. and Lawley, S. (2019), *Organizational Behaviour* (3rd edn). Oxford: Oxford University Press.

This textbook offers additional detail on organizational culture, as well as systems and learning within organizations if you wish to understand more in those areas.

REFERENCES

Arthur, M.B. and Rousseau, D.M. (1996). *The Boundaryless Career: A New Employment Principle for a New Organizational Era*. Oxford: Oxford University Press.

Barney, J.B. (1986). Organizational culture: can it be a source of sustained competitive advantage? *Academy of Management Review* **11**(3), 656–65.

Barney, J. (1991). Firm resources and sustained competitive advantage. *Journal of Management*, **17**(1), 99–120.

BBC (2016). Kids Company closure: What went wrong?' https://www.bbc.co.uk/news/uk-33788415 (accessed 12 June 2019).

Beale, I. (2017). Businesses need to prepare for full costs of cyber attacks: Lloyd's. https://www.lloyds.com/news-and-risk-insight/press-releases/2017/06/cyber-report-launch (accessed 12 June 2019).

Bennet, A. and Bennet, D. (2004). *Organizational Survival in the New World*. London: Routledge.

Birkinshaw, J. and Ridderstale, J. (2015). Adhocracy for an agile age. *McKinsey Quarterly*, **4**, 44–57.

Brant, T. (2016). Ballmer: Bill Gates didn't want Microsoft to make hardware. https://www.pcmag.com/news/349334/ballmer-bill-gates-didnt-want-microsoft-to-make-hardware (accessed 31 July 2019).

Bustamante, A.V. (2016). U-Form vs M-Form: how to understand decision autonomy under healthcare decentralization? Comment on 'Decentralisation of health services in Fiji: a decision space analysis'. *International Journal of Health Policy and Management*, **5**(9), 561–3.

Chandler, A.D. (1962). Strategy *and Structure: Chapters in the History of American Enterprise*. Boston, MA: MIT Press.

Chandler, A.D. (1990). *Strategy and Structure: Chapters in the History of American Enterprise* (reprint). Boston, MA: MIT Press.

Collinson, S., Narula, R., and Rugman, A.M. (2017). *International Business* (7th edn). Harlow: Pearson.

Davis S.M. and Lawrence P.R. (1978). Problems of matrix organisations. *Harvard Business Review*, May. https://hbr.org/1978/05/problems-of-matrix-organizations (accessed 27 July 2018).

Deal, T.E. and Kennedy, A.A. (1982). *Corporate Cultures: The Rites and Rituals of Corporate Life*. Reading, MA: Addison Wesley.

Denison, D.R. (1996). What is the difference between organizational culture and organizational climate? A native's point of view on a decade of paradigm wars. *Academy of Management Review*, **21**(3), 619-54.

Denison, D.R. and Mishra, A.K. (1995). Toward a theory of organizational culture and effectiveness. *Organization Science*, **6**, 204–23.

Desveaux, J.A. (2012). Adhocracy. https://www.britannica.com/topic/adhocracy (accessed 27 July 2018).

Dolan, T.E. (2010). Revisiting adhocracy: from rhetorical revisionism to smart mobs. *Journal of Future Studies*, **15**(2), 33–50.

Donaldson, L. (2001). *The Contingency Theory of Organisations*. Thousand Oaks, CA: Sage.

Dudovskiy, J. (2017). Alphabet Inc. organizational structure: divisional and flat. https://research-methodology.net/alphabet-inc-organizational-structure-divisional-and-flat/ (accessed 12 June 2019).

Edersheim, E.H. (2010). The BP culture's role in the Gulf Oil Crisis. https://hbr.org/2010/06/the-bp-cultures-role-in-the-gu (accessed 12 June 2019).

Eisenhardt, K.M. and Sull, D. (2001). Strategy as simple rules, *Harvard Business Review,* January.

Galunic, C. and Hermreck, I. (2012). How to help employees 'get' strategy. *Harvard Business Review*, **90**, 24.

Ganguly, D. (2012). Matrix evolutions: how GE underwent a fundamental change in its organisational and matrix structure. https://economictimes.indiatimes.com/matrix-evolutions-how-ge-underwent-a-fundamental-change-in-its-organisational-and-matrix-structure/articleshow/11921385.cms (accessed 12 June 2019).

Garvin, D.A. (1993). Building a learning organisation, *Harvard Business Review*, July–August, 78–91.

Ghemawat, P. (2003). Semiglobalization and international business strategy. *Journal of International Business Studies*. **34**(2), 138–52.

Glassman, B. (2013). What Zappos taught us about creating the ultimate client experience. https://www.forbes.com/sites/advisor/2013/05/13/what-zappos-taught-us-about-creating-the-ultimate-client-experience/#496f625820fb (accessed 12 June 2019).

Goold, M. and Campbell, A. (2002). Do you have a well-designed organization? *Harvard Business Review*, March.

Hickson, D.J., Miller, S.J., and Wilson, D.C. (2003). Planned or prioritized? Two options in managing the implementation of strategic decisions, *Journal of Management Studies,* **40**(7), 1803–36.

Hobday, M. (2000). The project-based organisation: an ideal form for managing complex products and systems? *Research Policy,* **29**, 871–93.

Ilott, O. (2016). Kids Company: an anatomy of failure. https://www.instituteforgovernment.org.uk/blog/kids-company-anatomy-failure (accessed 1 May 2019).

Johanson, J. and Vahlne, J. (1977). The internationalization process of the firm: a model of knowledge development and increasing foreign market commitments. *Journal of International Business Studies*, **8**(1), 23–32.

Johnson, G. (1988). Rethinking incrementalism. *Strategic Management Journal*, **9**(1), 75–91.

Johnson, G. (1992). Managing strategic change: strategy, culture, and action. *Long Range Planning,* **25**(1), 28–36.

Johnson, G. (2000). Strategy through a cultural lens: learning from managers' experience. *Management Learning*. **31**(4), 403–26.

Kaplan, R.S. and Norton, D.P. (1996). Using the balanced scorecard as a strategic management system. *Harvard Business Review*, January–February, 75–85.

Kodama, M. (2007). Project-based organization in the knowledge-based society. https://www.researchgate.net/publication/281445331_PROJECT-BASED_ORGANIZATION_IN_THE_KNOWLEDGE-BASED_SOCIETY_Project-based_Organizations_11_Why_Are_Project-based_Organizations_Necessary (accessed 27 July 2018).

Kogut, B. (1985). Designing global strategies: profiting from operational flexibility. *Sloan Management Review,* **27**(1), 27–38.

Kotter, J.P. and Heskett, J.L. (1992). *Corporate Culture and Performance*. New York: Free Press.

Kranias, D.S. (2000). Cultural control: the case of Japanese multinational companies and their subsidiaries in the UK. *Management Decision*, **38**(9), 638–49.

Looney, B. (2017). Digitally enabled. https://www.bp.com/en/global/corporate/news-and-insights/speeches/digitally-enabled.html (accessed 12 June 2019).

Miles, R.E., Snow, C.C., Mathews, J.A., et al. (1997). Organizing in the knowledge age: anticipating the cellular form. *Academy of Management Executive*, **11**(4), 7–24.

Mintzberg, H. (1979). The structuring of organisations. Adapted in Segal-Horn, S. (ed.) (2004). *The Strategy Reader* (2nd edn). Oxford: Blackwell.

Mintzberg, H. (1989). *Mintzberg on Management: Inside Our Strange World of Organisations.* New York: Free Press/Collier Macmillan.

Mintzberg, H. (1993). *Structure in Fives: Designing Effective Organizations*. Englewood Cliffs, NJ: Prentice Hall.

Montgomery, C.A. (2008). Putting leadership back into strategy. *Harvard Business Review*, **86**(1), 54–60.

Nadler, D., Tushman, M., and Nadler, M.B. (1997). *Competing by Design: The Power of Organizational Architecture*. Oxford: Oxford University Press.

Nystrom, P.C. and Starbuck, W.H. (1984). To avoid organizational crises, unlearn. *Organizational Dynamics*, **12**(4), 53–65.

Ogbonna, E. and Harris, L.C. (2002). Managing organisational culture: insights from the hospitality industry, *Human Resource Management Journal*, **12**(1), 33–53.

Open University (2010). B301: Making sense of strategy, Block 5. https://ccourse.arabou.edu.kw/LMS_eBooks/OU_Courses'eBooks/B301/B301_Block-5.pdf (accessed 20 July 2019).

Ouchi, W.G. (1981). *Theory Z*. New York: Avon Books.

Perlmutter, H.V. (1969). The tortuous evolution of the multinational corporation. *Columbia Journal of World Business*, **4**, 9–18.

Pongatichat, P. and Johnston, R. (2008). Exploring strategy-misaligned performance measurement. *International Journal of Productivity and Performance Management,* **57**(3), 207–22.

Porter, M.E. (1986). *Competition in Global Industries*. Boston, MA: Harvard Business School Press.

Renegade Inc. (2017). Kids Company—what happened? https://renegadeinc.com/kids-company-what-happened/ (accessed 12 June 2019).

Renteria, M. (2010). Executing a global strategy, locally: lessons from the world's local bank. https://brandleadership.wordpress.com/2010/11/23/executing-a-global-strategy-locally-lessons-from-the-worlds-local-bank/ (accessed 27 July 2018).

Rumelt, R. (2011). The perils of bad strategy. *McKinsey Quarterly,* June. https://www.mckinsey.com/business-functions/strategy-and-corporate-finance/our-insights/the-perils-of-bad-strategy (accessed 29 July 2018).

Schein, E.H. (2004). *Organizational Culture and Leadership* (3rd edn). San Francisco, CA: Jossey-Bass.

Segal-Horn, S. (ed.) (2004). *The Strategy Reader* (2nd edn). Oxford: Blackwell.

Segal-Horn, S. and Faulkner, D. (2010). *Understanding Global Strategy*. Andover: Cengage Learning EMEA.

Simons, R. (1995). *Levers of Control: How Managers Use Innovative Control Systems to Drive Strategic Renewal*. Boston, MA: Harvard Business School Press.

Stopford, J.M. and Wells, L.T. (1972). *Managing the Multinational Enterprise: Organization of the Firm and Ownership of the Subsidiary*. New York: Basic Books.

Sull, S. and Eisenhardt, K.M. (2012). Simple rules for a complex world. *Harvard Business Review*, September.

Tata Steel Europe (2019). Management control and compliance. https://www.tatasteeleurope.com/en/sustainability/environment/management-control-and-compliance (accessed 12 June 2019).

Taylor, F.W. (1911). *The Principles of Scientific Management*. New York: Harper & Brothers.

Tsoukas, H. (2005). Do we really understand tacit knowledge? In: Little, S. and Ray, T. (eds) (2nd edn), *Managing Knowledge: An Essential Reader.* London: Open University/Sage.

Twitter (2019). Our values. https://about.twitter.com/en_us/values.html (accessed 12 June 2019).

Watkins, M.D. (2013). What is organizational culture? And why should we care? *Harvard Business Review,* May. https://hbr.org/2013/05/what-is-organizational-culture (accessed 27 July 2018).

Wheelen, T.L. and Hunger, J.D. (2012). *Strategic Management and Business Policy.* Upper Saddle River, NJ: Prentice Hall.

Zappos (2019). What we live by. https://www.zappos.com/about/what-we-live-by (accessed 12 June 2019).

CHAPTER EIGHT

Strategies for Achieving Competitive Advantage

CONTENTS

LEARNING OBJECTIVES

By the end of this chapter, you should be able to:

- Define the nature and sources of competitive advantage
- Appreciate the link between the firm's business model, its strategic resources, and strategies for achieving competitive advantage
- Recognize the importance of isolating mechanisms, causal ambiguity, and dynamic capabilities in achieving and maintaining competitive advantage
- Explain generic strategies that organizations can apply to gain competitive advantage
- Consider the feasibility of maintaining a sustainable competitive advantage in highly competitive and dynamic environments

TOOLBOX

- **Business model**
  The rationale of how an organization creates, delivers, and captures value in a competitive environment.
- **Isolating mechanisms**
  The impediments to immediate imitation of a firm's resource position by competitors. Isolating mechanism are to a firm what entry barriers for new entrants are to an industry.
- **Generic strategies**
  Explanation of strategies that describe how a company pursues competitive advantage across its chosen market scope.
- **Strategy clock**
  A model that explores the options for the organization to strategically position its products and services, i.e. how a firm can position its product in a marketplace to give it a competitive advantage.

8

OPENING CASE STUDY AN EXTRAORDINARY TURNAROUND AT WATERSTONES

In 2012, Waterstones, the famous British high street bookseller, was at the brink of bankruptcy. Waterstones had grown rapidly, operating nearly 300 retail stores across the UK. However, the firm had come under severe pressure from the relentless growth of Amazon, the low price online megastore, and the increasing popularity of e-books that could be purchased at a lower price to that of physical books (McMaken 2012).

Just when it looked as if Waterstones would tumble into bankruptcy, the traditional paper book provided a lifeline. In the first half of 2015, industry figures showed a rise of 3% in sales of paperback and hardback books, and the sales of digital books and Kindle eReaders fell so significantly that Waterstones chose to remove them from most of its branches. In fact, for the whole of 2015, digital content sales had fallen from £563 million in 2014 to £554 million, while physical books had increased from £2.74 billion to £2.76 billion (Cain 2017). This trend accelerated further in 2016 when digital book sales declined by 4% and sales though shops increased by 7% (Cain 2017), and Waterstones announced that it had made its first annual profit since the global recession of 2008. In 2018 Waterstones reported an 80% jump in annual profits, after shifting away from low-margin products into more profitable products like stationery and toys.

According to James Daunt, Waterstones' CEO, that initial surge towards digital reading would not be sustainable, and eventually consumers would settle back into reading paperback and hardback books. He sees the experience of reading an e-book as less memorable, and the reader would feel less of an affiliation with an e-book, as you don't have that feeling of turning the pages and holding the weight of the book in your hands; you wouldn't treasure an e-book, and you cannot admire it on your bookshelf. He sees a value in the experience of reading a physical book, saying 'You are left with a memory; you've got something that has an enduring value. Why wouldn't you buy the physical book? You aren't even saving that much money by buying digital.' However, he admitted that e-books have been particularly popular in some genres, such as romance fiction and escapist reading.

However, nostalgia for words-on-paper books was only half the story in the recovery of Waterstones, which at the time of Daunt's appointment, was losing tens of millions of pounds a year. The main challenges for Daunt were to cut costs, and to entice shoppers into Waterstones branches, rather than buying books at a discount from Amazon or supermarkets.

In order to cut costs, Daunt implemented significant changes in staff numbers, meaning that thousands of staff lost their jobs, including managers and shop-floor staff. However, his experience of running a successful chain of independent, highly specialized bookshops in London, called Daunt Books, showed that people still wanted to visit well-run bookshops. Waterstones was the opposite of Daunt Books, but if he could create a store of cult status among booklovers, then the market was out there. He knew he had to move away from 'three for two' offers and heavy discounting and make Waterstones stores more appealing to the avid booklover.

One way he considered to increase local customer appeal was to give the remaining store staff the power to choose what books they stocked, which shifted Waterstones' relationship with publishers. Previously, publishers had been able to pay to get their books in prime spots in Waterstones' stores. Waterstones' bestseller charts reflected what was bought in based on publishers' priorities, rather than sales to the consumer.

Other incremental changes to make stores more appealing included the staff ditching their uniforms and putting an end to the three-for-two book offers that had created an image of a discount store. Cafés were also introduced into a number of stores, which encouraged customers to browse and read books off the shelves while sipping a latte. But the main focus was firmly on what a bookseller should actually do: recommend books that customers wanted to buy. If a customer could tell Waterstones what was the last book that they enjoyed reading, then the store would know exactly what to sell them next. Given that Waterstones stocks more than 150,000 titles, this was no mean feat.

These changes produced major benefits. Waterstones' shops now sold books that appealed to local customers, which supported increased sales, and because more books were selling, fewer unsold books were returned to the publisher. Under the previous system, some 23% of the books publishers sent to Waterstones were unsold and returned. In 2016 the return rate had fallen to less than 4%. Waterstones' recovery has since gathered momentum despite competitive pressures that have affected competitors, such as Borders, and as a result of Daunt's strategic positioning of the firm and continuous improvements in efficiency the firm reported a pre-tax profit of £20 million on sales of £386 million for the fiscal year ending April 2018. The company was confident that it would see continuing improvement in its business performance, but with new US fund manager Elliott now owning a controlling stake in the organization, the story of Waterstones' period of change continues.

Questions for discussion

1. What do you think are the differences between e-books and physical books in terms of a reading experience?
2. What are the pros and cons of reading an e-book and a physical book? You may want to think about your experience of reading a university e-book compared to a physical textbook?
3. Owning a physical high street store is expensive. What did Waterstones do to attract customers to their bookstores?
4. Do you think Waterstones have a competitive advantage? Why/Why not?

Sources

Ruddick, G. (2015). Waterstones prepares for new chapter as bookshop chain returns to profitability, 20 November. https://www.theguardian.com/business/2015/nov/20/waterstones-profit-books-amazon (accessed 31 July 2019).

Balancing the books: how Waterstones came back from the dead, *The Guardian*, 3 February 2017. https://www.theguardian.com/books/2017/feb/03/balancing-the-books-how-waterstones-returned-to-profit (accessed 31 July 2019).

James Daunt says pay row obscures 'decent progress' at Waterstones, *The Bookseller*, 2 April 2019. https://www.thebookseller.com/news/james-daunt-says-pay-row-obscures-decent-progress-waterstones-980056 (accessed 31 July 2019).

Waterstones' annual profits jump 80% as buyers loom, *The Guardian*, 18 January 2018. https://www.theguardian.com/books/2018/jan/18/waterstones-annual-profits-jump-80-percent-books-sale (accessed 31 July 2019).

New chapter for Waterstones as Elliott takes control, *FT*, 29 April 2018. https://www.ft.com/content/884e5acc-4a0a-11e8-8ee8-cae73aab7ccb

8.1 **Introduction**

An important task in strategizing is to clarify how the organization competes in a way that creates value for customers for which they are willing to pay more than the cost of creating that value. Therefore strategy practices that focus on debating how a firm competes—particularly when new information becomes available about shifting context—are a crucial feature of strategizing episodes. In market economies, few firms have the luxury of having no serious competitors or threats to their market position. More often than not, it is necessary for firms to change the way they compete in response to evolving competitive conditions and the threat of new competitors. Faced with ever-present competitive pressures, firms must develop business models that align with strategies that seek to produce a competitive advantage over their rivals. At the same time they must try to slow down the erosion of this advantage by existing competitors, potential new entrants to the market, or new product innovations and technologies.

Competitive success is achieved through the deployment of the firm's tangible and intangible resources, such as the firm's brand reputation and capabilities to produce a superior customer value proposition that cannot be copied or bettered by the firm's rivals. However, no competitive advantage lasts indefinitely. In highly competitive and dynamic environments, a firm can (at best) hope to achieve a temporary advantage until it is competed away, unless it is able to build barriers against rivals and continually renew its sources of competitive success to stay ahead of the competition to enjoy a sustainable competitive advantage. To do this, a firm must consistently be better or meaningfully different from its rivals.

As you study strategy it is important to understand the key sources of competitive advantage and how this can be achieved, sustained, or indeed eroded by competitors, as this is a main concern for managers. Being able to frame and explain an organization's situation in terms of theories of competitive advantage will increase your ability to lead effective debate and decision-making in strategizing episodes. We begin this chapter by considering what constitutes the nature and the sources of a firm's competitive advantage and how this advantage can be maintained in a competitive marketplace. We will then turn to critically evaluate the mechanisms that may protect an organization from competitive imitation and how strategy practitioners can slow down the inevitable competitive erosion in fast-moving competitive environments. In the chapter we will also consider the most common types of competitive advantage and hybrid strategies that a business can deploy. Building on the concepts introduced in Chapter 5, we emphasize the importance of finding ways for a firm to continually renew its value to stakeholders by creating resources and capabilities to stay ahead of the competition. We conclude the chapter with a critical evaluation of the implications of research (McGrath 2013a,b), which suggests that, in today's intensely competitive environments, firms can no longer maintain a sustainable competitive advantage indefinitely. Instead, firms can develop a series of temporary advantages that need to be re-created and protected through continual innovation and development. We encourage you to reflect on how the knowledge of new context and options generated by the analytical tools outlined in Section 8.3 might provide valuable inputs to debates on how an organization could and should compete.

8.2 The nature of competitive advantage

Companies such as Facebook in social media, Airbnb in owner-managed holiday rentals, Apple in mobile devices and laptops, Amazon in low-cost online retail and entertainment, and Dior in haute couture have become names that are recognized throughout the world. The prominence of these firms in their respective competitive spheres is not a result of a clever advertising campaign or a PR stunt. These businesses have become successful because they have created business models that enable them to offer something unique to their customers that their rivals cannot match. This uniqueness may be based on either these firms' ability to offer products or services to their customers at a better value for money, or by providing a highly desirable product or service at a premium price. It is the ability to be different in a meaningful way in the eyes of their customers which sets these firms apart from their closest rivals.

Business model

An organization's **business model**, its value-creating resources and activities, and its strategy for achieving competitive advantage are closely linked concepts. A successful business model defines the firm's economic logic, and a successful business strategy describes how the business model fits the firm's value-creating resources and capabilities with the opportunities in the external environment. Think about Waterstones in our opening case—how the firm developed a successful business model to attract customers to its high street physical bookstores by offering them targeted recommendations and a space to peruse books in comfortable surroundings.

In essence, a successful business model is the firm's guiding principle of how to make money. More specifically, the business model directs how the firm deploys its resources and undertakes activities that generate a valuable product or service to customers. It incorporates the whole range of the organization's activities from logistics and supplier relations, to production, to marketing, and after-sales customer care through which the value creation occurs. The greater the perceived value by customers and the lower the purchase price, the greater the firm's overall value proposition is to its customers. To be effective, however, the business model must also factor in the firm's costs of production. Thus the business model needs to incorporate an operating model that takes the costs of production into account in determining the price of the product or the service in relation to the perceived customer value, in order to achieve an attractive profit. Figure 8.1 shows how this relationship can be expressed.

We see from this equation that the lower the costs of production, given the firm's overall value proposition (perceived customer value - price), the higher the profit the business is able to earn. Managing the relationship between the overall value proposition and the costs of production is crucial to the firm's financial viability and success. The challenge for any business is to ascertain how to continually improve the overall customer value proposition while simultaneously maintaining or improving the firm's profitability. A business model is not sustainable if it does not enable an organization to operate profitably over an extended period of time. To do so, the firm has to have an advantage over (or at least match the performance of) its competitors which allows it to protect its revenue and profit streams.

Competitive advantage

A firm is said to have a competitive advantage when it is able to create, or has the potential of creating, more economic value than its competitors. Profit is frequently used to measure a firm's competitive advantage (Figure 8.1), but the concept of economic value added is a

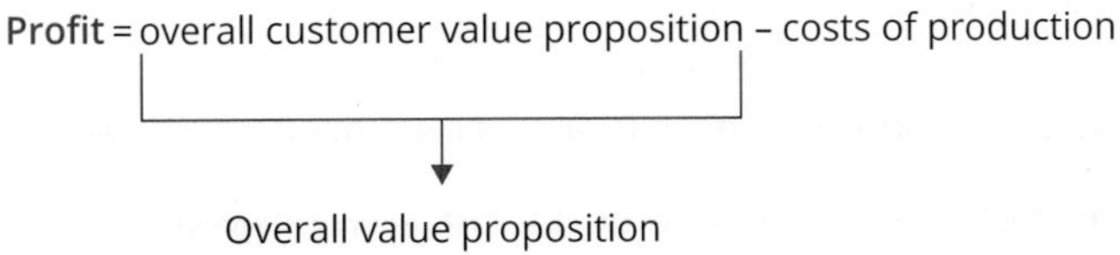

FIGURE 8.1 Business model equation.

8

more accurate indicator of the firm's advantage, as it takes into account the firm's total costs including the cost of capital. Economic value is the difference between the perceived benefits gained by customers when they purchase the firm's products and services, and the full economic cost of production of these products and services (Figure 8.2). Economic value differs from the traditional accounting profit as the latter only takes into account the explicit costs that are recorded in the firm's profit and loss statement, not the firm's cost of capital. Thus, as shown in Figure 8.3, the size of the firm's competitive advantage is the difference between the economic value the firm is able to create, and the economic value of its rivals (Peteraf and Barney 2003).

A firm's competitive advantage can be temporary or sustainable. A temporary advantage lasts for a finite period of time until it is competed away. A sustainable advantage, in contrast, may last much longer. A critique of the feasibility for companies to create and maintain sustainable competitive advantage is discussed in more detail in Section 8.4, but in mature and stable industries companies who are able to match and protect their internal resource strengths and align them with external key success factors may be able to maintain an advantage over their competitors for an extended period. For example, Levi Strauss began manufacturing denim overalls in the 1870s and the company created their first pair of Levi's 501 Jeans in the 1890s. Although the company's fortunes have been buffeted by the winds of fashion over the years, denim is an everyday staple for many and the company still possesses an enduring appeal. Its products have been worn by people from all walks of life from cowboys, to miners, and even to Nobel prize winners, including Albert Einstein whose Levi's leather jacket was sold at auction for over £110,000 in 2016 (www.stuarts.com).

We define a sustainable competitive advantage as a set of tangible and intangible resources and capabilities that allows a firm to consistently outperform their rivals. The emphasis in our definition is the idea of consistency in outperforming rivals. This does not mean that the firm merely matches the performance of its competitors, but the company should consistently be among the highest performing companies in its industry. Most firms are able to have a good year or two when they outperform the competition, but few firms are able to consistently produce performance above industry average year after year. Hence, it is important to analyse a firm's market position in terms of relative profitability over an extended period of time. The firm's market position may vary from one year to another, and profitability may even dip below the performance of its closest competitors for a short period of time. However, this does not necessarily mean that the firm has lost its competitive advantage, as a decision may be taken to forgo today's

Economic value = perceived customer benefit on purchase – costs of production (including capital)

FIGURE 8.2 Economic value equation.

Competitive advantage = economic value of the firm – economic value of rival

FIGURE 8.3 Competitive advantage equation. Source: Reproduced with permission from Peteraf, M.A. and Barney, J.B. (2003). Unraveling the resource-based tangle. *Managerial & Decision Economics*, **24**(4), 309–23. © John Wiley & Sons Ltd.

profitability by investing in the acquisition of market share, new technology development, or hiring and compensating talented people, with the expectation that these investments will result in superior future performance (Rumelt 2003).

To summarize, a firm can be said to possess a sustainable competitive advantage when the firm consistently outperforms its rivals by creating more economic value over a sustained period of time.

8.3 The sources of competitive advantage

Having defined competitive advantage, what are the potential sources of competitive advantage? Building on the MBV and RBV concepts introduced in Section 8.2, we will discuss three different sources of competitive advantage:

1. the firm's position in the industry (structural industry forces view)
2. its internal resources and capabilities (resource-based view)
3. impact of external and internal changes on competitive advantage.

The first view (the structural industry forces perspective), is based on the assumption that the firm's competitive advantage is derived from securing a defensible position in the most attractive segments of a given industry (Porter 1980.). Hence, the firm's competitiveness is greatly influenced by external industry and competitive factors. Porter's industry forces analysis is discussed in more detail in Chapter 5.

The second, resource-based view (Wernerfelt 1984; Barney 1991), in contrast with the industry forces perspective, considers competitive advantage to result from distinctive and socially complex combinations of the firm's internal resources and capabilities. As explained in Chapter 5, these resources and capabilities are developed over a long period of time, and so prove hard to transfer outside the firm or to imitate, which in turn creates value as they will not be available to competing firms. It is this resource specificity that may provide the firm with a competitive advantage until the its resource combinations either become obsolete, or are competed away through rival innovation if the firm is unable to continually renew its resource base to keep ahead of the competition (Dierickx and Cool 1989).

The third view is a more holistic way of thinking about the emergence of competitive advantage by considering the impact of both external and internal changes as a source of competitive advantage. External changes have a varying impact on firms in the same industry, as no firm, not even very close competitors, possesses identical resources and capabilities. This is frequently referred to as **resource heterogeneity**, meaning that firms in the same industry possess and compete with different resource and capability mixes. For example, both British Airways and Virgin Atlantic have similar tangible resources, such as airplanes, landing slots at airports, lounges, pilots and crew, catering services, jet fuel, and so on, but the way these similar resources are combined together produces flying experiences that are perceived to be different by travellers. The way that these resources are combined are a result of how the firm has produced the service in the past, but also a reflection of how the firm's strategists perceive the present and future state of air travel.

A seminal example of how resource heterogeneity influences competitive advantage of different firms in the same industry is the effect that the creation of OPEC in the early 1970s had on the automotive industry. The formation of the oil cartel resulted in a fourfold increase in the price of oil and gasoline within a year between 1973 and 1974. High gasoline prices almost brought the American automotive industry to its knees as the American carmakers produced almost exclusively large 'gas guzzling' cars which consumers began to shun because of the skyrocketing gasoline prices at the pumps, and the subsequent high running costs of the vehicles. In contrast, the high gasoline price was great news for the Japanese and European car manufactures, who were able to take advantage of this external change to enter the US market with small automobiles with frugal engines. The oil shock enabled the Japanese and European car manufactures to gain a foothold in the American market, and use that as a base to build their reputation as manufacturers of high-quality energy-efficient vehicles. Some argue that the US automotive manufacturers never fully recovered from the oil shock and were not able to catch up with the foreign manufacturers in terms of efficiency and quality. It is worth noting that not all external changes have the same magnitude as the 1973 oil crisis, but it is true that the greater the external change, the greater the entrepreneurial opportunities that become available for exploitation by organizations that are positioned to take advantage of them.

Opportunities presented by external changes must be accompanied by the firm's ability to take an advantage of these changes. Apple's late CEO Steve Jobs perceived that consumers would be willing to pay a dollar for a music download rather than 'stealing' tracks that had been made available by pirate sites. 'We believe that 80% of the people stealing stuff don't want to be, there's just no legal alternative. Therefore, we said: Let's create a legal alternative to this. Everybody wins. Music companies win. The artists win. Apple wins. And the user wins, because he gets a better service and doesn't have to be a thief' (Jobs 2003). Mr Jobs had spotted an emerging change in consumer attitudes and he was able to harness Apple's technological knowhow and innovative capability to create the iTunes music store to take an advantage of the change in consumer attitudes towards music piracy. There may have been other businesses who had also identified this new emerging consumer trend before Steve Jobs, but Apple was the first business to be able to mobilize its resources to take advantage of it.

In addition, Apple had introduced its first iPod in 2001 and the iTunes music download service provided added benefit and functionality to the customers who had purchased the firm's iPods. The additional music download service tied Apple's iPod customers even closer to the firm's product and service offer through the iTunes platform. This seamless hardware and software integration became a powerful protective mechanism for maintaining Apple's competitive advantage. Even today, rivals still have difficulty challenging Apple's dominance in music downloads with superior product/service features or quality. However, Apple's story did not end with iPods and iTunes. Having successfully launched the iPod, the company began actively thinking how else the firm could leverage the technological knowhow it had acquired by developing iPod and the music platform. Six years later, in 2007, Apple launched the world's first smart phone, iPhone, which revolutionized the mobile telephone industry, and in 2010 the firm launched the iPad, which redefined how we browse the web, watch movies and photos, and send and read

FIGURE 8.4 Sources of competitive advantage.

emails. It should not come as a surprise that iPad, iPhone, and the original iPod look uncannily similar, although with much improved and different functionality, as they all share the technological and design competencies of the firm. Apple is classic example of a firm that has managed to maintain its competitive advantage in a fast-moving competitive environment by marrying evolving external opportunities with continual development of its core competencies in technology and design (Schoemaker et al. 2018).

Figure 8.4 depicts the relationship between external and internal factors and competitive advantage.

Sustaining competitive advantage

From a process–practice perspective, the creation and maintenance of competitive advantage is a continuous cycle that is subject to erosion by competitor moves and changes in the external environment, as illustrated in Figure 8.5. Competitive erosion refers to a gradual destruction (or the chipping away) of a firm's competitive advantage. In a competitive environment, the firm has two main priorities:

1. The protection of the existing sources of competitive advantage from competitive erosion. This can be achieved by building barriers to imitation or avoiding resource mobility (preventing valuable resources from leaving the firm and ending up with rivals).
2. The process of resource renewal. This can be achieved by investing in new strategic resources and capabilities.

A firm's strategic value-adding resources and capabilities enable the business to achieve a favourable market position that underpins its competitive advantage. The benefits of competitive advantage may result in higher customer satisfaction and loyalty and increased market share, as well as a higher profitability levels. The improved financial performance should then enable the business to invest in the continuous development of new strategic resources and capabilities in order to maintain its advantage. As discussed in Case Example 8.1, Amazon used its experience and success in online retailing to branch into new digital content provision and even physical retailing that combines traditional stores with the firm's e-commerce technology. Similarly, Apple

CASE EXAMPLE 8.1 AMAZON—THE EVERYTHING STORE

Founded by entrepreneur Jeff Bezos in Seattle in 1994 as one of the first dotcom firms, Amazon's business model is built entirely around emerging digital technology. It has grown to become a $315.5 billion turnover e-commerce mega-retailer and cloud computing business, with a brand value that has quintupled in the past five years (*Financial Times* 2019).

As it started life as a small bookseller, at the heart of Amazon's success is the firm's ability to sell books at a significantly reduced price compared with more traditional book retailers by leveraging its e-commerce platform as a value-creating strategic resource. The more Amazon achieved increasing economies of scale, the more significant the cost savings it could make to its books, which allowed Amazon to sell its product at an unmatchable price compared with its competitors.

Additionally, Amazon was at helm of an emerging new technology, developing the Kindle, which gave booklovers the convenience of hundreds of book titles on a single device. Amazon sold Kindles at a break-even price, but the additional book downloads from Amazon's cloud server drove the firm's marginal costs down even further, and compensated for the lack of profits generated from Kindle sales. Amazon's ability to invest in emerging technologies put enormous pressure on other booksellers, who were struggling to compete. Had Waterstones in the UK not been able to reconfigure its activities to provide incentives for people to visit their stores rather than buy their books from Amazon (as discussed in the opening case study), Waterstones would have followed other well-known book retailers, such as Borders in the USA, into administration. Amazon remains a constant threat to many iconic independent bookshops today, despite a rise in the number of independent bookshops in the UK in more recent years.

Amazon has also expanded into new markets. It continues to react to changing external environments such as technological change and innovation, as well as changes in consumer tastes, which has led them to expand into grocery delivery services (Amazon Pantry) and cashierless grocery stores (Amazon Go), fashion retailing (Prime Wardrobe), movie entertainment production (Amazon Studios), everyday electronics (AmazonBasics), voice recognition technology (Echo- and Alexa-enabled smart speakers), and even book publishing by exploiting the opportunities to sell more physical and digital products to a loyal customer base. Most recently, Amazon has been experimenting with the use of drone technology to deliver purchases within 30 minutes of a customer order, calling it Prime Air. It even has plans to launch thousands of satellites to provide the entire globe with broadband internet access.

Amazon has also increased the rate of its acquisitions since 2015, with its most significant acquisition being Whole Foods, a premium grocery retailer, in 2017. This acquisition gives Amazon access to premium retail sites, and may allow Amazon to use Whole Foods to expand its own food offer and use the physical space for customers to pick up their Amazon orders and to sell items that may be less suitable for online retailing.

However, Amazon has not stopped there. Although Amazon continues to beat its competitors' customer order fulfilment times, its customers' shopping experience is limited to simply browsing a webpage. Amazon's competitors saw this as a potential for competitive advantage, and responded by enhancing their own customer experience by creating 'living spaces' beyond a traditional shopping experience, such as the cosy cafés in Waterstones. However, Amazon has counter-responded by disruptively opening bricks and mortar stores in a number of US cities. These stores are designed to meet the supercharged expectations of the modern-day consumer by rotating inventory out on a weekly basis as items become more or less popular on their website, and items are tagged with exclusive prices for Prime customers, and customer ratings and reviews. Through this new move, Amazon seeks not just to replicate other retailers' in-store experience, but also identify new ways to engage customers.

The company has truly become an 'everything store'. As Jeff Bezos is fond of saying, 'Amazon wants to continually give more to their customers without charging more'.

Questions for discussion:

1. What do you consider is/are Amazon's strategic resource(s)?
2. How does Amazon use these resources to create and sustain competitive advantage?
3. Do you consider Amazon's venture in physical retailing logical given the firm's source(s) of competitive advantage? If so, why, and if no, why not?

Sources

Amazon, the world's most remarkable firm, is just getting started. *Economist*, 25 May 2017. https://www.economist.com/leaders/2017/03/25/amazon-the-worlds-most-remarkable-firm-is-just-getting-started

Financial Times (2019). Amazon clinches top spot in world's most valuable brand ranking, 11 June 2019. https://www.ft.com/content/9dac0724-789f-11e9-b0ec-7dff87b9a4a2 (accessed 28 June 2019).

Unputdownable! The bookshops Amazon couldn't kill. *The Guardian*, 6 June 2019. https://www.theguardian.com/books/2019/jun/06/amazon-booksellers-beating-odds-book-shops (accessed 28 June 2019).

Amazon blamed as 'iconic' bookshops announce closure. *The Guardian*, 30 May 2019. https://www.theguardian.com/books/2019/may/30/amazon-blamed-as-iconic-bookshops-announce-closure(accessed 28 June 2019).

Here's Amazon's new transforming Prime Air delivery drone. *The Verge*, 5 June 2019. https://www.theverge.com/2019/6/5/18654044/amazon-prime-air-delivery-drone-new-design-safety-transforming-flight-video (accessed 28 June 2019).

Amazon plans to launch thousands of satellites to provide broadband, *Bloomberg*, 4 April 2019. https://www.bloomberg.com/news/articles/2019-04-04/amazon-plans-to-launch-thousands-of-satellites-for-broadband (accessed 28 June 2019).

Five reasons why Amazon is moving into bricks-and-mortar retail, *Forbes*, 19 December 2018. https://www.forbes.com/sites/annaschaverien/2018/12/29/amazon-online-offline-store-retail/#76bf35f51287 (accessed 28 June 2019).

Infographic: Amazon's biggest acquisitions, *CBInsights*, 19 June 2019. https://www.cbinsights.com/research/amazon-biggest-acquisitions-infographic/ (accessed 28 June 2019).

Amazon just opened a new store that sells popular items from its website. Here's what it looks like inside. *CNBC*, 27 September 2018. https://www.cnbc.com/2018/09/27/amazon-just-opened-its-4-star-store-in-new-york-heres-a-look.html (accessed 28 June 2019).

used their technology knowhow to launch successive products from iPod to iPad, and they are in the process of expanding their successful iTunes and App store to a games arcade subscription service (https://www.ft.com/content/44236e86-5ba3-11e9-9dde-7aedca0a081a).

Continual investment in developing resources and capabilities is vital, as any firm with a superior competitive position will be subject to competitive imitation, and unless it is able to stave off competition, its advantage will be lost or 'eroded'.

How fast is a firm's competitive advantage eroded by its competitors? This depends on how easy it is for the competition to imitate the leading company's strategic resources and capabilities, as imitation is the most direct form of competition. Imitation is particularly easy where the leading firm possesses no significant proprietary resources, technologies, or other barriers for competitive imitation, such as brand equity.

As will be discussed furthe in Chapter 11, rivals may also seek to divert resources and attention towards innovation, which may change the competitive landscape through new products, technologies, platforms, or ways of working. For example, as addressed in Chapter 6, a generation ago most people associated a 'Kodak moment' with happy events that were saved for posterity on film using an Eastman Kodak camera. Today, the name Kodak increasingly serves as a corporate blunder that warns managers of the need to stand up and respond when disruptive developments encroach on their market (Anthony 2016). As Kodak's core business was selling film, it is not hard to see why the last few decades proved challenging for the firm. Cameras went digital and then disappeared into smartphones. People went from printing pictures to

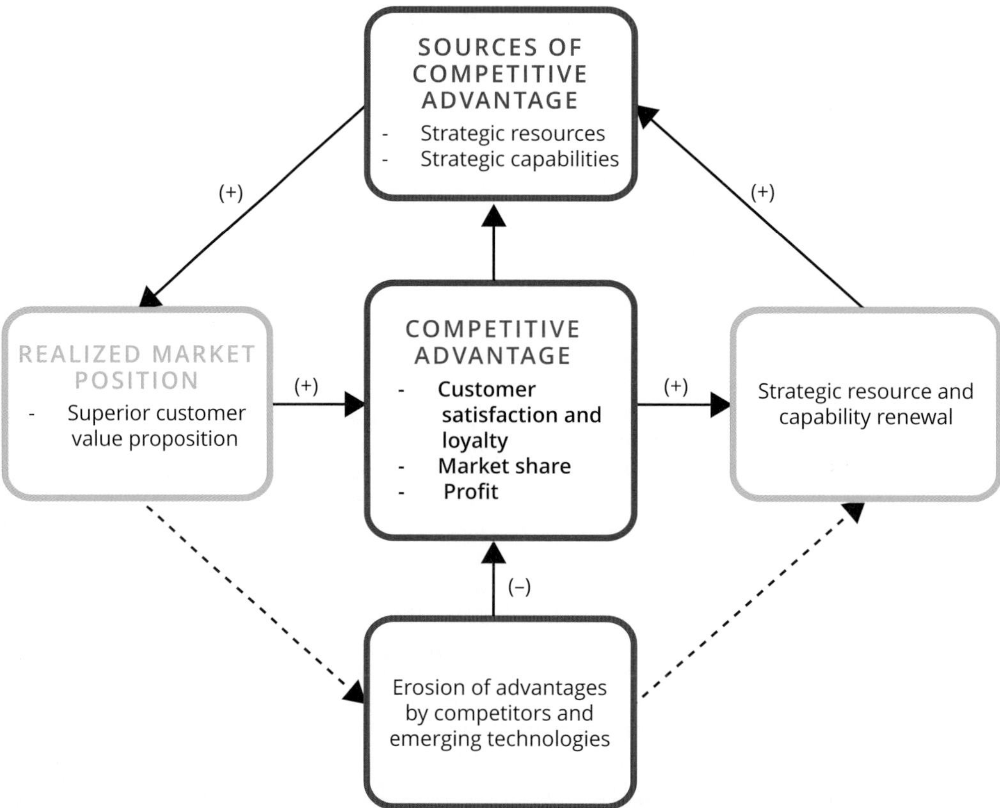

8

FIGURE 8.5 Cycle of competitive advantage. Source: Reproduced with permission from Day, G., Reibstein, D., and Gunther, R. (eds) (1997). *Wharton on Dynamic Competitive Strategy*. New York: John Wiley. Copyright © 1997, John Wiley & Sons.

sharing them online. Of course, some people do still print photo books and holiday cards, but that volume pales in comparison with Kodak's heyday. The company filed for bankruptcy protection in 2012, exited legacy businesses, and sold off its patents before re-emerging as a much smaller company in 2013. Once one of the most powerful companies in the world, the firm's market capitalization had plunged to $109 million in April 2019 (NYSE:KDK).

However, innovation can be costly, and at a minimum requires slack resources and involves a degree of risk, which is why imitation remains a more common mode of direct competition. This means that if a firm is to maintain a sustainable competitive advantage, it must have or develop effective barriers to imitation, which are referred to as **isolating mechanisms** (Rumelt 1984). The more effective these isolating mechanisms are, the longer the firm can expect to enjoy a competitive advantage.

Isolating mechanisms

Isolating mechanisms can take different forms. Some isolating mechanisms are a mixture of resource characteristics whereas others involve managerial practice, and each type offers varying success in protecting and sustaining competitive advantage, and combating competitive imitation. In this section we will examine the following examples of the most common isolating mechanisms and their effectiveness in protecting and sustaining competitive advantage:

- unique historical conditions
- path dependency
- patents
- social complexity
- causal ambiguity.

Unique historical conditions

As explained in the concept of path dependence (see Chapters 4 and 6), unique historical conditions may have been present at a time when a firm was able to acquire or develop a particular resource or a resource mix upon which its competitive advantage is based. This is often referred to as **time compression diseconomies**, as some resources are almost impossible to imitate because they have arisen from unique historical conditions (Dierickx and Cool 1989). For a competitor to imitate such a resource, it would require those same historical conditions. In other words, history would need to repeat itself. An example of time compression diseconomies is Caterpillar's global service and supply network which was created through US Federal Aid. When the USA entered the Second World War, the country needed a primary supplier of construction equipment to build and maintain military bases throughout the world. For a competitor to build and replicate a competing network of such a global reach and magnitude could potentially be prohibitively expensive and difficult, so Caterpillar sought to secure a competitive advantage within these unique historical conditions. The global service network was Caterpillar's strategic resource and the business managed to enjoy a leading position globally in earth-moving equipment.

8

This advantage lasted until Komatsu, a Japanese upstart, decided to challenge Caterpillar. It would have been financially impossible for Komatsu to replicate Caterpillar's service network. Instead, Komatsu adopted a long-term strategy by beginning to design and produce machinery that did not break down, or at least did not require as much servicing as Caterpillar's heavy-duty earth-moving equipment. By producing more reliable machinery, Komatsu effectively devalued Caterpillar's service network as a strategic resource and a source of competitive advantage.

Path-dependent competitive advantage

In Chapter 6, we explained that what an organization can do today depends on what it has done in the past—a concept known as path dependency. Path-dependent evolution of competitive advantage occurs when a firm gains a competitive advantage today, based on the acquisition or development of a resource or processes in the past. Returning to Case Example 8.1, when Jeff Bezos of Amazon first developed the company's online platform for selling books, he may not have been fully aware of the future value potential of leveraging the resource across different product categories. Once the value of Amazon's e-commerce platform became more widely known, Amazon had already moved down the learning curve and the cost of replicating the resource by potential imitators placed these rivals in a cost disadvantage. Path dependency is linked to the concept of **first-mover advantage**, which refers to circumstances when the first firm to market with a new product, process, technology, business model, or platform is able to gain such a solid foothold in the market by earning customer loyalty, economies of scale, or learning benefits that subsequent entrants are unable to successfully challenge the first mover's dominant position. This is a key question for practitioners involved in strategizing episodes considering innovation: 'Should we seek to capture first-mover advantage? Or should we let others go first, let them make the main mistakes, and then imitate the successful path?'

Isolating mechanisms are often examples of strategic resources, practices, and processes that have evolved over a long time, and therefore might make up much of the 'taken for granted' characteristics of the organization, its culture, and how business is conducted. They are also a part of the day-to-day experience of practitioners. If these resources, practices, and processes are valuable and inimitable by a firm's competitors, they can form the basis of the firm's sustainable competitive advantage. However, a downside to these mechanisms is that they can become the value-destroying 'core rigidities' (Leonard-Barton 1992) explained in Chapter 6. In other words they can deteriorate in value in competitive environments characterized by a significant degree of new product or process innovation. For example, Caterpillar lost its leading industry position in earth-moving machinery when competitors brought more reliable and less service-intensive products to the market. This eroded the value of Caterpillar's superior global service network. Similarly, Nokia lost its position in the market to smartphones when consumers began to attribute less value to the durability of Nokia phones than to the functionality offered by Apple's iPhone.

Patents

Another example of an isolating mechanism is **patents**. Patents can act as a powerful isolating mechanism as they can be used to exclude others from a product market for the duration of patent protection. Patents raise the cost of competitive imitation and protect the firm's revenue streams. The only way that potential competitors can challenge patent protection is by creating a substitute product or a new, more innovative product that does not infringe the existing patent protection of the leading firm.

However, some scholars argue that instead of cementing a firm's sustainable competitive advantage, patents may have the opposite effect (Barney 1986). Patents may, in effect, reduce the costs of imitation, especially for patents that seek to protect specific products from competitive imitation. When a patent application is submitted to the Patent Office, the firm must reveal significant details about the product, and this important information is then available to competitors. This information can effectively provide a blueprint for product imitation that is only temporarily protected by the patent. Moreover, patent infringements are very expensive to defend. In most cases, small to medium-sized firms lack the financial resources to defend against such infringements. Hence, some scholars (Rumelt 1984; Thurm 1998) question the wisdom of patent protection for new innovative products by small entrepreneurial firms.

Patent disputes and theft are by no means a new phenomenon. Individual inventors and entrepreneurs have always been at the risk of theft of their inventions. A famous case that underpins our digital world as we know it today involved Nikola Tesla and Guglielmo Marconi. In the 1890s, Tesla discovered that he could use electrically charged 'Tesla coils' to transmit messages over long distances by setting them to resonate at the same frequency. Tesla's patent for this design was accepted in 1900. At the same time, Marconi was working on his own device for transmitting signals over long distances. However, Marconi's patents were repeatedly turned down due to the priority of previous inventors. Undeterred, Marconi experimented with technologies like the Tesla oscillator to transmit messages over long distances. Tesla initially tolerated Marconi using his work. He is quoted as having said, 'Marconi is a good fellow. Let him continue. He is using seventeen of my patents'. Yet this changed in 1904, when the US Patent Office decided to award credit for the invention to Marconi. A furious Tesla attempted to sue Marconi, but he didn't have sufficient financial resources to prosecute successfully. The patent was not restored to Tesla until after the inventor's death in 1943 (http://www.businesscareers-guide.com/10-great-business-ideas-that-were-actually-stolen/).

Social complexity

A firm's resources may be difficult to imitate due to their **social complexity**. Social complexity arises because the composition and configuration of the firm's resources are a mix of socially complex phenomena such as interpersonal relationships among managers and employees (including tacit interactions between them), cultural norms, and the firm's reputation among customers and suppliers (Strebel 1996). It can be argued that socially complex resources such as a firm's culture can be a source of sustainable competitive advantage. Organization culture (see Chapter 4) has been cited, at least partially, as the source of the sustained superior performance of companies such as IBM, Hewlett-Packard, McDonald's, and Proctor & Gamble (Peters and Waterman 1982). Successful cultures are very difficult to imitate. Rivals who try to change their cultures to emulate a leading firm will rarely achieve sustainable advantage. Although the rivals may successfully incorporate valuable new attributes to their organizational cultures, such activities rarely result in sustained superior performance (Barney 1986).

Causal ambiguity

We have already seen that if a firm is to imitate the competitive advantage of another firm, it must understand the basis of the rival's success. If the firm's sources of success are transparent and there are no isolating mechanisms present, competitive imitation should be a relatively easy process. In such circumstances, sustainable competitive advantage is not possible. An increasing amount of research has focused on the implications that resource inimitability has on the sustainability of competitive advantage from the perspective of both the imitating firm and the firm that is the target of competitive imitation (Ambrosini and Bowman 2008).

Causal ambiguity (King 2007; McIver and Lengnick-Hall 2018) is a concept that describes the degree to which would-be imitators, as well as the managers of the firm that is being imitated, understand the relationships between resources and business results. Causal ambiguity exists when the value of the resource itself, the characteristic of the resource, or the linkage between the resource and business performance is not fully understood. If the link between the firm's resources and competitive advantage is opaque, it is difficult for competing firms to duplicate the resources through imitation, as they do not know which resources to imitate. The framework of causal ambiguity is depicted in Figure 8.6.

In quadrant A, the nature of the resource and its link to business performance is known to the firm's managers, and so both characteristic and linkage ambiguity are low. The resource can be imitated relatively easily by hiring away the firm's managers who understand the nature and linkage between resources and business performance, or by engaging in systematic intelligence

CASE EXAMPLE 8.2 COMPETITIVE ADVANTAGE FROM COMPLEX INTERACTIONS

Companies are increasingly aware that sustainable competitive advantage can no longer be based on tangible products and services that can be copied or substituted with relative ease by rivals. Firms are looking for intangible, socially complex resources within the organization to find ways to improve the effectiveness of solving their strategic business problems.

Tacit interactions between employees are becoming a focus of daily strategic activity, and are increasingly a fundamental part of organizations' way of working within particularly competitive markets. 'Tacit' activities involve the exchange of information, making judgements, and drawing on multifaceted forms of knowledge between coworkers, customers, and suppliers.

For example, at Toyota Motor Company, employees from different function groups, such as production workers, engineers, and managers, work together to establish cost-cutting strategies without risking product quality. Managers are an example of those employees within an organization who are primarily responsible for these types of collaborative activities. At Toyota, they make up 25–50% of the workforce, and typically have the highest salaries to reflect their involvement in shaping competitive strategies within a volatile external environment.

Companies that make these activities central to their strategy may not only raise their top and bottom lines, but this type of activity also enables organizations to establish a competitive advantage against its rivals through the collective talent of their workforce. Establishing competitive advantage is challenging, but in order to build on this competitive advantage, companies must channel this talent to evolve their strategy, design organizations, and maximize use of technology—this is no mean feat. The best way for executives to begin to think strategically about these socially complex resources and capabilities is to understand the nature of tacit interaction: the searching, coordinating, and monitoring activities required to exchange goods, services, and information.

The faster pace of specialization, globalization, and technical change that we see today has also significantly improved the way in which companies, their customers, and their supply chains interact. The result has been a dramatic increase in the volume and value of interactions. In most advanced economies, four out of five non-agricultural jobs involve interactions such as these, but only one in five of these roles in today's economy involves actually extracting raw materials or working on a production line, whereas pre-globalization this may have been more proportionate. What this tells us is that the number of jobs which require the more 'tacit' interactions between different highly paid function groups is growing faster than any other type of role within a supply chain. Examples of today's more 'tacit' roles include managing supply chains, managing the way customers buy and experience products and services, rebranding, and negotiating acquisitions.

Questions for discussion

1. If firms' competitive advantage is increasingly derived from intangible resources, such as employees and their social interactions, what managerial challenges do you consider such intangible resources present and why?
2. How do you think you could identify the link between the most valuable resources and business performance if they are intangible?

Source

Beardsley, S.C., et al. (2006) Competitive advantage from better interactions, *McKinsey Quarterly*, May. http://www.mckinsey.com/business-functions/organization/our-insights/competitive-advantage-from-better-interactions (accessed 10 April 2017).

gathering and analysis of the firm's competitive success. Once the resource becomes disseminated across the firms in the industry, it will be only be able to provide competitive parity (the resource won't provide a competitive advantage for any of the firms). The managerial challenge

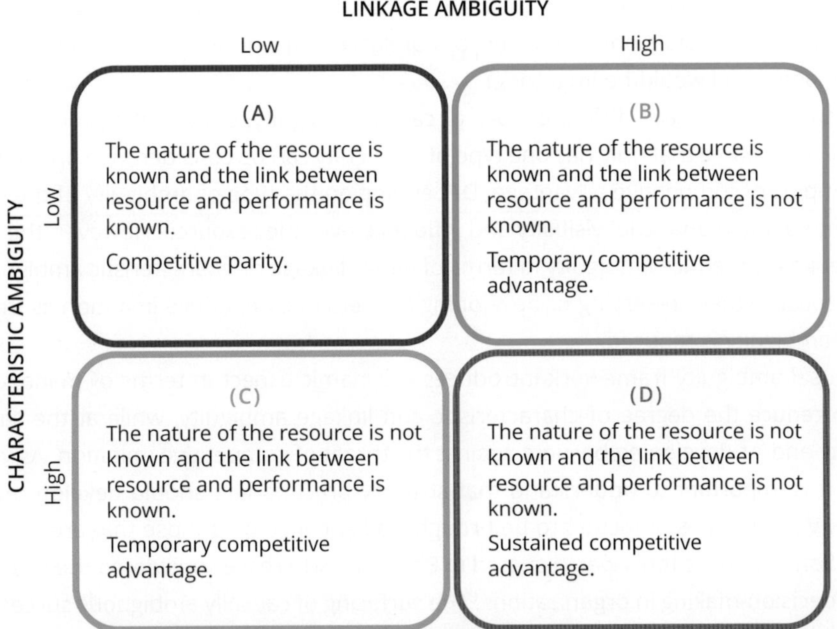

FIGURE 8.6 Characteristic and linkage ambiguity: the framework of causal ambiguity.

for the firm is to develop the existing resource or replace it with a new resource that possesses at least some inimitable characteristics in order to protect the firm's competitive position.

In quadrant D, sustained competitive advantage is possible as both the firm and its competitors face perfect characteristic and linkage ambiguity. In other words the nature of the competitive resource and the link between the resource and the firm's performance are not known (to either the firm or its competitors). Since imitation is not possible, sustained competitive advantage can only be destroyed through resource substitution where the competitor develops a competing product by using a different set of resources from that of the leading firm.

However, as the firm that possesses the valuable resource also faces perfect causal ambiguity, it does not have the means to develop the resource further. At worst, the firm may inadvertently destroy the resource because it does not understand its value and its link to performance (Barthelemy and Adsit 2003). This can happen when firms divest or outsource activities that may mistakenly be considered of secondary importance. For example, many banks rushed to cut their operating costs by offshoring their call centres. However, it was only once their customers had difficulties in communicating with the offshore call centre staff (due to language and cultural barriers) that the banks realized that domestic call centres were in fact the key differentiating service that customers valued the most.

The managerial challenge for the firm that faces perfect ambiguity is to reduce both characteristic and linkage ambiguity, but preserve or develop alternative barriers to competitive imitation as the degree of causal ambiguity is reduced.

(We should note that causal ambiguity presents a critique of the resource-based view which posits that competitive advantage is derived from firm's internal resources and capabilities. However, causal ambiguity makes it difficult for practitioners to identify and manage the firm's internal sources of success. And, as quadrant D shows, at least in theory, sustainable competitive advantage is possible only if the sources of success are perfectly ambiguous to both the firm's managers and would-be imitators.)

Quadrants B and C have differing types of causal ambiguity, either linkage or characteristic ambiguity. A resource that only has one type of ambiguity can be considered to provide the firm with a temporary competitive advantage. Depending on the type of ambiguity of the resource, the firm has some managerial visibility and influence over the resource. However, the managerial challenge is to reduce ambiguity in terms of either linkage or characteristic ambiguity, while simultaneously either preserving or developing barriers to competitive imitation as the degree of causal ambiguity is reduced.

The causal ambiguity framework introduces a dynamic aspect in terms of managerial processes to reduce the degree of characteristic and linkage ambiguity, while at the same time preserving and/or developing barriers against the threat of competitive imitation. As you study strategy, it is important to understand that strategy practitioners should develop techniques that allow various types of factors to be brought to light, including those that are causally ambiguous. Some of these tools were covered in Chapter 3 where we considered the challenges of strategic decision-making in organizations. The surfacing of causally ambiguous success factors may provide a trigger for organizational learning. The debate and the unpacking of what the causes of success are can facilitate the reframing of the basic assumptions underlying managers' beliefs about sources of success. This could ultimately lead to a reframing of managers' strategic choices, as they begin to understand the sources of the firm's success in more depth.

To illustrate the concept of causal ambiguity, consider Richard Branson's Virgin Group of companies. Having created more than 400 Virgin companies, Branson shared in a blog post (https://www.virgin.com/entrepreneur/richard-bransons-secrets-success?amp) his secrets of success and how others could replicate it. 'One of the tried-and-true methods of building a business is by offering such useful products and terrific service that you disrupt the local market, winning customers away from your competitors', he says. 'We at Virgin have done this with a particular focus on disruptive change.'

Virgin won't venture into a new business unless they believe they can offer something that is distinct from what already exists. 'From our first ventures, like our music stores and record label, to some of our flagship businesses today, including our airlines and space tourism companies, we have approached business development proactively and opportunistically, looking for openings where we can surprise and delight customers by offering something truly different.'

'Success in one area tended to lead to success in other fields, and so it has been sustained', he says. 'We built up an extensive network of relationships, and now entrepreneurs and companies often approach us with ideas for partnerships that will help them to start a new business, or to attract new customers.'

'There is a lot of cross-over between sectors in everything from technology and design to trends in customer preferences', he explains. 'The lessons we learn from one business can often be applied to another.' Companies across the Virgin Group often work together to achieve common goals, meeting at forums based around either a sector, like mobile technology, or a department, like communications.

But what is the real secret of Virgin's success? Branson says: 'Consider the importance of what seems to be the final magic ingredient: since we started Virgin over 40 years ago with such strong personal relationships, we have always also had close ties with our customers.'

It is clear that Virgin and Richard Branson have a clear strategy and, although there have been failures along the way, it has worked remarkably well. Eight businesses that have been created in eight completely different sectors have an enterprise value of more than $1 billion. However, the question remains as to whether, due to causal ambiguity, any would-be imitator, or even Branson himself, could replicate Virgin's success based on the insight provided by Branson.

Dynamic capabilities

The ability of firms such as Apple and Amazon to adopt and take advantage of changes in the competitive environment while some other firms stagnate implies differences in the capabilities of these firms. As introduced in Chapter 6, this capability to continually renew the firm's resource base and capabilities is referred to as **dynamic capabilities** (Teece et al. 1997). In relation to competitive advantage, we can think of dynamic capability as arising from:

> *... the firm's processes that use resources, specifically the processes to integrate, reconfigure, gain and release resources, to match or even create market change. Dynamic capabilities are the organisational and strategic routines by which firms achieve new resource configurations as markets emerge, collide, split, evolve, and die.*
>
> Eisenhardt and Martin (2000:1107)

This understanding of dynamic capabilities links a firm's resources to organizational processes that can be used for defending the basis of the firm's existing competitive advantage, as well as to dynamic processes of **creating market change** and creating new sources of advantage. Crucially, dynamic capabilities don't directly result in competitive advantage but instead create valuable new resource-base configurations through which competitive advantage might be gained (Wang and Ahmed 2007). In other words, the customer may be willing to pay us for the resource-based outcomes of deploying dynamic capabilities (e.g. new products from revised operational processes), but not the dynamic capabilities themselves (e.g. in-house R&D capabilities).

Recent research has categorized dynamic capabilities into four main processes:

- **Reconfiguration**—the transformation and recombination of resources (e.g. the consolidation of central support functions). Such consolidations often occur as a result of mergers and acquisitions or a reorganization of operations in large multinational corporations. Large-scale bank mergers such as that of J.P. Morgan and Chase Manhattan Bank (JP Morgan Chase & Co market capitalization $361 billion, NYSE:JPM) achieved significant economies of scale from the amalgamation and reconfiguration of their banking operations activities.
- **Leveraging**—replication of a system or a process from one business unit to another, or extending a resource by deploying it into a new domain (e.g. by applying an existing brand to a new set of products). The Virgin Group of companies have successfully leveraged their brand from an airline, to an internet and entertainment service provider, to a high street bank.
- **Learning**—allows tasks to be performed more effectively and efficiently as an outcome of experimentation, reflecting on both failures and successes. Amazon's Jeff Bezos has stated

that the firm explores all avenues, although some of them may lead into blind alleys. Prime Air is a future delivery system from Amazon designed to get packages safely to customers in 30 minutes or less using drones.

- **Creative integration**—relates to the ability of the firm to integrate its resources in a novel way that may result in new resource configuration. As we have already seen, Apple has used its technical and product design capabilities from iPod to launch iPad, a product that revolutionized the way people use the internet, view photos, send email, etc.

Dynamic capabilities also link with causal ambiguity and path dependence in explaining sustainable competitive advantage. As we already know, sustainable advantage can only be maintained if the firm's advantage is based on strategic resources including routines and capabilities that are difficult to imitate. The transfer of capabilities from one setting to another can be accomplished only if the capability that is being transferred is fully understood by the firm's managers. This could make it imitable, but in managerial practice this is not often the case. Not only does the tacitness of organizational routines hinder imitation, but also a change in an organizational routine in one part of the organization impacts a routine in another part of the firm, making competitive imitation even more difficult.

Zollo and Winter (2002) relate high causal ambiguity to 'learning investments', or learning by doing, which produce routines that govern organizational activity. These routines emerge over time and hence will be path-dependent and shrouded in ambiguity. The higher the degree of causal ambiguity between the emerging routines and business performance, the higher the likelihood that explicit articulation of such routines, if possible, will provide a better effectiveness in developing dynamic capabilities. In order to achieve this, in your future career as a strategy practitioner you must try to make explicit the link between routines and performance outcomes. This is a very difficult thing to do, but firms that are able to reduce causal ambiguity to gain an insight into the relationship between their resources, routines, and performance outcomes are better able to leverage these capabilities to gain and sustain a competitive advantage.

8.4 Types of competitive advantage

So far in this chapter we have considered the sources of competitive advantage. How, then, can firms compete effectively, given the nature of their strategic resources?

It is unlikely that any two firms will employ competitive strategies that are exactly alike in every sense. Even close competitors in the same industry possess slightly different resources and resource mixes that are used to produce a product or a service. Moreover, managers in different companies have different perceptions of industry driving forces, the nature of future threats and opportunities, and how best to deal with competitive pressures. Firms try to avoid competing head-on with rivals, as this ultimately results in price wars that are destructive to all industry participants. Even in the most competitive industries, companies try to find different customer segments and adjust their strategies in order to find ways to protect their business from cut-throat competition.

Porter's generic strategies and competitive scope

It is possible to classify firms by general strategic orientation. Porter (1985) identified two basic dimensions on which firms base their competitive strategies. The first dimension involves the firm's competitive scope: whether the firm's target market segment is broad or narrow. The second dimension is whether the firm pursues low-cost or product/service differentiation strategy. These strategy frameworks are referred to as Porter's Generic Strategies.

The four generic competitive strategy frameworks

Porter's two strategy dimensions give rise to four generic strategy options for establishing a market position to deliver value to customers. The four generic strategy options are broad low-cost strategy, broad differentiation strategy, low-cost focus strategy, and differentiation focus strategy. We will start by briefly explaining each strategy, before looking at the key considerations of low-cost and differentiation strategies in more detail. We will conclude by considering the possibility of hybrid strategies.

Broad low-cost strategy

Broad low-cost strategy aims to achieve the lowest overall costs in the industry by offering similar products to rivals' at better value for money for a broad range of buyers. An example of broad low-cost strategy is Timex. Timex is the original dollar watch company, which means that it is a high-volume provider of inexpensive, but stylishly branded, watches. The company constantly tries to drive down costs by exploiting low-cost manufacturing resources and using extensive advertising to drive up volumes to increase economies of scale. The firm produces hundreds of watch variations of its no-nonsense timekeepers so that customers can always have a fashionable Timex to match their outfits or activities from camping to Ironman competitions. This strategy has helped Timex to become one of the best known watch brands in the world.

Broad differentiation strategy

Broad differentiation strategy seeks to differentiate the firm's product/service offer from that of rivals so that it will appeal to a broad range of buyers who are willing to pay a premium price for the offering. An example of broad differentiation strategy is Starbucks. Starbucks' baristas are happy to prepare orders to meet their customers' wishes, no matter how detailed. The company is also well known for quality products, with strict guidelines on coffee roasting and brewing—a cup of espresso must be served within 23 seconds of brewing. Food offering and preparation is strictly controlled so as not to overpower the smell of coffee in its shops, which the company likes to call a 'third place'—a place alongside one's home and office. The quality of coffee, personal attention, and the network of 24,000 stores has made Starbucks the coffee lovers' choice in 70 countries.

Low-cost focus strategy

Low-cost focus strategy concentrates on a narrowly defined target market segment by out-competing rivals on costs by being able to offer a low-priced product to a customer segment whose needs may be slightly below average. Therefore the firm may use demographic profiling as a basis for identifying its target market. Papa Murphy's is a take-and-bake pizza company. It was formed in 1995 as the merger of two local take-and-bake pizza companies, Papa Aldo's Pizza and Murphy's Pizza. The company and its franchisees operate more than 1300 outlets in the USA and Canada. Papa Murphy's is authorized to accept food stamps as payment. This allows Papa Murphy's to attract customers who might not otherwise be able to afford a prepared pizza.

Differentiation focus strategy

Differentiation focus strategy concentrates on a narrowly defined target market segment who are willing to pay a premium for a product/service that meets their specific needs better than the rival product/service offerings. An example of differentiation focus strategy is Bang & Olufsen. Bang & Olufsen products are marketed as 'lifestyle' products, and they are carefully targeted at wealthy customers with particular tastes that reflect individualism, and self-expression, and motivation. Bang & Olufsen often refers to Mercedes Benz as their primary competitor, and perceive that they are competing for upper middle-class discretionary spending. The company's designs attract both men and women with their combination of high technology, spectacular and often audacious Danish modern styling, excellent performance, and extremely functional integration into the typical upper middle-class home.

Porter's generic strategies are directly linked to an organization's business model, as the strategy adopted must be aligned with the firm's overall business system through which the value creation occurs. This requires the organization's resources to be harnessed to deliver a satisfactory customer value proposition (refer to our discussion of the business model in Section 8.2). The nature of the organization's resources and isolating mechanisms largely determine which generic strategy is a feasible option for the firm. There would be little sense in identifying the product/service attributes that are valued by customers if the business is not able to supply those attributes. Similarly, there is little purpose in developing resources to deliver product/services with attributes that are not valued by customers. For example, the firm that pursues a low-cost strategy must possess resources and capabilities that are focused on delivering a product at an acceptable price which customers value for its value/quality at a lower cost than the firm's rivals. For example, the whole business model of Ryanair, the leading European low-cost airline, is based on a resource configuration that is focused on delivering an acceptable service at the lowest possible cost and price to the customer.

Low-cost strategy should not be equated with selling products and services that are perceived as 'cheap and nasty' or of inferior quality by customers. Companies that pursue low-cost strategies have to be able to offer products and services that are of acceptable quality and comparable to industry standards, but be able to do so at a lower overall cost than that of the rival firms. It is unlikely that any company can survive very long by offering a poor-quality product or service, however low the price.

Similarly, companies that pursue differentiation strategies must ensure that the firm's resources and any materials used in the production process are consistent with supplying a highly differentiated product/service for which customers would be willing to pay a premium price compared with rival offers. Firms that sell highly differentiated premium-priced products or services must have highly sophisticated market research, advertising, and promotion capabilities to provide customers with an appropriate justification to make a decision to pay a premium price for what is offered to them.

Low-cost strategies

Firms with costs that are lower than those of their rivals are likely to enjoy a competitive advantage in the marketplace because they can offer their customers lower prices and hence gain increases in sales and market share. Competitive advantage can be sustained as long as the firm is able to maintain their cost advantage over their competitors and as long as their customers will consider the firm's offer as value for money.

Companies that pursue the low-cost strategy on a broad market basis will be able to exploit economies of scale and learning effects that will drive the firms' costs even lower as the volume of production increases. In contrast with broad market based economies, a firm that follows the low-cost focus, or niche, strategy is not able to earn significant economies of scale or learning effects as its production volumes and market share are low as a result of the company's focus on a narrow market segment.

Achieving a low-cost position affords a firm with greater pricing flexibility than its rivals, which can be used as a tool for sustaining competitive advantage. It is important to note that cost and price are not used interchangeably here. A firm that achieves a low-cost position is able to maintain flexibility in its pricing strategy. In a less competitive market, the firm may choose to maintain the price at the same level as its competitors, thus earning a higher level of profit due to its low cost base. In a fiercely competitive market, the firm may wish to set the price below its rivals' price to maintain market share, given that competitors with a higher cost base would find it difficult to match the lower price without incurring losses.

Low-cost strategy is usually most effective in industries in which the material characteristic or the reputation of the product is less important than the price. This is especially true in commodity markets where competing products are virtually indistinguishable from each other. The airline industry has suffered from commoditization for a long time. Although airlines have tried to differentiate their services in the eyes of the travelling public, customers don't seem to value the airlines' differentiation efforts to build customer loyalty. Travellers usually make their buying decisions based on price, and choose an airline that best fits their travel schedule.

On the other hand, a low-cost strategy is less likely to be successful in industries or markets that are characterized by differentiation. This is particularly true for services such as legal advice, consulting advice, and medical care. Customers are more concerned about the reputation and quality of advice and care than the price of the service. Most customers would probably be wary of a lawyer or financial advisor who emphasized low fees.

To achieve an overall low-cost position, the main focus of the firm's operating activities is a relentless focus on improving efficiency and lowering the overall costs. Successful low-cost strategies are often characterized by:

- low labour costs achieved through capital-intensive production processes
- product design that that can be manufactured easily with shared components
- sophisticated inventory and supply chain management systems
- low-cost distribution networks.

Efficiency-focused production processes must be accompanied by a culture and management that emphasizes close supervision of labour, cost control in all activities across the organization, and incentives that are based on achieving cost and efficiency targets.

Differentiation strategies

Differentiation strategies aim to give a firm a competitive advantage by offering customers products that are perceived as unique on either a broad or narrow market basis. Differentiation strategy works best in industries and markets where the characteristics of products and services themselves offer opportunities for differentiation. Automotive, fashion, and consumer product industries are prime examples of industries where differentiation strategies work best. However, innovative differentiation strategies can be found in even the most basic commodity industries. Perhaps one of the best examples is Morton Salt, an old US brand and a very basic commodity. Morton Salt is packaged in a container with a distinctive blue label with a yellow illustration of a girl holding an umbrella (Figure 8.7).

The company's strapline 'When It Rains It Pours' implies that even in humid conditions Morton's salt pours without getting clogged up. Morton has recently launched its first major brand campaign in the firm's 168-year history, which sponsored the music video of OK Go's *The One Moment*. It was one of the breakout videos of 2016 and by 2019 it had attracted over 25 million YouTube and 24 million Facebook views. The video was just one small part of the brand's effort to recreate itself as a much more 'on trend' company that speaks directly to millennials who reputably value quality ingredients and foods. The strategy seems to work, as Morton Salt products usually retail at a premium of over 30% compared with competing salt products.

FIGURE 8.7 The evolution of the Morton Salt girl.

Differentiation is often based on real differences between competing products or services, but it is the customer's perception of the experience that the product or service offers that is critical to the long-term success of a differentiation strategy. Companies that are able to create an emotional bond with their customers are more likely to benefit from long-lasting customer loyalty towards their product. This is especially important in markets that are characterized by fickle trends or fads.

Morton Salt attempts to cement this type of emotional bond by creating an image of Morton Salt beyond the salt itself and make it what the firm calls an 'emotional lifestyle choice'. It is increasingly imperative for the Morton brand to connect on a more emotional level. This comes even as competition grows from other products like kosher salt or Himalayan pink salt, and as Morton tries to tell customers that its product is key to their everyday lives beyond food—for example, it is used in healthcare and farming.

The ability to innovate, in addition to strong marketing skills, is an important organizational capability for firms that pursue differentiation strategies. They must continuously be able to develop new products or product extensions that are perceived as unique by customers. Gillette has been the dominant firm in the wet-shaving market and they have maintained their lead by continuously launching new product iterations and extensions. Although online sellers like Dollar Shave Club have eaten into their market share in the USA, Gillette still controls 65% of the global blades and razors market with the slogan 'The Best a Man Can Get'. However, the main risk of differentiation strategies is that, in their attempts to constantly increase the functionality of their products in order to maintain or even increase premium pricing, companies may add features that are no longer considered of added value and price by customers. For example, in 2016, Philips launched a 'OneBlade' razor in the UK that mocks Gillette's strategy of introducing an ever-increasing number of blades into their shaver cartridges.

To sustain a differentiation advantage, firms must possess or be able to enhance their:

- innovation and research capabilities to improve the perceived value of their products and services by customers
- ability to coordinate R&D, manufacturing, and marketing to ensure a high-quality product or service
- ability to attract highly skilled and creative scientists, designers, marketers, and creative people.

The organization culture and management focus of successful differentiators is on ensuring that the firm produces products of the highest possible quality, and undertakes support activities in marketing and distribution to ensure superior customer satisfaction.

Hybrid strategies

Porter (1985) argues that successful firms must select and concentrate on effectively implementing the generic strategies. According to Porter, a firm that attempts to pursue low-cost and differentiation strategies simultaneously ends up 'stuck in the middle' without clear strategic focus, which will ultimately lead into failure.

This mutually exclusive strategy choice promoted by Porter has come under criticism. Empirical evidence suggests that while low-cost and differentiation strategies may be seen as mutually exclusive, successful strategies can be based on a mix of two. In the UK, John Lewis Partnership trades under the motto of 'Never Knowingly Undersold', while investing in attractive store layouts and prime locations as well as hiring very knowledgeable and specialized sales assistants and partners. While such a combination, or hybrid strategy, may not be easy to achieve, it is by no means impossible to achieve both low-cost and differentiation at the same time. Hendry (1990) argued that low-cost strategy is more of a position than a strategy. As there can only be one company that is the lowest-cost producer amongst its competitors, it is a precarious position if the firm ignores other opportunities for adding value. Other competitors are always likely to follow cost-reduction strategies and may over time challenge the position of the cost leader if it ignores opportunities for differentiation.

The development of a hybrid strategy is a complex task as it involves consideration of a trade-off between low cost and differentiation. As Porter (1985) has pointed out, the risk is that once profits accumulate, successful companies that follow the low-cost strategy will be tempted to relax their obsessive focus on costs and efficiency. Similarly, successful differentiators, having achieved a position where they are able to justify high prices based on the perceived value of their products, may be tempted to ease off on R&D, advertising, or even lower the quality of raw material inputs to lower their costs to maximize profits. In both cases the loss of the primary strategic focus may place the companies at risk of losing their long-term competitive advantage. The managerial challenge for organizations is to decide what activities are crucial to maintaining or improving the overall value proposition of the firm, and what activities could be cut as they make little impact on how the firm's offer is perceived by customers.

Bowman's strategy clock

Porter's concept, in terms of its simplicity and its assumptions about cost and differentiation, can be considered as an attempt to limit the options available to managers. The strength of Porter's model lies in its prescriptiveness for managers to focus on costs when competing against low-cost competitors, and on building unique differentiation capabilities when confronted with a competitive environment with a number of differentiated products or services on offer. But what about less clear-cut competitive environments? A more complex model has been put forward by Cliff Bowman which aims to reflect the competitive reality more effectively (Bowman 1988).

Bowman has developed what became known as 'the **strategy clock**' (Figure 8.8). In Bowman's framework, also referred to as 'the customer matrix' in later work (Bowman and Faulkner 1997), the two base strategies for competitive success are to reduce price relative to the firm's immediate competitors' products or services, but still provide the same perceived use value by the customer, or to increase the perceived use value of the product or service by customers, while maintaining price parity with the firm's closest competitors. Bowman realized that these two base strategies were too general for many firms, and that in practice there were a number of different perceived use value and price combinations that firms could pursue. Bowman's framework extends Porter's generic strategy model into eight strategic options for companies to follow when comparing their competitive basis against their competitors. The model identifies eight strategic options, and it explains the cost and perceived use value of the combinations that are available to firms, as well as identifying the likelihood of success for each strategic option. The eight price/perceived use value positions are detailed below.

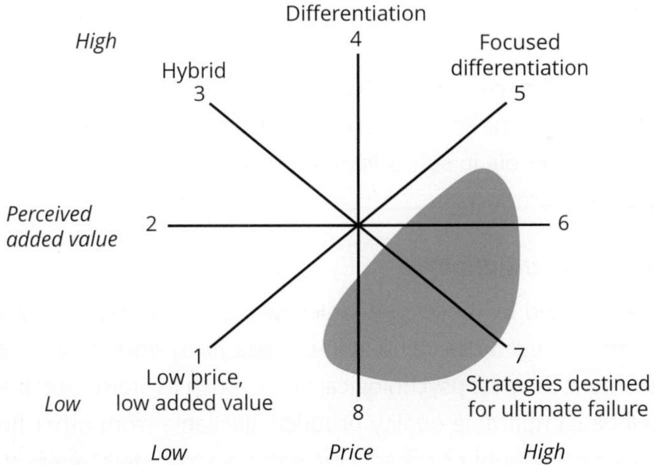

FIGURE 8.8 The strategy clock. Source: From Bowman, C. and Faulkner, D. (1997) *Competitive and corporate strategy*, Irwin, London. Reproduced with permission of McGraw-Hill School Education Group via Copyright Clearance Center.

Position 1. Low price/low perceived use value

This is likely to be a segment-specific 'no frills' position. Most firms do not wish to choose this option, but they may need to accept this position if their product lacks opportunities for any differentiation. In order to survive in this position, the firm must be able to drive its costs to the bare minimum and attract high volumes of new and potential customers. The business will probably not be able to command customer loyalty, but it may be able to sustain itself as long as the company stays one step ahead of the customers. Product quality for this position is likely to be low, but the prices are attractive enough to convince consumers to try them at least once. The firm may be able to move up on the clock to a more sustainable position by maintaining a low price but being able to improve the perceived use value.

Position 2. Low price/medium perceived use value

A firm can select this option for its products or services when it is the cost leader. When the business operates under the strategy of low prices, its profit margin will be very low, requiring the firm to generate a high sales volume. If the company is able to achieve significant sales volume that will drive its costs down even further as a result of economies of scale, it can become a powerful force in the market. Walmart in the USA and Lidl and Aldi in Europe are good examples of firms pursuing this strategy of providing their customers with a value proposition that is perceived as value for money.

Position 3. Hybrid

Hybrids are companies that are able to offer products or services to customers at a relatively low price, but at a higher perceived use value than low-cost competitors. In this strategy volume is an issue, but companies build a reputation for offering fair prices for reasonable goods and services. Some of the emerging economy car manufacturers such as Hyundai and Kia could be considered as following a hybrid strategy. As the quality and value of the product is perceived to be good, this combination often builds customer loyalty for a particular firm's product or services.

Position 4. Differentiation

The basis of differentiation strategy is to produce products and services that offer unique attributes that are highly valued by customers. Branding plays a key role in differentiation strategies as it allows a company to become synonymous with high quality as well as premium prices. Nike in sporting goods and Coca Cola in soft drinks have strong brand identities that communicate high quality and premium products.

Position 5: Focused differentiation

This strategy can be adopted by those companies whose customers may buy products or services purely based on perceived use value alone. These firms often have a brand identity that appeals to the customers' deepest psychological needs, such as status and the sense of belonging. There may well be comparable quality products available from other firms, but they lack the crucial psychological attribute of connecting with the customers' deepest desires. Focused differentiation companies often focus on very narrow market segments, otherwise they would lose their exclusiveness. Luxury brands such as American Express Centurion Black and Platinum cards in financial services, Aston Martin in automobiles, and Hubolt in watches are good examples of focused differentiation companies.

Positions 6, 7, and 8

The remaining positions, encompassing high price and low perceived use value, will only work in certain circumstances, such as a monopoly or if all competitors follow suit in increasing prices. These positions will result in ultimate failure as we assume a competitive environment where long-term collusion is not feasible and monopolies are not allowed to be formed or sustained. In these positions, the firms would attempt to charge a price for products or services that is not justified by their underlying quality.

In summary, Bowman's version of generic strategy positions suggests that, while cost is an important factor, it is not a position on its own, and for a generic strategy to be successful, it has to move beyond pure cost considerations. A successful strategy has to be based on something that customers can perceive in terms of the value of the product and the service and the price of the offer.

8.5 **The end of competitive advantage?**

Perceived value according to the customer can always change. Consider brands such as Kodak, Blockbuster, Circuit City, and HMV Records. These once admired organizations are either gone, or no longer relevant. According to Rita Gunther McGrath, in her book *The End of Competitive Advantage* (McGrath 2013a), their downfall was a predictable outcome of practices that were designed around the concept of sustainable competitive advantage. While the strategist could apply carefully informed structures and systems, the fundamental problem is that deeply ingrained structures and systems designed to extract maximum value from a competitive advantage can become a liability when the environment requires instead the capacity to ride through waves of short-lived opportunities (Denning 2013). As we have seen, to successfully compete in a volatile and fast-moving environment, firms may need to rethink their approaches to strategy.

The ingrained assumption in strategy literature and practice of sustainable competitive advantage creates a bias toward stability that can be detrimental to the continuing success of the firm. Stability, not change, is the state that is most dangerous in highly dynamic competitive environments. One of the biggest changes firms need to make in their assumptions is that within-industry competition is the most significant competitive threat (McGrath 2013a) This assumption has led companies to define their most important competitors as other companies within the same industry, meaning that those firms offering products that are in direct competition or close substitutes for one another. According to McGrath (2013a), this is a dangerous way to think about competition. In more and more markets, industries are seen competing with other industries, business models competing with business models even in the same industry (see Chapter 12 about born global business models), and entirely new industry categories emerging that may destroy existing industries.

Industries have not stopped being relevant, but using industry as a level of analysis is often not fine-grained enough to determine what is really going on at the level at which strategic decisions need to be made (McGrath 2013b). Firms must adopt a new level of analysis. A competitive arena rather than an industry is needed to make a connection between the firm's market segment, offer, and geographic location at a granular level. This is where decisions are made about the connections between a firm's customers and solutions offered to their problems. In other words, customers seek 'jobs to be done' rather than buying a particular product or service. IKEA sells cheap furniture and furnishing with Scandinavian design flair, but in reality most customers do not shop at IKEA to buy Scandinavian design. Instead, they have a job to be done—for example, furnish a rented apartment in a new city quickly and cheaply for a finite period of time without having to worry too much about what to do with the furniture once they move on.

To use a military analogy, competitive battles are fought in particular geographic locations, with particular equipment, to beat particular rivals. Increasingly, business strategies need to be formulated to that level of precision (McGrath 2013b).

The new strategy playbook

The end of competitive advantage means that the assumptions of what we used to believe about running organizations are no longer relevant. A new playbook is required that prompts companies to explore how they can build their capabilities to move from one competitive arena to another, rather than attempting to defend existing or ageing sources of competitive advantage. Companies that can do this show a remarkable degree of dynamism. Moving from one advantage to another advantage will become perceived as quite normal, not exceptional. Clinging to older advantages is seen as potentially dangerous. Disengagement from old advantages is seen as intelligent, and failures as potential harbingers of useful insight. Most importantly, companies develop a rhythm for moving from one arena to another, and rather than the wrenching downsizings and restructurings that are so common in business today, disengagements will occur in a steady rhythm, rather than as a result of radical change (McGrath 2013b).

Finally, as the pace of competition becomes faster, decisions that are made quickly, that are roughly right, and that are satisfactory are likely to beat a decision-making process that is more precise, but slower. Prediction and being right will be less important than reacting quickly and taking corrective action (see Chapter 3).

PRACTITIONER INSIGHT: DICK HOWESON, CEO OF UTALK

> We were not too concerned about competition as Andrew and I knew that we were going to be different—we have always been different.
>
> Richard Howeson, CEO

How would you like to learn 134 languages including Kinyarwanda, Greenlandic, Oromo, Cockney, or even Star Trek Klingon? This is what uTalk, a London-based educational publisher known primarily for its interactive language learning, is able to offer its globe- and galaxy-trotting customers.

The company was established in 1999 by Richard (Dick) Howeson and Andrew Ashe. uTalk is distinctive among language self-study programmes in teaching most of the target languages with a choice of over 130 base languages, so the programmes can be used all over the world. The company's products are sold worldwide through their website and a network of distributors; 70% of the firm's revenue comes from outside the UK. uTalk content is also sold under the Instant Immersion brand in the USA. As a differentiating feature, uTalk's customers have access to language learning programmes from uTalk's websites that have been localized for global audiences and through Apple's App Store.

Competition in the language learning market is fierce and most self-study programme businesses aim to provide their customers fluency, but 'We don't do that', says Dick Howeson, uTalk's CEO. Instead, the company focuses on providing solutions for a 'job to be done'—help people get by in a foreign country. 'If you ask anyone on the street if they would like to learn a foreign language most will say "Yes", but if you ask them how much time they have, the answer is "Not much", but most would like to learn enough to get by. That's what we do and we make learning a language fun and simple.'

Dick tells a story of landing at the airport in Hungary and needing to visit the restroom, and not being able to figure out which door was for men and which for women, as the doors did not have pictures on them. This was his Eureka moment as he realized that most travellers would love to learn the basics if only just being able to understand the restroom signage. People should be able to open up their laptop on the plane to their destination and learn the rudimentary basics by the time they landed. The focus should be on the spoken word, not writing or grammar. 'Many people have been telling us that we should add grammar courses, but we don't do that ... you can go and buy a grammar book if you are interested.' The company does not use focus groups, but they have begun running pop-up learning sessions in Costa Coffee shops in London. Participants get the app, which normally costs £49, free of charge. Although uTalk does not make a profit from the classes, they do help to build brand awareness, and the workshops give a chance to get feedback on the firm's language-teaching techniques.

Dick's airport Eureka moment occurred at the time when digital technologies and laptops with CD-ROM readers were becoming available to consumers at a reasonable price. Andrew trained himself as a multimedia designer and Dick visited a library to read everything he could find on learning a foreign language. He came across six different theories which all contradicted each other. Dick concluded that as there was no conclusive evidence of a best way to learn a language then uTalk would come up with its own language learning theory. Armed with Dick's insight and Andrew's programming skills, the pair set out to develop their own CD-ROM-based interactive language learning program. 'As Englishmen, we naturally began by designing a French course with English as a base language.' The course sold well, but soon uTalk began receiving inquiries from distributors and agents for an English language course with French as a base language and a French language course with German as a base language. 'We realised very early on that whenever we developed a new language learning course we also needed to make sure that this language could be used as a base language platform for another language program.'

Another differentiator for the firm is that thinking about languages both as a target and as a base language gave uTalk an unprecedented number of theoretical language programme combinations. With 134 languages and 130 base languages, the firm is able to offer 17,430 language combinations. To reach the maximum target audience for the most popular language combinations, uTalk hired website designers and coders to create websites in base languages that could be accessed by anyone with internet access, anywhere in the world in local language.

uTalk had always used Apple Mac-based technology and when Steve Jobs launched iPad in 2010, Andrew, uTalk's chief technologist, called it a truly revolutionary product that would permanently change how people learn things. The firm's CD-ROM-based product was still selling strongly alongside internet downloads, but the company saw apps as the way forward. By this time the company had a built an in-house technology development capability, and today most of uTalk's most popular languages are available in the Apple and Google App stores.

'Andrew and I have always been a bit different', says Dick. 'We have lunch out together every week and we think about the world, not only business, and come up with ideas to make the world a better place. When people say that something can't be done, we try to go and do it to prove people wrong.' Learning a language can be a step in making the world better. uTalk has developed Chatterbox, a classroom teaching tool for primary-aged children, that can be used world over, and the firm supports the charity onebillion.org to educate one billion children in maths and languages with the help of apps wherever they are in the world. 'The key to our success is to build a product that we are passionate about and that we know works.'

Dick's guide to uTalk apps can be found at https://youtu.be/fhxnNKNwd58

CHAPTER SUMMARY

In this chapter we addressed the following learning outcomes.

- **Define the nature and sources of competitive advantage**

  We defined competitive advantage as the difference between the economic value that the firm creates from its business model and the economic value created by its rivals. Two prominent views on competitive advantage show that advantage can arise from the firm's position in the industry and/or its internal resources and capabilities.

- **Appreciate the link between the firm's business model, its value-creating strategic resources, and strategies for achieving competitive advantage**

  The resource-based perspective of the firm states that the firm's competitive advantage arises from the exploitation of its strategic resources to produce a product or service that is different from a competitive offer. Such an offer has to be better in terms of either providing better value for money or by being significantly different so that customers are willing to pay a premium price for it. The firm's configuration of strategic resources will influence the firm's orientation to pursue either low-cost or differentiation strategies.

- **Recognize the importance of isolating mechanisms, causal ambiguity, and dynamic capabilities in achieving and maintaining competitive advantage**

  Imitation is the most direct form of competition. Isolating mechanisms (unique historical conditions, path dependency, patents, social complexity) and causal ambiguity can act as deterrents to such competitive erosion. Another threat to the firm's competitive advantage is competitive and technological innovation. Therefore it is imperative that the organization is continually able to renew its strategic resources and capabilities.

- **Understand generic strategies that organizations can apply to gain competitive advantage**
  We presented two main frameworks for a firm's strategic orientation: Porter's generic strategies of cost leadership, differentiation, and focus, and Bowman's strategy clock, also often referred to as the customer matrix. We also considered the feasibility of hybrid strategy. A firm's strategic orientation is greatly influenced by its business model and the configuration of its strategic resources and capabilities.
- **Consider the feasibility of maintaining a sustainable competitive advantage in highly competitive and dynamic environments**
  We demonstrated that in highly dynamic and competitive markets it may not be possible for firms to enjoy a sustainable competitive advantage for an extended period of time. Instead, firms should focus on earning successive temporary advantages, which requires them to continually reconfigure their business operations and even disengage from activities that no longer create value and a competitive advantage.

END OF CHAPTER QUESTIONS

Recall Questions

1. What is a business value proposition?
2. Define competitive advantage.
3. What is an isolating mechanism?

Application questions

A) What impact does resource heterogeneity have on how firms in the same industry compete?

B) What are the differences between characteristic and linkage ambiguity and what impact do they have on competitive imitation?

C) Compare and contrast the similarities and differences between Porter's generic strategies, the strategy clock, and hybrid strategies?

ONLINE RESOURCES

www.oup.com/he/mackay1e

FURTHER READING

Firm resources and sustained competitive advantage, by Jay Barney

Barney, J. (1991). Firm resources and sustained competitive advantage. *Journal of Management*, **17**(1), 99–120.

Understanding sources of sustained competitive advantage has become a major area of research in strategic management. Building on the assumptions that strategic resources are heterogeneously distributed across firms and that these differences are stable over time, this article examines the link between firm resources and sustained competitive advantage.

Dynamic capabilities: what are they?, by Kathleen M. Eisenhardt and Jeffrey A. Martin

Eisenhardt, K.M. and Martin, J.A. (2000). Dynamic capabilities: what are they? *Strategic Management Journal*, **21**(10–11), 1105–21.

This seminal paper focuses on dynamic capabilities and, more generally, on the resource-based perspective of the firm. The authors argue that dynamic capabilities are a set of specific and identifiable processes such as product development, strategic decision-making, and alliancing. They are detailed, analytic, stable processes with predictable outcomes.

The End of Competitive Advantage: How to Keep Your Strategy Moving as Fast as Your Business, by Rita Gunther McGrath

McGrath, R.G (2013). *The End of Competitive Advantage: How to Keep Your Strategy Moving as Fast as Your Business*. Boston, MA: Harvard Business School Publishing.

The book argues that it's time to go beyond the very concept of sustainable competitive advantage. Instead, organizations need to forge a new path to winning: capturing opportunities fast, exploiting them decisively, and moving on even before they are exhausted. McGrath shows how to do this with a new set of practices based on the notion of transient competitive advantage.

The causal ambiguity paradox: deliberate actions under causal ambiguity, by Derrick McIver and Cynthia Lengnick-Hall

McIver, D. and Lengnick-Hall, C. (2018). The causal ambiguity paradox: deliberate actions under causal ambiguity. *Strategic Organization*, **16**(3), 304–22.

Causal ambiguity describes a lack of understanding of cause and effect interactions between resources and competitive advantage. As a central construct in strategic management, causal ambiguity constrains a firm's ability to replicate valuable capabilities internally, yet simultaneously offers a means of protecting those capabilities from imitation by external agents. This shifts the attention from looking at casual ambiguity as a given characteristic within organizations and examines the causal ambiguity paradox by looking at how organizations can strategically act on causal ambiguity as a mechanism for extending advantages.

REFERENCES

Ambrosini, V. and Bowman, C. (2008). Surfacing tacit sources of success. *International Small Business Journal*, **26**(4), 403–32.

Anthony, S. (2016). Kodak's downfall wasn't about technology. *Harvard Business Review*, 15 July (Reprint H02ZWT).

Barney, J.B. (1986). Organizational culture: can it be a source of sustained competitive advantage? *Academy of Management Review* **11**(3), 656–65.

8

Barney, J. (1991). Firm resources and sustained competitive advantage. *Journal of Management*, **17**(1), 99–120.

Barthelemy, J. and Adsit, D. (2003). The seven deadly sins of outsourcing. *Academy of Management Executive*, **17**(2), 87–100.

Bowman, C. (1988). *Strategy in Practice*. Harlow: Prentice Hall.

Bowman, C. and Faulkner, D. (1997). *Competitive and Corporate Strategy*. London: Irwin.

Cain, S. (2017). EBook sales continue to fall as younger generations drive appetite for print. *The Guardian*. https://www.theguardian.com/books/2017/mar/14/ebook-sales-continue-to-fall-nielsen-survey-uk-book-sales (accessed 28 July 2017).

Denning, S. (2013). It's official! The end of competitive advantage, *Forbes*, 2 June. https://www.forbes.com/sites/stevedenning/2013/06/02/its-official-the-end-of-competitive-advantage/#3fbb9c831565 (accessed 17 July 2019).

Dierickx, I. and Cool, K. (1989). Asset stock accumulation and the sustainability of competitive advantage. *Management Science*, **35**(12), 1504–11.

Eisenhardt, K.M. and Martin, J.A. (2000). Dynamic capabilities: what are they? *Strategic Management Journal*, **21**(10–11), 1105–21.

Financial Times (2019). Amazon clinches top spot in world's most valuable brand ranking, 11 June. https://www.ft.com/content/9dac0724-789f-11e9-b0ec-7dff87b9a4a2 (accessed 28 June 2019).

Hendry, J. (1990). The problem with Porter's generic strategies. *European Management Review*, **8**(4), 443–50.

Jobs, S. (2003). Steve Jobs rare interview. 60-minutes. https://www.youtube.com/watch?v=ZUfzXz23ndo (accessed 28 July 2017).

King, A.W. (2007). Disentangling interfirm and intrafirm causal ambiguity: a conceptual model of causal ambiguity and sustainable competitive advantage. *Academy of Management Review*, **32**(1), 156–78.

Leonard-Barton, D. (1992). Core capabilities and core rigidities: a paradox in managing new product development. *Strategic Management Journal*, **13**(S1), 111–25.

McGrath, R.G. (2013a). *The End of Competitive Advantage: How to Keep Your Strategy Moving as Fast as Your Business*. Boston, MA: Harvard Business School Publishing.

McGrath, R. (2013b). The end of competitive advantage. *European Business Review*, 7 November. https://www.europeanbusinessreview.com/the-end-of-competitive-advantage (accessed 17 July 2019).

McIver, D. and Lengnick-Hall, C. (2018). The causal ambiguity paradox: deliberate actions under causal ambiguity. *Strategic Organization*, **16**(3), 304–22.

McMaken, M. (2012). E-books vs print books. http://www.investopedia.com/financial-edge/0812/e-books-vs.-print-books.aspx. (accessed 28 July 2017).

Peteraf, M.A. and Barney, J.B. (2003). Unraveling the resource-based tangle. *Managerial & Decision Economics*, **24**(4), 309–23.

Peters, T.J. and Waterman, R.H. (1982). *In Search of Excellence.* New York: Harper & Row.

Porter, M.E. (1980). *Competitive Strategy: Techniques for Analyzing Industries and Competitors*. New York: Free Press.

Porter, M.E. (1985). *Competitive Advantage: Creating and Sustaining Superior Performance*. New York: Free Press.

Rumelt, R.P. (1984). Toward a strategic theory of the firm. In: Lamb R. (ed), *Competitive Strategic Management*, pp. 556–70. Upper Saddle River, NJ: Prentice Hall.

Rumelt, R.P. (2003). *What in the world is competitive advantage*? Working paper, Anderson School, UCLA.

Schoemaker, P.J.H., Heaton, S., and Teece, D. (2018). Innovation, dynamic capabilities, and leadership. *California Management Review*, **61**(1), 15–42.

Strebel, P. (1996). Why do employees resist change? *Harvard Business Review*, **74**(3), 86–92.

Teece, D.J., Pisano, G., and Shuen, A. (1997). Dynamic capabilities and strategic management. *Strategic Management Journal*, **18**(7), 509–33.

Thurm, S. (1998). Copy this typeface? Court ruling counsels caution. *Wall Street Journal*, 15 July.

Wang, C.L. and Ahmed, P.K. (2007). Dynamic capabilities: a review and research agenda. *International Journal of Management Reviews*, **9**(1), 31–51.

Wernerfelt, B. (1984). A resource-based view of the firm. *Strategic Management Journal*, **5**, 171–80.

Zollo, M. and Winter, S.G. (2002). Deliberate learning and the evolution of dynamic capabilities. *Organization Science*, **13**(3), 339–51.

CHAPTER NINE

Functional Strategy and Performance

CONTENTS

LEARNING OBJECTIVES

By the end of this chapter, you should be able to:

- Describe the role of functional strategy in supporting organizational strategy
- Identify and outline the different types of functional strategy, such as financial strategy, HRM strategy, marketing strategy, operations strategy, and IT strategy
- Discuss the potential advantages and disadvantages of functional strategy
- Explain the role of strategic performance management tools, such as the Balanced Scorecard, in connecting functional strategy with the effective implementation of organizational strategy

TOOLBOX

- **Functional strategies: financial, HRM, marketing, operations, IT**
  Functional strategies are the strategies and plans adopted by each functional area of the organization, such as finance, human resource management, marketing, operations, and IT. Functional strategies need to be in line with the overall business or corporate strategy to help the organization to achieve its overall objectives.
- **McFarlan's Strategic Grid**
  McFarlan's Strategic Grid can help an organization to assess the relationship between IT projects, business operations, and business functions. One axis of the grid focuses on IT's relationship with the business strategy. The other axis focuses on IT's relationship with business operations. IT projects and initiatives, both current and proposed, are placed on the grid based on their expected impact.
- **Henderson and Venkatraman's strategic alignment model**
  The key message of this model is that, in a successful organization, the IT strategy should be fully aligned with the business strategy. The model can be used to analyse the goals, objectives, and activities of the IT function, and compare them with the goals, objectives, and activities of the organization as a whole.
- **IT maturity models**
  IT maturity models have been developed because it can be helpful to view the organization's IT capabilities through a maturity 'lens'. This means that managers can find it useful to look at the organization's IT capabilities as a portfolio that can be managed and improved to enable a more productive and innovative organization.

9

The Balanced Scorecard (Kaplan and Norton)
The Balanced Scorecard is a strategic performance measurement model. Its purpose is to help managers to translate an organization's mission and vision into functional plans and activities. It can help to provide information on the organization's performance against its chosen strategy, aiding feedback and learning processes. The organization's strategy is usually viewed from four perspectives: financial, customers, internal business processes, and learning/growth.

Strategy maps (Kaplan and Norton)
A strategy map is a diagram that can represent the organization's strategy on a single page. It can be a useful tool for making clear connections between the performance of each function and the performance of the organization as a whole. If a manager's goal is to manage the performance of their organization towards the successful achievement of its defined strategy, a strategy map can help people to see how their jobs affect the company's strategic objectives.

OPENING CASE STUDY VAIL RESORTS

Founded in the mid-1950s in the Vail Valley in Colorado, USA, Vail Resorts Inc. is the parent company for three 'highly integrated and interdependent business segments'—Mountain, Lodging, and Real Estate. The Mountain segment owns and operates 17 mountain ski resorts and three urban ski areas, and includes lift ticket, ski and snowboard school, dining, and retail and rental businesses. The Lodging segment includes a portfolio of luxury hotels under the RockResorts brand and a range of hotels and properties near mountain resorts. The Real Estate segment holds, develops, buys, and sells real estate in and around Vail's resort communities.

Vail Resorts Inc. describes itself as 'the premier mountain resort company in the world and a leader in luxury, destination-based travel at iconic locations'. Owning four of the top five visited mountain resorts in the US, Vail Resorts and its main competitor Alterra either own or partner at 58 mountain locations in North America.

In 2018, Vail reported revenue of $2.01 billion on a cost of goods sold of $1.35 billion, growing 5.5% from 2017. About 59 million skiers took to the snow in the USA in the 2018–2019 season, an 11% increase from the previous period and the fourth best season on record. The total number of season-to-date skier visits for Vail's North American mountain resorts climbed 6.8% from the prior season.

As reported by Bloomberg, an important innovation for Vail was 'the introduction of the Epic Pass in 2008 for unlimited lift rides at all of its (then five, now twenty) resorts for $579, roughly one-third the cost of other existing passes. It has an important catch: pass sales were offered only before the season hit its stride, closing right before Thanksgiving. By getting skiers to buy early, the company locked in a mass of customers and raked in a pile of revenue during its slowest months'. The company achieved a 22% increase in revenue in the first year, and over the subsequent decade invested in adding resorts across North America as a hedge against weather.

Building on the lock-in achieved by the 'pass' model, CEO Rob Katz reportedly realized that the key to making money in the ski industry isn't necessarily finding more skiers—it's getting more money from the ones you already have. In 2018, for every daily visit to a resort by a skier, it collected $168 and paid only $135, a 20% profit margin. Half the revenue came from lift passes, and the rest from ancillary products and services.

On a continuing basis, Vail describes a strategic intent to invest in resort acquisition and facilities upgrade to improve guest experience. The aim is to drive increased visitation, ancillary sales, and price growth based on an enhanced value proposition. As it grows, the team behind its luxury RockResorts brand 'drives the design, marketing, sales and management of planned new developments, which combines our strong expertise in real estate development and resort management while leveraging our strong brands and customers'.

Vail uses technology extensively throughout its operations. According to Bloomberg:

> Every Vail pass or ticket is embedded with a radio frequency identification chip, which is automatically scanned like an E-ZPass at every one of the company's 430 lifts. Vail knows how much, where, and with whom each guest skis. The data are used to predict how likely the person is to return to a Vail resort. It's a Big Data play in an historically analogue industry, and the machinery will only get smarter every time Vail swallows another resort.

Cross-functional work helps deliver gains for Vail. IT and marketing teams work together to brainstorm and realize new customer apps, express day tickets (digital downloads), lift wait-time transparency, and the creation of a new on-mountain digital assistant to keep visitors informed and happy. The IT function makes sure that the digital support structure exists to make marketing's understanding of what matters most to customers a reality.

Servicing Vail's businesses are about 40,000 full-time or seasonal staff. Vail prescribes a set of foundational values to be lived out 'every day in everything we do—Serve Others, Do Right, Drive Value, Do Good, Be Safe, Have Fun'. Further, Vail identifies five stakeholder groups which shape its strategy and activities—guests, employees, communities, the natural environment, and shareholders. To help manage growth and consistency of experience across locations, Vail has agreements with a number of corporate partners—for example, Pepsi for drinks, Verizon for communications, Helly Hansen for clothing, and a zero-waste partner, Eco-care.

Vail Resorts was awarded the 2019 Golden Eagle Award for Environmental Excellence by the National Ski Areas Association. Further, in 2019 Vail Resorts was recognized by Forbes as one of 'America's 500 Best Employers' and a 'Best Employer for Diversity' for efforts to advance women in a traditionally male-dominated industry. Katz commented on the awards: 'For us, it's all about creating a strong leadership culture where we continuously invest in the development of every employee at every level of our company.'

Questions for discussion

1. How would you summarize Vail Resorts' business model? What are the key resources and capabilities supporting that business model? Which resources and capabilities are owned (by the firm, in-house) and which are not?
2. How would you summarize Vail Resorts' business strategy?
3. How would you summarize Vail Resorts' IT strategy? How core is its competence in technology to its business strategy?
4. How would you summarize Vail Resorts' financial strategy? How does it manage the flow of funds to support its business strategy?
5. How would you summarize Vail Resorts' HR strategy? How important is the right corporate culture to its business strategy?

Sources

http://news.vailresorts.com/corporate/vailresorts/vail-resorts-wins-golden-eagle-award-environmental-excellence.htm

https://www.prnewswire.com/news-releases/vail-resorts-named-one-of-americas-best-employers-by-forbes-300835166.html

https://www.bloomberg.com/news/articles/2019-05-07/vail-resorts-sees-run-of-relief-on-american-ski-season-pick-up

https://www.forbes.com/sites/danielnewman/2019/05/16/cios-and-cmos-achieving-convergence-of-infrastructure-and-analytics/#41b8ea297d6e

https://www.marketwatch.com/investing/stock/mtn/financials

Stock, K. (2019). One pass to ski them all. *Bloomberg Businessweek* (4605), 56–61.

Fisher, D. (2016). Peak Performance. *Forbes*, **198**(8), 44–6.

MarketLine Company Profile: Vail Resorts, Inc. (2017).

9.1 Introduction

A discussion of strategic management often focuses at the level of the corporate, or the whole organization (see Chapter 1). However, strategizing can occur within elements of an organization, in which the aims and activities of the rest of the organization form part of the context influencing what people do in relation to strategy. The same dynamic frameworks of strategy identified in Chapter 2 still apply, but the practitioners involved in making and realizing decisions are focused on specific functional concerns. In this chapter we consider the functional strategies which, particularly in medium and large organizations, will need to be in place to support the organizational strategy and can help to ensure that it is delivered as intended. We can think of functional strategy as the organizational strategies and plans prepared for various functional areas of the organization, such as financial strategy, human resources management (HRM) strategy, marketing strategy, operations strategy, and information technology (IT) strategy. Functional strategies can be both part of the organization's overall strategy, and a key element of 'cascading' or implementing the organizational strategy within each functional area. In this chapter, we explore each of the main areas of functional strategy in turn (finance, HRM, marketing, operations, and IT), summarizing what each type of strategy involves and highlighting some of the key factors to be considered when developing a successful strategy in each area. In our final section on managing strategic performance (Section 9.8), we look at tools such as the Balanced Scorecard which can help us to understand the relationship between the organization's overall strategy and the operation of its key functions; we also explore how the firm can use functional strategies in order to manage the implementation of organizational strategy.

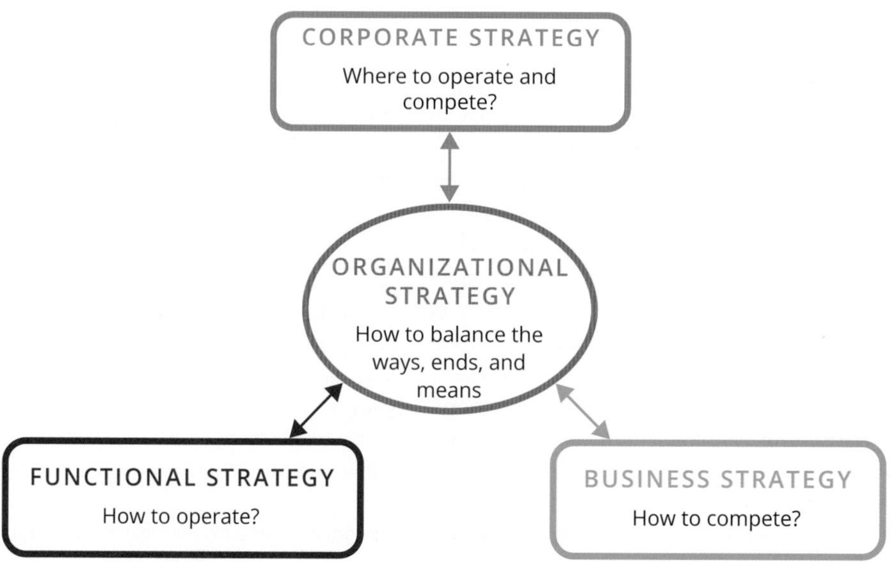

FIGURE 9.1 Components of organizational strategy.

9.2 **Types of functional strategy**

As discussed in Chapter 1, organizational strategy formation is made up of three main types of strategy (see also Figure 9.1):

- Corporate strategy: relating to the entire organization; asking the question, where should we operate and compete?
- Business strategy: strategies for individual business units or sectors of industry; asking how should we compete?
- Functional strategy: strategies for each function, such as finance, marketing, and operations; asking the question, how should we operate?

It is important to understand the role of functional strategy within the wider organizational strategy. However we can also break this functional strategy down into common areas (see Figure 9.2) in order to provide you with an understanding of how organizations should operate in order to be successful.

These common areas can be defined as follows:

- **Financial strategy**—this may include selecting the main source(s) of funding, the development of the organization's own funds, and so on.
- **HRM strategy**—this includes decisions about how staff are recruited and organized, such as the type of organizational structure, compensation system, etc.

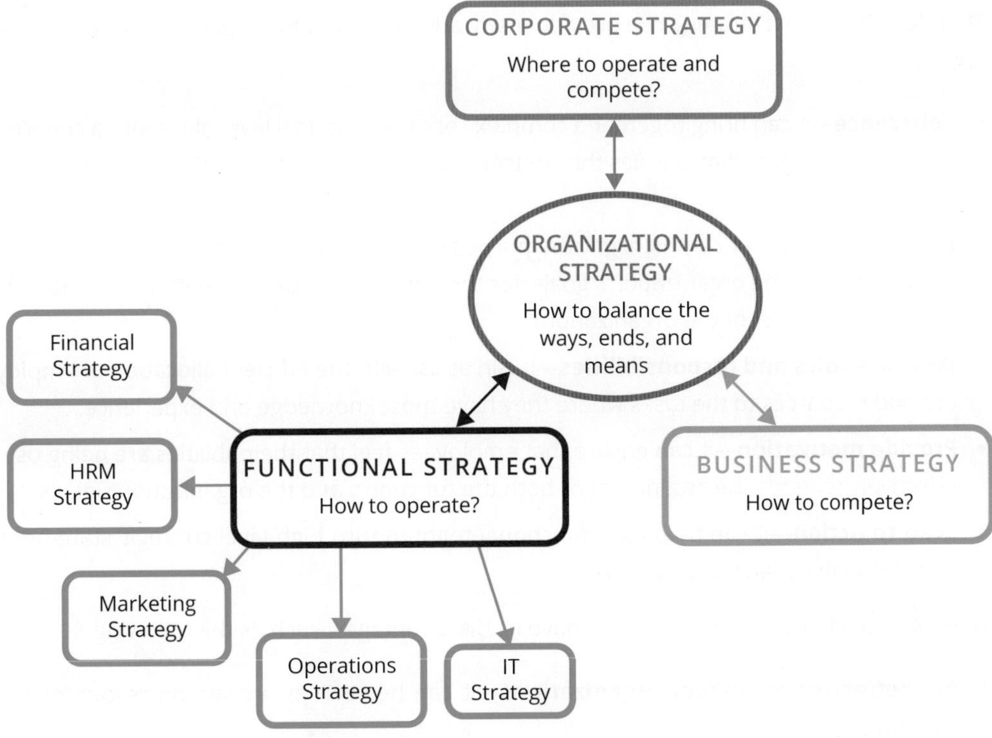

FIGURE 9.2 Components of functional strategy.

- **Marketing strategy**—this may include decisions around the pricing of products and services, their promotion and distribution, the image and public relations of the organization, and so on.
- **Operations strategy**—this may include the crucial 'make or buy' decisions that define what the company produces itself, what it purchases from suppliers or partners.
- **IT strategy**—this outlines how information technology should be used to help achieve the organization's goals; it may include an outline of current and future IT projects and initiatives, with timelines and milestones.

Advantages and disadvantages of functional strategy

Organizations with a strong functional strategy have recognized that it is a valuable tool in helping leaders and individuals within each function to understand the overarching strategy of the organization, and align with that strategy and help to deliver it. When many people encounter the notion of 'strategy' for the first time, they may assume that strategic thinking, formulation, and implementation are only for the senior executives of the organization. However, we might argue here that 'strategy is everyone's job', i.e. strategic thinkers are needed within every function of the organization—right from entry level. If a company can establish a difference at each level, or in each activity of the business, it is in a strong position to outperform its competitors. This highlights that functional and departmental leaders play a very demanding role, in that they must be in tune with the organization's senior management and strategy, and the needs and wants of customers, as well as the business conditions, environment, market, competitors, and so on.

Therefore functional strategy can provide many advantages to the organization, such as the following:

- **Coherence**—it can bring together a complex set of operational level plans into a coherent strategic statement that clarifies the contribution of each function to the overall organizational strategy.
- **Provide purpose**—it can highlight the purpose and contribution of each function to the achievement of the organization's goals, for the benefit of all parties (both within the function and in the rest of the organization).
- **Delegate roles and responsibilities**—it can assist with the efficient allocation of employees and resources to the tasks where they have most knowledge and experience.
- **Provide motivation**—it can ensure that employees feel that their abilities are being used effectively towards the attainment of both the function's and the organization's goals.
- **Lead to action**—it can help each functional team to turn high-level strategic statements into actionable plans.

However, functional strategy can also have its disadvantages, such as the following:

- **Be ineffective in smaller organizations**—it can be seen as a drain on resources and staff time.

- **Lead to potential conflicts**—it can cause conflict between the organization's overall strategy and one or more specific functional strategies, which must then be resolved.
- **Overstretch managers**—it can leave functional managers feeling that they are facing too many conflicting requests and that they are 'stretched too thinly' across a range of priorities.
- **Distract functional managers**—it can cause too much distraction for functional managers, to the point where they can lose sight of the main objectives of the organization.

To seek to maximize the potential advantages of functional strategy while avoiding the downsides, organizations might focus on developing actionable programmes in each functional area. These actionable programmes should be closely aligned with the higher-level strategic statements of their business unit and/or organization and help to bring such statements to life for staff in each function. For example, consider the Opening Case Study on Vail Resorts. Its financial strategy appears to include investing in and managing a portfolio of real estate, hotels, and other accommodation, and a sharp focus on revenue management with an innovative customer proposition—its early sale of passes for unlimited lift rides. Its HR strategy includes a clear focus on a set of foundational values to be lived out by all employees, and these values are seen as key to supporting the organization's mission. Its IT strategy includes gathering and analysing rich customer data by embedding chips in passes and tickets; the insights from this data are used to inform future marketing to customers and enhance the customer experience; and so on for each function. The point is that, in each functional area, there seems to be a clear sense of the purpose of that function and what it needs to do to support the overall organizational strategy. These functional strategies and action plans are not felt to be a distraction, a source of conflict, or a drain on resources; they are at the heart of what each function is about and exists to do.

In the next five sections, which together make up the main part of the chapter, we discuss each of the main areas of functional strategy in turn—financial strategy, HRM strategy, marketing strategy, operations strategy, and IT strategy.

9.3 **Financial strategy**

We have discussed what functional strategy is and considered some of its strengths and weaknesses. We now turn to exploring each of the types of functional strategy. We begin with financial strategy—a topic which is core to the start-up and ongoing operation of any successful organization. What is meant by financial strategy? And how does it add value to an organization's strategy? It is important for students of strategy to consider how organizations that are seeking to implement their strategies and track their progress need clear financial goals and metrics. Managers make important decisions on a daily basis, and those decisions have financial implications. Such decisions might include recruiting staff, planning a marketing campaign, scheduling the organization's operations, or approving investment in an IT project. In other words, they connect with all of the other aspects of functional strategy that we discuss in this chapter (HRM, marketing, operations, and IT). All of these decisions have important financial implications for the organization. In this section we consider what is meant by financial strategy in different kinds of organization, and how it can add value by supporting strategic planning and decision-making.

What is financial strategy?

Firstly, it is important to understand what financial strategy means. According to Bender (2014), financial strategy has two components:

- raising the funds needed by the organization in the most appropriate manner
- managing the employment of those funds within the organization, including whether to reinvest or distribute any profits, and how to do so in a way that is appropriate to the goals of the organization.

Imagine you are a manager in an organization, charged with making strategic decisions. In particular, your decisions are likely to impact upon the second component of Bender's definition of financial strategy, which concerns the appropriate use of funds within the organization. However, for a publicly listed company, we also need to remember the first component (raising funds), which leads us to consider the linkages between strategic decisions and the interests of shareholders, and hence the firm's relationship with capital markets. However, for any organization, a good financial strategy must reflect the interests of all of its internal and external stakeholders—as indeed the overall strategy should.

In Bender's definition of the two main components of financial strategy, she uses the term 'appropriate to the goals of the organization'. This highlights the importance of considering that the aim of the financial strategy is to add value for the organization, and not always to minimize costs. As such, Bender goes on to discuss the definitions of value in relation to a two-stage investment process for private firms as follows:

1. The **first step** in the investment process is for shareholders and others to decide to invest in a company. This leads to a definition of **investor value**, which reflects the required returns of the capital markets, and is mirrored in the financial value placed on the company's securities by the markets.
2. **The second step** in the investment process is the set of decisions by the organization with regard to how it invests in a portfolio of projects. This links to a definition of **corporate value**, which is the present value of the expected returns from a combination of the current business strategies and future investment programmes.

To put this another way, and elaborate on the first step in Bender's process: imagine that you are a venture capitalist—an investor who is interested in providing capital to a firm that is exhibiting high growth potential in return for an equity stake in the firm, as in *Dragon's Den* in the UK, or similar to *Shark Tank* in the USA. You might be interested in funding a start-up venture, or a small firm with an exciting business idea that wants to expand. What criteria will you be seeking to evaluate when you make your choice to invest in a particular firm? First, you will probably be looking for significant potential for earnings growth. However, venture capitalists have a range of questions in mind when choosing firms to invest in (Fried and Hisrich

1994; Mason and Stark 2004). Can the business idea be brought to market within a reasonable timescale (perhaps two or three years)? Can the business gain competitive advantage (see Chapter 8 for a longer discussion of competitive advantage)? And what is your opinion of the management of the firm? Do they have a good 'track record' in business? Do they exhibit leadership? Do they demonstrate an ability to identify risks and, when necessary, develop plans to deal with those risks?

Putting ourselves in the shoes of a venture capitalist can help to make the connection between the two stages in Bender's investment process. Most managers will tend to focus on the second step of improving the organization's (internal) investments in its project portfolio to make it a 'better business'. However, the aims of corporate financial strategy, as defined by Bender (2014), remind us to focus on the first step as well—on creating (external) shareholder value, and making the organization a better investment for shareholders or other potential investors. In the case of GE (Case Example 9.1), we shall see the extreme pressure put on CEOs who are not seen to be delivering in this way.

Drivers of value

Bender (2014) suggests that, from the perspective of financial strategy, there are seven drivers (based on Rappaport 1998) which can be utilized to create value. Bender argues that this is a very useful model, which is widely adopted to underpin most corporate valuations, and applied to explore sensitivity analysis and to evaluate synergies in mergers and acquisitions. The seven drivers can be outlined as follows:

1. **Increase sales growth**, for example launching new products or finding new markets for existing products (for further discussion, see Ansoff's matrix in Chapter 10).
2. **Increase the operating profit margin** (the relationship between money flowing in and expenses), for example cutting costs or achieving economies of scale (discussed further in Chapter 10), perhaps at the same time as boosting revenue.
3. **Reduce incremental investment in capital expenditure**, meaning the funds used to acquire and upgrade physical assets such as buildings, equipment, and technology.
4. **Reduce investment in working capital**, meaning the amount of money you need to expand your business and meet short-term responsibilities and expenses.
5. **Reduce the cost of capital**, i.e. the cost of the firm's funds.
6. **Increase the time period of competitive advantage**, such as the time period over which the business is expected to generate returns on incremental investment which exceed its cost of capital.
7. **Reduce the cash tax rate**, i.e. tax payments over a particular time period.

It is important to note that, if we look across different businesses, different drivers will be more or less important. In the hotel business, we may find that sales (i.e. the hotel occupancy rate) is the most important driver, because of high fixed costs of property ownership in that sector. However, for a bank lending to corporate clients, profits are derived from a slim margin between the rate at which the bank borrows money and the rate at which it lends money to its customers. Therefore the bank may create more value by seeking to improve interest margins and reducing its operating costs than by seeking to increase the volume of sales (lending).

So how do we identify the key drivers of value in a particular organization? Researchers offer advice on this (e.g. Marr et al. 2004), with most approaches to identifying value drivers starting from the resource-based view of the firm, given the importance of understanding an organization's resources and capabilities (see Chapter 6 for a longer discussion) when considering how it adds value. The work of Amit and Zott (2001) is particularly important to today's organizations in that it explores new business models in the digital economy, and argues that managers should focus on four interdependent dimensions of value creation:

- **Efficiency**: the greater the transaction efficiency gains that are enabled by a particular e-business, the lower the costs and hence the more valuable it will be.
- **Complementarities**: e-businesses can leverage the potential for value creation by offering bundles of complementary products and services to their customers.
- **Lock-in**: the greater the switching costs (i.e. the costs of switching to a rival firm), the lower the likelihood of customers and strategic partners migrating to competitors.
- **Novelty**: e-businesses innovate in the ways in which they do business, i.e. in the structuring of transactions.

Consider the company in our Opening Case Study, Vail Resorts. One of their value drivers is clearly 'novelty', in other words the introduction of the 'Epic Pass' (embedded with a radio frequency identification chip) offering unlimited lift rides at their ski resorts, and bringing valuable revenue before the height of the season by requiring skiers to buy early. Yet half of Vail's revenue comes from ancillary products and services, suggesting that they have also given careful thought to 'complementarities'. Their use of IT is likely to allow developments in the 'efficiency' category, and their focus on understanding and delighting their customers is intended to encourage loyalty and repeat purchase.

A more recent study has both confirmed Amit and Zott's (2001) dimensions of value creation, and found evidence of how they may interplay and reinforce one another. Visnjic et al. (2017) gave the example of Caterpillar (a leading manufacturer of construction and mining equipment, engines, etc.). Caterpillar collects valuable data on the performance of its equipment, such as engines; this can support powerful data analytics and give insight into the performance of a machine—a 'novelty' value driver. However, it can also represent an 'efficiency' value driver by supporting better cost management of expensive equipment over its lifetime, alongside other benefits such as better predictions of the future maintenance requirements of the machinery.

Finally, Marr (2005) advocates using Kaplan and Norton's strategy maps (Kaplan and Norton 2004a,b) to identify key resources; we will return to this point in Section 9.8 on managing strategic performance. But having discussed how an organization can create value, we should now think about how an organization protects the value it has created, which takes us to the topic of risk management.

Risk management

Risk is the possibility of losing something of value. Bender (2014) suggests that risk management is an important part of financial strategy. By changing the business risk profile of the organization, it is possible to change its financial strategy. If business risks are high, then it is likely that profits and cash flows will be volatile. This implies that lenders may be reluctant to lend to the organization unless rates are high, in which case the organization should probably avoid borrowing very much. A company may choose to adopt risk management tools such as insuring against adverse conditions, hedging currency flows, or buying/selling forward commodities to protect prices. Such tools can reduce the variability in profits and cash flows.

Kaplan and Mikes (2012) argue that a practical approach to risk management is provided by the following framework, which begins with the identification of three categories of risk:

- **Preventable risks** arise within the organization; they are controllable and should be eliminated or avoided by active prevention and monitoring of processes and actions. They include risks from the breakdown of processes, or from the behaviour of managers when taking actions that are unauthorized, illegal, unethical, incorrect, or inappropriate.
- **Strategy risks** are not necessarily undesirable. An organization will sometimes accept some risks as it seeks to generate superior returns from its strategy. They should be managed via a system where the probability of such events materializing is calculated, and actions planned to improve the organization's ability to manage the consequences.
- **External risks** arise outside the organization and are beyond its control, such as natural and political disasters and major macro-economic shifts. Management should focus on identifying these risks in advance, and mitigating their impact on the organization.

Kaplan and Mikes (2012) suggest that firms can enhance their risk management processes with the support of experts (independent and/or embedded in the organization), and by linking their discussion of risk to the organization's Balanced Scorecard (see Section 9.8 on managing strategic performance).

Financial strategy in different types of organization

Much of what we discuss in this section is applicable to all sorts of organizations. However, some of it only applies to publicly listed firms. In such a firm, the shareholders own the company and it is run by the directors. This raises a number of issues. First, there is a potential conflict of agency between the directors and the shareholders; directors' actions may not always be in line with shareholders' goals. Secondly, most publicly listed companies have thousands of shareholders, and in such situations it is not possible for the directors to determine and act upon the goals of so many individuals. Therefore we make assumptions about a generic 'shareholder value' as the company's target for performance—and we note that if a listed company's share price does not perform as well as expected, it may become a target for a threatened takeover bid. For example, in 2018 Melrose Industries, a London-based company that specializes in buying underperforming businesses, acquired GKN, a British multinational automotive and aerospace components company, for around £8 billion. About a year later the deal hit the headlines again when Melrose announced plans to close a GKN factory, leading to accusations of 'asset stripping' (*The Guardian* 2019). Critics were clearly questioning whether, if we look beyond a narrow definition of shareholder value, the steps taken by Melrose were in the interests of a wider set of stakeholders, such as the employees of the GKN factory in question.

As an alternative to the situation in publicly listed firms, consider the situation in a private company, which is rather different. The company is often owned by its directors. Where this is not the case, there is still likely to be a strong link between the owners and the directors, so the directors can still communicate directly with the key stakeholders to discuss their goals. The main objectives may be financial security for family shareholders, for example, and/or the creation and maintenance of a business that will be passed on to future generations of the family. Such companies may be reluctant to take on debt; and they may be in a strong position to respond to the threat of a hostile takeover bid. For example, for a number of years, LVMH (or Louis Vuitton, the luxury goods conglomerate) pursued Hermès, the French high fashion manufacturer that has been led by the same family since it was founded in the nineteenth century. LVMH slowly acquired shares in Hermès in what was seen as the start of a hostile takeover. Hermès responded by, amongst other things, 'locking up' just over 50% of its shares in a holding company, and challenging LVMH's actions in the French courts (Adams 2014). These tactics have been successful in supporting Hermès in its desire to remain as an independent family-led firm—but such challenges to private companies are not unusual, and illustrate the need to align financial strategy with the overall organizational strategy in different ways in different types of organization.

Linking financial strategy with business/corporate strategy

In this section, we have identified some of the important connections between financial strategy and the overall business strategy, including the impact of investment decisions in key strategic projects and the implications of those decisions for the organization's performance. We have explored the creation of value from a financial perspective (discussing the seven drivers), and the need to protect value once it has been created by paying attention to risk management. We have also touched on the different views of financial strategy that may emerge in different types of organization, such as publicly listed and private firms. In Case Example 9.1, we explore the financial strategy of GE (General Electric Company, a US-based multinational firm), before going on to consider the other functional strategies that organizations must consider and their interconnections—human resource management (Section 9.4), marketing (Section 9.5), operations (Section 9.6), and IT (Section 9.7).

In this section, we have considered key aspects of financial strategy, such as drivers of value and risk management. Case Example 9.1 gives us the opportunity to consider the financial strategy of GE, which includes a change in approach to paying dividends to shareholders and a sharp focus on managing the firm's costs. But GE also needs to consider changing other important elements of its business, such as how it rewards senior executives and how it holds staff accountable for targets to be met. This illustrates that financial strategy is pursued alongside other elements of functional strategy, such as human resource management—and we turn to this next.

CASE EXAMPLE 9.1 THE RIGHT MECHANIC? FLANNERY UNVEILS HIS STRATEGY TO REVIVE GENERAL ELECTRIC (GE)

General Electric is an American multinational conglomerate operating within a huge range of industries including aviation, healthcare, power, digital technologies, renewable energy, transportation, and capital. In 2001 GE's market value was over $400 billion, thanks to Jack Welch, the former CEO; during his tenure the company's value had risen by 4000%.

Following Welch's departure, Jeffrey Immelt became the new CEO in September 2001, four days before the attacks on the World Trade Center in New York. This, combined with the global financial crisis that followed some years later, had serious impacts on the aviation and financial services arms of the company. By 2018 the company hit a low point and was valued at only $60 billion.

GE leaders employed a strategy that drove productivity and cut costs. The company had a history of aggressive accounting and a reliance on multiple accounting standards, as well as opaque long-term service contracts. Financial analysts were unhappy with the lack of openness. Where Welch preferred organic growth, Immelt employed a different strategy focusing instead on acquisitions. Immelt's acquisition of large energy companies coincided with low oil and gas prices, which placed GE in serious financial trouble. In August 2017 he was succeeded by John Flannery, and in October 2017 the company revealed terrible third-quarter results, prompting Flannery to announce the need for urgent change. In November 2017 he unveiled his strategy to save GE. The plan had three main components: slash costs, sharpen the culture, and shrink to the core. In terms of costs, Flannery planned to cut a total of $3 billion in annual spending, reduce GE's dividend by half, and save money in the long term by taking advantage of low interest rates and borrowing £6 billion to repay pension obligations.

The second focus was on culture: Flannery said: 'Our culture needs to be driven by mutual candor and intense execution, and the accountability that must come with that.' Under Immelt, employees had complained that they felt adrift, and whilst innovation had been prioritized, investments in accountability and targets were not always as prominent as they should have been. Flannery also planned to realign pay for top executives and to reform the board of directors.

Flannery also pledged to sell $20 billion in assets. He sold GE's healthcare unit for $1 billion, and then announced that the majority of GE's transportation business would be sold for $11.1 billion. By disposing of other units as well as these, Flannery met the $20 billion goal. However, as GE had assets worth over $300 billion, this was a drop in the ocean. GE's shares fell by 12% following the plan's unveiling. Analysts were underwhelmed at the extent of the divestments, with one pointing out that $10 billion had already been spent on restructuring with little impact made to the bottom line.

Flannery's tenure was short; in October 2018 he was replaced by Laurence Culp. According to *The Economist*, while many felt that Flannery's instincts had appeared to be sound, and his principles of curbing costs, cultural clarity, and cutting to the core were surely the right ones, he was perhaps punished for his reluctance to wield the knife more aggressively. Culp served on the board under Flannery and so may not drastically change Flannery's approach. However, given that 90% of his annual salary and bonuses is contingent on GE's stock price rising between 50% and 150%, there may be some drastic plans in the works.

Questions for discussion

1. How would you summarize GE's financial strategy under CEO John Flannery?
2. How do you think GE's financial strategy under John Flannery differed from the company's financial strategy under the two previous CEOs, Jeffrey Immelt and Jack Welch?
3. How would you summarize GE's approach to strategic HR issues under John Flannery? Make sure that you discuss corporate culture and the CEO's approach to top management, for example.
4. How would you summarize GE's business strategy under John Flannery? Are there any

Continued

9

aspects of the strategy that seem to be missing, or are not covered in the extract above? What else would you like to know, before commenting on Flannery's approach?

5. Why do you think John Flannery's plans were criticized by some commentators, as reported in the extract above? Explain briefly whether or not you agree with the criticisms, giving reasons.

Sources

Adapted from *The Economist*, 16 November 2017, with additions from *Bloomberg*, 1 October 2018.

https://www.economist.com/business/2017/11/16/flannery-unveils-his-strategy-to-revive-ge

https://www.bloomberg.com/news/articles/2018-10-01/ge-taps-culp-to-replace-ceo-flannery-will-miss-profit-guidance

https://www.kornferry.com/institute/organizational-culture-ge-john-flannery

9.4 Human resource management strategy

In the previous section we discussed key aspects of financial strategy. We will now move on to the next of the functional strategies: human resource management (HRM) strategy. What is meant by HRM strategy? This aspect of functional strategy is generally considered to include an organization's plans for managing its people, their performance, and their training and development. It also covers the organization's culture, and its approach to determining how people and culture fit into the organization's future growth strategies and plans. We will explore what HRM strategy involves, how it can be framed around five key questions, and how it links to the organization's overall business strategy.

9

What is HRM strategy?

Human resource management has been defined as the process through which management builds the workforce and tries to create the human performance that the organization needs (Boxall and Purcell 2016). This definition immediately raises questions about the fit between the activities of the HR function and the organization's overall strategy. Boxall and Purcell (2016) argue that strategic analysis in HRM can be framed around five questions:

- **Talent**: can the firm recruit and retain the people it needs?
- **Performance**: is the model of HRM helping to deliver the kind of performance that the organization needs?
- **Strategic fit**: does the organization have a set of HRM models that fits its environment, its goals, and its configuration of activities?
- **Dynamic**: what economic and sociopolitical changes are likely to affect the firm's HR strategy and how should it prepare for them?
- **HR function**: how can HR departments contribute more strategically?

Managing HRM strategy

We will go through each of Boxall and Purcell's five questions in turn to explore how HRM strategy can be managed.

Managing 'talent' via HRM strategy

In Chapter 1 we introduced the idea that when considering how to build competitive advantage, an organization can use the RBV (or resource-based view of the firm, discussed further in Chapter 6) to consider the ways in which valuable resources can be built and barriers to imitation can be created. HRM issues are, of course, a very important element of the RBV perspective. Therefore we begin with the first of the five questions identified above, which is sometimes summarized as 'talent management'.

When we think about identifying and building the core distinctive capabilities of the organization, the role of the firm's workers and their skills has to be central to our thinking. The HR strategy of the organization should help it to survive, thrive, and 'add value'. This leads to key questions (Boxall and Purcell 2016), such as how to enhance the motivation and development of those individuals whose human capital is core to the firm's mission and renewal. And, how to build the kinds of organizational processes and/or social capital that enable individuals to function effectively. Therefore a first key aspect of HR strategy must be to build and maintain a workforce of appropriate quantity and quality. Such 'talent management' must be a critical concern of strategic HRM, even when the labour market may contain a surplus of jobseekers (Collings and Mellahi 2009; Lanvin and Evans 2013).

Managing 'performance' via HRM Strategy

If an appropriate workforce can be built, attention must next turn to the achievements of the workforce, including operating and financial outcomes such as the levels of productivity and quality that the organization can reach. In attempts to explain how HRM affects performance, the AMO model is a popular starting point (Boxall and Purcell 2016; Vroom 1964); it argues that performance depends on the individual's **ability**, **motivation**, and **opportunity** to perform (Blumberg and Pringle 1982; Guest 1997). Hence the role of any HRM process is to put in place the policies and practices that will enhance employee ability, motivation, and opportunity to perform (Boselie et al. 2005; Jiang et al. 2012). For example, a lot of attention has been paid to Google's policies of offering employees free meals, free shuttles to work, and other 'perks' (Quora 2018), which may result in staff feeling more highly valued, spending more time at work, and socializing with colleagues—perhaps leading to higher levels of productivity which benefit their employer. And in 2018, London transport organization TfL came top of a survey to find the best employers in the UK for work–life balance (McCulloch 2018), having introduced policies on flexible working hours and generous holidays for staff.

Managing 'strategic fit' via HRM Strategy

Turning to the third question around strategic fit, HR strategy must also reflect the context in which it is implemented, such as the type of organization in question. Let's briefly consider a number of examples—manufacturing, services, and public sector—in order to understand the variety of issues that HR strategy may need to address.

First, we might look at the context of manufacturing. HR strategy in manufacturing has had to address many challenges in recent decades, such as the development of lean manufacturing (Ohno 1988), a philosophy that combines high utilization of manufacturing capacity with low inventory, eliminating the buffers built into traditional approaches to mass production (Womack et al. 1990). In other words, where a traditional manufacturing process might have a stock of items waiting to be worked on at each stage in the process, a lean approach demands the elimination of any 'waste' so that the organization can focus only on activities that are directly 'adding value'. Lean production calls for the application of skills that are less important in traditional mass production, such as technical skills in the diagnosis of waste and quality problems, and team-working skills (Sterling and Boxall 2013).

Following on from lean manufacturing, the idea of agile manufacturing has also gained traction in many businesses. Agile manufacturing focuses on thriving in an unpredictable environment, reflecting the fact that most organizations now operate in dynamic markets with fast-changing customer requirements. Agility demands that staff are responsive to the market and able to integrate operational information and processes, for example across different partners such as suppliers, to create systems that are reliable, flexible, and capable of rapid change (Krishnamurthy and Yauch 2007; Soltan and Mostafa 2015; Yusuf et al. 1999). HRM strategy has an important role to play in building and mobilizing such core competencies. An exciting example is that of Wikspeed, a registered car manufacturing company that developed a functioning prototype within just three months (much faster than a 'traditional' approach to designing a new car) using an agile approach based on self-organizing teams and effective horizontal communications (Denning 2012).

Turning to the context of service industries, we can identify a number of differences between services and other industry sectors, leading to a different set of challenges for HRM strategy and the management of performance (Boxall and Purcell 2016). First, service firms are typically much more labour intensive than manufacturing firms (Frenkel 2000). Secondly, services differ from manufacturing in terms of the balance between tangibility and intangibility in the offering to the customer (Bowen and Ford 2002). Thirdly, services are typically produced and consumed as and when consumers demand them, and fourthly consumers are involved in co-producing a range of services (Lovelock et al. 2010). Consider the example of Vail Resorts, our Opening Case Study. With a workforce of 40,000, both full-time and seasonal, the challenges of managing performance are considerable for Vail. One approach that they adopt is the clear prescription of a set of values to be lived out 'every day in everything we do—Serve Others, Do Right, Drive Value, Do Good, Be Safe, Have Fun'. These values focus employees on key issues, from corporate value, safety, and customer service to the needs of a wider range of stakeholders such as the environment.

When considering service industries, we should not overlook the importance of HR strategy in the public sector. Under the 'New Public Management' (Greener 2013), HRM is regarded as 'one of the key ways that an organization can achieve a competitive edge over its rivals' (Greener 2013:197). This comprises aspects such as the determination of performance standards, measurement to ensure compliance, and intervention when performance falls below the expected standards; proactive recruitment of key individuals, sometimes from a global labour market; training and development, with a focus on new ways of working, the constant updating of skills and knowledge; and in some instances the adoption of performance-related pay as an element of individual appraisal (Boxall and Purcell 2016).

Managing in a dynamic environment via HRM strategy

Many organizations seek to anticipate important changes in the external environment—social, political, economic, and so forth—and to plan initiatives to help the organization to prepare for such changes. However, it is widely argued that many change initiatives are often judged to be unsuccessful. Ulrich (1997) suggests that the HR function has an important role as an agent of change, helping to identify and implement processes for change. This role, as a change agent, is highly strategic: 'the actions of change agents include identifying and framing problems, building relationships of trust, solving problems, and creating—and fulfilling—action plans' (Ulrich 1997:31).

According to Ulrich, HR professionals must help their organization to meet new objectives, and to do so quickly. They must enhance the ability of the organization to improve the design and implementation of its initiatives, and to reduce cycle time in all organizational activities. A key step in the process of change is to identify key success factors for building the capacity to change. This requires HR professionals to assist with aligning the internal culture to the desired market identity, understanding the process for creating a shared mindset, having a model of change that is used throughout the business, and keeping the pressure on the business to respond to change, even in the midst of creating new strategies (Ulrich 1997). Consider the example of GE (Case Study 9.1): the CEO identified a need to change the culture, to 'realign pay' for top executives, and to 'reform' the board of directors. Yet, the firm's poor performance suggests that the senior team were struggling to change the organization to meet its new goals and strategies in a challenging and dynamic environment.

How HRM can contribute strategically

Ulrich (1997) argues that HR will play a 'strategic partner' role when it has the ability to translate business strategy into action. To achieve this role, Ulrich advocates the design of an organizational 'architecture' and the assessment or audit of the organization against this architecture to identify areas of strength and weakness. Moreover, HR should be playing a role in leading improvement practices and setting priorities (Ulrich 1997). In this world view, HR managers collaborate with line managers to turn strategies into action.

Such advice can perhaps be fleshed out by considering the strategic role of HR in particularly challenging contexts. Consider the context of a multidivisional company, where HR strategy is likely to face a particular set of issues. For example, in such an organization, HR strategies may be required to deal with the restructuring and downsizing associated with strategic projects (discussed further in Chapter 10) such as acquisitions, mergers, and divestments (Boxall and Purcell 2016). In a multinational firm, HR strategy must address the tensions between global integration and local adaptation or decentralization (e.g. Dowling et al. 2013; Evans et al. 2002). Ulrich's (1997) notions of designing an organizational architecture, and assessing the organization against the desired framework, may be particularly pertinent in such a demanding setting where organizational strategy is facing many pressures and forces for change.

Linking HRM strategy with business/corporate strategy

To conclude, we return to the key issue of people as a critical (human) resource in any organization, and how resources are combined into capabilities to support the organization's strategy. Ulrich and Smallwood (2004) shed some light on the importance of organizational capabilities in a strategic HR context, and how leaders can evaluate the organization's capabilities and build the ones needed to create value for the business. They advocate the use of a 'capabilities audit' to build a high-level picture of an organization's strengths and areas for improvement (see Table 9.1). They suggest that such an audit is a powerful way to evaluate intangible assets and render them concrete and measurable.

In terms of how to proceed, Ulrich and Smallwood suggest that the first step is to select the focus for your study—it might be the whole organization, or just a business unit, division, region, etc. The second step is to assess the organization's performance against each of the 11 organizational capabilities proposed in Table 9.1. However, they note that these 11 areas are just a guide; the questions posed can be flexed to reflect the overall strategy of the organization. The assessment, via a survey, can be done by a small team or a large number of staff, depending on

TABLE 9.1 **How to perform a capabilities audit**

Organizational capabilities	Questions	Assessments	Ranking
Talent	Do our employees have the competencies and the commitment required to deliver the business strategy in question?		
Speed	Can we move quickly to make important things happen fast?		
Shared mindset and coherent brand identity	Do we have a culture or identity that reflects what we stand for and how we work? Is it shared by both customers and employees?		
Accountability	Does high performance matter to the extent that we can ensure execution of strategy?		
Collaboration	How well do we collaborate to gain both efficiency and leverage?		
Learning	Are we good at generating new ideas with impact and generalizing those ideas across boundaries?		
Leadership	Do we have a leadership brand that directs managers on which results to deliver and how to deliver them?		
Customer connectivity	Do we form enduring relationships of trust with targeted customers?		
Strategic unity	Do our employees share an intellectual, behavioural, and procedural agenda for our strategy?		
Innovation	How well do we innovate in product, strategy, channel, service, and administration?		
Efficiency	Do we reduce costs by closely managing processes, people, and projects?		

Source: From Ulrich, D. and Smallwood, N. (2004). Capitalizing on capabilities, *Harvard Business Review*, June, 119–27. By permission of Harvard Business Publishing.

the organization's particular needs. Respondents can make their assessments on a scale from 0 (worst) to 10 (best); they can also rank the capabilities in terms of improvement needed, where 1 represents the highest priority, 2 represents next highest, and so on.

To illustrate the power of the suggested approach, Ulrich and Smallwood give the example of InterContinental Hotels Group (IHG). A capabilities audit was undertaken by their executive team (see Figure 9.3 for a summary). Respondents were asked about the firm's 'actual state' and 'desired state' with regard to a set of key capabilities for IHG (similar to the 11 capabilities listed in Table 9.1, but adapted to meet the particular needs of IHG). The audit enabled the firm to identify areas where the respondents felt that there was a large gap between the current performance and the desired future performance of the firm. In the data, there was no difference between the scores for actual and desired capabilities categorized as 'shared mindset', and 'accountability', in which case, efforts can focus on efficiency and cost reduction. However, Figure 9.3 illustrates the data where there was a difference between actual and desired capabilities.

IHG's capabilities audit indicated that there were two priority areas where the team felt that current performance fell short and most investment was needed: 'collaboration' and 'speed'. They identified another four areas where moderate investment was needed: 'execution', 'leadership', 'talent', and 'learning'. Finally, the audit indicated two areas where the team felt that IHG was already on target: 'shared mindset' and 'accountability'. The results of such an audit can be used to summarize an organization's actual and desired position, and prioritize future attention and investment in relation to any of the key areas discussed in this section and highlighted by an organization's business strategy—managing talent, performance, strategic fit, and HR's contribution to strategy in a dynamic environment.

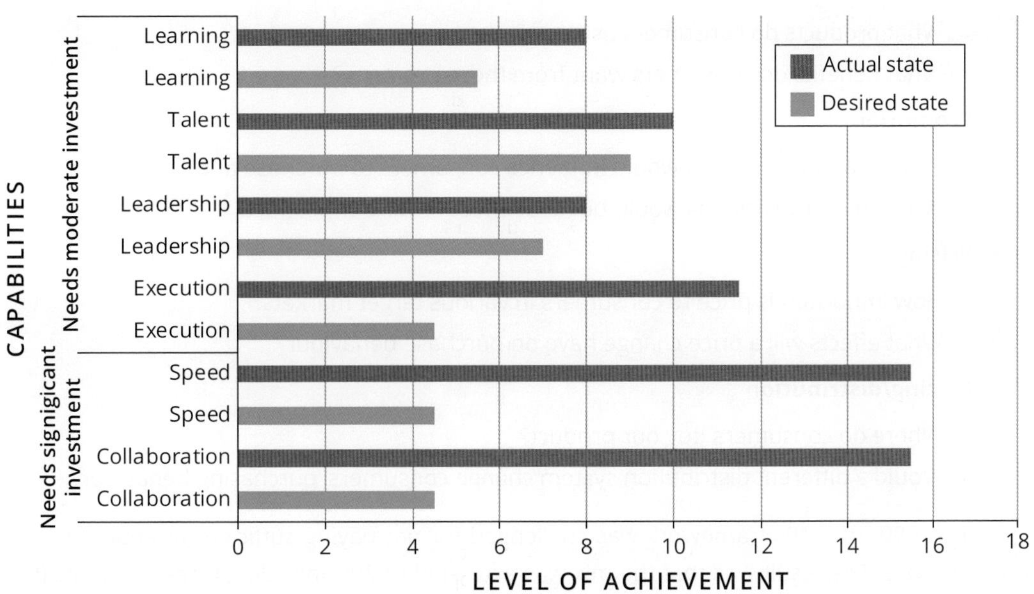

FIGURE 9.3 A snapshot of IHG's capabilities audit results. Source: From Ulrich, D. and Smallwood, N. (2004). Capitalizing on capabilities, *Harvard Business Review*, June, 119–27. By permission of Harvard Business Publishing.

9.5 **Marketing strategy**

Having considered two important areas of functional strategy (financial and HRM), we now turn to a third—marketing strategy. What is meant by marketing strategy and how does it link to the organization's business strategy? A marketing strategy for a firm aiming to make a profit sets out the firm's overall approach to reaching people and turning them into customers of the product or service that it offers; as well as its approach to retaining existing customers. A sound marketing strategy will be based on market research and a good knowledge of the firm's existing and target customers. When the managers of a company develop its marketing strategy, they have to think about the product or service that they are promising to deliver to customers, and how they plan to do so. This is typically followed by the development of a more detailed marketing plan, covering types and timing of marketing activities, key marketing messages, and so on.

What is marketing strategy?

A marketing strategy can be defined as 'a plan designed to influence exchanges to achieve organizational objectives', and 'typically ... intended to increase the probability or frequency of consumer behaviours, such as frequenting particular stores or purchasing particular products' (Peter et al. 1999: 10). The marketing plan is often accomplished by developing and presenting marketing 'mixes' directed at selected target markets. A marketing mix consists of elements such as product, promotion, pricing, and placing/distribution (Borden 1964), known as the 4Ps framework. Therefore Kotler and Armstrong (2017) argue that a marketing strategy needs to be based on a good understanding of a range of consumer issues that fall within these four Ps, such as:

- **Product**
  - What products do consumers use now?
  - What benefits do consumers want from these products?
- **Promotion**
  - What promotion appeal would influence consumers to purchase and use our product?
  - What advertising claims would be most effective for our product?
- **Pricing**
  - How important is price to consumers in various target markets?
  - What effects will a price change have on purchase behaviour?
- **Placing/distribution**
  - Where do consumers buy our product?
  - Would a different distribution system change consumers' purchasing behaviour?

In the 1980s, the 4Ps framework was challenged for not paying sufficient attention to customer service. The result was that the mix was extended to 7Ps, including three elements (the service mix) that better reflect service delivery: people, process, and physical evidence (Booms and Bitner 1981). The additional Ps can be illustrated as:

- **People**
  - What is the role of our staff in delivering our services to our customers?
  - What training and skills do they require? What recruitment policies should we adopt?
- **Process**
  - How should we design the process of delivering our services to our customers?
  - What role does IT play in the process of service delivery?
- **Physical evidence**
  - How do our customers experience our brand?
  - How is this experience embodied and delivered, for example through our staff, our product packaging, or our website?

Chaffey and Ellis-Chadwick (2019) summarize the 7Ps in an era of digital marketing (Figure 9.4). For example, they suggest that, under 'product', if a firm provides its services via the internet, its staff should understand customer behaviour, such as when the customer uses the online service. The firm then needs to consider factors such as the availability of the service and the provision of customer service and online support.

The elements of the marketing mix, summarized in Figure 9.4, can give us an insight into the key needs and wants of existing and potential customers. However, many markets are large, with diverse customer requirements. Next, we discuss how marketers can divide a broad market into sub-groups based on the shared characteristics of some customers. The elements of the marketing mix can then be varied to meet the distinct needs of different sub-groups or segments, enabling the organization to build a more targeted approach to marketing to its chosen customers.

USING THE INTERNET TO VARY THE MARKETING MIX

PRODUCT	PROMOTION	PRICE	PLACE	PEOPLE	PROCESS	PHYSICAL EVIDENCE
• Quality • Image • Branding • Features • Variants • Mix • Support • Customer service • Use occasion • Availability • Warranties	• Marketing communications • Personal promotion • Sales promotion • PR • Branding • Direct marketing	• Positioning • List • Discounts • Credit • Payment methods • Free or value-added elements	• Trade channels • Sales support • Channel number • Segmented channels	• Individuals on marketing activities • Individuals on customer contact • Recruitment • Culture/ image • Training and skills • Remuneration	• Customer focus • Business-led • IT-supported • Design features • Research and development	• Sales/staff contact experience of brand • Product packaging • Online experience

FIGURE 9.4 Using the internet to vary the marketing mix. Source: Reproduced with permission from Chaffey, D. and Ellis-Chadwick, F. (2019). *Digital Marketing: Strategy, Implementation and Practice* (7th edn). © Pearson Education Limited 2012, 2016, 2019.

Market segmentation

The buyers in a market typically differ in terms of their needs and wants. Companies use a process known as market segmentation to divide large heterogeneous markets into smaller segments. This is an integral part of marketing strategy (Baines et al. 2019). Market segmentation can allow a company to reach different segments of customers more efficiently and effectively with products and services that meet their varying needs. Table 9.2 outlines some of the criteria that can be used to segment customer markets.

For instance, in Case Example 9.2 (later in this section), we will explore Fiat Chrysler's approach to the segmentation of the global car market. In terms of geography, the company is clearly very well aware of the different needs and preferences of customers in different parts of the world—Europe, USA, China, and so on. Via their product range, with brands such as Fiat, Jeep, Alfa Romeo, Maserati, and Ferrari, the company aims to explore the needs and wants of consumers on a range of variables (demographic, behavioural, etc.)—from mass market to luxury cars, including SUVs, the 'pint-sized' Fiat 500, and so on.

As an example of a segmented **digital** marketing campaign, consider the targeting of young business professionals in the UK by the *Financial Times* (*Financial Times* 2014). In terms of the dimensions of the marketing mix (introduced above), their mix of 'product', 'place', and 'promotion' was all carefully chosen. The goal was to tempt readers (typically aged 24–34) who are unlikely to buy the print version of the newspaper, likely to be time poor, digital savvy, and tend to access news on the go, to use FT.com on their mobile phones, under the tagline 'Find your personalised Financial Times at FT.com'. The campaign ran at digital poster sites at London commuter stations alongside a digital media acquisition campaign across Facebook and Twitter, and it stressed a business-focused offering drawing on technology and exciting creative formats. This segmentation exercise sits at the intersection of a number of segmentation variables—geographic (focused on London commuters in the UK), demographic (many of the variables listed above, including age and level of education), psychographic (likely to appeal to young professionals with career aspirations), and behavioural (given patterns of accessing the news and likely benefits sought, etc.).

TABLE 9.2 **Criteria that can be used to segment customer markets**

Segmentation criteria	Example
Demographic	Age, sex/gender or gender identity, life-cycle stage, income, occupation, education, religion, ethnicity, social class
Geographic	Nations, regions, states, counties, cities, neighbourhoods, population density (urban, suburban, rural), climate, customs and traditions
Life stage	Childhood, adulthood, young couples, retired people
Psychographic (lifestyles)	Social demographic or culture, activities, interests, personality
Behavioural	Occasions, benefits, user status, usage (frequency, time of usage, or situations), loyalty status, media channels used

Source: based on Baines, P., Fill, C., Rosengren, S., and Antonetti, P. (2019). *Marketing*. Oxford: Oxford University Press.

Having identified some potentially attractive market segments to target, marketers need to understand how the customers in that segment make decisions about which products or services to try, and we turn to this issue next.

Understanding the decision-making behaviour of customers

To develop effective marketing strategies, and to reach a particular segment of customers that they wish to target, marketers also need to know the type of problem-solving process their customers use to make purchase decisions. These processes can vary widely. Marketers who want to target several customer segments with different problem-solving processes may have to develop multiple strategies to influence the different decision outcomes. A brief overview of three widely cited choice behaviours is given below (see, for example, Betsch et al. (2002) and Sirakaya and Woodside (2005) for a discussion of the decision-making behaviour of travellers/tourists).

- **Routinized choice behaviour** may occur when consumers think they know all they need to know about a product category, and are not motivated to search for more information. Their choice behaviour is based on a learned decision plan stored in their memory. Marketers of established brands may want consumers to continue to follow a routine choice approach, as they are already well positioned in the consumers' minds. Marketers of new brands, or brands with low market share, may be seeking to interrupt the consumers' automatic problem-solving process.
- **Limited decision-making** may occur when consumers already have a lot of information about the product. The basic marketing strategy is likely to be to make additional pieces of information readily available to consumers when and where they may need them.
- **Extensive decision-making** may occur when consumers' level of knowledge is low, and a wide range of information is being sought. Marketers will typically seek to make the necessary information available in a format and at a level that consumers can understand and use in the problem-solving process.

In Case Example 9.3 (in Section 9.7), we will explore IKEA's approach to opening new stores in city centres such as London and Paris. These stores are primarily 'planning centres' where money and goods will not be changing hands. Consider what, for most customers, will be a major purchase decision, such as choosing a new fitted kitchen. IKEA is seeking to provide an appropriate setting in which customers with a low level of knowledge can absorb the information they need, and staff can guide them through a problem-solving process towards making the right choices. This example indicates the importance of understanding the decision-making behaviour of consumers, as well as creating the right physical and social environment for the consumer with a purchase decision to make—and we turn to this issue, the consumer's environment, next.

Understanding the social and physical environment

As well as understanding the consumer's problem-solving process, marketers need to understand the social and physical environment in which consumers operate. Marketing strategies can then seek to alter aspects of the environment, with the intention of influencing consumers and their behaviour. Table 9.3 provides examples of how aspects of the physical environment can be changed.

TABLE 9.3 **Using Kotler and Armstrong's marketing strategy to explore examples of possible environmental changes to influence consumer behaviour**

Type of strategy	Example(s) of changes
Product strategies	New product design or new packaging
Pricing strategies	Notification of a 'sale' in the window of a high street store or online, or price labelling on physical products
Promotion strategies	Advertisements in magazines or on electronic displays in major railway stations
Place/distribution strategies	Design of websites, or the location or layout of a retail store

Based on Kotler and Armstrong (2017).

Other marketing strategies can seek to alter aspects of the social environment. For example, consumers are influenced by the behaviour of sales and service staff—whether their attitude is friendly, aggressive, or pushy, etc. A study of 48 branches of a major UK bank (Wilson 1997) showed that distinct subcultures existed across the different locations; this highlights the difficulties and complexities of designing and controlling a single style of 'corporate behaviour'. Going beyond the interactions between staff and customers, another increasingly important aspect of the social environment is interaction between customers themselves. Studies suggest that we are much more likely to believe word-of-mouth recommendations from our own friends and family than from other sources (Nielsen 2012). For example, providers of internet shopping might ask customers to invite friends to try their service at a special reduced rate, such as the campaign by Ocado, a UK-based online supermarket (Ocado 2019).

Understanding international/global marketing strategy

We should also consider the challenges of developing marketing strategy in an international and cross-cultural context. Even when cross-cultural differences have been understood, there has been some debate about how marketers should respond to those differences as they develop their strategies. The traditional view of international marketing (for organizations that are not 'born global') is that each local culture should be carefully researched for important differences from the domestic market (Peter et al. 1999). Differences in consumer needs, wants, preferences, attitudes, and values, as well as in behaviours when purchasing and consuming, should be carefully examined. The marketing strategy should then be tailored to fit the needs and wants of each distinct culture. However, alternative voices have called for a 'global marketing' approach. For example, Levitt (1983) has argued that, in an era of widespread travel and telecommunication capabilities, consumers across the world will think and make purchases in a similar way, as tastes, preferences, and motivations become more homogeneous. Such views have been hotly debated; for instance, de Mooij (2018) argues strongly for the important role of different cultures around the world in explaining differences in consumer behaviour which must in turn influence marketing and advertising strategies. A more 'middle ground' version of the global marketing argument (Peter et al. 1999) suggests that certain segments of consumers may be comparable across cultural boundaries (e.g. at the high end of many markets). Moreover, it is possible that some parameters of marketing may be standardized across cultures while others might not. For example, even across European countries, some automotive firms may have success in identifying common aspects of the appeal of their brands to international consumers, while some food companies may find that certain products are highly culturally sensitive. The concept of 'born global' is considered in Chapter 12, and culture is discussed in more detail in Chapter 4.

Linking marketing strategy with business/corporate strategy

In Chapter 8 we discussed how corporate strategy is summarized in an organization's business model (also discussed further in Chapter 11). As you study strategy, it is important to understand how an organization's marketing strategy connects with its business model. In order to do this, in Table 9.4 we explore the fit between a business model and marketing strategy, including some key questions that management should pose.

This summary clearly indicates that an effective marketing strategy is a strong complement to—and not a substitute for—a robust business model and organizational strategy. Marketing strategy can be seen as taking a desired organizational strategy and elaborating on the organization's interactions with its customers, and with its use of resources and capabilities, to achieve a desired position in the market.

TABLE 9.4 **The fit between an organization's marketing strategy and its business model**

	Business model	Marketing strategy
Definition	A business model can provide a template of how an organization interacts with other parties	Marketing strategy summarizes a pattern of managerial actions that are deployed to achieve competitive advantage through market positioning
Some key questions addressed	Which parties to bring together, and how to interact with them? What goods or information to exchange? What resources and capabilities to deploy?	What products/services to provide? Which customers to serve? What positioning to adopt against rivals? When to enter certain markets? Etc.
Unit of analysis	The organization and its partners	Primarily focused on the organization itself
Focus	Externally oriented: the exchanges between the organization and other parties	Internally oriented: how should the organization act in the light of competition?

Based on Zott and Amit (2008): 5.

CASE EXAMPLE 9.2 **FCA FIAT CHRYSLER'S NEW STRATEGY**

9

In 2018 Sergio Marchionne, the boss of Fiat Chrysler (FCA), was set to continue as CEO of the newly merged carmaker until at least 2018. However, he became gravely ill, was replaced as CEO of the carmaker in July 2018, and died only days later. Since 2014, Marchionne had intended to oversee a broad strategic plan that was designed to deliver a huge boost in sales and match the profitability of the best manufacturers in the business while eliminating the company's debt. The five-year strategic vision included plans to sharpen the brands, release new products, and expand its market presence in emerging (as well as established) markets, with a focus on China and India.

Alfa Romeo, Maserati, Fiat, and, of course, Ferrari were expected to perform well, but it was the American side of the company that was projected to deliver most of the growth. In 2018, FCA sold just under five million vehicles globally, which was an increase of around 2% from 2017—and nearly a third of the cars sold by FCA around the world were Jeeps.

Jeep, the original sports utility vehicle (SUV), started out as a niche product, but became a mainstream vehicle in the 1980s. Its popularity attracted attention and a number of companies produced their own SUVs. Jeep is no longer the market leader, and their competitors are also performing better in China.

In its 2018 full-year results report, FCA said its global net revenue went up by 4% year-on-year to 115.4 billion euros ($130.4 billion), and net profit increased by 3% to 3.6 billion euros ($4.07 billion), thanks to its record global sales of Jeep and Ram brands. However, in Asia and Pacific, including China, FCA suffered a 17% drop in net revenue. Increased competition, particularly in the SUV segments, and market weakness in 2018 were cited as the main reasons for its underperformance in China.

Among the new product plans was a new strategy for Chrysler. This brand was to move from being positioned as a luxury marque (or make of car) to targeting the mainstream market in North America. Dodge, another brand, was to continue building on the muscle cars it is known for, even if this meant a short-term dip in the volume of sales. Marchionne had envisioned significant growth for Alfa and Maserati, and in 2017 Alfa enjoyed rapid growth in the American marketplace after its return, thanks to the release of two new models.

The marque that comes first on the corporate masthead has been questioned by Fiat's brand boss, Olivier Francois, who suggested that it suffers from a 'dissociative identity disorder'. According to *The Economist*, this not only attempts to appeal to the mainstream European market, but also produces vehicles, such as versions of the pint-sized Fiat 500, for which consumers are willing to pay more. With Europe still struggling, and with little sign of a sustained recovery, Fiat will downplay the low-margin mainstream side of its business, at least in the home market.

The strategy was challenging: the targets set by Marchionne were incredibly ambitious, and the breadth was wide. However, this strategic vision helped FCA report a net profit of 3.6 billion euros in 2018.

Questions for discussion

1. How would you summarize FCA's overall business strategy? Make sure you discuss key customer markets internationally.
2. How would you summarize FCA's marketing strategy? How core is its marketing strategy to its business strategy?
3. How would you summarize the different challenges faced by each of the main marques (or makes of car) mentioned above: Jeep, Chrysler, Dodge, Alfa Romeo, Maserati, and Fiat?
4. What do you think are the main challenges facing FCA at the corporate level, as it seeks to develop its business in different countries around the globe?
5. Are there any aspects of FCA's strategy that seem to be missing, or are not covered in the extract above? What else would you like to know, before choosing whether to invest in FCA for example?

Sources

Adapted from *The Economist*,7 May 2014, with additions from *Bloomberg*, 4 January 2018; CNBC, 25 July 2018, and *China Daily*, 8 February 2019.

Fiat Chrysler's new strategy: Marchionne magic, *The Economist*, 7 May 2014. https://www.economist.com/schumpeter/2014/05/07/marchionne-magic (accessed 1 August 2019).

Auto industry legend CEO Sergio Marchionne dies at age 66, *CNBC*, 25 July 2018. https://www.cnbc.com/2018/07/25/fiat-chrysler-sergio-marchionne-dies.html (accessed 1 August 2019).

Fiat Chrysler takes measures to improve performance in China, *ChinaDaily*, 8 February 2019. http://www.chinadaily.com.cn/a/201902/08/WS5c5ce22ba3106c65c34e85a4.html (accessed 1 August 2019).

Alfa Romeo bets big on America and wins: the racy brand outperformed all others in U.S. sales last year, *Bloomberg*, 4 January 2018. https://www.bloomberg.com/news/articles/2018-01-04/alfa-romeo-bets-big-on-america-and-wins (accessed 1 August 2019).

9.6 **Operations strategy**

So far we have discussed three areas of functional strategy—financial, HRM, and marketing. Next we turn to the crucial area of operations strategy. What is meant by operations strategy and how does it impact on the organization's business strategy? An organization's operations strategy is the driver behind its operations, the part of the organization that produces and distributes its goods and services. Operations strategy addresses important issues, including the allocation of resources to ensure that the organization's infrastructure and activities, like production or distribution, are properly supported in a manner that is both effective and efficient.

What is operations strategy?

It has been noted that the term 'operations strategy' can at first sound like a contradiction. Slack and Lewis (2017) ask: How can the term 'operations', which is generally concerned with the day-to-day delivery of goods and services, be strategic? However, it can be argued that the effective management of an organization's operational resources (including workers, facilities, machines, and tools, etc.) is key to its long-term success. Operations strategy can be defined as the total pattern of decisions which shape the long-term capabilities of an operation, and their contribution to overall strategy. Operations strategy should certainly 'prevent strategic decisions being frustrated by poor operational implementation' (Slack and Lewis 2017:1); it should also be able to ensure that the management of operations resources can itself provide competitive advantage. This emphasizes the role of operations strategy in both facilitating planned strategic activity (e.g. supporting the delivery of a marketing plan) and potentially contributing to the ability of the organization to compete, survive, and thrive in the future via sustainable competitive advantage.

Operations strategy in different contexts

In order to understand operations strategy it is important to consider distinctions between operations strategy in different contexts. Two key contexts to compare are manufacturing and service industries.

Manufacturing industries

In a manufacturing context, Hill (2000) highlights the need to embed manufacturing strategy within a wider process of both corporate strategy development and marketing strategy, and advocates a five-step process for doing so. Having (1) defined corporate objectives and (2) determined marketing strategies to meet these objectives, manufacturing strategy should be developed by (3) assessing how different products qualify in their respective markets and win orders against competitors, (4) establishing the appropriate process to manufacture these products (i.e. process choice), and (5) providing the manufacturing infrastructure to support production.

Consider the automotive industry, which is under increasing pressure to customize its products for customers and is worth an estimated trillion dollars worldwide (Nathan 2019). This industry can provide a context for critical decisions about establishing appropriate manufacturing processes and providing infrastructure to support production. A key driver is the Industrial IoT, or Internet of Things (e.g. Boyes et al. 2018), a term which is widely applied to connected devices in consumer, domestic, business, and industrial settings. The Industrial IoT allows managers to gather machine data and analyse it against various key performance indicators, such as productivity, quality, and maintenance (see Table 9.5 for further examples).

Service industries

In the context of service industries, academics frequently stress the importance of the notion of customer experience. Pullman and Gross (2004:553) define an experience as occurring when:

9

> a customer has any sensation or knowledge acquisition resulting from some level of interaction with different elements of a context created by a service provider. Successful experiences

TABLE 9.5 **The Industrial Internet of Things in automotive manufacturing**

Potential area of benefit	Example
Productivity	Improved throughput, reduced cycle time, better understanding of bottlenecks in the manufacturing process
Predictive maintenance	Reduction in lost time due to equipment malfunctions
Predictive quality	Migration from statistical or sample-based control to online measurement of every part in a car, with alerts to management if the quality falls outside specified ranges
Energy monitoring and conservation	Sensors can monitor every stage in the manufacturing process to identify where energy is being wasted
Health and safety monitoring	The use of connected sensors and monitors can make compliance automatic and/or influence worker behaviour
Process traceability	In the case of failure of a part, manufacturers can trace the part to where it was manufactured and determine if it is a machine-level problem, a part-level problem, or a component-level problem, potentially limiting the scope of the recall

are those that the customer finds unique, memorable and sustainable over time, would want to repeat and build upon, and enthusiastically promotes via word of mouth.

Voss et al. (2008) propose a construct that they label experience capability, defined in terms of the firm's ability to choreograph customer experiences. Therefore their view of service operations strategy comprises three main classes of deliberate design choices, which are termed stageware (physical environment), orgware (management organization focused on customer experience), and customerware (the key role of customer contact employees). We can consider the example of IKEA (Case Example 9.3) in choosing to open smaller stores in city centres such as London and Paris. The company has clearly focused on stageware, in creating a new retail format for itself—from a large suburban warehouse to a smaller, high street 'planning centre'. However, the company needs to demonstrate that the other dimensions of operations strategy in the service sector—the key role of customer contact employees and the management organization focused on customer experience—have been adjusted to fit with their exciting new idea. The work of Voss et al. suggests that all three dimensions are important for service businesses.

These design choices (stageware, orgware, and customerware) emphasize the unique challenges faced by managers who are developing operations strategy in a service industry context. It has been argued (Roth and Menor 2003) that an operations strategy perspective is needed to determine the theoretical and practical insights, which will enable firms to effectively deploy their operations in order to provide the right offerings to the right customers at the right times. Organizations should consider the strategic alignment of three elements:

- their targeted market and customer segments
- the notion of the service concept as a complex bundle of offerings
- their choice of service delivery system design.

Each element combines with the others to influence the customer encounter and, in turn, the evoked customer response to the service delivery system (Roth and Menor 2003; Voss et al. 2008). As an example of outstanding customer experience, consider Zappos, the online shoe store frequently praised for its customer service (Solomon 2018). The excellent customer experience at Zappos is achieved via a mix of important elements (Glassman 2013), illustrated in Table 9.6.

Key dimensions of operations strategy

Having considered operations strategy in two distinct contexts (manufacturing and service industries) we now move on to discuss two key dimensions of operations strategy: servitization and outsourcing.

Servitization

The concept of servitization takes us beyond an overly simple view of operations strategy as being concerned with either products or services (but never both). Servitization is now widely recognized as the innovation of a manufacturer's capabilities and processes to move from selling products to selling integrated products–service offerings that deliver value in use (Baines et al. 2008;

TABLE 9.6 **Design choices at Zappos to deliver outstanding customer experience**

Category of design choice	Example	Result
Customerware: the key role of customer contact employees	Employees seek to create an emotional connection with customers, e.g. over the problems of finding a comfortable shoe for narrow feet, leading to variable call length	Future customer loyalty and word-of-mouth recommendations, e.g. customer delighted by a free delivery upgrade to ensure shoes arrive in time for a special event
Orgware: management organization focused on the customer experience	Low agent occupancy targets, i.e. the proportion of time spent on calls is typically 60–70%, compared with 80% or more in many other businesses	The communication style and actions of agents appear to be highly sympathetic to customers, and offer a customized service for each individual
Stageware: physical environment	Zappos spend a lot of time observing and tracking behaviour to understand exactly what customers want—enormous selection and convenience, with an interface and delivery package that is easy to use	Appropriate mix of technology and excellent human interface; customers find it easy to make purchases, and to return any that they are not entirely happy with

Vandermerwe and Rada 1988). Baines et al. (2008) argue that, in many organizations, operations strategy still suffers from a decoupling between product manufacture and service delivery. A decoupled approach to operations strategy is unsatisfactory, as it creates many challenges emerging from a traditional approach to product manufacture. Such an approach means that it is problematic for the firm to deliver its offering to the marketplace in an effective manner. An operations strategy that integrates a range of features is desirable (Baines et al. 2008), covering typical structural aspects of operations (such as process, capacity, facilities, and supply chains) as well as a range of infrastructure issues (such as human resources, customer relations, and supplier relations).

An innovative example of servitization is the relationship between Philips, the Dutch multinational technology company, and Amsterdam Airport Schiphol (Electronics360 2015). Philips provides lighting for the terminal buildings inside Schiphol and owns the fixtures and installations inside the airport, which were specifically designed for the purpose and are planned to last 75% longer than conventional fixtures. LED lighting is very efficient, but has high up-front purchase costs. Under this model of lighting as a service, Schiphol pays for the energy it uses, benefiting from low electricity usage while avoiding the cost of buying the lamps initially, and aims to be one of the most sustainable airports in the world. Philips and its partners will be responsible for the performance, durability, and re-use of the LED lamps that will be installed in the airport, with a predicted saving of 50% in electricity consumption.

Outsourcing

A key element of operations strategy for many organizations will be a consideration of its decisions around outsourcing. Outsourcing has been defined as the act of obtaining finished or semi-finished products or services from an outside company if these activities were traditionally performed internally (Dolgui and Proth 2013; Simchi-Levi et al. 2004). Outsourcing first came to prominence in the early 1990s, and was soon described as one of the most important new management ideas and practices of the twentieth century (Sibbert 1997). According to Corbett (2004), for outsourcing to be fully effective, it needs to be integrated into the organization's overall business strategy.

> *This means shifting from a view of outsourcing as a reactive tool—where opportunities are sought only in response to external pressures for change or a consultant's report on the latest opportunity—to one of weaving outsourcing into the very fabric of the business's decision-making and operations*
>
> Corbett (2004:77)

A top-down approach to identifying outsourcing opportunities involves making sourcing decisions an integral part of the organization's strategic decision-making. A more bottom-up approach suggests that the identification of external sourcing opportunities begins with those areas of the organization than can offer little opportunity for competitive advantage. For Corbett (2004), the most important factor is to elevate sourcing to the level of an important management decision. He argues that new sources of competitive advantage can be sought via the unique ways that a firm aims to blend its internal and external sources.

However, outsourcing is a controversial topic, particularly in the public sector. Its supporters point to money saved and innovations successfully introduced. The Forth Valley Royal Hospital, run by a company called Serco, was the first in the UK to use automated guided vehicles to move laundry and waste around in the basement, saving money by cutting about 40 jobs (*The Economist* 2018). A survey of evidence from around the world (Hodge 2000) found that outsourcing had resulted in an overall saving in government expenditure of between 6% and 12%. But critics argue that the average cost savings have fallen dramatically over time, as private contractors trim any 'slack' from the services that they now operate and public providers have arguably become more efficient.

Moreover, evaluating whether outsourcing has delivered improved services is a complex issue—particularly when we look beyond relatively simple services such as refuse collection, and consider more complex activities, such as the running of a prison. In the UK, some have recently pointed to a crisis in such outsourcing projects. For example Carillion, the giant construction firm, collapsed in January 2018, leading to, amongst other problems, delays in building new hospitals for the UK's National Health Service (Bowden 2019). Capita, the largest business process outsourcing and professional services company in the UK, has been criticized for its financial performance, along with its failure to deliver targets for Army recruitment and a website that 'cost three times its budget and was 52 months late' (BBC 2018).

Linking operations strategy with business/corporate strategy

As with marketing strategy, discussed in the previous section, it is important for you to understand how operations strategy links to business strategy. Slack and Lewis (2017) propose four perspectives on operations strategy, which can help to draw out some of its key dimensions. First, operations strategy must reflect the aims and objectives of the whole organization, and what it is seeking to achieve, i.e. a top-down perspective. Secondly, operations strategy must also adopt a bottom-up perspective; in this view, operational activities and improvements cumulatively help to build the organization's strategy. Thirdly, operations strategy should help to translate market requirements into operations decisions. Finally, operations strategy involves exploiting the capabilities of operations resources in chosen markets. This is highlighted in Figure 9.5.

FIGURE 9.5 Four perspectives on operations strategy: top-down, bottom-up, market requirements, and operations resources. Source: Reproduced with permission from Slack, N. and Lewis, M. (2017). *Operations Strategy* (5th edn), Harlow: Financial Times/ Prentice Hall. © Pearson Education Limited 2011, 2015, 2017.

CASE EXAMPLE 9.3 IKEA'S MOVE INTO THE HIGH STREET

The growth in e-commerce has triggered substantial changes to the retail industry in recent years. High street retailers are increasingly looking to build their online presence and sales in response to consumers moving a large amount of their purchases online. This is often at the cost of physical stores, and town and city centres are beginning to see drastic changes in the number and types of stores operating. However, rather than retreating from the high street, IKEA is entering it.

In October 2018 IKEA opened up a new 'planning studio' on Tottenham Court Road in London. Nothing is sold here. According to IKEA, the planning studio 'is a smaller store dedicated to kitchen and bathroom inspiration'; it is a space dedicated to ideas. IKEA is known for large out-of-town stores, so this marked a significant change in strategy. There are now plans to expand and open planning studios in 30 city centres.

Whilst this change is significant, IKEA sees these smaller concept stores as complimenting their existing offers—they hope that it drives more traffic to the website and its big shops in the long run. IKEA is known for being later than others in adapting its business model to reflect the growth in e-commerce, despite the key advantages this brings.

E-retailers are in a position to offer a wider range of goods, at better prices, with a more personalized service driven by data. E-commerce also changes the distribution system. Retailing used to be cash-and-carry, with shoppers taking their merchandise home with them. Now they often travel by different routes, unencumbered by shopping bags. In addition to sales, retailers have to factor in delivery, and this is where IKEA is devoting a lot of attention.

IKEA's head of retail argues that the company's strong brand and balance sheet give it freedom to have a 'test-and-fail' approach, rather than 'being in a panic to do something'. It has three major tasks ahead: redefining sales measures, logistics, and the whole concept of the store.

First let's consider sales measures in store. Online sales make up at most 10% of the total, and stores are still the best way of attracting customers, so these will remain integral to the business.

However, as IKEA ships more of its products to people's homes, it has to bear in mind online purchases, delivery, and assembly. In 2017, IKEA bought TaskRabbit, a gig economy start-up that can spare customers the grief of assembling furniture with an Allen key. Logistics is a second factor. Fast delivery has come to be expected by online shoppers. IKEA's large suburban stores, which are within easy reach of densely populated areas, can also function as part of the logistics network, shortening delivery times to meet shoppers' demands.

The final challenge relates to changing the concept of the store. Rather than always stocking the full range of products, the priority in smaller stores is to allow customers to 'touch and feel' items they have seen online. This means that stores can hold less stock and results in space being available to display full kitchen and other room designs. Staff in these stores are there to offer advice on furnishings, which is a more personalized service than is offered in the larger out-of-town stores.

In May 2019 IKEA opened a different type of store in Paris, selling goods across a floor space four times smaller than its typical store. It aims to attract local visitors more frequently, offering frequent range changes, fresh food, and events.

These new store formats respond not just to online pressure, but to generational trends like urbanization, demand for sustainability, and reduced car use. Shoppers already treat going to an IKEA store as an 'experience'—albeit not one for everyone. In an online world, it is vital to build on this to keep customers interested, and these new stores offer customers different experiences.

Questions for discussion

1. How would you summarize IKEA's business model? What are the key resources and capabilities supporting that business model?
2. How would you summarize IKEA's operations strategy?
3. How would you summarize IKEA's marketing strategy? Describe the customer's choices and 'experience' when shopping with IKEA. How important are the connections between its operations strategy and its marketing strategy?
4. How would you summarize IKEA's IT strategy? How core is its competence in technology to its business strategy?
5. How would you summarize IKEA's financial strategy? Discuss the ways in which the financial strategy can or should support the overall business strategy.
6. How would you summarize IKEA's overall business strategy, looking forward?

Sources

Based on *The Economist* (print edn) (2019). A topsy-turvy world, 26 Jan, with additions from Reuters, 6 May 2019.

https://www.economist.com/business/2019/01/26/as-retailers-abandon-the-high-street-why-is-ikea-moving-in

https://www.reuters.com/article/us-ikea-france-store/ikea-opens-central-paris-store-to-cater-for-changing-tastes-idUSKCN1SC0HL

https://www.ikea.com/gb/en/stores/planning-studios/

9

9.7 **IT strategy**

We have now discussed four of the five key functional strategies: financial, HRM, marketing, and operations. In this section we will consider the final functional strategy: IT (information technology) strategy. What is IT strategy and how does it align with business strategy? A number of frameworks have been developed to help managers analyse their organization's portfolio of IT projects, think through the problem of alignment with business strategy, and identify appropriate actions. In this section we will discuss a number of useful frameworks, and consider their strengths and weaknesses.

What is IT strategy?

We can think of IT strategy as the total pattern of decisions relating to the use of technology within an organization. An organization's IT strategy may be documented as a comprehensive plan, setting out how IT will be used to help the organization to meet its goals. IT strategy is often implemented via IT projects, where a project is a set of interrelated activities that are time limited and use a defined set of resources to achieve a particular objective (PMI 2019). Therefore in order to manage its IT strategy, an organization must typically monitor and control a set of projects, and ensure that IT strategy is fully supporting the organization's overall strategy. Next, we introduce two models that are designed to address these questions around how to manage a portfolio of IT projects and ensure that business strategy and IT strategy are aligned.

McFarlan's Strategic Grid

First, we consider McFarlan's Strategic Grid (McFarlan 1984). This framework was developed to assist managers with analysing the portfolio of IT projects that their organization might be pursuing. According to Burgelman et al. (2009:989), in a technology-intensive environment 'projects are where the action is. They're where the "rubber meets the road"'. This is because development projects can lead to a host of benefits from success in a new market to barriers to entry for competitors due to a new delivery system. Therefore the portfolio of IT projects can be an important indicator of an organization's priorities and strategic intent—and the changes that it is seeking to introduce. If important resources (such as money, people, time, and management attention) are being allocated to support current projects, the make-up of the project portfolio may shed light on changes in performance, productivity, returns, and innovation across the organization.

The Strategic Grid (McFarlan 1984) can help managers to analyse the portfolio of IT initiatives along two dimensions—the impact on business operations (focusing on the organization's current activities) and the impact on strategy (with a focus on future plans). The aim is to help managers to assess the alignment of IT with the organization's strategic goals, and also to ensure that the approaches for organizing and managing IT are appropriate, given the position of the projects on the Strategic Grid (Figure 9.6). We will now briefly review each of the four quadrants in Figure 9.6 to consider how the framework can be used to analyse different types of IT project.

- **Support (low impact on business operations/low impact on strategy):** projects and initiatives that fall within the 'support' quadrant of the grid have little impact on an organization's core strategy or operations. Such projects may aim to achieve local improvements or incremental cost savings, and are typically carried out by IT specialists in partnership with local end-users.
- **Factory (high impact on business operations/low impact on strategy):** IT projects that fall within the 'factory' quadrant are typically designed to improve the performance or reduce the costs of the core operations of an organization. Business unit managers and IT managers will work in partnership on such projects, given their high operating impact/risk.
- **Turnaround (low impact on business operations/high impact on strategy):** IT projects in the 'turnaround' quadrant are designed to exploit emerging strategic opportunities.

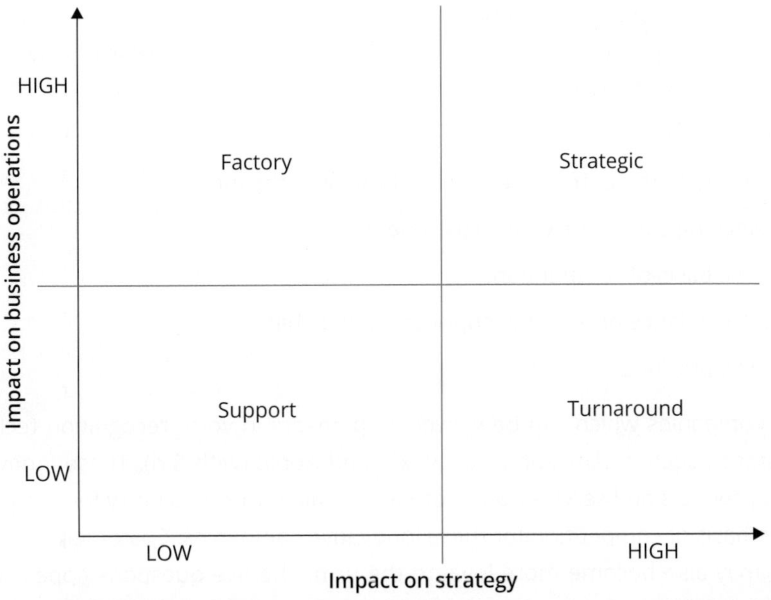

FIGURE 9.6 The Strategic Grid. Source: Reproduced with permission from Applegate, L., Austin, R. and McFarlan, F. (2007). *Corporate Information Strategy and Management: Text and Cases*. 7th ed. Boston: McGraw-Hill.

Such initiatives require input from business managers (e.g. those involved with business development), IT managers, and those with expertise in emerging technologies.

- **Strategy (high impact on business operations/high impact on strategy):** finally, firms which have important IT projects in the 'strategic' quadrant are making a commitment to use IT to enable both core operations and core strategy. Such projects are typically defined, implemented, and managed with key input from the most senior levels of the organization.

Overall, this framework can help managers to describe their current portfolio of IT projects, to understand whether the allocation of resources is appropriate, given the organization's overall goal, and to identify whether they wish to make changes to their stance on IT from a more defensive to an offensive approach. This is highlighted in a later study, where Nolan and McFarlan (2005) place 'need for reliable IT' (rather than 'current operational impact') on the vertical axis, and 'need for new IT' (rather than 'strategic/future impact') on the horizontal axis. Their point is that companies focusing on the left-hand side of the grid ('factory' and 'support' quadrants) are typically adopting a defensive stance with their IT, while companies on the right ('turnaround' and 'strategic' quadrants) are using IT in a more offensive manner to support and move their business strategy forward.

Some of the world's most innovative companies are using IT in this 'strategic' manner. The CEO of Alphabet/Google has described it as an 'AI first' company. AI (artificial intelligence) can be described as the simulation of human intelligence processes by machines, especially computer systems. For instance, users of Google's email software are becoming used to Gmail offering to finish their sentences for them (Ringel et al. 2019). This Smart Compose feature relies on Google's expertise in AI, and, for Google, such AI-driven initiatives are likely to represent projects on the right-hand side of McFarlan's Strategic Grid where impact on strategy is high.

In order to assess the strategic impact of IT, McFarlan suggested that we can pose five basic questions about IT applications, in relation to the competitive forces (Porter's Five Forces, introduced in Chapter 5), as follows.

Can IT applications:

- build barriers to the entry of new competitors into the industry?
- build switching costs for existing customers?
- change the basis of competition?
- change the balance of power in supplier relationships?
- create new products?

Consider companies which can be viewed as pioneers in voice recognition technology and virtual assistants, such as Amazon (with Alexa) and Apple (with Siri). These innovations have created new products and services, and potentially built barriers to entry for competitors while changing the basis of competition for these innovative companies. Customers who enjoy these innovations may also become more loyal to the firm. The five questions appear to focus our thinking on the right-hand side of the grid, i.e. the scope for the organization to use IT offensively as part of its strategic positioning.

Next we consider another 'classic' model for thinking about the alignment of IT and business strategy, which emphasizes both an outward-facing strategic perspective and a more internally focused view of the organization's capabilities.

Henderson and Venkatraman's strategic alignment model

Another framework for exploring the alignment of IT strategy and business strategy was developed by Henderson and Venkatraman (1993). This framework aims to assess business and IT alignment across all aspects of an organization's business model (see Figure 9.7), and has been described as the 'jewel in the crown' of important work on management and IT that emerged from the Massachusetts Institute of Technology (MIT) in the 1990s (MacDonald and Yapp 1992:256).

The model shown in Figure 9.7 has two dimensions: vertically it draws a distinction between the external domain focused on strategy, and the internal domain focused on capabilities. Horizontally it distinguishes between the business domain and the IT domain. The authors argue that organizations should seek alignment in both the horizontal and vertical planes, as depicted in the figure by black arrows between the four boxes; the first direction for alignment is between corresponding IT and business domains (horizontal black arrows) and the second is alignment of IT and business strategy with capabilities (vertical black arrows). The authors propose that value is ultimately created through alignment in four key directions, as shown by the four coloured arrows (yellow, red, blue, and green). The arrows identify four main perspectives on alignment.

- **Strategy execution** (arrow 1, yellow): business strategy is viewed as both the driver of organizational design choices and the logic of technology infrastructure. In this 'classical' view, senior managers formulate strategy and technology managers implement it.

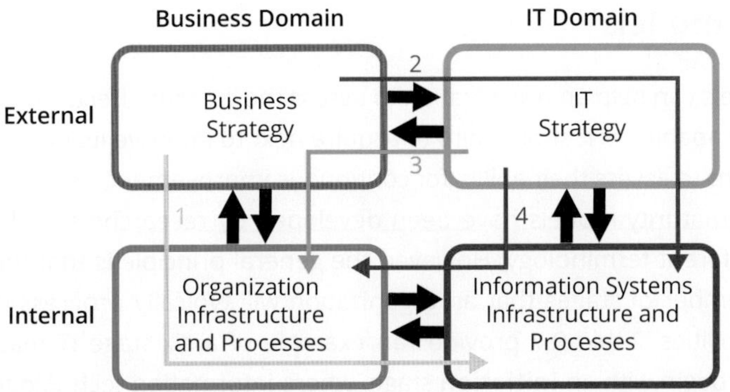

FIGURE 9.7 The strategic alignment model. Courtesy of International Business Machines Corporation, © 1993 International Business Machines Corporation.

- **Technology potential** (arrow 2, red): again, business strategy is the driver. However, an IT strategy is then articulated to support the business strategy. The IT strategy supports the specification of the required technology infrastructure and processes.
- **Competitive potential** (arrow 3, green): this perspective concerns the exploitation of IT capabilities to impact on new products and services, capabilities, and governance. Therefore the business strategy might be modified in the light of emerging IT capabilities.
- **Service level** (arrow 4, blue): this perspective can be seen as focusing on how to create a world class IT organization within the wider organization.

Many innovative companies are seeking new approaches to aligning their IT strategy and their business strategy. McDonald's uses an AI algorithm to serve digital menus that change in response to such factors as time of day, day of the week, restaurant traffic, and weather (Ringel et al. 2019). This provides an example of what Henderson et al. would refer to as 'technology potential', where business strategy is closely supported by IT strategy and IT capabilities. In 2018, Philips launched an AI platform that helps 'scientists, software developers, clinicians and health care providers access advanced analytic capabilities to curate and analyze health care data and offers them tools and technologies to build, maintain, deploy and scale AI-based solutions' (Ringel et al. 2019). This is an example of 'competitive potential' where the organization seeks to exploit its IT capabilities, with the potential of changing business strategy and new ways of working.

We have seen that both MacFarlan's Strategic Grid, and Henderson and Venkatraman's framework can be used by managers to assess the fit between their IT initiatives and the organization's strategy. As a result of the assessment, opportunities for amendments to existing IT strategy can be identified, and new initiatives can be created to improve alignment and value creation. Before moving on to discuss strategic opportunities and risks, we introduce one more set of models that have played an important role in IT theory and practice—maturity models.

IT maturity models

IT maturity models can help an organization to assess the current effectiveness of its IT capabilities, and which capabilities it should aim to acquire next to improve its performance. They can help organizations to assess their ability for continuous improvement, in terms of IT capabilities.

Numerous IT maturity models have been developed by researchers and businesses, each using slightly different terminology. However, the general principle is that the maturity model will set out a number of stages that an organization will typically progress through, in terms of their IT capabilities. Table 9.7 provides an example of a six-stage IT maturity model. The models typically begin with an **initiation** stage, where information technology is introduced to the organization. This may be followed by a **contagion** stage, including rapid proliferation of systems, technology, and supporting infrastructure. Next, a **control** stage often occurs when spending on IT has escalated and returns on investment are negligible. There may also have been disasters along the way, leading organizations to take back the control of IT spending by cutting budgets etc. Next, the beginnings of IT maturity occur, with the **integration** stage when the organization is beginning to address its difficulties and become more comfortable with IT and systems in general. Maturity progresses in the **entrepreneurial opportunity** stage, where effective use of information begins to add value for the organization. Finally, the **integrated harmonious relationship** stage is when IT becomes more fully integrated into the mainstream of the organization, and linkages between external and internal data sources can be put in place. The stages are elaborated in Table 9.7.

Wainwright and Waring (2000) illustrate the application of maturity models to the National Health Service (NHS) in the UK, and draw important conclusions about the readiness of the NHS to move through various stages of its IT strategy. They argued that the level of IT maturity

TABLE 9.7 **Six stages of IT maturity**

Stage	Characteristics
Initiation (adhocracy)	Lack of control and understanding of IT issues
Contagion (expansion/starting the foundations)	Increasing unsatisfied demand for IT services and technology; lack of business involvement in IT
Control (formalization/centralized dictatorship)	Conflict where IT department comes under scrutiny of senior management due to unsatisfactory service
Integration (maturity I/democratic dialectic and cooperation)	Lessons are learned and more cooperative business and IT relationships emerge
Entrepreneurial opportunity (maturity II/data administration)	Adding value to IT and systems through effective use of information
Integrated harmonious relationship (maturity III)	Lessons are absorbed with emphasis on linkages between internal and external data and integration of IT into the mainstream of the organization

Based on Nolan (1979), Galliers and Sutherland (1991), Wainwright and Waring (2000).

in the NHS was not sufficient to adopt certain initiatives that it was seeking to implement. For example, they discussed ambitious targets, unexpected effort in data collection, and the need for strong leadership when moving between stages.

In a further example, governments around the world are encouraging public agencies to join e-Government initiatives, in order to provide better services to their citizens in areas such as housing, education, health, and social services, etc. Therefore maturity models are being put to work to measure the e-Government preparedness of public agencies. For instance, in a study of 30 government agencies in Chile, researchers concluded that while the operational aspects of some IT services were improving, further work was needed in the development of human capital and redesign of business processes underlying the new e-Government activities (Valdés et al. 2011).

Therefore such maturity models provide managers with another tool for assessing the level of IT maturity in their organization and the suitability of its current strategy. Consider the Opening Case Study, Vail Resorts. Their extensive use of IT, including cross-functional working across marketing and IT teams, suggests that their IT capabilities are reaching a high level of integration and maturity.

Strategic opportunities and risks

Having discussed three frameworks for exploring IT strategy, we now move on to consider how IT can play a part in both strategic opportunities and strategic risks in an organization.

Strategic opportunities

IT can be an important part of an organization's search for new strategic opportunities (Applegate et al. 2007; Tidd and Bessant 2018).

- **IT can change the basis of competition:** for example, consider the automotive industry. Many customers focus on the features, function, and appearance of a car when making a buying decision. However, more recently, some customers have become more focused on both their experience at the dealership when making their purchase, and the quality of service after the purchase. This shift offers a potential advantage to companies who can use IT to support the customer experience, both during and after the sale.
- **IT can change** the nature of relationships and balance of power among buyers and suppliers. Today organizations in many sectors are allowing data, and knowledge of their operations, to flow through their supply chain as they collaborate more closely with suppliers. Data flows and collaborations, which would have been more difficult in the past, are now supported and facilitated by new technology; for example, manufacturers who can easily share information such as stock levels and specifications for particular parts with other firms in the supply chain. In addition, online communities are growing, allowing organizations to discover and collaborate more easily with new partners.
- **IT can build or reduce barriers to entry:** for example, Amazon initially took advantage of the fact that the internet had reduced barriers to entry in certain sectors, such as selling books; anyone who wanted to become a bookseller could do so via a website (no longer needing a shop on the high street). However, Amazon's business model required the

company to take ownership of physical inventory (i.e. stocks of books and other products, waiting for customer orders), and this required significant investment in infrastructure, such as buildings where stock could be stored.

- **IT can increase or decrease switching costs:** for example, the costs incurred when opening or closing an account with a financial services provider can be reduced by using new IT systems. NatWest attracted attention when it launched a 'paperless mortgage', allowing customers and staff to share and verify documents online (Finextra 2019), potentially cutting costs in terms of paper processing and staff time, as well as improving customer service.
- **IT can add value to existing products or services, or create new ones:** for example, the digitization of books, magazines, music, video games, etc. According to recent data, more than 487 million e-books are now sold in the USA each year, with Amazon recently capturing 83% of the market. In the UK, e-books currently account for around 34% of all book sales (PublishDrive 2017).

Strategic risks

However, Applegate et al. (2007) urge managers to also consider the role of IT in strategic risk. It is important for organizations to identify possible threats to their current strategies as their external environment shifts due to new technologies, leading, for example, to new forms of competitive pressure. Managers can identify potential risks by asking themselves:

- Can emerging technologies disrupt current business models?
- Are we too early or late to exploit an IT opportunity?
- Does IT lower entry barriers?
- Does IT trigger regulatory action?

Focusing on the first of these questions, established firms can face important challenges when confronted with disruptive technologies (Christensen 2003) (disruptive strategy is discussed further in Chapter 11). For instance, in the travel and tourism sector, the convergence of internet technologies has led to the development of peer-to-peer services such as Airbnb, challenging traditional providers of accommodation for leisure and business travel, and at the same time social media has given consumers a much stronger voice (Benckendorff et al. 2019). In order to identify an emerging technology as a disruptor, it is useful to consider some of the key features of disruptive technologies (Applegate et al. 2007):

- When technology evolves significantly faster than the evolutionary path of the dominant technology in the industry—for example, Netflix and other online TV/streaming services have changed the way that many people watch television at home, and some providers of 'traditional' TV are moving into the online space in an attempt to keep up.
- When technology enables new products, services, pricing, or business models that change the basis of competition in ways that are difficult for established players to match—for instance, Uber is a mobile platform connecting consumers who need rides with drivers willing to provide them, and it has challenged the business model of the 'traditional' taxi cab. Other ride-sharing services, such as zipcar and car2go, are also giving consumers a new perspective on the taxi and car hire businesses.

- When the emergence of the technology coincides with regulatory changes or significant customer dissatisfaction with the status quo that dramatically influences the competitive power of established players to respond—for instance, we have seen a growth in the popularity of open source software, such as Linux, at the same time as a dominant 'traditional' player, Microsoft, is accused of abusing its dominance in the market (*The Economist* 2013).

As an illustration of an issue that presents both opportunities and risks for many organizations in relation to their IT strategy, Christensen et al. (2002) return to the topic of outsourcing (as we discussed in relation to operations strategy in Section 9.6). They argue that outsourcing is a good example of a strategic topic where functional strategies, such as those pertaining to operations and IT, must come together. They question the apparently simple logic, often repeated, that firms should outsource components or services in areas that are not their core competence, or if somebody else can do it at a lower cost. Christensen and colleagues argue that this logic can lead a firm to outsource 'those pieces of value-added in which most of the industry's profit will be made in the future—and to retain activities in which it is difficult to create enduring, differentiable advantages versus competitors' (Christensen et al. 2002:986).

They suggest that the assemblers of modular items—for example, think of firms that make their products by putting together smaller parts supplied by other firms, whether the finished product is a car or a computer—are likely to struggle to earn attractive profits or achieve competitive advantage. They argue that attractive profitability seems to flow from the point of customer contact back through the system to the point at which unsatisfied demand for functionality exists. In other words, if our cars or computers tend to offer more functionality than most customers really need or use, it may be very challenging for many makers of cars or computers to operate profitably—and more likely that the suppliers of key components within products like cars or computers will play a critical and profitable role in the manufacturing and assembly process. This indicates that the point of attractive profitability is likely to shift over time as such dynamics work through an industry.

Linking IT strategy with business/corporate strategy: digital strategy

In an increasingly digital world, for many managers the term 'IT strategy' has become inextricably linked with 'digital strategy'. We will discuss digital strategy in greater depth in Chapter 11 when we explore innovation and disruption. However, for Dave Aron, an analyst at Gartner, the distinction between IT strategy and digital strategy can be explained as follows:

> - *IT Strategy is a technical answer to a business question: 'How will IT help the business win?' It assumes the business strategy is set, then considers how to use IT to make that strategy successful. IT Strategy is usually conducted after business strategy.*
> - *Digital Business Strategy is a business answer to a digital question: 'How should our business evolve to survive and thrive in an increasingly digital world?' It is not a separate strategy, but instead a lens on business strategy. All aspects of the business strategy should be informed by digital considerations.*
>
> Aron (2013)

For example, Kaiser Permanente, a provider of healthcare and not-for-profit health plans based in California (Ross et al. 2017), has a digital strategy that can be summarized using some of the elements of functional strategy we have discussed in this chapter:

- **Marketing:** Kaiser's approach begins with its customer engagement strategies. Data analytics are applied to achieve personalized medical outreach, and digital channels provide access to personal health records, secure messaging between patients and providers, and remote care.
- **HR:** Kaiser approaches its business as a collaboration between care providers and patients/members of the organization.
- **Operations:** Kaiser's operational 'backbone' starts with its electronic health records system, which facilitates meaningful patient interactions and enables new digital initiatives that require accurate, accessible patient data.

Looking to the future, Bharadwaj et al. (2013) suggest that there are four key themes that should guide our thinking on digital business strategy and may help to provide insights for the future. These themes are:

1. scope of digital business strategy
2. scale of digital business strategy
3. speed of decision-making
4. sources of value creation and capture.

As shown in Figure 9.8, there are a number of drivers of these four themes, including external digital trends and internal organizational changes or 'shifts'.

Examples of drivers for each of these four themes are as follows:

- **Scope of digital business strategy:** Netflix moves beyond being a subscription service to a wide range of content development
- **Scale of digital business strategy:** airline alliances such as Star Alliance and Oneworld can choose to share aspects of their business operations including reservation systems, loyalty programmes, and online cross-selling
- **Speed of decision-making:** organizations can respond to customer service requests in real time through Twitter, Facebook, and other social media platforms
- **Sources of value creation and capture:** Google's entry into the smartphone business based on giving away the software (Android) free and monetizing it through its ability to influence and control advertising.

Bharadwaj et al. (2013) also suggest a series of key questions for understanding digital business strategy (see Table 9.8), under the four key themes. These questions emphasize the important relationship between digital business strategy and the functional strategies we have discussed in this chapter, for example by asking whether the organization's digital business strategy transcends the traditional functional 'silos' (i.e. helping to break down barriers between business functions and departments), whether digital business strategy can speed up operational decision-making and supply chain orchestration, and whether digital business strategy is effective in creating and capturing value.

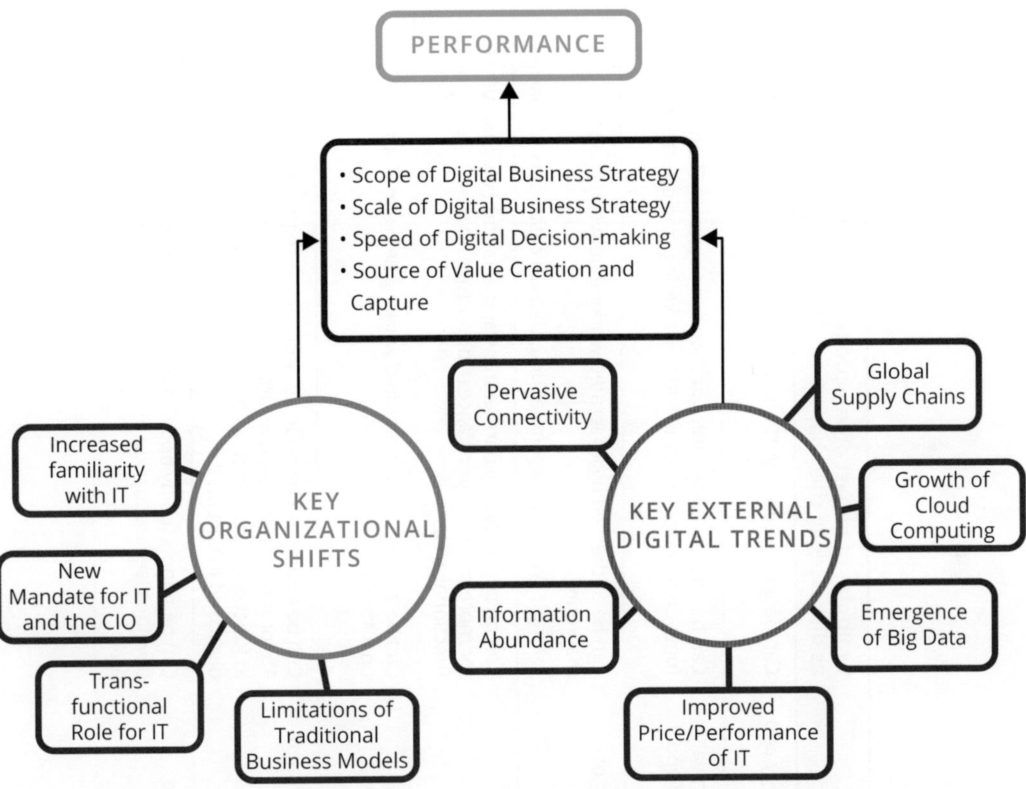

FIGURE 9.8 **Four key themes of digital business strategy, and their drivers.**
Source: Reproduced with permission from Bharadwaj, A., El Sawy, O.A., Pavlou, P.A., and Venkatraman, N. (2013). Digital business strategy: toward a net generation of insights, *MIS Quarterly*, **37**(2), 471–82, Figure 1.

9.8 Managing strategic performance

At the beginning of the chapter we explored how functional strategies play a key role in contributing to and delivering an organization's overall strategy (refer back to Figure 9.2 in Section 9.2). Having considered each of the types of functional strategy in detail in Sections 9.3–9.7, you should now be able to explain how different types of functional strategies can play this key role. For example, in summary:

- **Financial strategy**—ensuring that the organization raises the funds it needs, and deploys those funds in a manner that fits with its goals
- **HRM strategy**—ensuring that the organization recruits and retains the people it needs, and that those people work within a dynamic framework where they are supported to deliver the performance that the organization needs
- **Marketing strategy**—ensuring that the organization develops and presents marketing 'mixes' directed at selected target markets, in an international/global context where appropriate, based on a robust understanding of consumer decision-making behaviour and the importance of a range of key physical and social factors
- **Operations strategy**—ensuring that the organization's strategic decisions are not frustrated by poor operational implementation, and that the management of operational

TABLE 9.8 **Key questions on digital business strategy**

Key theme	Key questions	Examples of impact on functional strategies and impacts, as discussed in this chapter
Scope of digital business strategy	What is the extent of fusion and integration between IT strategy and business strategy?	Can be addressed with IT alignment models (Section 9.7)
	How encompassing is digital business strategy, and how effectively does digital business strategy transcend traditional functional and process silos?	Can be addressed by integrated working between IT and all of the functional areas—finance, HRM, marketing, and operations
	How well does digital business strategy exploit the digitization of products and services, and the information around them?	Can be addressed by integrated working between IT and marketing Example: Vail Resorts, embedding chips in customers' ski passes
	How well does digital business strategy exploit the extended business community?	Can be addressed by partnerships and alliances (see Chapter 10 for more on strategic alliances); opportunities may arise in any/all functional areas
Scale of digital business strategy	How rapidly and cost effectively can the IT infrastructure scale up and down to enable a firm's digital business strategy to bolster a strategic dynamic capability?	Can be addressed by integrated working between IT and operations
	How effective is digital business strategy in scaling volume through alliances and partnerships?	Can be addressed by alliances and partnerships (see Chapter 10 for more on strategic alliances); opportunities may arise in functional areas such as operations (e.g. outsourcing was discussed in Section 9.6)
	How well does digital business strategy take advantage of data, information, and knowledge abundance?	Can be addressed by building new capabilities as IT maturity develops; see discussion of IT maturity and capabilities (in Section 9.7)

Speed of digital business strategy	How effective is digital business strategy in accelerating new product launches?	Can be addressed by integrated working between IT and marketing Example: Vail Resorts, launch of Epic Pass
	How effective is digital business strategy in speeding up learning for improving strategic and operational decision-making?	Can be addressed by integrated working between IT and other functions Example: Vail Resorts, analysis of customer behaviour data to gain new insights
	How quickly does digital business strategy bolster the speed of dynamic supply chain orchestration?	Can be addressed by integrated working between IT and operations
	How quickly does digital business strategy enable the formation of new business networks that provide complementary capabilities?	Can be addressed by alliances and partnerships (see Chapter 10 for more on strategic alliances); opportunities may arise in functional areas such as operations (e.g. outsourcing was discussed in Section 9.7)
Sources of value creation and capture	How effective is digital business strategy in leveraging value from information?	Can be addressed by integrated working between IT and other functions Example: Vail Resorts, analysis of customer behaviour data to gain new insights
	How effective is digital business strategy in capturing value through coordinated business models in networks?	Can be addressed by new approaches to business models (see Chapters 8 and 11), alliances, and partnerships (see Chapter 10)
	How effective is digital business strategy in appropriating value through the control of the firm's digital architecture?	See Henderson and Venkatraman's model (Section 9.7), which gives different perspectives on alignment and value generation

Based on Bharadwaj et al. (2013:479).

resources itself provides advantage, with continuous improvements feeding back into strategy and market requirements being translated into operational decisions

- **IT strategy**—ensuring that the organization's technology-related activities support the business strategy, with a portfolio of IT projects that are well aligned to meet the organization's present and future needs, and adopting a proactive approach to the opportunities and risks associated with its chosen IT strategy.

But how can the firm use these functional strategies in order to manage the implementation of its organizational strategy? In this final section, we introduce tools to support the organization as it seeks to manage the implementation of its strategy through the activities of its various functions.

The link between organizational strategy and functional strategies

In order to understand how an organization can use functional strategies to manage the implementation of organizational strategy, we first need to understand the relationship between the organization's strategy on the one hand, and the operation of its key functions on the other. Kaplan and Norton (2008) argue that:

> *A visionary strategy that is not linked to excellent operational and governance processes cannot be implemented. Conversely, operational excellence may lower costs, improve quality, and reduce process and lead times; but without a strategy's vision and guidance, a company is not likely to enjoy sustainable success from its operational improvements alone.*
>
> Kaplan and Norton (2008:1)

Kaplan and Norton's proposition is that an organization is likely to fail at implementing a strategy or managing operations if they lack an overarching management system to integrate and align these two vital processes (the organization's strategy and the operation of its functions). They argue for a number of strategy execution processes that organizations need to put in place:

- translate the strategy, i.e. create a clear articulation of the organization's strategy and its accompanying measures
- manage (a limited number of) strategic initiatives
- align the organization's units (business units and support units) to deliver the strategy
- communicate the strategy
- review the strategy, i.e. regular meetings to report on and manage the strategy
- update the strategy regularly, to account for changing conditions.

Kaplan and Norton also stress the role of the functional strategies in working towards the overall organizational goals. For example, the financial strategy should link the strategic initiatives to the budget; the IT strategy may include the development of key service level agreements; the HR strategy is likely to address organizational development, and so on.

We will now discuss two tools that an organization can use to help it manage the implementation of its strategy through the activities of its various functions.

The Balanced Scorecard

Kaplan and Norton (1992) introduced the notion of the Balanced Scorecard as a set of measures that give senior managers a fast but fairly comprehensive view of key aspects of the organization. They suggest that the tool allows managers to look at the organization from four important perspectives (see Figure 9.9):

- Financial perspective: How do we look to shareholders?
- Customer perspective: How do customers see us?
- Internal business perspective: What must we excel at?
- Innovation and learning perspective: Can we continue to improve and create value?

The four perspectives of the Balanced Scorecard can clearly be linked to the areas of functional strategy that we have been discussing in this chapter. The first, the financial perspective, addresses the organization's financial strategy in a direct manner. The second, the customer perspective, is probably easiest to connect with marketing strategy in the first instance. The third, internal business, can perhaps be thought of as encompassing all of the functions that support the organization in the implementation of its strategy—HRM, operations, and IT. Finally, the fourth perspective, innovation and learning, emphasizes the importance of considering how the organization will continue to improve in all the above areas and create value in the future.

The framework also stresses the connections between the different perspectives. To give a simple example, if customers are satisfied (**customer perspective**), they are more likely to

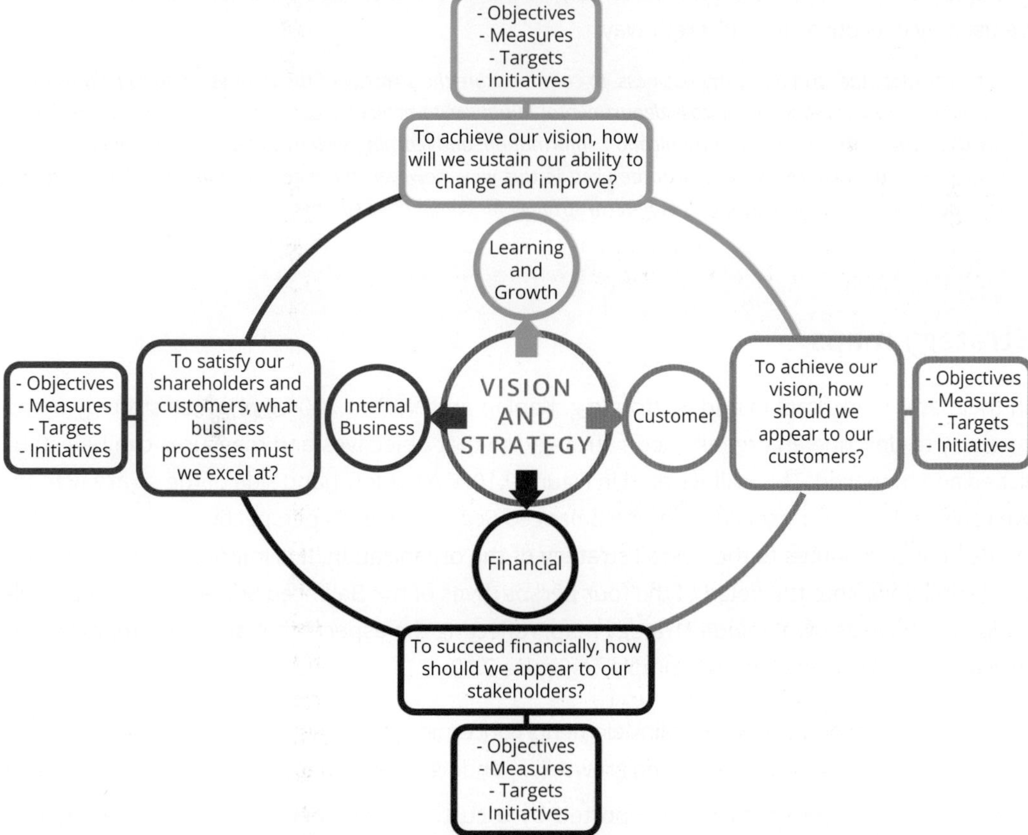

FIGURE 9.9 The Balanced Scorecard provides a framework to translate a strategy into operational terms. Source: Adapted from Kaplan, R.S. and Norton, D.P. (1996). *The Balanced Scorecard: Translating Strategy into Action*. Boston, MA: Harvard Business School Press. By permission of Harvard Business Publishing.

choose to spend more money with the firm, leading to increased revenue (**financial perspective**). And customers are more likely to be satisfied (**customer perspective**) if the firm's staff are well motivated and providing excellent service via smoothly running internal processes (**internal business perspective**).

Kaplan and Norton argue that the financial and non-financial measures on a Balanced Scorecard should be derived from the company's unique strategy (Kaplan and Norton 1996a,b). The Balanced Scorecard is viewed by many as a 'classic' model that has been widely applied in organizations in all sectors from banks (Balkovskaya and Filneva 2016) to local government (Sharma and Gadenne 2011). Kaplan and Norton (1996a:55) write that 'the Balanced Scorecard provides executives with a comprehensive framework that can translate a company's vision and strategy into a coherent and linked set of performance measures'. They suggest that the measures should include both outcome measures and the performance drivers of those outcomes. By articulating the outcomes desired by the firm, as well as the drivers of those outcomes, managers can channel the knowledge and energies of people throughout the organization towards achieving the business's long-term goals.

Kaplan and Norton insist that they reject the traditional view of measurement as a tool to control behaviour and evaluate past performance. While many systems of control and performance measurement attempt to keep individuals and organizational units in compliance with a pre-established plan, Kaplan and Norton argue that the measures on a Balanced Scorecard can be used by executives in a different way:

> *... to articulate the strategy of the business, to communicate the strategy of the business, and to help align individual, organizational, and cross-departmental initiatives to achieve a common goal. These executives are using the scorecard as a communication, information, and learning system, not as a traditional control system. For the Balanced Scorecard to be used in this way, however, the measures must provide a clear representation of the organization's long-term strategy for competitive success.*
>
> Kaplan and Norton (1996a:56)

Strategy maps

In their later work, Kaplan and Norton (e.g. Kaplan and Norton 2004a) propose strategy maps as a way to describe an organization's strategy, so that objectives and measures can be established and managed. This is illustrated in Figure 9.10. On the left-hand side of the strategy map, we can see the four perspectives of the Balanced Scorecard; each perspective has a 'row' of the model that contributes to the overall strategy of the organization. It is important to stress that, as we drill down into the detail of the four perspectives of the Balanced Scorecard, each organization will have its own unique strategy map, reflecting the aspects that are most important to its own unique strategy. As an example, in Figure 9.10:

- the financial perspective contains elements concerning productivity (improving the cost structure and utilization of assets) and growth (expanding revenue and enhancing customer value)
- the financial perspective is supported by a customer perspective showing the key elements of the customer value proposition—price, quality, and so on
- the customer perspective is supported by an internal perspective, which highlights the importance of sound processes for managing operations, managing customers, managing innovation, and so on

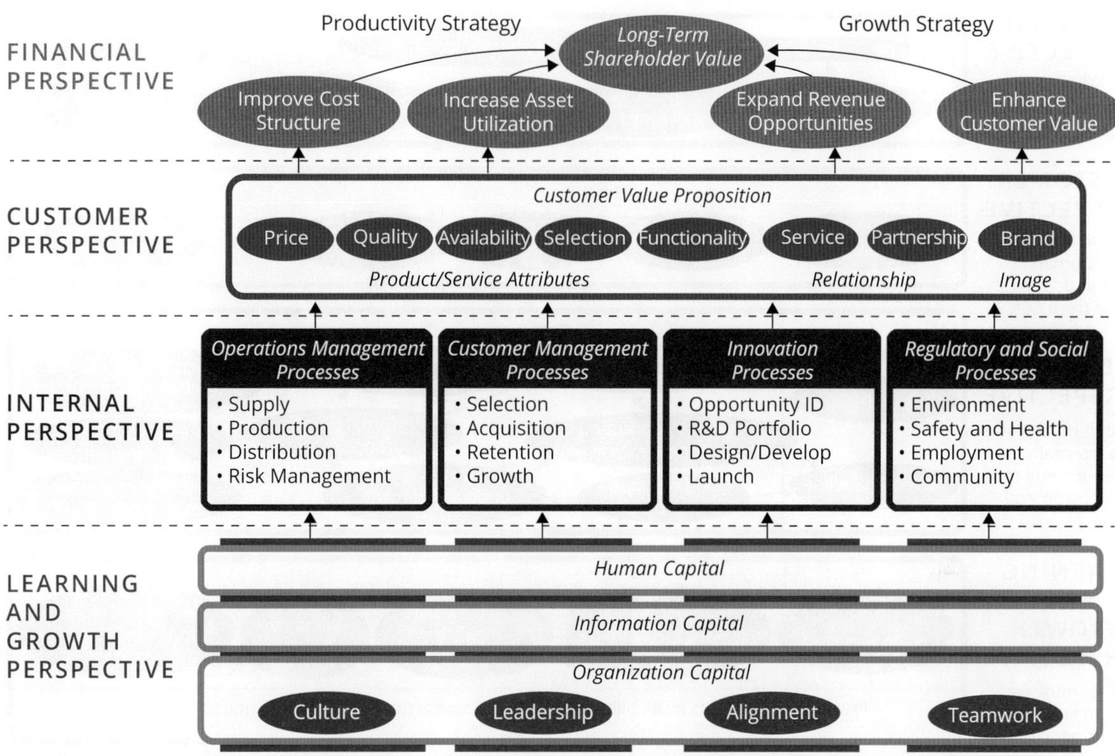

FIGURE 9.10 A strategy map represents how an organization creates value.
Source: Adapted with permission from Robert S. Kaplan, David P. Norton, (2004). The strategy map: guide to aligning intangible assets. *Strategy & Leadership*, Vol. 32 Issue: 5, pp.10–17, https://doi.org/10.1108/10878570410699825. Copyright © 2004, Emerald Publishing Limited.

- finally, all of the above is supported by a focus on learning and growth, which reflects the importance of human capital, information capital, etc.

Kaplan and Norton see the strategy map as 'the missing link between strategy formulation and strategy execution' (Kaplan and Norton 2004a:10). The map evolves from the Balanced Scorecard with its four perspectives introduced earlier in this section; it adds an additional layer of detail that illustrates the time-based dynamics of strategy. The intention, according to the authors, is to add granularity—and subsequently clarity and focus. The aim of a strategy map is to provide a framework that illustrates how strategy links intangible assets to value-creating processes. They describe the framework as follows:

> *A strategy map for a Balanced Scorecard makes explicit the strategy's hypotheses. Each measure of a Balanced Scorecard becomes embedded in a chain of cause-and-effect logic that connects the desired outcomes from the strategy with the drivers that will lead to the strategic outcomes. The strategy map describes the process for transforming intangible assets into tangible customer and financial outcomes. It provides executives with a framework for describing and managing strategy in a knowledge economy.*
>
> Kaplan and Norton (2001:69)

To illustrate the use of a strategy map in action, Figure 9.11 provides an example for Crown Castle, a large US-based technology firm.

If an organization's goal is to manage its performance towards the successful achievement of its defined strategy, a strategy map can be a useful tool in making clear connections between

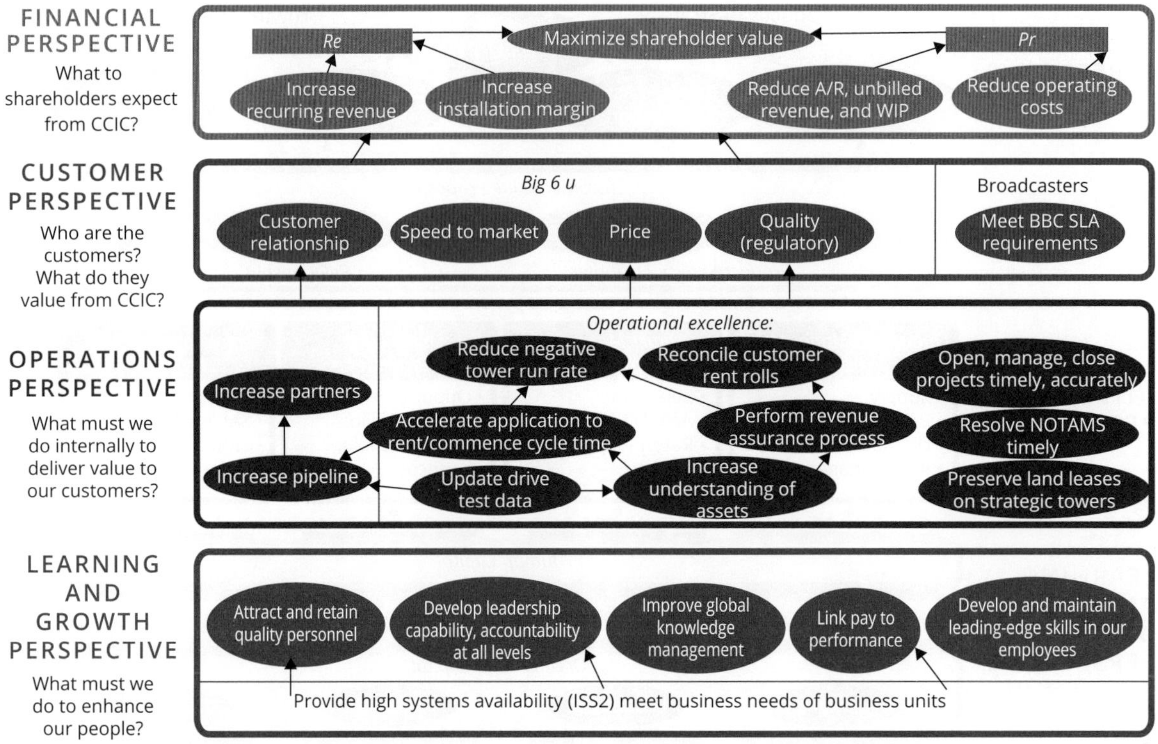

FINANCIAL PERSPECTIVE
What to shareholders expect from CCIC?
Re
Maximize shareholder value
Pr
Increase recurring revenue
Increase installation margin
Reduce A/R, unbilled revenue, and WIP
Reduce operating costs

CUSTOMER PERSPECTIVE
Who are the customers? What do they value from CCIC?
Big 6 u
Broadcasters
Customer relationship
Speed to market
Price
Quality (regulatory)
Meet BBC SLA requirements

OPERATIONS PERSPECTIVE
What must we do internally to deliver value to our customers?
Operational excellence:
Reduce negative tower run rate
Reconcile customer rent rolls
Open, manage, close projects timely, accurately
Increase partners
Accelerate application to rent/commence cycle time
Perform revenue assurance process
Resolve NOTAMS timely
Increase pipeline
Update drive test data
Increase understanding of assets
Preserve land leases on strategic towers

LEARNING AND GROWTH PERSPECTIVE
What must we do to enhance our people?
Attract and retain quality personnel
Develop leadership capability, accountability at all levels
Improve global knowledge management
Link pay to performance
Develop and maintain leading-edge skills in our employees
Provide high systems availability (ISS2) meet business needs of business units

FIGURE 9.11 Kaplan and Norton's strategy map applied to Crown Castle. Source: Adapted with permission from Robert S. Kaplan, David P. Norton, (2004). The strategy map: guide to aligning intangible assets. *Strategy & Leadership*, Vol. 32 Issue: 5, pp.10–17, https://doi.org/10.1108/10878570410699825. Copyright © 2004, Emerald Publishing Limited.

the performance of each function and the performance of the organization as a whole. Taking the Crown Castle strategy map (Figure 9.11) as an example, and comparing it with the functional strategies we have discussed in this chapter, we can see the following:

- **Financial strategy:** the strategy map illustrates the relationship between the customer perspective (with dimensions such as price and speed to market) and the financial perspective which emphasizes revenue, operating costs, margins, etc.
- **HRM strategy:** the strategy map illustrates the importance of HR in the learning and growth of the organization by highlighting aspects such as attracting and retaining personnel, developing leadership capabilities, linking pay and performance, etc. The strategy map indicates that these dimensions provide fundamental support to all of the other strategies that the organization is aiming to pursue.
- **Marketing strategy:** the customer perspective of the strategy map stresses the importance of building customer relationships in supporting the future financial success of the organization. It also identifies key dimensions of achieving customer satisfaction such as quality and speed to market.
- **Operations strategy:** the strategy map places key operational issues at the heart of the organization's strategic performance, highlighting a wide range of dimensions from successful project management to appropriate partnerships.

- **IT strategy:** Crown Castle is a technology-based company, with IT at the centre of all its activities, and Kaplan and Norton (2004b) stress that its operating environment is highly dynamic, competitive, and fluid. Therefore the strategy map needs to be updated regularly, for example to reflect shifting pressures in the external business environment for Crown Castle, as well as to respond to any changes required in the firm's portfolio of IT projects as suggested by McFarlan's Strategic Grid (Section 9.7).

In this section we have discussed how tools such as the Balanced Scorecard and strategy maps can be used to develop the relationship between the organization's strategy and the operation of its key functions. As discussed at the beginning of the section, tools like these are important as they orient organizational practices and help organizations to avoid failing to implement their strategy because of a lack of alignment between these two processes. We touched on the Balanced Scorecard in Chapter 4, when we discussed an organization's need for a set of key performance indicators to help deliver its strategic purpose.

PRACTITIONER INSIGHT: **ALAN WRIGHT, CENTRAL OPERATIONS DIRECTOR, ARCUS**

Arcus (www.arcusfm.com) is a facilities management (FM) company that was founded in 2009 as a joint venture between the supermarket Sainsbury's and a specialist FM company. Now employing around 3500 staff, it operates throughout the UK with clients including Sainsbury's, Argos, Capita, the Co-op, and Central Bedfordshire Council. Alan Wright is the central operations director for Arcus. In his current position, he is responsible for strategy and leadership of operations that support client-facing staff, including customer helpdesk, IT, and innovation functions. Previously he worked for IBM, Sanmina-SCI, Alfred McAlpine, and Carillion in a range of operations and project management roles.

Alan shares his views about how functional strategy can be made and managed.

Explaining facilities management

At Arcus we offer a total facilities management solution for our customers. This means that on a customer's behalf we undertake servicing of their infrastructure and buildings (such as mechanical, electrical, refrigeration, drainage, heating, ventilation, and air-conditioning systems). By engaging with us as specialists in FM, facilities can be managed more efficiently and effectively for the customer than by an in-house function whilst allowing the customer to focus on their core business. This is how we started as a joint venture with Sainsbury's. Working with us enables our customers to be agile in terms of their usage of facilities whilst benefiting from excellent cost performance and operational availability of infrastructure.

We are supporting customers in a rapidly changing retail environment. Consumer connectivity has given rise to online fresh food retailers such as Ocado and Amazon, meaning that traditional bricks-and-mortar supermarkets are having to digitalize rapidly. Aldi and Lidl are reshaping consumer expectations and eroding differentiation advantage for high-end brands such as Waitrose and M&S. Fewer people are visiting supermarkets, so incumbents are bringing in concessions (e.g. Tesco bringing in Arcadia outlets to their stores) to try to turn their superstores into destinations, similar to the approach of continental supermarkets. This changing customer context directly affects us, passing on cost challenges and service development requirements that we need to meet at strategic and operational levels.

Continued

How is strategy developed in Arcus?

We have assigned business plans with our customers which are linked to a contract. On a year-by-year basis, we refresh our views about how we can best deliver against that plan. This can be an incremental refresh, building upon the fundamentals that are already in place, or we may make more wholesale changes if the situation demands it or we decide that we want to explore new areas of business (e.g. propose new services to the client).

Our organizational strategy comes from the executive team, with a degree of input from the director team. Directors are then tasked with developing strategies for their functions. For example, for IT strategy, I'll work with the head of IT and his or her team to clarify the technical details, costs, operational requirements. etc. of potential initiatives. We'll evaluate risks, and fit with the business, cost, practicalities, and feasibilities of options, in order to make a compelling case for approval of our recommendations.

And we also draw on principles. For example, in HR strategy, when we invest in new hires, the decisive criterion is always attitude. You can teach people skills and you can train them in technology. But without the right attitude to fit into our culture, align with our values, and understand our strategic purpose, it won't be a long-term appointment. This is particularly true in a service industry. Our recruitment strategy, and our strategic investment in new hires, will always focus on behaviours and attitudes.

What drives your functional strategy?

At the core of our functional and organizational strategy work we have a number of consistent themes—shared areas of focus—which describe our purpose and approach. These themes are an expression of the strategic priorities we have held from day one. They are in some way the strategy of the business as they describe what we are trying to do. They sit alongside our values—'Do it well, do it simply, do it with passion'—as guiding principles for the organization.

How do you monitor functional strategy delivery?

Our strategy work identifies objectives annually that are cascaded down from the top team into the personal development plans of employees—this is how we motivate and set directions for individuals to contribute to the business plan. Thereafter, our system of key performance indicators (KPIs) is important for how we monitor and manage functional strategy implementation. We have no-miss, what we call gateway, KPIs relating to core governance and compliance targets for the client. They are the main focus—financial performance, compliance with the law—that need the tightest of control. They are also a key feature of how we differentiate ourselves through a customer service built on transparency, auditability, and performance. We then have KPIs that monitor important business function performance targets, for example infrastructure availability, such as lifts and fridges, for our customers. We monitor these on a continuing basis and make operational responses accordingly. Our final set of KPIs track progress versus annual business plan initiatives and projects. We use these KPIs to keep the client up to date on the implementation of functional change (e.g. projects to reduce energy consumption in stores from a baseline level).

What does the term strategy mean to you?

For me, strategy is the process by which you set a plan that consciously addresses what you want to be next and achieve as an organization or function. This can also include being clear about what you don't want to do. For example, we are an FM business, and that is what we do. If any business opportunities arise that don't fit in that remit, we will partner with others to realize that opportunity. You can draw a line between strategy and tactics when it comes to plans. Whilst your ideas may be simple or complex, strategy is looking at a longer-term horizon than operational plans. Making the decision to not make a plan can be a strategy in itself. However, that view doesn't work for me in the operations role—I always have to be thinking about what's next. At a functional level, a lot of what strategy comes down to is dealing with ambiguity and the variables that are in play.

I've learned not to be fearful of strategy. It seems, by reputation, to sit on a pedestal—it shouldn't! I've learned that you can incorporate valuable inputs from all throughout the organization, and that it is never too early in your career to get involved in strategy. Further, it is important not to get caught up with planning too far ahead. You can end up projecting a decade in advance, looking well beyond what is currently knowable or tangible. This can make you miss the opportunities that are right in front of you.

Of course, try to look ahead and stay ahead of the curve, but don't neglect the real opportunities that are there for the taking. And be mindful of the context in which you are operating.

In making strategy, I think it is important to listen to your customers and gain an understanding of their wants and needs, what they are trying to be, and how their context is changing. If you can do that and have trusted conversations with those around you, then you can create strategy that takes you forward. You need not seek perfection—the future is too unknowable. Instead make a strategy based on what you know and keep it regularly updated, learning as you go.

CHAPTER SUMMARY

In this chapter we addressed the following learning outcomes.

- **Describe the role of functional strategy in supporting organizational strategy**
  Functional strategy can help managers within each functional area of the organization to align their own activities with the organization's overall strategy—and hence ensure that the strategy is delivered. If successful, the functional strategy can bring the organization's operational plans together into a coherent strategic statement that clarifies the contribution of each function to the overall organizational strategy. It can highlight the contribution of each function to the achievement of the organization's goals, and assist with the efficient allocation of resources to the tasks where they can be most effective. A good functional strategy will help each functional team to turn high-level strategic statements into actionable plans, and ensure that employees feel that their abilities are being used effectively towards the attainment of both the function's and the organization's goals.
- **Identify and outline the different types of functional strategy**
  We have discussed functional strategy for five key areas of the organization—finance, HRM, marketing, operations, and IT—in relation to a number of case examples. For example, we saw that IKEA has refreshed its operations strategy in response to external factors such as shifting patterns of retail behaviour, we reflected on FCA's changing marketing strategy as it reconsiders the role of each of its brands, and we saw GE renew its approach to financial strategy, including a new approach to cost management, under the organization's new leadership. In our Opening Case Study of Vail Resorts, we see many of these elements come together, as they adopt innovative approaches to generating income from their target markets and their use of technology, as well as focusing on the values espoused by staff. We have noted the complex interactions between these dimensions, and their contribution to the overall strategy of the organization.
- **Discuss the potential advantages and disadvantages of functional strategy**
  We have discussed the potential value of functional strategy, for example in aligning functional areas with the organization's overall strategy, articulating and highlighting the contributions of the functional areas, assisting in planning and resource allocation,

and ensuring that the overall strategy is delivered. However, attention must also be paid to the context of the strategy, such as the type of the organization in question, and its unique needs. For example, functional strategy may be seen as ineffective in smaller organizations; managers may argue that functional strategy is an unnecessary drain on resources and staff time. In particular cases, it may lead to (real or perceived) conflicts between the organization's overall strategy and one or more specific functional strategies, which must then be resolved. Moreover, functional strategies may leave functional managers feeling that they are facing too many conflicting requests and that they are 'stretched too thinly' across a range of priorities; they may even distract functional managers to the point where they can lose sight of the main objectives of the organization.

- **Explain the role of strategic performance management tools, such as the Balanced Scorecard, in connecting functional strategy with the effective implementation of organizational strategy**

  We have introduced tools such as the Balanced Scorecard and strategy maps to help to elaborate the relationship between the organization's strategy on the one hand, and the operation of its key functions on the other. This is an important step as organizations often fail to implement their strategy because they lack an overarching management system to integrate and align these two processes. These tools illustrate the role of functional strategy in working towards the overall organizational goals. The Balanced Scorecard is a set of measures which give senior managers an overview of key aspects of the organization, while a strategy map can provide a framework to show how strategy links intangible assets to value-creating processes within the organization.

END OF CHAPTER QUESTIONS

Recall questions

1. What is functional strategy, and how might it be of value to an organization?
2. Describe the relationship between functional strategy, business unit strategy, and organizational/corporate strategy. Explain how the different levels of strategy may interact.
3. Draw Kaplan and Norton's Balanced Scorecard, labelling the four perspectives and giving examples of performance measures in each of the four quadrants.
4. Define the concept of market segmentation, and how the marketing mix can be used build customer insight and support marketing planning in an organization.
5. Describe the relationship between digital strategy, IT strategy, and business strategy.

Application questions

A) Describe some of the advantages and disadvantages of functional strategy, relating your comments to an organization that you know well.

B) Choose an organizational function that you are familiar with—finance, HR, marketing, operations, or IT. Make notes on the strategy of that function within an organization that you know well or can research online. Highlight the key topics and issues that the functional strategy covers, and any that it might be missing. How does the functional strategy influence, and how is it influenced by, the organization's overall strategy?

C) Develop a strategy map for an organization that you know well, or can research online. Make notes on the connections that the map highlights between the strategies of the functions within the organization, and the organization's strategy as a whole. What does your work tell you about how functional strategy should be developed and managed in organizations?

ONLINE RESOURCES

www.oup.com/he/mackay1e

FURTHER READING

Strategic dissonance, by Robert A. Burgelman and Andrew S. Grove

Burgelman, R.A. and Grove, A.S. (1996). Strategic dissonance. *California Management Review*, **38**(2), 8–28.

Robert Burgelman and Andrew Grove point out that aligning corporate strategy and strategic action is a key management responsibility. Focusing on high tech industries, they explore how management can make strategic decisions in highly dynamic environments. They emphasize strategic dissonance (divergence between strategic intent and actions), inflection points (when one type of industry dynamic gives way to another), and strategic recognition (the capacity of managers to appreciate the importance of managerial initiatives after they have come about but before unequivocal feedback is available).

Ambidextrous organizations: managing evolutionary and revolutionary change, by Michael L. Tushman and Charles A. O'Reilly III

Tushman, M.L. and O'Reilly, C.A., III (1996). Ambidextrous organizations: managing evolutionary and revolutionary change. *California Management Review*, **38**(4), 8–30.

Michael Tushman and Charles O'Reilly ask why anything but incremental change is so difficult in most successful organizations. They argue that, to remain successful, managers and organizations must be ambidextrous, i.e. able to implement both incremental and revolutionary change.

See also Tushman, M.L. and O'Reilly, C.A., III (1997). Winning Through Innovation: A Practical Guide to Leading Organizational Change and Renewal. *Boston, MA: Harvard Business School Press.*

The power of strategic integration, by Robert A. Burgelman and Yves L. Doz

Burgelman, R.A. and Doz, Y.L. (2001). The power of strategic integration. *Sloan Management Review*, **42**(3), 28–38.

Robert Burgelman and Yves Doz explore the challenges of strategic integration, when issues of scope (of the existing strategy) are positioned against issues of reach (in other words, extending the current strategy). They discuss the tensions that can be caused when managers try to both reinforce the core (existing strategy) and aim for redirection (new strategic intent). They argue that what they call complex strategic integration requires a range of management skills—cognitive, political, and entrepreneurial.

Big Data consumer analytics and the transformation of marketing, by Sunil Erevelles, Nobuyuki Fukawa, and Linda Swayne

Erevelles, S., Fukawa, N., and Swayne, L. (2016). Big Data consumer analytics and the transformation of marketing. *Journal of Business Research*, **69**(2), 897–904.

This paper seeks to understand the impact of Big Data on various marketing activities. The authors argue that three resources—physical, human, and organizational capital— impact on the process of collecting and storing evidence of consumer activity as Big Data, the process of extracting consumer insight from Big Data, and the process of utilizing consumer insight to enhance dynamic/adaptive capabilities.

9

Global talent management and global talent challenges: strategic opportunities for IHRM, by Randall S. Schuler, Susan E. Jackson, and Ibraiz Tarique

Schuler, R.S., Jackson, S.E., and Tarique, I. (2011). Global talent management and global talent challenges: strategic opportunities for IHRM, *Journal of World Business*, **46**(4), 506–16.

The authors discuss the vital role of international human resource management for international organizations. The management of talent, in a global setting, can entail dealing with talent shortages, talent surpluses, locating and relocating talent, and compensation levels of talent. They label these issues as 'global talent challenges', and discuss their implications for organizations.

Internet marketing capabilities and international market growth, by Shane Mathews et al.

Mathews, S., Bianchi, C., Perks, K.J., et al. (2016). Internet marketing capabilities and international market growth. *International Business Review*, **25**(4), 820–30.

This study explores how the internet, combined with marketing capabilities, can drive international market growth. It suggests that internet marketing capabilities indirectly lead to international market growth when the firm has a high level of international strategic orientation and international network capabilities. Overall, internet marketing capabilities enhance the firm's ability to generate other internal capabilities within the firm.

REFERENCES

Adams, S. (2014). Hermès and LVMH make peace. *Forbes*. https://www.forbes.com/sites/susanadams/2014/09/11/hermes-and-lvmh-make-peace/#3c844d0d6288 (accessed 26 May 2019).

Amit, R. and Zott, C. (2001). Value creation in e-business, *Strategic Management Journal*, **22**, 493–520.

Applegate, L.M., Austin, R.D., and McFarlan, F.W. (2007). *Corporate Information Strategy and Management* (7th edn). New York: McGraw-Hill.

Aron, D. (2013). The difference between IT strategy and digital strategy. *Gartner*, https://blogs.gartner.com/dave-aron/2013/11/12/the-difference-between-it-strategy-and-digital-strategy/ (accessed 19 May 2019).

Baines, P., Fill, C., Rosengren, S., and Antonetti, P. (2019). *Marketing* (5th edn). Oxford: Oxford University Press.

Baines, T., Lightfoot, H., Peppard, J., et al. (2008). Towards an operations strategy for product-centric servitization. *International Journal of Operations & Production Management*, **29**(5), 494–519.

Balkovskaya, D. and Filneva, L. (2016). The use of the Balanced Scorecard in bank strategic management. *International Journal of Business Excellence*, **9**(1), 48–67.

BBC (2018). Army's £113m recruitment website 'was 52 months late'. https://www.bbc.co.uk/news/uk-46561779 (accessed 22 May 2019).

Benckendorff, P.J., Xiang, Z., and Sheldon, P.J. (2019). *Tourism Information Technology* (3rd edn). Wallingford: CABI Tourism Texts.

Bender, R. (2014). *Corporate Financial Strategy* (4th edn) London: Routledge.

Betsch, T., Haberstroh, S., and Hohle, C. (2002). Explaining routinized decision making: a review of theories and models. *Theory & Psychology*, **12**(4), 453–88.

Bharadwaj, A., El Sawy, O.A., Pavlou, P.A., and Venkatraman, N. (2013). Digital business strategy: toward a net generation of insights. *MIS Quarterly*, **37**(2), 471–82.

Blumberg, M. and Pringle, C. (1982). The missing opportunity in organizational research: some implications for a theory of work performance. *Academy of Management Review*, **7**(4), 560–9.

Booms, B.H. and Bitner, M.J. (1981). Marketing strategies and organization structures for service firms. In: Donnelly, J.H. and George, W.R. (eds), *Marketing of Services*, pp. 47–51. Chicago, IL: American Marketing Association.

Borden, N.H. (1964). The concept of the marketing mix, *Journal of Advertising Research*, **2**, 7–12.

Boselie, P., Dietz, G., and Boon, C. (2005). Commonalities and contradictions in HRM and performance research. *Human Resource Management Journal*, **15**(3), 67–94.

Bowden, G. (2019). A year since Carillion's collapse. The NHS faces a multi-million pound headache. https://www.msn.com/en-gb/money/companies/a-year-since-carillion%E2%80%99s-collapse-the-nhs-faces-a-multi-million-pound-headache/ar-BBSfStO (accessed 22 May 2019).

Bowen, J. and Ford, R. (2002). Managing service organizations: does having a 'thing' make a difference? *Journal of Management*, **28**(3), 447–69.

Boxall, P. and Purcell, J. (2016). *Strategy and Human Resource Management* (4th edn). London: Palgrave Macmillan Education.

Boyes, H., Hallaq, B., Cunningham, J., and Watson, T. (2018). The Industrial Internet of Things (IIoT): an analysis framework. *Computers in Industry*, **101**, 1–12.

Burgelman, R., Christensen, C., and Wheelwright, S. (2009). *Strategic Management of Technology and Innovation*. New York: McGraw-Hill.

Chaffey, D. and Ellis-Chadwick, F. (2019). *Digital Marketing: Strategy, Implementation and Practice* (7th edn). Harlow: Pearson.

Christensen, C. (2003). *The Innovator's Solution: Creating and Sustaining Successful Growth*. Boston, MA: Harvard Business School Press.

Christensen, C., Verlinden, M., and Westerman, G. (2002). Disruption, disintegration, and the dissipation of differentiability. *Industrial and Corporate Change*, **11**(5), 955–93.

Collings, D. and Mellahi, K. (2009). Strategic talent management: a review and research agenda. *Human Resource Management Review*, **19**(4), 304–13.

Corbett, M.F. (2004). *The Outsourcing Revolution: Why It Makes Sense and How to Do It Right*. New York: Kaplan Publishing.

de Mooij, M. (2018). *Global Marketing and Advertising: Understanding Cultural Paradoxes* (5th edn). Thousand Oaks, CA: Sage.

Denning, S. (2012). Transformational leadership in agile manufacturing: Wikispeed. *Forbes*. https://www.forbes.com/sites/stevedenning/2012/08/01/transformational-leadership-in-agile-manufacturing-wikispeed/#3f4826db6df3 (accessed 18 May 2019).

Dolgui, A. and Proth, J. (2013). Outsourcing: definitions and analysis. *International Journal of Production Research*, **51**(23-24), 6769–77.

Dowling, P.J., Festing, M., and Eagle, A. (2013). *International Human Resource Management* (6th edn). Andover: Cengage Learning EMEA.

The Economist (2013). Sin of omission. https://www.economist.com/business/2013/03/09/sin-of-omission (accessed 18 May 2019).

The Economist (2018). Britain's outsourcing model, copied around the world, is in trouble. https://www.economist.com/britain/2018/06/28/britains-outsourcing-model-copied-around-the-world-is-in-trouble (accessed 18 May 2019).

Electronics360 (2015). Philips to supply lighting for Dutch airport. https://electronics360.globalspec.com/article/5276/philips-to-supply-lighting-for-dutch-airport (accessed 18 May 2019).

Evans, P., Pucik, V., and Barsoux, J.-L. (2002). *The Global Challenge: Frameworks for International Human Resource Management*. New York: McGraw-Hill.

Financial Times (2014). *Financial Times* targets younger readers with new digital advertising campaign. https://aboutus.ft.com/en-gb/announcements/financial-times-targets-younger-readers-with-new-digital-advertising-campaign/ (accessed 18 May 2019).

Finextra (2019). NatWest paperless mortgage process picks up 100,000 customers. https://www.finextra.com/pressarticle/78431/natwest-paperless-mortgage-process-picks-up-100000-customers?utm_medium=rssfinextra&utm_source=finextrafeed (accessed 25 May 2019).

Frenkel, S. (2000). Introduction: service work and its implications for HRM. *International Journal of Human Resource Management*, **11**(3), 469–76.

Fried, V.H. and Hisrich, R.D. (1994). Toward a model of venture capital investment decision making, *Financial Management*, **23**(3), 28–37.

Galliers, R.D. and Sutherland, A.R. (1991). Information systems management and strategy formulation: the stages of growth model revisited. *Journal of Information Systems*, **1**, 89–114.

Glassman, B. (2013). What Zappos taught us about creating the ultimate client experience. *Forbes*. https://www.forbes.com/sites/advisor/2013/05/13/what-zappos-taught-us-about-creating-the-ultimate-client-experience/#165626220fbd (accessed 18 May 2019).

Greener, I. (2013). *Public Management* (2nd edn). London: Red Globe Press.

Guest, D. (1997). Human resource management and performance: a review and research agenda. *International Journal of Human Resource Management*, **8**(3), 263–76.

The Guardian (2019). Melrose plan to shut GKN Aerospace factory is 'breach of faith'. https://www.theguardian.com/business/2019/apr/05/melrose-plan-to-shut-gkn-aerospace-factory-is-breach-of-faith (accessed 26 May 2019).

Henderson, J.C. and Venkatraman, N. (1993). Strategic alignment: leveraging information technology for transforming organizations. *IBM Systems Journal*, **32**(1), 472–84.

Hill, T. (2000). *Manufacturing Strategy: Text and Cases* (2nd edn). Basingstoke: Palgrave.

Hodge, G.A. (2000). *Privatization: An International Review of Performance.* Boulder, CO: Westview Press.

Jiang, K., Lepak, D., Hu, J., and Beer, J. (2012). How does human resource management influence organizational outcomes? A meta-analytic investigation of mediating mechanisms. *Academy of Management Journal*, **55**(6), 1264–94.

Kaplan, R.S. and Mikes, A. (2012). Managing risks: a new framework. *Harvard Business Review*, **90**(6), 48–60.

Kaplan, R.S. and Norton, D.P. (1992). The Balanced Scorecard: measures that drive performance. *Harvard Business Review*, **70**, 71–9.

Kaplan, R.S. and Norton, D.P. (1996a). Linking the Balanced Scorecard to strategy. *California Management Review*, **39**(1), 53–79.

Kaplan, R.S. and Norton, D.P. (1996b). *The Balanced Scorecard: Translating Strategy into Action*. Boston, MA: Harvard Business School Press.

Kaplan, R.S. and Norton, D.P. (2001). *The Strategy-Focused Organization: How Balanced Scorecard Companies Thrive in the New Business Environment*. Boston, MA: Harvard Business School Press.

Kaplan, R.S. and Norton, D.P. (2004a). *Strategy Maps: Converting Intangible Assets into Tangible Outcomes*. Boston, MA: Harvard Business School Press.

Kaplan, R.S. and Norton, D.P. (2004b). The strategy map: guide to aligning intangible assets. *Strategy & Leadership*, **32**(5), 10–17.

Kaplan, R.S. and Norton, D.P. (2008). *The Execution Premium: Linking Strategy to Operations for Competitive Advantage*. Boston, MA: Harvard Business School Press.

Kotler, P. and Armstrong, G. (2017). *Principles of Marketing* (17th edn). Harlow: Pearson.

Krishnamurthy, R. and Yauch, C.A. (2007). Leagile manufacturing: a proposed corporate infrastructure. *International Journal of Operations & Production Management*, **27**(6), 588–604.

Lanvin, B. and Evans, P. (2013). *The Global Talent Competitiveness Index*. https://www.insead.edu/sites/default/files/assets/dept/globalindices/docs/GTCI-2018-report.pdf (accessed 13 December 2019).

Levitt, T. (1983). The globalization of markets. *Harvard Business Review*, May–June, 92–102.

Lovelock, C., Patterson, P., and Wirtz, J. (2010). *Services Marketing: An Asia–Pacific and Australian Perspective* (5th edn). Sydney: Pearson Australia.

McCulloch, A. (2018). TfL tops league table of best organisations in UK for work–life balance, *Personnel Today*. https://www.personneltoday.com/hr/tfl-tops-league-table-of-best-organisations-in-uk-for-work-life-balance/ (accessed 18 May 2019).

MacDonald, K.H. and Yapp, C. (1992). IT strategies: issues and prescriptions. In: Brown, A. (ed.), *Creating a Business-based IT Strategy*, pp. 243–60. London: Chapman & Hall.

McFarlan, F.W. (1984). Information technology changes the way you compete. *Harvard Business Review*, **62**(3), 98–103.

Marr, B. (2005). Strategic management of intangible value drivers. *Handbook of Business Strategy*, **6**(1), 147–54.

Marr, B., Schiuma, G., and Neely, A. (2004). The dynamics of value creation: mapping your intellectual performance drivers. *Journal of Intellectual Capital*, **5**(2), 312–25.

Mason, C. and Stark, M. (2004). What do investors look for in a business plan? A comparison of the investment criteria of bankers, venture capitalists, and business angels. *International Small Business Journal*, **22**(3), 227–48.

Nathan, V. (2019). Auto makers are improving operations with help from Industrial IoT. *Forbes*. https://www.forbes.com/sites/vinaynathan/2019/03/29/the-iiot-is-driving-results-for-the-automotive-industry/#43ef318634ad (accessed 18 May 2019).

Nielsen (2012). Global trust in advertising and brand messages. https://www.nielsen.com/us/en/insights/reports/2012/global-trust-in-advertising-and-brand-messages.html (accessed 18 May 2019).

Nolan, R. (1979). Managing the crises in data processing. *Harvard Business Review*, **57**(2), 115–26.

Nolan, R. and McFarlan, F.W. (2005). Information technology and the board of directors. *Harvard Business Review*. **83**(10), 96–106.

Ocado (2019). Invite a friend and share something nice. https://www.ocado.com/webshop/recommendFriends.go?clkInTab=inviteAFriend (accessed 18 May 2019).

Ohno, T. (1988). *Just-in-Time: For Today and Tomorrow*. Cambridge, MA: Productivity Press.

Peter, J.P., Olson, J.C., and Grunert, K.G. (1999). *Consumer Behaviour and Marketing Strategy*. London: McGraw-Hill.

PMI (2019). What is project management? https://www.pmi.org/about/learn-about-pmi/what-is-project-management (accessed 20 July 2019).

PublishDrive (2017). Amazon e-book market share 2017: is it big enough? https://publishdrive.com/amazon-ebook-market-share/ (accessed 20 July 2019).

Pullman, M.E. and Gross, M.A. (2004). Ability of experience design elements to elicit emotions and loyalty behaviors. *Decision Science*, **35**(3), 531–76.

Quora (2018), Are Google employees more productive because of company perks? *Forbes*. https://www.forbes.com/sites/quora/2018/07/09/are-google-employees-more-productive-because-of-company-perks/#7a0e3e474b4d (accessed 18 May 2019).

Rappaport, A. (1998). *Creating Shareholder Value*. New York: Free Press.

Ringel, M., Grassi, F., Baeza, R., et al. (2019). Innovation in 2019: the most innovative companies 2019. https://www.bcg.com/en-gb/publications/2019/most-innovative-companies-innovation.aspx (accessed 25 May 2019).

Ross, J.W., Sebastian, I.M., and Beath, C.M. (2017). How to develop a great digital strategy. *Sloan Management Review*, **58**(2), 6–9.

Roth, A.V. and Menor, L.J. (2003). Insights into service operations management: a research agenda. *Production Operations Management*, **12**(2), 145–64.

Sharma, B. and Gadenne, D. (2011). Balanced Scorecard implementation in a local government authority: issues and challenges. *Australian Journal of Public Administration*, **70**(2), 167–84.

Sibbert, D. (1997). 75 years of management ideas and practice 1922–1997. *Harvard Business Review*, **75**, 2–12.

Simchi-Levi, D., Kaminsky, P., and Simchi-Levi, E. (2004). *Managing the Supply Chain: The Definitive Guide for the Business Professional*. New York: McGraw-Hill.

Sirakaya, E. and Woodside, A.G. (2005). Building and testing theories of decision making by travellers. *Tourism Management*, **26**, 815–32.

Slack, N. and Lewis, M (2017). *Operations Strategy* (5th edn). Harlow: Financial Times—Prentice Hall.

Solomon, M. (2018). How Zappos delivers wow customer service on each and every call. *Forbes*. https://www.forbes.com/sites/micahsolomon/2018/09/15/the-secret-of-wow-customer-service-is-breathing-space-just-ask-zappos/#7b527d521b2c (accessed 18 May 2019).

Soltan, H. and Mostafa, S. (2015). Lean and agile performance framework for manufacturing enterprises. *Procedia Manufacturing*, **2**, 476–84.

Sterling, A. and Boxall, P. (2013). Lean production, employee learning, and workplace outcomes: a case analysis through the ability–motivation–opportunity framework. *Human Resource Management Journal*, **23**(3), 227–40.

Tidd, J. and Bessant, J.R. (2018). *Managing Innovation: Integrating Technological, Market, and Organizational Change* (6th edn). Chichester: John Wiley.

Ulrich, D. (1997). *Human Resource Champions: The Next Agenda for Adding Value and Delivering Results*. Boston, MA: Harvard Business School Press.

Ulrich, D. and Smallwood, N. (2004). Capitalizing on capabilities. *Harvard Business Review*, **82**(6), 119–27.

Valdés, G., Solar, M., Astudillo, H., et al. (2011). Conception, development, and implementation of an e-government maturity model in public agencies. *Government Information Quarterly*, **28**, 176–87.

Vandermerwe, S. and Rada, J. (1988). Servitization of business: adding value by adding services. *European Management Journal*, **6**(4), 314–24.

Visnjic, I., Jovanovic, M., Neely, A., and Engwall, M. (2017). What brings the value to outcome-based contract providers? Value drivers in outcome business models. *International Journal of Production Economics*, **192**, 169–81.

Voss, C., Roth, A.V., and Chase, R.B. (2008). Experience, service operations strategy, and services as destinations: foundations and exploratory investigation. *Production and Operations Management*, **17**(3), 247–66.

Vroom, V. (1964). *Work and Motivation*, New York: John Wiley.

Wainwright, D. and Waring, T. (2000). The information management and technology strategy of the UK National Health Service: determining progress in the NHS acute hospital sector. *International Journal of Public Sector Management*, **13**(3), 241–59.

Wilson, A. (1997). The culture of the branch team and its impact on service delivery and corporate identity. *International Journal of Bank Marketing*, **15**(5), 163–8.

Womack, J., Jones, D., and Roos, D. (1990). *The Machine that Changed the World: The Triumph of Lean Production*. New York: Rawson Macmillan.

Yusuf, Y.Y., Sarhadi, M., and Gunasekaran, A. (1999). Agile manufacturing: the drivers, concepts, and attributes. *International Journal of Production Economics*, **62**(1–2), 33–43.

Zott, C. and Amit, R. (2008). The fit between product market strategy and business model: implications for firm performance. *Strategic Management Journal*, **29**, 1–26.

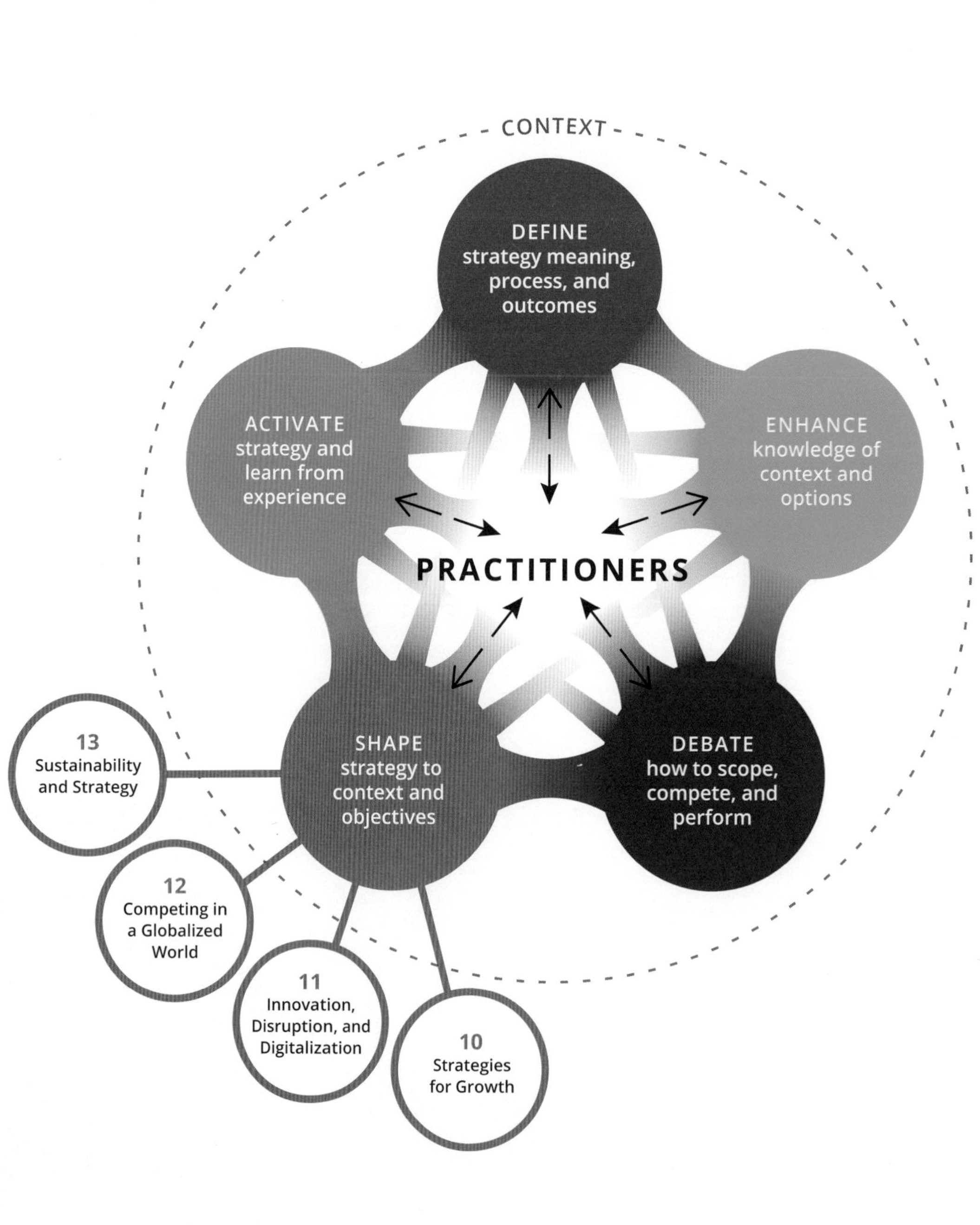
CONTEXT
DEFINE
strategy meaning, process, and outcomes
ENHANCE
knowledge of context and options
ACTIVATE
strategy and learn from experience
PRACTITIONERS
SHAPE
strategy to context and objectives
DEBATE
how to scope, compete, and perform
13
Sustainability and Strategy
12
Competing in a Globalized World
11
Innovation, Disruption, and Digitalization
10
Strategies for Growth

PART FOUR

Shape strategy to context and objectives

In Part 4 we address contemporary concerns of wide relevance to organizations during strategy development to meet specific situational needs. Chapter 10 extends corporate strategy thinking by examining how organizations—as multi-business enterprises—might strategize about growth in ways that include both related and unrelated diversification strategies. In Chapter 11 we examine how incorporating innovation and digitalization in strategizing might sustain organizational relevance, improve efficiency, or create new sources of value creation with disruptive market potential. Strategic options for internationalization of the organization's operations, including a consideration of various business models to manage global expansion and the emerging strategy of 'born global' organizations, are discussed in Chapter 12. Finally, Chapter 13 examines the strategic importance of sustainability to organizations, industries, societies, and nations. Successful organizations of the future will need build their sustainability capabilities and credentials to be able to take an advantage of new opportunities arising from the sustainability mega-trend.

By the end of Part 4, you should have enhanced abilities to think, talk, and act like a practitioner, shaping strategy in response to organization-specific influences and opportunities.

CHAPTER TEN

Strategies for Growth

CONTENTS

LEARNING OBJECTIVES

By the end of this chapter, you should be able to:

- Analyse the role of 'corporate parenting' in supporting strategy for single- and multi-business organizations
- Explain the concepts of economies of scale and scope
- Appreciate the role of relatedness and synergy in the development of corporate strategy
- Recognize, develop, and evaluate strategic options based on related and unrelated diversification, vertical and horizontal integration, mergers and acquisitions, joint ventures, and other forms of alliance
- Assess the risks and rewards associated with a range of approaches to diversification
- Apply a range of tests of suitability to potential strategic options

TOOLBOX

- **Economies of scale and scope**
  Economies of scale and economies of scope are two concepts that can be used to help an organization think about the possible benefits of a growth strategy, such as reducing its costs. Economies of scale focus on the cost advantages that can arise when the organization increases the level of production of a particular product or service. Economies of scope focus on the cost advantages that can arise when the organization's costs are shared across a variety of goods or activities.

- **The Ansoff matrix, also known as Ansoff's growth vectors**
  The Ansoff matrix is a tool which can help an organization identify and plan its product and market growth strategies. We can think of the organization's products as new or existing, and its target markets as new or existing. As part of our strategic planning, the Ansoff matrix helps us to see the possible growth strategies, or growth vectors, for an organization—market penetration, market development, product development, and diversification.

- **Diversification: related and unrelated**
  A diversification strategy involves expanding or adding to the organization's current range of products and markets. A related diversification is one in which the organization expands its activities into products and/or services that are similar to those it currently offers. Unrelated diversification involves entering a new line of business that lacks any important commonalities with the organization's existing industry or industries.

- **Synergy**
  Synergies occur when the whole is greater than the sum of its parts. It refers to the situation where two or more business units or organizations combine their efforts,

and find that they can accomplish more together than they can separately. Achieving synergy is often an important goal within a growth strategy, for example when two companies are planning a merger or alliance of some kind.

- **Vertical and horizontal integration**
  When an organization engages in a growth strategy of horizontal integration, it acquires a similar organization in the same industry to increase its size and perhaps achieve economies of scale. An organization adopting a growth strategy of vertical integration acquires an organization that operates in the production process of the same industry, either before or after it in the supply chain process, perhaps to strengthen its supply chain or capture upstream or downstream profits.

- **Different approaches to diversification**
  An organization seeking a suitable growth strategy might consider a merger, where two organizations combine into a single legal entity, or an acquisition, where one organization purchases a portion or all of another. A range of cooperative strategies can also be considered, including a joint venture, where two or more organizations create a new entity, a strategic alliance, which is a less formal agreement between two or more organizations to cooperate, and a consortium, which is a set of relationships between a variety of organizations, often concerned with bidding for and delivering a large and complex project. Finally, an organization might choose to pursue a strategy of divestment—selling or otherwise disposing of one or more of its activities.

- **Testing and evaluating strategic options**
  Having generated a set of possible growth strategies for the organization, the strategist can apply a set of tests to evaluate how the organization should proceed. For example, does a particular strategic option seem to be consistent with any prior strategic analysis of the organization's external environment and internal resources? Is the strategy likely to work well in practice, and how difficult will it be to achieve? And how acceptable is any new strategic option to the organization's range of stakeholders?

OPENING CASE STUDY NORWEGIAN AND A POTENTIAL MERGER WITH THE IAG

Since 2013, Norwegian, a low-cost airline carrier, has been trying to make 'no frills' long-haul flights (particularly on transatlantic routes) a reality. From humble beginnings in 1993 (starting off with only three aircraft), the company grew to become Europe's third largest low-cost carrier, focusing first on domestic routes in Norway, and then on short-haul routes across Europe. After enjoying strong financial results for a few years, Norwegian decided to branch out and expand into the long-haul market. The company ordered an additional 222 new aircraft, and by the end of 2017 had 145 aircraft operating on over 500 routes. According to *Aviation International News*, in 2018 Norwegian had overtaken British Airways (BA) to become the largest non-US airline on transatlantic routes to and from the New York area.

However, the jets that Norwegian ordered cost several times the value of the company, and in order to be competitive in this new market Norwegian had significantly reduced ticket prices for the new long-haul routes. It wasn't long before it started to suffer the financial consequences. According to *The*

Economist, Mr Kjos (founder and CEO) revealed that the airline had lost NKr299 million (£30.6 million) in 2017, compared with profits of NKr1.14 billion the previous year. Unsurprisingly, the share price of Norwegian dropped.

The vulnerable financial position of Norwegian presented an opportunity to the International Airlines Group (IAG). The IAG was formed in 2011 and is a group of carriers including BA, Iberia, Aer Lingus, Vueling, and Level. In April 2018 the IAG bought 4.6% of Norwegian, which was thought to be a sign that they were interested in a takeover. As *The Economist* points out, the IAG has also launched a low-cost long-haul brand of its own, so adding Norwegian to its portfolio could strengthen that venture. However, the IAG could also choose to remove a rival which has contributed to lower fares on routes flown by the other airlines within its portfolio. *The Economist* notes:

> According to experts, a takeover would therefore offer a mix of possible advantages and disadvantages for fliers. It would ensure that the weakness of Norwegian's balance-sheet does not kill off low-cost long-haul flying. But it would take out the biggest disruptive threat to IAG and other flag-carrier rivals.

In January 2019 the IAG stated that it did not intend to make an offer for Norwegian, and would sell its stake in the airline after having had two bids rejected by Norwegian's board. Such a deal might have been challenged on competition grounds anyway—the IAG is one of the five largest airline groups in the world, and adding Norwegian would increase its market share and further add to its influence. Following the news, Kjos said: 'Norwegian's plans and strategy remain unchanged ... The company's goal is to continue building a sustainable business to the benefit of its customers, employees and shareholders.' There are still options on the table as Norwegian has reportedly received several expressions of interest from 'serious players', including rival airlines such as Lufthansa. 'We are happy to have IAG as an investor. Needless to say, they are not the only interested party that has approached us', Kjos added.

The Economist stated: 'From a competition perspective, a takeover by a low-cost rival such as Ryanair would be preferable. It does not yet do long-haul and would have no qualms about carrying on disrupting the flag carriers'. However Ryanair's boss, Michael O'Leary, was cautious about the bid from the outset, predicting that the carrier would be 'bust this winter' (which did not happen). It is harder to boost aircraft utilization (the amount of time an airplane is in flight per 24-hour period) on longer flights, which is what makes Ryanair so cheap on shorter routes. Moreover, Mr O'Leary is convinced that Europe's three big flag carriers and their partners, which now control 78% of transatlantic flying, will do everything they can to destroy low-cost rivals, including, perhaps, buying them.

Questions for discussion

1. What do you think motivated IAG to consider making a merger deal with Norwegian? What do you think they hoped to achieve by it?
2. Can you identify other strategic options that IAG could have pursued, apart from a merger with Norwegian? Do you think that those options would have achieved the same objectives?
3. Consider the proposed merger deal from the perspective of Norwegian. What potential benefits and risks can you think of?
4. Consider the possibility of merger deals in the airline industry from the perspective of existing and potential customers of the companies concerned. What possible pros and cons of such deals can you identify?

Sources

The Economist, 19 April 2018

https://www.ainonline.com/aviation-news/air-transport/2018-10-09/norwegian-now-non-us-leader-transatlantic-nyc-market

https://www.forbes.com/sites/michaelgoldstein/2019/01/30/financial-infusion-to-keep-norwegian-air-flying/

https://www.ft.com/content/19a19188-1fd5-11e9-b126-46fc3ad87c65

10

10.1 **Introduction**

To begin our discussion of strategies for growth, it is helpful to establish a distinction between **corporate strategy** and competitive strategy. Bourgeois (1980) offers the following definitions:

- corporate strategy discusses **where** a company seeks to compete, a decision sometimes known as 'domain selection'
- competitive strategy discusses **how** a company seeks to compete, a decision sometimes known as 'domain navigation'.

Therefore corporate strategy occurs at a higher level than business or competitive strategy. It involves choices such as which industries, markets, or segments an organization should compete in, and whether and how an organization should collaborate with another organization. Competitive strategy follows these decisions. Having decided where to compete, competitive strategy focuses on how this can be done. For example, a firm may intend to compete in a particular market, but what will be the basis of its competitive advantage (we introduced the important idea of competitive advantage in Chapter 5)? Will it be differentiation, for example? Or perhaps price? Before we can analyse and engage in strategic decisions about which growth strategies to pursue, we need to consider both of these 'levels' of strategy. We also need to reflect for a moment on what we mean by 'growth' in this context. Many organizations will reach a point in their development or life cycle when they want to consider whether and how to expand. This may be about a desire to increase profits, or to serve more clients. It might be driven by new opportunities present in the external environment, or the financial ambitions of the owner of a firm. In any case, in this chapter we will be exploring questions of **where** to compete and **how** to compete from the perspective of an organization that is interested in increasing the scale of its current activities.

In this chapter we will focus on some classic questions of corporate strategy. We begin by exploring the role of the 'corporate parent' in supporting strategy. This is often an important corporate strategy issue, as the 'headquarters' of a large organization is typically responsible for high-level decisions around what business the organization participates in. We introduce some important ideas that the strategist should consider when planning growth strategies, as they help us to understand the pros and cons of a range of strategic options. The first is economies of scale and scope; this addresses the potential benefits of either increasing business volumes to reduce unit costs, or sharing costs across multiple lines of business. The second is synergy—when two business units find that they can achieve more working together than they can independently. We also discuss strategies of diversification—when the organization moves into products and markets that are new to it—and we explore diversification strategies that are both related and unrelated, depending on the degree of similarity between the existing and new lines of business. We explore a range of approaches to growth, including integration, mergers and acquisitions, joint ventures, and other forms of alliance. These decisions are typically viewed as important corporate strategy decisions. Finally, we will consider tests for evaluating whether such options are suitable, and explore some of the issues around their implementation.

10.2 **The role of corporate parenting**

We begin our discussion of corporate strategy by considering the role of **corporate parenting**. As mentioned briefly in Section 10.1, a corporate 'parent' is the head office of a business and its senior managers. In a multi-business organization, this is often a separate entity from the business units themselves. In a small or medium-sized company (SME), it may simply be one person. In any case, 'parenting' is about the influence of the corporate centre on its business units and the type of relationship it has with them, both in strategy formulation and in potentially controlling or enhancing the sources of competitive advantage of the business units within the organization's portfolio. Before understanding the different types of growth strategy, it is important for the student of strategy to understand the impact of the corporate parent on corporate strategy. Therefore in this section we will focus on two key aspects of the 'corporate parenting' role (Furrer 2016):

- the responsibility of the corporate parent for value creation
- the corporate parent's role as a bridge between the corporate- and business-level strategies.

Parenting in single- or multi-business organizations

First, it is helpful to distinguish between single- and multi-business organizations. A single-business organization focuses upon a single industry or product market. The organization may be based around the exploitation of a single technology or product, or even an individual owner–manager. This type of organization is common amongst new start-ups, such as a local hairdresser or beauty salon, and across the small and micro organizational sectors, such as a local restaurant or coffee roaster that has ambitions to grow the scale of its business. It is also possible to identify medium or large single-business organizations, such as a retailer, IT firm, or law firm that confines itself to a core set of products or services, perhaps in a well-defined geographic market.

In contrast, a multi-business organization operates in multiple markets through several distinct units (Paroutis and Pettigrew 2007). It may be organized around different geographical markets, such as Unilever which operates in 190 countries around the world with key units in Europe, the USA, and Asia, different product markets, like Samsung Electronics with its presence in consumer electronics, mobile communications, etc., or different vertical stages, such as ExxonMobil's structure which includes 'upstream' businesses that cover searching and drilling for oil and gas, through to 'downstream' businesses that involve refining, distributing, and selling fuel. Therefore a multi-business organization is an organization which has chosen to diversify away from its original product, market, or industry focus, and engages in a number of subsidiary activities. These activities could take place in different markets, or possibly with different modes of operation.

The role of the corporate parent

The role of the corporate parent in a single-business organization, such as an SME, is relatively clear. The single-business organization is its own corporate parent and there will be no separation in practice between business and corporate levels of strategy, although they remain conceptually distinct. In a single-business organization, the parent is present at all stages of the strategy process, and can influence the operation of the organization at first hand. Inevitably, as organizations grow, their processes tend to become more complex. And as complexity grows, the role of the corporate parent changes.

In multi-business organizations, the focus is not upon controlling day-to-day activities across the managerial hierarchy, but on making a significant contribution to the overall performance of the organization. The key strategic issue for the organization becomes the evaluation of how the corporate centre adds value. In a 'typical' multi-business organization, the parent is likely to be located in a corporate headquarters (HQ). This HQ will provide a hub around which a variety of subsidiary activities in separate business units will revolve. What is the relationship between the HQ and the business units? Traditionally, the corporate parent has performed a largely functional role aimed at assisting its business units. Based on Porter (1987), Henry (2018) identifies four such areas:

1. **Standalone influence:** this concerns the parent company's impact upon the strategies and performance of each business the parent owns. Stand alone influence includes such things as the parent company setting performance targets and approving major capital expenditure for the business. There is an opportunity here for the parent to create substantial value. However, where the parent imposes inappropriate targets or fails to recognize the needs of the business for funds, it will destroy value.
2. **Linkage influence:** this occurs when the parent seeks to create value by enhancing the linkages that may be present between different businesses. For example, this might include transferring knowledge and capabilities across business units. The aim is to increase value through synergy.
3. **Functional and services influence:** the parent can provide functional leadership and cost-effective services for the businesses. The parent company creates value to the extent that they provide services which are more cost effective than the businesses can undertake themselves or purchase from external suppliers.
4. **Corporate development activities:** this involves the parent creating value by changing the composition of its portfolio of businesses. The parent actively seeks to add value through its activities in acquisitions, divestments, and alliances. In reality, the parent company often destroys value through its acquisitions by paying a premium which it fails to recover.

However, the parent can do more than perform these functional tasks in order to add value to the organization. It can also manage the relationships between the business units more actively. Authors such as Furrer (2016) and Goold et al. (1998) discuss the question of how corporate parents can identify synergy (see Section 10.6), and the circumstances in which they might encourage value creation. As an example, consider economies of scope. You can find a further discussion of economies of scale and scope in Section 10.3, but a brief definition of economies of scope is the cost savings that the firm creates by successfully transferring some of its capabilities and competencies that were developed in one of its businesses to another of its businesses. Therefore economies of scope are made possible when an organization moves from being a single- to a multi-business organization. This is particularly relevant when an organization engages in related diversification (see Section 10.7 for a fuller discussion of diversification). A related diversification is one that occurs within the same product, market, or industry area. Therefore it should offer opportunities for activities to be shared, or for core competencies and skills to be transferred across businesses (as in the Opening Case Study of IAG and Norwegian).

If an organization is pursuing a strategy based on diversification (we will define diversification when we introduce the Ansoff matrix in Section 10.4, and discuss it further in Section 10.7), it will be part of the role of the corporate parent to ensure that value is added by the effective implementation of any possible economies of scope offered by the diversification. This is what is meant by potential 'synergies' which may be attainable as a result of a diversification, i.e. any potential economies of scope that can be achieved across two businesses. The parent can assume a coordinating role, aiming to explore and exploit interrelationships amongst business units.

Considering all this, how might the HQ add value, rather than just using up the time and resources of the managers of the business units? One way they could add value is through their responsibility to encourage strategic decisions to be taken as close as possible to its markets. In the public sector this has been illustrated by trends towards deregulation and privatization of local government services or public utilities. The aim of this kind of deregulation is to shift responsibility for the development of capabilities and competitive strengths down to the business unit level, and away from the corporate parent who, in this case, is the government. However, this is a controversial topic. For example, studies of the deregulation of public transport in the UK report a mixed picture of success, with bus travellers outside the capital city London facing rising prices and a falling number of journeys (*The Guardian* 2014), leading critics to question whether all the intended benefits of the deregulation have been achieved in this case.

10.3 **Understanding economies of scale and scope**

We have discussed the impact of the corporate parent on corporate strategy for growth. What are the benefits of growth that a corporate parent might look to achieve? When an organization pursues a strategy of growth, there are a number of potential advantages of growth that it may be pursuing. In this section we discuss two such benefits—economies of scale and scope, which have already been mentioned briefly. These are important ideas which can help the student of strategy to understand why some organizations seek to implement growth strategies—and why it can be difficult to achieve all the potential benefits of such strategies in practice.

Economies of scale

Economies of scale are the cost advantages that an organization can achieve when it increases the scale of its operations. Put simply, economies of scale occur when the cost per unit of output decreases as output increases. For example, this may occur when a manufacturing business makes improvements to its production process, allowing faster production of goods at lower unit costs. Economies of scale apply to a variety of situations and at various levels, such as a business or manufacturing unit, a plant or an entire enterprise. When average costs start falling as output increases, economies of scale are occurring.

One possible source of economies of scale is that the firm may be able to purchase inputs at a lower cost per unit when they are purchased in large quantities. Examples include a large supermarket that has the buying power to negotiate a significant 'bulk discount' when purchasing from farmers and other suppliers, or an energy firm negotiating its supply contracts for large quantities of coal and gas.

It's important to remember that economies of scale often have limits. An example might be when the firm's demand for a particular raw material exceeds nearby supply. For example, 'rare earths' are a group of 17 similar chemical elements (BBC 2012), crucial to the manufacture of many high tech products. Ninety-five per cent of global production of rare earths takes place in China, a fact that occasionally leads to expressions of concern in other parts of the world (Blau 2010). Similarly, a firm may reach a point when its local markets are saturated, and therefore transport costs rise because of having to transport its products over greater distances to reach its customers. Another example might arise when its defect rate increases; in other words, a higher proportion of goods produced are faulty. For example, changes to a production process—intended to allow higher volumes and lower unit costs—may result in an increase in the percentage of output that fails to meet the desired quality target, such as the precise specifications for the dimensions of a car axle in the automotive industry.

Economies of scope

Economies of scope operate in a similar way to economies of scale, except that where economies of scale result from increasing the volume of production of a single product, economies of scope can be seen as the cost benefits resulting from using the same resource across a range of outputs. They are the result of a more intensive use of a shared resource across business units rather than within a single business unit. Clark (1988) explains the difference between economies of scale and economies of scope as follows:

- economies of scale are associated with firm size (i.e. as output rises, production costs, either per unit or on average, decline)
- economies of scope are associated with the joint production of two or more products.

Farsi et al. (2007) discuss economies of scope in the case of local public transport in the Swiss marketplace, where a single operator may offer trolley bus, motor bus, and tramway systems. Shareable inputs are labour, capital, and energy. 'Local public transport companies that combine several transport modes use similar equipment such as wires, overhead lines, and similar skills such as driving, management, and network maintenance. Such synergies also apply to activities such as advertising, scheduling, and ticketing' (Farsi et al. 2007:347).

Achieving economies of scope can clearly have an impact upon cost if, for example, they permit the sharing of primary activities, such as marketing or operations, or support activities, such as human resources or IT functions. For example, it is easier for large firms to carry the overheads of sophisticated research and development (R&D). R&D is crucial in the pharmaceuticals industry. Yet the cost of discovering the next blockbuster drug is enormous and increasing. Several of the mergers between pharmaceuticals companies in recent years have been driven by the desire of companies to spread their R&D expenditure across a greater volume of sales (*The Economist* 2008).

10.4 **Corporate strategy: Ansoff's growth vectors**

Having explored the key ideas of economies of scale and scope as potential benefits of the implementation of growth strategies, what are the growth options that are available to an organization? In this section we will introduce a classic strategy framework, the Ansoff matrix, which allows the student of strategy to begin to generate and evaluate the various growth options that an organization might consider.

In Section 10.1, we noted Bourgeois' definition of corporate strategy as being concerned with domain selection. In other words, corporate strategy is about where (not how) an organization chooses to compete. So, as we discuss corporate strategy, we are interested in the options available to an organization when they come to choose the industry or market segments that they will compete in. At the simplest level, this may mean that an organization chooses to stay within its original market or product area. However, in a complex global environment, an organization may feel that it is faced with a very wide range of options for extending its activities into new markets or product sectors.

The Ansoff matrix

To begin, we consider the work of Ansoff (1965, 1987) in identifying that there are a number of broad alternative approaches to growth that an organization may decide to implement. His work establishes the idea of the 'strategic portfolio strategy' which will assist an organization in mapping out the 'business we are in'. Ansoff suggests that we can think of any organization as an 'assembly of distinctive strategic business areas (SBAs), each of which offers different future growth/profitability opportunities and/or will require different competitive approaches' (Ansoff 1987:108). It is worth noting that Ansoff seems to assume that the organization we are considering is relatively complex, and so his notion of the organization as an assembly of SBAs is probably less appropriate for a relatively simple single-business firm, and more useful when we are thinking about larger multi-business organizations. However, more recent research has also emphasized that analysis based on the ideas behind the Ansoff matrix, such as the four growth vectors, can also be insightful for small organizations (Byrom et al. 2003)—by exploring an appropriate growth strategy for an SME, for example.

Ansoff's work encourages us to be clear about where each SBA is located, and how SBAs can be distinguished from each other. This is an important contribution which is explored by introducing the idea of a growth vector. A growth vector is defined as 'the direction in which growth can occur'. It is argued that growth vectors arise when we consider two important criteria:

- **The geographical scope of the firm**, meaning either the organization's existing 'present market' or an alternative 'new market', or both at the same time in complex organizations.
- **The scope of the firm's mission**, meaning the dominant product sector it is seeking to serve. This can be focused on either its existing product market, or an alternative different product market ('diversification'), or both its existing market and a number of different markets for more complex organizations.

For the purposes of this discussion, Ansoff's matrix is being utilized to highlight the possible strategic options that a firm may wish to pursue in the future. However, it is important to remember that Ansoff himself describes his ideas as addressing growth, i.e. as focusing upon the opportunities for an organization to consider where it should be located in the future, based on the assumption that every organization is always keen to pursue growth (Open University 2010). Of course, this may not always be true. For instance, some firms may be focused on survival rather than growth, and some very small organizations may not be actively pursuing opportunities for growth at all. But what we can assume is that most organizations, once established, are interested in pursuing growth opportunities, and, with that, we can use Ansoff's matrix to explore their strategic options.

Ansoff suggests that there are four broad approaches to growth, or growth vectors, based on whether or not the organization is going to extend beyond its existing market, and whether or not it is going to extend its product range. These are depicted in Figure 10.1 and explained in Table 10.1. A market penetration strategy is focused on increasing market share for its present products in its present markets. A strategy of market development seeks new markets (for existing products), and a strategy of product development introduces new products (in existing markets). Finally, a strategy of diversification focuses on both new products and new markets.

Having identified these categories of corporate strategic options, it is useful for you to develop an understanding of how an organization might pursue some or all of these options. This will allow you to analyse the current strategies that you can observe in organizations around the world, and to begin to evaluate the range of strategic options that an organization might or should be considering.

Market penetration

This strategic option emphasizes stability, at least in terms of the products or services provided and the market where the organization has chosen to operate. However, as described by Ansoff, it also stresses that the organization is seeking to increase the amount or value (or both)

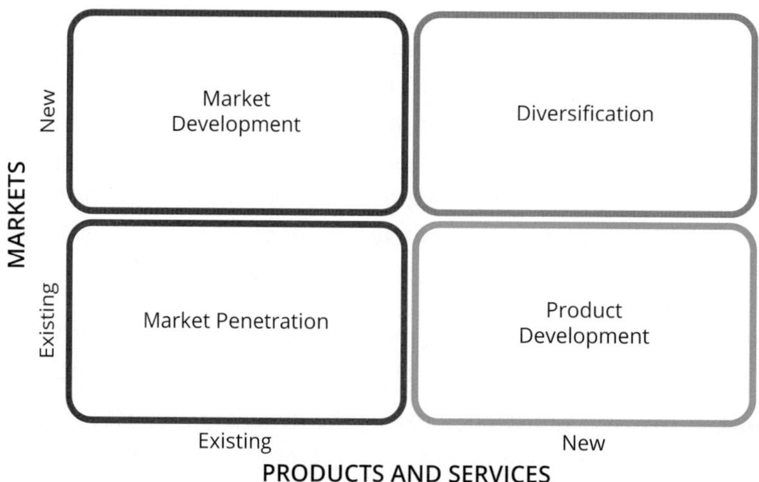

FIGURE 10.1 The Ansoff matrix.

TABLE 10.1 **Ansoff's growth vectors**

Growth vector	Aim	Target market	Strategic action
Market penetration	Identifies a direction for growth based upon an organization increasing the market share for its present product market	Its existing market with existing products	Selling more of its existing products and services to its existing customers
Market development	Identifies new missions for the firm's products	A new market with its existing products	Selling its existing products or services to new customers
Product development	Creates new products to replace or add to current ones	Its existing market with new products	Anticipating changes in existing customer needs and developing the appropriate products to meet those needs
Diversification	Both products and missions are new to the firm	A new market with a new product	Moving into a completely new market or product area to that in which it is used to competing

of the products or services that it sells as a means of achieving growth. For example, if we look at a list of firms spending the most on advertising in the UK during 2017–2018, supermarkets such as Tesco (the UK's biggest supermarket) and Lidl (a German discounter) are amongst the biggest spenders. These firms are battling to protect their current positions, to sell more to their current customers, and to take market share from each other. In 2018, as an important tactic in this competitive battle, Tesco launched Jack's (Barrie 2018), a discount chain which is seeking to compete more directly with the rapidly expanding discounters Aldi and Lidl, both of which are eating into the market share of the traditional supermarkets.

The potential of a market penetration strategy may be determined by a number of factors, including the prospects for growth in the sector, the organization's capabilities in delivering more of its products or services to meet increased demand, its ability to resist the challenges it faces with regard to existing or new entrants who may be attracted by the prospects for growth or evidence of growing demand, and so on. Additionally, it is important to remember that selling to existing customers has often been shown to be considerably cheaper than attracting new customers (Gallo 2014).

A growing market is likely to attract a market penetration strategy on the part of existing participants. However, market penetration may also be viable in mature or stable markets, where competition is likely to be well established and the focus is on obtaining market share at the expense of competitors. Market penetration may even be possible in declining markets, where existing firms aim to 'harvest' the remaining opportunities in the sector as other firms decide it is no longer economically viable to compete there. For example, although the car industry in the USA has struggled during 2017 and 2018, its major players, such as Ford and General Motors, continue to spend heavily on advertising to promote their brands and shore up their positions.

The concept of market penetration is also applicable in a not-for-profit (NFP) context, even if describing the strategy as 'market penetration' seems inappropriate, as many NFP organizations do not see themselves as 'serving markets' as such. However, voluntary organizations might aim to provide a more complete service to the same group of beneficiaries that they currently serve. For example, under its 'Change Please' programme, the *Big Issue* (perhaps best known for its magazine sold by homeless or marginalized people) is backing a scheme to offer homeless people the opportunity to work as baristas at coffee carts across London (Burns 2017). This initiative enables the organization to help more homeless people and get them into work faster.

Market development

In a market development strategy, the organization takes its existing products and services into new markets. These may be new geographic markets, or new segments of existing markets where the firm has identified customer needs that are currently unmet or unexpected.

Motivations for pursuing a market development strategy vary by firm. For instance, it may be an appropriate way to secure a foothold in a sector that is currently small, or where the extent of demand is as yet unknown. Alternatively, the firm may undertake a major launch of an established brand in a new area. Well-known firms may seek to establish a presence in mature but profitable markets where they have no presence to date. For instance, outside the USA, Amazon's second biggest market is Germany, followed by Japan and the UK (we will discuss Amazon's international goals further in Case Example 10.1). In 2017, Amazon spent $580 million to acquire the e-commerce platform souq.com in order to establish a strong presence in the Middle East market, which it believes is poised for strong growth. In May 2019, as it announced that souq.com would be rebranded amazon.ae in the UAE, the company said that it was proud that its team in the region had grown to more than 3600 employees since 2017, and that its customers would now have access to a wider range of products and be able to opt to shop online using the Arabic language for the first time (Maceda 2019).

For some companies, market development can be a key feature of a corporate strategy based upon a competitive approach to building global brands as a vital source of product differentiation for what are essentially commodity products. Consider the international strategies of leading footwear firms like Adidas, Nike, and Reebok. These companies have entered international markets for the purposes of expansion. For example, Adidas points to urbanization as a global mega-trend driving its strategy, and identifies 'six key cities in which we want to over-proportionally grow share of mind, share of market and share of trend: London, Los Angeles, New York, Paris, Shanghai and Tokyo' (Adidas 2019). This approach can also be viewed as a differentiation strategy as a firm like Adidas seeks to build and maintain a strong global brand.

In terms of understanding the risks associated with this option, it is worth noting that market development is usually viewed as second only to market penetration in terms of cost advantage and risk avoidance. This is because the emphasis is typically upon marketing existing products (or in Ansoff's (1987) terms, finding a new mission for these products), possibly in a marginally modified form, to customers in related market areas, primarily through adding new channels of distribution. For example, consider a manufacturer of electric vehicles that is currently based in Europe and wants to sell its existing products (perhaps slightly modified) to new customers by setting up a branch in Asia.

Once again, the concept of market development is also applicable to an NFP context, albeit with some modification. Market development for a voluntary organization may involve extending the range of coverage of its activities. For instance, Depaul (a charity that focuses on helping homeless, vulnerable, and disadvantaged people) began in the UK, but has expanded its operations internationally to include Slovakia, Ukraine, USA, and France, allowing it help more people beyond the UK (Depaul 2019).

Product development

In contrast with market development, where an existing product enters a new market, product development (or service development) offers a strategic route to growth in areas where existing product ranges do not fully exploit all the available existing opportunities, where there are advantages to offering a full range of products, or where the demand for a product or service is evolving. For example, Blizzard Tecnica, who produce ski gear, have received a great deal of positive coverage for redesigning items of ski equipment (such as boots and skis, which are traditionally designed with men in mind) to offer a product range that is better suited to female customers who now make up a large part of the market for such goods (CSGA 2017). In 2019, it was reported that, thanks to the Blizzard Black Pearl, the best-selling ski in the USA was, for the first time, one aimed at women (Kestenbaum 2019).

NFP organizations may alter the nature of the service they offer as needs and circumstances change. For example, Marie Curie is a UK-based charity best known for giving care and support to the terminally ill via hospices and nursing staff. However, its strategic plan describes a broadening in the range of services it offers to include information, helpers, and support for the bereaved (Marie Curie 2014). It launched information and support services in 2015; each year the information and support pages on its website are viewed more than 1.4 million times and around 10,000 enquiries are answered through the Marie Curie Support Line and live web chat (Marie Curie 2019).

10

CASE EXAMPLE 10.1 **AMAZON VS ALIBABA**

Amazon, the world's leading e-commerce company based in the USA, has recently been competing for dominance in foreign markets with Alibaba, a Chinese multinational company also specializing in e-commerce. In 2014, CEO Jeff Bezos announced that Amazon would be investing heavily in India, and very shortly afterwards Jack Ma (co-founder of Alibaba) voiced similar intentions. So far, Amazon has invested $300 million of the $5 billion committed into the Indian business by Bezos. In 2015 Alibaba put $500 million into PayTM, an Indian digital payments company.

India is a source of fierce competition because of its market potential. It is a growing economy and its online retail market is expected to expand from $15 billion in 2016 to $200 billion in 2026, according to a report by Morgan Stanley. Being successful in growing economies such as India is vital to the ambitions of each company.

Alibaba's goal is to serve two billion customers around the world within 20 years, creating 100 million jobs. In some cases it has begun with digital payments, as in India with PayTM. In others it has invested in e-commerce sites, as with Lazada in South-East Asia. Alibaba aims to build a broad range of services within each market, including payments, e-commerce, and travel services, and then link local platforms with Alibaba's platforms in China. Alibaba helps Chinese companies sell in places such as Brazil and Russia, and assists foreign firms with marketing, logistics, and customs in China. In May 2019, Alibaba announced that it is overhauling the business model of AliExpress and, as part of this, the company launched an initiative which will allow

Continued

small to medium-sized overseas vendors from Russia, Turkey, Italy, and Spain to use its platform to sell to other countries in the AliExpress network. It hopes to eventually use its technology to link logistics networks around the world so that any product can reach any buyer anywhere within 72 hours.

Amazon, on the other hand, already earns more than a third of its revenue from e-commerce outside North America. Its second-largest market is Germany, followed by Japan and the UK. In 2017 it bought Souq.com, an e-commerce firm in the Middle East. Its criteria for expansion elsewhere include the size of the population and the economy, and the density of internet use; India has been one of its main testing grounds. Amazon also wants to help suppliers in any country to sell their products abroad.

However, there is no guarantee that strategies that have worked in the organizations' home countries will succeed elsewhere. It may be that Amazon and Alibaba will need to adapt their business models in these newer markets, and in doing so their models may start to look more similar. So far the companies have differed in significant ways. Amazon owns inventory and warehouses; Alibaba does not. However, Alibaba has a broader reach than Amazon, particularly with Ant Financial's giant payments business. Given the huge market opportunities, both companies will be watching carefully to see if other technology firms will invest in e-commerce, and what partnerships might emerge from that. At the time of writing, Amazon and Alibaba remain each other's fiercest international rivals. Success in e-commerce requires scale, which needs lots of capital. Big firms also have a natural advantage as they expand, because technologies developed for one market can be introduced across many.

Questions for discussion

1. Analyse the growth strategies of Amazon and Alibaba using Ansoff's matrix (Figure 10.1). Identify and describe any elements of the four growth vectors—market penetration, product development, market development, and diversification—that you think are informing their plans.
2. Do you think that economies of scale currently play an important part in the strategies of either business? Explain your answer.
3. Do you think that economies of scope currently play an important part in the strategies of either business? Explain your answer.
4. What role do you think the corporate parent could, or should, be playing in the strategic development of the two businesses?

Sources

Adapted from *The Economist*, 28 October 2017.

https://www.ft.com/content/ac3fd8f8-ae5f-11e7-beba-5521c713abf4

https://www.ft.com/content/3d25007c-713d-11e9-bbfb-5c68069fbd15

Diversification

The first three of Ansoff's growth vectors (see Figure 10.1) represent strategic decisions linked to familiar products, services, or missions (markets). The final vector, diversification, suggests diversifying slightly from the familiar. Therefore it is important to consider what this 'diversification' actually means, as well as the variety of different strategic options available to an organization through diversification. Let's remind ourselves of the definition of diversification provided by Ansoff (1987). He suggests that diversification represents a situation where both products and missions are new to the firm, such that the firm moves into a completely new market and product area than that in which it is used to competing. Given our discussion of resources and capabilities, you may be asking why, if it is true to say that there is a close link between an organization's existing capabilities and competitive advantage, would a firm opt to explore opportunities in areas where it has no prior experience, and where its resources and capabilities may not be well suited or might not offer any potential to create value for the firm? This is a very important question, and leads us to a discussion of two key concepts, relatedness and synergy (see Sections 10.5 and 10.6), before we go on to a fuller discussion of different strategic options that may represent diversification strategies (Section 10.7). In order to explore the potential reasons for, and drivers of, growth strategies such as diversification, we first explore the idea of related and unrelated diversification in multi-business organizations (Open University 2010).

10.5 **Corporate strategy in multi-business organizations: understanding related and unrelated diversification**

We have learned about Ansoff's four growth vectors: market penetration, market development, product development, and diversification. In the next three sections we will develop our understanding of the final vector—diversification.

A diversification strategy generally emphasizes both a move away from a single industry approach and some interrelationship with one or more other organizations. There are also different degrees of diversification that an organization can pursue. For example, if 95% of its revenue were generated by a single business, it would be undertaking a low level of diversification. This contrasts with highly diversified multi-business organizations where no single business unit is responsible for the majority of revenues. For example, Johnson & Johnson produce a wide range of prescription and over-the-counter drugs. They also make medical devices and run a sports performance research institute for athletes. This example demonstrates how there can also be different degrees of relatedness within diversified organizations. But what types of relatedness can an organization pursue, and how does this relate to the strategy's ability to create value? In this section we will consider two main areas of relatedness—corporate and operational relatedness—before considering the question of synergy in Section 10.6.

Corporate and operational relatedness

The opportunity to create value through diversification is usually achieved by identifying economies of scope (see Section 10.3). Put simply, economies of scope exist where a proportionate saving is made by producing two or more distinct goods together, when the cost of doing so is less than that of producing each good separately (Teece 1980). If economies of scope can be realized, potential synergies can also be achieved.

In order to understand how an organization can realize economies of scope, it is useful to think about exactly where in the organization the costs savings can be made or synergies achieved. Hitt et al. (2007) point out that we should consider whether two organizations are related at the corporate level or the operational/business unit level. Figure 10.2 illustrates the types of value-creating opportunities that are offered by different types of diversification.

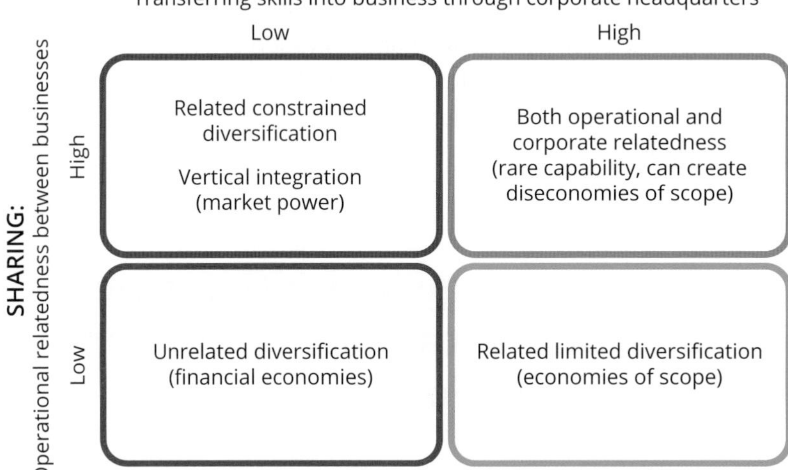

FIGURE 10.2 Hitt et al.'s 2×2 matrix on 'value-creating strategies of diversification'. Source: Adapted from MacMillan, I. (1988). Controlling Competitive Dynamics by Taking Strategic Initiative. *Academy of Management Perspectives*, **2**(2):111–118. https://doi.org/10.5465/ame.1988.4275518. © Academy of Management Perspectives.

Figure 10.2 has two axes. The first (vertical axis, labelled 'sharing') considers the potential offered by the diversification to share assets. This emphasizes the operational relatedness between the two organizations. The second (horizontal axis, labelled 'corporate relatedness') considers the potential offered by the diversification to combine capabilities and pursue asset creation or improvement. We will now briefly review each of the four quadrants of Figure 10.2 to consider how they offer the opportunity to add value.

Low opportunity for sharing assets/low corporate relatedness

With no relatedness of either kind, diversification in this quadrant can be considered to be 'unrelated diversification'. For this type of diversification, the only opportunities for value creation are likely to lie in the area of financial economies, i.e. cost savings realized through the improved allocation of financial resources. These can be based on investments inside or outside the firm. The motivation here may be to build a portfolio of businesses, each of which possesses a different profile of risk and reward, with the aim of reducing the total business risk to the organization as a whole. This type of thinking, leading to a portfolio approach, was particularly popular among large diversified conglomerates during the 1970s. While it can be argued that the popularity of the concept of synergy (Goold and Campbell 1998) has undermined this approach, conglomerates continue to exist. Consider the success of the Virgin Group, which began in the 1970s as a record mail order and record store business, and has since engaged in unrelated diversification into the airline industry (Virgin Atlantic), the travel sector (Virgin Trains), the financial services sector (Virgin Money), and so on. However, not every initiative has been a success. For example in the mid-1990s, the Virgin Group launched Virgin Cola, and achieved a very low level of market share and rapidly exited the market. The reason for this unsuccessful example of diversification is that existing powerful players in the soft drinks market were able to make distribution difficult for Virgin and engage in expensive advertising campaigns.

High opportunity for sharing assets/low corporate relatedness

For a good example of a firm adopting strategies of diversification where corporate relatedness is low yet there are good opportunities for asset sharing, consider Procter & Gamble, the American multinational consumer goods corporation. With around 65 brands across ten product categories (dishwashing, laundry detergents, haircare, skincare, and so on), this company has the potential to take advantage of considerable economies of scope. The cost of undertaking many of its activities (around manufacturing, distribution, etc.) can be shared across a number of business units; hence the average cost is lower than if each business unit operated in isolation. In this quadrant we also find firms that are seeking to achieve market power through vertical integration. An example is the US retailer Target, which has a wide range of 'own brand' products—hence controlling manufacturing and distribution.

Low opportunity for sharing assets/high corporate relatedness

A similar position occurs in this quadrant, but the opportunities for economies of scope emerge from relatedness at the corporate level. These opportunities are based on the ability to transfer skills across a range of businesses through the activities of the corporate parent. An intriguing example is provided by the transformation that is taking place at GE—from a 'classic conglomerate', with a portfolio that had been described as opaque and too broad, to a 'digital industrial company', according to its CEO (Imelt 2017). GE now sees itself as a global technology company, has doubled its R&D investment, and has divested slower-growth, lower-tech, non-industrial businesses in favour of higher growth, manufacturing-based products and services.

High opportunity for sharing assets/high corporate relatedness

Finally, we consider the situation where significant opportunities exist for both operational and corporate relatedness; this situation may offer the greatest potential for value creation. For example, the Honda Motor Company began in the motorcycle business, before moving into cars and trucks, arguably drawing on both operational relatedness and corporate relatedness across the different lines of business.

In summary, Hitt et al.'s matrix helps us to think through the different types of relatedness that might exist between two organizations, and the different types of diversified strategies that might be open to an organization when pursuing growth strategies.

10.6 **Corporate strategy in multi-business organizations: understanding synergy**

In the previous section we set out different types of diversification strategies an organization might pursue, based on how related they are to another organization at corporate and/or operational level. Each of the quadrants offers different opportunities to add value. But why might achieving the added value be very challenging? To understand more about this question, we need to discuss further the concept of synergy which underpins the strategies of diversification that we discussed in the previous section.

To emphasize the importance of the idea that the organization should be clear about the potential benefits of a diversified strategy, we now explore the concept of synergy in more depth in this section before going on in Section 10.7 to set out the different approaches to diversification that an organization might consider.

Synergy 'exists when the value created by business units working together exceeds the value those units create working independently' (Hitt et al. 2007:211). It is the concept of the whole being greater than the sum of the parts, and it is sometimes the key driver behind mergers and acquisitions, or other collaborative arrangements between organizations. For example, a company that is excellent at manufacturing—having the latest manufacturing technology, and able to make one of the best products on the market—may be quite poor at logistics, with inefficiencies in its systems for getting products to customers. Therefore it might choose to merge with another firm that is excellent at logistics but has a rather outdated manufacturing operation. Thus synergy can be an explanation for, and/or a driver of, diversification strategies.

Synergy sounds like a relatively simple concept, although it can be difficult to realize and sustain in reality. If it is successful it creates greater value, as the definition suggests. On the other hand, it also creates interdependence between separate business units, which may in turn limit their flexibility and make them less effective as a source of competitive advantage. For example, a decision to pursue synergy may lead an organization to limit itself to the use of certain technologies in order to achieve the synergistic benefits associated with activity sharing. The organization may become more risk averse and less willing to experiment or innovate, and this may be unwise in a dynamic competitive environment. In the discussion of dynamic capabilities in Chapter 9, it was clear that it was the relationship between such capabilities and strategic flexibility that delivered potential competitive advantage. Any search for synergy could result in this kind of flexibility being undermined.

To overcome this contradiction between flexibility and synergy, the concept of co-evolution (from Eisenhardt and Galunic (2000)) suggests ways of reconnecting flexibility and synergy. They argue that successful firms adopt a flexible approach to building synergy. For example, relationships between two organizations should be allowed to emerge at business unit level, rather than dictated from the top of the organization; and the links between two organizations should be allowed to evolve over time, with new links emerging and old ones ceasing to exist. The ability to manage synergies in this flexible way is likely to represent a type of capability that is probably rare, difficult to imitate, and therefore valuable.

Discussion of synergy relates very closely to our discussion of resources and capabilities. Resources offer routes to competitive advantage, but the nature of that advantage may be uncertain since the sustainability of resources over time is uncertain. Part of the corporate parenting responsibility must include a responsibility for management to create corporate-level capabilities. Diversification also offers managers the potential—through exploiting operational relatedness and, more particularly, corporate relatedness—to identify ways in which 'strategic assets' can be enhanced (Markides and Williamson 1994). This is also what Hamel and Prahalad (1993) mean when they talk about 'stretch and leverage'. They note that we often describe strategy as being about the 'fit' between an organization and its environment, and the 'allocation' of resources. However, they argue that it's also an important management task to think about the 'misfit' between the organization's resources and its aspirations (their concept of 'stretch'). In addition, senior managers need to go beyond the simple allocation of resources (often while lamenting their scarcity) to really 'leveraging' existing resources—thinking creatively about how resources can be conserved and/or concentrated on the organization's key strategic goals. As an example of leveraging marketing resources, an organization might build its corporate level capabilities in engaging its customers via social media—enabling it to achieve more by building on synergies across its business units, with potentially scarce marketing resources.

10.7 **Corporate strategy: understanding different approaches to diversification**

We have discussed **why** organizations might choose to diversify—for example, to obtain synergies or economies of scope, or to improve the long-term value of their strategic assets, resources, and capabilities. But **how** might an organization pursue a strategy of diversification? This is what we turn to in this section.

We have already introduced Ansoff's (1987) definition of diversification (see Table 10.1), involving a situation where an organization pursues new opportunities where both products and missions are new to the firm. In other words, it enters a completely new market and product area from the area in which it usually competes. But what does this mean in practice? One option is that the organization could create a presence in the new market itself, or begin to produce a new product in order to enter a new market. This would be a more organic approach, and would usually result in a conglomerate, or a corporation made up of a number of seemingly unrelated businesses formed over time. Alternatively, the organization could recognize that it does not have all the required resources or capabilities to undertake all aspects of diversification by itself. This means that it might opt to take a more collaborative approach, i.e. working with another organization.

In order to begin to answer questions about how diversification might work in practice, we should first acknowledge how rapidly the external environment is changing for organizations today. In the past, seeing an organization move into new product and market territories organically (i.e. without any help from external organizations) would seem much more feasible than it would today because of a more stable external environment. Jardine Matheson and the Swire Group were both founded in the nineteenth century, and successfully grew in this 'organic' way into new markets and territories, to form conglomerates. However, that isn't to say that this 'old style' of forming conglomerates cannot be found today. Alphabet, the parent company of Google, is a well-known example of a company founded more recently (in 2015) which has developed into a new conglomerate. However, in more modern changing environments, most major corporations tend to pursue the value-added potential offered by encouraging their SBUs to work collaboratively through a search for synergy prompted by a strategy of related diversification. We recognize that in today's increasingly complex environment, it has become extremely difficult for firms to pursue growth strategies in new territories without some form of partnership with an external organization, so our focus here is on the options for organizations looking to achieve diversification through collaborative means (Open University 2010), as discussed further throughout this section of the chapter.

Collaborative approaches to diversification

In this section we focus on approaches which permit an organization to overcome resource deficiencies, mitigate risk, or take advantage of opportunities by diversification through a number of collaborative approaches. The main options are introduced in Table 10.2. We can think about the decision whether to engage in diversification or not (and if so, which approach to adopt) as being based upon a number of criteria:

- **risk:** the risk of deciding to pursue diversification or the risk to the organization of doing nothing
- **cost:** the cost of the decision to diversify or not to diversify
- **reward:** the potential benefits of a decision to diversify
- **control:** the degree to which the organization is prepared to share control over the diversification approach.

In this section we explore strategies that affect the interrelationships between business units, either within the corporate portfolio or among business units across different organizations. The strategies we describe here look at opportunities for an organization to seek potential competitive advantage from shared activities with other organizations. We include vertical and horizontal integration, mergers and acquisitions (M&A), joint ventures, strategic alliances, and consortia. These strategic options differ on the basis of the levels of risk and control that they involve; they also reflect requirements in terms of the organization's resources, such as resource gaps or deficiencies, a lack of market power, or an ability to overcome barriers to entry. These ideas are summarized in Table 10.2.

We now discuss each of the approaches mentioned in Table 10.2 in more depth.

Vertical and horizontal integration

Consider the situation where a manufacturer decides to set up a chain of retail outlets to sell its products. This could be regarded as related diversification into retailing. We might also refer to it as 'forward vertical integration', as the firm has acquired control of a business activity that lies nearer to the end-user market than its core activity as a manufacturer. In contrast, a firm may choose to 'integrate backwards' towards the raw material or other supply inputs that go into making its own products. This issue, sometimes called the 'make-or-buy' decision, leads managers to consider, for example, the costs of a transaction. Is it cheaper for an organization to perform an activity, such as distributing its products, itself or to pay another organization to do it? These questions will also lead managers to consider the boundaries of the firm.

In contrast with vertical integration, a firm which acquires a provider of complementary products or services is said to be engaging in 'horizontal integration'. For example, in 2012, Facebook acquired Instagram. The two companies operate in the same sector (social media), but Instagram was seen as a social networking app with particular strengths in the area of sharing photos and videos from a smartphone, so its resources and capabilities could be seen as complementary to those of its acquirer. Facebook's aims in acquiring Instagram included growing its market share and reducing competition.

TABLE 10.2 **Different approaches to diversification**

Approach to diversification	Features	Possible rewards	Possible risks
Vertical or horizontal integration	**Vertical integration**: an organization extends its operations closer to its customers (forward vertical integration) or its suppliers (backward vertical integration) **Example**: Netflix has moved from distributing content to owning and producing its own content **Horizontal integration**: an organization takes over one of its main competitors **Example**: Disney's acquisition of Pixar in 2006	• Increased control over its own operations • Greater potential for economies of scale and scope • Greater effectiveness of value-chain operations • Improved value appropriation • Increased market share in a growing industry or increased ability to 'harvest' in a declining industry	• Reduction in organizational flexibility • The potential benefits of outsourcing to third parties, such as access to higher quality or cost reduction, may not be realized
Mergers and acquisitions (M&A)	A **merger** is a decision between two companies to integrate their operations on a relatively equal basis **Example**: Daimler and Chrysler in 1998, or AOL and Time Warner in 2000 An **acquisition** involves one organization taking over another **Example**: Amazon bought the food retailer Whole Foods in 2017	• Increased market power • Overcoming entry barriers • Reduced cost of new product development • Increasing speed to market • Increased diversification • Avoidance of excessive competition • Organizational learning and development of new capabilities	• Integration difficulties • Inadequate evaluation of the target firm • Large or extraordinary debt • Inability to achieve synergy • Too much diversification • Managers becoming too focused upon the M&A deal itself • Organization becoming too large (e.g. Hitt et al. 2007)
Cooperative strategies: joint ventures (JVs)	A **JV** is a new corporate entity created by two separate organizations; it may be created to serve a specific purpose, enter a new market, or exploit new or complementary capabilities **Examples**: In 2011, Ford and Toyota (motor industry rivals) agreed to work together on the development of hybrid trucks; Vodafone and Telefonica entered into a JV in 2012	• Combination of expertise, to the benefit of both 'parent' organizations • If a home government is unwilling to allow foreign organizations unlimited access to its markets, a JV may be the only way for a foreign firm to access particular industries • The JV shares the risks associated with a new venture between the partners	• The JV shares the control between the partners, as well as the ability to appropriate value; this lack of control may be a cause for concern (e.g. control of proprietary information)

Continued

TABLE 10.2 *Continued*

Approach to diversification	Features	Possible rewards	Possible risks
Cooperative strategies: strategic alliances (SAs)	A **strategic alliance** is a decision by two or more organizations to cooperate in the development, manufacture, or sale of products or services; there are a range of types of alliance **Examples**: For marketing, licensing and knowledge, Barnes & Noble (bookstore) have an alliance with Starbucks (coffee) In 2014, Google and Samsung signed a broad agreement to cross-license a range of each other's patents Disney use Hewlett Packard's technology platforms in ride creation, animation, etc.	• A strategic alliance is less formal than a JV, so there is typically less risk associated with a strategic alliance • Access to new technology and/or intellectual property rights • Improved agility • Reduced costs (administration or R&D)	• Sharing of resources and profits, possibly also skills and know-how • Focusing and committing to an SA may lead the firm to overlook other opportunities • In an uneven alliance, the weaker partner may be forced to act according to the will of the stronger partner • Difficulties and costs associated with coordination and resolving disputes
Cooperative strategies: consortia	A **consortium** is a set of relationships between a number of organizations, often with the intention of collaborating on a large and complex project for a fixed, short term **Examples**: Airbus is a European aerospace consortium that manufactures and sells aerospace products worldwide In the travel and tourism sector, independent travel agencies collaborate in order to increase their purchasing power	• Less rigid than a JV or an SA • The partners can benefit from each other's skills, knowledge, expertise, and experience • No equity stake is required • All partners retain their independent legal status • The activities of partners are not constrained outside the remit of the consortium itself	• Time-consuming to build such a partnership • Partners may not have sufficient control of the project or the activities of other partners • Resources, such as profits and knowledge, are likely to be shared • Difficult to ensure consistency and quality across the project • Difficult to coordinate between partners and resolve disputes • Reputation of all partners may be damaged if one partner fails to deliver

Figure 10.3 provides an illustration of vertical and horizontal integration in the car industry. If one manufacturer buys another, this is an example of horizontal integration. If a car manufacturer buys one of its suppliers, this is (backward) vertical integration. If a car manufacturer buys a chain of outlets that sell vehicles directly to customers, this is (forward) vertical integration. These strategic options can provide the organization with a range of benefits including increased market share, greater control over its own operations, and increased opportunities for economies of scale and scope. On the downside, vertical or horizontal integration may make the organization less flexible. It may also lose out on the benefits of outsourcing to third parties (such as higher quality or lower costs), as it has effectively brought some activities 'in house'.

Both vertical and horizontal integration can be achieved by another type of diversification strategy, i.e. mergers and acquisitions—and we turn to this strategy now.

Mergers and acquisitions

Before looking at mergers and acquisitions (M&A) as strategic options, we should first clarify the differences between the two. A merger involves a decision taken by two organizations to integrate their operations on a relatively equal basis. An acquisition, on the other hand, involves one organization buying a controlling interest in another organization. The acquisition often becomes a subsidiary of the acquiring organization, operating within its portfolio of other business units. If the acquisition was not agreed with the managers and owners of the acquired organization, this is known as a (hostile) takeover. For example, during 2018 GKN (a maker of car and plane parts) was the target of a hostile takeover bid from a buy-out firm called Melrose

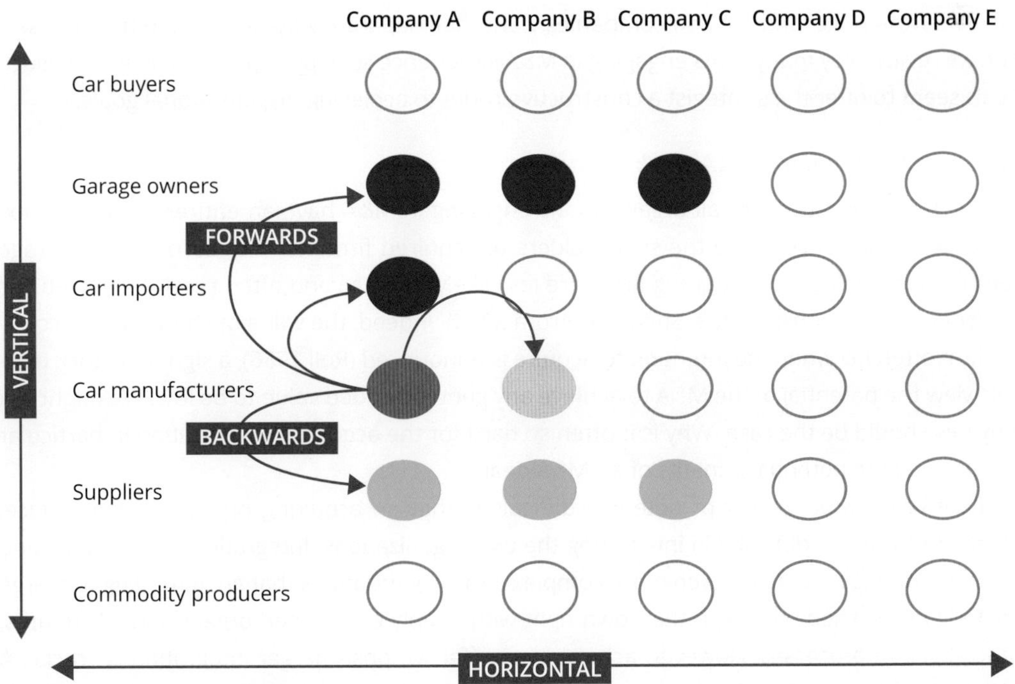

FIGURE 10.3 Example of vertical and horizontal integration in the car industry.

(*The Economist* 2018a). Melrose found itself facing a campaign led by customers, politicians, and industry groups, but the deal was completed, and Melrose is predicted to break up GKN in order to sell off some business units.

The popularity of M&A as a corporate strategy, or rather the view that M&A can provide a route by which organizational goals and objectives can be achieved, is cyclical in nature. M&A activity tends to come in waves. In fact, seven waves of M&A activity have been identified since the late nineteenth century. The most recent wave (since 2007) has recently led to three peak years (2015–2017), with more than 50,000 M&A transactions worldwide each year (Boyden 2019). In 2017 the value of global M&A deals amounted to $3.66 trillion (Statista 2019).

An advantage of M&As is that they can provide growth opportunities. An M&A can increase an organization's market power through horizontal integration. It may achieve entry into a new market, because either an organization possesses excess resources it cannot profitably use in its own market, or its existing market is declining and revenue growth is slowing. It may spread an organization's exposure to risk across a variety of industries. It may secure resources not currently possessed by the acquiring firm. M&A, in theory at least, should achieve two key objectives: improve competitiveness and deliver superior shareholder value.

Having mentioned some of the potentially beneficial outcomes of acquisitions, we should note that considerable evidence exists to suggest that pursuing an M&A strategy is both risky and uncertain to satisfy the desired objectives. The business world is full of examples of large-scale mergers that have failed to deliver the intended outcomes. Perhaps the biggest disaster of all was the purchase of AOL by Time Warner in 2000, for $165 billion. Time Warner was attracted by AOL's online presence and subscriber base. Shortly after the deal, the 'dot com bubble' burst (the price of leading technology shares reached their peak, and then fell very sharply (Madslien 2010)) and the economy went into recession. Over the next few years, the losses resulting from the deal were huge, and the two companies went their separate ways in 2009. In the next section we review why many firms engaging in M&A experience such poor performance when such deals seem to offer the strategist a constructive route to achieving organizational goals.

Problems with making M&A work

Research suggests that not all organizations engaging in M&A have an entirely successful experience; for instance, while the shareholders of acquired firms tend to earn above average returns, shareholders of acquiring firms are less likely to do so and often receive zero returns (Fuller et al. 2002; Jensen 1988; Shah and Arora 2014). Indeed, the value of shares in an acquiring firm often fall when the intention to acquire is announced (Roll 1986), a sign that stock markets view the potential of the M&A to achieve any genuine added value to be low. We might ask why this should be the case. Why is it often so hard for the acquiring organization in particular to realize all the potential benefits of an M&A deal?

There are a wide variety of potential difficulties that an acquiring organization may face. The first of these is difficulty in integrating the two organizations. Integration is a complex and time-consuming task, made even more complex if the organizations that are intending to merge are long-established entities in their own right with deeply entrenched organizational cultures, practices, and processes. However, achieving an effective post-merger integration is crucial. A high level of organizational resources needs to be allocated to the M&A activity. Acquisition targets need to be carefully chosen, and considerable effort needs to be focused upon integrating technical, financial, and human resources into the acquiring organization. Some organizations appear to build, over time, a valuable capability in post-merger integration management. For example, Danaher Corporation is a global conglomerate that has grown via hundreds of acquisitions since its formation in 1984—an example of a successful 'serial acquirer'. However, in other successful organizations, an M&A can act as a distraction, undermining the recipe that has brought them success in the first place. Similarly, managers who are primarily focused on assimilating new acquisitions into the organization may lose sight of the core business, leading to an overall deterioration in performance. There is also a risk that acquisitions may simply produce an organization that is too large for its control systems, or for a consistent culture to emerge.

Poor choice of takeover target is a common problem, reflecting a failure in due diligence. For example, Sprint acquired a majority stake in Nextel Communications in 2005, creating the world's third largest telecommunications provider. However, the two networks had very different technologies, very different customers, and very different brand positioning. Compromises were made, staff left citing cultural differences and incompatibility, and the merger generally came to be viewed as a disappointing failure (Forbes 2012).

Other acquisitions have been undermined by taking on too much debt to pay for the deal; for example, the acquisition by Cnooc, the Chinese state-owned oil company, of Nexen, a Canadian oil producer, for US$15 billion, which hit trouble when global oil prices slumped. This is especially serious if the revenue-generating effect of the acquisition has been overestimated, and sufficient income does not exist to service the debt.

A failure to deliver any expected synergies could also undermine the M&A and ultimately lead to **divestment**. For example, in the financial services sector, two merging banks often plan to achieve cost savings by consolidating their branch networks. However, in practice, estimated cost savings may be difficult to achieve in full, and calculations should also be made about the likely loss of revenue, such as if customers choose to leave the target bank.

So, what are the other growth strategies that two organizations that want to collaborate without making the major and potentially risky step of a merger or acquisition explore? Next we consider some cooperative strategies, where two or more organizations choose to work together while remaining separate entities.

Cooperative strategies

Both strategic alliances and joint ventures involve the formation of some sort of partnership with another organization, and this involves losing some degree of control over the organization's operations on the part of senior managers. These strategic approaches are of particular importance for organizations operating in global, fast-moving, or technology-driven environments, but the principles underlying the use of partnership approaches are relevant to all such strategic options. We will first examine joint ventures.

Joint ventures

A joint venture (JV) can be seen as the child of two organizational parents. The JV may be created to deliver a specific project, to pursue a particular market opportunity, or to capitalize on complimentary resources which would otherwise not be utilized effectively. For example, in 2012 Jaguar Land Rover (JLR), a British automotive company and subsidiary of the Indian

CASE EXAMPLE 10.2 TRANSATLANTIC TRYSTS: BRITISH LAW FIRMS SEEK MERGER PARTNERS IN AMERICA

Allen & Overy is a London-based international law firm and a member of the UK's 'magic circle'—a collection of the top five most prestigious law firms. Most firms within this group have made a concerted effort to expand their businesses internationally, opening offices across the world. However, there is one market in particular where it has proved quite difficult to get a foothold—the USA. The legal market in the USA is worth a total of $437 billion; it is the most litigious market in the world.

Like other firms, Allen & Overy understandably want a share of this immense market. In March 2019 it was reported that Allen & Overy was in the final stages of discussions around a merger with US firm O'Melvenry & Myers. There is no formal proposal document yet, but partners have been given access to information about the proposed terms. If the two firms merged it would create one of the world's largest law firms (according to revenue). A partner at one of the firms added that following meetings between partners at both firms, they felt that there was a good cultural fit between the two sides.

Entering the American market would further boost Allen & Overy's presence beyond the USA. Judgements made in American courts often have ramifications beyond its borders; for example, New York law (as with English law) is a common choice of governing law for international business transactions. Gaining a foothold in the USA via this merger would give Allen & Overy the chance to exploit these opportunities through an American outpost.

However, such opportunities rarely come without challenges. The American market is very difficult to crack; clients have strong relationships with their lawyers/firms and the market is already very crowded with US firms. The other issue is around pay; as the profits of leading US firms are generally twice the profits of their UK counterparts, they can afford to pay their partners substantially more. The 'magic circle' firms are further restricted by the 'lockstep' model which broadly remunerates partners on the basis of seniority. The scope for large awards tends to be limited, whereas in the USA they have greater freedom to award substantial pay increases if an individual brings in significant new business.

One of the key issues of this merger, if it happens, will be around talent retention. Big differences in pay and culture can lead to partners leaving, taking with them clients who are willing to switch firms to stay with their partner. If too many partners leave, taking with them too many clients, this can negate the benefits of the merger in the first place. So whilst the merger presents these two firms with a huge opportunity, it does not come without serious risk.

Questions for discussion

1. Case Example 10.2 suggests that a top London law firm may be in merger talks with an American law firm. Before deciding to pursue such a deal, what alternative options (other than an M&A deal) would you recommend the UK firm to consider before selecting a merger as its preferred strategic choice?
2. What benefits is the London law firm likely to be seeking to achieve via a merger deal? For example, what synergies might it be able to achieve?
3. Compare the sector that the firm operates in (i.e. law and professional services) with another industry sector with which you are familiar (for example, air travel, the subject of this chapter's opening case study concerning IAG and Norwegian). Do you think that there are any characteristics of this industry sector that might make the deal particularly attractive or particularly difficult to implement successfully?
4. What do you see as the key challenges that the UK firm may face if the deal proceeds? What risks should it plan for?

Sources

The Economist, 12 April 2018.

https://www.law.com/americanlawyer/2019/03/13/allen-overy-and-omelveny-hone-in-on-key-merger-terms-405-33350/

10

firm Tata Motors, and Chery, a Chinese automobile manufacturer, began to put in place a joint venture to build a new plant in China which would bring together strengths in manufacturing, production, and logistics with local R&D and an iconic British brand. In 2018, it was announced that the JV will invest 7 billion yuan (over 900 million euros) in the development and production of electric cars—as well as producing more than 200,000 conventional cars per year at its local facility—suggesting that the two partners are continuing to see the benefits of their collaborative activities (Manthey 2018).

At the time of its JV with Chery, JLR saw China as a fast-growing market where it was aiming to achieve better access. In some instances, JVs may be the only way for an organization to access a new market. Governments of some countries can insist upon local JV partners before allowing market entry to foreign companies to minimize the threat of foreign domination and to enhance the development of skills, employment opportunities, and revenue generation within the host economy of the JV. One such example is the Chinese government's approach to protecting key industries such as its financial services sector. Late in 2018, American Express (AmEx) became the only foreign payment provider allowed to work in China through a 50–50 partnership with a domestic company LianLian Group. In 2019, Visa and Mastercard, the world's two leading credit card brands, were still waiting for the go-ahead to process yuan payments; the Chinese central bank had not acknowledged or formally accepted their applications, more than a year after the applications were submitted (Pham 2018). Visa and Mastercard can only issue co-branded cards in China, typically in collaboration with China UnionPay, the largest card services organization in the world. AmEx is now able to compete with UnionPay inside China, and aims to win business in UnionPay's home market.

In JVs, both risk and control are shared. They are consequently viewed with some caution by many managers, who value the opportunities that they can provide and appreciate the ability to share risk, but dislike having to giving up a degree of control over the new venture. Public–private partnerships (PPPs) have been used widely to deliver public sector services in the UK and elsewhere. Such partnerships can involve complex JVs between public and private sector organizations. Researchers have argued that one such project, Building Schools for the Future, entailed 'limited and aggregated financial reporting and patchy oversight and scrutiny, leading to a loss of control over public expenditure' (Shaoul et al. 2013), as well as a loss of accountability. This illustrates the need to design and implement appropriate structures for managing risks and rewards in JV projects.

Strategic alliances

One key difference between joint ventures and strategic alliances (SAs) is that while JVs involve joint ownership, SAs do not. According to Das and Teng (2000a), strategic alliances are voluntary cooperative inter-firm agreements aimed at achieving competitive advantage for the partners. In practice, this typically means that two or more independent organizations have decided to cooperate in the development, manufacturing, or sale of products and services: 'The proliferation of strategic alliances in recent years marks a shift in the conception of the intrinsic nature of competition, which is increasingly characterized by constant technological innovations and speedy entry into new markets' (Das and Teng 2000a:34).

An SA is less formal than a JV, so there is typically less risk associated with an SA; it is easier for an organization to end the partnership if it wishes to do so. The alliance may provide an organization with access to new technology or intellectual property rights (see the Google–Samsung and Disney–Hewlett Packard examples in Table 10.2). It may make the organization more agile in its capacity to move into new product lines or markets; and it may reduce costs in certain areas, for example in R&D, if that activity is now being shared as part of the SA. However, alliances inevitably involve additional costs, such as the cost of searching for and selecting a suitable partner.

An SA can also bring some inherent disadvantages. For instance, the need to focus on, and commit to, a strategic alliance may lead an organization to overlook other opportunities, such as other growth strategies in different markets to the SA being undertaken. Organizations may feel that they can no longer act solely in their own interests, as they must consider the interests of the alliance, and a 'stronger' partner may be able to force a 'weaker' partner to do its bidding. The frustrations of working in partnership can be considerable. They may include the need for trade-offs and compromise, and the need to take account of partners' different cultures, practices, and processes. For instance, a four-year dispute between VW and Suzuki was settled in court in 2015. The two automotive firms established an SA in 2009, working together on fuel-efficient cars, but 'cultural differences' were cited as one of the reasons for the termination of the alliance, after Suzuki accused VW of withholding information it had promised to share, and VW objected to a Suzuki deal to buy diesel engines from Fiat (BBC 2015). There may be difficulties and costs associated with coordination or dispute resolution between two organizations in an SA. Of course, profits and other resources must be shared, perhaps even skills and know-how, and organizations may feel that they are at risk of having to disclose proprietary knowledge relating to their own activities, which may weaken their own ability to capture value in the future.

Management issues affecting strategic alliances

Particular demands are placed upon the managers in an SA, and the record of running successful alliances is somewhat mixed. The success of an alliance may lie more in its management than in the circumstances of its initial creation (Elmuti and Kathawala 2001; Harrigan 1984). Managers from partner companies often come from different national and corporate cultures and have difficulty in understanding or approving of their new allies' practices and ways of operation. In addition they may have been trained to operate in hierarchically organized firms and are somewhat disadvantaged when faced with the need to cooperate and act through consensus. That is why SAs are often referred to as 'cooperative strategies', rather than competitive ones. This often implies a need to focus upon the operational issues, rather than the strategic ones. According to Das and Teng (2000b), alliances become unstable due to three key kinds of internal tension: cooperation versus competition, rigidity versus flexibility, and short-term versus long-term orientation.

It has been estimated that large firms (e.g. the Fortune 500 list in the USA) have an average of 50–70 strategic alliances each (*The Economist* 2009). This suggests that there is scope for organizations to learn from their own experiences of strategic alliances over time, and to improve their capabilities at managing such relationships. Kale et al. (2002:747) argue that 'firms with greater alliance experience and, more importantly, those that create a dedicated alliance function (with the intent of strategically coordinating alliance activity and capturing/disseminating alliance-related knowledge) realize greater success with alliances'. Faulkner (1995) found that four factors play a key role in the successful management of alliances:

- **Positive attitudes between the partners** Alliances are likely to fail when a lack of trust develops and relationships between partners become negative, as in the example of VW and Suzuki.
- **Clear organizational arrangements for the alliance** For instance, Hewlett Packard has an approach to SAs that is very formal, structured, and well organized, based on a 400-page binder with tools, checklists, policies, and procedures (Elmuti and Kathawala 2001).
- **A philosophy of organizational learning** For partners such as Google–Samsung and Disney–Hewlett Packard with collaborations around innovative technology and intellectual property, learning from each other provides an important objective of the alliance.
- **Congruent long-term goals** For example, consider the alliance between Starbucks and Pepsico to create the coffee-flavoured drink Frappacino. This allowed both firms to meet their goals, as Starbucks moved into the bottled beverage market while PepsiCo gained an innovative product with a well-branded partner.

Making international alliances work

There are difficulties involved not just in setting up international strategic alliances, but also in maintaining positive cooperative attitudes as the alliance progresses. The actions that must be taken to ensure that the gap between organizations in an alliance is bridged are known as 'boundary-spanning'. Some organizations possess greater skills than others in the area of boundary-spanning. These enhanced capabilities make the alliances that they are engaged in more likely to work both formally and informally, and more likely to achieve their objectives (Albers et al. 2013). Boundary-spanning is a crucial aspect of alliances, and the skill with which it is carried out seems to have considerable impact upon the success of the alliance.

An example of a boundary-spanning action is a 'gateway' system (Badaracco 1991; Killing 1992). This is a system in which, at least in the early months of the alliance, all communications must pass through the office of only one 'gatekeeper' in each partner company in order to avoid the risk of misunderstandings, such as through the duplication of contacts. The gatekeeper is normally the sole interface between the companies, and is kept informed of all contacts and therefore, by implication, any areas of potential dispute. By careful selection of appropriate boundary-spanners, and by gradually increasing areas of involvement as the partners get to know each other, the effects of organizational incompatibilities may be reduced. This is a strategic role, and the human resource function is likely to play an important part in it. For instance, Søderberg and Romani (2017) discuss the complexity of global IT development projects where Western firms outsource to Indian service companies. In such situations, key boundary-spanners play an important role in developing trustful and sustainable client relationships and coordinating highly complex projects.

A common example of an alliance objective is to encourage the absorption of know-how, embedded knowledge, tacit routines, and organizational practices from the partner (e.g. the alliance between Hewlett Packard and Disney mentioned in Table 10.2). Many alliances are set up for short-term gains in order to deal with temporary situations such as resource deficiencies or lack of market knowledge. Specific short-term objectives may be perfectly satisfactory. Alliances are, of course, not confined to the private sector. CRUK, a cancer research and awareness charity based in the UK, works with a wide range of strategic partners including pharmaceutical companies, technology companies, and bodies from the public and charity/not-for-profit sectors, both in the UK and internationally. The aims of such partnerships include co-funding of research, sharing expertise, and investing in people and training (Cancer Research UK 2014). Many of these aims, such as a pooling of certain training and expertise, or conducting a specific research project, can potentially be met over a relatively short timescale, such as between one and three years, with a plan to dissolve the alliance at that point.

Whilst a strategic alliance can bring many benefits to organizations, ending a strategic alliance can be a painful and lengthy process. As noted earlier, VW and Suzuki established a strategic alliance in 2009, but in 2015 a court ruling was required to settle a four-year dispute between the two firms (BBC 2015). In order to avoid this sort of dispute, many successful alliances form an agreement at formation, in anticipation of their eventual dissolution—a sort of a 'divorce' procedure. This can help to reduce anxiety about the costs of potential failure.

Ultimately, it is helpful for the student of strategy to understand the degree to which the management of an alliance involves constant negotiation to find overlaps between goals rather than to clarify totally congruent goals. As Walter et al. (2012:1582) note, 'alliance-related decision processes have to balance each partner's self-interest on one hand and collective actions on the other hand, with both partners being dependent on each other's collaboration'. The potential problem of conflicting objectives is ever present, since perhaps the key characteristic of alliances is the wish of the partners to obtain the advantages of joint activity, while retaining their individual autonomy. Therefore a substantial contribution to success must depend upon the management of internal tensions (Das and Teng 2000b; Powell 1990). Both partners must remember that they are partners, and not seek to achieve advantages which benefit one at the expense of the other.

A less contentious form of strategic alliance that you should be aware of involves licensing agreements. Under a licensing agreement, the rights to use a brand, product, process, or other trademarked or patented resource is passed to an alliance partner for the payment of a fee or a share in revenues. Licensing agreements are frequently used to allow major brands to migrate across borders, as a rapid and cheap way to establish themselves as global brands. For instance, the Coca-Cola Corporation licenses regional bottling companies to manufacture and distribute soft drinks under the Coca-Cola and other brand names. Strategic alliances can permit organizations to establish manufacturing plants in new territories, and to outsource some activities for a variety of reasons; operating in partnership can allow an organization to tap into local knowledge in a new market, managing its risks and lowering its expenditure on fixed costs such as manufacturing plant, without losing focus on its core business.

Consortia

To end our discussion of cooperative strategies, we consider the possibility of engaging in a consortium to support strategic growth. A consortium is an interconnecting set of relationships between a variety of organizations, often with the intention of bidding for, and then delivering, large and complex projects. While it may sound similar to a JV or an SA, it is likely to be a much less rigid arrangement, established for a limited period of time to achieve a particular goal shared by all the partners, and then disbanded. For example, as mentioned in Table 10.2, Airbus is a European aerospace corporation, registered in The Netherlands and trading shares in multiple European countries. The current company is the product of consolidation in the European aerospace industry dating back to 1970. It designs, manufactures, and sells civil and military aerospace products worldwide. A consortium like Airbus allows the partners to benefit from each other's skills, knowledge, expertise, and experience, but no equity stake is required. All partners retain their independent legal status (unlike in a JV), and the activities of the partners are not constrained outside the remit of the consortium itself.

In the travel and tourism sector, for example, consortia are quite common. Independent travel agents and agencies get together with the aim of increasing their purchasing power and improving amenities for their customers. Such an arrangement can allow the partners to retain their independence, while sharing skills and experience, and working towards a common goal. However, potential partners need to be aware of the possible downsides of engaging in a consortium. Such a partnership may be time-consuming to build. Partners may feel that, because of the relative flexibility of the arrangement, they do not have sufficient control of the project or the activities of the other partners—yet resources, such as profits and knowledge, are likely to be shared. Partners may struggle to ensure consistency and quality across the project; it can be difficult to coordinate effectively between partners or resolve disputes. And the reputation of all partners may be damaged if one partner fails to deliver as expected.

To sum up, a strategist who is considering pursuing a cooperative strategy should be aware of the range of options available, including JVs, SAs, and consortia. Their relative advantages and disadvantages are associated with a spectrum of flexibility and formality.

CASE EXAMPLE 10.3 **SOUTH KOREA'S CHAEBOL**

South Korea has developed into one of Asia's most affluent countries; its economy is now the fourth largest in Asia, and the twelfth largest in the world. It has a mixed economy which is dominated by family-run conglomerates known as 'chaebol'; there are several dozen chaebol, including organizations such as Samsung, LG, Hyundai, SK, and Lotte. To provide an idea of their size, the top ten chaebol own 27% of all business assets in South Korea. Establishing chaebol was seen as a way to fast track the development of the country's economy; however, in recent years the chaebol has been under scrutiny following a corruption scandal so significant it led to the impeachment, and eventually arrest, of the then president of South Korea, Park Geun-hye.

In January 2017 Jay Y. Lee, the vice-chairman of Samsung, was accused of bribery, embezzlement, and perjury by special prosecutors. One month later Mr Lee was arrested for handing bribes to Park Geun-hye and her associate Choi-Soon-sil that were reportedly worth almost £30 million. Mr Lee handed over the bribe to try to win government support for a smooth leadership transition in his bid to achieve greater control of the company. He was sentenced to five years imprisonment, but following appeal Seoul's high court reduced that sentence and allowed him to walk free after serving less than a full year.

The public were angry about his release; this was not the first time a business leader had been convicted for corruption only to be let off. According to Bloomberg, public discontent with chaebol has long been brewing; in December 2017, the 95-year-old founder of the Lotte retail group was sentenced to four years in jail for embezzlement and breach of fiduciary duty. In February 2018, Lotte's chairman was convicted in a separate corruption trial. At a hearing in 2016, nine chaebol leaders faced a barrage of questions from lawmakers, and anger from hundreds of thousands of protesters. Sixteen months later, former president Park was sentenced to 24 years in prison after being found guilty of crimes ranging from bribery to coercion, abuse of power, and the leaking of state secrets. In November 2018 more than 150,000 workers walked out of work in protest at the lack of progress in reforming the chaebol.

Continued

The cross-shareholdings and intragroup deals within chaebol has led to a perception of cronyism by investors across the world. There is, in fact, a phenomenon known as 'the Korea discount' where stock is depressed (compared with the value of similar stock in the USA, Europe, or Japan) partly due to investors' concerns over the undue influence the chaebol system allows.

South Korea's chaebol have similarities to Japan's keiretsu, as explored in Case Example 7.1. However, there are some key differences between them. Chaebol are still mainly controlled by the founding families, whereas keiretsu are controlled by professional managers. Another key difference pertinent to this case is that chaebol do not have their own financial institutions and were more heavily dependent on government loans—they still have a closer relationship with government than the Japanese keiretsu.

Questions for discussion

1. List some of the possible ways that being a member of a chaebol might help a firm to survive and thrive in a competitive economy. Can you think of any disadvantages of being a member of a chaebol?
2. What other strategic options might be open to such firms, other than being a member of a chaebol? What might be some of the advantages and disadvantages of those alternative options?
3. Consider our discussion of related and unrelated diversification, and asset sharing (refer to the axes of the 2×2 matrix on value-creating strategies of diversification shown in Figure 10.2). How do these ideas help us to understand the mix of firms that are members of a particular chaebol?
4. Consider our discussion of corporate parenting. How does this help us to understand how a chaebol might operate in offering benefits to its member firms?

Sources

Bloomberg.com, 29 May 2014, updated 6 April 2018. https://www.bloomberg.com/quicktake/republic-samsung

Wall Street Journal

https://www.wsj.com/articles/a-presidential-scandal-transfixes-south-korea-1480112351?mod=article_inline

Financial Times

https://www.ft.com/content/b55b2d6a-ed43-11e8-89c8-d36339d835c0

The Economist

https://www.economist.com/business/2017/01/21/lee-jae-yong-dodges-arrest-on-charges-of-bribery

The Telegraph

https://www.telegraph.co.uk/business/2017/02/16/south-korean-court-issues-warrant-arrest-samsung-heir/

10.8 **Divestment**

We have discussed a range of strategies for growth including market penetration, market or product development, and diversification. We have looked in depth at a range of options for diversification that involved collaborating with another organization, whether through integration, M&As, joint ventures, or strategic alliances. But, in contrast with all these strategies for growth, might there be an argument to **reduce** an organization's activities? Could that alternative track also provide opportunities for growth? In this section we will explain one such possibility, known as divestment. Divestment refers to the sale or disposal of one of a corporation's activities. Divestments may occur when corporate synergies no longer exist, when under-utilized corporate assets can be better deployed elsewhere, or if finance is needed to invest elsewhere in the portfolio. Many divestments occur when subsidiary businesses show decline; for example, a soft drinks company may terminate investment in declining areas of its product range in order to reallocate funds to a new line of energy drinks.

Divestment, core competencies, and outsourcing

Various rationales for divestment decisions can be identified. In Chapter 5 we discussed the ways in which organizations identify businesses and activities that they see as core. The concept of core competencies can therefore provide a rationale to determine which activities should be retained within the organization, and which might be divested or outsourced. If a competence is core to a corporation, it is a strategic focus for longer-term competition for market share of core products. A corporation would not normally seek to divest activities that enhance its core competencies. However, if an activity or business does not involve a core competence, an organization can consider whether to divest that activity. It is here that 'make-or-buy' tests of transaction costs can be used to test divestments. Can the activity be more efficiently carried out within the organization, or by outside partners or contractors? The test of efficiency is not measured in purely financial terms, but should include all potential managerial efficiencies.

'Outsourcing' is a divestment strategy which recognizes that improved effectiveness might come from buying in non-core competencies. Such improved effectiveness rests on the better skills, resources, and expertise of partners or contractors for whom particular activities do constitute core competencies, or on the opening up of a non-core activity to market-based competition, rather than continuing an internal monopoly. Outsourcing provides opportunities for both divestors and suppliers of services. For example, suppliers can build a business around the fast and expert provision of particular services, while divestors may find that outsourcing allows them to achieve cost reduction while focusing on core rather than supporting processes.

However, the outsourcing of information systems can raise serious questions for organizations over what constitutes a strategic asset, the competitive security of information and knowledge, and what are, or are not, core competencies. For instance in Europe, where new rules governing the protection of personal data came into effect in May 2018 (known as GDPR) (*The Economist* 2018b), it has been noted that many organizations are likely to outsource the task of handling personal data as it becomes increasingly challenging to comply with stricter regulation. Critics of this approach to outsourcing personal data argue that organizations need to remain mindful of the data that they hold, on their customers for example, and how that data is handled. If data is potentially a key resource for the organization, then outsourcing data handling may lead to missed opportunities. The organization will fail to build its own core competencies in data handling, or to gain key insights into customers which can lead to new ideas for strategic growth and potentially competitive advantage for the organization.

Divestment in the public sector

The issue of what constitutes a proper activity to be outsourced also underpins much controversy surrounding the privatization and deregulation of public services—a form of divestment by the state. Public sector divestment activities have many forms. For instance, in India, one in every six rupees spent goes to a so-called 'public sector undertaking' (PSU) (*The Economist* 2017), and commentators frequently debate whether many such PSUs should be sold or closed. Despite providing jobs for disadvantaged segments of Indian society, such as certain castes and ex-servicemen, PSUs are often criticized for being unproductive and a drain on public finances.

Divestment of state activities is often controversial, not least because it is heavily influenced by political ideologies which differ in the extent to which they believe that the state should be involved in economic and social activity at all. It also generates public concern about the potential impact on employment, and unemployment. This makes it difficult for managers to apply the tests of diversification, discussed in Section 10.4, in a rational manner. For instance, when the UK-based firm Carillion collapsed in early 2018 (its activities ranged from construction projects for hospitals and roads to the provision of school meals), the UK government was subjected to strong demands for a re-examination of their procurement processes (*The Economist* 2018c).

CASE EXAMPLE 10.4 **EBAY AND PAYPAL**

In 2015 the relationship between eBay and PayPal ended, 13 years after eBay acquired the payment platform in 2002 for $1.5 billion. This is one example of a number of 'tech divorces' in the works as organizations are repositioning themselves in response to major market changes, such as mobile and cloud technologies.

The Economist notes that, as technology and markets change increasingly rapidly, it helps to be independent, and shareholders tend to be enthusiastic about spin-offs. The eBay Inc Board of Directors stated the following: 'The benefits of the existing relationships between eBay and PayPal will naturally decline over time and can be optimized in arm's length operating agreements between the two entities.' The split will allow both companies to be much more flexible and better able to respond to the movements of competitors such as Apple Pay (in PayPal's case). Being so closely associated with eBay has made rival e-commerce sites reluctant to engage in a partnership with PayPal. An operation agreement will be in place until 2020. However, both companies have already started looking to their separate futures.

PayPal is a leading digital payment service ranking 222nd on the 2018 Fortune 500 (a list of the largest US corporations in terms of revenue). Perhaps surprisingly, PayPal is much larger and stronger than eBay. As of July 2019, the share price of eBay Inc. was valued at $39.92 compared with a value of $119.71 for PayPal. Since splitting with eBay, PayPal has gone on to acquire nine companies, the largest of which was iZette, a Swedish fintech company, at a cost of $2.2 billion. In 2019 PayPal also announced a new partnership with Instagram as part of the company's new checkout feature.

Meanwhile, eBay announced in 2018 that PayPal is being replaced by Adyen—a relatively small Netherlands-based e-commerce company founded in 2006. Beginning life as a privately held start-up, Adyen went public in 2018 and it now provides the payment technology behind sites such as Uber, Netflix, and Spotify.

The Economist notes:

> What made eBay one of the winners of the dotcom boom is now holding it back. Having been an early mover in online auctions in the late 1990s, for example, today consumers prefer the certainty of quickly completing an online purchase. Today 80% of items are sold at a fixed price, but many still view eBay mainly as an auction site. Being a marketplace where others list their wares has spared the firm costly investments in warehouses and logistics, but today this lack of 'vertical integration' makes it difficult to meet the increasing demands of buyers who expect rapid purchase and delivery.

Questions for discussion

1. What advantages do you think eBay was seeking to achieve when it bought PayPal in 2002?
2. How would you summarize some of the key changes in the market that have taken place since 2002?
3. Can you identify any other strategic options that you think the two firms should be considering at this point? What might the pros and cons of such options be?

4. The Case Example suggests that eBay should perhaps consider greater 'vertical integration' in the future. What might this look like, and what risks and benefits might it entail?

Sources

Adapted from *The Economist*, 18 July 2015.

https://investor.paypal-corp.com/static-files/d7789358-2196-4799-8e0e-a3c3355407f3

https://www.ebayinc.com/stories/news/ebay-paypal-become-independent-companies-2015/

10.9 **Testing and evaluating strategic options**

Having discussed a range of possible strategies that present opportunities for growth of the organization, how can strategists evaluate the set of strategic options that are open to them? In what ways might they assess how successful the strategies might be in serving the purposes of the organization? In this section we will consider a range of tests that strategists might use to evaluate strategic options. As a student of strategy it is important to know a range of tests available to the strategist and to gain an understanding of how these tests can be applied in practice.

It is worth noting that, while a number of tests are suggested in this section, they are not mutually exclusive. A strategist could consider applying all the suggested tests in order to help them evaluate their strategic options.

Johnson and Scholes' tests of suitability, feasibility, and acceptability

The first perspective on evaluating strategic options for growth comes from Johnson and Scholes (2003). They suggest three sets of generic testing criteria: suitability, feasibility, and acceptability (SFA). A matrix can be used to summarize the results of the strategist's assessment of each strategic option that's open to the organization against each of the three areas suitability, feasibility, and acceptability (see Figure 10.4). For example, an organization might be considering three options for strategic growth into a new international market:

Option A: acquisition of an established player in the new market

Option B: joint venture with another organization also wanting to expand into the new market

Option C: strategic alliance with another organization also wanting to expand into the new market.

We will now examine each of the tests and the steps involved.

	Option A	Option B	Option C
Suitability	4	4	3
Feasibility	2	3	4
Acceptability	1	3	5
Total	7	10	12

FIGURE 10.4 Example of the SFA matrix.

Suitability

The suitability of a proposed strategy can be assessed by the extent to which it matches the needs identified from a strategic analysis. Such a test of suitability can be regarded as a test of consistency with the environmental and resources analyses, and their fit with the organizational objectives. In order to assess the suitability of a possible strategic option, the strategist can consider the following set of four questions:

1. Is the proposed strategy consistent with, and does it fulfil, the market key success factors (KSFs) (see the discussion of competitive advantage in Chapter 5)? The KSFs apply to the industry within which the organization operates, and represent the minimum entry requirements of that market.
2. Does the proposed strategy address the strategic problem or opportunity identified in the strategic analysis? Does it overcome an identified resource weakness or environmental threat?
3. Does the proposed strategy capitalize on the organization's identified resources and capabilities, and the ways in which they relate to the external opportunities?
4. Does the strategy fit the organization's objectives, such as required rates of return on capital, profitability measures, and other non-financial performance indicators? These may involve considerations of the organization's role in a wider context, including an acknowledgment of social responsibility.

Having considered each of these questions, the strategist can arrive at an assessment of the suitability of each strategic option that the organization is considering—and record the results in the first row of the SFA matrix (see Figure 10.4), perhaps using a scale of 1 to 5, where 5 indicates that the option is highly suitable and 1 indicates that it is not suitable at all. For instance, in the example above, the firm may feel that an acquisition or a JV would be more suitable than an SA, as these options may give more controlled access to new resources and capabilities.

Next, we consider the second test, which concerns the feasibility of the organization's strategic options.

Feasibility

A second test applied by the strategist would be the test of feasibility. This test of a proposed strategy considers how well the strategy will work in practice, and how difficult it might be to achieve. The steps for this test are:

1. Can the strategy be resourced? Even the most brilliant strategy cannot be implemented if, for example, the organization's financial position is too weak to raise the necessary capital.
2. Can the organization actually achieve the required level of operational performance, say in quality and service levels? For example, a strategy aimed at cutting costs in a manufacturing environment may run into problems associated with inadequate managerial resources, insufficient numbers of trained staff, insufficient plant, or inadequate process and product technologies.

3. How will the competition react, and how will the organization cope with that reaction? For example, a strategy to increase market share by reducing prices may lead to a fierce response from competitors.

Having considered each of these questions, the strategist can arrive at an assessment of the feasibility of each strategic option that the organization is considering—and record the results in the second row of the SFA matrix (see Figure 10.4), perhaps using a scale of 1 to 5, where 5 indicates that the option is highly feasible and 1 indicates that it is not feasible at all. In the example above, the organization may feel that an acquisition would be the most difficult to achieve, and an SA would be the least difficult.

Acceptability

This third and final criterion addresses the issue of how stakeholders might feel about the expected outcomes of the strategy—typically in terms of risk, profitability, reward, ethics, and the effect on relationships. Meeting reasonable stakeholder expectations would appear to be a crucial test for the acceptability of any new strategy. The steps involved in the test of acceptability are:

1. What will be the financial or cost–benefit performance? Is there an unacceptable risk of endangering overall liquidity or affecting capital structure?
2. Is there a risk that the organization's relationships with its stakeholders could be unacceptably affected? The proposed strategy may be unpopular with employees, institutional shareholders, existing customers/clients, or governmental organizations.
3. What is the effect of the proposed strategy on the internal systems and procedures? Even if feasible, will there be an unacceptable level of additional pressure upon staff?

Having considered each of these questions, the strategist can arrive at an assessment of the acceptability of each strategic option that the organization is considering and record the results in the third row of the SFA matrix (see Figure 10.4), perhaps using a scale of 1 to 5, where 5 indicates that the option is highly acceptable and 1 indicates that it is not acceptable at all. For instance, in the example above, the firm may feel that an SA would be the most acceptable to key stakeholders, and an acquisition the least acceptable.

A total score can then be calculated for each option, giving the strategist an indication of which strategies perform well on the three tests, and which do not. Of course, in practice, it may not be as simple as then choosing the option with the highest score. For instance, a particular strategic option may score well because of its suitability and feasibility, but managers may judge that it cannot be pursued because it is unacceptable to key stakeholders, or this exercise may lead managers to debate how they can take an option that is both suitable and feasible, and adapt it so that it is also more acceptable.

These three tests of suitability, feasibility, and acceptability provide an initial set of screening tools for possible strategic options. They prompt managers to be explicit about the rationale that underpins potential strategies, and to assess the associated risks and uncertainties. The criteria can also guide the softer process of assessing how acceptable the proposed strategies might be to stakeholders. However, it is usually helpful to test proposed strategies from a number of perspectives. Rumelt proposes an alternative perspective to consider.

Rumelt's tests of consistency, consonance, advantage, and feasibility

Rumelt (1995) suggests four tests of consistency, consonance, advantage, and feasibility. In comparison with the set of tests put forward by Johnson and Scholes (2003), we find some similarities; both sets of tests explore 'feasibility', and, for Rumelt, the test of 'consistency' appears to cover the same broad set of issues as 'suitability' in the set of tests by Johnson and Scholes (2003). However, Rumelt proposes a test for advantage instead of acceptability, and he adds a test of consonance. He acknowledges that it may be impossible to demonstrate conclusively that a particular strategy can or will work, let alone that it is an 'optimal' strategy. However, he points out that all strategies could be tested for these four types of problem.

Consistency

First, the proposed strategy must not present goals and policies that lack consistency. You may feel that failing this test is unlikely, but it may be a particularly necessary test for strategies that have emerged over time, rather than being explicitly formulated. Even deliberate strategies may contain compromises between different power groups within the organization for example.

Inconsistency in strategy is not simply a flaw in logic. A key function of strategy is to provide a coherent framework for organizational activity, and a clear sense of vision, direction, and purpose for the organization. Sears Holdings, the parent of US retailer Kmart, finally filed for bankruptcy in October 2018. For some years Kmart had been widely criticized for a lack of focus in comparison with key competitors such as Walmart ('always lowest prices') and Target ('cheap-chic clothing styles'). It can be argued that Kmart's strategy was unsuccessful because it lacked the clear sense of vision and purpose that Rumelt refers to, at least in comparison with the coherent and consistent approach to the market adopted by its competitors.

Rumelt goes on to argue that an organization relates to its environment in two main aspects, which we will consider next. First, its products or services must create more value than they cost (leading us to consider a criterion around consonance). Secondly, it must compete with other organizations that are also trying to adapt and prosper (hence a concern for advantage, discussed after consonance).

Consonance

This test is focused on the creation of social value. For Rumelt, the test seeks to evaluate the economic relationships that are the key characteristics of the business. The aim of the test is to explore whether sufficient value is being created to sustain the demand for the firm's strategy over the longer term. An evaluation of consonance is a difficult task, not least because many of the critical threats from the external environment will also threaten the firm's entire industry. The firm's senior team may be so intent on doing battle with existing rival firms that a serious threat to the whole industry is only recognized at a relatively late stage. According to Rumelt, many forecasting techniques do not help managers to identify potentially critical changes that arise from interactions between combinations of trends. In order to apply this test effectively, we have to ask ourselves why the organization exists, and question the basic economic foundations that support and define it. We can then explore the consequences of significant changes in the firm's external environment. As a classic example, consider Blockbuster, the former movie rental chain. In 2004 its revenue was around $6 billion, but just six years later it was bankrupt, having failed to respond to a changing business landscape and adapt its operating model.

Advantage

Rumelt's third test is about competitive advantage, or whether the organization can capture enough of the value it creates. Competitive strategy can be viewed as the art of creating and exploiting those advantages that are most enduring and most difficult to duplicate. The strategy must provide for the creation and/or maintenance of a competitive advantage from one or more of three sources: superior skills, superior resources, or superior position.

Feasiblity

As discussed above, feasibility refers to how well the strategy might work in practice, and how difficult it might be to achieve. Once again, we might ask whether the strategy can be resourced, whether the organization can actually achieve the required level of performance, such as quality, and how competitors might react.

Rumelt's four tests of consistency, consonance, advantage, and feasibility provide an alternative set of screening tools for possible strategic options to those proposed by Johnson and Scholes. These can be used instead of or in addition to Johnson and Scholes' three tests of suitability, feasibility, and acceptability. Other tests that would be useful to consider alongside those already discussed include testing for business risk and for shareholder/stakeholder interests. We will move on to these next.

Testing for business risk and for shareholder/stakeholder interests

Two final tests that are valuable for most businesses are tests of business risk and tests of shareholder/stakeholder interests. We will consider tests of business risk first.

Business risk

According to Lynch (2018), the analysis of business risk is made up of two key elements. Each element is supported by a range of relevant approaches to exploring business risk. The two elements are:

- financial risk analysis
- scenario building.

Financial risk analysis focuses on the financial risks that may be associated with the strategic options that the organization is interested in pursuing. Types of financial risk analysis include cash flow analysis, break-even analysis, company borrowing requirements, financial ratio analysis, and currency analysis. Scenario building seeks to question all the basic assumptions behind each option. The key assumptions are varied to understand their impact on various company objectives. Changes are assessed in relation to their possible impact on the types of financial risk measure mentioned earlier (Open University 2010). For example, some level of fluctuation in foreign exchange rates may be acceptable, but within what range? How sensitive are costs or revenues to variations outside the acceptable range?

Attractiveness to shareholders and other stakeholders

When exploring the interests of shareholders and other stakeholders, techniques may be employed to judge the appropriateness of strategic options when measured against different types of value. These may include:

- shareholder value added, i.e. how will the proposed strategic option contribute towards the aim of maximizing the long-term cash flow of the business unit it affects?
- cost–benefit analysis, which is a broader appraisal method seeking to determine how a strategic decision will perform against a wider set of criteria than sales, profits, or costs.

Cost–benefit analysis tends to be applied in situations where a broader range of stakeholder interests is being considered, rather than in instances where returning shareholder value is the principal concern. For example, in 2005 the UK government undertook an analysis of a number of options for investment in childcare. The choice was between higher-cost 'integrated' childcare centres, providing a range of services to both children and parents, or lower cost 'non-integrated' centres that provided basic child care facilities. The analysis included both a 'hard exercise' and a 'soft exercise'. The hard exercise identified, quantified, and monetized direct costs and benefits. The soft exercise identified and described qualitatively non-financial outcomes, leading to option ranking (Better Evaluation 2014). This illustrates an approach designed to analyse the full range of benefits of different options to a range of stakeholders—including non-financial benefits.

Not-for-profit and public organizations: testing for efficiency, effectiveness, economy, and equity

Public and private not-for-profit organizations may question whether all the above tests apply to them. For example, a test of 'advantage' may not seem appropriate to managers who feel that they are not in a competitive situation. It has been suggested that such organizations may choose to test proposed strategies against objectives that are founded on the **'four Es'**: efficiency, effectiveness, economy, and equity (Norman-Major 2011). We should note that there can be conflicting objectives if, for example, both efficiency and effectiveness are to be served. Take the example of something as simple and uncontroversial as filling potholes in the road: using a cheaper mix to fill the holes may be economical in the short term; however, it may not be effective, efficient, or even economical in the long term if the potholes need constant refilling (Norman-Major 2012).

In this section we have explored a range of tests that strategists can use to evaluate possible strategic options for growth. As you study strategy it is important to understand how strategists can use tests to ensure that they select the most suitable option. These tests can be seen as complementing each other, and a skilled strategist will use a variety of tests when considering their strategic options.

PRACTITIONER INSIGHT: **KIERAN PHELAN, GLOBAL SUSTAINABILITY AND COMPLIANCE DIRECTOR, WILLIAM GRANT & SONS**

Kieran is Global Sustainability and Compliance Director with William Grant & Sons (WG&S). He has previously worked for several multinationals in operational improvement, environmental affairs, and international health and safety roles. He is part of the leadership team that contributes to the strategy process in WG&S.

The company started in 1887 in Dufftown in Speyside, when the founder William Grant wished to make 'the best dram in the valley' (a dram is a measure of whisky). From an initial malt whisky distillery has grown the diverse organization of today. Alongside malt whisky and grain whisky, WG&S now produces premium vodka, gins, tequila, rums, and liqueurs. WG&S has distilleries throughout Scotland and bottling facilities in the UK, Ireland, the US, and Mexico, as well as a large network of third-party bottling support across the globe. Still family-owned, WG&S has grown rapidly in recent decades to be one of Scotland's largest family-owned businesses, with revenues of more than £1 billion.

Kieran shares his views on strategy, systems, and growth in WG&S.

Growth strategy

Our strategy is to be the market leader in the whisky sector and challenge the premium spirit categories in which we compete. As a growing organization, we're always looking at the brand portfolio to ensure that it fits with our aspirations as a business. We have a continual debate about brands that may need to be refreshed, extended, or retired. We focus on the premium end of the spirits market. Some of the pressures that apply at the other end of the sector don't affect us. We aren't in a race for high-volume, low-price output. We're about exclusivity, quality, and premiumization—a commitment to these product traits drives our growth.

The company has diversified in part through acquisitions to address what we consider gaps in our portfolio. For instance, we recently acquired Drambuie, which is a great fit for the business as a premium liqueur. We also bought Tullamore D.E.W., an Irish whiskey, in 2010 and invested behind the strong heritage of the brand, building a new distillery and bottling facility in Tullamore.

We have also systematized our approach to innovation and now have a pipeline of product development to fuel organic growth in a robust way based on the high-quality liquids we hold. Glenfiddich is the most-awarded Scotch malt whisky brand in the world, and this is a result of the amazing liquid and how we have continued to innovate around it.

Trends affecting the organization

In terms of external factors that affect growth, there are many parts of the world (e.g. China and India) that are now opening up to the increasing tastes of Western premium products through burgeoning middle classes with disposable incomes. These are exciting markets for us and we find ourselves responding to rising demand.

Like many businesses, we also have to respond to cyclical availability of raw materials, such as agave. We use this to produce tequila and it grows on a seven- or eight-year cycle where availability affects price. At present, it's scarce and thus particularly expensive. We try to mitigate those cycles by having a diverse portfolio of products.

Another factor, which is a big societal trend, is an increasing focus of the effects of alcohol on health. We manufacture products for special occasions and don't subscribe to the 'pile it high, sell it cheap' philosophy. Low- and no-alcohol drinks, experiencing high uptake from the younger generation, is another trend that's looming on the innovation horizon for our business and the whole industry.

Adapting to diverse customer needs

We sell to more than 180 countries worldwide directly or through distributors, and demand often outstrips supply. We are a branded business that aims to appeal to specific consumer needs in different parts of the world. For example, in China, the number eight is of high significance, and therefore

Continued

we will develop 18 or 28 Year Old spirits to meet those consumer needs.

We are very fortunate to be in position where we have stocks of liquids that have been x sourced very carefully and laid down over the years, a position to which larger organizations may not have paid enough attention. This is a real benefit of being a family business and means that we can make the best decisions for the long term, not just to hit quarterly results. That long-term perspective is vital in an industry where the age of the product has been an authenticator of quality.

Systems supporting growth

As our company has expanded to locations around the world, growth has been enabled by the introduction of processes and systems. This is vital for repeatability and reliability of operations as the scale of the business grows.

As we have grown, maintaining a clear commitment to quality has been vital. As there is ever more emphasis on the standards of product, yet increasing demands for volume, having control of operations through systems and processes is crucial for us.

We are currently rolling out the William Grant Way—our operational excellence programme—which means that we are investing significantly in systems and technologies to make sure that we are fit for the next 30 years. For example, we have invested in a new global quality team in the last two years to help ensure that our standards are maintained as we grow around the world through in-house and partner operations.

Alliancing and collaborations

An important alliance for us is the Scotch Whisky Association (SWA), which is the umbrella organization that ensures that industry standards and legal definitions are maintained for Scotch whisky.

The SWA will resist calls from other nations seeking to open up the legal definition to retain geographical exclusivity to Scotland, much in the same way that champagne has a protected heritage and definition. Although, having said that, as globalization continues an evolution of industry boundaries is inevitable over time and the SWA can help to minimize the possibility of major disruption.

In operations, we deal with many partners and stakeholders. Akin to the SWA, we work with the Tequila Board in Mexico and the Irish Whiskey Association in Ireland. We have a number of partners with whom we co-pack and bottle our products, and several third-party supply chain organizations that service our significant distribution needs around the world. These partners give us global production capacity and flexibility which support our growth needs. In an ever more complex world the necessity to have strong relationships with all stakeholders is a critical factor for the continued success of our business.

CHAPTER SUMMARY

In this chapter we addressed the following learning outcomes.

- ○ **Analyse the role of 'corporate parenting' in supporting strategy for single- and multi-business organizations**

  We have looked at the role of the 'corporate parent' for a small organization, where that role might be played by a single person, or a large organization, where the corporate parenting role is complex and multifaceted. We have discussed the responsibility of the corporate parent for value creation, and examined its role as a bridge between the corporate- and business-level strategies.

- ○ **Comprehend the concepts of economies of scale and scope**

  We have introduced the idea that economies of scale are the cost advantages that an organization can achieve when it increases the scale of its operations. We also noted that economies of scope are the cost benefits that can result from using the same resource across a range of outputs.

- **Appreciate the role of relatedness and synergy in the development of corporate strategy**
  The idea of relatedness was explored, both at the corporate and operational level. The notion of related and unrelated diversification was also set out in the context of the framework proposed by Hitt et al. (2007) showing value-creating strategies of diversification. We have introduced the concept of synergy, which may help the organization to decide whether to pursue a particular strategic option. We noted that synergy exists when the value created by business units working together exceeds the value that those units create working independently. If a firm is successful in pursuing synergy, it may create greater value.
- **Recognize, develop, and evaluate strategic options based on related and unrelated diversification, vertical and horizontal integration, mergers and acquisitions, joint ventures, and other forms of alliance**
  We have explored a range of strategic options that may be open to an organization that is seeking to survive and thrive in a challenging external environment. We introduced the Ansoff matrix as a tool for mapping the various growth options that an organization might choose to pursue—under the headings of market penetration, market or product development, and diversification.
- **Assess the risks and rewards associated with a range of approaches to diversification**
  We have looked at a range of strategies for growth under the headings of related and unrelated diversification, including vertical and horizontal integration, mergers and acquisitions, and collaborative initiatives such as joint ventures, strategic alliances, and consortia. We also discussed divestment—the sale or disposal of one of an organization's activities. We have explored the risks and rewards that these options may entail for the organization.
- **Apply a range of tests of suitability to potential strategic options**
  Finally, we looked at a range of tests of suitability that a management team might apply when deciding which strategies to pursue. These tests address consistency, consonance, advantage, and feasibility (Rumelt 1995), as well as suitability, feasibility, and acceptability (Johnson and Scholes 2003).

? END OF CHAPTER QUESTIONS

Recall questions

1. Give definitions of both 'corporate strategy' and 'competitive strategy', highlighting the main differences between the two. Give examples of both levels of strategy from an organization that you know well.
2. Explain what is meant by the term 'corporate parent'. Outline some of the functions that an effective corporate parent can perform.
3. Give definitions of 'economies of scale' and 'economies of scope', with an example in each case. What is the key difference between the two concepts?
4. Explain what is meant by the term 'synergy'. Give some examples of possible synergies in a range of organizations, and outline why synergies are sometimes difficult to achieve.

5. Give definitions of the terms 'related diversification' and 'unrelated diversification', with an example in each case. List some of the strategic options for diversification (related or unrelated) that a firm might pursue.

Application questions

A) Select an organization that you can research online. Imagine you have been assigned to lead a strategy team within that organization. Your task is to apply Ansoff's matrix (Figure 10.1) to identify opportunities for growth. Generate ideas for possible new strategies in each of the four quadrants of the matrix. Make brief notes to share with other students on your course about the likely benefits and risks associated with the possible new strategies in each quadrant.

B) Research five different large organizations online and describe the activities of the corporate parent in each of them. Identify some of the ways in which corporate parenting might be improved in the organizations in question in order to increase the benefits for the business units concerned and the organization as a whole.

C) Choose an organization that you know well (or one you can research online) and identify a strategic option that is, or could be, under consideration in that organization at present. Use the tests covered in this chapter (suitability, feasibility, and acceptability, etc.) to evaluate whether or not the strategic option is appropriate.

ONLINE RESOURCES

www.oup.com/he/mackay1e

FURTHER READING

Cracking frontier markets, by Clayton M. Christensen, Efosa Ojomo, and Karen Dillon

Christensen, C.M., Efosa, O., and Dillon, K. (2019). Cracking frontier markets. *Harvard Business Review*, **97**(1), 90–101.

In this paper, Clayton Christensen (professor at Harvard Business School) and colleagues note that as 'emerging market giants', such as Brazil, Russia, India, and China, are experiencing economic slowdowns, investors and multinational corporations are considering the challenges of seeking growth in 'frontier economies' such as Nigeria and Pakistan.

The characteristics of partnership success, by Jakki Mohr and Robert Spekman

Mohr, J. and Spekman, R. (1994). The characteristics of partnership success. *Strategic Management Journal*, **15**, 135–52.

This study explores vertical partnerships between manufacturers and dealers, and finds that important characteristics of partnership success include partnership attributes of commitment, coordination, and trust, communication quality and participation, and the conflict resolution technique of joint problem solving. It offers insights into how to manage partnerships more effectively to increase the chances of success.

When a thousand flowers bloom: structural, collective, and social conditions for innovation in organizations, by Rosabeth M. Kanter

Kanter, R.M. (1988). When a thousand flowers bloom: structural, collective, and social conditions for innovation in organizations. *Research in Organisational Behaviour*, **10**, 169–211.

Rosabeth Moss Kanter is a professor at Harvard Business School. In this paper she considers the tasks that individuals and organizations undertake to generate innovation, and the conditions which might best support the cultivation of innovation. She argues that inter-organizational ties, and connections between the organization and its environment, can facilitate and enrich the process of innovation.

To diversify or not to diversify, by Constaninos C. Markides

Markides, C. (1997). To diversify or not to diversify. *Harvard Business Review*, **75**, 93–9.

Constantinos Markides, professor at London Business School, argues that before diversifying, managers must think not about what their company does, but what it does better than its competitors, and whether their strategic assets are transportable to the industry that they want to target.

REFERENCES

Adidas (2019). Our strategic choices. https://www.adidas-group.com/en/group/strategy-overview/ (accessed 14 June 2019).

Albers, S., Wohlgezogen, F., and Zajac, E.J. (2013). Strategic alliance structures: an organization design perspective. *Journal of Management,* **42**(30), 582–614.

Ansoff, H.I. (1965). *Corporate Strategy*. New York: McGraw-Hill.

Ansoff, H.I. (1987). *Corporate Strategy* (revised edn). London: Penguin.

Badaracco, J.L. (1991). Alliances speed knowledge transfer. *Planning Review*, **19**(2), 10–16.

Barrie, J. (2018). Tesco launching Jack's, a new discount chain to compete with Aldi and Lidl. https://inews.co.uk/news/consumer/jacks-tesco-new-discount-store-when-open-lidl-aldi/ (accessed 14 June 2019).

BBC (2012). What are 'rare earths' used for? https://www.bbc.co.uk/news/world-17357863 (accessed 14 June 2019).

BBC (2015). VW and Suzuki settle four-year dispute. https://www.bbc.co.uk/news/business-34103944 (accessed 14 June 2019).

Better Evaluation (2014). Cost benefit analysis. https://www.betterevaluation.org/en/evaluation-options/CostBenefitAnalysis (accessed 14 June 2019).

Blau, J. (2010). Europe worries over raw materials. https://www.dw.com/en/europe-worries-over-raw-materials/a-5731662 (accessed 14 June 2019).

Bourgeois, L.J. (1980). Strategy and environment: a conceptual integration. *Academy of Management Review*, **5**(1), 25–39.

Boyden (2019). Industry insights: a supersized year for M&A. https://www.boyden.com/media/a-supersized-year-for-ma-3770192/index.html (accessed 14 June 2019).

Burns, A. (2017). Big Issue-backed Change Please coffee now available nationwide. https://www.bigissue.com/latest/big-issue-backed-change-please-coffee-now-available-nationwide/ (accessed 14 June 2019).

Byrom, J., Medway, D., and Warnaby, G. (2003). Strategic alternatives for small retail businesses in rural areas. *Management Research News*, **26**(7), 33–49.

Cancer Research UK (2014). Strategic partnerships. https://www.cancerresearchuk.org/sites/default/files/cruk_strategic_partnerships_brochure.pdf (accessed 14 June 2019).

Clark, J.A. (1988). Economies of scale and scope at depository financial institutions: a review of the literature. *Economic Review*, **73**, 16–33.

CSGA (2017). Blizzard Tecnica 'Women to Women Initiative'. https://csga.ca/blizzard-tecnica-women-women-initiative/ (accessed 14 June 2019).

Das, T.K. and Teng, B. (2000a). A resource-based theory of strategic alliances. *Journal of Management*, **26**(1), 31–61.

Das, T.K. and Teng, B. (2000b). Instabilities of strategic alliances: an internal tensions perspective. *Organization Science*, **11**(1), 1–117.

Depaul (2019). About us. https://uk.depaulcharity.org/about-us (accessed 14 June 2019).

Eisenhardt, K.M. and Galunic, D.C. (2000). Coevolving: at last, a way to make synergies work. *Harvard Business Review*, **78**(1), 91–101.

Elmuti, D. and Kathawala, Y. (2001). An overview of strategic alliances. *Management Decision*, **39**(3), 205–18.

The Economist (2008). Idea: economies of scale and scope. https://www.economist.com/news/2008/10/20/economies-of-scale-and-scope (accessed 14 June 2019).

The Economist (2009). Idea: strategic alliance. https://www.economist.com/news/2009/11/10/strategic-alliance (accessed 14 June 2019).

The Economist (2017). Business and bureaucracy: most of India's state-owned firms are ripe for sale or closure. https://www.economist.com/business/2017/06/01/most-of-indias-state-owned-firms-are-ripe-for-sale-or-closure (accessed 14 June 2019).

The Economist (2018a). Dogfight: Melrose's bid for GKN raises questions about Britain's defence industry. https://www.economist.com/britain/2018/01/25/melroses-bid-for-gkn-raises-questions-about-britains-defence-industry (accessed 14 June 2019).

The Economist (2018b). The joys of data hygiene: Europe's tough new data-protection law. https://www.economist.com/business/2018/04/05/europes-tough-new-data-protection-law (accessed 14 June 2019).

The Economist (2018c). Cleaned out: where did Carillion go wrong? https://www.economist.com/britain/2018/01/18/where-did-carillion-go-wrong (accessed 14 June 2019).

Farsi, M., Fetz, A., and Filippini, M. (2007). Economies of scale and scope in local public transportation. *Journal of Transport Economics and Policy*, **41**(3), 345–61.

Faulkner, D. (1995). *International Strategic Alliances: Co-Operating to Compete.* Maidenhead: McGraw-Hill Education.

Forbes (2012). Was Sprint buying Nextel one of the worst acquisitions ever at $35b? https://www.forbes.com/sites/quora/2012/11/29/was-sprint-buying-nextel-one-of-the-worst-acquisitions-ever-at-35b/#317d267448e3 (accessed 14 June 2019).

Fuller, K., Netter, J., and Stegemoller, M. (2002). What do returns to acquiring firms tell us? Evidence from firms that make many acquisitions. *Journal of Finance*, **57**(4), 1763–93.

Furrer, O. (2016). *Corporate Level Strategy: Theory and Applications.* Abingdon: Routledge.

Gallo, A. (2014). The value of keeping the right customers. *Harvard Business Review,* October. https://hbr.org/2014/10/the-value-of-keeping-the-right-customers (accessed 14 August 2018).

Goold, M. and Campbell, A. (1998). Desperately seeking synergy. *Harvard Business Review,* September/October, 131–43.

Goold, M., Campbell, A., and Alexander, M. (1998). Corporate strategy and parenting theory. *Long Range Planning*, **31**(2), 308–14.

The Guardian (2014). Bus deregulation outside London has been a failure—thinktank report. https://www.theguardian.com/uk-news/2014/aug/26/bus-deregulation-outside-london-failure-thinktank (accessed 14 June 2019).

Hamel, G. and Prahalad, C.K. (1993). Strategy as stretch and leverage. *Harvard Business Review,* March/April, 75–84.

Harrigan, K. (1984). Joint ventures and global strategies. *Journal of World Business,* Summer, 7–16.

Henry, A.E. (2018). *Understanding Strategic Management* (3rd edn). Oxford: Oxford University Press.

Hitt, M.A., Ireland, R.D., and Hoskisson, R.E. (2007). *Strategic Management: Competitiveness and Globalisation: Concepts* (7th edn). Mason, OH: Thomson/South-Western.

Imelt, J.R. (2017). How I remade GE and what I learned along the way. *Harvard Business Review*, September/October, 42–51.

Jensen, M.C. (1988). Takeovers: their causes and consequences. *Journal of Economic Perspectives,* **1**(2), 21–48.

Johnson, G. and Scholes, K. (2003). *Exploring Corporate Strategy*. Harlow: Pearson.

Kale, P., Dyer, J.H., and Singh, H. (2002). Alliance capability, stock market response, and long-term alliance success: the role of the alliance function. *Strategic Management Journal*, **23**(8), 747–67.

Kestenbaum, R. (2019). Active outdoor sports may have a new group of customers: women. https://www.forbes.com/sites/richardkestenbaum/2019/02/24/women-in-action-outdoor-sports-ski-snowboard-climbing-hiking-camping-fishing-rei-camber-outdoor/#1e13047c4c80 (acccessed 14 June 2019).

Killing, P.J. (1992). How to make a global joint venture work. *Harvard Business Review*, May-June, 120–7.

Lynch, R. (2018). *Strategic Management* (8th edn). Harlow: Pearson.

Maceda, C. (2019). Amazon officially launches in UAE, replaces Souq.com. https://gulfnews.com/business/retail/amazon-officially-launches-in-uae-replaces-souqcom-1.1556686706424 (accessed 14 June 2019).

Madslien, J. (2010). Dotcom bubble burst: 10 years on. http://news.bbc.co.uk/1/hi/business/8558257.stm (accessed 14 June 2019).

Manthey, N. (2018). JLR & Chery turn China factory into EV centre. https://www.electrive.com/2018/11/27/jlr-chery-to-turn-china-factory-into-e-mobility-centre/ (accessed 14 June 2019).

Marie Curie (2014). Our charity's future: strategic plan 2014–19. https://www.mariecurie.org.uk/globalassets/media/documents/who-we-are/strategicplanbooklet2014-19_full.pdf (accessed 14 June 2019).

Marie Curie (2019). Vision and strategic plan. https://www.mariecurie.org.uk/who/plans-reports-policies/vision-strategic-plan (accessed 14 June 2019).

Markides, C. and Williamson, P. (1994). Related diversification, core competencies, and corporate performance. *Strategic Management Journal*, **15**(S2), 149–65.

Norman-Major, K. (2011). Balancing the Four Es: or can we achieve equity for social equity in public administration? *Journal of Public Affairs Education*, **17**(2), 233–252.

Norman-Major, K. (2012). The Four Es of great governance. *Minnesota Cities*, May/June, 13.

Open University (2010). B301: making sense of strategy, block 3. https://ccourse.arabou.edu.kw/LMS_eBooks/OU_Courses'eBooks/B301/B301_Block-3.pdf (accessed 15 July 2019).

Paroutis, S. and Pettigrew, A. (2007). Strategizing in the multi-business firm: strategy teams at multiple levels and over time. *Human Relations*, **60**(1), 99–135.

Pham, S. (2018). China gives American Express first shot at its huge payments market. https://edition.cnn.com/2018/11/09/business/american-express-china/index.html (accessed 14 June 2019).

Porter, M.E. (1987). From competitive advantage to corporate strategy. *Harvard Business Review*, **65**(3), 43–59.

Powell, W.W. (1990). Neither market nor hierarchy: network forms of organisation. *Research in Organisational Behaviour*, **12**, 295–336.

Roll, R. (1986). The hubris hypothesis of corporate takeovers. *Journal of Business*, **59**(2), 197–216.

Rumelt, R. (1995). The evaluation of business strategy. In: Mintzberg, H., Quinn, B.J., and Ghoshal, S. (eds), *The Strategy Process*. Hemel Hempstead: Prentice Hall.

Shah, P. and Arora, P. (2014). M&A announcements and their effect on return to shareholders: an event study. *Accounting and Finance Research*, **3**(2), 170–90.

Shaoul, J., Shepherd, A., Stafford, A., and Stapleton, P. (2013). Losing control in joint ventures: the case of building schools for the future. https://www.icas.com/__data/assets/pdf_file/0006/7782/98-Losing-Control-in-Joint-Ventures-Building-Schools-for-the-Future-ICAS.pdf (accessed 14 June 2019).

Søderberg, A.M. and Romani, L. (2017). Boundary spanners in global partnerships: a case study of an Indian vendor's collaboration with Western clients. *Group & Organization Management*, **42**(2), 237–78.

Statista (2019). Value of mergers and acquisitions (M&A) worldwide from 1985 to 2018 (in billion US dollars). https://www.statista.com/statistics/267369/volume-of-mergers-and-acquisitions-worldwide/ (accessed 14 June 2019).

Teece, D. (1980). Economies of scope and the scope of the enterprise. *Journal of Economic Behavior & Organization*, **1**(3), 223–47.

Walter, J., Kellermanns, F.W., and Lechner, C. (2012). Decision making within and between organizations: rationality, politics, and alliance performance. *Journal of Management*, **38**(5), 1582–1610.

CHAPTER ELEVEN

Innovation, Disruption, and Digitalization

CONTENTS

LEARNING OBJECTIVES

By the end of this chapter, you should be able to:

- Appraise the relevance and usefulness of innovation to organizational strategy
- Explain how an organization can take steps towards building strategically valuable innovation culture, capacity, and capabilities
- Explain how different types of innovation might influence organizational strategy
- Assess the relative merits of different ways of developing innovation strategy
- Critically evaluate how digitalization and data strategy should drive innovation and transformation in an organization

TOOLBOX

- **Business model canvas**
  A method to systematically map the components of a current business model in order to identify ways in which the business model might be changed.
- **Value net**
  A method that helps identify opportunities for enhanced collaboration with other players—competitors, customers, suppliers, and complementors—within an organization's network.
- **Blue ocean strategy**
  An approach to innovation strategy that searches for uncontested market space. Guides exploration of cost reduction and differentiation options, and identification of new value propositions that render the competition irrelevant.
- **Innovation portfolio strategy**
  A framework to identify the different ways in which innovation is being attempted by an organization. Provides clarity around technical and commercial modes of innovating.
- **Innovation portfolio risk matrix**
  Creates a visual representation of the level of risk inherent in an organization's approach to innovation. Aids management of expectations about the likely returns from strategic innovation.
- **Platform strategy**
  An action-oriented framework for developing an innovation strategy that creates or develops an ecosystem. Organizations may direct this towards achieving platform leadership—a network position with maximum influence on the ecosystem.
- **Data strategy orientation**
  A checklist-based approach to align data strategy—data architecture, objectives, and activities—with broader organizational objectives. Sets a platform for digital transformation which in turn enables organizational strategy.

OPENING CASE STUDY **REINVENTING THE REINVENTOR—INNOVATION AT W.L. GORE**

W.L. Gore, one of the world's most innovative companies, is hunting for new product lines—and reinventing itself in the process

W.L. Gore & Associates Inc. is a manufacturer best known for Gore-Tex, the waterproof membrane used in high-end outerwear. The company also makes air filters, headlight vents, heart stents, guitar strings, and more. Gore has long been lauded less for 'what it makes' than for 'how it makes'—a workers' democracy where engineers unencumbered by short-sighted investors and middle managers perform feats of materials wizardry. The company has grown steadily over the years to $3.7 billion revenue in 2018. Yet in the past decade the markets for Gore's most successful products have matured and the company is seeking new directions.

Gore's origins are in the late 1950s, when Wilbert Lee Gore, a DuPont research chemist, became obsessed with a durable and inert substance called polytetrafluoroethylene (PTFE), commercialized by DuPont in 1945 under the brand name Teflon. DuPont were only interested in manufacturing PTFE rather than innovating with it. In 1958, Gore quit his job and set up his own business applying PTFE to new product lines. W.L. Gore's earliest products were PTFE-insulated wires and cables, some of which went on the first manned Moon landing in 1969.

Through extensive experimentation, Gore discovered a way to make expanded PTFE (ePTFE)—a lighter and stronger version of PTFE. Over time, Gore engineers perfected a set of techniques to refine the ePTFE molecular structure and product capabilities. ePTFE technical know-how now underpins diverse offerings from Gore, from hazmat suits to high-tension ropes for deep-water oil rigs to premium dental floss. In 1976, the first Gore-Tex 'waterproof and breathable' rain gear went on sale. This was a commercial innovation for Gore as it chose not to make most of the clothing incorporating its technology, instead selling the membrane to licencees who turn it into garments for major brands such as North Face and Patagonia. The agreements strictly mandate how Gore-Tex is incorporated into the final products; for example, ensuring that its logo is always visible.

For all ePTFE's versatility, Gore's leaders and admirers tend to credit human, not molecular, structure with the company's success. Gore's founders organized the growing global business like a set of tribes, intending to optimize the human creative and social potential of its associates. From the 1970s onwards, the company opened a new plant whenever an existing one expanded past a couple of hundred workers (so everyone in the plant could know each other). Associates chose and committed to the projects on which they wished to work. As Gore employees followed their instinct to find new applications for PTFE in seemingly unconnected markets, the organization diversified and added new divisions and plants to organize production operations.

Although Gore now has about 10,000 associates, this approach still largely holds. Ideas live and die on collective enthusiasm; authority is temporary and contingent on the job at hand. Digital technologies are deployed to create collaboration opportunities and flow between projects. The company routinely finds itself on lists of the best places to work, and its highly trained, eminently employable employees rarely leave—turnover in its North American offices is 2%. But despite Gore's organizational flexibility, it is heavily reliant on its ePTFE-related technologies, and competition is growing. For example, eVent, NeoShell, and OutDry Extreme fabrics challenge the once supreme Gore-Tex brand. And today an automobile firm or appliance maker looking for a basic ePTFE membrane for one of its products can choose from a plethora of suppliers who will sell it cheaper than Gore.

In 2015 then CEO Terri Kelly, believing that Gore had grown too conservative and incremental in its innovation, began looking for ways to stimulate a new approach. Gore commissioned support from Steve Blank, an innovation adviser known in Silicon Valley for the lean start-up concept in which companies are pushed to go to market early and often in order to let the resulting customer feedback guide their product refinement.

Lean start-up thinking has been introduced in Gore through a new innovation management approach. Its engineers can now pitch their ideas to investment committees of colleagues with relevant technical, financial, and market expertise. The process is 'survival of the fittest'. Concepts without clear market appeal are dropped, while those that show promise get additional funding rounds and more resources. So far so good for Gore's re-invention prospects—ideas are flowing into the investment process and new beta-products are already being sold in fabrics, electronics, and healthcare markets. Blank is already talking about Gore as a success story. 'The big idea that I see large companies getting wrong and Gore getting right', Blank says, 'is that innovation is not a point activity, it's an end-to-end process. You need a pipeline'. For W.L. Gore, after some internal reflection and strategic re-invention, the pipeline is filling back up.

Questions for discussion

1. Drawing on the definitions in the introduction, identify examples of technological, organizational, and strategic innovations in the W.L. Gore story.
2. The polymer PTFE arguably forms a technological platform upon which a wide range of further innovation activity occurs at Gore. What are the apparent advantages and disadvantages of having such a platform?
3. To what extent will 'lean start-up' thinking and processes be part of how innovation is conducted in Gore in the long term? Explain your answer.

Sources

This example is based on an article by D. Bennett, 'They're coming for your eyeballs' in *Bloomberg Businessweek European Edition*, 13 May 2019, pp. 38–45.

11.1 **Introduction**

Innovation—the successful exploitation of new ideas—refers to the process and outcomes of how new ideas are realized in practice (Dodgson et al. 2008). In this chapter, we consider how innovation might feature in organizational strategy. The strategic intent of innovation activity may be to improve operating efficiency, find new sources of value creation for stakeholders, or both. Further, innovation within an industry changes the competitive landscape for rivals, customers, and suppliers. Innovation provides a means for organizations to cope with the 'creative destruction' of the cumulative effects of innovation occurring in its context, and to find new ways to increase the performance of its resource base.

The scale and scope of innovation can vary from a small-scale change within an organizational team to a wholesale transformation of national institutions. Innovation may occur within the closed confines of an organization, or in a more open way through a network of collaborating stakeholders. The nature of innovation can also vary. **Technological innovation** involves conversion of new knowledge and technology into advances in products, services, operational processes, and infrastructure. **Organizational innovations** are new processes by which we can organize firm activities, coordinate human resources, and revise management approaches. **Open innovation** involves ideas flowing to and fro between an organization and its network to be exploited in novel collaborative ways to the benefit of all involved. **Strategic innovation** describes innovation in an organization's business model, altering how it creates value whilst possibly disrupting how a current market operates or creating uncontested new market space. And **platform innovation**—the creation or growth of a foundation for an ecosystem of activity—increasingly features as a topic of strategic interest in a networked world.

In keeping with a process–practice perspective, we consider how an organization's situation will impact its capacity for innovation and how it might respond to the innovative activities of others. Disruption describes an event or trend which unsettles stable competitive or operating conditions. Disruptive innovation might arise from the activities of start-ups, existing firms, or new players entering a market from adjacent industries. We will examine possible approaches to innovation to keep or set the pace in a shifting organizational context through market-creating 'blue ocean', risk-managing 'portfolio', and ecosystem-defining 'platform-leader' strategies.

We also review the implications for strategy of digital technology's increasing role as an enabler and outcome of innovation activity. We consider how digitalization—the process of exploiting digital technologies and resources for operational improvement or new value creation—might feature in organizational strategy. Once a peripheral issue, how data is collected, stored, analysed, distributed, and deployed is now a central strategic concern for most organizations. We will examine how organizations of all types are responding to disruption from digital transformation and big data through planned and emergent innovation activity.

11.2 **Innovation and strategy**

In this section we explain how innovation can be understood from a process–practice perspective, delivering enhanced value as a focus of attention in strategizing in an ever-changing world. We consider contemporary challenges that may trigger or inhibit innovative strategic initiatives, before concluding with a discussion of how innovation strategy might be made and managed.

A process interpretation of innovation

A process–practice model of innovation

A widely used term, innovation is subject to multiple interpretations in practice. Innovation can mean a novel product, service, or way of organizing (i.e. an output), a way of preparing for the future, or a mindset focused on exploiting novelty. In keeping with a process–practice perspective, we focus on innovation as a continual process in which individuals or groups of individuals attempt to exploit new ideas successfully (Fagerberg 2006).

As will be explored in the section on types of innovation, the types of new ideas addressed by innovation activities can vary widely. Broadly though, innovation as a continual process can be understood through several related activities as shown in Figure 11.1.

Triggers for creative responses and innovation potential arise from continuing search and scanning activities (through the application of methods as detailed in Chapters 5 and 6). New ideas may arise from external factors such as customer feedback, competitor monitoring, or macro-trends (e.g. changing regulations); purposeful internal exploratory activities such as R&D and design; or learning acquired from previous organizational innovation activity. This learning may even be an unintended consequence of organizational activity directed towards an alternative target outcome (e.g. chewing gum being created during a search for a new type of adhesive).

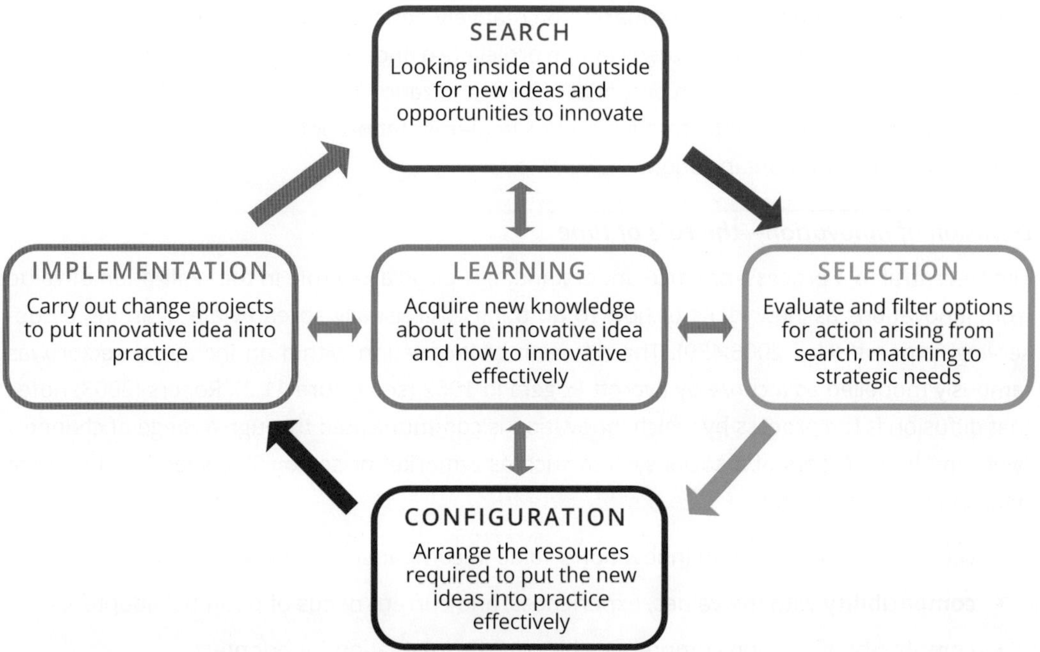

FIGURE 11.1 **A process–practice model of innovation.**

Novel ideas and suggestions arising from search activities are then filtered through selection. This funnelling of ideas from many options to a limited selection of active innovation interests (Wheelwright and Clark 1992) typically involves a combination of expert judgement and cost–benefit analysis, such as through financial modelling methods. If an idea is selected, resource allocation activities are undertaken (e.g. assigning staff to work on implementation, allocating a budget, etc.). Selected ideas are then implemented as change projects, which embed the innovation into revised organizational practices in order that the innovation might be sustained as part of continuing organizational life.

Through all activities, practical learning occurs which influences current and future actions. This learning helps decision-makers decide whether to continue to support the current innovation idea. For example, an innovation idea may be stopped if configuration activity uncovers a need for additional complementary resources not anticipated during selection that reduces the possible financial benefits. Learning can also occur about how the innovation activities are conducted—using insights acquired from the 'doing' of innovation to improve how future activities happen.

The role of creativity in innovation

Learning acquired through innovation, or indeed any organizational activity, can act as a source of creative inspiration or insight for new ideas. Often falsely used as substitutable terms, innovation and creativity are two distinct but related concepts. Creativity underpins innovation, referring to original thinking and inventiveness that generates new ideas. Innovation requires such novel ideas, but then implies an attempt to put them into practice. One can be creative without necessarily being innovative (von Stamm 2008). As such, the organizational capacity to innovate is determined by the capacity to creatively generate new ideas **multiplied** by the capacity to implement the associated change project (Govindarajan and Trimble 2010). If either capacity is lacking, the innovation potential of an organization is diminished. Collaborating with other organizations to tap into creative and/or implementation potential can help improve innovation results for an organization.

Diffusion of innovation—the role of time

Time—central to a process-practice understanding—plays a key role in the realization of value from innovations as 'new ideas of how to do things will usually spread via a "learning by observing" process' (Hall 2006:459). The diffusion of innovation within an industrial sector was famously modelled as a curve by Everett Rogers in 1962 (see Figure 11.2). Rogers (2003) notes that diffusion is the process by which innovation is communicated through a range of channels over time by members of a social system such as a market or sector. The speed and scale of diffusion is influenced by:

- **relative advantage** of an innovation's value in comparison to the status quo
- **compatibility** with the values, experiences, and current needs of potential adopters
- **complexity** of use and comprehensibility of the innovation for adopters
- **trialability**—the extent to which adopters can experiment with the innovation
- **observability**—the extent to which the effects of an innovation are apparent to others.

Rogers (2003:17) notes that the greater the perceived relative advantage, compatibility, trialability, and observability of an innovation, and the lower its perceived complexity, the faster and more widely it will diffuse within a social system.

Rogers noted how, over time, innovations diffuse throughout a system according to the reaction of those within each 'phase' of adoption. Rogers coined the phrase 'early adopters' to describe the influential opinion leaders who encourage or dissuade the majority of users to

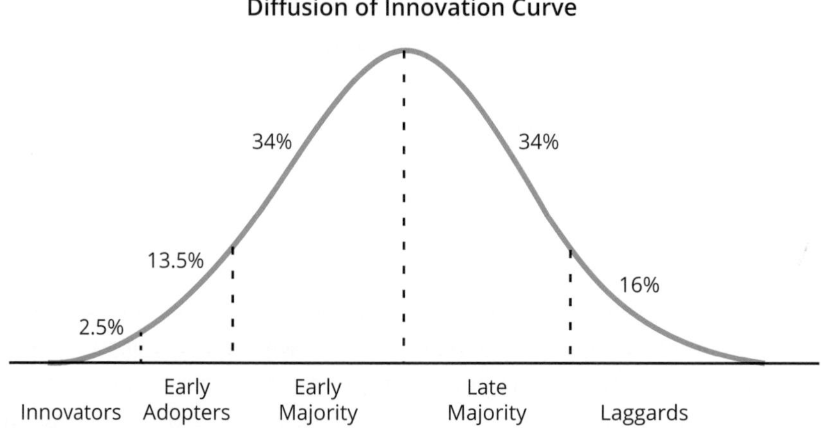

FIGURE 11.2 Rogers' innovation diffusion curve. Source: Rogers, E.M. (1962). *Diffusion of Innovations*. New York: Free Press.

adopt an innovation. Winning over early adopters—whether for internal innovations such as new operating methods or externally facing innovations such as new products or services—is vital to an innovation being sustainable. Innovation strategy should address how 'early adopters' will be reached and influenced as part of planning for successful exploitation of new ideas.

Responding to creative destruction

Innovation as a continuing process helps to explain how organizations might contribute to, survive, and indeed thrive in the face of creative destruction. As articulated by the economist Joseph Schumpeter, creative destruction describes 'a process of industrial mutation that incessantly revolutionizes the economic structure from within, incessantly destroying the old one, incessantly creating a new one' (Schumpeter 1942). Schumpeter explained that continuing entrepreneurial actions and technological advances—probing for more effective ways of creating value, replacing old practices with new in pursuit of profit—will eventually render any technology, product, or organizational approach irrelevant (Gilbert et al. 2012).

Creative destruction can rapidly reconfigure a sectoral landscape or ecosystem, but is easier to understand after it has occurred than whilst you are immersed in it (Bettis and Hitt 1995). As innovative organizational conduct is preferred by customers during creative destruction, the superior performance that follows changes the players and relationships within an ecosystem. Consider the evolution from video cassette players to DVDs to Blu-Ray to streaming technologies that occurred within the space of 30 years. JVC—the original 'winners' of the video cassette standards war—are one of many technology providers now in the media streaming technology industry. The consumer media industry is unrecognizable from its video tape origins, transformed several times over by creative destruction within a few decades.

Organizational innovation is of increasing importance in all walks of life as a means of continuously refreshing products, services, and processes to keep pace with creative destruction. Public sector organizations and governments must innovate services and policies as they compete with other nations to retain citizens, sustain economic activity, and attract new investment. Equally, third-sector organizations competing for funding, attention, and legitimacy need to be innovative in order to continue to deliver on their mandates. For leaders in all types of organizations, creative destruction makes it imperative that innovation is addressed as a routine aspect of strategy work.

Dealing with disruption

Disruption refers to an event or shift in a context that unsettles the status quo. In organizational life, disruption can be understood as an acceleration in the creative destruction process that 'occurs when an innovation creates a new market and business model that cause established players to fall' (Kim and Mauborgne 2019:46). Disruptive innovations typically 'challenge industry incumbents by offering simpler, good-enough alternatives to an underserved group of customers' (Christensen et al. 2006:96).

For example, the streaming service Spotify disrupted the music industry, challenging long-established high-street music retailers such as HMV and Virgin Megastores, supermarket retailers, and even online retailers such as Apple. All these incumbents had business models based on selling customers music. At a low monthly fee (no adverts) or no fee (with adverts), Spotify's launch offered consumers access to a massive library of streaming-quality music rather than ownership of high-quality music. This popular service has many imitators now, has changed the flow of revenues in the music industry, and had grown to 100 million paying subscribers by April 2019 (Jolly and Sweney 2019).

Disruption can occur from start-ups, such as Spotify, from industry incumbents, such as First Direct (a division of HSBC that disrupted the banking sector in the UK in the late 1990s with the first internet banking offering), or from well-resourced competitors in adjacent industries—what Downes and Nunes (2013) refer to as 'Big Bang' disruption. As the name suggests, Big Bang disruption can be devastating for incumbents. For example, consider the speed with which sat-nav manufacturers (e.g. Tom-Tom, Garmin) were negatively impacted by the release of free high-performance navigational tools integrated into iOS and Android devices. Google and Apple had far larger resource bases than GPS mapping sector incumbents and a flexible technical platform to distribute their services to a large user base.

You may detect the possibility of disruption, or be disruptive, for your organization when applying the external analysis tools in Chapter 5. In developing a strategic response, specific modes of innovation can provide options for consideration. Acquiring capabilities in business model innovation will provide a means to respond to disruptive potential by (a) being the disruptor, (b) keeping pace with disrupting organizations, or (c) finding uncontested market space. Equally, platform innovation activity might provide some defence against Big Bang disruption. What these specific modes of innovation mean, and how they might be approached, will be discussed later in this chapter.

Understanding strategic capacity for innovation

As a mechanism for creating value, reducing costs, or preserving performance in a shifting external context, innovation is likely to be of continuing strategic interest to leaders. However, an organizational capacity to innovate is not a given. Being aware of general and specific innovation capabilities, enduring innovation culture, and strategic resource constraints can help you gauge the potential for an organization to incorporate innovation initiatives into strategy work.

Possessing adequate innovation capabilities

If an organization is described as having innovation capability, this broadly means it has formal or informal innovation processes, sufficiently knowledgeable staff, and a supportive environment in which innovation activities can be carried out. Bayley (2019) proposes that innovation capability can be nurtured by: constantly streamlining organizational processes; 'clearing out' non-value-adding activities in order to create capacity for change and free resources for new investments; investing in creating a work environment that encourages innovation at all levels of the organization, building process expertise for when it is required; and looking for ways in which to connect and integrate new innovative, even disruptive, business activities and technologies with the existing organization.

However, even if an organization can claim high-level innovation capability, each attempt to implement a specific new idea will require an evaluation of circumstances. This is because each novel idea considered as part of innovation will require specific knowledge and resources to support implementation. For example, successfully launching a new product doesn't mean that the organization should assume it has the capability to implement a new business model.

From a process–practice perspective, innovation capability should be evaluated according to circumstances. The nature of the organization's history and culture, its ever-changing operating environment, resource base, and focal activities, as well as the intended scope, scale, and focus of innovations under consideration will need to be understood in order to grasp situational innovation potential.

Managing with a finite resource base

Awareness of available resource stocks (see Chapter 6) is important in understanding specific innovation capabilities in any situation (Burgelman and Doz 2001). Every organization has a finite resource base to support continuing operations, and needs to plan around these limitations when considering any strategic initiatives or innovation activity (Kaplan and Norton 2008). Freeing resources for innovation that, in the short term, don't generate returns can be hard to justify for managers. Less resource intensive, small-scale 'incremental' innovations are often attractive as they are easier to accommodate alongside operational demands. For lower possible returns, incremental innovations tend to be less complex than more ambitious 'radical' innovations that require the firm to develop new situation-specific competencies in technological, commercial, organizing, and project-managing domains (Vanhaverbeke and Peeters 2005). Considering resource scarcity, a series of incremental innovations rather than a radical innovation initiative can seem like a prudent low-risk way to improve the organization. However, an organization may become obsolete with this approach if more risk-seeking competitors succeed with game-changing radical innovation. As a means of addressing resource scarcity, innovating in collaboration with others in its network can enable an organization to achieve innovative outcomes which otherwise would have been too resource intensive for it to achieve on its own (Powell and Grodal 2006).

Nurturing an innovation culture

Innovation culture refers to patterns in the way innovation activity tends to be perceived and enacted in an organization. With the activity focus of the process–practice model of innovation (Figure 11.2), innovation culture will play a significant role in regulating what might be achieved through innovation in an organization.

In the Opening Case Study, we reviewed how W.L. Gore has a strong track record of innovation and is working hard to revise and sustain an innovation culture. Ex-CEO Teri Kelly suggested a need for organizational leaders to constantly focus on the question 'How do we create the right environment where collaboration happens naturally—that people actually want to work together, that they actually like to be part of something greater than just the individual contribution?' (cited in Mangelsdorf 2009).

This view is echoed by IDEO, a world-leading design consultancy whose innovation successes range from creating the first mouse for Apple to redesigning complex healthcare systems. However, IDEO and W.L. Gore are organizational outliers in how innovation is understood and

VALUES
Being entrepreneurial, promoting creativity, and fostering continuous learning

BEHAVIOURS
Willngness to change, communicate, and take action; tenacity and improvization

CLIMATE
Leadership attitude encourages engagement, experimentation, and independent thinking

INNOVATION CULTURE
how innovation activity is perceived, enacted, and reacted to in an organization

RESOURCES
Allocation of the right people to innovation, funding of projects, and supportive systems

PROCESSES
Capture and filter ideas, review and prioritize options, and implement initiatives

SUCCESS
Externally recognized success, positive business outcomes, and individual rewards

FIGURE 11.3 Factors shaping innovation culture.

enacted as part of their culture. For most organizations, innovation culture will present issues and development areas that inhibit the strategic exploration and exploitation of new ideas. According to Rao and Weintraub (2013), innovation culture will be shaped by the extent to which the six factors shown in Figure 11.3 are present.

Rao and Weintraub (2013:30) comment that:

When it comes to fostering innovation, enterprises often give more attention to resources, processes and measuring success—the more easily quantified, tools-oriented innovation building blocks—but less to the harder-to-measure, people-oriented determinants of innovative culture—values, behaviors and climate.

Analysing the innovation culture, using the categories of influencing factors outlined in Figure 11.4 to organize data, can make a useful addition to resource base profiling (as described in Chapter 6). Insights into the nature of the innovation culture in an organization will be of value as an input into strategic decision-making.

11.3 **Types of innovation**

As you engage in strategy analysis, you will encounter different types of innovation. Each type has specific characteristics and strategic implications. Being aware of these types can help you understand your options in terms of instigating innovation through strategy and also the innovation activity of others to which you might have to respond. In this section, we describe a range of innovation types and how they might feature in strategy.

Technological innovation

Technological innovation describes the application of new practical knowledge to exploit, extend, or create physical processes, products, services, or infrastructure. Technological innovation draws on learning by doing (such as experimentation) or learning by using (identifying gaps in existing product and process effectiveness) (Dosi et al. 2006). As an option for strategy, technological innovation might be used to improve efficiency or find new ways to compete (Dodgson et al. 2008). Henderson and Clark (1990) define a well-known typology of technological innovation, shown in Table 11.1. In Table 11.1, 'core concept' refers to the main technology used in a design, such as jet propulsion in aircraft engines, and 'components' are the peripherals (e.g. turbine housing) included in the design to allow the core technology to function. Linkages refer to how core concepts and components are configured as a system.

An **incremental innovation** is one which improves existing products, services, or ways of working by better or further exploiting existing capabilities or resources (Henderson and Clark 1990). For example, Netflix commissioning a new book series adaption into a mini-series is an incremental innovation—creating a new product offering valued by customers that draws on existing technical capabilities without transforming how the organization operates.

In contrast, a **radical innovation** is defined as 'highly revolutionary in nature, competence destroying, and induces major transformations of existing products, technologies, or services' (Obal et al. 2016:137), based on introducing entirely novel thinking to an organization. For example, the introduction of a digital platform and services to local government processes in Singapore fits the radical innovation definition as it requires a new set of technical competences to operate and revolutionizes the way in which citizens are served.

Modular innovation refers to a change of a core design concept within a largely unchanged product architecture. For example, electric vehicles represent a modular innovation to internal combustion engine alternatives—requiring a new set of competences to deliver propulsion and drive train technology, whilst drawing on established competences for the remaining vehicle design.

Architectural innovation is 'the reconfiguration of an established system to link together existing components in a new way' (Henderson and Clark 1990:12). This often involves a change in the scale of application of technology. Domestic wind turbines, for example, are an architectural innovation from industrial wind turbines—the underlying technology is the same, but the size and arrangement of the components differs to meet the different scale of use.

As you weigh up options for strategic initiatives, thinking about the technological innovation options available to your organization or currently being attempted by competitors will give you useful insights to feed into the decision-making process.

TABLE 11.1 **Types of technological innovation**

		Core concepts	
		Reinforced	**Replaced**
Linkages between core concepts and components	Unchanged	Incremental innovation	Modular innovation
	Changed	Architectural innovation	Radical innovation

Based on Henderson and Clark 1990:12.

Organizational innovation

Organizational innovation, also known as managerial or administrative innovation, refers to:

> *Changes in the organization's structure and processes, administrative systems, knowledge used in performing the work of management, and managerial skills that enable an organization to function and succeed by using its resources effectively.*
>
> Damanpour et al. (2009:655)

New knowledge underpinning organizational innovation doesn't arise from R&D and therefore doesn't have a technological component (Edquist et al. 2001). Instead, it is a change in the social processes and configuration of an organization enabled by management insights (Damanpour 2014). Organizational innovation may involve shifting between organizational designs, such as Rolls-Royce's restructuring as described in Chapter 7. It might mean allocating resource and focus in a different way, such as the GEA switch from functional to customer divisions in the Haier case vignette in Chapter 6. And it might involve introducing different management philosophies, as Gore attempted with a move to a lean start-up approach to innovating. The underlying novelty of lean start-up versus the traditional innovation approach is illustrated in Table 11.2. As can be seen, this organizational innovation requires the implementation of novel management ideas that channel organizational activities in new ways.

Organizational innovation may might be undertaken to increase the potential for creativity, learning, and knowledge flows in the organization (Lam 2006). Organizational innovation may be triggered by changes in the external environment, or as part of a broader strategic initiative (such as internationalizing). And organizational innovation might happen as a reflection of a new leader's own management philosophy and long-term vision for an organization.

Strategic innovation

Strategic innovation, also referred to as business model innovation, involves 'a fundamental reconceptualization of what the business is all about that, in turn, leads to a dramatically different way of playing the game' (Markides 1998:32). In Chapter 8 we explained that a business model is the organization's guiding principle of how to make money or deliver value for money (if a non-profit organization). Amit and Zott (2012) propose that by reconfiguring or modifying the activity system of how an organization engages with customers, partners, and vendors, inexpensive ways in which to increase value created from the same or fewer resources might be identified.

The impact of strategic innovation can vary. Undertaking business model innovation might bring an organization into line with the business models of competitors (e.g. Apple launching a music streaming service to match Spotify). Alternatively, strategic innovation might be disruptive to an existing market, such as when the low-cost business model of Ryanair challenged established national carriers such as British Airways and Aer Lingus (Charitou and Markides 2003). Strategic innovation may also establish entirely new markets in a non-disruptive way; for example, the micro-finance business model of organizations such as the Grameen Bank emerged to address problems for customers who didn't use established banks anyway

TABLE 11.2 **Lean start-up versus traditional innovation approaches**

Lean	Traditional
Strategy	
Business model	Business plan
Hypothesis-driven	Implementation driven
New product process	
Customer development	Product management
Get out of the office and test hypothesis	Prepare offering for market following a linear step-by-step plan
Engineering	
Agile development	Waterfall development
Build the product iteratively and incrementally	Fully specify the product before building it
Organization	
Customer and agile development teams	Departments by function
Hire for learning nimbleness and speed	Hire for experience and ability to execute
Financial reporting	
Metrics that matter	Accounting
Customer acquisition cost, lifetime customer value, churn, viralness	Income statement, balance sheet, cash flow statement
Failure	
Expected Fix by iterating on ideas and pivoting away from ones that don't work	Exception Fix by firing executives
Speed	
Rapid	Measured
Operates on good enough data	Operates on complete data

Source: Blank (2013:69).

(Kim and Mauborgne 2019). We will explore how non-disruptive new market creation might be undertaken in the section on the blue ocean strategy.

A popular method for exploring strategic innovation is the business model canvas shown in Table 11.3. The elements of the canvas represent different aspects of the business model which, if adjusted, might represent a strategic innovation (Osterwalder and Pigneur 2010). The current business model for an organization can be described by answering the questions in each category (insights from the tools outlined in Chapters 5 and 6 will help you do this). Reviewing the output, options for changing elements of the business model can be identified, evaluated, and possibly enacted.

TABLE 11.3 **The business model canvas**

Key partners	Key activities	Value propositions	Customer relationships	Customer segments
Who are our key partners? Who are our key suppliers? Which key resources are we acquiring from our partners? Which key activities do partners perform?	What key activities do our value propositions require? Our distribution channels? Customer relationships? Revenue streams?	What value do we deliver to the customer? Which one of our customers' problems are we helping to solve? What bundles of products and services are we offering to each segment? Which customer needs are we satisfying? What is the minimum viable product?	What key activities do our value propositions require? Our distribution channels? Customer relationships? Revenue streams?	For whom are we creating value? Who are our most important customers? What are the customer archetypes?
	Key resources		**Channels**	
	What key resources do our value propositions require? Our distribution channels? Customer relationships? Revenue streams?		Through which channels do our customer segments want to be reached? How do other companies reach them now? Which ones work best? Which ones are most cost efficient? How are we integrating them with customer routines?	

Cost structure	Revenue streams
What are the most important costs inherent in our business model? Which key resources are most expensive? Which key activities are most expensive?	For what value are our customers really willing to pay? For what do they currently pay? What is the revenue model? What are the pricing tactics?

Source: https://www.strategyzer.com/canvas/business-model-canvas

Open innovation

Open innovation is defined as 'the use of purposive inflows and outflows of knowledge to accelerate internal innovation, and expand the markets for external use of innovation, respectively' (Chesbrough 2008:1). Open innovation implies two complementary kinds of openness: drawing in ideas and technologies from outside the organization, or allowing an organization's ideas, technologies, and processes to be accessed externally by others, such as customers, suppliers, or even competitors (Chesbrough 2011).

Intellectual property describes intangible resources—such as know-how, product designs, and brand assets—that can be shared, licensed, or sold. A traditional approach to managing new ideas and intellectual property has been to maintain secrecy, and retain exclusive ownership within the strict control of the organization. Collaborative communities—collections of individuals embracing open innovation thinking—such as Wikipedia challenge this mindset by accepting use of external ideas and sharing of internally generated ideas with others for mutual advantage as a normal part of innovating (Kolbjørnsrud 2017). For all organizations, bringing outside ideas in might create new value through complementary combinations with existing organizational resources. And by taking ideas out from the organization, the potential of valuable internal resources might be exploited on a larger scale than the organization could achieve on its own.

For example, LEGO has created highly successful new product ranges based on licensing intellectual property, such as the right to use Star Wars and Batman brand assets, for combination with its unique brand and play system manufacturing capabilities. Equally, LEGO has licensed its own brand to be used by others in creating a diverse range of products such as theme parks, clothing, and computer games. These examples of open innovation show how the organization can benefit from managing knowledge flows across the traditional organizational boundary.

The possibilities of open innovation can be explored through the **value net** tool (see Figure 11.4). This method, proposed by Brandenburger and Nalebuff (1996), draws attention to the relationships an organization has or could have, and looks for new ways in which to collaborate, share ideas, and create mutual beneficial value with this network. To work with a value net,

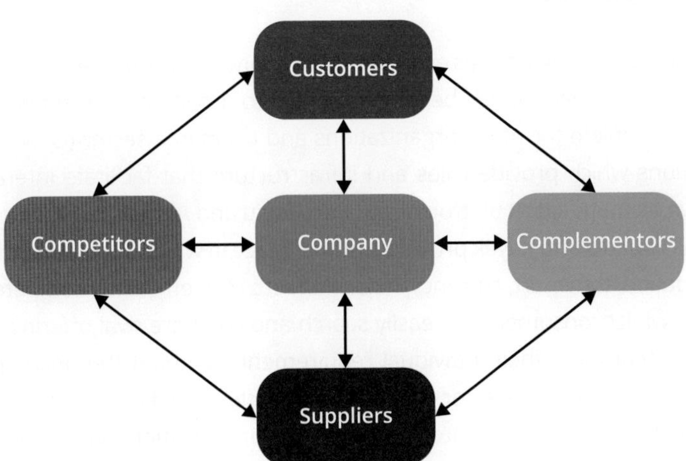

FIGURE 11.4 The value net framework. Source: Brandenburger, A. and Nalebuff, B. (1996). *Coopetition*. New York: Doubleday Business.

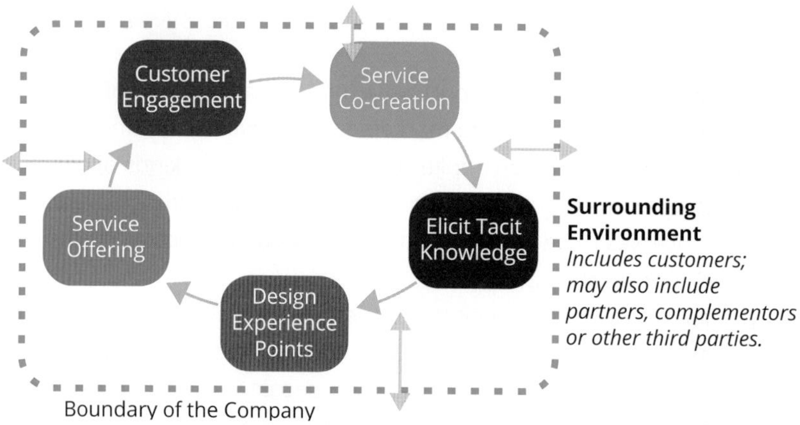

FIGURE 11.5 Open service innovation: value web. Source: Reproduced with permission from Chesbrough, H. (2011). Bringing open innovation to services. *MIT Sloan Management Review*, **52**(2), 85–90.

start by identifying the current and possible players in each of the boxes. Paying attention to possible complementors from other sectors can generate many useful possibilities. Then identify valuable ideas or capabilities that each player has (including your own organization). Being mindful of any rules governing relationships, identify possible initiatives that could be taken to collaborate and engage in open innovation with any combination of players in the value net. You can prepare well for using this method by carrying out Five Forces, strategic group analysis (see Chapter 5 for both), and value chain analysis (see Chapter 6).

As an alternative to the value chain for service organizations, Chesbrough (2011:87) proposes a value web method to understand how value is created (see Figure 11.5). By modelling the iterative processes commonly involved in providing a service, points of interaction (shown with yellow arrows) where open innovation might occur can be identified.

Platform innovation

Platform innovation, also referred to as ecosystems innovation, involves creating products, services, infrastructure, or technologies which become essential to a system of commercial activity whilst solving a strategic problem for many organizations and users in a sector (Gawer and Cusumano 2008). Organizations which provide rules and infrastructure that facilitate interactions between parties are known as multi-sided platforms (MSPs) (Hagiu and Altman 2017). For example, online platforms such as Expedia and Kayak provide a marketplace in which all manner of travel organizations (accommodation, transport, currency, insurance, etc.) can efficiently compete to fulfil specific consumer needs, whilst consumers can easily search and compare rival offerings to quickly build travel experiences that meet their individual requirements. Without the online platform, higher transaction costs (in the form of greater expense and hassle) would be incurred for all involved.

Platforms change how value is created for and by an organization, but are not a new concept. When first introduced, the shopping mall was a platform innovation, providing the physical and commercial infrastructure to bring together vendors and shoppers on an unprecedented scale. However, platform innovation has increased significantly in recent times through the possibilities of building commercial networks through digital technologies. Accordingly, platform innovation is a topic of increasing focus and influence in organizational strategy. Adopting agile ways of operating and embracing a strategy as plasticity perspective (see Chapter 1) can help organizations capitalize on the potential of platform innovation (Denning 2018).

Van Alstyne et al. (2016:57) note that 'with a platform, the critical asset is the community and the resources of its members. The focus of strategy shifts from controlling to orchestrating resources, from optimising internal processes to facilitating external interactions, and from increasing customer value to maximising ecosystem value'.

Platforms may have an internal focus, such as the Unreal Engine underpinning multiple product innovations for Epic (see Chapter 2), or an organization's information management system allowing internal business processes to occur across functions (Gawer and Cusumano 2014). Many examples of digital platform innovation (e.g. Alibaba, Booking.com, Careem, etc.) are emerging in ecosystems where activity is reshaped, often in an overlapping way, with other industries. As Gawer and Cusumano observe:

> *Industry platforms and associated innovations, as well as platforms on top of or embedded within other platforms have become increasingly pervasive in our everyday lives (for example, microprocessors embedded within personal computers or smart phones that access the Internet, on top of which search engines such as Google and social media networks such as Facebook exist, and on top of which applications operate, etc.).*
>
> Gawer and Cusumano (2014:418)

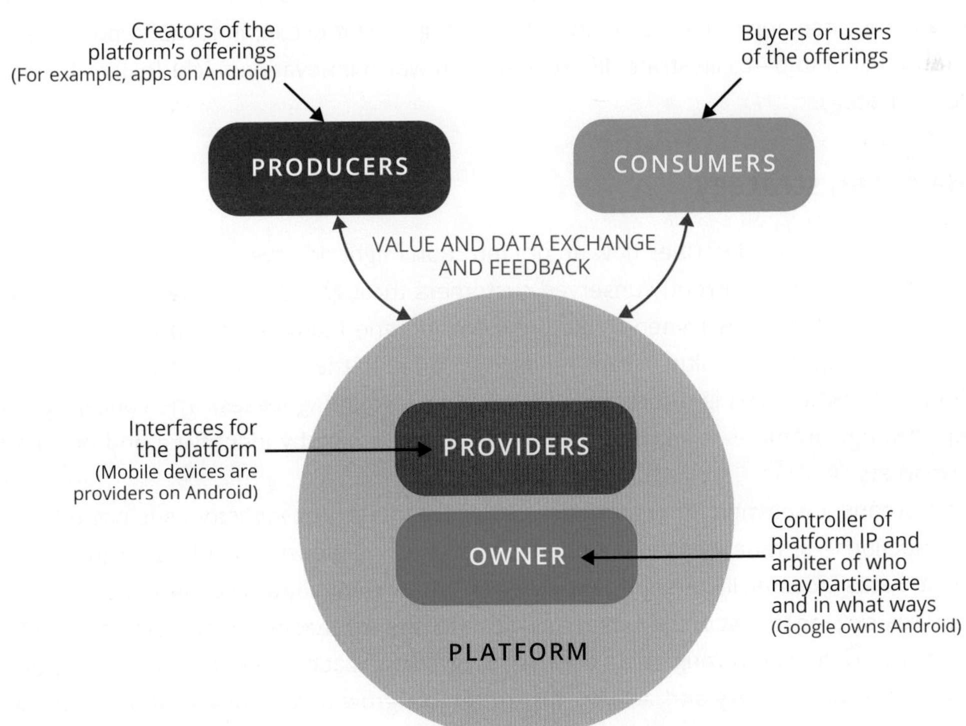

FIGURE 11.6 Common platform ecosystem structure. Source: Van Alstyne et al. (2016:58).

Van Alstyne et al. (2016:58) note that all platforms have an ecosystem with the same basic structure, comprising four types of players as shown in Figure 11.6: 'The owners of the platform control their intellectual property and governance. Providers serve as the platforms' interface with users. Producers create their offerings, and consumers use those offerings.' Complementary innovation by producers and providers is vital to the growth and health of the platform.

Whether as an owner, provider, producer, or consumer, platform innovation and its implications will be an essential consideration for organizational strategy on a continuing basis. We will explore platform innovation strategy in the next section.

11.4 Innovation strategy

An innovation strategy—akin to a functional strategy—describes the balance of ways, ends, and means for how innovation will contribute to broader organizational outcomes. Innovation strategy should guide the use of resources, time, and attention towards specific modes and intended outcomes from innovating. Further, innovation strategy should describe how to build capacity for innovation in the organization for future advantage.

Innovation activity can vary in scale, scope, and approach, with equally variable consequences and potential for the organization. An innovation strategy can clarify the principles and intentions by which different types and foci of innovation are to be pursued. Whilst not guaranteeing success, having a coherent view in the senior team as to how innovation is to be approached increases the likelihood of a range of new ideas being successfully exploited. In this section, we examine three approaches to innovation strategy—blue ocean, innovation portfolio, and platform leadership—to illustrate different ways in which innovation might feature in organizational strategy.

Blue ocean strategy

A blue ocean strategy describes how an organization might achieve profitable growth by addressing the needs of currently unserved customers through strategic innovation. The term 'blue ocean strategy' was coined by Kim and Mauborgne (2004) as a metaphor for uncontested market space. The blue ocean stands in contrast to the typical 'red ocean' competitive environment (where red is the colour of ink noting accounting losses). The concept of blue ocean strategy promises to make the competition 'irrelevant' by identifying and/or creating new markets

Blue oceans arise when an organization either creates a new industry—such as eBay with online auctions—or redefines the boundaries of an existing industry—such as Cirque du Soleil with the circus industry. Incumbents and new entrants are equally as capable of being the blue ocean creators, regardless of the extent to which they are succeeding or failing in other endeavours at any given time. Through blue ocean strategy, organizations can draw in non-customers of the traditional industry and achieve fast profitable growth without having to fight skilled competitors for a share of an existing market. Kim and Mauborgne (2019:47) suggest that blue ocean strategy is an example of non-disruptive creation that 'taps into the immense potential for creating new markets where none existed before. This is creation without disruption or destruction. All the demand generated by this kind of innovation is new'.

Apply blue ocean

Blue ocean strategic initiatives focus on creating or re-imagining business models. A crucial framework for doing so is the Eliminate–Reduce–Raise–Create (ERRC) grid, as shown in Table 11.4.

The ERRC grid breaks the Porterian view of competitive strategy requiring a choice between differentiation or low-cost focus (see Chapter 8). When making blue ocean strategy, using ERRC thinking forces you to consider how to do both simultaneously. New value is created through the provision of features not previously offered, and cost savings often arise from eliminating features or activities important to red ocean competition. As a non-competitive environment in which high growth is achieved, economies of scale quickly deliver further cost savings for the organization.

To illustrate this method, we consider how Cirque du Soleil created untapped market space (see Kim and Mauborgne (2004) for background information about this organization). Table 11.5 shows ERRC applied to the typical profile of organizations in the circus industry before Cirque du Soleil formed. The entries in the table describe how a new customer offering might be created.

TABLE 11.4 **The ERRC grid**

Eliminate	Raise
Which of thes factors that the industry takes for granted should be eliminated?	Which factors should be raised well above the industry's standard?
Reduce	**Create**
Which factors should be reduced well below the industry's standard?	Which factors should be created that the industry has never offered?

Source: Kim and Mauborgne (2004:28).

TABLE 11.5 **ERRC applied to Cirque du Soleil**

Eliminate	Raise
Star performers Animal shows Aisle concession sales Multiple show arenas	Unique venue
Reduce	**Create**
Fun and humour Thrill and danger	Theme Refined environment Multiple productions Artistic music and dance

Source: Kim and Mauborgne (2004:30).

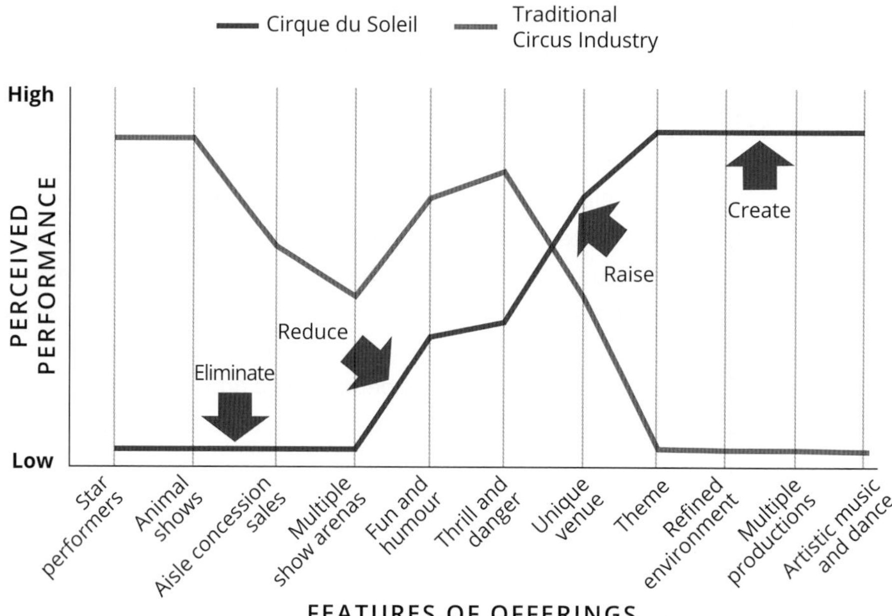

FIGURE 11.7 Blue ocean canvas applied to Cirque du Soleil.

The outcomes of completing the ERRC grid can then be transferred onto a blue ocean canvas (see Figure 11.7). The *x*-axis maps the features identified in ERRC against a *y*-axis showing how your organization competes against others in the industry; competitive analysis (Chapter 5) can inform this comparison. Alterations to the profile of your intended performance (known as the value curve) can be used to communicate and plan for the creation of a new offering to meet currently unserved customers.

According to Kim and Mauborgne (2015a), for a blue ocean strategy to be sustainable requires three new intertwined propositions to be developed in a coherent way:

- value proposition—provide an offering that attracts customers to pay for it
- profit proposition—deploy a business model that allows revenues to exceed costs
- people proposition—motivate people working for or with the organization to execute it.

An organization might attempt a blue ocean strategy whilst continuing to service its core market through different competitive strategies. A blue ocean perspective as part of organizational strategy might help an organization break out of myopic thinking and play an active role in shaping industries of the future to its long-lasting benefit.

Innovation portfolio strategy

Pisano (2015) suggests that a lack of innovation strategy aligned with organizational strategy aims is at the root cause of the failure of many organizations to benefit fully from innovation activity. In response, an innovation portfolio—comprising a deliberate mix of varying types of risk, reward, and resource requirements—might be defined. As shown in Figure 11.8, Pisano

CASE EXAMPLE 11.1 **THE BLUE OCEAN CREATED BY COMIC RELIEF**

Comic Relief is a charity fundraising organization based in the UK. Founded in 1985 by Richard Curtis (writer of the film *Love Actually*) and friends, the organization has received over £1 billion in donations through its subsequent activities. All of its donations are deployed to support a wide range of initiatives supporting vulnerable people and communities in the UK and internationally. Its continuing themes are of humour and hope, and achievement through community of action.

The charity was launched in a third-sector red ocean of competition for funding from potential donors. The analysis by Kim and Mauborgne (2007, 2015b) identifies blue ocean moves through which the Comic Relief organization was able to (a) attract donors who had not previously been involved in charity work, achieving 96% brand awareness in a saturated market, (b) generate a high margin for the cause through achieving an ultra-low-cost structure able to efficiently mass process micro-donations, and (c) sustain participation from across highly diverse stakeholder groups.

Value proposition

When Comic Relief was launched, the charitable donation sector red ocean was characterized by many organizations targeting fundraising efforts at gaining sizeable donations from a small number of wealthy donors. Emotive advertising was used on a continuing basis throughout the year to encourage guilt-based giving. Comic Relief approached fundraising in a different way. A star-studded comedy telethon was instituted every two years to avoid donors becoming bored or feeling hassled. Fundraising events are encouraged in all walks of life—from schools to workplaces to retirement homes—with an emphasis on comedy, fun, wackiness, and community events. Promoted by many celebrities, participants are educated as to how even the smallest donations will make a difference to others at home and abroad.

Profit proposition

Comic relief maximizes funding flowing to the causes it supports by achieving an ultra-low-cost structure. Those involved in the main telethon event donate their time and resources. The fundraising participants are all volunteers as well. PR support means that there is not a need to engage in expensive advertising. And for distribution of participant materials and receipt of micro-donations, Comic Relief taps into the existing physical infrastructure of participating supermarkets, retail outlets, and social organizations. Comic Relief does not implement any of the initiatives it supports; rather, it provides grants for other charitable organizations to do so, meaning that continuing operating costs are very low.

People proposition

Comic Relief utilizes free PR in national media to communicate effectively with the diverse network of celebrities, supporting organizations, and fundraising public that make the bi-annual event happen. Highly visible and distinctive 'red-nose' branding previously allows all stakeholders to gain a sense of community, achievement, and legitimacy from their involvement in Comic Relief. Supporting organizations and participating celebrities achieve positive free publicity through association with a moral cause which delivers local as well as international social benefits.

These three propositions intertwine and are mutually constitutive of a coherent strategy for the organization. At its founding, Comic Relief created blue ocean space and established itself as a national brand. Its success has attracted followers of its format (e.g. the BBC's Children in Need campaign), such that it is now one of several organizations 'competing' for donations and participant attention in a similar way. Those leading Comic Relief will no doubt remain vigilant for new blue ocean opportunities and the chance to create new value for the causes supported by the organization.

Continued

Questions for discussion

1. What would be the impact on the value, profit, and people propositions if Comic Relief started delivering initiatives rather than funding other charities?
2. Would Comic Relief have still been worthwhile pursuing if it had had to pay for infrastructure and celebrity and fundraiser participation? Explain your answer with reference to red and blue oceans.
3. If you were running Comic Relief, what would be your future focus for the organization's innovation strategy? Draw on the innovation considerations and types of innovation described in the first half of this chapter when making your response.

Source

https://www.comicrelief.com/what-your-money-does

suggests that this strategy might create a portfolio across varying degrees of novelty in technical competences (the bodies of knowledge and operating capabilities that reside in the organization) and the business model approach (how the organization creates value for stakeholders).

Pisano's framework identifies four different modes of innovating that strategists might consider. Routine innovation—corresponding to incremental technological innovation—is the most common form of innovating that exploits existing technical competences to reach existing customers in a novel way (e.g. ever more powerful microprocessor chips from Intel). Radical innovation involves introducing new technical competences into the organization in

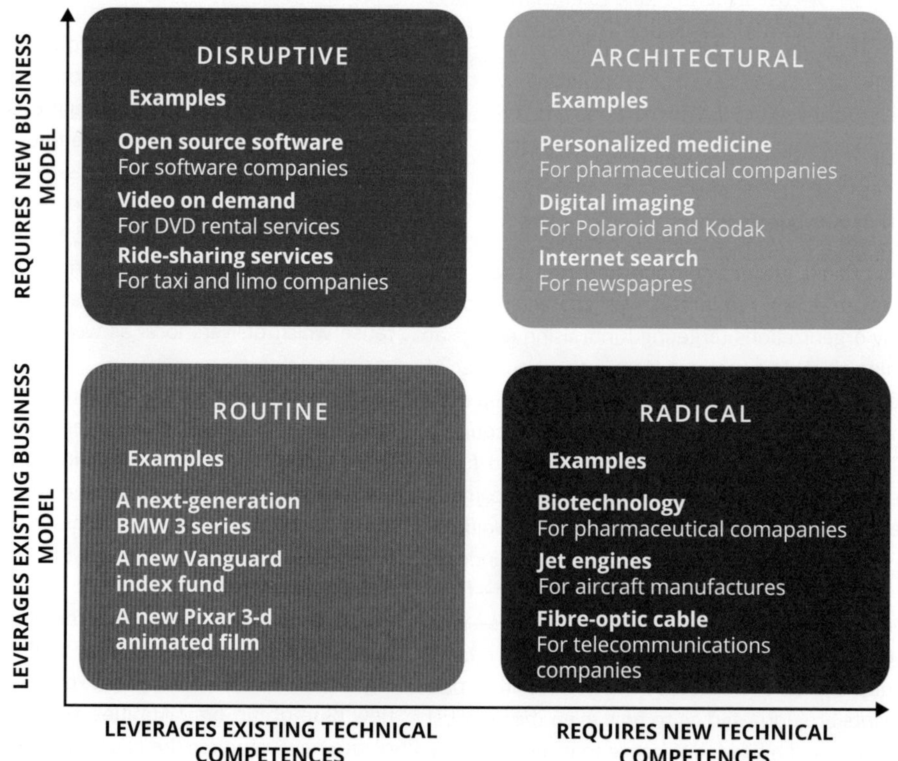

FIGURE 11.8 Innovation portfolio strategy (from Pisano 2015:51) Source: Reproduced with permission from Pisano, G. (2015). You Need an Innovation Strategy. *Harvard Business Review* **93**, no. 6 (June 2015): 44–54. By permission of Harvard Business Publishing.

order to serve existing customers in a transformational way (e.g. the introduction of enzyme technology to create a new category of biological washing powders by P&G). Disruptive innovation might draw on business model, open, or platform innovations to finding new ways to create value for new and/or existing customers using existing technical competences; for example, releasing Android for free disrupted the marketplace for mobile operating systems, and created significant new value for a wide range of stakeholders. Architectural innovation (more comprehensive than technological architectural innovation) is new technical competences and business models reshaping an entire industry; for example, the introduction of the Kindle by Amazon required a new division of the organization to be launched, deployed a new commercial model for book purchase, and reshaped the nature of publishing.

Pisano (2015) challenges strategists to consider the question of 'How much resource should be dedicated to each of these categories?' Routine innovations will be the easiest and least risky projects to instigate. However, a routine approach leaves the organization exposed to radical, disruptive, or architectural changes from competitors. By clarifying how each of the 'portfolio' elements is to be explored, a guiding framework of innovation strategy can be prepared for an organization. The balance of the innovation portfolio can be evaluated using a risk matrix method.

Innovation portfolio risk matrix method

Proposed by Day (2007), the innovation portfolio risk matrix uses the degree of newness of product technology and the degree of newness of the target market to evaluate the extent to which an innovation carries risk for an organization. By plotting where innovations lie against these two axes, a visual representation of innovation portfolio risk is created.

To prepare an evaluation matrix, innovation attributes should be rated using the two tables in Figure 11.9. The ratings are combined to create a total score for each innovation. The innovations are then plotted onto a risk matrix as shown in Figure 11.10 (which has been completed using imaginary data).

Each dot represents a possible innovation project. The size of the dot indicates either the size of the possible revenue or the financial investment required. At a glance, this matrix allows the strategist to evaluate the level of risk anticipated in an organization's innovation portfolio (see Day (2007:112) for an explanation of how the matrix was developed). If too much or too little ambition is being shown in relation to organizational strategy objectives, the innovation portfolio strategy can be revised.

According to Day (2007), it is typical for organizations to have a cluster of innovations in the bottom left of the matrix, with a few further outliers distributed across the remainder of the chart. This profile may be adequate for maintaining an organization's position in a stable industry. However, this profile of incremental adjustment may threaten the sustainability of an organization in the face of disruptive or radical innovation from competitors.

Platform strategy

Platform strategy describes the deliberate innovative actions an organization can make to either create a new platform or grow an ecosystem in which the organization is embedded. Creation of a new platform is to innovate a technology or service that acts as an essential foundation for an ecosystem of organizations. Platform ecosystems deliver benefits to all participants through network effects (see Chapter 5)—the more producers and consumers transacting through the

	INTENDED MARKET					
	... be the same as in our present market		... partially overlap with our present market		... be entirely different from our present market or are unknown	
Customers' behaviour and decision-making processes will ...	1	2	3	4	5	
Our distribution and sales activities will ...	1	2	3	4	5	
The competitive set (incumbents or potential entrants) will ...	1	2	3	4	5	
	... highly relevant		... somewhat relevant		... not at all relevant	
Our brand promise is ...	1	2	3	4	5	
Our current customer relationship are ...	1	2	3	4	5	
Our knowledge of competitors' behaviour and intentions is ...	1	2	3	4	5	
					TOTAL (*x*-axis coordinate)	

	PRODUCT/TECHNOLOGY					
	... is fully applicable		... will require significant adaptation		... is not applicable	
Our current development capability ...	1	2	3	4	5	
Our technology competency ...	1	2	3	4	5	
Our intellectual property protection ...	1	2	3	4	5	
Our manufacturing and service delivery system ...	1	2	3	4	5	
	... are identical to those of our current offerings		... overlap somewhat with those of our current offerings		... completely differ from those of our current offerings	
The required knowledge and science bases ...	1	2	3	4	5	
The necessary product and service functions ...	1	2	3	4	5	
The expected quality standards ...	1	2	3	4	5	
					TOTAL (*y*-axis coordinate)	

FIGURE 11.9 Innovation risk assessment tables. Source: Reproduced with permission from Day, G.S. (2007). Is it real? Can we win? Is it worth doing? *Harvard Business Review*, **85**(12), 112. By permission of Harvard Business Publishing.

platform, the greater the value of the platform to all involved. In platform innovation strategy, scale trumps differentiation as a target outcome (Van Alstyne et al. 2016).

Gawer and Cusumano (2008:32) describe an action-oriented approach to delivering platform strategy as outlined in Table 11.6. Depending on whether the aim is to create or to grow a platform, an organization should develop a plan which considers how best to address these action points according to their specific context and broader organizational aims.

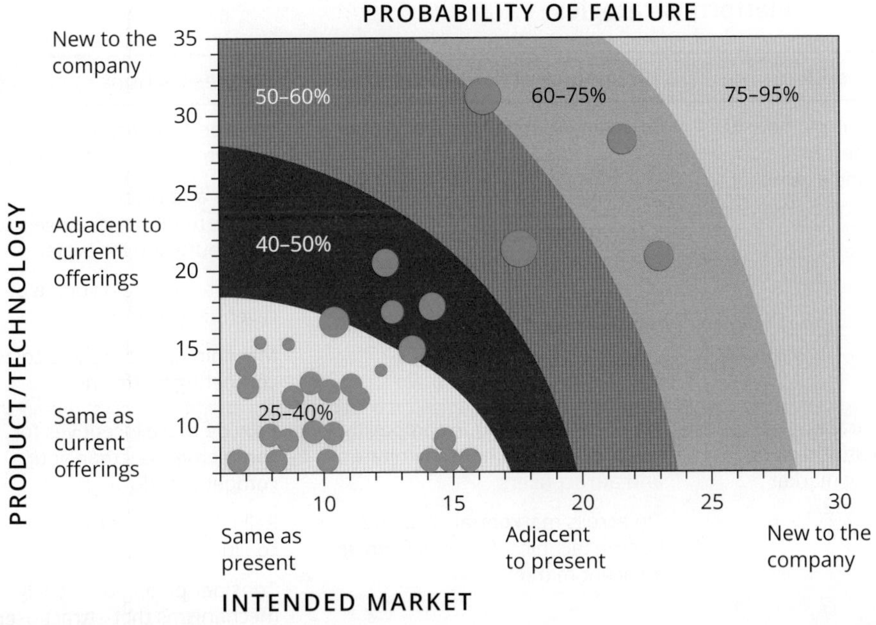

FIGURE 11.10 A sample innovation portfolio risk matrix. Source: Reproduced with permission from Day, G.S. (2007). Is it real? Can we win? Is it worth doing? *Harvard Business Review*, **85**(12), 112. By permission of Harvard Business Publishing.

Platform leaders

When developing a platform strategy, an organization may target the establishment of a platform leadership position.

> *Platform leaders are organizations that successfully establish their product, service, or technology as an industry platform and rise to a position where they can influence the trajectory of the overall technological and business system of which the platform is a core element. When done properly, these firms can also derive an architectural advantage from their relatively central positions*
>
> Gawer and Cusumano (2014:423)

This architectural advantage is synonymous with a keystone advantage in an ecosystem, as described in Chapter 5. This may be highly lucrative—an IBM study of 2148 CEOs from around the world in 2018 found that platform business models were resulting in faster revenue growth and the generation of more profit than other strategies, and that up to $1.2 trillion is planned to be invested in platform working by the surveyed firms in the next three years (Berman et al. 2018).

To become an effective platform leader, organizations need to address both the business and technology aspects of platform strategy. Platform leaders need to ensure that their innovation strategy allows them to balance generation of revenue (e.g. from transaction fees or supplying support services) with the ability of other players in the ecosystem to receive sufficient gains so as to stay part of the ecosystem (Gawer and Cusumano 2008). This will involve making decisions about the extent to which platform architecture will be open, allowing all involved access to platform resources (e.g. app developer tools). Further, the extent to which platform governance will be open, allowing non-owners to shape the rules of trade and reward sharing on the platform, also needs to be decided.

TABLE 11.6 **Platform strategies**

Strategic option	Technology actions to consider	Business actions to consider
Coring strategy: how to create a new platform where none existed before	Solve an essential 'system' problem Facilitate external companies' provision of add-ons Keep intellectual property closed on the innards of your technology Maintain strong interdependencies between platform and complements	Solve an essential business problem for many industry players Create and preserve complementors' incentives to contribute and innovate Protect your main source of revenue and profit Maintain high switching costs to competing platforms
Tipping strategy: how to win platform wars by building market momentum	Try to develop unique compelling features that are hard to imitate and attract users Tip across markets, absorb and bundle technical features from an adjacent market	Provide more incentives for complementors than your competitors do Rally competitors to form a coalition Consider pricing or subsidy mechanisms that attract users to the platform

Source: Gawer and Cusumano (2008:32).

Cusumano and Gawer (2002) offer a set of practical advice for those making platform strategy based on research on how Intel sustains a platform leadership position. They list the following lessons from Intel's platform leadership:

- protect the core technology but share interface technology
- sacrifice short-term interests in favour of the industry's common good
- do not step carelessly onto partners' turf
- when pushing the platform in a particular direction, test the waters in a low-key way
- help complementors protect their intellectual property
- separate internal groups that produce complements from those that assist complementors
- leverage internal processes, such as senior-management arbitration of conflicting goals
- communicate diligently with partners and internal stakeholders.

11.5 **The strategic influence of digitalization on innovation**

Contemporary innovation strategy and innovating activity are closely tied to the concept of digitalization. Incorporating concepts of digital transformation, big data, business intelligence, information, and data analytics, digitalization is a process that is of increasing relevance to organizational strategy.

Digitalization

Digital indicates a virtual electronic format for a platform, service, product, communication, or piece of data. Digitization—the process of converting physical or analogue assets into digital form—is occurring in all sectors, governments, and societies around the world (Parviainen et al. 2017). The phenomenon of digitalization—harnessing digitization for process improvement, innovation, and new value creation—is transforming organizations worldwide at an increasing pace (Bughin and Catlin 2017). A Gartner survey of Fortune 500 companies in 2018 found that 87% of senior business leaders identified digitalization as either a key strategic priority or a do-or-die imperative for their organization (Gartner 2018).

Data and digital resources

Digital resources are assets owned or accessed by the organization which support 'virtual' electronic modes of working and creating value. The physical IT infrastructure in an organization, its website, a software product, an online 'bot' responding to customer queries, and a supplier database are all examples of digital resources. Recently the Academy of Management (2018) noted that digital technologies can be broadly identified against four functional aims: efficiencies technologies (e.g. 'cloud technologies'), connectivity technologies (e.g. 5G technologies and IoT), trust disintermediation technologies (e.g. Blockchain), and automation technologies (e.g. big data and artificial intelligence).

Within an organization's digital resource base, data refers to discrete pieces of knowledge/things that are known. Data can be structured—organized into an easily searchable indexed form such as a customer relationship management system—or unstructured—such as images of failed components on a service engineer's phone. According to DalleMule and Davenport (2017:114) 'more than ever, the ability to manage torrents of data is critical to a company's success [however] ... most companies remain badly behind the curve ... to remain competitive, companies must wisely manage quantities of data'.

Digital resources are fuelled and controlled by data. 'Data was once critical to only a few back-office processes, such as payroll and accounting. Today it is central to any business, and the importance of managing it strategically is only growing' (DalleMule and Davenport 2017:121). Digital processes create, manipulate, distribute, or store data; for example, a customer making an online purchase of a train ticket will trigger digital processes in the banking system, the rail company, station ticketing operations, the intermediary seller, etc.

The strategic value of data science and business analytics

Data is distinct from information, where information is 'data endowed with relevance and purpose' (Peter Drucker). Raw data about individual transactions or physical process steps are of limited use until aggregated or combined with other data into an informational format that can aid decision-making. For example, sales figures combined with market trends are far more instructive to those making organizational strategy than individual customer purchase records. Data architecture describes how data is collected, stored, transformed, and deployed in an organization (DalleMule and Davenport 2017). Data architecture is an influential enabler of the extent to which an organization can generate value from its data.

As all manner of human interactions and activities convert to digital processes and systems, organizations can access vast new flows of data (McAfee and Byrnjolfsson 2012). This phenomenon is referred to as big data which, according to the analytics firm SAS, 'is a term that describes the large volume of data—both structured and unstructured—that inundates a business on a day-to-day basis'. Big datasets are too voluminous, rapidly changing, or varied in format to be processed by conventional linear computational techniques. Instead, data science and analytics techniques are required.

Analytics refers to processes that convert big data into meaningful information known as business intelligence. Analytics uses a mix of machine learning, programming, communications, statistics, mathematics, and visualization methods in alignment with the data architecture and strategic objectives of the organization to create powerful insights from big data. Data science holds significant new potential for strategic decision-makers to address wicked problems too complex for conventional computational methods to unlock (Ketter et al. 2016).

Backward-looking descriptive analytics examines historical data to offer business intelligence about events that have happened in the past (e.g. to explore consumer responses to a new product launch). Forward-looking predictive analytics extrapolates from descriptive insights and experimental data to generate business intelligence anticipating what is likely to happen in the future. Descriptive and predictive analytics can form powerful aids to strategic decision-making.

As part of analytics processes, data science is the application of experimental methods and computational systems to generate new insights from big datasets. How an organization engages with digitalization, big data, data science, business intelligence, and the management of its digital resource base should be set out in a digital strategy.

Digital strategy

A digital strategy refers to the coherent set of decision-making principles, investments, and priorities that guide digitalization in line with broader organizational objectives. A digital strategy will address how data and digital technologies can solve customer problems, create new solutions that customers find valuable, and deliver discontinuous operational improvements (Ross 2018a).

If business models are how an organization creates value, digital business models are how they do so through the exploitation of digital technology. Transitioning to a digital business model involves rethinking what is possible and required from a customer's point of view, not just replicating the capabilities an organization currently has in a digital format (Anthony 2015).

Ross et al. (2017) suggest that an organization's digital strategy should push it towards either customer engagement or a digitized solution focused on business strategy. A customer engagement digital strategy focuses on customer needs first and foremost. Digital resources are harnessed to offer 'seamless, omnichannel customer experiences, rapid responses to new customer demands, and personalised relationship built upon deep customer insights ... constantly identifying new opportunities to connect with their customers' (Ross et al. 2017:8). Kaiser Permanente, a Californian not-for-profit healthcare firm, adopt this approach to facilitate the delivery of its patient-centred care services. Digital resources allow information to flow between patients and all organizations involved in care provision, analytics monitor patient behaviours, and social media engages families in patient care in carefully controlled way.

Alternatively, a digitized solution strategy prioritizes digital product development and the creation of integrated digital customer offerings. This approach delivers support for customers throughout the life cycle of the product, moving away from arms-length transactions to sophisticated offerings that generate recurring revenue in multiple ways. Schindler group—the manufacturer of elevators, escalators, and supporting services, has integrated real-time condition monitoring to reduce maintenance costs and increase the availability of its products to its clients around the world. For Schindler's clients, operating cost is reduced and product availability is enhanced. Alongside gains in revenue from increased customer loyalty, Schindler accumulates valuable product performance data that helps with the design of future products and services.

Digital strategies may differ between different divisions or geographical locations of an organization according to localized needs. Over time, digitized solutions and customer engagement approaches might converge (e.g. Schindler have developed a mobile app to communicate elevator status to facilities managers). Having a sense of the customer or product priorities for digital resource deployment sets an important platform for digital innovation activities.

Digital strategy also addresses the 'building of an operational backbone' in which efficient reliable transactions and processes are assured. This will typically require investment in open infrastructure capable of integrating new technologies, enterprise-wide capabilities and systems for customer and operation management, and a clear data strategy. The use of digital resources to improve operating efficiency is fast becoming a threshold capability within many industries (Ross et al. 2017). Without a digitalized operating approach, an organization may be unable to compete with others that have digitally transformed their organizations.

Data strategy

It is common practice now for data to be treated as a class of economic asset akin to oil and gold where 'an abundance of data is a valuable asset; a dearth of data is increasingly seen as a damning liability' (Farboodi 2018). Yet cross-industry studies show that:

> *on average, less than half of an organization's structured data is actively used in decision making—and less than 1% of its unstructured data is analysed or used at all. More than 70% of employees have access to data they should not, and 80% of analysts' time is spent simply discovering and preparing data. Data breaches are common, rogue data sets propagate in silos, and companies' data technology often isn't up to the demands put on it.*
>
> DalleMule and Davenport (2017:114)

As a component of digital strategy, a data strategy sets out the objectives, core activities, and orientation for how data—as a valuable strategic resource—is to be managed in an organization. DalleMule and Davenport (2017) identify two principal modes of managing data—adopting a defensive orientation focused on data control, or an offensive orientation targeting flexibility and creativity (Table 11.7).

A defensive orientation deploys data management policies that ensure security and privacy, maintain compliance with regulations, and ensure that governance standards, data integrity, and quality are maintained. This approach places a premium on optimizing data extraction, standardization, storage and access activities, and building a single source of truth (SSOT) dataset.

TABLE 11.7 **Assessing data strategy orientation**

Data strategy	# ID	Organizational strategic objective
Data defence Strong defence is characterized by single source of truth (SSOT) architecture, robust data governance and controls, and a more centralized data management organization	1	Reduce general operating expenses
	2	Meet industry regulatory requirements
	3	Prevent cyberattacks and data breaches
	4	Mitigate operational risks such as poor access controls and data losses
	5	Improve IT infrastructure and reduce data-related costs
	6	Streamline back-office systems and processes
	7	Improve data quality (completeness, accuracy, timeliness)
	8	Rationalize multiple sources of data and information (consolidate and eliminate redundancy)
Data offence Strong offence is characterized by multiple versions of the truth (MVOTs) architecture, high data flexibility, and a more decentralized data management organization	9	Improve revenue through cross-selling, strategic pricing, and customer acquisition
	10	Create new products and services
	11	Respond rapidly to competitors and market changes
	12	Use sophisticated customer analytics to drive business results
	13	Leverage new sources of internal and external data
	14	Monetize company data (sell as a product or service)
	15	Optimize existing strong bench of analytics and data scientists
	16	Generate return on investments in big data and analytics infrastructure

Based on DalleMule and Davenport (2017:120).

An offensive orientation seeks to use data to improve competitive position, revenue generation, and profitability, prioritizing flexibility of use over security. This approach emphasizes activities that optimize data analytics, modelling, prediction, visualization, and business intelligence as data-related outcomes. An offensive approach encourages multiple versions of the truth (MVOT) datasets to be created in the organization (where datasets are customized and mined for local applications).

Organizations may look to their strategic priorities when defining the defence/offence balance of their data strategy. DalleMule and Davenport (2017:120) suggest reviewing the strategic objectives in Table 11.7 to help determine data-related priorities. For example, an organization that identifies with objectives 1, 2, 4, 6, 7, 11, and 12 will be skewed towards a defensive data strategy; whereas an organization prioritizing objectives 5, 10, 13, 14, and 15 would be better adopting an offensive data strategy.

The balance of an organization's data strategy will be determined in part by the organization's industry and its competitive and regulatory environment in combination with its specific strategic objectives. In balancing defensive and offensive approaches, many organizations will require a hybrid SSOT–MVOT data architecture in order that data and digital strategies can support the ambitions of the organization. This is achieved through a data lake—agile scalable data infrastructure and architecture that can hold a secure and reliable SSOT whilst hosting as many MVOTs as are required to meet the value-creating needs of the organization.

Data strategy will ensure that the needs of the organization are understood, and systems, infrastructure, and capabilities are developed in order to meet those needs. Data strategy matters because of the increasing importance of data as a strategic asset, and of data management capabilities as threshold or even competitive capabilities in many sectors. As Dalle-Mule and Davenport (2017:121) note: 'Companies that have not yet built a data strategy and a strong data management function need to catch up very fast or start planning for their exit.'

Already, organizations are starting to reap the benefits of effective data strategies. Figure 11.11 shows the outcomes of a survey of the Fortune 1000 companies about the impact that their data strategies and initiatives are yielding (Anon 2017). The 27% of organizations that have not started to decrease their operating expense or the 45% of organizations that have not started adding revenue through data strategy initiatives would seem to be putting themselves at a competitive disadvantage.

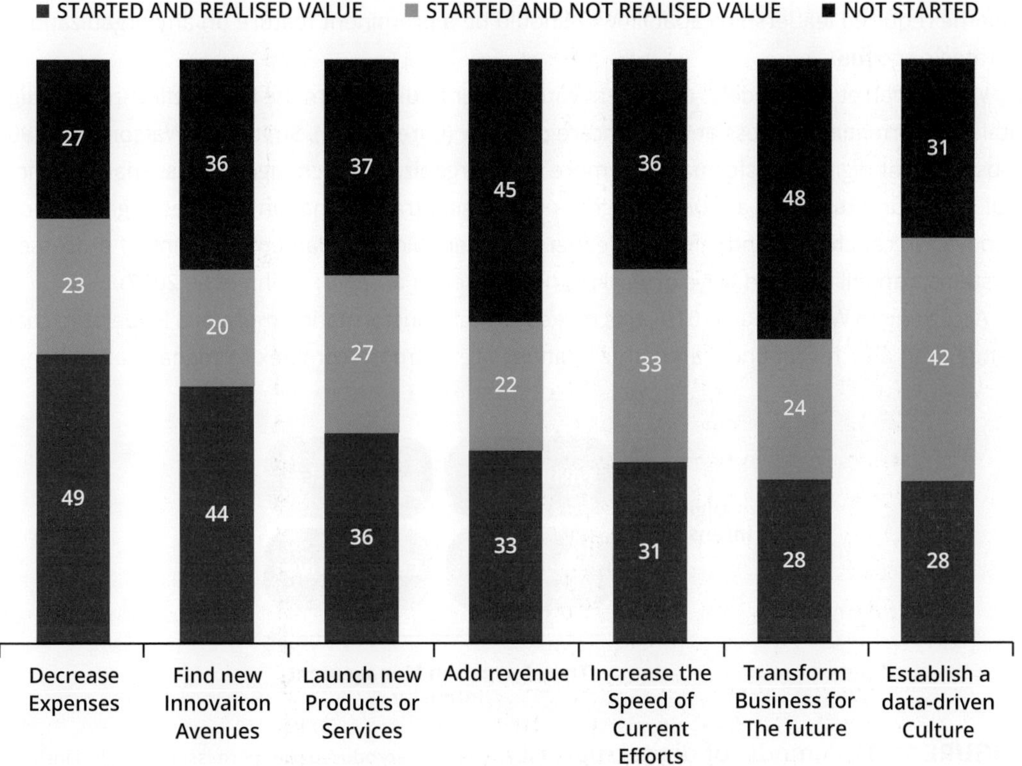

FIGURE 11.11 Realized benefits of data strategy. Source: Anon (2017).

Digital transformation

Digitalization, strategy, and innovation concepts coincide in the concept of digital transformation. A digital transformation occurs when bundles of digital technologies are used to change the way the organization operates, particularly around customer interactions, in the creation of new stakeholder value and in accordance with organizational objectives (Libert et al. 2016).

As digitalization increasingly acts as a driving force in creative destruction across sectors, digital transformation might reasonably be assumed to be an inevitable part of the strategic plans of most organizations (Loonam et al. 2018). However, an early study by McKinsey in 2016 found that only 16% of companies had embraced or prepared for digital transformation (Bughin and Catlin 2017:2).

Westerman et al (2019) introduce the concept of digital maturity to explain why digital transformation might not be happening at the same pace as technological change. Figure 11.12 represents digital maturity as a combination of digital intensity—the level of investment in technology-enabled initiatives—and transformation management intensity—the level of investment in leadership capabilities for digital transformation. Palmié et al (2016) note that, from an attention-based view, what organizations do in relation to digital transformation will be determined by how decision-makers direct attention to digitalization and digital strategy. This matters, as, according to the research by Westerman et al. (2012), 'digirati' organizations are already outperforming competitors in all sectors, and organizations not building towards digital maturity risk being left behind. They suggest that it takes several years to build maturity and that it is transformation management capabilities that are constraining digital maturity more than digital intensity. Their advice is that digital transformation—with a focus on developing the required leadership capabilities—should be a prominent feature on any organization's strategic agenda.

Westerman et al.'s model is consistent with further findings from the field. Reflecting on a digital transformation process at a healthcare provider (Carestream), Smith and Watson (2019:96) observe that digital transformation is more of an organizational change process than a technical shift. For strategists, a crucial insight is that digital transformation requires organizational innovation capabilities and informed leadership to enable a fundamental rethink of processes, systems, capabilities, and ways of working (Parviainen et al. 2017; Svahn et al. 2017).

According to Westerman (2019), this makes 'digital transformation more of a leadership challenge than a technical one. Large organizations are far more complex to manage and change

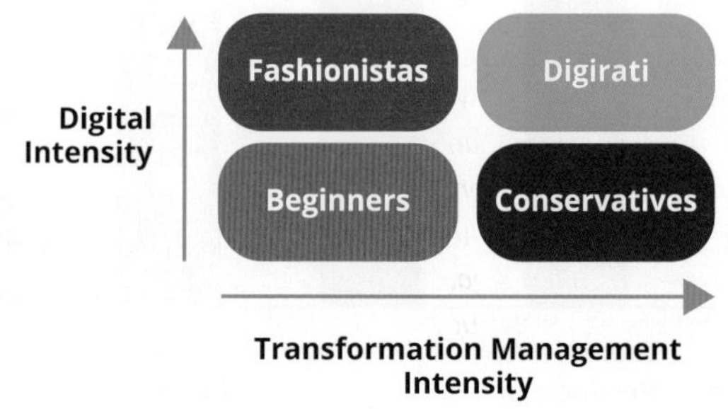

FIGURE 11.12 A model of digital maturity. Source: Reproduced with permission from Birkinshaw, J. and Gibson, C. (2004). Building Ambidexterity Into an Organization. *MIT Sloan Management Review*.

CASE EXAMPLE 11.2 **TRANSFORMING PUBLIC SERVICES IN SINGAPORE**

Singapore is a successful country according to national indicators such as GDP per capita (11th in the world) and the Human Development Index (9th in the world)—a measure of level of education, housing, health, and life prospects. The World Economic Forum (WEF) ranks Singapore first in the world for national infrastructure, and fourth for information and communications technology (ICT) adoption by the population, creating a strong framework for the future of the nation. Despite this success, the Government of Singapore is seeking to transform public services and national digital capabilities.

On 5 March 2019, the Government issued an update on their efforts to keep the public services relevant and agile in times of change. The update acknowledged the fact that Singapore's public services faces a number of challenges such as 'an ageing population and shrinking workforce, fiscal constraints, rising citizenship expectations, and technological disruption'.

The Government is planning to increase its digital transformation efforts to ensure that Singapore continues to be successful and vibrant in the future: 'We want to think and act boldly to tackle challenges and exploit new opportunities. We also know that citizens want to have a part in finding solutions, and digital solutions can help improve productivity.'

The update outlined by the Government lists four areas they intend to focus on over the next few years:

Improving service delivery: *We will redesign services involving many agencies to be more customer-centric. One example is the Moments of Life project, which resulted in a digital application launched in June 2018. Citizens now have seamless interactions with the Public Service during key life moments, starting with families with young children.*

Building a Digital Government as part of Singapore's vision to be a Smart Nation: *We will better use data and new technologies and drive broader efforts to build a digital economy and digital society. The Digital Government Blueprint outlines how the Government will reorganise itself to deliver public services better through the use of technology.*

Working with citizens closely: *We will create more opportunities to partner with citizens, businesses and non-government organizations to improve our policy-making. For example, in 2017 the Ministry of Health organised a Citizens' Jury for the War on Diabetes, mobilising citizens to discuss and make recommendations on how to better manage and prevent diabetes as a nation.*

Preparing every officer for the future: *Every public officer will learn and reskill in how to adapt to changes. Every officer will pursue innovation and be open to new ways of working. The Civil Service College has launched LEARN, a mobile platform to enable officers to learn anytime, anywhere.*

In transforming Singaporean public services, a structured innovation process is used that is inclusive, data-driven, and intended to shape future-proof outcomes (see Figure 11.13).

The head of the civil service, Leo Yip, describes the next phase of public sector transformation (PST): 'We in the public service must always strive to create a better Singapore and a better life for Singaporeans, and that means we must have a strong sense of ambition for Singapore.' Mr Yip highlights that better outcomes can only be achieved through coordinated aligned action between ministries or agencies and a shared agenda for the future as 'a thousand flowers blooming doesn't give you a garden'. Action is also crucial as 'No ministry becomes better by just talking about new ideas ... every ministry becomes better only when it gets things done in a better way—and having the public benefit from that'.

Digital Government is a central component of the national strategy for delivering public sector reform in Singapore. Combining excellent national infrastructure and citizen capabilities, Digital Government is intended to set the global standard for government–citizen relations and enable Smart Nation development.

On a national scale of digital transformation, innovative applications of data science to public sector 'big data' are being explored through the Smart Nation initiative. According to the Singaporean Government's Technology Team: 'Singapore is putting in place systems to collect data, perform analytics to interpret real-time data as far as possible, and ultimately, to visualise insights to help public agencies make better planning decisions, and enhance their operations.' The team further note that under an initiative entitled Pulse of the Economy, the Singaporean Government is drawing on real-time big data sources to create

Continued

11

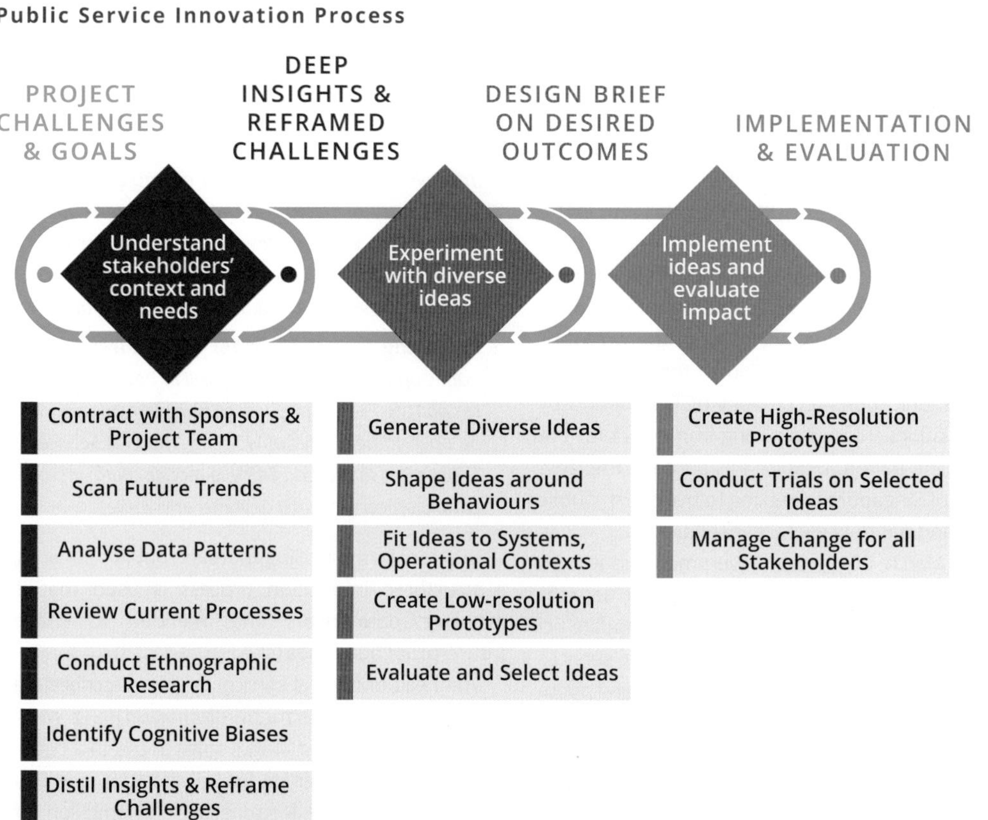

FIGURE 11.13 Public sector innovation process deployed in Singapore. Source: Innovation Lab, Public Sector Transformation Group, Public Service Division, Prime Minister's Office, Singapore.

11

detailed insights into the state of the economy and offering early warning signals as to where intervention in specific locations and sectors may be required.

Looking forward, the team comment:

> *As more meaningful big data sources become available, new ways of improving people's lives will become possible. For example, we can use crowd density data to understand how people commute and access key social amenities (for example, parks, healthcare, places of worship), and thus improve the distribution and accessibility of these amenities. Similarly, better data could improve transport modelling to relieve congestion and enhance public transport options.*

As Singapore continues to transform its public services, coping with technology disruption and national challenges, innovation and digitalization seem certain to remain at the heart of national renewal strategy for a long time to come.

Sources

https://www.weforum.org/reports/the-global-competitveness-report-2018

https://www.psd.gov.sg/what-we-do/transforming-the-public-service-to-build-our-future-singapore

https://www.psd.gov.sg/challenge/people/profile/hcs-leo-yip-the-way-forward-for-public-sector-transformation

https://www.tech.gov.sg/digital-government-blueprint/?utm_source=top_nav

Questions for discussion

1. With such strong existing national infrastructure, why does Singapore's national strategy urge public sector transformation and the building of further digital and economic capabilities?
2. Critique the 'public sector innovation process' shown in Figure 11.13—how effective do you

think it will be in supporting the Digital Government vision of Singapore and the digital transformation required as part of the Pulse of the Economy initiative? Draw on any relevant insights from the whole of this chapter in explaining your answer.

3. What are the main challenges that you believe the Singapore Government will have to address as it progresses on its Digital Transformation journey in the next 5–10 years?

than technologies. They have more moving parts, and those parts, being human, are much harder to control'. With digital transformation, there is a need to manage transformation tensions across organizational levels (Eden at al. 2019), and the limitations of innovation culture and organizational capabilities must be considered alongside technical concerns. For those involved in organizational strategy, the digital transformation imperative offers further justification for an investment in organizational innovation capability.

11.6 **Where next? Digital strategy challenges**

Between 66% and 84% of digital transformation efforts fail to deliver the desired results (Libert et al. 2016:2). Digital innovation and transformation are fraught with challenges as legacy cultures and operating models struggle to accommodate new digital technologies and ways of working. Digital strategy needs to address a number of challenging factors including, but not limited to, human resource issues, increased operational complexity, limitations of maturity, cybersecurity, and remaining relevant.

Human resource challenges

The biggest employee concern raised by digitalization is a near-universal demand for digital dexterity—a set of beliefs, mindsets, and behaviours that help employees deliver faster and more valuable outcomes from digital initiatives (Gartner 2018). To maintain commitment from employees anxious about being left behind, digital strategy will need to allocate resources towards, upskilling employees and modernizing work practices (Roth and Keller 2019). More generally, digital transformation is often accompanied by workforce stress, fatigue, and the need to continually respond to unexpected events. Strategic investment is required to build a strong innovation culture foundation that enables the workforce to cope with the demands of digital transformation (Eden et al. 2019:14). This approach to building digital skills should also preserve valuable components of traditional culture, and seek to maintain the morale, integrity, and values of the organization (Westermann et al. 2019). Organizational investment is also required in sourcing and nurturing skilled employees who are able to act as data translators—sufficiently skilled in data science, data analytics, and business intelligence, but also with business management credentials that give them legitimacy in discussions with organizational leaders (Brady et al. 2017).

A further source of human resource challenge is the fatigue associated with customer expectations for constant connectivity and service. Siggelkow and Terwiesch (2019) report that continuous connectivity will quickly become the new normal, to the extent that organizations should develop a connected strategy. For employees of organizations that remain under cost pressure, this may mean less downtime and increased demands to remain connected to work themselves.

Blended approaches and increased complexity

The rise of business intelligence has led to the rise of data hubris—'the often-implicit assumption that big data are a substitute for, rather than a supplement to, traditional data collection and analysis' (Lazer et al. 2014). Digital and data strategies must seek to balance the use of analytics and first-hand observations in a complementary way to form strategic decisions (Brady et al. 2017).

More generally, Vermeulen (2017) and Svahn et al. (2017) suggest that digitalization outputs will tend to supplement existing ways of working rather than replace them (except where there is direct substitution, such as budget airlines using online booking portals only). This means that digital transformation may increase customer choice and business model complexity for an organization; for example, desktop computing existing alongside cloud computing for a company like Microsoft, or online service capacity for a local council existing in parallel with a service desk at a council building.

The main counter to this view is the emergence of cognitive technologies—artificial intelligence and technological processes by which machines learn to embody the skills, knowledge, and capabilities that are performed in a cognate way by humans (Davenport and Mahidhar 2018). Very few organizations have a cognitive strategy—a plan to capitalize on or mitigate the possibilities of cognitive technologies—leaving themselves vulnerable to competitor activities in this technological space.

A need to start simply and build carefully

As a digitalization gap grows between organizations and their competitors, it is tempting to propose a radical digital innovation strategy. But digital transformation can't be rushed (Ross 2018b). Stephen Andriole (2017), former director of the Cybernetics Technology Office of the US Defense Advanced Research Projects Agency (DARPA), comments that many organizations lack the systems maturity and process knowledge to be able to transform digitally, and that to attempt to do so would be ruinous to the organization. According to Andriole, digital transformation requires in-depth knowledge of current business processes in order to successfully model and enhance them in a digital format, which will typically employ conventional 'known' technology with proven capabilities. Therefore staying realistic but persevering with digital aspirations will be a key challenge for digital strategists. As Jeanne Ross, principal research scientist for MIT's Center for Information Systems Research, notes, 'digital is about speed, but it takes time' (Ross 2018b).

Cybersecurity

Cybersecurity is the preservation of the security of digital systems in the face of cybercrime. Analysis by CyberSecurity Ventures predicts that annual global cybercrime costs will rise to $6 trillion by 2021(Gregersen 2018). As digitalization unfolds, there is an increasing need to ensure the security of transactions, relationships, and systems. This is not just a technical challenge— where human interaction occurs, digital systems are vulnerable to scams such as phishing (Gartner 2018). Thus investment in digital transformation brings with it a parallel obligation to invest in cybersecurity.

PRACTITIONER INSIGHT: **NED PHILLIPS, FOUNDER AND CEO, BAMBU**

Founded in March 2016, Bambu is a Singapore headquartered financial technology (fintech) company. Clients turn to Bambu for their digital innovation capability, financial technology expertise, and process knowledge of how to digitalize and digitally transform to create high-quality digital customer experiences.

Three years into its journey, Bambu has hired 53 people, raised $5 million in funding, with $10 million more in the pipeline, and built a portfolio of 16 global financial institution clients including HSBC, Standard Chartered, CIMB, and Franklin Templeton. Growing rapidly, Bambu now has offices in San Francisco, London, Kuala Lumpur, Hong Kong, and Jakarta, in addition to the head office in Singapore. Bambu has already won seven awards, including the best Singapore start-up, best Hong Kong start-up, and best Asian start-up, and has also reached the final of Alibaba's tech search.

Founder and CEO Ned Phillips shares his views on digitalization, disruption, growth, and innovation in banking and finance:

Digital-led creative destruction

Ten years ago if you'd told a bank you have to have internet banking, they would have said 'Well, maybe'. But today, it's impossible to be a bank without internet banking. The same with e-payments in many countries. For example, in China if you don't have an Ali-wallet or a TenCent wallet, you can't operate. And I think that in 10 years' time, the idea that your savings and investment are not digital will be crazy. People will marvel that it used to be normal to meet a financial advisor, and have paperwork or multiple savings and investment accounts rather than an integrated digital portfolio. For financial institutions, FOMO—fear of missing out—is a significant driver of adoption of digital technologies as the sector evolves.

Big bang disruption and digital transformation

Banks are petrified that private wealth management and savings and investment will go to the likes of Amazon, Apple, Facebook, Alibaba—all of these e-commerce, e-wallet apps to which people are moving their wealth. And I think all financial institutions are trying to digitize not because they think it will increase margin, but because they realize customers want digital and if they don't react rapidly, they could lose out in a big way.

Responding to threats from big tech firms, financial institutions are asking 'What is the best and quickest way in which to digitally transform?' Quite often it is not building an in-house team but using external experts like us, accessing our technology platform and know-how. We can deliver a fully working digital solution in six months that would take a client two years to build themselves. Equally, companies like Apple represent a huge opportunity for banks, as tech companies don't really want to manage money—they want to partner with financial institutions. The entrance of big tech companies is only a threat to financial institutions that don't think about it, and don't partner up. The Apple credit card launch in partnership with Goldman's is an example of mutually beneficial partnering.

In our industry I think that step-by-step digital transformation doesn't work as you will not even be changing at the speed of the environment. To digitally transform means building capability to radically alter what you are doing. Step-by-step for me is actually digital improvement—upgrading not transforming. If that's what you want, fine. But if you want to transform, you need to go for the home run.

On innovation culture

It is super-hard for a large corporate that is not a tech company to be disruptive or transform on their own, as financial incentives and job security mean that employees don't want to get fired, and the easiest way not to get fired is not to do anything crazy or bold. That is why our sector lacked a disruptive presence until a few years ago—finance is a very well paid and conservative industry. People were tending to innovate just enough not to get fired.

Continued

It was the work environment/culture that stifled innovation—if we go to a large bank, there are lots of people in there capable of being disruptive, clever people with good ideas. We operate in a different way—we also have clever people but we remove negative outcomes for attempting to be innovative and disruptive, and our physical space encourages great teamworking to achieve breakthroughs.

On strategy

I like the idea of strategy as process, influencing flow to build momentum. As the market is changing so quickly, if we take daily decisions to preserve our momentum, that is more valuable than any fixed plan. We formed this view from hard experience. Trying to work out what our long-term strategy should be—each time we've tried we've got it wrong. So we stopped and we just said, 'When opportunities come let's analyse them in real time and decide if we should pursue them. Yes or no'. For example, after setting up international offices in different ways, we realized 'We've got a global operation now!' It is the planned way in reverse—we didn't try to build a global structure; it just happened as a result of our day-to-day decisions. It works for us, and we are going to keep growing like that.

Remaining relevant

Ever-increasing digitalization and digital transformation organizational activity is creating permanent VUCA conditions in many sectors (Millar et al. 2018). As new waves of digital technology from fields such as artificial intelligence, machine learning, the Internet of Things, block chain, and autonomous vehicles progress towards mainstream adoption, a constant need for digital innovation will be required in order to remain relevant as an organization (Schoemaker et al. 2018).

For example, banking and financial services sectors around the world are being disrupted by fintech—digital financial technologies that deliver operational improvements, innovation, and new sources of customer value. The rise of fintech has created a situation where 'banks may freeze, fight, form alliances with challengers, or be forced into flight by the Big Tech companies' (Ashta and Biot-Pacquerot 2018:301). Equally, regulators are faced with a continual challenge to renew legislation in the face of the digital transformation of the banking and finance sector.

CHAPTER SUMMARY

In this chapter we addressed the following learning outcomes.

- **Appraise the relevance and usefulness of innovation to organizational strategy**
  Innovation—the successful exploitation of new ideas—is a process by which novelty is realized as a product of creativity and execution capabilities. As creative destruction and disruption incessantly replace old with new ways of working in an industry, innovation provides a mechanism through which organizations can keep pace with or instigate change in their operating environment. Innovation might enable lower operating costs, the creation of new customer value, and even new markets. Innovation is a crucial mechanism of renewal that all organizations need to consider as a routine aspect of their strategy work.

- **Explain how an organization can take steps towards building strategically valuable innovation culture, capacity, and capabilities**
  Organizational innovation capability describes the potential of an organization to successfully exploit new ideas. Innovation process capability can be nurtured by involving a relevant mix of people, setting effective parameters for activities, and creating a supportive environment according to the needs of the innovation. Innovation culture refers to the way innovation tends to be perceived and enacted in an organization. Innovation culture can be shaped by ensuring that resources, processes, values, behaviour, climate, and success are all invested in or managed according to organizational needs. Over time, organizational strategy might prioritize investment in addressing innovation capability gaps that build the capacity for innovation as a strategic resource.
- **Explain how varying approaches to technical competence and business model innovations can be used to enact different innovation strategies**
  Technical competence (the bodies of knowledge and operating capabilities in an organization) and the business model (how the organization creates value for stakeholders) are two key strategic dimensions that can be used to understand innovation strategy. Without changing the business model, an organization can use existing technical competences for routine innovation or add new technical competence for radical innovation. With existing technical competences, changing the business model leads to disruptive innovation. Changing the business model whilst adding new technical competence is described as architectural innovation. The strategic value of each approach differs, as does the risk–reward profile. The challenge for the strategist is to instigate a portfolio of innovation approaches that match the risk profile and broader ambitions of the organization.
- **Explain how different types of innovation might influence organizational strategy**
  Different types of innovation initiative offer different potential contributions that might be considered as part of organizational strategy. Technological innovations offer the potential to create or adapt products, services, operational processes, and infrastructure. Organizational innovations can alter how organizations are structured and managed. Open innovation enhances how knowledge-flows between the resource base and network of an organization can be used to create new value. Strategic innovation finds new ways for the organization to create value and platform innovation enables an organization to compete based on powerful network effects.
- **Critically evaluate how digitalization and data strategy should drive innovation and transformation in an organization**
  Digitalization is the process of exploiting digital formats and technologies for operational improvement or new value creation. Digitalization is transforming how industries and sectors operate and serve customers around the world. Digital capabilities and data-informed ways of working take time to build, however, and digital transformation is a slow process that is as much an organizational cultural change as it is a technical initiative. Harnessing the potential of digitalization and data for innovation, transformation, and performance is a complex and challenging task which requires strategic learning, leadership, and vision if success is to be a possibility. Equally, forces of creative destruction suggest that non-participation in the digital revolution is not an option.

END OF CHAPTER QUESTIONS

Recall questions

1. Describe innovation from a process–practice perspective. What are the key activities and how do they interface?
2. Explain why innovation might be considered a topic of high strategic importance to an organization, given the ongoing phenomena of creative destruction and disruption.
3. Describe what is meant by innovation culture and explain how it might influence organizational strategy.
4. Describe five different types of innovation and explain what potential each offers to those making strategy.
5. Define platform leadership and explain how it might be achieved through platform innovation strategy approaches.
6. Describe how digitalization is both a strategic threat and an opportunity for organizations.

Application questions

A) Pick an organization you know well and for which you can access product innovation launch data. Evaluate their product innovation successes and failures of the last 5–10 years. Use the risk matrix and innovation portfolio tools to map their approach and explain performance outcomes, and explain their attempted innovation portfolio with reference to their organizational strategy.

B) Apply the blue ocean method to an organization you are familiar with, to identify possible uncontested market space. Take notes on how easy or not it is to deploy blue ocean thinking as you go. Reflecting on your experience, write a short critique of the possibilities and limitations of blue ocean strategy that you could use to advise a strategist considering using the method.

C) Deploy the data strategy orientation method to identify the required approach for three organizations—an environmental charity, an online retailer, and a government driving licence agency. Compare your findings, looking for common challenges and points of difference. What does your effort tell you about how data strategy should be made and managed in organizations?

ONLINE RESOURCES

www.oup.com/he/mackay1e

FURTHER READING

The Innovator's Dilemma: When New Technologies Cause Great Firms to Fail, by Clay Christensen

Christensen, C. (2016). *The Innovator's Dilemma: When New Technologies Cause Great Firms to Fail*. Boston, MA: Harvard Business Review Press.

This latest edition of a seminal text by Clay Christensen examines the concepts of disruptive technology and innovation, and proposes an up-to-date version of disruptive innovation theory. Not without its critics, this book provides many examples and a popular take on how disruption is both a problematic and potentially highly valuable feature of organizational strategy.

Blue Ocean Strategy, Expanded Edition: How to Create Uncontested Market Space and Make the Competition Irrelevant, by W. Chan Kim and Renée Mauborgne

Chan Kim, W. and Mauborgne, R. (2015). *Blue Ocean Strategy, Expanded Edition: How to Create Uncontested Market Space and Make the Competition Irrelevant*. Boston, MA: Harvard Business Review Press.

This updated version of a famous business text explores how new sources of creation can drive business performance. Explaining in depth the value of exploring new ways to lower operating costs whilst pursuing differentiation, the authors provide many examples from their consulting work for students wishing to know how to apply blue ocean strategy in practice.

Data-driven city management: a close look at Amsterdam's smart city initiative, by Michael Fitzgerald

Fitzgerald, M. (2016). Data-driven city management: a close look at Amsterdam's smart city initiative. *MIT Sloan Management Review*, **57**(4), 3–10.

'Smart city' refers to a redesign of urban living spaces in which information technology is tightly integrated into public services, spaces, and infrastructure. Smart city trends are predicted to be a main driver behind the next global wave of creative destruction at a macro-level that will affect government, third-sector and private-sector organizations, and citizens around the globe. This report by Michael Fitzgerald, in collaboration with Ernst & Young, gives insights into how this is already happening in Amsterdam through data analytics, digital transformation, innovation process, and systems and public strategizing.

Value Proposition Design: How to Create Products and Services Customers Want, by Alex Osterwalder, Yves Pigneur, Greg Bernarda, and Alan Smith

Osterwalder, A., Pigneur, Y., Bernarda, G., and Smith, A. (2014). *Value Proposition Design: How to Create Products and Services Customers Want*. Hoboken, NJ: John Wiley.

This book develops thinking about how the business model canvas and related ideas might be applied in organizational innovation and strategy. The business model canvas is extremely popular because of its simplicity and ease of use. Familiarizing yourself with how to lead a value proposition design session creates a useful employability skill that blends innovation, strategy, and business model capabilities.

The A to Z of Innovation Management, by Mike Kennard

Kennard, M. (2018). *The A to Z of Innovation Management: The Essential Guide to 26 Key Innovation Management Theories, Models, and Frameworks*. York: York Publishing Services.

This is a useful, compact text which takes the reader through a range of classical innovation management tools and challenges (e.g. first-mover advantage and user centred innovation) alongside how innovation features as a contextual factor of relevance to strategy (e.g. clusters, triple helix). This will be of interest to students wanting to explore the ways in which innovation can be managed from a process–practice perspective or how decision-maker attention might be usefully directed towards innovation as a source of strategic options.

REFERENCES

Academy of Management (2018). Call: Digital transformation: what is new if anything? *Academy of Management Discoveries*, **4**(3), 378–87.

Amit, R. and Zott, C. (2012). Creating value through business model innovation. *MIT Sloan Management Review*, **53**(3), 41–9.

Andriole, S.J. (2017). Five myths about digital transformation. *MIT Sloan Management Review*, **58**(3), 20–2.

Anon (2017). How companies really use big data. *Harvard Business Review*, **95**(5), 26.

Anthony, S. (2015). How understanding disruption helps strategists. *Harvard Business Review Digital Articles*, 2–4.

Ashta, A. and Biot-Pacquerot, G. (2018). Fintech evolution: strategic value management issues in a fast changing industry. *Strategic Change*, **27**(4), 301–11.

Bayley, N. (2019). Harnessing the power of disruption. *Rotman Management Magazine*, January, 112–14.

Berman, S., Davidson, S., Ikeda, K., and Marshall, A. (2018). Navigating disruption with ecosystems, partners, and platforms. *Strategy & Leadership*, **46**(5), 26–35.

Bettis, R.A. and Hitt, M.A. (1995). The new competitive landscape. *Strategic Management Journal*, **16**, 7–19.

Blank, S. (2013). Why the lean start-up changes everything. *Harvard Business Review*, **91**(5), 63–72.

Brady, C., Forde, M., and Chadwick, S. (2017). Why your company needs data translators. *MIT Sloan Management Review*, **58**(2), 14–16.

Brandenburger, A. and Nalebuff, B. (1996). *Coopetition*. New York: Doubleday Business.

Bughin, J. and Catlin, T. (2017). What successful digital transformations have in common. *Harvard Business Review Digital Articles*, 1–5.

Burgelman, R.A. and Doz, Y.L. (2001). The power of strategic integration. *MIT Sloan Management Review*, **42**(3), 28–38.

Charitou, C.D. and Markides, C.C. (2003). Responses to disruptive strategic innovation. *MIT Sloan Management Review*, **44**(2), 55–63.

Chesbrough, H.W. (2008). Open innovation: a new paradigm for understanding industrial innovation. In: Chesbrough, H.W., Vanhaverbeke, W., and West, J. (eds), *Open Innovation: Researching a New Paradigm*, pp. 1–12. Oxford: Oxford University Press.

11

Chesbrough, H. (2011). Bringing open innovation to services. *MIT Sloan Management Review*, **52**(2), 87.

Christensen, C.M., Baumann, H., Ruggles, R., and Sadtler, T.M. (2006). Disruptive innovation for social change. *Harvard Business Review*, **84**(12), 94–101.

Cusumano, M.A. and Gawer, A. (2002). The elements of platform leadership. *MIT Sloan Management Review*, **43**(3), 51–8.

DalleMule, L. and Davenport, T.H. (2017). What's your data strategy? *Harvard Business Review*, **95**(3), 112–21.

Damanpour, F. (2014). Footnotes to research on management innovation. *Organization Studies*, **35**(9), 1265–85.

Damanpour, F., Walker, R.M., and Avellaneda, C.N. (2009). Combinative effects of innovation types and organizational performance: a longitudinal study of service organizations. *Journal of Management Studies*, **46**(4), 650–75.

Davenport, T.H. and Mahidhar, V. (2018). What's your cognitive strategy? *MIT Sloan Management Review*, **59**(4), 19–23.

Day, G.S. (2007). Is it real? Can we win? Is it worth doing? *Harvard Business Review*, **85**(12), 110–20.

Denning, S. (2018). The emergence of agile people management. *Strategy & Leadership*, **46**(4), 3–10.

Dodgson, M., Gann, D., and Salter, A. (2008). *The Management of Technological Innovation: Strategy and Practice*. Oxford: Oxford University Press

Dosi, G., Llerena, P., and Labini, M.S. (2006). The relationships between science, technologies, and their industrial exploitation: an illustration through the myths and realities of the so-called 'European Paradox'. *Research Policy*, **35**(10), 1450--64.

Downes, L. and Nunes, P.F. (2013). Big-bang disruption. *Harvard Business Review*, **91**(3), 44–56.

Eden, R., Burton-Jones, A., Casey, V., and Draheim, M. (2019). Digital transformation requires workforce transformation. *MIS Quarterly Executive*, **18**(1), 1–17.

Edquist, C., Hommen, C.L., and McKelvey, M. (2001). *Innovation and Employment: Process Versus Product Innovation*. Cheltenham: Edward Elgar.

Fagerberg, J. (2006). Innovation: a guide to the literature. In: Fagerberg, J., Mowery, D.C., and Nelson, R.R. (eds), *Oxford Handbook of Innovation*, pp. 1–26 Oxford: Oxford University Press.

Farboodi, M. (2018). The problem with big data. https://sloanreview.mit.edu/article/the-problem-with-big-data/ (accessed 19 December 2019).

Fitzgerald, M. (2016). Data-driven city management. *MIT Sloan Management Review*, **57**(4), 3–10.

Gartner (2018). Every organizational function needs to work on digital transformation. *Harvard Business Review*, 27 November, 6–9.

Gawer, A. and Cusumano, M.A. (2008). How companies become platform leaders. *MIT Sloan Management Review*, **49**(2), 28–35.

Gawer, A. and Cusumano, M.A. (2014). Industry platforms and ecosystem innovation. *Journal of Product Innovation Management*, **31**(3), 417–33.

Gilbert, C., Eyring, M., and Foster, R.N. (2012). Two routes to resilience. *Harvard Business Review*, **90**(12), 65–73.

Govindarajan, V. and Trimble, C. (2010). *The Other Side of Innovation: Solving the Execution Challenge*. Boston, MA: Harvard Business Review Press.

Gregersen, H.B. (2018). Digital transformation opens new questions—and new problems to solve. *MIT Sloan Management Review*, **60**(1), 27–9.

Hagiu, A. and Altman, E.J. (2017). Finding the platform in your product: four strategies that can reveal hidden value. *Harvard Business Review*, **95**(4), 94–100.

Hall, B.H. (2006). Innovation and diffusion. In: Fagerberg, J., Mowery, D.C., and Nelson, R.R. (eds), *Oxford Handbook of Innovation*, pp. 459–85 Oxford: Oxford University Press.

Henderson, R.M. and Clark, K.B. (1990). Architectural innovation: the reconfiguration of existing product technologies and the failure of established firms. *Administrative Science Quarterly*, **35**(1), 9–30.

Jolly, J. and Sweney, M. (2019). Spotify reaches 100m paying subscribers worldwide. https://www.theguardian.com/technology/2019/apr/29/spotify-paying-subscribers-streaming-us-canada (accessed 15 May 2019).

Kaplan, R.S. and Norton, D.P. (2008). Mastering the management system. *Harvard Business Review*, **86**(1), 62–77.

Kennard, M. (2018). *The A to Z of Innovation Management: The Essential Guide to 26 Key Innovation Management Theories, Models, and Frameworks*. York: York Publishing Services.

Ketter, W., Peters, M., Collins, J., and Gupta, A. (2016). Competitive benchmarking: an IS research approach to address wicked problems with big data and analytics. *MIS Quarterly*, **40**(4), 1057–89.

Kim, W.C. and Mauborgne, R. (2004). Blue ocean strategy. *Harvard Business Review*, **82**(10), 76–84.

Kim, W.C. and Mauborgne, R. (2007). How strategy shapes structure. *Harvard Business Review*, **87**(9), 72–80.

Kim, W.C. and Mauborgne, R. (2015a). Red ocean traps. *Harvard Business Review*, **93**(3), 68–73.

Kim, W.C. and Mauborgne, R. (2015b). Closing the gap between blue ocean strategy and execution. *Harvard Business Review Digital Articles*, 2–8.

Kim, W.C. and Mauborgne, R. (2019). Nondisruptive creation: rethinking innovation and growth. *MIT Sloan Management Review*, **60**(3), 46–55.

Kolbjørnsrud, V. (2017). Agency problems and governance mechanisms in collaborative communities. *Strategic Organization*, **15**(2), 141–73.

Lam, A. (2006). Organizational innovation. In: Fagerberg, J., Mowery, D.C., and Nelson, R.R. (eds), *Oxford Handbook of Innovation*, pp. 115–47. Oxford: Oxford University Press.

Lazer, D., Kennedy, R., King, G., and Vespignani, A. (2014). The parable of Google flu: traps in big data analysis. *Science*, **343**(6176), 1203–5.

Libert, B., Beck, M., and Wind, Y. (2016). 7 questions to ask before your next digital transformation. *Harvard Business Review Digital Articles*, 2–5.

Loonam, J., Eaves, S., Kumar, V., and Parry, G. (2018). Towards digital transformation: lessons learned from traditional organizations. *Strategic Change,* **27**(2), 101–9.

McAfee, A. and Brynjolfsson, E. (2012). Big data: the management revolution. *Harvard Business Review*, October. https://hbr.org/2012/10/big-data-the-management-revolution (accessed 19 December 2019).

Mangelsdorf, M.E. (2009). Creating a culture of innovation. https://sloanreview.mit.edu/article/creating-a-culture-of-innovation (accessed 19 December 2019).

Markides, C.C. (1998). Strategic innovation in established companies. *Sloan Management Review,* **39**(3), 31–42.

Millar, C.C.J.M., Groth, O., and Mahon, J.F. (2018). Management innovation in a VUCA world: challenges and recommendations. *California Management Review*, **61**(1), 5–14.

Obal, M., Kannan-Narasimhan, R., and Ko, G. (2016). Whom should we talk to? Investigating the varying roles of internal and external relationship quality on radical and incremental innovation performance. *Journal of Product Innovation Management*, **33**, 136–47.

Osterwalder, A. and Pigneur, Y. (2010). *Business Model Generation: A Handbook for Visionaries, Game Changers, and Challengers*. Hoboken, NJ: John Wiley.

Osterwalder, A., Pigneur, Y., Bernarda, G., and Smith, A. (2014). *Value Proposition Design: How to Create Products and Services Customers Want*. Hoboken, NJ: John Wiley.

Palmié, M., Lingens, B., and Gassmann, O. (2016). Towards an attention-based view of technology decisions. *R&D Management*, **46**(4), 781–96.

Parviainen, P., Tihinen, M., Kääriäinen, J., and Teppola, S. (2017). Tackling the digitalization challenge: how to benefit from digitalization in practice. *International Journal of Information Systems and Project Management*, **5**(1), 63–77.

Pisano, G.P. (2015). You need an innovation strategy. *Harvard Business Review*, April, 44–55.

Powell, W.W. and Grodal, S. (2006). Innovation and diffusion. In: Fagerberg, J., Mowery, D.C., and Nelson, R.R. (eds), *Oxford Handbook of Innovation*, pp. 56–85. Oxford: Oxford University Press.

Rao, J. and Weintraub, J. (2013). How innovative is your company's culture? *MIT Sloan Management Review*, **54**(3), 29–37.

Rogers, E.M. (2003). *Diffusions of Innovation* (5th edn). New York: Free Press.

Ross, J. (2018a). Let your digital strategy emerge. *MIT Sloan Management Review*, October. https://sloanreview.mit.edu/article/let-your-digital-strategy-emerge/ (accessed 19 December 2019).

Ross, J. (2018b). Digital is about speed — but it takes a long time. *MIT Sloan Management Review*, April. https://sloanreview.mit.edu/article/digital-is-about-speed-but-it-takes-a-long-time/ (accessed 19 December 2019).

Ross, J.W., Sebastian, I.M., and Beath, C.M. (2017). How to develop a great digital strategy. *MIT Sloan Management Review*, **58**(2), 7–9.

Roth, M. and Keller, B. (2019). Modernization through digital transformation. *TD: Talent Development*, **73**(1), 32–7.

Schoemaker, P.J.H., Heaton, S., and Teece, D. (2018). Innovation, dynamic capabilities, and leadership. *California Management Review*, **61**(1), 15–42.

Schumpeter, J. (1942). *Capitalism, Socialism, and Democracy*. New York: Harper and Row.

Siggelkow, N. and Terwiesch, C. (2019). The age of continuous connection. *Harvard Business Review*, **97**(3), 64–73.

Smith, H.A. and Watson, R.T. (2019). Digital transformation at Carestream Health. *MIS Quarterly Executive*, **18**(1), 86–98.

Svahn, F., Mathiassen, L., Lindgren, R., and Kane, G.C. (2017). Mastering the digital innovation challenge. *MIT Sloan Management Review*, **58**(3), 14–16.

Van Alstyne, M.W., Parker, G.G., and Choudary, S.P. (2016). Pipelines, platforms, and the new rules of strategy. *Harvard Business Review*, April, 54–60.

Vanhaverbeke, W. and Peeters, M. (2005). Embracing innovation as strategy: corporate venturing, competence building, and corporate strategy making. *Creativity and Innovation Management*, **14**(3), 262–73.

Vermeulen, F. (2017). What so many strategists get wrong about digital disruption. *Harvard Business Review Digital Articles*, 2–5.

von Stamm, B. (2008). *Managing Innovation, Design, and Creativity* (2nd edn). Chichester: John Wiley.

Westerman, G. (2019). The first law of digital innovation. *MIT Sloan Management Review*, April. https://sloanreview.mit.edu/article/the-first-law-of-digital-innovation/ (accessed 19 December 2019).

Westerman, G., Bonnet, D., and McAfee, A. (2012). The advantages of digital maturity. *MIT Sloan Management Review*, November. https://sloanreview.mit.edu/article/the-advantages-of-digital-maturity/ (accessed 19 December 2019).

Westerman, G., Soule, D.L., and Eswaran, A. (2019). Building digital-ready culture in traditional organizations. *MIT Sloan Management Review*, May. https://sloanreview.mit.edu/article/building-digital-ready-culture-in-traditional-organizations/ (accessed 21 July 2019).

Wheelwright,. S.C. and Clark, K.B. (1992). *Revolutionizing Product Development*. New York: Free Press.

CHAPTER TWEVLVE

Competing in a Globalized World

CONTENTS

LEARNING OBJECTIVES

By the end of this chapter, you should be able to:

- Recognize the nature of globalization and examine how this influences strategy
- Explore the drivers for globalization and their impact on organizations
- Recognize the cultural and practice challenges in global strategy implementation
- Evaluate the motivations and models for internationalization
- Examine the phenomenon of 'born global'
- Compare and contrast the generic global strategy orientations

TOOLBOX

- **Yip's industry globalization drivers**
  Four sets of 'industry globalization drivers' which underlie conditions in each industry that create the potential for that industry to become more global and, as a consequence, for the potential viability of a global approach to strategy.
- **Porter's diamond framework of national advantage**
  A model that is designed to help understand the emergence of competitive advantage of nations or industry clusters as a result of certain factor conditions available to them, and how strategists can apply the tool to identify attractive markets or locations to situate their production activities.
- **CAGE Distance framework**
  A framework that identifies Cultural, Administrative, Geographic, and Economic differences or distances between countries that companies should address when crafting international strategies. It may also be used to understand patterns of trade, capital, information, and people flows.
- **Foreign market entry modes**
  These are the channels ranging from export strategies to direct foreign investment that an organization can employ to gain entry to a new international market.
- **Three international strategy orientations**
  The three main international strategy orientations are: (1) multidomestic, (2) global, and (3) transnational. Each strategy involves a different approach to trying to build efficiency across national markets while remaining responsive to variations in foreign customer preferences and local market conditions.
- **Born global firms**
  A born global firm is an organization that, from its inception, seeks to derive significant competitive advantage from the use of resources and the sale of the firm's outputs in multiple countries. Born global firms are usually small technology-oriented companies that operate in international markets from the very beginning.

12

OPENING CASE STUDY FROM $80 AIR MATTRESS NIGHTS TO A $10,000 A NIGHT VILLA

In less than a decade, Airbnb has transformed the lives of millions of travellers by building a global marketplace around short-term apartment and room rentals. Airbnb connects people to places, at any price point, in more than 65,000 cities and 191 countries, and in over 3000 castles, 1400 tree-houses (The Verge 2016), or even a $10,000 a night villa where Beyoncé stayed after performing at the 2016 Super Bowl in San Francisco (The Verge 2016). The company has become a real threat to the hotel industry—a threat that is likely to intensify as Airbnb expands its global reach.

It all started in 2007, when room-mates Brian Chesky and Joe Gebbia noticed that there were surprisingly few hotel vacancies in their city of San Francisco. Taking advantage of an influx of visitors to the city, and the lack of hotel rooms available, Chesky and Gebbia created a website, airbedandbreakfast.com, to advertise modest accommodation on their apartment floor. They promised an air mattress and a cooked breakfast, and for $80 a night, they housed three guests. From this moment, Airbnb was born.

After the first weekend, Chesky and Gebbia realized that visitors could not search (in real time) for available accommodation and book on the spot. They realized that in order to monetize their business idea, and to avoid being limited to operating merely as a messaging site, airbedandbreakfast.com needed to handle payments. They enlisted the help of Gebbia's former room-mate, Nathan Blecharczyk, to develop the website to enable the exchange of payments between the hosts and guests.

However, it was the success in the late summer of 2008 which marked a turning point in the development of Airbnb. The business concept gained traction as a serious business which brought better chance of attracting investors. This allowed their listings to grow substantially, attracting nearly 10,000 registered users and offering approximately 2500 listings. During 2009, a night of lodging was booked on Airbnb on average every five minutes, but it did not stop there. During its second full year of business in 2010, Airbnb became a global phenomenon; listings were available in more than 8000 cities and 166 countries by the autumn, by which time Airbnb had booked more than 700,000 night stays since its launch two years earlier.

Rapid growth continued throughout 2011 and shifted focus to addressing the needs of a multinational audience, which Blecharczyk considered to be one of Airbnb's biggest challenges. Their strategy was to expand Airbnb's international operations by making the site available in 10 languages and streamlining transactions for owners with 34 country-specific payment options. At this point, Airbnb had just celebrated the millionth night booked through its service.

In June 2011 Airbnb acquired its German counterpart Accoleo, which gave the company its first subsidiary based outside the USA. International travel accounted for more than half the company's annual revenues by the time Accoleo was purchased, a portion that increased with every move made by Airbnb overseas. In September 2011 the company announced 'the next step in the evolution of Airbnb' (The Verge 2016)—its entry into offering monthly rentals, a strategy which sought to redefine the multibillion dollar sublet market. By the end of the year, after averaging a night of stay every minute in 2010, Airbnb's website was used to book a night of stay every 10 seconds.

At the start of 2012, the company's website booked its five millionth night of stay, and, in the space of a month, opened offices in London, Paris, Barcelona, Milan, Copenhagen, and Moscow, each charged with helping to support the more than 200,000 bookable properties offered on its website. In April, the company opened a South American office in São Paulo, Brazil. In June, five months after booking its five millionth night of stay, the company doubled the achievement by booking its 10 millionth guest midway through the month.

At the end of 2012, Chesky kept his focus on Airbnb's international presence. To foster greater growth, the company opened an office in Sydney, Australia, capitalizing on Australia's potential as Airbnb's second-largest market (trailing only the USA). The Sydney office was Airbnb's 11th satellite location. Chesky also looked to increase the company's business in Asia through a new office in Singapore. During that year, a night of stay was booked every two seconds through the company's website.

Since November 2016, Airbnb has become the world's second-largest lodging company with one million rooms or listings, behind leading hotel chain Marriott International. However, Airbnb has enjoyed a substantial lead in a market it had created, holding sway as a global force.

Questions for discussion

1. How would you describe Airbnb's business model (refer to our discussion of business models in Chapter 8)?
2. What do you think are the similarities and differences, if any, between Airbnb's business model and that of a more traditional global company such as McDonald's?
3. What factors do you think have contributed to Airbnb's rapid international expansion?
4. Critically evaluate Airbnb's sources of competitive advantage, if any.

Sources

The Verge (2016). https://www.theverge.com/2016/2/9/10949134/beyonce-super-bowl-airbnb-photos-los-altos (accessed 2 August 2019).

Statista (2017). Number of Airbnb overnight stays in the United States and Europe from 2015 to 2020. https://www.statista.com/statistics/795964/airbnb-room-nights-2015-2020/ (accessed 19 December 2019).

The Telegraph (2018). Airbnb abandons humble flat-sharing origins with move to offer hotel stays, 23 February. https://www.telegraph.co.uk/travel/comment/airbnb-to-offer-luxury-hotels/ (accessed 31 July 2019).

The Growthhackers (2018). Airbnb: the growth story you didn't know. https://growthhackers.com/growth-studies/airbnb (accessed 2 August 2019).

12.1 **Introduction**

Global strategy development has traditionally started with companies gradually building an international presence by taking their best products and services to markets where foreign customers share similar needs and characteristics as the home market customers. With the increasing connectivity and digitization of business, some firms, both small and large, are beginning to explore new ways of launching international ventures. Although the traditional routes to foreign markets are unlikely to disappear anytime soon, we see a trend that will increasingly involve business-model-grounded globalization ('born global' businesses) compared with the more traditional product- and service-led global expansion.

Traditional **multinational enterprises (MNEs)** have become global entities having evolved and developed their international operations over decades. Examples of MNEs include firms such as Siemens, Toyota, and Rolls-Royce Engines, among many other well-known enterprises. However, in our globally connected digital world, new innovative and entrepreneurial business models such as those of Alibaba, Airbnb, Facebook, and Uber may challenge the dominance of the widely known and applied internationalization strategies. We are likely to see an increasing number of start-up companies that were 'born global'—firms that enter international markets from their inception, or very early on after their founding—in contrast with the traditional MNEs.

In order to better understand international strategy and the challenges that organizations face when competing internationally, we start by exploring the changing landscape of global markets and businesses. We will consider globalization as a phenomenon and take a critical look at its advantages and disadvantages on both economic and societal levels. Globalization has become an emotionally and politically charged concept that has made and will continue to make a significant impact on how global companies operate and conduct themselves in a whole host of areas, including employment and tax practices, corporate social responsibility, executive compensation, and so on. Next, we will consider factors that may act as drivers for the globalization of industries, and finally we will assess the impact of these drivers at an organizational level. We will consider the challenges and decisions that organizations face when they evaluate opportunities for expanding their operations internationally. These sorts of strategic issues involve decisions, such as how does the firm get its product to the foreign market, and to what extent (if at all) does the product have to be adapted to meet local customer needs?

To help us explore these issues, we introduce analytical concepts and frameworks to develop our understanding of how and why organizations look to compete in a globalized world. More specifically, we will use Porter's diamond of national advantage to position an organization in the global economy within the context of its home nation, and identify competitive advantage from that perspective. We will apply the CAGE Distance framework, which will help us evaluate cross-border challenges to consider when evaluating foreign market entry strategies. We will also analyse the mechanics of becoming international, and the three main international strategic orientations (multidomestic, global, and transnational). Finally, we will evaluate the conditions for creating sustainable competitive advantage globally and consider the concept of 'born global' firms as an emerging strategic orientation.

12.2 **Globalization**

Globalization can be considered as an ongoing process of international integration that results from and supports the interchange of products, ideas, culture, and institutions. Many national economies today benefit from a form of globalization that is governed by both national laws and international agreements and treaties, such as the trade rules of the World Trade Organization (WTO).

The term 'globalization' began to become more commonly used in the 1980s, reflecting technological advances that made it easier and quicker to complete international transactions, both trade and financial flows (Ashenfelter et al. 2018). More specifically, globalization encompasses economic globalization: the increasing integration of economies around the world, particularly through free trade in goods, services, and the movement of capital across borders. The term often includes the free movement of people (labour) and knowledge (technology), as well as broader cultural, political, and environmental dimensions (IMF 2008).

According to the IMF (2008), there is substantial evidence from countries of different sizes and regions to suggest that, as countries globalize, their citizens benefit in the form of access to a variety of goods and services, lower prices, increased numbers of better-paying jobs, improved health, and higher overall living standards. As the number of countries which have become more open to global economic forces increases, the percentage of the developing world living in extreme poverty has reduced dramatically.

In 1820 only a tiny elite enjoyed higher standards of living, while the vast majority of people lived in conditions that we would call extreme poverty today. Since then the share of extremely poor people has fallen continuously. More and more world regions industrialized and thereby increased productivity, which made it possible to lift more people out of poverty. In

1950 two-thirds of the world population were living in extreme poverty; in 1981 it was still 42%. In 2015, the last year for which we currently have data, the share of the world population in extreme poverty has fallen below 10% (Our World in Data 2019).

A number of factors underpin the overall improvement in prosperity. One of the key factors has been greater direct foreign investment (FDI). This may include acquisitions, establishment of local manufacturing operations, or other forms of permanent investments made by foreign firms or individuals from one country into business interests located in another country. Other factors include the spread of technology, strong societal institutions, sound macroeconomic policies, an educated workforce, and the existence of a market economy (UN 2016). Fundamentally, however, all these advances are underpinned by what *The Economist* calls the 'competitive spirit of meritocracy' that has 'created extraordinary prosperity and wealth of new ideas.' In the name of efficiency and economic freedom, governments have opened up markets to competition and globalization has lifted hundreds of millions of people in emerging markets out of poverty (*The Economist* 2018).

Globalization has also opened up unprecedented opportunities for firms to trade internationally. As a result of the removal of trade barriers, deregulation of financial transactions, and harmonization of product standards and legal frameworks, it is now relatively easy for companies to sell what they produce in their home countries to foreign markets, source raw materials and products globally, or even locate their value-chain activities in one or more foreign countries. Globalized trading possibilities present a firm with strategic opportunities upon which it can build its competitive advantage.

De-globalization

While some countries have embraced globalization and experienced significant income increases, other countries that have rejected globalization, or only embraced it tepidly, have fallen behind (IMF 2008). A similar phenomenon is at work within individual countries, where some people have been bigger beneficiaries of globalization than others. In fact, rising incomes around the world have been accompanied by increasing inequality within individual countries across both developing and advanced economies (Kuttner 2018).

The World Bank (2016) reports that between 2008 and 2013 income gaps widened in 34 of the 83 countries as income grew more quickly for those in the wealthiest 60% of the income distribution than for those in the poorest 40%, and in 23 countries people in the poorest 40% saw their income decline.

It is against this backdrop that trade policies such as those of the Trump Administration have come to dominate the current discourse about the pros and cons of globalization. For workers in globalized industries in America who have experienced stagnating real wages, having been forced to compete for hourly wages with workers in Asia, a de-globalization trend is viewed as a relief (*The Economist* 2018). However, this is only a part of the story. The thinking of globalization where mainly US and European corporations shifted their supply chains to take advantage of cheaper Asian labour is coming to an end as wages in previously cheap labour cost countries are rising steadily. Hence, it will only make sense for global firms to relocate their manufacturing abroad if they save on tax or if such relocations bring the firm closer to the market that it is trying to sell to (*The Economist* 2018). In the new twenty-first century world, supply chains in

Europe, North America, and Asia will be increasingly based on producing goods closer to the home of the customer. In Asia and Europe most trade is already intra-regional, such as in the EU and other intra-regional trading blocks. It is especially noteworthy that Asian firms made more foreign sales within Asia than in the USA in 2017, indicating a shift in global trade flows (D'Urbino 2019).

Whatever form globalization will take in terms of regionalization and relocation of supply chains as well as political interventions, global trade is here to stay. In fact it will probably accelerate further with the digitization of trade and an increasing shift from manufacturing to service production. Digitization will make it easier for smaller firms and start-ups as 'born global' enterprises to participate in a global economy through e-commerce.

Digital data flows are already estimated to contribute as much as $450 billion to global growth annually (Pinkus et al. 2017). However, this also means that there are workers who will invariably be left behind by the onward march of globalization. It is suggested that retraining workers who have been affected by trade and globalization is not a solution on its own. In addition to retraining, where that is possible, policy responses will require a concerted effort by both governments and businesses to reinvest in dislocated communities, match smaller firms with foreign markets, match communities with foreign investors, ensure unfettered access for small firms and start-ups to cross-border digital platforms, and provide adequate safety net measures (Pinkus et al. 2017).

Finally, we should be clear that globalization is not the same thing as global strategy. Global strategy is effectively the means by which a firm achieves its international expansion of their objectives and scope. However, economic globalization is a phenomenon that firms cannot ignore, and, in general terms, the larger the firm, the more extensive is its global reach, and the more the business has to consider the impact of its operations on the local markets in which it operates.

CASE EXAMPLE 12.1 WORLD'S GLOBAL RETAILER

Walmart, founded in 1969, is the world's ultimate bargain basement retailer, selling over 140,000 food and non-food items in its superstores. The retailer's promise of 'everyday low prices' certainly resonates with bargain hunters, as the company serves 270 million customers every week in its 11,700 stores in 280 countries. This makes Walmart the world's largest bricks and mortar retailer, although over 70% of the company's sales are still generated from their US operations. In 2017 the firm's total revenue amounted to $500.3 billion with an operating cash flow of $28.3 billion (Walmart 2018).

Walmart's competitive advantage is based on its ability to consistently keep its cost base below that of its competitors. Beyond the economies of scale, the tight supply chain management processes, the purchasing power that Walmart is able to exercise over its suppliers, and the sourcing of cheap manufactured goods for sale in its stores has allowed the firm to become the world's largest bricks and mortar retailer. Its revenues are only eclipsed by Alibaba, the Chinese online retailer.

Sam Walton, the founder of Walmart, thought that many American produced goods were no longer competitive and he began looking for opportunities to procure goods cheaper internationally. By 2004 Walmart had ordered $18 billion worth of goods from China, and it has been estimated that in the decade since then Walmart's annual spending on Chinese manufactured goods amounted to $50 billion (David 2018). Although Walmart is a significant retailer of Chinese electronics and other goods, its sales of Chinese-made goods only accounted for only one in ten dollars spent by the US consumers on Chinese-made products.

China is currently the largest goods trading partner of the USA with $659.8 billion in total (two-way) goods trade during 2018. Goods exports totalled $120.3 billion, and goods imports totalled $539.5 billion. The US goods trade deficit with China was $419.2 billion in 2018 (Office of the United States Trade Representative 2019).

Some studies (David 2018) estimate that Walmart has destroyed some 400,000 manufacturing jobs in the USA over the last 12 years. The company denies this and cites the benefits of the Chinese imports to the USA: creating new jobs in distribution and logistics, and keeping bills down so that customers have money left over to spend on eating out or going to the cinema, thus boosting the takings elsewhere in the economy. However, it is argued that the new jobs that have been created may not be manufacturing jobs or may not pay as well as the old manufacturing jobs. Hence, one justification for tariffs on Chinese imports that is being considered by the current US Administration is the claim that trade protection protects and creates jobs. Taxing foreign goods increases demand for domestic products, bolstering production and sending more Americans to work.

There are some numbers that support this argument. New jobs have been added in every month of Trump's presidency, averaging 200,000 per month. This includes roughly 450,000 manufacturing jobs. After shedding five million jobs between 2001 and 2010, the manufacturing sector has enjoyed a soft rebound. In addition, there is anecdotal evidence of new employment in protected industries, including 1100 jobs at US Steel's Fairfield Works. Supporters of the Trump Administration's trade protection policy claim that job creation outpaces losses from tariffs by 20:1. However, this may not be the result of tariffs. The USA has enjoyed over 100 straight months of uninterrupted job growth. This means that strong performance under the Trump Administration cannot be attributed to recent policy shifts. Furthermore, most of those jobs are in services, not manufacturing. Services employment grew dramatically after the Great Recession of 2008–2009, increasing by about 17 million (*Washington Post* 2019).

Economists point out that trade deficits are mainly driven by macroeconomic factors. In particular, if a country has a high savings rate relative to investment, that country will send some of its excess savings to others by exporting more goods than it imports. China, Japan, and Germany, all with high savings rates, have trade surpluses. The USA, with low savings and high consumption, has a deficit. In other words, the trade deficit is mostly home grown, and the Trump Administration's economic policies are likely to increase it. A large tax cut and increases in government spending have temporarily boosted consumption and economic growth. To help meet the new demand, the USA has started importing more, further increasing the trade imbalance (Irwin 2019).

Questions for discussion

1. Why do you think it is imperative for Walmart to import goods from China to maintain its competitive advantage?
2. What impact would import tariffs on Chinese goods have on Walmart's business?
3. Do you think that the imposition of tariffs on Chinese imports would make an American consumer and worker better off? If so, why and how? If not, why not?

Sources

Walmart (2018). *2018 Annual Report*. http://www.corporatereport.com/walmart/2018/ar/Walmart_2018_Annual%20Report.pdf (accessed 19 December 2019).

David, D. (2018). *The Almighty Dollar*. London: Elliott & Thompson.

Office of the United States Trade Representative. The People's Republic of China. https://ustr.gov/countries-regions/china-mongolia-taiwan/peoples-republic-china (accessed 24 April 2019).

Washington Post (2019). Trump may be ending the trade war with China. Who won? 27 February. https://www.washingtonpost.com/politics/2019/02/27/trump-may-be-ending-trade-war-with-china-who-won/?utm_term=.ce6d0d0597c1 (accessed 24 April 2019).

Irwin, D. (2019). Understanding Trump's trade war. *Foreign Policy*, Winter. https://foreignpolicy.com/gt-essay/understanding-trumps-trade-war-china-trans-pacific-nato/ (accessed 24 April 2019).

12

12.3 Drivers of industry globalization

We have considered globalization as a phenomenon and taken a critical look at its advantages and disadvantages on both economic and societal levels. At the centre of economic globalization are businesses that have become increasingly global in their outlook and reach. However, global firms traditionally operate in a number of business environments, both national and global. The complexity of this operating environment is depicted in Figure 12.1, which incorporates both the macro- and industry-level environments that global firms have to manage effectively when competing in multiple markets, and even across traditional industry boundaries. Figure 12.1 shows that in a global business environment a firm is a participant not only in a domestic industry and market of a national economy, but a participant in a global industry and market that is influenced by the global macro-environment. And even if one particular firm itself would not have cross-border operations, it is very likely that the firm would face competition in its domestic market from international competitors.

What factors act as drivers for the globalization of industries? And how do these drivers impact on firms at an organizational level? In this section, we consider how globalization affects firms' competitive activities. We begin our discussion by exploring the globalization of industries to identify if there are any common factors that may act as enablers for an emergence of a global industry. We then develop a more specific understanding of why firms choose to compete in international markets, given the opportunities offered by the globalized nature of the industry in which the business operates.

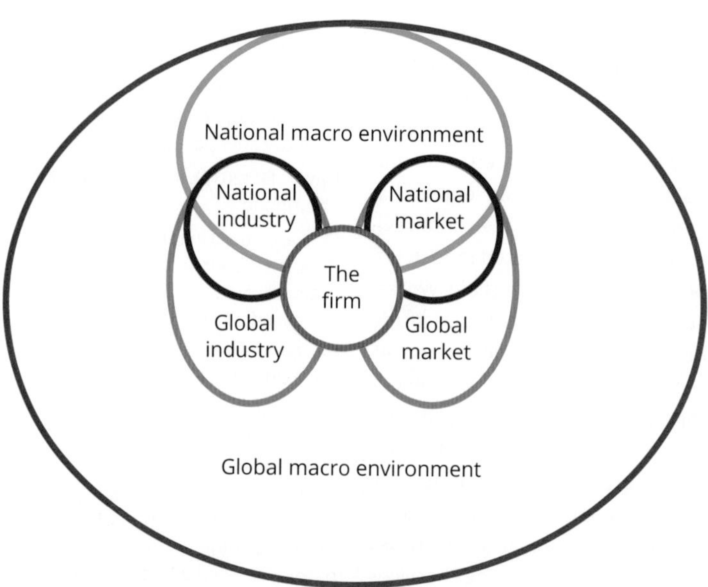

FIGURE 12.1 Global business environment.

Drivers of industry globalization and their effects on competitive activity

In his seminal book, *Total Global Strategy: Managing for Worldwide Competitive Advantage*, George Yip identified four generic sets of 'industry globalization drivers' (Yip 1995). According to Yip, these industry globalization drivers may create conditions for industries to globalize and, as a consequence, for the potential viability of adopting a global approach to a firm's strategy development. Yip's framework (see Figure 12.2) proposes four main drivers for industry globalization:

- market drivers
- cost drivers
- competition drivers
- government drivers.

We will consider each of these drivers in turn.

Market drivers

One of the key drivers for industry globalization is a convergence of customer needs and tastes internationally. Think about how Coca-Cola is sold in 200 countries regardless of national culture or income levels, or think how many teenagers across the world, regardless of the language they speak, do not wish to use Apple or Samsung's smartphones to communicate with their friends. As customers across the world increasingly demand similar products and services, opportunities for economies of scale and scope arise through the production and marketing of more or less standardized offerings. How common needs, tastes, and preferences vary by

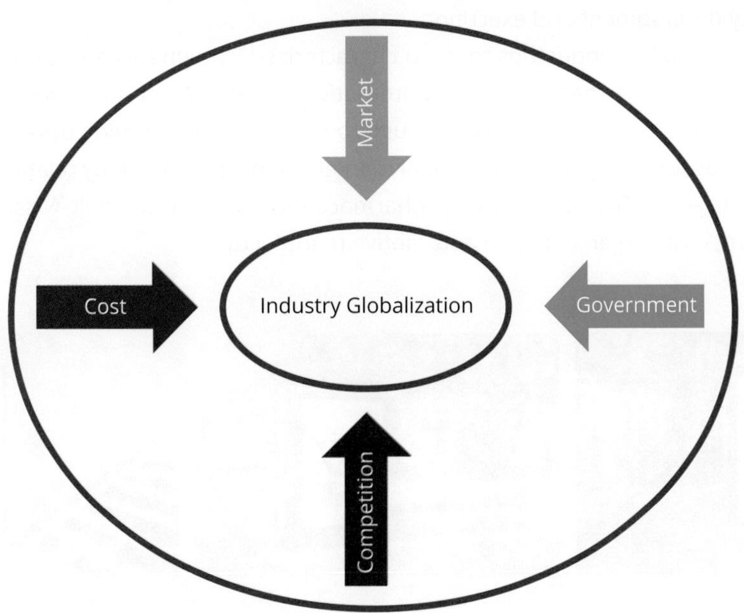

FIGURE 12.2 Industry globalization drivers.

12

product depend on such factors as the importance of cultural variables, disposable incomes, and the level of consistency of the conditions in which the product is consumed or used. This applies to consumer as well as industrial products and services. For example, McDonald's, while adapting to local tastes and preferences, has standardized many elements of its operations to ensure maximum operating efficiency, and standardized the quality of its products across its global outlets. Increasingly, products such as software, oil and lubricants, and accounting services look alike, no matter where they are purchased.

Similarly, large corporations such as Airbus, DuPont, GE, HSBC, or Toyota demand the same level of quality in the products and services they buy, no matter where in the world they are procured. In many industries, global distribution channels are emerging to satisfy an increasingly global customer base, further causing a convergence of needs and tastes that results in further standardization of products and services. Finally, as consumption patterns become more consistent, global branding and marketing as a differentiating factor from competitor organizations, in the eyes of the consumer, will become increasingly important to global success. To further gain economies of scale and scope, many global companies (especially in consumer goods industries) run standardized advertising campaigns across their global markets, which are designed by advertising companies which themselves are increasingly global in their reach.

Figure 12.3 shows examples of an advertising campaign that was run by Ontario Maple Syrup Producers Association, advertising a standardized product. In order to take local tastes into consideration, the advertising hoardings were adapted to local market tastes and conditions in various international markets. However, the advertiser was able to earn economies of scope as the general theme of the campaign remained the same across the various markets.

Cost drivers

Economies of scale and scope, learning effects, and the exploitation of differences in factor costs for product development, manufacturing, and sourcing are important determinants in global strategy development and execution.

Global reach is vital for industries that are characterized by high research and development (R&D) costs, such as pharmaceutical and automotive industries. For such industries, a single domestic market will no longer be large enough to recapture the accruing development costs. Therefore it is not surprising to see the global markets being dominated by relatively few global firms such as Pfizer and GlaxoSmithKline in pharmaceuticals and the Renault–Nissan–Mitsubishi alliance and the Volkswagen Group in automotive manufacturing.

FIGURE 12.3 Ontario Maple Syrup Producers Association advertisements. Source: Courtesy of the Ontario Maple Syrup Producers' Association 2019.

The size of the national economy of the firm or industry can also act as a driver for globalization. For example, the mobile communications industry first emerged primarily in the Nordic region, spearheaded by Ericsson of Sweden and Nokia of Finland. Both countries are small: Sweden has a population of approximately ten million and Finland approximately five million. Given the small size of the domestic markets that would not have been able to absorb the R&D costs, the emerging mobile telecommunications industry and firms had to think globally from the start in order to be able drive down the unit production costs through economies of scale to make the product affordable.

Many of the Scandinavian firms followed what is known as the Uppsala model of internationalization (as discussed in Chapter 7). Swedish researchers (Johanson and Wiedersheim-Paul 1975) from Uppsala University in Sweden found that companies normally start their expansion by selling to markets near their home base, such as the trade between the Nordic countries. It is only after they become more knowledgeable about selling to a foreign market that they gradually expand to more 'distance markets'. Distance markets is a term used to refer to the cultural distance as well as the differences in language, politics, and geography, and the difficulty in acquiring knowledge of and information about the market. The Uppsala model is in sharp contrast to a company such as Airbnb which became a global firm almost from the outset based on its 'born global' digital platform business model.

Competitive drivers

Industry characteristics, such as the diversity of competitors in terms of their national origin and the extent to which major players have globalized their operations, also affect the globalization potential of an industry. Consider a firm that operates in a globalized industry with a wide diversity of competitors. That firm risks being crowded out of the market by global competitors who may have achieved a lower cost structure, unless it enjoys such a strong position in its domestic market that it cannot be challenged. In reality such a protected position in a free-trade environment is likely to be temporary at best. Therefore, if a nationally focused firm's competitors are global, the national firm is likely to be forced to become global in order to survive.

Government drivers

Government drivers, such as trade policies, technical standards, and other regulatory frameworks, are important drivers in shaping the global competitive environment. As the politics and economics of global competition become more closely intertwined, both national governmental and supranational regulations and policies will have an impact on firms' global strategies. (Supranational regulations are those that go beyond national boundaries.) Firms often engage with policy-makers with the aim of shaping the global competitive environment to their advantage by lobbying local governments and international institutions. Examples of policy initiatives that attract lobbying by businesses are trade restrictions, investment subsidies, tax rebates, etc. This broadening of the scope of global strategy reflects a subtle but real change in the balance of power between national governments and global corporations, and it is likely to have important consequences for how differences in policies and regulations affecting global competitiveness will be settled in the years to come.

Additional globalization drivers

Yip's framework of industry globalization drivers (Yip 1995) is by no means an exhaustive list. In a review of literature on economic globalization, Bang and Markeset (2012) identified additional globalization drivers that may affect firms' competitive situation:

1. lower transportation costs
2. lower communications costs
3. ICT development
4. technology development and penetration.

All these factors, especially information and communications technologies, enable firms to manage their global operations more efficiently and, with the reach of internet technology, almost in real time.

Reasons for organizations to enter international markets

We have seen that globalization drivers are benign factors that encourage and, in some cases (such as cost considerations), force organizations to expand outside their domestic markets. Table 12.1 highlights the six main reasons that may prompt firms to seek international expansion.

Given that globalization has become such a major phenomenon, a new orthodoxy has risen which assumes that businesses of all types and sizes have to embrace it and the pressure to do so is likely to intensify further. Although the motivations for entering international markets listed in Table 12.1 make a compelling case for organizations to enter international markets, we should be very clear that to do so successfully is difficult. There are a number of very large and well-managed companies that have tried to take advantage of the opportunities and have failed in their globalization efforts. In the financial services industry, a Dutch banking group, ABN Amro, set out to create a global financial powerhouse by acquiring banks in numerous countries. However, the banking group failed to integrate the banking institutions acquired in order to generate value with its international network. ABN Amro was eventually broken up and parts of the group were acquired by the Royal Bank of Scotland, a bank that itself became a high-profile casualty and contributor to the financial crisis of 2008–2009.

In the automotive industry, one of the largest mergers of recent times was that between Daimler–Benz and Chrysler in 1998. The two companies intended to create Welt AG, a world corporation. However, this ambition was never realized as the merged entity failed to acquire the power over the market and suppliers that the firms' global ambitions were supposed to deliver. The merger failed, and in 2014 Chrysler became a part of the Fiat Group.

Many failures could be avoided if firms seriously addressed three seemingly simple questions (Alexander and Korine 2008):

1. Are there potential benefits for our firm?

Just because it makes sense for a firm's rival to globalize, does it make sense, given the firm's own market position and the resources and capabilities available to it, to do so as well? Perhaps most importantly, is the firm in a position to leverage its technology and know-how beyond the

TABLE 12.1 **Reasons for organizations to enter international markets**

Aim of entering an international market	Motivation or reason for entering international market	Benefit or opportunity
To gain access to new customers	The firm's home market is mature, or nearing saturation	Opportunities for increased revenues and profits in markets at a growth stage of the firm's product life cycle
	The firm sits in an industry: with high R&D costs with products that can be quickly imitated by competitors where profits are dependent on high sales volumes	Opportunity to earn returns on investments more quickly or in higher volumes
To achieve lower costs through economies of scale, scope, learning effects, and increased purchasing power	The firm is not able to recapture development, manufacturing, and marketing costs through economies of scale offered in their domestic markets	Opportunity to gain experience, which enables the firm to move down the learning curve Producing and selling higher volumes may increase the organization's purchasing power
	The home market is too small to earn sufficient economies of scale	Achieving lower costs are a 'push' factor for firms in small countries to internationalize
To exploit core competencies	The firm has a competitive advantage in a given industry in one country	Opportunity to gain further leverage from their core competencies in another country
To gain access to global resources and capabilities	The firm needs access to resources that are not available in the firm's home market	Opportunity to access new expertise; expertise is often found in clusters, and by having a presence in one of the many clusters, companies can access the required expertise
To spread business risk across a wider operating base	The firm needs to reduce risk	Opportunity for organizations to spread their business risk by operating in multiple markets as opposed to a single market
To follow their customers abroad	The firm needs to secure loyalty and commitment from their own internationally operating clients that the business depends on	Companies that are suppliers to organizations that operate internationally will often need to follow their customers abroad, which builds two-way loyalty and commitment with the client

home market, or should the organization concentrate its efforts on developing and defending its position within the home market?

2. **Do we have the requisite management skills?**

Theoretical aspects such as economies of scale are very difficult to realize in practice. Realization of economies of scale is often one of the most common incentives for firms to pursue globalization strategies. However, firms often lack the managerial skills to deliver such an elusive benefit. Also, in many cases, making organizational and cultural change can become an unsurmountable barrier. In order to succeed, the organization and its component parts should necessarily be able to achieve seamless coordination and collaboration across national boundaries. Both ABN Amro and Daimler–Chrysler made a failed attempt to unlock the prize of economies of scale.

3. **Will the costs outweigh the benefits?**

Going global is costly. Companies often underestimate the cost of globalization. Some of these costs are not direct costs but hidden opportunity costs. For example, would the effort to harmonize practices and products across the firm's global operating network drive existing customers away or distract national management teams from the local market needs?

12.4 **Complexity of cross-border strategy-making**

We have already seen that developing and implementing competitive cross-border strategy is a complex undertaking. But what are the reasons for this complexity and how do they differ between countries? There are a number of factors that increase the level of complexity as firms expand their international reach:

- differing competitive conditions between countries
- differing availability of resources required for business operations
- differing political and economic conditions
- volatility of exchange rates
- differing demographics, social norms and behaviours, cultures, and religions.

These factors are additional to the organization's internal capabilities in managing and coordinating a highly complex global operation. In this section we consider the cross-border variation in factors that affect industry competitiveness and outline factors that govern decisions for locating value-chain activities in different countries. We also consider the impact of variations in wider economic, social, and cultural conditions on the organization's cross-border strategy.

National variation in factors that affect industry competitiveness

Certain countries are often perceived to possess strengths in particular industries. Japan is known for its excellence in consumer electronics, with companies such as Sony and Canon, Switzerland for its precision watches, such as Swatch and Rolex, Australia for mining companies, such as the Anglo-Australian mining giant Rio Tinto, and Germany for its excellence in car manufacturing including Volkswagen, one of the largest automotive manufacturing groups. These countries are said to possess a national advantage in these particular industries. A number of factors may influence the likelihood of a country developing a competitive advantage. Porter (1990) developed a **theory of national advantage**, often referred to as Porter's Diamond model, which helps us understand the competitive advantage that nations possess due to certain factors available to them. It also helps us to explain how governments can act as catalysts to improve a country's competitive position in the global economy. The original model included only four factors:

- firm strategy, structure, and rivalry
- related and support industries
- demand conditions
- factor conditions.

However, two additional forces can be considered to affect national competitiveness:

- the role of the government
- the role of chance.

The Diamond model (with the two added factors), is depicted in Figure 12.4.

Porter's Diamond model is visually represented by a diagram that resembles the four points of a diamond. The four points represent four interrelated determinants that Porter considers to be the deciding factors of national competitive advantage. Porter defines these interrelated determinants as follows:

- **Firm strategy, structure, and rivalry** refers to the basic fact that competition leads to businesses finding ways to increase production and to the development of technological innovations.
- **Related supporting industries** refers to upstream and downstream industries that facilitate innovation through exchanging ideas.

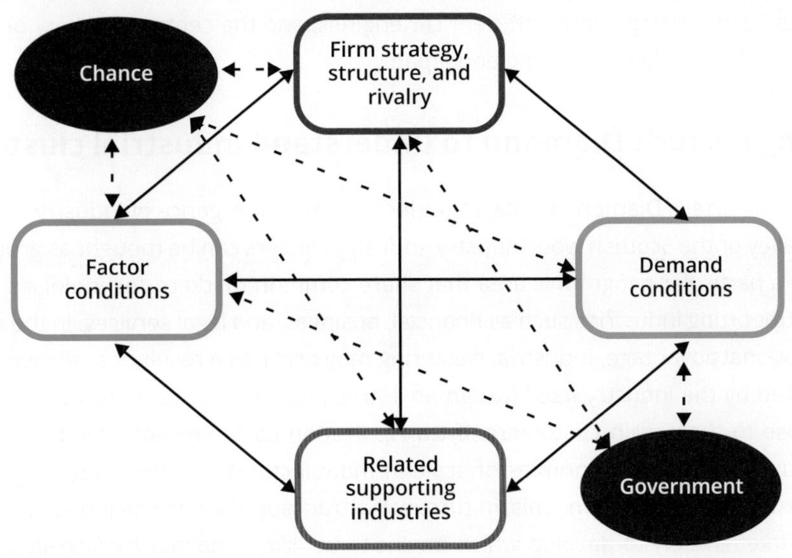

FIGURE 12.4 Porter's Diamond model of national advantage. Adapted from Porter, M. (1990). *The Competitive Advantage of Nations*. New York: Free Press. By permission of Harvard Business Publishing.

- **Demand conditions** refer to the size and nature of the customer base for products, which also drives innovation and product improvement.
- **Factor conditions** are elements that Porter believes a country's economy can develop for itself, such as a large pool of skilled labour, technological innovation, infrastructure, and capital.

Factor conditions are the most important, according to Porter's theory. He argues that the elements of factor conditions are more important in determining a country's competitive advantage than naturally inherited factors such as land and natural resources. For example, Japan has developed a competitive global economic presence beyond the country's inherent natural resources, in part by producing a very large number of engineers who have helped drive technological innovation by Japanese industries (Chappelow 2019).

Porter further suggests that the primary role of **government** in driving a nation's economy is to encourage and challenge businesses within the country to focus on creation and development of factor conditions. One way for government to accomplish that goal is to stimulate competition between domestic companies by establishing and enforcing anti-trust laws. However, it is important to note that **government interventions** must be considered in terms of their impact on domestic company activities, because the underlying view in the Diamond model is that 'firms, not nations, compete in international markets' (Porter 1990:33).

Finally, Porter also suggests that in most markets **chance** plays an important role. However, the influence of chance is, by its very nature, not predictable. For example, chance influences the creation of new ideas or new inventions. Additionally, international (or national) conflicts, significant shifts in world financial markets, discontinuities in input costs (e.g. oil price shocks), major technological breakthroughs, and major shifts in foreign market demand can all have a significant impact on a nation's competitive advantage. For example, as discussed in Chapter 8, it could be argued that the American automotive industry never recovered from the oil shock of 1973 when OPEC was formed. The US car industry was ill prepared to respond to sky-rocketing petrol prices by producing energy-efficient car engines, and the centre of gravity of car manufacturing excellence shifted to Europe and Japan.

Extending Porter's Diamond to understand industrial clustering

We can extend Porter's Diamond model to understand the emergence of industry clusters such as Silicon Valley or the Scottish wool industry. Industry clusters can be thought as groups of similar firms in a particular geographic area that share common markets, technologies, employee skills, and supporting industries such as financial, business, and legal services. In the absence of a natural national advantage, industrial clustering may occur as a result of a relative advantage that is created by the industry itself (Krugman 1993). Producers tend to locate manufacturing facilities close to their main customers. If transportation costs are not prohibitive and there are opportunities to earn economies of scale in manufacturing, a large geographic area can be served from a single location. This, in turn, will attract suppliers to the industry. In addition, a labour market is likely to develop which begins to act like a magnet for 'like' industries that require similar skills. This locating together—clustering—of 'like' industries can lead to technological interdependencies, which will further encourage clustering. Therefore clustering is the natural outcome of economic forces and it is very closely the product of the factors detailed in Porter's Diamond model.

Another example of industrial clustering is the semiconductor industry. American and Asian firms supply most of the world's semiconductors needed for the production of digital equipment from cameras to super-computers. The industry is capital intensive, research and development costs are high, and the manufacturing process is highly complex, but transportation costs are minimal which means that semiconductors can be shipped globally relatively cheaply. Technology interdependencies encourage producers and suppliers to be located close together, whereas cost and learning curve effects can result in economies of scale efficiencies.

Only when transportation costs are prohibitive or scale economies are difficult to realize (i.e. when there are disincentives to clustering) do more decentralized patterns of industry location define the natural order. The appliance industry illustrates this. Companies such as GE and Whirlpool have globalized their operations in many respects, but the fundamental economics of the industry make clustering unattractive. For example, the production of certain value-added components, such as compressors or electronic parts, can be concentrated to some extent, but the bulky nature of the product and high transportation costs make further concentration economically unattractive.

Applying Porter's Diamond as a tool for strategy-making

Porter's Diamond model has been critiqued since it was first published in 1990. We highlight some of the criticisms but, despite the framework's shortcomings, it is important in your studies to understand the Diamond model, as it can still be used by strategists as an effective strategy-making tool.

The most significant critique of Porter's Diamond model is that it has an almost exclusive focus on the home country. In Porter's model, the home country is perceived as the place from where the competitive advantages of a nation can be derived (Porter 1990). However, as Rugman and D'Cruz (1993) found, that was not the case for countries outside the USA, the EU, and Japan. Cartwright (1993), in his research on New Zealand, concluded that Porter's Diamond model could not explain the success of export-dependent and resource-based industries. Porter's model failed to understand that for small open trading economies, where firms earn the majority of their revenues outside their home country, the diamond of their target markets is more relevant than their own home diamond (Rugman and D'Cruz 1993).

Another critical dimension that is missing in Porter's model is the influence of national culture, as pointed out by Van den Bosch and Van Prooijen (1992). Porter himself noted that many aspects of a nation, such as attitude towards authority, norms of interpersonal interaction, and attitude towards management and social norms, influence the way firms are organized and managed (Porter 1990). Many of such social and political aspects of a nation originate from the national culture. How national culture influences competitiveness through the Diamond model was a key issue, which Porter did not explore in his work. We will consider the impact of socio-cultural factors in our discussion of the CAGE Distance framework later in this section.

Despite these shortcomings, it is important for you to understand the model when studying strategy. Managers can apply the Diamond model to find answers to important questions for competing internationally.

1. The model can be used to predict where foreign entrants into a firm's industry are likely to come from. This information may enable managers to develop entry barriers for foreign competitor entry, as the Diamond analysis will reveal some information about the foreign competitors' strengths and weaknesses.
2. The analysis may reveal the countries where international competitors are the weakest. This may help managers to decide which markets they should enter as competition is perceived to be weakest.
3. The Diamond model highlights countries where a certain industry has a competitive advantage or where a certain cluster of excellence is located. This signals that the country with world-leading industries or clusters of excellence has qualities that allow an industry to flourish. This may help managers of international firms to decide where they could gain access to valuable knowledge and resource, or even locate some of their firm's value-chain activities in such countries.

CASE EXAMPLE 12.2 IDENTIFYING OPPORTUNITIES FOR MOBILE TECHNOLOGY BASED RETAIL BANKING SERVICES

A European retail bank known for their mobile banking apps is considering opportunities for international expansion. The managers of the bank have identified a rapidly growing emerging economy with a large population and an emerging prosperous middle class. Porter's Diamond analysis reveals the following information:

Demand conditions

- Evolving mobile commerce possibilities
- Growing number of smartphone owners
- Data usage is becoming cheaper so smartphones will become available for most people in the country
- Emerging prosperous middle class

Factor endowments

- Technology workforce is developing and growing
- Level of competence of using mobile and Internet technology is high
- The country has geographical technology advantages
- Upcoming online businesses including app builders
- Poor national fixed telephone line networks, and lower usage of landlines
- Limited number of physical bank branches that do not cover the country fully

Related and supporting industry

- The country is the regional leader in the microchip market
- The county is the regional leader in mobile network and technology
- The banking system of the country is in need of new technology infrastructure

Firm strategy and structure

- Emerging venture capital firms investing in technology start-ups
- Small and medium-sized technology businesses
- Market competition in mobile telecommunications
- Continuous development and improvement of mobile technologies

Government

- The government has stated that it will promote mobile communications technology over fixed-line communications
- The government is planning to invest in mobile R&D and technology development
- The government is in the process of developing mobile commerce regulatory frameworks
- The government provides attractive tax incentives for foreign investors

Questions for discussion

1. Does the above information support a further investigation of mobile banking opportunities? Why/Why not?
2. What additional information would you need before considering a decision to expand your operations to this market?

CAGE Distance framework

The CAGE Distance framework (Ghemawat 2001, 2007; Ghemawat and Siegel 2011) identifies Cultural, Administrative, Geographic, and Economic (CAGE) distance or differences between countries that organizations should address when developing international strategies. The framework can also be used to understand patterns of trade, capital, information, and people flows. Unlike Porter's Diamond model, which makes an attempt to identify the sources of national advantage, the CAGE Distance framework considers the distance between countries as the main contributing factors to the level of trade between countries. Approaching international trade and business relationships from different perspectives makes the Diamond model and the CAGE Distance framework complementary analytical strategy tools.

The CAGE Distance framework defines four major categories of 'distances', and considers that the differences along these dimensions generally have a negative effect on many cross-border interactions between countries and businesses (Ghemawat and Siegel 2011).

- Cultural distance includes differences in religious beliefs, race/ethnicity, language, and social norms and values. Countries can even differ in their social attitudes to the market power of firms and income inequality, which may have implications on the economic policies of the individual countries.
- Administrative distance covers historical and political associations between countries include colonial links, free trade agreements, and the length of bilateral relationships.
- Geographic distance encompasses more than how far two countries are from each other geographically. Other factors include a country's physical size, within-country distances to borders, access to ocean, topography, and even time zones.
- Economic distance includes consumer wealth and labour costs, but other factors that impact the economic distance include differences in availability of resources, infrastructure, and organizational capabilities.

The CAGE Comparator, which covers 163 home countries and 65 industries, and allows users to customize the impacts of 16 types of CAGE distance, is included in the **online resources**.

Some research quantifies the impact of these distances on bilateral trade (Ghemawat and Mallick 2003). Table 12.2 shows the effects of similarities versus differences on bilateral trade between two country pairs. Some of these factors probably make sense intuitively, such as the cultural factor of a common language. If there is a common language between two countries, communication channels are more straightforward and therefore trade is likely to be facilitated. This can be seen in the first row of Table 12.2, which shows a 42% increase in bilateral trade under these circumstances. However, not all factors are so straightforward. An example of a more surprising change in trade, according to the data in Table 12.2, is the magnitude of the impact of colonial ties. The data in the second row in Table 12.2 indicates that countries with colonial ties are almost three times as likely to trade as countries without them (188%). Ghemawat and Mallick (2003) state that such a relationship is even more pronounced if one takes into account the role of colonial ties in generating cultural similarities. This is especially significant as one considers that the impact of colonial ties on trade persists decades or even centuries after colonial relationships were dissolved.

The CAGE framework in strategy implementation

Ghemawat (2018) offers advice on how the CAGE framework can help managers to consider their options for international strategy development:

- It makes distance visible for managers.
- It helps pinpoint the differences across countries that might handicap multinational companies relative to local competitors.

12

TABLE 12.2 **Effects of similarities versus differences on bilateral trade**

Dimensions of distance/proximity	Determinant	Change in trade
Cultural	Common language	+42%
Administrative	Common regional trading block	+47%
	Colony–colonizer links	+188%
	Common currency	+114%
	Differences in corruption	–11%
Geographic	Physical distance	–1.1%
	Physical size	–0.2%
	Landlockedness	–48%
	Common land border	+125%
Economic	Economic size: GDP	+0.8%
	Income level: GDP per capita	+0.7%

Source: Ghemawat and Mallick (2003).

CASE EXAMPLE 12.3 **STARTV'S MISCALCULATION**

Many strategists recognize the importance of geographic distance. For example, geography and distance are significant factors in shipping goods internationally. So are economic distance, differences among nations in labour costs, and so on. But strategists often underestimate the influence held by administrative or cultural distances.

A powerful example of where cultural distance was not accounted for is StarTV, which was acquired by Rupert Murdoch's News Corporation in the early 1990s. Back in the 1990s, satellite television was a new development, and this novel digital technology destroyed geographic distance as a boundary factor. This meant that broadcasting could become international. A broadcaster no longer needed a TV tower on the ground; instead, a satellite source, about 23,000 miles above the Earth's surface, could cover a hemisphere. StarTV launched pan-Asian English-language programming, targeting Asia's wealthiest 5% as its audience. However, while geographic distance was no longer an issue for StarTV, their venture into the Asian market was still a step too far.

Culturally, people prefer to watch TV programmes in their own language. This was already established in research, and it seems an obvious obstacle that even the invention of satellite TV could not overcome. However, the real barrier to StarTV's success was the barrier of administrative distance. When Murdoch gave a speech in 1993 about satellite TV being 'an unambiguous threat to totalitarian regimes everywhere', the Chinese government reacted by banning the ownership of satellite dishes—which effectively choked StarTV's business in that key country.

Question for discussion

How could Murdoch make such a miscalculation? According to one News Corporation executive, the firm's operating experience was in the USA, the UK, and Australia. In none of these markets was it considered a big deal to rail against authoritarian regimes. 'We weren't thinking. We just figured that this was a harmless little bit of filler.'

Source

Strategy+Business, 26 February 2008.

- It can shed light on the relative position of multinationals from different countries. For example, it can help explain the strength of Spanish firms in many industries across Latin America compared with UK multinational firms operating in the same geographic market.
- It can be used to compare markets from the perspective of a particular company. One method to conduct quantitative analysis of this type is to discount (specifically, divide) raw measures of market size or potential with measures of distance, broadly defined.

Ghemawat emphasizes that different types of distance matter to different extents depending on the industry. For instance, because geographic distance affects the costs of transportation, it is of particular importance to companies dealing in heavy or bulky products. A cement manufacturer that is considering a globalization strategy would be ill advised to ship cement around the world from a central manufacturing location as the transportation costs relative to the value of a heavy shipment of cement would be uneconomical. Instead, the cement company should consider exporting its special technological know-how or open manufacturing operations in local markets. Conversely, high value but low weight items such as microchips can be shipped at low cost from one location across vast geographic distances. Cultural distance, on the other hand, affects consumers' product preferences. This should be a crucial consideration for a consumer goods or a media company as such a distance is more psychological than physical, but by no means less important.

12.5 Entering international markets

Once a business has decided to expand its operations beyond domestic markets, in what ways can it enter foreign markets? In this section we consider six internationalization options available to existing organizations. But first we recognize that there are increasingly exceptions to the traditional idea that a firm starts in its domestic market and later on expands into foreign markets. These exceptions, often referred to as 'born global' firms, achieve international sales from an early stage in their development (Knight and Cavusgil 2005) without a gradual progression of their international activities.

Born global firms

Much of international strategy literature has focused on the evolutionary nature of firm internationalization which has assumed an orderly expansion from exporting to strategic alliances and joint ventures to wholly owned foreign subsidiaries (Johanson and Vahlne 1977), which we discuss later in this section.

In contrast with the orderly development of international operations, from the outset born global firms consider opportunities that are present in international markets and they develop their resources and capabilities accordingly to take advantage of such opportunities. Born global firms are not a new phenomenon, however. For example, the East India Company, which was founded in 1601, was a global firm from its inception which was founded to trade with the East Indies. Today, the likely firms that can be viewed as born global will not be major domestic trading companies but digital enterprises. Many companies in the digital economy are by their nature born global from the outset. We have already seen the explosive international expansion of Airbnb from a small start-up to the second-largest accommodation provider in the world. Other born global firms that are familiar to most of us are Facebook, Uber, Amazon, and LinkedIn from the USA and Skype from Denmark, which was acquired by Microsoft in 2011 for $8.5 billion.

The 'born global' concept was first used by Rennie (1993) and describes the development that a firm does not need to evolve into a large organization in order to internationalize. In a digital economy e-commerce companies can overcome barriers to internationalization and can do so quickly and cheaply.

In their review of the literature on born global companies Rasmussen and Tanev (2015: 13) identify six characteristics and entrepreneurial challenges of early internationalization.

1. The decision of a born global firm to engage in a systematic internationalization process is usually determined by its nature—the type of technology that is being developed or the firm's specialization within the specific industry sector, value chain, or market (Jones et al. 2011).
2. Born global firms tend to be relatively small and have far fewer financial, human, and tangible resources compared with the large multinational enterprises that have been considered as dominant in global trade and investment.
3. Many born global firms are technology firms, although the born global phenomenon has spread widely beyond the technology sector (Moen 2002).

4. Born global firms have managers possessing a strong international outlook and international entrepreneurial orientation. The skills of top management teams have been found to be very important for the enablement of a more intense internationalization, particularly in the knowledge-based sectors (Andersson and Evangelista 2006; Johnson 2004; Loane et al. 2007).
5. Born global firms tend to adopt differentiation strategies focusing on unique designs and highly distinctive products targeting niche markets which may be too small for the tastes of larger firms (Cavusgil and Knight 2009).
6. Many born global firms leverage information and communication technologies to identify and segment customers into narrow global market niches and skilfully serve highly specialized buyer needs. Such technologies allow them to process information efficiently and communicate with partners and customers worldwide at practically zero cost (Maltby 2012; Servais et al. 2006).

By definition, born global firms are multinational enterprises. In the changing global landscape that is characterized by increasing digitization of products and services and e-commerce capabilities, we are likely to see an increasing number of born global firms. Some of them are likely to become household names. Further emergence of born global enterprises can be encouraged by universities and other knowledge clusters by channelling technology and business expertise to prospective entrepreneurs. This is especially important in countries with small domestic markets that force embryonic firms to think globally from the outset, and for entrepreneurs in developing economies to reach out to global markets with innovative technologies and products that may be ahead of their time in their domestic markets.

Six internationalization options

In contrast with the born global firms just described, most traditional companies begin life as a domestic firm. If they choose to enter foreign markets, they have six options. These strategies, in the order of their complexity and business risk, are as follows.

1. Maintain a domestic production base, but export goods from the home market to foreign buyers and markets either indirectly or directly.
2. Enter into a licence agreement with a foreign firm to manufacture and distribute the company's products in a foreign market.
3. Enter into a franchise agreement with a foreign franchisee to carry out specific production and/or sales activities for the company in the franchisee's own home market.
4. Enter into a cooperative agreement with a foreign partner through a joint venture or strategic alliance.
5. Enter a foreign market through an acquisition.
6. Enter a foreign market by establishing a presence through a wholly owned subsidiary.

The organization's choice of the foreign market entry strategy depends on factors such as the business potential offered by the foreign markets, the resources available for international expansion, and the previous experience of the firm in international business. For example, it is unlikely that a small to medium-sized firm operating in a national market will have the resources and expertise available to enter a foreign market immediately by establishing international operations, unless the firm is acquired by a larger firm with resources and expertise in international markets. For example, the UK-based coffee chain, Costa Coffee, a medium-sized firm, was acquired in the summer of 2018 by Coca-Cola for £3.9 billion. It remains to be seen if Coca-Cola will attempt to build Costa Coffee into a global brand to challenge the dominance of Starbucks.

The six strategies for international expansion can be arranged in terms of the degree of control the firm has over the internationalization process relative to the degree of risk and return from such activities. This degree of control–risk/reward relationship is depicted in Figure 12.5, where it can be seen that exporting either indirectly or directly to a foreign market represents the lowest level of risk/return but also the lowest level of control that an exporting firm has over how the product is positioned or represented in the foreign market. Conversely, having a wholly owned subsidiary in a foreign market affords the firm the highest level of control and return, but the firm also carries all the risk if the internationalization venture fails. The characteristics of each international expansion strategy and their advantages and disadvantages are detailed in Table 12.3.

When considering whether to internationalize, firms have to take into account not only the managerial and financial resources available to them, but also factors that are beyond their control such as the globalization drivers which affect the industry that the business operates in. In addition, companies have to take into account geographical, national, cultural, and other legacy factors such as psychological distance between the firm's home country and the possible foreign markets.

Once a decision has been made to internationalize, companies are faced with a number of different foreign market entry strategies ranging from exporting to establishing wholly owned operations abroad. There is no single 'right' entry strategy. It will depend on the resources available to the firm, and in some cases the foreign country regulations may dictate what type of operating presence is available for foreign company entrants. Most companies have to make trade-offs that are often based on the assessment of risk of the proposed entry strategy. As we have seen, different international expansion strategies have varying degrees of risk. The more control a firm has over its international operations, the more business risks are associated with

FIGURE 12.5 International expansion options.

TABLE 12.3 **International expansion strategies**

Expansion strategy	Characteristics	Advantages	Disadvantages
Indirect exporting	• A firm sells its product to a foreign intermediary based in the company's home country. • Requires little or no knowledge of foreign markets.	• Particularly attractive for small to medium-sized companies as indirect exporting requires no international experience and no commitment of resources for foreign operations. • Low risks as indirect exporting is a domestic transaction with a buyer located in the firm's home country. • No foreign exchange risk, unlike in other international expansion strategies, as the firm is paid in its local home currency.	• The firm has limited control over how the product is marketed and sold in the foreign market. • The firm has limited knowledge of the foreign buyers of the product. • Less profit is earned by the firm when a number of intermediaries are involved, which may include foreign buying agents, brokers, trading companies, and distributors.
Direct exporting	• Unlike indirect exporting, the firm sells directly to a distributor or end-user located in a foreign market. • Direct exporting is a suitable strategy for firms that expect foreign export markets to form a significant portion of the firm's total sales. • In the UK, BP, Rio Tinto, and GlaxoSmithKline are the top three export companies.	• Better control over the distribution, marketing, and sale of the firm's product to foreign buyers. • Improved feedback from foreign customers that provides the firm with insight into the foreign market conditions and how the product is perceived by the foreign buyers. • Low-cost strategy to build economies of scale. • Better protection of trademarks and brand. • Fewer intermediaries involved in direct exporting provides the firm with a larger share of the profit.	• Higher risk in terms of foreign counter-party risk as the firm is trading with intermediaries or buyers in a foreign market, which may involve both economic and political risks. • Limited knowledge of foreign market conditions based on arm's length experience.
Licensing	• A firm may use licensing in the transfer of patented information and trademarks, information and know-how, including specifications, written documents, and computer programs, as well as information needed to sell a product or service in a foreign market (Mottner and Johnson 2000).	• Particularly attractive for small to medium-sized companies as licensing affords international expansion with very limited resource commitment in the foreign market.	• The licensor may lose control of the quality of the product that is manufactured by the licensee. • The licensor may lose control of the marketing and distribution of the product in the foreign market.

Continued

TABLE 12.3 *Continued*

Expansion strategy	Characteristics	Advantages	Disadvantages
	• Walt Disney is the world's largest licensor with the firm's portfolio of Star Wars and Mickey and Minnie Mouse characters.	• Allows speedy entry to a foreign market and can be used as a stepping stone for a more committed entry to the foreign market in the future.	• Licensing may encourage opportunistic behaviour by a licensee copying the licensor's technology, know-how, or product. • Licence agreements are based on royalty payments made to the licensor by the licensee. It may be difficult for the licensor to enforce agreements in some markets.
Franchising	• Franchising is a 'contract-based organizational structure for entering new markets' (Teegen 2000) • The franchisor agrees to transfer to a franchisee a business concept that it has developed with corresponding product, technologies, and operational guidelines. • UK's BodyShop is probably one of the best known franchisors which achieved quick global presence in the 1980s under the founders Anita and Gordon Roddick. • 81% of MacDonald's outlets are franchises.	• Requires moderate resources that are committed to a foreign market but allows speedy market entry. • A steady cashflow of royalty payments and management fees made by a franchisee to the franchisor.	• The main risk is that the franchisee does not follow the directives set by the franchisor. This can damage the overall reputation and brand of the franchisor. • Requires detailed vetting and continuous monitoring of the franchisees.
Strategic alliance/ joint venture	• A firm may enter into a strategic alliance that is a cooperative agreement between firms in different countries. • A strategic alliance involves exchange, sharing, or co-development for achieving significant objectives that are mutually beneficial and beyond what a single firm could achieve alone (Frynas and Mellahi 2015). • A strategic alliance does not result in the creation of a separate corporate entity but it may be a precursor to a joint venture.	• A strategic alliance may allow both partners to respond quickly to a changing business environment and contribute complementary knowledge and strengths to seize emerging opportunities quickly. • A joint venture as a formalized agreement through the creation of a separate entity allows complementary strengths to be leveraged more permanently.	• As strategic alliances and joint ventures are based on a shared risk, the profits are shared between the partners. • Disagreements between partners may arise from disputes over management approaches, organizational cultures, differing levels of resource contribution to the partnership efforts, and lack of trust among the employees and managers of the partner firms.

	• Joint venture is a cooperative agreement that has been created as a separate entity by two or more partners. A joint venture may result from a strategic alliance. • Refer to Case Example 12.4 as an example of a complex alliance.	• In some markets, such as China, a joint venture with a local Chinese partner may be the only legal way to enter the market.	
Wholly owned subsidiary	• Compared with other international expansion strategies, wholly owned subsidiaries involve the highest level of risk. • A firm can either enter a market by building a wholly owned subsidiary in a foreign market from scratch (greenfield strategy) or establishing a presence through a merger or acquisition (M&A strategy). • For a firm to choose an acquisition rather than a greenfield entry strategy, the cost of constructing new facilities, installing equipment, and hiring a new labour force must exceed the cost of purchasing and recasting existing properties.	• Low risk to appropriation of the firm's know-how. • Full control of operations. • Ability to appoint managers who are loyal to the parent firm. • No need to share profits with outside partners.	• High risk as all business risks are borne by the parent company. • Could be perceived as a foreign firm by the local market, especially for greenfield strategy. • Possible problems in recruiting qualified employees and managers from a local market. • Problems in integrating management and operating systems in an M&A strategy.

Source: Barkema and Vermeulen (1998).

12

CASE EXAMPLE 12.4 WHAT'S IN STORE FOR THE WORLD'S LARGEST CAR MANUFACTURING ALLIANCE?

The new emerging technology of driverless cars is at the forefront of car manufacturers' agendas looking to the future. However, despite the close alliance that has bound them together for over 20 years, Renault and Nissan are said to be pursuing their own paths towards the future of mobility.

In 2016, Renault and Nissan formed an alliance with Mitsubishi, making them collectively the world's biggest passenger car manufacturer in 2017, ahead of the nearest competitor, Volkswagen Group.

The nature of this three-company alliance is complex. Renault, Nissan, and Mitsubishi have not entered into a full merger, as each firm remains (to an extent) autonomous while sharing a growing number of links into each other's supply chains.

The alliance seemed to be working well for the trio, but analysts were wary of the venture, and controversy has hit the company surrounding alleged financial misconduct, several failed merger attempts between the French and Japanese carmakers, and the breakdown of talks between Renault and Fiat Chrysler in 2019. Unsurprisingly, reports have suggested that the alliance is facing a difficult decision about its future. However, the announcement of a new partnership with Waymo, hailed by Waymo CEO Joh Krafcik as a way to bring Waymo's 'autonomous technology to a global stage', may suggest new hope as the alliance works together to explore and develop long-term profitable driverless mobility solutions.

But how does this complicated structure work, and how will the partnership with Waymo fit into the existing alliance? The complex collaborative structure means that Renault owns a controlling 43.4% of Nissan, and Nissan has a non-voting 15% stake in Renault. However, Mitsubishi is controlled by Nissan through a 34% stake. The trio are governed by a chairman, Jean-Dominique Senard, who presides over an operating board of the alliance, with the CEOs of Nissan, Renault, and Mitsubishi Motors all joining the board.

The firms of the alliance are exploring implementing a simpler and tighter structure, which could cut costs and shore up profits for the alliance. Whatever happens, the logic of the tie-up, which fills gaps in the partners' businesses and cuts costs, is clear. Renault's strength in Europe complements Nissan's in China and America. Nissan brings a premium brand, Infiniti. Mitsubishi offers expertise in plug-in hybrids.

Tying the alliance members together more tightly based on the three firms' complementary resources and competencies could make the alliance 'irreversible'. Yet that brings problems of its own. The alliance has survived where full mergers such as Daimler–Chrysler have failed because the firms did not have to work too closely together. One former executive recounts how Renault and Nissan engineers could not agree on anything. 'There is tension in the system' admits Trevor Mann, another former Nissan executive who is now Mitsubishi's chief operating officer, 'but positive tension'.

Managing internal friction may keep the alliance growing. So far it has experienced growth, despite challenges facing the mass market. Scale is vital to be able to invest in electric and autonomous vehicles. Max Warburton of Bernstein, an equity research firm, likens the alliance to a 'hustler' for its skills in sniffing out opportunities. With German carmakers dominating the most profitable segments of the European market, Renault pushed Dacia, its successful low-cost brand. Early investments in electric cars will ensure that the alliance is the first to turn a profit from them, according to Union Bank of Switzerland. A big bet on emerging markets and new mobility solutions looks inspiring, but will the alliance survive the re-engineering of the alliance structure while allowing alliance partners to pursue their own opportunities?

Questions for discussion

1. Identify key business drivers for the alliance.
2. What do you consider are the main difficulties for managing the alliance?
3. Critically consider the feasibility of continued future success of the alliance. What recommendations would you make to the management of the alliance?

Sources

The Economist, 17 March 2018. https://www.economist.com/business/2018/03/17/renault-nissan-mitsubishi-has-become-the-worlds-biggest-carmaker (accessed 2 August 2019).

Digital Trends (2019). Nissan and Renault are the latest automakers to ally themselves with Waymo, 20 June. https://www.digitaltrends.com/cars/waymo-and-renault-nissan-mitsubishi-alliance-partnership/ (accessed 31 July 2019).

FT (2019). Ex-Nissan executive points to CEO's role in Ghosn's pay decision, 20 June. https://www.ft.com/content/2b701806-8a9e-11e9-a1c1-51bf8f989972 (accessed 2 August 2019).

Bloomberg (2019). Divorce? Merger? Renault–Nissan Alliance Faces a Crossroads, 11 June. https://www.bloomberg.com/news/articles/2019-06-11/what-may-happen-next-in-renault-s-20-year-alliance-with-nissan (accessed 31 July 2019).

The Alliance (2019). Groupe Renault and Nissan sign exclusive alliance deal with Waymo to explore driverless mobility services, 20 June. https://www.alliance-2022.com/news/groupe-renault-and-nissan-sign-exclusive-alliance-deal-with-waymo-to-explore-driverless-mobility-services/ (accessed 31 July 2019).

FT (2019). Renault-Nissan: how long can the fractured alliance last?, 7 July. https://www.ft.com/content/504e1682-9e76-11e9-9c06-a4640c9feebb (accessed 2 August 2019).

Group Renault International Media Website, 12 March 2019. https://media.group.renault.com/global/en-gb/renault-nissan-mitsubishi/media/pressreleases/21222895/jean-dominique-senard-president-de-renault-hiroto-saikawa-ceo-de-nissan-thierry-bollore-ceo-de-renault (accessed 31 July 2019).

such strategies. Hence the managers have to make an honest appraisal of their own capabilities to manage complex international operations and choose an appropriate expansion strategy accordingly.

12.6 **Three generic international strategy options**

In Section 12.5 we saw that companies may choose to expand internationally in a number ways, ranging from export-driven strategies to establishing fully owned subsidiaries in foreign markets. Once a firm moves from just exporting its domestically produced products to more complex involvement in foreign markets, it will need to balance the conflicting pressures of product standardization with drivers for local responsiveness. The firm does this by adapting its products to local market conditions. Selling a fully standardized product across multiple markets will most likely allow the firm to earn efficiency gains in the form of economies of scale and scope (see the discussion in Section 12.3 of the Ontario Maple Syrup Producers Association which sells a standardized product across a number of markets with minimally adapted advertising campaigns). Should firms adapt their competitive approach in each market? And if so, how should they do this? In this section we will consider three generic international strategy options that provide answers to these questions.

One of the key strategic decisions firms that compete internationally have to make is whether and how they have to adapt their competitive approach in each of the host countries to take into account the specific market conditions and customer preferences. Companies have three generic strategic options to solve this dilemma:

- a multidomestic strategy
- a global strategy
- a transnational strategy.

A multidomestic strategy is a strategy that is based on differentiating the firm's products on a country by country basis in an effort to be responsive to the local market conditions and customer tastes and preferences. A company that follows a multidomestic strategy takes the approach of thinking local and acting local. A high responsiveness to local market needs is appropriate when there are significant cross-country differences in demographic, cultural, and market conditions, and where opportunities for earning economies of scale and scope are limited. In order to be successful, local managers have to be given a significant degree of autonomy and decision-making power to address the local market needs and implement activities and policies accordingly. An example of multidomestic strategy is that white goods companies have to be highly responsive to local market conditions. In the USA, customers prefer large two-door fridge-freezers as people tend to do their shopping weekly in bulk and homes are often bigger than in Europe. In contrast, Southern Europeans prefer small refrigerators as people tend to do their food shopping daily.

Global strategy is very different to multidomestic strategy. Companies that follow global strategy are said to 'think global, act global'. Such an organization employs the same competitive approach regardless of the markets where it operates. The firm attempts to sell the same product across all markets by developing a global brand with strong control from the company's headquarters in terms of product, marketing, and distribution standardization. A prerequisite for successful global strategy execution is that customer needs and preferences are relatively homogenous across markets. Examples of companies that follow a global strategy can be found in the pharmaceuticals industry, as some human diseases are common across the world, or consider Apple Inc. that sells a standardized smartphone across the world either online or in store.

In contrast, a **transnational strategy** is an approach that incorporates elements of both multidomestic and global strategy. This 'think global, act local' approach is often referred to as 'glocalization'. This hybrid strategy is appropriate when there is a relatively high need for local responsiveness, but the firm can realize benefits from a degree of standardization. McDonald's is a good example of a firm that implemented a mass customization technique which allows it to address local market preferences in its menu selection in an efficient semi-standardized manner. Another example of semi-standardization is Disneyland Paris, although some Disney fans insist that the Paris amusement park failed to replicate the authentic Disney experience of their US parks.

As is the case in all strategy development, there is no one size fits all approach. Table 12.4 highlights both the advantages and the disadvantages of each of the three strategy options.

Each of the three generic international strategy options involves distinct advantages and disadvantages. Which option is appropriate for the firm is dependent not only on the product attributes produced by the firm, but also on the resources and capabilities of the firm and its management. Transnational strategy is probably the most difficult option to implement in practice. In order for such a strategy to succeed, not only should the firm be able to adapt to local market conditions by empowering local managers to make strategic decisions, but at the same time the firm's management should be able to ensure global coordination of activities in order to gain possible economies of scale and scope without restricting local responsiveness. As is often the case, theory is easy, but the implementation of theory in practice is difficult. When evaluating opportunities for international expansion, in your future career as a strategist you should conduct an honest appraisal of what resources are available to the firm, including access to local management expertise and the ability of the top management team to manage a complex global organization effectively.

TABLE 12.4 Advantages and disadvantages of generic international strategy options

International strategy option	Advantages	Disadvantages
Multidomestic strategy	• Ability to meet specific market needs and tastes • Ability to respond quickly to changes in local market conditions • Ability to respond better to local competitive opportunities and threats • Potential for a development of a market-specific competitive advantage	• Sharing of resources and knowledge across markets is difficult • Higher production, marketing, and distribution costs • Not conductive for development of a global brand and global competitive advantage
Global strategy	• Lower costs as a result of economies of scale and scope • Improved efficiency as knowledge is shared across markets • Global brand recognition and standardized promotion and distribution strategies • Potential for the development of a global competitive advantage	• Inability to meet specific market needs and tastes • Limited ability to respond to changes in local market conditions • Higher transportation costs than in multidomestic strategy • Possible exposure to import tariffs
Transnational strategy	• Benefits from being locally responsive but globally integrated • Ability to transfer and share some resources and knowledge across markets, such as manufacturing • Potential benefits from global coordination of activities, such as marketing and brand strategy • Potential for the development of a global competitive advantage	• Complex strategy that may be difficult to implement • High implementation costs due to the complexity of strategy • Difficult to assess the trade-off between conflicting goals of local responsiveness and global integration

PRACTITIONER INSIGHT: **FIONA LOGAN, CEO, INSIGHTS**

Fiona Logan is CEO of Insights, a multi-award-winning global learning and development organization (https://www.insights.com). Its diverse client base includes LinkedIn, the NHS, Danone, Philips, AstraZeneca, Microsoft, and the Danish Football Association. Fiona became chief operating officer of Insights in 2015 before taking over as CEO in 2018. She started her career in marketing for Unilever, holding roles in Amsterdam and Australia, before moving to New Zealand to work for Greenpeace and then IBM, where she progressed to the role of marketing director for Asia–Pacific operations. She returned to Scotland as the CEO of the Trossachs National Park, a role she held for six years before joining Insights.

Fiona shares her views on internationalization, strategy, and running a global company in an ever-changing world.

Continued

What does Insights do and where do you operate?

Insights is a global learning and development (L&D) organization. We create insights for our clients' people and breakthroughs for their organizations. We do this through a portfolio of programmes and services that combine our IP and practical methodologies. Our flagship offering is Insights Discovery, a psychometric tool based on the psychology of Carl Jung which helps people understand themselves, understand others, and make the most of the relationships that affect them in the workplace. Discovery was deployed in over 90 countries in 2018. We manage our operations through Insights offices in 15 countries, controlling networks of regional distributors.

What drives the business to enter new countries and regions?

Insights started with a global mindset from day one. We wanted to work with large organizations in order to make the biggest difference. Our earliest clients were in the USA as well as in the UK—this meant that we were effectively 'born global'. In terms of expansion now, we follow our clients—we set up and deliver the high-quality Insights service wherever they locate their operations. We then build up a local client base from that foundation. Our initial growth was enabled by setting up joint venture partners—effectively like-minded learning and development organizations—all over the world. We have recently bought them out to return international operations to be wholly under our control. After that intensely entrepreneurial start-up phase, I would say that we are now far more intentional in our approach to internationalization, such as our recent expansion in the Asia–Pacific region.

What are the key strategic challenges that you have had to manage as you've expanded internationally?

We put a lot of energy into localization. The regional offices and practitioner community help us figure out how to localize. We learned quickly about the nuances of language, country, and culture and the importance of adapting to them. We keep consistent to the core of our brand, proposition, values. But beyond that we always need to adapt to local circumstances and client needs.

More broadly, as we've scaled, maintaining the right blend of people, processes, and capabilities is a continuing challenge. A key criterion is that we maintain capability in our international human resources. As a provider of L&D services, having high-performing people to sell and deliver our services is paramount. And as we add many new staff, how do we sustain the Insights culture? We give this matter a lot of attention.

Further, we are always striving to ensure that our processes and systems remain robust as we expand. Staying still isn't an option—we need to be at the cutting edge. Ensuring scalable processes to support service delivery and the client experience is a key managerial focus.

And finally, how do we innovate and remain creative around the product? Insights Discovery has been highly successful. What opportunities do we have to adapt our product to capitalize on new platform technologies and the data that we hold and share? How can we leverage our economy of scope and tap into megatrends of digital and data through our global operations?

How would you describe the global environment at present?

The global environment is exciting! It is disrupting organizations everywhere, but that creates massive opportunity. That is our mindset. You can always find potential in a disruptive context. For example, take GDPR (the EU legislation on data protection). On one hand we had to dedicate significant effort to address new regulations. But we also took full advantage of GDPR to focus on the depth of our client relationships and understand the possibilities of the information we hold about them. From the learning gained, we have been able to refine what we do and put clear blue water between us and our competitors.

We are also interested in the possibilities of digital technology and disruption in learning. Again, there is massive opportunity. The rise of digital may be disruptive for our client, but we can help them grow their human capital around the world to meet the challenges.

Finally, we are also exploring the theme of 'rediscovering human' in the face of disruption. There is something about the dehumanizing nature of being simultaneously more connected and lonelier in the modern context that we want to help our clients address. For wellbeing, mental health, and personal effectiveness, equipping our clients' people—around the world—to deal with the human aspects of social, technological, and environmental disruption is an area we want to develop further.

CHAPTER SUMMARY

In this chapter we addressed the following learning outcomes.

- **Recognize the nature of globalization and examine how this influences strategy**
  Globalization is an ongoing process of international integration that results from, and supports, the interchange of products, ideas, culture, and institutions. The results of the removal of trade barriers, deregulation of financial transactions, harmonization of product standards, and legal frameworks present strategic opportunities upon which firms can build their competitive advantage by operating internationally. The shifting patterns in global trade, such as increasing regionalization of trade, require firms to anticipate such macro-level shifts in their strategic decision-making over issues such as where to locate their value-chain activities.

- **Explore the drivers for globalization and their impact on organizations**
  There are four generic sets of 'industry globalization drivers': market, cost, competition, and government drivers. These industry globalization drivers may create conditions for industries to become global and, as a consequence, for the firms in such a global industry to adopt a global approach to their strategy development.

- **Recognize the cultural and practice challenges in global strategy implementation**
  When considering an internationalization strategy, a firm has to make a decision as to what extent its product or service can be standardized across multiple foreign markets, or to what extent the firm has to adapt its offer to conform to local market, social, and cultural conditions. An ability to sell a standardized product across multiple markets will earn the firm economies of scale, but this is has to be balanced with prevailing foreign market conditions and characteristics.

- **Evaluate the motivations and models for internationalization**
  When considering whether to internationalize by adopting activities that range from exports to direct foreign investment, firms have to consider both the managerial and financial resources available to them, and factors that are beyond their control such as the globalization drivers that affect the industry in which the business operates. In addition, organizations have to take into account geographical, national, cultural, and other legacy factors such as psychological distance between the firm's home country and the possible foreign markets. There is no single 'right' entry strategy. It will depend on the resources available to the firm, and in some cases the foreign country regulations may dictate what type of operating presence is available for foreign company entrants. Most companies have to make trade-offs that are often based on the assessment of risk of the proposed entry strategy.

- **Examine the phenomenon of 'born global'**
  Born global firms are organizations that from early in their founding seek superior international performance from the application of knowledge-based resources to the sale of outputs in multiple foreign markets. From the outset such firms consider opportunities that are present in international markets, and they develop their resources and

capabilities accordingly to take an advantage of these opportunities. Today, the firms that are most likely to be viewed as born global are digital enterprises.

- **Compare and contrast the generic global strategy orientations**
The three generic global strategy orientations are multidomestic, global, and transnational. Each of the three generic options involve distinct advantages and disadvantages. Which option is appropriate for a firm depends not only on the product attributes produced by the firm, but also on the resources and capabilities of the firm and its management. When evaluating opportunities for international expansion, strategists should conduct an honest appraisal of what resources are available to the firm, including access to local management expertise and the ability of the top management team to manage a complex global organization effectively.

END OF CHAPTER QUESTIONS

Recall questions

1. What is the difference between globalization and the firm's global strategy?
2. Identify Yip's industry globalization drivers.
3. What are the different internationalization options available to firms?
4. What is understood by the concept born global?

Application questions

A) What do you consider to be the advantages and disadvantages of globalization?

B) Conduct an analysis of an industry of your choice using Yip's globalization drivers. Does your analysis support the globalization of your choice of industry? Why/Why not?

C) Identify companies that followed multidomestic, global, and transnational strategies. Why do you think that the firms adopted such a strategy?

D) It is often assumed that firms internationalize gradually. Identify firms that became global almost from the start. Why do you think that these firms were born global?

ONLINE RESOURCES

www.oup.com/he/mackay1e

FURTHER READING

Viewing global strategy through a microfoundations lens, by Farok Contractor et al.

Contractor, F., Foss, N.J., Kundu, S., and Lahiri, S. (2019). Viewing global strategy through a microfoundations lens. *Global Strategy Journal*, **9**(1), 3–18.

Studies of corporate strategies have focused on the firm as a unit of analysis, as if the firm could decide or think on its own, neglecting the fact that it is practitioners who think, decide, and act. The underlying motivations, interactions, and characteristics of individual managers of companies have often been missing in explanations of global strategy formulation. This introductory paper refines and enunciates strategic practice theory in its application to global business.

Global Strategic Management, by Jedrzej George Frynas and Kamel Mellahi

Frynas, J.G. and Mellahi, K. (2015). *Global Strategic Management*. Oxford: Oxford University Press.

This specialized textbook on global strategic management provides insight into the corporate strategies of organizations operating on a global scale and explains the analysis, decision-making, and development processes behind securing competitive advantage.

Systematic literature review on born global firms, by Sinan Nardali

Nardali, S. (2017). Systematic literature review on born global firms. *Journal of Management & Economics*, **24**(2), 563–78.

Born global firms enter the global marketplace soon after their inception, bypassing the domestic market in many cases. Sometimes these firms grow largely in their home markets before they rapidly reach high percentages of international revenues. This paper offers a systematic literature review on born global firms.

The Competitive Advantage of Nations, by Michael E. Porter

Porter, M.E. (1998). *The Competitive Advantage of Nations* (11th edn). New York: Free Press.

This seminal book presents a theory of competitiveness based on the causes of the productivity with which companies compete. The author shows how traditional comparative advantages such as natural resources and pools of labour have been superseded as sources of prosperity, and how broad macroeconomic accounts of competitiveness are insufficient. The concept of 'industry clusters' outlines a new way for companies and governments to think about economies, assess the competitive advantage of locations, and set public policy.

Globalization and Its Discontents Revisited: Anti-Globalization in the Era of Trump, by Joseph E. Stiglitz

Stiglitz, J.E. (2017). *Globalization and Its Discontents Revisited: Anti-Globalization in the Era of Trump*. New York: W.W. Norton.

The book addresses globalization's new discontents in the USA and Europe. The Nobel Prize winning author demonstrates how the International Monetary Fund, other major institutions like the World Bank, and global trade agreements have often harmed the developing nations they are supposedly helping. The author argues that globalization continues to be mismanaged today, and now causes damage as exemplified by the increasing inequality to which it has contributed.

REFERENCES

Alexander, M. and Korine, H. (2008). When you shouldn't go global. *Harvard Business Review*, December.

Andersson, S. and Evangelista, F. (2006). The entrepreneur in the born global firm in Australia and Sweden. *Journal of Small Business and Enterprise Development*, **13**(4), 642–59.

Ashenfelter, O., Engle, R.F., McFadden, D.L., and Schmidt-Hebbel, K. (2018). Globalization: contents and discontents. *Contemporary Economic Policy*, **36**, 29–43.

Bang, K.E. and Markeset, T. (2012). Identifying the drivers of economic globalization and the effects on companies' competitive situation. In: Frick, J. and Laugen, B.T. (eds), *Advances in Production Management Systems. Value Networks: Innovation, Technologies, and Management*. Berlin: Springer.

Barkema, H. and Vermeulen, F. (1998). International expansion through start-up or through acquisition: a learning perspective. *Academy of Management Journal*, **41**, 7–26.

Cartwright, W.R. (1993). Multiple linked 'diamonds' and the international competitiveness of export-dependent industries: the New Zealand experience. *Management International Review*, **33**(2), 55–70.

Cavusgil, S.T. and Knight, G. (2009). *Born Global Firms: New International Enterprise*. New York: Business Expert Press.

Chappelow, J. (2019). Porter Diamond. https://www.investopedia.com/terms/p/porter-diamond.asp (accessed 17 July 2019).

David, D. (2018). *The Almighty Dollar*. London: Elliott & Thompson.

D'Urbino, L. (2019) The steam has gone out of globalisation. *The Economist*, 24 January.

The Economist (2018). A manifesto for renewing liberalism, 13 September. https://www.economist.com/leaders/2018/09/13/a-manifesto-for-renewing-liberalism (accessed 20 December 2019).

Frynas, J.G. and Mellahi, K. (2015). *Global Strategic Management* (3rd edn). Oxford: Oxford University Press.

Ghemawat, P. (2001). Distance still matters: the hard reality of global expansion. *Harvard Business Review*, September.

Ghemawat, P. (2007). Managing differences: the central challenge of global strategy. *Harvard Business Review*, March.

Ghemawat, P. (2018). *The New Global Road Map: Enduring Strategies for Turbulent Times*. Boston, MA: Harvard Business Review Press.

Ghemawat, P. and Mallick, R. (2003). The industry-level structure of international trade networks: a gravity-based approach. Working paper. Harvard Business School.

Ghemawat, P. and Siegel, J. (2011). *Redefining Global Strategy: Crossing Borders in a World Where Differences Still Matter*. Boston, MA: Harvard Business School Press.

IMF (2008). Issues Brief, IMF, Issue 02/08, May 2008. https://www.imf.org/external/np/exr/ib/2008/pdf/053008.pdf.

Johanson, J. and Vahlne, J. (1977). The internationalization process of the firm: a model of knowledge development and increasing foreign market commitments. *Journal of International Business Studies*, **8**(1): 23–32.

Johanson, J. and Wiedersheim-Paul, F. (1975). The internationalization of the firm: four Swedish cases. *Journal of Management Studies*, **12**, 305–323.

Johnson, J.E. (2004). Factors influencing the early internationalization of high technology start-ups: US and UK evidence. *Journal of International Entrepreneurship*, **2**, 139–54.

Jones, M.V., Coviello, N.E., and Tang, Y.K. (2011). International entrepreneurship research (1989–2009): a domain ontology and thematic analysis. *Journal of Business Venturing*, **26**(6), 632–59.

Knight, G.A. and Cavusgil, S.T. (2005). A taxonomy of born global firms. *Management International Review*, **45**, 15–35.

Krugman, P.R. (1993). On the relationship between trade theory and location theory. *Review of International Economics*, **1**, 110–22.

Kuttner, R. (2018). *Can Democracy Survive Global Capitalism*. London: W.W. Norton.

Loane, S., Bell, J.D., and McNaughton, R. (2007). A cross-national study on the impact of management teams on the rapid internationalization of small firms. *Journal of World Business,* **42**(4), 489–504.

Maltby, T. (2012). Using social media to accelerate the internationalization of startups from inception. *Technology Innovation Management Review*, **2**(10), 22–6.

Moen, O. (2002). The born globals. *International Marketing Review*, **19**(2), 156–75.

Mottner, S. and Johnson, P.J. (2000). Motivations and risks in international licensing, a review and implications for licensing to transitional and emerging economies. *Journal of World Business* **35**(2): 171–88.

Our World in Data (2019). https://ourworldindata.org/a-history-of-global-living-conditions-in-5-charts (accessed 24 April 2019).

Pinkus, G., Manyika, J., and Ramaswamy, S. (2017). We can't undo globalization, but we can improve it. *Harvard Business Review*, 10 January.

Porter, M. (1990). *The Competitive Advantage of Nations*. New York: Free Press.

Rasmussen, E.S. and Tanev, S. (2015). The emergence of the lean global startup as a new type of firm. *Technology Innovation Management Review*, **5**(11), 12–19.

Rennie, M.W. (1993). Global competitiveness: born global. *McKinsey Quarterly*, **4**(1), 45–52.

Rugman, A.M. and D'Cruz, J.R. (1993). The 'double diamond' model of international competitiveness: the Canadian experience. *Management International Review*, **33**(2), 17–32.

Servais, P., Madsen, T.K., and Rasmussen, E.S. (2006). Small manufacturing firms' involvement in international e-business activities. *Advances in International Marketing,* Vol. 17. *International Marketing Research.* Bingley: Emerald Publishing, pp. 297–317.

Teegen, H. (2000). Examining strategic and economic development implications of globalising through franchising. *International Business Review*, **9**(4), 497–521.

UN (2016). United Nations Development Programme, Human Development Report, 2016. http://hdr.undp.org/sites/default/files/2016_human_development_report.pdf.

Van Den Bosch, F.A.J. and Van Prooijen, A.A. (1992). European management: an emerging competitive advantage of European nations. *European Management Journal*, **10**(4), 445–8.

Walmart (2018). Annual Report. http://www.corporatereport.com/walmart/2018/ar/Walmart_2018_Annual%20Report.pdf.

World Bank (2016). Poverty and shared prosperity 2016: taking on inequality. https://openknowledge.worldbank.org/bitstream/handle/10986/25078/9781464809583.pdf.

Yip, G. (1995). *Total Global Strategy: Managing for Worldwide Competitive Advantage*. Upper Saddle River, NJ: Prentice Hall.

CHAPTER THIRTEEN

Sustainability and Strategy

CONTENTS

LEARNING OBJECTIVES

By the end of this chapter, you should be able to:

- Appraise the importance of sustainability as a factor in organizational strategy processes and outcomes
- Evaluate the relevance and possible impact of the triple bottom line and sustainable development goals concepts to an organization's strategy and stakeholder group
- Explain how sustainability trends in the macro-environment and shifting stakeholder views of sustainability are impacting on strategy-making
- Appraise the relative merits and limitations of corporate social responsibility, creating shared value, and beyond compliance approaches to sustainability strategy
- Appreciate and explain trends in sustainability strategy practice

TOOLBOX

- **Triple bottom line (TBL)**
  TBL is a model of sustainable performance in which a balance is achieved within a system of objectives addressing people-, profit-, and planet-related outcomes. TBL can be used as a framework to evaluate and enhance organizational objectives and initiatives towards achieving sustainability.
- **Sustainable development goals (SDGs)**
  Proposed by the United Nations, SDGs are a framework of interrelated goals and objectives intended to influence national, local, and organizational strategies for driving sustainable development. Alignment of objectives with the SDGs framework can help communicate and explain how sustainability is prioritized in organizational strategy and practice.
- **Corporate social responsibility (CSR)**
  CSR is a management philosophy in which an organization's obligations to society at large are prioritized over other business objectives to varying degrees. Applied to strategy, CSR will influence the sustainability outcomes achieved by an organization.
- **Creating shared value approach (CSV)**
  CSV is a management philosophy focused on growing total value created for an organization and its stakeholders, and splitting the benefits fairly. CSV is increasingly entering organizational strategy processes as a means of enhancing sustainability outcomes and communicating alignment of sustainability strategies to the long-term purpose and obligations of the organization.

Beyond compliance
An emerging managerial perspective in which the full environmental and social costs of operating are considered alongside creating shared value during the development of sustainable organizational strategy. It is at an early stage of development, but is likely to gather strong governmental and regulatory support—and associated opportunities—for adopting organizations.

OPENING CASE STUDY SUSTAINABILITY AT UNILEVER

Founded in 1929 by the merger of Lever Bros and United Margarine, Unilever is an Anglo-Dutch multinational consumer goods firm jointly headquartered in London and Rotterdam. Every day, over 2.5 billion people use one of over 400 Unilever products around the world. Across beauty and personal care, food and refreshment, home care and water purification categories, Unilever owns many well-established global and regional brands, including Axe, Dove, Birds Eye Wall's, Hellmans, Persil, Domestos, and PG tips. Unilever employs over 161,000 people globally, and in 2017 58% of its €53.7 billion sales were recorded in emerging economies.

In 2019, Alan Jope took over as CEO of Unilever. Under the leadership of the previous CEO, Paul Polman, Unilever became known as an active promoter of sustainability as a strategic driver for organizational activity and business success. As an expression of this intent, all group functions and divisions align behind a 'Sustainable Business Plan', which was launched in 2012. The rationale behind this approach is explained as follows.

> We want our business to grow but we recognise that growth at the expense of people or the environment is both unacceptable and commercially unsustainable. Sustainable growth is the only acceptable model for our business.
>
> Our Unilever Sustainable Living Plan (USLP) is central to our business model. It sets out how we are growing our business, whilst reducing our environmental footprint and increasing our positive social impact.
>
> Our USLP has three big goals:
>
> 1. Help more than a billion people to improve their health and wellbeing.
> 2. Halve the environmental footprint of our products.
> 3. Source 100% of our agricultural raw materials sustainably and enhance the livelihoods of people across our value chain.
>
> We know that our products must be sustainable at every stage in their life-cycle, not just in our factories. That means working with others, including our suppliers, consumers, governments, NGOs and other businesses to help create the major changes that are needed to address the biggest challenges facing our world.
>
> https://www.unilever.com/about/who-we-are/about-Unilever/

Through the sustainable business plan, Unilever manages a suite of 'sustainable living' brands—products that are made, marketed, and sold in ways that minimize environmental impact, contribute to social initiatives, and deliver financial benefits to Unilever and its supply chain. According to Polman, in 2017 its 26 Sustainable Living brands grew 46% faster than the rest of the business and delivered 70% of its turnover growth. In addition to financial performance, Unilever tracks performance towards sustainable development outcomes that 'decouple our growth from our environmental footprint, while increasing our positive social impact'.

Unilever's strategic focus on sustainability is described by Polman as part of a long-term vision to 'make purpose pay'. Critiquing organizational leadership approaches that treat sustainability as a peripheral concern or subordinate function, Polman comments:

> The CEO has to lead the charge. In multiple companies and change efforts, when the development of the sustainable business model

is delegated to the corporate social responsibility office or another task force, it fails or happens only halfheartedly.

https://www.brandchannel.com/2018/05/10/unilever_sustainable_living_brands_good_business/

In Polman's view, sustainability must be woven into strategy and all aspects of the organization's functioning if it is to be successful as a long-term driver of success. Organizational leadership is crucial in making this happen. The handover from Polman to Jope will be the first test of whether sustainability is engrained in the leadership culture of Unilever.

In addition to his role with Unilever, Polman demonstrated his conviction to this cause by taking on the role of chairman of the World Business Council for Sustainable Development, a collaborative endeavour of around 200 organizations seeking business solutions to the most pressing sustainability challenges. Through Polman's involvement, Unilever contribute to, and benefit from, the generation of sustainable developments and technology through this network.

The realization of Unilever's sustainability-focused business strategy has not been without setbacks. For example, it was strongly criticized for the social impacts of decommissioning the historic site of one its most famous brands, allegations of linkages to negative environmental practices were levelled by third-sector groups, and a hostile takeover had to be defended in 2017 with implications for cost-cutting and strategic performance. Nonetheless, as Unilever refines and evolves its business practices towards achieving the three big goals of the USLP, it continues to break ground in exemplifying how established multinationals can drive strategic business performance through sustainability.

Questions for discussion

1. What does sustainability seem to mean in the context of Unilever's strategy?
2. Despite Polman's criticism of the approach, might it still be to an organization's advantage to engage with sustainability as a peripheral concern, rather than not at all?
3. Consider the focus areas highlighted for incorporating sustainability into organizational strategy and practice. Which of the suggestions seem most important, and why?

Sources

https://www.unilever.com/about/who-we-are/about-Unilever/

https://www.brandchannel.com/2018/05/10/unilever_sustainable_living_brands_good_business/

Bhattacharya, C.B. and Polman, P. (2017). Sustainability lessons from the front lines. *MIT Sloan Management Review*, **58**(2), 1–13.

https://www.wbcsd.org/

https://www.theguardian.com/business/2018/jan/04/unilever-to-close-160-year-old-colmans-mustard-factory-in-norwich

https://www.theguardian.com/environment/2017/jul/21/pepsico-unilever-and-nestle-accused-of-complicity-in-illegal-rainforest-destruction

https://www.theguardian.com/business/2017/feb/17/unilever-rejects-kraft-heinz-mega-merger

https://www.theguardian.com/business/nils-pratley-on-finance/2017/feb/22/humbled-unilever-show-shareholders-values-loyalty

13.1 **Introduction**

The concept of sustainability increasingly features in organizational communications about strategy in a wide range of ways. A review of any sample of organizational websites is as likely to identify sustainability as a core value, strategic objective, business function, or key operating principle. Sustainability also appears to be a matter of importance to an organization's stakeholders. Increasingly, shareholders and institutional investors (Winston 2018) are concerned with sustainability as:

- an indicator of long-term value-creation potential
- whether new and existing talent consider an organization's attitude to sustainability as an influencing factor in their choice of employer

- whether local communities and non-governmental organizations (NGOs) seek assurances about the sustainability and responsibility of an organization's way of doing business
- how local and national government regulate and encourage commitment to enhanced sustainability.

In this chapter we examine what sustainability means and how it influences those making and managing strategy. For some, the concept of sustainability presents a set of wicked problems for which there are no easy or practical solutions in a consumption-focused world (Dentoni et al. 2016). There is a growing view that sustainability is a 'megatrend'—meaning a global shift, such as globalization or digital technologies—that is reshaping the world and changing the way we live and do business (PWC 2019); sustainable approaches will increasingly impact all organizations, industries, societies, and nations (Lubin and Esty 2010). Those organizations that build their sustainability capabilities and credentials now will be well placed to benefit from many new opportunities arising from the sustainability megatrend in the next decade (NCE 2018).

We consider external drivers—in the international and national policy-making arenas—which are creating an environment in which sustainability needs to be managed through strategy. Further, we examine how sustainability relates to competitive advantage in both differentiation and cost leader strategies for organizations, and as a threshold capability required for participation in a market.

We also consider internal factors influencing how sustainability is understood and practised in organizations. We review how sustainability attitude and practices shape an organization's culture, thus enabling and constraining strategy options. We consider the extent to which sustainability is incorporated into strategy work or expressed through the creation of separate sustainability strategies. Drawing on a range of illustrative case examples, we introduce a range of useful concepts and challenges that can be deployed through strategy practice to ensure appropriate consideration of sustainability in strategy.

13.2 What does sustainability in strategy mean?

In common usage, the term sustainability means 'able to be maintained'. To refer to an idea or situation as being 'unsustainable' means that one has a sense that, sooner or later, the idea or situation will fail unless some aspect of it changes. A formal definition proposed by the United Nations describes sustainability as 'meeting the needs of the present without compromising the ability of future generations to meet their own needs'. This definition is often applied to international actions and initiatives, such as the Paris agreement on climate change (UNFCCC 2019). However, it can be applied to the actions and systems of organizations, communities, and even individuals.

Sustainability describes the capacity of a system to continue over time. If we adopt the perspective that the sole purpose of an organization is to generate economic value for shareholders, questions of sustainability focus on the potential to deliver financial returns and expenditure on a continuing basis. Sustainability in this context means taking actions and financial decisions in the present which don't jeopardize the future capability of the firm to create economic value for shareholders (Elkington 2017). However, if we consider organizations to be part of a broader ecosystem with natural, commercial, and social strands, sustainability can only be achieved with a broader set of objectives. With this stakeholder view, sustainability implies understanding and managing the impact of actions taken today by an individual or organization on the future of the financial, social, and natural environmental systems in which they are embedded (Eccles and Serafeim 2013).

The attitude to sustainability described in organizational strategy or reflected in the practices of employees and leaders can be considered an attribute of an organization's culture that influences the possibilities of sustainability (Wickert and de Bakker 2019). For some organizations, a commitment to a stakeholder view of sustainability is so woven into the fabric of organizational practice and strategic decision-making that it is taken for granted (see Case Example 13.1 on CMS Windows). For others, sustainability is treated as a cost that needs to be managed through exceptional organizational practice and isolated strategic decision-making.

Understanding how sustainability is viewed in an organization is a crucial piece of contextual understanding for the strategy practitioner. Attitude to sustainability will have a bearing on which strategic options are best suited to the organizational culture and sense of purpose (Geradts and Bocken 2019). Further, strategy practitioners may be called upon to produce a sustainability strategy. In this chapter our aim is to equip you as a strategy student to be able to engage with the concept of sustainability as part of any strategy process, and to be able to develop a sustainability strategy if required.

The triple bottom line

A well-known conceptual model for sustainability is the **triple bottom line (TBL)** shown in Figure 13.1. First articulated by Elkington in 1994, the TBL proposes that systemic sustainability should be evaluated on the combined basis of economic, social, and environmental performance which delivers profit-, people-, and planet-related outcomes, respectively (Elkington 1998). At an organizational level, it is argued that the TBL delivers more value for shareholders over time as a managerial decision-making framework than an exclusive focus on traditional bottom line thinking.

Profit focus

The profit focus remains a key component of the performance criteria of any private organization. For organizations in the public sector or third sector, profit can be read as financial performance. Every organization needs to be mindful of its sources of income/funding and its cost base. Over time, an organization cannot indefinitely sustain a cost base that exceeds levels of income. Therefore, to be able to continue as a viable entity, financial sustainability must be given due consideration as part of organizational strategizing (Santos and Williamson 2015). In the strategy process, financial sustainability implies the use of cost–benefit analysis and business case thinking in the review of possible projects, and a review of organizational finances and cash flow for continuing operations. However, a profit focus doesn't preclude people or planet gains. As Kurt Kuehn, the chief financial officer of the multinational delivery firm UPS, notes, socially and environmentally beneficial initiatives that emphasize efficiency can also contribute to financial sustainability (Kuehn and McIntire 2014).

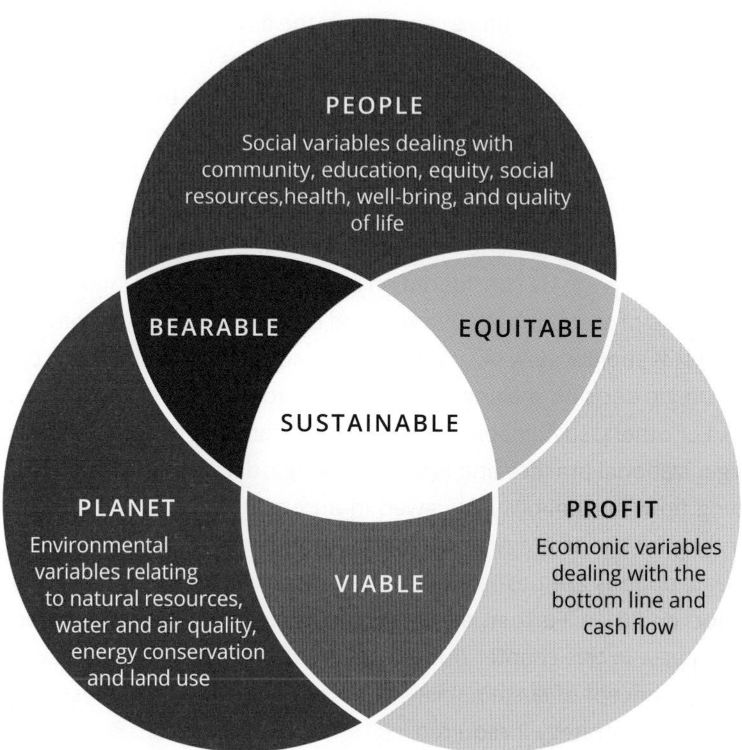

FIGURE 13.1 The triple bottom line: balancing people, planet, and profit.
Source: Copyright © 2019 All Rights Reserved by BNAC Environmental Solutions Inc.

13

People focus

A people focus directs attention to how organizations impact on their stakeholders such as employees, shareholders, owners, customers, and suppliers. Each person with a 'stake' in the organization will have a sense of the fairness and acceptability of how the organization operates, its viability over time, and whether their individual relationship with the organization can be maintained. A people focus can result in positive outcomes for an organization. For instance, in an examination of a selection of social enterprises—businesses with a social or environmental mission—in Vietnam, Truong and Barraket (2018:2963) found that considerate treatment of staff and their families by the employer led to reciprocal goodwill and effort from employees which enabled the organizations to grow in a resource-constrained environment.

A positive impact on the local communities in which an organization is embedded can arise from a people focus. Caesar's Entertainment, one of the world's largest gaming companies, has won more than 50 awards for its sustainability leadership efforts to 'act responsibly with its customers, support local communities, treat employees with respect and support them in building satisfying careers' (Posner and Kiron 2013:65). However, as users of infrastructure and resources, and as inhabitants of local spaces and places, there is also a potential for organizations to be a nuisance. Community influence on politicians and regulators can be impactful, and therefore many organizations deem it prudent to consider how to maintain a positive relationship with local communities as part of strategy and sustainability thinking.

Planet focus

A planet focus is about the relationship between an organization and the natural environment—how finite resources and energy are used, how waste is created and managed, and how climate change is impacted by organizational activities. The concept of natural capital—natural resources linked to location and geographical conditions (introduced in Chapter 6)—is highly relevant to a planet focus. For an organization to be considered sustainable, the land it owns and the physical environment it inhabits must be maintained to at least a minimum threshold level. Others go further and focus on planet outcomes as a key feature of their business. For instance, Bureo is a Chilean start-up that recycles discarded fishing nets into its Netplus range of affordable nets for the fishing industry, whilst reclaiming hundreds of tonnes of marine plastic pollution.

Further, all organizations are embedded in, impacted by, and have an impact on climate. Climate describes the patterns in weather conditions in any given area. Climate change describes a shift in weather conditions in an area over time, often with consequences for natural environmental conditions. Climate change can have a profound impact on natural ecosystems, including systems of human behaviour and organizational activity. With implications for living standards around the world, climate change is also a major international concern for governments and intergovernmental organizations such as the United Nations (UN). Increasingly, environmental sustainability is a core topic for organizations to consider because of government policy and regulation. Further, consideration of how to manage organizational inputs and outputs, energy, waste, pollution, and emissions, and the relationship with the natural ecosystems and climate, is becoming a mandatory feature of strategy practice. For example, Fairtrade requires the adoption of sustainable agricultural practices as part of its support for coffee farmer groups, minimizing climate impact whilst protecting the fertility of the land and future production potential (Fairtrade 2019).

Sustainability as a system

An important feature of the TBL model is that each component is interrelated—sustainability is thought of as a dynamic system requiring management of profit, people, and planet factors in a coherent way. For example, having a keen focus on the natural environment and impact on individuals and societies might create an organization with apparent high moral standing. However, if this leads to neglect of financial viability, the organization will have a short lifespan, limiting the positive impact and outcomes it might achieve. Equally, a focus on the planet as an instrumental means of enhancing profit might create a viable organization in the physical sense, but not one that is sustainable in terms of relationships with local communities, politicians, and talented employees if social factors are not considered.

Novo Nordisk, a Danish multinational pharmaceutical company, describes the triple bottom line as 'how they do business' (see Figure 13.2). On their website, the company writes:

> *By promoting responsible and ethical business practices throughout our global value chain and continuously reducing the negative environmental impacts generated by our activities, we stimulate economic growth that is socially just and environmentally sustainable. TBL makes good business. It delivers long-term growth for our business by building trust, protecting and enhancing our licence to operate and attracting and retaining the best people.*
>
> Novo Nordisk (2019)

13

TBL is how we do business

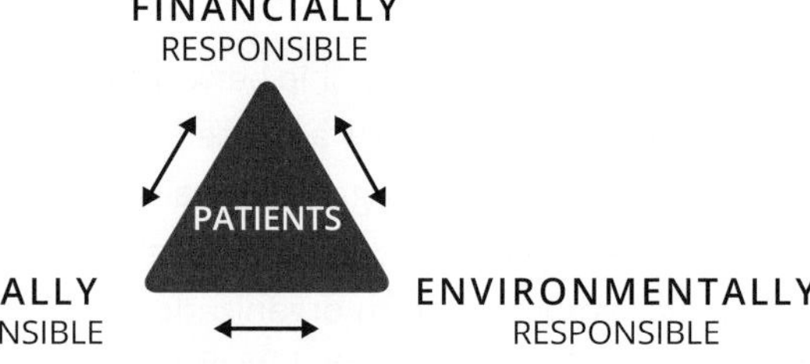

FIGURE 13.2 Triple bottom line at Novo Nordisk.

Effectively the TBL describes sustainability as a system of interlocking priorities. This system works in balance between ensuring economic viability, positive social impact, and environmental stewardship. When too much emphasis is placed on any of these, organizational performance will not be delivered in a sustainable way. This doesn't mean instant failure for an organization that doesn't balance its priorities. Instead, it means that habits and culture that have a finite lifespan become embedded in the organization that will ultimately limit its capacity to continue operating.

TBL—the way forward or time for a product recall?

The TBL has entered political discourse in relation to organizational profits and performance. Global pronouncements on climate change bring increasingly stark warnings about the need to modify our relationships with the planet and each other, and the notions of unfettered capitalism and growth for growth's sake are becoming politically toxic. Organizations that don't give due consideration to TBL outcomes are unlikely to be viewed favourably in political circles (Slaper and Hall 2011). As will be discussed, sustainability credentials are increasingly required to operate as part of supply chains, or to tender for publicly funded work. Consequently, sustainability is a threshold or even competitive capability feature in the strategy work of many organizations.

However, John Elkington—originator of the TBL concept— recently issued what he described as a 'product recall'. Observing the misuse of TBL as a measuring rather than an action framework, he comments: 'It was never supposed to be just an accounting system. It was originally intended as a genetic code, a triple helix of change for tomorrow's capitalism, with a focus on breakthrough change, disruption, asymmetric growth (with unsustainable sectors actively sidelined), and the scaling of next-generation market solutions' (Elkington 2018a:4).

Elkington's views reflect the challenge of bringing about systemic change towards sustainable organizational practice, and the ease with which concepts can be misappropriated. Therefore, as we consider theories and practical examples of sustainability, it is valuable for you to adopt a critical 'strategic perspective', as described in Chapter 1. In other words, be sceptical of how sustainability might be interpreted and enacted within established organizational practice and try to consider how strategic initiatives need to be undertaken to yield holistic benefits.

CASE EXAMPLE 13.1 **CMS WINDOWS: A 'BORN SUSTAINABLE' COMPANY?**

CMS Windows is a privately owned manufacturer of PVCu and aluminium windows, doors, and curtain-walling. From its establishment in January 2006 in Cumbernauld, Scotland, CMS has grown based on principles of triple bottom line sustainability. Housed in state-of-the-art facilities, the company's aim is provide 'energy efficient and environmentally friendly products and systems that not only benefit our customers but have minimal negative impact on the environment too'.

Prizing efficiency in business processes, CMS has always been profitable, remaining economically viable even throughout the financial downturn of 2007–2008 and its lingering impact on the construction sector in the UK. This success has been recognized in recent years by the business press, such as the *Sunday Times*, and the London Stock Exchange. The social impact of the organization is significant—creating hundreds of jobs, education, and career advancement for local people in an area of high unemployment, paying a living wage and signing up to anti-modern slavery initiatives, and promoting equal opportunities and personal advancement for staff. The organization's approach to environmental management has a clear alignment with sustainable development. Their products are designed for remanufacture (future recycling or repair) and use recycled materials from old windows wherever possible. Product performance meets industry green standards for thermal efficiency, minimizing user environmental impact.

CMS has a wide range of industry standard, staff well-being, and health, safety, and environmental accreditations. It has won many awards from local, national, and international bodies in recognition of its sustainable development approach. This includes winning the management award for medium and large entities at the prestigious European Business Awards for the Environment (EBAE) in 2016. CMS's way of operating has also attracted a wide range of industry incumbents, suppliers, and customers to set up a base near CMS in order to be part of its collaborative 'innovation hub' development centre.

An interesting feature of this organization is the extent to which staff and management take sustainability for granted as a factor of strategy and organizational practice. Quite simply, they have always acted in a 'triple bottom line' sustainable way, and to try to do otherwise would meet with high levels of internal cultural resistance. The core value of sustainability, which for CMS means 'We strive to make a positive contribution to the communities in which we live and work as well as trying to achieve environmental sustainability, for current and future generations', has served them well so far, and seems set to carry the organization forward successfully in the foreseeable future.

Questions for discussion

1. What advantages might CMS have over competitors that don't operate with the same focus on sustainability?
2. Comparing CMS with the commentary on Unilever at the start of the chapter, what should be the role of the leaders in CMS in relation to sustainability?
3. Imagine that CMS is presented with an opportunity to use a new material in its windows which costs 15% less than current materials and maintains user environmental performance, but is produced by a process that generates carcinogenic by-products. Should the organizational leadership consider using the new material? Explain your answer using triple bottom line and sustainability concepts.

Acknowledgement: Thanks to Professor George Burt for suggesting the strategy concept of 'born sustainable'.

Sources

https://www.cmswindows.com/

http://www.bqlive.co.uk/scotland/2018/04/23/news/cms-window-systems-lands-record-contract-31897/

13

13.3 **Sustainability as a factor of influence in strategy work**

In this section we consider how attitudes and priority initiatives arising in the international and national political and competitive environments exert pressure on organizations to engage with sustainability. We also examine how views of sustainability within ownership, leadership, and staff populations might impact on organizational strategy. Building your understanding of the priorities and attitudes of different stakeholder groups will help you determine the ways in which sustainability concerns should be incorporated into strategy activity according to the specific nature and circumstances of an organization.

External drivers of sustainability

International community

The term 'international community' refers to collaboration between nations. Typically, this collaboration is brokered by an intergovernmental organization, formed to coordinate collective agreement and initiatives on a specific topic of shared interest. Sustainability is one such key concern for the international community. For example, in the *World Economic Forum Global Risks Report* for 2019, extreme weather and climate change policy failures are seen as the gravest threats to global stability and peace, closely followed by economic stand-offs and political conflicts. In 2018, the Intergovernmental Panel on Climate Change issued the stark warning that uncontrollable and irreversible climate change impacts will be reached in 2030 without significant adjustment of human activity with regard to emissions and environmental management. The UN has highlighted that the loss of biodiversity should be a major cause for concern for the international community. Biodiversity describes the variety and variation in the species of life on the planet. Local and global ecosystems are finely balanced, and as species are lost as a consequence of human activity, the system can be damaged leading to further harm to all species (including humans).

The consequences of unsustainable development threaten life and living standards around the world. Climate change may render regions uninhabitable in the near future—from rising sea levels destroying coastal communities to temperature increases to life-threatening levels in locations with little rainfall (such as the Middle East and Australia). As swings in weather patterns arising from climate change destroy farming traditions and subsistence living in many, typically poor, regions of the world, the human consequences can be drastic. The health, well-being, livelihood, and ways of life of vast numbers of people are placed in jeopardy.

Equally, the concept of **sustainable development**—i.e. human progress that doesn't harm future generations or the planet—promises new ways of global interaction, cooperation, and understanding whilst raising living standards. Taking the lead in the international community, in September 2015 the UN authorized 17 **sustainable development goals (SDGs)**, as illustrated in Figure 13.3 (UN 2019). Each of the goals is a high-level topic of common interest that nations from around the world might collaborate on to bring a halt to unsustainable human activity. Each of the goals has a set of specific aims and solutions proposed by the UN.

FIGURE 13.3 The UN sustainable development goals. Source: United Nations Sustainable Development Goals. Copyright © United Nations.

These SDGs might be relevant to the organizational strategist in several ways (Lamach 2017). Increasingly, the SDGs are featuring in organizational strategy work as an external reference benchmark to explain and justify internal sustainability initiatives. Aligning with the SDGs gives a common language to unite stakeholders in understanding how and why the organization is responding to global sustainability challenges (Schramade 2017). Aligning with the SDGs might also open access to funding initiatives, where part of the requirements is that sustainable development is in evidence. Further, the SDGs are being interpreted and used to shape national governmental policy. As the laws and regulatory expectations of nation states are being aligned with SDGs, ease of doing business and commercial opportunities are increasing for organizations that embrace the SDGs in their strategy work and communications. Therefore strategy practitioners and their organizations stand to benefit from engaging with governments and regulators in relation to sustainability (Santos and Williamson 2015).

National governments

Governments are key stakeholders for organizations in relation to sustainability. Governments contribute to international communities, and so have a vested interest in the sort of initiatives described in the previous section. Organizations that align with programmes such as the sustainable development goals are likely to find routes to productive dialogue with national governments. For example, the Colombian Government has established a forum to engage organizations and citizens in planning how to best implement the SDGs in the country (Mead 2019).

Further, governments have a strong interest in triple bottom line outcomes from their industrial base and from public- and third-sector organizations. It is in a government's interest

CASE EXAMPLE 13.2 **SDGs IN IBERDROLA**

Iberdrola is a global energy firm headquartered in Spain. Owning energy-related companies in many countries, Iberdrola cites a group vision of 'creating a sustainable, greener energy future'. Shaping the group strategy and delivery of this vision is a firm commitment to the SDGs. An extract from the group's website is displayed in Figure 13.4.

> In line with our activity, the Iberdrola group is focusing its efforts on supplying affordable and clean energy (goal 7 in Figure 13.3) and fighting against climate change (goal 13). It has created a specific long-term incentive plan to achieve this. In addition, the group makes a direct contribution to guarantee clean water and sanitation (goal 6), has increased its investment in R&D activities (goal 9), promotes respect to life on land (goal 15) and works to establish partnerships for the goals (goal 17). The company also makes an indirect contribution to all other sustainable development goals and has launched the first credit line with a sustainable indicator to achieve them. The group's contribution to social and economic development of the communities in which it operates and to protect the environment is articulated through its sustainable energy business model.
>
> https://www.iberdrola.com/sustainability/committed-sustainable-development-goals

Drawing on the perspectives of strategy introduced in Chapter 1, we can identify several related ways in which the SDGs have permeated group strategy in Iberdrola:

- **Strategy as priority**. Rather than attempt to do everything, Iberdrola identifies focal SDGs

SUSTAINABLE DEVELOPMENT GOALS

THE SDGs, PART OF THE IBERDROLA'S GROUP BUSINESS STRATEGY

MAIN FOCUS

DIRECT CONTRIBUTION

INDIRECT CONTRIBUTION TO ALL OTHER SGDs

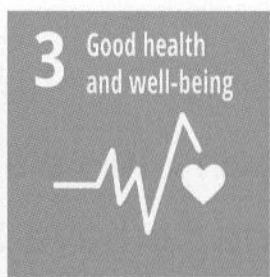

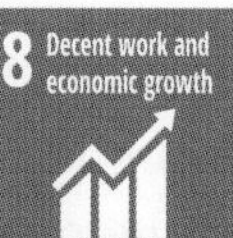

FIGURE 13.4 Iberdrola's deployment of the SDGs. Source: United Nations Sustainable Development Goals. Copyright © United Nations.

and goals where the greatest direct contribution can be achieved. The SDGs identified are best aligned with the core business of the organization, bringing a realism and focus to the subsequent connection of SDGs with organizational strategy.

- **Strategy as possession**. In presenting the SDGs within their strategy work, Iberdrola reapply the original UN artwork and terminology. This use of imagery makes the Iberdrola sustainability strategy instantly recognizable, and aids stakeholder communication of what the organization is working on and why.
- **Strategy as purpose**. The articulation of the commitment to sustainability uses the SDGs to define part of the future vision of the organization. How the SDGs will connect with core business is described with reference to individual SDGs, and long-term aims of positive social and environmental impact are identified.
- **Strategy as problem-solving**. Through strategy work tied to a selection of the SDGs, Iberdrola is directly tackling sustainability problems that have arisen, in part, as a consequence of energy production in the past. By showing industry leadership in addressing these sectoral issues, Iberdrola might create competitive advantage and threshold competencies.
- **Strategy as preparation for the future**. Iberdrola identifies a future in which energy production has to be sustainable, as defined by the triple bottom line. By building capacities and creating resources to meet this future state now, including embedding sustainability within the organizational culture, Iberdrola is preparing for the future.

Regardless of the extent to which one agrees with Iberdrola's approach, sustainability can be seen to be a core concern for the business—deliberately woven into the fabric of its strategic work. For the strategists in Iberdrola, engagement with the concept of 'sustainability' will be a crucial consideration for the foreseeable future.

Questions for discussion

1. If you were a shareholder in Iberdrola, how might you feel about the organization's commitment to sustainability in general, and engagement with the SDGs in particular?
2. If you were an employee in Iberdrola, how might you feel about the organization's statements about a sustainable future?
3. If you were a government official in a country in which Iberdrola operates, how might you feel about Iberdrola's public commitment to addressing a targeted set of SDGs?

to balance the preservation of natural heritage, wildlife, infrastructure, industries, and ways of life in rural and urban communities. In effect, this is a sustainability agenda. A government will also be liable for addressing the negative impacts associated with sustainability barriers, such as climate change. Take for example the cost and disruption to businesses and communities associated with flooding. As flooding arises from a combination of factors, such as climate change, mass agricultural practices, river management, and urban development, local and national governments will typically foot the bill for flooding incidents. In England, for instance, 1136 flood and coastal erosion projects are being undertaken in the five financial years up to 2020–2021 at a projected total cost of just over £6 billion of public funds. To avoid such negative financial outcomes, a government might legislate and regulate organizational practice towards sustainable approaches.

As a consequence of international trends, many governments also sense opportunity in relation to sustainability. As technological solutions to environmental challenges create new industries and jobs (e.g. renewable energy from sources such as wind power and biomass), and

FIGURE 13.5 Anticipated global gains of sustainable development. Source: Global Commission on the Economy and Climate (2018). https://newclimateeconomy.report/2018/wp-content/uploads/sites/6/2018/08/18_NCE_iconwheels-05.png

as social initiatives build national capabilities (e.g. raising education and living standards for all citizens), an emphasis on sustainable development has the potential to contribute to many national objectives. Figure 13.5 shows the possible global benefits of engaging with sustainable development rather than 'business as usual'.

13

Benefits also include global reputation within the international community. In engaging with existing organizations, government may incentivize organizational practice to evolve towards sustainable approaches through funding, tax breaks, and procurement initiatives. For example, a study of local council performance measures in New Zealand in the build-up to more stringent government sustainability laws coming into force showed an embrace of social and environmental practices by the councils. This anticipatory action was, in part, driven be a desire to maximize funding potential after the new laws were introduced (Othman et al. 2017).

Such government activity may be viewed as a constraint on the strategy process. Mandatory responses to local and national government sustainability policies, laws, and regulations may be understood as part of the cost of doing business. Equally, if sustainability can be incorporated into the everyday operation of the organization, government incentives and opportunities, which are withheld from competitors, may be available to the organization. In this way, organizations that go 'beyond compliance' might create competitive advantage—doing well whilst 'doing good'. For instance, Superglass, a UK-based manufacturer of home insulation materials, has transformed its business performance by pioneering sustainability practices that push well beyond the minimum regulatory requirements.

It is useful to note that there is extensive variation in practice between the attitudes of nation states to sustainability. As you examine the macro-context for an organization, PESTEL can serve as a valuable framework through which to understand the trajectory of sustainability within a country. When conducting PESTEL analysis, how government currently legislates—and is likely in the future to legislate—on sustainability might affect organizational strategy. Direct connection between the organizational aims of the triple bottom line and the trends of the macro-environment can be found in the PESTEL framework (Economic, Social, and Environmental). Indirectly, movement in the Political, Legislative, and Technological aspects of macro-trends will also have a bearing on how sustainability and strategy are managed within organizations.

Non-governmental organizations and community pressures

Organizations may be subject to powerful pressures to engage with sustainability from NGOs (Hart et al. 2003). NGOs are non-profit groups organized at a local, national, or international level around a common purpose. NGOs focus on providing services and information to citizens or advocating on their behalf with government and organizations (Conley and Williams 2005). NGOs may monitor organizational activity, praising exemplars of what they deem good practice, and criticizing or actively mobilizing against practice which they deem unacceptable. The actions of NGOs can affect an organization's reputation and relationship with government, and limit possible options for action (Eccles and Serafeim 2013).

An example of a sustainability-related NGO is the B-Lab (https://bcorporation.uk/about-b-lab). Headquartered in Pennsylvania, USA, B-Lab is a non-profit organization that 'serves a global movement to redefine success in business so that all companies compete not only to be the best in the world, but the best for the world, and as a result, society enjoys a shared and durable prosperity'.

B-Lab has developed an audit structure that examines the impact of an organization's practices against governance, workers, community, and environment impact criteria. Organizations showing sufficient sustainable practices and capabilities can then be registered for **Benefit Corporation (B-Corp)** status as a public symbol of their sustainability credentials. At the start of 2019, 2300 B-Corps of all sizes and sectors had been certified in over 50 countries (https://bcorporation.uk/directory).

B-Lab is engaging with governments, businesses, and the UN to develop a digital platform to expand the reach of B-Corp certification and the availability of free-to-use sustainability management tools, as well as lobbying for legislative changes around the world that encourage sustainability-positive regulatory environments.

Community pressures can also have an influence on an organization's practices. The priorities of the local community may differ from those of the organization. Typically, local communities will be interested in preserving habitat, infrastructure, and ways of life. Organizations may be interested in deploying habitat and infrastructure to productive ends and changing ways of life for economic return. Tensions may arise in relation to specific initiatives proposed by organizations. For example, proposals to route waste streams from a production process into a river—even within legal limits for pollution—may lead to protest and disruption from members of a local community.

Local communities may be more amenable to the activities of social enterprises that 'pursue a social mission while relying on a commercial business model' (Santos et al. 2015:36). Social enterprises are characterized by having a clear social and/or environmental mission, generating the majority of income through commercial trade, and reinvesting the majority of profits to further the social mission (Social Enterprise 2019). When business acumen is used to ensure financial viability, social enterprises have the potential to create significant societal and environmental value (Powell et al. 2019).

Social enterprises tend to generate goodwill in the communities in which they operate through outcomes such as local job creation and meeting specific social needs. For example, Divine Chocolate is a fair trade chocolate company co-owned by the 85,000 cocoa farmers of

CASE EXAMPLE 13.3 **NATURA: A B-CORP THRIVING BY DOING GOOD**

Natura Cosméticos SA is a multinational company headquartered in Brazil that makes cosmetics, hygiene products, and beauty products. Founded in 1969 by Antônio Luiz Seabra, currently the company's biggest shareholder, the Natura & Co group owns the Natura, Aesop, and Body Shop brands and companies. In addition to 6400 employees, Natura operates a network of 1.8 million direct sales consultants in Brazil. As a complement to its direct sales operation, the company is currently expanding the footprint of its wholly owned stores and partnerships with drugstore chains, as well as investing in an expanding digital platform. It has an on the ground presence in Argentina, Chile, Colombia, France, Mexico, Australia, and Peru.

Natura & Co is the fourth-largest pure-play beauty group in the world, with a gross turnover of 13.4 billion Brazilian reals (€3.2 billion) in 2018. Natura has expressed a public commitment to sustainable development since its creation (Santos and Williamson 2015). It has strategic objectives targeting a positive environmental, social, and economic impact by 2020. Among key commitments in this strategy are helping to preserve the Amazon and Atlantic Forest ecosystems and ways of life, protecting the climate with 100% carbon neutral products, providing funding to support the education of 500,000 children annually, advocating on behalf of women's rights and well-being, and reducing waste whilst promoting the use of recyclable materials.

A commonly expressed view in the organization is that the company's values remain a fundamental source of competitive advantage (Jones 2012). On its website, Natura comments: 'Thanks to its commitment to sustainable development since its creation and its objective by 2020 to generate a positive environmental, social and economic impact, Natura has become the world's largest certified B-Corp company and the first publicly traded company to receive this certification in December 2014.'

The B-Corp listing for Natura describes it as 'A cosmetics company that is conscious about well-being and sustainable development by cultivating better relationship within the community as well as with nature. They work with sustainable practices in their operations, bringing awareness to better choices for a better future ... Their own plants are

13

located in Cajamar, São Paulo and Benevides, Pará, in which the soap factory is located in an industrial complex that enables them to expand production and attract other companies interested in sustainable business development.'

Natura's leadership appear to be committed to living out their values. Guilherme Leal, the co-chair of Natura's board is a board member of the Brazilian Fund for Biodiversity, the World Wildlife Foundation in Brazil, and the UN Global Compact, a sustainability initiative. He also founded the Instituto Arapyaú, which is focused on promoting the 'green economy'.

When Natura bought The Body Shop from L'Oréal for €1 billion in 2017, Mr Leal commented: 'Natura and the Body Shop have always walked in parallel, and today their paths meet. The complementarity of our international footprints, the sustainable use of biodiversity in our products, a belief in ethics in management and fair relations with communities and a high degree of innovation constitute the pillars of the journey on which we are now embarking.'

Natura are also embarking on developing Brazil's international commercial presence. According to Mr Leal, 'Brazil needs to globalise itself. There are, in fact, very few Brazilian retail brands with global relevance today. We expect to be one of the first'. In May 2019, it took a further step in this direction, agreeing to an all-shares $2 billion merger with Avon in a move that would leave 75% of the new group owned by Natura & Co.

Questions

1. What do you think the strategic rationale was for Natura pursuing B-Corp certification in 2014? How might B-Corp certification help Natura on a continuing basis?
2. What benefits and issues might arise from pursuing an internationalization agenda as a company built on sustainable development?
3. In what ways could you describe Natura's strategy as an expression of Mr Leal's leadership attitudes to sustainable development?

Sources

Natura co-founder cements global ambitions with $2bn Avon deal. https://www.ft.com/content/40c0989e-7cf1-11e9-81d2-f785092ab560 (accessed 26 May 2019).

https://www.naturabrasil.fr/en-us/about-us/cosmetics-leader-in-brazil (accessed 26 May 2019).

https://www.theguardian.com/business/2017/jun/09/loreal-body-shop-natura-aesop (accessed 26 May 2019).

https://www.theguardian.com/business/2019/may/22/body-shop-aesop-owner-natura-takeover-avon (accessed 26 May 2019).

https://bcorporation.uk/directory/natura-cosmeticos-sa (accessed 26 May 2019).

Jones, G. (2012). The growth opportunity that lies next door. *Harvard Business Review*, **90**(7/8), 141–5.

Santos, J.F.P. and Williamson, P.J. (2015). The new mission for multinationals. *MIT Sloan Management Review*, **56**(4), 45–54.

the KuapaKokoo cooperative in Ghana: 'As owners, they get a share in the profits, a say in the company, and a voice in the global marketplace' (Divine Chocolate 2019).

The scale of social enterprise activity is growing. A research report by Social Enterprise UK (an NGO) in 2018 found that there were over 100,000 social enterprises contributing £60 billion to the UK economy and employing two million people, considerably higher than previous estimates. We will discuss the impact of social enterprises on organizational strategy in the 'Trends and strategic directions of sustainability' section later in this chapter.

Shareholder attitude

An increasing concern for owners, shareholders, and investors is the role that sustainability plays in organizational strategy. Lubin and Esty (2010) note a growing disconnect between the importance of sustainability to those setting organizational strategies and the perceived relevance of sustainability to mainstream investors. They suggest that transparent sustainability reporting and the active management of sustainability concerns—as expressed through strategy—is vital to reassuring those who own the company of its long-term prospects. Indeed, Mark Carney, the outgoing Governor of the Bank of England, and incoming United Nations special envoy for climate action and finance has warned financial institutions that the climate crisis may render many of their assets worthless (BBC 2019).

Further, a new type of investment approach, known as sustainable investing, has emerged to meet the needs of shareholders for whom sustainability is a moral and ethical concern. UBS, a Swiss global investment and financial services firm, defines sustainable investing as 'a way to invest for the returns you expect while staying true to your values. That's whether you care about a cause, driving social change, or how a company or country conducts itself' (UBS 2019). Sustainable investing appears to be gaining traction as a consequence of increased societal awareness of sustainability and topics such as climate change and business impact (Cubas-Díaz and Martínez Sedano 2018). The SDGs are increasingly providing a useful common framework with which investors can interpret the sustainability plans and actions of organizations when they consider how to invest (Schramade 2017). Also, for institutional investors, a desire to avoid embarrassing revelations about investments in industries with conflicting values is changing shareholder attitudes. For example, in 2018 the Church of England attracted media criticism when it was revealed that it invested in organizations under scrutiny for underwhelming tax contributions, zero hours contracts, and environmental impacts—all running against the professed values of the Church.

UBS identify three ways in which to achieve sustainable investing:

- **Exclusion**—avoiding companies and industries that don't reflect your values from your investment portfolio.
- **Integration**—select organizations that actively engage with environmental, social, and corporate governance as part of your portfolio.
- **Impact**—alongside financial returns, track the measurable difference made to environmental and social outcomes by the companies you invest in.

Sustainability is increasingly a topic of scrutiny for shareholders of publicly listed firms seeking to attract investment and maintain share price. Morgan Stanley, an investment bank, concluded from the first three years' experience of operating a '**sustainable investment** foundation' that 'sustainability concerns will prove more than just a temporary trend and assume a prominent, and permanent, position in the dialogue between companies and investors' (Choi 2016:62). As you consider how sustainability might influence organizational strategy, the trend towards sustainable investing implies that the owners of the firm, or funders of public- and third-sector organizations, will expect at a minimum strategy options, initiatives, and objectives to be able to be explained in terms of sustainability impacts and implications (Eccles and Klimenko 2019).

Competitive pressures

Competitive advantage—the potential to outperform the break-even competitor in a chosen sector—is increasingly impacted by the topic of sustainability. Whether adopting cost-leadership, differentiation, or focus strategies, an organization's response to attitudes to sustainability within a sector will influence its competitive advantage.

The cost base of organizations adopting a cost-leadership strategy may be reduced by sustainability initiatives. Initiatives that reduce waste, such as minimizing logistics through local sourcing and reducing energy usage can have a triple bottom line impact whilst maintaining a focus on cost leadership; for example, Ryanair report that their commitment to fuel-efficient jets is principally to keep costs down. Further, ensuring that minimum regulatory requirements are met in all aspects of an organization avoids any costs associated with non-compliance. For organizations that compete on differentiation, financial benefits can also arise from sustainability initiatives. For instance, 3M—a global manufacturing conglomerate—instituted the Pollution Prevention Pays (3P) initiative which focused engineering resource on designing out sources of pollution from its production processes. Over 20 years of the initiative, 3M reported a reduction in toxic releases by 99% and greenhouse gas emissions by 72%, saving billions of dollars (Winston 2012).

For organizations deploying differentiation strategy, sustainability initiatives may offer the potential to enhance the value of offerings to customers; for example, Natura's portfolio of sustainability initiatives enhances its differentiation advantage (Rodríguez Vilá et al. 2017). Consumers or customers concerned with climate change, such as local government tenders, may seek—and be willing to pay more for—products from organizations with green credentials and sustainable operational processes. This consumer behaviour of making purchasing decisions to express morality and values is referred to as **consumer activism**, and it has an increasingly powerful presence in brand management (Chatzidakis and Shaw 2018).

For example, in early 2019 Gillette gained a high level of publicity for aligning their traditionally stereotypically 'macho' marketing approach with evident support for the #metoo movement, and disregarding the idea of toxic masculinity (*The Guardian* 2019). Sustainability is a topic which features heavily in consumer activism campaigns. Further, an overt commitment to sustainable products and ethical processes can create a sense of pride for employees (Epley and Kumar 2019) This makes the organization more attractive to talented potential employees and helps to retain that talent within an industry, as well as boosting creativity in product development (Posner and Kiron 2013).

Within an industrial sector, new niches may emerge from sustainable practice, such as Method's environmentally friendly cleaning products within the home care sector (https://methodhome.com/). Equally, there is scope for disruptive innovation in relation to sustainability that might eliminate significant costs of production. For example, British Recycled Plastics (https://britishrecycledplastic.co.uk/) reclaim the raw materials used to make their external furniture products, providing a lower cost base than competitors that use non-recycled equivalents, and allowing them to price their offerings keenly.

Competitive advantage is a relative measure (organization versus break-even competitor). In other words, the actions of competitors in parallel with the organization's own actions define competitive advantage. For organizations electing not to evolve towards sustainable practice, whilst others in the sector do, competitive disadvantage may arise at some point in the future. Competitive disadvantage is when an organization is unable to break even as customers are only willing to pay less than the cost of providing them with goods or services (Bowman and Ambrosini 2007). This may be the fate of organizations that fail to comply with legal standards for, or keep pace with, changing customer perspectives on sustainability.

For those organizations that embrace sustainability, performance aims such as revenue growth or increased profitability may arise as a consequence of incorporating sustainability into organizational strategy work. Whelan and Fink (2016) articulate that enhanced sustainability efforts are highly likely to lead to lower cost of capital, better operational performance, and high stock price. Further, given macro-trends in the international community and local and national government priorities, building a capacity for and track record in sustainability will increase the resilience, efficiency, and relevance of the organization.

Internal perspectives on sustainability

Leadership attitude

A recent survey of executives (Kiron et al. 2017) identified that a crucial factor in the success of sustainability initiatives—from individual projects, to building a culture of sustainability, to delivering triple bottom line outcomes—relies on getting buy in from the board and making a solid business case. How leaders describe sustainability to others in the organization has a direct impact on the traction that sustainability initiatives can gather (Elkington 2017). Without collective leadership support, sustainability will likely remain on the periphery of an organization's way of working.

Within organizations, the attitude of leaders towards sustainability has a significant impact on the extent to which it is reflected as a key concern in organizational practice (Arena et al. 2018). As already highlighted in this chapter, Unilever has received recognition as a multinational aiming to improve its sustainability performance. Unilever's former CEO Paul Polman reflects on the role of leadership and management in embedding sustainability into the organization:

> *Sustainability is a grand goal for multinational companies that have been focused for years on quarterly profits and shareholder value. But financial performance and sustainability are not mutually exclusive, if the very significant barriers to aligning them can be identified and surmounted with impassioned management. Once companies start on a path toward sustainability, momentum takes hold and the organizations can move forward, with the majority of their employees striving toward sustainability.*
>
> Bhattacharya and Polman (2017:12)

For leaders, finding ways in which to work with sustainability—and implement sustainability initiatives effectively—remains a significant challenge. Having experience working with sustainability initiatives plays a significant role in a leader's willingness to promote sustainability in their own organization (Schaltenbrand et al. 2018). Being willing to learn, open to critical feedback, taking the first action steps despite uncertainty, and attempting to engage staff in an holistic way are identified as leadership approaches that will define the extent to which sustainability is nurtured in an organization (Elkington 2018b). Regardless of approach adopted, ignoring sustainability as a topic of core leadership concern is not an option. Sustainability is an imperative that organizational leadership must address (Lubin and Esty 2010).

Employee attitude

Studies have found that corporate engagement with sustainability and the triple bottom line objectives over time leads to enhanced staff job satisfaction, and an increase in staff behaviours that contribute to TBL outcomes (Perez et al. 2018). This may be attributable to an enhanced sense of purpose for employees, and pride at working for an organization that recognizes the shared challenges of meeting sustainable development goals (Casey and Sieber 2016). For organizational leaders, improved business performance and profitability are likely to follow from high employee engagement in developing and implementing sustainability practices.

As sustainability has gained traction as a topic of interest in the mainstream media and in published organizational strategies and corporate communications, employee awareness of sustainability has grown (Onkila et al. 2018). Further, the human resources function within an organization can play a key role in attracting prospective employees by promoting sustainability credentials as a proxy for the values of the organization, and to gauge the personal fit with the organization before making a recruitment choice (de Stefano et al. 2018).

A positive employee attitude towards sustainability is not a given, however, and may need to be developed through engagement work, including communication, education, and incentivization activities, backed up by the availability of supporting tools and work methods (Bhattacharya 2018). The adoption of Environmental Management Systems—operating frameworks that explain how to design and operate business processes with minimal environmental impact—encourage shared sustainable practices and make it clear to employees that sustainability is a necessary part of everyday life (Lyon and Maxwell 2011).

As an aspect of organizational culture, changing employees' attitudes to sustainability takes time and effort. Organizations that aim to build deep employee commitment and capabilities in sustainable practices should expect progress that is gauged in months and years (Spicer and Hyatt 2017). Without a commonly held attitude amongst employees that places sustainability as a core concern for the organization, it is highly unlikely that sustainable outcomes will be delivered in a significant way (Geradts and Bocken 2019). Therefore strengthening and aligning employee attitudes to sustainability is a matter of strategic concern for organizations. Equally, understanding existing attitude to sustainability as part of the cultural resources of the organization will help you in evaluating options for action in strategy work.

Sustainability as a factor of influence: summary

In Chapters 5 and 6, we reviewed how external and internal environmental factors might be analysed, understood, and incorporated into strategy work. In this section, we have examined how—from international initiatives, through governmental policies, to pressure from competitors, NGOs, and communities—sustainability as an external consideration is increasingly a factor of relevance and interest to those making strategy in organizations. Further, we have considered how 'internal' stakeholder views from shareholders, leaders, and employees are increasingly elevating the importance of sustainability in strategy work. In the next section, we will examine ways in which sustainability might be embedded and enacted in organizational strategy.

13.4 Embedding sustainability in strategy

If sustainability is now an imperative in organizational strategy, what routes might be available for you to embed it in strategy? In this section, we discuss the concept of **corporate social responsibility**, examine the newer concept of **creating shared value** as a strategic initiative, and consider some practical guides nominated by business practitioners for embedding sustainability in strategy.

Corporate social responsibility

Corporate social responsibility (CSR) describes the organizational attitude towards going beyond the profit motive and delivering positive social and environmental impacts (Vashchenko 2018). Initiatives undertaken through CSR programmes can generate goodwill, enhanced reputation, and legitimacy to communities in which the organization operates (Choi et al. 2018). CSR programmes can also be a simple way to engage staff and leaders in addressing strategic sustainability concerns (Wickert and de Bakker 2019). However, the extent to which CSR programmes make an adequate contribution to triple bottom line outcomes remains an open question.

Freeman and Dmytriyev (2017) propose that the sustainability needs of stakeholders and the scope of CSR only partially overlap. Both CSR and stakeholder theory argue for the importance of incorporating societal interests into business activity, as firms are an integral part of any society. However, whilst stakeholder theory considers responsibility to the wider society important, but only as one part among the firm's other corporate responsibilities, CSR theory prioritizes the firm's responsibility to society over other business responsibilities. Figure 13.6 illustrates the relationship between stakeholder theory and CSR.

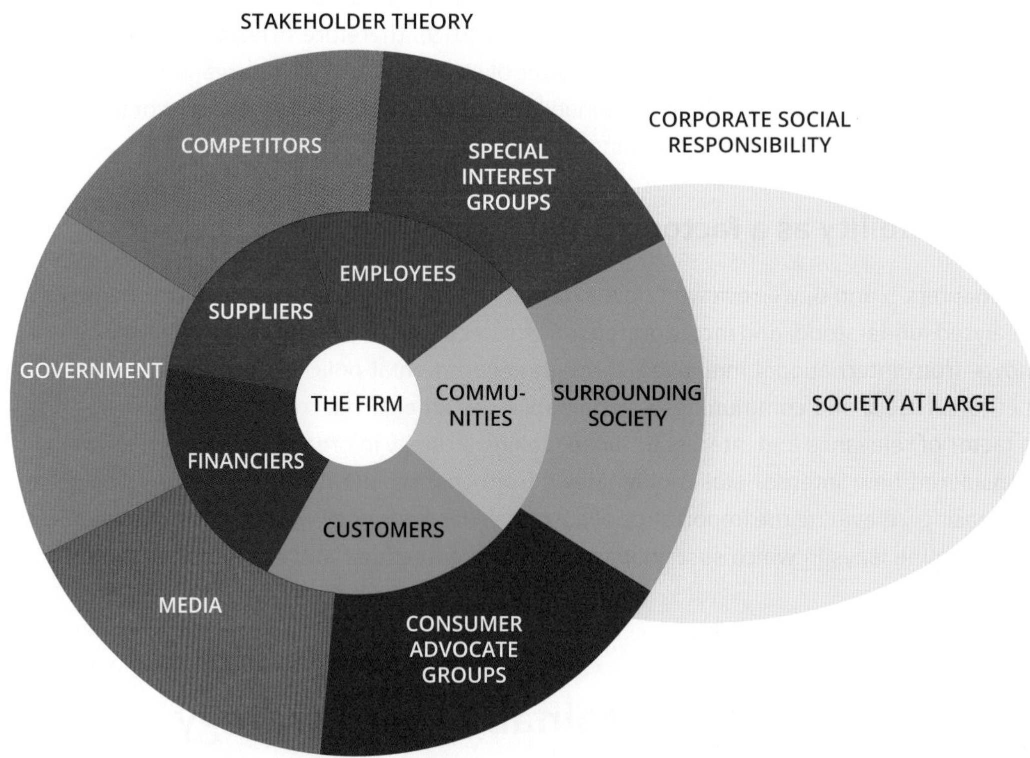

FIGURE 13.6 The relationship between stakeholder theory and CSR. Source: Reproduced from Freeman, R.E. and Dmytriyev, S. (2017). Corporate social responsibility and stakeholder theory: learning from each other. *Emerging Issues in Management*, **2**, 7–15. http://dx.doi.org/10.4468/2017.1.02freeman.dmytriyev. CC BY 4.0.

13

In Figure 13.6, the inner ring represents the organization's immediate stakeholders over which it has some degree of control. The outer ring includes groups of secondary stakeholders which, as described in Chapter 4, may exercise a powerful influence over the activities of the organization, but over which the organization has little control. With an ever-growing interest in the activities of organizations by NGOs, consumer groups, and communities, as described earlier in this chapter, there is a need to identify organizational strategy approaches with the potential to manage and influence all stakeholders appropriately. In this regard, CSR can help but only in a limited way, as certain stakeholders are prioritized over others, as shown in Figure 13.6.

Depending on its governance approach and values, an organization may undertake CSR initiatives for reasons ranging from pure philanthropy, to environmental concerns, to an active pursuit of enhanced value for all (Rangan et al. 2015). For example, Sheth and Babiak (2010) find that the attitude to winning in professional sports organizations has an impact on motivations for CSR (see also Babiak and Kihl (2018) for a case study of CSR engagement with a range of stakeholders by a baseball team). Whilst CSR may be core to an organization, it is not uncommon for CSR programmes to be viewed as unrelated activities detached from the overall strategy of the firm and without top management sponsorship. In order to make CSR initiatives impactful and sustainable, organizations must develop coherent strategies that tie CSR into their business models and avoid unnecessarily compromising continuing operations (Costa et al. 2015). For this to succeed, economic issues should not be separated from social, business, ethical, and environmental factors. Crucially, profit-making and societal gain should not be perceived to be moving in opposite directions (Freeman 1984; Harris and Freeman 2008).

Creating shared value

For those involved in organizational strategy, how might engagement with the 'secondary' stakeholders identified in Figure 13.6 be managed through CSR as part of organizational practice and strategy? Porter and Kramer (2011) state that most firms remain stuck in a 'social responsibility' mindset in which societal issues remain on the periphery, and are not an integral part of strategy (yet, paradoxically, the more that organizations embrace a stakeholder view, the more they are blamed for society's failures). In response, they advocate a new business model of creating shared value (CSV) (Porter and Kramer 2011). The key principle of a CSV strategy is that it must explain how economic value can be created in a way that creates social value, and that social value initiatives deliver economic returns—for example, investing in a wellness programme that boosts the health of employees and their families, reducing absenteeism and raising productivity.

As a management philosophy, CSV considers that the concept of value is defined as benefits relative to costs, not benefits alone. Those costs could be to the natural environment or local communities, typically not considered within the boundaries of accounting conventions. Therefore organizations increasingly need to create new business and/or operating models that take into account society's needs whilst building a profitable enterprise (Pfitzer et al. 2013).

With a CSV approach, novel ways of achieving economic success which delivers societal benefits may be uncovered, such as Samsung has achieved by embracing CSV (albeit with an initial aim of helping to boost its reputation) (Lee 2019). If CSV thinking can be incorporated in an organization's strategy, then profitability and competitive position which create economic value by creating social value can be delivered. In this way, CSV is not about sharing or redistributing the value that has already been generated. Instead, it is about expanding the overall pool of value created.

For example, the Fairtrade movement aims to increase the proportion of revenue that goes to poor farmers by paying a higher price for the same crops, meaning that a redistributionist approach is taken rather than expanding the overall value that is being created. A CSV perspective would focus on improving crop cultivation techniques and improving efficiency, crop yields, product quality, and sustainability. This would lead to the expansion of the total revenue and profit pool, which benefits both farmers and the companies that buy from them. Studies of cocoa farmers in the Côte d'Ivoire indicate that while Fairtrade agreements may increase farmers' incomes by 10%–20%, shared value investments can increase their incomes by more than 300% (Porter and Kramer 2011). The differences between CSR and CSV are highlighted in Table 13.1.

Unilever and Iberdrola, discussed in the Opening Case Study and in Case Example 13.2, respectively, highlight their commitment to a CSV approach. Skandia, a Swedish insurance and financial services firm, provides an example of how CSV can be applied in the service industries. In 2002, Skandia faced significant losses of up to SEK 2.6 billion ($308 million) as a result of an unprecedented volume of claims against its employee long-term sick leave insurance product. Adopting a CSV mentality, it then spent several years researching how healthy organizations work and piloting initiatives that tackled the root causes of long-term absenteeism. Based on this research, Skandia piloted a 'rehab hotline' to refer at-risk employees to appropriate therapists for physiological and psychological support through career advice services.

In 2009, Skandia rolled out the 'rehab' package free of charge as part of its broader occupational pension and insurance package, and employers' premiums were linked to the health status of each client firm. This innovative insurance product in a highly competitive market

TABLE 13.1 **The difference between corporate social responsibility and creation of shared value**

Corporate social responsibility	Creation of shared value
Values: doing good Citizenship, philanthropy, sustainability	Values: economic and societal benefits relative to costs
Discretionary by the firm, or in response to external pressure	Joint company and community value creation—integral to competing in a marketplace
Separate from profit maximization	Integral to profit maximization
Agenda is determined by external reporting to stakeholders and personal preferences	Agenda is company specific
Impact is limited by corporate CSR budget	Realigned to the entire corporate budget

Source: Based on Porter and Kramer (2011:76).

CASE EXAMPLE 13.4 **NESTLÉ IN SOCIETY**

> We believe that our company will be successful in the long term by creating value for both our shareholders and for society as a whole. This approach, called Creating Shared Value (CSV), is the principle for how we do business. It enables us to bring our purpose to life: enhancing quality of life and continuing to a healthier future
>
> Nestlé in Society, Annual Review Extract, 2017

Nestlé is a leading nutrition, health, and wellness company with around 308,000 employees worldwide, more than 2000 brands in 189 countries, and sales of CHF91.4 billion in 2018 (Annual Report 2018). The company was ranked as the world's largest fast-moving consumer goods company by revenue in 2018 (Statista.com).

For most of the twentieth century, Nestlé enjoyed high levels of profitability, having early on established factories in developing countries and worked with local farmers to improve infrastructure, crop yields, and productivity. However, in the early 1980s Nestlé became subject to scrutiny that resulted in a call for a boycott by some NGOs that blamed the company for 'aggressive marketing techniques' of breast milk substitutes in developing countries, particularly among the poor, who did not always have access to safe drinking water. Furthermore, in the 1990s the entire processed food and beverage industry began to face severe challenges as a result of increasing health consciousness by consumers who began switching from processed products to healthier organic alternatives. Major food companies were blamed for causing a global epidemic of obesity and diabetes, and governments stepped up their regulations to force food manufacturers to reduce the sugar and salt content in their products and improve the quality of their food labelling, often based on a form of traffic light system.

In light of these changes Nestlé has started to reposition its business as a nutrition, health, and wellness company by reformulating its products, adding micronutrients, developing disease-specific nutritional supplements, and expanding into skin health. As a logical extension of this repositioning strategy, Nestlé has embraced the CSV approach to improve nutrition, conserve water, and improve the productivity of its smallholder farmers and their communities. Through a CSV approach, Nestlé has attempted to integrate sustainable development into its business activities which is still perceived to be increasingly important for the company's long-term investors. CSV is designed to bring business and society together in creating economic returns as part of generating value for both the shareholders and society at large. An example of Nestlé's CSV approach is the way the company sources raw materials such as cocoa, coffee, and milk from more than 680,000 farmers worldwide. In some cases, a lack of investment in the social and agricultural infrastructure in a region or country may make it difficult for farmers to supply Nestlé with high quality crops. But, to address these difficulties, Nestlé provides farmers with access to the knowledge and information that they need to increase productivity and establish sustainable production systems (Kruschwitz 2013).

Every two years Nestlé invite an independent third party to conduct a formal review of the activities and the issues that matter the most to the business and the firm's stakeholders. This review is designed to support the firm's strategic decision-making. The issues of concern are evaluated to determine both the risks and opportunities for Nestle's reputation, revenues, and costs. The most important material issues in 2017 were identified as the following (Nestlé in Society, Annual Review Extract, 2017):

- over- and undernutrition
- water stewardship
- human rights
- food and product safety
- responsible marketing and influence
- business ethics
- resource efficiency and food waste
- responsible sourcing and traceability
- climate change
- rural development and poverty alleviation.

Nestlé has attempted to integrate the CSV approach throughout the firm's operations. The company does not have a 'sustainability officer',

Continued

but CSV-related objectives and activities are put into key performance indicators (KPIs) of every employee, from the shop floor to the top management team. Through this consistent performance measurement approach, the CSV philosophy is increasingly embedded into the firm's organization culture, shaping the functional activities of the organization.

Questions for discussion

1. Apply the CSV framework described in Table 13.2 to this Nestlé case by identifying an example of how Nestlé have approached CSV against each of the five practices.
2. What activities can you detect in the Nestlé case that correspond to the profit, people, and planet aspects of the triple bottom line?
3. If you were a shareholder in Nestlé, why might you approve of the CSV approach, and why might you challenge it?
4. Thinking as a strategist, why might it be in Nestlé's long-term interest to try to encourage a cultural shift towards adopting the 'Creating Shared Value' way of doing business?

provided Skandia with a differentiation advantage. Moreover, major value was created for Skandia's clients as sick leave rates declined. By 2014, the percentage of sick-leavers relative to overall employees stood at 2% in Skandia's clients compared with the national average of 7%. Skandia benefited, shareholders were rewarded, clients saw productivity improvements, and clients' employees felt significant societal benefit.

Pfitzer et al. (2013) describe five practices of implementing CSV, which are exemplified by Skandia as outlined in Table 13.2. These steps give you a framework by which you can consider how CSV might be applied in an organization. The optimal balance between these practices, and the way in which they are implemented, will depend on the organization's culture and specific circumstances.

From CSR and CSV to beyond compliance?

Management research continues to explore ways in which sustainability concerns, such as expressed in the SDGs, might be further incorporated into organizational strategy and practice (Rosati and Faria 2019). In parallel, public bodies and regulators—such as the Scottish

TABLE 13.2 **Skandia practices of implementing a CSV approach**

Practice	Skandia example
Embedding a social purpose	Made it a company aim to reduce employee absenteeism—a societal challenge in Sweden—for its clients
Defining the social need	Research the underlying causes of absenteeism
Measuring shared value	Track the change in absenteeism rates and the impact on premium claims
Creating the optimal innovations structure	Allocate organizational resources to research problem and pilot solutions
Co-creating shared value with external stakeholders	Establish a new product, in collaboration with therapy organizations, endorsed by clients for their employees

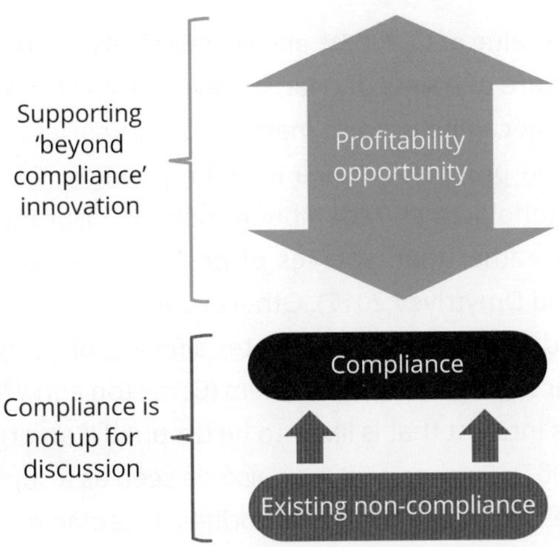

FIGURE 13.7 Beyond compliance. Source: Reproduced with permission from Scottish Environment Protection Agency (2016). *One Planet Prosperity: Our Regulatory Strategy*.

Environment Protection Agency (SEPA)—continue to seek practical ways in which regulatory activities can enhance sustainability performance.

In 2016, SEPA started promoting a strategic organizational approach referred to as 'Beyond compliance'. 'At SEPA, we are changing the way we regulate', commented Chief Executive Terry A'Hearn (see Practitioner Insight at the end of this chapter for further comments from Mr A'Hearn). Unveiling a new regulatory strategy entitled 'One Planet Prosperity,' he outlined how SEPA would be providing expert support and advice to organizations to go **beyond compliance** to help Scotland tackle the challenge of reducing the overuse of the planet's resources. He commented 'The most successful businesses and organizations in the 21st century will be those that are low carbon, low materials use, low water use and low waste. For these businesses, the environment will be an opportunity, not a problem' (see Figure 13.7). 'It won't be an easy journey but SEPA's One Planet Prosperity approach is leading the way; creating the regulatory framework for businesses to go beyond compliance and bringing the goal of one planet prosperity within our grasp.'

As regulatory organizations increasingly examine how to encourage organizations to go 'beyond compliance', there are implications for organizational strategy. Tracking the attitude, initiatives, and frameworks of social, environmental, and other governmental regulators will continue to be an important task for those monitoring external environmental trends as an informant of strategy. This will certainly reveal evolving 'costs of non-compliance' and possible shifting of the boundaries of what may be legally permissible to externalize from value-creation costs. Equally, it reveals that there may be strategic opportunities and competitive advantage for organizations willing to engage with regulators in pushing the boundaries of how to address the SDGs, or implement CSV, and going beyond compliance to deliver superior triple bottom line returns.

The dark side of CSR, CSV, and sustainability arguments

As you reflect on the possible value of CSR, CSV, and sustainability approaches to organizational strategy, it is helpful to be aware of points of criticism levelled at these concepts.

Earlier, we outlined how CSR can be used to make a positive societal contribution. Based on how CSR has been misused in practice, it has a mixed reputation. CSR programmes may be viewed with cynicism by stakeholders as 'redemption tools' or 'insurance' against reputational damage and negative press, rather than sources of positive social or environmental impact (Choi et al. 2018; Freeman and Dmytriyev 2017). Others have criticized CSR for 'moral licensing', which means that doing good in the community creates a feeling of being excused for behaving at a lower standard of conduct with other stakeholders (Ormiston and Wong 2013). CSR is often seen as a 'non-core' business interest that is likely to be dropped if an organization experiences financial issues (Campbell 2007). Further, CSR may also be seen as a superficial act to pre-empt stricter regulations of business activities by the authorities (Freeman and Dmytriyev 2017).

CSV was an attempt by Porter and Kramer (2011) to repair some of the trust issues associated with CSR and capitalism in general. However, it has ended up being subject to similar criticism as CSR. Jackson and Limbrick (2019) note that CSV retains a focus on self-interest above everything else. Crane et al. (2014:130) comment that CSV is 'unoriginal; it ignores the tensions inherent to responsible business activity; it is naive about business compliance; and it is based on a shallow conception of the corporation's role in society'. Bansal and DesJardine (2014) observe that CSV can still lead to unsustainable growth activities that borrow resources from future needs, and Dembek et al. (2016) suggest that CSV is more a management 'buzzword' than a concrete set of practices.

Further, the principles of environmental sustainability have long been plagued by the malpractice of greenwashing—deliberately misleading consumers about the environmental practices of a company or the environmental traits or benefits of a product or service (Parguel et al. 2011). To boost sales or avoid activist scrutiny, organizations may misuse terms such as 'eco', 'environmentally friendly', 'green', 'earth friendly', and 'sustainability' when describing their products or business practices to give a false impression of their sustainability (Chen and Chang 2013:489). This may be particularly true for organizations seeking to build market share in new locations or sectors (Maniora 2018). The rise in social media usage has driven down more overt forms of greenwashing, as organizational claims can now be rapidly checked and debunked by activist networks. (Lyon and Montgomery 2013).

These criticisms seem to be at odds with organizational reality, given the many and varied examples of sustainability, CSV, and CSR practice discussed in this chapter. But the overarching issue is perhaps that practice fails to live up to theory in too many cases—giving the appearance of positive action whilst in reality failing to deliver social or environmental impact. Bansal and DesJardine (2014) observe that a short-term focus on results in strategy is at odds with the long-term view of sustainability required to take CSV and CSR seriously. It is this lack of concrete results that prompted Elkington (2018a) to issue his product recall for the 'triple bottom line' concept. These issues might be reversed by deliberately and systematically adopting sustainability practices that have been shown to deliver organizational performance as an integral and normal part of how your organization functions (Ioannou and Serafeim 2019).

TABLE 13.3 **Lessons from practice in applying sustainability through strategy**

Lesson	Survey finding	Example from this chapter
1. Set your sustainability vision and ambition	90% of executives see sustainability as important, but only 60% of companies have sustainable strategy	Iberdrola's articulation of a sustainability vision linked to the SDGs
2. Focus on material issues	Companies that focus on material issues report up to 50% added profit from sustainability. Those that don't focus on material issues struggle to add value from their sustainability activities	Bureo's use of reclaimed fishing net material as a sustainable basis for their business
3. Set up the right organization to achieve your ambition	Building sustainability into business units doubles an organization's chance of profiting from its sustainability activities	CMS's core focus on sustainability in all aspects of the business lives out sustainable practice every day
4. Explore business model innovation opportunities	Nearly 50% of companies have changed their business models as a result of sustainability opportunities	Nestlé's adoption of a CSV model to refocus as a nutrition, health, and wellness company
5. Develop a clear business case for sustainability	While 60% of companies have a sustainability strategy, only 25% have developed a clear business case for their sustainability efforts	Unilever's switch to focus on Sustainable Living Brands that outperform regular brands
6. Get the Board of Directors on board	86% of respondents agreed that boards should play a strong role in their company's sustainability efforts, but only 48% say their CEOs are engaged, and fewer (30%) agreed that their sustainability efforts had strong board-level oversight	Natura's highly engaged chairman and executive team acting as advocates for sustainable practice
7. Develop a compelling sustainability value-creation story for investors	75% of executives in investment companies think sustainability performance should be considered in investment decisions, but only 60% of corporate executives think investors care about sustainability performance	SEPA's promotion of the business opportunities of 'going beyond compliance' with the assistance of the regulator
8. Collaborate with a variety of stakeholders to drive strategic change	90% of executives believe collaboration is essential to sustainability success, but only 47% say their companies collaborate strategically	Skandia working with health professionals and clients to deliver new initiatives

Practical lessons for integrating sustainability in strategy

To help you consider how sustainability might be embedded in organizational life and rendered a core consideration in organizational strategy, we draw on the findings of a large-scale survey of sustainability strategy practice (Kiron et al. 2017) which was conducted in collaboration with the Boston Consulting Group, a global strategy consultancy. Eight high-level lessons were identified from reviewing survey responses from 60,000 organizations around the world as to how sustainability might be approached in and through strategy activity (see Table 13.3).

These high-level findings can act as a checklist for you to consider strategic initiatives which might embed sustainability within an organization. To do so, you could redraw this table, and fill the third column with a response to the question: 'How could we respond to this key lesson?'

The outcome of the study by Kiron et al. (2017) and further practitioner-oriented sustainability research (e.g. Geradts and Bocken 2019; Lubin and Esty 2010; Posner and Kiron 2013) seems to give a clear message that sustainability can no longer be treated as a peripheral concern in an organization. Instead, concepts of sustainability must be embedded in strategy processes, practices, and objectives, and sustainability strategy should be tightly integrated with other functional strategies of the organization. Leadership plays a crucial role in making this happen, by creating clear businesses cases for enhanced sustainability, engagement of staff, stakeholders, and collaboratives, and the communication of benefits and supportive narratives. For many organizations, transformation of structure, ways of working, systems and methods, attitudes, and even products and services may be implied by a strategic sustainability agenda. And no organization seems able to do this alone—it takes engagement, collaboration, and open innovation with an organization's value chain and external stakeholders to deliver sustainability-focused strategy.

Trends and strategic directions of sustainability

Sustainability-related challenges, trends, practical methods, and strategic options are constantly evolving. The regular cycle of reports and initiatives from the international community drive change, alongside organizational activity, government priorities and law-making, and consumer interests and demands. As you engage in strategy work, it is crucial that you monitor the external context for changes in the sustainability landscape on a continuing basis.

Whilst it is impossible to predict exactly how sustainability will drive change for organizations, emerging trends in sustainability research and practice include the following.

1.5°C

1.5°C above pre-industrial levels will be a crucial target for limiting global warming in the next decade, influencing international and national policies, regulations, and initiatives, and thus organizational operating environments and sustainability strategies. The Intergovernmental Panel on Climate Change (IPCC) is the UN body for assessing the science related to climate change. The IPCC doesn't carry out research—instead it peer reviews and issues regular reports collating the latest research outcomes from around the world relating to climate (IPCC 2019). Its latest report reaffirms the importance of halting the man-made contribution to warming of the

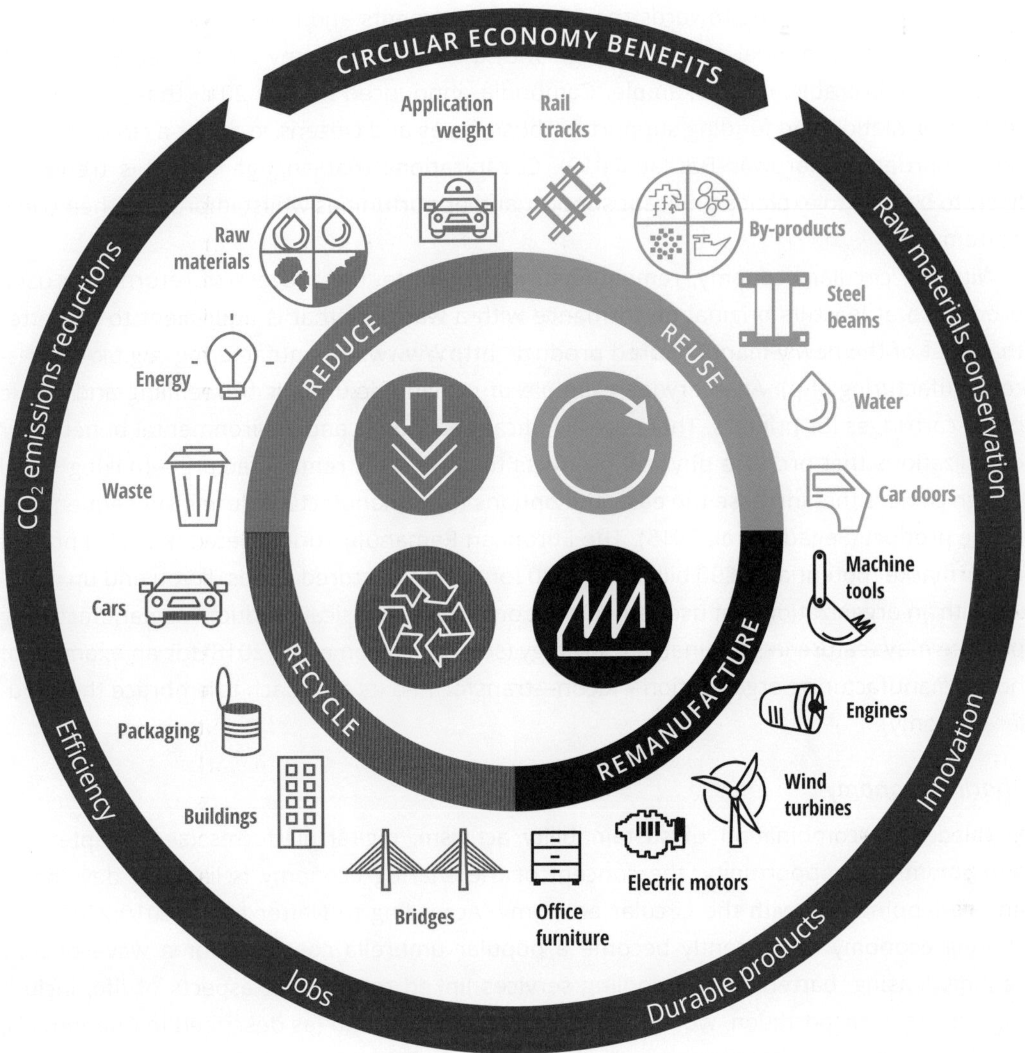

FIGURE 13.8 Benefits of the circular economy approach. Source: From *Circular Economy*, by the United Nations Conference on Trade and Development, © 2019 United Nations. Reprinted with the permission of the United Nations.

planet by various means (https://www.ipcc.ch/sr15/). The implication for organizational strategy is that legislation and regulation will only become more stringent as time passes and inadequate progress is made towards the 1.5°C target. Preparing for that near inevitable outcome now would be prudent business practice.

Circular economy

The international community, through the UN and other intergovernmental organizations, is promoting a move towards what is known as the circular economy (see Figure 13.8):

> *A circular economy is an alternative to a traditional linear economy (make, use, dispose) in which we keep resources in use for as long as possible, extract the maximum value from them whilst in use, then recover and regenerate products and materials at the end of each service life.*
>
> WRAP (2019)

13

As a means of working towards the SDGs, governments and regulators will increasingly incentivize organizational activity to align with a circular economy model (see Figure 13.8 for focus deliverables). For example, Cambodia announced in May 2019 that it would be setting legislation and funding support for businesses and citizens to adopt a circular economy approach (Chorowan-Basilan 2019). Organizations that engage with this trend are likely to be able to exploit significant support and opportunities whilst improving their triple bottom line.

With the circular economy, remanufacturing refers to 'the process of returning a used product to at least its original performance with a warranty that is equivalent to or better than that of the newly manufactured product' (http://www.remanufacturing.org.uk/what-is-remanufacturing.php). An everyday example of remanufacturing is the refilling and resale of ink cartridges for printers. There are significant economic and environmental benefits for organizations that produce physical products to 'design for remanufacture'—making initial design choices that increase the ease and options for remanufacture during subsequent use of the product (Fegade et al. 2015). The European Remanufacturing Network (2019) predict an EU market potential of €90 billion by 2030 for remanufactured goods. If you end up working with an organization that uses equipment or supplies physical products, remanufacturing practice may feature in sustainability strategy (see Hopkinson et al. (2018) for an example of how a manufacturing organization—Ricoh—transformed its approach to embrace the circular economy).

Sharing economy

Enabled by a combination of sustainability activism, digital platforms (see Chapter 11) and commercial opportunity, the concept of the sharing economy is likely to develop in an overlapping way with the circular economy. According to Netter et al. (2019:2240) 'the sharing economy has recently become a popular umbrella construct for a wave of new renting, leasing, bartering, and pooling services linked to different aspects of life, including lodging, transportation, work, leisure, and fashion'. Airbnb (as described in Chapter 12), BlaBlaCar, and Couchsurfing are all examples of digitally enabled platforms that operate on the principles of the sharing economy. A local platform example is a 'library of things' in which everyday items can be borrowed or traded for a minimum fee within a local community. Examples of this sort of social enterprise are springing up all over the world, offering an alternative to make–use–dispose habits (https://www.shareable.net/the-library-of-things-8-spaces-changing-how-we-think-about-stuff/).

The sharing economy fits with a sustainability agenda as sharing, reusing, renting, and leasing are ways of acting that reduce environmental impact, increase social exchange and community, and offer low-cost access to goods and services. There are multiple possible implications for organizational strategy, from options to build or exploit 'sharing' platform innovations to ways in which sharing economy thinking and practices might be harnessed to lower costs of production (Chatterjee and Matzler 2019). As the circular economy gains traction with governments, incentives to engage with sharing economy approaches are likely to grow. However, tensions may also grow between profit-oriented sharing organizations and those with more of a social focus (Almiral et al. 2016).

Eco-innovation

In line with the circular economy, 'eco-innovation refers to all forms of innovation—technological and non-technological—that create business opportunities and benefits to the environment by preventing or reducing their impact, or by optimizing the use of resources' (European Commission 2014). The UN provides a field manual to enable organizations large and small to implement an eco-innovation approach to the design of its products and services (UN Environment Programme 2017). The manual outlines how business model, open, and technological innovation modes (see Chapter 11) are deployed to innovate on the principles of the circular economy, delivering benefits as outlined in Figure 13.9.

In organizational strategy, eco-innovation is likely to be able to attract government funding or tax breaks, and will boost the organization's sustainability credentials. When you are considering innovation initiatives in future as part of strategy work, aligning with eco-innovation standards may end up delivering significant value-creation potential for the organization.

Hybrid organizations

Social entrepreneurs are practitioners who are morally motivated to create social value from entrepreneurial behaviour (Bacq and Janssen 2011). At the convergence of sustainability and social economy trends, social entrepreneurs tap in to resources of a public, market, and community nature to deliver impact (Picciotti 2017). Also referred to as hybrid organizations, social enterprises 'pursue a social mission while relying on a commercial business model' (Santos et al. 2015:36). Porter and Kramer (2011:70) suggest that social entrepreneurs are

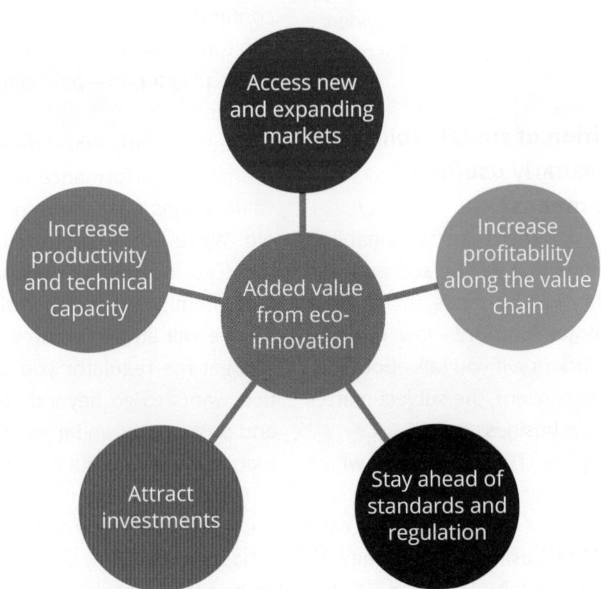

FIGURE 13.9 Anticipated value add from eco-innovation. Source: United Nations Environment Programme (2016). *Eco-I Manual: Eco Innovation Implementation Process*. Copyright © United Nations Environment Programme 2017.

PRACTITIONER INSIGHT: **TERRY A'HEARN, CEO, SEPA**

Terry A'Hearn is CEO of the Scottish Environment Protection Agency (SEPA). With a budget of about £80 million and around 1300 staff, SEPA is Scotland's principal environmental regulator. An accountant and economist by training, Terry worked at the Environment Protection Agency (EPA) in the State of Victoria, Australia, for 17 years, rising to the role of deputy CEO before moving to London in 2010 as an environmental consultant. In 2012 he became CEO of the Northern Irish EPA before moving to SEPA in 2014. Terry shares his views on business success, the environment, and strategy.

What is the role of SEPA in the Scottish economy?

Every human activity takes inputs from the environment (e.g. air, water, materials) to produce outputs, which will result in waste returning to the environment. EPAs were set up to tackle that waste and reduce industrial pollution. There is a clear statutory purpose for SEPA—protect and improve the environment. In addition to regulating the industrial base, we regulate non-businesses such as hospitals and local councils, and manage the flooding service (warnings, prevention systems, etc.). We also provide evidence and expert opinion as inputs to the policy-making process.

Is there any definition of sustainability that you find particularly useful for explaining what it means?

I tend talk about success rather than 'sustainability' as the only organizations that will be successful in the twenty-first century will be those that have a minimized environmental footprint—low material use, low waste, high efficiency. If you talk about sustainability as a separate concern, the subject matter isn't core enough to your business model.

I used triple bottom line (TBL) extensively whilst in Australia. It was brilliant for the time, as it put sustainability on the agenda in a way that made it easy for government and the business community to grasp. But now, I agree with John Elkington (2018a) that the TBL needs to be 'recalled'. If you've got a TBL report, you are thinking about your impact in the wrong way. Take it seriously and TBL is woven all the way through your annual report.

In contrast, the Sustainable Development Goals (SDGs) are a key focus for us. Working with businesses and NGOs, we have created a reporting forum in Scotland to help shift the system in all walks of life as guided by the SDGs. For me, they provide a universally relevant framework for how we can succeed as a human species.

What do 'One Planet Prosperity' and 'beyond compliance' mean?

One Planet Prosperity (OPP) firstly reflects that we only have 'One Planet' but it would take three Earths to continue to support our current production–consumption levels. OPP is about finding ways to drive systemic change that allows us to prosper, but within a vastly different relationship with the planet. We have a climate crisis, a biodiversity crisis, a marine plastic crisis. The one that worries me most is a collapse in the insect population—if this continues, the food chain will be devastated. We can turn it round but we need all segments of society to play a part—politicians, citizens, businesses, EPAs, etc.

'Beyond compliance' means improving the environmental performance of organizations and their value chains past the minimum legislated threshold. We're not going to tell any organization they must go 'beyond compliance'—instead we try to help them see that it is in their own interest to do so. We will always enforce regulation, but equally you get the regulator you deserve. If an organization wants to go beyond compliance with the law and push the boundaries of environmental performance, we will go out our way to help them.

For me, strategy means working out what you are trying to achieve and figuring out how to make it happen. In SEPA, our strategic aims are to help organizations go 'beyond compliance' and for systems of human activity in Scotland to go from three to one planet's worth of impact. One Planet Prosperity is our gauge of success. Within our mandated powers, we focus our energy and efforts guided by these aims, and we adapt what we choose to do as our context changes.

What do you see as the trends in the sustainability landscape over the short, medium and long term?

We are trying to help organizations see the environment as a driver of economic success, not a barrier to it. That conversation is increasingly happening at a strategic level with the people making decisions about how organizations fundamentally operate. More broadly, a shared sense of a need to change our system is growing. Take the Extinction Rebellion events—these are people who have never protested before, and they aren't being ignored. And the consequences of climate disintegration will increasingly affect our daily lives, driving further change in societal views. As politicians respond to voters, laws, regulations, and organizational practice will all move in a direction that enhances environmental performance.

What would be your 30-second pitch to organizational leaders?

Scotland's environmental impact is at 'three planets'. Imagine that you start your next executive meeting with the headline 'Last year our costs were three times our revenue. It's been like that for the last few years, and the projection for next year is that it will be 3.1'. Would you spend your executive meeting looking for incremental changes? No, you'd say, 'This is existential—we need to look at fundamental change in our business model or we are going out of business soon'. If you frame your thinking about your organization's relationship with the environment in this way, then you'll take strategic steps that set you up for future success.

What would be your 30-second pitch to business and management students?

Ongoing, managing environmental impact will be a fundamental aspect of organizational life, in the same way as a response is required to megatrends such social media use or the rise of digital technologies. But you don't need to act as an environmental evangelist. Talk in the language of success that business colleagues care about and act as a knowledgeable practitioner who can help an organization thrive, because managing environmental impact is good business.

often ahead of businesses in 'finding profitable solutions to social problems', whilst being better able to 'grow and become self-sustaining' than purely public or charitable organizations.

There are many organizational forms that social entrepreneurs might adopt in order to benefit from public sector support, and to fit the nature and scope of the social opportunity (Haigh et al. 2015). In this chapter we have already examined several examples of social enterprises and B-Corps (corporations with sustainability obligations built into their legal constitutions), exhibiting to varying degrees social entrepreneurial characteristics. A trend towards social enterprises is growing—Battilana et al. (2015:1658) comment that 'over the last 30 years, we have witnessed an unprecedented increase in the number of organizations that operate at the intersection of the social and commercial sectors'.

Hybrid organizations are also a topic of increasing interest to organizational strategists. With continuing government moves towards the delivery of SDGs creating fertile conditions for social entrepreneurial start-ups, it is highly likely that you will encounter social enterprises within your business ecosystem. Experimenting with how best to engage with social enterprises to optimize your own organizational performance is a strategic move you may have to make. Further, there are options for traditionally structured organizations to 'hybridize' and 'use a flexible approach to their own legal structure to push their CSR or corporate sustainability initiatives forward' (Haigh et al. 2015:78).

CHAPTER SUMMARY

In this chapter we addressed the following learning outcomes.

- **Appraise the importance of sustainability as a factor in organizational strategy processes and outcomes**

  Sustainability has been shown to be an increasingly important facet of organizational strategy. Increasingly, external stakeholders seek assurances about an organization's approach to sustainability. The operating environments shaped by governments, NGOs, and communities set constraints and reward progress towards sustainable operating approaches. Sustainability is a dynamic topic, and the trends point towards it gaining in prominence as required feature of organizational strategy.

- **Evaluate the relevance and possible impact of the triple bottom line and sustainable development goals concepts to an organization's strategy and stakeholder group**

  The triple bottom line was shown to be a system for measuring business performance that balances people, profit, and planet considerations. It is increasingly a common concept used in strategy and business management. As sustainability grows as a topic of concern for stakeholders, the triple bottom line increases in relevance for organizational strategy. However, caution is required in ensuring that it leads to concrete action and the realization of sustainable outcomes. The sustainable development goals (SDGs) defined by the UN were shown to be a valuable common framework which sets out a sustainable development agenda that is influencing the plans and practices of nations, organizations, and individuals.

- **Explain how sustainability trends in the macro-environment and shifting stakeholder views of sustainability are impacting on strategy-making**

  Organizational strategy is subject to influence from macro-environmental pressures raising sustainability as a topic of concern. The international community unites regularly through intergovernmental organizations such as the UN and the IPCC to influence national and local governmental policy on sustainability. Further championed by NGOs and local communities, sustainability is increasingly seen as a cause demanding organizational responses, strategies, and changing practice. These expectations mirror shifting internal stakeholder views, from shareholders, leaders, and employees alike, that sustainability is increasingly understood as a necessary component of organizational strategy and performance reporting.

13

- **Appraise the relative merits and limitations of corporate social responsibility, creating shared value and beyond compliance approaches to sustainability strategy**

  Corporate social responsibility (CSR) is a commonly understood term referring to how an organization understands and adapts its obligations to society through strategic initiatives. Not without benefit, CSR is also subject to significant criticism. Creating shared value (CSV) is a management philosophy which extends CSR to improve benefits for a wider range of stakeholders whilst enhancing sustainability outcomes. However, CSV arguably is subject to the same underlying issues as CSR. 'Beyond compliance' is a nascent perspective that promises further integration and balancing of triple bottom line outcomes through organizational strategy and strong collaboration with a broad group of stakeholders (including government and regulators).

- **Appreciate and explain trends in sustainability strategy practice**
  Sustainability is an increasingly central concern for organizational strategy. Concepts of sustainability are becoming embedded in strategy processes (such as data analysis and option generation), and sustainability strategy needs to be an integral part of any suite of functional strategies. Strategic leadership is vital from the board down in embedding sustainability in organizational culture and practice. Systems, methods, and decision-making processes also need to evolve to support sustainability as a crucial organizational capability. To deliver sustainability impact seems to demand capacity for effective collaboration, open innovation, and stakeholder management practices. Monitoring, understanding, and being able to respond creatively to sustainability trends will be a core component of strategy practice for the foreseeable future.

END OF CHAPTER QUESTIONS

Recall questions

1. Define the term sustainability as it might be used within the context of organizational strategy.
2. Describe and explain the difference between a financial bottom line and the triple bottom line.
3. What are the SDGs, and how are they shaping strategy communications for some organizations?
4. List a range of stakeholder pressures being exerted on organizations to adopt sustainability as focus of organizational strategy and practice.
5. What are the main similarities, differences, benefits, and deficiencies of CSR and CSV?
6. What trends might impact sustainability as a topic of strategic concern in the next 10 years?

Application questions

A) Think of an organization (of any type, sector, or size) you know well and evaluate its triple bottom line performance. What could it do to improve its performance? Use any concepts or perspectives from the chapter to help you decide, and draw on the practical sustainability guides in making suggestions of options for action.

B) Search online for trends in sustainability. Based on your research, nominate three trends which you think will be most influential on organizational strategy in a sector or territory that you are familiar with. Describe how an organization might gain an advantage by anticipating and preparing for the unfolding of the identified sustainability trends.

ONLINE RESOURCES

www.oup.com/he/mackay1e

FURTHER READING

UN Sustainable Development Goals

https://www.un.org/sustainabledevelopment/sustainable-development-goals/

In this chapter, the SDGs were identified as a valuable framework for the alignment and communication of sustainability objectives in organizational strategy. As an increasingly influential framework in policy and regulatory environments around the world, and as a framework that is permeating organizational strategy practice, it is well worthwhile exploring the detail behind the SDGs further. The best place to start is to explore the information on the website—underneath each of the 17 SDGs is a wealth of information. For students of strategy, the SDGs will provide much stimulus about strategic initiatives that organizations you are studying might have to take. Knowing about the SDGs is also excellent interview preparation. When you are a practising manager, being knowledgeable about the SDGs will help you contribute to organizational strategy and the effective delivery of sustainability impacts.

IPCC Special Report on Global Warming of 1.5°

https://www.ipcc.ch/sr15/

To understand future pressures and trends in sustainability (driven by climate change science and implications in particular), the IPCC Special Report on Global Warming makes for sobering reading. This report (and indeed any of the IPCC publications) contains summary statements that will provide you with excellent insights about factors that will shape international and national government policy in the years to come. There is also significant detail and information behind the summary statements, should you wish to dig further. Whilst alarming, you will further appreciate the challenges and opportunities presented by sustainability in organizational strategy.

The New Climate Economy report

https://newclimateeconomy.report/2018/

Briefly referenced in the chapter, this is a compelling read about the future of topics such as climate reporting, international action, crucial economic systems—clean energy, cities, food and land use, water and industry—and a 'new growth agenda' for development that is 'strong, sustainable, balanced, and inclusive'. This report is full of useful information and perspective that will help you make sense of the sustainability megatrend.

The B-Corp Directory

https://bcorporation.net/directory

This online database, made available free by B-Lab, lists the 2300+ organizations from around the world that have gained B-Corp certification. If you are needing inspiration from how other organizations approach sustainable development, you will be able to derive many ideas from browsing this resource. When you click into a company, you can see their audit report and a breakdown of their sustainability performance by categories. This is very useful for students wishing to build insight through diverse examples from practice.

Solar Impulse Foundation

https://solarimpulse.com/

The Solar Impulse Foundation aims to identify 1000 eco-innovations, 'bringing together protection of the environment and financial viability to show that these solutions are not expensive fixes to problems, but rather opportunities for clean economic growth'. Many interesting examples of technological and business model innovations are made available through this site.

REFERENCES

Almirall, E., Wareham, J., Ratti, C., et al. (2016). Smart cities at the crossroads: new tensions in city transformation. *California Management Review*, **59**(1), 141–52.

Arena, C., Michelon, G., and Trojanowski, G. (2018). Big egos can be green: a study of CEO hubris and environmental innovation. *British Journal of Management*, **29**(2), 316–36.

Babiak, K. and Kihl, L.A. (2018). A case study of stakeholder dialogue in professional sport: an example of CSR engagement. *Business and Society Review*, **123**(1), 119–49.

Bacq, S. and Janssen, F. (2011). The multiple faces of social entrepreneurship: a review of definitional issues based on geographical and thematic criteria. *Entrepreneurship and Regional Development*, **23**(5/6), 373–403.

Bansal, P. and DesJardine, M. (2014). Business sustainability: it is about time. *Strategic Organization*, **12**(1), 70–8.

BBC (2019). Bank of England chief Mark Carney issues climate change warning, 30 December. https://www.bbc.co.uk/news/business-50868717 (accessed 7 January 2020).

Battilana, J., Sengul, M., Pache, A.-C., and Model, J. (2015). Harnessing productive tensions in hybrid organizations: the case of work integration social enterprises. *Academy of Management Journal*, **58**(6), 1658–85.

Bhattacharya, C.B. (2018). How to make sustainability every employee's responsibility. *Harvard Business Review Digital Articles*, 2–5.

Bhattacharya, C.B. and Polman, P. (2017). Sustainability lessons from the front lines. *MIT Sloan Management Review*, **58**(2), 1–13.

Bowman, C. and Ambrosini, V. (2007). Identifying valuable resources. *European Management Journal*, **25**(4), 320–9.

Campbell, J.L. (2007). Why would corporations behave in socially responsible ways? An institutional theory of corporate social responsibility. *Academy of Management Review*, **32**(37), 946–67.

Casey, D. and Sieber, S. (2016). Employees, sustainability, and motivation: increasing employee engagement by addressing sustainability and corporate social responsibility. *Research in Hospitality Management*, **6**(1), 69–76.

Chatterjee, S. and Matzler, K. (2019). Simple rules for a network efficiency business model: the case of Vizio. *California Management Review*, **61**(2), 84–103.

Chatzidakis, A. and Shaw, D. (2018). Sustainability: issues of scale, care, and consumption. *British Journal of Management*, **29**(2), 299–315.

Chen, Y.-S. and Chang, C.-H. (2013). Greenwash and green trust: the mediation effects of green consumer confusion and green perceived risk. *Journal of Business Ethics*, **114**(3), 489–500.

13

Choi, A. (2016). Morgan Stanley perspectives on sustainable investing: acceleration and integration. *Journal of Applied Corporate Finance*, **28**(2), 62–5.

Choi, J.J., Jo, H., Kim, J., and Kim, M.S. (2018). Business groups and corporate social responsibility. *Journal of Business Ethics*, **153**(4), 931–54.

Chorowan-Basilan, M. (2019). Cambodia is taking big steps in adopting a circular economy. https://en.businesstimes.cn/articles/112728/20190527/cambodia-is-taking-big-steps-in-adopting-a-circular-economy.htm (accessed 27 May 2019).

Conley, J.M. and Williams, C.A. (2005). Engage, embed, and embellish: theory versus practice in the corporate social responsibility movement. *Journal of Corporation Law*, **31**(1), 1–38.

Costa, C., Lages, L.F., and Hortinha, P. (2015). The bright and dark side of CSR in export markets: its impact on innovation and performance. *International Business Review*, **24**(5), 749–57.

Crane, A., Palazzo, G., Spence, L.J., and Matten, D. (2014). Contesting the value of 'creating shared value'. *California Management Review*, **56**(2), 130–51.

Cubas-Díaz, M. and Martínez Sedano, M.Á. (2018). Measures for sustainable investment decisions and business strategy: a triple bottom line approach. *Business Strategy and the Environment*, **27**(1), 16–38.

De Stefano, F., Bagdali, S., and Camuffo, A. (2018). The HR role in corporate social responsibility and sustainability: a boundary-shifting literature review. *Human Resource Management*, **57**(2), 549–66.

Dembek, K., Singh, P., and Bhakoo, V. (2016). Literature review of shared value: a theoretical concept or a management buzzword? *Journal of Business Ethics*, **137**(2), 231–67.

Dentoni, D., Bitzer, V., and Pascucci, S. (2016). Cross-sector partnerships and the co-creation of dynamic capabilities for stakeholder orientation. *Journal of Business Ethics*, **135**(1), 35–53.

Divine Chocolate (2019). About us—owned by cocoa farmers. made for chocolate lovers. http://www.divinechocolate.com/us/about-us (accessed 20 December 2019).

Eccles, R.G. and Klimenko, S. (2019). The investor revolution. *Harvard Business Review,* **97**(3), 106–16.

Eccles, R.G. and Serafeim, G. (2013). The performance frontier. *Harvard Business Review*, **91**(5), 50–60.

Elkington, J. (1998). Accounting for the triple bottom line. *Measuring Business Excellence*, **2**(3), 18–22.

Elkington, J. (2017). The 6 ways business leaders talk about sustainability. *Harvard Business Review Digital Articles*, 2–5.

Elkington, J. (2018a). 25 years ago I coined the phrase 'triple bottom line.' Here's why it's time to rethink it. *Harvard Business Review Digital Articles*, 2–5.

Elkington, J. (2018b). Climate change is an overwhelming problem: here are 4 things executives can do today. *Harvard Business Review Digital Articles*, 2–5.

Epley, N. and Kumar, A. (2019). How to design an ethical organization. *Harvard Business Review*, **97**(3), 144–50.

European Commission (2014). Eco-innovation. http://ec.europa.eu/environment/pubs/pdf/factsheets/ecoinnovation/en.pdf (accessed 27 May 2019).

European Remanufacturing Network (2019). https://www.remanufacturing.eu/ (accessed 27 May 2019).

Fairtrade (2019). Fairtrade and sustainability. http://www.fairtrade.org.uk/What-is-Fairtrade/Fairtrade-and-sustainability (accessed 26 May 2019).

Fegade, V., Shrivatsava, R.L., and Kale, A.V. (2015). Design for remanufacturing: methods and their approaches. *Materials Today: Proceedings*, **2**(4), 1849–58.

Freeman, R.E. (1984). *Strategic Management: A Stakeholder Approach*. Cambridge: Cambridge University Press.

Freeman, R.E. and Dmytriyev, S. (2017). Corporate social responsibility and stakeholder theory: learning from each other. *Emerging Issues in Management*, **2**, 7–15.

Geradts, T.H.J. and Bocken, N.M.P. (2019). Driving sustainability-oriented innovation. *MIT Sloan Management Review*, **60**(2), 9–16.

Global Commission on the Economy and Climate (2018). The new growth agenda. https://newclimateeconomy.report/2018/the-new-growth-agenda/ (accessed 26 May 2019).

The Guardian (2019) Gillette MeToo ad on toxic masculinity cuts deep with men's rights activists. https://www.theguardian.com/world/2019/jan/15/gillette-metoo-ad-on-toxic-masculinity-cuts-deep-with-mens-rights-activists (accessed 25 May 2019).

Haigh, N., Walker, J., Bacq, S., and Kickul, J. (2015). Hybrid organizations: origins, strategies, impacts, and implications. *California Management Review*, **57**(3), 5–12.

Harris, J.D. and Freeman, R.E. (2008). The impossibility of the separation thesis. *Business Ethics Quarterly*, **18**(4), 541–8.

Hart, S.L., Milstein, M.B., and Caggiano, J. (2003). Creating sustainable value: executive commentary. *Academy of Management Executive*, **17**(2), 56–69.

Hopkinson, P., Zils, M., Hawkins, P., and Roper, S. (2018). Managing a complex global circular economy business model: opportunities and challenges. *California Management Review*, **60**(3), 71–94.

Ioannou, I. and Serafeim, G. (2019). Yes, sustainability can be a strategy. *Harvard Business Review Digital Articles*, 2–4.

IPCC (2019). https://www.ipcc.ch/ (accessed 25 May 2019).

Jackson, I. and Limbrick, L. (2019). Creating shared value in an industrial conurbation: evidence from the North Staffordshire ceramics cluster. *Strategic Change*, **28**(2), 133–8.

Jones, G. (2012). The growth opportunity that lies next door. *Harvard Business Review*, **90**(7/8), 141–5.

Kiron, D., Unruh, G., Kruschwitz, N., et al. (2017). Corporate sustainability at a crossroads. *MIT Sloan Management Review,* May.

Kruschwitz, N. (2013). Creating shared value at Nestlé. https://sloanreview.mit.edu/article/creating-shared-value-at-nestle/ (accessed 20 December 2019).

Kuehn, K. and McIntire, L. (2014). Sustainability a CFO can love. *Harvard Business Review*, **92**(4), 66–74.

Lamach, M.W. (2017). How our company connected our strategy to sustainability goals. *Harvard Business Review Digital Articles*, 1–4.

Lee, Y.W. (2019). Enhancing shared value and sustainability practices of global firms: the case of Samsung Electronics. *Strategic Change*, **28**(2), 139–45.

Lubin, D.A. and Esty, D.C. (2010). The sustainability imperative. *Harvard Business Review*, May, 42–51.

Lyon, T.P. and Maxwell, J.W. (2011). Greenwash: corporate environmental disclosure under threat of audit. *Journal of Economics & Management Strategy*, **20**(1), 3–41.

Lyon, T.P. and Montgomery, A.W. (2013). Tweetjacked: the impact of social media on corporate greenwash. *Journal of Business Ethics*, **118**(4), 747–57.

Maniora, J. (2018). Mismanagement of sustainability: what business strategy makes the difference? Empirical evidence from the USA. *Journal of Business Ethics*, **152**(4), 931–47.

Mead, L. (2019). Paper describes Colombia's efforts to localize, achieve SDGs. https://sdg.iisd.org/news/paper-describes-colombias-efforts-to-localize-achieve-sdgs/ (accessed 26 May 2019).

NCE (2018). The 2018 Report of the Global Commission on the Economy and Climate. https://newclimateeconomy.report/2018/ (accessed 26 May 2019).

Netter, S., Pedersen, E.R.G., and Lüdeke-Freund, F. (2019). Sharing economy revisited: towards a new framework for understanding sharing models. *Journal of Cleaner Production*, **221**, 224–33.

Novo Nordisk (2019). http://www.novonordisk.co.uk/about-novo-nordisk-in-uk/corporate_overview/sustainability.html (accessed 26 May 2019).

Onkila, T., Mäkelä, M., and Järvenpää, M. (2018). Employee sensemaking on the importance of sustainability reporting in sustainability identity change. *Sustainable Development*, **26**(3), 217–28.

Ormiston, M.E. and Wong, E.M. (2013). License to ill: the effects of corporate social responsibility and CEO moral identity on corporate social irresponsibility. *Personnel Psychology*, **66**, 861–93.

Othman, R., Nath, N., and Laswad, F. (2017). Sustainability reporting by New Zealand's local governments. *Australian Accounting Review*, **27**(3), 315–28.

Parguel, B., Benoît-Moreau, F., and Larceneux, F. (2011). How sustainability ratings might deter 'greenwashing': a closer look at ethical corporate communication. *Journal of Business Ethics*, **102**(1), 15–28.

Perez, S., Fernández-Salinero, S., and Topa, G. (2018). Sustainability in organizations: perceptions of corporate social responsibility and Spanish employees' attitudes and behaviors. *Sustainability*, **10**, 1–15.

Pfitzer, M.W., Bockstette, V., and Stamp, M. (2013). Innovating for shared value. *Harvard Business Review,* September.

Picciotti, A. (2017). Towards sustainability: the innovation paths of social enterprise. *Annals of Public and Cooperative Economics*, **88**(2), 233–56.

Porter, M.E. and Kramer, M.R. (2011). Creating shared value. *Harvard Business Review*, January–February.

Posner, B. and Kiron, D. (2013). How Caesars Entertainment is betting on sustainability. *MIT Sloan Management Review*, **54**(4), 63–71.

Powell, M., Gillett, A., and Doherty, B. (2019). Sustainability in social enterprise: hybrid organizing in public services. *Public Management Review*, **21**(2), 159–86.

PWC (2019). Megatrends. https://www.pwc.co.uk/issues/megatrends.html (accessed 25 May 2019).

Rangan, V.K., Chase, L., and Karim, S. (2015). The truth about CSR. *Harvard Business Review*, May–June.

RodrÍguez Vilá, O., Bharadwaj, S., and Knowles, J. (2017). Competing on social purpose: interaction. *Harvard Business Review*, **95**(6), 94–101.

Rosati, F. and Faria, L.G.D. (2019). Addressing the SDGs in sustainability reports: the relationship with institutional factors. *Journal of Cleaner Production*, **215**, 1312–26.

Santos, J.F.P. and Williamson, P.J. (2015). The new mission for multinationals. *MIT Sloan Management Review*, **56**(4), 45–54.

Santos, F.M., Pache, A.-C., and Birkholz, C. (2015). Making hybrids work: aligning business models and organizational design for social enterprises. *California Management Review*, **57**(3), 36–58.

Schaltenbrand, B., Foerstl, K., Azadegan, A., and Lindeman, K. (2018). See what we want to see? The effects of managerial experience on corporate green investments. *Journal of Business Ethics*, **150**(4), 1129–50.

Schramade, W. (2017). Investing in the UN Sustainable Development Goals: opportunities for companies and investors. *Journal of Applied Corporate Finance*, **29**(2), 87–99.

SEPA (2016). Beyond compliance. https://www.sepaview.com/2016/12/beyond-compliance/ (accessed 26 May 2019).

Sheth, H. and Babiak, K. (2010). Beyond the game: perceptions and practices of corporate social responsibility in the professional sport industry. *Journal of Business Ethics*, **91**(3), 433–50.

Slaper, T.F. and Hall, T.J. (2011). The triple bottom line: what is it and how does it work? http://www.ibrc.indiana.edu/ibr/2011/spring/article2.html (accessed 26 May 2019).

Social Enterprise UK (2018). The Hidden Revolution. https://www.socialenterprise.org.uk/wp-content/uploads/2019/05/The_Hidden_Revolution_-_FINAL-1.pdf (accessed 20 December 2019).

Social Enterprise (2019). Can I register to become a social enterprise? https://www.socialenterprise.org.uk/pages/faqs/category/faqs (accessed 26 May 2019).

Spicer, A. and Hyatt, D. (2017). Walmart's emergent low-cost sustainable product strategy. *California Management Review*, **59**(2), 116–41.

Truong, A. and Barraket, J. (2018). Engaging workers in resource-poor environments: the case of social enterprise in Vietnam. *International Journal of Human Resource Management*, **29**(20), 2949–70.

UBS (2019). Sustainable investing. https://www.ubs.com/uk/en/wealth-management/sustainable-investing/education.html (accessed 26 May 2019).

UN (2019). Sustainable development goals. https://www.un.org/sustainabledevelopment/sustainable-development-goals/ (accessed 26 May 2019).

UN Environment Programme (2017). Eco-innovation field manual. http://unep.ecoinnovation.org/wp-content/uploads/2017/06/UN_Environment_Eco-i_Manual_Pack.zip.

UNFCCC (2019). The Paris agreement. https://unfccc.int/process-and-meetings/the-paris-agreement/the-paris-agreement (accessed 25 May 2019).

Vashchenko, M. (2017). An external perspective on CSR: what matters and what does not? *Business Ethics: A European Review*, **26**(4), 396–412.

Whelan, T. and Fink, C. (2016). The business case for sustainability. *Harvard Business Review*, October, 1–10

Wickert, C. and de Bakker, F.G.A. (2019). How CSR managers can inspire other leaders to act on sustainability. *Harvard Business Review Digital Articles*, 2–5.

Winston, A. (2012). 3M's sustainability innovation machine. *Harvard Business Review Digital Articles*, 2–4.

Winston, A. (2018). Does Wall Street finally care about sustainability? *Harvard Business Review Digital Articles*, 1–5.

WRAP (2019). Circular economy. http://www.wrap.org.uk/about-us/about/wrap-and-circular-economy (accessed 26 May 2019).

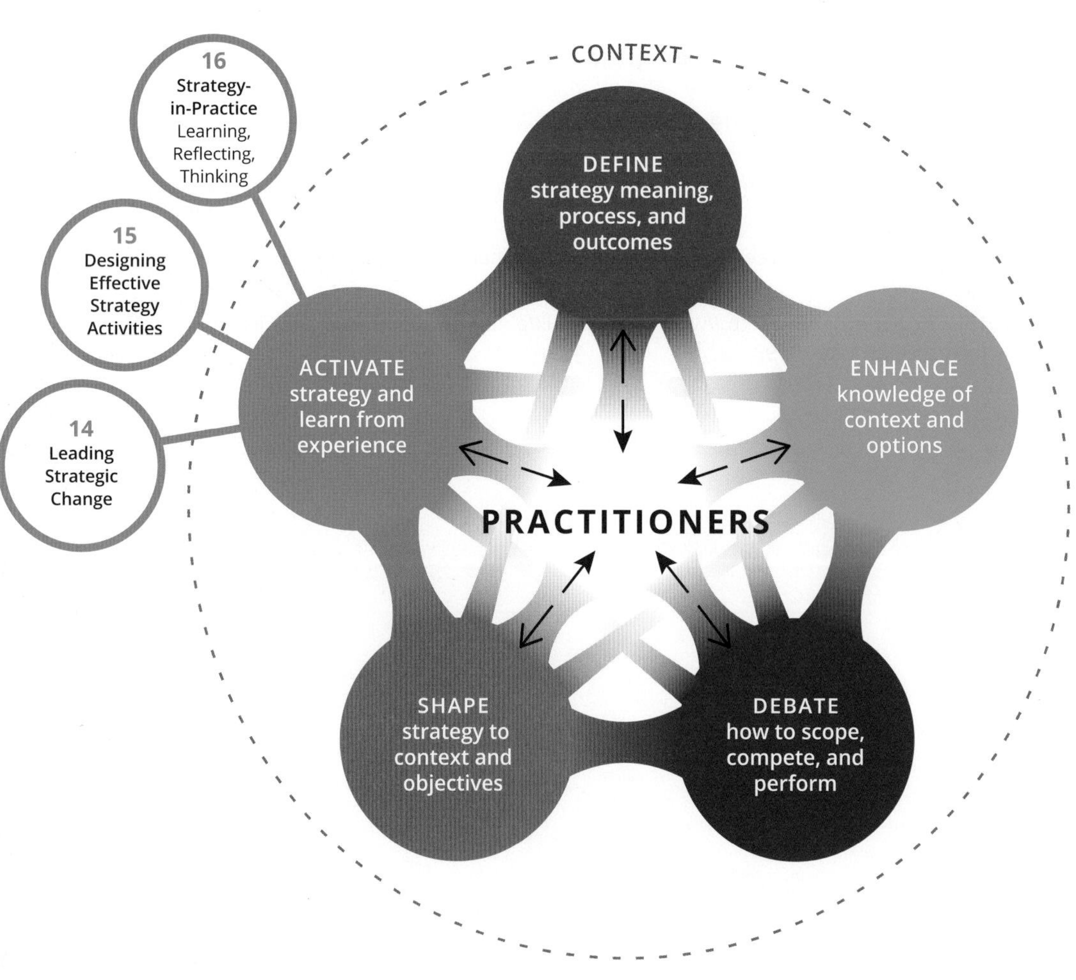
16
Strategy-in-Practice
Learning, Reflecting, Thinking
15
Designing Effective Strategy Activities
14
Leading Strategic Change
CONTEXT
DEFINE
strategy meaning, process, and outcomes
ENHANCE
knowledge of context and options
DEBATE
how to scope, compete, and perform
SHAPE
strategy to context and objectives
ACTIVATE
strategy and learn from experience
PRACTITIONERS

PART FIVE

Activate strategy and learn from experience

In this concluding section, we examine how strategic decisions can be activated through change initiatives, tailored design of activities, and knowledge and insights gained from multiple learning experiences.

To enhance your understanding and vocabulary, in Chapter 14 we introduce models of strategic change that can meet a wide range of strategy implementation needs, in Chapter 15 we explain how design thinking and inclusivity principles can develop blueprints for highly effective strategy activities, and in Chapter 16 we examine theories of strategic learning and reflection that enable continuous improvement of strategy practice.

To support your capacity to apply these insights, in Chapter 14 we review methods for the strategic leadership of change and implementation initiatives, in Chapter 15 we show how you can design effective strategy activities, and in Chapter 16 we describe techniques for undertaking individual or group reflective activity that drives experiential learning and practical impact during strategy work.

By the end of Part 5, you should have enhanced abilities to think, talk, and act like a practitioner, activating strategy and learning from experience.

CHAPTER FOURTEEN

Leading Strategic Change

CONTENTS

LEARNING OBJECTIVES

By the end of this chapter, you should be able to:

- ○ Evaluate the importance of organizations to be able to manage in the present while simultaneously preparing for the future
- ○ Understand the concept of strategic change and the types of strategic change
- ○ Critically evaluate the different approaches to strategic change management
- ○ Examine the processes and tools available for managers to effectively manage and implement strategic change
- ○ Recognize the role of sensemaking and sensegiving in leading change
- ○ Understand the special cases of change: turnaround and crisis management

TOOLBOX

- ○ **Strategic drift**
  A framework that can be applied to understand the consequences of the organization failing to keep pace with changes in the external environment.
- ○ **Forcefield analysis**
  An analytical tool to identify forces in the organization that may drive and restrain change.
- ○ **Step-based models for managing strategic change**
  Models that have been developed to enable managers to approach the task of strategic change as a logical step-by-step process. This includes forcefield analysis, Lewin's model of change, Kotter's eight-step model of change, and Kotter's Accelerate model.
- ○ **Sensemaking and sensegiving**
  A cognitive process that individuals use to make sense of complex situations and influence others to share their perceived world view.

OPENING CASE STUDY **BLOCKBUSTER AND NETFLIX**

Founded in 1985, Blockbuster became the dominant company in the video rental industry. Within three years of its founding, the firm had become the largest video rental chain in the word, and by 1991 Blockbuster owned 3600 stores worldwide each crammed with up to 13,000 pre-recorded videotapes (*New York Times* 8 January 1994). In 1994 Blockbuster was acquired by Viacom, a multinational media and film conglomerate, in a merger valued at $8.4 billion. Blockbuster expanded rapidly and at its peak the company operated 10,000 stores (Downes and Nunes 2013). However, by 1996 Blockbuster had lost half its value. By the time Viacom decided to divest Blockbuster in 2004, the company had lost $984 million despite $5.9 billion revenue (Davis and Higgins 2013). No longer able to service its debt, Blockbuster filed for bankruptcy protection in September 2010, and the firm finally ceased trading in 2014 (Downes and Nunes 2013).

For years Blockbuster seemed unbeatable. Then, in 1997, Netflix came to market. The start-up firm built a distribution model that was based exclusively on mailing DVDs to customers which was almost as convenient as a Blockbuster's neighbourhood retail store. Netflix charged a flat monthly fee but did not charge late rental return fees. In contrast, Blockbuster's revenue model relied on earning enormous amounts of money by charging its customers late fees. Blockbuster's customers found the late fees a major irritant, and this became the company's Achilles heel as the firm's profits were highly dependent on penalizing its patrons. Blockbuster continued to charge late fees, even after the company began charging a monthly fee for rentals. By the time Blockbuster started competing by mail subscription service in 2004, Netflix had already cut into its customer base.

The main disruption came in 2007 with the advent of Netflix's streaming video service. At that time less than 50% of US households had a broadband connection, but Netflix's CEO Reed Hastings clearly saw the that streaming content onto a flat screen at customers' homes represented the future of on-demand entertainment. Unlike Blockbuster, Netflix reacted quickly enough to take an advantage of the digital technology transformation by offering customers all the movies and television programmes that they wanted to watch, whenever they wanted to watch them, all for a flat monthly fee.

Blockbuster was caught out by the speed of digital transformation and the company was slow to launch its own digital download service. By this time Blockbuster's one-time core assets which underpinned the firm's competitive advantage—the retail stores—had become expensive liabilities. Customers no longer needed to rent physical videotapes as they could stream or download content in the convenience of their own homes. Moreover, Blockbuster's business model, which was based on generating cash from late fees, became outdated as a flat monthly fee for digital content became the industry norm.

Blockbuster tried to renew its business model by dropping late fees, but this cost the firm $200 million in lost revenue, and the cost of launching Blockbuster Online amounted to additional $200 million. Although Blockbuster Online was able to slow down Netflix's advance, the company tried to replace its lost profits from the scrapping of the late fees by significantly increasing the price for their online customers, reducing marketing spend, and intensifying in-store operations with products to replace the physical video tapes. Part of the in-store operation was the acquisition of Circuit City, a large consumer electronics chain, which became bankrupt soon after the acquisition.

Questions for discussion

1. What factors contributed to Blockbuster's demise and why?
2. Blockbuster's senior management team members were very experienced in retailing and Blockbuster was the dominant company in the video rental industry. Why do you think that they failed to defend the firm's market position against Netflix's challenge?
3. How feasible do you think it is for a firm to radically change its business model?

4. What obstacles did Blockbuster encounter in changing its business model after it had become clear that it had become outdated?

Sources

Antioco, J. (2011). How I did it: Blockbuster's former CEO on sparring with an activist shareholder. *Harvard Business Review*, April.

Davis, T. and Higgins, J. (2013). Chapter 11 Bankruptcy Case Studies. A Blockbuster failure: how an outdated business model destroyed a giant. https://trace.tennessee.edu/utk_studlawbankruptcy/11 (accessed 20 December 2019).

Downes, L. and Nunes, P. (2013). Blockbuster becomes a casualty of big bang disruption. *Harvard Business Review*, November.

Satell, G. (2014). A look back why Blockbuster really failed and why it didn't have to. *Forbes*, 5 September.

14.1 **Introduction**

Managing strategic change is not easy. Within an ever-changing environment, organizations need to be able to manage and reconcile their current activities to protect their current market position while simultaneously adapting to the future. Any adaptation from the way the organization operates currently will entail change, and any change is bound to encounter resistance. Organizations are composed of people, and people are highly resistant to any change in their routines as well as protective of their positions, spheres of influence, and power. Therefore change is perceived as disruptive, uncomfortable, and costly. Moreover, managers must consult a multitude of stakeholders and often convince them to change their behaviours and attitudes, not to mention changing and realigning organizational processes and routines to new organizational realities. Additionally, with conflicting priorities and objectives among the various stakeholder groups, change management can become a socio-political process that the strategists need to navigate. Considering these difficulties, Balogun et al. (2016) unsurprisingly estimate that approximately 70% of organizational change programmes fail to achieve their stated aims and outcomes.

In this chapter our focus is on exploring how strategists can approach the strategic change management process in organizations as a consequence of the changes in the external environment. We open the chapter by considering the concept of organizational ambidexterity, the tension between managing for the short term within the current competitive environment while at the same time developing longer-term organizational capabilities to be able to compete successfully in the future; we also describe how strategic leadership is needed in an ambidextrous organization. We then offer a definition of what constitutes strategic change, discuss the types of change, and outline the sources of organizational inertia that makes strategic change difficult. We then turn our attention to the change process and evaluate various prescriptive models of how strategic change can be managed and implemented. As an integral part of this discussion is the role that leadership plays in strategic change, and we consider sensemaking and sensegiving as fundamental skills in leading change. We conclude the chapter by considering two change management situations: corporate turnaround and crisis management.

14.2 **Organizational ambidexterity and strategic leadership**

One of the biggest challenges that strategists face is how to develop an organizational capability to explore future opportunities while simultaneously working on exploiting their organization's current competencies and capabilities in the existing markets. Essentially, strategists have to consider future opportunities and current activities and performance at the same time, so it is important for the student of strategy to understand how strategists might go about doing this. Abell (1993) states that running a successful business requires a clear strategy in terms of defining target markets, paying attention to those factors that are critical to the organization's success, and changing the business in anticipation of the future. This requires a vision of how the future will unfold and a strategy for how the organization will have to adapt or anticipate future challenges. In this section we will explore the idea of being adaptable to this challenge (a concept known as organizational ambidexterity) and consider how strategic leadership is needed to deal with this challenge successfully.

Organizational ambidexterity

Most successful businesses are better at refining their current offerings than at pioneering radically new future products and services (O'Reilly and Tushman 2004). A number of theories have been put forward to explain this conundrum—for example that established companies simply lack the flexibility to explore new opportunities, and that firms find it difficult to reconcile 'mastering the present' with 'pre-empting the future'. However, in turbulent markets, firms need be able to move quickly towards new opportunities, adjust to volatile markets, and avoid complacency (Birkinshaw and Gibson 2004). O'Reilly and Tushman (2004) have termed such adaptability as organizational ambidexterity, which can be defined as a capability of the organization to simultaneously exploit existing competencies (exploitation) and explore new opportunities (exploration).

O'Reilly and Tushman (2004, 2011) argue that the ability of a firm to be ambidextrous is at the core of dynamic capabilities. Ambidexterity requires senior managers to accomplish two critical tasks. First, they must be able to accurately sense changes in their competitive environment, including potential shifts in technology, competition, customers, and regulation. Secondly, they must be able to act on these opportunities and threats—to be able to seize them by reconfiguring both tangible and intangible assets to meet new challenges. As a dynamic capability, ambidexterity combines a complex set of routines, including decentralization, differentiation, and integration, with the ability of senior leadership to coordinate the complex trade-offs required when pursuing exploitation and exploration at the same time. Developing these dynamic capabilities is a central task of executive leadership.

Birkinshaw and Gibson (2004) have identified two forms of organizational ambidexterity: structural ambidexterity and contextual ambidexterity. In structural ambidexterity, exploitation and exploration are undertaken in separate organizational units with different types of activity. For example, business units have the responsibility for exploiting the current market opportunities, while research and development (R&D) and business development units have the responsibility for exploring new markets, developing new products and services, and keeping abreast of the emerging market trends. In contrast, contextual ambidexterity entails the same organizational units with their members pursuing both exploratory and exploitative activities. Contextual ambidexterity requires individuals to take the initiative and remain alert to opportunities beyond the boundaries of their own jobs. This could mean working collaboratively with a colleague from another area of the organization to combine their skills and efforts.

Strategic leadership

Research (O'Reilly and Tushman 2011) indicates that the most successful ambidextrous organizations have leaders who develop a clear vision and common identity, build senior teams that are committed to organizational agility, and are incentivized to both explore and exploit, employ distinct and aligned subunits to focus on either exploration or exploitation, and build teams that can deal with the resource allocations and conflicts associated with exploration and exploitation. It is important to understand that change is a constant feature in organizations, although the intensity of change may vary from time to time. Regardless of the magnitude of change, the role of the top management is to actively engage with changes in strategy, organization structures, systems, and processes of the organization, as well as to create an environment that embeds organizational agility in the culture and activities of the business.

We can term such managerial competency as **strategic leadership**, which refers to the influencing of events and outcomes within the continuing stream of organizational strategy activity. As Hughes (1998:7) comments, 'strategic leadership is an interpersonal process, not an administrative procedure'. It arises from the efforts of groups within the organization working together to deliver initiatives and achieve aims, while 'building healthy and constructive norms, systems, climate and an agenda for the whole organisation' (Hughes 1998:4). The process–practice framework (Chapter 2) identifies five types of strategy practices which might be used to lead others towards this type of continuing collective accomplishment.

Focusing on strategy practitioners and what they do, Schoemaker et al. (2013:131) describe a strategic leader as 'someone who is both resolute and flexible, persistent in the face of setbacks but also able to react strategically to environmental shifts'. These authors describe how the capacity of a strategic leader can be gauged by the degree of mastery of six skill areas, namely abilities to:

anticipate—constantly vigilant and honing their ability to anticipate by scanning their environment for signals of change.

challenge—questions the status quo. They challenge their own and others' assumptions and encourages divergent points of view. Only after careful reflection and examination of a problem through many lenses do they take decisive action.

interpret—able to deal with complex and conflicting information, they avoid just seeing or hearing what they expect, but rather look for patterns, push through ambiguity, and seek new insights. They are able to take supposed facts and rethink them to expose hidden implications.

decide—makes tough calls with incomplete information, often quickly while thinking on their feet. They will typically follow a robust decision process that balances rigour with speed, considers trade-offs, and takes short- and long-term aims into account.

align—adept at finding common ground and achieving buy-in among stakeholders who have disparate views and agendas. Actively reaches out though proactive communication, trust-building, and frequent engagement.

learn—promotes a culture of inquiry, searching for the lessons in both successful and unsuccessful outcomes. They study failures—their own and those of their teams—in an open constructive way to find the hidden lessons, learning, and ideas for improvement.

14.3 **What is strategic change?**

Having considered the need for organizational ambidexterity and agility in continually changing environments and the critical leadership qualities required, we now turn our discussion to what constitutes strategic change, before going on to identify organizational factors that make change difficult to manage and implement.

How do we decide whether change is strategic or not? At any given point in time, an organization may have a number of change initiatives under way. For example, the firm's finance department may be in the process of installing a new invoicing system, while the marketing department is considering outsourcing some of its marketing material development to a specialist content development firm. All these initiatives will involve change that may result in new organizational processes and even redundancies among the people who will be affected by these changes. However, the litmus test of what constitutes strategic change is whether the changes will have an impact on the overall direction, competitive position, and scope of the organization's activities. As we saw in Chapter 4, organizations are a collection of stakeholder groups that may have conflicting interests, objectives, and even their own organization cultural norms which may constitute a series of subcultures within the organization. Hence, the kind of change which is deemed to be strategic is a result of a political process in organizations. This is not the only indication of a strategic change. For example, we can consider change to be strategic if it results in:

- changes to the competitive position of the firm
- changes to the firm's overarching business model
- changes to the firm's product and service offer
- development of new organizational capabilities
- changes to the geographic scope of the firm through international expansion
- outsourcing of activities or bringing activities in-house that have previously been carried out by outside suppliers
- changes to the nature and overall structure of the organization through the formation of strategic alliances, mergers and acquisitions, divestments, etc.

While this level of impact may feel significant to those experiencing the strategic changes, it is worth understanding that not all strategic change is disruptive or revolutionary. Incremental changes that take place gradually in the organization may have a strategic impact on the firm's competitive position over an extended period of time. As we saw in the previous section, employees may simultaneously engage in exploitation and exploration, meaning that changes might be implemented either gradually over time or more suddenly as a result of breakthrough discoveries.

Why is change difficult?

All approaches to change management are based on the recognition that change and its implementation are difficult due to organizational inertia or resistance to change. Five common barriers to change are presented in Table 14.1.

Given these common barriers to change, it is not surprising that the majority of organizational change programmes fail to deliver their aims (Balogun et al. 2016). Most managers have a rational understanding that change is an ever-present phenomenon and is essential if organizations are to survive in an environment that is characterized by technological innovation, globalization, and new business models such as 'born global' (Chapter 12). However, few organizations are

TABLE 14.1 **Barriers to change**

Common barriers to change	Why this factor is a barrier to change
Social and political structures	Organizations are both social and political constructs. As social systems, organizations develop shared practices and processes that make change disruptive and stressful for organizational participants. As political systems, organizations have concentrations of power and authority. Any change that may threaten the position of those in power will meet resistance.
Organizational routines	Routines and processes that have been developed over a long period of time and become embedded in the way the organization operates are difficult to change. Organizations fall into competency traps where exiting core competencies become core rigidities (see Chapter 4, section on path dependency).
Institutional isomorphism	**Isomorphism** is a similarity of the processes or structures of one organization to those of another. It can result from competitive imitation or independent development under similar competitive conditions. It can also emerge from external pressures by investors, lenders, or regulators that encourage firms in a particular industry to develop similar strategies and structures. Change under institutional isomorphism will be difficult as managers may be concerned that, by moving away from the processes and structures of their competitors, they may lose their competitive position in the industry.
Bounded rationality and satisficing	Decision-makers engage in a limited information search due to the concepts of bounded rationality and satisficing. These behaviours lead decision-makers to find solutions to problems from their existing knowledge and competencies. This is also a reason why organizations have a bias towards exploitation over exploration when doing things in a new way or seeking new opportunities. (See Chapter 3 on strategic decision-making in organizations.)
Equilibrium-seeking behaviour	Organizations develop a fit between their strategy, structure, management systems, culture, and competencies and their external competitive environment. If the environment changes, it might not be sufficient to change only some of the elements of the organization in response. (See Chapter 4 on organizational culture.) Hence organizations tend to operate in an equilibrium state until such a time that the gap between the external environment and the organization grows to a stage where a complete realignment of the organization and its environment is required (as explored in the opening case study on Blockbuster).

capable of successfully managing change, and the consequences of this failure to deliver and manage change means that organizations will eventually lose their competitive position.

There are countless examples of once leading companies that have completely vanished. Goh (2017) identifies two well-known firms that were not able move with the times: Kodak and Toys 'R' Us. Kodak (1889–2012) failed to keep up with the digital revolution for fear of cannibalizing its strongest product lines in film. Even though Kodak invented digital photography, the firm was caught off guard with the change from film to digital photography. The company was blindsided by its core business of selling silver halide film. Kodak, as the leader of design, production, and marketing of photographic equipment, had a number of opportunities to renew itself, but the firm's hesitation to fully embrace the transition to digital led to its demise. For example, Kodak invested billions of US dollars into developing technology for taking pictures using mobile phones and other digital devices. However, it held back from developing digital cameras for the mass market for fear of eradicating its all-important film business. Competitors, such as the Japanese firm Canon, jumped at this opportunity. Kodak filed for bankruptcy in 2012 and, after exiting most of its product streams, re-emerged in 2013 as a much smaller consolidated company focused on serving commercial customers.

Toys 'R' Us (1948–2018) is a recent story about the firm's financial struggle. The company was once one of the world's largest toy store chains. With the benefit of hindsight, Toys 'R' Us may have been the architect of its own downfall when it signed a 10-year contract to be the exclusive vendor of toys on Amazon in 2000. Amazon began to allow other toy vendors to sell on its site in spite of the deal, and Toys 'R' Us sued Amazon to end the agreement in 2004. As a result, Toys 'R' Us missed the opportunity to develop its own e-commerce presence early on. Far too late to the e-commerce retail revolution, Toys 'R' Us announced in May 2017 its plan to revamp its website as part of a $100 million, three-year investment to jump-start its e-commerce business. However, under pressure from its debt and fierce online retail competition, the company ceased trading in 2018.

The important point to take away from this section is that what is deemed to constitute strategic change is a result of an organization's socio-political processes, and there are a number of factors that make the management of change very difficult. Moreover, what is clear is that if organizations are not able to manage change and stay relevant in the changing environment, they will ultimately fail regardless of their current position in the industry. This idea is reinforced by Jeff Bezos, CEO of Amazon, who famously said that he is under no illusion that at some point in time Amazon's business model will be disrupted by a new competitor; it is inevitable, but he will fight to make sure that that day will not be soon (https://www.youtube.com/watch?v=32rCNumOu4E).

14.4 Types of change

We have discussed what strategic change is and why it is difficult. But how do organizations realize that they need to implement change? And how can we categorize different sorts of change? In this section, we will discuss how the need for change emerges and will identify four main types of change.

How the need for change emerges

Rational managerial decision-making models (see Chapter 3) assume that change is a rational outcome in organizations. Such a perspective attempts to explain change as a process where strategists adjust the firm's strategy as a result of continuous **environmental scanning** which detects changes in the organization's competitive environment, changes in customer tastes, emerging new technologies, and so on. Analytical tools such as PESTEL and SWOT analysis provide managers with the ability to engage in environmental scanning, and adjust the firm's strategy based on the results of such analysis through the application of change management tools and techniques.

However, in practice, strategic change does not always occur in such a measured way. The concept of **strategic drift** lies at the core of organizational change management. Often, the environment changes gradually without any detectable revolutionary shocks. Political and economic changes do not generally occur overnight, nor do new technologies, and changes in customer preferences do not emerge without some warning. However, if the firm is not able to keep pace with such incremental evolutionary changes, strategic drift occurs. This is because the firm's strategy becomes detached from the changes happening in the external competitive environment. Figure 14.1 illustrates the concept of strategic drift.

Figure 14.1 illustrates how the organization is initially able to keep up with the changing environment (shown by the blue line) by implementing incremental change (shown by the orange line). However, as environmental change accelerates (in the middle section of the graph), the firm is beginning to fall behind the changing environment resulting in strategic drift. This is demonstrated in the graph by the widening gap between the red and blue lines in the middle

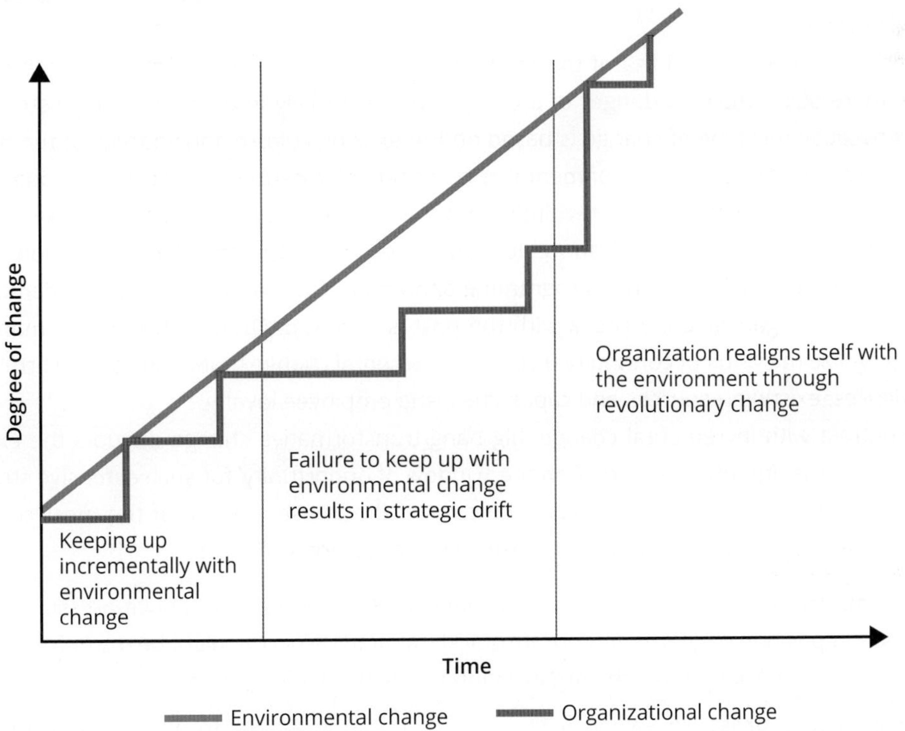

FIGURE 14.1 Strategic drift.

section of the graph. Over a period of time it becomes clear that incremental change is no longer sufficient, but more transformational revolutionary change is required if the organization is to recover its competitive position in a changing competitive environment. If successful, the firm is able to make a step change where the orange line closes the gap with the blue line as the organization catches up with the environmental change.

In our opening case we saw Blockbuster lose its leadership position in the video rental industry by failing to change its strategy in light of the emerging digital download and streaming technology. The company made an attempt to adapt to change, but this change was made within Blockbuster's main business paradigm based on charging customers late return fees by replacing them with high membership subscription fees, cost-cutting programmes, and adding additional services that were offered to customers from the firm's retail outlets. In a fairly short period of time Blockbuster's strategic drift had become so severe that radical revolutionary change was the only option for the firm's survival. Unfortunately, by this time Blockbuster had been overtaken by its rivals and the organization's attempt to launch its own online service and divest itself of extensive physical retail outlets came too late. The change that was required of Blockbuster was too big for the firm to close the gap with their competitors, and the environment had evolved beyond Blockbuster's reach, given the resources and capabilities available to them.

The speed and extent of change

Balogun et al. (2016) identify two dimensions of organizational change: the speed and extent of change that is required. These two dimensions give rise to four main types of strategic change: adaption, evolution, reconstruction, and revolution. The nature of these types of change is explored in Table 14.2.

We should keep in mind that if the approach of incremental change in the organization is taken, there still remains a danger of strategic drift, especially in adaptive change strategies. This is because this type of change is based on the existing culture and strategy of the organization, and it might be that environmental or competitive pressures require more fundamental transformative (reconstructive or revolutionary) change than the organization is making.

When selecting an approach to strategic change, managers struggle with the question of how extensive and how fast a change programme should be. On the one hand, to fundamentally transform the organization, a break with the past is required. On the other hand, managers also recognize the value of continuity through incremental change that builds on the firm's past experiences, existing resources and capabilities, and employee loyalty.

In contrast with incremental change, big bang/transformative change disrupts the existing paradigm of the organization and often the 'window of opportunity' for such extensive strategic change can be narrow, as witnessed in the case of Blockbuster. Some of the most common triggers that necessitate big bang/transformative change are as follows:

- **Competitive pressure**—when a firm comes under intense competitive pressure and its market position begins to deteriorate quickly, a rapid response might be the only approach possible, especially when the organization is threatened by insolvency.
- **Regulatory pressure**—when a firm comes under pressure from the government or regulatory agencies to push through major changes within a short period of time. Such externally imposed revolutions can be witnessed in public sector organizations, such as

TABLE 14.2 **Types of strategic change**

Speed of change	Extent of change	
	Realignment	**Transformation**
Incremental	Adaptation is the most common form of organizational change. Change is undertaken incrementally within the existing cultural norms and strategy to realign the organization to the changes in the competitive environment. It builds on the existing strategy rather than fundamentally changing the existing strategy. May include changes that are made to the current methods of production, new product introductions, or related diversification of activities.	Evolution is perhaps the most challenging form of strategic change. It involves exploiting and building on the organization's existing strategic capabilities, while also exploring new opportunities and developing new capabilities (organizational ambidexterity, as we discussed earlier in this chapter).
Big bang/ transformative	Reconstruction is rapid change. It may involve major structural changes and cost-cutting programmes to address a decline in the organization's financial performance or difficult market conditions. Reconstruction does not fundamentally change the culture or the prevailing strategy. Reconstruction is often referred to as turnaround, which is discussed later in this chapter.	Revolution is urgent transformational change. It requires a change in both culture and strategy. The pressure for change is often extreme as the future viability of the organization is at stake. For example, a hostile takeover may threaten the very existence of the firm. Revolution differs from reconstruction, as in revolutionary change it is often necessary to change both the culture and the strategy of the organization (as in the case of Blockbuster).

Source: Adapted from Balogun et al. (2016).

hospitals and schools that fail official quality inspections, and highly regulated industries, such as utilities and telecommunications that may come under scrutiny for exercising too much monopolistic market power.

- **First mover advantage**—when a firm adopts a more proactive reason for instigating revolutionary change. The firm places itself under pressure to be the first firm to introduce a new product or technology to build up barriers to entry for competitors who may follow the first mover with competing products or technologies.

14.5 **Models for managing change**

In the previous section, we explored four main types of change. Regardless of the type of change the organization adopts, it needs to be managed. What processes and tools can managers use in practice when confronted by a need for change? The most common change management frameworks consider change as a series of rational steps and processes that the organization takes to pivot from one state into another. In this section we consider three such models:

- Lewin's change model
- Kotter's eight-step model of change
- Kotter's Accelerator model for increased agility and innovation.

Lewin's model of change management

Lewin's model is probably one of the best known and most widely applied models of change management. Lewin (1947) was a social psychologist who was interested in group dynamics and how individuals relate to and become influenced by others. As a social psychologist his primary interest was to understand how social groups changed for the worse, and what could be done to effect recovery and improve group interaction and performance. The fundamental assumptions of Lewin's theory of change are as follows:

- Change is the result of dissatisfaction with the current state of the organization (e.g. financial performance, deteriorating market position, failure to meet set objectives).
- Change does not happen by itself. It is critical for the organization to develop a vision of a better future.
- Management needs to formulate strategies to implement change.
- Any change will inevitably meet resistance, but it is not impossible to overcome.

Based on these assumptions, what does Lewis' model actually entail? We will go through it step by step, starting with **forcefield analysis**.

Forcefield analysis

The first stage of Lewin's model is to conduct a forcefield analysis which provides an overview of the problems that need to be tackled by the organization, splitting factors into forces that act for and against change. The cultural web (Chapter 4) or causal mapping (Chapter 3) could be useful frameworks to conduct the analysis.

Lewin's forcefield model in Figure 14.2 identifies driving and restraining forces for change. Where there is an equilibrium between the two sets of forces, no change takes place. In order

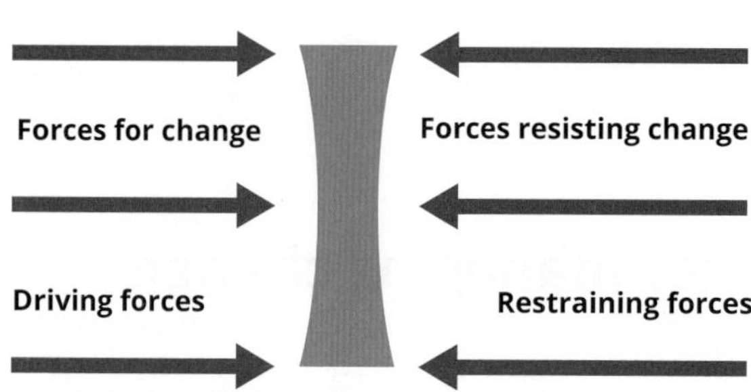

FIGURE 14.2 Forcefield analysis. Source: Lewin, K. (1951). *Field Theory in Social Science*. New York: Harper and Row.

for change to occur, the driving forces must be stronger than the restraining forces and can then be leveraged to overcome the restraining forces. In undertaking forcefield analysis, all forces for change and forces resisting change should be identified. Each force should then be assigned a relative weighting. Based on the relative weighting of the forces, a strategist can identify the critical forces that can be leveraged for maximum effect and the restraining forces that must be eliminated for change to take place.

Examples of forces for change are:

- new management and/or employees
- changing market and customer tastes
- new technology
- competition
- changing regulatory environment
- public opinion.

Examples of forces resisting change are:

- individual's fear of failure
- organizational politics and turf wars
- organizational apathy and inertia
- hostility to management
- change fatigue.

Lewin's change as three steps (CATS)

Having conducted the forcefield analysis and identified the critical forces to be addressed, the next stage in Lewin's change model is to effect 'change as three steps' (CATS): unfreezing, moving, and refreezing (adapted from Burnes 2004).

Step 1. Unfreezing

As we have seen from the forcefield analysis, Lewin believed that the stability of human behaviour is based on an equilibrium (or state of balance), supported by a complex field of driving and restraining forces. He argued that the equilibrium needs to be destabilized (unfrozen) before old behaviour can be discarded (unlearnt) and new behaviour successfully adopted (refreezing).

The key to 'unfreezing' is to recognize that change, whether at individual or group level, is a psychological dynamic process. In fact, three simultaneous actions are necessary to achieve unfreezing:

- statement that the current state of affairs or behaviours is no longer acceptable (disconfirmation of the validity of the status quo)
- the introduction of a sense of survival anxiety should the change not succeed
- the creation of a sense of psychological safety to institute a shared belief that the group is safe from negative consequences that may arise from interpersonal and group risk-taking.

CASE EXAMPLE 14.1 FOOD AND AGRICULTURE ORGANIZATION OF THE UNITED NATIONS

The Food and Agriculture Organization of the United Nations (FAO) adopted forcefield analysis by adding an extra element of the organization's control over a reforestation programme. In an attempt to improve the success of afforestation (planting trees to make a new forest) and reforestation (restocking forest areas) programmes, the FAO agency listed all the driving forces and restraining forces. It then rated each force by its importance and by the degree of control the agency exerted over any given force. The totals were then calculated (see Table 14.3). For each force, the higher the total of importance and control, the more impact the agency could have in trying to address that force. In addition, if the agency could find some forces that had a correlation with other forces, the effectiveness of the agency's interventions could be greater. For example, 'improved operational planning' was deemed to reduce 'losses to fires and grazing', and to address 'poor procedures for hiring and paying field workers'. The agency decided to focus its attention on 'operational planning' as it had the highest overall score as well as having a cross-force impact on 'losses to fires and grazing' and 'poor procedures for hiring and paying field workers' (Hovland 2005).

Questions for discussion

1. Why do you think it is important to identify and assign weightings to both driving and restraining forces?
2. Choose an organization that you know and conduct forcefield analysis. Assign a weighting on a scale of 1 (least important) to 5 (most important) for each force you have identified and calculate the total scores.
3. Based on your forcefield analysis, what are the most important forces that can be leveraged for change and what restraining forces must be eliminated?

TABLE 14.3 **Forcefield analysis for success in afforestation and reforestation programmes**

	Importance	Agency control	Total
Driving forces			
Rising prices of wood products	2	2	4
Genetically improved planting stock	2	4	6
Improved operational planning	4	5	9
Increasing public support	2	2	4
Restraining forces			
Decreasing agency budget	2	2	4
Irregular annual precipitation	5	1	6
Poor procedures for hiring and paying field workers	4	4	8
Losses to fires and grazing	5	3	8

Source: Hovland (2005).

Unless sufficient psychological safety is created among the organization members, the disconfirming information will be denied or in other ways defended against. If so, no survival anxiety will be felt and, consequently, no change will take place. In other words, those organization members who are most affected by change have to feel safe from potential loss and humiliation before they can accept the desired new state of affairs and reject old behaviours.

Step 2. Moving

Unfreezing creates motivation to learn, but it does not generate change. Any attempt to predict or identify a specific outcome from planned change is very difficult because of the complexity of the driving and restraining forces. Instead, strategists should seek to take into account all the forces at work and identify and evaluate, on a trial and error basis, all the available options to pivot the organization from its existing state to a new state of affairs. Using an iterative approach of developing viable options and testing them enables groups and individuals to move from a less acceptable to a more acceptable set of behaviours.

Step 3. Refreezing

Without continuous reinforcement, change could be short-lived. Refreezing seeks to stabilize the group at a new state of balance in order to ensure that the new behaviours are relatively safe from reverting to the old behaviours. The main point about refreezing is that new behaviours must be, to some degree, consistent with the rest of the behaviours, personality, and environment of the members of the organization. If not, it will simply lead to a new round of disconfirmation. To avoid this happening, Lewin saw successful change as a group activity. This is because unless group norms and routines are also transformed, changes to individual behaviours will not be sustained. Therefore, in organizational terms, refreezing often requires changes to organizational culture, norms, policies, and practices.

Critiques of Lewin's CATS model

In recent years, some scholars have critiqued Lewin's CATS model as being too simplistic (Cummings et al. 2016). Kanter et al. (1992) suggest that Lewin's CATS model is too linear and treats an organization as an 'ice cube', and therefore is 'so wildly inappropriate that it is difficult to see why it has not only survived but prospered' (Kanter et al. 1992:10). Child (2005:293) also critiques Lewin's rigid idea of 'refreezing' as inappropriate in today's complex environments, as organizations change constantly, which requires flexibility and adaptation. Furthermore, Clegg et al. (2005) critique the way in which Lewin's framework of unfreezing, moving, and refreezing has become the template for most change programmes. For them, it would just be a matter of repackaging the Taylorian concept of scientific management that is based on mechanistic analysis of workflows to identify and implement optimum performance and maximization of efficiency.

Despite the critiques, these scholars acknowledge that Lewin's CATS model, as well as other step-based change management models, have an enduring appeal to managers. This popularity can be explained by the perception of certainty that such models offer that there is one 'correct way' to manage change, however simplified the models are in real life.

Kotter's eight-step process of leading change

Another influential step-based model is based on John Kotter's work *Leading Change* (Kotter 1996), *Leading change: why transformation efforts fail* (Kotter 2007), and *Accelerate: building strategic agility for a faster-moving world* (Kotter 2014). Kotter's change process model is inspired by Lewin's work, but instead of effecting change in three steps, change is described as an eight-step process.

Eight steps to transforming the organization

Kotter's eight steps are as follows (Kotter 2007):

1. **Establish a sense of urgency** Create a sense of urgency by examining market and competitive realities and develop business scenarios around crises, potential crises, or major opportunities. Use these discussions to communicate that the status quo of the organization is not sustainable.
2. **Form a powerful guiding coalition** Assemble a group of influential change leaders with enough power to help direct the change effort. Encourage this diverse group of people to work as a change management team.
3. **Create a vision** Develop a clear vision to help direct the change effort to communicate why change is needed and develop viable strategies for achieving the vision.
4. **Communicate the vision** Communicate the vision continually and embed every possible communication vehicle in everyday activities of the organization that goes beyond organization-wide communications events. Teach new behaviours by example of the guiding coalition.
5. **Empower others to act on the vision** Identify obstacles to change. Change organizational systems or structures that undermine the change vision. Encourage risk-taking and non-traditional ideas and experimentation.
6. **Plan for and create short-term wins** Plan for and create visible performance improvements as short-term wins. Publicly recognize and reward employees involved in delivering these improvements.
7. **Consolidate improvements and produce still more change** Use increased credibility derived from short-term wins to change organizational systems, structures, and policies that do not fit the change vision. Hire, promote, and develop employees who share and can implement the vision. Continually reinvigorate the change vision with new projects, themes, and change agents.
8. **Institutionalize new approaches** Articulate the connections between the new behaviours and organization success and develop the means to ensure leadership development and succession.

Kotter's model offers a rational and systematic process for effecting change by clear, predominately top-down leadership interventions. However, as with any theoretical framework, there are some limitations to the model. Change is a complex process that does not necessarily follow a linear step-by-step progression. In addition, the strong focus on top-down leadership in the model does not fully account for the financial, political, and external forces that impact the success of a change effort. Research by Pettigrew (1985) found that formal change management plans bore little relationship to what actually happened in the organization, as the way that change unfolded was influenced by complex interplay between organizational history, culture, and politics. Moreover, as Mintzberg (1987) points out in his discussion of realized and unrealized strategies, planned change is not always implemented, and some strategies emerge without formal planning.

Kotter's eight accelerators

Kotter has further developed his model to take into account the increasing complexity and dynamism of today's competitive environment with a view to improving organizational agility and propensity to innovate.

The premise of Kotter's new change model, Accelerate, is that although traditional organizational hierarchies and processes that form a company's 'operating system' are optimized for day-to-day business, they are too rigid to adjust to the quick shifts in today's complex and rapidly changing competitive environments. Therefore a second operating system that is built on a fluid network-like structure is needed to continually formulate and implement strategy (Kotter 2012). Accelerate describes a more agile structure that operates alongside the hierarchy to create a 'dual operating system' which is designed to bridge the gap between evolutionary and revolutionary innovation (see Chapter 11). This network is dynamic and free from bureaucratic layers. At its core is a guiding coalition that represents each level and department in the hierarchy, and its drivers are a 'volunteer army' of people energized by and committed to the coalition's vision and strategy.

Kotter suggests that instead of focusing on the problem to be solved, managers should focus on 'the big opportunity' to create new value. That feeds into a 'change vision' which in turn informs the required 'strategic initiatives'. The key to making the dual operating system work is alignment and that the big opportunity is used to rally people round in both systems concurrently. This should not be an either/or choice between the hierarchy and the network. If the organization only manages the day-to-day hierarchy, it has no hope of seeing revolutionary innovations. On the other hand, if all the focus is on the network, revolutionary innovations will never see the light of day, as a hierarchy is needed to realize the innovations in practice. Therefore this justifies the dual operating system in Kotter's model.

The accelerators are quite similar to Kotter's original eight-step change process, but it is important to distinguish the revised principles and accelerators that define Kotter's dual operating system.

The five principles

Kotter's eight accelerators are based on five principles:

1. Get buy-in from more than 50% of the organization for the initiative.
2. Create a 'get-to' environment that generates an army of volunteers for the initiative.
3. Involve people's hearts (not just heads). Their passion brings more power to the initiative.
4. Invite, encourage, and promote many small acts of leadership.
5. Ensure that all those involved are in alignment.

The eight accelerators

The eight accelerators are as follows (adapted from Kotterinc.com and Kotter 2012):

Step 1 Create a sense of urgency around a single big opportunity. Heighten the organization's awareness that it needs continual strategic adjustments that should be aligned with the biggest perceived opportunity.

Step 2 Build and maintain a guiding coalition. Create a group of volunteers whom the leadership trusts and is able to see inside and outside the organization. These volunteers know the detail and the big picture and use information to make good organization-wide decisions about what strategic initiatives to launch and implement.

Step 3 Formulate a strategic vision and develop change initiatives designed to capitalize on the big opportunity. Develop a well-formulated vision that is focused on taking advantage of the big make-or-break opportunity.

Step 4 Communicate the vision and the strategy to create buy-in and attract a growing volunteer army. Develop a communications strategy that can go viral and attract employees to buy in to the ambition of the message and begin to share commitment to it.

Step 5 Accelerate movement toward the vision and the opportunity by ensuring that the network removes barriers. As design and implementation of the big opportunity occur in the network but are instituted in the hierarchy, ensure that the network and the hierarchy truly operate closely together.

Step 6 Celebrate visible significant short-term wins. To ensure success, the best short-term wins should be obvious, unambiguous, and clearly related to the vision. Celebrating the wins of the volunteer army will prompt more employee volunteers to join the effort.

Step 7 Never let up—keep learning from experience and don't declare victory too soon. Carry through on strategic initiatives and create new ones to adapt to shifting business environments to enhance the firm's competitive position. Be aware that when an organization lets up, cultural and political resistance arise.

Step 8 Integrate changes in the organization culture. Institutionalize the new direction, processes, and methods into the organization culture. This can be done as long as the initiative produces visible results and sends the organization into a strategically better future.

See kotterinc.com for a workbook and a discussion guide on how to improve organizational agility through the development of the dual operating system (https://www.kotterinc.com/research-and-perspectives/8-steps-accelerating-change-ebook/).

As we discussed earlier, step-based models have an enduring appeal to managers as such frameworks maintain that there is a universal approach to the management of change using an orderly process. In reality, however, managerial practice differs from theoretical abstractions. Dunphy and Stace (1988, 1993) and Balogun et al. (2016) argue that there are no universal 'one size fits all' models for managing change. The management of change is contingent on the context, such as the type of change needed and the nature of the organization, including social, cultural, and political considerations as well as its operating environment. Depending on the context of change, strategists have to decide to what extent the change has to be incremental or transformational, and to what extent it is necessary to hold consultation with employees. A more consultative approach to managing change may be more appropriate in the context of incremental change where the organization is adopting or evolving with the environment and its survival is not

CASE EXAMPLE 14.2 **FROM AN IDEA TO A PRODUCT LAUNCH IN SIX MONTHS**

Sometimes, a light-bulb moment brings a new idea to an employee for a new opportunity or product that should be shared with their manager. However, sometimes it takes particular perseverance to demonstrate the potential of the opportunity, and get the backing (and funding) to pursue it.

A first step to get this managerial backing might be to present the opportunity to a general manager. However, no matter what the opportunity is, the general manager might focus on current business rather than look to expanding into new areas. As a response to this rejection, an employee might choose to go away and prepare evidence to support the case put forward for the new product or opportunity.

Once a supportive case has been collated, the employee might present the idea to their manager a second time, using financial projections that would substantiate their idea within a business context. However, this still might not necessarily convince a manager that the idea is a lucrative business opportunity. In fact, it might even convince a manager to refuse the idea a second time in favour of concentrating on current business.

Using some real tenacity by this point, as well as some willing team resources, the employee might look for ways to strengthen the support for their idea beyond financial projections. This might involve mocking up a campaign for the opportunity or product, perhaps involving branding, advertising material, and samples. At this point, a manager might accept the potential of the opportunity, but only so far as to allow the employee financial support, rather than any further team support, in order to pursue the idea.

This would be enough to launch a product. This process, from idea to launch, could take as little as six months. But why would the manager push back if they could see the opportunity was so worthwhile for their business? Essentially, the manager might seek to set up a dual operating system. This would involve focusing one side of their team on managing the core business, continue to grow business steadily with safe evolutionary innovation, and simultaneously allow the other side of the team to work in an opportunity-driven mindset, with opportunity-driven volunteers who wouldn't take no for an answer and were freed up to experiment and try completely new things and new ways of taking them to market.

Questions for discussion

1. What are the two Kotter's operating systems in the case?
2. How did the operating systems interact in this case?
3. How would you describe the elements of the culture of the organization in this case? (You may wish refer to the discussion about culture in Chapter 4 and innovation in Chapter 11.)

Source

Bradt, G. (2014). Leverage John Kotter's 'dual operating system' to accelerate change in large organizations. *Forbes*, 14 May. https://www.forbes.com/sites/georgebradt/2014/05/14/leverage-john-kotters-dual-operating-system-to-accelerate-change-in-large-organizations/#66fadda1aef8 (accessed 24 July 2019).

an issue. In contrast, where radical change is the only option for corporate survival, the change effort will most likely require a directive approach set by the management. In practice, however, many change programmes involve both managerial approaches of consultation and direction.

Research by Dunphy and Stace (1993) suggests that a comprehensive approach to managing change should incorporate transformational change, as well as incrementalism, but also that change management should accommodate both directive and consultative means for achieving change. Rather than evolution and transformation being incompatible strategies, and collaboration, consultation, and more directive approaches being incompatible modes, they are in fact complementary.

Dunphy and Stace's research findings suggest that for most organizations undergoing transformational change at the corporate level, a directive management style is required to begin the process of repositioning the organization. However, these scholars go on to suggest that once the basis for organizational renewal is in place, there is a choice to be made at the corporate level in terms of mixing the directive and consultative management approaches that are needed to keep up the momentum of change. If the change programme is to be successful, while it may be started with a directive, there must also be a predominance of consultative practices at the business unit level in order to win commitment to the implementation of change. Essentially, if people at the business level do not feel properly consulted, they may find it more difficult to get on board with the changes that have been imposed on them. Hence, effective organizational change necessitates that strategists design organizational change programmes with flexibility, rather than relying on rigid change management models.

14.6 Leading change through sensemaking and sensegiving

In the previous section we considered change management models that were based on the assumption that the management of change was a rational step-by-step process. However, we concluded that there was no universally 'correct' way of managing change. It is context dependent, and managers have to deal with organizational complexity that is compounded by the uncertainty and ambiguity of the information they have to rely on in their decision-making (a more detailed discussion of complexity, uncertainty, and ambiguity in strategic decision-making is given in Chapter 3). Given this complexity, how can strategists make sense of the situation they find themselves and the organization in? In this section we will consider how strategists try to gain an understanding of the organization's resources and capabilities, the dynamics of the competitive environment, and the urgency of the change that is needed. Rouleau and Balogun (2011) refer to this as sensemaking (an individual's understanding of the world filled with uncertainty and ambiguity) and sensegiving (an individual influencing others' perspectives). Recent research by Rouleau and Balogun (2011) and Balogun et al. (2015) highlights that managerial sensemaking and sensegiving are critically important leadership skills in the management of change.

Sensemaking and sensegiving in managing change

It is generally accepted that organizations find it difficult to manage changes in their environment, be they technical innovations, regulatory changes, or market crises (Kaplan 2008). Although some organizations are more adaptable, many are subject to strong forces that restrain change. It is not necessarily the environmental changes themselves that make change hard to manage, but rather the ambiguity that makes it difficult for managers to assess what the changes mean. This creates a challenge for strategy-making and the management of change, which require managers to match strategic choices to their understanding of the external environment (Bower 1970).

Research in managerial cognition has suggested that cognitive frames, or mental maps, are the means by which managers try to deal with these uncertainties and ambiguities (Walsh 1995). This psychological perspective is based on the view that strategic action is influenced by how managers make sense of and interpret change, and how they translate these perspectives into strategic choices (Daft and Weick 1984).

Sensemaking is a process through which individuals make an effort to understand novel, unexpected, or confusing events, and it has recently become a critically important topic in the study of organizations (Maitlis and Christianson 2014). When organizational members are faced with moments of ambiguity or uncertainty, they seek to understand what is going on by interpreting signals from their internal and external environment. They then use these signals as the basis for constructing a plausible account that provides order and 'makes sense' of what has occurred, and through which they continue to enact or construct their understanding of these environments (Brown 2000; Maitlis 2005; Weick 1995; Weick et al. 2005). Sensemaking is not a passive activity but an active interpretation and construction of events and frameworks for understanding, as people play a role in constructing the very situations they attempt to comprehend (Weick 1995; Weick et al. 2005).

Sensegiving is an opposite activity to sensemaking. In sensegiving, the person who is trying to give sense is making an attempt to influence other people to perceive and interpret certain actions and events in a particular way. In their work on strategic change processes, Gioia and Chittipeddi (1991) found that sensegiving was concerned with the process of managers attempting to influence the sensemaking and meaning construction of others towards

CASE EXAMPLE 14.3 **SUCCESSFUL STRATEGIC CHANGE AT MULCO**

In 2005, a new president was recruited to MulCo, a family-owned 100-year-old global firm operating in construction and the construction technology industry. The new president came from a global telecommunications company, where he had been the executive director of strategy development. It was highly unusual for MulCo to recruit the president externally, since the previous presidents had largely been promoted from within the company.

In the mid-2000s MulCo employed about 27,000 people with €4 billion Euros in net sales. Although MulCo's business was cyclical, reflecting global trends in the construction industry, the company had successfully balanced this by growing its servicing business, which accounted for more than 50% of the company's net sales. MulCo was recognized as a technology developer in the industry and its employees took a lot of pride from its leadership position in innovation. MulCo ranked fourth in its industry globally, although it struggled to rise from this position. The new president observed:

> At the turn of 2004 and 2005, MulCo was a good company and it had a healthy culture in many ways. However, its profitability was lagging behind its competitors and its global market share was not strengthening anymore. Therefore, it was easy to arrive at the conclusion that firm needed to get onto a new path of growth—profitable growth in particular. The first task was, hence, to create a shared understanding of the existing situation, the need for change, and to define the new strategy.

The president wanted to refocus the employees' perceptions to become more customer-oriented and

Continued

pursue profitable growth by becoming more global in their thinking to achieve competitive advantage. He was also determined to restructure MulCo from functional departments to cross-functional collaboration. Moreover, the president wished the company to become more agile.

The president's first task was to create a sense of urgency for change through communication. He observed the importance of communication in ensuring that the employees maintained their sense of pride in their work and the company, following this change. In fact, for the first time in MulCo's history, the new strategy was communicated to the entire global workforce. The president's dedication to involve and engage everyone in the strategic change placed his communication efforts at centre stage at MulCo. He stated that 'the way we put strategy into practice was ... through the entire organization. It was essential ... to mobilize the entire company ... In this respect, the must-win battles ... connected every employee to the change at least in some way. Nobody was left outside the change ... We "planted" the must-win battles deeply into the organization'.

However, MulCo's historical growth through acquisitions and its decentralized management structure did not fit well with the firm's goal of global alignment, which was at the base of the new strategy. Previously acquired companies had been allowed to keep their own local processes, cultures, and languages until the beginning of the strategic change process. This posed challenges for top management. A large gap was identified between global and local functions in the firm, and the business processes were fragmented and inconsistent. A new process architecture was required to improve global alignment. In addition, the company's corporate values, which originated from the family-firm background, and its entrepreneurial culture presented a challenge in the face of change.

As a result, the strategic change process called for an extensive global communication programme involving both direct top-down communication as well as local communication efforts between managers, supervisors, and employees in the form of a dialogue. These communication efforts were aimed at reaching everyone in MulCo in the spirit of inclusiveness. Historically, communication in the company had been rigid and impersonal, so this degree of communication was unprecedented. The president had to find his own 'voice', and he did so mainly through letters which he sent directly to all organization members in English. These letters were meant to support two-way strategy dialogue between all managers and supervisors and their teams on a personal level. This personal communication provided opportunities to discuss new change-related topics, such as asking: 'What's in it for me?' In order to support the communication within the organization, the president chose strategy facilitators—experts from the middle of the organization, often energized and highly motivated early adaptors—to support local management to facilitate open conversations.

MulCo proved a challenging environment to communicate the new strategic direction towards global alignment. The history of the company as a multi-domestic federation of autonomous subsidiaries had led to fragmented processes and little communication across these units. Additionally, the very contextual engineering language in the firm meant that conveying meanings from the top of the organization was cumbersome, especially early on in the change process. In addition, the lack of urgency for change shaped the way the president's sensegiving efforts unfolded.

Questions for discussion

1. Using forcefield analysis, identify the driving and restraining forces of change in MulCo.
2. Why do you think that the new president adopted a consultative approach to the management of change?
3. How was language used to create a frame for change?
4. What evidence of sensemaking and sensegiving does the case offer?
5. If anything, what would you have done differently, and why?

Source

Adapted from Logemann et al. (2019).

a preferred definition of organizational reality. The sensegiving process bridges the top and middle manager levels as well as the gap between managers and employees.

Initiatives can also be taken at the organizational macro-level to give sense to organizational change processes through corporate storytelling. This provides a narrative framing of the current state of the organization, and the preferred future position, by sensegiving. Essentially, this develops shared values among organization members in understandable and evocative terms. Hence, strategists leading change processes have to have strong communication skills in order to convince others of the necessity of change, and to shape the interpretations of the employees of the preferred future direction and state of the organization (Logemann et al. 2019). Therefore language provides a frame for change. Framing is a process through which people construct a meaning or experience through the use of symbolic constructs, metaphors, and images.

It is important for the student of strategy to understand that sensemaking and sensegiving are critical skills for leading and implementing strategic change. Unfortunately, the skills and talents needed for strong verbal and non-verbal communication do not come pre-packaged in a step-by-step process framework. The development of these skills requires holistic professional and personal growth, but they are a powerful combination when applied along with the prescriptive change management models. For example, the cultural web (discussed in Chapter 4) can be used as a framework for making sense of the existing and the future desired culture of an organization. In addition, the cultural web of the future paradigm of the organization can be used as a framework for creating a sensegiving narrative.

14.7 **Turnaround and crisis management**

We have considered the important leadership skills of sensemaking and sensegiving in the management of change. Before we close this chapter, we will consider two special change management situations: turnaround and crisis management. How can strategists approach particularly complex situations that deal with troubled organizations and managerial practice? There are strategists and consultants who specialize in crisis and turnaround management, and we will discuss the techniques they apply in these difficult situations. We conclude the chapter with a Practitioner Insight featuring one such professional strategist.

Turnaround management

Turnaround management is a process dedicated to organizational renewal. It uses analysis and planning to save troubled organizations, and often seeks to return businesses to financial solvency. It identifies the reasons for failing performance and tries to rectify the problems identified. Turnaround management can involve a management review, including a root analysis of the causes of organizational failure, and a SWOT analysis to determine why an organization is failing based on internal and external factors. Once an analysis is completed, long-term strategic plans and short-term restructuring plans can be created and implemented.

Turnaround managers

Turnaround managers are also called turnaround practitioners. They are often interim managers who stay with the organization for as long as it takes to achieve the turnaround. Assignments typically last from 3 to 24 months, depending on the size of the organization and the complexity of the situation. Hence, turnaround managers are often freelancers working on a daily rate basis, although others work for large organizations and have permanent positions.

Turnaround management does not only apply to distressed companies. It may help in any situation where a new direction, strategy, or general change in the ways of working needs to be implemented. Therefore turnaround management is closely related to change management and post-merger integration management. Turnaround management may also help in high-growth situations, for example where an organization needs to adopt a new approach in order to make the most of some emerging opportunities.

Techniques for repositioning during a turnaround

Seminal work by Mayes, McKiernan and Grinyer (1988), amongst other researchers, has shown that the four main stages/techniques adopted when seeking to create a turnaround are typically known as:

- retrenchment
- repositioning
- replacement
- renewal.

We will discuss each of these stages in turn.

Stage 1. Retrenchment

The retrenchment stage of turnaround management comprises wide-ranging short-term actions intended to reduce any financial losses, stabilize the organization, and, where possible, solve any immediate problems that are causing poor performance. The essential content of the retrenchment stage is often to reduce the scope and size of the organization by selectively shrinking it. This can be done by selling assets, abandoning difficult markets, halting unprofitable lines of production, downsizing, outsourcing, and so forth. These actions can generate resources, with the intention of redirecting the firm's attention towards more productive activities and preventing or reducing further financial losses. Retrenchment is often orientated towards efficiency and a refocusing of the organization on its core business(es).

Stage 2. Repositioning

14

The repositioning stage attempts to generate revenue by introducing innovations and making changes in product portfolios and market positioning. This may include the development of new products, entry into new markets, exploring alternative sources of revenue, and/or modifying the image or the mission of a company. Therefore it is a very different phase from the previous (retrenchment) phase, which typically focuses on efficiency. In the repositioning phase, the leadership is focused on more positive and entrepreneurial strategic thinking.

Stage 3. Replacement

During a turnaround, a decision may be made to replace the chief executive officer (CEO) and/or other senior managers. The thinking behind the **replacement** stage of a turnaround is typically that new managers will help to introduce strategic change, and resulting recovery, based on their different experiences and backgrounds. Top teams, such as the board of directors, may also be concerned that the current CEO and/or other senior managers will have an entrenched view of the organization and its situation, meaning that they cannot view the organization's problems with fresh eyes. If they rely too heavily on their past experience of running the organization, the current leadership may fail to recognize that significant change is necessary to turn the organization around. However, introducing a change of CEO can clearly bring new problems, such as the potential resignation of other well-qualified and experienced employees that the organization would have preferred to retain.

Stage 4. Reorganization/renewal

Within the **reorganization/renewal** stage of a turnaround, the leadership team should begin to pursue long-term actions that are intended to return the organization to a more successful level of performance. The first step may be to analyse the existing strategies and structures within the organization. This examination may end with a closure of some divisions, a development of new markets or business areas, and an expansion into new initiatives and projects. A reorganization/renewal stage may lead the organization to remove inefficient routines or make better use of existing resources. If core competencies are identified and more widely implemented, this may lead to an increase in knowledge sharing and a stabilization of the organization's value.

This stage is sometimes merged into the first two, leaving a '3Rs' strategy of retrenchment, repositioning, and reorganization. It important for the student of strategy to understand that

CASE EXAMPLE 14.4 **A MEDIA MAKEOVER: *THE GUARDIAN* HEADS BACK TO PROFITABILITY**

The media is one of the industries suffering the most from the news being freely available online, and as a multi-century-old publication, *The Guardian* has had to adapt significantly to the changing landscape of newspaper journalism. Considering the degree of turbulence in the external environment, and the cost-cutting that has come with it in order to survive, it is arguably an impressive achievement for *The Guardian* to still publish the news for free online. What's their story?

In January 2016, Katharine Viner, the new editor-in-chief of *The Guardian*, and David Pemsel, the new chief executive of Guardian Media Group (GMG), informed staff that in just six months, the source of money to ensure the financial security of the paper (GMG's endowment fund), had lost £100 million ($140 million) taking it to £740 million. To survive, industry peers advised Mr Pemsel to reduce outgoings, and to put online news behind a paywall. The pair worked to cut costs by 20%, which equated to more than £50 million, and within only two years, they had to reduce their workforce by almost a third.

They did not stop there. On 15 January 2018, *The Guardian* revealed its new format, relinquishing its Berliner design to a format associated more with tabloid newspapers, such as *The Sun* or *The Daily Mirror* in the UK, alongside a new logo in black type. However, they did refuse to introduce a paywall. As an alternative, *The Guardian* provides a membership model,

Continued

14

which asks online readers to contribute whatever they feel is appropriate. The model offers options of either recurring payments, or one-off amounts, and approximately 600,000 subscribers now pay for the content. GMG says the total figure amounts to tens of millions of pounds per year, and the paper receives higher revenue from its readership (including 200,000 print subscribers) than it does from advertisers. In fact, 55% of the company's income now comes from digital activities, which is higher proportionally than other British news outlets.

After several years of losses, GMG is finally starting to break even. In fact, recorded losses have declined from £57 million in the financial year 2015–2016, to £38 million in 2016–2017, to less than £25 million in 2017–2018, and finally to operating at a profit of £800,000 in 2018–2019. In 2018, Mr Pemsel credited the design overhaul in helping to save several million pounds a year, so while the paper looks more like its competitors than ever, its story remains ever more distinct.

Questions for discussion

1. How would you summarize the range of factors driving the management of *The Guardian* to implement their 'media makeover'?
2. Do you see it as a company in distress, a company facing new emerging opportunities, or both?
3. We suggested that the first stage of a turnaround is often 'retrenchment'. What aspects of retrenchment can you identify in *The Guardian*'s story?
4. Can you also identify aspects of 'repositioning' and 'reorganization/renewal'?
5. How would you summarize the business model that *The Guardian* is now operating with?
6. Where do you think *The Guardian* currently is, in terms of its journey towards turnaround? What are the next steps that you would recommend?

Sources

The Economist, 20 January 2018 (the article appeared in the 'Britain' section of the print edition under the headline 'Back in black').

https://www.economist.com/britain/2018/01/20/the-guardian-heads-back-into-the-black (accessed 11 March 2019).

https://www.techworld.com/business/how-guardian-is-hacking-its-business-model-in-digital-world-3694559/ (accessed 20 December 2019).

https://www.theguardian.com/media/2019/may/01/guardian-breaks-even-helped-by-success-of-supporter-strategy (accessed 20 December 2019).

these stages do not address the costs or impact of a turnaround strategy on the organization's employees. Neither do they address the potential impact on the culture of the organization.

Turnaround management in the public sector

Much has been written about turnaround management in the private sector—but what about public sector organizations? Problems of public service 'failure' are high on the political agenda (Boyne 2004, 2006) in the UK and other countries, and national policy-makers and local service managers in the public sector also need strategies to improve the performance of organizations that are struggling or failing.

Boyne (2006) developed a model of the turnaround process (Figure 14.3), and reviews evidence on the effectiveness of different turnaround strategies. There are a substantial number of studies of decline and recovery in private firms—and fewer studies on public sector organizations. The private sector evidence suggests that recovery from failure is associated with strategies of retrenchment, repositioning, and reorganization, as already outlined. In fact, it appears that turnaround is more likely in companies that pursue these approaches. Boyne (2004, 2006) analyses the relevance of this '3Rs' strategy to the public sector, and broadly supports the approach. However, he notes that the replacement stage can be particularly sensitive in the public sector for the following reasons.

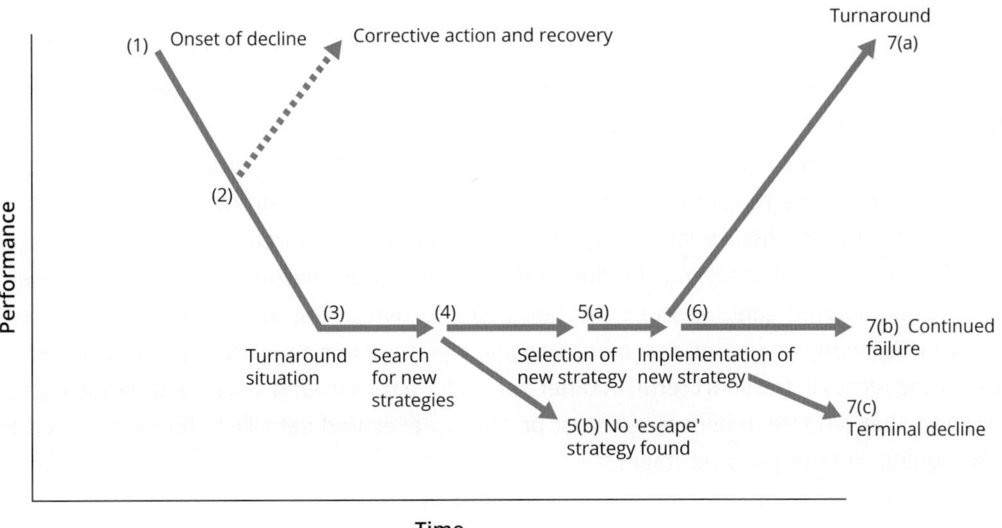

FIGURE 14.3 Stages of organizational turnaround. Source: Reproduced with permission from Boyne, G.A. (2006). Strategies for public service turnaround: lessons from the private sector? *Administration & Society*, **38**(3), 365–388. https://doi.org/10.1177/0095399705286004.

- A new senior management team may revive a private sector company through the comprehensive implementation of strategies of retrenchment and repositioning. However, the scope for the pursuit of these strategies is likely to be more limited in the public sector.
- New executives in the private sector may be able to achieve turnaround through financial incentive schemes for staff and more flexible approaches to human resource management. However, these options are less likely to be available to new senior managers in a public sector organization.
- Leadership in the public sector is political, as well as managerial (e.g. in local government). To identify whether executive succession is likely to lead to turnaround, it is first necessary to discover whether any weakness of leadership is attributable to appointed officials or elected politicians. Service improvement may hinge on democratic as much as managerial processes.

Turnaround management in smaller organizations

Many of the existing studies of turnarounds focus on large organizations. But what about turnarounds in small organizations? Small business owners experiencing decline in performance are typically faced with a choice between growth and retrenchment as turnaround strategies. Rasheed (2005) asks whether such a choice depends upon the owner/manager's perceptions of performance and resource availability during a period of decline. The study finds that they are likely to choose a growth strategy when their perceptions of resource availability and past financial performance are high or low, indicating that small business owners/managers remain aggressive when faced with adverse conditions.

Existing studies have tended to focus on successful turnarounds—so what can we learn from unsuccessful ones? Chathoth et al. (2006) use a case study approach to analyse the turnaround actions of two restaurant firms, comparing their actions with the '3Rs' model we explored earlier in this section. These authors argue that such work is needed, as many small firms in sectors such as tourism and hospitality perish after failing to implement turnaround strategies. In the cases studied, the restaurant businesses did not wait for the retrenchment measures to stabilize the situation before launching into repositioning and reorganizing strategies. Turnaround failure in these cases may be due to the simultaneous execution of the retrenchment and repositioning/reorganizing strategies. Successful turnaround strategies in such businesses should focus clearly on operational measures initially—for example, putting in place stringent cost-cutting tactics in the short term. In other words, for a turnaround strategy to be successful, it appears that a retrenchment stage must be sharply executed initially, before moving on to repositioning and reorganizing stages.

Crisis management

Crisis management is the process by which an organization deals with disruptive and unexpected events that threaten to harm the organization or its stakeholders. The study of crisis management originated with large-scale industrial and environmental disasters in the 1980s. A crisis mindset requires the ability to think of the worst-case scenario while simultaneously suggesting a range of feasible solutions. There are many types of crisis, but some that are important to consider and prepare for include the following:

- **Natural disaster:** including environmental phenomena such as earthquakes and tsunamis.
- **Technological crisis:** caused by human applications of science and technology, including systems failure or human error.
- **Confrontation crisis:** such as boycotts and strikes.
- **Crisis of malevolence:** use of criminal means or other extreme tactics by opponents of the organization (e.g. product tampering or kidnapping).
- **Crisis of deception:** when management conceals or misrepresents information about itself and its products when dealing with consumers and others.
- **Crisis of organizational misdeeds or skewed management values:** when management takes action it knows will harm or place stakeholders at risk of harm, or when management favours short-term economic gain and neglects broader social values and stakeholders other than investors.

We can categorize these crises into three common elements:

- a threat to the organization
- the element of surprise
- a short decision time.

Within an organization, crisis can also be viewed as a process of transformation, where the 'old system' can no longer be maintained. Therefore it has been argued that there is a fourth defining quality of a crisis—the need for change. If change is not needed, the event could perhaps be described as a failure or incident, rather than a crisis. In contrast with risk management, which involves assessing potential threats and finding the best ways to manage and avoid them, crisis management involves dealing with threats before, during, and after they have occurred.

Crisis management is often viewed as a situation-based management system that includes clear roles, responsibilities, and process-related requirements across an organization. The set of responses within the crisis management system will often include actions in the areas of crisis prevention, crisis assessment, crisis handling, and crisis termination. The aim of crisis management is to be well prepared for any crisis situation: to ensure a rapid and adequate response to the crisis; to maintain clear lines of reporting and communication when a crisis occurs; and to agree rules for crisis termination.

Crisis management techniques

But how does a strategist manage a crisis? A strategist should implement the following techniques of crisis management:

- Design and adopt strategies for preventing, alleviating, and overcoming different types of crisis.
- Maintain up-to-date lists of contingency plans; always remain on the alert for potential crisis situations.
- Assess a potential crisis situation and gain an understanding of its influence on the organization.
- Establish metrics to define what scenarios constitute a crisis and should consequently trigger the necessary response mechanisms.
- Deploy a set of methods used to respond to both the reality and the perception of crisis.
- Establish clear communication throughout the response phase of crisis management scenarios.

Crisis management is considered to be a very important process in public relations, as organizations must seek to communicate effectively, as well as taking effective action, during periods of crisis. The credibility and reputation of organizations is strongly influenced by the internal and external perceptions of their responses during crisis situations. The ability to communicate effectively while responding to a crisis in a timely fashion often presents organizations with a significant challenge. There must be open and consistent communication throughout the hierarchy to contribute to a successful crisis communication process.

Crisis management in the public sector

Comfort (2007) argues that 'cognition' is central to performance when seeking to manage crises and emergencies by public administrative agencies. Comfort writes that 'cognition' is defined as the capacity to recognize the degree of emerging risk to which a community is exposed and to act on that information. Using the case of Hurricane Katrina and how the public agencies and crisis responders managed the environmental crisis, Comfort proposes a dynamic system with four main decision points:

- **awareness stage:** detection of risk
- **cognition stage:** recognition and interpretation of risk for the immediate context
- **communication stage:** communication of risk to multiple organizations in a wider region
- **engagement stage:** self-organization and mobilization of a collective community response system to reduce risk and respond to danger.

In practice, it is at these four main decision points, with escalating requirements for action, that human cognitive, communicative, and coordinating skills frequently fail—and this means that organizations are likely to lose control of the situation. In particular, if the first three steps are not successfully completed, the fourth—engagement—is unlikely to succeed.

Crisis management across sectors

Crisis management should also be considered in the particular context of different industries. For example, the hospitality and tourism industry is highly susceptible to crises and disasters of different kinds, so it is particularly important for that industry to have a good understanding of crisis management. The sector is relatively fragmented, and often impacted by a range of external factors. However, an improved analysis of the nature of crises provides insights into how they can be managed, while adopting a more strategic, holistic, and proactive approach (Ritchie 2004). For example, the strategist in this industry should:

- develop proactive scanning and planning
- implement strategies when crises or disasters occur
- evaluate the effectiveness of these strategies to ensure continual refinement of crisis management strategies.

Flexibility and continual monitoring is required by organizations and destinations to design and implement effective strategies to deal with crises. Organizations should take a holistic approach to managing crises, and may have to reconfigure their management structure and consider aspects related to resource allocation and organizational culture, all of which may influence the effectiveness of crisis management. Furthermore, there is a need for cooperation between a wide number of stakeholders, both internal and external to the organization, to effectively plan and manage crises and disasters. Leadership is required to provide direction to the industry in times of crisis and to bring stakeholders together at an organizational and destination level for integrated crisis/disaster management (Ritchie 2004).

Coombs and Holladay (2006) point out that crisis managers believe in the value of a favourable pre-crisis reputation. The prior reputation of the organization can create a 'halo' effect that protects it during a crisis. Coombs and Holladay (2006) undertook two studies—one based on an amusement park, and another on a major retailer—to test if the halo effect seemed to occur in practice. Their study suggests that the 'halo' effect for prior reputation can indeed be a valuable attribute for organizations in crisis, and that the 'halo' may operate within a limited range for organizations with very favourable prior reputations, acting as a shield that deflects the potential reputational damage from a crisis.

PRACTITIONER INSIGHT: **KATHRYN KERLE**

Kathryn Kerle is a senior executive in the financial services industry. She is currently Chair of Greater London Mutual Limited (GLM), which is part of an emerging UK-wide network of 18 mutually owned cooperatives that aim to become regional savings and loans banks, designated to serve the financial needs of people of ordinary means, local community groups, and small and medium sized companies. Prior to her appointment as Chair of GLM, Ms Kerle worked at Moody's Investor Services credit rating agency, and the Royal Bank of Scotland where she was Head of Enterprise Risk Reporting and Chair of the Decision-Making Committee responsible for adjudicating loan cases in a high-profile strategic remediation project at the bank. Ms Kerle discusses the types of change in organizations, but more specifically the role of strategists as leaders in transformational change and crisis situations.

Drawing on her experience in global financial services, Ms Kerle says that change in organizations is about doing new things, such as Goldman Sachs, a Wall Street investment bank, becoming a commercial bank and launching Marcus, a banking service targeted at individual retail customers, or doing things in a new way, such as replacing organizations' legacy IT systems with new systems.

'Given the rate of change in financial services, one of my favourite questions to ask is: what business are you in? Unless firms understand what exactly customers buy from them, you may be confronted with potentially the most dangerous type of competitors: those who look at the problem in a different way. If one were to ask banks in the UK who their competitors were, Royal Bank of Scotland would probably say Lloyds, HSBC, Santander, etc., but until recently they wouldn't necessarily have thought that iTunes might be a competitor through Apple Pay: iTunes could conceivably just exchange payments between people who are already connected, because they're all customers of Apple. Companies such as Apple think of payments as a technical problem, not a banking problem, and therefore they bring tech expertise to it. And who knows, it might turn out to be a technological, as opposed to a banking problem. So, I think dealing with a new competitor might make us think we've looked at this in the wrong way. And do we have the wherewithal to look at it and compete on an entirely different basis?'

Organizational crisis presents its own challenges, but as Ms Kerle says, 'Never allow a good crisis go to waste'. The key thing in the management of radical change is for the leader to 'provide a vision, move forward, and not dwell in the past'.

The traditional approach to change management in crisis has been to adapt very much of a dictatorial style of management. However, if we rely only on diktat and coercion, change management won't work. Ms Kerle refers to a conversation she had with an executive coach about this. She had asked the coach if she had ever worked with a company where an individual was put into an executive role because they were good at managing people. 'She thought about that long and hard. And she said, no, I can't think of a single one. So, we often think that the dictator is the leader. And the person who has a strong ego, loud voice, can command a room, or whatever, is best placed to make things happen. I would really challenge this—if you want lasting change where people are happy to be part of it, and bring their skills and knowledge, that is precisely the wrong way to do it.'

This is quite possibly the case, especially in crisis: 'You may need someone to point out that the house is on fire. Not that people don't already know it, but people very often need to have a focal point. And I think having someone articulate what the issue is, is absolutely useful. But then to actually mobilize people to solve the problem, I don't think that has to be done by diktat at all.' In terms of senior management teams, 'the most effective company boards and the most effective chairs will typically be people who facilitate the arrival at a good decision by the members of the board, not those who inform the board of what their view is.' To be an effective change leader is a difficult skill that requires a 'need to hear all the voices in the room and arrive

Continued

at a solution; there's an art to arriving at a plan. But what is being decided and what the plan for change is should be something that everyone can at least live with because you can't do it yourself. Change is implemented through people and if they're not sold on it, it's just not going to happen.'

Finally, management style has to be flexible and listening. As for the leader, one has to remain calm. 'Different people respond to crisis in different ways. But if you can remain calm, or if you're a naturally calm person, and certainly not reacting in a negative way, then that calms everybody else down.'

CHAPTER SUMMARY

In this chapter we addressed the following learning outcomes.

- **Evaluate the importance of organizations to be able to manage in the present while simultaneously preparing for the future**
  The only constant in our twenty-first century world is change, and no organization is immune to it. We considered the dual task of exploiting the firm's existing resources and capabilities while simultaneously exploring future opportunities and developing new capabilities. Organizational ambidexterity and agility are crucial competencies if a firm is going to survive in highly dynamic competitive environments. This requires strategists to possess a vision of how the future will unfold and a strategy for how the organization can adapt or anticipate future challenges while continuing to manage for the present, e.g. strategic leadership.

- **Understand the concept of strategic change, and the types of strategic change**
  Change can be considered to be strategic if it has an impact on:
  - the competitive position of the firm
  - changes to the firm's overarching business model
  - changes to firm's product and service offer
  - development of new organizational capabilities
  - changes to the geographic scope of the firm through international expansion
  - outsourcing of activities or bringing activities in-house that have previously been carried out by outside suppliers
  - changes to the nature and overall structure of the organization through the formation of strategic alliances, mergers and acquisitions, divestments, etc.

  Organizations can approach implementing change incrementally and consultatively over a period of time or radically through more directive big bang/transformational means. However, recent research has shown that most successful change management initiatives apply both consultative and directive approaches regardless of the type of change effected.

- **Critically evaluate the different approaches to strategic change management**
  Given the importance and difficulty of managing change, a number of change models have been developed to help managers in this task. Most of these models consider the management of change as a rational process and we outlined the benefits as well as the problems with some of the most commonly used change management frameworks. We challenged the assumption that change is a rational linear step-by-step process and

suggested that there is no one correct way to manage change. Change and the management of it are context specific, contingent to the circumstances of the organization.

- **Examine the processes and tools available for managers to effectively manage and implement strategic change**
  Using the prescriptive rational process approach to change management, we considered how forcefield analysis can be used to identify forces that either drive or constrain chance. Once these forces have been identified, there are a number of step-by-step process tools available to strategists to implement change in organizations. These are useful tools for strategists, but we need to bear in mind that change is always context specific.
- **Recognize the role of sensemaking and sensegiving in leading change**
  Successful change management requires skills of sensemaking and sensegiving through which change is conceived and implemented. However, sensemaking and sensegiving skills require strong verbal and non-verbal communication that do not come prepackaged in frameworks. The development of these skills requires holistic professional and personal growth, but they are a powerful combination when applied along with the prescriptive rational change management models.
- **Understand the special cases of change: turnaround and crisis management**
  Turnaround and crisis management are special cases that involve significant and, in some cases, immediate change. Turnaround management is a process dedicated to organizational renewal and it uses analysis and planning to save a troubled organization. Distressed organizations often appoint interim turnaround managers who have experience in returning organizations to financial health. In contrast with turnaround management, crisis management deals with disruptive and sudden unexpected events that threaten to harm the organization or its stakeholders. A crisis management mindset requires an ability to think of the worst-case scenario, while simultaneously suggesting a range of feasible solutions that can be implemented without delay.

END OF CHAPTER QUESTIONS

Recall questions

1. What is understood by organizational ambidexterity?
2. What are the most common barriers to change?
3. What is the purpose of forcefield analysis?
4. What is the difference between sensemaking and sensegiving?
5. What is the difference between turnaround and crisis management?

Application questions

A) What do you consider to be the biggest obstacles for successful change management and why?

14

B) What are the different types of change and how would you approach each change situation with the models outlined in this chapter?

C) Consider an organization that you know well, such as your university. In groups, create a cultural web of the organization in its current form. (You can find a more detailed discussion of the cultural web framework in Chapter 4.) Discuss together in your group what the resulting paradigm tells you about the organization. Assuming that all organizations can change for the better, identify a cultural web of the organization for the future. Comparing the two paradigms, conduct a forcefield analysis for effecting change and discuss how you would conduct a change management initiative.

D) Sensemaking and sensegiving are important leadership skills in change management. Based on the work you have undertaken for Question C, in groups discuss the process that you went through in developing the two cultural webs and create a sensegiving narrative for the future paradigm of the organization that you analysed.

ONLINE RESOURCES

www.oup.com/he/mackay1e

FURTHER READING

Exploring Strategic Change, by Julia Balogun, Veronica Hope Hailey, and Stefanie Gustafsson

Balogun, J., Hailey, V.H., and Gustafson, S. (2016). *Exploring Strategic Change* (4th edn). Harlow: Pearson.

This is one of the most comprehensive books on change management. Written in an accessible style yet drawing on solid theoretical foundations, this latest edition includes up-to-date case examples and new insights in topical areas such as employee engagement.

Unfreezing change as three steps: rethinking Kurt Lewin's legacy for change management, by Stephen Cummings, Todd Bridgman, and Kenneth G. Brown

Cummings, S., Bridgman, T., and Brown, K.G. (2016). Unfreezing change as three steps: rethinking Kurt Lewin's legacy for change management. *Human Relations*, **69**(1), 33–60.

Lewin's model is regarded by many as the fundamental approach to managing change. Lewin has been criticized by scholars for oversimplifying the change process and has been defended by others against such charges. However, what has remained unquestioned is the model's foundational significance. Based on a comparison of what Lewin wrote about change as three steps (CATS) with how this is presented in later works, the paper argues that he never developed such a model and it took form after his death. The authors investigate how and why CATS came to be understood as the foundation of change management and to influence change theory and practice to this day.

Accelerate: Building Strategic Agility for a Faster Moving World, by John P. Kotter

Kotter, J. (2014). *Accelerate: Building Strategic Agility for a Faster Moving World.* Boston, MA: Harvard Business Review Press.

Kotter explains how traditional organizational hierarchies have evolved to meet the daily demands of running an enterprise. For most companies, the hierarchy is the singular operating system at the heart of the firm. In practice, however, this system is not built for an environment where change has become the norm. Kotter advocates a more agile, network-like structure that operates in concert with the hierarchy to create what he calls a 'dual operating system' for change.

Sensemaking in organizations: taking stock and moving forward, by Sally Maitlis and Marlys Christianson

Maitlis, S. and Christianson, M. (2014). Sensemaking in organizations: taking stock and moving forward. *Academy of Management Annals*, **8**(1), 57–125.

This paper develops a definition of sensemaking that is rooted in recurrent themes from the literature and integrates existing theory and research, focusing on two key bodies of work. The first explores how sensemaking is accomplished, unpacking the sensemaking process by examining how events become triggers for sensemaking, how meaning is created, and the role of action in sensemaking. The second body considers how sensemaking enables the accomplishment of other key organizational processes, such as organizational change, learning, and creativity and innovation.

Organizational ambidexterity in action: how managers explore and exploit, by Charles A. O'Reilly III and Michael L. Tushman

O'Reilly, C.A. and Tushman, M.L. (2011). Organizational ambidexterity in action: how managers explore and exploit. *California Management Review*, **53**(4), 5–21.

Conceptually, the need for organizations to both explore and exploit is convincing, but how do managers and firms actually do this? The focus of this paper is to gain a deeper understanding of the challenges of ambidexterity for managers and organizations, and what, in practice, differentiates the more successful attempts at ambidexterity from the less successful organizational efforts in developing ambidexterity.

Sensemaking in Organizations, by Karl E. Weick

Weick K.E. (1995). *Sensemaking in Organizations*. London: Sage.

The teaching and research of organization theory have been dominated by the treatment of strategy and change as a rational process. However, the rational model ignores the inherent complexity and ambiguity of real-world organizations and their environments. This seminal book highlights how the 'sensemaking' process shapes organizational structure and behaviour. The process is seen as the creation of reality as an ongoing accomplishment that takes form when people make retrospective sense of the situations in which they find themselves.

REFERENCES

Abell, D.F. (1993). *Managing with Dual Strategies*. New York: Free Press.

Balogun, J., Bartunek, J.M., and Do, B. (2015). Senior managers' sensemaking and responses to strategic change. *Organization Science*, **26**(4), 960–79.

Balogun, J., Hailey, V.H., and Gustafson, S. (2016). *Exploring Strategic Change* (4th edn). Harlow: Pearson.

Birkinshaw, J. and Gibson, C. (2004). Building ambidexterity into an organization. *MIT Sloan Management Review*. **45**(4), 47–55.

Bower, J.L. (1970). *Managing the Resource Allocation Process: A Study of Corporate Planning and Investment* (2nd edn). Boston, MA: Harvard Business School Press.

Boyne, G.A. (2004). A '3Rs' strategy for public service turnaround: retrenchment, repositioning, and reorganization. *Public Money and Management*, **24**(2), 97–103.

Boyne, G.A. (2006). Strategies for public service turnaround: lessons from the private sector? *Administration & Society*, **38**(3), 365–88.

Bradt, G. (2014). Leverage John Kotter's 'dual operating system' to accelerate change in large organizations. https://www.forbes.com/sites/georgebradt/2014/05/14/leverage-john-kotters-dual-operating-system-to-accelerate-change-in-large-organizations/#23096fffaef8 (accessed 19 May 2019).

Brown A.D. (2000). Making sense of inquiry sensemaking. *Journal of Management Studies*, **37**(1), 45–75.

Burnes, B. (2004). Kurt Lewin and the planned approach to change: a reappraisal. *Journal of Management Studies*, **41**(6), 977–1002.

Chathoth, P.K., Ching-Yick Tse, E., and Olsen, M.D. (2006). Turnaround strategy: a study of restaurant firms. *International Journal of Hospitality Management*, **25**(4), 602–22.

Child, J. (2005). *Organization: Contemporary Principles and Practice*. Oxford: Blackwell.

Clegg, S.R., Kornberger, M., and Pitsis, T. (2005). *Managing & Organizations: An Introduction to Theory and Practice*. London: Sage.

Comfort, L.K. (2007). Crisis management in hindsight: cognition, communication, coordination, and control. *Public Administration Review*, **67**, 189–97.

Coombs, W.T. and Holladay, S.J. (2006). Unpacking the halo effect: reputation and crisis management. *Journal of Communication Management*, **10**(20), 123–37.

Cummings, S., Bridgman, T., and Brown, K.G. (2016). Unfreezing change as three steps: rethinking Kurt Lewin's legacy for change management. *Human Relations*, **69**(1), 33–60.

Daft, R.L. and Weick, K.E. (1984). Toward a model of organizations as interpretation systems. *Academy of Management Review*, **9**(2), 284–95.

Dunphy, D. and Stace, D. (1988). Transformational and coercive strategies for planned organizational change: beyond the OD model. *Organization Studies*, **9**(3), 317–34.

Dunphy, D. and Stace, D. (1993) The strategic management of corporate change. *Human Relations*, **46**(8), 905–20.

Gioia, D.A. and Chittipeddi K. (1991). Sensemaking and sensegiving in strategic change initiation. *Strategic Management Journal*, **12**(6), 433–48.

Goh, F. (2017). 10 companies that failed to innovate, resulting in business failure. https://www.collectivecampus.com.au/blog/10-companies-that-were-too-slow-to-respond-to-change (accessed 8 February 2019).

Hovland, I. (2005). *Successful communication: a toolkit for researchers and civil society organizations*. ODI Working Paper 227, Overseas Development Institute, London.

Hughes, R.I. (1998). Strategic leadership. *Leadership in Action*, **18**(4), 1–8.

Kanter, R.M., Stein, B., and Jick, T. (1992). *The Challenge of Organizational Change*. New York: Free Press.

Kaplan, S. (2008). Framing contests: strategy making under uncertainty. *Organization Science*, **19**(5), 729–52.

Kotter, J. (1996). *Leading Change*. Boston, MA: Harvard Business Press.

Kotter, J. (2007). Leading change: why transformation efforts fail. *Harvard Business Review*, January.

Kotter, J. (2012). Accelerate: how the most innovative companies capitalize on today's rapid-fire challenges—and still make their numbers. *Harvard Business Review*, November.

Kotter, J. (2014). *Accelerate: Building Strategic Agility for a Faster Moving World*. Boston, MA: Harvard Business Review Press.

Lewin, K. (1947). Frontiers in group dynamics. In: Cartwright, D. (ed.), *Field Theory in Social Science.* London: Social Science Paperbacks.

Lewin, K. (1951). *Field Theory in Social Science*. New York: Harper and Row.

Logemann, M., Piekkari, R., and Cornelissen, J. (2019). *Long Range Planning*, **52**(5), 101, 852.

Maitlis, S. (2005). The social processes of organizational sensemaking. *Academy of Management Journal*, **48**, 21–49.

Maitlis, S. and Christianson, M. (2014). Sensemaking in organizations: taking stock and moving forward. *Academy of Management Annals*, **8**(1), 57–125.

Mayes, D., McKiernan, P., and Grinyer, P.H. (1988). *Sharpbenders: The Secrets of Unleashing Corporate Potential*. Oxford: Blackwells.

Mintzberg, H. (1987). *Crafting Strategy*. Boston, MA: Harvard Business School Press.

O'Reilly, C.A. and Tushman, M.L. (2004). The ambidextrous organization. *Harvard Business Review*, April.

O'Reilly, C.A. and Tushman, M.L. (2011). Organizational ambidexterity in action: how managers explore and exploit. *California Management Review*, **53**(4), 5–21.

Pettigrew, A. (1985). *The Awakening Giant: Continuity and Change at ICI*. New York: Basil Blackwell.

Rasheed, H.S. (2005). Turnaround strategies for declining small business: the effects of performance and resources. *Journal of Developmental Entrepreneurship*, **10**(3), 239–52.

Ritchie, B.W. (2004). Chaos, crises, and disasters: a strategic approach to crisis management in the tourism industry. *Tourism Management*, **25**(6), 669–83.

Rouleau, L. and Balogun, J. (2011). Middle managers, strategic sensemaking, and discursive competence. *Journal of Management Studies*, **38**(5), 953–83.

Schoemaker, P.J.H., Krupp, S., and Howland, S. (2013). Strategic leadership: the essential skills. *Harvard Business Review*, **91**(1/2), 131–4.

Walsh, J.P. (1995). Managerial and organizational cognition: notes from a trip down memory lane. *Organization Science*, **6**(3), 280–321.

Weick K.E. (1995). *Sensemaking in Organizations*. London: Sage.

Weick, K.E., Sutcliffe, K.M., and Obstfeld, D. (2005). Organizing and the process of sensemaking. *Organization Science*, **16**(4), 409–21.

CHAPTER FIFTEEN

Designing Effective Strategy Activities

CONTENTS

LEARNING OBJECTIVES

By the end of this chapter, you should be able to:

- ◯ Critically evaluate the usefulness of 'design thinking' in strategizing
- ◯ Explain how strategy activities can be designed to deliver target outcomes whilst building stakeholder engagement
- ◯ Evaluate the possibilities of inclusivity in strategy activities, considering social and practical acceptability and procedural justice and rationality factors
- ◯ Explain the importance of prioritization in strategy work
- ◯ Appraise the value of accessible language, mediating artefacts, and customized methods in designing strategy activities for a diverse group of stakeholders

TOOLBOX

- ◯ **Design thinking**
  A human-centred set of methods and attitudes for creating products, services, solutions, and experiences based on the needs of stakeholders. It is increasingly used in organizations around the world to design strategizing activities.
- ◯ **Knowledge loop**
  An inclusive design method that tests prototypes of planned approaches with a wide range of users in order to refine activity designs for inclusivity. Builds ownership for strategy activities within different stakeholder groups when executed well.
- ◯ **Inclusive design principles**
  A set of principles that can be used to guide design choices towards maximum inclusivity of participants within the practical constraints of the situation.
- ◯ **Activity design checklist**
  A knowledge resource highlighting considerations for the design of strategy activities.
- ◯ **TOWS framework**
  An integrating method for collating contextual insights and strategy options arising from the use of analytical methods. Serves as a platform for creative development of options, and as an input to evaluative methods.
- ◯ **Multi-criteria decision analysis**
  A highly structured rational approach to evaluating and prioritizing options. Creates a detailed explicit record of the reasoning behind decision-making which can aid the resolution of contentious issues, or support groups learning to work together through a strategy activity.

OPENING CASE STUDY **IDEO: TAKING DESIGN THINKING TO THE WORLD**

IDEO is a global design company employing over 700 staff and operating out of nine offices around the world. The organization has its roots in what is known as industrial design—providing contract design services to organizations seeking to develop new products and services. IDEO's industrial design work can be found in many households and offices around the world—from computers and video games to sunglasses and clothing, IDEO has led the design of hundreds of well-known products. A key insight gained early on for the founders of IDEO was the need for design practices to put the user–product interaction at the centre of the process, rather than create products based on the capabilities or preferences of the designer.

According to the IDEO website:

> Since day one, human-centred design has been at the core of everything IDEO does. Drawing upon decades of collective experience in human-centred design, IDEO now applies human-centred methodologies to the world's most complex systemic challenges, from healthcare to government to education and more.

IDEO refers to the philosophy and tools of its human-centred methodology as 'design thinking'.

Despite being a leading organization in the global design industry, IDEO has sought to diversify its offerings in order to protect its future. IDEO now provides a range of online and in-person training products in the use of design thinking. It has also increasingly moved into strategy consulting, competing with the likes of the Boston Consulting Group, Accenture, and McKinsey who have added design thinking methods to their strategy consulting.

Current IDEO CEO Tim Brown comments:

> It's remarkable how often business strategy, the purpose of which is to direct action toward a desired outcome, leads to just the opposite: stasis and confusion. Strategy should bring clarity to an organization; it should be a signpost for showing people where you, as their leader, are taking them—and what they need to do to get there. But the tools executives traditionally use to communicate strategy—spreadsheets and PowerPoint decks—are woefully inadequate for the task. You have to be a supremely engaging storyteller if you rely only on words, and there aren't enough of those people out there. What's more, words are highly open to interpretation—words mean different things to different people, especially when they're sitting in different parts of the organization. The result—in an effort to be relevant to a large, complicated company, strategy often gets mired in abstractions.

His views are a swipe at the traditional approaches of the consulting sector, stereotypically portrayed as conservative, detached, and ineffective compared with the engaged, simple, and practical human-centric approaches of IDEO. Brown (2019:93) proposes design thinking 'as a tool with the power and flexibility to tackle enormously complex social systems' through strategy and solutions. Brown (2019:94) believes that design thinking will be ever more useful to strategists 'as the business models of social media, artificial intelligence, and the internet reveal their dark sides', and organizations, institutions, and governments need an approach to strategy that allows them to transform.

Brown (2019:95) notes that 'The continuous eruptions of new technology and the relentless integration of today's connected universe are driving us to apply design thinking to ever more complex systems'. For example, IDEO is playing a leading in role in researching and consulting about the design of augmented reality products, where digital services are integrated with consumer goods. Brown's aim is that IDEO's involvement will 'ensure that the next generation of smart products—our phones, our cars, our clothing, our medications, our services—will engage with us in ways that are dynamic, flexible, and responsive to the rhythms of everyday life'.

A further societal challenge that IDEO is addressing is how design thinking can enable the circular economy—a sustainable model of economic activity that massively reduces waste and the consumption of resources and energy (see Chapter 13). Brown comments:

> The transition to a regenerative circular economy is now a declared objective of the

European Union and China, and a growing list of companies with global reach, such as Apple, Philips, Steelcase, and L'Oréal, have committed themselves to its implementation. In 2017, IDEO partnered with the Ellen MacArthur Foundation with the goal of producing a practical road map for businesses. Through our Circular Economy Guide, which we've made freely available online, we have begun to engage industry leaders in the pursuit of a business model that creates new value, delivers long-term economic prosperity and ecological stability—and turns a profit. And we are now in a position to propose concrete, practical measures that can be prototyped, piloted, and scaled.

Where IDEO goes next is unclear as it seems there are no 'wicked problems' or intractable challenges that they are unwilling to address. What is clear, though, is how the organization will approach the next venture. As Brown (2015:3) comments, 'Whenever I'm faced with a tough business challenge, rather than trying to use some prescribed CEO logic, I tackle it as a design problem. That's not an inborn ability, it's a skill—OK, a mastery—learned over many years of doing.'

Questions

1. Why might established strategy consultants be concerned at IDEO's entry into their market?
2. Why do you think that IDEO is exploring global/societal challenges, rather than simply focusing on remaining at the leading edge of industrial design for private organizations?
3. Is there a risk in the long term of the organization for IDEO being so centred/reliant on design thinking?
4. Why might IDEO have given away its circular economy guide free of charge?

Sources

www.ideo.com

https://www.ideo.com/news/strategy-by-design

Brown, T. (2015). When everyone is doing design thinking, is it still a competitive advantage? *Harvard Business Review Digital Articles*, 2–3.

Brown, T.J. (2019). Strategic design or design strategy? Effectively positioning designers as strategists. *Design Management Review*, **30**(1), 38–45.

15.1 **Introduction**

Strategy happens through the actions and interactions of practitioners and stakeholders. As we described in Chapter 2, strategy is something people do—a social and political process (Ackermann and Eden 2011a,b). People's history, skills, relationships, and motivations shape strategy outcomes to the extent that they are included and engaged in strategy activity.

As you attempt to activate strategy, choices you make about how and with whom you work will go a long way to determining the outcomes that you achieve. In this chapter, we examine how you can approach the design of strategy activities—and specifically strategizing activities—as defined in the dynamic frameworks discussed in Chapter 2.

We introduce **design thinking**—a design philosophy that is increasingly featuring in strategizing activities across industries, sectors, and countries (Micheli et al. 2019). Design thinking is 'a human-centred, creative, iterative, and practical approach to finding the best ideas and ultimate solutions' to complex challenges such as those faced in strategy (Brown 2008:92).

As discussed in Part 1 of the book, strategy happens through a continuing combination of planned and emergent activities. Without denying that much of strategy is unplanned and organic, we will examine how you can apply design thinking to activate planned activities in an effective way. We will review the principles and methods of design thinking by which strategy can be made inclusive and engaging for stakeholders—drawing on the full range of talents available whilst building commitment to the outcomes from all involved (McGahan and Leung 2018).

In deploying design thinking, having a guiding structure helps to keep participants focused on what matters to everyone, and not just themselves. When shaped according to design thinking principles, strategizing activities can flow in a way that draws the best out of people in an efficient manner whilst mitigating many of the traditional challenges of strategy work (Liedtka 2018b). In the second half of the chapter, we'll examine a generic blueprint for strategizing activities incorporating design thinking that you can adapt to the needs of any specific situation you face when leading strategizing activity in your career.

In short, design thinking gives you a way to approach the design of strategizing activities or strategic change initiatives as described in Chapter 14. Design thinking can also be applied to many other problem-solving, innovation, and change situations and is increasingly associated with strategic leadership practice (Bason and Austin 2019). Design thinking is not an inborn ability—it is a skill acquired through practice (Brown 2015). Gaining insights about design thinking and how it might be applied to the design of business processes in general is increasingly a feature of management education and training that appeals to employers (Kurtmollaiev et al. 2018). The insights you acquire in this chapter should have broader applicability for the development of your practice capabilities.

15.2 **Designing strategy activities**

What is design thinking?

Definition

Design thinking is a set of methods and attitudes for creating products, services, solutions, and experiences based on the needs of stakeholders. Design thinking methods are borrowed from human-centred design practices that define user needs, creatively develop options, and then narrow those options down to valuable, implementable solutions. The attitude of the design thinker will be to emphasize connection with others, integrative thinking, optimism, experimentalism and collaboration in approach (Brown 2008).

A useful way to understand design thinking is as a management philosophy or 'social technology'—like total quality management—that has the potential to change how people work in organizations (Liedtka 2018a). The principles of design thinking encourage empathy, accessibility, and practicality—aiming to see the world as others see it, involving and engaging users, and producing workable solutions through methods of high practical value. As a result, an organization that embraces design thinking will be human centric in its internal operations and customer focused in its approach to providing products and services (Bason and Austin 2019). Indra Nooyi, CEO of Pepsi from 2001 to 2018, credits an embrace of design thinking as a key reason why she was able to drive growth in Pepsi's revenue and share price during her tenure (Ignatius 2015). More broadly, design thinking has been deployed in the strategy work of organizations of all types, sizes, and sectors around the world to design products and services, rethink business processes, and plan for the future (Liedtka 2014; Liedtka et al. 2018b).

Applied to strategy

Design thinking is recognized as a valuable way of approaching strategy development (McGahan and Leung 2018). Applied over time, design thinking enables the development and curation of a portfolio of strategic initiatives by which existing operations can be incrementally improved whilst experimenting with more radical adaptions (Liedtka and Kaplan 2019).

In this chapter, we will examine **how** design thinking might be applied to specific strategizing episodes in which a group of practitioners formulate a response to a perceived strategic need (as defined in Chapter 2). From a design thinking perspective, such episodes are approached as complex problems set within a context that might have many possible solutions (Brown 2019).

For those involved in strategizing, many practical issues may be encountered which can be addressed through the application of design thinking. Table 15.1 shows typical problems facing practitioners during strategizing, design thinking responses, and possible benefits to the strategizing outcome.

As can be seen in Table 15.1, design thinking provides a means of bringing creative contributions into the strategy process by engaging and integrating a wide range of relevant stakeholder talents in a structured way (Brandenburger 2019). This involvement builds momentum and commitment from stakeholders such that the boundaries between strategizing and implementation

TABLE 15.1 **Design thinking in strategy**

Problem facing practitioners during strategizing	Design thinking applied to strategy	Impact on strategy outcome
Trapped in their own experience and expertise	Involve a range of diverse views and perspectives, using a range of methods	A richer set of outcomes that are better attuned to the needs of a wide range of stakeholders
Overwhelmed by the volume and messiness of qualitative data	Organize data using frameworks into themes, patterns, and implications	New insights and possibilities emerge from the data
Divided by differences in team members' perspectives	Build alignment by developing data into options for action	Convergence of agreement on plausible ways forward
Confronted by too many disparate but similar ideas	Use evaluative frameworks to eliminate, combine, and simplify ideas	A limited but diverse set of well thought through options/ initiatives for further review
Constrained by existing biases about what works and what doesn't work	Use common evaluation criteria rather than personal opinion to filter options	Clarity and traceability of why recommendations have been made
Lacking a shared understanding of good ideas and access to user feedback	Engage others in reviewing the work of the team	Credible solutions that are connected with reality
Afraid of change and ambiguity about the new future	Provide a process framework, endorsed by a leader/sponsor, that encourages participation	Shared commitment and confidence in the process

Adapted from Liedtka (2018a:76).

become blurred and the potential for the realization of intended strategy outcomes is increased (Lafley et al. 2012)

When design thinking is applied, the strategizing approach will be characterized by creativity and innovation, user-centredness and involvement, problem solving, iteration and experimentation, interdisciplinary collaboration, visualization, behavioural observations, intuitive reasoning, and tolerance of failure and ambiguity (Micheli et al. 2019:132). In the following sections we will examine how these traits are brought to life for strategizing activities.

Design thinking principles for effective strategy activities

Building engagement and commitment to strategy outcomes

Liedtka and Kaplan (2019:8) observe that traditional strategy 'typically does really badly at engaging employees and fails to build emotional commitment to the outcomes'. The two failures in this statement are connected. Engagement means involvement and inclusion in the activity. Being invited to participate is in itself a sign of respect that increases a stakeholder's positive perception of the strategy activity (Gergen 2009). If the activity seems sensible and appropriate, and the stakeholder perceives that they are able to contribute in a meaningful way, they are likely to participate and make a contribution to the outcomes.

Once that contribution is made, the participant has moved from being a recipient to being a co-creator of the strategizing outcomes. This is the crucial difference, and the participant is likely to feel an emotional commitment to the strategizing outcome from their role in its development. That will make them an advocate for the outcomes and a voluntary agent for change in the subsequent implementation work (Markides 2000). In effect, inclusion in strategizing can connect employees with a sense of organizational purpose, whilst fostering pride and ownership of strategizing outcomes (Bartlett and Ghoshal 1994). If this can be achieved, the boundary between strategy formulation and implementation dissolves as momentum, understanding, and commitment are built through the way in which strategizing is carried out.

This can enable the achievement of intended strategy outcomes. For example, as part of organizational transformation following a difficult period in their history, IBM deployed design thinking to the redesign of the organizational performance management system (see the vignette 'When fixed strategy goes wrong' in the **online resources**).

Through a digital platform, all employees (377,000 at the time) were invited to participate in this strategic initiative. With this inclusive invitation, 18,000 shared their views on the first day alone, and over 100,000 had contributed by the end of the five-month project. Repeated cycles of engagement and questioning with employees led to a system design and name that was a co-creation between the leadership team and the workforce.

The initiative was delivered faster than previous consultant-led 'exclusive' approaches, with consistently favourable feedback from the workforce. According to Diane Gherson, Head of HR at IBM:

> *Our employees created their own program, and there is pride in that ... Their overall message has been 'This is what we wanted ... And more important, they are not feeling like spectators in our transformation; they are active participants ... That's the power of engaging the whole workforce—people are much less likely to resist the change when they've had a hand in shaping it.*
>
> Burrell (2018:57–8).

Strategizing engagement framework

How can we achieve engagement in strategy through design thinking? Four interrelated concepts from the strategy and design literatures can be used to define stakeholder perceptions that will influence engagement:

- **Procedural justice:** perception of the fairness of the activity (Kim and Mauborgne 1998).
- **Procedural rationality:** perception of the activity as sensible and based on well-articulated reasoning (Eden and Ackermann 1998).
- **Social acceptability:** perception of the activity as attuned to the social needs of stakeholders in a trustworthy way (Keates 2007).
- **Practical acceptability:** perception of feasibility and cost effectiveness of the activity (Keates and Clarkson 2003a).

The extent to which a stakeholder holds a positive perception of the activity on these four dimensions will determine the extent to which they will be able to engage and commit with 'heart' (i.e. emotionally) and 'mind' (i.e. cognitively). These dimensions of engagement are shown in Table 15.2. Each dimension is likely to have more influence over either emotional or cognitive commitment.

With a stakeholder focus, design thinking can be applied to plan strategizing activities which are perceived to be fair, sensible, attuned, and doable. If perceptions as outlined in Figure 15.1 are achieved, stakeholder engagement and commitment to outcomes may well enhance the prospects for successful implementation.

The importance of inclusion

For strategizing, design thinking will drive inclusion and participation from a wide range of stakeholders and seek to represent the broadest range of stakeholder needs in the outcomes arising (McGahan and Leung 2018).

We have established that being invited to participate in strategizing is the first step to building engagement and commitment to outcomes. Wide inclusion of stakeholders also increases the diversity of creative inputs to strategizing, increases the likelihood of outcomes that meet stakeholder needs, and prevents potential negative consequences for implementation that might arise by excluding stakeholders.

TABLE 15.2 **Engagement factors in the design of strategizing activities**

Factor	The design of strategizing activity ...	Leading to commitment from:
Procedural justice	... seems fair and involves all those that should have a voice in proceedings	HEART > head
Procedural rationality	... involves sensible steps and targets appropriate valuable outcomes	HEAD > heart
Social acceptability	... seems trustworthy and attuned to our culture and situation	HEART > head
Practical acceptability	... seems a worthwhile use of time and resources that we will actually be able to do	HEAD > heart

FIGURE 15.1 Strategy engagement framework.

It is normal for business processes to be designed to serve the needs of the people that created them, rather than the people they serve (Bason and Austin 2019). Consider Figure 15.2, which shows two approaches to designing strategizing activities. Approach 1 is the traditional approach with a senior management focus. By design, and probably unintentionally, groups of stakeholders will be excluded from participation. Approach 2 is a design thinking approach, which focuses on the needs of all stakeholders and excludes no-one. By default, lead user needs are accommodated.

To move from approach 1 to approach 2 means designing the strategizing activity (the methods, timescale, location, tasks, etc.) to be suitable for all stakeholder needs as an enabler of inclusion and participation. Such an inclusive strategizing design would be the natural outcome of design thinking's 'simplifying and humanizing' methods (Kolko 2015:70). As the British Design Council (2006) suggest, 'inclusive design is good design' that will typically benefit all users and lead to enhanced system performance.

With an inclusive design in place, a diverse set of stakeholders can be invited to participate. From a design thinking perspective, involving a wide range of stakeholders increases the diversity of inputs and the likelihood of novel value-adding outcomes being created (Liedtka 2018b). The more challenging and complex the stakeholder needs, the more benefit that will be derived from inviting a representative set of stakeholders to participate.

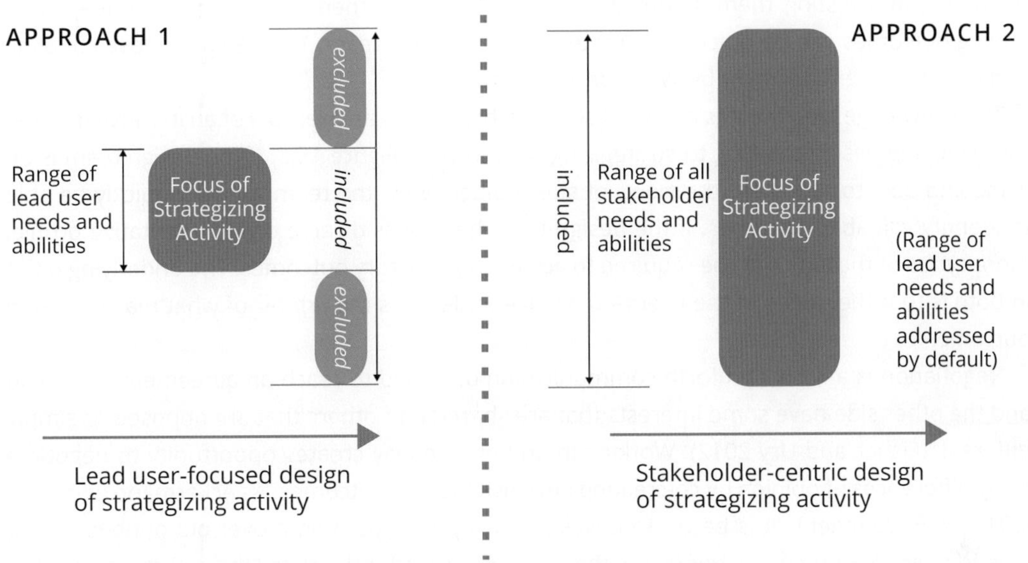

FIGURE 15.2 Approaches to inclusion in strategizing.

A dual aim of design thinking is to enable 'superior solutions' in parallel to 'buy-in' (Liedtka 2018b). Inclusive strategizing efforts benefit from accessing a wider range of capabilities in the organization as well as creating 'interlocking rationales' between stakeholder groups about what needs to be done (Canales 2013). This can prove vital to implementation efforts. As Brown and Martin (2015) observe, when stakeholders aren't involved in the preparation of a strategy they will likely critique the solutions and focus of the strategy to the point of rejecting the outcomes on the basis that it is someone else's work. This rejection is highly likely to happen when the strategy outcomes propose significant change.

In a recent consultancy engagement, one of the authors of this textbook was working with a regional bank in the UK. In a workshop session with the managerial team one level below the board, the management team were highly critical of recent strategic recommendations by the board. The author hijacked the rest of the workshop to go through a strategizing activity with the managerial team. The team produced an identical set of recommendations to those proposed by the board! To be fair, the managerial team had a reflective moment and laughed about how their perspective had changed in such a short space of time. But the issue was significant. By excluding the managerial team from strategizing, the board had inadvertently created political opponents and organizational resistance to plausible recommendations.

Negotiating outcomes

Design thinking encourages an experimental 'fail-fast' attitude from participants. Experimental approaches are an effective way of exploring creative possibilities (Binns et al. 2014). Prototypical approaches—in which ideas are shared in draft format, using rough descriptions, sketches, and approximate models—to engage others in design work can foster shared ownership of outcomes (Comi and Whyte 2018). Further, by working in an iterative way—suggesting ideas, discussing and testing them, learning and improving, and then repeating the cycle—value-adding outcomes can be quickly co-created by the 'design' team. This requires close coupling and continuous engagement between designers and users.

The knowledge loop (Keates and Clarkson 2003b:76–83) is an example of an iterative method for deploying design thinking to strategizing, as shown in Figure 15.3. If the design team is diverse and able to represent the views of stakeholders well, the team will very quickly be able to identify valuable outcomes. If the design team has a less diverse or representative profile, more cycles of the loop may be required to achieve satisfactory outcomes. The underlying point in both is that the needs of the users—the stakeholders—is the arbiter of what makes a good outcome.

Negotiation is a 'back and forth communication designed to reach an agreement when you and the other side have some interests that are shared and others that are opposed or simply different' (Fisher and Ury 2012). Working in an iterative way creates opportunity to negotiate away differences of opinion by co-creating new insights and outcomes. As Ackermann and Eden (2011b:296) comment, 'it is better to develop new options than fight over old options'. Being able to negotiate outcomes reinforces the sense of procedural justice ('the activity is fair—I've been listened to') and procedural rationality (better outcomes are achieved by the collective than the individual could manage) of participants. These perceptions enhance what is known as the 'political feasibility' of the strategy. Political feasibility means that participants won't subvert or work against the implementation of an outcome because they feel a sense of ownership and anticipated benefit in making it happen (Ackermann and Eden 2011a).

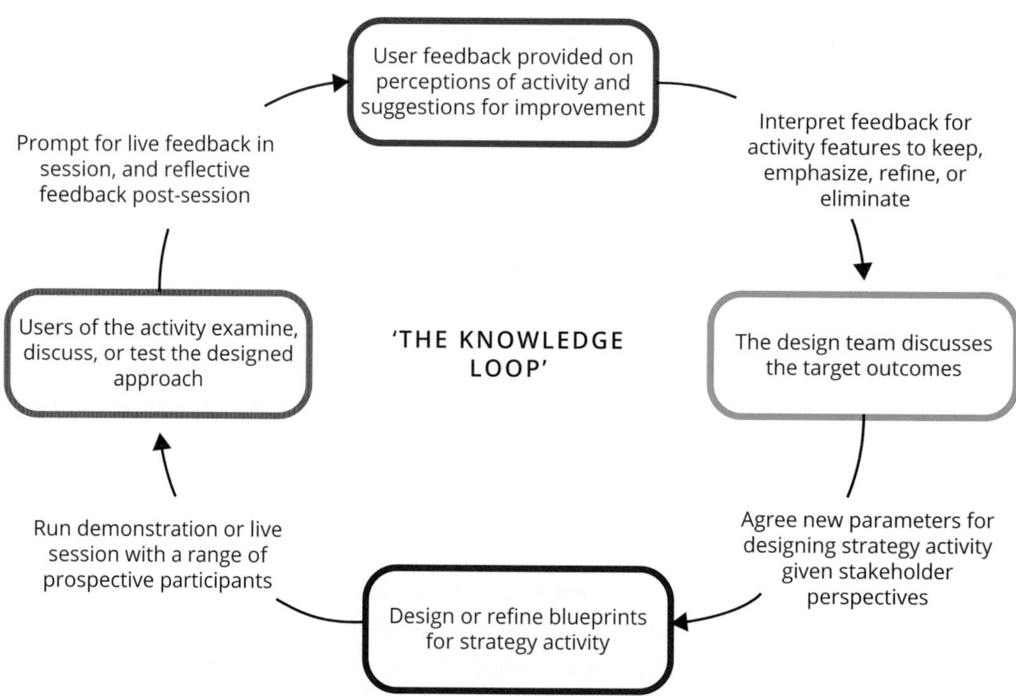

FIGURE 15.3 Knowledge loop method. Source: Reproduced with permission from Keates S., Clarkson J. (2004) Knowledge transfer in inclusive design. In: *Countering design exclusion*. Springer, London. Copyright © 2004, Springer-Verlag London.

15

CASE EXAMPLE 15.1 **DESIGN THINKING IN STRATEGIZING AT C-CHANGE**

C-Change is a supported-living organization that works with and for adults with learning difficulties, disabilities, and/or mental health issues. With a strong interest in the preservation of human rights, C-Change's aim is to allow people to live the lives they choose. Founded in Glasgow in 2001, but now working at localities across Scotland, C-Change employs about 250 staff providing services for about 50 individuals (https://c-change.org.uk/).

In 2012, the CEO Dr Sam Smith decided to approach the organization's strategy renewal in a more inclusive way than previous versions (see the Practitioner Insight at the end of this chapter for more insights from Sam). Engaging with a member of the author team of this textbook, Sam commissioned a redesign of strategy-making activities to conform with the following parameters:

1. the methods used should be the same for everyone
2. a wide range of stakeholder groups should be included—from service users to the board
3. outputs should be generated that are meaningful to all involved
4. the communication throughout should be accessible
5. the work should be completed within six months.

Working with a range of stakeholders from C-Change, changes to the design of the strategy activities were instituted, as per Table 15.3. The exact changes were agreed iteratively using the 'knowledge loop' approach to produce prototype methods, gain feedback from stakeholders, refine thinking, and retest until satisfactory outcomes were achieved. For example, as some of the service users struggled with the language of the process, as well as document formatting (font type and size), the documentation was rewritten to accessible standards. This involved simplifying the language, adding visual images to accompany the text, and increasing the font size.

Applying design thinking principles made the methods and language of the strategizing activity accessible to all stakeholders. This wasn't just a gimmick to satisfy an engagement criterion. Board members and management participants from the previous strategy exercises reported that it was easier to follow the strategy process and make improved contributions with the revised design.

After several weeks of design, five initial strategy ideas gathering sessions were activated over a period of three months at Strathclyde University. The use of a graphic artist, in a novel setting away from the office, in parallel with analytical data capture through causal mapping guided by a facilitated conversation, gathered a rich set of stakeholder perspectives.

Further, participant motivation and interest were raised, and intermediate outcomes were generated in the forms of graphic and causal maps (see Figure 15.4 and the discussion on causal mapping in Chapter 3, including Figure 3.1 which illustrates a causal map). Within the organization, the word spread about the strategy sessions as participants returned with stories of being listened to and achieving tangible progress. The use of parallel methods didn't extend the time taken to gather data. A marginal cost was incurred, which delivered engagement and inclusivity outcomes as well as analysable data.

The outputs of the live strategy sessions were compiled, drawing heavily on the analytical data gathered from causal mapping to identify patterns and priorities. The intermediate outcomes were then presented back to the full organization for review, priority voting, and rating of options. This was done in an open manner with a day-long display of options and manual voting methods by which all stakeholders could offer an opinion on the strategy options identified (see Figure 15.4). Upon completion of the prioritization review, the outcomes were written up and a range of outcomes produced. A vision, mission, and statement of strategic priorities were prepared in an inclusive format, along with action plans to start delivering against the priorities. A multimodal output video was created to communicate with all stakeholders (https://www.youtube.com/watch?v=nXiM8oka8n8).

Continued

TABLE 15.3 **A sample of adjustments made by applying inclusive design principles to strategy activities**

Aspect	Original	Adjusted	Reasoning
Involvement of 'users'	Strategy sessions with management team and board	Strategy sessions across hierarchical levels and with service users	Rethink 'users' of strategy as all with a direct stake in the organization's future, not just senior management
Accessibility of instructions	Use plain written English in business language for email instruction, post-session feedback, etc.	Revise format of paperwork templates for accessibility and introduce 'multimodality' for communications	Design out unnecessary barriers to understanding the process; make the materials more engaging, and better prepare all users for what to expect in the sessions and to contribute their views
Accessibility and usability of strategy prototyping mechanism	Use computer-generated causal map as transitional object/ prototyping mechanism	Augment computer-generated causal map with visual display prepared live in parallel by a graphic artist	Causal mapping retained to protect functionality of process (capacity to analyse outcomes); addition of visual displays provided engaging alternative representation
Location of sessions	Run all aspects at C-Change	Run initial workshops at the university and host collective event at C-Change	Enhance user engagement with novel off-site experience, maximize promotion of research project, and enable user participation in final collective session
Accessibility of collective feedback mechanism	Use computer voting session to evaluate collective outcomes	Use simple manual methods to gather collective outcomes	Avoid introducing barriers to participation—cognitive, sensory, or time availability—and maximize the potential for social interaction

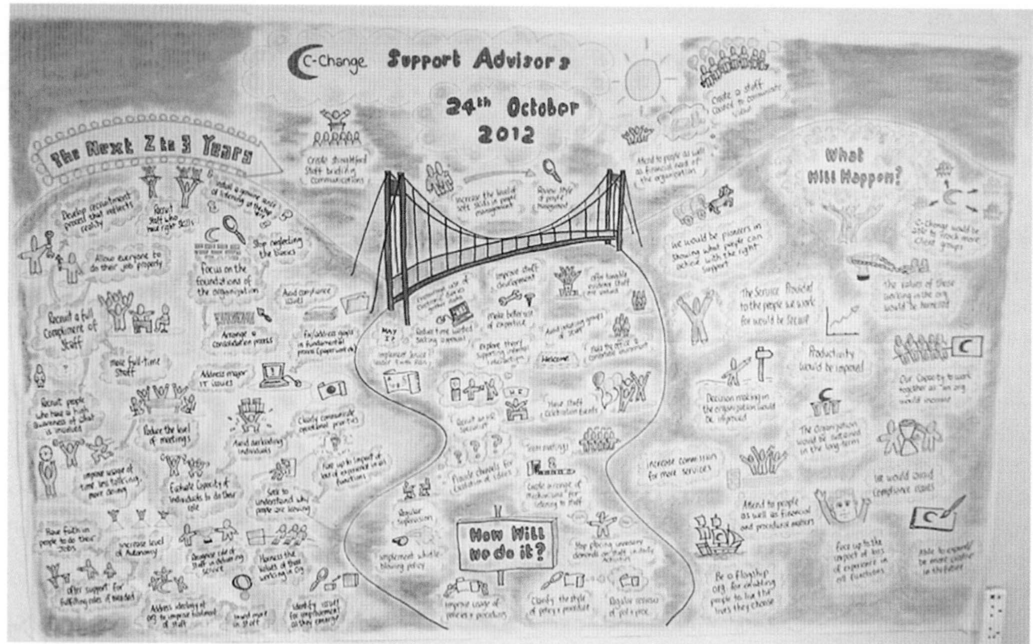

FIGURE 15.4 A visual display capture of a strategy ideas session.

'This was a good process as it is really important that everyone has their say and that the people who C-Change work for are able to contribute to decisions about the future.' - Improvement Council Member

'The graphical mapping technique was ideal to ensure that there was equity in capturing the information of all the group which meant the reporting took account of everyone that contributed. It removed any room for excluding views of any one individual or group, making it a fair and open process.' - Functional Manager

'I think the process really works to allow people across the whole organisation to have a voice. I have worked as a personal development worker and now manage others as a support adviser—these two groups make up the majority of C-Change staff so it's important to see that they can influence strategy work and take the same ownership of C-Change's destiny as the people we work for and the central management team.' - Support Adviser

'We meant to ensure that the people who use the services of C-Change could fully participate in setting the strategic direction of the organisation. As it turns, we could then see that the process could yield better outputs for the organisation by enabling us to draw on the full range of talents and expertise of all stakeholders.' - Functional Manager

'The final session allowed us all to see what had been said by others—the voting was great as it gave us another chance to say what we think, even if we hadn't attended a workshop.' - Personal Development Worker

'Everybody involved in these sessions matters to the future of C-Change—not just managers—that's why everyone needed to be asked what they thought.' - Improvement Council Member

'The mapping session was amazing! I love the combination of the visual and the analytical—it was fascinating to be involved in this and it has got to be an approach that other organizations are going to want to do too.' - Board Member

'It was great to go to the University—people'll be thinking I'm a professor!'- Improvement Council Member

'The project achieved what it set out to do—the unique perspectives and contributions of people who receive support was valued and included along with other stakeholders and strategy development was richer and more considered as a result of their input. This work shows that individuals who have been assigned reputations for challenging services can contribute to strategic planning when supported by a process that is inclusive & accessible.' - CEO

'I found the voting session very accessible and didn't feel any barriers to contributing to the process.' - Improvement Council Member

FIGURE 15.5 Participant comments on the inclusive strategy process.

Figure 15.5 contains the views of participants as to how design thinking principles influenced the attainment of fair, sensible, engaging, and practical strategy activities. Six years later, the co-created vision and mission for the organization endure, as do some of the organizational priorities. New priorities have also been added, and old ones renewed, as the organization continues to provide a valuable service in the face of a continually changing external environment. When the time comes for the next major strategy engagement, C-Change will be seeking to find further ways to apply inclusive methods to create meaningful and engaging strategy outcomes that benefit and guide the organization in the long term.

Questions for discussion

1. From a design thinking perspective, critique the strategy design approach in this case example.
2. Do you think that this design thinking approach to strategizing was only feasible because C-Change is a third-sector organization? Explain your answer.
3. What seem to be the main advantages and costs associated with applying a design thinking approach?
4. In what way could it be claimed that the design thinking approach has led to effective strategy outcomes?

15.3 Applying design thinking principles

To design a strategizing episode is to lay down a blueprint for how a set of strategy decision outcomes are to be achieved through the work of practitioners. This blueprint will include details of practical matters, such as how data will be sourced, what methods will be deployed by whom and by when, and how stakeholders will be communicated with and engaged towards achieving the target outcomes. These matters are non-trivial contributors to achieving productive outcomes from strategizing (Battilana et al. 2019). This blueprint may also address how activities can be designed in a way that delivers maximum benefit. Through design thinking, strategizing activities can be enacted that are meaningful to, and representative of, the needs of as wide a range of stakeholders as possible. This application of design thinking connects with the notion of 'attentional design' introduced in Chapter 2.

If you are leading the design of a strategizing activity, it is useful to be aware of a range of parameters (Glaser 2017). These parameters will include, but may not be limited to, the matters identified in Table 15.4. We have presented this prompting table in question format in keeping with a theme in the design thinking literature. Questions are highlighted as more powerful than statements in generating creative and value-adding contributions from participants (Liedtka 2014). As you practise using design thinking, you may wish to attempt a 'question burst' with participants in a brainstorming session. This involves setting a rule that participants can only speak

TABLE 15.4 **Strategy activity design considerations**

Parameter	Design questions
Scope of activity	What decisions need to be made through this strategy process? How much time do we have available? What resources—people, funding, materials, locations—will we be able to use in this strategy work? How much power do we have to decide about the process design?
Inputs and participation	Which informational inputs are required for this strategy activity? Which groups of stakeholders need to be represented in this process? Who has relevant knowledge from within those stakeholder groups to feed into this process? Who needs to be involved for political/influencing reasons? Who needs to be involved in order to lay the foundations for successful implementation?
Language and communication	What language and terminology will be effective? What terminology and concepts can we use that will be meaningful and understood by all stakeholders? How can we write communications in a way that meets the needs of all strategy 'users'? How should this strategy activity be explained to participants?
Analytical methods	What methods will help us achieve target outcomes from the strategy activity? What ways of working will fit organizational culture and history? What design of methods will enable participation within time and resource constraints?
Integration methods	How can data and insights gathered from analytical methods be compiled and integrated? How can a platform for prioritization and decision-making best be created?
Prioritization methods	What approach will we use to deliver prioritized 'rational' outcomes? How do we make appropriate decisions from analytical outputs? How do we keep a record of our decision-making?

in questions (e.g. 'what if we could ... ?') when responding to a shared challenge. The tentative nature of questions encourages greater creativity in participant contributions (Gregersen 2018).

Aside from grappling with the requirements in Table 15.4, according to Breene et al. (2007:88) being a lead facilitator of strategizing requires you to be trusted, a multi-tasker, a jack of all trades, a doer not just a thinker, able to focus on multiple horizons, an influencer not a dictator, comfortable with ambiguity, and objective, as far as possible. The lead facilitator also has a responsibility to ensure clear communication of session objectives with participants as an enabler of successful attainment of strategizing outcomes (Healey et al. 2015).

In the following sections, we will explore the parameters highlighted in Table 15.4, with sample illustrations, to provide insights as to how strategy activities might be designed in practice from a design thinking perspective.

Investigate scope of activity

Planned strategy activities will typically have a sponsor—an individual or group of individuals that purposefully initiate the activity. This is a crucial ingredient for success from a design thinking perspective, encouraging candour and creativity from those involved (Bason and Austin 2019). The sponsor will provide political support for the activity—what is often referred to as 'air cover' (Dunne 2019:122). This support provides participants with the required sense of psychological safety to accept a tolerance of failure and ambiguity in iterative experimental working (Kupp et al. 2019).

As strategy has many possible definitions, scopes, and interpretations, it is important to clarify with sponsoring stakeholders the exact boundaries, what they mean to achieve by the strategy activity from the outset, and the scope implications, as suggested in Figure 15.6. For example,

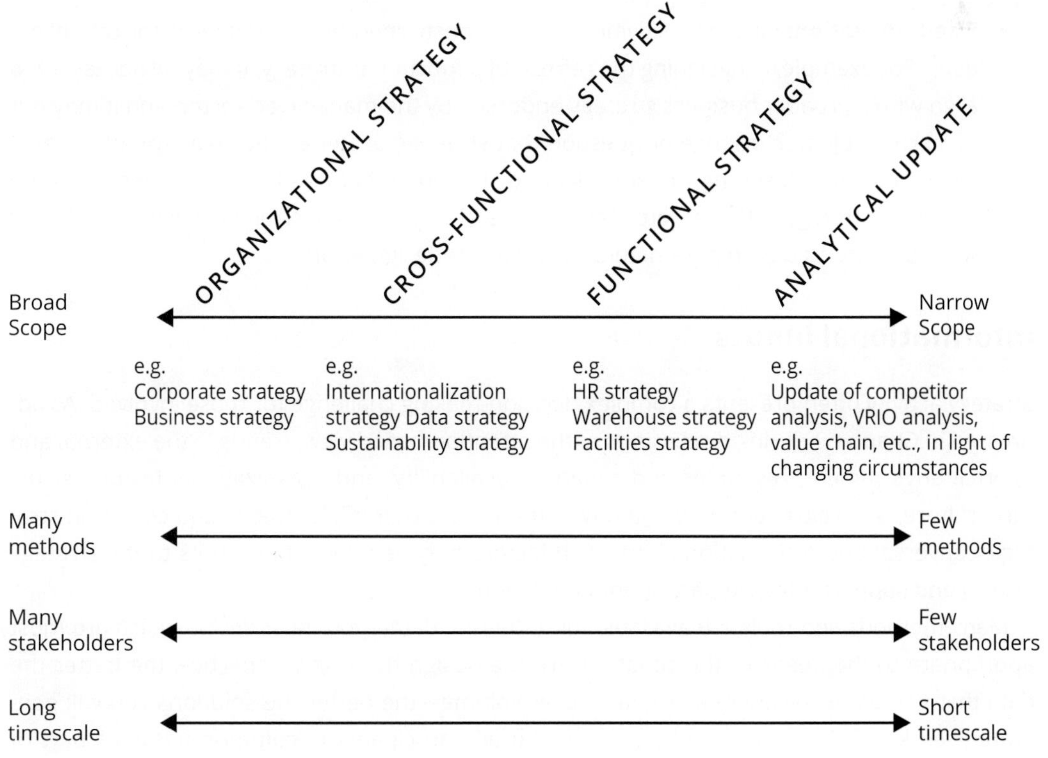

FIGURE 15.6 Sponsor scope considerations.

'I'd like us to update our functional HR strategy', 'I'd like to create a new three-year business strategy for this division', 'I'd like to develop a data strategy for our production operations', etc. It is also important to engage the sponsor from the outset to clarify what 'success' looks like for the work. This means defining the nature and formats of outputs, the timescale, the resource requirements, and any fixed criteria for method or involvement:

- **Nature and formats of outputs** Sponsors may well have a clear idea as to what the output of a strategy activity should 'look like'—whether it is a document, Gantt chart, video, set of verbal agreements, illustrations, booklet, website update, etc. This may also include criteria about social outcomes, such as changes in awareness, engagement levels, and learning within affected stakeholder groups.
- **Timescale** Sponsors may have a fixed end date by when a strategy activity needs to yield agreed outputs; for example, a divisional strategy might need to be completed by a certain date in order to feed into a broader organizational strategy process. If this is the case, the design of activities would have to work backwards from the endpoint to identify optimal arrangements. If no fixed end date is in place, a timescale can be proposed to the sponsor during design work, to check that it is acceptable to their needs.
- **Resource requirements** Strategy activities involve stakeholder time, managerial attention, organizational effort, and often financial expenditure. These resource requirements may well have to be approved by the sponsor in advance, and an available budget of resources may constrain the design options available. Knowing the budget for resources—and discussing the possibilities of different levels of resource constraint—is an important design parameter to agree up front. This includes the extent to which different stakeholders may be called upon to participate.
- **Fixed obligations** Strategy activities may be constrained by cultural or historical obligations. For example, in designing the refresh of a functional strategy, it may be necessary to align with a broader business strategy endorsed by the managing director, and it may not be permissible to challenge or question that strategy, or there may be a style of engagement in a cultural setting (organizational or national) that needs to be respected in the design of strategy activities, etc. Being aware of any fixed constraints which the sponsor wishes to use as design parameters saves later redesign efforts.

Informational inputs

Strategy activity often presents a complex decision-making challenge for those involved. As addressed in Chapter 2 during discussions of the attention-based view, trends in the external and internal environment, resources and capability availability, and organizational history, structure, culture, and values are among a few of the factors that might enable and constrain strategic conversations. Information about such factors may be relevant as inputs to the strategy activity and support effective participant interaction.

Many methods and tools are available for gathering data—you must decide which are most appropriate to the needs of the situation. From a design thinking perspective, the better the data that you gather—variety and quality over volume—the better the solutions you will generate (Liedtka 2018b). Data can be shared with all participants in common packs as part of strategizing (Sull et al. 2018). Data might be obtained from the organization's own research, or existing sources such as trade or academic journals, government publications, market or industry research firms, internet searches, or media companies. Often, industry bodies and forums will undertake research on trends, issues, and opportunities affecting their members. Such publications can be invaluable sources of insights that can be fed into strategy activities. There is much information in the public domain that may be of use—the boundaries of the strategy activity identified can put helpful limits on the scope of information searches.

Equally, internal sources of information may be called upon to support strategy activities. This can include operational and commercial performance data, such as process efficiencies, operating costs, customer revenue and sales trends, product profitability, etc. This may be in a raw format (i.e. large quantities of data as collected) or in the form of 'business information'. Business information is obtained by analysing raw business data to look for patterns, trends, or derivatives that provide insights about organizational performance.

The design thinking literature also strongly advocates spending time 'in the field', sharing experiences with stakeholders in order that you can gain first-hand insights as to their needs. (Kolko 2015). Data gathered from the field may reveal surprising or even shocking insights. Bason and Austin (2019) cite an example of a Danish insurance agency that had won awards for the productivity of its business processes. However, upon conducting design thinking fieldwork, the process owners discovered that customers found their approach stressful and challenging to engage with.

Who should participate in strategy activities?

'Who to involve?' will always arise as a question to be addressed during strategy activity design. Developing Barnett's (2008:612) model of how decisional outputs are reached from a set of informational inputs, Figure 15.7 shows an inclusive architecture of participation mirroring the design thinking principles on inclusion. Senior management ideas and data from internal and external sources are included alongside matter from experts, experienced colleagues, representatives of different stakeholder interests (including possibly customers and suppliers, local communities, trade unions, etc.), and different levels of the organization (from operational staff through to owners).

Dobusch et al. (2019) describe the advantages of such an inclusive approach as including increased diversity of input and enhanced commitment to the outputs from those involved, and stronger stakeholder comprehension of decision outputs increasing the likelihood of successful implementation. By including inputs from a diverse range of stakeholders, the strategy activity is more likely to incorporate organizational wisdom—reflecting operational and commercial realities—without sacrificing senior management ambition, stretch, and political considerations, or compromising data sensitivity. Mixing a broader range of inputs also increases the potential for novel combinations of ideas, breakthrough thinking, and making creative options available for consideration.

An interesting tactic that we have seen deployed in practice is to invite an 'informed third party' to offer their input as a way of stimulating new thinking. McGahan and Leung (2018:112) describe the case of Telus, a Canadian telecoms firm. In aiming to create a 'stakeholder centric strategy', Telus involve external stakeholders as partners in the process. Judy Mellett, the Service Design Director at Telus, comments on the benefits: 'Broad stakeholder engagement not only garners diversity of input and builds advocacy for resulting solutions and strategies, it also identifies linkages that were previously unarticulated—ultimately lowering uncertainty and risk.'

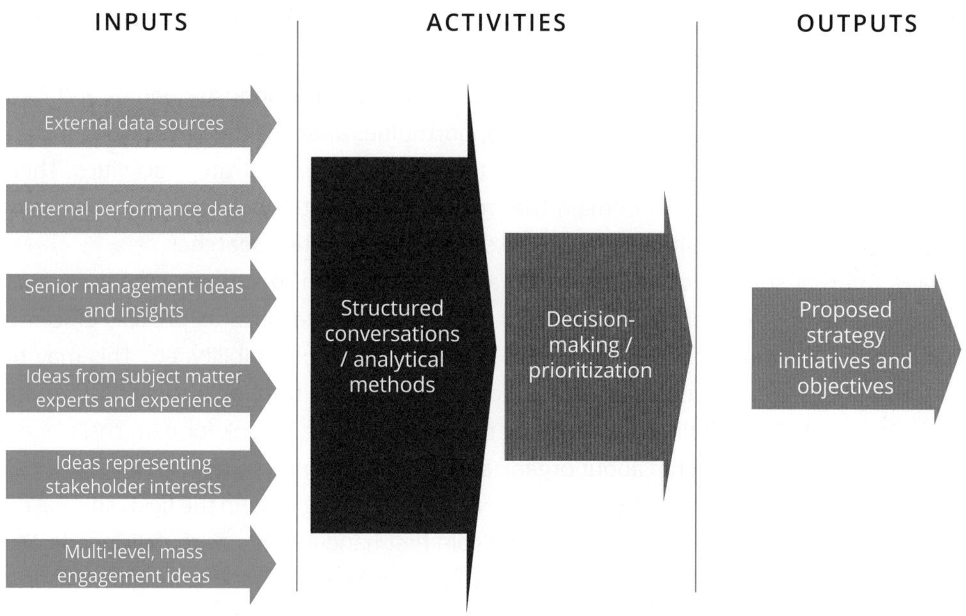

FIGURE 15.7 Broadening participation in strategy-making approach.

Opting for a broader participative approach to strategy activities requires a leadership team that is open to the thinking of others and willing to invest the additional time and organizational resource required. A study of deployment of design thinking in a US Government department showed such leadership support was crucial to embedding new ways of working (Liedtka et al. 2018b). From a design thinking perspective, leaders should consider the broader involvement of stakeholders as a 'positive loss of control' (Bason and Austin 2019:89).

Accessible language

The language, concepts, and theories of strategy can limit the contribution of many participants in a strategy activity (Belmondo and Sargis-Roussel 2015). In other words, participants may be unable to engage with strategy activities, even if they are motivated to do so, because of unfamiliarity with the way strategy is communicated and explained (Mantere and Vaara 2008). For those designing strategy activities, broadening stakeholder engagement brings this issue to the fore. Strategy activities designed for those at the top of an organization's hierarchy may deploy sophisticated methods and management technologies peppered with acronyms and abstract business concepts (Suominen and Mantere 2010). This sort of language can be impenetrable to 'outsiders', even from within the same organization.

This sort of barrier to participation goes against design thinking principles. Whether targeting objectives, deciding methods, communicating with participants, or facilitating discussions, the language used will have a strong influence on the level of inclusivity that can be achieved. As far as the situation will allow, communication with participants should be in plain English, avoiding jargon, and in a format that matches organizational norms (Liedtka et al. 2018b). As with many inclusive approaches, in our practical experience the use of accessible language tends to be well received by all stakeholders, including the 'typical' strategy users in senior management roles.

Multimodal communication

Design thinking encourages what is known as multimodality in communication. Multimodality is the use of multiple means, in parallel, of achieving the same user utility or outcome. Multimodality adds redundancy to designs that would suit the typical user, but enables a broader range of user participation (Baskinger 2008).

For example, the 'typical' user of a television uses the audio and visual outputs. However, there are further groups within the user population that can't engage with either the audio or visual outputs. Adding closed captioning and audio description features allows the aurally or visually impaired to be able to engage with television programmes. These features are in addition to, rather than in place of, the core audio and visual features of the programme. The user can decide which format suits them best, referring to any combination of the audio and visual feeds, captions, or audio descriptions, according to how they can best engage with the programme for the most effective user experience.

It takes time and effort to include multimodality in designs, and therefore it incurs a cost. It is not always necessary, as sometimes a single design solution can be found that meets the needs of all in the user population (e.g. a ramped entrance to a building can be a single design solution that will meet the access requirements of all users). However, when a single design solution is not possible, multimodal design can be considered to meet multiple stakeholder needs (Arnaud et al. 2016).

In strategy work, multimodality of communication plays a key role in achieving inclusivity. For example, from a traditional design perspective, strategy activity outputs will be communicated in line with the anticipated needs of the typical user, such as a senior management team member. From an inclusive design perspective, strategy outcomes will be communicated in however many modalities are required to meet the needs of all stakeholders (Steinfeld and Maisel 2012). For example, modalities of output might include an action plan, verbal agreements, or Gantt charts.

From a design thinking perspective, multimodality of methods is also worth considering in strategy work in order to gather as wide a range of inputs and stakeholder perspectives as possible (Liedtka 2017). For example, some participants may not be comfortable participating in a workshop activity. Instead, they may wish to share views by anonymous survey or suggestion box. Whilst these different modes of engagement take extra effort, the benefits gained are an increased diversity and volume of inputs to the strategy work and engagement from the stakeholder population. Using video, audio, or any other means that makes it easy for participants to understand and engage in the work is to be encouraged (Bason and Austin 2019).

Designing effective methods

A specification of the methods to be used as part of the strategy activity is a crucial design consideration. We will review design choices to be made in relation to analytical methods (to better understand the situation), integrative methods (to organize insights and options), and evaluative methods (to review and prioritize options).

Selecting analytical methods

Analytical methods are procedures which, focusing on a limited aspect of the organization's situation, provide a framework for organizing external data and/or capturing participant views and uncovering deeper understanding of trends and implications through structured conversations (Demir 2015). From a design thinking perspective, the selection of analytical methods that suit the situation and the participants is vital. Crucially, these should be deployed in a way that encourages conversations and dialogue to occur and new ideas and possibilities to emerge (Liedtka 2017).

Many of the methods described in this book have been examples of such 'analytical methods': for example, Five Forces enables analysis of industry profitability, VRIO enables analysis of resource-based competitive advantage, etc. Analytical methods will typically be used as a first step in social interaction in a strategy activity—guiding sharing of ideas and building an as complete as possible shared view of some aspect of the organization's situation. A combination of analytical methods can be used to build sufficient insights about an organization's situation so as to be able to meet the activity target outcomes in full.

Drawing on the design thinking insights presented in Table 15.1, Figure 15.8 shows a range of questions that can be used to guide the selection and refinement of analytical methods during strategy activity design. Analytical methods can be used in the generic format prescribed in academic papers/journals. Alternatively, methods can be refined to suit situational factors such as participant needs and practical constraints (Ashkenas 2013).

It is important to select methods that match the 'scope' of the strategy activity. This means that the methods selected must generate adequate insights to be able to meet target outcomes and sponsor needs in an intellectually sound and valid way. This might imply using a combination

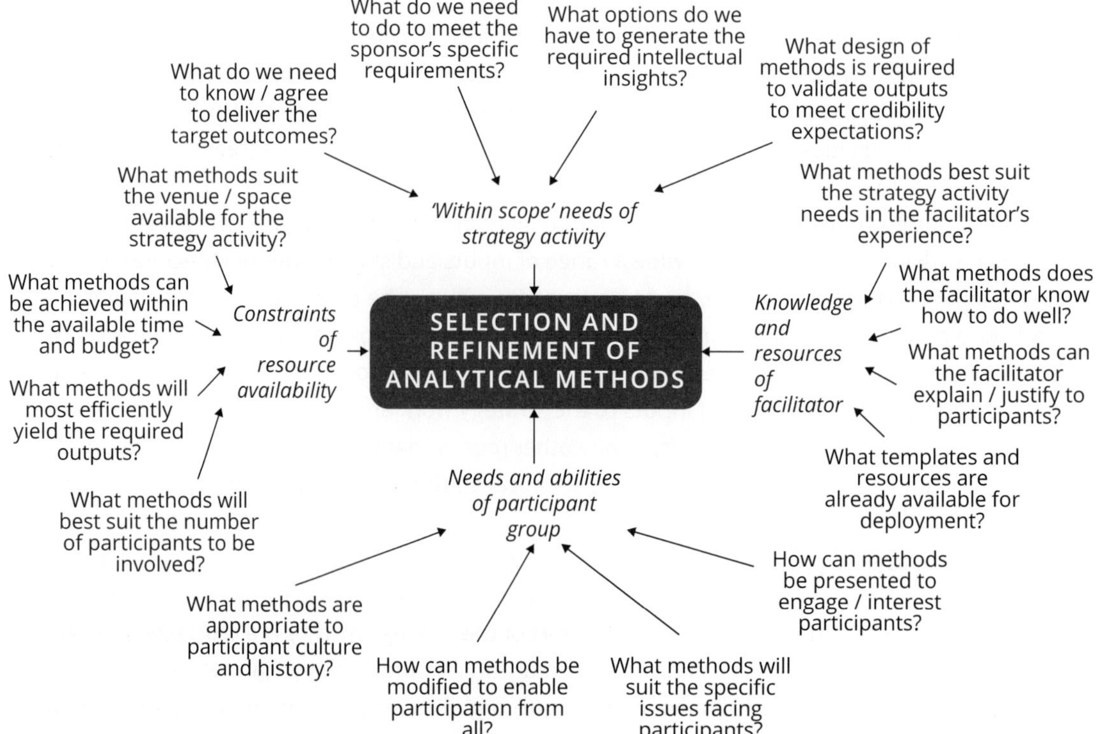

FIGURE 15.8 Selecting and refining methods to use in strategy activity.

15

of methods (see discussion of triangulation of methods in Chapter 5), the collective strengths of which will give the sponsor confidence in the outcomes of the strategy activity.

The 'geosocial space'—the physical environment and spaces used for social interaction—influence the strategizing outcomes that might be achieved (Arnaud et al. 2016:54). However, the principle of practical acceptability means that the selection and refinement of methods should also take account of resource constraints—time, budget, facilities, and number of participants to be involved. Overlaying these considerations with the scope requirements may rule out some methodological options or identify how others could be refined to make them possible, given situational practicalities.

The needs and abilities of participants should also shape method design. Consideration should be given to how participant engagement can be enabled and made appealing. According to participant preferences, strategy making can involve sticky notes, strategy tool templates, paperboards, technological devices, or texts as material support to conversations and interactions (Garreau et al. 2015).

The appropriateness of methods in the current organizational, as well as the historical and cultural, context of participants should also be reviewed. Participants may wish to draw from fields adjacent to strategy in selecting methods. For example, Gavrilova et al. (2018:369) propose that tools from fields as diverse as 'operations research, enterprise modeling, knowledge engineering, and artificial intelligence have potential to enrich the strategizing process'. Refinement considerations might also address how methods can be tailored to maximize participant contributions.

Finally, the capabilities, experience, knowledge, and available resources of the facilitator/designer should be considered. Those leading strategy activities have an important role to play in realizing outcomes, and their strengths and limitations can be an important factor in method selection (Gulati 2018).

From our experience in practice, most organizations have 'go to' methods that they use to initiate strategy conversations. These range from SWOT analyses to PESTEL, value-chain, business model canvas, stakeholder analysis, and forcefield analysis. They tend to use the same methods to initiate the conversations for efficiency reasons—participants understand what is expected of them, facilitators know how to adapt them to meet the needs of a situation, and prior experience has shown that they deliver required results and are 'acceptable' to the organization's culture. The 'go to' methods are then supplemented with methods that guide exploration of specific issues according to the focus of the strategy activity. For consultants seeking to design effective strategy activities, connecting with historical strategy practice can help build a trusting relationship with a client.

Selecting an integration method

Insights about organizational context and options for actions/objectives accrue as participants deploy analytical methods. Integration methods can be used to organize such insights into a framework for further analysis, development, or decision-making. Integration may not be required for activities with a very narrow scope that can be satisfied by simple means. However, for most strategy activities, some form of integration will be required once multiple analytical methods are deployed.

Integration involves transferring the ideas and insights arising from individual analytical methods into a common framework. This framework can take any form that suits participants' needs and the volume/type of data to be integrated. As illustrated in Figure 15.9, examples of

ID	Title	Type	Tags
3	We need to establish new mechanisms for how our organisation will generate income	Actions / Initiatives	add finances
4	The entire company is switching to a single medical record	Actions / Initiatives	modify systems
5	Dealing with change fatigue	Actions / Initiatives	modify employee wellbeing
9	We need to do the upfront work of change leadership more efficiently (fast and effective)	Actions / Initiatives	modify mngt/leadership
10	We need to focus more on the upfront planning for change - we can identify structures, processes, procedures but not the human side (social and political).	Actions / Initiatives	modify change capabilities
11	How we are going to be paid e.g. we need to create payment models that multiple stakeholders will buy into e.g. physicians, patients, insurers	Actions / Initiatives	add finances
12	Looking at either old, current or new problems with 'new eyes'	Actions / Initiatives	modify innovation

Online ideas forum with integrating categories and tags

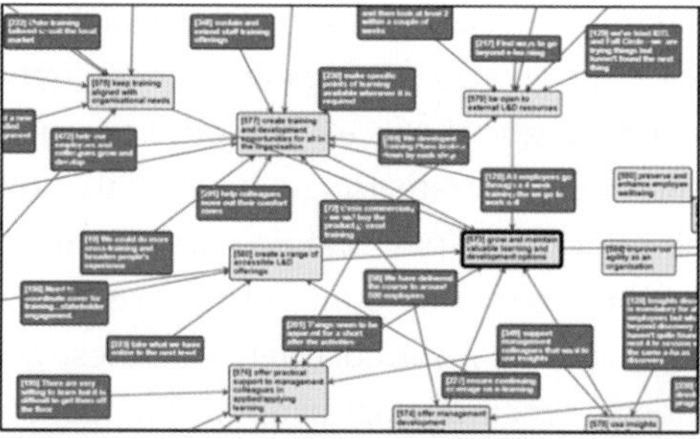

Software mapping of integrating clusters of insights

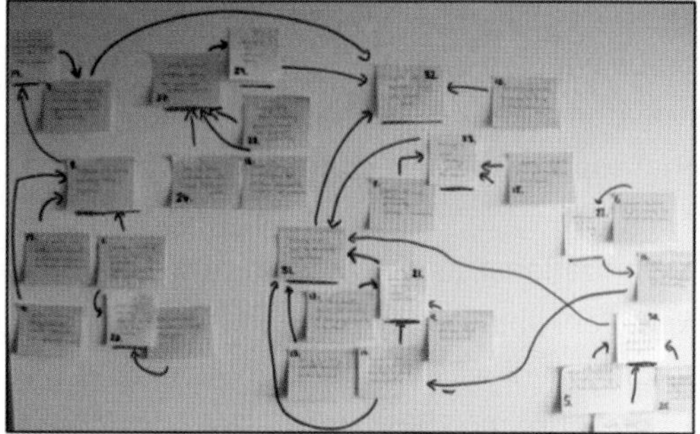

Manual integration of ideas on a whiteboard

Options for Action	Organizational Implications	Supporting Data
Arrange and manage financial position to fend off takeovers	Prepare to fend off takeovers	Market overcapacity trends-PESTEL
Commission scanning of market for merger & acquisition targets	Prepare to exploit M&A activity, and benefit from industry shakeout	Market overcapacity trends-PESTEL
Explore joint venture options in top 10 growing emerging markets	Position the organization to effectively compete in high growth markets	Market growth trends - PESTEL
Invest in marketing intelligence for all emerging markets	Develop insights as to which markets to target in the long term	Market growth trends - PESTEL
Build superior compliance and funding access message into marketing dialogue with potential customers	Ensure that superior compliance capability is understood by target customers in the mass market	Competitive advantage - competitive analysis
Ramp up efforts to capture market share, building brand reputation and customer loyalty	Exploit the current phase of the industry lifecycle to establish an market share that might endure	Lifecycle and market structure trends - Industry Forces
Prioritise investment in electric vehicle R&D activity	Prepare technical competence and production capabilities for new era of auto	Technology development trends - PESTEL
Continue to invest in 'in-house' R&D for EV specific components and technology	Prevent bargaining power drifting towards the EV supply chain; and enhance ability to compete against rivals	Low supplier power and trending rise in competitive rivalry - Industry Forces
Invest in aesthetic design teams and R&D activity to move EV beyond 'prototypical' look, feel and features towards a mainstream design	Address a customer need that is currently not well served to avoid it becoming a competitive disadvantage in future	Competitive performance-competitive analysis
Continue to invest in alternative technological portfolio options - hybrid and clean ICE	Manage risk of price-performance trade-off switches for customers to substitutes to electric vehicles	Threat of substitutes- Industry Forces
Maintain investment in range performance technology and EV reliability R&D activity	Keep pace with competitors and preserve strong technical performance that positions products well	Competitive performance-competitive analysis
Source tech partner firms for AV technology	Prepare technical competence and production [illegible]	Technology development trends - [illegible]

Simple tabulation of insights and options arising

FIGURE 15.9 Examples of approaches to integrating analytical findings.

integrating methods include cluster maps, sticky note clusters on flipcharts, tabulation of ideas, online sharing forums, etc. The common characteristic of these methods is that they provide only a general organizing framework, as opposed to analytical frameworks which focus on specific concepts and aspects of an organization's situation.

To illustrate the application of an integration method, we will examine a variation of a well-known tool. **SWOT** analysis, as illustrated in Figure 15.10, is subject to extensive criticism as a limited static strategy tool. If it is used on its own as a sole basis for 'strategy', the criticisms are arguably fair. However, when used as an integrating framework to compile outcomes of analytical methods, SWOT can serve a useful purpose (Kaplan and Norton 2008).

The categories of a SWOT framework are sufficiently generic to accommodate the insights arising from more specific analytical methods. Strengths and weaknesses capture implications for the resource base of the organization, and the opportunities and threats can accommodate organizational context insights from all manner of analyses. As an implication or insight about an organization's context is identified from analytical methods, it can be added to the relevant section in the SWOT table. For example, imagine a new piece of environmental legislation is identified in PESTEL work that initial analysis suggests will have a negative impact on production costs once compliance becomes mandatory. This might correspond to a 'threat' and the organization's current non-compliance status be considered a 'weakness'.

The SWOT framework acts as a repository in which analytical insights can be organized. It doesn't easily allow for the integration of options for action/objectives that might arise during conversations around analytical methods. As we have highlighted in the previous chapters, these implied options are a crucial component of strategy activity in practice.

+ Perceived strengths + Enablers + Source of value creation **STRENGTHS**	+ Perceived weaknesses + Constraints + Limiters of value creation **WEAKNESSES**
+ Perceived opportunities + Enabling trends + New sources of value creation **OPPORTUNITIES**	+ Perceived threats + Constraining trends + New sources of value limitation **THREATS**

FIGURE 15.10 SWOT analysis.

To integrate options for action/objectives in addition to contextual insights, the SWOT framework can be extended to a **TOWS** framework format (see Table 15.5). The ideas captured in the SWOT framework are re-created as column and row headings for four additional organizing categories. These quadrants (labelled SO, WO, ST, and SW, as in Figure 15.11) are based on combinations of 'internal' strengths and weaknesses and 'external' opportunities and threats. It is in these additional categories that strategic options might be organized and integrated. Option ideas emerging through analytical conversations can be allocated to the best-fitting quadrant. Returning to the example of new legislation being identified as a threat (T), and non-compliance as a weakness (W), in the WT box, possible options for action could be noted. The organization might (WT1) work to develop alternative production methods to avoid the impact of the legislation, (WT2) bring existing production methods into alignment to avoid non-compliance costs, (WT3) outsource production activity to a legislation-compliant third party, etc.

This simple act of organizing can help participants identify multiple lines of argument in support of the various options for action. Further, as contextual insights and options for action are added to the integrating framework, new options for action might be identified either from scratch or through creative refinement of existing options for action. This exploration of options for action is enabled by bringing all the insights into a single location. It will also be fully customized to the organization's situation, as the column and row headings keep a focus on specific analytical outputs. In this way, the arguments in support of different options for argument are also accrued.

TABLE 15.5 **TOWS integrating framework**

	Strengths	Weaknesses
Opportunities	SO—How might we seize opportunities using our strengths?	WO—How might we mitigate our weaknesses in order to better seize opportunities?
Threats	ST—How might we defend against threats using our strengths?	WT— How might we mitigate our weaknesses in order to better defend against threats?

15

	STRENGTHS	WEAKN
The tagging shows that this option, SO1, is supported by lines of argument from strength 1 and 5, and opportunities 1, 8 and 10	1. Strong R & D focus and investment from parent company 2. Diverse product portfolio (Truck, Cars) 3. Globally recognised strong brand 4. Existing hybrid range - from 2019 all new cars launched will be hybrid or all electrics Vehicles 5. High focus on innovation and world-leading safety technology 6. Year on Year growth on car sales in UK	1. Behi compe 2. No f 3. Volv image 4. Gaps 5. Prod 6. Decli 7. High househ 8. Mark 9. Trad remain 10. Ma 11. Exp parts a 12. Ger
OPPORTUNITIES 1. Build on reputation for safety incorporated in new technology 2. Economic uptick and customer spending 3. Lower inflation rate 4. New customers from online channels 5. Manufacturing in the UK and Re-Manufacturing/ Recycle of parts and vehicles 6. Growth of the UK Market Share from current 20th position 7. Grow Care by Volvo (Rent a Car Service, Car Sharing) 8. Autonomous Car with Enhanced Volvo Safety 9. Deliver more fuel-efficient models 10. Tap into the automotive council R&D funding	SO1 – Develop autonomous car with enhanced Volvo safety, tapping into support from UK Automotive Council (S1, S5, O1, O8, O10) SO2 – Grow UK market through Hybrid & Electric Vehicles – UK is largest ULEV market in EU (S4, O6) SO3 – Grow UK market by expanding Care by Volvo and offer on all new hybrids and electric cars (S3, S6, O7) SO4 – Improve electric charging infrastructure to broaden appeal of electric vehicles through possible collaboration with supermarket or fuel station chain (S1, S3, S4, O6, O9)	WO1 – price (V WO2 – adverti fuel eff WO3 conside remanu W11, C WO4 – O5) WO5 custom custom
THREATS 1. UK to ban sale of all diesel and petrol cars by 2040	ST1 – Offer AR/VR experience to meet changing consumer behaviours when purchasing (S1, T4, T5)	WT1 – compo

FIGURE 15.11 Sample of TOWS tagging of options.

In practice, we have found it possible to make this SWOT/TOWS method of integration work in a wide variety of circumstances. However, any of the other integration options highlighted earlier might be better suited to the needs of the situation (client needs, traditional ways of working, participant abilities, etc.). It is most important that the integrating method adopted is optimized to the needs of the situation.

The generation of options is a crucial component of a design thinking approach. Bason and Austin (2019:90) cite an example from Boeing:

> We saw Larry Loftis, then a manufacturing executive at the aerospace giant, insist that process-improvement teams use an approach called the seven ways—identifying at least seven options when brainstorming possible solutions. 'The first two or three come very easily', Loftis said, 'but then it becomes very difficult to come up with those other solutions. You have to unanchor [from your initial thoughts] and open up your mind.'

Applying prioritization methods

Once an integrating framework is prepared, the options identified can be prioritized and proposed outputs clarified. Prioritization methods are approaches for determining the relative importance of individual ideas within a broader set. The ordering of options occurs by considering the extent to which ideas conform to evaluative criteria, which will vary according to organizational circumstance (Camillus 1996). When prioritization has taken place, a set of options can be explained in terms of their relative ordering of importance. Resources can then be allocated towards a limited set of top priorities at the expense of lesser priorities.

When executed well, prioritization delivers strategic efficiency—the optimization of results for a whole organization and the maximization of return on effort. This is as opposed to naïve efficiency, in which each stakeholder group strives to maximize their own results to the detriment of the whole organization. Prioritization methods enable strategic coordination—providing guiding parameters for teams and individuals about how to contribute to an overall direction. With a sense of the overall priorities for the organization, individuals, teams, and divisions can organize their work to contribute towards what matters most for all (Sull and Turconi 2019). Without prioritization, resources may be deployed according to the interests of individual managers or groups.

Prioritization can be conducted inclusively, extending engagement in the strategy activity across stakeholder groups. Involving stakeholders in prioritization gives voice to a range of views that enhances the quality of option evaluation by subjecting options to scrutiny from a wide range of perspectives. Further, prioritization doesn't mean eliminating options from future consideration. Instead, prioritization elevates certain options for priority consideration at the current time. When conducting evaluative work, it is advisable that previously deprioritized options are not considered taboo but instead reconsidered on their merits in the current context (Hoon and Jacobs 2014). Through transparent involvement in a prioritization, stakeholders are more likely to support the ordered outcomes, and let go of their own preferences, than if they had not been included in the activity.

Criteria for prioritization

Prioritization involves sorting possible options for either initiatives or objectives according to relative importance. What constitutes 'importance' will depend on the nature of the organization and its situation. From a design thinking perspective, it is important to articulate and evaluate the relative attractiveness and feasibility of competing options (Liedtka 2018b:78). What those terms mean, however, will have to be agreed with those undertaking the prioritization work. Following suggestions from Hambrick and Fredrickson (2001:59), and drawing on our own experiences facilitating evaluation in strategizing, prioritization will typically evaluate options for initiatives or objectives on a combination of factors such as those presented in Table 15.6.

Evaluation criteria can be used to prioritize options in many ways. The simplest means is to discuss available options and create an ordered list of options through debate. In consultancy practice, we have encountered many organizations that conduct evaluation and prioritization through group discussion without capturing a record of the decision process. Kahneman et al. (2019) caution that whilst such an approach is certainly quick and commonplace, it is also most susceptible to bias and risks failing to engage stakeholders fully as the arguments behind options aren't made transparent.

TABLE 15.6 **Example prioritization criteria**

Criteria	Associated questions
Impact What difference will this option make to the long-term direction of the organization?	Are new sources of value creation enabled by this option? Is enhanced cost management enabled by this option? To what extent does this option allow us to continue to operate by meeting a legal or regulatory obligation?
Urgency Does this option address a pressing or time bound need?	Does this option help us capture or exploit an opportunity that is available for only a limited period of time? Does this option help us address a mandatory requirement to which we need to work to an externally imposed timescale? Does this option help us address a competitor move, operational issue, or customer difficulty that is harming the organization at present?
Practicality Is it realistic to expect that this option can be delivered?	Do we have the available knowledge and resources to address this option? Do we have a track record in achieving this sort of option? Do we have capacity to be able to deliver this option and continue to deliver existing operations?
Sustainability Is this option viable on a continuing basis?	What is the environmental impact of this option? How does this option impact on the stakeholders and local communities associated with the organization? To what extent is this option financially viable? Will this option harm our ability to survive and thrive in the long term?
Fit How well does this option align with internal and external stakeholder expectations?	Does this option fit with our existing strategies, sense of purpose, and overall strategic direction? How well does this option align with our existing ways of working and internal stakeholder expectations? How well does this option align with our external stakeholder expectations and the competitive/operating environment?

Alternatively, participants may be invited to use voting mechanisms to indicate the extent to which they think different options best meet the evaluative criteria. Manual 'dot-voting' or voting card methods have low barriers to participation and can be organized at short notice. Whilst requiring a degree of preparation, technology-enabled voting (via device/smartphone apps) can be used to quickly capture and compile many stakeholder votes during prioritization (see Figure 15.12).

When there is an interest in evaluating options against a range of considerations, a simple form of 'multi-criteria decision analysis' (MCDA) is a useful possibility for the strategist to consider. MCDA involves listing all possible options in the left-hand column of a table and using agreed evaluative criteria as column headers in the same table.

With a grid prepared as in Figure 15.13, insights from data collection and stakeholder engagement can be used to qualitatively or quantitatively evaluate each of the options. Using MCDA draws together the insights, wisdom, and arguments of the participants into a traceable resource that underpins collective decision-making. The act of completing option evaluation can often prompt the need for additional analysis and conversation as gaps in shared understanding are identified. As option 'scores' are co-created by participants using a sensible

ID	Title	Voting	Impact	Feasibility
1	Increase the size of the marketing budget		★★★★	★★
2	Introduce a system for measuring production performance		★★★	★★★
3	Improve communications between the managerial team and employees		★★★	★★★
4	Introduce an HSE training system		★★★★★	★★★★
5	Explore the possibilities of setting up a sales operation in mainland Europe		★★★	★★
6	Upgrade our documented roles and responsibilities		★★★	★★★
7	Develop our dialogue with customers		★★★★	★★★★

FIGURE 15.12 Example of a technology-enabled voting and rating approach.

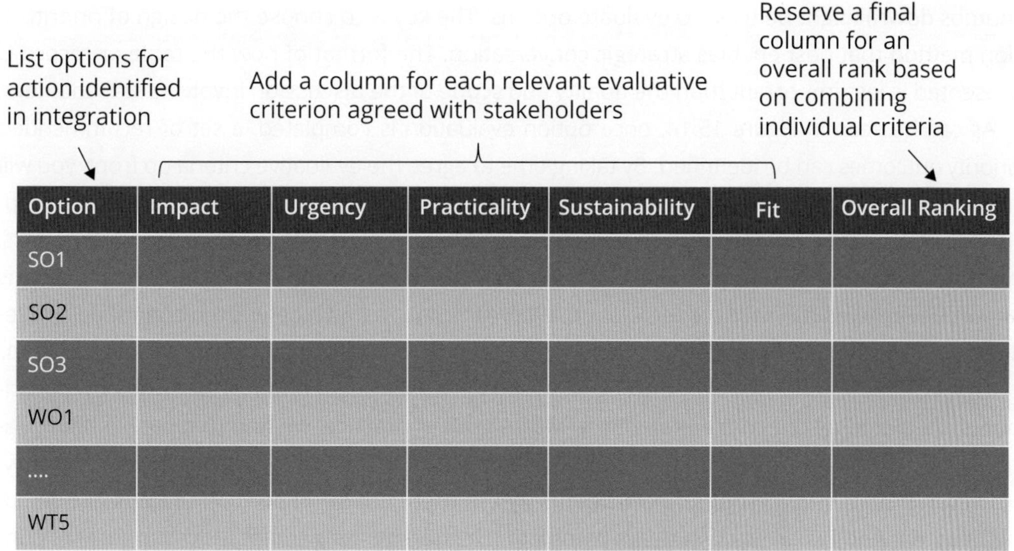

Option	Impact	Urgency	Practicality	Sustainability	Fit	Overall Ranking
SO1						
SO2						
SO3						
WO1						
....						
WT5						

FIGURE 15.13 Preparing for MCDA option evaluation.

operational procedure, a tangible record of supporting arguments and diverse views is generated whilst driving towards prioritization of outcomes. The effect on participants is that the process is seen as fair and rational, with buy-in to the collective outcome being more likely to be achieved.

Figure 15.14 shows an example of how option evaluation might be completed. Each option is evaluated against each of the categories and assigned a score between 1 (low) and 5 (high) according to stakeholder insights and data collected. A total score can then be proposed for each option. In Figure 15.14, this is achieved by simply totalling up the score in the preceding columns. Depending on the relative importance of the different evaluative criteria to those involved, this total could be weighted (e.g. 2× for impact, 0.5× for urgency, etc.).

Option	Impact	Urgency	Practicality	Sustainability	Fit	Total Score	Ranking
SO3	5	5	4	4	4	22	1
SO2	3	2	5	3	3	16	2
WO1	4	2	2	2	3	13	3
WT5	2	3	1	4	3	13	
....	....	....	....	....	....	....	....
SO1	1	4	3	1	1	10	last

Recommend

Reserved

Top rank

Reordered by total score

Lowest rank

Each category for each option given a score between 1 (low) – 5 (high) based on data collected and stakeholder insights

In this case, a simple tally of the previous columns' values

FIGURE 15.14 Illustrative completed MCDA option evaluation.

The approach shown in Figure 15.14 is a structured method using simple quantification as the basis for prioritization. Different scales and qualitative indicators (such as thumbs up, thumbs down) might be used to evaluate options. The key is to choose the design of prioritization method that best enables strategic conversation. The format of how the table or record is presented is less important than the quality and scope of the discussion involving stakeholders.

As can be seen in Figure 15.14, once option evaluation is completed, a set of recommended priority outcomes can be identified. By taking time to agree the evaluative criteria up front, you will have a set of options that everyone has created, and that has been vetted by clearly stated assumptions (Liedtka 2018a:78). Options can be ranked according to total score or participant consensus, and then a decision taken about which options to recommend for the strategy and which options should be reserved for future consideration. Where the line is drawn between recommend and reserve will likely be determined by available resources and the change capacity of the organization.

This evaluation and decision-making approach enables negotiation of priorities by participants, mediated by the co-creation of the MCDA grid. In practice, we find that such a highly rational, structured approach tends not to be used by groups that have a strong working history. However, it does suit a group of participants where there are strong or contentious options to be debated. And it also suits students completing a strategy assignment, as the arguments underpinning choices for recommendation are made explicit.

Reflecting on the design

Once the design parameters are understood and initial design decisions have been taken, a draft blueprint for the strategy activity can be prepared. For example, Figure 15.16 shows a sample blueprint for a student group strategy assignment activity. Imagine that the group has been tasked with undertaking a strategizing episode for a case organization, using methods from the module and producing a set of recommendations. The group has spoken to the tutor to clarify the assignment criteria and also the tutor's views from experience.

The diagram shows how the student group plan to address the assignment. The main tasks and phases of the activity are presented in the central column, and the decreasing width of the steps indicates the group converging on recommendations. The arrows at the side of the diagram, going up as well as down, indicate the flows of insights and feedback between the

CASE EXAMPLE 15.2 **APPLYING DESIGN THINKING IN OMAN VISION 2040**

Oman 2040 is a national vision-setting exercise with inclusivity at its heart. Oman 2040 arose from a Royal Decree issued by His Majesty Sultan Qaboos bin Said to provide a guide to future national planning over the next two decades under three key themes: People and Society, Economy and Development, and Governance and Institutional Performance.

In the Royal Decree, involvement of all walks of society in all phases of the vision development was mandated. We were involved as strategy activity design consultants in phase 3 of the vision process, in which strategic directions, initiatives, and national level key performance indicators (KPIs) were to be developed.

The blueprint for activities was shaped following the design parameters framework and inclusive design thinking. Initial scoping meetings were held with sponsoring stakeholders from the Supreme Council for Strategic Planning. These meetings clarified the target outputs and formats, the rules of engagement with participants, the practical constraints, and the stakeholders to be invited (about 220 participants from all walks of Omani public, business, and civic life).

Although the main language of the vision exercise was English, many participants were more comfortable in Arabic. Therefore multimodality of communication was introduced through dual language production of all written materials and hiring a team of bilingual facilitators to support interactions. For example, Figure 15.15 shows the strategy engagement framework (see Figure 15.1) translated into Arabic, ready to be explained by a facilitator in a participant information session.

As the design work progressed, multiple test workshops of prototype methods were conducted over several weeks. This led to significant simplification and refinement of methods used.

The outputs required were the selection and agreement of 45 KPI targets and 18 strategic directions within the three themes. Informational inputs for each possible KPI and strategic direction were prepared and issued in advance for participants to review and prepare for workshop sessions. This was done in a multimodal way—presenting the same information in graph, chart, and text format, with all materials offered in Arabic and English.

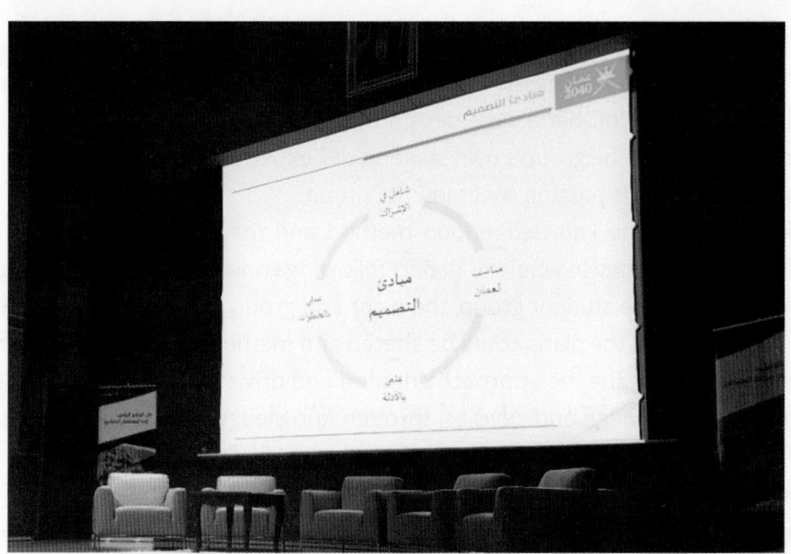

FIGURE 15.15 **The inclusive design considerations presented in Arabic.**

Continued

With a confirmed and refined design, implementation workshops were activated. As 220 participants were involved, a large venue was required. A significant up-front effort was necessary to ensure that the activity design was feasible within the practical constraints of the layout and infrastructure of the facilities.

For the benefit of participants and the large facilitator team, the language and communication of the sessions had to be simple, clear, and multimodal—combining flow diagrams, animations, text, and verbal explanations of the steps involved and the target outputs.

Simple analytical, integrative, and evaluative methods were used across 14 working groups to guide structured conversations between participants. Simple manual methods of participation—sticky notes, sticky dots, and voting grids filled in with a pen—were used to ensure that all could participate as fully as they wished.

The inclusive session blueprints opened up a 'space' for working in which a sense of fairness and engagement was high, and Omani cultural considerations for social interaction were respected. In keeping with the initial design parameters, participants were able to share and listen to each other's ideas, co-authoring outputs and giving full attention to proceedings. The activation of methods wasn't identical between groups—each group felt able to refine their working according to their own preferences and the needs of the topic under discussion. The overall activity structure kept participants working to time and ensured preparation of mediating artefacts on schedule.

In addition to within-group working, all groups had a chance to review their proposed outcomes with other teams in order to learn from and harmonize the overall outputs. At the end of a 1.5 day workshop, all target outputs were agreed and participant satisfaction with the process was high. The outputs of the successful session are now ratified as part of the Oman 2040 Vision, to which all involved in the workshops have a co-authorship claim.

Questions for discussion

1. Identify and analyse examples of the ways in which the strategy engagement framework seems to have influenced the activity design. How did these examples help meet the initial brief?
2. Reflect on the impact that having to accommodate over 200 participants had on the design of the strategy activity. How did the design of activities have to be altered from a workshop with, say, 20 participants? What general lessons can you extract for the impact that the number of participants will have on any strategy activity design?

stages. Each pair of blue–yellow arrows between levels is an instance of the knowledge loop (see Figure 15.3). This represents the potentially iterative nature of the development of recommendations. On the left-hand side, design-thinking-inspired notes are captured. These are all intended to improve the group's own stakeholder experience and deliver an assignment output that meets or exceeds passing assessment criteria.

In keeping with the knowledge loop method and the strategy evaluation framework, this blueprint can be refined in whole or in part following conversations and trialling with stakeholders. In the case of the student group, the tutor and group members would be consulted on the initial plans. Further, the plans could be shared and methods trialled in collaboration with other student groups to refine the approach adopted and drive towards improved performance.

Being open to change and revision through knowledge loop conversations is a useful attitude for the designer team to adopt. Further, through reflective conversations the design team should challenge themselves about the extent that the activity blueprint conforms with inclusive design considerations in a balanced way, and the extent to which the blueprint addresses all the design parameters. Once stakeholder feedback and team reflections have been considered, and there are no more changes to include, implementation can be activated.

During implementation, innovation around the blueprint can also occur. For example, imagine that the student group have prepared an integrative TOWS grid following completion of the

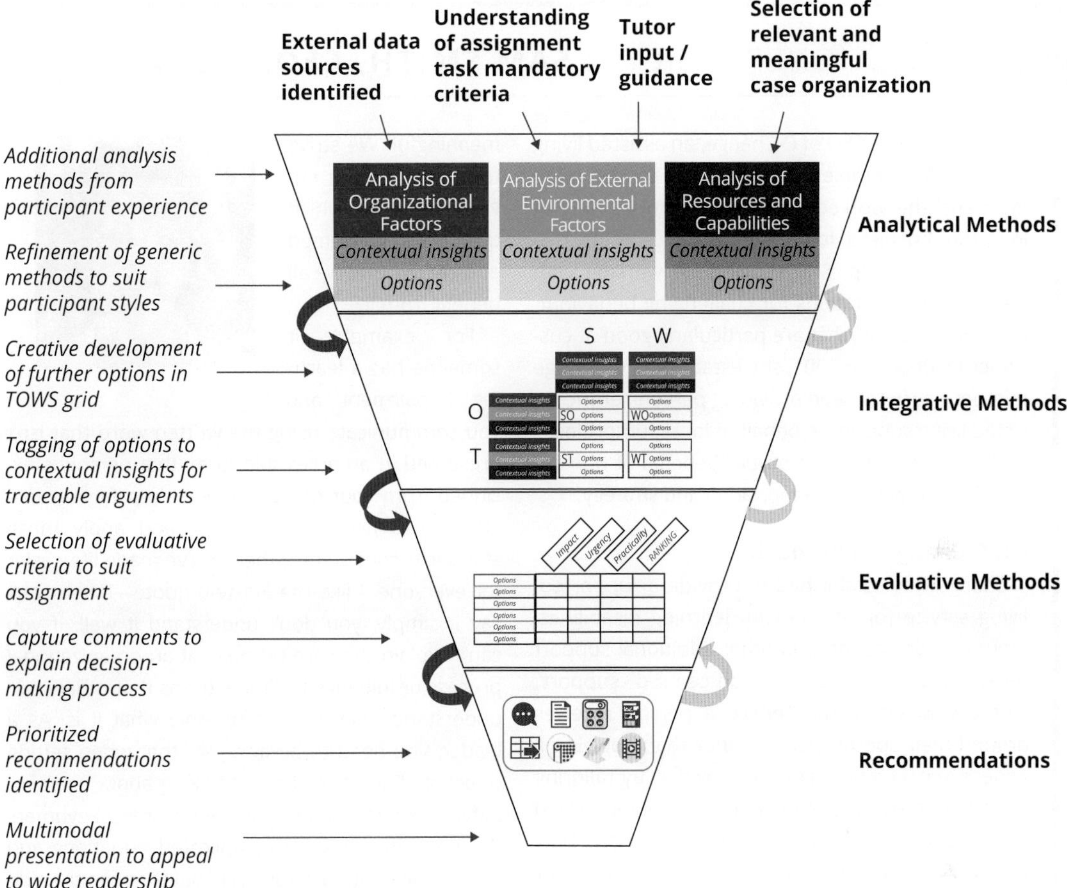

FIGURE 15.16 Example blueprint for a student group strategy case assignment.

analytical methods highlighted in Figure 15.16. Upon review of the TOWS grid, sustainability and internationalization seem to be important themes emerging for the case organization. The team also feel that there are gaps in their knowledge about the case organization in relation to these themes. The team may then elect to conduct further analysis (going back 'up' a phase), drawing on theories, concepts, or methods addressed in their strategy module (as per Chapters 12 and 13), or from further reading on the topic outside the scope of the class. This practical decision can easily be explained to stakeholders based on the evidence of the work-in-progress TOWS framework, and can be agreed as a good use of participant time.

In summary, the preparation of a blueprint for strategy activities creates an initial guiding framework based on design thinking methods and parameters. Through knowledge loop approaches, participants may consider themselves to have a stake in the design. Participants will also have a positive sense of fairness, rationality, engagement, and practicality considerations built into the blueprint. This sets the activity up for success before implementation is activated in full. However, once implementation is under way, the blueprint should be subject to review in order that the quality of output can be raised based on the wisdom, creativity, and value-adding efforts of participants. In this way, the rational frameworks and plans support rather than restrict the attainment of target outcomes through an inclusive social process that respects and capitalizes on the capabilities of a broad set of stakeholder talents.

PRACTITIONER INSIGHT: SAM SMITH, CEO, C-CHANGE

Sam Smith is the CEO of C-Change, an assisted living charity. After completing a doctorate in risk management, she worked on the decommissioning of long-stay hospitals for the Glasgow Learning Disability Partnership. She focused on working with people with reputations for challenging behaviour, or, as Sam puts it, 'that are particularly good at customer feedback'. In 2001, she established C-Change to meet a societal need providing person-centric assisted living support on behalf of local authorities.

She shares her views on the benefits of human-centric approaches in organization and strategy.

On C-Change's approach

C-Change was established to provide a supported-living service for people with learning disabilities, mental health issues, and other additional support needs. We pioneered 'person-centred support', where you design the service a person receives around their specific needs rather than applying a generic service that suits the provider. By tailoring support to the needs of the individual, our intention is to allow people to live the life they choose, having their own home and place in a community. Our aim from the start was to ensure that our service led to social inclusion, and that we would deliver it at the same or lower cost than keeping people in an 'institution'. Working on behalf of local authorities, our approach delivers on this aim. Right from the start, we've found that if you support people in a person-centric way, they no longer challenge you as you are listening harder and providing assistance that meets their needs.

Organizing for inclusivity

For me, inclusion means that 'everyone's in'. If you start from there, it is not for the person to fit—the onus is on the organization to make sure that everyone can contribute. If you invest in making processes accessible and easy to follow, everyone benefits from it. If people know and understand your processes, they can follow them and contribute to improving them. It is about picking your language and mode of communicating—be empathic, how would others feel trying to make sense of what you are doing. The onus is on the organization to ensure that engagement and communication with stakeholders is meaningful. We strive to create a work environment in which diversity is welcomed and valued, and we all benefit from it.

For example, if someone has a learning impairment and you communicate using the written word that isn't presented in an accessible form, that person is excluded from your process. If you simplify your language, use accessible formats, and apply those standards consistently, then you've made life easier for everyone. I like the Einstein quote—if you can't say it simply, you don't understand it well. If you can't explain the core purpose of an organizational process or initiative in simple terms that others can understand, then you don't know what it is. As a leader, you need to be aware of that when setting direction. For clarity, I'm not talking about oversimplifying things that are complex. Richard Feynman, the physicist, took his complicated equations and turned them into diagrams. He put them on the side of his camper van! I've always thought, if he could do something like that then we should be able to make what we do understandable in organizations. That is where we can use tools and processes that help us all engage with complex ideas in an accessible way.

We borrow tools from a wide range of external parties that you might call the inclusion movement. We'll use anything that helps us focus on the needs of the people we work for. We do our best to organize ourselves optimally around the most crucial relationship—between the person we work for, and the colleague who supports them. That is why we use person-centred planning tools to design our services and for organizational planning.

On inclusion and strategy

I dread the prospect of an inclusivity strategy and the inclusivity team that rolls it out! Inclusivity is not about some separate initiative—it is about a way of being that creates a culture that will not accept people being excluded. I can't imagine strategy without inclusivity. Why would anyone think that I or the board have all the answers, or that somewhere away from the lived experience of our people a small group would come up with plans for what the organization will do? It's an unreasonable expectation of me as a CEO, and a waste of the opportunity of gathering in all the ways of thinking that may not have crossed your mind. By not involving others you narrow down your options before you even start. Inclusivity is about valuing different perspectives.

For example, we have a dating service called 'Dates 'n' Mates' which is for, and run by, people with learning disabilities. We are often asked for media comment and colleagues say to me 'You should do that—you're the CEO'. I am the least powerful person to do that! We have directors of 'Dates 'n' mates' who are people with learning disabilities. They live and breathe it and have a power of emotional connection and aspiration that I could never bring to a media comment. As a strategic leader, I think that if you get over your ego and operate with greater humility you will be able to recognize the value of different perspectives and contributions. If you get that insight, then you wouldn't dream of developing a strategy without ensuring that those voices are part of it. Why would you waste that resource—that different knowledge, that different wisdom?

CHAPTER SUMMARY

In this chapter we addressed the following learning outcomes.

- **Critically evaluate the usefulness of design thinking in strategizing**

  Design thinking refers to a set of methods and attitudes for creating rationally designed products, services, solutions, and experiences based on the needs of stakeholders. Design thinking can help to create strategizing activities that overcome typical challenges facing strategy practitioners. Design thinking places a premium on empathy, accessibility, and practicality of approach. Design thinking does require training, leadership support, and the freeing up of stakeholders for participation. If achieved, by involving stakeholders widely, strategizing built on design thinking principles can build commitment to outcomes and increase the likelihood of successful implementation.

- **Explain how planned strategy activities can be designed to deliver target outcomes whilst building stakeholder engagement**

  When designing a planned activity, we should avoid unnecessarily prescriptive details that restrict participation for arbitrary reasons. Instead we can aim to produce guiding frameworks that steer participation and encourage 'co-authorship' of outcomes, raising stakeholder engagement. This can generate valuable commitment to strategy activity outcomes, increasing the likelihood of successful implementation. This impact is enhanced by involving a wide range of stakeholders. Quality of outcomes is also enhanced by diverse inputs from a range of stakeholders. Through high awareness of target outcomes and activity sponsor needs, a thoughtful selection of participants, use of clear language, and communication methods that accommodate all user needs, and an effective combination of analytical, integrative, and evaluative methods, a design of planned activity can be prepared that increases the likelihood of high-quality outcomes being realized.

- **Evaluate the possibilities of inclusivity in strategy activities, considering social and practical acceptability and procedural justice and rationality factors**
  The philosophy of an inclusive design approach is to align blueprints for planned methods and outcomes with the needs of the whole user population rather than 'typical' user needs. In terms of strategy, this means selecting methods and targeting outcomes for planned activities that meet as broad a range of stakeholder needs as possible, rather than just the needs of senior management users. Inclusive design can be enacted by close-coupling design efforts with stakeholder feedback using the knowledge loop method. Inclusive design decisions are guided by social and practical acceptability and procedural justice and rationality considerations. These principles aim to make strategy activities fair, sensible, and engaging within practical limitations, delivering maximum buy-in and quality of target outcome. Effort towards deploying these principles can build positive relationships between stakeholders, shared comprehension of organizational circumstances, and commitment towards implementing strategy decisions.
- **Appraise the value of accessible language, mediating artefacts, and customized methods in designing strategy activities for a diverse group of stakeholders**
  Without forethought, approaches to strategy work can be excluding. As unfamiliar concepts and terminology can create barriers to participation, deliberate use of simple straightforward language in stakeholder communications is a key consideration in inclusive design. Purposefully involving participants—at least to some extent—in the creation of analytical, integrative, and evaluative outcomes (mediating artefacts) can build perceptions of inclusion and outputs reflective of a wide range of talents and perspectives. And customizing methods to suit the needs of the situation—including the sponsor, participants, and facilitators—can enhance the efficiency and effectiveness of the strategy activity.
- **Explain the importance of prioritization in strategy work**
  Prioritization describes the ordering of options in terms of relative importance. This ordering is done in relation to evaluative criteria (such as impact, practicality, urgency, etc.). Prioritization entails identifying what will not be done, as well as what will, thus enabling coordinated actions between stakeholders towards agreed outcomes. Prioritization guides the deployment of resources and can bring effective closure to strategy conversations and analysis. Without prioritization, stakeholders may end up working at cross-purposes to the detriment of organizational performance.

? END OF CHAPTER QUESTIONS

Recall questions

1. Explain what is meant by design thinking and how it might be applied to planned strategy activities.
2. Describe the business case for inclusivity in strategy activities.

3. List inclusive design considerations and explain what the key terms mean.
4. Summarize the parameters that need to be addressed during the design of strategy activities.
5. Define multimodal communication and provide an example of effective use of multimodal practice for inclusivity.
6. Describe factors that are useful to consider when selecting or refining analytical methods.
7. Explain the possible value of adding an integrative framework to the design of strategy activity.
8. What is prioritization and why is it important in formal strategy activities?

Application questions

A) Think of a process or activity from which you felt excluded or unable to contribute to your full potential. Drawing on design thinking, identify how the design of the process or activity could have been improved to enable you to make your contribution. Explain your answer.

B) Find a piece of strategy text for an organization you know well or in which you are interested. Create further types of output, such as visual representations or infographics, for that text. Reflecting on your experiences, comment on how challenging this exercise was. What did you learn about the ease of multimodal working in strategy?

C) Imagine that you are starting up a new business enterprise with five colleagues. Create a blueprint design for the activity of preparing a business strategy for the new venture. Write a commentary to accompany your blueprint explaining the design choices you've made throughout. Connect your commentary with inclusive design thinking and the design parameters highlighted in this chapter.

ONLINE RESOURCES

www.oup.com/he/mackay1e

FURTHER READING

IDEO's online circular economy resource

https://www.ideo.com/post/designing-a-circular-economy

To develop a sense of design thinking in practice, and also to compare with insights from Chapter 13, it is worth reviewing IDEO's online circular economy resource. This will provide you with a range of tools and methods that can be borrowed and adapted, and give you a specific detailed example of how design thinking can be used to strategize and innovate in relation to highly complex problems.

Change by Design: How Design Thinking Transforms Organizations and Inspires Innovation, by Tim Brown

Brown, T. (2019). *Change by Design: How Design Thinking Transforms Organizations and Inspires Innovation* (2nd edn). New York: Harper Business.

A recognized design thinking guru, Tim Brown writes lucidly on design thinking and how it might be applied widely. This is for students who are interested in deepening their understanding of the theory and history of design thinking, and its value as a skill to consultants.

Countering Design Exclusion: An Introduction to Inclusive Design, by Simeon L. Keates and John Clarkson

Keates, S. and Clarkson, J. (2003). *Countering Design Exclusion: An Introduction to Inclusive Design.* London: Springer.

Inclusion is an important topic in design thinking. This handbook compiles a wide range of contributions—all practical—about how inclusion can be fostered through design methods and approaches in a wide variety of settings. This will be a useful reference source for students wishing to creatively explore how to nurture inclusivity.

Designing for Growth: A Design Thinking Toolkit for Managers, by Jeanne Liedtka and Tim Ogilvie

Liedtka, J. and Ogilvie, T. (2011). *Designing for Growth: A Design Thinking Toolkit for Managers.* New York: Columbia University Press.

Jan Liedtka is a widely published author in design thinking and a key influence on the content in this chapter. Writing here with Tim Ogilvie, she covers a range of methods that are very useful for deploying design thinking in innovation and strategy development. This book is a useful source for students looking to test methods through an applied session.

A structured approach to strategic decisions, by Daniel Kahneman, Dan Lovallo, and Olivier Siboney

Kahneman, D., Lovallo, D.A.N., and Sibony, O. (2019). A structured approach to strategic decisions. *MIT Sloan Management Review*, **60**(3), 67–73.

Daniel Kahneman won a Nobel Prize for his work on the psychology of decision-making. In this paper, he offers a compelling argument for the use of a structured approach to making strategic decisions in order to reduce bias, noise, and poor judgement. Many useful points for those seeking to design a strategizing activity are covered.

REFERENCES

Ackermann, F. and Eden, C. (2011a). *Making Strategy: Mapping Out Strategic Success*. London: Sage.

Ackermann, F. and Eden, C. (2011b). Negotiation in strategy making teams: group support systems and the process of cognitive change. *Group Decision and Negotiation*, **20**(3), 293–314.

Arnaud, N., Mills, C.E., Legrand, C., and Maton, E. (2016). Materializing strategy in mundane tools: the key to coupling global strategy and local strategy practice? *British Journal of Management*, **27**(1), 38–57.

Ashkenas, R. (2013). Four tips for better strategic planning. *Harvard Business Review Digital Articles*, 2–4.

Barnett, M.L. (2008). An attention-based view of real options reasoning. *Academy of Management Review*, **33**(3), 606–28.

Bartlett, C.A. and Ghoshal, S. (1994). Changing the role of top management: beyond strategy to purpose. *Harvard Business Review*, **72**(6), 79–88.

Baskinger, M. (2008). Pencils before pixels: a primer in hand-generated sketching. *Interactions*, **15**(2), 28–36.

Bason, C. and Austin, R.D. (2019). The right way to lead design thinking. *Harvard Business Review*, **97**(2), 82–91.

Battilana, J., Pache, A.-C., Sengul, M., and Kimsey, M. (2019). The dual-purpose playbook. *Harvard Business Review*, **97**(2), 124–33.

Belmondo, C. and Sargis-Roussel, C. (2015). Negotiating language, meaning, and intention: strategy infrastructure as the outcome of using a strategy tool through transforming strategy objects. *British Journal of Management*, **26**, S90–104.

Binns, A., Harreld, J.B., O'Reilly, C.A., and Tushman, M.L. (2014). The art of strategic renewal. *MIT Sloan Management Review*, **55**(2), 21–3.

Brandenburger, A. (2019). Strategy needs creativity. *Harvard Business Review*, **97**(2), 58–65.

Breene, R.T.S., Nunes, P.F., and Shill, W.E. (2007). The chief strategy officer. *Harvard Business Review*, **85**(10), 84–93.

British Design Council (2006). The principles of inclusive design. https://www.designcouncil.org.uk/resources/guide/principles-inclusive-design (accessed 30 May 2019).

Brown, T. (2008). Design thinking. *Harvard Business Review*, **86**(6), 84–92.

Brown, T. (2015). When everyone is doing design thinking, is it still a competitive advantage? *Harvard Business Review Digital Articles*, 2–3.

Brown, T. (2019). *Change by Design: How Design Thinking Transforms Organizations and Inspires Innovation* (2nd edn). New York: Harper Business.

Brown, T. and Martin, R. (2015). Design for action. *Harvard Business Review*, **93**(9), 56–13.

Burrell, L. (2018). Co-creating the employee experience. *Harvard Business Review*, March–April.

Camillus, J.C. (1996). Reinventing strategic planning. *Strategy & Leadership*, **24**(3), 6–12.

Canales, J.I. (2013). Constructing interlocking rationales in top-driven strategic renewal. *British Journal of Management*, **24**(4), 498–514.

Comi, A. and Whyte, J. (2018). Future making and visual artefacts: an ethnographic study of a design project. *Organization Studies*, **39**(8), 1055–83.

Demir, R. (2015). Strategic activity as bundled affordances. *British Journal of Management*, **26**, S125–41.

Dobusch, L., Dobusch, L., and Müller-Seitz, G. (2019). Closing for the benefit of openness? The case of Wikimedia's open strategy process. *Organization Studies*, **40**(3), 343–70.

Dunne, D. (2019). Design thinking: mastering the tensions. *Rotman Management*, 121–3.

Eden, C. and Ackermann, F. (1998). *Making Strategy: The Journey of Strategic Management*. London: Sage.

Fisher, R. and Ury, W. (2012). *Getting to Yes: Negotiating an Agreement Without Giving In.* New York: Random House.

Garreau, L., Mouricou, P., and Grimand, A. (2015). Drawing on the map: an exploration of strategic sensemaking/giving practices using visual representations. *British Journal of Management*, **26**(4), 689–712.

Gavrilova, T., Kubelskiy, M., Kudryavtsev, D., and Grinberg, E. (2018). Modeling methods for strategy formulation in a turbulent environment. *Strategic Change*, **27**(4), 369–77.

Gergen, K. (2009). *An Invitation to Social Construction.* London: Sage.

Glaser, V.L. (2017). Design performances: how organizations inscribe artifacts to change routines. *Academy of Management Journal*, **60**(6), 2126–54.

Gregersen, H.A.L. (2018). Better brainstorming. *Harvard Business Review*, **96**(2), 64–71.

Gulati, R. (2018). Structure that's not stifling. *Harvard Business Review*, **96**(3), 68–79.

Hambrick, D.C. and Fredrickson, J.W. (2001). Are you sure you have a strategy? *Academy of Management Executive*, **15**(4), 48–59.

Healey, M.P., Hodgkinson, G.P., Whittington, R., and Johnson, G. (2015). Off to plan or out to lunch? Relationships between design characteristics and outcomes of strategy workshops. *British Journal of Management*, **26**(3), 507–28.

Hoon, C. and Jacobs, C.D. (2014). Beyond belief: strategic taboos and organizational identity in strategic agenda setting. *Strategic Organization*, **12**(4), 244–73.

Ignatius, A. (2015). How Indra Nooyi turned design thinking into strategy. *Harvard Business Review*, September, 80–85.

Kahneman, D., Lovallo, D.A.N., and Sibony, O. (2019). A structured approach to strategic decisions: reducing errors in judgment requires a disciplined process. *MIT Sloan Management Review*, **60**(3), 67–73.

Kaplan, R.S. and Norton, D.P. (2008). Mastering the management system. *Harvard Business Review*, **86**(1), 62–77.

Keates, S. (2007). *Design for Accessibility: A Business Guide to Countering Design Exclusion.* Mahwah, NJ: Lawrence Erlbaum.

Keates, S. and Clarkson, J. (2003a). Design exclusion. In: Clarkson, J., Coleman, R., Keates, S., and Lebbon, C. (eds), *Inclusive Design: Design for the Whole Population*, pp. 88–107. London: Springer.

Keates, S. and Clarkson, J. (2003b). *Countering Design Exclusion: An Introduction to Inclusive Design*. London: Springer.

Kim, W.C. and Mauborgne, R. (1998). Procedural justice, strategic decision making, and the knowledge economy. *Strategic Management Journal*, **19**, 323–38.

Kolko, J. (2015). Design thinking comes of age. *Harvard Business Review*, **93**(9), 66–9.

Kupp, M., Anderson, J., and Reckhenrich, J.R. (2019). Why design thinking in business needs a rethink. *MIT Sloan Management Review*, **60**(2), 4–6.

Kurtmollaiev, S., Pedersen, P.E., Fjuk, A., and Kvale, K. (2018). Developing managerial dynamic capabilities: a quasi-experimental field study of the effects of design thinking training. *Academy of Management Learning & Education*, **17**(2), 184–202.

Lafley, A.G., Martin, R.L., Rivkin, J.W., and Siggelkow, N. (2012). Bringing science to the art of strategy. *Harvard Business Review*, **90**(9), 56–66.

Liedtka, J. (2014). Innovative ways companies are using design thinking. *Strategy & Leadership*, **42**(2), 40–5.

Liedtka, J. (2017). Evaluating the impact of design thinking in action. *Academy of Management Annual Meeting Proceedings*, 2017(1), 1–6.

Liedtka, J. (2018a). Innovation, strategy, and design: design thinking as a dynamic capability. *Academy of Management Annual Meeting Proceedings*, 2018(1), 74–9.

Liedtka, J. (2018b). Why design thinking works. *Harvard Business Review*, **96**(5), 72–9.

Liedtka, J. and Kaplan, S. (2019). How design thinking opens new frontiers for strategy development. *Strategy & Leadership*, **47**(2), 3–10.

Liedtka, J., Salzman, R., and Azer, D. (2018a). Design thinking for the greater good. *Rotman Management*, 48–53.

Liedtka, J., Sheikh, A., Gilmer, C., et al. (2018b). The use of design thinking in the US Federal Government. *Academy of Management Annual Meeting Proceedings*, 2018(1), 1–6.

McGahan, A.M. and Leung, M. (2018). Strategy + design thinking = stakeholder-centric design. *Rotman Management,* 110–12.

Mantere, S. and Vaara, E. (2008). On the problem of participation in strategy: a critical discursive perspective. *Organization Science*, **19**(2), 341–58.

Markides, C.C. (2000). *All the Right Moves: A Guide to Crafting Breakthrough Strategy*. Boston, MA: Harvard Business School Press.

Micheli, P., Wilner, S.J.S., Bhatti, S.H., et al. (2019). Doing design thinking: conceptual review, synthesis, and research agenda. *Journal of Product Innovation Management*, **36**(2), 124–48.

Steinfeld, E. and Maisel, J. (2012). *Universal Design: Creating Inclusive Environments*. Hoboken, NJ: John Wiley.

Sull, D. and Turconi, S. (2019). How to recognize a strategic priority when you see one. *MIT Sloan Management Review*, 32–35.

Sull, D., Turconi, S., Sull, C., and Yoder, J. (2018). How to develop strategy for execution. *MIT Sloan Management Review*, **59**(2), 47–53.

Suominen, K. and Mantere, S. (2010). Consuming strategy: the art and practice of managers' everyday strategy usage. In: Joel, A.C.B. and Lampel, J. (eds), *Advances in Strategic Management: The Globalization of Strategy Research*, pp. 211–45. Bingley: Emerald.

CHAPTER SIXTEEN

Strategy-in-Practice: Learning, Reflecting, Thinking

CONTENTS

LEARNING OBJECTIVES

By the end of this chapter, you should be able to:

- Appraise the value of different models of learning in explaining how strategy happens in practice
- Explain how reflection is a crucial mechanism of experiential learning that contributes to evolving strategic thought and activity
- Critically evaluate your own views of the role of learning and reflection in strategy

TOOLBOX

- **Kolb's experiential learning cycle**
  A model of learning that highlights how concrete experience can be transformed into learning, which in turn can drive experimental action and new experiences.
- **Argyris and Schön's double-loop learning model**
  A framework that aids evaluation of the likely impact of learning activities on future organizational performance. Single-loop learning alters our strategies and tactics; double-loop learning casts new light on our values, assumptions, and beliefs.
- **Situated learning perspective**
  A framework to help us understand how contextual, environmental, and social factors will influence learning.
- **Feelings, facts, proposals**
  A reflective writing tool from practice that is intended to guide an individual to collect their thoughts and feelings on a matter, seek external perspectives and data on the same, and uncover new insights to guide future actions.

16

16.1 Introduction

When working with strategy in practice, how can we adapt and modify our approach as we go? In this final chapter, our aim is to provide you with insights about how learning and reflection will support you as you develop your effectiveness in strategy activities.

Commenting on a survey of 400 chief executives from around the world, Vona et al. (2019:97) note:

> In this age of disruption, learning has an ever more critical role to play in supporting business strategy and transformation. Developing new skills is the top priority across the workforce. The challenge is correctly identifying those skills generically and in the context of each business.

Relating this comment to the process–practice framework of strategy, 'generic skills' correspond to the categories of practices that we have explored throughout this book. Learning and reflection processes will give you a means by which to keep those practices adapted and attuned to the needs of the organizational situations you face as you build your career.

In this chapter, we flip the normal running order by starting with a set of reflective practitioner writings. This is to create a learning resource which means that any reader, whether a seasoned manager or an undergraduate yet to acquire work experience, will have a point of reference by which to engage with the subsequent discussions on learning and reflection in strategy.

We have deliberately presented a diverse set of practitioner perspectives. By so doing, we re-emphasize the point that multiple competing opinions and perspectives underpin strategy-in-practice. The opinions and insights expressed by each practitioner have been developed from their own unique history of study, experience, working with others, and reflecting on why they do what they do. None is more right or wrong than the others, and all writing combines thoughts and emotions. However, you will identify with some perspectives more than others. Figuring out why you are drawn to certain views will help you engage with the theory, concepts, and methods that follow.

Following the practitioner perspectives, we consider how learning might support current and future strategic actions and initiatives, potentially leading to enhanced organizational performance (Thomas et al. 2001). To explain how such strategic learning might occur, and to what effect, we present a range of models of learning that might be applied in strategy.

We then examine reflection—a learning mechanism which involves looking back on an episode in life to better understand the flow of events, how outcomes emerged, and our role in proceedings. Reflection is a mechanism which drives deep understanding and an improvement in personal effectiveness. We will look at reflection in the context of strategy, but it is also a personal learning skill that will benefit you more broadly.

We explore the possible value of reflection in strategy, and what it means to be a reflective strategy practitioner. We consider reflection that occurs after an activity (**reflection-on-action**) as well as reflection that occurs in the moment as we are taking action (**reflection-in-action**). This will help you explain how changes to any strategy approach can occur between and within activities. We examine why it might benefit you to make time for reflection, and barriers, enablers, and methods that will influence the extent to which that is possible.

Once you understand the principles of reflection, you will have a means by which to purposefully modify how you carry out activities through the process–practice framework. During or after each activity, reflection gives you a way to learn from experience—becoming more effective in how you act as a strategist and improving the outcomes that you can achieve for yourself and your organization. This chapter aims to equip you with insights that enable you, as you activate strategy, to draw on your experiences from yesterday to guide your practices today, and to be better prepared for the challenges of tomorrow.

16.2 **Reflective insights from strategy practitioners**

In this section, we present reflective writing from six practitioners in response to three questions:

1. What does strategy mean to you?
2. How has learning shaped your views of strategy?
3. What strategy practices would you advise others to consider?

We asked these questions without any further prompts, and we have recorded the responses as received from the practitioners.

Question 1 is intended to give you a sense of how each practitioner interpreted strategy, which you should be able to relate to the perspectives of strategy described in Chapter 1. (You might want to practice applying the strategy scoping method from Chapter 1 to the practitioner responses.)

Question 2 asks for opinions about learning—how new knowledge is acquired—in strategy. You will see that both successes and failures feature in the responses. Further, comments vary in how they address the process of learning, learning outcomes, and priority insights. This information will help us examine strategic learning theory.

Question 3 asks for justified advice about what is important to do in strategy activity. Apart from giving you useful insights, this question was intended to prompt practitioner reflection on their own practice. You will notice some points of commonality in what is proposed, but you should also be able to see how the practitioner advice is strongly grounded in their own experiences and paths through life.

Essential preparation

To make the most of the practitioner reflections as a learning resource that supports this chapter's aims, we suggest a set of activities to complete before moving on:

1. **Read each of the perspectives** Make time to read and comprehend each of the perspectives. Keep a notepad handy (paper or virtual) and write down any points of significance that jump out at you upon reading each perspective. You should decide what 'significant' means.

2. **Select two perspectives to compare** Based on your initial reactions, select the two practitioner perspectives you find the most and least relevant to your views of strategy. Don't overthink this—use your gut instinct.
3. **Complete a contrastive grid** Contrastive means 'to show the difference between two things when you compare them'. Re-reading your selected perspectives, complete the contrastive grid (see Table 16.1) with as many ideas as seem relevant in each of the cells.
4. **Interpret your answers** Focusing on the differences and similarities between your reviews of the practitioner perspectives, note down what you think your answers tell you about how you understand strategy. What preferences do you seem to have about how strategy should be understood, expressed, or put into practice? How will these views influence how you approach strategy in future?

Going further

If you can complete the essential preparation, you will be in a position to be able to engage fully with the rest of the chapter. Equally, if you find the contrastive process useful, you may wish to undertake further optional review steps:

(a) **Extend the grid** Add a further practitioner perspective to engage in a comparison of three views. Whilst this is more challenging, you may be able to add depth to your personal insights with a further frame of reference. Consider picking a practitioner that you think differs in views from where your first two practitioners seem to agree. Alternatively, compare the practitioner reflections in this section with any of the practitioner insights at the end of each chapter.

(b) **Change the selection criteria** Complete a second contrastive grid in which you compare the two or more practitioners that you consider to be 'most different', regardless of whether you liked their views or not. Once you have completed this contrastive grid, ask yourself if the comparison process was more or less useful when you selected practitioners on more 'objective' criteria.

TABLE 16.1 **Contrastive grid for practitioner reflections**

	What do you feel about their writing? What is it that you feel most strongly about—either agree or disagree? Explain why you hold these views.	How does this practitioner interpret strategy? How do the views and proposed actions relate to the process–practice framework? How has learning influenced this practitioner's view of strategy?	Which of the practitioner recommendations for action would you, or do you, put into practice? Why do you think that advice is appealing to you?
Practitioner 1			
Practitioner 2			

(c) Change the questions Either extend or replace the question set in the contrastive grid with different points of comparison. You can generate your own questions according to what interests you. Alternatively, you could use some of the following questions that relate directly to the content of this chapter.

(i) How has practical experience shaped this person's view of strategy?

(ii) What personal 'values' seem to be reflected in this practitioner's advice?

(iii) To what extent does the person seem to be influenced by the external environment or social context in which they are strategizing?

(iv) How do emotions and feelings seem to impact on this person's views of strategy?

(v) To what extent, and through what means, is engaging with others raised as important by this practitioner?

(vi) To what extent does this person value time and space to think in strategy work?

(vii) How does being able to improvise and change direction feature as important in this practitioner's views?

Interested in further views? You can search the Chapter 16 **online resources** for a wide range of further practitioner perspectives.

16.3 Practitioner views

This section contains six practitioner perspectives. They are not arranged in any particular order. Each piece of reflective writing is organized by the three common questions.

PRACTITIONER VIEW 1: **GORDON RAMSAY, PLANT LEADER, P&G, WEST VIRGINIA, USA**

1. What does strategy mean to you?
Strategy is the approach you are going to take to achieve something—a set of choices that you believe are the best approaches to achieving results. We must make choices as we always have options. Equally, resources are always limited and so we need to decide what to prioritize and what we aren't going to do. To work together on this, my team and I find the terms strategy and tactics useful. For us, strategy defines your long-term goals and how you're planning to achieve them. Strategy gives you the path you need to follow to contribute towards achieving your organization's mission. Tactics are much more concrete and oriented toward smaller steps and shorter time frames. Tactics involve best practices, specific plans, resources, etc. For me, 'tactics' correspond to 'initiatives'.

Continued

2. How has learning shaped your views of strategy?

I've learned from experience that (1) strategy has to be simple, (2) it takes 100 times more effort to align the organization to the strategy than it does to create it, and (3) it is vital to get the organization engaged in the development of the strategy to create ownership and accountability. I've also found that it is very important to communicate to the organization 'The Why'. In other words, for any strategy 'Why are we doing this?' 'Why is it important?' 'Why are we chasing this versus another strategy?' When people grasp 'The Why' they will take over ownership of the strategy, align efforts behind, it and drive it through.

3. What strategy practices would you advise others to consider?

For me, there are five elements to strategy practice that are essential to implement initiatives successfully and deliver your goals.

1. Be clear on your success criteria and measures. Have you defined what success looks like? How are you going to check that what you are doing is working?
2. Have an action plan that outlines who will do what by when. The action plan must tie back to the success criteria.
3. Be clear on roles and responsibilities for every part of the strategy, and know who is responsible for each aspect of your strategy work.
4. Set a review cycle—organize meetings on an appropriate frequency to review the action plan, check the measures, and adjust initiatives if required.
5. Ensure that everyone knows the cultural behaviours that are expected in strategy tactics work. Define them, communicate them, and tie them to your reward and recognition programme.

PRACTITIONER VIEW 2: ANN-MAREE MORRISON, BUSINESS OWNER, AND CHAIR, WOMEN IN ENTERPRISE, SCOTLAND

1. What does strategy mean to you?

Strategy to me means a planned approach to how you will run and build or change your business, and your lifestyle as well, over the next year, three years, and five years. This is a written document accompanied by a mission and a vision, and a more detailed plan. This plan might be prepared by mind mapping, list writing, SWOT, and any other analysis methods that you prefer to use, and a variety of these, not just one.

2. How has learning shaped your views of strategy?

The most significant experience I have had is that strategy can change the next day! One day it's all sorted, and the next day you get a phone call or email that can turn everything on it's head. You need to be willing to be both proactive and reactive. Too many people treat strategy as something set in stone. They have a written strategy just like a business plan, or indeed the business plan is their strategy in a lot of cases, and then they file it. Then suddenly when something happens, such as a key staff member leaving or a large client going out of business, the strategy is out the window and yet it is never revised. Strategy needs to be ongoing and continually updated.

3. What strategy practices would you advise others to consider?

The most important practices on a regular basis are as follows.

- Monitor and take necessary action on monthly statistics—costs, clients, new sales, lost sales, search engine optimization, product lines, operations successes and problems, staff successes and problems, customer feedback.

- Watch competition online and offline in the press and check their sites from product ranges to pricing and strategic moves.
- Read widely in your field about new technology and take action to keep ahead where possible.
- Invest in technology and staff within your means, including investment in coaching, mentoring, repositioning, training, and replacing 'dead wood' if necessary.

I find that SWOT analysis, monthly accounts analysis, online research, and reading widely are the most commonly used and successful strategy analysis methods for me and the team.

PRACTITIONER VIEW 3: **TARIQ IBRAHIM, STRATEGY CONSULTANT, OMAN**

1. What does strategy mean to you?

I would define strategy as 'a set of big decisions with extended impact'—your response to environmental drivers that you anticipate will develop a preferential future position. The stress here is on the words 'response', which can vary in nature, and 'preferential position', which defines a competitive endpoint. A good strategy attempts to anticipate influential environmental factors before they become current and to develop a preferential position relative to competitors as early and for as long as possible.

2. How has learning shaped your views of strategy?

Originally educated as an engineer, I used to think that there was a 'right way' to do strategy, in the same way there is a 'right way' to design a physical system. However, working with many organizations I have learnt to appreciate the difference between the collaborative nature of 'strategy in motion' as ideas are formulated and 'strategy at rest' once decisions have been made and shared. You have to approach strategy work differently in each of these states. I have also learnt that information systems can usefully facilitate strategy work if used in the right way. I choose my strategy formulation approach after carefully examining the way and with whom it is going to be implemented. For example, whilst working on a national level strategy the formulation approach was designed to guarantee involvement and buy-in from the wider segments of society—activities and methods were designed in alignment with that priority.

3. What strategy practices would you advise others to consider?

For me, effective strategic management mixes art and science, drawing appropriately from the hundreds of strategy tools available. I think practitioners benefit from a rounded knowledge of the different strategy schools and perspectives available to be able to tackle the situation in hand, especially for strategy consultants working in different environments. As a consultant, an important practice is to develop a generic starting design for strategy process, and then plug in the right strategy tools customized to meet the needs of each situation. Knowing how to do this can be an invaluable skill—add technology capability which makes it all efficient and you become indispensable!

PRACTITIONER VIEW 4: DR STEVE GRAHAM, CEO, ROYAL COLLEGE OF PHYSICIANS AND SURGEONS

1. What does the term strategy mean to you?

For me, strategy is about having a clear and shared vision of where the business or organization sees itself, to which all resources are allocated towards achieving. Strategy should be inspirational and should answer questions on why it sees itself there, what it needs to do, how it will do it, etc.

2. How has learning shaped your views of strategy?

I have learned three things—externality and perspective, adaptability, and engagement—from getting strategy wrong! It is vital to draw on externality and perspective. For me, this means seeking out relevant objective external advice to test out assumptions and challenge your firmly held beliefs, the 'doability' of your plans, learning about competitive pressures, and questioning financial constraints. Working with external voices can help you take off any organizational blinkers that are stopping you from seeing reality in a rounded way. And external views are vital in knowing how your strategy will realize value for your customers.

In terms of adaptability, I've learned that it is vital that there is enough flexibility in your approach to allow plans to change. Things around you invariably do change, and the test of a good strategy and plan is the ability to move quickly to address these changes and/or seize opportunities.

And I've learned that engagement with the strategy message is crucial. Your stakeholders—externally and internally—need to have a clear grasp and understanding of your strategy. For me, the best strategy will be able to be articulated in 10 seconds or less.

3. What strategy practices would you advise others to consider?

I would advise that when working with strategy, have the courage to set out on a journey, ensuring that you have enough expertise around you to build a compelling vision whilst being prepared to listen to constructive dissenters.

As you go, spend time communicating, listening, and engaging to keep all focused on why this strategy makes sense, and the ways in which it creates value to your end-customer. The what, how, and who often follow quickly, because people invariably know their business or organization.

And finally, don't get blind-sided by continually seeking external perspectives and advice!

PRACTITIONER VIEW 5: CATHERINE TILLEY, EX-DIRECTOR OF OPERATIONS, STRATEGY & TREND ANALYSIS CENTRE, MCKINSEY

1. What does the term strategy mean to you?

There are lots of definitions of strategy, but the idea I've found most consistently helpful is that the essence of strategy is a clear and differentiated point of view that supports forceful and coherent action. This communicates well that strategy is based on a way of seeing that is distinctive, and that strategy tells people how to act in a way that is coherent so that the actions build upon each other.

This is helpful for several reasons. First, it's clear that strategy is different from target-setting or planning, as it answers the question 'How?', rather than 'What?'. Second, it suggests that there are choices involved; if strategy informs coherent action, then there are some things that you won't be able to do. Third, it implies that creativity is involved in the strategic process. Differentiated points of view are, by definition, not the usual ones.

2. How has learning shaped your views of strategy?

There are two lessons that have been very important to me. The first is that strategy formulation is essentially a creative act, but it is often framed in quite a technocratic way. As Rumelt says, strategy is based on a 'differentiated point of view'. For me, this means going beyond the industry forecasts, competitor data, and so on that you tend to start with in a company to see if you can find a new way of looking at things. This can mean finding new insights into consumer behaviour or asking what the future would be like if some critical aspect of the present were different. Many of the frameworks that people rely on to develop strategies fail to encourage this sort of creative thinking. I think that some of my most significant learning experiences while working with strategy have come from finding new ways of engaging with the world. For example, many years ago I was working on developing strategies for a consumer products organization and all the major insights came from us really understanding what people wanted from their bathrooms. This wasn't information we were going to find in an industry report or spreadsheet.

The second is that strategies have significant human implications. Creating strategy is a social act; people need to understand the world view on which it is based, and then act accordingly. This means that strategists need a broad understanding of the organization—including its culture and identity as well as its more formal structures—as part of the basis for their recommendations. A strategy that is beautiful on paper but doesn't command the attention of the organization has failed.

3. What strategy practices would you advise others to consider?

There are three that spring to mind.

First, understand the nature of the strategic decision itself—especially the level of uncertainty around it, and the particular boundary conditions. Are you actually solving the right problem? In particular it's important to understand the type of uncertainty that is involved, and the time frame for the strategy—there's a huge difference in the way you'd think about a two-year plan compared with a ten-year strategy.

Second, bring in interesting data. Given that strategy is based on having a particular view of the world, you need to ground this data that other people might not have understood. Of course you need to understand your own performance and that of your competitors, you need data about the market and the possible technological and regulatory upheavals, but you need to keep asking what else? How would these data look to other people? What would someone from outside the industry who didn't share your norms see here?

Third, involve the right people and manage the process thoughtfully. Strategy rarely needs to be completed on a short time-frame so make sure that all involved are able to absorb the ideas and engage deeply with the topic. It's important to run a process where people are comfortable having their preconceptions challenged, and to find that they are wrong—something that most people find uncomfortable. This means that you need effective and explicit processes to help people 'think out loud' and to challenge potential biases. An effective process will also help to balance the effort between creating the distinctive view of the situation and identifying the set of actions to take. I've often found it helpful to be explicit at this point about what people won't be able to do as part of the strategy—this is a great way to test your thinking.

PRACTITIONER VIEW 6: AILEEN MCLEOD, HEAD OF BUSINESS PLANNING, COMMERCIAL AND PERFORMANCE, TRANSMISSION AT SSE PLC

1. What does the term strategy mean to you?

As a practitioner, for me strategy is forward planning. Strategy contends with the certainty that the future of a corporation is largely exogenous, and hence is uncontrollable and unpredictable. In addition, the people involved in strategy have biases and are influenced by their prevailing business environment. Evidently, strategy is not science.

Recognizing this, the day-to-day practice of strategy iterates qualitative inputs to derive probable outcomes. The resultant range of possible forward plans is then assessed in the context of the risk appetite and resilience of the organization. While this work does not determine the future, it can give insight to possible futures and so inform and improve business decisions made today.

2. How has learning shaped your views of strategy?

From my work in strategy, a strong and consistent theme over many years has been learning about the dynamics of the people in the organization. It is commonplace to hear that the greatest asset of an organization is its people. As a strategy practitioner, I find it equally commonplace to hear from employees that 'there is no strategy' or 'the strategy doesn't make sense'. It can require a thick skin and open mind to work in strategy. Further, I've learned that there is merit in the truism that any forward plan will fail without the organization's people working towards that goal. There is huge satisfaction, and relief, when the ethos of the organization integrates a long-developed strategy.

3. What strategy practices would you advise others to consider?

- Adopting and maintaining an open inquisitive mind.
- Adapt as you go. The development and implementation of strategy is not a sequential activity. Strategy is continually tested by new information—that includes the information revealed by putting the strategy into effect and the information revealed by exposure to others' experiences and opinions. In response, when required and sometimes quickly, strategy must adapt.
- Be careful not to become paralysed by the noise of information and the false security of perpetual analysis.

16.4 The influence of learning on strategy-in-practice

In this section we explore how learning might influence strategy. In Chapter 6, learning was identified as a dynamic capability that might enable the creation of new change capabilities and adaption of operating capabilities. Therefore learning is a topic of high relevance and potential usefulness to strategy practitioners. The aim of this section is to raise your awareness of a range of theories that explain how learning plays a role in strategy. We will illustrate the relevance of these theories through examples from the practitioner reflections. By understanding how learning can inform and improve strategy practices over time, you will enhance your ability to lead the delivery of effective strategy activities.

What do we mean by learning?

As a general definition, learning is 'the acquisition of knowledge or skills through study, experience, or being taught' (Oxford Living Dictionary 2019). As Senge (1990:13) observes, learning has become synonymous with 'taking in information', whereas it should really refer to a shift in our thinking or way of seeing the world. For example, absorbing the information from a competitor report isn't learning—learning refers to new insights arising from that information that help us understand competitors in a different way.

In this section we will aim to focus on ways in which strategic learning can be stimulated. Strategic learning refers to learning which informs and influences the identification and enactment of strategic initiatives intended to deliver future capacity for organizational growth and survival (Mackay and Burt 2015:546). According to Ambrosini and Bowman (2005:493), 'strategic learning relates directly to the key management question of how organizations change their strategy'.

In relation to the process–practice framework, strategic learning might arise when we derive insights from information flowing to us from our context. We can stimulate information flows through deliberate action. In his reflective comments, Steve Graham highlights the importance of seeking external perspectives and 'dissenting voices' as a way of testing the validity of your plans. This is an example of strategic learning that arises because of purposeful action (Figure 16.1): (1) Steve decides to ask for external perspective about his strategy; (2) dialogue with a trusted adviser takes place; (3) the adviser offers an opinion; (4) Steve decides to listen; (5) Steve processes the adviser's views into new insights about this strategy.

Strategic learning is of high value to strategy practitioners as it helps us to think in new ways and improve the effectiveness of the strategic practices we use. The strategy consultant Kenichi Ohmae explains that strategic thinking is central to the success of organizational leaders in continuing to steer their organizations.

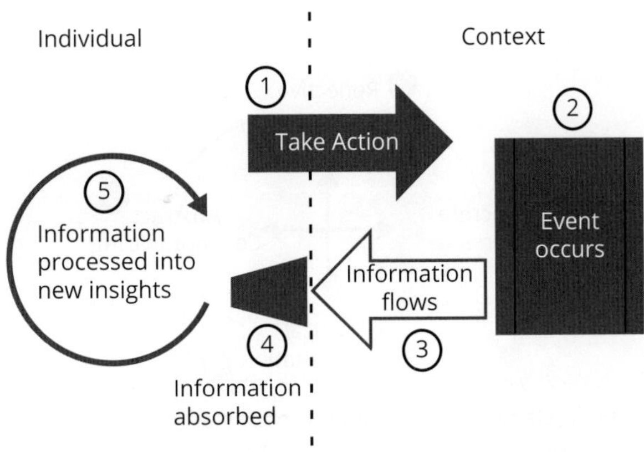

FIGURE 16.1 Taking action to generate learning potential.

In strategic thinking, one first seeks a clear understanding of the particular character of each element of a situation and then makes the fullest possible use of human brainpower to restructure the elements in the most advantageous way. Phenomena and events in the real world do not always fit a linear model. Hence the most reliable means of dissecting a situation into its constituent parts and reassembling them in the desired pattern is not a step-by-step methodology such as systems analysis. Rather, it is that ultimate non-linear thinking tool, the human brain.

Ohmae (1982:304)

While his central insight is as true today as it was in 1982, our knowledge of strategic thinking and how it is supported by learning has come a long way. This section gives an overview of several of the most influential perspectives on strategic learning, the tools they use, and recent advances in research.

Experiential learning cycle

Learning can arise from our experience of individual events or patterns of events happening over time. For example, in his practitioner reflection, Gordon Ramsay comments that he has 'learned from experience that strategy has to be simple'. This means that based on his previous activity in strategy and his observations of how different approaches lead to different levels of success in outcomes, he has developed refined knowledge about how to act effectively.

This refinement of strategic practice can be described by the **experiential learning cycle** (ELC), first articulated by Kolb (1984). As shown in Figure 16.2, the ELC consists of four phases. Applied to Gordon's comment:

1. try to make strategy with others to varying degrees of success (concrete experience)
2. absorb information about context, actions, and outcomes (reflective observation)
3. generate insights from the absorbed information by trying to figure out plausible explanations for how actions taken led to the outcomes observed in the given context (abstract conceptualizing)

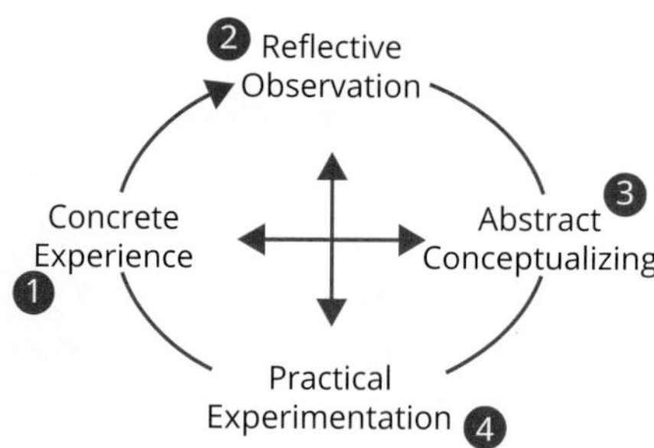

N.B. the cycle is continuous and without start or end point—the numbers are purely for reference to points in the text

FIGURE 16.2 The experiential learning cycle. Adapted from Kolb, D.A. (1984). *Experiential Learning: Experience as the Source of Learning and Development*. Englewood Cliffs, NJ: Prentice Hall.

4. refine the new insights arising from small-scale actions or debate with others in readiness for full deployment in future (practical experimentation).

In Gordon's case, after several iterations of the ELC, he has refined his practical knowledge about strategy to favour simplicity based on personal experience.

Through the ELC, individuals will generate new insights in different ways according to their preferred learning styles. Kolb (1984) proposes that we favour learning by either doing or observing, and we tend to favour how we feel or what we think as we learn. We will maximize learning when we figure out our learning preferences and attempt to follow them.

The ELC emphasizes the need for considered reflection and reflective practice as a way of improving strategizing performance—we explore how you might do this later in this chapter. As you engage in strategy activity, knowledge of the ELC will enable you to design purposeful learning experiences and experiments for you and your colleagues that deliver practical impact (Renshaw 2017) and deep personal insights (Tomkins and Ulus 2016). The ELC itself has been subject to criticism as representing learning as a neat orderly cycle that always follows a fixed routine in contrast with how learning might occur in reality (Coffield et al. 2004; Smith 2001). Nevertheless, the ELC continues to be an evolving and influential model (see also Kolb and Kolb 1999, 2005, 2008; Kolb et al. 2001), and is a useful starting point for thinking about how to become a more reflective and effective strategy practitioner.

Single- and double-loop learning

Figure 16.3 shows a well-established model of single- and double-loop learning first developed by Argyris (1976) and Argyris and Schön (1974). These authors noted that, through the course of life, it is easy to end up in a situation where our mental models go unchallenged for a long period of time, creating blind spots in our strategic thinking. Senge (1990:8) describes mental models as 'deeply ingrained assumptions, generalisations, or even pictures or images that influence how we understand the world and how we take action'. As Marshak (2019) explains, double-loop learning is when we gain new insights about 'why?' we are doing something, allowing us to change our mental models as well as our practices. In contrast, single-loop learning is when we gain insights about 'what we are doing' only, such that we refine our practice without changing our mental models.

To illustrate these concepts, consider Tariq Ibrahim's practitioner reflections. Tariq comments that he now believes strategy practice is 'a blend of art and science', and that it is vital to vary one's approach to strategy depending on whether it is 'in motion' or 'at rest'. However, this wasn't always Tariq's view. Early in his strategy career, his mental models developed through engineering education led him to apply the predictable rules of the physical world to the ambiguous social world in which strategy is made. Tariq's subsequent work with a range of organizations led to him experiencing double-loop learning and changing his taken-for-granted assumptions about there being one way to 'do strategy'. His new mental model emphasizes flexibility, contingency, and reacting to circumstances. Over time, he has still refined and developed his range of strategy practices—what he does—through single-loop learning experiences. But this single-loop learning takes place within a very different mindset from his original engineering perspective of the world.

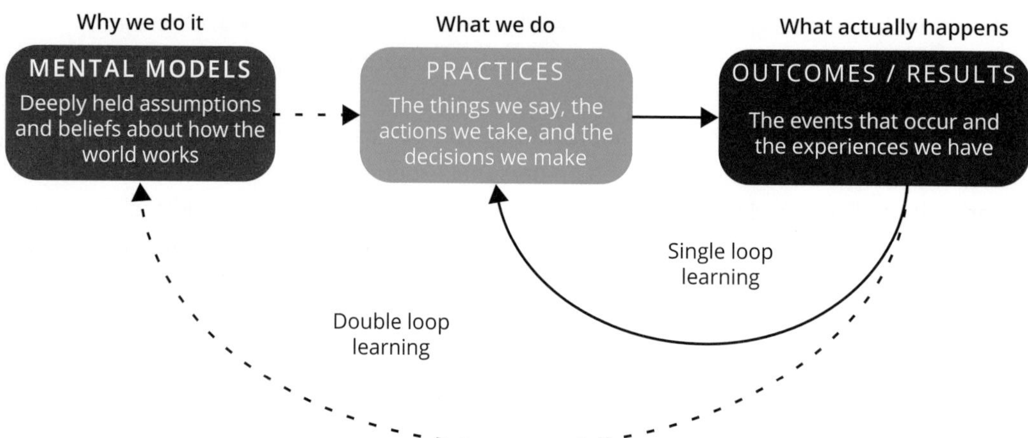

FIGURE 16.3 Single- and double-loop learning. Adapted from Argyris, C. and Schön, D. (1974). *Theory in Practice: Increasing Professional Effectiveness*. San Francisco, CA: Jossey Bass, and Argyris, C. (1976). Single-loop and double-loop models in research on decision making. *Administrative Science Quarterly*, **21**(3), 363–75.

This matters in strategy practice, as what people say and what they really believe and do are often different. Argyris and Schön (1974) refer to this as the difference between espoused theories, which people will use to justify the logic behind their behaviours and decisions, and the unstated theories-in-use that really drive their behaviours and decisions. In a strategic context, a rationale will normally be given for making a particular decision—the espoused theory—but what people actually do, sometimes unconsciously, is based on what they believe, which is frequently connected to intuition or 'gut feeling'. Strategic learning may require focus on improving our practices, but periodically strategic learning may be required to refresh our mental models too (Markides 2000).

Jarzabkowski and Kaplan (2015) have adapted concepts of theories-in-use to help to shed light on the experience and practice of using strategy tools (see the section on tools in Chapter 2). They argue that, from a practice perspective, the interaction of people and tools—the selection, application, and outcomes of using tools—creates opportunities for acting, but also results in feedback loops that shape each other. In other words, strategy tools are not neutral, but have choices embedded within them about which information to privilege and which to exclude, thus playing a role in what learning is activated. As Tariq commented, effective strategic management comes from 'drawing appropriately from the hundreds of strategy tools available'. Learning not just what practices and methods exist but also but why you might use them is vital to developing your capacity as a strategy practitioner.

Situated learning

Learning can be embedded in activity, context, and culture (Lave and Wenger 1991). This means that the new knowledge we acquire is tied into the situation in which we acquire it. This perspective is known as a situated learning approach. Situated learning theory recognizes that strategic knowledge derived from cognitive learning processes is not static but has 'a dynamic aspect in both formation and content' (Clancey 1997:4). This means that the learning and new knowledge we acquire in one situation may not be valid when we change context and may need

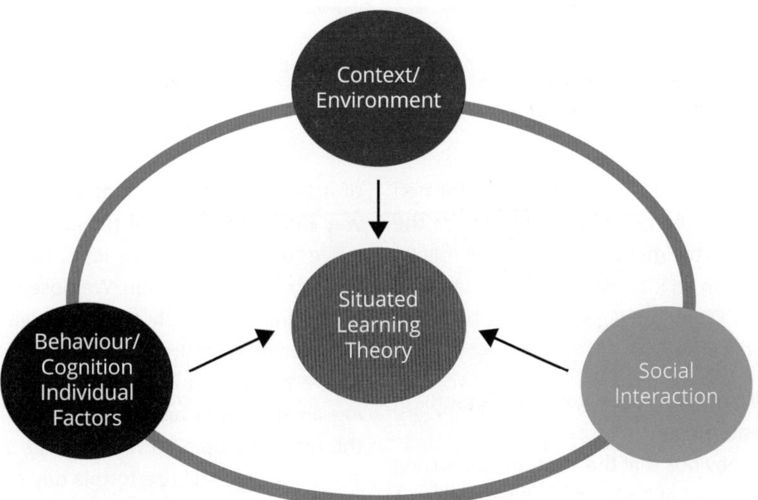

FIGURE 16.4 The situated learning perspective. Adapted from Greeno, J.G. (1994). Gibson's affordances. *Psychological Review*, **101**(2), 336–42, and Greeno, J.G. (1998). The situativity of knowing, learning, and research. *American Psychologist*, **53**(1), 5–26.

to be revisited. Therefore a situated learning perspective 'brings the context back in' to our understanding of how learning occurs (Hotho et al. 2014:60). A situated learning perspective also recognizes the influence of the macro and organizational context and culture, as well as social groups in which interaction occurs, in determining what learning can take place (Brown et al. 1989; Zhu and Bargiela-Chiappini 2013).

A model of situated learning is shown in Figure 16.4. Learning occurs where we undertake activities in a social context that resides within a broader environment. As we work with different groups, change companies or countries, or as time passes and we acquire new behaviours, previously acquired learning may become outdated.

In her practitioner reflections, Catherine Tilley articulates why situated learning might matter to strategists. Catherine comments that it is necessary to go 'beyond the industry forecasts, competitor data and so on that you tend to start with in a company to see if you can find a new way of looking at things. This can mean finding new insights into consumer behaviour or asking what the future would be like if some critical aspect of the present were different'. By interacting with consumers in their homes, rather than reading market research reports in the office, new situated learning was gained. This proved highly valuable to the strategy in which 'all the major insights came from us really understanding what people wanted from their bathrooms. This wasn't information we were going to find in an industry report or spreadsheet'.

The implication of a situated learning perspective is that as your context changes—working with a different set of colleagues, a new organization, a new type of strategy (e.g. IT strategy to business strategy)—don't assume that what you've learned to be effective strategy practice in a different setting still applies. Approach the situation tentatively and with humility, and establish how the social, organizational, and cultural contexts differ from the situations in which you've operated before (Jordan 2010). In Chapter 1 for example, the strategy scoping exercise gives you a method of establishing how those you are working with understand strategy in the situation you are looking to address. If you can be tentative in your initial approach, you will be able

CASE EXAMPLE 16.1 AN INTERVIEW WITH 'THE MAN WHO SAVED LEGO'

Between 2003 and 2012, Lego was transformed from a business on the point of bankruptcy to the global leader in the toy market. Consider the following comments from an interview with 'the man who saved Lego', ex-CEO Jorgen Vig Knudstorp, by Adam Burns of *Meet the Boss TV*.

(Interviewer) What have been your key lessons in adapting the enterprise?

I think it was obvious that the strategy was wrong but we didn't know what it should be. It looked like it was the right strategy on paper. So for the first two years of this new transformation we said 'We don't have a strategy—we just have a plan of detailed actions that we intend to carry through', and by doing that we could start to build confidence again. Only then did we develop a new strategy for Lego as a second phase of adaptation.

And I think the major distinction we made—and maybe we could do it because we were a family owned business—many companies in this situation will say 'Let's grow. Once we get growing, we'll get profitability'. We said 'For the next three years, there is going to be no growth but productivity will be many-fold increased'. It's kind of like if you look at a national economy, and the government goes out and says 'there's not going to be any growth in the economy but we're going to make this country far more competitive than it is today'. That's what we did with the Lego group.

(interviewer) That clear plan was yours?

People said 'That must be the Knudstorp survival plan'. I said 'No, its super-generic'. Leadership is not about these conceptual ideas. The difference between good and bad leadership is that you actually do it! And its like your New Year's Resolutions—too many leaders think the idea 'I must lose weight' is the insight. That's not the insight ... the insight is actually knowing how to make it happen through 8000 people.

(interviewer) How did you coalesce your executive team at the time around your insights?

The major thing I learned is that too often you believe you need to think your way into a new way of acting, but actually what you do is you act your way into a new way of thinking. This was a challenge for me as I think a lot ... for us it was about less talk and more action. We closed offices, we sold off businesses, we shut down activities, we started introducing measures. For instance, in the factories where we weren't in control, rather than introducing an IT system and elaborate reporting, we put the reporting up on a white board, and we created something we still use to this day called 'the visual factory'. Every Friday morning we get together as a management team, and each manager writes down how their bit of the factory is performing in front of us all. Green numbers for good outcomes, red numbers for bad outcomes. And people look at that and say 'When are you going to put that in an IT system?' And I say 'It's never going to go into the IT system!, Because it is all in the doing. The sharing of data and how are we doing is a social mechanism that starts driving change. Because once you have written that red number up there, you don't need to be told you need to change it, you start changing it.

My favourite motto is that the CEO needs any avenue to the truth that he or she can find. And some of those avenues are candid dialogue with employees, which means nine out of ten times they may tell you something you know or consider vaguely relevant. But if you dismiss those nine times, you don't get the tenth time where they tell you something that is crucial. You were never aware of it, and if they didn't tell you you'd only learn later, once it is too late.

(Interviewer) We live in a 24/7, always-connected world. But if you don't make time for yourself to plan change, then your leadership is only a reaction to change. How do you make time for yourself to plan?

Well what you do, which is harder to do than to just say it, is that you have to build your defences. I have periods where I don't get disturbed by phone calls or emails. And that means sometimes there is a long log of things that are fairly important or urgent that I'm not touching, as I want to make sure that I have room for the not urgent but extremely important stuff. At times I turn off my

Continued

mobile—absolutely! Leave it in the car, it's a great solution! But you may also have a day where you tell your staff 'I'm not reachable. I'm going to spend some time reflecting today'. You need to carve out that time. And it is hard, as you will say no to things where you are thinking 'Shoot! I really ought to do this'. But you don't.

Questions for discussion

1. In what ways did the context of the organization shape how the CEO responded to the strategic challenges facing Lego?
2. How does learning appear to happen for the CEO and the senior management team?
3. How open does the CEO seem to be to having his thinking challenged? Why do you think he has this attitude?
4. Why might it be important for the CEO of a firm like Lego to take time out from the business, in which they can't be contacted, on a regular basis?

Source

Interview: *The Man Who Rescued Lego—Meet the Boss TV* https://www.youtube.com/watch?v=JlVyiFqlg0w

to adapt your approach to best suit the situation. Equally, you may wish to purposefully change your context (as Catherine did in the example in Section 6.3) in order to broaden your insights by taking action in a different setting.

This view is highly relevant to a process–practice model of strategy. In Chapter 2, we defined strategy practice as situated activity, recognizing the influence of context and time on how activity is carried out. Situated learning aligns with that view.

16.5 The possibilities of reflection for strategy-in-practice

Experiential, double-loop, and situated learning perspectives give us different ways of understanding how learning might occur for practitioners which translates, through their subsequent strategy practice, into strategic learning for the organization. A central concern that links these three learning perspectives is the importance of critical reflection. In this section we will examine reflection and related concepts as an important enabler of strategic learning for individuals and organizations.

As a possible driver of individual and organizational performance, reflection is an increasingly common focus in the academic and practitioner literature. Reflection is seen as a learning mechanism that can distil valuable insights from moments of experience and shed light on how we might improve future performance or comprehension.

The term reflection is often used interchangeably with critical reflection, reflexivity, and reflective practice. However, Bolton and Delderfield (2018:2–3) suggest that it is more helpful to draw a distinction between these terms, as follows.

Reflection—in-depth focused attention.
Critical reflection—giving in-depth focused attention to questions of how political and social context shape values, assumptions, judgements, and beliefs.
Reflexivity, or critical self-reflection—focused in-depth reflection upon one's own perspective, values, and assumptions.

Reflective practice—the development of insight and practice through critical attention to practical values, theories, principles, assumptions, and the relationship between theory and practice which inform everyday actions.

These definitions intersect the models of learning addressed earlier in the chapter: reflective observation is part of the experiential learning cycle; reflection, critical reflection, and reflexivity all might play a role in single- and double-loop learning; critical reflection underpins situated learning; reflective practice might arise through learning from any of the three perspectives.

Characteristics of reflection

As in-depth focused attention, reflection is a practice of inquiry by which learning from experience can occur. Unlike physical reflection of light by a mirrored surface, through which an exact replica of an original image is produced in reverse, reflection as a contemplative learning process is more complex. Reflection is characterized by 'engaging in comparison, pondering alternatives, taking diverse perspectives and drawing inferences' (Jordan 2010:393).

Reflection can focus attention on events, decisions, and actions that have happened, are currently taking place, or are yet to occur. Reflection can be useful to us in any setting by helping us generate new insights and learning that can inform future practice (Jordan et al. 2009). Reflection is situated—involving the cognition and feelings of a person in context at a moment in time in the flow of events (Jordan 2010). From a process–practice perspective of strategy, reflection provides a means by which we can adapt strategic initiatives within and between activities, incorporating new insights from our immersion in strategy practice.

As individuals or collectives, reflection requires a purposeful focus of our attention on the exploration of a specific matter, an opening up to new possibilities, and the application of effort in order to discover new insights. And it may not be an easy process—as Gosling and Mintzberg (2004:20) comment, 'the key to learning is thoughtful reflection ... [involving] wondering, probing, analysing, synthesising—and struggling'.

Connecting with the challenge of double-loop learning, reflection is important as 'it allows us to critique our taken-for-granted assumptions, so that we can become receptive to alternative ways of reasoning and behaving' (Gray 2007:496). As you deal with complex challenges involving multiple stakeholders in strategy, a capacity for reflection may act as an enabler of 'better' outcomes. If you are able to keep an open mind whilst asking searching questions, without always reverting to familiar routines, new practices or ways of thinking might become apparent within or between strategy activities (Keevers and Treleaven 2011:517).

The value of reflection

As you study strategy, reflection is a valuable addition to the toolkit that enables personal development and improvement based on learning from experience (Gilmore and Anderson 2012). Reflection enables us not only to better understand what we have done or experienced in the past, but also to evaluate what we are considering doing in the future. As the management guru Peter Drucker once commented: 'Follow effective action with quiet reflection. From the quiet reflection, will come even more effective action'.

Aside from creating new insights, reflection is also an individual capacity that boosts employability. Reflection often features in the recruitment checklist of organizations (Wharton 2017). If an organization invests in a new hire, and that new hire has the capacity to reflect, learn, and improve, the effectiveness and contribution of that potential employee will grow over time. Regardless of your level of experience, you can improve your capacity for reflection through practice, which in turn will enable you to learn and develop your effectiveness as a (strategy) practitioner.

Reflection-on-action and reflection-in-action

Reflection is often characterized as the practice of purposefully stepping back to consider the meaning of recent events involving or affecting us and those around us in our immediate environment. By challenging our assumptions and understanding of how an event unfolded, we can deepen our understanding of the mechanisms at play in the world, illuminating new ways of thinking and being (Raelin 2002). This approach to reflection is what Schön (2016) defines as 'reflection-on-action'—looking backwards, occurring after an event.

Schön (2016:55) contrasts reflection-on-action with 'reflection-in-action', in which a practitioner reflects on 'patterns of action, situations in which they are performing, and the know-how implicit in their performance' to make adjustments to events as they occur. Reflection-in-action is synonymous with phrases such as 'thinking on your feet' and 'keeping your wits about you'—drawing on your experience, capabilities, and observations about 'the stuff at hand' to effectively navigate a situation. Reflection-in-action is a mechanism for instant situational learning that aids coping and development of solutions that are appropriate to the situation in hand.

Figure 16.5 offers an illustration of reflection-on-action compared with reflection-in-action as it might occur in relation to ongoing strategizing activity. Reflection-in-action takes place as the events of strategizing episode 1 unfold. The learning arising from reflection-in-action is immediately put into play to adjust how the practitioner participates in the strategizing episode. In comparison, after strategizing episode 1 has finished, the practitioner looks back on events through reflection-on-action. New learning arising here isn't immediately deployed, but rather is available for use by the practitioner as an informant of practice and reflection-in-action in subsequent strategizing episodes.

Critical reflection and reflexivity

Management students are often faced with the challenge of applying critical reflection to ideas. Connecting with the concept of 'double-loop' learning, this means moving beyond cognitive gains to challenging the feelings, emotions, values, and beliefs that influence actions or events in a given context.

For strategists, critical reflection might provide a first step in bringing stakeholders together when attempting to build shared views of how to progress strategy work.

> *Critical reflection can transform perspectives. People recognize that their perceptions may be flawed because they are filtered through unexamined views, beliefs, attitudes and feelings inherited from one's family,*

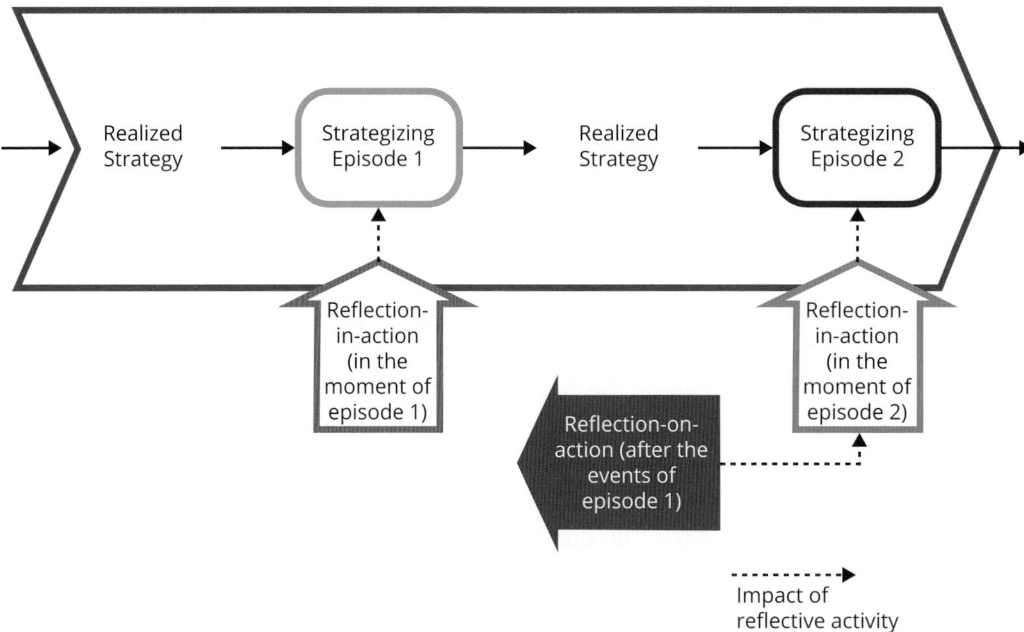

FIGURE 16.5 Reflection-on-action versus reflection-in-action relating to strategizing.

> *school and society. Flawed perceptions distort one's understanding of problems and situations ... critical reflection can also go beyond the individual participant's underlying assumptions and can lead specifically to the examination of organizational norms.*
>
> Marsick and O'Neil (1999:163)

By working with others—through discussions, questions, probing, and respectful challenge—we can encourage a deep learning about how and why we perceive situations, cause and effect, and future actions in a given way (Lai 2017). Such insights may open the possibility of self-realizing changes that we would like to make to those views and finding new paths to personal development and collaboration with others.

This sort of learning can be challenging to achieve. Reflection and critical reflection are often described in terms of 'taking a helicopter view' or 'standing on the cliff' to see the world from afar in a detached objective way (Keevers and Treleaven 2011). However, 'in a world that is practically experienced rather than abstractly theorised, the idea of reflection as stepping back from unfolding processes into a disengaged position becomes impossible' (Zundel 2013:110).

Instead, we can learn to reflect in a situated immersed way. And when reflecting, we shouldn't set ourselves the challenge of being objective and clear, expecting to find new truths. Instead, without ignoring the role of cognition and logic, reflection might be most effective when we recognize that we are emotional, spiritual, and physical beings too, immersed in an unfolding world. By taking account of the vital role of emotions alongside cognition in our learning we can engage in critical reflectivity—the surfacing and critiquing of tacit or taken-for-granted assumptions and beliefs (Gray 2007:496)—to spur on the development of our management and strategy capabilities, and our personal effectiveness in making organizational contributions.

The reflective practitioner

When a person describes themselves as a 'reflective practitioner', this typically means that they are characterized by:

> *the ability and willingness to question routinized ways of thinking and acting, either after having acted (reflection-on-action) or in the midst of acting (reflection-in-action). The latter makes it possible to alter one's current course of action by framing the problem in a new way (problem setting) or by improvising on new ways of solving the problem at hand.*
>
> Jordan (2010:393)

The reflective practitioner will have a willingness to engage in reflection-on-action—'passionate humility, recognition of multiple truths, scepticism about one's own ways of thinking and acting' and a capacity to reflect-in-action 'ability to experiment, engage in backtalk and interactive practices of informing and questioning' (Jordan 2010:408).

Aileen McLeod's reflections provide an example of this dual capability. Aileen highlights the importance of 'learning about the dynamics of the people in the organization' as well as their 'biases' and reactions to the 'prevailing business environment'. This sort of learning occurs after the fact through reflection-on-action. Equally, Aileen recognizes that 'strategy is continually tested by new information—that includes the information revealed by putting the strategy into effect and the information revealed by exposure to others' experiences and opinions. In response, when required and sometimes quickly, strategy must adapt'. A capacity to respond and adapt with a 'thick skin and open mind' to employees saying 'there is no strategy' or 'the strategy doesn't make sense' requires reflection-in-action.

Aileen's reflective practice illustrates that we are not separate from the world or the actions of others. Gosling and Mintzberg (2004:20) note that reflection occurs effectively when those reflecting are 'engaged, curious and alert on a personal level and in a social process' that draws on the ideas and activities of others.

Barriers to and enablers of reflection

Reflection is not necessarily a natural activity for any of us to undertake, and the prospect can be anxiety inducing for many reasons. Porter (2017) highlights the following challenges that prevent people reflecting:

1. We don't know how to reflect—we lack knowledge of processes or methods that enable reflection.
2. We don't like reflection as it goes against 'normal' fast-paced, well-defined routine activities, and can feel like a 'wasted' or inefficient use of time.

3. We don't like the results that can emerge from reflection—whilst it may affirm our approach, equally it may lead to uncomfortable new insights about us or our situation.
4. We have a strong bias for action which overrides our willingness to ponder.
5. We can't see an immediate return on the time invested when there are other more pressing matters to be addressed.

Time management is a major barrier to reflection. Cross et al. (2018:135) cite a study by the consultancy firm Connected Commons suggesting that:

> most managers now spend 85% or more of their work time on email, in meetings, and on the phone, and the demand for such activities has jumped by 50% over the past decade. Companies benefit, of course: Faster innovation and more seamless client service are two by-products of greater collaboration. But along with all this comes significantly less time for focused individual work, careful reflection, and sound decision making.

This emphasis on action privileges the exploitation of reflection-in-action over the investment of time in reflection-on-action. Ultimately, this is a short-term approach, as without making time for reflection-on-action, individual and organizational learning and improvement potential is diminished. In contrast, organizations that encourage and support regular allocation of time for reflection and learning for employees will benefit from enhanced performance and productivity (Garvin et al. 2008).

For personal and organizational learning, it is as important to understand negative events and outcomes as it is to understand positive ones in order to avoid future issues and costly errors (Bouquet et al. 2018). Reflection gives us a means by which to do such 'post-mortems', but it requires us to be honest with ourselves and others (Healey and Hodgkinson 2017). Achieving the required honesty levels can be a major challenge in organizations where admitting errors, failures, or weaknesses can lead to ridicule or retaliation. Therefore a degree of psychological safety—'being able to show and employ one's self without fear of negative consequences of self-image, status or career' (Kahn 1990:708) is a major factor in determining the extent to which reflection can occur in an organization.

Organizational leaders can influence the extent to which reflection can occur through their attitude to challenge and competing views. Reflection is enabled by the comparison of opposing ideas—often our own versus the ideas of others. Organizational leaders who 'recognise the value of competing functional outlooks and alternative worldviews can increase energy and motivation, spark fresh thinking, and prevent lethargy and drift' (Garvin et al. 2008:112), creating conditions for 'a reflective culture'. This can be a valuable, but fragile, strategic asset that drives organizational improvement by making 'it possible for people to constantly challenge without fear of retaliation. Yet, a culture that permits questioning of assumptions is difficult to tolerate because it requires that people in control lose their grip on the status quo' (Raelin 2002:68).

Inclusive approaches as described in Chapter 15 might unlock the potential for reflection in strategy. Lowering barriers to participation in organizational processes, and inviting and engaging a range of stakeholders to become involved, will increase the diversity of competing views to which we are exposed. Further, it reduces the pressure on the organizational leader to have all the answers, and thus enables them to better 'let go' of formal power.

CASE EXAMPLE 16.2 MORE FOR LESS? TRIALLING THE FOUR-DAY WEEK

A precedent has been set. Should other companies follow Perpetual Guardian in switching to a four-day working week? Not only has the move appeared to have increased profits, but staff wellbeing has risen and productivity has apparently risen by as much as 20%. Is it really the case that less is more when it comes to time in work? Based on the findings of Perpetual Guardian's innovative trial, it could well be that millions of working people across the world could benefit from a better work–life balance in parallel with the organizations making performance gains from moving to a four-day working week.

The change made by Perpetual Guardian, a financial services company in New Zealand, meant that employees' wages were maintained, but the working week was reduced from five to four days for its 240 members of staff. Monitored by the University of Auckland and Auckland University of Technology, the trial recorded increased productivity, stating that there was no drop in the work completed despite the lower number of days at the office.

Data showed that leadership, stimulation, and empowerment were rated higher by Perpetual Guardian employees compared with a survey conducted the previous year under the traditional system of a five-day week, with commitment and empowerment the most improved. Moreover, staff stress levels were down from 45% to 38%, and work–life balance scores increased from 54% to 78%.

'This is an idea whose time has come', said Andrew Barnes, Perpetual Guardian's founder and chief executive. 'We need to get more companies to give it a go. They will be surprised at the improvement in their company, their staff and in their wider community.'

Perpetual Guardian released a how-to guide for other organizations, including findings from the trial and implementation. 'We've been treated like adults and I think as a result everyone is behaving like adults', said Tammy Barker, a branch manager who was part of the trial that cut the working week from 37.5 hours to 30.

The eight-week experiment was closely watched by employers and policy-makers around the world. More than 350 requests were received by Perpetual Guardian from 28 countries, such as the UK, Australia, the USA, and Germany, and recently trials have taken place in Brighton-based tax consultancy Accordance VAT, Irish recruitment, training, and outsourced services company ICE GROUP, and London start-up Upgrade Pack.

It is true to say that this way of working won't suit everyone. Questions have been raised about how far people working in front-line occupations, such as nursing or the police, could cut their hours without reducing the public service they provide, or how it would work in industries such as retail, where being present is a key part of the job. But where it would possibly be realistically practical to implement a four-day working week, Tammy Barker says 'the biggest concern from an employer point of view is ensuring that the full-time introduction of the policy doesn't lead to complacency, with the risk that people's productivity will slip back'. In order 'to guard against this happening we've spent a lot of time making sure every person in every team has their own plan as to how they're going to maintain and even improve their productivity'. Drawing on her own experience, Barker said 'I did find that my productivity increased purely by being more aware of my work processes and thinking about how I was doing things and why I was doing them. At the same time, I didn't feel any more stressed at work, probably because I was really focusing on the tasks at hand and because I had the extra day off to compensate for the increased work rate.'

But in the UK, for example, where average working hours have been increasing since the financial crisis, workers might envy their Australasian cousins using the additional day off for some of the same leisure activity they would have done at the weekend. In the Perpetual Guardian trial, people used the additional day off for some of the same leisure activity they would have done at the weekend, such as golf or watching Netflix, but new activities emerged as well. According to Jarrod Haar, a professor of human resource management at Auckland University of Technology, these included 'spending time with parents', 'spending much-needed time studying', and 'cleaning the house on a Wednesday and then having the weekend free'.

Continued

'Managers reported their teams were more creative after the trial', he said. 'It involved them finding solutions to doing their work in four days, so this reflected well. Importantly, they rated their teams as giving better customer service—they were more engaging and focused when clients and customers called'. He said that significantly lower job stress and burnout was reported, with work–life balance levels achieving record highs.

'Beyond wellbeing, employees reported their teams were stronger and functioned better together, more satisfied with their jobs, more engaged, and they felt their work had greater meaning,' he said. 'They also reported being more committed to the organization and less likely to look elsewhere for a job.'

Questions for discussion

1. In what ways might spending less time at work have increased the potential for reflection-on-action and reflection-in-action for Perpetual Guardian staff?
2. How applicable is the learning from Perpetual Guardian to other contexts. Would we expect to see the same outcomes in different settings? Explain your answers.
3. What are the common messages between Perpetual Guardian and the views of Jurgen Knudstorp earlier in Case Example 16.1?
4. What are the strategic opportunities and risks for Perpetual Guardian's competitors in adopting, and not adopting, a four-day week?

Sources

https://www.theguardian.com/money/2019/feb/19/four-day-week-trial-study-finds-lower-stress-but-no-cut-in-output

https://www.accordancevat.com/press-room/accordance-vat-pilots-four-day-working-week/

https://www.prolificlondon.co.uk/marketing-tech-news/tech-news/2019/06/london-startup-marks-first-anniversary-four-day-week-trial

https://4dayweek.ie/

16.6 **Methods of strategic learning and reflection**

There are many ways in which reflection and strategic learning can occur, and it is important that we find specific reflective approaches that work for us and the situations we encounter. In this section we examine considerations and options for students or managers who wish to engage in reflective learning as part of strategy-in-practice.

Dedicate time to reflection

Reflection needs time dedicated to allowing it to happen, as with any purposeful activity. The need to dedicate time implies two main considerations. First, on a practical basis, Cross et al. (2018) comment that it is vital to make time for reflection and to be clear to those around you when you are available, and when you are not. Boyatzis et al. (2002:91) suggest that it is valuable to build 'reflective structures' in your schedule which give 'time and space for self-examination, whether a few hours a week, a day or two a month, or a longer period every year'. Reflective structures that provide time to be with your own thoughts can include activities such as meditation, walking, going for a bike ride, and exercise.

Secondly, dedicating time also means that once reflection is under way, it is crucial to 'fight against framing and action biases that might encourage you to accept the issue as presented and rush into problem solving' (Bouquet et al. 2018:108). By not rushing to conclusions and allowing adequate time to allow reflective insights to mature, reflection might enrich our knowing in a more complete way. Ingrid Johnson, the CEO of Nedbank Group, South Africa, found that instigating 'pause and reflect' sessions boosted the rate at which transformation occurred within the organization, as members of the management team found the space to connect change targets to daily priorities (Binns et al. 2014).

Ann-Maree Morrison's practitioner reflections further illustrate the benefits of making time for strategic reflection in a disciplined way. Ann-Maree makes time to read widely about technology in order to identify and absorb relevant insights, staying aware of trends so that she can respond in a selective and measured way. She also invests time in mentoring others as a way of building the strategic capabilities in her organization. And on a monthly schedule, her reviewing and revaluation of business metrics through tried and tested strategy analysis methods provides a reflective structure in her business leadership role.

Provoke thought

Posing questions to ourselves or others can direct reflection towards aspects of organizational life where learning or improvement is required (Felin and Zenger 2018). As we define the scope of activities and consider possible options for action based on evaluation activities, challenging questions can help increase the potential for strategy to deliver valuable gains to the organization.

Lindh and Thorgren (2016) suggest that simple reflective questions such as 'What did we do?', 'How did we do it?', 'What would we do differently?', 'What does this experience mean?', and 'How can we explain it?', can usefully direct learning activities. A common organizational activity that poses these sorts of questions is a 'project wash-up' or after-action review (AAR) (Darling and Parry 2001). An AAR is a collective reflection-on-action activity that occurs at the end of an initiative. Project stakeholders gather to discuss the implementation of the initiative, reflecting on (a) what went well and should be reinforced in future work, (b) what didn't work well and needs to be improved, and (c) what was missing and needs to be added in future. The aim of an AAR is to learn and drive enhanced performance of future strategic initiative working (Gino and Staats 2015).

Lindh and Thorgren (2016) also propose that by pushing ourselves to ask critical or creative questions—What impact might we have on the broader communities in which we are entangled? What are the effects of differences generated by our practice? How do strategy practices appear to be changing? What is differing from what we expected to happen?—the value of reflection can be enhanced. Reflective questions that examine how we are entangled in a context—how we maintain relationships, co-produce outcomes, and interact with others—can stimulate deep learning about our own practice as well as our situation and context (Keevers and Treleaven 2011).

As has been suggested throughout this book, strategy from a process–practice perspective is enhanced by incorporating a wide range of stakeholder perspectives into activities. So too with reflection—taking into account external perspectives and data can help with the reflective process (Gino and Staats 2015). By listening or observing carefully how others describe a phenomenon which you think you know a lot about, or are ready to act upon, it is possible to find new perspectives for framing the problem or exploring possible actions.

Reflective dialogue and conversations can bring to the surface honest and well-rounded insights that fuel reflection, revealing the 'challenging material shoved into boxes mentally labelled *do not open*' (Bolton and Delderfield 2018:3). By engaging in dialogue with other stakeholders you can build valuable insights into your practice and be stimulated to reflect. Individual and collective reflective activity can be usefully provoked by engaging with '(1) the plurality of values and interests, and the multiplicity of situations; (2) the inclusion and active involvement of stakeholders in the process of learning; and (3) dialogue as a vehicle for discussing what it is right to do in a given situation' (Abma 2003:222).

Use a reflective method/technique

The use of methods can create fertile conditions to spur reflection. Gray (2007:500–2) notes a range of tools that can be deployed to aid reflection-on-action in any situation:

- **Storytelling**—individually or collectively preparing a narrative about an event or aspect of organizational life. The act of preparing the 'story' in a way that is coherent necessitates us attempting to make sense of something that has occurred, bringing forth experiential learning (Baker et al. 2005). Storytelling workshops can enable learning from others about how they approach a common topic of interest (Abma 2003). The more time and effort dedicated to retelling organizational narratives that connect past, present, and future, the more likely that creative reflective learning will be uncovered by a team (Kaplan and Orlikowski 2014).
- **Reflective conversations**—working with a trusted facilitator or coach, discuss an event, activity, behaviour (etc.) about which we would like to learn. An external facilitator can push us to be honest with ourselves and go beyond the superficial in our reflection and learning (Gino and Staats 2015). Through deep questioning, we can have our assumptions and understanding challenged towards finding new insights of practical relevance (Garvin et al. 2008).
- **Reflective dialogue**—with colleagues, perhaps at a function or in a project team or interest group, debating a shared issue. If this can be achieved in a respectful but honest manner (such as by following the formalisms of a strategy analysis method), productive collective learning might be generated from the diversity of perspectives shared. Reflective dialogue can build a trusting community over time, providing continuing support for those leading in an organization (Boyatzis et al. 2002).
- **Reflective writing**—noting insights, feelings, and events as they occur in a written format such as a log book, personal journal, or learning diary. Over time, a stimulus for and aid to reflection is collated (Bolton and Delderfield 2018). Audio or video diaries also offer a mechanism for the creation of powerful reflective records by individuals or groups (Zundel et al. 2018). Writing might be backward looking, recording events, or forward looking, envisioning possible futures (Boyatzis et al. 2002).
- **Cognitive maps**—for individuals, cognitive maps are a useful way to explore how we see cause and effect in the world—capturing our thinking in a visible format that invites critical reflection.

Beyond these techniques, any of the strategic analysis methods in this book have the potential to foster reflection. The crucial question we encouraged in the method sections of Chapters 5 and 6 was 'What are the implications?' of the data added to frameworks. This is intended to provide focused attention for conversations arising from the strategy tool, and to guide learning towards practical outcomes. Further, as described in Chapter 15, if a strategy activity is designed to actively involve stakeholders in an inclusive way, the potential for valuable learning from rich reflective dialogue is enhanced.

An applied method of reflection

Table 16.2 shows a reflective feedback tool that was used to prepare for group reflective dialogue for one of our previous corporate employers. Known as the FFP—**Feelings, Facts, Proposals**—framework, this tool challenges an individual to first free-write their feelings about a particular event or situation. This should be a personal account of their thoughts, emotions, and feelings. Once that is completed, the second column challenges the individual to seek out alternative perspectives and data to establish what might be the 'facts' of the situation. With this additional information, the participant is invited to reflect on what productive actions might be taken to learn and change behaviour. This is a method for reflecting-on-action that can incorporate a combination of reflective tools (e.g. reflective conversations, critical incident analysis, reflective journal).

TABLE 16.2 **Illustration of the Feelings, Facts, Proposals framework**

	Feelings	Facts	Proposals
Description of activity	Freeform writing of what the individual thinks and feels about an event or moment in organizational life	A summary of alternative perspectives and data available about the event or moment in organizational life	A set of suggestions to resolve any immediate difficulties and also to learn/find better ways of working in future
Purpose of activity	To bring to the surface as complete a sense of perspective from the participant as can be articulated	To seek alternative views and further information that can be compared, compiled, and used to evaluate the author's feelings, thinking about the event or moment in a focused and deep way	To provide an actionable conclusion to the reflective process that focuses on what the individual can influence and to seek to positively impact future practice potential
Example content	'I felt my views weren't listened to in production meeting A ... I was offering an opinion with the best of intentions, and from technical expertise that could have prevented issue X arising, but colleague CW did his usual and steamrollered the meeting' 'In my view, issue X was totally preventable ... I feel angry and disrespected by the behaviour of CW, and frustrated that I now have to fix an even bigger issue, etc.'	'CW is under a huge amount of time pressure' 'Colleagues DE, GH, and ST were present at the meeting and didn't notice me trying to speak up' 'Issue X didn't end up disrupting production outputs as we had planned maintenance scheduled for the time issue X happened' 'Colleagues DE, GH, and ST are all keen to work with me in resolving the current challenge'	'Schedule a meeting with CW to arrange quality time for a productive conversation about the technical aspects of issue X' 'Convene a short-term working group with DE, GH, and ST to resolve the impact of issue X' 'Discuss how to raise points well/be effective in communicating with meetings with personal mentor'

16

PRACTITIONER PERSPECTIVE: SANDY WILSON

Sandy Wilson is an independent strategy consultant, educator, and executive coach. Previously Sandy was head of Group Sales and Operations for Enterprise Holdings, and director of Executive Education at the University of Strathclyde. He works with organizational leaders to support their reflective learning, and with organizations across a wide range of sectors in the design and activation of strategy, including supporting small and medium-sized enterprises on behalf of a regional development agency.

Sandy shares his views about learning and reflection for individual development, and as an integral component of strategy process and practice.

What is strategy?

Strategy is about identifying a system of initiatives, objectives, and challenges that you want to focus on and establishing how you are going to address that system through action. In practice, strategy is a dynamic concept that is always shifting, although the common way in which it is described is as a periodic activity. Through strategy we plan actions and initiatives, but they are rarely if ever realized in the way that they are envisaged in the planning stage ... they tend to be refined and revised multiple times on the way to conclusion. From my work with organizations, I find strategy to be a far more soluble concept than it is often presented in theory.

Strategic success more often arises from regular incremental extension of quite a simple core idea leading to a robust well-tuned organization. Full-scale transformation can happen but requires very high levels of managerial and leadership capabilities—more often, strategic action as thoughtful continual stewardship of the organization is successful. Through many integrated smaller-scale initiatives, you retain flexibility whilst building capability, and create the potential to engage those within and outwith your organization in a significant way.

Supporting strategy work

In relation to strategy, I facilitate—help a group to have a better conversation than they could achieve themselves—and coach—help individuals to understand their situation differently and find new ways of thinking and acting to overcome the challenges they are facing.

In supporting individuals or groups, there are lots of lenses—RBV, MBV, culture, business performance, customer focus, etc.—through which you can stimulate strategic thinking. Over time, I have developed a pragmatic sense of what lenses are going to be helpful in any given context based on the personalities and cultural norms of the senior team. Those I work with seem to value my practical experience blended with knowledge of strategy theory. A lot of executives don't know many strategy frameworks—they sense value in the theory, but as they lack the time to explore it in depth themselves they want to import it through an external source.

Learning

I think that there is often an untapped potential to learn from diverse data sources—customer feedback, operational performance, market trends, etc.—to drive investment in new capabilities that have long-term strategic benefit. Instead there is a real tendency—often because of time constraints—not to seek to validate or challenge the veracity of our decisions. A commitment to learning can help build our potential for effective informed strategic decision-making. Further, learning things you don't know about yourself, either through reflective insight or external feedback, can aid effectiveness of development as a strategy practitioner.

Reflection

As a coach, I have conversations with executives that help them understand more deeply how and why they do what they do. This can be a challenging conversation—whilst you are unequivocally on the side of the person you are working with, and they can trust you, you are unlikely to be adding value if you are constantly agreeing with them. New strategic insights arise when deep-rooted beliefs are challenged, often from an external perspective.

Focused action, driven by performance measures and KPIs, can often lead to the attainment of results at the expense of other possible outcomes. Through reflection, we can do our best to be conscious of the implications and compromises implied in our choices. Equally, if you aren't reflecting, you might not be aware of the alternatives and downsides to your decisions.

A useful way in which to make a positive reflective challenge in strategy work is when discussing options, asking participants 'If that is an option, what is another way to achieve the same (or a better) outcome ... in my experience we tend to stop thinking through options as soon as we believe we have identified one that works'. Often, a few days after you have had a reflective conversation with someone, the next time you meet they thank you for the provocation—'You helped me open up my ideas—I was thinking that that option was the only way to do that, and I had no real reason for thinking that'.

Value of learning and reflection

I don't have any trouble getting people to agree that they are living in an uncertain turbulent world, or that the pace of change is increasing. But the number of strategists that haven't yet made the connection between that shifting context and the need to enhance their ability to learn is surprising. If we want to thrive in a turbulent world, why would we not be giving priority to learning to learn and reflect? For some, there are emotional obstacles to wanting to look in the mirror. However, it is not difficult to grasp that reflecting on our shortcomings is the first step in a long journey to doing something about them. And if we can make that first move, the benefits of even small steps can be pretty significant. In a leadership role, a huge amount of what will drive your success is how you create the environment for others to thrive. If you aren't aware of the effect that how you operate has on other people, it's a real limiter on your prospects of being successful.

Working with executive teams, I notice that the activities that support reflection are normally constricted. It is normal for senior leaders in organizations to be under significant time pressure from multiple competing demands. Also, it is normal for senior leaders to be action-oriented and often interventionist with their teams. In that situation, reflection can feel like 'not doing something', creating a reflection-hostile context. Further, it is common for leaders to not really have a sense of how to go about reflecting, and there can be limited understanding of the returns on reflection. However, if you can get beyond that, there is huge opportunity for individuals to grow by looking at decisions and actions they have taken, how it could have played out differently, and how their approach affected other people.

CHAPTER SUMMARY

In this chapter we addressed the following learning outcomes.

- **Appraise the value of different models of learning in explaining how strategy happens in practice**

  It was suggested that strategic learning—learning that informs the selection of initiatives and goals that might sustain the organization in the long term—aids explanation and understanding of how strategy happens in practice and can improve future effectiveness. Several strategic learning theories were reviewed—the experiential learning cycle, double-loop learning, and situated learning theory. These models were all shown to helpfully shine a spotlight on aspects of how strategic learning can occur, providing a framework with which to evaluate the extent to which learning occurs, or might occur, in an organization. By combining theories of strategic learning, we can cast light on how strategy-in-practice evolves over time.

- **Explain how reflection is a crucial mechanism of experiential learning which contributes to evolving strategic thought and activity**

  Reflection is a vital learning mechanism which allows us to extract new insights by directing focused attention to aspects of our experiences. It is also a common theme in

16

the strategic learning theories reviewed in this chapter. Critical reflection is a related activity in which we consider the impact of the social and political context on a matter. Critical self-reflection, or reflexivity, is when the focus of our critical reflection is our own values and way of being. By enabling us to learn from experience, reflection creates the possibility of improving our capacity for effective strategy practice, comprehension and anticipation of the flow of organizational activities, and the ability to steer strategy activities on an ongoing basis. It was recognized that both reflection-on-action—after the event reflective activities—and reflection-in-action—thinking on your feet, drawing on all available learning—help to explain how the process–practice framework of strategy operates.

- **Critically evaluate your own views of the role of learning and reflection in strategy**
  Reflective capacity and an ability to learn about strategy can be fostered through practice, drawing on external perspectives as stimulus to reviewing our own thoughts, beliefs, assumptions, and values. In this chapter, we presented a range of practitioner perspectives reflecting on their strategy practice. By interrogating those views and using them to make sense of our own preferences and intuitions, new insights can be generated. Methods and advice that can enable (critical) reflection—as an individual or as part of a collective—were also highlighted for future reference.

END OF CHAPTER QUESTIONS

Recall questions

1. Define what is meant by strategic learning and draw on learning theories to explain how strategic learning might occur.
2. Define the similarities and differences between reflection, critical reflection, and critical self-reflection.
3. Explain the value of reflection to strategy practitioners. With reference to reflection-on-action and reflection-in-action, discuss how reflection might aid the strategist (a) at different stages of their career and (b) at different points during strategy activity.
4. Discuss the barriers and enablers to a 'reflective culture', and how strategic leaders in an organization play a role in fostering a collective capacity for reflection.

Application question

A) Think about a concept of strategy (e.g. competitive advantage) that you have learned about recently. Using a method that suits you, reflect on the difference between your understanding of that concept before and after the learning event. Comment on how this learning occurred, and what you feel are the remaining gaps in your understanding of the concept. How will your new understanding of the concept influence future practice? How do you plan to further develop your knowledge of the concept?

ONLINE RESOURCES

www.oup.com/he/mackay1e

FURTHER READING

The Fifth Discipline: The Art and Practice of the Learning Organization, by Peter Senge

Senge, P. (2006). *The Fifth Discipline: The Art and Practice of the Learning Organization*. London: Random House Business Books.

This is a seminal text about the strategic value of learning, learning systems and processes, and how learning might occur in an organization. Following the work of Deming, Senge highlights 'systems thinking' as the eponymous fifth discipline that enables four other disciplines—personal mastery, mental models, shared vision, and team dialogue—to create a 'learning organization'. In a learning organization the configuration of people, processes, and systems focuses on enabling the learning process, which in turn drives continual improvement in strategic performance.

Reflective Practice: Writing and Professional Development, by Gillie Bolton and Russell Delderfield

Bolton, G. and Delderfield, R. (2018). *Reflective Practice: Writing and Professional Development* (5th edn). London: Sage.

This is the fifth edition of a practical guide to the application of a range of reflective methods. The authors focus on ways in which writing might enable enhanced personal performance through reflective learning. Further, the value of reflection to individuals and organizations is addressed in a comprehensive way. It is useful for students who wish to experiment with building their own personal reflective capacity.

The Reflective Practitioner: How Professionals Think In Action, by Donald Schön

Schön, D.A. (2016). *The Reflective Practitioner: How Professionals Think In Action* (paperback edn). Abingdon: Routledge.

This latest edition of a core text on reflective practice will provide students with further detailed insights into 'reflection-on-action' and 'reflection-in-action'. Schön also provides food for thought about how we are embedded in the 'swamp' of everyday life, and how reflection-on-action and reflection-in-action can help us cope in different settings.

REFERENCES

Abma, T.A. (2003). Learning by telling. *Management Learning*, **34**(2), 221–40.

Ambrosini, V. and Bowman C. (2005). Reducing causal ambiguity to facilitate strategic learning. *Management Learning*, **36**(4), 493–512.

Argyris, C. (1976). Single-loop and double-loop models in research on decision making. *Administrative Science Quarterly*, **21**(3), 363–75.

Argyris, C. and Schön, D. (1974). *Theory in Practice: Increasing Professional Effectiveness*. San Francisco, CA: Jossey Bass.

Baker, A.C., Jensen, P.J., and Kolb, D.A. (2005). Conversation as experiential learning. *Management Learning*, **36**(4), 411–27.

Binns, A., Harreld, J.B., O'Reilly, C.A., and Tushman, M.L. (2014). The art of strategic renewal. *MIT Sloan Management Review*, **55**(2), 21–3.

Bolton, G. and Delderfield, R. (2018). *Reflective Practice: Writing and Professional Development* (5th edn). London: Sage.

Bouquet, C., Barsoux, J.-L., and Wade, M. (2018). Bring your breakthrough ideas to life. *Harvard Business Review*, **96**(6), 102–13.

Boyatzis, R., McKee, A., and Goleman, D. (2002). Reawakening your passion for work. *Harvard Business Review*, **80**(4), 86–94.

Brown, J.S., Collins, A., and Duguid, S. (1989). Situated cognition and the culture of learning. *Educational Researcher*, **18**(1), 32–42.

Clancey, W.J. (1997). *Situated Cognition: On Human Knowledge and Computer Representations*. Cambridge: Cambridge University Press.

Coffield, F., Moseley, D., Hall, E., and Ecclestone, K. (2004). *Learning Styles and Pedagogy in Post-16 Learning: A Systematic and Critical Review*. London: LSR.

Cross, R.O.B., Taylor, S., and Zehner, D.E.B. (2018). Collaboration without burnout. *Harvard Business Review*, **96**(4), 134–7.

Darling, M.J. and Parry, C.S. (2001). After-action reviews: linking reflection and planning in a learning practice. *Reflections*, **3**(2), 64–72.

Felin, T. and Zenger, T. (2018). What sets breakthrough strategies apart. *MIT Sloan Management* Review, **59**(2), 86–8.

Garvin, D.A., Edmondson, A., and Gino, F. (2008). Is yours a learning organization*? Harvard Business Review*, **86**(3), 109–16.

Gilmore, S. and Anderson, V. (2012). Anxiety and experience-based learning in a professional standards context. *Management Learning*, **43**(1), 75–95.

Gino, F. and Staats, B. (2015). Why organizations don't learn. *Harvard Business Review*, **93**(11), 110–18.

Gosling, J. and Mintzberg, H. (2004). The education of practicing managers. *MIT Sloan Management Review*, **45**(4), 19–22.

Gray, D.E. (2007). Facilitating management learning developing critical reflection through reflective tools. *Management Learning*, **38**(5), 495–517.

Greeno, J.G. (1989). A perspective on thinking. *American Psychologist* **44**, 134–41.

Greeno, J.G. (1994). Gibson's affordances. *Psychological Review*, **101**(2), 336–42.

Healey, M.P. and Hodgkinson, G.P. (2017). Making strategy hot. *California Management Review*, **59**(3), 109–34.

Hotho, J.J., Saka-Helmhout, A., and Becker-Ritterspach, F. (2014). Bringing context and structure back into situated learning. *Management Learning*, **45**(1), 57–80.

Jarzabkowski, P. and Kaplan, S. (2015). Strategy tools-in-use: a framework for understanding 'technologies of rationality' in practice. *Strategic Management Journal*, **36**(4), 537–58.

Jordan, S. (2010). Learning to be surprised: how to foster reflective practice in a high-reliability context. *Management Learning*, **41**(4), 391–413.

Jordan, S., Messner, M., and Becker, A. (2009). Reflection and mindfulness in organizations: rationales and possibilities for integration. *Management Learning*, **40**(4), 465–73.

Kahn, W (1990). Psychological conditions of personal engagement and disengagement at work. *Academy of Management Journal*, **33**(4), 692–724.

Kaplan, S. and Orlikowski, W. (2014). Beyond forecasting: creating new strategic narratives. *MIT Sloan Management Review*, **56**(1), 23–8.

Keevers, L. and Treleaven, L. (2011). Organizing practices of reflection: a practice-based study. *Management Learning*, **42**(5), 505–20.

Klein, G. (2004). *The Power of Intuition*. London: Crown Business.

Kolb, A. and Kolb, D.A. (1999). *Bibliography of Research on ELT and the Learning Style Inventory*. Cleveland, OH: Department of Organisational Behaviour, Weatherhead of School of Management, Case Western Reserve University.

Kolb, A.Y. and Kolb, D.A. (2005). Learning styles and learning spaces: enhancing experiential learning in higher education. *Academy of Management Learning and Education*, **4**(2), 193–212.

Kolb, A.Y. and Kolb, D.A. (2008). Experiential learning theory: a dynamic holistic approach to management learning, education and development. In: Armstrong, S.J. and Fukami, C. (eds), *Handbook of Management Learning, Education and Development*, London: Sage.

Kolb, D.A. (1984). *Experiential Learning: Experience as the Source of Learning and Development*. Englewood Cliffs, NJ: Prentice Hall.

Kolb, D.A., Boyatzis, R.E., and Mainemelis, C. (2001). Experiential learning theory: previous research and new directions. In: Sternberg, R.J. and Zhang, L.F. (eds), *Perspectives on Cognitive Learning and Thinking Styles*, pp. 227–48. Mahwah, NJ: Lawrence Erlbaum.

Lai, L. (2017). Being a strategic leader is about asking the right questions. *Harvard Business Review Digital Articles*, 2–4.

Lave, J. and Wenger, E. (1991). *Situated Learning: Legitimate Peripheral Participation*. Cambridge: Cambridge University Press.

Lindh, I. and Thorgren, T. (2016). Critical event recognition: an extended view of reflective learning. *Management Learning*, **47**, 525–42.

Mackay, D. and Burt, G. (2015). Strategic learning, foresight and hyperopia. *Management Learning*, **46**(5), 546–64.

Markides, C.C. (2000). *All the Right Moves: A Guide to Crafting Breakthrough Strategy*. Boston, MA: Harvard Business School Press.

Marshak, R.J. (2019). Dialogic meaning-making in action. *OD Practitioner*, **51**(2), 26–31.

Marsick, V. and O'Neil, J. (1999). The many faces of action learning. *Management Learning*, **30**(2), 159–76.

Ohmae, K. (1982). *The Mind Of The Strategist: The Art of Japanese Business*. New York: McGraw Hill Professional.

Oxford Living Dictionary (2019). Definition of learning. https://en.oxforddictionaries.com/definition/learning (accessed 28 May 2019).

Porter, J. (2017). Why you should make time for self-reflection (even if you hate doing it). *Harvard Business Review Digital Articles*, 2–4.

Raelin, J.A. (2002). 'I don't have time to think!' versus the art of reflective practice. *Reflections*, **4**(1), 66–75.

Renshaw, J. (2017). Learning design for impact. *Training & Development*, **44**(5), 18–19.

Schön, D.A. (2016). *The Reflective Practitioner: How Professionals Think In Action* (paperback edn). Abingdon: Routledge.

Senge, P. (1990). *The Fifth Discipline: The Art and Practice of the Learning Organization*, New York: Doubleday.

Smith, M.K. (2001). David A. Kolb on experiential learning. *The Encyclopaedia of Informal Education*. www.infed.org/biblio/b-explrn.htm (accessed 20 December 2019).

Thomas, J.B., Sussman, S.W., and Henderson, J.C. (2001). Understanding 'strategic learning': linking organizational learning, knowledge management, and sensemaking. *Organization Science*, **12**(3), 331–45.

Tomkins, L. and Ulus, E. (2016). 'Oh, was that "experiential learning"?!' Spaces, synergies, and surprises with Kolb's learning cycle. *Management Learning*, **47**(2), 158–78.

Vona, M.K., Woolf, M., and Sugrue, B. (2019). Learning's value in the era of disruption. *Training*, **56**(2), 94–7.

Wharton, S. (2017). Reflection in university and the employability agenda: a discourse analysis case study. *Reflective Practice*, **18**(4), 567–79.

Zhu, Y. and Bargiela-Chiappini, F. (2013). Balancing emic and etic: situated learning and ethnography of communication in cross-cultural management education. *Academy of Management Learning and Education*, **12**(3), 380–95.

Zundel, M. (2013). Walking to learn: rethinking reflection for management learning. *Management Learning*, **44**(2), 109–26.

Zundel, M., MacIntosh, R., and Mackay, D. (2018). The utility of video diaries for organizational research. *Organizational Research Methods*, **21**(2), 386–411.

GLOSSARY

Acceptability Test of a proposed strategy which addresses how stakeholders might feel about the expected outcomes of the strategy

Acquisition A transaction when one company purchases most or all of another company's shares to gain control of that company

Activity That which is actually done by practitioners, individually or collectively

Activity outcomes The consequences of individual or organizational activities

Activity system The ongoing system of resource stocks and flows through which the organizational resource base changes shape as activity outcomes are realized through the deployment of capabilities grounded in existing resources

Adhocracy A form of organization that is flexible, informal, and adaptable, lacking a formal structure and operating in a manner that contrasts with a traditional bureaucracy

Advantage This test of a proposed strategy is about competitive advantage, or whether the organization can capture enough of the value it creates

Affective conflict Concerns interpersonal relationships or incompatible personalities; arises from emotions and frustration in conflict situations that may have a detrimental impact on group decision-making and the acceptability of the group decision outcome

Affordances All the possible ways in which a user might use a tool or object in everyday strategy activity

Agency The ability of humans to be creative and exhibit independently minded choices

Agility Being able to organize and respond to situations quickly and nimbly

Analytical methods Procedures which, focusing on a limited aspect of the organization's situation, provide a framework for organizing external data and/or capturing participant views and uncovering deeper understanding of trends and implications through structured conversations

Ansoff matrix (Ansoff growth vectors) A strategy tool that can help managers devise strategies for future growth

Architectural innovation Innovation involving the reconfiguration of an established system to link together existing components in a new way

Artefact An object, such as a piece of media, drawing, or other physical construct, made by human activity; in the case of strategy, an object arising from strategic activities (e.g. a causal map can be considered an artefact built by a decision-making group)

Attentional design Using tools and procedures to deliberately channel the attention of decision makers to consider a broad and representative set of information in order that they can better understand the context in which they are operating

Attentional structures Communication channels, knowledge flows, organizational procedures, and opportunities for interaction with others that influence how information reaches the attention of decision-makers

Attention-based view A set of concepts and theoretical contributions that help explain how organizations behave, adapt to changing environments, develop capabilities, and strategize according to how the attention of decision-makers is informed and directed

Balanced Scorecard A strategic performance management model used to help managers translate an organization's mission and vision into operational plans and actions

Benefit Corporation (B-Corp) A type of for-profit corporate entity which includes in its constitution positive impacts on society, workers, the community, and the environment as legally defined goals alongside profit aims

Beyond compliance An emerging managerial perspective in which the full environmental and social costs of operating are considered alongside creating shared value during the development of sustainable organizational strategy

Big data The vast information flows available to organizations from multiple sources on a daily basis

Biodiversity The variety and variation in the species of life on the planet

Blue ocean strategy An approach to innovation strategy that searches for uncontested market space; it guides exploration of cost reduction and differentiation options, and identification of new value propositions that render the competition irrelevant

Born global A term used to describe companies that from very early on pursue a vision of becoming global and globalize rapidly without any preceding gradual internationalization of activities; born global companies are usually small technology-oriented companies that operate in international markets from the earliest days of their founding

Born sustainable A term used to describe organizations which, from their inception, operate on the basis of principles of sustainability in everything they do

Bounded rationality An idea that when individuals make decisions, their rationality is limited by the availability of information, their capability to understand the decision problem, the cognitive limitations of their minds, and the time available for decision-making

Budgeting Development of a plan for deploying financial resources

Bundles (of resources) A term used to describe the use of resources in combination during organizational activities

Business analytics Processes that convert big data into meaningful information which can inform strategic and operational decision-making

Business ecosystem A complex network of relationships, interactions, and influences within which a business is embedded and in which the prosperity of the ecosystem affects the prosperity of the business

Business model The overarching logic and rationale of how an organization creates, delivers, and captures value in a competitive environment

Business model canvas A method to systematically map the components of a current business model in order to identify ways in which it might be changed

Business performance The financial and non-financial results achieved by an organization against a set of standards or expectations within a given time frame

Business strategy Answering the question 'How to meet customer needs?', this strategy addresses how to gain an advantage over competitors in selected geographies and sectors

Buyer power The bargaining power that the entity purchasing a good or service has over the supplier

CAGE Distance framework An analytical framework that identifies Cultural, Administrative, Geographic, and Economic differences or distances between countries which companies should address when developing international strategies

Capabilities What an individual or organization is able to do to a threshold level of performance, based on the potential inherent in accumulated resources

Capabilities audit A method for identifying the capabilities currently being used by the organization to undertake activities and deliver outcomes

Causal ambiguity Where the causes of a phenomenon are unknown or unknowable; for example, the relationship between the firm's resources and capabilities and competitive advantage may be causally ambiguous, which makes the management of resources difficult

Causal map Provides a visual explanation of why an incident occurred or what the consequences of a decision would be; it contains a visualization of individual cause-and-effect relationships to reveal the system of causes within a given issue or decision problem (sometimes referred to as a concept or cognitive map)

Chaebol A large industrial conglomerate in South Korea that is run and controlled by an owner or family

Change management A collective term for all management approaches to prepare, support, and help individuals, teams, and organizations in effecting organizational change through deliberate planned efforts

Circular economy An alternative to a traditional linear economy (make, use, dispose) in which resources are kept in use for as long as possible, extracting the maximum value from them whilst they are in use, and then recovering and regenerating products and materials at the end of their service life

Climate The patterns in weather conditions in any given area

Climate change A shift in weather conditions in an area over time, often with consequences for natural environmental conditions

Cognitive bias A systematic pattern of deviation from the norm or rationality in judgement; inferences about other people, situations, or problems may be made in an illogical fashion. Individuals create their own mental map of 'subjective social reality' based on their perception of the situation

Cognitive conflict Arises when a group focuses on a task or a problem and debate to come to a solution. Group members might argue and exchange views vigorously, yet there is two-way communication and an openness to hearing each other. The goal is to find the best possible solution rather than to win the argument. Alternative solutions to the problem are seen as valuable rather than threatening (see definition of affective conflict)

Cognitive strategy A plan to capitalize on or mitigate the possibilities of cognitive technologies

Cognitive technologies Artificial intelligence and technological processes by which machines learn to embody the skills, knowledge, and capabilities that are performed in a cognate way by humans

Collaboration The act of cooperating with one or more other parties in order to achieve a shared outcome

Collaborative community An increasingly popular organizational form in which participants collaboratively solve problems and integrate their contributions (e.g. Wikipedia)

Communication practices Approaches to giving or receiving information within an organization

Competence Individual or collective potential to take action to a superior level of performance

Competitive advantage The capacity of an individual, organization, or nation to outperform competitors in attaining some outcome of interest (often financial performance)

Competitive strategy Describes how a company seeks to compete; sometimes known as 'domain navigation' (compare with corporate strategy, which focuses on where to compete)

Competitor profiling A method that guides evaluation of how competitors operate, and how they might act/react to future strategic initiatives by your own organization

Complementarity When two separate resources, products, or services enhance the qualities and usefulness of each other when present together (e.g. the gaming and console markets are complementarities)

Complex structure In contrast with a simple structure, the term complex structure refers to a set of more complex organizational forms such as multidivisional, holding, matrix, network, and transnational structures

Configuration The way in which an organization arranges its activities to create a particular organizational structure; configurations are the result of grouping the key elements of a structure and combining them in a particular manner

Connected strategy A plan to deal with the new normal of customer expectations for continuous connectivity to service providers

Consensus decision-making A group decision-making process in which group members develop, and agree to support, a decision in the best interest of the whole group or organization. Consensus decision can be defined as an acceptable and satisfactory solution to a problem that is acceptable to all group members, even if is not the favourite solution of each individual decision-making group member

Consistency This test of a proposed strategy points out that the strategy must not present goals and policies that lack consistency

Consonance This test of a proposed strategy is focused on the creation of social value

Consortium An association of two or more organizations, created with the objective of participating in a common activity or pooling their resources for achieving a common goal (often a large and complex project) for a fixed short term

Consultancy Provision of expert advice on a given topic, typically on a commercial basis as an external party to an organization

Consumer activism A process by which activists seek to influence the way in which goods or services are produced or delivered, by spending of money on goods, services, or organizations that align with the purchaser's values

Context The circumstances which form the setting for strategy activity to occur

Contextual ambidexterity When individuals are able to make choices between either exploitation-oriented or exploration-oriented activities in their work. To enable this, it is necessary for the organization to be more flexible, permitting employees to use their own judgement in pursuing both exploratory and exploitative activities

Contingency theory This theory suggests that there is no single 'best way' to run an organization or make decisions; the 'best' course of action is contingent, or depends, on the internal and external situation

Control system A system that manages or directs the behaviour of other parties; it aims to ensure that individuals, locations, and activities are governed by strategic decisions, and are accountable for their performance

Cooperative strategies Strategies where two or more organizations choose to work together, for example in a strategic allance or joint venture, while remaining separate entities (i.e. not engaging in mergers, acquisitions, or other strategies that create a single entity)

Core competences Competences that recur throughout an organization, underpinning value creation and strategy across all aspects of operations

Core dynamic capabilities Capabilities to create, extend, or modify the resource base which are continually engaged in an organization

Core rigidities Resources which were once valuable, and are still considered so in strategy work, but in actuality are a hindrance to organizational performance

Corporate parent/parenting Corporate parenting looks at the relationship between 'head office' (i.e. the corporate parent) and the strategic business units that report to head office; it explores how the head office can add value to the individual business units

Corporate relatedness Considers the potential offered by a strategy of diversification to combine capabilities and pursue asset creation or improvement across two or more organizations

Corporate social responsibility (CSR) A management philosophy in which an organization's obligations to society at large are prioritized over other business objectives to varying degrees

Corporate strategy Sets out where a company seeks to compete; sometimes known as 'domain selection' (compare with competitive strategy, which focuses on how to compete and operate)

Costs An outlay or deployment of resources (often financial) towards some specific end or activity

Creating shared value (CSV) A management philosophy focused on growing the total value created for an organization and its stakeholders, and splitting the benefits fairly

Creative destruction A process of industrial mutation which incessantly revolutionizes the economic structure from within—incessantly destroying the old one, and incessantly creating a new one

Creativity Original thinking and inventiveness that generates new ideas

Crisis management A process by which an organization deals with a major event that threatens to harm the organization, its stakeholders, or the general public—often considered to be one of the most important processes in public relations

Critical reflection In-depth focused attention given to questions of how political and social context shape values, assumptions, judgements, and beliefs

Cultural web An analytical framework to identify the components of an organization's culture. Cultural web is a power tool in change management (see definition of change management)

Culture The habitual and patterned ways in which activity is done in a social setting, such as how work is carried out in an organization

Cyber-security The preservation of the security of digital systems in the face of cyber-crime

Data Discrete pieces of knowledge/things that are known

Data hubris The often implicit assumption that big data is a substitute for, rather than a supplement to, traditional data collection and analysis

Data lake An agile scalable data infrastructure and architecture which can hold a secure and reliable single source of truth whilst hosting as many versions of the truth as are required to meet the value-creating needs of the organization

Data science The application of experimental methods and computational systems to generate new insights and business analytics from big datasets

Dynamic capability analysis A method for figuring out how new resource configurations might be created to develop a capability profile that is fit for the future

Dynamic capability view (DCV) A set of concepts and theoretical contributions that helps explain how organizations can purposefully create, extend or modify their resource base over time; an extension of the resource based view

Dynamic control systems Robert Simons argues that, for a control system to be effective in a fast-changing context, it must be dynamic, i.e. it must promote the strategic flexibility and innovative capabilities that the organization needs to adapt to change in a controlled manner

Eco-innovation All forms of innovation that create business opportunities and benefits to the environment by preventing or reducing their impact, or by optimizing the use of resources

Economic value The financial measure of the benefit of a good, service, or course of action to interested parties

Economic value added (EVA) A measure of a company's economic profit, which is the profit earned by the company minus the cost of financing the company's capital; EVA = net operating profit after tax – (invested capital × weighted average cost of capital) is used to calculate true shareholder value. Unlike accounting net income, EVA is used to measure the amount of a company's returns in excess of its cost of capital

Economies of scale The cost advantages that an organization can achieve when it increases the scale of its operations. Economies of scale occur when the cost per unit of output decreases as output increases

Economies of scope The cost benefits resulting from using the same resource across a range of outputs

Ecosystem A complex network of relationships, interactions, and influences in which an individual or organization is embedded

Ecosystems View A theoretical perspective that considers organizations as embedded in a complex network of relationships, the prosperity of which directly affects the prosperity of the organization

Efficacy A gauge of effectiveness—the extent to which an activity (one off, or continuing) achieves desired outcomes

Efficiency The extent to which organizational activity can achieve target outcomes with minimal use of resources; often described as a rate measured by 'output divided by input'

Embedded approach An approach to strategic thinking in which the organization's strategic options are influenced by, but also have the potential to influence, the environment in which the organization is embedded

Emergence The process of activities, events, or outcomes happening in a non-planned way, arising through the natural course of events

Emotional commitment A willingness to advocate on behalf of ideas or decision outcomes based on positive feelings of ownership to the ideas

Engagement Involvement as an active participant in a process, with a stake and interest in process outcomes

Entrepreneurial Showing initiative, a sense of opportunity, and a capacity to access and organise resources in order to exploit situations profitably

Episode A period of time, with a defined start and end-point, within which a set of activities involving practitioners, practices, context, and outcomes can be examined

Espoused theories The narratives we use to justify the logic behind our behaviours and decisions

Experiential learning cycle A model of learning that highlights how concrete experience can be transformed into learning, which in turn can drive experimental action and new experiences

External context All aspects of an organization's situation which exist beyond the boundaries of its direct control

Facilitation Creation of conditions in which activities, interactions, decisions, or a flow of events can occur in an effective and/or efficient manner

Feasibility This test of a proposed strategy considers how well the strategy will work in practice, and how difficult it might be to achieve

Feelings, Facts, Proposals (FFP) A reflective writing tool from practice that is intended to guide an individual to collect their thoughts and feelings on a matter, seek external perspectives and data on the same matter, and uncover new insights to guide future actions

Financial control systems Financial control systems are based on hard data ('numbers') as key metrics used to define budgetary activities and financial targets, and support financial planning and budgetary review to control organizational performance

Financial strategy Includes the organization's approach to both raising the funds it needs and managing the employment of those funds within the organization

Fintech Digital financial technologies that deliver operational improvements, innovation, and new sources of customer value

First-mover advantage Circumstances when the first firm to market with a new product, process, technology, business model, or platform is able to gain such a solid foothold by earning customer loyalty, economies of scale, or learning benefits that subsequent entrants are unable to successfully challenge the first mover's dominant position

Five Forces A framework for evaluating the profit potential of an industrial sector or market through analysis of its structure, considering buyer, supplier, and competitor factors, alongside the threats of new entrants and substitutes

Flow A continuous stream of activity or movement

Forcefield analysis An analytical tool to identify forces in the organization that may drive and restrain change

Foreign direct investment (FDI) The activities of multinational corporations are based on FDI, i.e. locating part of the firm's activities in countries other than the firm's domestic market

Foreign market entry modes The channels ranging from export strategies to direct foreign investment that an organization can employ to gain entry to a new international market

Formulation Activity or effort dedicated to generating new strategy ideas, plans, and initiatives

Four Es Particularly in public and not-for-profit organizations, a proposed strategy may be tested against objectives that are founded on the 'four Es': efficiency, effectiveness, economy, and equity

Functional strategy Addresses the question 'How to operate?' in order to deliver an optimal contribution to corporate and business strategy from functions such as human resources, finance, and operations

Functional structure The simplest form of organizational structure which typically divides responsibilities according to the organization's primary functions, such as operations, finance, marketing, human resources, and IT

Generic strategies An explanation of strategies (differentiation, cost-leadership, and focus strategies) which describe how a company pursues competitive advantage across its chosen market scope

Global strategy The opposite of a multidomestic strategy—it sacrifices responsiveness to local requirements within each of its markets in favour of emphasizing efficiency. Some minor modifications to products and services may be made in various markets, but a global strategy stresses the need to gain economies of scale by offering essentially the same products or services in each market

Globalization A continuing process of integration and movement of people, companies, goods and services, and finance, and harmonization of rules and regulations between governments globally

Greenwashing The act of deliberately misleading consumers about the environmental practices of a company or the environmental traits or benefits of a product or service

Groupthink A cognitive phenomenon that occurs within a group of people in which the desire for harmony or conformity in the group results in an irrational or dysfunctional decision-making outcome. Group members try to minimize conflict and reach a consensus decision without critical evaluation of alternative viewpoints

Growth An organization seeking growth may be aiming to increase profits or serve more clients Strategies for growth may be driven by new opportunities present in the external environment, or by the financial ambitions of the owner of a firm

Heuristics An approach to problem solving that uses a practical method, not guaranteed to be optimal, perfect, or rational, but instead sufficient for reaching an immediate goal. Heuristics can be speedy mental shortcuts that ease the cognitive burden of deciding, such as a gut feeling or extrapolating from previous experience

Holding structure This structure brings together a number of diverse businesses under a central head office These diverse businesses may have come together through diversification activities such as mergers or acquisitions

Horizontal integration This strategy involves the combination of two businesses operating in the same industry and at the same stage of the supply chain

HRM strategy This aspect of functional strategy typically includes an organization's plans for managing its people, their performance, and their training and development. It may also cover the organization's culture, and its approach to determining how people and culture fit into the organization's future growth strategies and plans

Human-centred design An approach to design activities that puts the user–product interaction at the centre of the process rather than the capabilities or preferences of the designer

Implementation Activity and effort directed towards turning strategy ideas into reality

Inclusive design A set of principles that can be used to guide design choices towards maximum inclusivity of participants within the practical constraint of the situation

Inclusive strategizing An approach to designing strategizing activity in which the methods, timescale, location, tasks, etc. meet all stakeholder needs as an enabler of inclusion and participation

Incremental innovation An innovation that improves existing products, services, or ways of working by better or further exploiting existing capabilities or resources

Industry A group of organizations engaged in a particular type of commercial or economic activity (e.g. the smartphone industry)—potentially related markets which can be grouped together according to similarity in products and/or geographies

Industry forces analysis A method of examining the organizational implications of how a market is structured and interacts now and in the future

Industry life cycle The historical development of an industry from birth through growth to maturity and then decline

Industry structure The number of entities and their transactional relationships within a sector

Information asymmetry Where one party has more or better information than the other

Innovation The process and outcome of the successful exploitation of new ideas

Innovation capability Capacity to innovate arising from adequate formal or informal innovation processes, sufficiently knowledgeable staff, and a supportive environment in which innovation activities can be carried out

Innovation culture Patterns in the way innovation activity tends to be perceived and enacted in an organization

Innovation-oriented structures Flexible and dynamic structures, such as project-based structures and adhocracies, associated with an intention to innovate

Innovation portfolio risk matrix Creates a visual representation of the level of risk inherent in an organization's approach to innovation. Aids management of expectations about the likely returns from strategic innovation

Innovation portfolio strategy A framework to identify the different ways in which innovation is being attempted by an organization. Provides clarity around technical and commercial modes of innovating

Innovation strategy Akin to functional strategy, it describes the balance of ways, ends, and means in which innovation will contribute to broader organizational outcomes

Integration methods Procedures which can be used to organize data and insights into a framework for further analysis, development, or decision-making

Integrative review A method for consolidating and improving initial insights and options generated by external analysis techniques

Intergovernmental Panel on Climate Change (IPCC) An organization comprised of global scientists who compile the latest research on climate change, and make the aggregated findings freely available

International community Collaboration between nations, typically brokered through intergovernmental organizations

Internationalization The process by which an organization interacts across national borders through import or export trade, or the flow of capital/investment in other geographical locations

Interpretation A way of understanding or assigning meaning—in relation to strategy, part of the way in which a stakeholder comprehends what strategy means or should involve

Isolated interpretation An approach to strategic thinking in which the organization is considered separately from its external environment, which acts as a constraint of strategic choice

Isolating mechanism The impediments to immediate imitation of a firm's resource position, equivalent to entry barriers to an industry. Can include privileged access to scarce resources, time lag for competitive resource acquisition, and information asymmetries

IT maturity models A set of models which can help an organization to assess the current effectiveness of its IT capabilities, and which capabilities it should aim to acquire next in order to improve its performance

IT strategy This aspect of functional strategy includes the total pattern of decisions relating to the use of technology within an organization

Joint venture A new organization created by two separate organizations, perhaps for a specific purpose such as entering a new market or exploiting complementary capabilities

Keiretsu This structure, traditionally seen in many major companies in Japan, results in a grouping of organizations which take equity stakes in one another and sometimes collaborate and share projects

Keystone advantage The position of a leading firm that provides a stable and predictable set of common assets to an ecosystem, and therefore is in a position of influence over all others in the ecosystem

Key performance indicators (KPIs) A type of performance measurement used to evaluate the success of an organization or a particular activity in which it engages

Knowledge loop An inclusive design method that tests prototypes of planned approaches with a wide range of users in order to refine activity designs for inclusivity

Learning Acquisition of knowledge or skills through study, experience, or being taught

Licencing A business arrangement involving a firm authorizing another firm to temporarily access its intellectual property rights, such as a manufacturing process or a brand name; for example, Coca-Cola and Pepsi are globally produced and sold by local bottlers in different countries, under licence

M&A A general term used to describe the consolidation of organizations and their assets through a financial transaction such as a merger or an acquisition

McFarlan's strategic grid A model developed to assist managers to analyse the portfolio of IT projects that their organization might be pursuing

Market The individuals, organizations, and activities involved in the provision or consumption of a product or service within a defined geography

Market-based view (MBV) A collection of concepts and theoretical contributions intended to explain how an organization can effectively gain and sustain competitive advantage by adopting strategies for organizational conduct appropriate to its external environment—also known as the 'outside-in' approach to strategy

Market development A growth strategy based on an organization identifying new markets for its existing products

Marketing mix (4Ps or 7Ps) A model for exploring the components of the organization's marketing options, such as price, product, promotion, place, and other key dimensions

Marketing strategy This aspect of functional strategy typically sets out the firm's overall approach to reaching people and turning them into customers of the product or service that it offers, as well as its approach to retaining existing customers

Market penetration A growth strategy based on an organization increasing its market share in its present market(s)

Market position How the organization compares with rivals on key performance dimensions (such as price and product features) in the minds of customers

Market segmentation The process of dividing a market of potential customers into groups, or segments, based on different customer characteristics

Matrix structure This structure sets up reporting relationships as a grid, or matrix, rather than a traditional hierarchy. Employees are likely to have dual reporting relationships—for example, to both a functional manager and a product manager

Megatrend A global shift, such as globalization or digital technologies, that is reshaping the world and changing the way we live and do business

Mental models Deeply ingrained assumptions, generalizations, or even pictures or images that influence how we understand the world and how we take action

Merger An agreement that unites two existing organizations into one new organization

Method A technique or approach to undertaking activity designed to achieve an outcome in an effective manner

Mission The current main focus of organizational effort towards a set of coherent goals and objectives

Mission statement A short and memorable statement defining why an organization exists, its overall goal, and the extent of its operations—what kind of product or service is provided, to whom, and in what markets

Modular innovation An innovation that involve changing a core design concept within a largely unchanged product architecture

Monopoly A situation in which a single individual or organization is the exclusive supplier of a product or service

Monopsony A situation in which a single individual or organization is the exclusive buyer of a product or service

Multi-business organization A diversified organization, where no single business unit is responsible for the majority of the revenue

Multi-criteria decision analysis A highly structured, rational approach to evaluating and prioritizing strategy options which can aid the resolution of contentious issues, or support groups learning to work together through a strategy activity

Multidivisional form or multidivisional structure (M-form) An organizational structure separating an organization into several discrete units which are guided and controlled by targets from the corporate centre

Multidomestic strategy A strategy by which companies try to achieve maximum local responsiveness by customizing both their product offer and marketing strategy to match different national conditions. This strategy sacrifices efficiency in favour of emphasizing responsiveness to local requirements within each of its markets

Multimodality The use of multiple means, in parallel, of achieving the same user utility or outcome, such as in the communication of information

Multinational company/corporation (MNC) A business that operates in more than one country, i.e. it has business operations in two or more countries This goes beyond selling goods and services in more than one country, and involves FDI

Multinational enterprise (MNE) An alternative term for MNC—MNC and MNE are interchangeable terms

Multi-sided platform (MSP) An organization that provides rules and infrastructure that facilitate interactions between parties

Network structure A flexible and non-hierarchical organizational structure that brings together a number of strategic business units (SBUs), or even independent organizations, linked together by formal or informal relationships which change over time

Non-governmental organization (NGO) A non-profit group organized at a local, national, or international level around a common purpose, providing advocacy and information on an issue of societal or environmental importance

Objectives Desirable outcomes targeted by an organization or individual for attainment in the future

Open innovation The flow of ideas to and fro between an organization and its network to be exploited in novel collaborative ways to the benefit of all involved

Operational relatedness If two organizations have a high level of operational relatedness, there may be the opportunity to share assets at the business unit level

Operational systems Mechanisms, working practices, or routines that underlie the efficient use and deployment of resources and capabilities, for example the order fulfilment system in a warehouse where customer orders that have been placed online are picked and prepared for distribution

Operations strategy This aspect of functional strategy addresses the efficient and effective allocation of resources to ensure that the organization's infrastructure, and activities like production or distribution, are properly supported

Opportunism Reacting swiftly and effectively—often in an unplanned way in response to emerging circumstances—in order to achieve desirable outcomes as situations unfold and opportunities are presented

Ordinary capabilities Capabilities that have a direct impact on the production of goods or provision of services

Organizational ambidexterity An organization's ability to be efficient in its management of current business activities whilst adapting to changing operating conditions; requires the use of exploration and exploitation techniques in parallel

Organizational change A process that focuses on the stages that organizations go through as they evolve or attempt renewal. The principles of organizational change theory apply to both short- and long-term changes as well as the speed and urgency of change in adverse business operating conditions

Organizational conduct The choices taken and activities attempted by an organization out of the many options available to it

Organizational culture A set of the underlying beliefs, assumptions, values, and ways of interacting that contribute to the unique social and psychological environment of an organization

Organizational design The purposeful design of how work is conducted in an organization through structures, systems, and procedures, including reporting lines and allocation of responsibilities to employees and teams

Organizational innovations New processes by which we can organize firm activities, coordinate human resources, and revise management approaches—also known as managerial or administrative innovation

Organizational learning The continuing process of generating, retaining, flowing, and deploying knowledge within an organization, as opposed to the same effect in individuals

Organizational strategy Organizational effort, initiative, and attention towards maintaining a balance between ends, ways, and means of surviving and thriving—providing a framework for making choices and trade-offs, and identifying resources, methods, actions, and value-creating objectives that sustain the organization over time within an ever-changing context

Organizational structure The particular structure adopted by a given organization

Organizational survival An organization remains financially viable in the long term and can continue in its current form without merging, being taken over, or having to shut down

Outsourcing The practice of hiring a party outside an organization to perform activities that were traditionally performed in-house by the organization's own employees

Path dependency Refers to the effect that what an organization is capable of doing in the present is a function of what has happened in the past; for example, a firm may gain competitive advantage today based on past acquisition and development of resources and capabilities

Paths, positions, processes framework Associated with the dynamic capability view—a framework for understanding what an organization can do today based on its historical paths, and what it might do today in order to create future options

People focus Goals and activities directed towards improving the impact of an organization on its stakeholders, such as employees, shareholders, owners, customers, and suppliers

Performance management A system for managing employees, teams, and aspects of an organization towards the attainment of quantified targets

PESTEL A framework for describing the state and trajectory of the non-market macro-environmental context in which strategy is made, addressing Political, Economic, Social, Technological, Environmental, and Legislative factors

Planet focus Goals and activities directed towards improving the relationship between an organization and the natural environment—how finite resources and energy are used, how waste is created and managed, and how climate change is impacted by organizational activities

Plasticity The characteristic of being able to adapt or be moulded to meet changing needs or circumstances

Platform A product, service, infrastructure, or technology that becomes essential to a system of commercial activity whilst solving a strategic problem for many organizations and users in a sector

Platform innovation The creation or growth of a foundation for an ecosystem of activity—increasingly features as a topic of strategic interest in a networked world. Also referred to as ecosystems innovation

Platform leadership An organization's position in a network from which it can exert maximum influence on the ecosystem—relates to keystone advantage

Platform strategy The deliberate innovative actions an organization can make to either create a new platform or grow an ecosystem in which the organization is embedded

Policy Formal principles or rules which are to be followed by an organization through its decisions and activities

Political process Strategy as a political process means that decisions and interactions reflect the use of formal and informal power and the vested interests of individuals and groups

Porter's Diamond framework of national advantage A theoretical model that is designed to help understand the emergence of competitive advantage of nations or industry clusters as a result of certain factor conditions available to them, and how strategists can apply the tool to identify attractive markets or locations to situate their production activities

Practical acceptability Perception of the feasibility and cost effectiveness of a strategy activity within given practical constraints (time, cost, effort, etc.)

Practice An ongoing stream of activity occurring over time; that which is actually done

Practices The ways of working adopted by practitioners when trying to accomplish a type of task

Practitioners Those who 'do' or are involved in the 'doing' of strategy work—either employed by the organization or external parties contracted or included on a temporary basis

Prescriptive models Step-by-step guides to strategy work that indicate exactly how strategy activity and processes should take place

Prioritization methods Approaches for determining the relative importance of individual ideas within a broader set of ideas

Private sector The part of the economy that is owned by private individuals, rather than the government, comprising organizations that need to make profit to endure

Procedural justice Perception of the fairness of the way a strategy activity is conducted

Procedural rationality Perception that a strategy activity and its outcome is sensible and based on well-articulated reasoning

Process A flow of events, experiences, and activities occurring over time and in context

Process studies Research that addresses how human factors such as errors, learning, culture, habit, power, and politics play a role in how strategy happens over time and in context

Product development A growth strategy based on an organization creating new products to replace or add to current ones in its existing markets

Profit The difference between the financial income received by an organization and its operating costs

Profit focus Goals and activities directed towards generating profit or financial performance for an organization

Project-based structure An organizational structure where teams are created, undertake their work (usually for a fixed timespan), and are then dissolved

Prospect theory A foundational concept in behavioural economics—describes the way people choose between alternatives that involve risk, where the probabilities of decision outcomes are known. The theory states that people make decisions based on the potential value of losses and gains rather than the final outcome, and that people evaluate these losses and gains using certain heuristics.

Psychological Safety A context for social activity in which participants feel able to give their candid views on a subject without fear of retribution or negative outcomes

Public sector Organizations and aspects of an economy which are funded and controlled by local or central government

Question burst A method for encouraging a group to creatively and positively engage in a discussion task by framing all contributions in the form of questions

Radical innovation Innovation that involves the introduction of entirely new thinking into an organization

Rational decision-making A process or sequence of activities that involves the stages of problem recognition, information search, definition of alternatives, and selection of an optimal outcome from two or more alternatives that are consistent with the decision-makers ranked preferences

Rational plans Plans developed based on data-based analysis of a situation, where the situation is modelled, options identified, and an optimal option selected as the logical way forward

Reflection A learning mechanism which gives in-depth focused attention to the examination of an episode in life to better understand the flow of events, how outcomes emerged, and our role in proceedings

Reflection-in-action Reflection that occurs during the moment of activity

Reflection-on-action Reflection that occurs after an event

Reflective practice Development of insight and practice through critical attention to practical values, theories, principles, assumptions, and the relationship between theory and practice which inform everyday actions

Reflexivity Focused in-depth reflection on one's own perspective, values, and assumptions—also known as critical self-reflection

Regulation The act of controlling the flow of strategy activities in order to best meet perceived organizational needs

Related diversification The process that takes place when an organization expands its activities into products/services that are similar to those it currently offers

Relatedness The commonality between any two products, companies, or industries (see also corporate relatedness and operational relatedness)

Remanufacturing The process of returning a used product to at least its original performance with a warranty that is equivalent to or better than that of the newly manufactured product

Reorganization/renewal In the reorganization/renewal stage of turnaround management, the leadership team should begin to pursue long-term actions that are intended to return the organization to a more successful level of performance

Replacement In the replacement stage of turnaround management, senior managers may be replaced by new managers who will help to introduce strategic change, and resulting recovery, based on their different experiences and backgrounds

Repositioning The repositioning stage of turnaround management attempts to generate revenue by introducing innovations and making changes in product portfolios and market positioning

Resource base The total set of resources that an organization has, or has access to on a preferential basis

Resource base profiling A method of building up a clear shared picture of what an organization currently has available in terms of resources

Resource-based view (RBV) A collection of concepts and theoretical contributions intended to explain how an organization can effectively gain and sustain competitive advantage by adopting strategies to identify and organize around value-creating distinctive resources

Resource deployment The allocation of organizational resources towards a specific activity or long-term aim

Resource flows The incremental changes in resource stocks that occur over time

Resource heterogeneity Acknowledging that different firms, even in the same industry, possess different bundles of resources (where firms are thought of as bundles of value-creating resources)

Resources What an organization has, or has access to, that it can use to undertake activities or attempt to achieve objectives—synonymous with assets

Resource stocks The current level of resources available to the organization

Retrenchment Stage of turnaround management comprising wide-ranging short-term actions, intended to reduce any financial losses, stabilize the organization, and solve any immediate problems

Risk management The process of identifying and evaluating risks, as well as procedures to avoid or minimize their negative impact

Routines Semi-patterned ways of working in which activity is undertaken in a predictable way, embedding learning from previous activities, in order to improve effectiveness and efficiency of effort

Satisficing A combination of the words 'satisfy' and 'suffice'—a decision-making process that entails searching for available alternatives until an acceptable solution to a problem is found. Satisficing can explain the behaviour of decision-makers under circumstances in which an optimal solution cannot be determined

Scenario planning A method of modelling alternative plausible futures, deriving learning about the nature of those futures, and undertaking initiatives today in order to be ready to meet the challenges of multiple possible future scenarios

Scenario thinking A method of exploring the possible future implications of current trends and trajectories for an organization

Scope The range of activities, geographical territories, products, and services that an organization attempts to address

SCP The structure–conduct–performance framework of the market-based view that explains how the external environment and firm strategies interact

Sector A part or subdivision of an economy or industry (such as the public sector, private sector, etc.) that it is useful to analyse separately from the whole

Sensegiving The process of attempting to influence a target audience's perception of meaning. It can be used as a powerful process to set forth a desired future state of an organization and motivate people to deliver that vision

Sensemaking A process by which people give meaning to their individual or collective experiences. Often used to describe individuals' ongoing retrospective development of plausible mental frames to rationalize what they are doing

Servitization Involves organizations developing the capabilities they need to provide services and solutions that supplement their traditional product offerings

Shareholder An individual or organization that owns some or all of an organization

Shareholder value maximization A management philosophy which implies that the ultimate measure of a company's success is the extent to which it enriches shareholders

Sharing economy An umbrella term for a wave of new renting, leasing, bartering, and pooling services linked to different aspects of life, including lodging, transportation, work, leisure, and fashion (e.g. Air BnB is based on a sharing model)

Simple structure At an early stage in its development, an organization is likely to have a simple structure that reflects how work is divided between a number of sections or departments according to function (also known as a functional structure)

Single business organization An organization that operates in a single industry

Single-loop learning Learning in which our strategy and methods are enhanced without challenging our assumptions and beliefs

Situated activity Activity that occurs within, and is influenced by, context at a certain moment in time

Situated attention The influence of context on the direction of attention

Situated learning perspective A framework to help us understand how contextual, environmental and social factors influence learning

Situation The set of circumstances which provide the context for the activity of an individual or organization at any given moment in time

Social Occurring between individuals or groups of individuals—strategy as a social process is enacted through multiple interactions between individuals and groups

Social acceptability Perception that a strategy activity is attuned to the social needs of stakeholders in a trustworthy way

Social complexity Resources and capabilities that have evolved over time as a result of social interaction within the organization, for example interpersonal relationships among managers, the firm's culture, and its reputation among customers and suppliers

Social enterprise An entity that pursues a social mission while relying on a commercial business model—also known as a hybrid organization

Social entrepreneur An individual or organization that finds a profitable solution to social problems

Sponsor An individual or group of individuals who purposefully initiate a strategizing activity based on their formal position and allocated ownership of the outcomes

Stakeholder mapping An analytical framework and process to identify and prioritize the stakeholders in the organization

Stakeholders Those individuals or groups affected by, and with the power to influence, the outcomes of organizational activities

Stakeholder value maximization A management philosophy that regards maximization of the interests of all its stakeholders (customers, employees, shareholders, and the community) as its highest objective

Step-based models for managing strategic change Popular frameworks in managerial practice that have been developed to help managers approach the task of strategic change as a logical step-by-step process

Strategic activity Work done by practitioners towards attaining some sort of strategy-related outcome

Strategic alignment model The key message of this model is that an organization's IT strategy should be fully aligned with its business strategy

Strategic alliance An agreement by two or more organizations to cooperate in the development, manufacture, or sale of products or services without becoming a single entity

Strategic Business Unit (SBU) A fully-functional unit of a business that has its own vision and direction

Strategic drift A concept in change management that can be applied to understand the consequences of the organization failing to keep pace with changes in the external environment

Strategic group A collection of organizations adopting broadly the same strategy to service the needs of the same group of customers

Strategic group analysis A method of identifying clusters of competitors in a market that are following broadly similar strategies to serve similar groups of customers

Strategic innovation Innovation in an organization's business model, altering how it creates value whilst possibly disrupting how a current market operates or creating uncontested new market space

Strategic leader An organizational leader who is resilient and flexible, capable of drawing on talents in anticipating, challenging, interpreting, deciding, aligning, and learning to lead an organization successfully regardless of contextual events

Strategic leadership An individual or group's ability to articulate a strategic vision for the organization, and to motivate and persuade others to buy into and execute that vision

Strategic learning Learning which informs and influences the identification and enactment of strategic initiatives intended to deliver future capacity for organizational growth and survival

Strategic perspective Capacity of an individual or group to be able to think about and perceive holistically a system of events or activities and how they interrelate over time, rather than just understanding individual components of that system

Strategizing The enactment of activity relating to strategy

Strategy The best word we have to describe how we maintain a balance between ends, ways, and means; identifying objectives and the resources and methods available for meeting such objectives within the context of the drama and challenge of the inherent unpredictability of human affairs

Strategy-as-practice A collection of concepts and theoretical contributions intended to explain how strategy can be considered a continuing achievement, the outcomes of which are influenced by who is involved, when they are involved, and which tools and practices they use

Strategy clock A theoretical model that explores the options for the organization to strategically position its products and services in a competitive market, i.e. how a firm can position its product in a marketplace to give it a competitive advantage

Strategy map A diagram intended to illustrate the organization's strategy and performance, identify relationships between key strategic concepts, and communicate the organization's objectives and where employees contribute and fit in

Structural ambidexterity The creation of separate organizations or structures for different types of activities. Such organizations or structures are either fully explorative or exploitative. In these organizations or structures, employees have clearly defined responsibilities

Structuralist approach An approach to strategic thinking in which the organization's strategic options are bounded by the environment

Structures The enduring physical, social, and institutional settings in which an organization's activity occurs

Substitute In terms of market strategy, an alternative product or service that provides equivalent utility through very different means (e.g. an encyclopaedia compared with a Google search)

Suitability The suitability of a proposed strategy can be assessed by the extent to which it matches the needs identified from a strategic analysis

Supplier power The bargaining power that the entity selling a good or service has over the purchaser

Supply chain The network of organizations involved in the creation and sale of a product, from the delivery of source materials from the supplier to the manufacturer, through to the delivery of the product to the end-user

Sustainability The capacity of a system to continue over time at a global level, defined by the UN as meeting the needs of the present without compromising the ability of future generations to meet their own needs

Sustainable development Human progress that doesn't harm future generations or the planet

Sustainable Development Goals (SDGs) Proposed by the UN, the SDGs are a framework of interrelated goals and objectives intended to influence national, local, and organizational strategies for driving sustainable development

Sustainable investment Also known as ethical investment or green investment, an approach to managing an investment portfolio where the stocks and shares owned reflect the investor's sustainability, moral, and ethical concerns

SWOT A framework for describing and comparing the internal strengths and weaknesses of an organization with the external opportunities and threats presenting in its environmental context

Synergy The idea that the whole is greater than the sum of the parts, or that the value created by business units working together can exceed the value of those units create working independently

Systems Systems are the micro-structures that make organizations work. They tell people and machines what to do, monitor performance, and provide the basis for an overall evaluation of the organization's performance

Tangible and intangible assets The two main asset classes of an organization: tangible assets include both fixed resources, such as machinery, buildings and land, and current assets, such as inventory; intangible assets are non-physical resources, such as patents, trademarks, copyrights, goodwill, and brand recognition

Technological change Possibilities for new ways of working and interacting driven by advances in technical know-how, products, and equipment

Technological innovation New knowledge and technology being converted into advances in products, services, operational processes, and infrastructure

Theory A set of ideas that helps explain something—often set out in a format that can be tested through field research

Theories-in-use The thought processes that actually drive our behaviours and decisions, regardless of how we make explanations to others

Third sector Organizations fulfilling a social purpose that are not exclusively profit focused or controlled by government, such as charities, voluntary organizations, social enterprises, and community groups

Threshold capabilities Capabilities that an organization is required to maintain to a minimum performance level in order to compete in an industry

Time compression diseconomies The time and space needed to acquire or develop resources by an organization. Once time and space pass, firms that do not possess the same or similar time- and space-dependent resources may face significant cost disadvantages in acquiring and developing matching resources, because doing so would require these disadvantaged firms to re-create history

Tools The techniques, methods, models, and frameworks which support interactions and decision-making in strategy activity

Tools-in-use How strategy tools are actually deployed—exploiting the potential of affordances—in an effort to effectively meet the needs of strategy activity in any given situation

TOWS An integrating method for collating contextual insights and strategy options arising from the use of analytical methods. Serves as a platform for creative development of options and as an input to evaluative methods

Transnational strategy A middle ground between a multidomestic strategy and a global strategy A firm that pursues transnational strategy seeks to balance the desire for efficiency with the need to adjust to local preferences within the various countries in which it operates

Transnational structure This configuration is a means of managing internationally which can be effective in making good use of knowledge spread across geographic borders (see transnational strategy)

Triangulation A method for combining different data sources in order to establish a richer understanding of a matter of interest

Triple bottom line (TBL) A model of sustainable performance in which a balance is achieved within a system of objectives addressing people, profit, and planet-related outcomes

Turnaround management A process of corporate renewal, using analysis and planning to save troubled companies and return them to solvency, and to identify the reasons for failing performance in the firm's markets and rectify them

United Nations (UN) A global organization comprising representatives from the nations of the world which seeks to addressed shared challenges with policies, initiatives, and cooperative action

Unrelated diversification The process of entering a new industry that lacks any important similarities with the firm's existing businesses; often accomplished through a merger or acquisition

Utility The usefulness or advantage of a product or service to a user in providing a function or experience

Value Relative worth—often the extent to which an individual is willing to pay for a good or a service

Value-chain analysis A method which models an organization's direct activities that create value and indirect activities that shape the environment for value creation

Value creating The quality or attribute of a resource that describes the extent to which it can be used to achieve outcomes which a customer is willing to pay for

Value net A method that helps identify opportunities for enhanced collaboration with other players—competitors, customers, suppliers, and complementors—within an organization's network

Values Characteristics which describe how behaviour and conduct of individuals and teams should be consistently carried out, in compliance with ethical and moral codes of the organization

Vertical integration This strategy involves a firm extending its operations within its value chain, for example acquiring businesses in its supply chain

Vision A loose description of where an organization should aspire to be in a (typically far-off) future time that can be used to motivate, guide, and include organizational stakeholders in a collective effort to move in a certain direction

VRIO A framework for identifying resources which might act as a source of competitive advantage for an organization, by the extent which they are

Valued by the customer, Rare, Imperfectly imitable, and can be used within the Organization

VUCA An acronym for Volatile, Uncertain, Complex and Ambiguous circumstances that describe the challenging conditions facing many strategists

Wicked problem A problematic situation which is so complex and interwoven with influential factors that it is impossible to 'solve it' fully, and instead the challenge is to try to mitigate or deal with the situation in a better way

Yip's industry globalization drivers Four sets of 'industry globalization drivers' which underlie the conditions in each industry that create the potential for that industry to become more global and, as a consequence, for the potential viability of a global approach to strategy

Zero-order capabilities The operational capabilities of an organization that provide the potential to produce goods or provide services

NAME INDEX

Note: Tables and figures are indicated by an italic *t* and *f* following the page number.

A

B

C

M

N

O

P

Q

R

Y

Z

SUBJECT INDEX

Note: Tables and figures are indicated by an italic *t* and *f* following the page number.

E

H

I

N

Q

R

S

T

U